STREET ATLAS Birmingham and West Midlands

Contents

III Key to map symbols
IV Key to map pages
VI Route planning
VIII Administrative and Postcode boundaries
1 **Street maps** at 3½ inches to 1 mile
163 **Street maps of centres of Wolverhampton, Birmingham and Coventry** at 7 inches to 1 mile
166 **Index** of towns and villages
169 **Index** of streets, hospitals, industrial estates, railway stations, schools, shopping centres, universities and places of interest

First published in 1998 by
Philip's, a division of
Octopus Publishing Group Ltd
2-4 Heron Quays, London E14 4JP

Third colour edition 2006
First impression 2006
BWMCA

ISBN-10 0-540-08836-6 (spiral)
ISBN-13 978-0-540-08836-2 (spiral)

Printed by Toppan, China

Digital Data

The exceptionally high-quality mapping found in this atlas is available as digital data in TIFF format, which is easily convertible to other bitmapped (raster) image formats.

The index is also available in digital form as a standard database table. It contains all the details found in the printed index together with the National Grid reference for the map square in which each entry is named.

For further information and to discuss your requirements, please contact Philip's on 020 7644 6932 or james.mann@philips-maps.co.uk

Key to map symbols

22a	**Motorway** with junction number
	Primary route – dual/single carriageway
	A road – dual/single carriageway
	B road – dual/single carriageway
	Minor road – dual/single carriageway
	Other minor road – dual/single carriageway
	Road under construction
	Tunnel, covered road
	Rural track, private road or narrow road in urban area
	Gate or obstruction to traffic (restrictions may not apply at all times or to all vehicles)
	Path, bridleway, byway open to all traffic, road used as a public path
	Pedestrianised area
DY7	**Postcode boundaries**
	County and unitary authority boundaries
	Railway, tunnel, railway under construction
	Tramway, tramway under construction
	Miniature railway
Walsall	**Railway station**
	Private railway station
South Shields	**Metro station**
	Tram stop, tram stop under construction
	Bus, coach station

Acad	**Academy**	Inst	**Institute**	Recn Gd	**Recreation Ground**
Allot Gdns	**Allotments**	Ct	**Law Court**	Resr	**Reservoir**
Cemy	**Cemetery**	L Ctr	**Leisure Centre**	Ret Pk	**Retail Park**
C Ctr	**Civic Centre**	LC	**Level Crossing**	Sch	**School**
CH	**Club House**	Liby	**Library**	Sh Ctr	**Shopping Centre**
Coll	**College**	Mkt	**Market**	TH	**Town Hall/House**
Crem	**Crematorium**	Meml	**Memorial**	Trad Est	**Trading Estate**
Ent	**Enterprise**	Mon	**Monument**	Univ	**University**
Ex H	**Exhibition Hall**	Mus	**Museum**	W Twr	**Water Tower**
Ind Est	**Industrial Estate**	Obsy	**Observatory**	Wks	**Works**
IRB Sta	**Inshore Rescue Boat Station**	Pal	**Royal Palace**	YH	**Youth Hostel**
		PH	**Public House**		

■ The small numbers around the edges of the maps identify the 1 kilometre National Grid lines

■ The dark grey border on the inside edge of some pages indicates that the mapping does not continue onto the adjacent page

	Ambulance station
	Coastguard station
	Fire station
	Police station
	Accident and Emergency entrance to hospital
H	**Hospital**
	Place of worship
i	**Information Centre** (open all year)
	Shopping Centre
P P&R	**Parking, Park and Ride**
PO	**Post Office**
	Camping site, caravan site
	Golf course, picnic site
Prim Sch	**Important buildings, schools, colleges, universities and hospitals**
	Built up area
	Woods
River Medway	**Water name**
	River, weir, stream
	Canal, lock, tunnel
	Water
	Tidal water
Church	**Non-Roman antiquity**
ROMAN FORT	**Roman antiquity**
87 / 237	**Adjoining page indicators and overlap bands** The colour of the arrow and the band indicates the scale of the adjoining or overlapping page (see scales below)

Enlarged mapping only

	Railway or bus station building
	Place of interest
	Parkland

The scale of the maps on the pages numbered in blue is 5.52 cm to 1 km • 3½ inches to 1 mile • 1: 18103

0 – ¼ – ½ – ¾ – 1 mile

0 – 250 m – 500 m – 750 m – 1 kilometre

The scale of the maps on pages numbered in red is 11.04 cm to 1 km • 7 inches to 1 mile • 1: 9051

0 – 220 yards – 440 yards – 660 yards – ½ mile

0 – 125 m – 250 m – 375 m – ½ kilometre

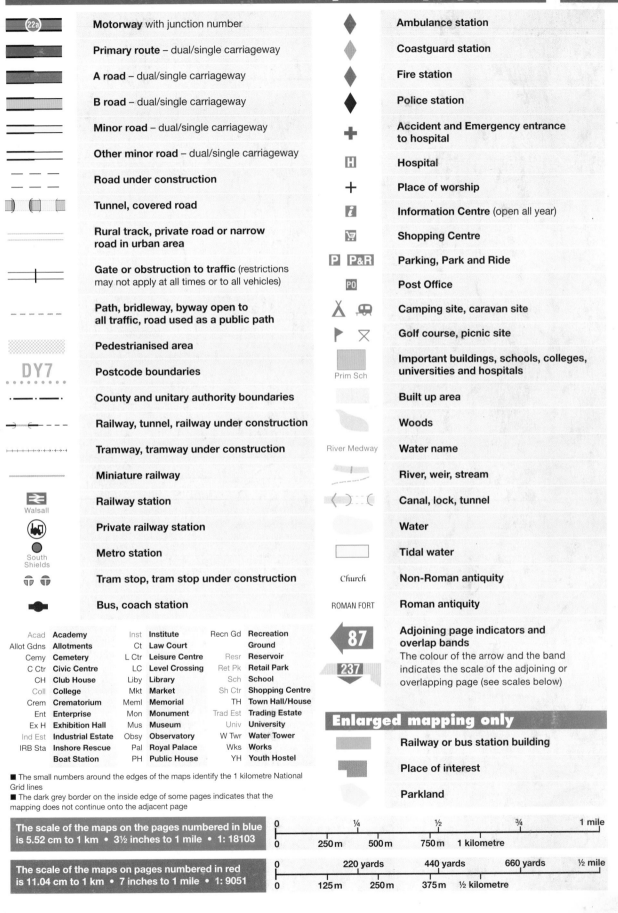

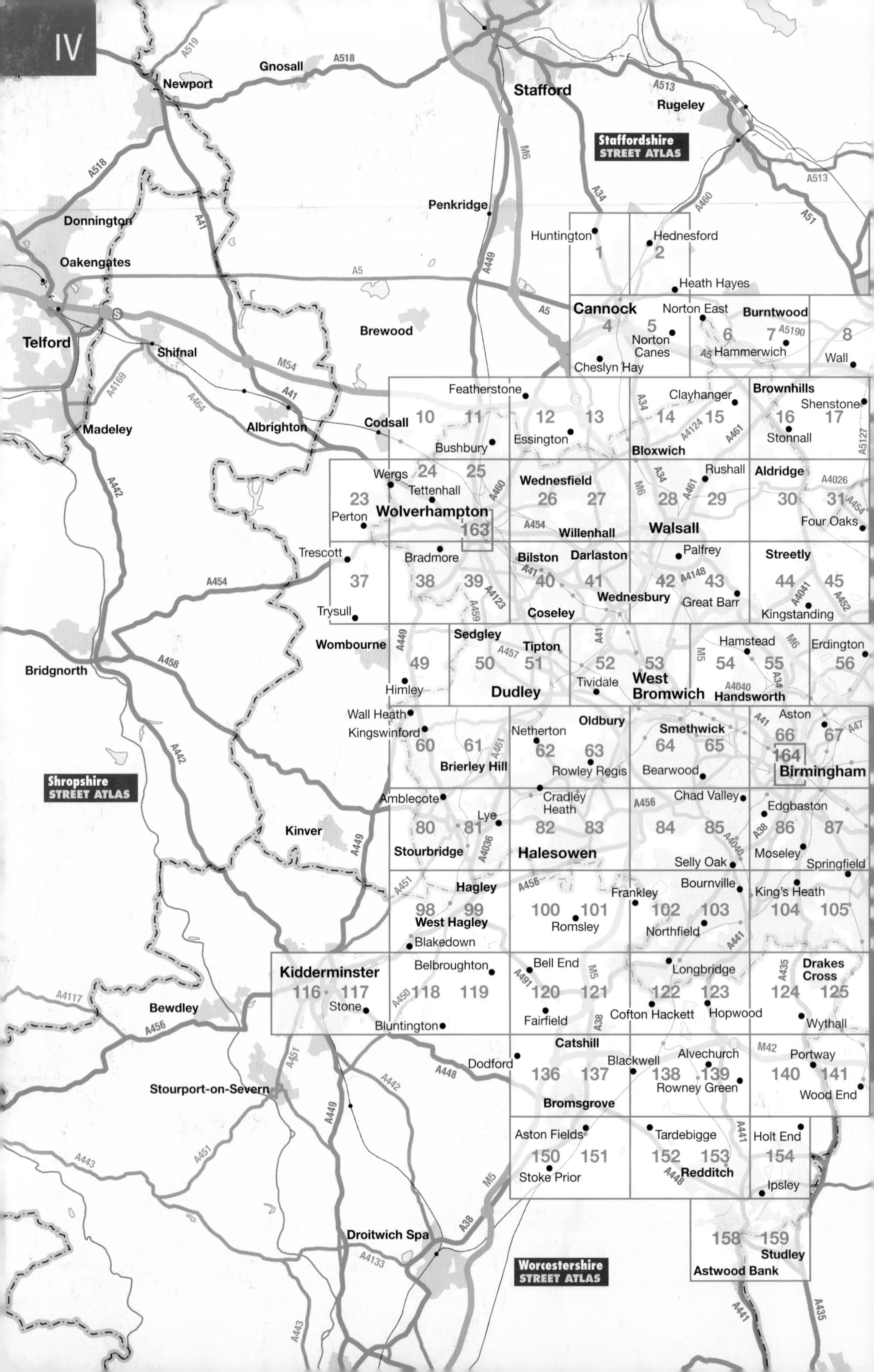
Staffordshire STREET ATLAS
Shropshire STREET ATLAS
Worcestershire STREET ATLAS
Stafford
Gnosall
Newport
Rugeley
Penkridge
Donnington
Oakengates
Telford
Shifnal
Madeley
Albrighton
Codsall
Brewood
Huntington
Hednesford
Heath Hayes
Cannock
Norton East
Burntwood
Norton Canes
Hammerwich
Cheslyn Hay
Wall
Featherstone
Clayhanger
Brownhills
Shenstone
Bushbury
Essington
Stonnall
Bloxwich
Wergs
Tettenhall
Wolverhampton
Perton
Wednesfield
Willenhall
Walsall
Rushall
Aldridge
Four Oaks
Trescott
Bradmore
Bilston
Darlaston
Palfrey
Streetly
Trysull
Coseley
Wednesbury
Great Barr
Kingstanding
Wombourne
Sedgley
Tipton
Hamstead
Erdington
Bridgnorth
Himley
Dudley
Tividale
West Bromwich
Handsworth
Wall Heath
Kingswinford
Brierley Hill
Netherton
Oldbury
Rowley Regis
Smethwick
Bearwood
Aston
Birmingham
Amblecote
Cradley Heath
Chad Valley
Edgbaston
Kinver
Lye
Stourbridge
Halesowen
Selly Oak
Moseley
Springfield
Hagley
West Hagley
Blakedown
Frankley
Romsley
Bournville
Northfield
King's Heath
Kidderminster
Belbroughton
Bell End
Longbridge
Drakes Cross
Stone
Bluntington
Bewdley
Fairfield
Cofton Hackett
Hopwood
Wythall
Catshill
Dodford
Blackwell
Alvechurch
Rowney Green
Portway
Wood End
Stourport-on-Severn
Bromsgrove
Aston Fields
Stoke Prior
Tardebigge
Redditch
Holt End
Ipsley
Droitwich Spa
Astwood Bank
Studley
1 2 4 5 6 7 8 10 11 12 13 14 15 16 17 23 24 25 26 27 28 29 30 31 37 38 39 40 41 42 43 44 45 49 50 51 52 53 54 55 56 60 61 62 63 64 65 66 67 80 81 82 83 84 85 86 87 98 99 100 101 102 103 104 105 116 117 118 119 120 121 122 123 124 125 136 137 138 139 140 141 150 151 152 153 154 158 159 163 164
M6 M54 M5 M42 A5 A34 A38 A41 A47 A51 A449 A454 A456 A458 A460 A461 A513 A518 A519 A442 A443 A448 A451 A441 A435 A459 A457 A4123 A4124 A4148 A4041 A4026 A452 A5127 A5190 A4040 A4036 A4169 A464 A4117 A4133 A491 A450 A4540

Key to map pages

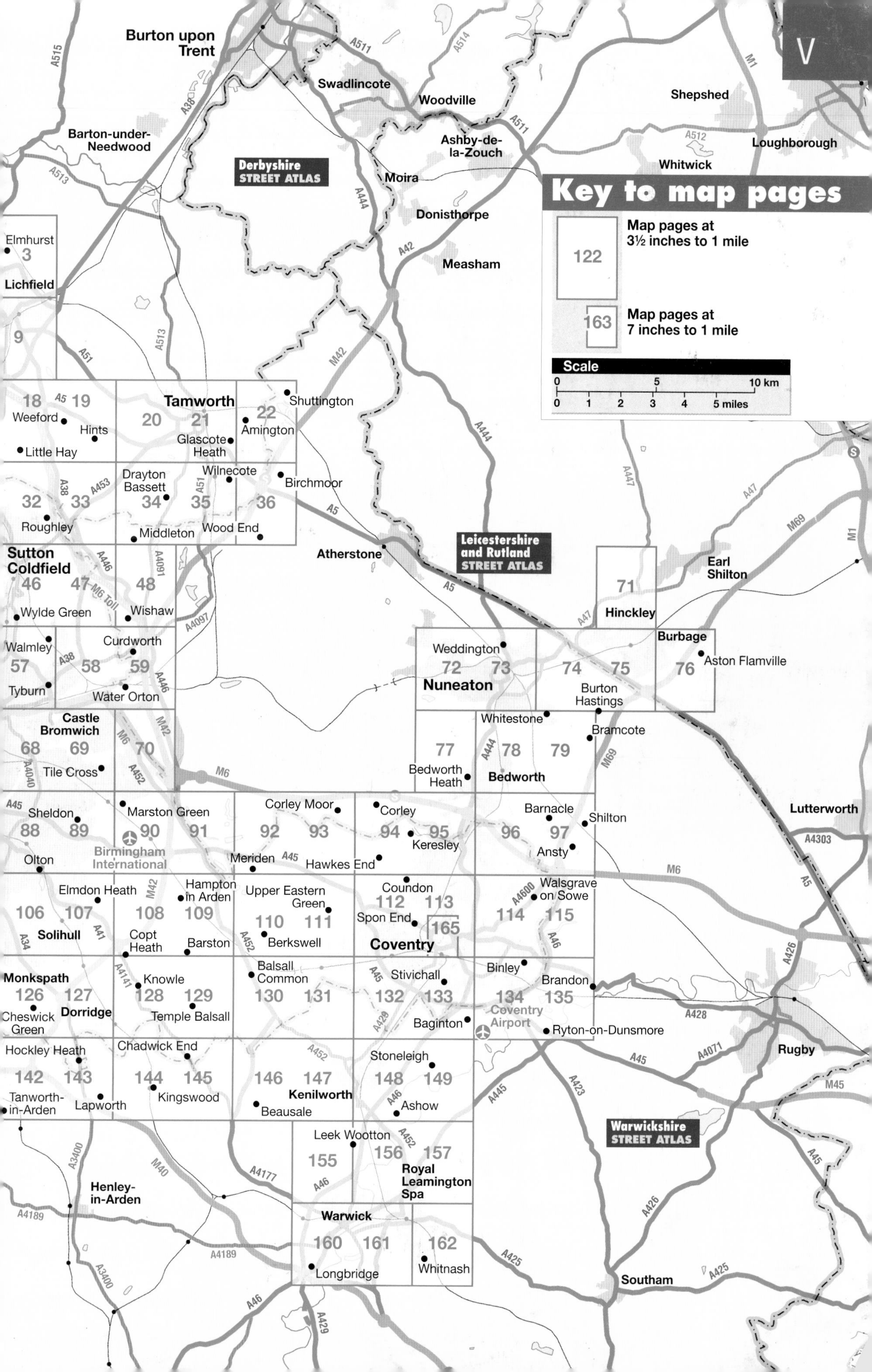
Map pages at 3½ inches to 1 mile
122
Map pages at 7 inches to 1 mile
163
Scale
0 5 10 km
0 1 2 3 4 5 miles
Derbyshire STREET ATLAS
Leicestershire and Rutland STREET ATLAS
Warwickshire STREET ATLAS
Burton upon Trent
Swadlincote
Woodville
Shepshed
Loughborough
Whitwick
Barton-under-Needwood
Ashby-de-la-Zouch
Moira
Donisthorpe
Measham
Elmhurst
3
Lichfield
9
18 19
Weeford
Hints
Little Hay
Tamworth
20 21 22
Glascote Heath
Amington
Shuttington
Drayton Bassett
Wilnecote
Birchmoor
32 33 34 35 36
Roughley
Middleton
Wood End
Atherstone
Sutton Coldfield
46 47 48
Wylde Green
Wishaw
Walmley
Curdworth
57 58 59
Tyburn
Water Orton
Castle Bromwich
68 69 70
Tile Cross
71
Hinckley
Earl Shilton
Burbage
Aston Flamville
Weddington
72 73 74 75 76
Nuneaton
Burton Hastings
Whitestone
Bramcote
77 78 79
Bedworth Heath
Bedworth
Lutterworth
Sheldon
Marston Green
Corley Moor
Corley
Barnacle
Shilton
88 89 90 91 92 93 94 95 96 97
Keresley
Ansty
Olton
Birmingham International
Meriden
Hawkes End
Elmdon Heath
Hampton in Arden
Upper Eastern Green
Coundon
Walsgrave on Sowe
106 107 108 109 110 111 112 113 114 115
165
Spon End
Solihull
Copt Heath
Barston
Berkswell
Coventry
Monkspath
Knowle
Balsall Common
Stivichall
Binley
Brandon
126 127 128 129 130 131 132 133 134 135
Cheswick Green
Dorridge
Temple Balsall
Baginton
Coventry Airport
Ryton-on-Dunsmore
Rugby
Hockley Heath
Chadwick End
Stoneleigh
142 143 144 145 146 147 148 149
Tanworth-in-Arden
Lapworth
Kingswood
Beausale
Kenilworth
Ashow
Leek Wootton
155 156 157
Royal Leamington Spa
Henley-in-Arden
Warwick
160 161 162
Longbridge
Whitnash
Southam
A515 A38 A511 A514 M1 A512 A513 A444 A42 M42 A5 A51 A453 A4091 A446 M6 Toll A4097 A447 A47 M69 A4040 A452 M6 A45 A4303 A41 A34 A4141 A4600 A46 A426 A429 A428 A4071 M45 A445 A423 A3400 M40 A4177 A4189 A425

West Midlands
Worcestershire
BIRMINGHAM
SUTTON COLDFIELD
Wolverhampton
Walsall
West Bromwich
Dudley
SMETHWICK
HALESOWEN
Stourbridge
Kidderminster
Bromsgrove
Redditch
Worcester
Droitwich Spa
Cannock
Lichfield
Rugeley
Brownhills
Bridgnorth
Stourport on Severn
Bewdley
Shifnal
Albrighton
Codsall
Penkridge
Brewood
Tettenhall
Wednesfield
Willenhall
Bilston
Darlaston
Wednesbury
Sedgley
Coseley
Tipton
Oldbury
Rowley Regis
Brierley Hill
Kingswinford
Wombourne
Wordsley
Kinver
Hednesford
Heath Hayes
Burntwood
Cheslyn Hay
Aldridge
Streetly
Great Barr
Kingstanding
Erdington
Handsworth
Aston
Harborne
Edgbaston
Selly Oak
Bournville
Northfield
Longbridge
King's Norton
Shirley
Olton
Studley
Alcester
Feckenham
Inkberrow
Broadwas
Wyre Forest
Oakengates
Donnington
Hagley
Catshill
Alvechurch
M5
M6
M6 TOLL
M42
M54
A5
A34
A38
A41
A449
A456
A491

VII
Route planning
Scale
0
5
10 km
0
1
2
3
4
5 miles
Yoxall
Woodhouses
Barton-under-Needwood
Walton-on-Trent
Church Gresley
Woodville
Smisby
Lount
Osgathorpe
Shepshed
Castle Gresley
Caldwell
Linton
Mount Pleasant
Blackfordby
Norris Hill
Newbold
Coleorton
Thringstone
Shelthorpe
Nanpantan
Rosliston
Orgreave
Alrewas
Ashby-de-la-Zouch
Swannington
Coton in the Elms
Overseal
Moira
COALVILLE
Fradley
Croxall
Donisthorpe
Packington
Oakthorpe
Ravenstone
Edingale
Lullington
Netherseal
Measham
Normanton le Heath
Elford
Harlaston
Haunton
Clifton Campville
Chilcote
Appleby Magna
Swepstone
Heather
Ibstock
Stanton under Bardon
Markfield
Field Head
Newtown Linford
Anstey
No Man's Heath
Appleby Parva
Snarestone
Newton Burgoland
Battram
Whittington
Thorpe Constantine
Norton-Juxta-Twycross
Bagworth
Thornton
Hademore
Shackerstone
Odstone
Nailstone
Groby
Wigginton
Seckington
Newton Regis
Austrey
Congerstone
Barton in the Beans
Barlestone
Ratby
Botcheston
Glenfield
Hopwas
Leyfields
Shuttington
Tamworth
Alvecote
Bilstone
Carlton
Newtown Unthank
Kirby Muxloe
Amington
Warton
Twycross
Market Bosworth
Glascote
Orton-on-the-Hill
Wellsborough
Newbold Verdon
Desford
Leicester Forest East
Leicester
Hints
Bonehill
Fazeley
Polesworth
St Helena
Birchmoor
Sheepy Magna
Sheepy Parva
Cadeby
Peckleton
Drayton Bassett
Wilnecote
Tamworth Services
Grendon
Sibson
Leicester Forest East Services
Dosthill
Dordon
Shenton
Sutton Cheney
Kirkby Mallory
Grendon Common
Ratcliffe Culey
Upton
Middleton
Wood End
Baddesley Ensor
Atherstone
Witherley
Dadlington
Stapleton
Thurlaston
Enderby
Bodymoor Heath
Baxterley
Mancetter
Fenny Drayton
Stoke Golding
Barwell
Earl Shilton
Narborough
Kingsbury
Bentley
Higham on the Hill
Elmesthorpe
Huncote
Littlethorpe
Hurley
Croft
Wishaw
Marston
Ridge Lane
Oldbury
Hinckley
Stoney Stanton
Cosby
Over Green
Lea Marston
Hartshill
Sutton in the Elms
Curdworth
Nether Whitacre
Church End
Camp Hill
Weddington
Sapcote
Whiteacre Heath
Chapel End
Sketchley
Primethorpe
Minworth
Galley Common
Burbage
Aston Flamville
Broughton Astley
Water Orton
Furnace End
Ansley
Stockingford
Nuneaton
Sharnford
Over Whitacre
Dunton Bassett
Shustoke
Church End
Old Arley
Chilvers Coton
Attleborough
Burton Hastings
Frolesworth
Leire
Ashby Magna
Castle Bromwich
Coleshill
Astley
New Arley
Whitestone
Smockington
Claybrooke Magna
Kitt's Green
Griff
Collycroft
Bramcote
Claybrooke Parva
Ashby Parva
Tile Cross
Maxstoke
Fillongley
Bedworth Heath
Bedworth
Copston Magna
Wibtoft
Ullesthorpe
Marston Green
Corley Ash
Corley Services
Bulkington
Wolvey
Chapel Green
Corley
Ash Green
Hawkesbury
Barnacle
Withybrook
Bitteswell
Lutterworth
Sheldon
Birmingham International
Butler's End
Corley Moor
Neal's Green
Longford
Shilton
Willey
Misterton
Elmdon
Keresley
Ansty
Cross in Hand
Hawkes End
Little Heath
Foleshill
Monks Kirby
Cotesbach
Bickenhill
Meriden
Coundon
Walsgrave on Sowe
Pailton
Elmdon Heath
Hampton in Arden
Allesley
Eastern Green
Spon End
Great Heath
Wyken
Stretton under Fosse
Churchover
Gibbet Hill
Four Oaks
Shawell
Eastcote
Berkswell
Whoberley
Coventry
Brinklow
Easenhall
Harborough Magna
Copt Heath
Earlsdon
Pinley
Binley
Binley Woods
Newbold on Avon
Newton
Catthorpe
Barston
Tile Hill
Bretford
King's Newnham
Knowle
Balsall Common
Stivichall
Willenhall
Brandon
Church Lawford
Long Lawford
Bentley Heath
Catchems Corner
Balsall
Clifton upon Dunsmore
Temple Balsall
Fen End
Burton Green
Tollbar End
Wolston
New Bilton
Dorridge
Ryton-on-Dunsmore
Bilton
Rugby
Hillmorton
Baginton
Hockley Heath
Meer End
Crackley
Chadwick End
Stoneleigh
Bubbenhall
Baddesley Clinton
Honiley
Stretton-on-Dunsmore
Wroxall
Kenilworth
Kingswood
Beausale
Dunchurch
Kilsby
Lapworth
Ashow
Stareton
Princethorpe
Bourton on Dunsmore
Thurlaston
Barby
Rowington
Weston under Wetherley
Wappenbury
Frankton
Draycote
Draycote Water
Leek Wootton
Eathorpe
Marton
Kites Hardwick
Shrewley Common
Old Milverton
Cubbington
Hunningham
Birdingbury
Woolscott
Lowsonford
Haseley
Lillington
Leamington Hastings
Willoughby
Hatton
Milverton
Braunston
Henley-in-Arden
Royal Leamington Spa
Grandborough
Preston Bagot
Budbrooke
Sawbridge
Broadwell
Hampton on the Hill
Offchurch
Claverdon
Warwick
Radford Semele
Long Itchington
Bascote
Stockton
Nethercote
Wootton Wawen
Whitnash
Flecknoe
Longbridge
Lower Shuckburgh
Daventry
Langley
Norton Lindsey
Edstone
Ufton
Southam
Wolverton
Heath End
Staverton
Sherbourne
Napton on the Hill
Bearley
Barford
Bishop's Tachbrook
Chapel Green
Upper Catesby
Snitterfield
Harbury
Wasperton
Ladbroke
Badby
Chesterton
Ingon
Warwick Services
Marston Doles
Wilmcote
Hampton Lucy
Newbold Pacey
Hellidon
Bishopton
Ashorne
Cross Green
Bishop's Itchington
Priors Marston
Alveston
Moreton Morrell
Charlecote
Charwelton
Priors Hardwick
Tiddington
Wellesbourne
Lighthorne
Shottery
Stratford-upon-Avon
Oxford Canal
Knightcote
Binton
Gaydon
Wormleighton
Upper Boddington
Byfield
Coventry Canal
Grand Union Canal
Ashby Canal

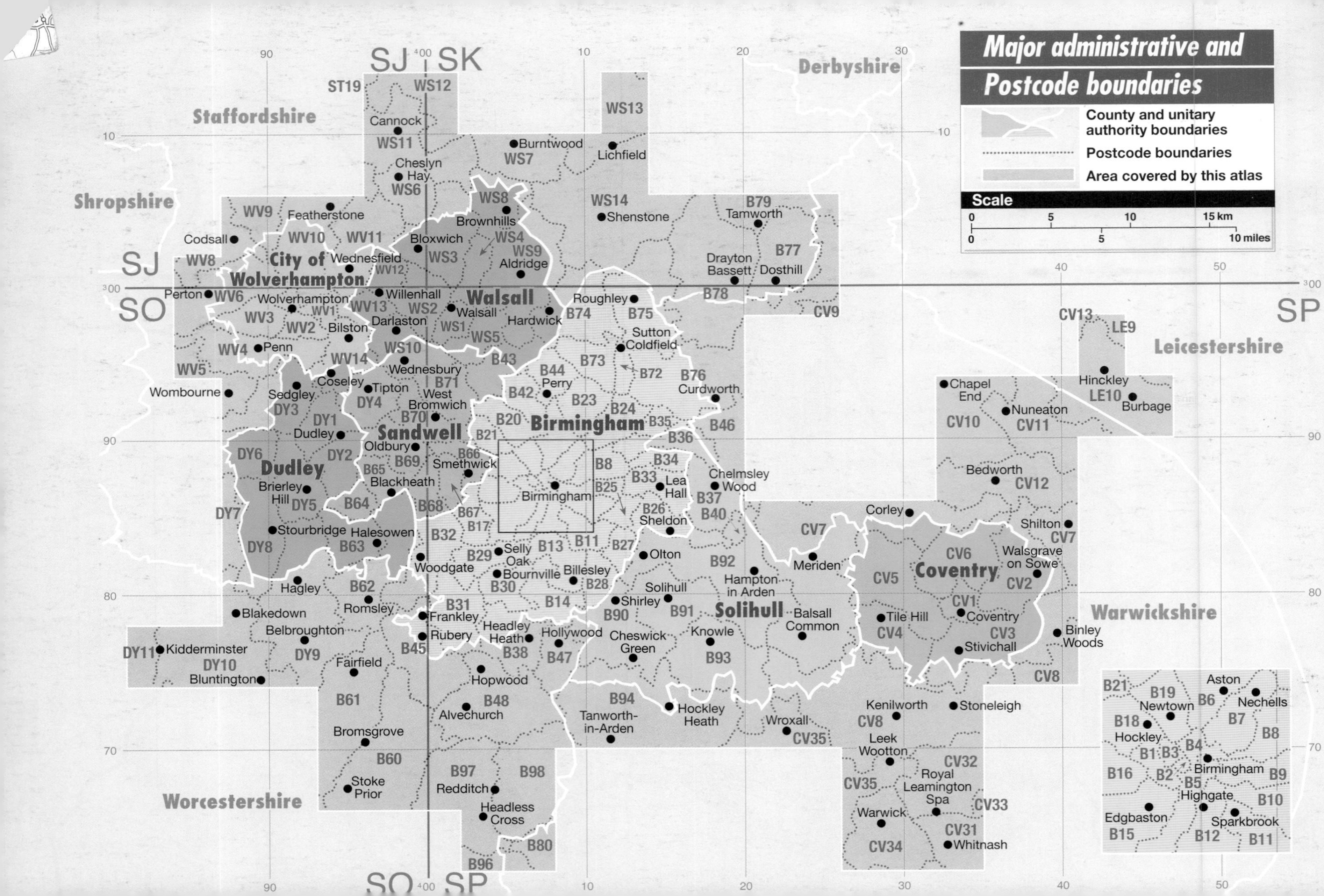
Major administrative and
Postcode boundaries
County and unitary authority boundaries
Postcode boundaries
Area covered by this atlas
Scale
0 5 10 15 km
0 5 10 miles
SJ SK
SO SP
Staffordshire
Shropshire
Derbyshire
Leicestershire
Warwickshire
Worcestershire
City of Wolverhampton
Walsall
Sandwell
Dudley
Birmingham
Solihull
Coventry
Cannock
Burntwood
Lichfield
Cheslyn Hay
Featherstone
Codsall
Brownhills
Shenstone
Tamworth
Bloxwich
Aldridge
Wednesfield
Drayton Bassett
Dosthill
Perton
Wolverhampton
Willenhall
Walsall
Hardwick
Roughley
Sutton Coldfield
Darlaston
Bilston
Penn
Wombourne
Sedgley
Coseley
Tipton
Wednesbury
West Bromwich
Perry
Curdworth
Dudley
Oldbury
Smethwick
Blackheath
Brierley Hill
Stourbridge
Halesowen
Chelmsley Wood
Lea Hall
Sheldon
Olton
Meriden
Corley
Chapel End
Nuneaton
Hinckley
Burbage
Bedworth
Shilton
Walsgrave on Sowe
Coventry
Tile Hill
Stivichall
Binley Woods
Selly Oak
Bournville
Billesley
Woodgate
Hagley
Romsley
Frankley
Rubery
Headley Heath
Hollywood
Shirley
Solihull
Hampton in Arden
Balsall Common
Cheswick Green
Knowle
Blakedown
Belbroughton
Kidderminster
Bluntington
Fairfield
Hopwood
Alvechurch
Bromsgrove
Stoke Prior
Redditch
Headless Cross
Tanworth-in-Arden
Hockley Heath
Wroxall
Kenilworth
Stoneleigh
Leek Wootton
Royal Leamington Spa
Warwick
Whitnash
Aston
Nechells
Newtown
Hockley
Birmingham
Highgate
Edgbaston
Sparkbrook
ST19 WS12 WS11 WS6 WS7 WS13 WS14 WS8 WS4 WS3 WS9 WS2 WS1 WS5 WS10
WV9 WV10 WV11 WV8 WV12 WV6 WV13 WV1 WV3 WV2 WV4 WV14 WV5
DY1 DY2 DY3 DY4 DY5 DY6 DY7 DY8 DY9 DY10 DY11
B79 B77 B78 B74 B75 B73 B72 B76 B44 B42 B43 B23 B24 B20 B21 B35 B46 B36 B71 B70 B69 B66 B65 B64 B68 B67 B17 B8 B34 B33 B25 B26 B37 B40 B32 B29 B13 B11 B27 B92 B63 B62 B30 B28 B14 B31 B90 B91 B45 B38 B47 B93 B61 B48 B94 B60 B97 B98 B80 B96
B21 B19 B6 B18 B7 B8 B1 B3 B4 B16 B2 B5 B9 B10 B15 B12 B11
CV9 CV13 LE9 LE10 CV10 CV11 CV12 CV7 CV6 CV5 CV2 CV1 CV4 CV3 CV8 CV35 CV32 CV33 CV31 CV34

2

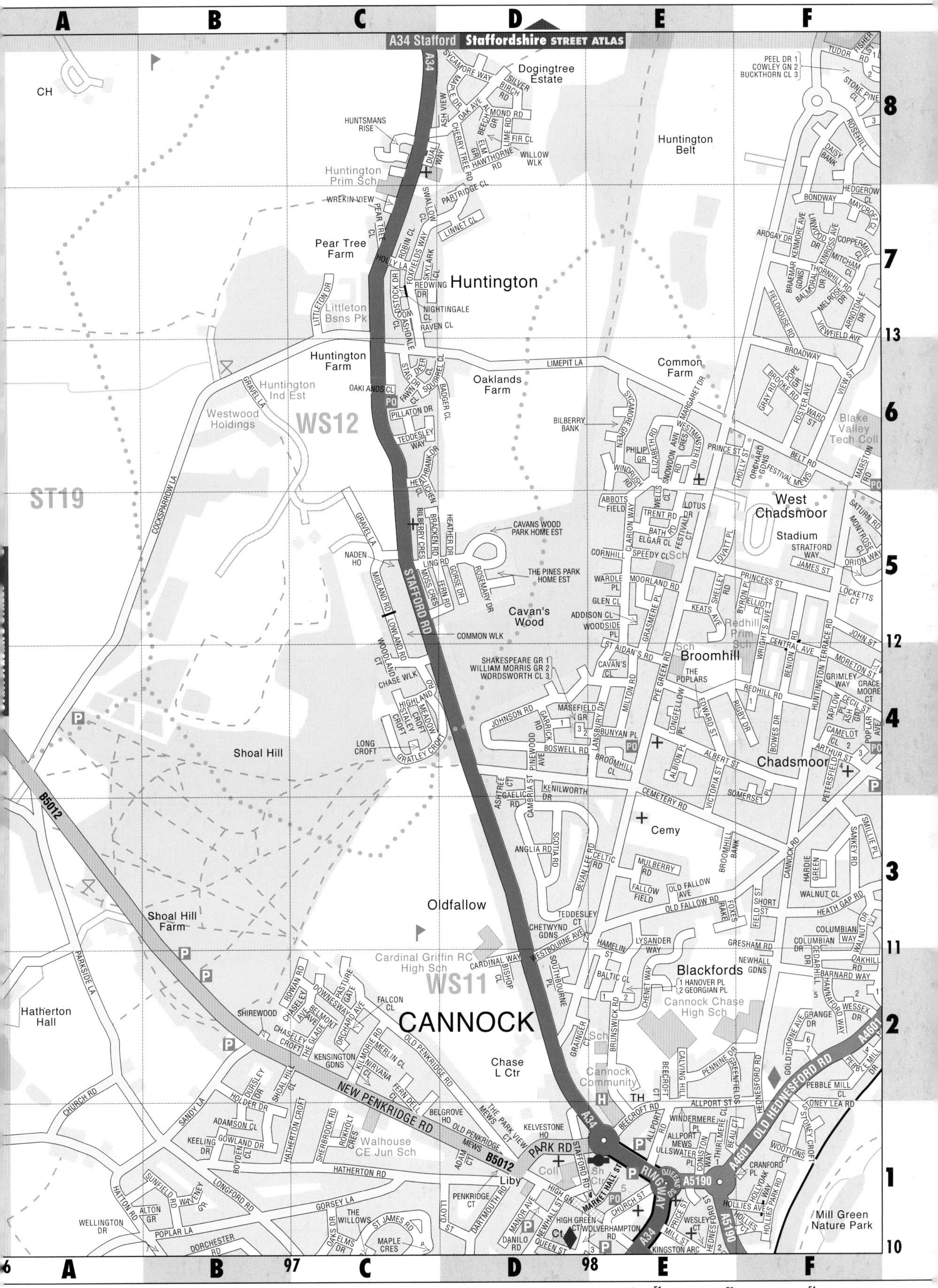

4
2

E1
1 WEAVING GDNS
2 KENILWORTH CT
3 BACKCROFTS
4 MARKET PL
5 The Forum

F2
1 MELBURY WAY
2 MELCHESTER WLK
3 STONEYFIELDS CL
4 MILLBROOK CL
5 EXONBURY WLK
6 STRATHMORE PL
7 HAWKESVILLE DR

F4
1 WOODFORD END
2 AVALON HO
3 HORTON CL
4 BETHANY MEWS

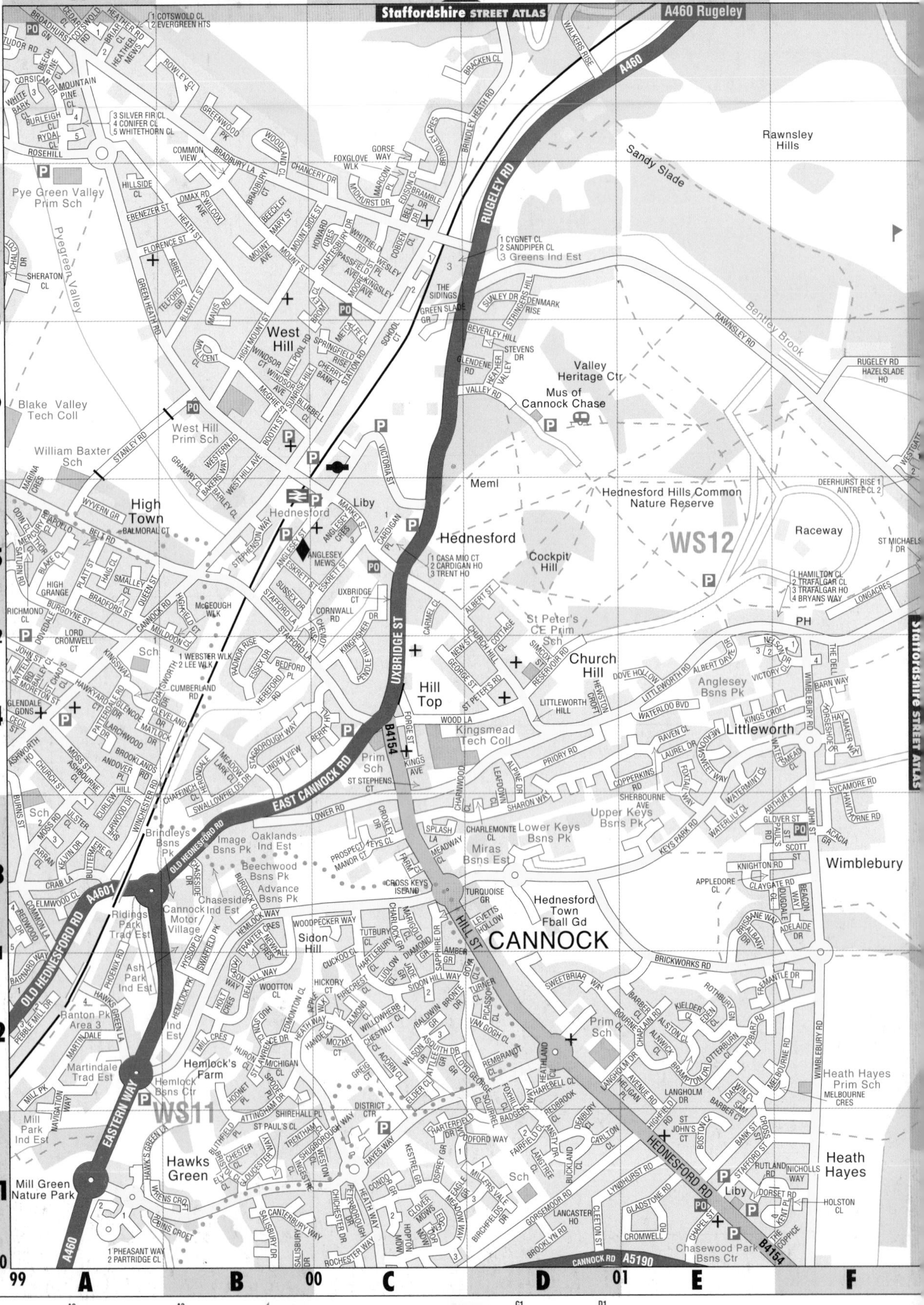

A2
1 D'UBERVILLE WLK
2 MARSHWOOD CL
3 RIDINGS BROOK DR
4 THE FIRS MOBILE HOME PK

A3
1 GLENDAWN CL
2 PATRICK HO
3 FIRCROFT CL
4 VERMONT GN
5 MEADOW HILL DR

1

5

C1
1 WHEATLANDS CL
2 GREEN MDWS
3 BUCKINGHAM PL

C2
1 PRIMROSE MDW
2 ROSE BAY MDW
3 CALLAGHAN GR

D1
1 SPINDLEWOOD CL
2 LAWNSWOOD CL
3 THISTLEDOWN DR

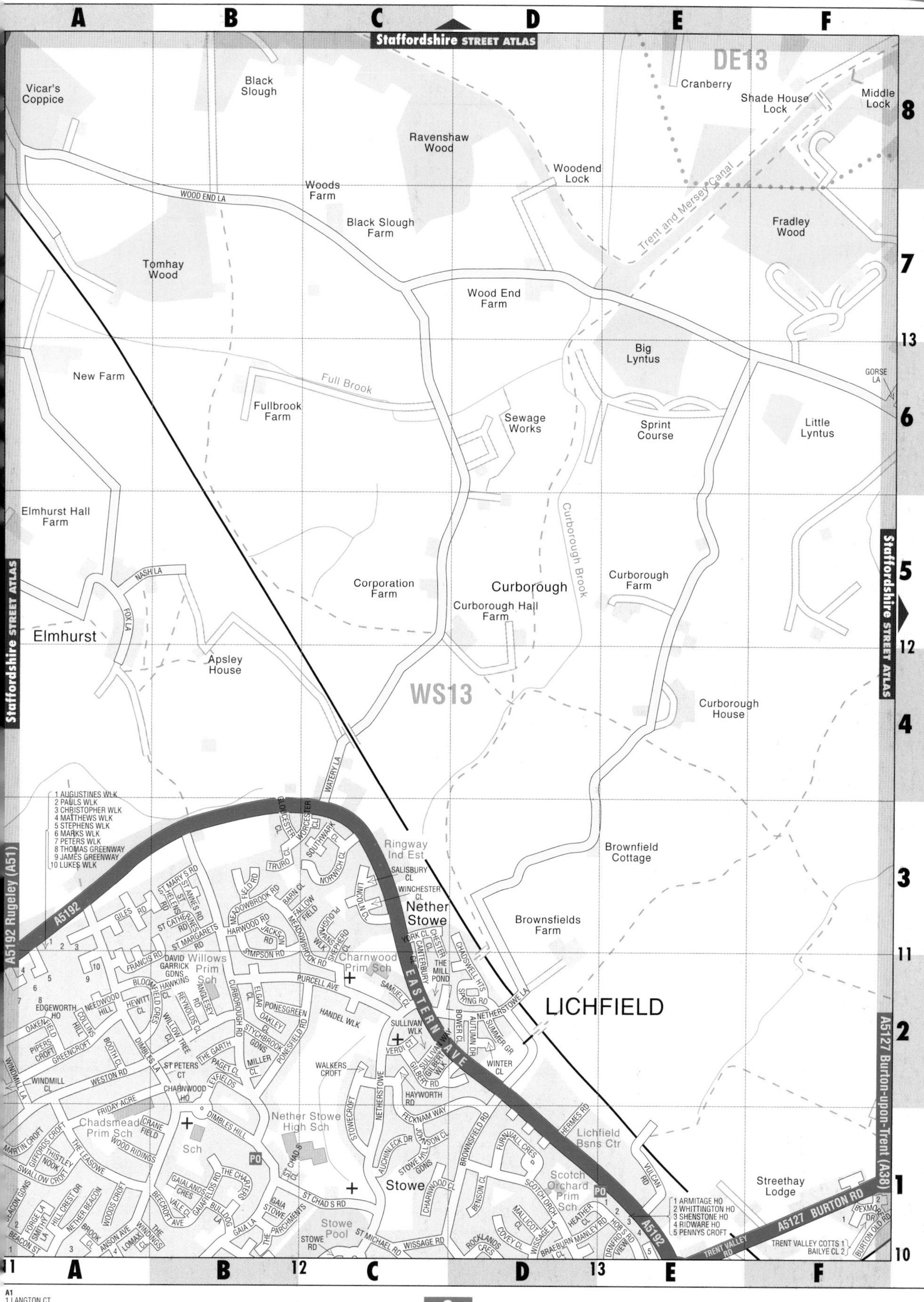

A1
1 LANGTON CT
2 CLEAVELAND MEWS
3 LITTLE BARROW WLK
4 DARWIN CL

1

E8
1 BACKCROFTS
2 HALLCOURT CRES
3 HALLCOURT CL
4 CAXTON CT
5 FAIRMOUNT DR
6 NEW ST

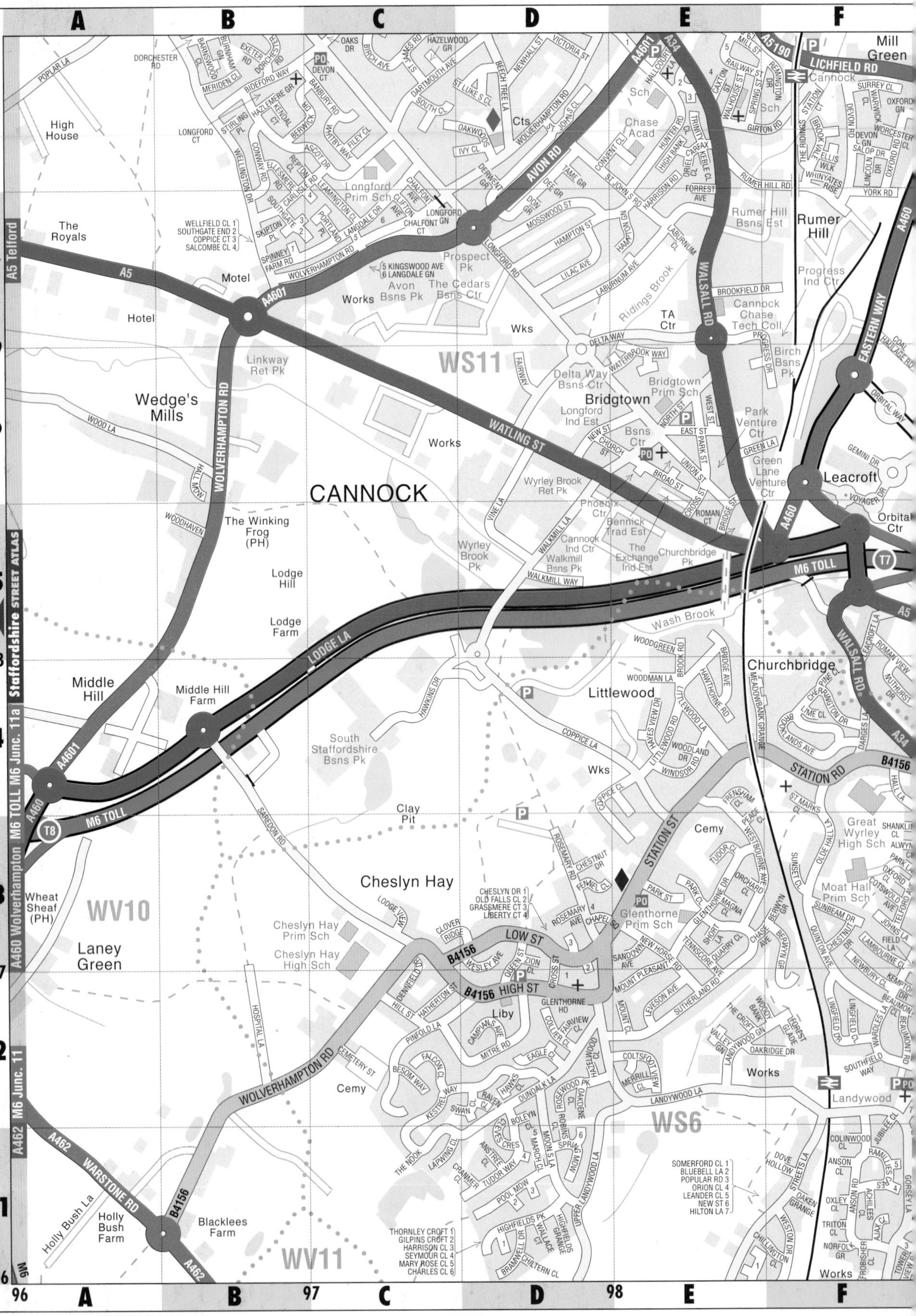

13

2
6
A B C D E F
CANNOCK RD
LICHFIELD RD
A5190
A460
EASTERN WAY
WS12
WS11
WS6
WS3
Newlands Lane
NEWLANDS LA
OLD HALL LA
NORTON LA
Tip
Leacroft
ORBITAL WAY
Streetway Farm
Norton Canes
Long Lane
Newlands Brook
WASHBROOK LA
STOKE'S LA
B4154 NORTON RD
HEDNESFORD RD
Jerome Prim Sch
CHAPEL ST
NORTON GREEN LA
CHURCH RD
NORTON HALL LA
Toll
WATLING ST
M6 TOLL
Fleur de Lys (PH)
Norton Green
Turf Inn (PH)
A5
Works
Apex Bsns Pk
WALSALL RD
Great Wyrley
St Thomas More RC Prim Sch
KINGSWOOD COLLIERY CVN SITE
HAZEL LA
Mine (dis)
Gains Brook
GAINS LA
SCHOOL LA
Yates Ind Est
LIME LA
GORSEY LA
Gorsey Lane Farm
Pelsall Road Bridge
JONES LA
Home Farm
JACOB'S HALL LA
Jacob's Hall
DARK LA
Cadman's Lane
WYRLEY LA
Hall Farm
GROVE LA
A34
Liby
PH
00
01
06
07
08
09
1 2 3 4 5 6 7 8
14
6

5

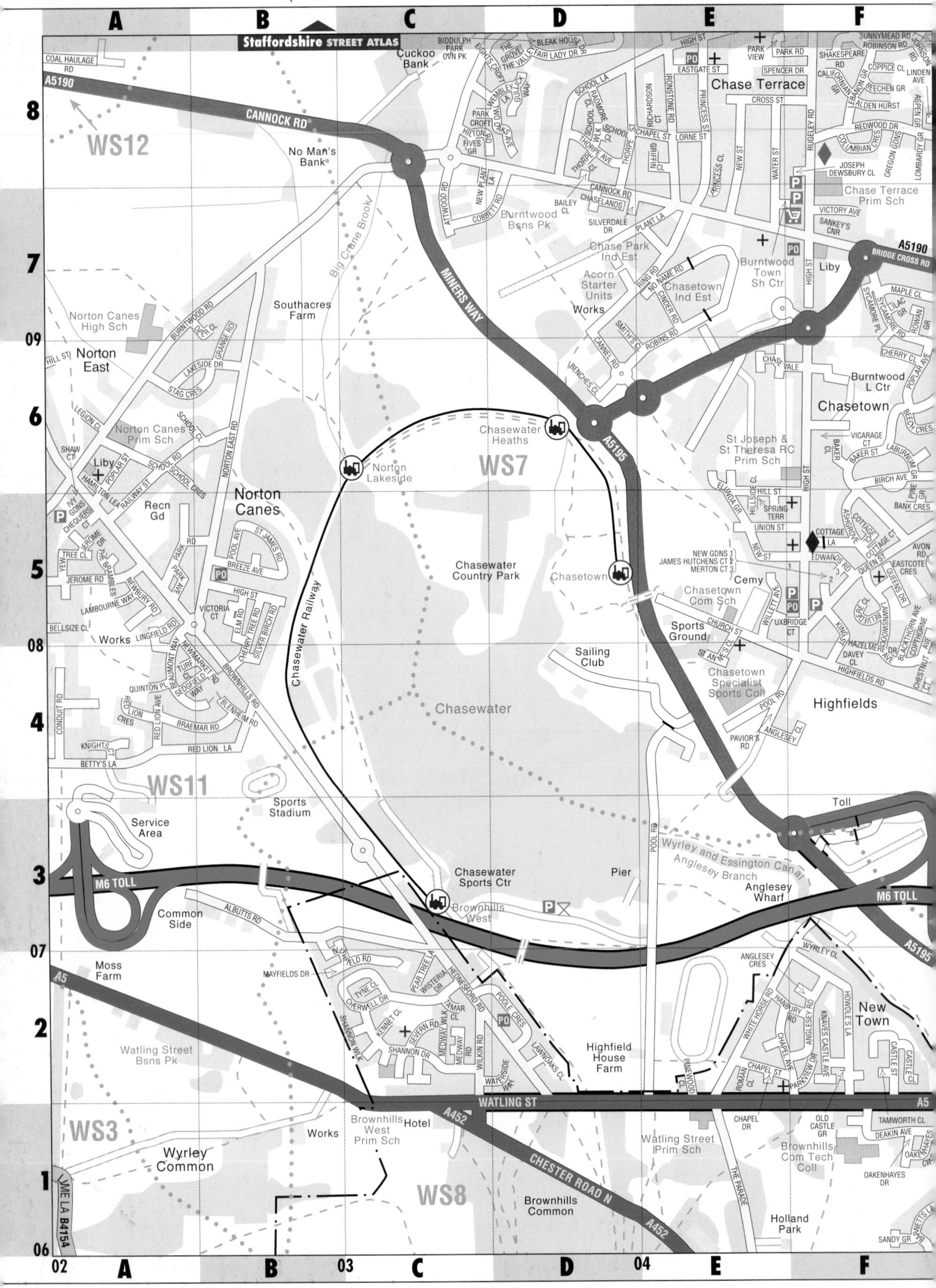
A
B
C
D
E
F
Staffordshire STREET ATLAS
8
7
09
6
5
08
4
3
07
2
1
06
02
03
04
COAL HAULAGE RD
A5190
CANNOCK RD
WS12
Cuckoo Bank
BIDDULPH PARK
OVN PK
EIGHTS CROFT
THE GROVE
THE VALLEY
BLEAK HOUSE DR
FAIR LADY DR
WEMBLEY LA
TWO OAKS AVE
GULLICK WAY
PARK CROFT
HILTON RD
FIVES GR
No Man's Bank
ATTWOOD RD
NEW PLANT LA
COBBETT RD
Burntwood Bsns Pk
SCHOOL LA
RADMORE CL
SCHOOL WLK
SCHOOL CL
THORPE AVE
THORPE CL
THORPE ST
RICHARDSON CT
CHAPEL ST
GRIFFIN CL
IRONSTONE RD
PRINCESS ST
LORNE ST
PRINCESS CL
NEW ST
WATER ST
HIGH ST
EASTGATE ST
PO
PARK VIEW
PARK RD
SPENCER DR
Chase Terrace
CROSS ST
RUGELEY RD
SUNNYMEAD RD
ROBINSON RD
JOHNSON RD
SHAKESPEARE RD
COPPICE CL
CALIFORNIAN GR
LEBANON GR
LINDEN AVE
BEECHEN GR
ALDEN HURST
REDWOOD DR
COLUMBIAN CRES
OREGON GDNS
ASPEN GR
LOMBARDY GR
JOSEPH DEWSBURY CL
Chase Terrace Prim Sch
VICTORY AVE
SANKEY'S CNR
BAILEY CL
CANNOCK RD
CHASELANDS
SILVERDALE DR
PLANT LA
Chase Park Ind Est
Acorn Starter Units
Works
RING RD
NO NAME RD
CINDER RD
Chasetown Ind Est
SMITH'S CL
ROBINS RD
CANNEL RD
BENCHES CL
Burntwood Town Sh Ctr
HIGH ST
Liby
A5190
BRIDGE CROSS RD
MAPLE CL
SYCAMORE PL
LILAC GR
SYCAMORE RD
ROWAN GR
CHERRY CL
POPLAR AVE
CHASE VALE
Burntwood L Ctr
Chasetown
BEECH CRES
VICARAGE CT
BAKER CL
BAKER ST
LABURNUM GR
BIRCH AVE
PINE GR
BANK CRES
St Joseph & St Theresa RC Prim Sch
ELMDALE GR
HILLSIDE CL
HILL ST
SPRING TERR
UNION ST
NEW ST
COTTAGE LA
COTTAGE ST
ASHGROVE
AVON RD
EASTCOTE CRES
QUEEN ST
QUEENS DR
NEW GDNS 1
JAMES HUTCHENS CT 2
MERTON CT 3
EDWARDS RD
Cemy
Chasetown Com Sch
WILLETT AVE
UXBRIDGE CT
CHURCH ST
BELVEDERE CL
LAWNSWOOD AVE
BLACKTHORN AVE
COPTHORNE AVE
KING ST
HAZELMERE DR
DAVEY CL
CHESTNUT CL
HIGHFIELDS RD
Sports Ground
ST ANNE'S CL
Chasetown Specialist Sports Coll
POOL RD
Highfields
PAVIOR'S RD
ANGLESEY CL
MINERS WAY
Big Crane Brook
Southacres Farm
Norton Canes High Sch
HILL ST
Norton East
BURNTWOOD RD
DYER CL
GRANGE RD
LAKESIDE DR
STAG CRES
LEGION CL
Norton Canes Prim Sch
SCHOOL CL
SHAW CT
Liby
POPLAR ST
SCHOOL RD
SCHOOL CRES
NORTON EAST RD
HAMILTON LEA
RAILWAY ST
IVY GDNS
CHEQUERS CT
Recn Gd
Norton Canes
POOL AVE
ST JAMES RD
BREEZE AVE
PARK RD
PARK AVE
YEW TREE CL
JEROME DR
THE BRAMBLES
JEROME RD
NEWBURY RD
LAMBOURNE WAY
HIGH ST
VICTORIA CT
ELM RD
CHERRY TREE RD
SILVER BIRCH RD
BELLSIZE CL
Works
LINGFIELD RD
BEAUMONT WAY
NEWMARKET RD
TURF CL
SEDGEFIELD WAY
QUINTON PL
BROWNHILLS RD
BLENHEIM RD
CONDUIT RD
RED LION CRES
RED LION AVE
BRAEMAR RD
KNIGHTS CT
BETTY'S LA
RED LION LA
WS11
Chasewater Heaths
Norton Lakeside
WS7
Chasewater Country Park
Chasetown
A5195
Chasewater Railway
Sailing Club
Chasewater
Sports Stadium
Service Area
Toll
POOL RD
Wyrley and Essington Canal Anglesey Branch
Chasewater Sports Ctr
Pier
Anglesey Wharf
M6 TOLL
Brownhills West
Common Side
ALBUTTS RD
M6 TOLL
A5195
Moss Farm
MAYFIELDS DR
FIELD RD
TYNE CL
CHERWELL DR
PEAR TREE LA
WISTERIA DR
HEDNESFORD RD
TAMAR CL
POOLE CRES
KENNET CL
SEVERN RD
SHANNON WLK
SHANNON DR
MEDWAY WLK
MEDWAY RD
WILKIN RD
WATERSIDE WAY
LAWNOAKS CL
Highfield House Farm
PINEWOOD CL
ANGLESEY CRES
WYRLEY CL
WHITE HORSE RD
HANBURY RD
ANGLESEY RD
KNAVES CASTLE AVE
HOWDLES LA
New Town
CHAPEL AVE
ROMAN CL
CHAPEL ST
PARKVIEW DR
CASTLE ST
CASTLE CL
A5
Watling Street Bsns Pk
WATLING ST
A5
WS3
Brownhills West Prim Sch
Hotel
A452
Works
CHAPEL DR
OLD CASTLE GR
TAMWORTH CL
DEAKIN AVE
OAKENHAYES CRES
Wyrley Common
Watling Street Prim Sch
Brownhills Com Tech Coll
OAKENHAYES DR
CHESTER ROAD N
WS8
Brownhills Common
THE PARADE
Holland Park
LIME LA B4154
A452
SANDY GR
BARRETTS LA

5
15

A8
1 SUNNYMEAD RD
2 SHELLEY RD
3 RYECROFT DR
4 BAMPTON AVE

8

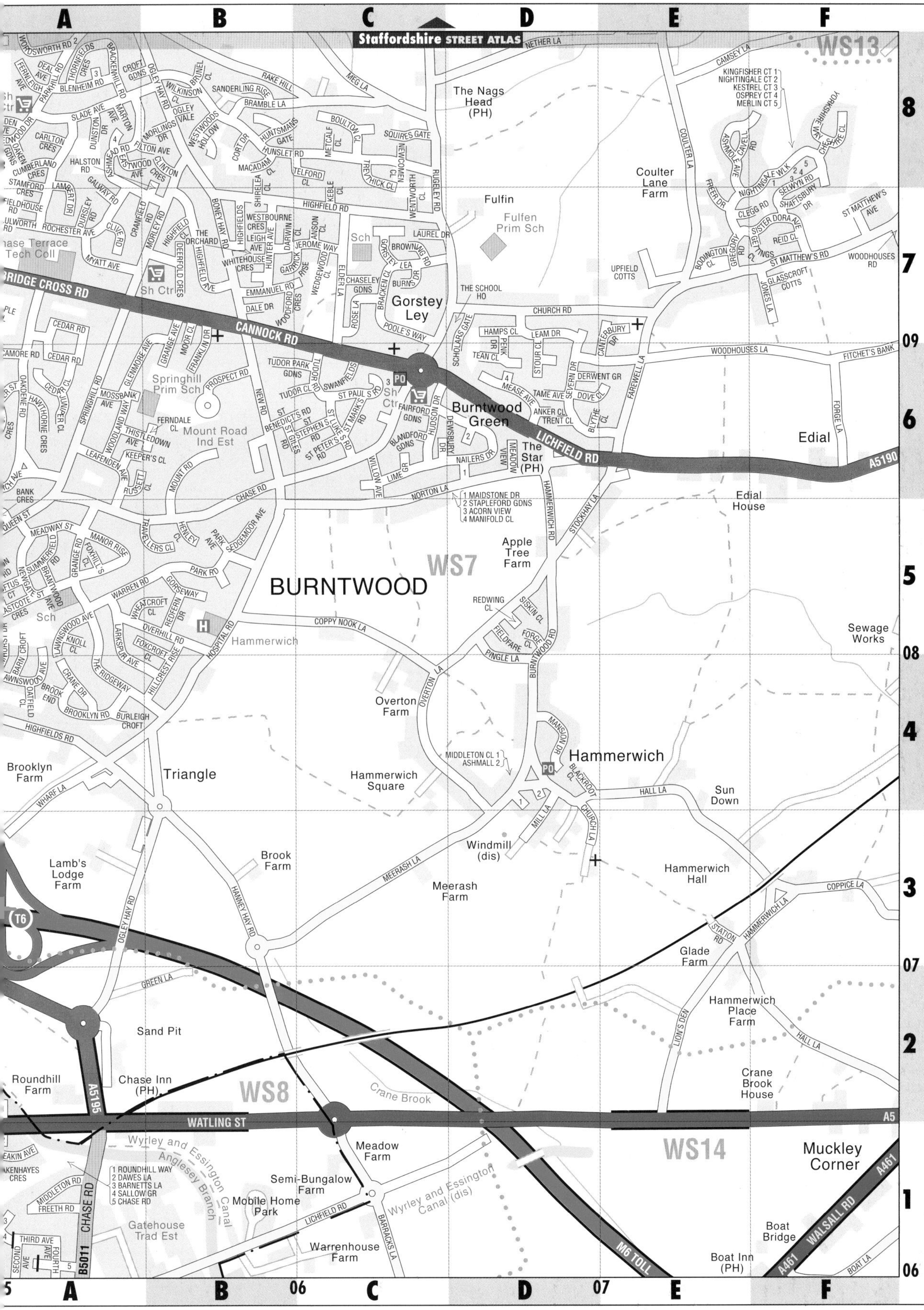

7

F6
1 BROADBENT CL
2 CATERBANCK WAY
3 COLLINS DR
4 MADDOCKE WLK
5 ALLINGTON AVE

7
17

A8
1 BEACONFIELDS
2 LILLINGTON CL
3 SECKHAM RD
4 JORDAN CL
5 BEACON MEWS

B7
1 CITY ARC
2 SARAH SIDDONS HO
3 TUDOR ROW
4 LEVETTS SQ
5 BAKER'S LA
6 CASTLE DYKE
7 HOMELODGE HO
8 GREEN CT
9 FORREST CT

B8
1 LOMBARD GDNS
2 ASHWORTH HO
3 ST CHADS CT
4 CATHEDRAL CT
5 THE CORN EXCHANGE

C8
1 HOULBROOKE HO
2 WILLIAM LUNN'S HOMES
3 THE CHEQUERS
4 DRAKE CROFT
5 MALLARD CROFT

E8
1 WITLEY DR
2 ASPEN CL
3 MULBERRY DR
4 LAMBOURNE CL
5 THE CROSSING

3

18

A B C D E F
Staffordshire STREET ATLAS
8 7 05 6 5 04 4 3 03 2 1 02
87 88 89
Long Birch Farm
Hunting Bridge
The Old Hattons
M54
M54 Telford
Staffordshire Way
PORT LA
The Middle Hattons
Lower Hattons Bridge
Ash Coppice
Ring Hill Covert
Gunstone Farm
Gunstone
WHITEHOUSE LA
Gunstone Hall
The Upper Hattons
River Penk
LAWN LA
UPPER HATTONS COTTS
PENDEFORD HALL LA
Upper Hattons Bridge
WV9
WV8
Monarch's Way
Shropshire Union Canal
WATERY LA
TEVIOT GDNS
RIVERSIDE GDNS
BROOKMEADOW
BROOK MDWS
MILLENNIUM WAY
THE FIELDS
OLD FARM DR
MAYTHORN GDNS 1
MEADOWS GR 2
SPRING MEADOWS CL 3
CHILLINGTON DR
CROMPTON CT
Moat Brook
Pendeford Mill Nature Reserve
Cvn Pk
MIDDLE LA
SANDY LA
ROSEVILLE GDNS
REEVES GDNS
SCHOOL CL
BILLBROOK RD
MILL STREAM CL
RAVENHILL DR
BROMLEY GDNS
YEW TREE GDNS
HAZEL GDNS
GLEN CT
SLADE GDNS
SHERBORNE GDNS
ELLIOTTS LA
L Ctr
Codsall Com High Sch
MANOR CL
ACACIA CRES
LIME TREE RD
COTTAGE VIEW
BEECROFT
MANOR HOUSE PK
Bilbrook
Sewage Works
WOBASTON RD
Lane Green Fst Sch
Bilbrook CE Mid Sch
JOEYS LA
HOMEFIELD RD
MILL GR
WITHERS RD
PENDEFORD MILL LA
Pendeford Bridge
Pendeford Bsns Pk
SIDESTRAND
OVERSTRAND
Gladman Bsns Quarter
Codsall
WILLOW DR
CEDAR GR
ORCHARD LA
LIME TREE GDNS
ASH CL
ELM GR
OAKLEIGH DR
WALNUT AVE
CHERRY TREE LA
CHERRY TREE GDNS
BILBROOK CT
ALEXANDER RD
Lane Green
LANE GREEN RD MASIONETTES
FLORENCE RD
CLIFTON GDNS
DOWNIE RD
PRIMROSE GDNS
Codsall Mid Sch
JASMINE GR
FORSYTHIA GR
CARTER AVE
PENDINAS DR
DUCK LA
BILBROOK GR
HEATH GR
LANE GREEN CT
BROOKFIELD RD
WOODSIDE
HISTONS HILL
WOLVERHAMPTON RD
PENDRELL CL
MAGNOLIA GR
AZALEA CL
Sch
Balliol Bsns Pk
Upper Pendeford Farm
CAMELLIA GDNS
FUCHSIA DR
JASMINE CL
IVY CROFT
CLEMATIS DR 1
LAVENDER CL 2
HATTONS GR
BROOK GR
RINGHILLS RD
Lane Green Shopping Par
PRINCES DR
PRINCES GDNS
Bilbrook
FARM RD
HEATH FARM RD
GREEN OAK RD
WESLEY RD
PRINCETON GDNS 1
QUADRILLE LAWNS 2
FARMSIDE GN 3
SOLENT CL 4
EXBURY CL 5
HAYWAIN CL 6
TYNING CL 7
THE DROVEWAY
TRAMWELL CL
WEYHILL CL
PAGHAM CL
SONNING DR
LEYBOURNE CRES
MARHOLM CL
SUCKLING GREEN LA
WHITEFIELD CL
WESLEY AVE
OAKFIELD RD
LANE GREEN RD
Lane Green Farm
Turnover Bridge
NEWCOTT CL
TEBWORTH CL
TIFFANY LA
HOWLAND CL
ELDRIDGE CL
OAKEN PARK
BIRCHES PARK RD
PARKES AVE
KYNASTON CRES
MADEIRA AVE
BIRCHES RD
BARNHURST LA
SMALLWOOD RD
FALLOWFIELD
TORFIELD
MIDDLEFIELD
WAYSIDE
SHEPHERDS WLK
DEER WLK
Pendeford
CORNFIELD
HALESWORTH RD
GREENACRE
MEADOW VALE
SOUTH VIEW CL
PALMERS CL
PALMERS WAY
CHARTERS AVE
Bilbrook Bridge
River Penk
THE COVERT
HARVESTERS WLK
BLANEFIELD
GLENFIELD
PLOUGHMANS WLK
KEEPERS LA
Birches Fst Sch
BIRCHES AVE
EASTWARD GLEN
LANE GREEN AVE
Aldersley High Sch
RUSSET WLK
BRACKEN CL
BARNWOOD RD
BARLEY CL
HEDGEROW WLK
RYEFIELD
Sch
GRANGEFIELD CL
REAPERS WLK
DUFFIELD CL
BRIDGEFOOT WLK
SHOLING CL
GAINFORD CL
PORTSWOOD CL
COATSGATE WLK
CATISFIELD CRES
HILSEA CL
Bedford Gorse
COLDRIDGE CL
LONG FURROW
GRANARY RD
THE GLADE
CROFTERS WLK
WHEATSHEAF RD
FORGE CL
THE HAYMARKET
COSGROVE WLK
CODSALL RD
WV6
FULLERTON CL
DROXFORD WLK
Sewage Works

12

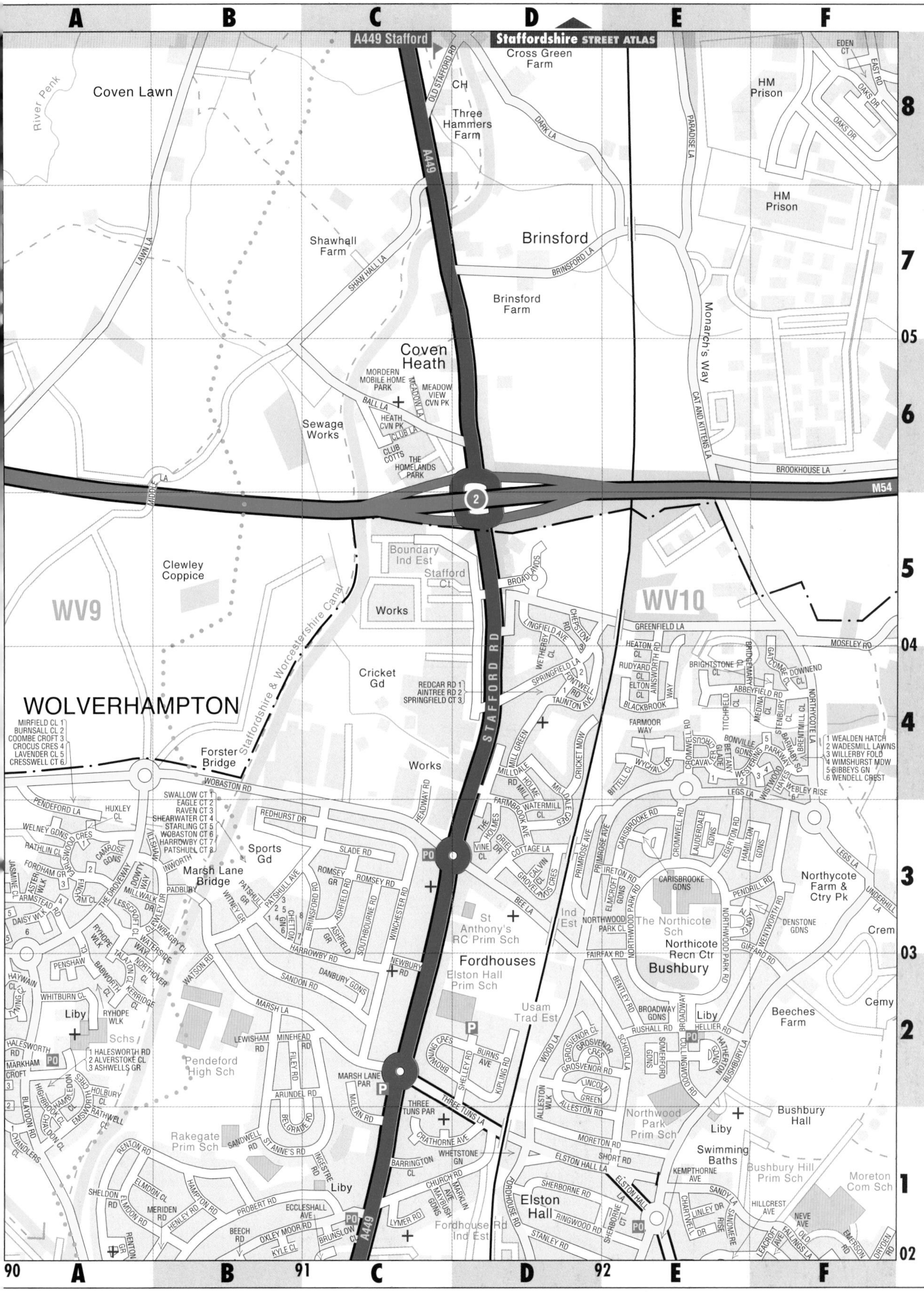

A449 Stafford
Staffordshire STREET ATLAS
Coven Lawn
River Penk
Cross Green Farm
CH
Three Hammers Farm
OLD STAFFORD RD
DARK LA
PARADISE LA
HM Prison
EDEN CT
EAST RD
OAKS DR
A449
Shawhall Farm
SHAW HALL LA
LAWN LA
Brinsford
BRINSFORD LA
Brinsford Farm
Monarch's Way
Coven Heath
MORDERN MOBILE HOME PARK
MEADOW LA
MEADOW VIEW CVN PK
BALL LA
HEATH CVN PK
CLUB LA
CLUB COTTS
THE HOMELANDS PARK
Sewage Works
CAT AND KITTENS LA
BROOKHOUSE LA
M54
MIDDLE LA
2
Boundary Ind Est
Stafford Ct
Works
BROADLANDS
Clewley Coppice
WV9
WV10
Staffordshire & Worcestershire Canal
Cricket Gd
REDCAR RD 1
AINTREE RD 2
SPRINGFIELD CT 3
STAFFORD RD
LINGFIELD AVE
CHEPSTOW RD
WETHERBY CL
SPRINGFIELD LA
FONTWELL RD
TAUNTON AVE
GREENFIELD LA
HEATON CL
RUDYARD CL
ELTON CL
AINSWORTH RD
BLACKBROOK WAY
BRIGHTSTONE CL
BRIDGEMARY CL
GATCOMBE CL
DOWNEND CL
MOSELEY RD
ABBEYFIELD RD
WOLVERHAMPTON
MIRFIELD CL 1
BURNSALL CL 2
COOMBE CROFT 3
CROCUS CRES 4
LAVENDER CL 5
CRESSWELL CT 6
Forster Bridge
Works
MILL GREEN
CRICKET MDW
FARMOOR WAY
WYCHALL DR
CROMWELL RD
CAVALIER CIRCUS
BONVILLE GDNS
WESTERING PARKWAY
1 WEALDEN HATCH
2 WADESMILL LAWNS
3 WILLERBY FOLD
4 WIMSHURST MDW
5 BIBBEYS GN
6 WENDELL CREST
WOBASTON RD
PENDEFORD LA
HUXLEY CL
SWALLOW CT 1
EAGLE CT 2
RAVEN CT 3
SHEARWATER CT 4
STARLING CT 5
WOBASTON CT 6
HARROWBY CT 7
PATSHULL CT 8
REDHURST DR
HEADWAY RD
MILLDALE RD
HOLME MILL
FARMBROOK AVE
WATERMILL CL
MILLDALE CRES
THE HOLMES
LEGS LA
WEBLEY RISE
Sports Gd
Marsh Lane Bridge
SLADE RD
ROMSEY GR
ROMSEY RD
PO
VINE CL
ORIEL CL
COTTAGE LA
CALVIN CL
GROVELANDS CRES
PRIMROSE AVE
CARISBROOKE RD
IRETON RD
CARISBROOKE GDNS
LAUDERDALE GDNS
EGERTON RD
HAMILTON GDNS
Northycote Farm & Ctry Pk
LEGS LA
UNDERHILL LA
THE DROVEWAY
DOWTY WAY
MILLWALK DR
INWORTH
PADBURY
PATSHULL AVE
BRINSFORD RD
ASHFIELD RD
SOUTHBOURNE RD
WINCHESTER RD
St Anthony's RC Prim Sch
BEE LA
Ind Est
NORTHWOOD PARK CL
The Northicote Sch
Northicote Recn Ctr
Bushbury
PENDRILL RD
WENTWORTH RD
DENSTONE GDNS
Crem
FAIRFAX RD
GIFFARD RD
HARROWBY RD
SANDON RD
DANBURY GDNS
NEWBURY RD
Fordhouses
Elston Hall Prim Sch
Usam Trad Est
BENTLEY RD
BROADWAY GDNS
RUSHALL RD
Liby
HELLIER RD
Beeches Farm
Cemy
WATSON RD
MARSH LA
LEWISHAM RD
MINEHEAD RD
FILEY RD
Pendeford High Sch
Liby
Schs
1 HALESWORTH RD
2 ALVERSTOKE CL
3 ASHWELLS GR
MARSH LANE PAR
P
BROWNING CRES
SHELLEY RD
BURNS AVE
KIPLING RD
WOOD LA
GROSVENOR CL
GROSVENOR CRES
GROSVENOR RD
LINCOLN GREEN
SCHOOL LA
SOMERFORD GDNS
BROADWAY
COLLINGWOOD RD
HATHERTON GDNS
BUSHBURY LA
ARUNDEL RD
BELGRADE RD
McLEAN RD
THREE TUNS PAR
THREE TUNS LA
ALLESTON WALK
ALLESTON RD
Northwood Park Prim Sch
Bushbury Hall
Rakegate Prim Sch
SANDWELL RD
ST ANNE'S RD
INGESTRE RD
CRATHORNE AVE
WHETSTONE GN
MORETON RD
SHORT RD
ELSTON HALL LA
Swimming Baths
KEMPTHORNE AVE
Bushbury Hill Prim Sch
Moreton Com Sch
RENTON RD
HAMPTON RD
HENLEY RD
MERIDEN RD
ELMDON CL
ELMDON RD
SHELDON RD
PROBERT RD
ECCLESHALL AVE
Liby
BARRINGTON CL
CHURCH RD
MARKLIN AVE
MAYBUSH GDNS
Fordhouse Rd Ind Est
FORDHOUSE RD
Elston Hall
SHERBORNE RD
RINGWOOD RD
STANLEY RD
SHERBORNE CT
CHARTWELL DR
LINLEY DR
SANDY LA
SANDMERE RISE
HILLCREST AVE
NEVE AVE
LEACROFT AVE
FALLINGS OLD
EMERSON RD
DRYDEN RD
BEECH RD
OXLEY MOOR RD
KYLE CL
BRUNSLOW CL
LYMER RD
RENTON GR
BLAYDON RD
CHANDLERS CL
CHALDON CL
HIGHBROOK CL
HAMBLEDON CL
EMSWORTH CRES
HOLBURY CL
RATHWELL CL
WHITBURN CL
HAYWAIN CL
PENSHAW CL
BARWORTH CL
KERRIDGE CL
NORTHOVER CL
TALATON CL
RYHOPE WLK
WATERSIDE CL
LESSCROFT CL
DAISY WLK
ARMSTEAD RD
JASMINE CL
ASTER WLK
FORDHAM GR
RATHLIN CL
WELNEY GDNS
CAMROSE GDNS
A B C D E F
8 7 05 6 5 04 4 3 03 2 1 02
90 91 92

25

12

11

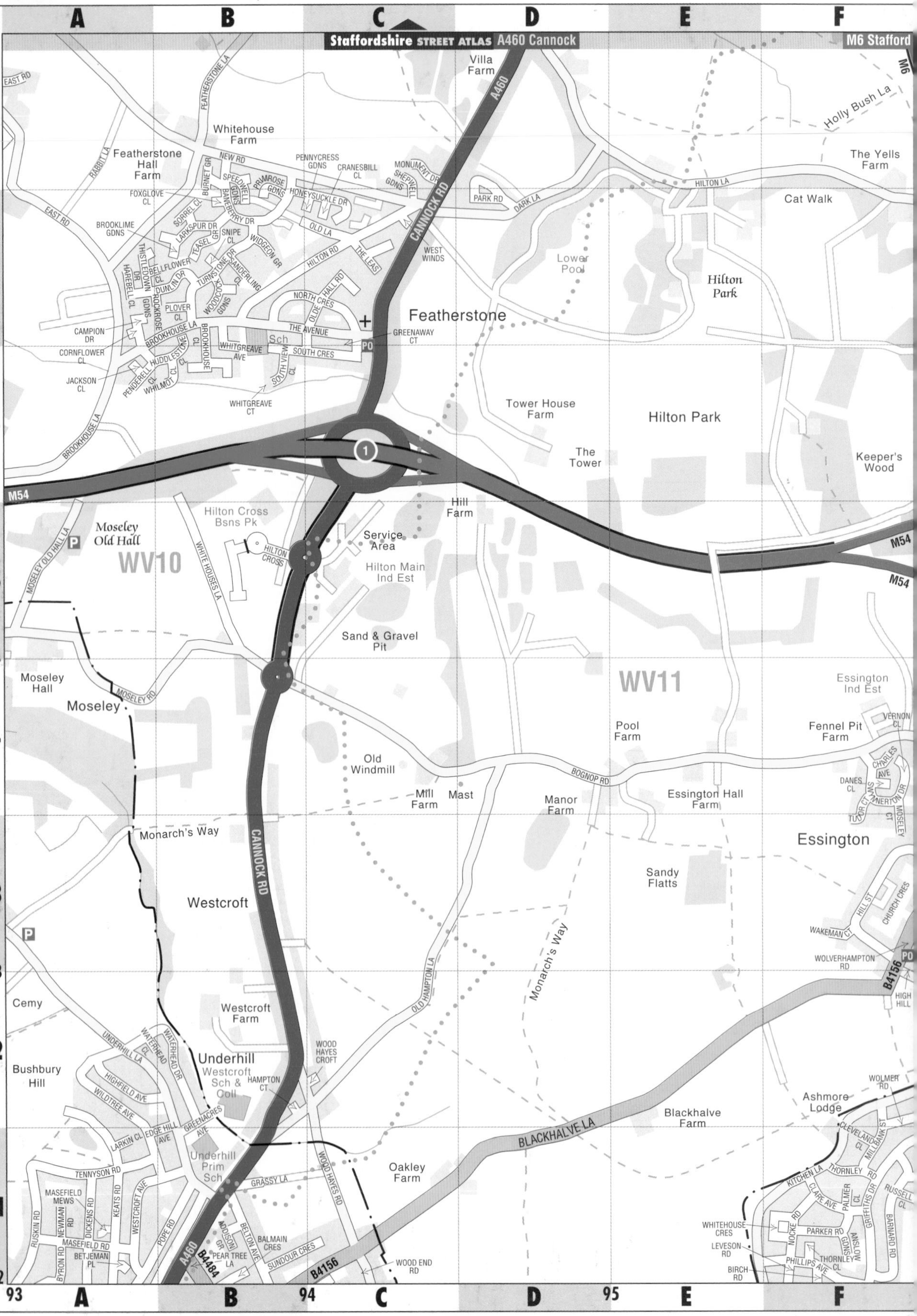
Staffordshire STREET ATLAS
A460 Cannock
M6 Stafford
Featherstone
Hilton Park
Featherstone Hall Farm
Whitehouse Farm
Villa Farm
The Yells Farm
Cat Walk
Lower Pool
Tower House Farm
The Tower
Keeper's Wood
Hill Farm
Service Area
Hilton Cross Bsns Pk
Hilton Main Ind Est
Sand & Gravel Pit
Moseley Old Hall
WV10
WV11
Moseley Hall
Moseley
Old Windmill
Mill Farm
Mast
Manor Farm
Pool Farm
Essington Hall Farm
Essington Ind Est
Fennel Pit Farm
Essington
Sandy Flatts
Monarch's Way
Westcroft
Westcroft Farm
Cemy
Bushbury Hill
Underhill
Westcroft Sch & Coll
Underhill Prim Sch
Oakley Farm
Blackhalve Farm
Ashmore Lodge
M54
A460
CANNOCK RD
BLACKHALVE LA
B4156
B4484
BOGNOP RD
HILTON LA
Holly Bush La
OLD HAMPTON LA
WOOD HAYES RD
MOSELEY RD
WHITE HOUSES LA
BROOKHOUSE LA
EAST RD
RABBIT LA
FEATHERSTONE LA
NEW RD
HILTON RD
THE AVENUE
SOUTH CRES
NORTH CRES
OLD LA
DARK LA
PARK RD
UNDERHILL LA
GRASSY LA
KITCHEN LA
WOLVERHAMPTON RD
WAKEMAN CT
HILTON CROSS
MOSELEY OLD HALL LA

A
B
C
D
E
F
8
7
05
6
5
04
4
3
03
2
1
02
97
98
WV10
WV11
WV12
WS6
WS3
M6
M54
10a
A462
B4210
B4156
A4124
Works
Warstone
Sewage Wks
HILTON LA
OLD WARSTONE LA
WARSTONE RD
Hilton Park Service Areas
Clay Pit
Ride Farm
Burns Wood
Holly Bank Farm
Chapel Farm
Mast
Springhill
PH
School Farm
St John's CE Prim Sch
HOBNOCK RD
BURSNIPS RD
BROAD LA
CH
Wood Farm Golf Range
Springhill Covert
Long Lane Bridge
LONG LA
The White House
NEW LANDYWOOD LA
OLD LANDYWOOD LA
UPPER LANDYWOOD LA
STRAWBERRY LA
Upper Landywood
SOMERFORD CL
WESTON DR
DUNSTON CL
PENDREL CL
STREETS LA
HOLLY HILL
HOLLY LA
Landywood Ent Pk
Landywood Prim Sch
GORSEY LA
TOWER VIEW RD
LILAC LA 1
PENNY CT 2
Wyrley and Essington Canal (disused)
Cemy
COXMOOR CL 1
TREVOSE CL 2
COALMEADOW CL 3
ROMSEY WAY 4
BOLTON WAY 5
FURNESS CL 6
TURNBERRY RD 7
FOUNTAINS WAY 8
PERSHORE WAY 9
EASBY WAY 10
MARGAM WAY 11
MARGAM TERR 12
GLASTONBURY WAY 13
SNEYD HALL RD 14
Bloxwich North
Abbey Prim Sch
Sneyd Farm
Sneyd Com Sch
BLOXWICH
Sneyd Resr
Farbrook Farm
RED LA
WITHYWOOD CL 1
BROCKERIDGE CL 2
FALCONDALE RD 3
CRANLEIGH CL 4
DORCHESTER RD 5
DORCHESTER CL 6
FAIRLAWN WAY 7
ARGYLL CT 8
GAIRLOCH RD 1
LONG MYND CL 2
HEBDEN GR 3
HIGH HILL
Holly Bank House
UPPER SNEYD RD
Ashmore Park
KITCHEN LA
DRUMMOND CL
ESSINGTON RD
SNEYD LA
LICHFIELD RD
WOLVERHAMPTON RD
ST JOHNS RD
FORREST AVE
KINGSWAY
HOLLYBANK AVE
MITRE CL
BROWNSHORE LA
BIRCHWOOD CL
GORSEMOOR WAY
BUTTERMERE DR
THIRLMERE DR
Sch
Mast
Farbrook Farm
BROOKHILL WAY
CRAB LA
LYNWOOD CL
VERNON WAY
MULBERRY RD
CROXDENE AVE
SHREWSBURY CL
KIRKSTALL CL
SELSDON RD
INGESTRE CL
WALTON HEATH
WHITBY CL
EVESHAM CRES
TEWKESBURY RD
WAVERLEY RD
ABBEY SQ
NETLEY RD
NEATH RD
ROCHE RD
FISHER RD
BUILDWAS CL
CHEPSTOW RD
CHEPSTOW WAY
SNEYD HO
HILTON RD
FAIRLAWN WAY
ASTORIA GDNS
RADSTOCK RD
KEWSTOKE RD
DRUID PARK RD
APPLEBY GDNS
TORRIDON RD
LOCHALSH GR
HEANTUN ROW
SIMMONS RD
SNAPE RD
HIGGS RD
GRIFFITHS DR
ROGERS CL
PERKS RD
ST ALBANS CL
GURNARD CL
BARGERY RD
BUCKNALL RD
HILL PL
ACORN RD
COPPICE CL
FERGUSON ST

13
5

A
B
C
D
E
F
8
7
05
6
5
04
4
3
03
2
1
02
99
00
01
Landywood
Oakenhayes Farm
Newtack Farm
WALSALL RD
A34
Cvn Site
HOBBLE END LA
LONG LA
Hobble End
Hobble End Farm
WS6
Cadman's La
DARK LA
Lower Farm
Little Wyrley Hall
Home Farm
Little Wyrley
WYRLEY LA
Wyrley Common Bridge
Wyrley Grove Bridge
Cannock Extension Canal
Green Bridge
Pelsall Common Bridge
Golf Range
CADMAN'S LA
Newtown
Pear Tree Farm
FISHLEY LA
Fishley Bridge (No 1)
Wood Common
Friar Bridge
Wyrley and Essington Canal
Pelsall Junction
Pelsall Wood
PH
Ivy House (PH)
Newtown Farm
WS3
Cemy
STAFFORD RD
Yieldfields Hall
Fishley
Beacon Way
Lower Farm Prim Sch
CH
WIGGIN HO
Little Bloxwich
Little Bloxwich CE Prim Sch
WOLVERHAMPTON RD
A4124
Pelsall Village Sch
1 DOWNFIELD CL
2 LYTHAM GR
3 WENTWORTH RD
4 ASTBURY CL
5 HOLLINWELL CL
6 THE BERKSHIRE
7 ALDEBURGH CL
8 MAXSTOKE CL
9 KEDLESTON CL
Broad Lane Farm
The Hills
Wallington Heath
B4210
BROAD LA
Walsall Acad
LICHFIELD RD
Goscote House Farm
Field House Farm
SHOWMANS CVN SITE
Works
1 DAVIES HO
2 CARTWRIGHT HO
3 CLARKE HO
4 WILKINS HO
BELL LA
SNEYD LA
A4124
SAND BANK
St Peter's RC Prim Sch
1 WIGHTWICK CL
2 ROCKINGHAM CL
3 QUEENS PAR
4 SAMUEL HO
5 CHURCH MOAT WAY
Cemy
HAMILTON HO
Green Rock Prim Sch
Works
Bloxwich
BLOXWICH
ELMORE GN RD
HIGH ST
Liby
PO
Sch
1 COALWAY RD
2 CROXSTALLS CL
Goscote Ind Est
Goscote Hall Bridge

13
28

6
16

A
B
C
D
E
F
8
7
05
6
5
04
4
3
03
2
1
02
03
04
WS11
WS8
WS3
WS9
WS4
BROWNHILLS
Wyrley Common
Engine Lane Spinney
Clay Pit
Coppice Side Ind Est
Wyrley Hayes
Big House Farm
The Slough
Beck's Bridge
Works
Beacon Way
Coopers Bridge
Wyrley and Essington Canal
Catshill Junction Bridge
High Bridge Bridge
Highbridge
York's Bridge
Holy Trinity CE Prim Sch
Recn Gd
Clayhanger
Brownhills Bsns Pk
Maybrook Ind Est
Ryder's Hayes Farm
Sewage Works
Ryder's Hayes Crossing
Railswood Farm
Ford Brook
Grange Farm
Oak Park
L Ctr
Walsall Wood
Dairy Farm
Liby
Sch
Pelsall
Pelsall Common
High Heath
Shelfield Sports & Com Coll
Barons Court Trad Est
Cemy
Vigo
Highfield Farm
Hotel
Lathams Bridge
Pit (dis)
Brick Kiln Pool
Daw End Branch
Clay Pit
Brick Works
Empire Ind Est
Heath End
Rushall JMI Sch
Nursery
Shelfield
St Bernadette's RC Prim Sch
St James Prim Sch
Superstore
PH
CHESTER ROAD N
PELSALL RD
LICHFIELD RD
WOLVERHAMPTON RD
NORTON RD
LIME LA
WALSALL RD
HIGH ST
COPPICE RD
LINDON RD
A452
A4124
A461
B4154
B4155
B4152
B4153
29
16

15
7

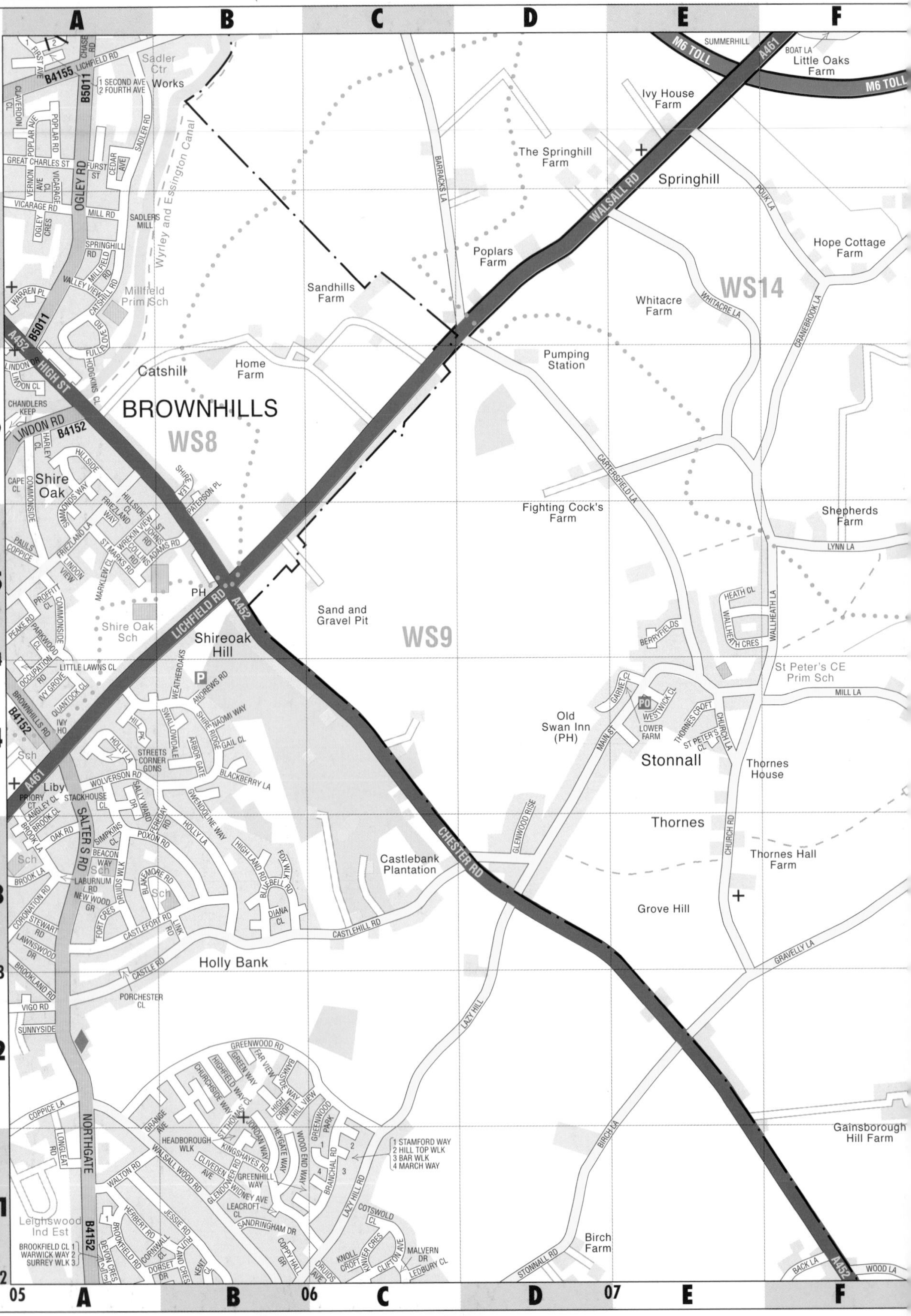
A
B
C
D
E
F
8
7
6
5
4
3
2
1
05
04
03
02
06
07
BROWNHILLS
WS8
WS9
WS14
Sadler Ctr
Works
Wyrley and Essington Canal
M6 TOLL
SUMMERHILL
BOAT LA
Little Oaks Farm
Ivy House Farm
The Springhill Farm
Springhill
WALSALL RD
A461
BARRACKS LA
POUK LA
Hope Cottage Farm
Poplars Farm
Sandhills Farm
Whitacre Farm
WHITACRE LA
CRANEBROOK LA
Pumping Station
Catshill
Home Farm
Millfield Prim Sch
CARTERSFIELD LA
Fighting Cock's Farm
Shepherds Farm
LYNN LA
HEATH CL
WALLHEATH CRES
WALLHEATH LA
BERRYFIELDS
St Peter's CE Prim Sch
MILL LA
Old Swan Inn (PH)
GARNET CL
WESTWICK CL
LOWER FARM
THORNES CROFT
ST PETER'S CL
CHURCH LA
MAIN ST
Stonnall
Thornes House
Thornes
CHURCH RD
Thornes Hall Farm
Grove Hill
GRAVELLY LA
Sand and Gravel Pit
Castlebank Plantation
CHESTER RD
A452
GLENWOOD RISE
LAZY HILL
Shireoak Hill
LICHFIELD RD
Shire Oak Sch
PH
HIGH ST
LINDON RD
B4152
B5011
B4155
LICHFIELD RD
CHASE RD
FIRST AVE
1 SECOND AVE
2 FOURTH AVE
CLAVERDON CL
POPLAR AVE
POPLAR RD
OGLEY RD
GREAT CHARLES ST
FURST ST
CEDAR AVE
SADLER RD
VERNON AVE
VICARAGE CL
VICARAGE RD
MILL RD
SADLERS MILL
OGLEY CRES
SPRINGHILL RD
MILLFIELD RD
VALLEY VIEW
CATSHILL RD
WARREN PL
FULLBROOK RD
HODGKINS CL
LINDON DR
LINDON CL
CHANDLERS KEEP
HARLEY CL
HILLSIDE
Shire Oak
CAPE CL
COMMONSIDE
SIMMONDS WAY
FRIEZLAND WAY
FRIEZLAND LA
HILLSIDE CL
WREKIN VIEW RD
ST JOHNS RD
COLLINS RD
ST MARKS RD
ADAMS RD
SHIRE LEA
PATERSON PL
PAULS COPPICE
LINDON VIEW
MARKLEW CL
PROFFITT CL
PEAKE RD
PARKWOOD CL
OCCUPATION RD
LITTLE LAWNS CL
IVY GROVE
QUANTOCK CL
BROWNHILLS RD
IVY HO
Sch
WEATHEROAKS
ANDREWS RD
NAOMI WAY
SWALLOWDALE
SHIRE RIDGE
GAIL CL
HILL PK
HOLLY LA
STREETS CORNER GDNS
ARBOR GATE
BLACKBERRY LA
Liby
WOLVERSON RD
PRIORY CT
ANGLEY CL
BROOK CL
BROOK LA
STACKHOUSE CL
SALLY WARD DR
FEREDAY RD
GWENDOLINE WAY
HOLLY LA
SIMPKINS CL
OAK RD
POXON RD
BEACON WAY
SALTERS RD
HIGH LAND RD
FOX WLK
BLUEBELL RD
DIANA CL
LABURNUM RD
DRUIDS WLK
BLAKEMORE RD
NEW WOOD GR
FORT CRES
CASTLEFORT RD
LINK RD
CASTLEHILL RD
CORONATION RD
STEWART RD
LAWNSWOOD DR
BROOKLAND RD
Holly Bank
CASTLE RD
PORCHESTER CL
VIGO RD
SUNNYSIDE
GREENWOOD RD
HIGHFIELD WAY
GREEN WAY
FAR VIEW
CHURCHSIDE WAY
BARNSIDE WAY
HIGH CROFT
HILL VIEW
GREENWOOD PARK
ST THOMAS CL
JORDAN WAY
HEYGATE WAY
WOOD END WAY
GRANGE AVE
HEADBOROUGH WLK
KINGSHAYES RD
CLIVEDEN AVE
GLENDOWER RD
GREENHILL WAY
WIDNEY AVE
LEACROFT CL
SANDRINGHAM DR
BRANCHAL RD
LAZY HILL RD
1 STAMFORD WAY
2 HILL TOP WLK
3 BAR WLK
4 MARCH WAY
COPPICE LA
LONGLEAT RD
NORTHGATE
WALTON RD
WALSALL WOOD RD
HERBERT RD
JESSIE RD
RUTLAND CRES
KENT CL
CORNWALL CL
DORSET DR
BROOKFIELD RD
DEVON CRES
COPPY HALL GR
DRUIDS AVE
KNOLL CROFT
KINVER CRES
CLIFTON AVE
COTSWOLD CL
MALVERN DR
LEDBURY CL
Leighswood Ind Est
BROOKFIELD CL 1
WARWICK WAY 2
SURREY WLK 3
B4152
BIRCH LA
Birch Farm
STONNALL RD
Gainsborough Hill Farm
BACK LA
WOOD LA

15
30

A
B
C
D
E
F
M6 TOLL
Barn Farm
Hilton
Hilton Farm
CRANEBROOK LA
Bullmoor Lane Covert
BULLMOOR LA
HORSLEY LA
Chesterfield Lodge
Chesterfield Farm
Chesterfield
Lawton Grange
Crane Brook
Raikes Covert
ASHCROFT LA
Cranebrook Farm
Gayley Cottage
RAIKES LA
Poultry Houses
Keeper's Cottage
Ashcroft Farm
ESSINGTON CL
THORNYHURST LA
Lynn Lane House
Malkin's Coppice
FODEN CL
MILLBROOK DR
GROSVENOR CT
PINFOLD HILL
HOLM VIEW CL
LINCROFT
ASTON CL
PO
LYNN LA
BIRCH BROOK LA
Shenstone
STATION RD
TRINITY CL
MAIN ST
Dairy Farm
Birchbrook Ind Pk
STATION COTTS
NEW RD
CHURCH RD
ADMIRAL PARKER DR
The Bungalow
Owletts Hall Farm
RICHARD COOPER RD
FOOTHERLEY RD
ST JOHNS HILL
Lynn
The Nurseries
Footherley Rough
HOLLY HILL RD
THE FARTHINGS
CHESTNUT DR
WS14
HOLLYHILL LA
ST JOHNS DR
Laurels Farm
Swan Farm
MILL LA
Keeper's Cottage
COURT DR
Spinney Farm
Lower Stonnall
FOOTHERLEY LA
Footherley Hall
Shenstone Court
HOOK LA
NEW BARNS LA
Home Farm
GRAVELLY LA
FOOTHERLEY LA
Footherley
New Barns Farm
Griffin's Covert
Footherley Brook
WS9
Cockheath Coppice
Footherley Farm
Croft Farm
White's Farm
Bagot's Barn
WOOD LA
MOOR LA
Biddle's Field Wood
Bosses
BACK LA
FORGE LA
8
7
05
6
5
04
4
3
03
2
1
02
08
09
10

17
9

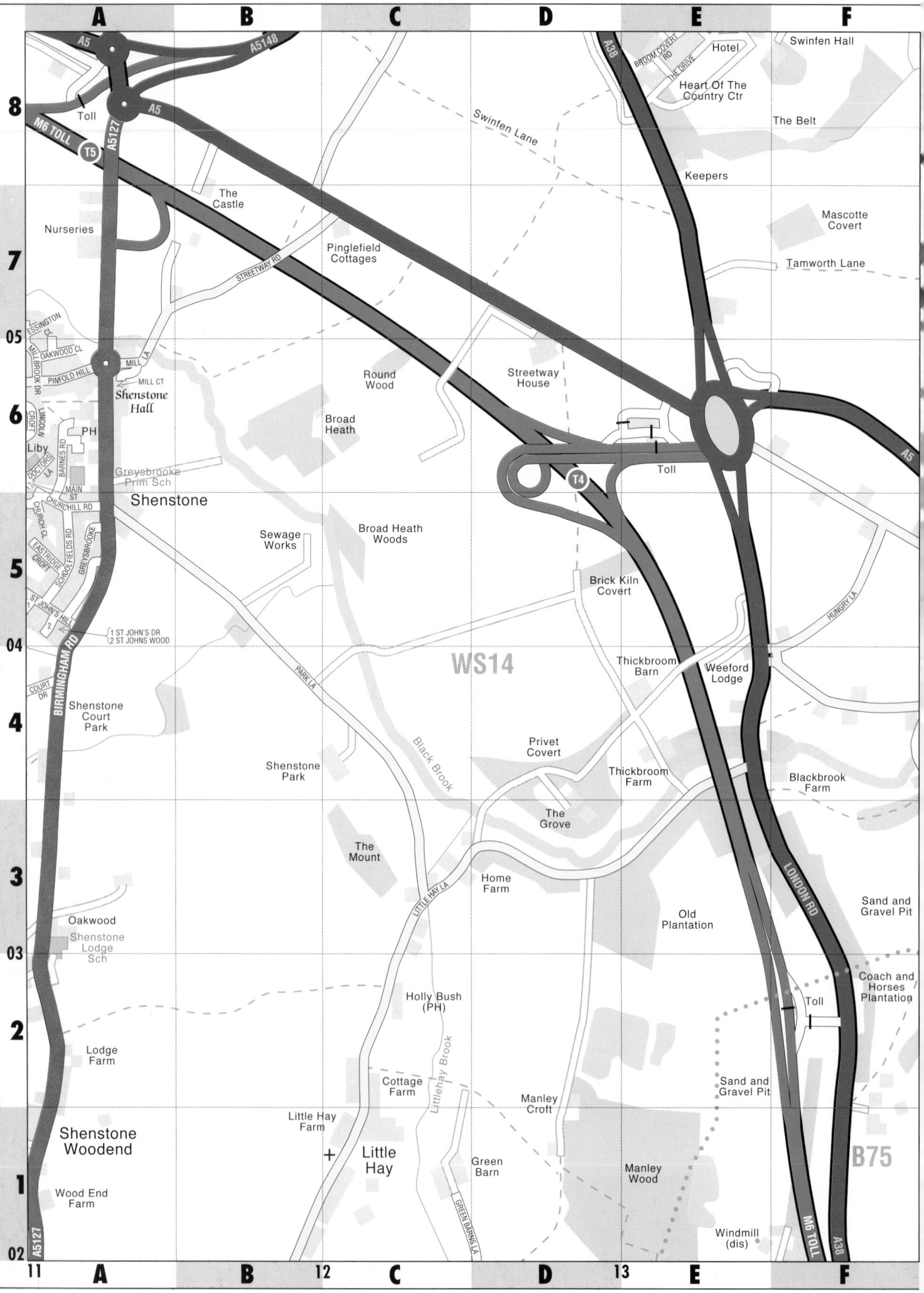
A5
A5148
A5127
A5
Toll
M6 TOLL
T5
8
Swinfen Lane
A38
BROOM COVERT RD
THE DRIVE
Hotel
Swinfen Hall
Heart Of The Country Ctr
The Belt
Keepers
The Castle
Nurseries
7
STREETWAY RD
Pinglefield Cottages
Mascotte Covert
Tamworth Lane
ESSINGTON CL
OAKWOOD CL
MILLBROOK DR
PINFOLD HILL
MILL LA
MILL CT
05
Shenstone Hall
Round Wood
Streetway House
6
CROFT
LINCOLN
PH
Broad Heath
Liby
DOCTORS LA
BARNES RD
Greysbrooke Prim Sch
MAIN ST
CHURCHILL RD
Shenstone
Toll
T4
A5
CHURCH CL
EASTRIDGE CROFT
SCHOOLFIELDS RD
GREYSBROOKE
Sewage Works
Broad Heath Woods
5
ST JOHN'S HILL
1 ST JOHN'S DR
2 ST JOHNS WOOD
Brick Kiln Covert
HUNGRY LA
04
COURT DR
BIRMINGHAM RD
PARK LA
WS14
Thickbroom Barn
Weeford Lodge
Shenstone Court Park
4
Black Brook
Privet Covert
Thickbroom Farm
Shenstone Park
Blackbrook Farm
The Grove
The Mount
3
Home Farm
LONDON RD
LITTLE HAY LA
Sand and Gravel Pit
Old Plantation
Oakwood
Shenstone Lodge Sch
03
Coach and Horses Plantation
Holly Bush (PH)
Toll
2
Lodge Farm
Littlehay Brook
Sand and Gravel Pit
Cottage Farm
Manley Croft
Little Hay Farm
Shenstone Woodend
Little Hay
B75
Green Barn
Manley Wood
1
Wood End Farm
GREEN BARNS LA
Windmill (dis)
M6 TOLL
A38
A5127
02
11
12
13
A B C D E F

17
32

20

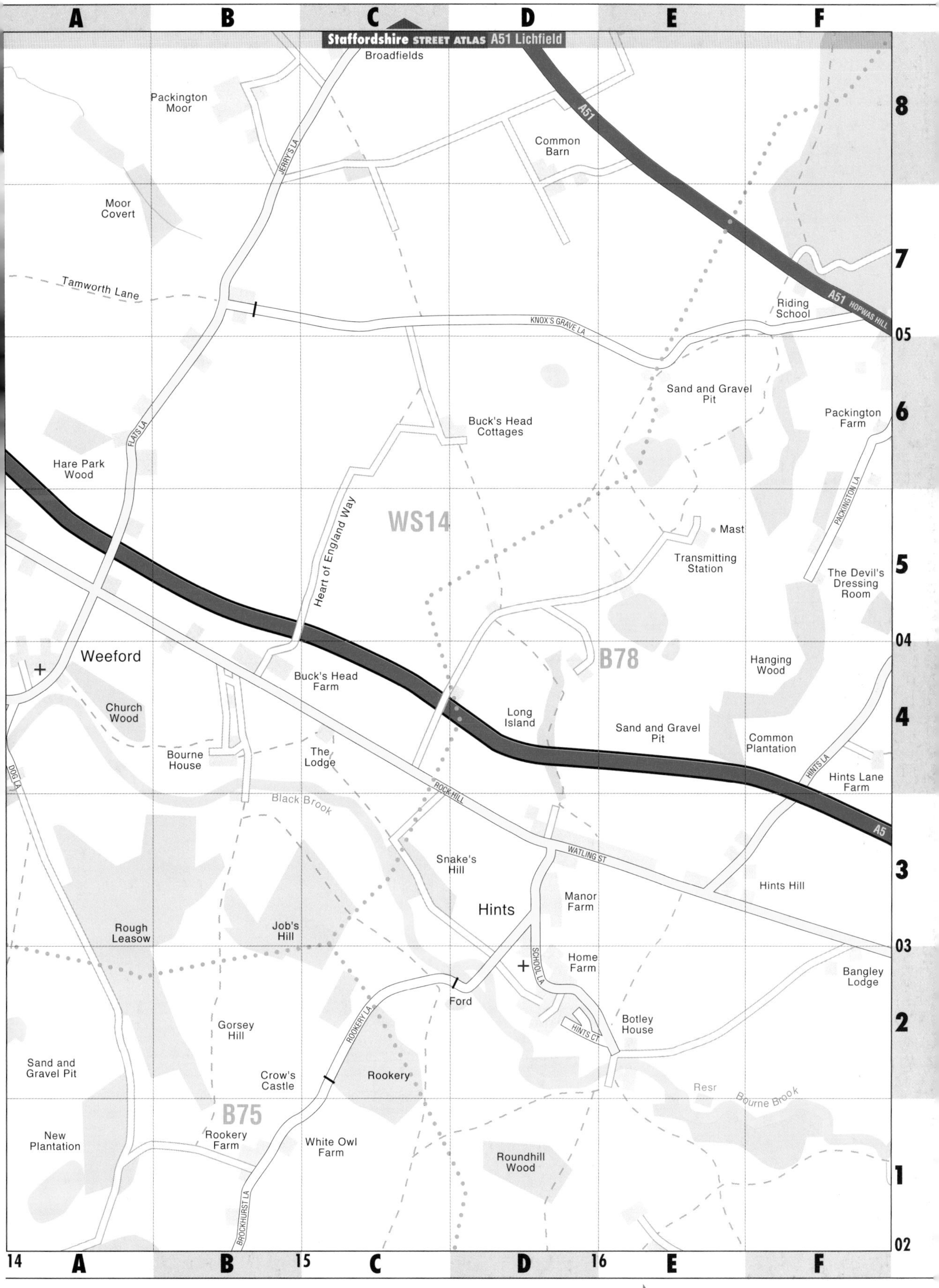

A B C D E F
Staffordshire STREET ATLAS A51 Lichfield
Broadfields
Packington Moor
Common Barn
A51
JERRY'S LA
Moor Covert
Tamworth Lane
KNOX'S GRAVE LA
Riding School
A51 HOPWAS HILL
Sand and Gravel Pit
Buck's Head Cottages
Packington Farm
FLATS LA
Hare Park Wood
Heart of England Way
WS14
Mast
Transmitting Station
PACKINGTON LA
The Devil's Dressing Room
Weeford
B78
Hanging Wood
Buck's Head Farm
Church Wood
Long Island
Sand and Gravel Pit
Common Plantation
Bourne House
The Lodge
HINTS LA
Hints Lane Farm
DOG LA
Black Brook
ROCK HILL
A5
WATLING ST
Snake's Hill
Hints Hill
Manor Farm
Hints
Rough Leasow
Job's Hill
Home Farm
SCHOOL LA
Bangley Lodge
Ford
Gorsey Hill
ROOKERY LA
Botley House
HINTS CT
Sand and Gravel Pit
Crow's Castle
Rookery
Resr
Bourne Brook
B75
New Plantation
Rookery Farm
White Owl Farm
Roundhill Wood
BROCKHURST LA
8 7 05 6 5 04 4 3 03 2 1 02
14 A B 15 C D 16 E F

33
20

19

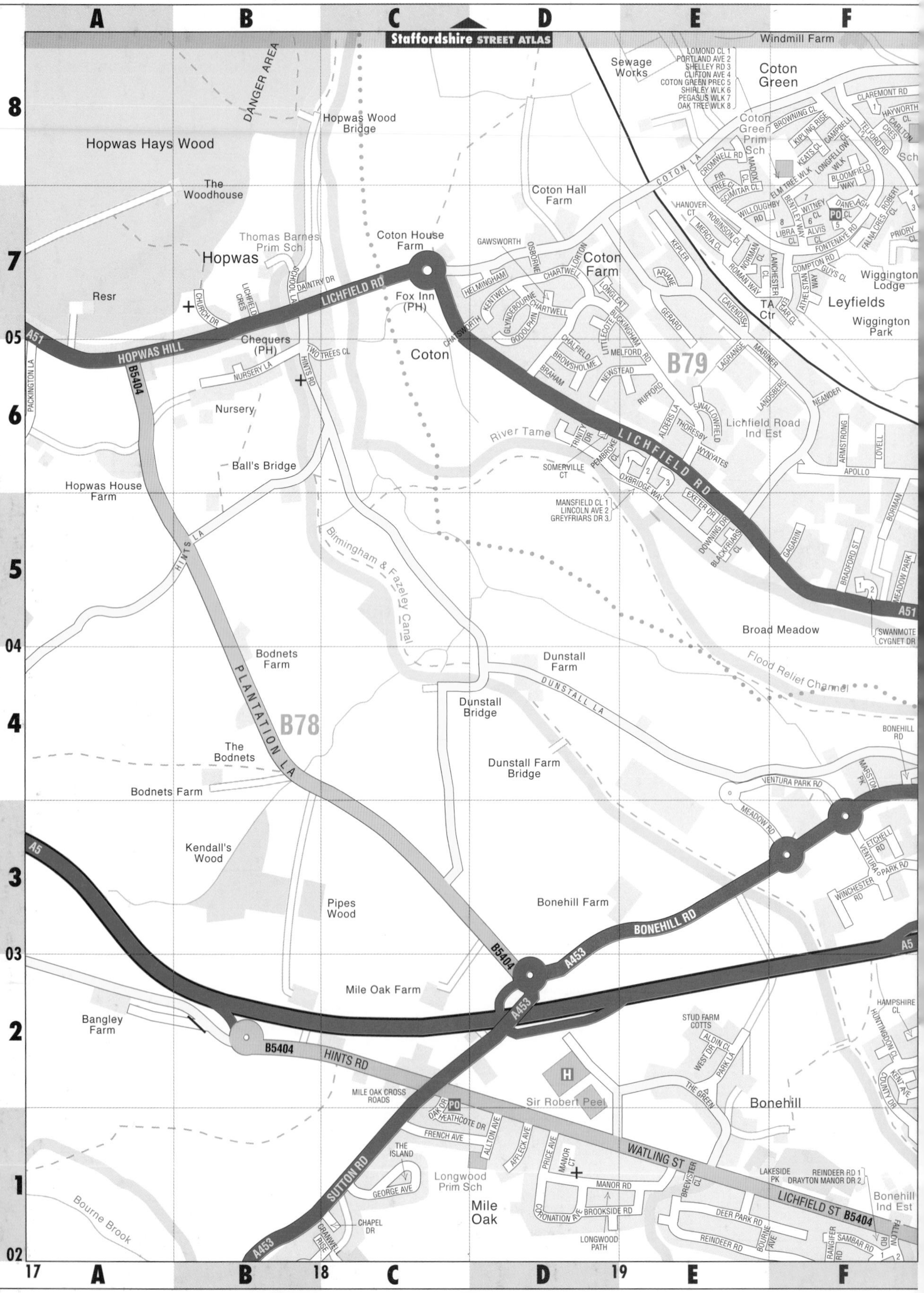
Staffordshire STREET ATLAS
A
B
C
D
E
F
8
7
6
5
4
3
2
1
05
04
03
02
17
18
19
Windmill Farm
Sewage Works
LOMOND CL 1
PORTLAND AVE 2
SHELLEY RD 3
CLIFTON AVE 4
COTON GREEN PREC 5
SHIRLEY WLK 6
PEGASUS WLK 7
OAK TREE WLK 8
Coton Green
Coton Green Prim Sch
DANGER AREA
Hopwas Wood Bridge
Hopwas Hays Wood
The Woodhouse
Thomas Barnes Prim Sch
Hopwas
Resr
Coton House Farm
Coton Hall Farm
Coton Farm
Fox Inn (PH)
Chequers (PH)
Coton
LICHFIELD RD
HOPWAS HILL
A51
B5404
PACKINGTON LA
NURSERY LA
HINTS RD
TWO TREES CL
DAINTRY DR
SCHOOL LA
CHURCH DR
LICHFIELD CRES
Nursery
Ball's Bridge
Hopwas House Farm
River Tame
Birmingham & Fazeley Canal
HINTS LA
PLANTATION LA
B78
B79
Bodnets Farm
The Bodnets
Kendall's Wood
Pipes Wood
Mile Oak Farm
Bangley Farm
Dunstall Farm
Dunstall Bridge
DUNSTALL LA
Dunstall Farm Bridge
Bonehill Farm
BONEHILL RD
A453
A5
Flood Relief Channel
Broad Meadow
Lichfield Road Ind Est
Leyfields
Wiggington Lodge
Wiggington Park
TA Ctr
SOMERVILLE CT
MANSFIELD CL 1
LINCOLN AVE 2
GREYFRIARS DR 3
SWANMOTE
CYGNET DR
BONEHILL RD
VENTURA PARK RD
MEADOW RD
STUD FARM COTTS
Bonehill
Sir Robert Peel
HINTS RD
MILE OAK CROSS ROADS
WATLING ST
SUTTON RD
THE ISLAND
GEORGE AVE
Longwood Prim Sch
Mile Oak
CHAPEL DR
MANOR RD
BROOKSIDE RD
CORONATION AVE
LONGWOOD PATH
LICHFIELD ST
LAKESIDE PK
REINDEER RD 1
DRAYTON MANOR DR 2
Bonehill Ind Est
DEER PARK RD
REINDEER RD
SAMBAR RD
Bourne Brook

19

34

22

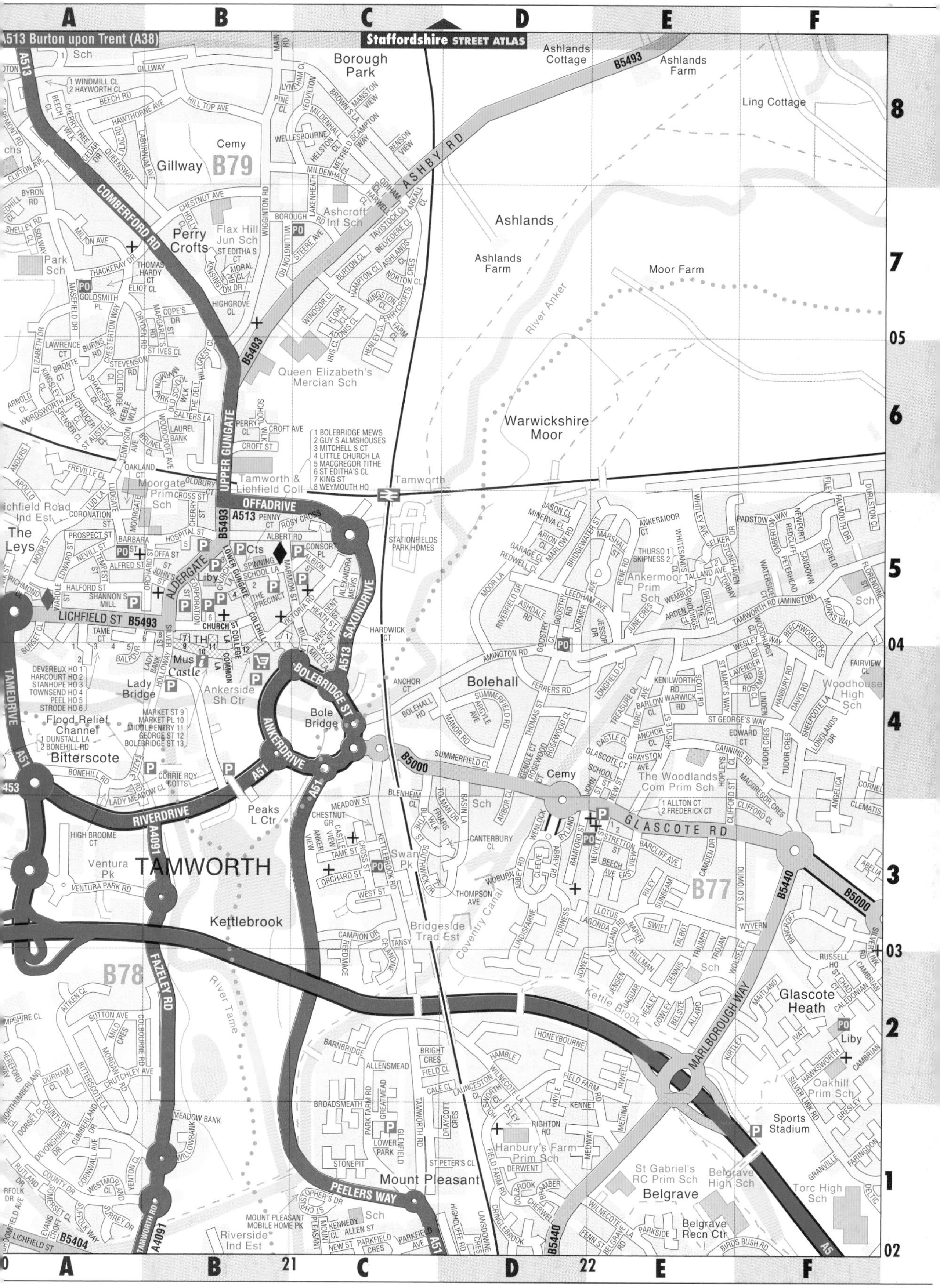
A
B
C
D
E
F
A513 Burton upon Trent (A38)
Staffordshire STREET ATLAS
Borough Park
Ashlands Cottage
B5493
Ashlands Farm
Ling Cottage
8
Gillway
Cemy
B79
ASHBY RD
COMBERFORD RD
Ashcroft Inf Sch
Ashlands
Perry Crofts
Flax Hill Jun Sch
Park Sch
Ashlands Farm
Moor Farm
7
River Anker
05
Queen Elizabeth's Mercian Sch
Warwickshire Moor
6
UPPER GUNGATE
1 BOLEBRIDGE MEWS
2 GUY S ALMSHOUSES
3 MITCHELL S CT
4 LITTLE CHURCH LA
5 MACGREGOR TITHE
6 ST EDITHA'S CL
7 KING ST
8 WEYMOUTH HO
Tamworth & Lichfield Coll
Tamworth
Moorgate Prim Sch
Lichfield Road Ind Est
OFFADRIVE
A513
The Leys
STATIONFIELDS PARK HOMES
5
Cts
Liby
Ankermoor Prim Sch
Sch
LICHFIELD ST
B5493
SAXONDRIVE
TAMWORTH RD (AMINGTON)
04
Mus
Castle
Lady Bridge
Ankerside Sh Ctr
BOLEBRIDGE ST
Bole Bridge
Bolehall
Woodhouse High Sch
DEVEREUX HO 1
HARCOURT HO 2
STANHOPE HO 3
TOWNSEND HO 4
PEEL HO 5
STRODE HO 6
MARKET ST 9
MARKET PL 10
MIDDLE ENTRY 11
GEORGE ST 12
BOLEBRIDGE ST 13
Flood Relief Channel
1 DUNSTALL LA
2 BONEHILL RD
TAMEDRIVE
4
Bitterscote
ANKERDRIVE
A51
B5000
Cemy
The Woodlands Com Prim Sch
1 ALLTON CT
2 FREDERICK CT
RIVERDRIVE
Peaks L Ctr
GLASCOTE RD
A4091
Ventura Pk
TAMWORTH
Swan Pk
B77
3
B5440
B5000
Kettlebrook
Bridgeside Trad Est
Coventry Canal
03
B78
FAZELEY RD
River Tame
Sch
Kettle Brook
Glascote Heath
2
MARLBOROUGH WAY
Liby
Oakhill Prim Sch
Sports Stadium
Hanbury's Farm Prim Sch
St Gabriel's RC Prim Sch
Belgrave High Sch
Torc High Sch
Mount Pleasant
PEELERS WAY
Belgrave
1
Riverside Ind Est
Belgrave Recn Ctr
B5404
A4091
A5
02
21
22

35

22

21

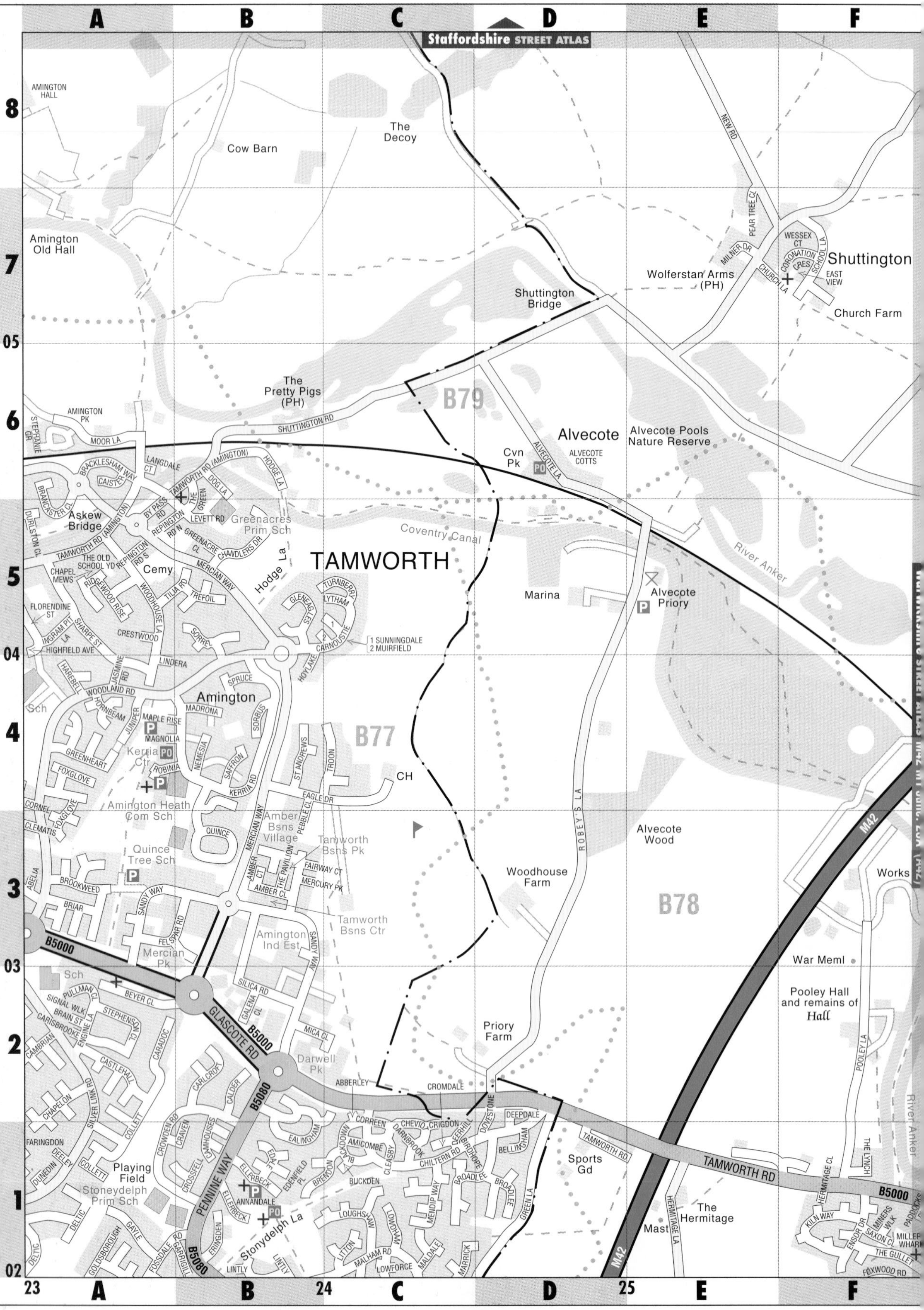

A
B
C
D
E
F
8
7
05
6
5
04
4
3
03
2
1
02
23
24
25
Staffordshire STREET ATLAS
AMINGTON HALL
Cow Barn
The Decoy
NEW RD
PEAR TREE CL
WESSEX CT
CORONATION CRES
SCHOOL LA
Shuttington
MILNER DR
CHURCH LA
EAST VIEW
Wolferstan Arms (PH)
Church Farm
Amington Old Hall
Shuttington Bridge
The Pretty Pigs (PH)
B79
AMINGTON PK
STEPHANIE GR
MOOR LA
SHUTTINGTON RD
Cvn Pk
ALVECOTE LA
Alvecote
ALVECOTE COTTS
Alvecote Pools Nature Reserve
BRACKLESHAM WAY
LANGDALE CT
TAMWORTH RD (AMINGTON)
HODGE LA
CAISTER
BRANCASTER CL
THE GREEN
DOG LA
BY PASS RD
LEVETT RD
Greenacres Prim Sch
Coventry Canal
River Anker
Askew Bridge
DURLSTON CL
REPINGTON RD N
REPINGTON RD S
GREENACRE CL
CHANDLERS DR
TAMWORTH RD (AMINGTON)
TAMWORTH
Hodge La
THE OLD SCHOOL YD
Cemy
MERCIAN WAY
CHAPEL MEWS
RIDGEWOOD RISE
TILIA RD
TREFOIL
WOODHOUSE LA
TURNBERRY
LYTHAM
GLENEAGLES
Marina
Alvecote Priory
FLORENDINE ST
INGRAM PIT LA
SHARPE ST
CRESTWOOD
SORREL
CARNOUSTIE
1 SUNNINGDALE
2 MUIRFIELD
HIGHFIELD AVE
LINDERA
HOYLAKE
HAREBELL
JASMINE RD
SPRUCE
WOODLAND RD
Amington
Sch
HORNBEAM
JUNIPER
MADRONA
SORBUS
MAPLE RISE
MAGNOLIA
B77
Kerria Ctr
NEMESIA
SAFFRON
ST ANDREWS
TROON
GREENHEART
ROBINIA
KERRIA RD
CH
FOXGLOVE
EAGLE DR
CORNEL
FOXGLOVE
Amington Heath Com Sch
MERCIAN WAY
Amber Bsns Village
PEBBLE CL
ROBEY'S LA
Alvecote Wood
M42
CLEMATIS
QUINCE
Tamworth Bsns Pk
ABELIA
Quince Tree Sch
AMBER CT
THE PAVILION
FAIRWAY CT
Woodhouse Farm
Works
BROOKWEED
SANDY WAY
MERCURY PK
AMBER CL
B78
BRIAR
Tamworth Bsns Ctr
FELSPAR RD
Amington Ind Est
SANDY WAY
B5000
Mercian Pk
War Meml
Sch
PULLMAN CL
SILICA RD
BEYER CL
GALENA CL
Pooley Hall and remains of Hall
SIGNAL WLK
BRAIN ST
STEPHENSON CL
CARISBROOKE
ENGINE LA
CARADOC
GLASCOTE RD
B5000
MICA CL
Priory Farm
CAMBRIAN
CASTLEHALL
Darwell Pk
POOLEY LA
CARLCROFT
CALDER
ABBERLEY
CROMDALE
B5080
CHAPELON
SILVER LINK RD
DOVESTONE
DEEPDALE
River Anker
EALINGHAM
CORREEN
CHEVIOT
CRIGDON
DEERHILL
FARINGDON
COLLETT
CROWDEN RD
CRAVEN
CAMHOUSES
BLACKDOWN
DARNBROOK
AMICOMBE
BIRDHOPE
BELLINGHAM
THE LYNCH
DEELEY
DUNEDIN
COLLETT
Playing Field
CROSSFELL
EDALE
EDENFIELD PL
BREDON
CLEASBY
CHILTERN RD
BROADLEE
TAMWORTH RD
Sports Gd
TAMWORTH RD
HERMITAGE CL
Stoneydelph Prim Sch
PENNINE WAY
ELLERBECK
ANNANDALE
BUCKDEN
MENDIP WAY
BROADLEE
GREEN LA
B5000
DELTIC
ELLERBECK
LOUGHSHAW
LOWDHAM
The Hermitage
KILN WAY
MINERS WLK
PADDOCKS
Stonydelph La
ENSOR DR
SAXON CL
MILLERS WHARF
Mast
HERMITAGE LA
THE GULLET
DELTIC
GOLDSBOROUGH
GAYLE
FOSSDALE RD
GARRIGILL
EHINGDEN
B5080
LINTLY
LINTLY
LITTON
MALHAM RD
LOWFORCE
MALDALE
MARRICK
M42
FOXWOOD RD

21

36

24

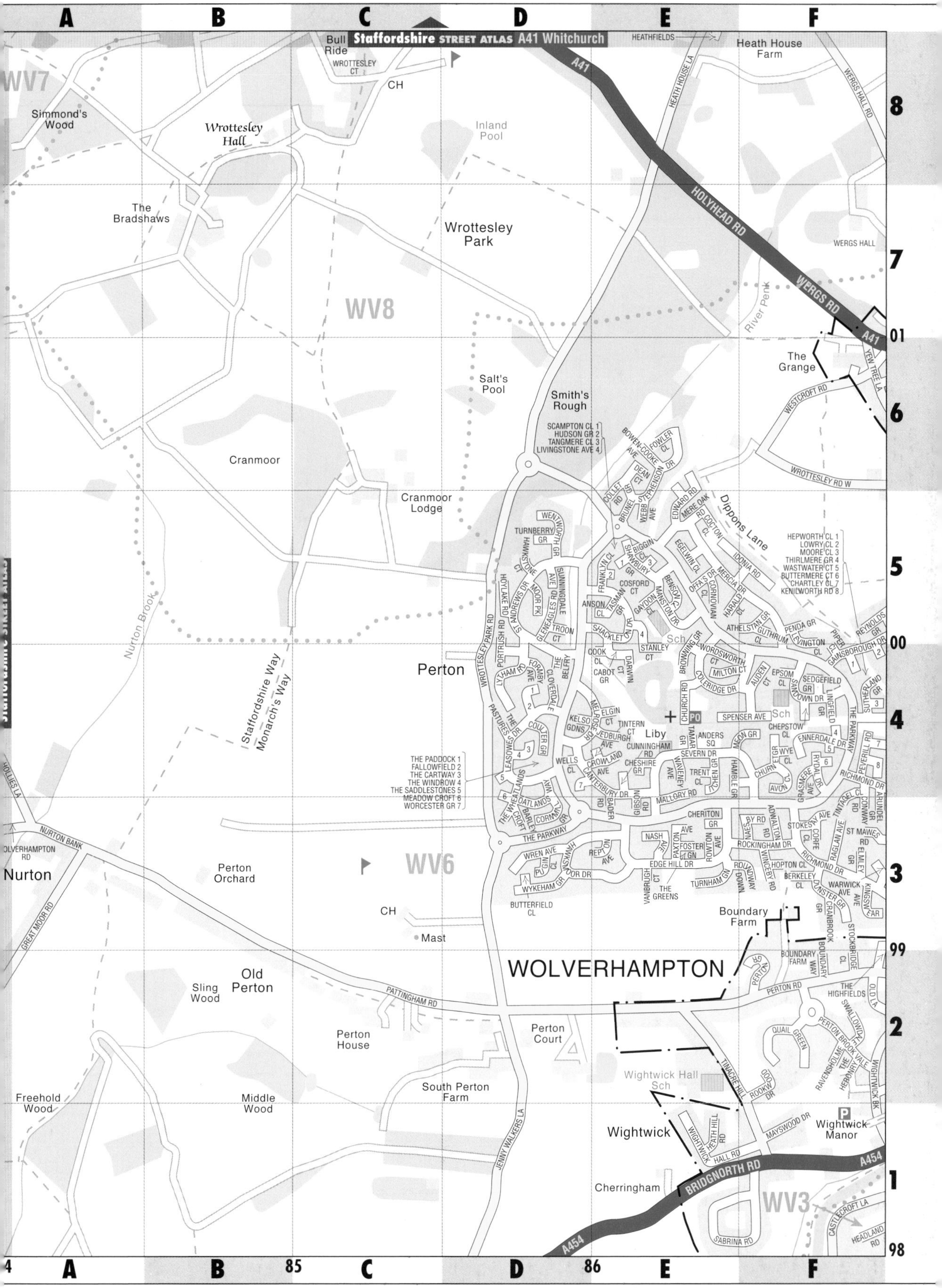

Staffordshire STREET ATLAS A41 Whitchurch
A B C D E F
8 7 01 6 5 00 4 3 99 2 1 98
85 86
WV7
WV8
WV6
WV3
Bull Ride
WROTTESLEY CT
CH
HEATHFIELDS
Heath House Farm
A41
HEATH HOUSE LA
WERGS HALL RD
Simmond's Wood
Wrottesley Hall
Inland Pool
The Bradshaws
HOLYHEAD RD
Wrottesley Park
WERGS HALL
WERGS RD
River Penk
The Grange
YEW TREE LA
Salt's Pool
Smith's Rough
WESTCROFT RD
Cranmoor
SCAMPTON CL 1
HUDSON GR 2
TANGMERE CL 3
LIVINGSTONE AVE 4
BOWEN-COOKE AVE
FOWLER CL
DEAN CT
STEPHENSON DR
WROTTESLEY RD W
Cranmoor Lodge
Dippons Lane
WENTWORTH GR
TURNBERRY GR
HAWKSTONE CT
BRUNEL GR
WEBB AVE
EDWARD RD
MERE OAK RD
COCTON CL
IDONIA RD
HEPWORTH CL 1
LOWRY CL 2
MOORE CL 3
THIRLMERE GR 4
WASTWATER CT 5
BUTTERMERE CT 6
CHARTLEY CL 7
KENILWORTH RD 8
HOYLAKE RD
ST ANDREWS DR
SUNNINGDALE AVE
MOOR PK
GLENEAGLES RD
FRANKLYN CL
BIGGIN CL
SHAWBURY GR
COSFORD CT
ANSON CL
TASMAN GR
GAYDON CL
MANSTON DR
BENSON CL
EGELWIN CL
OFFA'S DR
CORNOVIAN CL
MERCIA DR
HARALD CL
ATHELSTAN GR
GUTHRUM CL
PENDA GR
LEVINGTON CL
PIPERS
REYNOLDS
GAINSBOROUGH DR
Nurton Brook
WROTTESLEY PARK RD
PORTRUSH RD
TROON CT
SHACKLETON DR
STANLEY CT
Sch
COOK CL
CABOT GR
DARWIN CT
BROWNING GR
WORDSWORTH CT
MILTON CT
COLERIDGE DR
AUDEN CT
EPSOM CL
SANDOWN DR
SEDGEFIELD GR
LINGFIELD GR
THE PARKWAY
SUTHERLAND GR
Perton
LYTHAM RD
FORMBY AVE
THE BELFRY
CLOVERDALE
Staffordshire Way
Monarch's Way
THE PASTURES
COULTER GR
KELSO GDNS
MELROSE
ELGIN CT
JEDBURGH AVE
TINTERN CT
Liby
PO
CHURCH RD
SPENSER AVE
CHEPSTOW CL
ENNERDALE DR
PEVERILL RD
THE PADDOCK 1
FALLOWFIELD 2
THE CARTWAY 3
THE WINDROW 4
THE SADDLESTONES 5
MEADOW CROFT 6
WORCESTER GR 7
LEASOWES DR
WELLS CL
CROWLAND AVE
CUNNINGHAM RD
ANDERS SQ
TAMAR GR
SEVERN DR
MEON GR
WYE CL
RYDAL DR
CHESHIRE GR
WAVENEY AVE
TRENT CL
ITCHEN GR
HAMBLE GR
CHURNET GR
AVON CL
GRASMERE AVE
RICHMOND DR
ARUNDEL GR
CONWAY RD
HOLLIES LA
THE WHEATLANDS
OATLANDS WAY
BARLEY CROFT
CORNWALL GR
CANTERBURY DR
BADER RD
GIBSON RD
MALLORY RD
CHERITON GR
ADWALTON RD
TINTAGEL CL
NURTON BANK
WOLVERHAMPTON RD
Nurton
THE PARKWAY
NASH AVE
PAXTON AVE
FOSTER GN
ROWTON AVE
BY RD
NAES
ROCKINGHAM DR
STOKESAY AVE
CORFE CL
RAGLAN AVE
ST MAWES RD
ELMLEY GR
WREN AVE
HAWKSMOOR DR
REPTON AVE
EDGE HILL DR
HOPTON CL
Perton Orchard
WV6
PUGIN CL
WYKEHAM GR
VANBRUGH CT
THE GREENS
TURNHAM GN
ROUNDWAY DOWN
WINCEBY RD
BERKELEY CL
RICHMOND DR
DUNSTER GR
WARWICK AVE
KINGSWAY
CAR
BUTTERFIELD CL
GREAT MOOR RD
CH
Boundary Farm
CRANBROOK GR
STOCKBRIDGE CL
Mast
BOUNDARY FARM
BOUNDARY WAY
WOLVERHAMPTON
PERTON GR
Old Perton
Sling Wood
PATTINGHAM RD
PERTON RD
THE HIGHFIELDS
OLD LA
Perton Court
Perton House
QUAIL GREEN
PERTON BROOK VALE
SWALLOWDALE
RAVENSHOLME
THE HERONRY
WIGHTWICK BK
Wightwick Hall Sch
TINACRE HILL
ROOKWOOD DR
South Perton Farm
Freehold Wood
Middle Wood
JENNY WALKERS LA
Wightwick
WIGHTWICK HALL RD
HEATH HILL RD
MAYSWOOD DR
Wightwick Manor
P
A454
BRIDGNORTH RD
Cherringham
CASTLECROFT LA
HEADLAND RD
SABRINA RD

37 24

23

10

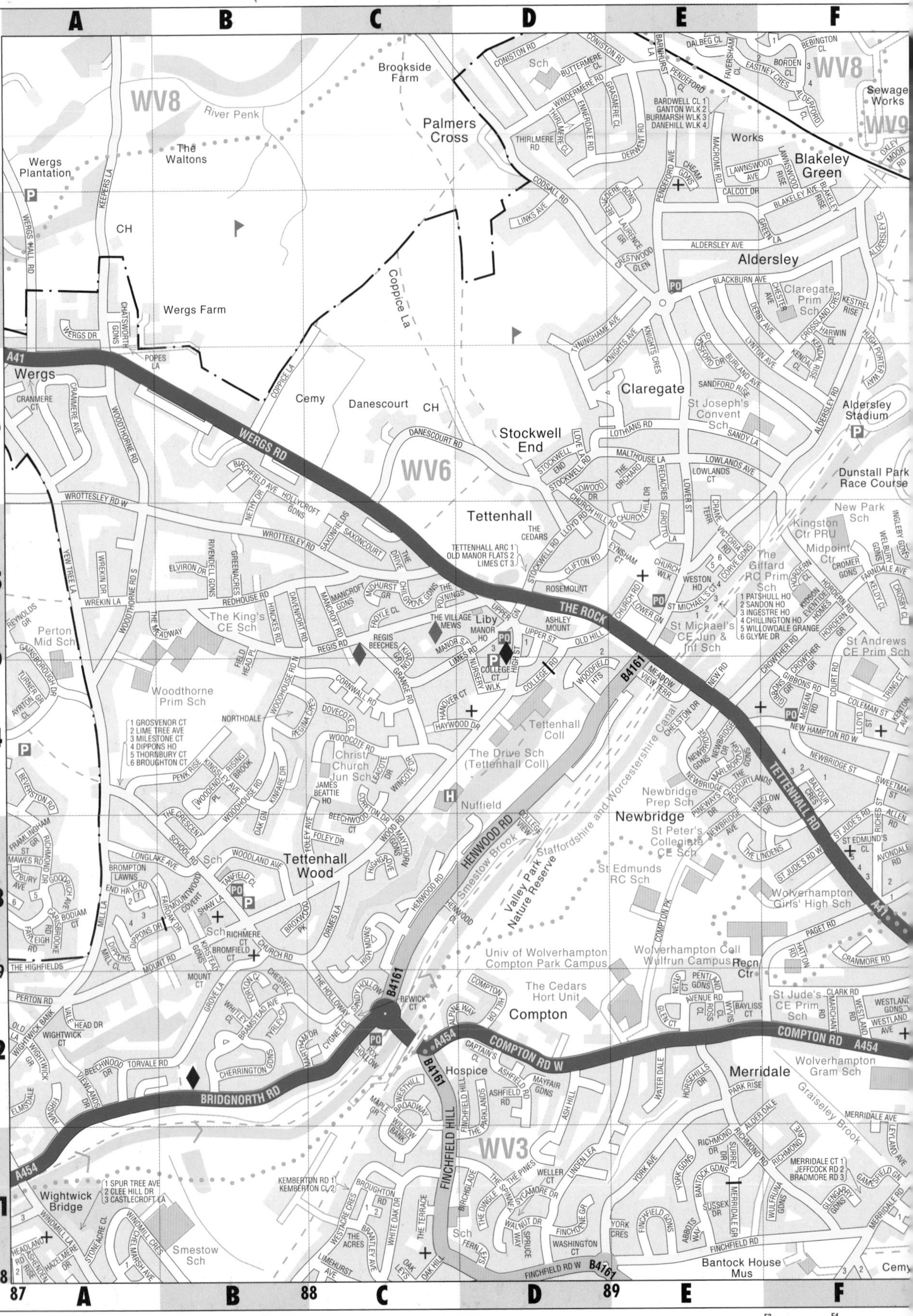

23

38

F3
1 ALBERT RD
2 BROMFORD DALE
3 SLADE HILL
4 ST JUDES'S CT
5 THE CEDARS

F4
1 BRIMFIELD PL
2 BALFOUR CT
3 NEWBRIDGE MEWS
4 GRAFTON CT

11
26

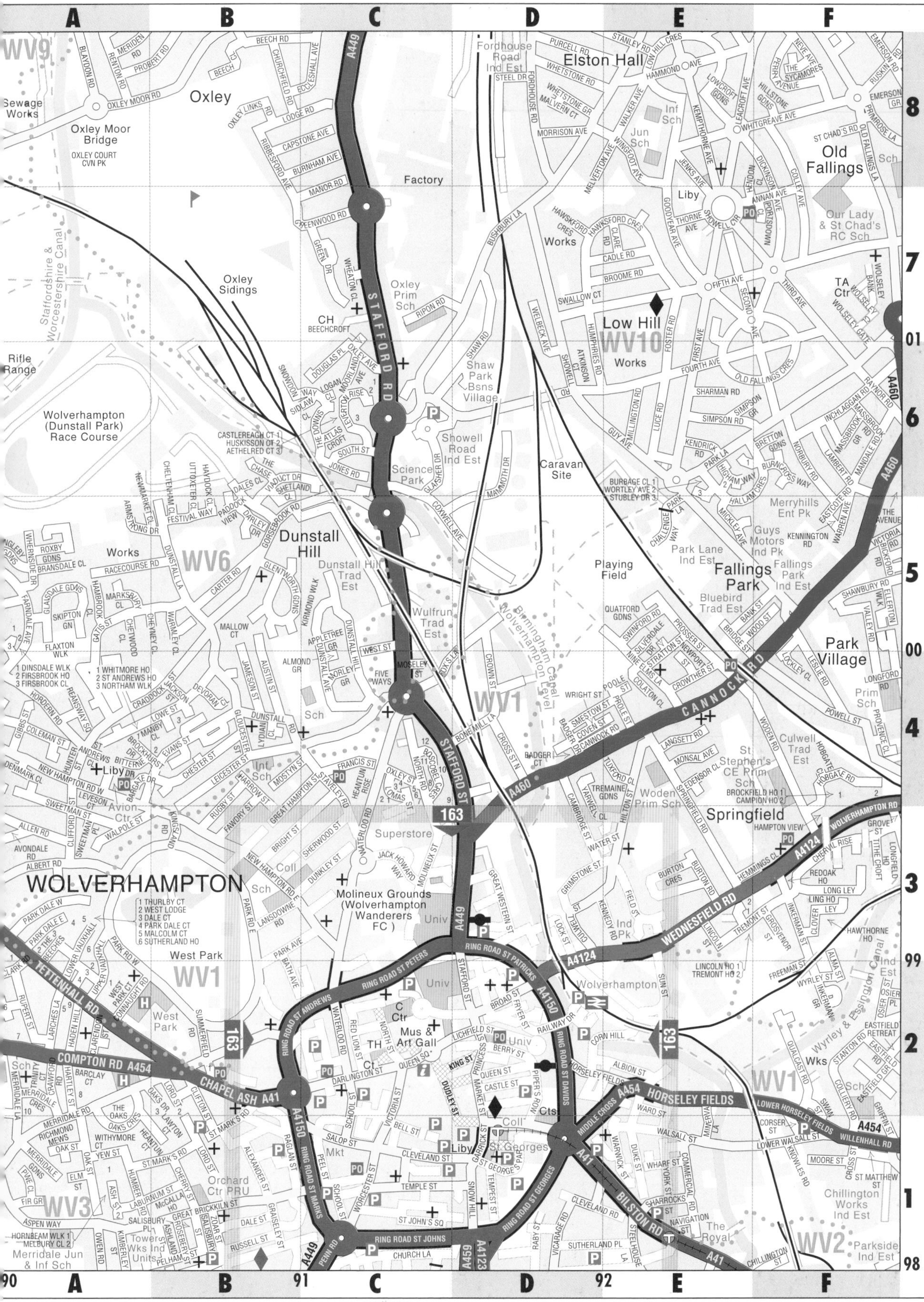

A2
1 CONNAUGHT HO
2 VAUXHALL HO
3 VAUXHALL AVE
4 MIDDLE VAUXHALL
5 HADEN CT
6 WESTLAND GDNS
7 COMPTON CT
8 BRIGHTON MEWS
9 TETTENHALL GATE

A2
10 BEECHWOOD HO

B2
1 MEADOW ST
2 ROTARY CT
3 OAKLEIGH CT

C4
1 DURHAM HO
2 ESSEX HO
3 FLINT HO
4 GLOUCESTER HO
5 ARGYLL HO
6 BEDFORD HO
7 CUMBERLAND HO
8 LANE CT
9 TONG CT
10 WESTON CT
11 BIRCH CT
12 KILSALL CT

39
26
For full street detail of the highlighted area see page 163.

25
12

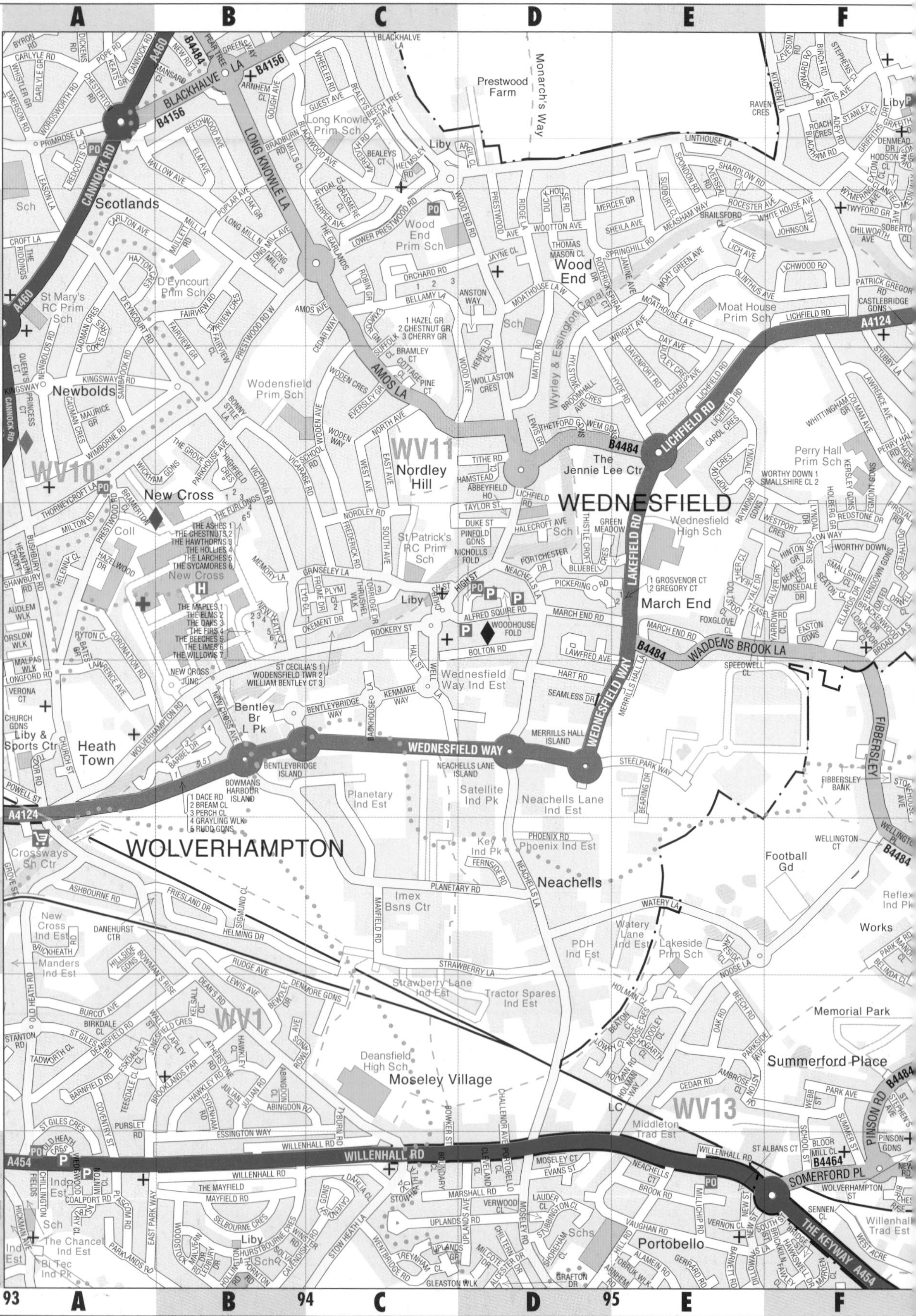
A
B
C
D
E
F
8
7
01
6
5
00
4
3
99
2
1
98
93
94
95
Prestwood Farm
Monarch's Way
Long Knowle Prim Sch
Scotlands
Wood End Prim Sch
Wood End
D'Eyncourt Prim Sch
St Mary's RC Prim Sch
Moat House Prim Sch
Wodensfield Prim Sch
Newbolds
Wyrley & Essington Canal
WV11
Nordley Hill
WV10
The Jennie Lee Ctr
Perry Hall Prim Sch
New Cross
WEDNESFIELD
Wednesfield High Sch
St Patrick's RC Prim Sch
March End
Wednesfield Way Ind Est
Bentley Br L Pk
Liby & Sports Ctr
Heath Town
WEDNESFIELD WAY
Planetary Ind Est
Satellite Ind Pk
Neachells Lane Ind Est
WOLVERHAMPTON
Crossways Sh Ctr
Key Ind Pk
Phoenix Ind Est
Neachells
Football Gd
Imex Bsns Ctr
New Cross Ind Est
Manders Ind Est
PDH Ind Est
Watery Lane Ind Est
Lakeside Prim Sch
Strawberry Lane Ind Est
Tractor Spares Ind Est
WV1
Memorial Park
Deansfield High Sch
Moseley Village
Summerford Place
WV13
Middleton Trad Est
WILLENHALL RD
The Chancel Ind Est
Bi Tec Ind Pk
Portobello
THE KEYWAY A454
A4124
A460
B4484
B4156
A454
B4464
LICHFIELD RD
LAKEFIELD RD
WADDENS BROOK LA
CANNOCK RD
LONG KNOWLE LA
AMOS LA
BLACKHALVE LA

25
40

13
28

A2
1 LEVESON CT
2 CROFT APARTMENTS
3 ST MARY'S CT
A1
1 ST STEPHEN'S GDNS
2 CROSS ST
3 CHEAPSIDE
4 ATLANTIC CT

B2
1 FREDERICK WILLIAM ST
2 CHARLES HOLLAND ST
3 KNIGHTS CL
4 SQUIRES GATE RD
5 WITTERSHAM CT
6 KING ST

41
28

A5
1 MURDOCK WAY
5 BALL HO
6 LEADBEATER HO

B8
1 CHURCH MOAT WAY
2 CARL EYNON CT
3 APPLEDORE CT
4 The Crossings Ind Est

27

C6
1 LUDLOW HO
2 HARLECH HO
3 KENILWORTH HO
4 PEMBROKE HO

14

F6
1 WARNER PL
2 DARTMOUTH HO
3 CARTBRIDGE WLK

27

C1
1 Brineton Ind Est
C2
1 PARGETER CT
2 MANOR ROAD PREC
3 FORRESTER STREET PREC

D2
1 CAVELL CL
2 WATERFRONT WAY

D3
1 TIBBITS HO
2 RICHARDS HO
3 WINN HO
4 BROCKHURST HO
5 FARRINGDON HO
6 REGENT HO
7 BURROWS HO

42

E1
1 THE OLD SQUARE
2 SISTER DORA BLDGS
3 THE BRIDGE
4 NEWPORT ST
5 LITTLE NEWPORT ST
6 UPPER HALL LA
7 THE HERITAGE
8 SISTER DORA GDNS
9 VICARAGE WLK

E2
1 GALLERY SQ
2 QUASAR CTR
3 BUTLERS PREC
4 PARK ST ARC
5 ST PAUL'S CL
E3
1 RYECROFT PK
2 RYECROFT ST
3 BATE ST

F1
1 ACORN CTR
2 CROFT HO
3 BROOKES HO
4 PRESTON HO
5 BYWATER HO
6 MILLSUM HO
7 THE GUILDHALL MEWS
8 CHURCH HILL
9 WHISTON HO

F2
1 WOLLASTON CT
2 JERVIS CT
3 DOG KENNEL LA
4 ST GEORGE'S PL
5 ST GEORGES CT
6 WALHOUSE CL
7 SOVEREIGN WLK
8 WAREWELL CL
9 WAREWELL ST
10 WEDGE ST
F3
1 THORNBROOK CT
2 THE ARCHWAY
3 COTTERELL CT
4 VICTORIA TERR

15
30

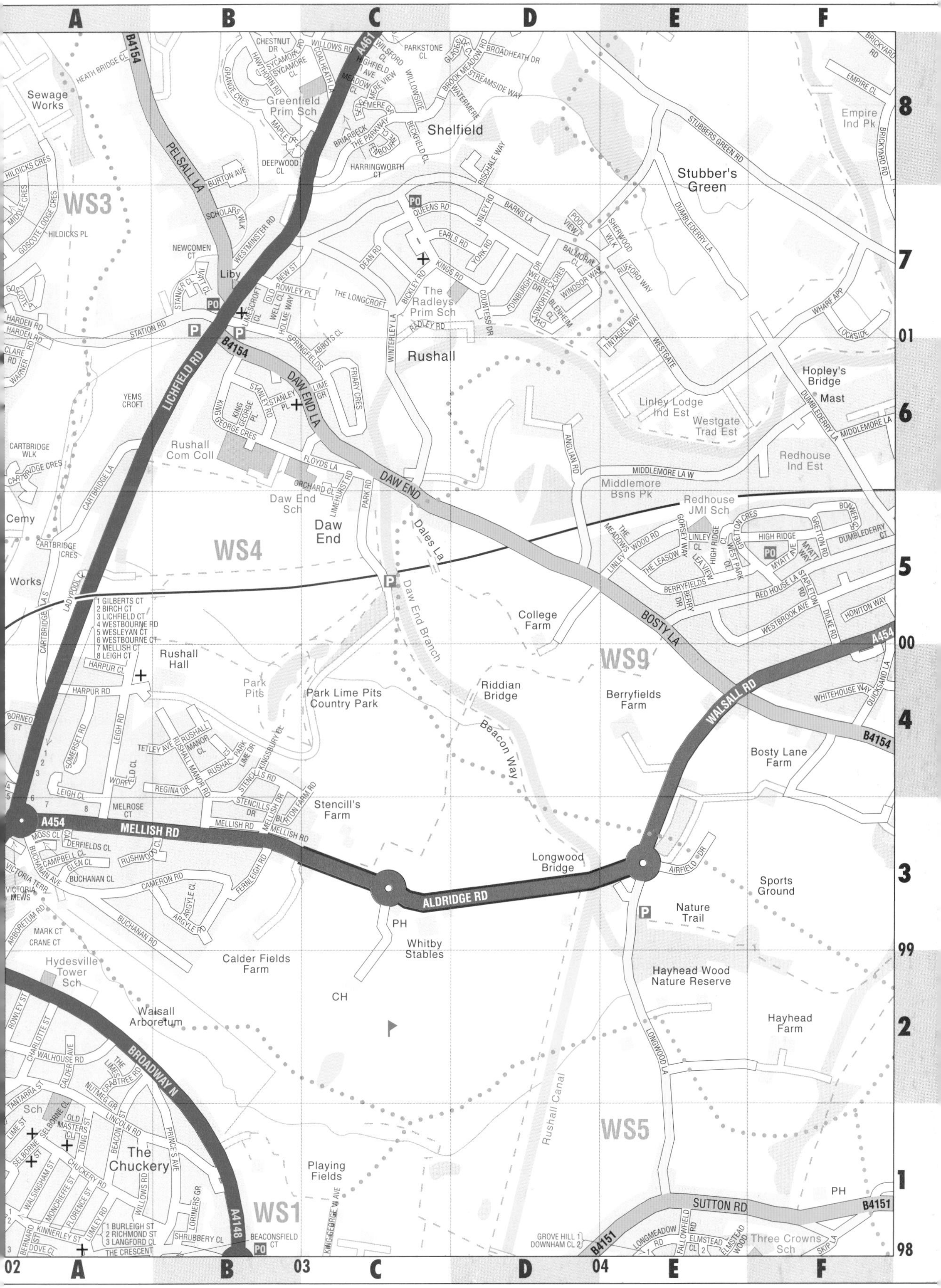
A
B
C
D
E
F
8
7
01
6
5
00
4
3
99
2
1
98
02
03
04
Sewage Works
WS3
Greenfield Prim Sch
Shelfield
Stubber's Green
Empire Ind Pk
Liby
The Radleys Prim Sch
Rushall
Hopley's Bridge
Mast
Linley Lodge Ind Est
Westgate Trad Est
Redhouse Ind Est
Middlemore Bsns Pk
Redhouse JMI Sch
Rushall Com Coll
Daw End Sch
Daw End
WS4
Cemy
Works
Rushall Hall
Park Pits
Park Lime Pits Country Park
Riddian Bridge
College Farm
WS9
Berryfields Farm
Bosty Lane Farm
Stencill's Farm
Longwood Bridge
Sports Ground
Nature Trail
Whitby Stables
PH
Calder Fields Farm
Hydesville Tower Sch
Walsall Arboretum
CH
Hayhead Wood Nature Reserve
Hayhead Farm
The Chuckery
Playing Fields
WS1
WS5
Three Crowns Sch
Rushall Canal
Daw End Branch
Beacon Way
Dales La
PELSALL LA
LICHFIELD RD
DAW END LA
DAW END
BOSTY LA
WALSALL RD
MELLISH RD
ALDRIDGE RD
BROADWAY N
SUTTON RD
LONGWOOD LA
STUBBERS GREEN RD
DUMBLEDERRY LA
MIDDLEMORE LA W
STATION RD
B4154
A461
A454
A4148
B4151
1 GILBERTS CT
2 BIRCH CT
3 LICHFIELD CT
4 WESTBOURNE RD
5 WESLEYAN CT
6 WESTBOURNE CT
7 MELLISH CT
8 LEIGH CT
1 BURLEIGH ST
2 RICHMOND ST
3 LANGFORD CL

29
16

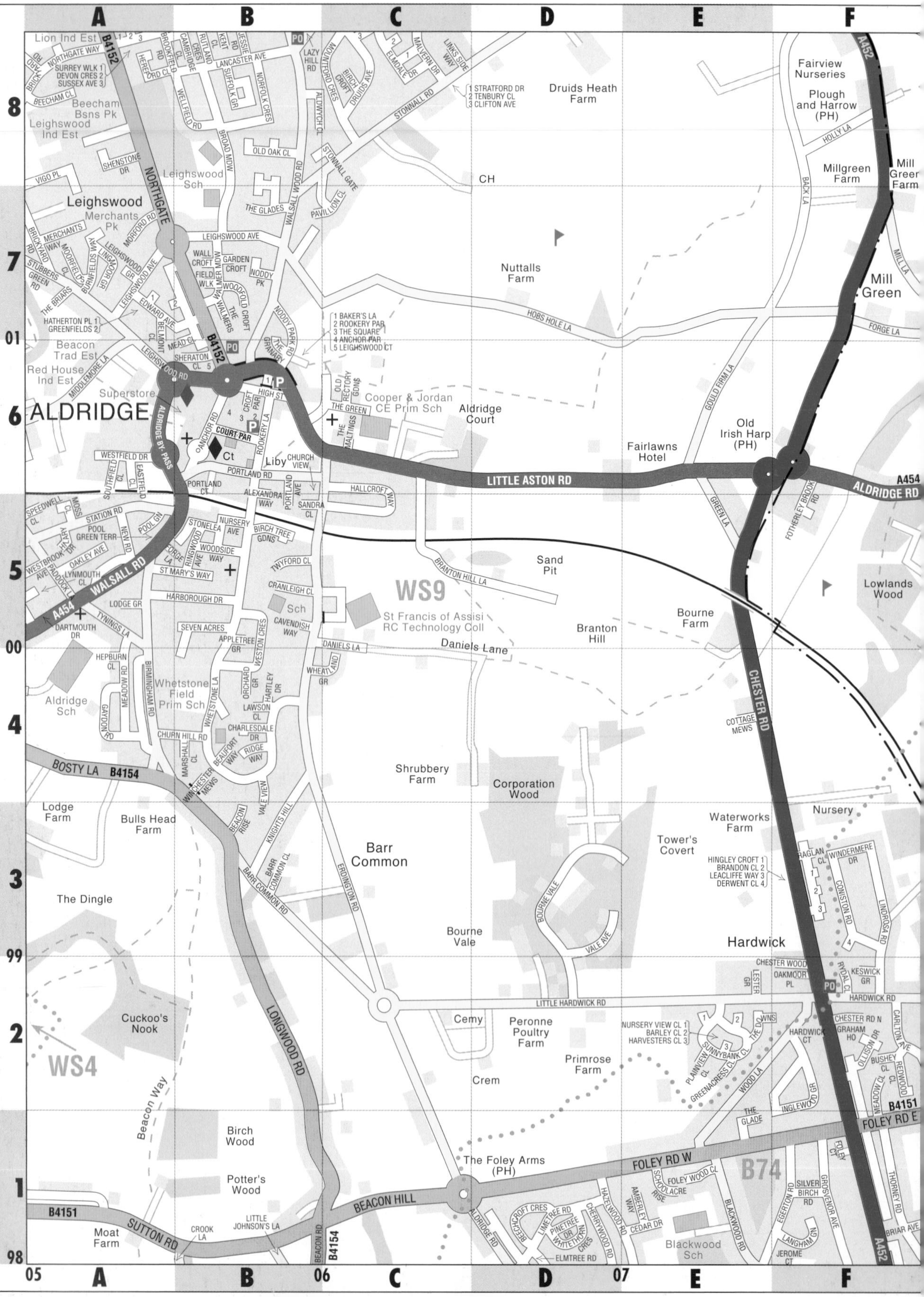
A
B
C
D
E
F
8
7
01
6
5
00
4
3
99
2
1
98
05
06
07
Lion Ind Est
B4152
NORTHGATE
SURREY WLK 1
DEVON CRES 2
SUSSEX AVE 3
BEECHAM CL
Beecham Bsns Pk
Leighswood Ind Est
SHENSTONE DR
VIGO PL
Leighswood
Merchants Pk
Leighswood Sch
LANCASTER AVE
NORFOLK CRES
SUFFOLK GR
WELLFIELD RD
BROAD MDW
OLD OAK CL
THE GLADES
WALSALL WOOD RD
STONNALL GATE
PAVILLION CL
STONNALL RD
LAZY HILL RD
ALDWYCH CL
MALVERN DR
ELMDALE DR
LINKS SIDE WAY
1 STRATFORD DR
2 TENBURY CL
3 CLIFTON AVE
Druids Heath Farm
CH
Fairview Nurseries
Plough and Harrow (PH)
HOLLY LA
Millgreen Farm
Mill Greer Farm
BACK LA
A452
MILL LA
Mill Green
FORGE LA
Nuttalls Farm
HOBS HOLE LA
LEIGHSWOOD AVE
MORFORD RD
MERCHANTS WAY
BRICKYARD RD
STUBBERS GREEN RD
THE BRIARS
HATHERTON PL 1
GREENFIELDS 2
Beacon Trad Est
Red House Ind Est
MIDDLEMORE LA
EDWARD AVE
BELMONT CL
LEIGHSWOOD RD
SHERATON CL
MEAD CL
WALL CROFT
FIELD WLK
GARDEN CROFT
NODDY PK
WOODFOLD CROFT
THE WALMERS
NODDY PARK RD
THE GRANARY
1 BAKER'S LA
2 ROOKERY PAR
3 THE SQUARE
4 ANCHOR PAR
5 LEIGHSWOOD CT
PO
P
HIGH ST
Superstore
ALDRIDGE
ALDRIDGE BY-PASS
ANCHOR RD
COURT PAR
CROFT PAR
ROOKERY LA
Ct
Liby
CHURCH VIEW
OLD RECTORY GDNS
THE GREEN
THE MALTINGS
Cooper & Jordan CE Prim Sch
Aldridge Court
GOULD FIRM LA
Old Irish Harp (PH)
Fairlawns Hotel
LITTLE ASTON RD
A454
ALDRIDGE RD
WESTFIELD DR
SOUTHFIELD CL
EASTFIELD
PORTLAND RD
PORTLAND CT
ALEXANDRA WAY
PORTLAND AVE
SANDRA CL
HALLCROFT WAY
GREEN LA
FOTHERLEY BROOK RD
SPEEDWELL CL
MOSS CL
STATION RD
POOL GREEN TERR
POOL GN
NEW RD
STONELEA
NURSERY AVE
BIRCH TREE GDNS
WOODSIDE WAY
RINGWOOD AVE
FORGE LA
WESTBROOK AVE
OAKLEY AVE
LYNMOUTH CL
PADDOCK LA
ST MARY'S WAY
TWYFORD CL
CRANLEIGH CL
WALSALL RD
BRANTON HILL LA
Sand Pit
WS9
Lowlands Wood
HARBOROUGH DR
LODGE GR
Sch
CAVENDISH WAY
St Francis of Assisi RC Technology Coll
Bourne Farm
Branton Hill
DARTMOUTH DR
TYNINGS LA
SEVEN ACRES
APPLETREE GR
WESTON CRES
DANIELS LA
Daniels Lane
WHEATLAND GR
HEPBURN CL
MEADOW RD
BIRMINGHAM RD
Whetstone Field Prim Sch
WHETSTONE LA
ORCHARD GR
HARTLEY DR
LAWSON CL
Aldridge Sch
GAYDON RD
CHURN HILL RD
CHARLESDALE DR
MARSHALL CL
BEAUFORT WAY
RIDGE WAY
WINCHESTER MEWS
COTTAGE MEWS
CHESTER RD
BOSTY LA
B4154
Lodge Farm
Bulls Head Farm
BEACON RISE
VALE VIEW
KNIGHTS HILL
Shrubbery Farm
Corporation Wood
Nursery
Waterworks Farm
Tower's Covert
BARR COMMON CL
BARR COMMON RD
ERDINGTON RD
Barr Common
HINGLEY CROFT 1
BRANDON CL 2
LEACLIFFE WAY 3
DERWENT CL 4
RAGLAN CL
WINDERMERE DR
CONISTON RD
LINDRIDGE RD
The Dingle
BOURNE VALE
VALE AVE
Bourne Vale
Hardwick
CHESTER WOOD
OAKMOOR PL
LESTER GR
RYDAL CL
KESWICK GR
HARDWICK RD
LITTLE HARDWICK RD
Cuckoo's Nook
WS4
LONGWOOD RD
Cemy
Peronne Poultry Farm
NURSERY VIEW CL 1
BARLEY CL 2
HARVESTERS CL 3
SUNNYBANK CL
THE DOWNS
PLAINVIEW CL
GREENACRESS CL
WOOD LA
HARDWICK CT
CHESTER RD N
GRAHAM HO
OLLISON DR
CARLTON AVE
BUSHEY CL
REDWOOD RD
MEADOW CL
Primrose Farm
Crem
INGLEWOOD GR
THE GLADE
B4151
FOLEY RD E
Beacon Way
Birch Wood
The Foley Arms (PH)
FOLEY RD W
B74
FOLEY CT
Potter's Wood
SCHOOLACRE RISE
FOLEY WOOD CL
AMBERLEY WAY
SILVER BIRCH RD
EGERTON RD
GROSVENOR AVE
THORNEY RD
BEACON HILL
B4151
SUTTON RD
CROOK LA
LITTLE JOHNSON'S LA
BEACON RD
ALDRIDGE RD
BEECHCROFT CRES
LIMETREE RD
PINETREE DR
WHITETHORN CRES
CHERRYWOOD RD
HAZELWOOD RD
CEDAR DR
BLACKWOOD RD
Blackwood Sch
LANGHAM GN
JEROME CT
BRIAR AVE
ELMTREE RD
Moat Farm

17
32

A B C D E F
WOOD LA
French Croft Farm
Forge Farm
Forge Wood
Sewage Works
Forge Cottages
Riding Stables
BACK LA
FOOTHERLEY LA
8
WS9
The Belt
New Wood
FORGE LA
WS14
7
MILL LA
Mill Farm
Home Farm
Aston Prim Sch
Claypit Rough
Cottage Farm
CH
Blake Street
BLAKE ST
A4026
01
6
ALDRIDGE RD
LITTLE ASTON LA
A4026
A454
HILL HOOK HO 1
BICKLEY HO 2
PO
Hill Hook
THE SPINNEY
LAKESIDE
LITTLE ASTON HALL DR
1 BEECH HO
2 OAK HO
3 CEDAR HO
4 BIRCH HO
5 MAPLE HO
LITTLE ASTON HALL
Little Aston
ROMANS GRANGE
WOODSIDE DR
Hornton Manor
BEECHWOOD CROFT
SQUIRREL WLK
KEEPERS RD
BEECH GATE
THE GROVE
POPLAR RISE
ROSEMARY NOOK
B4138
REGENCY WLK
VERNON CL
BICKLEY AVE
BIRCH DR
LOXTON CL
HORNTON CL
CHERRYWOOD WAY
SILVER BIRCH COPPICE
KNIGHTON RD
WAVENHAM CL
Mill Pond
BRADGATE DR
NETHERSTONE GR
MARLBOROUGH CL
STATION APP
HILL HOOK RD
5
CAMPION 1
CELANDINE 2
BRYONY 3
ASPHODEL 4
GERMANDER 5
MULLEIN 6
ST GEORGES CT
KESTERTON RD
HARRISON RD
AYLESFORD DR
A5127
LICHFIELD RD
00
Little Aston
CH
LONGACRES
LONGFIELD DR
PARK DR
SELWYN WLK
ROSEMARY HILL RD
ROSEMARY CT
CHARTWELL DR
BERKSWELL CL
EDGE HILL RD
Four Oaks Jun & Inf Schs
WINGATE CT
PACKINGTON CT
BLACKBERRY LA
WHITE FARM RD
CLARENCE RD
Sch
TANSY 7
VALERIAN 8
GENTIAN 9
4
Roundabout Wood
ROMAN PK
ROMAN RD
STONEHOUSE DR
ENDWOOD DR
JERVIS PK
WOODSTOCK DR
THE BEECHES
TALL TREES CL
WALSALL RD
CLAVERDON DR
ROMAN LA
BARNS CROFT
ALDERHITHE GR
ROSEMARY DR
THE HEADLANDS
WAYSIDE DR
ROUNTON CL
STREETLY DR
RUSSELL CT
RUSSELL BANK RD
LONGDON DR
HOOK DR
HARCOURT DR
Four Oaks
HILLMORTON RD
MEADOWSIDE RD
ROYSTON CHASE
VERCOURT
FALLOW FIELD
JERVIS CRES
PARK VIEW RD
STREETLY CRES
PINEWAYS 1
FOREST LAWNS 2
HIGHBURY RD
ST MARGARET'S
3
NEWICK AVE
BENNETT RD
MELLOR DR
FOUR OAKS COMMON RD
HELLABY HO
GROUNDS RD
ORCHARD GR
BUTLERS LA
WELFORD GR
KITTOE RD
TALBOT AVE
LITTLE ASTON PARK RD
LEAFY GLADE
CHESTNUT CL
THISTLE DOWN CL
KIMBERLEY CL
GRASMERE AVE
Streetly
WATERS DR
HIGHCROFT DR
CROWN LA
SEYMOUR GDNS
WOODSIDE
FARNCOTE DR
KNIGHTON DR
KNIGHTON CL
HERMES CT
CLARENCE GDNS
VESEY CL
ALL SAINTS DR
99
HARDWICK RD
STREETLY LA
B74
SETON HO
LESLIE RD
BURNETT RD
ROMAN PL
HORSLEY RD
MARWOOD CROFT
CARLTON CROFT
ELFORD CL
FEATHERSTON RD
FOLEY CHURCH CL
STREETLY WOOD
EASTMOOR CL
B4151
2
FOLEY RD E
B4151
A454
CARLTON AVE
Sutton Park
GREENSLEEVES
Sports Ctr
1 THORNEY RD
2 OAKDALE
3 PARKSIDE WAY
ASTOR RD
REDLANDS WAY
MIDDLETON RD
HIGHGATE
THORNHILL RD
Streetly Lodge
LINKS VIEW
FAIRGREEN WAY
CH
Streetly Belt
Mayor's Arbour
Gum Slade
Bracebridge Pool
SUTTON COLDFIELD
THE COPSE
1
BRIAR AVE
HAWTHORN RD
Manor Prim Sch
ICKNIELD CL
MANOR RD
B4138
Streetly Wood
HARTOPP RD
APPLECROSS
CLIVEDEN COPPICE
LUTTRELL RD
98
08 A B 09 C D 10 E F

45
32

E3
1 CROWN CT
2 ST JOHNS HO
3 CHERRYL HO
4 AUSTIN CT
5 OAK PARK CT

F2
1 ETON CT
2 THE SYCAMORES
3 MARLBOROUGH CT
4 WINCHESTER CT
5 HARROW CT
6 DENSTON CT
7 OUNDLE CT
8 MALVERN CT
9 WREKIN CT
10 THE WILLOWS
11 PARK WOOD CT
12 BRACEBRIDGE HO
13 LONGMOOR HO
14 BURCOT CT
15 BELWELL LA
16 FOUR OAKS RD
17 PARK DR

F3
1 COMPTON CT
2 TUDOR PARK CT

31
18

A B C D E F
8 7 01 6 5 00 4 3 99 2 1 98
11 12 13
WS14
B74
B75
Joburns Cottages
Alder Farm
Brookfield
GREEN BARNS LA
LITTLE HAY LA
Green Wood
M6 TOLL
A38
The Highwayman (PH)
BIRMINGHAM RD
A5127
Black Fir Wood
WOODLAND CT
SMARTS AVE
Blossom Hill Farm
LONDON RD
Camp Farm
BLAKE ST
WATFORD GAP RD
Biddles Farm
WATFORD GAP
LICHFIELD RD
WYNDLEY MANOR
Hovel Covert
Weeford Park Farm
Pine Tree Cottage
CAMP RD
Springhill Farm
Hill Common
HILLWOOD COMMON RD
Mast
Hill Farm
Television Station
Manorial Farm
HILLWOOD RD
Manorial Wood
Springhill Plantation
Hill Wood
Spreading Tree Hill
Hill
BYRON CL
HAYCROFT DR
KEATING GDNS
WARDLE
DUNTON CL
STRINGER CL
WESTFIELD MANOR
BEECH CL
DAWNEY DR
HATHAWAY RD
OAKLAND HO
HIGHOVER DR
GLANVILLE DR
GRESLEY CL
HILLSIDE RD
1 CHEVIOT CT
2 CHILTERN CT
3 BREDON CT
4 COTSWOLD CT
Hill Wood Farm
Hillside Farm
WORCESTER LA
1 PLOUGHMANS PL
2 TILLER GR
3 SOWERS CT
4 COMBINE CL
Hilltop Farm
TURF PITTS LA
Woodside Farm
Dale Farm
Piggery
CANWELL GATE
DUTTON'S LA
MAYALL DR
LOXLEY RD
ST JOHN CL
HARVEST FIELDS WAY
WHEATSHEAF CL
SCARECROW LA
WEEFORD RD
TURF PITTS LA
SHERIFOOT LA
CROCKFORD DR
HILL VILLAGE RD
BUTLERS LA
Butlers Lane
HENLEY DR
PEGASUS CT
BEATON RD
KITTOE RD
SARA CL
HOBART CT 1
BALFOUR CT 2
HARLAND RD
HOLLY LA
DUNCALFE DR
DUGDALE CRES
PUDSEY DR
GIBBONS RD
BODINGTON RD
HOMESTEAD DR
RANDLE DR
CARTWRIGHT RD
DARNEL HURST RD
EDWARDS RD
WOODSTILE CL
AMINGTON CL
WORCESTER LA
ST BLAISE RD
Little Sutton Prim Sch
WILLMOTT CL
WILLMOTT RD
CROFTERS LA
B4151
SLADE RD
E3
1 MARLPIT RISE
2 WEEFORD DELL
3 WHEATCROFT CL
4 SHEARERS PL
5 WOODMAN GR
6 FARM HOUSE LA
7 BLACKSMITH DR
8 WEAVER CT
MANORIAL RD
ROUGHLEY FARM RD
THE DOVECOTES
KINGS CT
BRENTNALL DR
WALCOT CL
DRAYTON CL
TOWER RD
GRANGE LA
REDHALL DR
CLARENDON RD
Roughley
PH
BISHOPS MDW
Mere Green
CHURCH TERR
WILMCOTE DR
GRANGE AVE
WHEATLEY CL
ELDRED CL
ELISABETH CT
The Arthur Terry Sch
Mere Green Comb Sch
PO
MARLPIT LA
COBURN DR
BRADWELL CROFT
BODICOTE GR
BLAYDON AVE
BUCKTON CL
MORDAUNT DR
AULTON RD
MAIN WARING DR
CHARNLEY DR
FOX HILL RD
ALL SAINTS DR
CLARENCE RD
BELWELL DR
BELWELL LA
CARLTON HO
Liby
FARN BOROUGH CT
ST JAMES RD
MERE GREEN RD
MERE GREEN CL
ROUGHLEY DR
HARVEY DR
LITTLE SUTTON RD
HOLTE DR
PEROTT DR
Moor Hall Prim Sch
SHARRAT FIELD
SHEPHERDS POOL RD
MERE POOL RD
CLIVE CL
B4151
BELWELL GDNS
1 DEVONSHIRE CT
2 HARBOROUGH CT
3 TUDOR CT
NURSERY LA
ALSTON CL
LE MORE
MIDGLEY DR
MERE DR
CREMORNE RD
ARLESCOTE CL
HOMER RD
ROWALLAN RD
A454
HARTOPP RD
THE FORDROUGH
CREMORNE WLK
KINGSLEIGH CROFT
JORDAN RD
STREATHER RD
HAREWELL DR
ESSEX RD
FERRERS CL
Fox Hill Farm
FOUR OAKS RD
GREENSLEVES
CRESSINGTON DR
BEECHCROFT CT
HANSON MAN
FOXTON MAN
IRNHAM RD
Ley Hill
HAWKESFORD CL
JORDAN CL
WENTWORTH CT
DOWER RD
QUEENS RD
DEVEREUX RD
LITTLE SUTTON LA
GROSVENOR CL
HEATH CROFT RD
BROCKHURST RD
WYRLEY RD
SUTTON COLDFIELD
Moor Hall
Hotel
MOOR HALL DR
CH
Ashfurlong Hall
A453 TAMWORTH RD
THE COPSE
LUTTRELL RD
FOUR OAKS CT
PINE LEIGH
LADYWOOD RD
HAZLEMERE DR
CEDARWOOD
LAUREATES WLK
RIDGEWOOD DR
TRINITY RD
LEY HILL RD
LOCKHART DR
Coppice Prim Sch

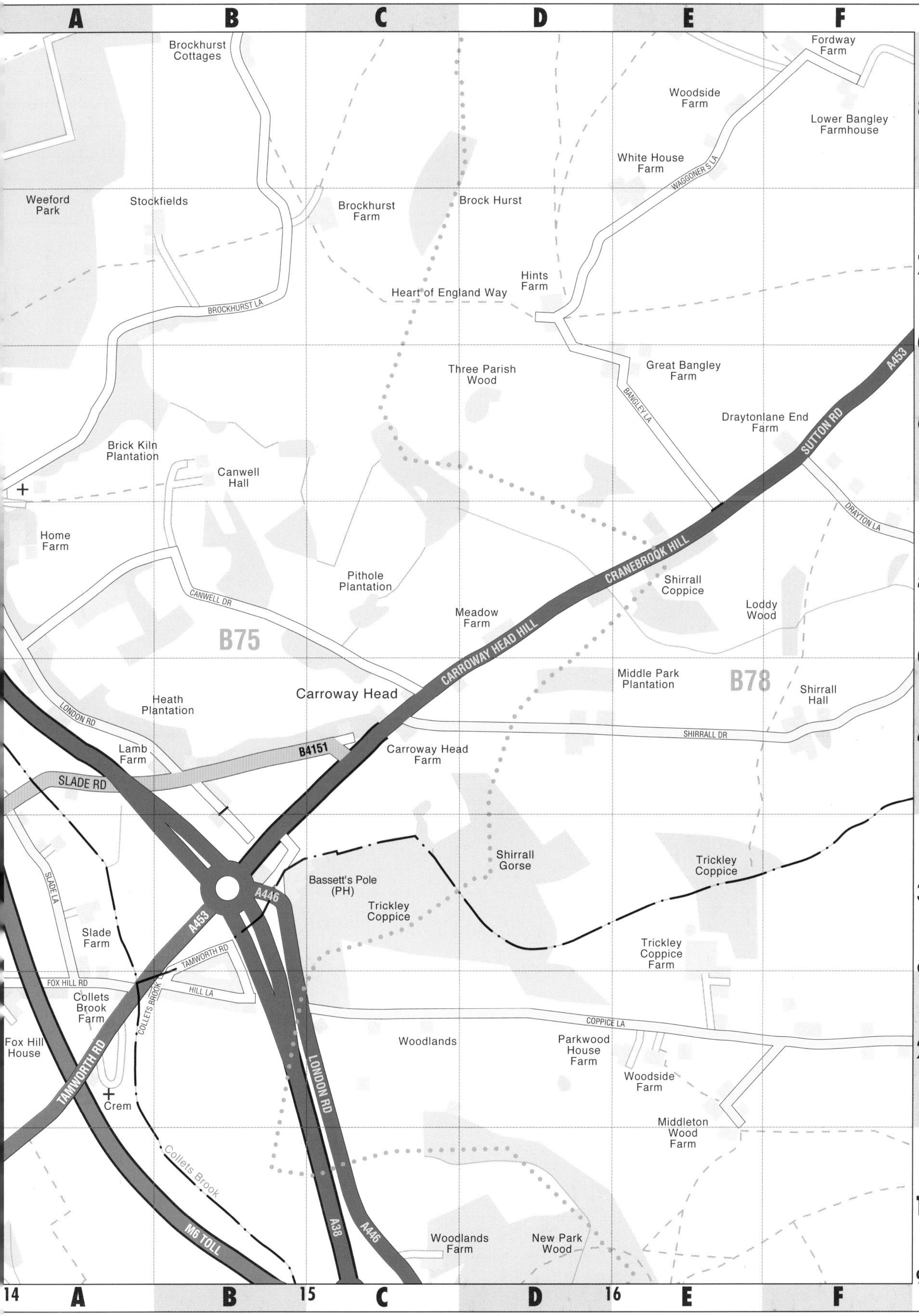
A
B
C
D
E
F
Brockhurst Cottages
Fordway Farm
Woodside Farm
Lower Bangley Farmhouse
White House Farm
WAGGONER'S LA
Weeford Park
Stockfields
Brockhurst Farm
Brock Hurst
Hints Farm
Heart of England Way
BROCKHURST LA
Three Parish Wood
Great Bangley Farm
BANGLEY LA
Draytonlane End Farm
SUTTON RD
A453
Brick Kiln Plantation
Canwell Hall
DRAYTON LA
Home Farm
CRANEBROOK HILL
Shirrall Coppice
Pithole Plantation
Loddy Wood
CANWELL DR
Meadow Farm
B75
CARROWAY HEAD HILL
Middle Park Plantation
B78
Shirrall Hall
Heath Plantation
Carroway Head
LONDON RD
SHIRRALL DR
Lamb Farm
B4151
Carroway Head Farm
SLADE RD
Shirrall Gorse
Trickley Coppice
Bassett's Pole (PH)
A446
Trickley Coppice
SLADE LA
A453
Slade Farm
Trickley Coppice Farm
TAMWORTH RD
FOX HILL RD
HILL LA
Collets Brook Farm
COLLETS BROOK LA
COPPICE LA
Fox Hill House
Woodlands
Parkwood House Farm
TAMWORTH RD
LONDON RD
Woodside Farm
Crem
Middleton Wood Farm
Collets Brook
M6 TOLL
A38
A446
Woodlands Farm
New Park Wood
8
7
01
6
5
00
4
3
99
2
1
98
14
15
16

33
20

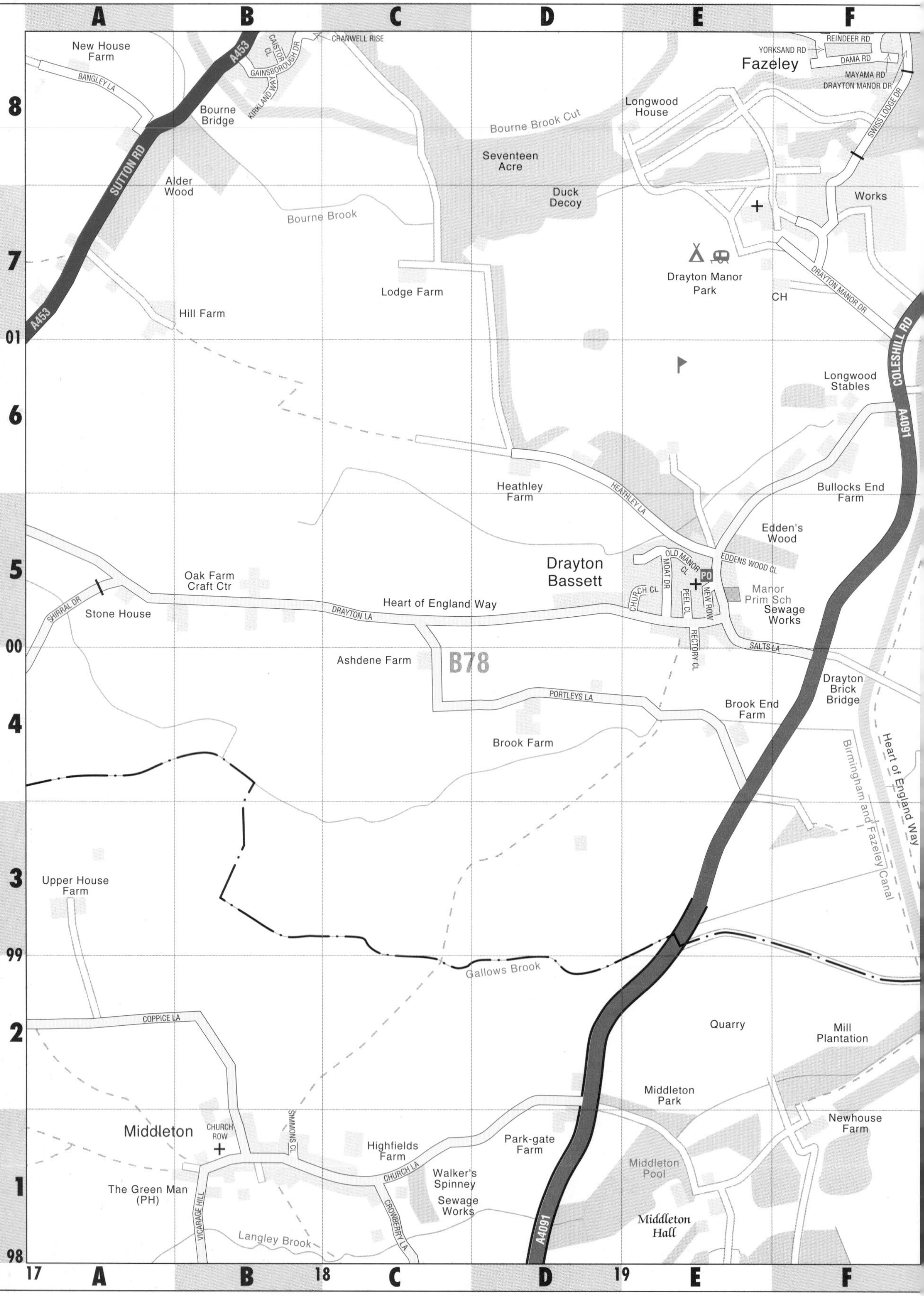
A
B
C
D
E
F
New House Farm
BANGLEY LA
A453
CAISTOR CL
GAINSBOROUGH DR
KIRKLAND WAY
CRANWELL RISE
REINDEER RD
YORKSAND RD
DAMA RD
Fazeley
MAYAMA RD
DRAYTON MANOR DR
SWISS LODGE DR
Bourne Bridge
Longwood House
Bourne Brook Cut
SUTTON RD
Seventeen Acre
Alder Wood
Duck Decoy
Works
Bourne Brook
Drayton Manor Park
CH
DRAYTON MANOR DR
Lodge Farm
Hill Farm
COLESHILL RD
Longwood Stables
A4091
Heathley Farm
HEATHLEY LA
Bullocks End Farm
Edden's Wood
Drayton Bassett
OLD MANOR CL
MOAT DR
EDDENS WOOD CL
PO
Oak Farm Craft Ctr
CHURCH CL
PEEL CL
NEW ROW
Manor Prim Sch
Sewage Works
SHIRRAL DR
Stone House
Heart of England Way
DRAYTON LA
RECTORY CL
SALTS LA
Ashdene Farm
B78
Drayton Brick Bridge
PORTLEYS LA
Brook End Farm
Brook Farm
Birmingham and Fazeley Canal
Heart of England Way
Upper House Farm
Gallows Brook
COPPICE LA
Quarry
Mill Plantation
Middleton Park
Newhouse Farm
Middleton
CHURCH ROW
SIMMONS CL
Highfields Farm
Park-gate Farm
Middleton Pool
CHURCH LA
Walker's Spinney
The Green Man (PH)
Sewage Works
VICARAGE HILL
CROWBERRY LA
Middleton Hall
Langley Brook
8
7
01
6
5
00
4
3
99
2
1
98
17
18
19

33
48

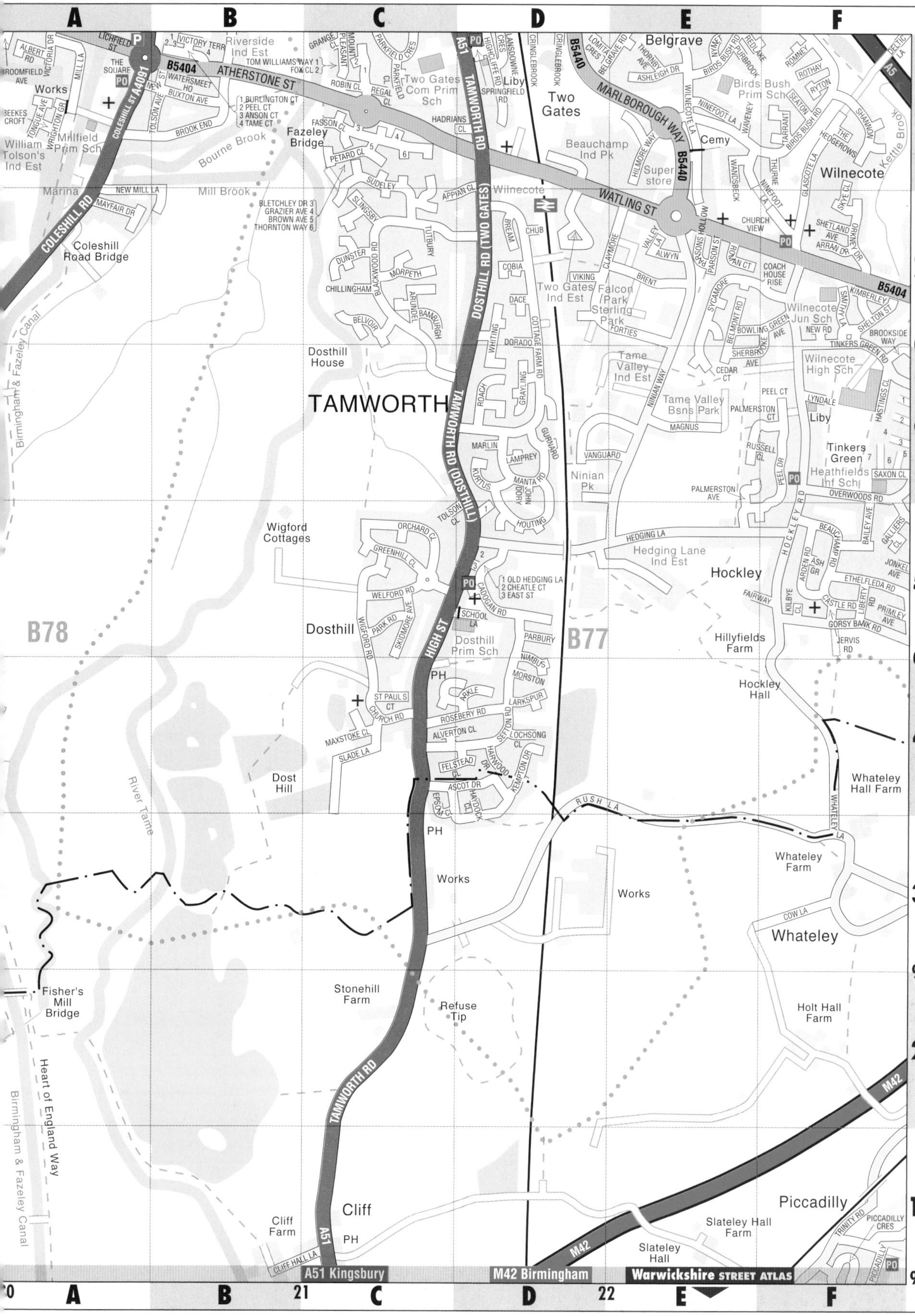
A B C D E F
8 7 01 6 5 00 4 3 99 2 1 98
TAMWORTH
Two Gates
Belgrave
Wilnecote
Fazeley Bridge
Dosthill
Hockley
Whateley
Piccadilly
Cliff
B78
B77
B5404
A4091
A51
B5440
A5
M42
ATHERSTONE ST
WATLING ST
MARLBOROUGH WAY
COLESHILL RD
TAMWORTH RD
DOSTHILL RD (TWO GATES)
TAMWORTH RD (DOSTHILL)
HIGH ST
Riverside Ind Est
Two Gates Com Prim Sch
Birds Bush Prim Sch
Beauchamp Ind Pk
Super store
Cemy
Millfield Prim Sch
William Tolson's Ind Est
Marina
Bourne Brook
Mill Brook
Coleshill Road Bridge
Dosthill House
Wigford Cottages
Two Gates Ind Est
Falcon Park
Sterling Park
Tame Valley Ind Est
Tame Valley Bsns Park
Wilnecote Jun Sch
Wilnecote High Sch
Liby
Tinkers Green
Heathfields Inf Sch
Ninian Pk
Hedging Lane Ind Est
Hillyfields Farm
Hockley Hall
Dosthill Prim Sch
Dost Hill
Whateley Hall Farm
Whateley Farm
Works
Stonehill Farm
Refuse Tip
Holt Hall Farm
Fisher's Mill Bridge
River Tame
Birmingham & Fazeley Canal
Heart of England Way
Cliff Farm
Slateley Hall Farm
Slateley Hall
Kettle Brook
1 BURLINGTON CT
2 PEEL CT
3 ANSON CT
4 TAME CT
BLETCHLEY DR 3
GRAZIER AVE 4
BROWN AVE 5
THORNTON WAY 6
1 OLD HEDGING LA
2 CHEATLE CT
3 EAST ST
A51 Kingsbury
M42 Birmingham

35
22

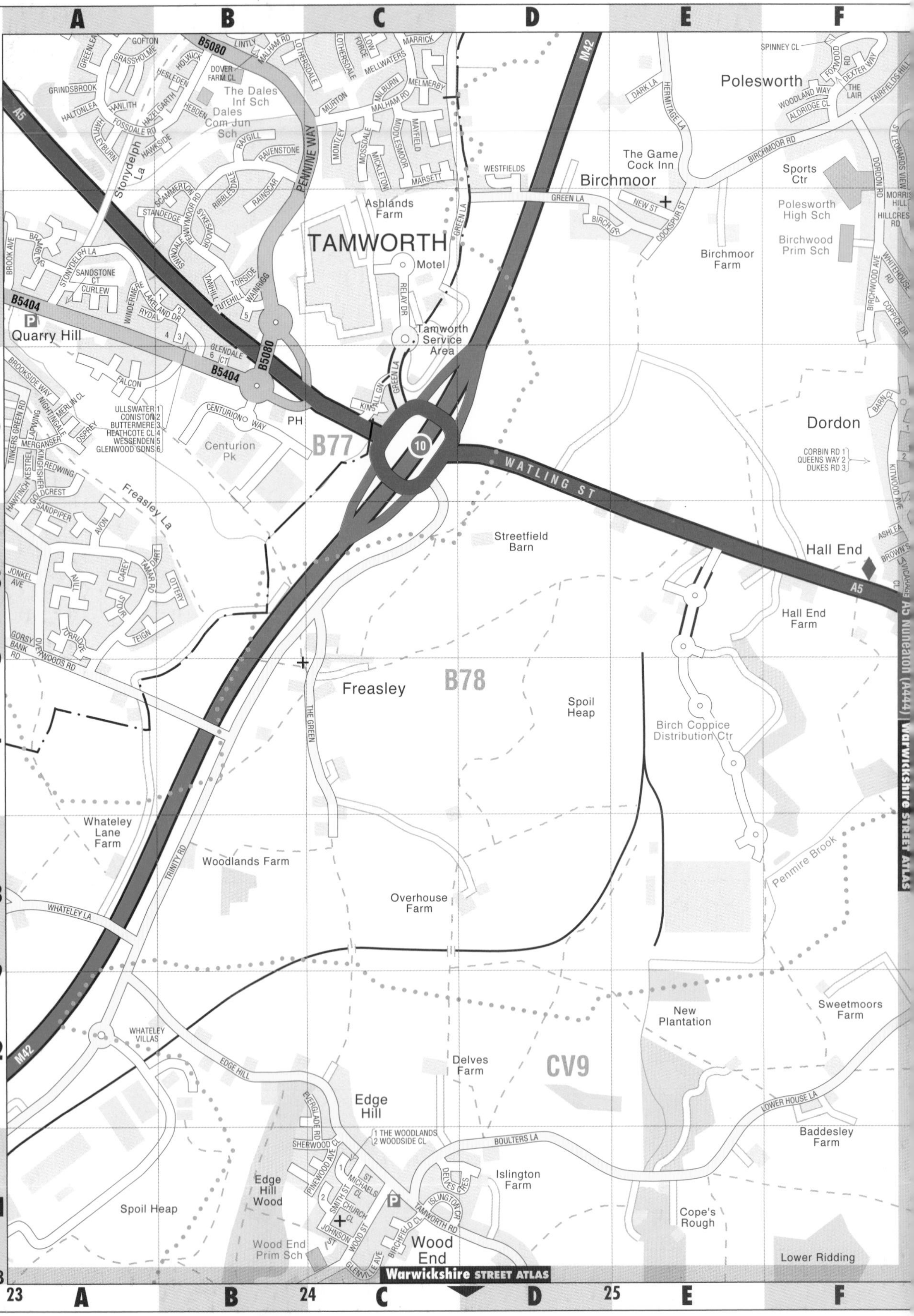
A
B
C
D
E
F
8
7
01
6
5
00
4
3
99
2
1
98
23
24
25
TAMWORTH
Polesworth
Birchmoor
Dordon
Hall End
Freasley
Quarry Hill
Edge Hill
Wood End
B77
B78
CV9
A5
M42
B5080
B5404
WATLING ST
PENNINE WAY
The Dales Inf Sch
Dales Com Jun Sch
Stonydelph La
Ashlands Farm
Motel
Tamworth Service Area
Centurion Pk
PH
Freasley La
The Game Cock Inn
Sports Ctr
Polesworth High Sch
Birchwood Prim Sch
Birchmoor Farm
Streetfield Barn
Hall End Farm
Spoil Heap
Birch Coppice Distribution Ctr
Whateley Lane Farm
Woodlands Farm
Overhouse Farm
Penmire Brook
New Plantation
Sweetmoors Farm
Delves Farm
Baddesley Farm
Islington Farm
Cope's Rough
Lower Ridding
Edge Hill Wood
Wood End Prim Sch
Spoil Heap
WHATELEY LA
WHATELEY VILLAS
EDGE HILL
TRINITY RD
THE GREEN
GREEN LA
RELAY DR
WESTFIELDS
NEW ST
BIRCH GR
COCKSPUR ST
DARK LA
HERMITAGE LA
BIRCHMOOR RD
BOULTERS LA
LOWER HOUSE LA
EVERGLADE RD
SHERWOOD CL
PINEWOOD AVE
ST MICHAELS CL
CHURCH CL
SMITH ST
JOHNSON ST
WOOD ST
GLENVILLE AVE
BIRCHFIELD CL
DELVES CRES
ISLINGTON CR
TAMWORTH RD
1 THE WOODLANDS
2 WOODSIDE CL
CORBIN RD 1
QUEENS WAY 2
DUKES RD 3
ULLSWATER 1
CONISTON 2
BUTTERMERE 3
HEATHCOTE CL 4
WESSENDEN 5
GLENWOOD GDNS 6
CENTURION WAY
FALCON
GLENDALE CT
GORSY BANK RD
OVERWOODS RD
JONKEL AVE
TEIGN
Warwickshire STREET ATLAS

35

23
38

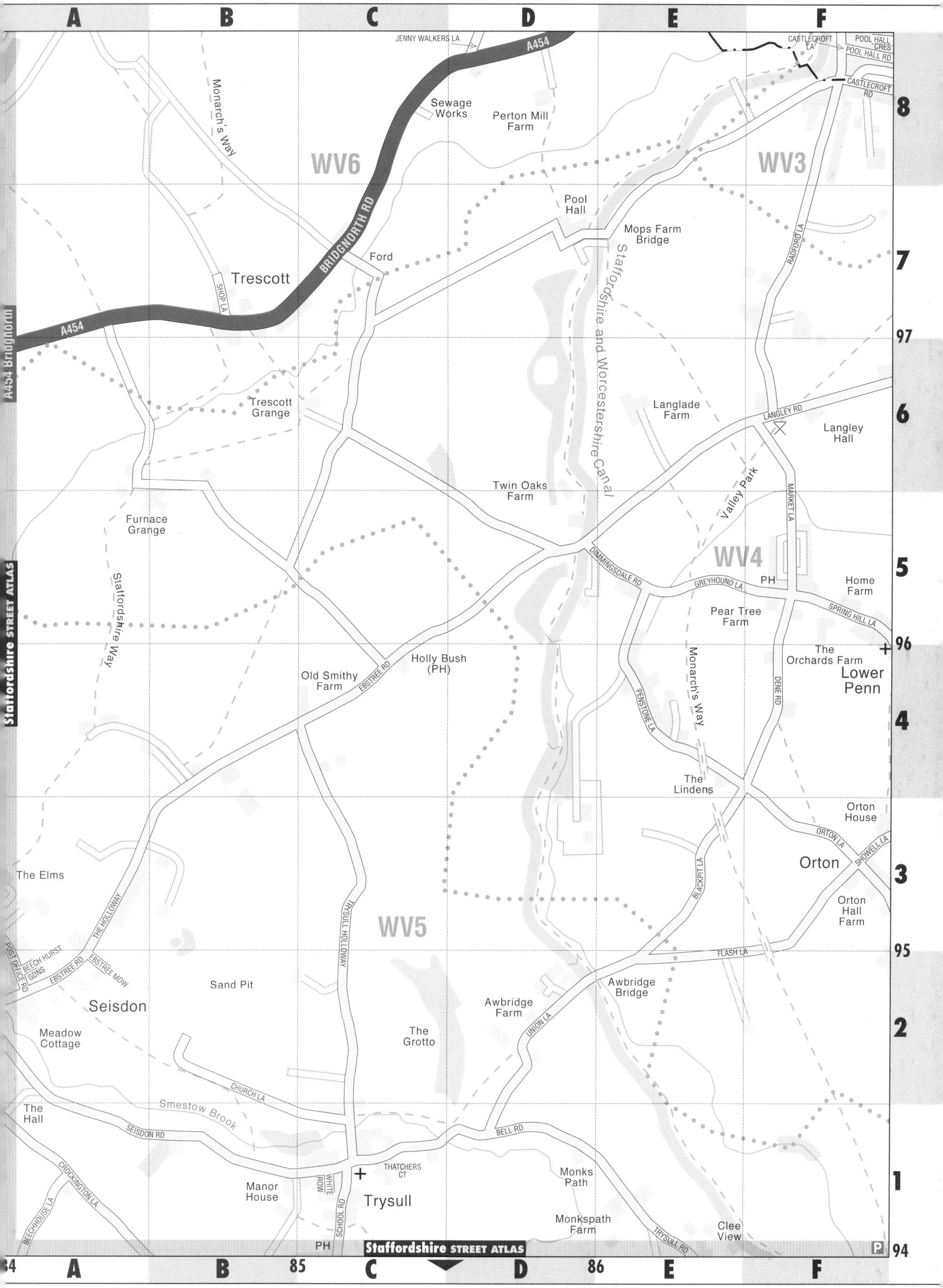
A
B
C
D
E
F
8
7
97
6
5
96
4
3
95
2
1
94
84
85
86
JENNY WALKERS LA
A454
CASTLECROFT LA
POOL HALL CRES
POOL HALL RD
CASTLECROFT RD
Monarch's Way
Sewage Works
Perton Mill Farm
WV6
WV3
BRIDGNORTH RD
Pool Hall
Mops Farm Bridge
Ford
Trescott
SHOP LA
RADFORD LA
Staffordshire and Worcestershire Canal
A454 Bridgnorth
Trescott Grange
Langlade Farm
LANGLEY RD
Langley Hall
Twin Oaks Farm
Valley Park
MARKET LA
Furnace Grange
WV4
DIMMINGSDALE RD
GREYHOUND LA
PH
Home Farm
Staffordshire STREET ATLAS
Staffordshire Way
Pear Tree Farm
SPRING HILL LA
The Orchards Farm
Lower Penn
Old Smithy Farm
EBSTREE RD
Holly Bush (PH)
PENSTONE LA
DENE RD
The Lindens
Orton House
ORTON LA
SHOWELL LA
Orton
BLACKPIT LA
The Elms
THE HOLLOWAY
TRYSULL HOLLOWAY
WV5
Orton Hall Farm
POST OFFICE RD
BEECH HURST GDNS
EBSTREE RD
EBSTREE MDW
FLASH LA
Sand Pit
Seisdon
Awbridge Bridge
Awbridge Farm
UNION LA
Meadow Cottage
The Grotto
CHURCH LA
Smestow Brook
The Hall
SEISDON RD
BELL RD
CROCKINGTON LA
Manor House
WHITE ROW
THATCHERS CT
Monks Path
Trysull
SCHOOL RD
BEECHHOUSE LA
Monkspath Farm
TRYSULL RD
Clee View
PH
P

38

37
24

A B C D E F

87 A B 88 C D 89 E F

37
49

For full street detail of the highlighted area see page 163.

25
40

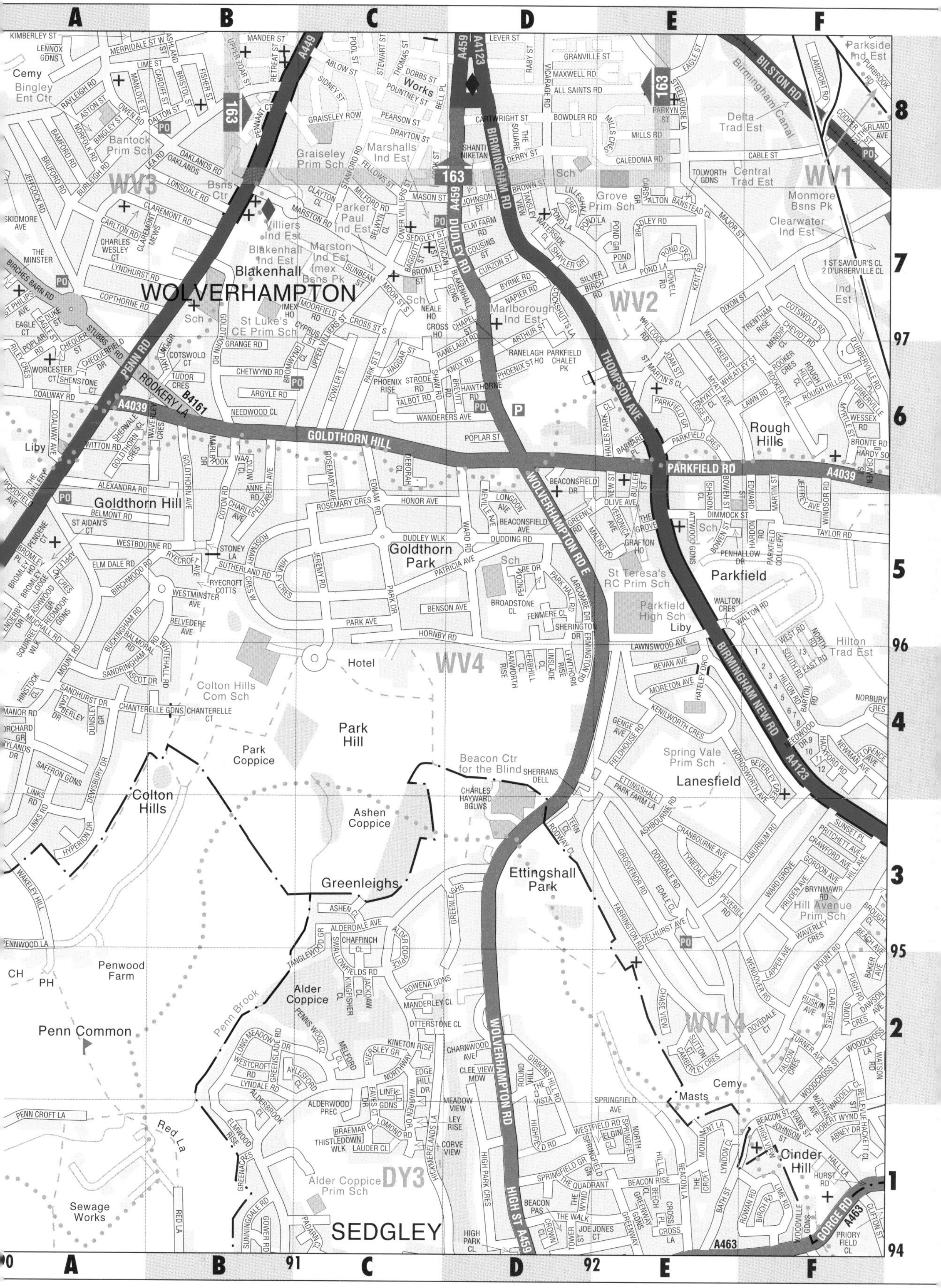

F4
1 ELLIOT CT
2 HARDIE CT
3 MERIDEN CT
4 MORRIS CT
5 WESLEY CT
6 WARWICK CT
7 RYLCROFT
8 AVONCROFT
9 FIRCROFT
10 HOLMCROFT
11 GENTHORN CL
12 ASHCROFT
13 CENTRAL AVE

50
40

39
26

F8
1 CHARLECOTE RISE
2 RAGLEY DR
3 PETWORTH CL

39
51

A7
1 TRAMWAY CL
2 DARTMOUTH CRES
3 JOHNSON PL
4 BARN FARM CL

C6
1 ALBERT HO
2 VICTORIA HO
3 ALLEN DR
4 WHEELWRIGHT CL

27

D6
1 THE LEYS
2 GREAT CROFT HO
3 JOHN WOOTON HO
4 PICTUREDROME WAY
5 CASTLE CT
6 REGENT CT

42

E3
1 MONWAY BLDGS
2 CINDER WAY
3 THE MEETING HO

F2
1 UPPER RUSSELL ST
2 SHAMBLES
3 GREGORY CL
4 RAILWAY TERR
5 ST JOHNS CT
6 TALBOT HO

F3
1 CHURCH HILL CT
2 GEORGIAN GDNS
3 ST BARTHOLOMEW TERR
4 PARTRIDGE CT
5 LOVER'S WLK
6 CHURCH HILL
7 SQUIRE'S WLK

52

42

B7
1 DAWLEY CL
2 HORSESHOE CL
3 SHERIDAN CL
B8
1 SOUTHBOURNE AVE
2 SCARBOROUGH CL

C7
1 SCRIMSHAW HO
2 DARBY HO
3 WESLEY HO
4 TAYLOR HO
5 CALEDON ST
6 ROCHFORD CL

41

C8
1 VICARAGE TERR
2 BLAKE HO
3 STANSBURY HO
4 MARSHALL HO

28

D7
1 THELMA ST
2 TRUDA ST
E7
1 WOOD HO
2 WHITEHALL RD

E8
1 SISTER DORA GDNS
2 MARYVALE CT
3 BARLEYFIELD HO
4 ORLANDO HO
5 NEWHALL HO
6 LITTLE CALDMORE
7 HAYDN SANDERS SQ
8 THE WHITE HART
9 HUMARA GHAR
10 NOELE GORDON GDNS
F7
1 LITTLE LONDON HO

F8
1 SANDWELL HO
2 MARET CT
3 LYSWAY CT
4 HIGHGATE CT
5 SPRINGHILL CT
6 ELMSDALE CT
7 RIDGEWOOD CL
8 SANDWELL WLK
9 HIGHVIEW
10 BIRMINGHAM RD

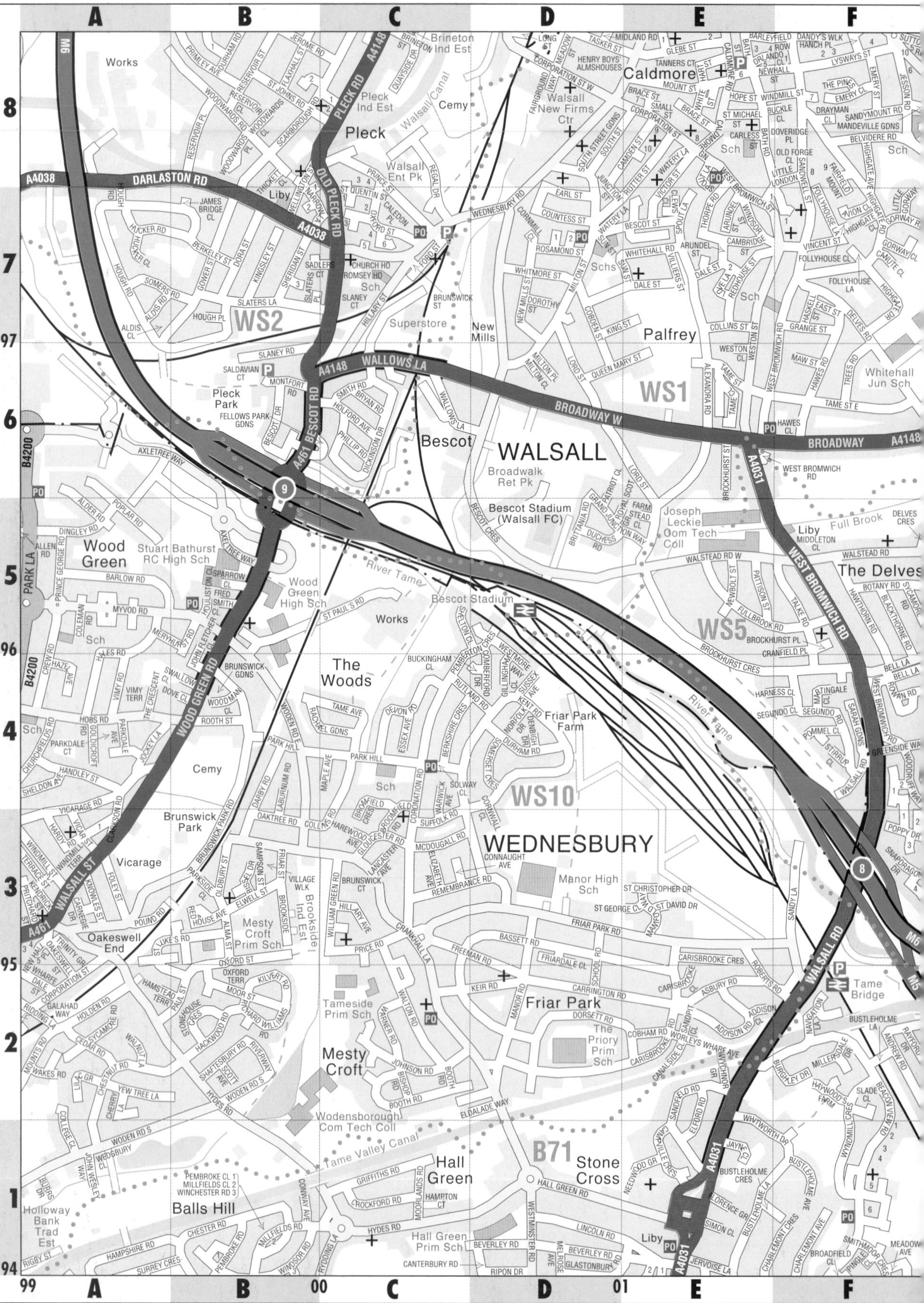

41

53

A3
1 LONGCROFT AVE
2 MOATFIELD TERR
3 JENNYNS CT
4 HOPKINS CT
5 COMBERFORD CT

E1
1 STONELEA CL
2 CANTERBURY RD

F1
1 SHEAPECOATE HO
2 STANTON HO
3 BROOM HO
4 BEACONVIEW HO
5 BRIARLEY HO
6 CAMBERLEY

F4
1 MAGNOLIA DR
2 WISTERIA DR
4 COLUMBINE CL
F3
1 BELLFLOWER DR
2 LAVENDER CL
3 ELDERBERRY CL

29
44

54
44

F1
1 BEACON MEWS
2 BEACON CT
3 SANDRINGHAM CT

43
30

A
B
C
D
E
F
8
7
97
6
5
96
4
3
95
2
1
94
05
06
07
WS5
WS9
B74
B73
B43
B44
B42
Beacon Hill Farm
Pool House Farm
Crook Cottage Farm
Beacon Farm
Mast
War Meml
Barr Beacon
Beacon Park Farm
Barr Common Farm
Blue House Farm
Crook House
Beacon Dairy Farm
Doe Bank Wood
Meadow View JMI Sch
Doe Bank Farm
The Old Hall Farm
Barr Beacon Language Coll
The Duckery
Pheasey Park Farm Prim Sch
Pheasey
High Wood
King George's Field
Lindens Prim Sch
Streetly
St Anne's RC Prim Sch
Gilbert's Wood
Holly Wood
Whitecrest Jun & Inf Sch
Superstore
Queslett
Kings Bsns Pk
Century Ind Est
Winster Grove Ind Ctr
Kingstanding Ctr
BIRMINGHAM
Recn Gd
Great Barr Sch
Great Barr Prim Sch
Maryvale Prim Sch
Old Oscott
Cardinal Wiseman Tech Coll
BEACON RD
BEACON WAY
QUESLETT RD
QUESLETT RD E
KING'S RD
KINGSTANDING RD
A452 CHESTER RD
B4154
B4149
B4138
A4041
M6
BRIDLE LA
DOE BANK LA
PINFOLD LA
OLD HALL LA
CROOK LA
BODENS LA
CHAPEL LA
SUTTON'S DR
HANDSWORTH DR
SHADY LA
OSCOTT SCHOOL LA
ALDRIDGE RD
OLD OSCOTT HILL
OLD OSCOTT LA

43
55

31
46

A
B
C
D
E
F
8
7
97
6
5
96
4
3
95
2
1
94
08
09
10
B4138
THORNHILL RD
CHESTER RD
Warden's Belt
A4041
The Streetly Sch
Pool Hollies
Darnel Hurst
Lady Wood
Upper Nut Hurst
Blackroot Pool
B74
Meml
Lower Nut Hurst
Keeper's Pool
Sutton Park
Hill Hurst
Rowton's Well
Hotel
Holly Hurst
SUTTON OAK RD
Westwood Coppice
Longmoor Pool
King's Standing
Banners Gate Jun & Inf Schs
Banners Gate
Liby
B73
KINGSTANDING RD
Longmoor Sch
CHESTER RD N
SUTTON COLDFIELD
La Reserve
Wyndley Wood
Powell's Pool
New Oscott Prim Sch
CH
MONMOUTH DR
New Oscott
KINGS RD
A453
JOCKEY RD
B4149
Superstore
BEGGAR'S BUSH
B4142
BOLDMERE RD
B44
Kingstanding
Twickenham Prim Sch
COLLEGE RD
A452
Oscott Coll
B23
Boldmere Jun & Inf Schs
Kingsthorne Sch
WINDLEY HO 1
BRACEBRIDGE HO 2
BLACKROOT HO 3
KEEPERS HO 4
POWELLS HO 5

56
46

45
32

F6
1 ALDERMORE DR
2 TRICKLEY DR
3 ST SIMONS CL
4 ST JUDES CL
5 YEOMANS GRANGE
6 MOORLANDS CL
7 RECTORY PARK C
8 WHITEHOUSE CT
9 WOLLERTON GR

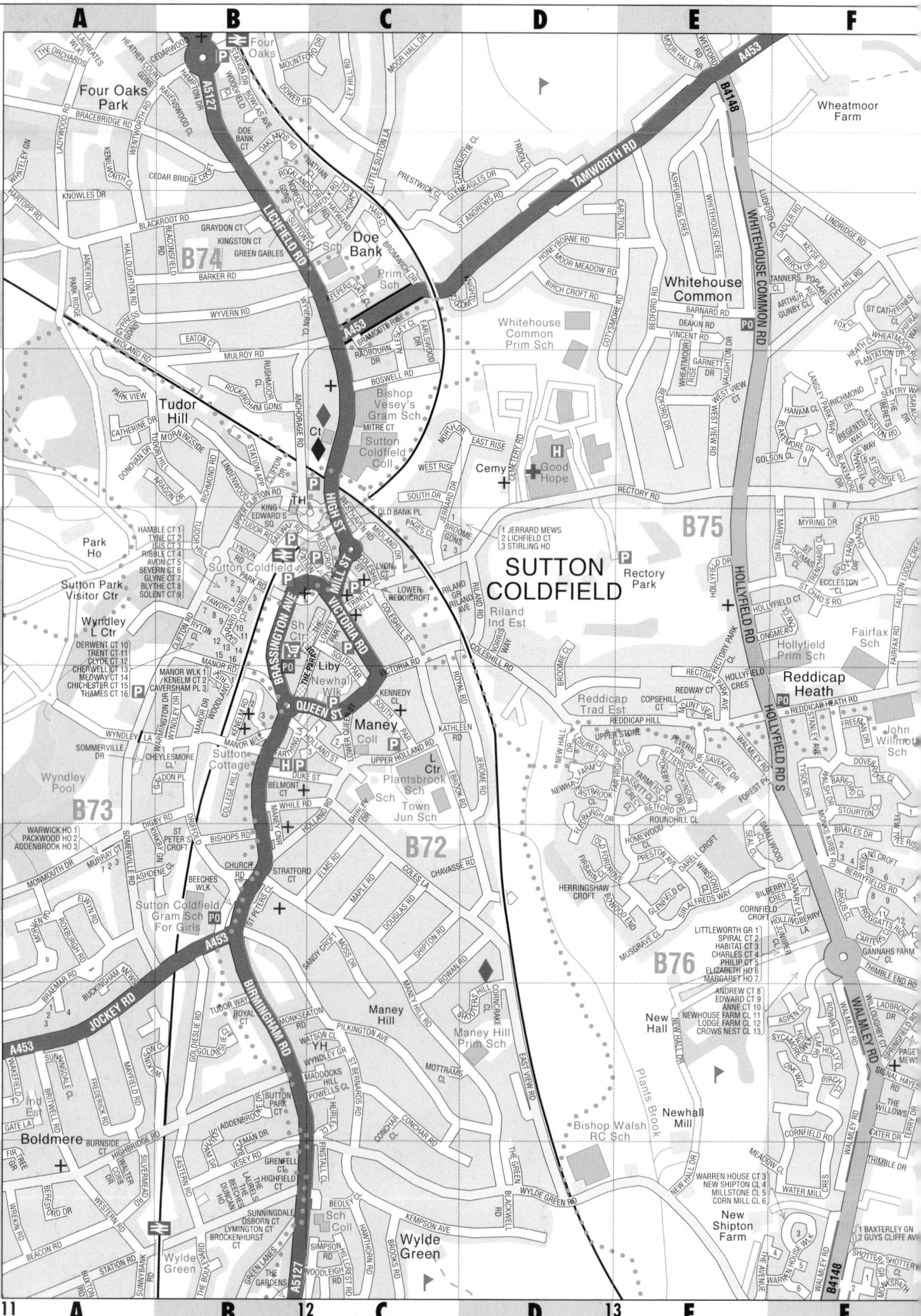

A2
1 BLACKETT CT
2 SOMERVILLE CT
3 BIDDULPH CT
4 TEDDINGTON CL

C4
1 FARTHING POOLS CL
2 DEEPLOW CL
3 HELLABY CL

45
57

33
48

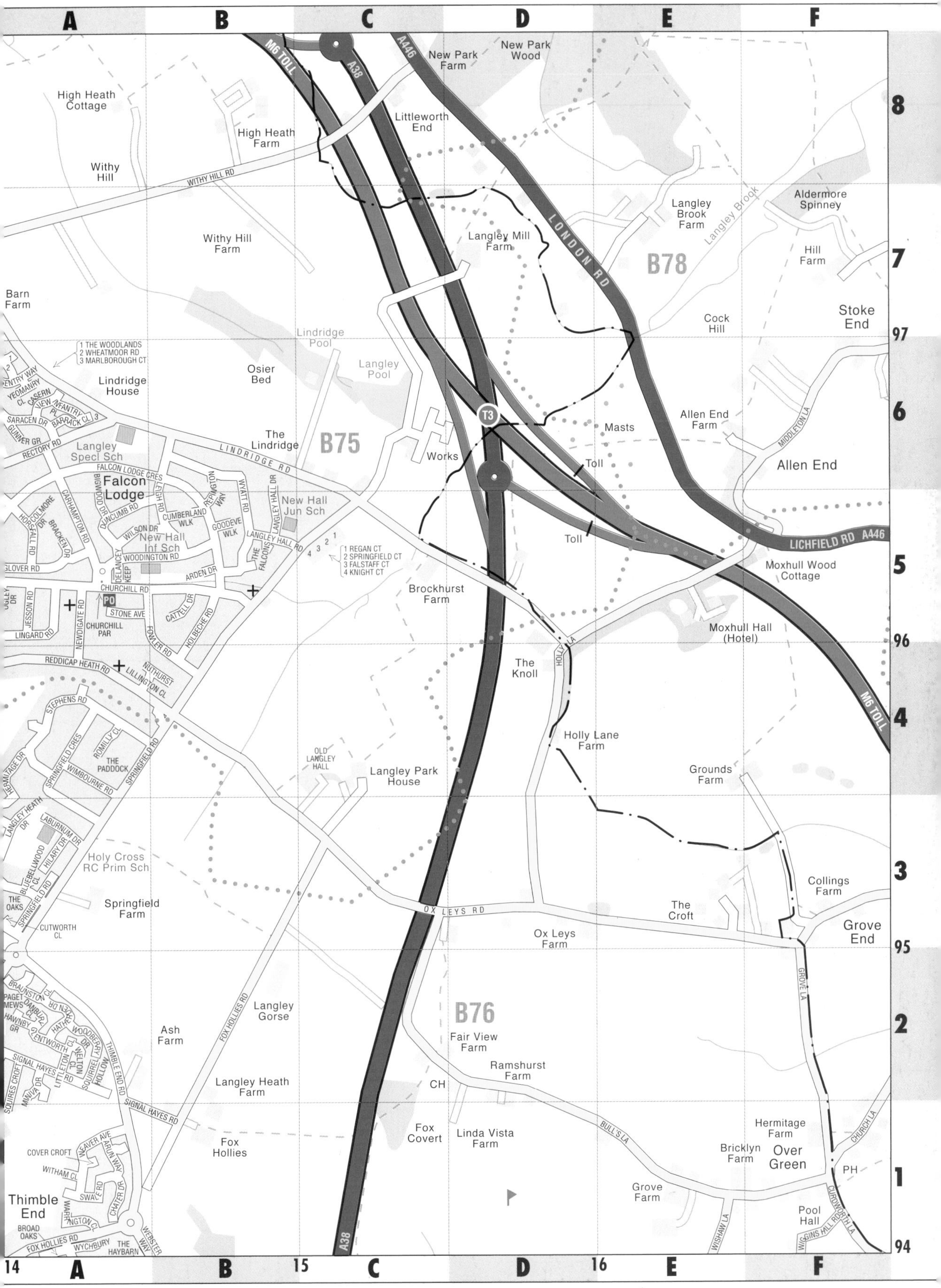
A
B
C
D
E
F
8
7
97
6
5
96
4
3
95
2
1
94
14
15
16
M6 TOLL
A38
A446
New Park Farm
New Park Wood
High Heath Cottage
High Heath Farm
Littleworth End
Withy Hill
WITHY HILL RD
Langley Brook Farm
Langley Brook
Aldermore Spinney
Langley Mill Farm
LONDON RD
B78
Hill Farm
Withy Hill Farm
Barn Farm
Cock Hill
Stoke End
Lindridge Pool
Langley Pool
1 THE WOODLANDS
2 WHEATMOOR RD
3 MARLBOROUGH CT
Lindridge House
Osier Bed
Allen End Farm
MIDDLETON LA
T3
Masts
The Lindridge
B75
Works
Langley Specl Sch
LINDRIDGE RD
Toll
Allen End
Falcon Lodge
FALCON LODGE CRES
New Hall Jun Sch
New Hall Inf Sch
LANGLEY HALL RD
1 REGAN CT
2 SPRINGFIELD CT
3 FALSTAFF CT
4 KNIGHT CT
LICHFIELD RD A446
Moxhull Wood Cottage
GLOVER RD
CHURCHILL RD
PO
STONE AVE
CHURCHILL PAR
LINGARD RD
Brockhurst Farm
Moxhull Hall (Hotel)
REDDICAP HEATH RD
LILLINGTON CL
The Knoll
HOLLY LA
STEPHENS RD
Holly Lane Farm
THE PADDOCK
OLD LANGLEY HALL
Langley Park House
Grounds Farm
Holy Cross RC Prim Sch
Springfield Farm
OX LEYS RD
The Croft
Collings Farm
Grove End
Ox Leys Farm
CUTWORTH CL
GROVE LA
Langley Gorse
B76
Ash Farm
Fair View Farm
Ramshurst Farm
Langley Heath Farm
CH
SIGNAL HAYES RD
BULL'S LA
Hermitage Farm
Fox Covert
Linda Vista Farm
Fox Hollies
Bricklyn Farm
Over Green
CHURCH LA
PH
Grove Farm
Thimble End
Pool Hall
WISHAW LA
CUDWORTH LA
FOX HOLLIES RD
WYCHBURY
THE HAYBARN
WEBSTER WAY
COVER CROFT
WITHAM CL
BROAD OAKS

58
48

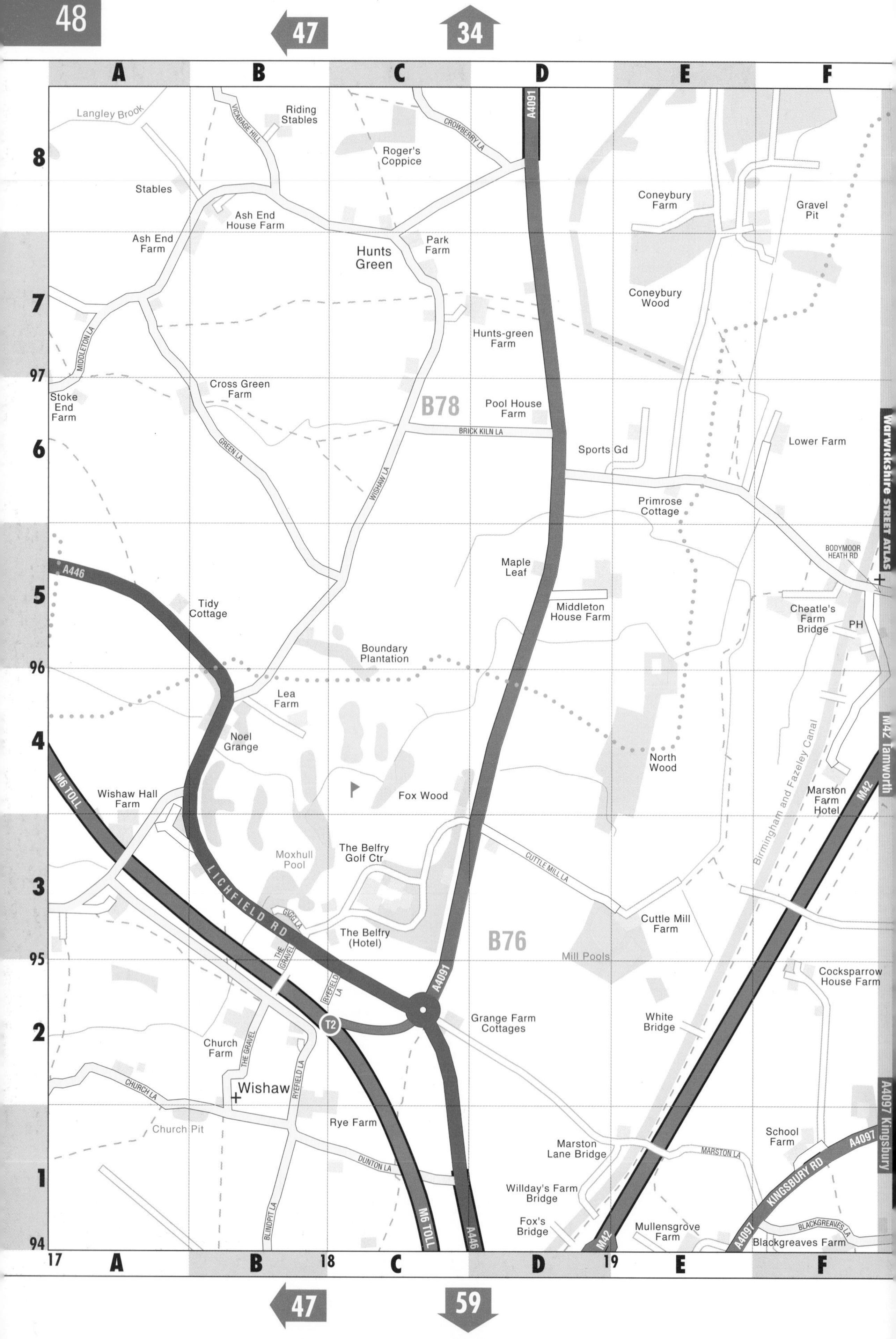
47
34
A
B
C
D
E
F
8
7
97
6
5
96
4
3
95
2
1
94
17
18
19
Langley Brook
Riding Stables
VICARAGE HILL
CROWBERRY LA
A4091
Roger's Coppice
Stables
Ash End House Farm
Ash End Farm
Hunts Green
Park Farm
Coneybury Farm
Gravel Pit
Coneybury Wood
MIDDLETON LA
Hunts-green Farm
Stoke End Farm
Cross Green Farm
B78
Pool House Farm
BRICK KILN LA
Sports Gd
Lower Farm
GREEN LA
WISHAW LA
Primrose Cottage
BODYMOOR HEATH RD
A446
Maple Leaf
Tidy Cottage
Middleton House Farm
Cheatle's Farm Bridge
PH
Boundary Plantation
Lea Farm
Noel Grange
North Wood
M6 TOLL
Wishaw Hall Farm
Fox Wood
Birmingham and Fazeley Canal
Marston Farm Hotel
M42
Moxhull Pool
The Belfry Golf Ctr
CUTTLE MILL LA
LICHFIELD RD
GIGG LA
The Belfry (Hotel)
Cuttle Mill Farm
B76
Mill Pools
THE GRAVEL
RYEFIELD LA
Cocksparrow House Farm
T2
Grange Farm Cottages
White Bridge
Church Farm
CHURCH LA
Wishaw
Church Pit
Rye Farm
Marston Lane Bridge
MARSTON LA
School Farm
A4097
DUNTON LA
KINGSBURY RD
Willday's Farm Bridge
Fox's Bridge
BLINDPIT LA
Mullensgrove Farm
BLACKGREAVES LA
Blackgreaves Farm
Warwickshire STREET ATLAS
M42 Tamworth
A4097 Kingsbury
47
59

38
50

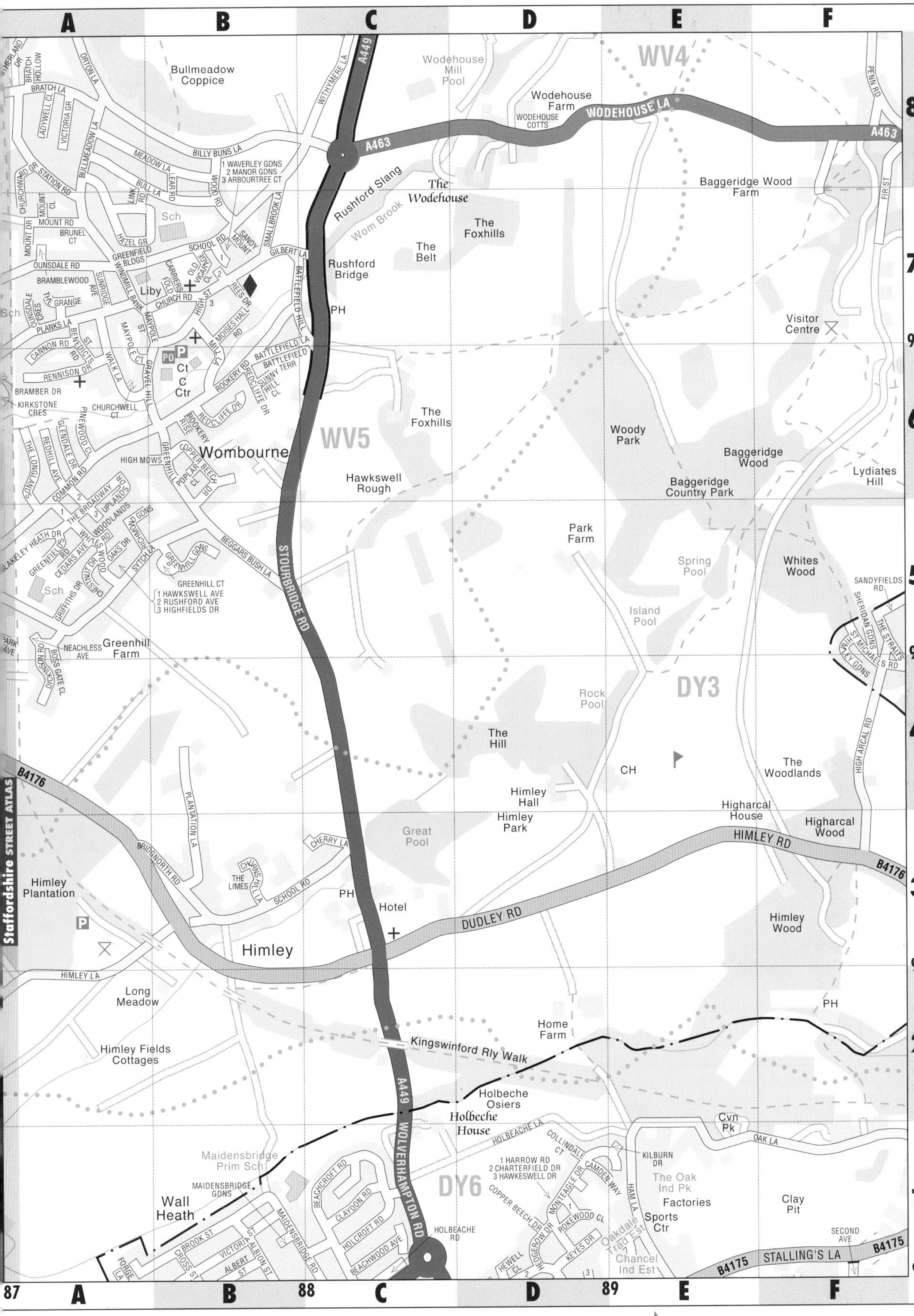
A
B
C
D
E
F
8
7
93
6
5
92
4
3
91
2
1
90
87
88
89
A449
A463
WODEHOUSE LA
WV4
WV5
DY3
DY6
Bullmeadow Coppice
Wodehouse Mill Pool
Wodehouse Farm
WODEHOUSE COTTS
Baggeridge Wood Farm
The Wodehouse
Rushford Slang
Wom Brook
The Foxhills
The Belt
Rushford Bridge
PH
Visitor Centre
Woody Park
Baggeridge Wood
Baggeridge Country Park
Lydiates Hill
Hawkswell Rough
Wombourne
Park Farm
Spring Pool
Whites Wood
Island Pool
Rock Pool
The Hill
CH
The Woodlands
Himley Hall
Himley Park
Higharcal House
Higharcal Wood
HIMLEY RD
B4176
Great Pool
DUDLEY RD
Hotel
Himley
Himley Plantation
Himley Wood
Long Meadow
Home Farm
Kingswinford Rly Walk
Himley Fields Cottages
Holbeche Osiers
Holbeche House
Cvn Pk
OAK LA
Maidensbridge Prim Sch
Wall Heath
The Oak Ind Pk
Factories
Sports Ctr
Clay Pit
Oakdale Trad Est
Chancel Ind Est
STALLING'S LA
B4175
WOLVERHAMPTON RD
STOURBRIDGE RD
BRIDGNORTH RD
PLANTATION LA
SCHOOL RD
CHERRY LA
HIMLEY LA
Greenhill Farm
BEGGARS BUSH LA
Liby
Sch
1 WAVERLEY GDNS
2 MANOR GDNS
3 ARBOURTREE CT
GREENHILL CT
1 HAWKSWELL AVE
2 RUSHFORD AVE
3 HIGHFIELDS DR
1 HARROW RD
2 CHARTERFIELD DR
3 HAWKESWELL DR
Staffordshire STREET ATLAS

60
50

49
39

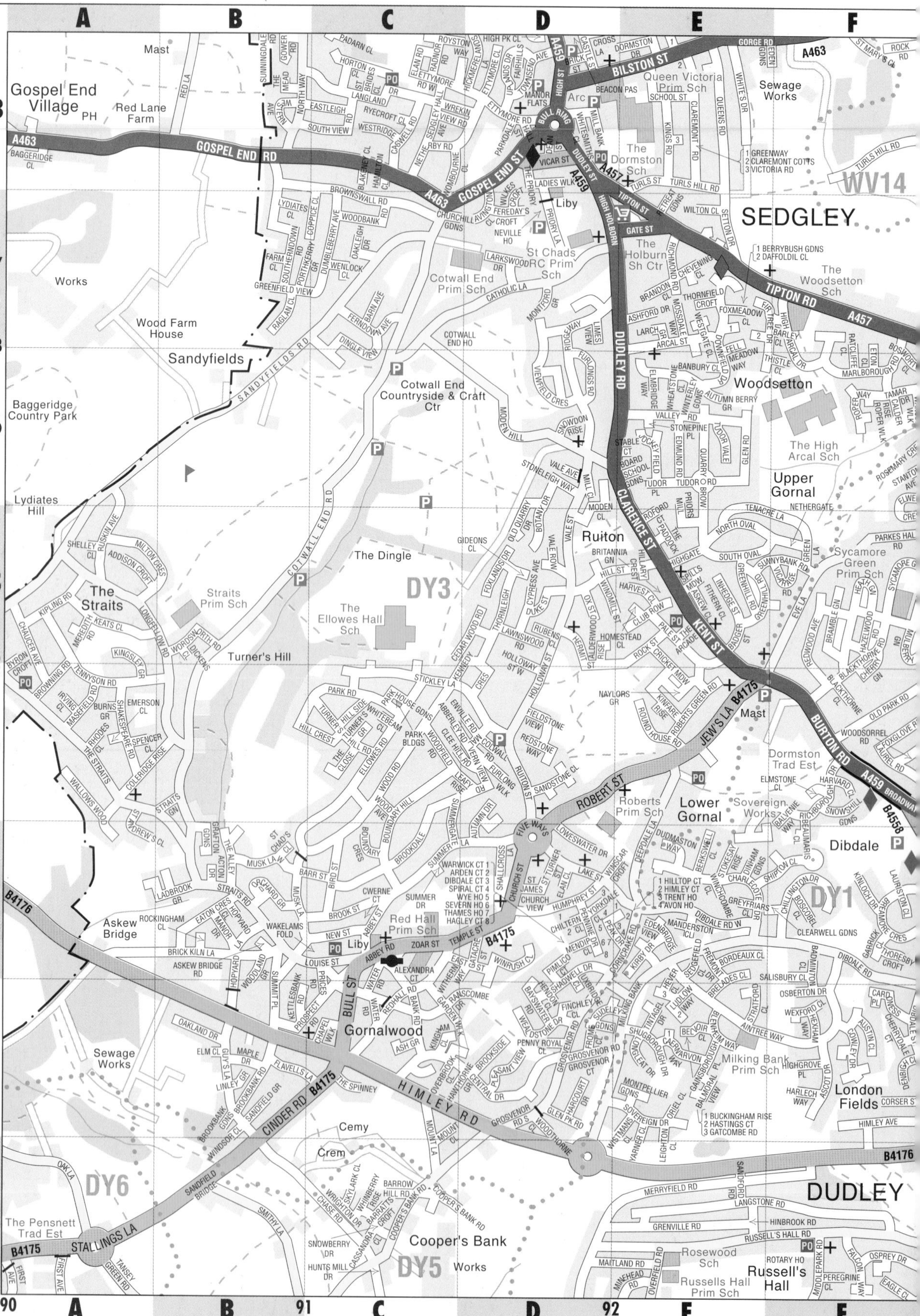
A
B
C
D
E
F
8
7
6
5
4
3
2
1
93
92
91
90
Gospel End Village
Mast
Red Lane Farm
GOSPEL END RD
A463
Works
Wood Farm House
Sandyfields
SANDYFIELDS RD
Baggeridge Country Park
Lydiates Hill
The Straits
Straits Prim Sch
Turner's Hill
Cotwall End Countryside & Craft Ctr
Cotwall End Prim Sch
COTWALL END RD
The Dingle
DY3
The Ellowes Hall Sch
Askew Bridge
B4176
Sewage Works
Gornalwood
Red Hall Prim Sch
Liby
HIMLEY RD
CINDER RD
B4175
Cemy
Crem
DY6
The Pensnett Trad Est
STALLINGS LA
Cooper's Bank
DY5
Works
BULL RING
A459
HIGH ST
Queen Victoria Prim Sch
The Dormston Sch
BILSTON ST
A457
SEDGLEY
WV14
Sewage Works
GOSPEL END ST
St Chads RC Prim Sch
The Holburn Sh Ctr
TIPTON RD
The Woodsetton Sch
Woodsetton
DUDLEY RD
The High Arcal Sch
Upper Gornal
Ruiton
CLARENCE ST
KENT ST
Sycamore Green Prim Sch
JEW'S LA
Mast
BURTON RD
Dormston Trad Est
Lower Gornal
Sovereign Works
Roberts Prim Sch
ROBERT ST
FIVE WAYS
Dibdale
DY1
Milking Bank Prim Sch
London Fields
DUDLEY
Rosewood Sch
Russells Hall Prim Sch
Russell's Hall

C8
1 COSELEY HALL
2 SCHOOL ST W
3 JACK NEWELL CT
4 ROSEVILLE CT
5 ROSEVILLE PREC
6 GROUCUTT ST

40

52

E5
1 Eclipse Ind Est
2 CAMPION CT
3 WADES CL
4 BEEHIVE WLK
5 BRINDLEY CT
6 HORSESHOE WLK
7 DOWNES CT

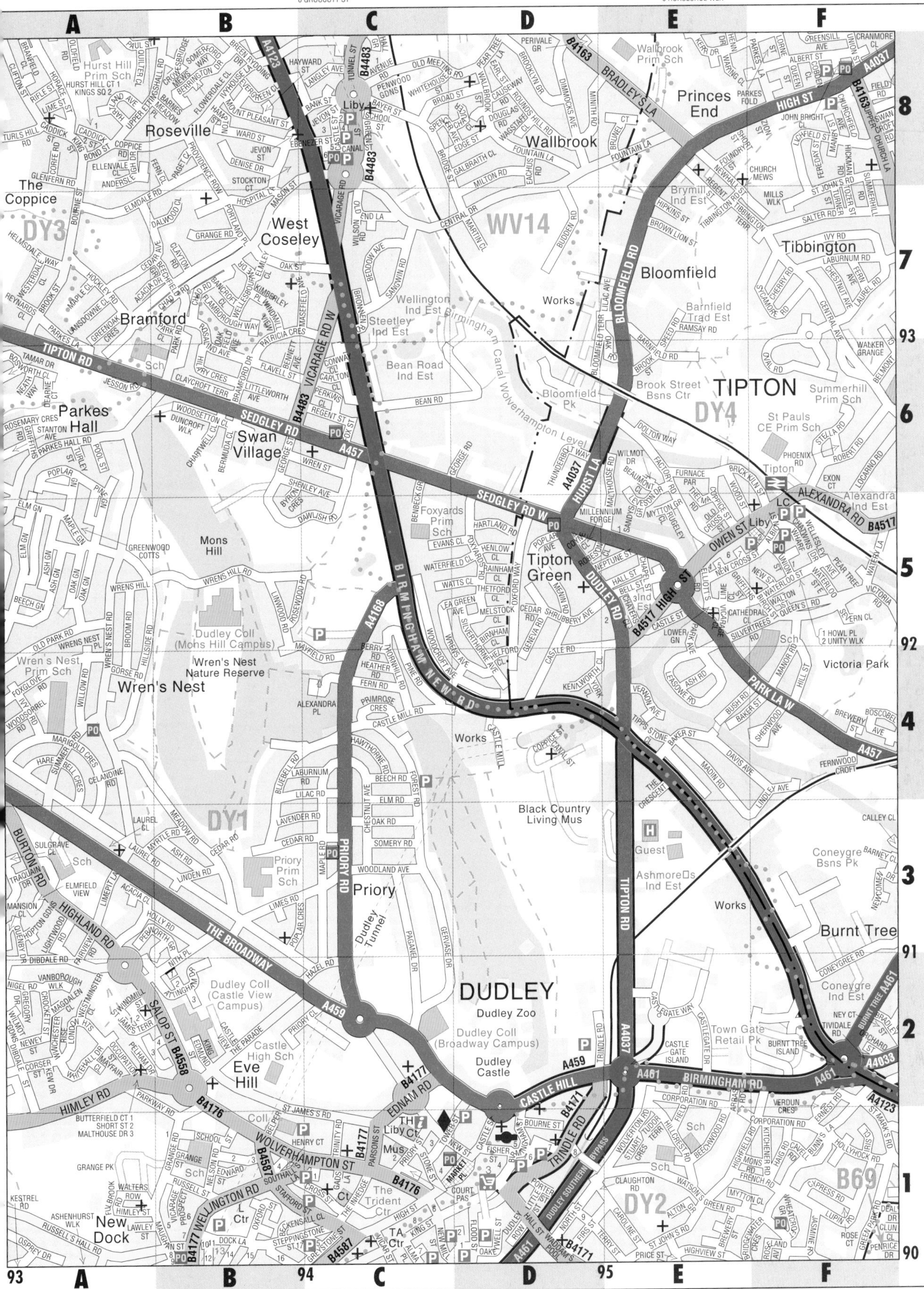

93
A
B
94
C
D
95
E
F

B1
1 GRANGE CT
2 ALEXANDRA ST
3 EDWARD ST
4 CHARLTON ST
5 CLENT CT
6 CLAVERLEY CT
7 FARTHINGS LODGE
8 HOLLAND ST
9 SWANCOTE RD
10 DOCK LA
11 LUDGATE ST
12 TURNER ST
13 Dock Lane Ind Est
14 CLEVELAND ST
15 CHARLOTTE ST
16 GREYSTONE PAS
17 PITFIELD ROW
B2
1 KING EDMUND ST
2 NORTHGATE CL
3 SOUTHGATE WAY
4 THE SHRUBBERY
C1
1 TINCHBOURNE ST
2 HERALD CT
3 PRIORY CT
4 FOUNTAIN ARC
5 PITFIELD ST
6 UNION ST

62

C1
7 NEW KING ST
8 RUTLAND PAS
D1
1 THE MINORIES
2 KING STREET PAS
3 Churchill Sh Ctr
4 BIRDCAGE WLK
5 GATEHOUSE FOLD
6 PORTERS FIELD
7 ST JOSEPH ST

52

D1
8 CLAUGHTON ROAD N
9 PORTER STREET S

A8
1 RIDGEWAY RD
2 KINGSBURY RD
3 BURBERRY CT
4 JOHN F KENNEDY WLK
5 CHURCHILL WLK
6 LANSBURY WLK
7 STOKES AVE
8 KINGSWAY AVE
9 JELLICOE HO
10 SWANN HO
11 SWANCROFT HO

51

C6
1 BROAD CROFT
2 COCHRANE CL
3 DEELEY DR
4 COBURG CROFT
5 CINQUEFOIL LEASOW
6 CLOVER PIECE

41

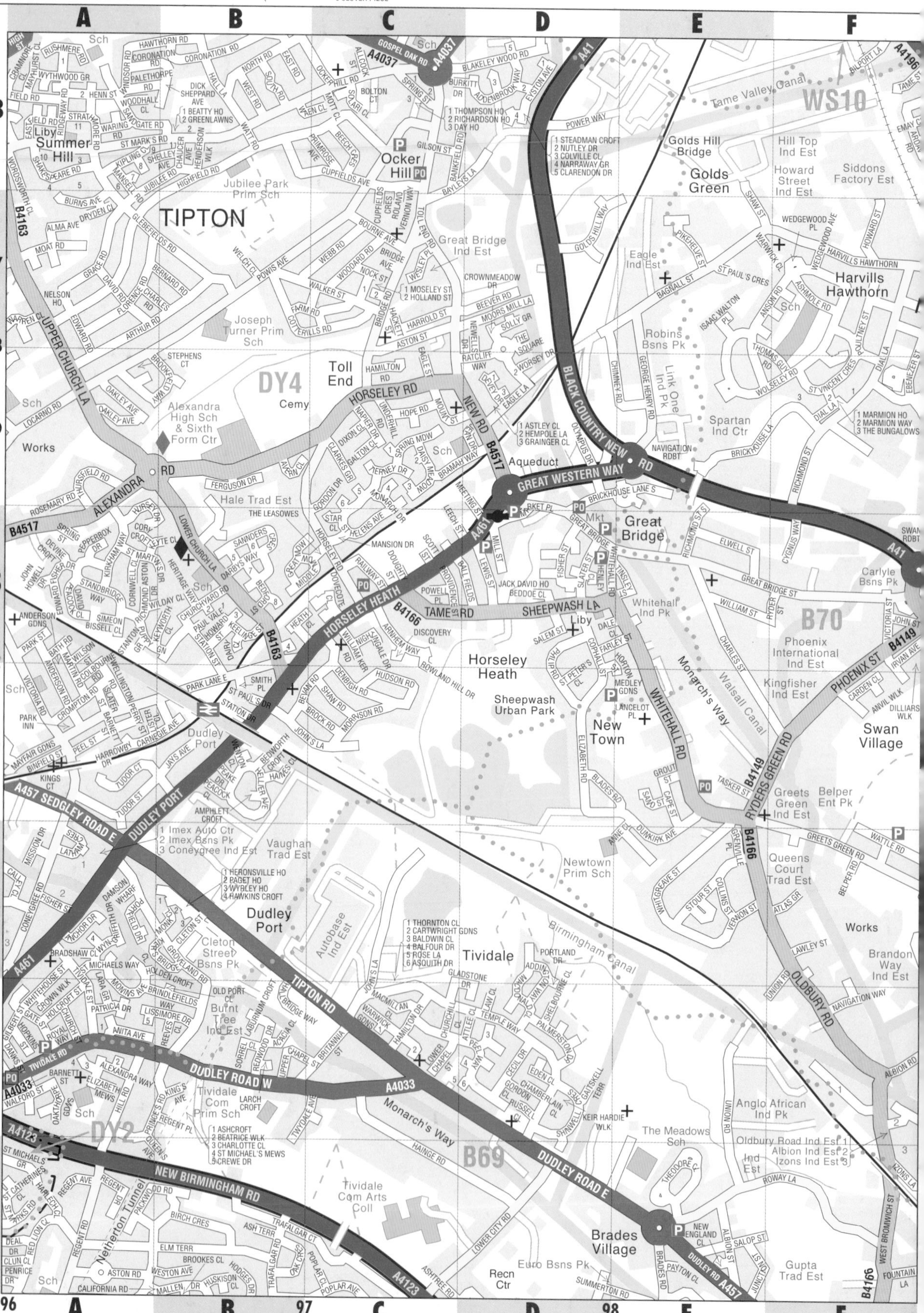

A B C D E F
8 7 93 6 5 92 4 3 91 2 1 90
96 97 98
TIPTON
Summer Hill
Ocker Hill
Jubilee Park Prim Sch
Great Bridge Ind Est
Golds Hill Bridge
Golds Green
Hill Top Ind Est
Howard Street Ind Est
Siddons Factory Est
Tame Valley Canal
WS10
Harvills Hawthorn
Eagle Ind Est
Robins Bsns Pk
Link One Ind Pk
Spartan Ind Ctr
Joseph Turner Prim Sch
Toll End
DY4
Cemy
Alexandra High Sch & Sixth Form Ctr
Works
Hale Trad Est
THE LEASOWES
Aqueduct
GREAT WESTERN WAY
BLACK COUNTRY NEW RD
Great Bridge
Mkt
Carlyle Bsns Pk
B70
Whitehall Ind Pk
Phoenix International Ind Est
Kingfisher Ind Est
Swan Village
Horseley Heath
Sheepwash Urban Park
New Town
Monarch's Way
Walsall Canal
Dudley Port
Vaughan Trad Est
1 Imex Auto Ctr
2 Imex Bsns Pk
3 Coneygree Ind Est
Greets Green Ind Est
Belper Ent Pk
Queens Court Trad Est
Newtown Prim Sch
Autobase Ind Est
Dudley Port
Tividale
Birmingham Canal
Cleton Street Bsns Pk
Burnt Tree Ind Est
Brandon Way Ind Est
Tividale Com Prim Sch
DY2
B69
Anglo African Ind Pk
The Meadows Sch
Oldbury Road Ind Est
Albion Ind Est
Izons Ind Est
Tividale Com Arts Coll
Netherton Tunnel
NEW BIRMINGHAM RD
DUDLEY ROAD W
DUDLEY ROAD E
TIPTON RD
HORSELEY HEATH
HORSELEY RD
A457 SEDGLEY ROAD E
OLDBURY RD
RYDERS GREEN RD
PHOENIX ST
Brades Village
Euro Bsns Pk
Recn Ctr
Gupta Trad Est
A4037 A41 A4196 A461 A4033 A4123 A457 B4163 B4517 B4166 B4149

B5
1 OLD CANAL WLK
2 JORDAN LEYS
3 RYLAND CL
4 MILLWRIGHT CL
5 NEAR HIGH DR
6 FAR HIGH DR
7 JEVONS DR
8 POTTERS BROOK

51

63

F8
1 BROADFIELD CL
2 GORSTY CL
3 EDNAM CL
4 BROGDEN CL
5 SPENCER CL

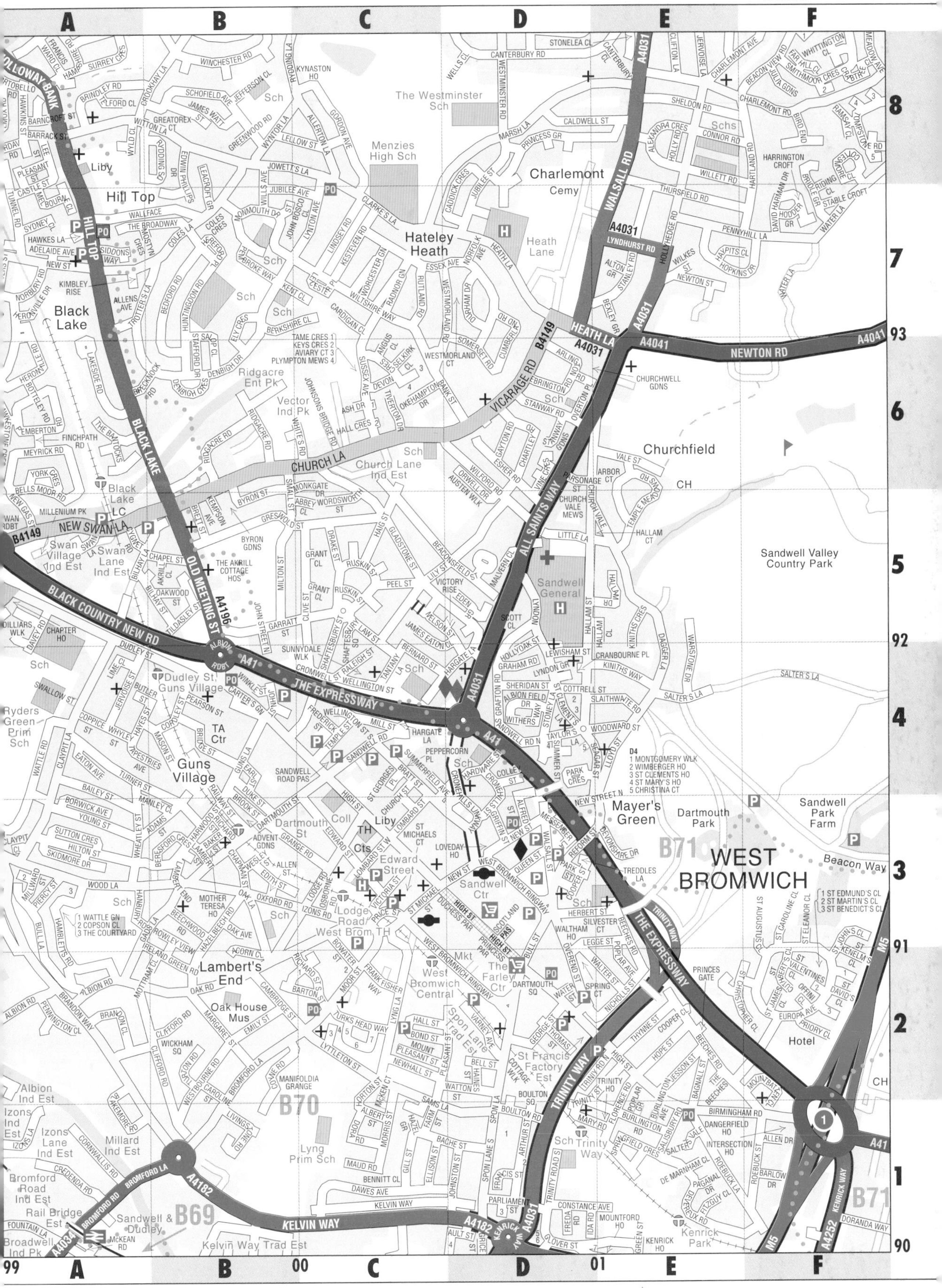

C2
1 RICHARD STREET W
2 BOWATER HO
3 BLACKSMITH WAY
4 VANTAGE POINT
5 THE SIDINGS
6 OLD FLOUR MILLS
7 CHARITY BICK WAY

D1
1 BOULTON HO
2 NINE PAILS WLK
3 WALPOLE WLK
4 BULLOCK ST
5 MACAULAY HO
6 NEALE HO
7 GREENFORD HO

53
43

D8
1 BURRELTON WAY
2 GLENDENE DR
3 FAIRDENE WAY
4 GARSTON WAY

A
B
C
D
E
F
8
7
93
6
5
92
4
3
91
2
1
90
02
03
04
M5
A4041
NEWTON RD
A34
WALSALL RD
B4124
B4167
Newton
Bishop Asbury Cottage
B43
Tame Valley Canal
HAMSTEAD RD
Crem
Haypits
FORGE LA
Forge Farm
Forge Mill Farm
Sandwell Valley Nature Ctr
Hamstead Jun & Inf Sch
Hamstead
Garden Grove
Superstore
Ferndale Prim Sch
OLD WALSALL RD
FARRAN WAY 1
CROMANE SQ 2
FREEMOUNT SQ 3
LATHAM AVE 4
STAFFORD CT 5
RUSHALL CT 6
ALLEN HO 7
PEPYS CT 8
SUTTON CT 9
BOLDMERE CT 10
HAMSTEAD HO 1
SCOTT HO 2
GROVE CT 3
Sandwell Valley Country Park
B71
Beacon Way
River Tame
Hamstead Hall Sch
Hamstead
Wks
Swan Pool
Park Farm
CH
B20
Grestone Prim Sch
HAMSTEAD HILL
Liby
Brown's Green
PARK LA
Sports Gd
SILVERCROFT AVE
B4124
HANDSWORTH WOOD RD
B70
Allot Gdns
Hamstead Campus
Handsworth Hall
St John Wall RC Sch
St Augustine's RC Prim Sch
B21
Cemy
OXHILL RD
CHURCH LA A4040
SANDWELL RD
ROOKERY RD
A4040
Recn Gd
Handsworth
Raleigh Ind Est
Park Lane Ind Est
B66
A41
BIRMINGHAM RD
HOLYHEAD RD
A4040 ISLAND RD
The Hawthorns (West Bromwich Albion FC)
MALVERN RD 1
PADDINGTON RD 2
St James CE Prim Sch
Rookery Sch
Wilkes Green Sch
Sch

53
65

F3
1 HAWTHORN PARK DR
2 CASSOWARY RD
3 QUORN HO
4 ALBRIGHTON HO
5 MEYNELL HO
6 PYTCHLEY HO
7 COTTESMORE HO

A8
1 BARDFIELD CL
2 HARRIS DR
3 BLOOMFIELD CT
4 MALHAY GDNS

44
56

66
56

D1
1 BIRCHFIELD TWR
2 CALDER TWR
3 CLARENDON GDNS
4 BENJAMIN GDNS

F1
1 LOWER GROUND CL
2 STAFFORDSHIRE POOL CL
3 HOLYOAK CL
4 McGREGOR CL

B7
1 LAVENDER GDNS
2 MALLOW RISE
3 ROYAL GR
4 QUEENS GDNS

55
45

A
B
C
D
E
F
8
7
93
6
5
92
4
3
91
2
1
90
08
09
10
BIRMINGHAM
Perry Common
Short Heath
Upper Witton
Witton Lakes
Stockland Green
Witton
Gravelly Hill
Brookvale Park
Salford Park
Highcroft
Erdington
B44
B23
B24
B6
B73
A453
A452
A4040
A5127
A38(M)
A38
M6
B4531
B4137
B4142
COLLEGE RD
CHESTER RD
MARSH HILL
MARSH LA
RESERVOIR RD
GRAVELLY HILL
GRAVELLY LA
TYBURN RD
WITTON RD
BROOKVALE RD
ASTON EXPRESSWAY
WOOD END RD
SUTTON NEW RD
HIGH ST
WITTON LODGE RD
PERRY COMMON RD
SHORT HEATH RD
SOMERSET RD
ROBERT AVE
ANDERSON RD
GOOSEMOOR LA
Cemy
Superstores
Hawthorn Prim Sch
The College High Sch
Wilson Stuart Sch
Court Farm Prim Sch
St Margaret Mary RC Jun & Inf Sch
Featherstone Prim Sch
Brookvale Prim Sch
Stockland Green Sch
Boating Lake
Tame Valley Canal
River Tame
Brookvale Trad Est
Atlas Est
Wyrley Trad Est
Deykin Ave Jun & Inf Sch
Junction 6 Ind Pk
Westwood Bsns Pk
Yew Tree Com Jun & Inf Sch
Tame Road Ind Est
Electra Park Ind Est
Erdington Hall Prim Sch
Queensbury Sch
Glover's Trust Homes
Allot Gdns
Recn Gd
Coll
Works
1 GREENFORD HO
2 LYNTON HO
3 KINGSBRIDGE HO
4 HUNTINGTON HO
1 LAPWING CROFT
2 SYCAMORE CT
3 SKYLARK CL
4 NIGHTINGALE CL
5 SANDPIPER WAY
CARTMEL CT 1
BRINDLE CT 2
DALTON CT 3
WATERFORD CT 4
1 ODDINGLEY CT
2 PENDOCK CT
3 NEWLAND CT
4 MALVERN CT
5 LEIGH CT
6 KNIGHTON CT
7 EXHALL CT
CHERITON WLK 1
UPTON CT 2
TEME CT 3
SEVERN CT 4
RUSHWICK CT 5
1 ABBERTON CT
2 BECKFORD CT
3 CHURCHDOWN CT
4 ELMLEY CT
5 HANLEY CT
6 FERNHILL CT
7 GRAFTON CT
8 DUNLEY CT
9 DUNLIN CL
10 DENHAM CT
11 CHILTON CT
CRANLEIGH HO 6
REPTON HO 7
STOKESAY HO 1
BERKELEY HO 2
WINDSOR HO 3
ARUNDEL HO 4
ALNWICK HO 5

E2
1 CHISWICK CT
2 HUNTON CT
3 WOODVILLE CT
4 GRAVELLY CT
5 WHEELWRIGHT CT
6 NEWCHURCH GDNS

F3
1 COPPICE CL
2 MAPLE CT
3 RESWOOD CT

F4
1 OSBORNE RD S
2 POPLAR AVE
3 SALISBURY HO
4 GLOUCESTER HO
5 TALBOT HO
6 WARWICK HO
7 BEDFORD HO
8 EXETER HO

B6
1 ADRIAN CT
2 ABBEY MANS
3 SUTTON CT
4 KENTMERE TWR
5 GLENDALE TWR

B7
1 The Lanes Sh Ctr
2 RICHMOND CT
3 HERON CT
4 FLORENCE DR
5 FLORENCE AVE

46 58

68 58

57
47

A
B
C
D
E
F
8
7
93
6
5
92
4
3
91
2
1
90
14
15
16
SUTTON
BIRMINGHAM
Peddimore Hall
The Cottage
Vine Cottage
Peddimore Lane
PEDDIMORE LA
B76
WISHAW LA
Wiggins Hill Cottages
WIGGINS HILL RD
Wiggins Hill Farm
Hurst Green Farm
Wiggins Hill Road Bridge
Birmingham & Fazeley Canal
A4097
A38
Minworth Greaves
Kingsbury Bsns Pk
SUTTON SQ
THE GREAVES
Liby
Ind Pk
KINGSBURY RD
KINGSBURY CL
HURST GREEN RD
LAWRENCE DR
SUMMER LA
COTTAGE LA
KIMBERLEY WLK
WHITEHEAD DR
LONGLEY AVE
FARVALE RD
THORNLEY GR
LINDRIDGE DR
REDMOOR WAY
OAKENHAYES CRES
OLD KINGSBURY RD
WATER ORTON LA
OXSTALL CL 1
CONEYBURY WLK 2
ARBURY WLK 3
Minworth
PO
Minworth Jun & Inf Sch
ROBINSON'S WAY
Midpoint Park Ind Est
Sewage Works
Hypermarket
WALMLEY ASH LA
WALMLEY ASH RD
Walmley Jun & Inf Schs
1 THE HAYBARN
2 HARVINGTON WAY
1 OAKLANDS CROFT
2 BEAUCHAMP CL
3 GEOFFREY CL
4 HUMBER AVE
5 LEVEN CROFT
BROMYARD AVE
FOXES MDW
GREENACRES
MAPLEWOOD
LEDBURY WAY
HIDCOTE AVE
KINVER CROFT
MALVERN DR
THE BRAMBLES
BROOKHUS FARM RD
LAWNSWOOD
POOL MDW
ROCHFORD CL
THE SAPLINGS
FOLDYARD CL
FAIRLAWNS
WEBSTER WAY
THE RIDDINGS
THE MOOR
BATES CL
CHURCHILL DR
LANE CROFT
JONES WOOD CL
PYTMAN DR
THE CROFTS
GALDER DR
OAK FARM CL
HANWELL CL
FALSTAFF CL
PATTERTON DR
JUNIPER DR
LATYMER CL
NEW LEASOW
TUDMAN CL
FOWEY CL
BOVEY CROFT
DOVEY DR
WELLAND WAY
WYE CL
TAMAR DR
MOAT CROFT
EASTLEIGH CROFT
HEMLINGFORD RD
ANTON DR
LYNEHAM GDNS
DENEGATE CL
DELMORE WAY
ASHSTEAD CL
HADLEIGH CROFT
OVERSLEY RD
NEWMARSH RD
WINTON GR
MARFIELD CL
LYTHAM CL
STAPLETON CL
COLEVILLE RD
FORGE CROFT
HARBURY CL
WALMLEY ASH RD
WILFORD GR
MORELAND CROFT
CHESWOOD DR
ORTON AVE
WINDYRIDGE RD
ROSSLYN RD
PLANTS BROOK RD
MAYTHORN AVE
FORGE LA
Minworth Ind Pk
FULFORD DR
STOCKTON CL
Metalloys Ind Est
MAYBROOK RD
Castle Vale Ind Est
FORGE LA
Nature Park
FIRST AVE
SELCO WAY
WATERSIDE CL
B24
HANSON'S BRIDGE RD
WOODLANDS FARM RD
HEYFORD WAY
BICESTER SQ
MANBY RD
BAGINTON RD
HEDLEY CROFT
STORNOWAY RD
CROY DR
GEESON CL
ST MAWGEN CL
PARK LA
SQUADRON CL
RUISLIP CL
WATTISHAM SQ
FILTON CROFT
RENFREW SQ
PRESTWICK RD
LUCE CL
LYDD CROFT
BARRA CROFT
GATWICK RD
Sch
NORTHHOLT DR
TURNHOUSE RD
MORAR CL
VALENCIA CROFT
UPAVON CL
DONIBRISTLE CROFT
MARTLESHAM SQ
INNSWORTH DR
DYCE CL
YATESBURY AVE
HAWKINGE DR
SUMBURGH CROFT
MONTROSE DR
KEMBLE DR
SHAWBERRY AVE
MERE AVE
HIGH ST
THOMAS WLK
Castle Vale Sch
RAWLINS CROFT
DAVENPORT DR
NEWCASTLE CROFT
SCHOOL CL
Castle Vale Ent Pk
MELKSHAM SQ
CRANWELL WAY
Castle Vale
BIGGIN CL
ABINGDON WAY
COSFORD CRES
LOCKING CROFT
BROOK PIECE WLK
ST ATHAN CROFT
PIXHALL WLK
FARNBOROUGH RD
PHOENIX CT
BOVINGDON RD
TANGMERE DR
CHIGWELL CL
MERLIN CL
WATTON GN
SHERIDAN WLK
PADGATE CL
RHOOSE CROFT
KESTREL CL
1 LONG CLOSE WLK
2 RYE GRASS WLK
3 ORCHARD MEADOW WLK
4 WORTHY DOWN WLK
5 SQUIRES GATE WLK
6 OAKINGTON DR
B35
LONGCROFT CL
ROUND MOOR WLK
NEVILLE WLK
AVRO WAY
LYSANDER WAY
JAVELIN AVE
TRIDENT BLVD
HIND CROFT
DREM CROFT
ROUGH COPPICE WLK
WATTON GN
WELLINGTON DR
VISCOUNT DR
AVELIN AVE
PIONEER WAY
SOPWITH CROFT
CHIVENOR HO
BLENHEIM WAY
LANCASTER DR
Vale Stadium
The Fort Ctr
Sch
DIXON CL
VISCOUNT CL
BROOKS CROFT
JACKSON WLK
HOWES CROFT
BERWOOD PK
SPITFIRE WAY
CLAYTON WLK
BEALE CL
CADBURY DR
River Tame
Parkhill Wood
Parkhall Wood
B46
BIRMINGHAM RD
B4118
Works
MYTTON RD
Langley Hill Wood
7 HALFPENNY FIELD WLK
8 DE HAVILLAND DR
9 HURRICANE WAY
10 KENRICK CROFT
ORTON WAY
Castle Bromwich Bsns Pk
LANGLEY DR
TAMESIDE DR
Caravan Site
M6
A452
5
TIDDINGTON CL 1
BROWNSOVER CL 2
KYTER LA 3
KINGSLEIGH DR
SUDELEY CL
DANZEY GREEN RD
WHITTLEFORD GR
BEECHCROFT RD
PARK HALL CRES
HUNGERFIELD RD
HODNELL CL
HILLHURST GR 1
REDLIFF AVE 2
DELAMERE CL 3
BOWSHOT CL 4
FOXFORD CL 5
KINGSFORD CL 6
HIPSLEY CL
FLECKNOE CL
CRAWSHAWS RD
MUSBOROUGH CL
WATCHBURY CL
PARKFIELD DR
TACKFORD CL
ASPBURY CROFT
CASTELLO DR
BLEWITT CL
PIKEHORNE CROFT
CHADSHUNT CL
MILESBUSH AVE
STONEYMOOR DR
HARBOROUGH DR
BRADWELL RD
SPRINGBROOK CL
FAIRCROFT RD
WATER ORTON RD
Park Hall Sch
GRANMORE RD
TOMLINSON RD
RONALD GR
NEVILLE RD
B36
BLANDFORD AVE
FARNWORTH GR
Forest Oak Sch
Lanchester Park
LANCHESTER WAY
SINGER CROFT
HILLMAN GR
DAIMLER CL
ALVIS WLK
MARCOS DR
ROVER DR
MORRIS CROFT
AUSTIN CROFT
ELVA CROFT
HUMBER GR
COWLEY CL
ARMSTRONG DR
SUNBEAM
VAUXHALL CRES
Bosworth Wood Prim Sch
M6
A452
WATER ORTON LA

57
69

48

A
B
C
D
E
F
Dunton Wharf Bridge
Dunton Wood
Dunton Coppice
Baylis's Bridge
Dunton Hall
Birmingham & Fazeley Canal
Dunton Park
Curdworth Tunnel
Fairview Ind Est
Chantry Ind Est
Highfield Farm
Curdworth Bridge
Curdworth Church Bridge
Moat
Curdworth Hall Farm
Curdworth
Curdworth Prim Sch
PH
B76
Spring Farm
Newlands Farm
Sewage Works
Curdworth Bridge
River Tame
Sewage Works
Water Orton
Jack O'Watton Bsns Pk
Liby
B46
Coleshill Ind Est
THE COURTYARD
Chattle Hill
Coleshill
Roman Pk
Temple Ct
Water Orton Prim Sch
Gilson Hall
Attleboro Farm
Gilson
Grimstock Hill
B36
M6 TOLL
A446
LICHFIELD RD
M42
A4097
KINGSBURY RD
BLINDPIT LA
WISHAW LA
MARSH LA
COLESHILL RD
FARADAY AVE
HAMS LA
EDISON RD
B4118
WATER ORTON LA
STONE CROSS
OLD CHURCH RD
MINWORTH RD
MANOR HOUSE LA
MERCER AVE
WAKEFIELD GR
DIGBY CRES
BIRMINGHAM RD
B4117
NEW RD
HARGRAVE CL
SALISBURY DR
GEORGE RD
OVERTON DR
EDWARD RD
MAUD RD
TURNPIKE DR
PARK GR
HOLLYHURST
WATTON LA
GYPSY LA
SMITHS WAY
ORTON CL
ADDISON PL
MICKLE MEADOW
CHURCH AVE
COTTRELLS MEWS
LONG LEYS CROFT
WELAND CT
WELAND CL
VESEY CL
ST PETER'S CL
JAQUES CL
WOODLANDS AVE
ST BLAISE AVE
OPENFIELD CROFT
VICARAGE LA
PLANK LA
LUDGATE CL 1
ST PAULS CT 2
STATION BLDGS 3
ALBION TERR 4
ALBION COTTS 5
LONG LEYS CT 6
ATTLEBOROUGH LA
GORSEY LA
GORSEY WAY
CHATTLE HILL
IMPERIAL RISE
ROMAN WAY
CAESAR WAY
BRUTUS DR
CENTURION CL
CONSTANTINE LA
AUGUSTUS CL
JULIUS DR
STATION RD
WANTAGE RD
HADRIAN DR
TEMPLE WAY
TRAJAN HILL
TIBERIUS CL
NORTON RD
ARDEN CROFT
BATEMAN RD
BGLWS
ENNERSDALE
ENNERSDALE RD
ENNERSDALE CL
MEADOWBANK DR
GILSON DR
GILSON RD
LANCHESTER WAY
RILEY DR
TRIUMPH WLK
WOLSELEY CL
A452
M6
4a
8
9
T1
ORCHARD CL
GLEBE FIELDS
ST NICHOLAS WLK
CHURCH LA
BREEDEN DR
BEEHIVE LA
SAXON CL
ASHLEIGH MEWS COTTS
FARTHING LA
THE MOUNT
OAKLANDS
COLESHILL RD
Warwickshire STREET ATLAS
8
7
93
6
5
92
4
3
91
2
1
90
17
18
19

70

49

D8
1 FRANCIS CL
2 TRESHAM RD
3 GLADSTONE GR
4 HAWKESWELL DR

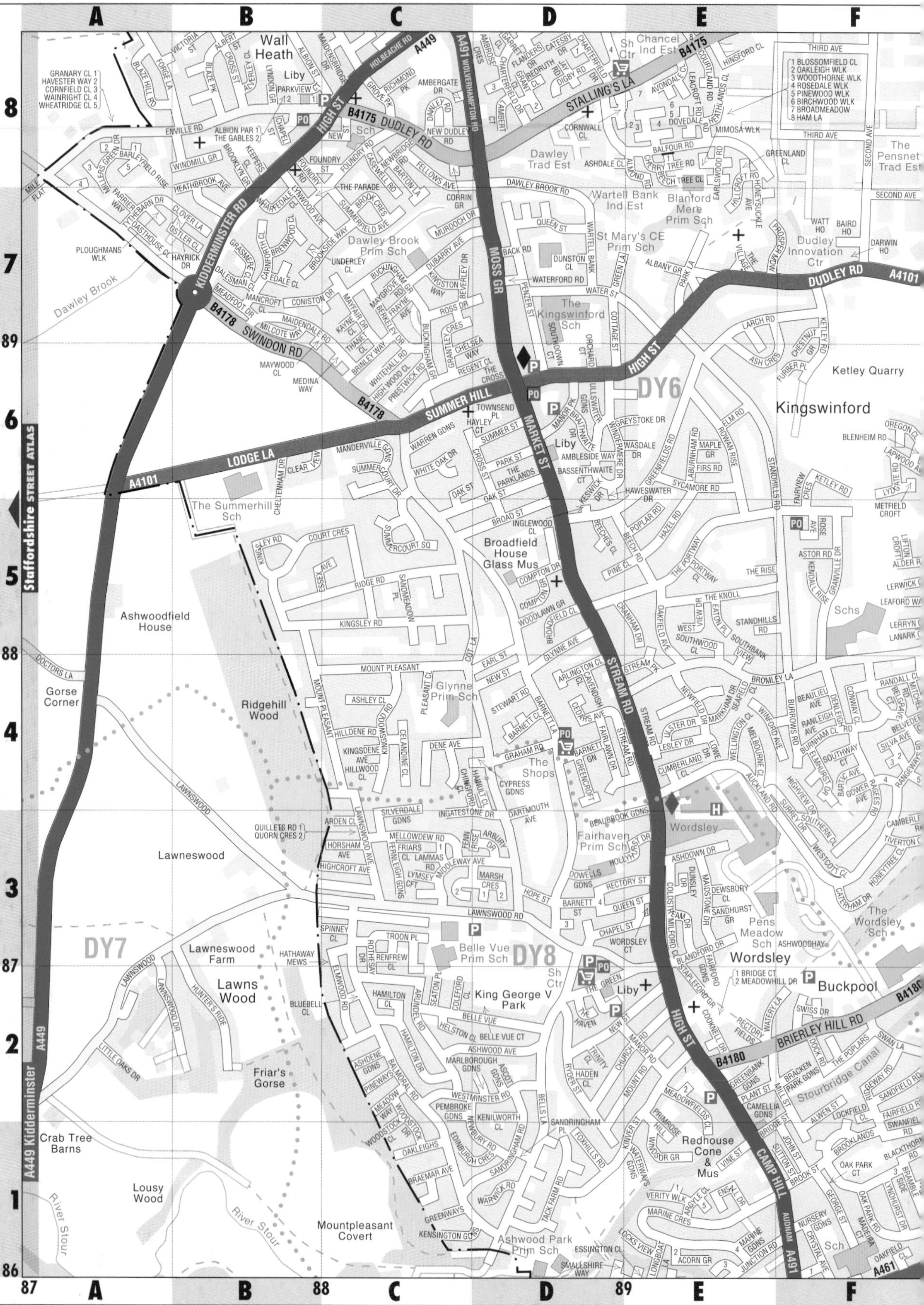

80

D3
1 MUIRVILLE CL
2 QUAYLE GR
3 ROSE COTTAGE DR
4 CROSS ST

E1
1 BRINDLEY CL
2 GREENWAY AVE
3 DIAMOND PARK DR
4 SWEETBRIER DR
5 GILBEYS CL

F1
1 MAGNOLIA WAY
2 WHITEHORN RD
3 DEWBERRY RD

F4
1 SUNNYMEDE RD
2 ANDOVER CRES
3 FREELAND GR
4 GRANGE LA
5 MADELEY RD

E8
1 ESK HO
2 AVON HO
3 BRENT HO
4 FROME HO
5 KENNET HO
6 LEA HO
7 CAM HO
8 DEE HO

A1
1 SYCAMORE PADDOCK
2 OAK TREE GDNS
3 AMELAS CL
4 OAK PARK RD

D2
1 MAPLE ROW
2 BRICKILN CT
3 ADELPHI CT
4 CHAPEL CT
5 DEAN CT
6 OAKFIELD CT
7 NEW CT
8 POTTER CT
9 NORTHWOOD CT

D2
10 LOWTHER CT
11 KNOTT CT
12 ST MARYS CT
13 GIFFORD CT
14 BRIAR CT
15 YEOVIL CT
16 BODMIN CT
17 BOOTH CT
18 BURNHAM CT
19 PLANT CT
20 ST JOHNS CT
21 RAVEN CT
22 WESTBURY CT

B8
1 HOLLAND ST
2 TURNER ST
3 CLIFFORD ST
4 CLEVELAND ST
5 CHARLOTTE ST
6 WESTLEY ST
7 HIGH ST

61

51

D8
1 CONSTITUTION HILL E
2 NEW BOND ST
3 SHEDDEN ST
4 SPRING GDNS
5 ROLLASON RD

E8
1 OLIVER CL
2 PRICE ST
3 SHARINGTON CL
4 LAMBERT FOLD
5 LEVESON WLK
6 HARLEY GRANGE
7 DIXONS GREEN CT
8 ASHLEIGH CT
9 OAKHAM CT

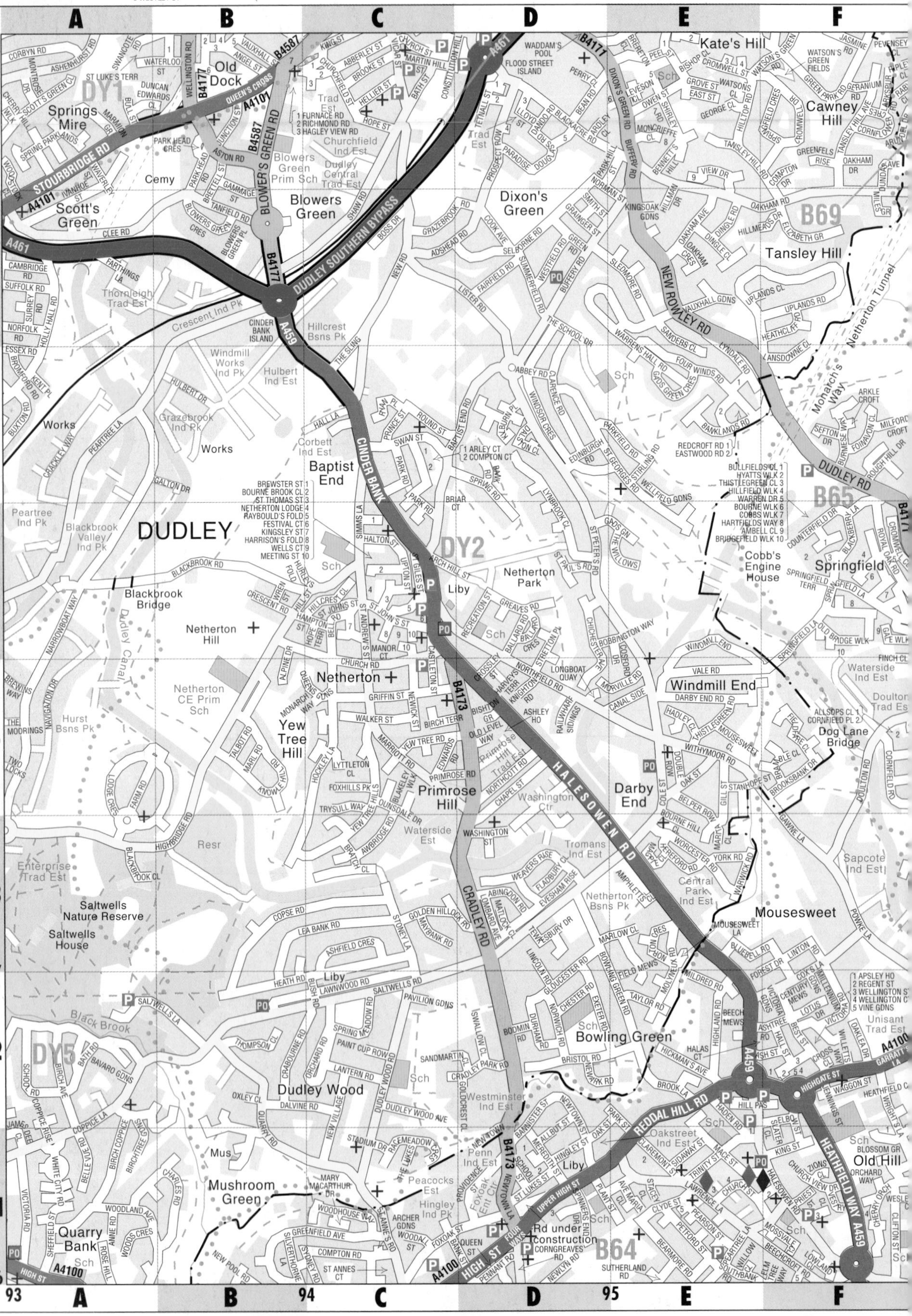

D1
1 CRAWLEY WLK
2 HOLLYBUSH WLK
3 DIAMOND CT

E1
1 TRINITY CTR
2 CLAREMONT CT
3 CHURCH CT
4 TRINITY CT
5 SKYE WLK

F1
1 CHERRY DR
2 COURT ST
3 SPRING MEADOW
4 BUTTERFLY WAY
5 APPLEWOOD GR

61

82

52
64

F7
1 RATCLIFF WLK
2 TIPPERARY WLK

83
64

C1
1 BASSANO RD
2 THE HEATHLANDS
3 BEN WILLETTS WLK
4 CROSS ST
5 FRANK TOMMEY CL
6 DOWNING CL

C3
1 MOUNTFORD CL
2 OLD SCHOOL DR
3 RAGLEY WLK
4 HADEN WLK
5 HARVINGTON WLK

D5
1 NEWBURY HO
2 LAING HO
3 JAMES CLIFT HO
4 ULLSWATER HO
5 DERWENT HO
6 RYDAL HO
7 CONISTON HO
8 WALLACE HO
9 HARRY PRICE HO

D5
10 HACKWOOD HO
11 WINDERMERE HO
12 BURNETT HO
13 GRASMERE HO
14 KESWICK HO
15 KENDALL HO

E4
1 INKBERROW CL
2 STANFORD WAY
3 RICHARDS HO
4 BLAKEDOWN WAY
5 STAULTON GN
6 WHITEHEATH CT
7 LANCASTER HO
8 WINCHESTER CL
9 CANTERBURY CL

F4
1 UNCLE BEN'S CL
2 PUMPHOUSE WAY
3 ST MICHAEL'S CRES

A7
1 DE SOMERLEY HO
2 HACKETT CT
3 RATCLIFF WLK
4 CHURCH SQ
5 LADY BRADES HO
6 LOW TOWN
7 DAVIES HO
8 PARKES HO
9 JACKSON HO
10 SHOWELL HO
11 JEFFRIES HO
12 WHEELER HO

63
53

C4
1 SHELLEY HO
2 KEATS HO
3 TENNYSON HO
4 WORDSWORTH HO

63
84

A5
1 KILMET WLK
2 METRIC WLK
3 REGENT CT
4 FEARON PL
5 ST MICHAEL'S CT

B5
1 CHAMBERLAIN WLK
2 ALLAN CL
3 SALCOMBE RD
4 SHALDON WLK
5 WALNUT DR
6 KINGSBRIDGE WLK
7 HONITON WLK
8 CHESHIRE HO

C5
1 PARK HO
2 THOMAS CRES
3 PRINCE OF WALES WLK
4 ASHCROFT
5 ELMCROFT
6 BIRCHCROFT
7 PAINTERS CNR
8 NASH WLK
9 UNETT CT
10 BRINDLEY WAY
11 CUIN WLK
12 APOLLO WAY

54
66

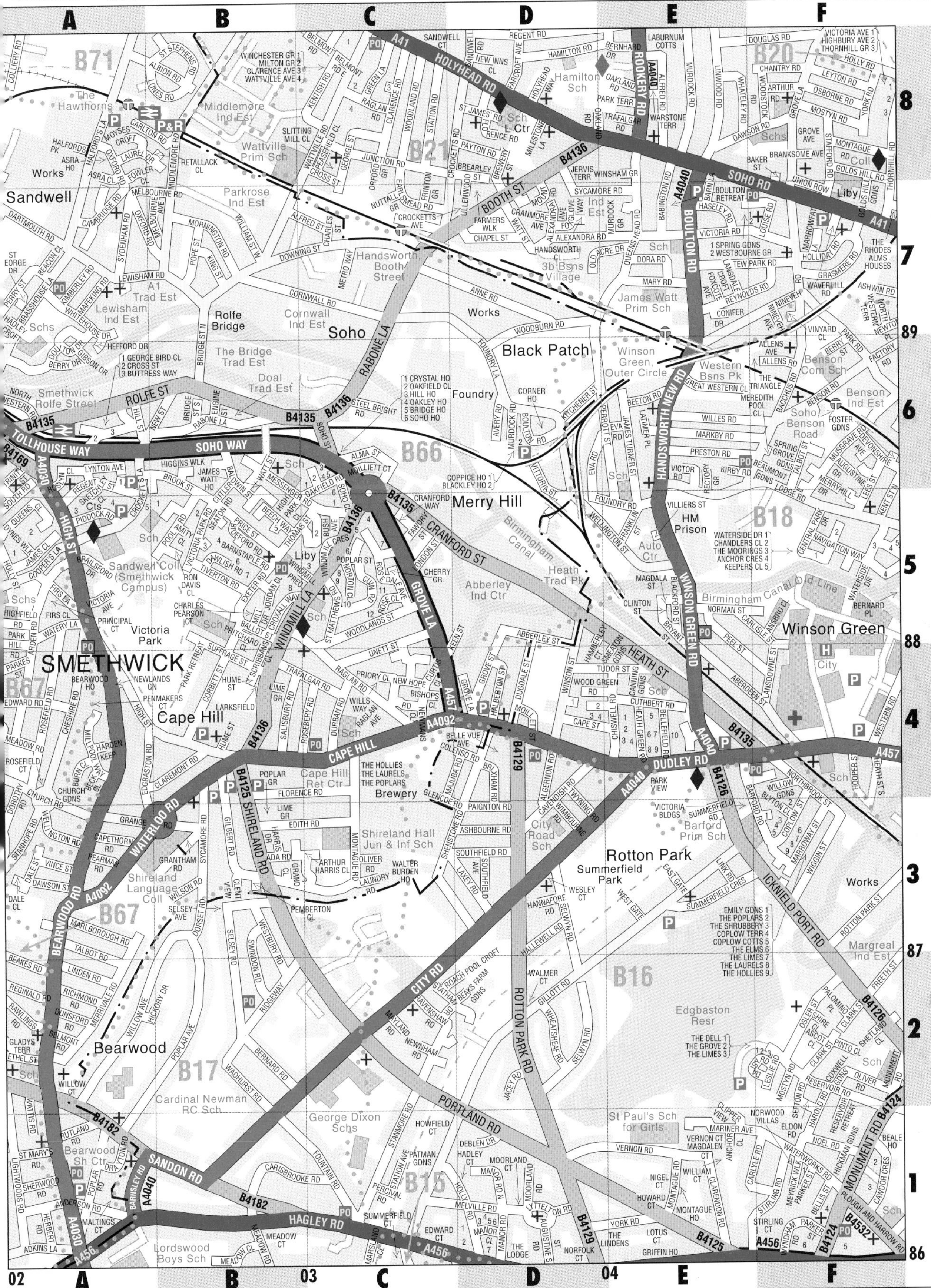

D1
1 MELVILLE HALL
2 WESTFIELD HALL
3 ST MICHAEL HO
4 ST HELLIER HO
5 ST DENNIS HO
6 ST LAWRENCE HO
7 HOLLY MOUNT

D4
1 SHIRELAND BROOK GDNS
2 WEST HEATH RD
3 BEWDLEY VILLAS
4 ARLEY VILLAS

85
66

E4
1 VICTORIA GR
2 FLORENCE GR
3 PEARL GR
4 HEATH GREEN GR
5 SUMMERFIELD GR
6 DUDLEY GR
7 HALIFAX GR
8 ASHOVER GR
9 ENDERBY GR
10 BELLEFIELD AVE

F1
1 BARROW HO
2 BALFOUR HO
3 CLAYTON HO
4 EDGWOOD CT
5 WINDSOR TERR
6 MONUMENT HO

A5
1 CLAREMONT PL
2 LANDSDOWN PL
3 LOUISA PL
4 BREDON TERR
5 RUTLAND TERR
6 PORTLAND TERR

B7
1 HEATHFIELD CT
2 LOZELLS WOOD CL
3 WELLINGTON TERR
C7
1 GRAFTON GR
2 STRETTON GR

65

C7
3 FLADBURY PL
4 RUCKLEY AVE
5 SEVERN GR
6 WESTON AVE
7 PATSHULL PL
8 SEVERN GR

C8
1 FINCHLEY AVE
2 THE AVENUE
3 ROLAND TERR
4 ROLAND GR
5 ROLAND GDNS
6 POPLAR AVE

55

C8
7 POPLAR GR
8 ARDEN GR
9 HAWTHORN GR
10 MYRTLE GR
D7
1 SANDHILL FARM CL

2 SHIRE BROOK CT
3 CLYDE TWR
4 GUILDFORD ST
D8
1 TRINITY CL
2 NEW INN RD
3 WESTON TERR

4 BEDFORD TERR
5 LEONARD AVE
6 LEONARD GR
7 CHERWELL GDNS
8 BIRCHFIELD GDNS

E8
1 DOVEHOUSE POOL RD
2 HOLYROOD GR
3 ASHBOURNE GR
4 HALISCOMBE GR
5 HAZELDENE GR

F6
1 RUDGEWICK CROFT
2 SAPPHIRE TWR
3 DUNSFOLD CROFT
4 CHILWORTH CL
5 LEATHERHEAD CL
6 HOLLAND RD W

65

A2
1 BRECON TWR
2 TRURO TWR
3 DARNLEY RD
4 KNOLLCROFT
5 BOTANY WLK
B1
1 BROADFIELD WLK
2 THE SQUARE
3 GARDEN CT

4 CALTHORPE MANS
5 AUCHINLECK SQ
6 ST MARTIN'S ST
7 ROSELAND WAY
8 SHEPHERDS GDNS
B2
1 LIBERTY PL
2 WATERMARQUE
3 BELLCROFT
4 VICTORIA HO

5 LADYCROFT
6 WATERSIDE CT
7 BRINDLEY POINT APARTMENTS
B3
1 CANTERBURY TWR
2 Summer Hill Ind Pk
3 DURHAM TWR
4 Sandpits Ind Est
5 TOWNSEND WAY

C1
1 WATERSIDE

2 LONGLEAT AVE
3 BEXHILL GR
4 TRIDENT HO
5 BROADWALK
6 FRIDAY BRIDGE
7 SATURDAY BRIDGE
C3
1 LOUISA ST
2 HELENA ST
3 JOHN SMITH HO

86

C3
4 LESLEY BENTLEY HO
5 RICHARD LIGHTON HO
6 SLOANE HO
7 SOVEREIGN CT
8 FARTHING CT
9 NEWHALL CT
C4
1 HOCKLEY CTR
2 WARSTONE MEWS

3 CHAMBERLAIN CT
4 CARPATHIAN CT
5 THE CARPATHIAN
F1
1 CHAPEL HOUSE ST
2 Bull Ring Trad Est
3 Cheapside Ind Est

For full street detail of the highlighted area see page 164.

B5
1 BLOOMSBURY WLK
2 BODMIN GR
3 LITTLE FRANCIS GR

C7
1 RAMSEY RD
2 OLD STABLES WLK
3 LITTLE CLOVER CL
4 JAMES MEML HOMES THE
5 ROBERTSONS GDNS

56
68

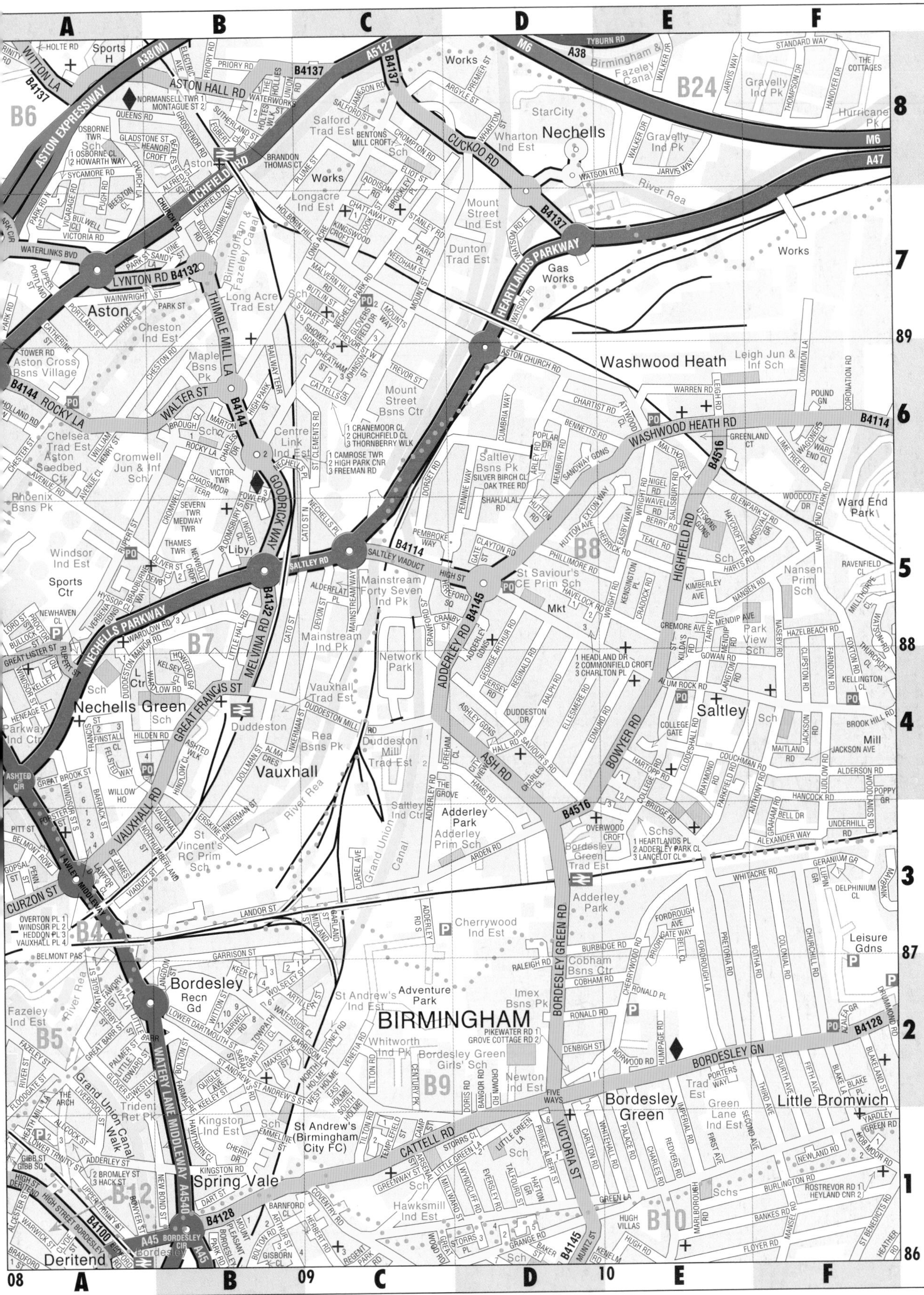

A1
1 RENAISSANCE CT
A4
1 HOBART CROFT
2 HUMBER TWR
3 TRENT TWR
4 REVESBY WLK
5 MOORCROFT PL
6 HENEAGE PL

B1
1 MOUNT PLEASANT CT
2 ST ANDREWS CT
3 DARNEL CROFT
4 PRITCHETT TWR
B2
1 ISBOURNE WAY
2 MEASE CROFT
3 MILL BURN WAY
4 ALPORT CROFT
5 GORDON ST
6 HOFF BECK CT
7 BORDSLEY CT
8 BARWELL CT
9 GARRISON CT
10 PARK VILLAS
11 ASH GR

C1
1 BROSELEY BROOK CL
2 TEMPLEFIELD GDNS
3 HARMONY HO
C4
1 Cornwall Ind Est
2 Adderley Trad Est

87

D1
1 NORTH WARWICK ST
2 EVERSLEY RD
3 HOLMWOOD RD
4 GRANEFIELD CT
5 BERTRAM RD
6 REGENCY CL
7 HAWKES ST

68

67
57

E8
1 VANGUARD CL
2 AYALA CROFT
3 BAYLEY TOWER
4 STONEYCROFT TOWER
5 BRIDGEMEADOW HO
6 KINGSPIECE HO

67
88

A B C D E F
Castle Bromwich Hall
Gardens
Castle Bromwich
B36
CHESTER RD
WATER ORTON RD
B4118
B4119 CHESTER RD
BRADFORD RD
B4114
Buckland End
Brownmead Jun & Inf Sch
Timberley Prim Sch
B34
Shard End
Liby
Hillstone Prim Sch
Colehall
York's Wood
Yorkswood Prim Sch
Playing Fields
River Cole
Babb's Mill
Recn Gd
Sheldon Hall
B37
Glebe Farm
Works
Kitt's Green
The Int Sch and Com Coll
The Archbishop Grimshaw RC Sch
Ridpool Prim Sch
Hallmoor Sch
B33
Lea Hall
RC Prim Sch
Shirestone Com Prim Sch
Tile Cross
Hatchford Com Prim Sch
Gossey Lane Jun & Inf Sch
Ace Bsns Pk
Central Bsns Pk
HRS Bsns Pk
Granby Bsns Pk
Blakenhale Jun & Inf Schs
B26
Garrett's Green
Coll
Tile Cross Trad Est
Whitesmore Sch
8 7 6 5 4 3 2 1
89 88 87 86
14 15 16

69
59

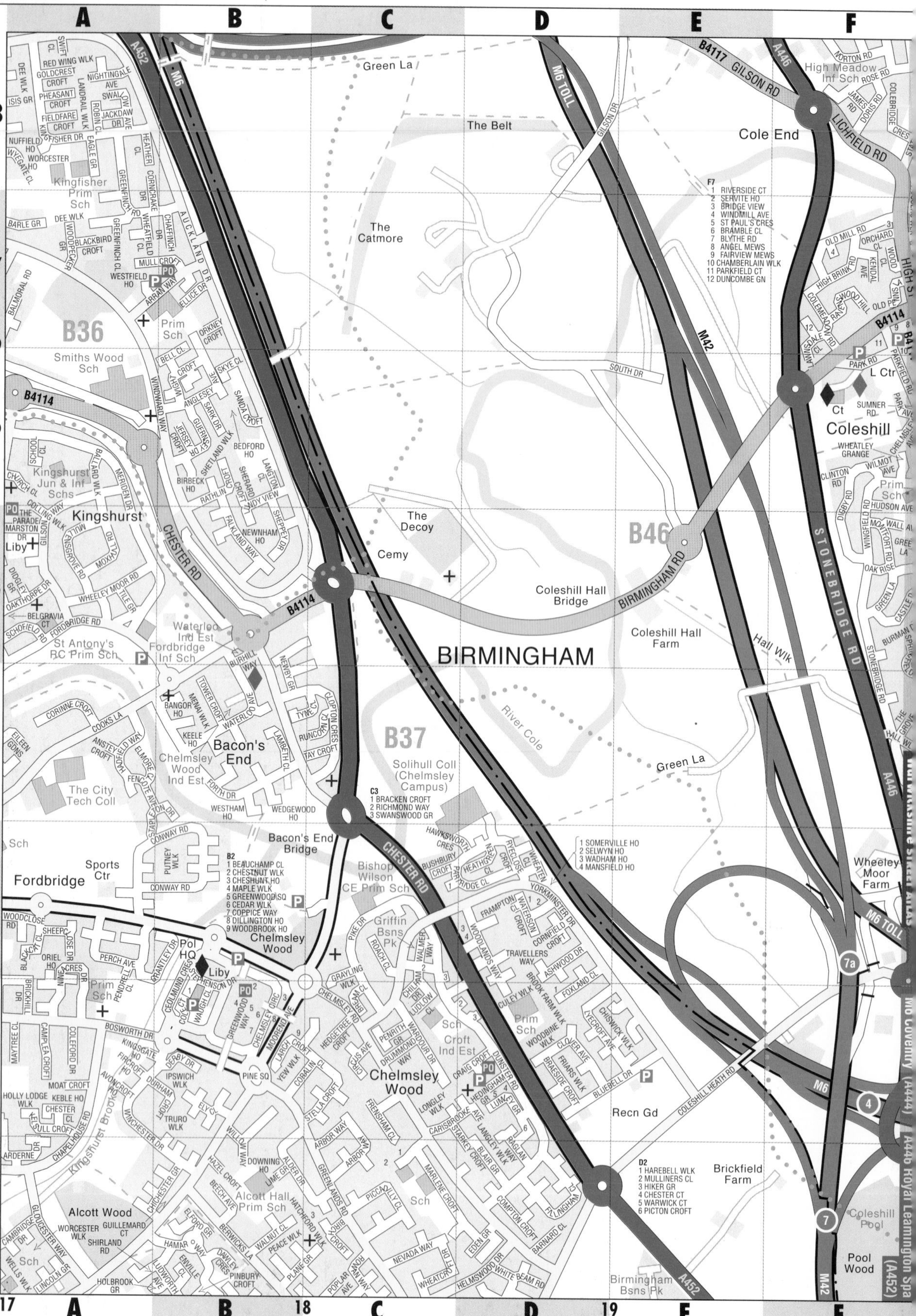
A
B
C
D
E
F
8
7
89
6
5
88
4
3
87
2
1
86
17
18
19
B36
B37
B46
BIRMINGHAM
Kingshurst
Coleshill
Cole End
Bacon's End
Chelmsley Wood
Fordbridge
The Catmore
The Decoy
The Belt
Green La
Cemy
Coleshill Hall Bridge
Coleshill Hall Farm
River Cole
Hall Wlk
BIRMINGHAM RD
CHESTER RD
STONEBRIDGE RD
B4114
B4117 GILSON RD
LICHFIELD RD
M6
M6 TOLL
M42
A452
A446
Kingfisher Prim Sch
Smiths Wood Sch
Kingshurst Jun & Inf Schs
St Antony's RC Prim Sch
Fordbridge Inf Sch
Waterloo Ind Est
Chelmsley Wood Ind Est
The City Tech Coll
Solihull Coll (Chelmsley Campus)
Bishop Wilson CE Prim Sch
Griffin Bsns Pk
Bacon's End Bridge
Sports Ctr
Croft Ind Est
Alcott Wood
Alcott Hall Prim Sch
Recn Gd
Brickfield Farm
Birmingham Bsns Pk
Wheeley Moor Farm
Coleshill Pool
Pool Wood
High Meadow Inf Sch
L Ctr
F7
1 RIVERSIDE CT
2 SERVITE HO
3 BRIDGE VIEW
4 WINDMILL AVE
5 ST PAUL'S CRES
6 BRAMBLE CL
7 BLYTHE RD
8 ANGEL MEWS
9 FAIRVIEW MEWS
10 CHAMBERLAIN WLK
11 PARKFIELD CT
12 DUNCOMBE GN
C3
1 BRACKEN CROFT
2 RICHMOND WAY
3 SWANSWOOD GR
B2
1 BEAUCHAMP CL
2 CHESTNUT WLK
3 CHESHUNT HO
4 MAPLE WLK
5 GREENWOOD SQ
6 CEDAR WLK
7 COPPICE WAY
8 DILLINGTON HO
9 WOODBROOK HO
1 SOMERVILLE HO
2 SELWYN HO
3 WADHAM HO
4 MANSFIELD HO
D2
1 HAREBELL WLK
2 MULLINERS CL
3 HIKER GR
4 CHESTER CT
5 WARWICK CT
6 PICTON CROFT
M6 Coventry (A444)
A446 Royal Leamington Spa (A452)

69
90

C1
1 TREVELYAN HO
2 RICHMOND HO
3 DARWIN HO

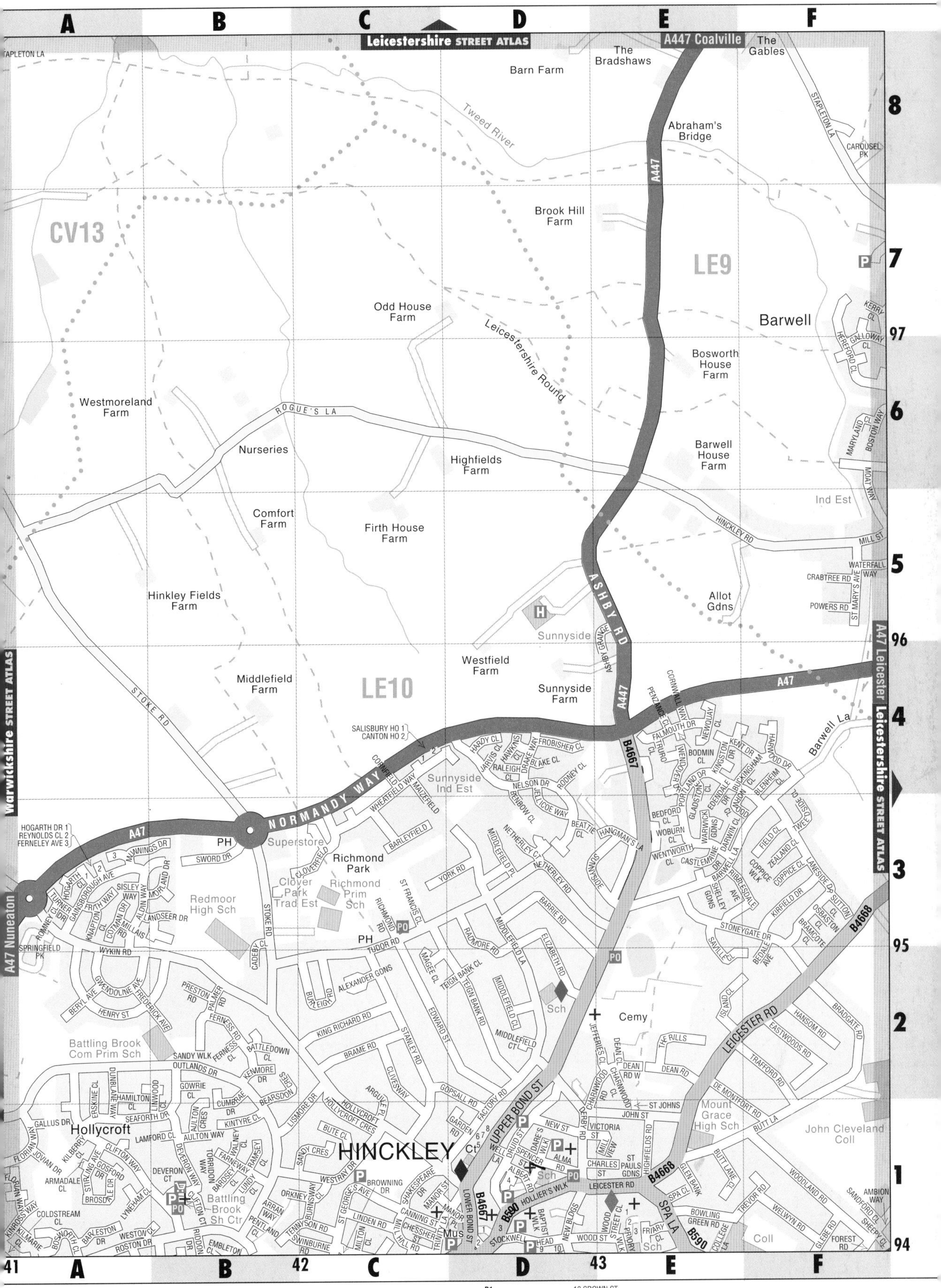

75

D1
1 BAINES' LA
2 KING ST
3 COUNCIL RD
4 QUEEN VICTORIA CT
5 JURIST HO
6 CONSUL HO
7 TRIBUNE HO
8 PRAETOR HO
9 EALES YD
10 CROWN CT

E1
1 APPLEBY HO
2 ST PETERS CT
3 BOSWORTH HO

Warwickshire STREET ATLAS
A
B
C
D
E
F
8
7
93
6
5
92
4
3
91
2
1
90
32
33
34
Hartshill
Michael Drayton Jun Sch
Hartshill Sch
Nathaniel Newton Inf Sch
Chapel End
Hartshill Quarries
Mast
Marina
Hill House
Wood Bridge
River Anker
Coventry Canal
Caldicote Hill
Mill
Judkins Quarry
B4111 NUNEATON RD
MANCETTER RD B4111
OLDBURY RD
ELM WAY
HILLSIDE
SPRINGHILL
DRAYTON CL
CHURCH CL
CHURCH RD
ROWAN WAY
MULBERRY WAY
OAK DR
ASH DR
WOOD CRES
HAYES RD
MOORWOOD LA
MOOR RD
MEADOW RD
LAUREL DR
SCHOOL HILL
VICTORIA RD
ORCHARD CL
MOORBROOKE 1
SILVERBIRCH CL 2
ANSLEY COMM
B4114
COLESHILL RD
CHANCERY CT
CHANCERY LA
WILLOW CL
ALDERS LA
BRETTS HALL EST
WAGGESTAFF DR
Nuneaton Common
PLOUGH HILL RD
PH
Plough Hill
SUTTON PK
GRANGE CL
CAMP HILL RD
HILLSIDE DR
BERRINGTON RD
CLEVELEY DR
ARLON AVE
WINDMILL RD
SALISBURY DR
LINCOLN AVE
WESTMINSTER DR
SMALLMAN RD
LILLEBURNE DR
REUBEN AVE
SKEY DR
DRAYTON WAY
CRADDOCK DR
CRADDOCK CT
RYDERS HILL CRES
NEWHAM GN
GREEN LA
HIGHBURY GN
HEDGE WAY
CHARLOTTE CL
RAMSDEN CT
BIRCHTREE RD
ALMOND AVE
KENSINGTON CT
ORCHARD WAY
TUDOR RD
RAMSDEN AVE
OAKROYD CRES
St Anne's RC Prim Sch
CAMP HILL DR
KAREN CL
PLANE GR
WHITEBEAM WAY
SPRUCE RD
WALNUT CL
CYPRESS WAY
Camp Hill Prim Sch
TUTTLE HILL
HOLLYSTITCHES RD
Cemy
BUCKS HILL
ROWAN RD
SPRING HILL RD
LUDFORD RD
EDINBURGH RD
BEECHWOOD RD
CEDAR RD
SYCAMORE RD
IVY GR
LABURNUM GR
THE DINGLE
PEAR TREE AVE
CHERRY TREE AVE
CHESTNUT CRES
LIME GR
ASHWOOD RD
WINDSOR CT
SANDRINGHAM CT
BALMORAL CT
THE HEDGEROWS
THE EVERGREENS
PLEASANT TERR
MOUNT PLEASANT TERR
HAWTHORNE TERR
WILLOW RD
DALE END
B4114
FREESLAND RISE
HILTON AVE
MERLIN AVE
FRASER CL
TRAFFORD DR
MALLARD AVE
FISHER AVE
MELFORT CL
Camp Hill
HAZEL RD
HILLCREST RD
QUEEN ELIZABETH RD
GORSY WAY
HOLYROOD CT
Hill Farm
Galley Common
Whittleford
CV11
Pool Road Ind Est
Pool Road Bsns Ctr
POOL RD
HILARY RD
MAPLE RD
ADDISON CL
BROWNING CL
RUSKIN CL
BLAKE CL
CHESTERTON DR
FIELDING WAY
ORWELL CL
KEATS CL
BETTINA CL
LORRINA CL
FRENSHAM DR
GARNETTE CL
MALLERIN CROFT
BURNABY CL
SWINBURNE CL
SELBY WAY
WIMBOURNE CL
SUNART WAY
LAGGAN CL
RANNOCH DR
ARKLET CL
LOMOND WAY
KATRINE CL
CV10
ACACIA RD
BLACK-A-TREE CT
BLACK-A-TREE RD
VERNONS MEWS
BEAUMONT RD
HARDY CL
CHAUCER DR
KIPLING CL
DICKENS CL
CAMPBELL CL
THACKERAY CL
WALTHAM CRES
HAMPTON AVE
SHERBOURNE AVE
BEVERLEY AVE
COOMBE DR
PORTLAND DR
BARONS CROFT
KNOWLES AVE
SPINNEY LA
WHITTLEFORD RD
WOODFORD CL
HAMILTON CT
VALE VIEW
WINDSOR GDNS
TRYAN RD
VERNONS LA
BYFORD ST
1 VERNONS CT
2 BYFORD CT
BEAUMONT PL
BARPOOL RD
THE CIRCLE
WOOD ST
Recn Gd
King's Wood
ST MICHAEL'S WAY
CHURCHDALE CL
KINGSWOOD GDNS
KINGSWOOD RD
QUARRY YD
SHORT ST
HILL ST
EADIE ST
FREEMAN CL
HAUNCHWOOD RD
RANDLE RD
MELDRUM RD
BEDE RD
CULPEPPER CL
FORD ST
VALE VIEW
WESTMORELAND DR
SOMERSET DR
TOMKINSON RD
RUTLAND AVE
CLIFTON RD
KINGS MDW
BERWYN WAY
THE SPIRES
ST LUKES CL
ST MARKS CL
ST MATTHEWS CL
ST THOMAS'S CT
RATCLIFFE CT
DANIEL AVE
CROSS ST
WHITEHOUSE CRES
WARWICK GDNS
HEREFORD CL
NORFOLK CRES
CUMBERLAND DR
MONMOUTH GDNS
NORTHUMBERLAND AVE
DEVON CL
DORSET CL
GRANBY RD
NORTH ST
THORNTONS WAY
SNOWDON CL
PRESCELLY CL
PENNINE WAY
CLENT DR
QUANTOCK DR
MENDIP DR
WENLOCK WAY
ASHE RD
TOWER VIEW CRES
COTSWOLD CRES
CHEVIOT CL
WYCLIF WAY
ST PAUL'S RD
Liby
Stockingford Inf & Jun Schs
WESTBURY RD
HUNTINGDON WAY
SUFFOLK CL
KILN CL
BERKSHIRE CL
VIRGINIA PL
MONTANA WLK
MARSDALE DR
Croft Jun Sch
HELENA CL
SUNNYSIDE CT
B4102
CROFT RD
SILVER WLK
ROBINS WAY
PARK LA
BRENDON WAY
CROMDALE CL
St Paul's CE Prim Sch
ARBURY CT
Stockingford
PADDIFORD PL
WEBB ST
MALVERN AVE
ARBURY GARTH
PRIORY ST
GROVE PL
GROVE RD
THE POPLARS
SUSSEX CL
SURREY CL
CAMBRIDGE DR
BELLE VUE
HERBERT ST
ALBERT ST
ST JOHN ST
WESTWOOD CL
DENEHURST WAY
RUNNYMEDE GDNS
HEATHER CL
B4112
ANSLEY RD
Park Lane Prim Sch
Tower Farm
B4102
ARBURY RD
SEESWOOD CL
Alderman Smith Sch
ROSSENDALE WAY
FOREST WAY
KIELDER DR
RADNOR DR
CHARNWOOD AVE
ATHOLL CRES
ATHOLL CT
B4112
HEATH END RD
Heath End
Heath End Farm
Centenary Way
Glendale Inf Sch
Ind Est
LEAWARD CL
BRACKENDALE DR
LINGWOOD DR
BROOMFIELD RISE
BRODICK WAY
MONTROSE DR
THE HAYWOODS
STROMA WAY
FAIR ISLE DR
KINROSS CL
SKYE CL
ORKNEY
OLDANY WAY
ASHDOWN DR
GLENDALE
CRES
WINTERBORNE GDNS
HASELBURY
SHILLINGSTONE DR
CHRISTCHURCH
Centenary Way
Seeswood Pool
Coton Lawn
Coton Lawn Farm
Sees Wood
ASTLEY LA
B4102

74

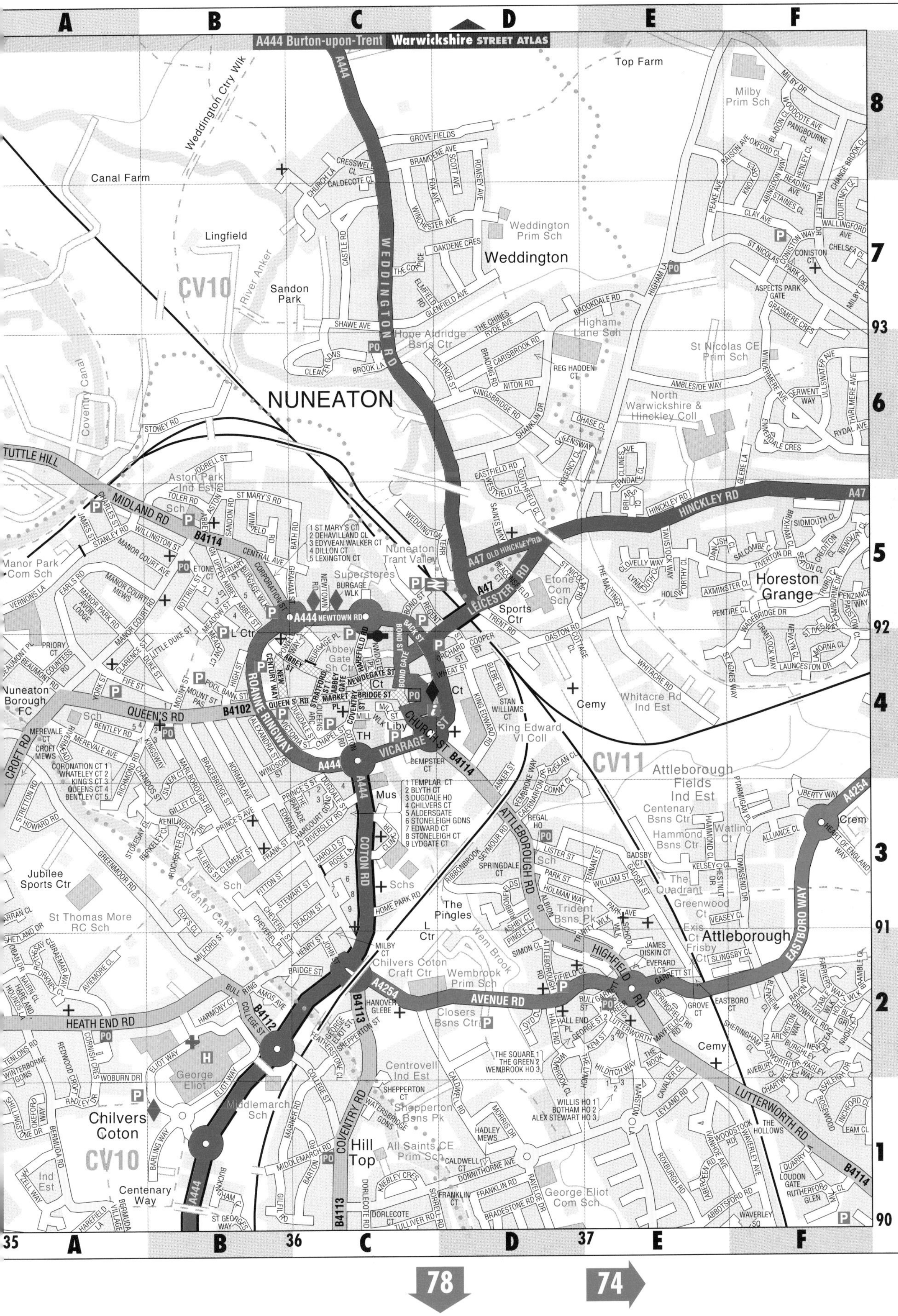
A444 Burton-upon-Trent
Warwickshire STREET ATLAS
A B C D E F
8
7
93
6
5
92
4
3
91
2
1
90
35
36
37
Top Farm
Milby Prim Sch
Canal Farm
Weddington Ctry Wlk
Lingfield
CV10
River Anker
Sandon Park
Weddington Prim Sch
Weddington
WEDDINGTON RD
Hope Aldridge Bsns Ctr
Higham Lane Sch
St Nicolas CE Prim Sch
NUNEATON
Coventry Canal
North Warwickshire & Hinckley Coll
TUTTLE HILL
MIDLAND RD
B4114
HINCKLEY RD
A47
Aston Park Ind Est
Manor Park Com Sch
Nuneaton Trant Valley
Superstores
LEICESTER RD
Etone Com Sch
Sports Ctr
Horeston Grange
Nuneaton Borough FC
QUEEN'S RD
B4102
ROANNE RINGWAY
A444 NEWTOWN RD
Abbey Gate Sh Ctr
VICARAGE ST
CHURCH ST
Cemy
Whitacre Rd Ind Est
King Edward VI Coll
CV11
Attleborough Fields Ind Est
Centenary Bsns Ctr
Hammond Bsns Ctr
Crem
Jubilee Sports Ctr
St Thomas More RC Sch
COTON RD
The Pingles
ATTLEBOROUGH RD
Trident Bsns Pk
The Quadrant
Attleborough
EASTBORO WAY
A4254
Chilvers Coton Craft Ctr
Wembrook Prim Sch
AVENUE RD
HIGHFIELD RD
HEATH END RD
B4112
B4113
Closers Bsns Ctr
George Eliot
Centrovell Ind Est
Middlemarch Sch
Shepperton Bsns Pk
Chilvers Coton
CV10
Hill Top
All Saints CE Prim Sch
George Eliot Com Sch
LUTTERWORTH RD
Centenary Way
Ind Est
1 ST MARY'S CT
2 DEHAVILLAND CL
3 EDYVEAN WALKER CT
4 DILLON CT
5 LEXINGTON CT
1 TEMPLAR CT
2 BLYTH CT
3 DUGDALE HO
4 CHILVERS CT
5 ALDERSGATE
6 STONELEIGH GDNS
7 EDWARD CT
8 STONELEIGH CT
9 LYDGATE CT
CORONATION CT 1
WHATELEY CT 2
KING'S CT 3
QUEENS CT 4
BENTLEY CT 5
THE SQUARE 1
THE GREEN 2
WEMBROOK HO 3
WILLIS HO 1
BOTHAM HO 2
ALEX STEWART HO 3

78

74

73

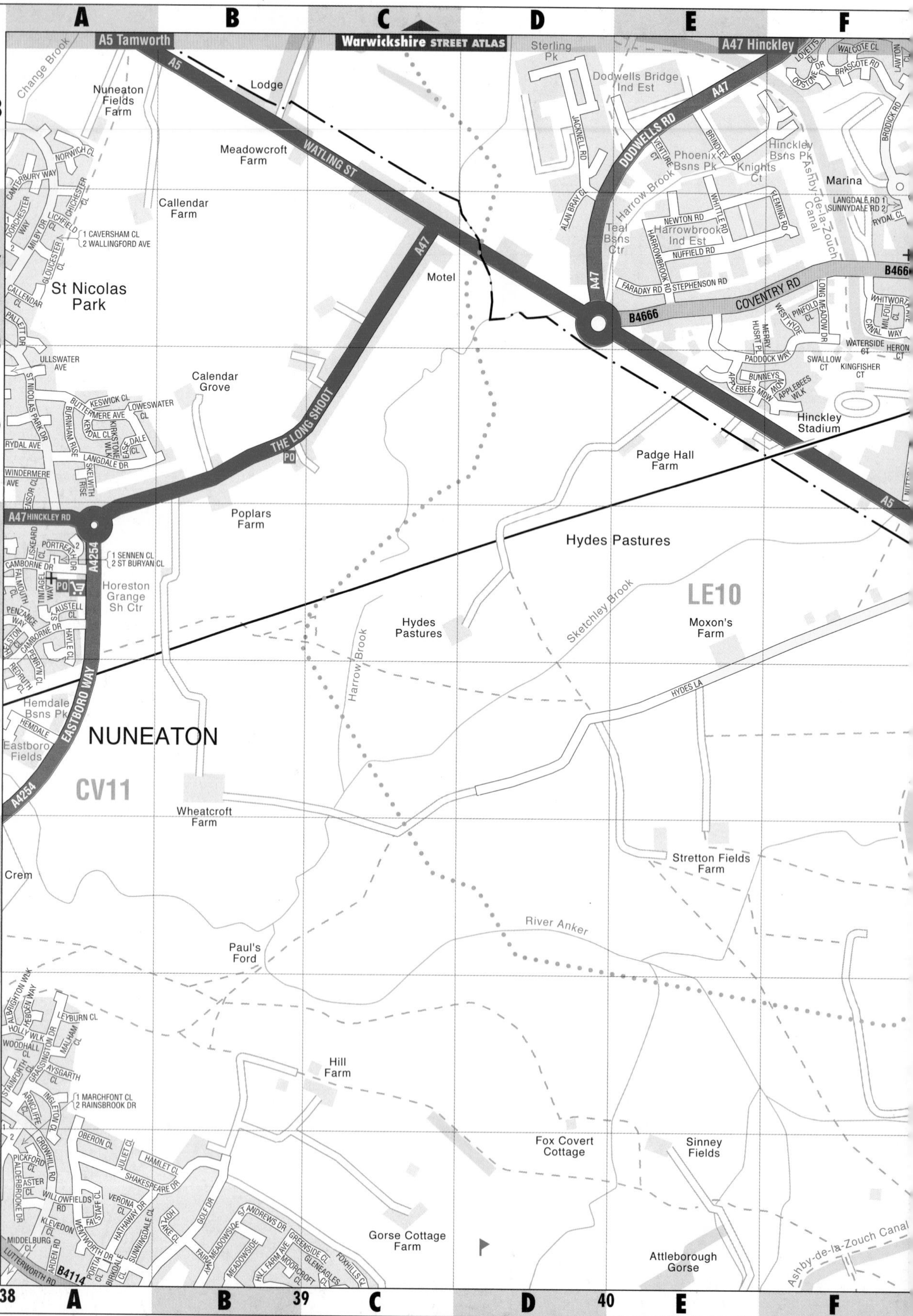
A5 Tamworth
Warwickshire STREET ATLAS
A47 Hinckley
Change Brook
Nuneaton Fields Farm
Lodge
Meadowcroft Farm
WATLING ST
Callendar Farm
St Nicolas Park
Motel
Sterling Pk
Dodwells Bridge Ind Est
DODWELLS RD
Phoenix Bsns Pk
Knights Ct
Hinckley Bsns Pk
Marina
Harrowbrook Ind Est
Teal Bsns Ctr
Ashby-de-la-Zouch Canal
COVENTRY RD
B4666
Hinckley Stadium
Calendar Grove
THE LONG SHOOT
Padge Hall Farm
Poplars Farm
Hydes Pastures
A47 HINCKLEY RD
Horeston Grange Sh Ctr
LE10
Moxon's Farm
Sketchley Brook
Harrow Brook
HYDES LA
Hemdale Bsns Pk
EASTBORO WAY
NUNEATON
Eastboro Fields
CV11
Wheatcroft Farm
Stretton Fields Farm
Crem
River Anker
Paul's Ford
Hill Farm
Fox Covert Cottage
Sinney Fields
Gorse Cottage Farm
Attleborough Gorse
Ashby-de-la-Zouch Canal
LUTTERWORTH RD
B4114

73
79

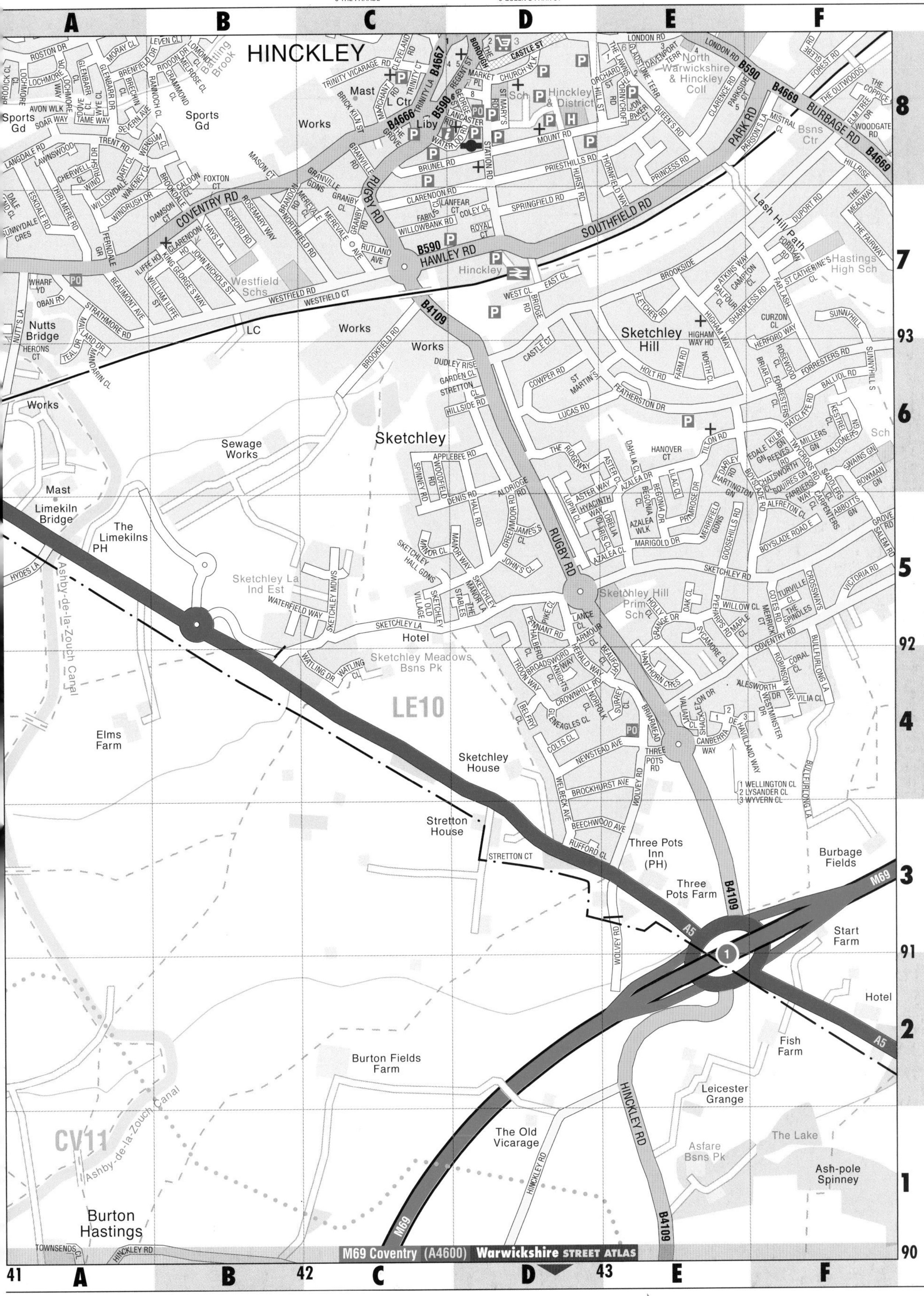
A
B
C
D
E
F
HINCKLEY
Sports Gd
Sports Gd
Works
Mast
L Ctr
Liby
Hinckley & District
North Warwickshire & Hinckley Coll
Bsns Ctr
COVENTRY RD
RUGBY RD
HAWLEY RD
SOUTHFIELD RD
BURBAGE RD
PARK RD
LONDON RD
CASTLE ST
B590
B4666
B4667
B4669
B4109
Hinckley
Westfield Schs
WESTFIELD RD
WESTFIELD CT
LC
Works
Works
Nutts Bridge
Lash Hill Path
Hastings High Sch
Sketchley Hill
Works
Sewage Works
Sketchley
Mast
Limekiln Bridge
The Limekilns PH
Sketchley La Ind Est
Sketchley Hill Prim Sch
Hotel
Sketchley Meadows Bsns Pk
LE10
Elms Farm
Ashby-de-la-Zouch Canal
Sketchley House
Stretton House
STRETTON CT
Three Pots Inn (PH)
Three Pots Farm
Burbage Fields
Start Farm
Hotel
A5
M69
Fish Farm
Burton Fields Farm
Leicester Grange
The Old Vicarage
HINCKLEY RD
Asfare Bsns Pk
The Lake
Ash-pole Spinney
CV11
Burton Hastings
TOWNSENDS CL
1 WELLINGTON CL
2 LYSANDER CL
3 WYVERN CL
8
7
93
6
5
92
4
3
91
2
1
90
41
42
43
M69 Coventry (A4600)
Warwickshire STREET ATLAS

75

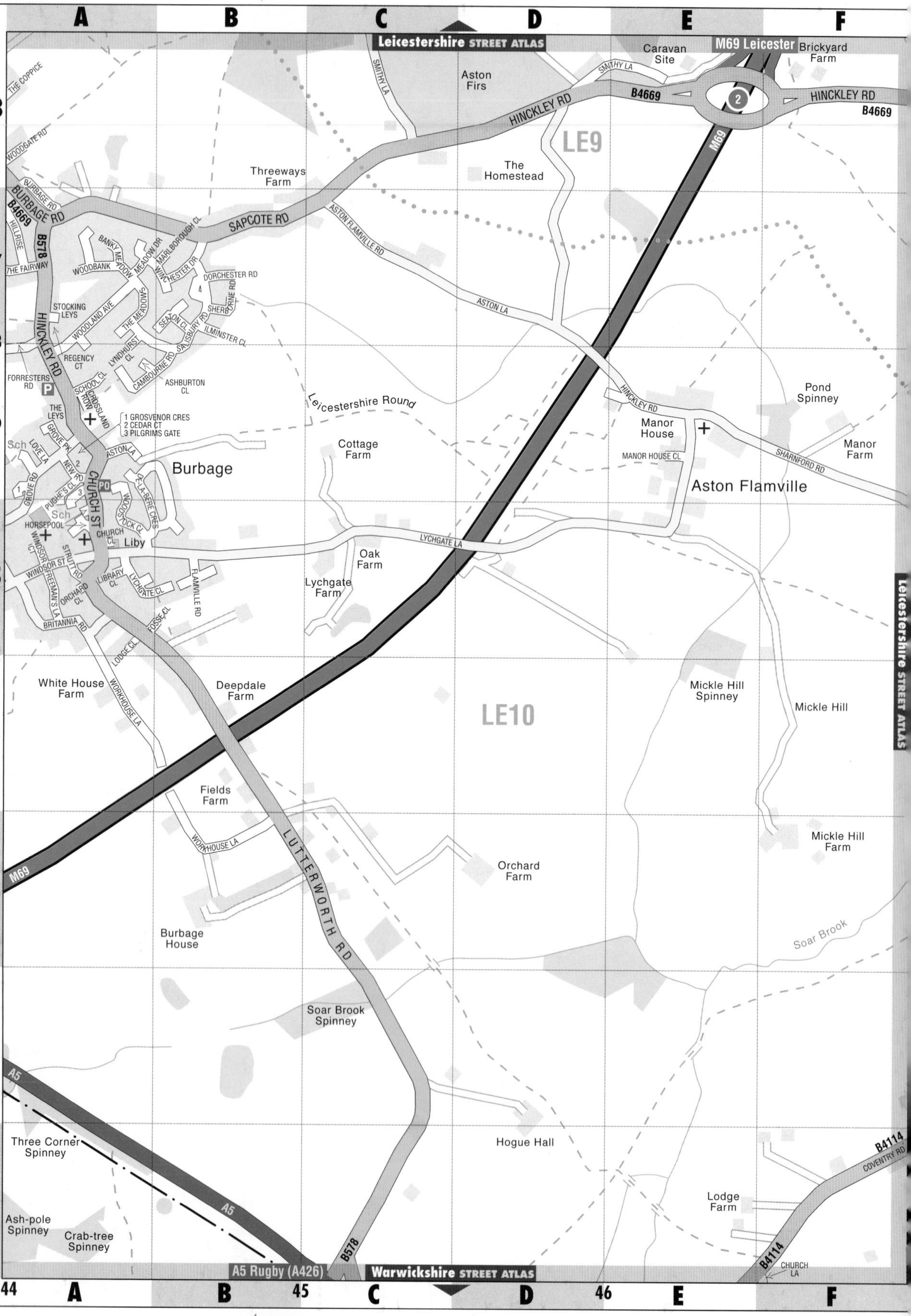
A
B
C
D
E
F
8
7
93
6
5
92
4
3
91
2
1
90
44
45
46
Leicestershire STREET ATLAS
Warwickshire STREET ATLAS
M69 Leicester
A5 Rugby (A426)
Caravan Site
Brickyard Farm
SMITHY LA
Aston Firs
HINCKLEY RD
B4669
M69
LE9
LE10
THE COPPICE
WOODGATE RD
Threeways Farm
The Homestead
BURBAGE RD
B578
HILLRISE
SAPCOTE RD
MARLBOROUGH CL
ASTON FLAMVILLE RD
THE FAIRWAY
WOODBANK
BANKY MEADOW
MEADOW DR
WINCHESTER DR
DORCHESTER RD
SHERBORNE RD
ASTON LA
STOCKING LEYS
WOODLAND AVE
THE MEADOWS
SEATON CL
SALISBURY RD
ILMINSTER CL
REGENCY CT
LYNDHURST CL
CAMBOURNE RD
ASHBURTON CL
FORRESTERS RD
SCHOOL CL
CROSSLAND ROW
THE LEYS
1 GROSVENOR CRES
2 CEDAR CT
3 PILGRIMS GATE
Leicestershire Round
Pond Spinney
Manor House
Manor Farm
SHARNFORD RD
MANOR HOUSE CL
Aston Flamville
Sch
LOVE LA
GROVE PK
NEW RD
GROVE RD
PUGHE'S CL
CHURCH ST
PO
DE-LA-BERE CRES
WOODSTOCK CL
Burbage
Cottage Farm
HORSEPOOL
CHURCH CL
Liby
LYCHGATE LA
Oak Farm
WINDSOR CT
STRUTT RD
WINDSOR ST
FREEMAN'S LA
ORCHARD CL
LIBRARY CL
LYCHGATE CL
FLAMVILLE RD
Lychgate Farm
BRITANNIA RD
FOSSE CL
LODGE CL
White House Farm
WORKHOUSE LA
Deepdale Farm
Mickle Hill Spinney
Mickle Hill
Fields Farm
LUTTERWORTH RD
Mickle Hill Farm
Orchard Farm
Burbage House
Soar Brook
Soar Brook Spinney
A5
Three Corner Spinney
Hogue Hall
B4114
COVENTRY RD
Lodge Farm
Ash-pole Spinney
Crab-tree Spinney
CHURCH LA

75

72
78

95
78

D2
1 WILDEY RD
2 HIMLEY RD
3 CAMPION WAY
4 DAFFODIL DRIVE
5 LARKSPUR GR
6 SPEEDWELL CL

F2
1 SYDNEY CT
2 CANBERRA CT
3 MELBOURNE CT
4 QUEENSLAND GDNS

77
73

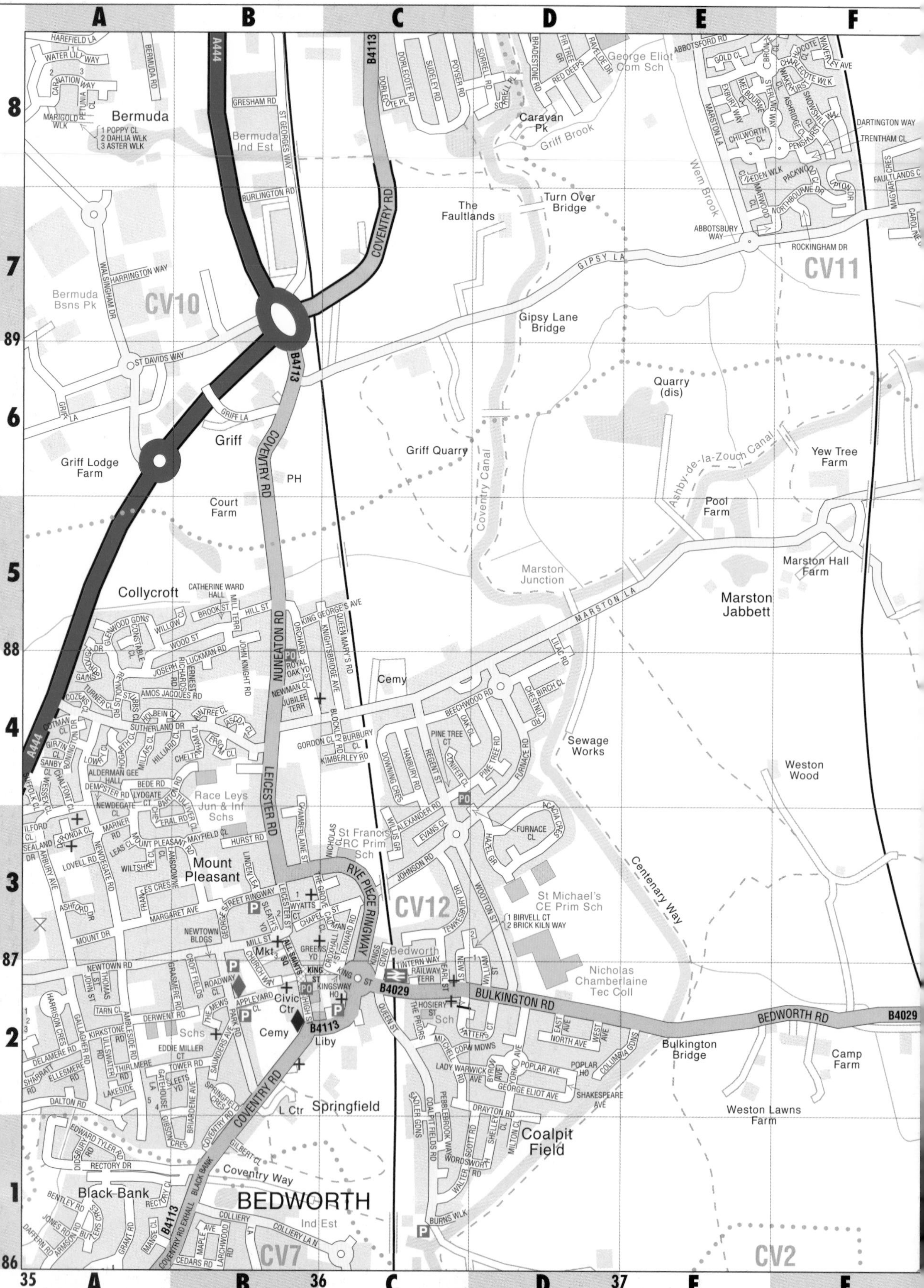
A
B
C
D
E
F
8
7
89
6
5
88
4
3
87
2
1
86
35
36
37
A444
B4113
B4029
Bermuda
Bermuda Ind Est
Bermuda Bsns Pk
CV10
CV11
CV12
CV7
CV2
George Eliot Com Sch
Caravan Pk
Griff Brook
Wem Brook
The Faultlands
Turn Over Bridge
Gipsy Lane Bridge
GIPSY LA
Quarry (dis)
Griff
Griff Lodge Farm
Griff Quarry
Coventry Canal
Ashby-de-la-Zouch Canal
Yew Tree Farm
Pool Farm
PH
Court Farm
Marston Junction
Marston Hall Farm
Marston Jabbett
MARSTON LA
Collycroft
Cemy
Sewage Works
Weston Wood
Race Leys Jun & Inf Schs
St Francis RC Prim Sch
Mount Pleasant
St Michael's CE Prim Sch
Centenary Way
Nicholas Chamberlaine Tec Coll
Bedworth
Mkt
Civic Ctr
Schs
Sch
Liby
Bulkington Bridge
BULKINGTON RD
BEDWORTH RD
Camp Farm
L Ctr
Springfield
Weston Lawns Farm
Coalpit Field
Coventry Way
Black Bank
BEDWORTH
Ind Est
COVENTRY RD
NUNEATON RD
LEICESTER RD
RYE PIECE RINGWAY
1 POPPY CL
2 DAHLIA WLK
3 ASTER WLK
1 BIRVELL CT
2 BRICK KILN WAY

A2
1 DARWIN CT
2 BRISBANE CT
3 ADELAIDE CT
4 OLD PENN'S YD
5 BUCKLER'S YD

B3
1 OLD MEETING YD
2 BEDE ARC
3 CONGREVE WLK

77
96

74

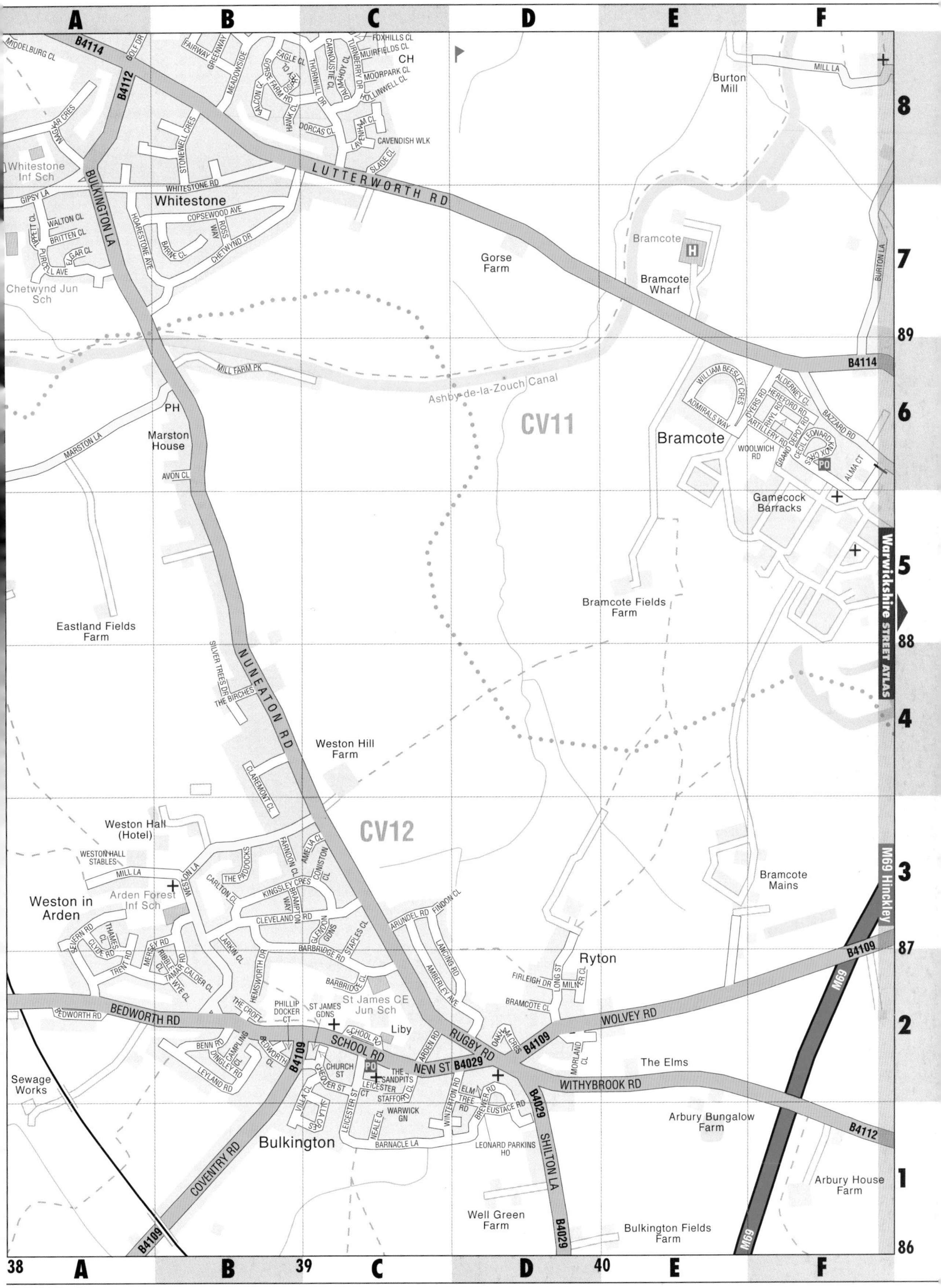

A
B
C
D
E
F
8
7
89
6
5
88
4
3
87
2
1
86
38
39
40
B4114
MIDDELBURG CL
GOLF DR
FAIRWAY
GREENWAY
MEADOWSIDE
EAGLE CL
FOXHILLS CL
MUIRFIELDS CL
CH
MOORPARK CL
HOLLINWELL CL
TURNBERRY DR
CARNOUSTIE CL
THORNHILL DR
FALCON CL
GORSE FARM RD
HAWK CL
DORCAS CL
CAVENDISH WLK
SLADE CL
B4112
MAGYAR CRES
STONEWELL CRES
Whitestone Inf Sch
WHITESTONE RD
LUTTERWORTH RD
BULKINGTON LA
GIPSY LA
Whitestone
COPSEWOOD AVE
WALTON CL
BRITTEN CL
ELGAR CL
PURCELL AVE
HOARESTONE AVE
BARNE CL
ROSS WAY
CHETWYND DR
Chetwynd Jun Sch
Burton Mill
MILL LA
Bramcote
Bramcote Wharf
Gorse Farm
BURTON LA
MILL FARM PK
Ashby-de-la-Zouch Canal
PH
Marston House
MARSTON LA
AVON CL
CV11
WILLIAM BEESLEY CRES
ADMIRALS WAY
DYERS RD
HEREFORD RD
ALDERNEY CL
RHYL RD
ARTILLERY RD
BAZZARD RD
Bramcote
WOOLWICH RD
GRAND DEPOT RD
CECIL LEONARD KNOX CRES
ALMA CT
PO
Gamecock Barracks
Bramcote Fields Farm
Eastland Fields Farm
Warwickshire STREET ATLAS
SILVER TREES DR
THE BIRCHES
NUNEATON RD
Weston Hill Farm
CLAREMONT CL
CV12
Weston Hall (Hotel)
WESTON HALL STABLES
MILL LA
WESTON LA
THE PADDOCKS
FARNDON CL
AMELIA CL
CONISTON CL
CARLTON CL
KINGSLEY CRES
BRAMPTON WAY
Weston in Arden
Arden Forest Inf Sch
CLEVELAND RD
GLENDON GDNS
STAPLES CL
ARUNDEL RD
FINDON CL
SEVERN RD
THAMES CL
CLYDE RD
TRENT RD
MERSEY RD
RIBBLE CL
TAMAR RD
CALDER CL
WYE CL
LARKIN CL
HEMSWORTH DR
BARBRIDGE RD
LANCING RD
AMBERLEY AVE
Bramcote Mains
M69 Hinckley
Ryton
FIRLEIGH DR
LONG ST
MILNER CL
BRAMCOTE CL
B4109
WOLVEY RD
BEDWORTH RD
BEDWORTH RD
THE CROFT
PHILLIP DOCKER CT
ST JAMES GDNS
St James CE Jun Sch
Liby
SCHOOL RD
RUGBY RD
OAKHAM CRES
MORLAND CL
The Elms
M69
BENN RD
CAMPLING CL
DINGLEY RD
LEYLAND RD
BEDWORTH CL
B4109
CHURCH ST
CHEQUER ST
LEICESTER ST
THE SANDPITS
STAFFORD CL
NEW ST
B4029
ARDEN RD
WITHYBROOK RD
Sewage Works
VILLA CL
VILLA CRES
NEALE CL
WARWICK GN
WINTERTON RD
ELM TREE RD
BREWER RD
EUSTACE RD
Arbury Bungalow Farm
B4112
Bulkington
BARNACLE LA
LEONARD PARKINS HO
SHILTON LA
COVENTRY RD
Arbury House Farm
Well Green Farm
Bulkington Fields Farm
B4029
B4109

97

60

E8
1 THE JUNCTION
2 ALDRIDGE CL
3 LONGBOAT LA
4 STEWKINS CT

F8
1 CRYSTAL AVE
2 SURREY HO
3 WILTSHIRE HO
4 DEVON HO
5 LANCASTER HO
6 HANOVER HO
7 ALLAN CL
8 CORBETT HO
9 DENNIS HALL

98

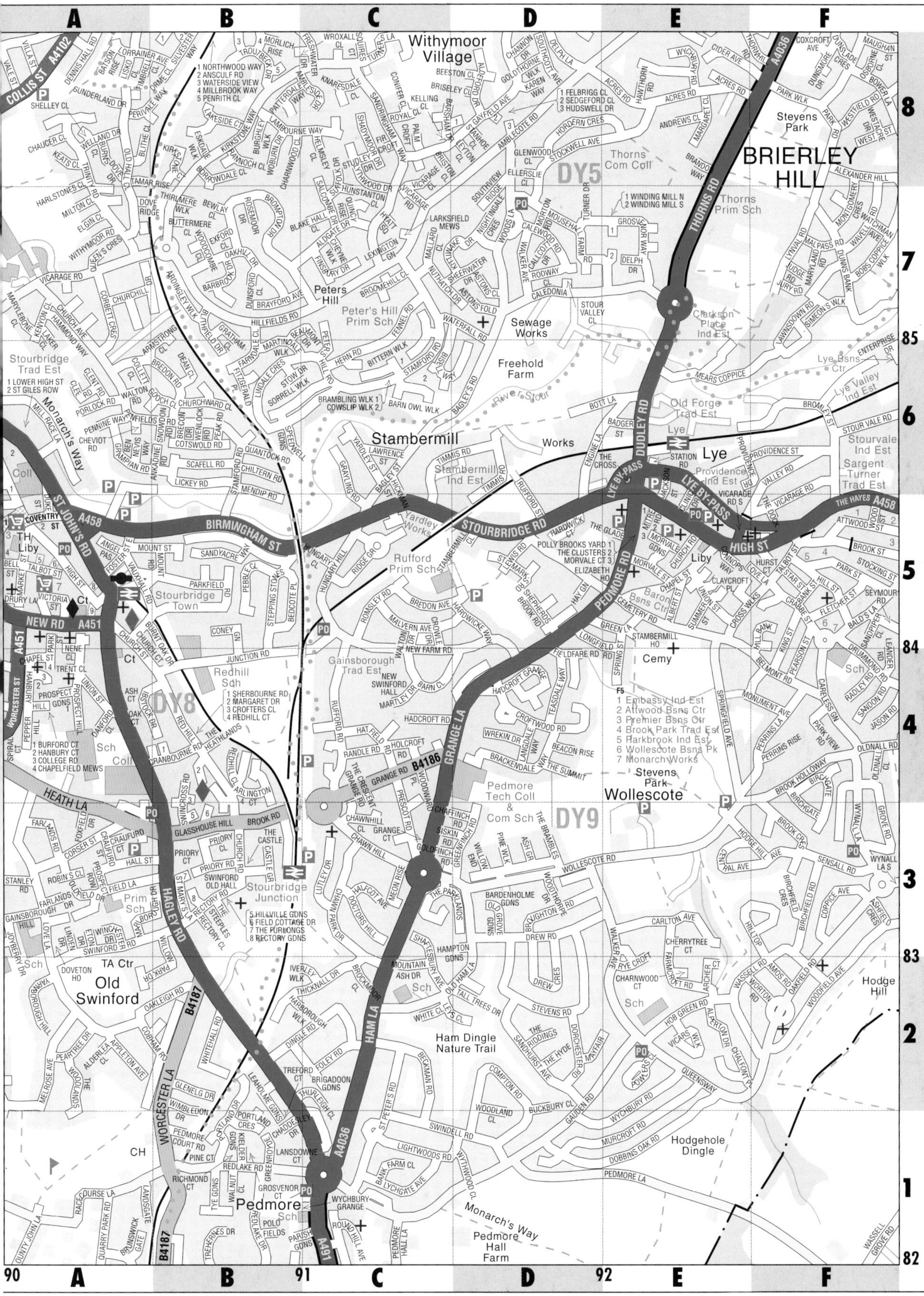
A
B
C
D
E
F
8
7
85
6
5
84
4
3
83
2
1
82
90
91
92
Withymoor Village
BRIERLEY HILL
Stevens Park
Thorns Com Coll
Thorns Prim Sch
DY5
Peters Hill
Peter's Hill Prim Sch
Sewage Works
Freehold Farm
Clarkson Place Ind Est
Lye Bsns Ctr
Lye Valley Ind Est
Old Forge Trad Est
Stambermill
Stambermill Ind Est
Works
Lye
Providence Ind Est
Stourvale Ind Est
Sargent Turner Trad Est
Stourbridge Trad Est
1 LOWER HIGH ST
2 ST GILES ROW
Monarch's Way
River Stour
Stourbridge Town
Yardley Works
Rufford Prim Sch
Gainsborough Trad Est
Redhill Sch
1 SHERBOURNE RD
2 MARGARET DR
3 CROFTERS CL
4 REDHILL CT
DY8
Liby
Baron Bsns Ctr
Cemy
F5
1 Embassy Ind Est
2 Attwood Bsns Ctr
3 Premier Bsns Ctr
4 Brook Park Trad Est
5 Parkbrook Ind Est
6 Wollescote Bsns Pk
7 Monarch Works
Stevens Park
Wollescote
DY9
Pedmore Tech Coll & Com Sch
Stourbridge Junction
5 HILLVILLE GDNS
6 FIELD COTTAGE DR
7 THE FURLONGS
8 RECTORY GDNS
1 BURFORD CT
2 HANBURY CT
3 COLLEGE RD
4 CHAPELFIELD MEWS
Old Swinford
TA Ctr
Ham Dingle Nature Trail
Hodgehole Dingle
Hodge Hill
Pedmore
Pedmore Hall Farm
1 NORTHWOOD WAY
2 ANSCULF RD
3 WATERSIDE VIEW
4 MILLBROOK WAY
5 PENRITH CL
1 FELBRIGG CL
2 SEDGEFORD CL
3 HUDSWELL DR
1 WINDING MILL N
2 WINDING MILL S
BRAMBLING WLK 1
COWSLIP WLK 2
POLLY BROOKS YARD 1
THE CLUSTERS 2
MORVALE CT 3
A458
A451
A4036
A4102
B4186
B4187
A491
BIRMINGHAM ST
STOURBRIDGE RD
ST. JOHN'S RD
HAGLEY RD
GRANGE LA
HAM LA
PEDMORE RD
DUDLEY RD
THORNS RD
LYE BY-PASS
HIGH ST
NEW RD
HEATH LA
GLASSHOUSE HILL
WORCESTER LA
WOLLESCOTE RD
PEDMORE LA
COLLIS ST
THE HAYES

A8
1 QUEEN STREET PAS
2 CHAPEL ST
3 HAMPDEN CL

E8
1 MORGAN CL
2 DELINGPOLE WLK
3 DOROTHY ADAMS CL

F8
1 SHERWOOD HO
2 EDGEWOOD CL
3 ADDENBROOK HO
4 WESLEY CT
5 MEADOW ST
6 PENN ST

81
62

81
100

63
84

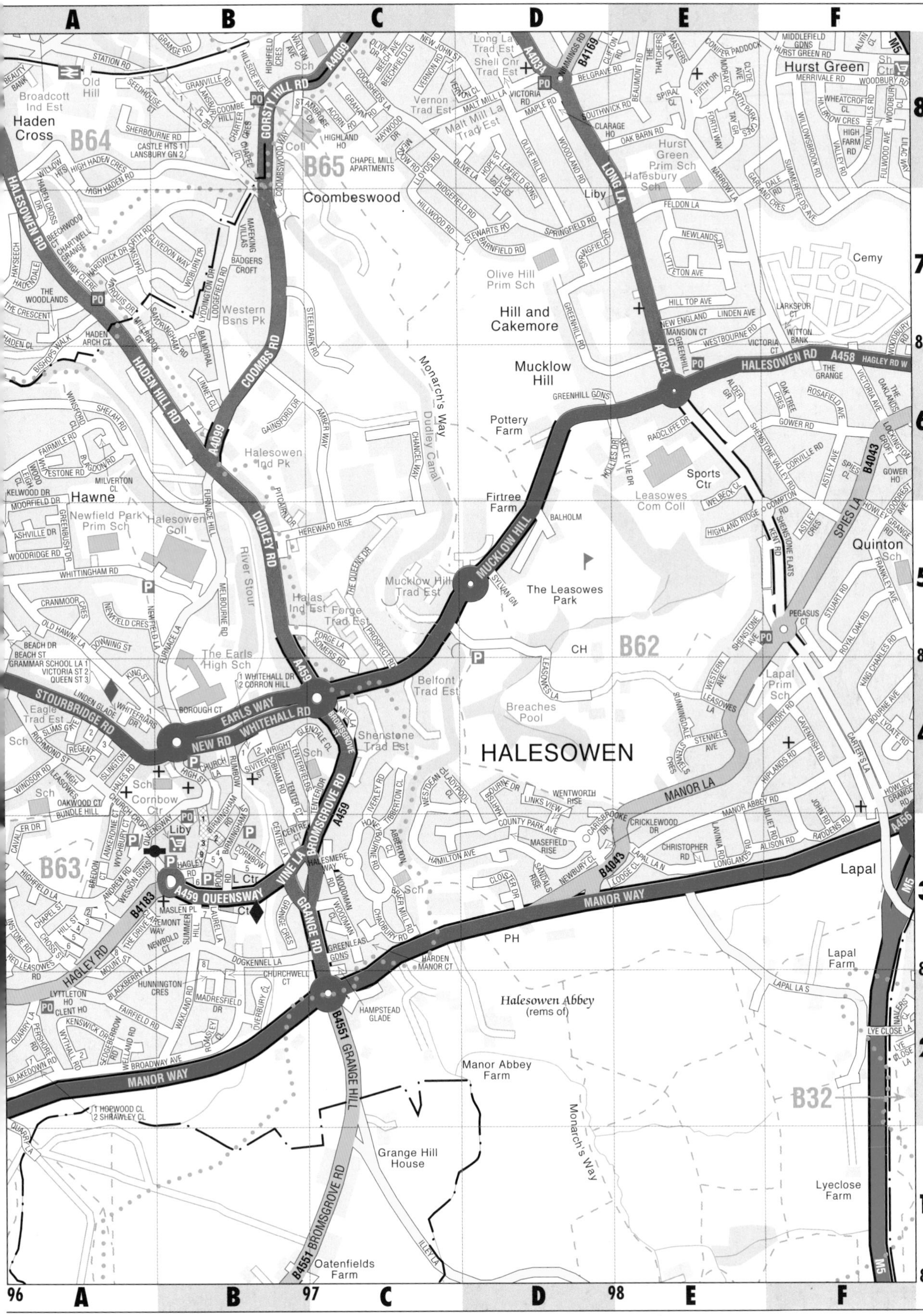

A3
1 HIGHFIELD LA
2 TENBURY HO
3 HONEYBOURNE CL
4 WORCESTER HO
5 BROOME CL
6 PICKERSLEIGH CL
7 MALVERN HO
8 HOLLYBERRY CL

B3
1 HIGH ST
2 PECKINGHAM ST
3 HAGLEY ST
4 BULL RING
5 GREAT CORNBOW
6 SUMMER HILL
7 POWELL ST
8 PEACHLEY CL
9 SOMERS SQ

101
84

A6
1 BEVERLEY CT
2 HICKMANS CL
3 LOMBARDY CROFT
4 THE GREEN

A7
1 ALBANY CT
2 WILLES CT
3 MILVERTON CT
4 REGENT CT
5 MANOR CT
6 VICTORIA CT

83

B7
1 ASTBURY CT
2 DOWNING CT

64

B8
1 ARROW HO
2 STOUR HO
3 AVON HO
4 SEVERN HO
5 RUSKIN CT
6 LAWRENCE CT
7 HENDERSON CT
8 OLD CRESCENT CT

F7
1 WALMEAD CROFT
2 GIMBLE WLK
3 PEEL WLK
4 GREEN WLK
5 HAZELEY CL

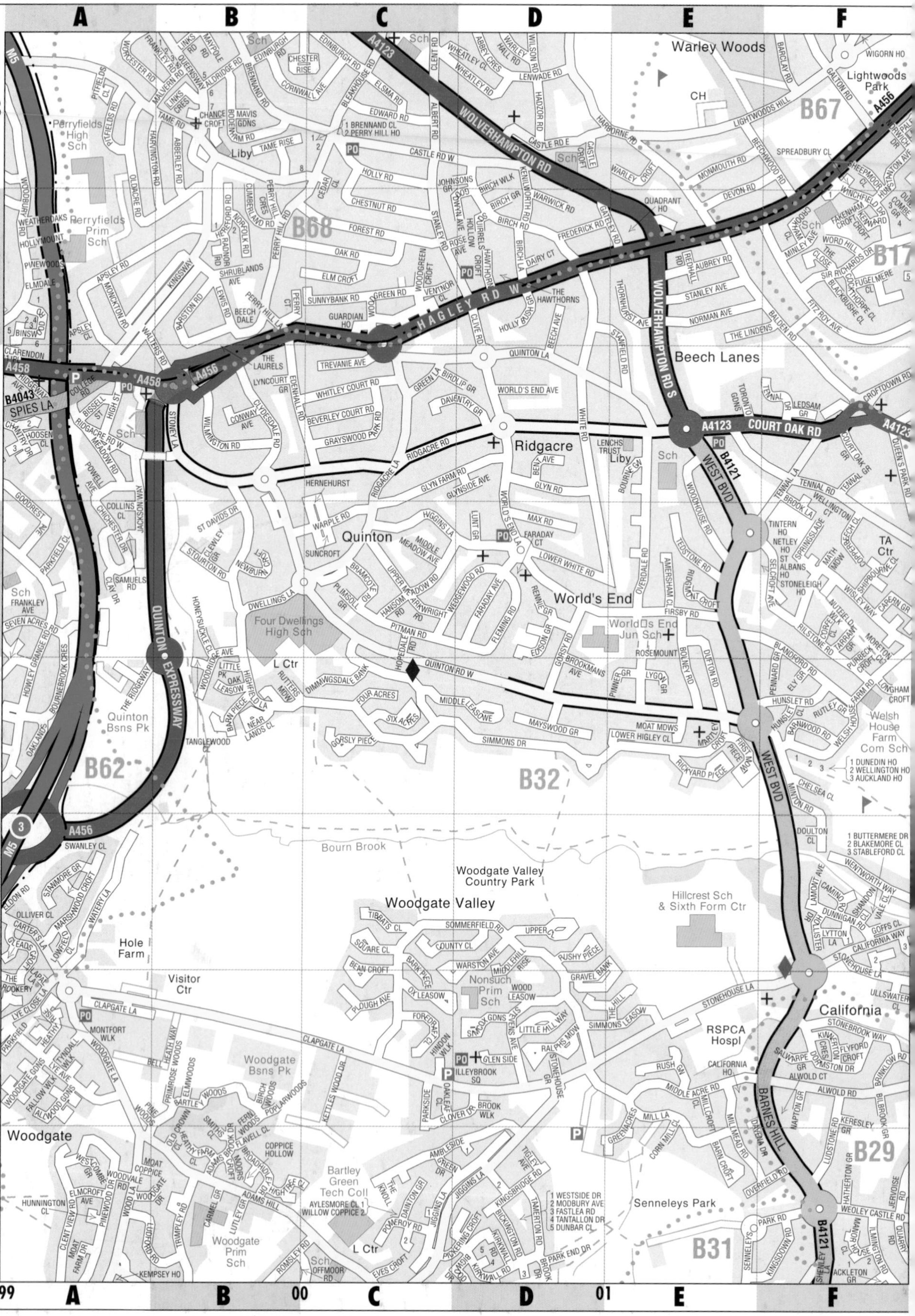

83
102

F1
1 PACKWOOD CT
2 HONNINGTON CT

65

86

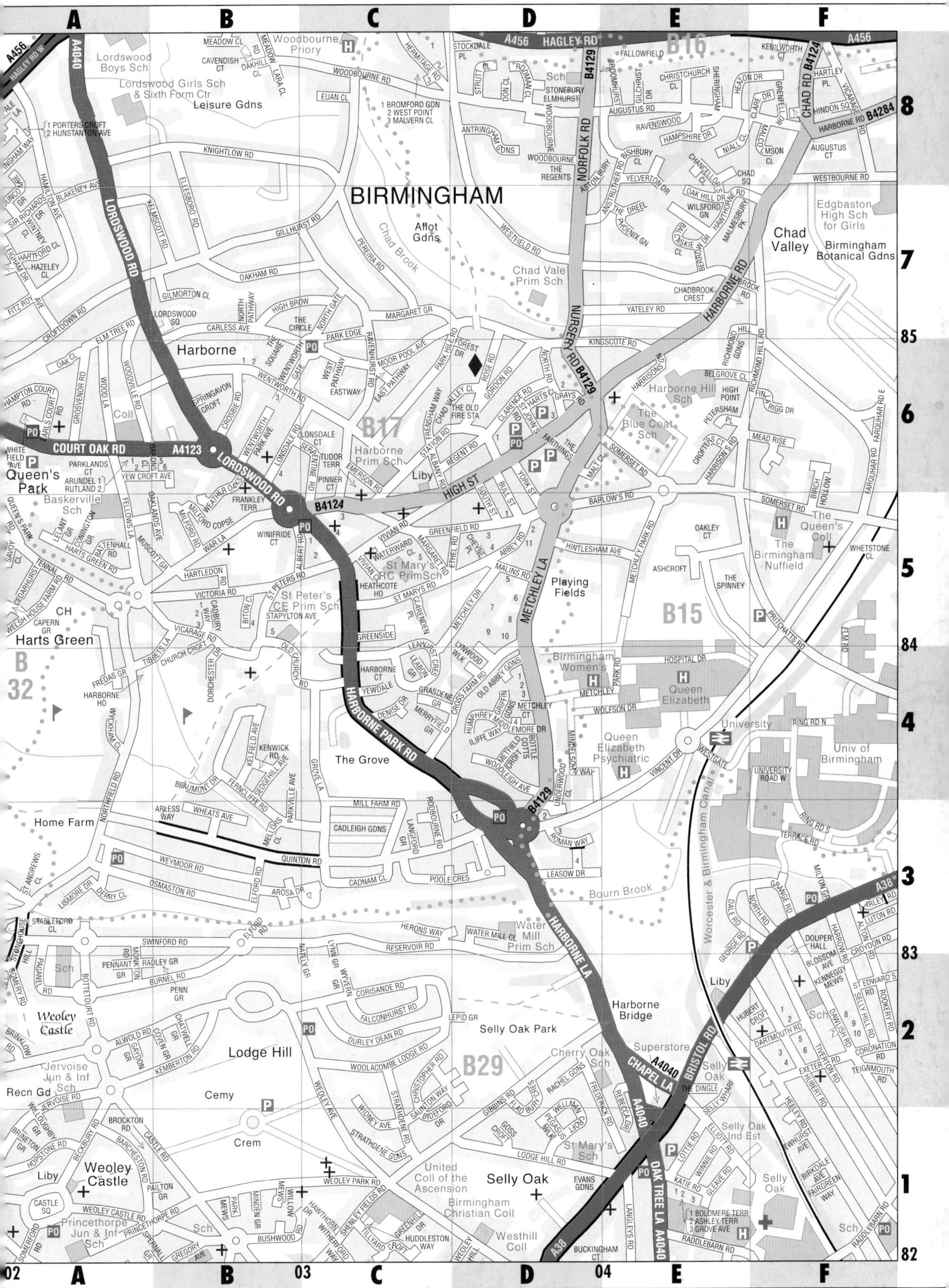

A B C D E F
8 7 85 6 5 84 4 3 83 2 1 82
02 03 04
BIRMINGHAM
B16
B17
B15
B29
B 32
A456 HAGLEY RD
A4040
LORDSWOOD RD
A4123
COURT OAK RD
B4124
HIGH ST
B4129
NORFOLK RD
NURSERY RD
METCHLEY LA
HARBORNE RD
CHAD RD B4124
B4284
HARBORNE PARK RD
HARBORNE LA
CHAPEL LA
BRISTOL RD
OAK TREE LA A4040
A38
Woodbourne Priory
Lordswood Boys Sch
Lordswood Girls Sch & Sixth Form Ctr
Leisure Gdns
Harborne
Queen's Park
Baskerville Sch
Harts Green
Home Farm
Weoley Castle
Lodge Hill
Cemy
Crem
Liby
Allot Gdns
Chad Brook
Chad Vale Prim Sch
Chad Valley
Edgbaston High Sch for Girls
Birmingham Botanical Gdns
Harborne Hill Sch
The Blue Coat Sch
The Queen's Coll
The Birmingham Nuffield
Playing Fields
Harborne Prim Sch
St Mary's RC Prim Sch
St Peter's CE Prim Sch
The Grove
Birmingham Women's
Queen Elizabeth
Queen Elizabeth Psychiatric
University
Univ of Birmingham
Worcester & Birmingham Canal
Bourn Brook
Water Mill Prim Sch
Selly Oak Park
Harborne Bridge
Superstore
Cherry Oak Sch
Selly Oak
Selly Oak Ind Est
St Mary's Sch
United Coll of the Ascension
Birmingham Christian Coll
Westhill Coll
Jervoise Jun & Inf Sch
Recn Gd
Princethorpe Jun & Inf Sch
1 PORTERS CROFT
2 HUNSTANTON AVE
1 BROMFORD GDN
2 WEST POINT
3 MALVERN CL
1 BOLDMERE TERR
2 ASHLEY TERR
3 GROVE AVE

103

86

C8
1 AUDLEIGH HO
2 CHISWICK HO
3 LEOFRIC CT
4 ALFRYTH CT
5 FARADAY HO
6 HOGARTH HO
7 BRADSHAW CL
8 Bell Barn Sh Ctr
9 WATERSIDE
D7
1 ST LAWRENCE CL
2 OTTAWA TWR

85

D8
1 HADDON TWR
2 NEWHOPE CL
3 KERRIA CT

66

E5
1 CANNON HILL PL
2 CANNON HILL GR
3 BEACONSFIELD CRES
E7
1 EARLSWOOD HO
2 ELMSTEAD TWR
3 CUMBERLAND AVE
E8
1 HIGHGATE HO
2 CHARLBURY TWR
3 WELLESBOURNE TWR
4 DUNCHURCH HO
F5
1 PARK AVE
2 HEATH CT
3 MINTON HO
F7
1 WILLIAM EDWARD ST
2 CANTLOW HO
3 LENCH'S TRUST ALMSHOUSES
4 BRINKLOW TWR
5 WILMCOTE TWR
6 UPPER CONYBERE ST
7 JAMES SAMUEL PL
8 THOMAS BENSON PL
9 Highgate Sq Craft Ctr
F8
1 HANWOOD HO
2 DARFIELD WLK
3 RADCLIFFE TWR
4 CANBERRA WAY

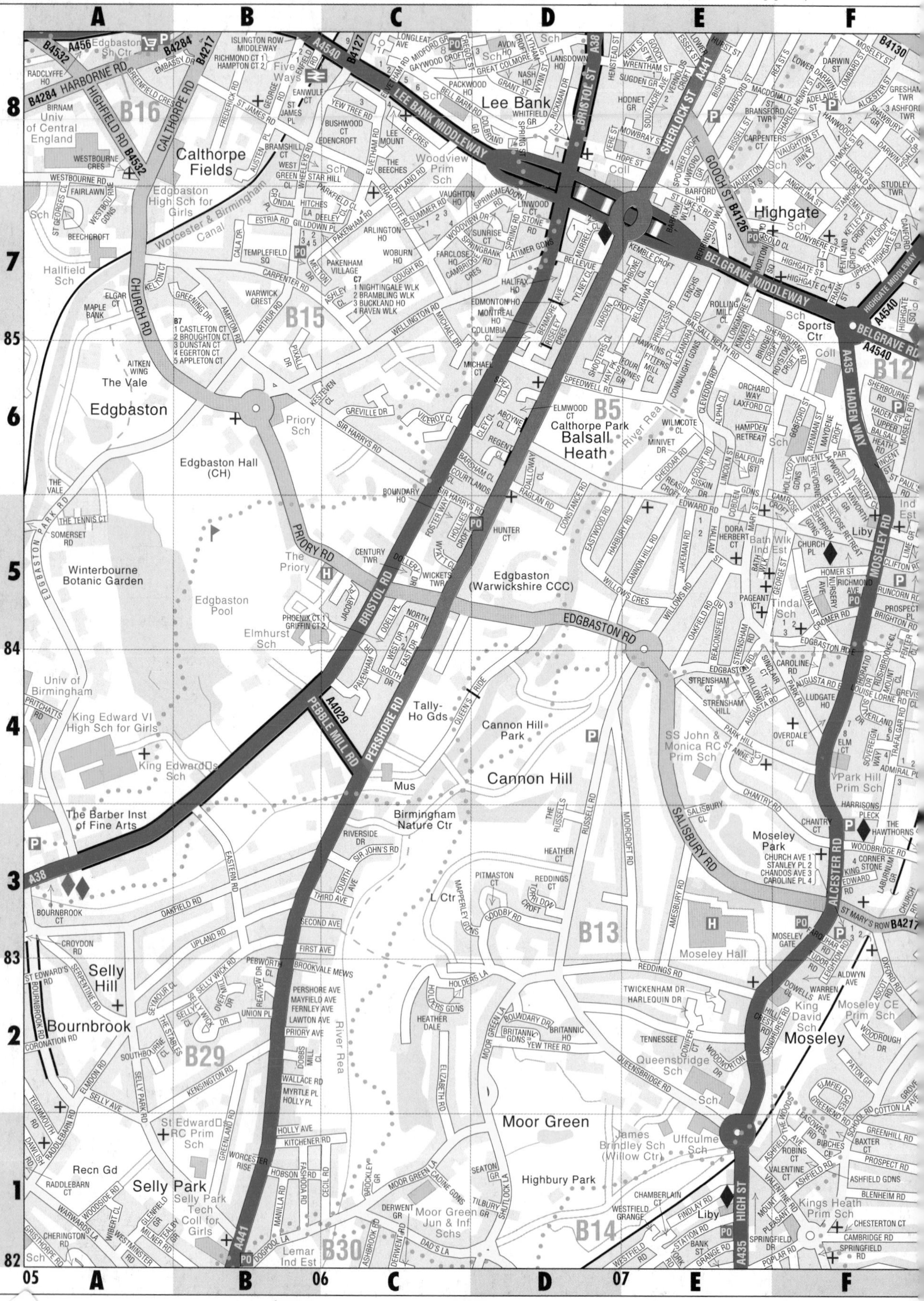

85
104

F4
1 HAMILTON CT
2 VICTORIA CT
3 FLEETWOOD HO
4 HARDY CT
5 NELSON CT
6 VICTORY HO
7 WILLIAM CT
8 HELEN DIXON CT

5
LILAC AVE
COPPERBEACH DR
MAY AVE
MYRTLE AVE
BEECH AVE

A6
1 ALBERT AVE
2 MILTON AVE
3 MILFORD AVE
4 BEWDLEY AVE
5 HEREFORD AVE
6 SPRINGFIELD AVE
7 CARPENTER PL
8 GROSMONT AVE
9 OAKFIELD AVE
10 FLORENCE PL
11 MILLICENT PL
12 BRADGATE PL

A8
1 WARNER ST
2 TRINITY TERR
3 LENCH'S TRUST ALMSHOUSES
4 NEW MOSELEY RD

B5
1 HANLEY VILLAS
2 MATLOCK VILLAS
3 IVY AVE
4 TINTERN VILLAS
5 CHEPSTOW VILLAS

B6
1 BEECHFIELD AVE
2 STANLEY GR

67

B6
3 LADYPOOL AVE
4 SOUTH RANGE

C5
1 ROSARY VILLAS
2 LABURNUM VILLAS
3 INGLESIDE VILLAS
4 ORIEL VILLAS

88

C8
1 WARNERS WLK
2 VANN CL
3 ST AIDANS WLK
4 TUDORS CL
5 CYRIL GR
6 HENSHAW GR

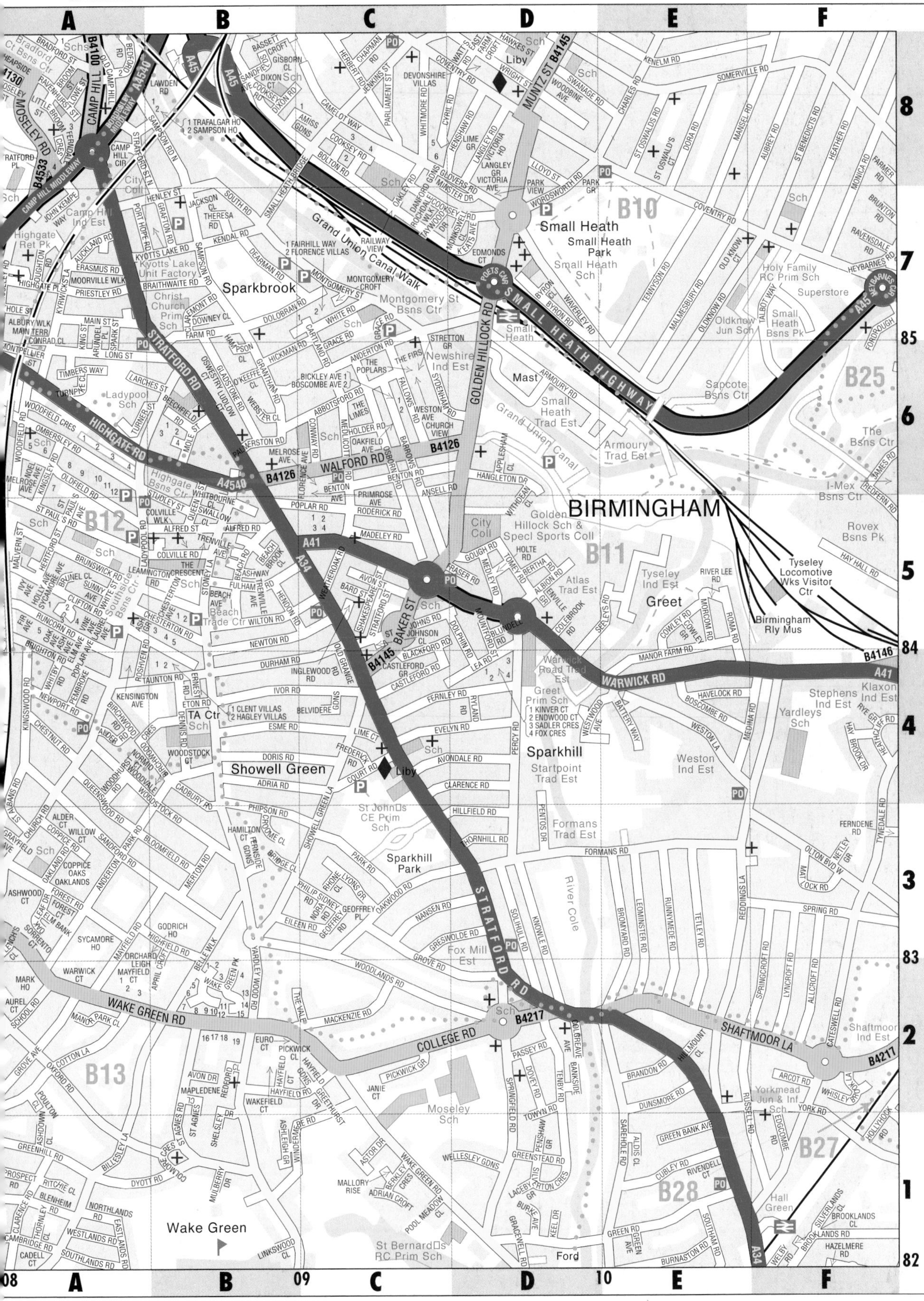

105

88

A2
1 PETERHOUSE MEWS
2 KINGS HALL
3 DARWIN HO

B2
1 WALLIS CT
2 VENICE CT
3 BROMFORD PARK HO
4 BOWEN CT
5 ROBERT CT
6 MAJOR CT
7 ROYSTON CT
8 CHARLES CT
9 STANLEY CT
10 MICHAEL BLANNING HO
11 BROWN'S CT
12 OULSNAM CT
13 JAMES CT
14 GALLAGHER CT
15 BUCKNALL CT
16 CLEVELAND CT
17 INGOLDSBY CT
18 BURFORD CT
19 MOSELEY CT

87
C5
1 SYCAMORE WAY
2 CYPRESS SQ
3 LAUREL GDNS
4 ASH MEWS
5 CHERRY TREE CROFT
6 SNOWBERRY GDNS

68
C5
7 RYE CROFT
8 HONEYSUCKLE GR
9 BLOSSOMVILLE WAY

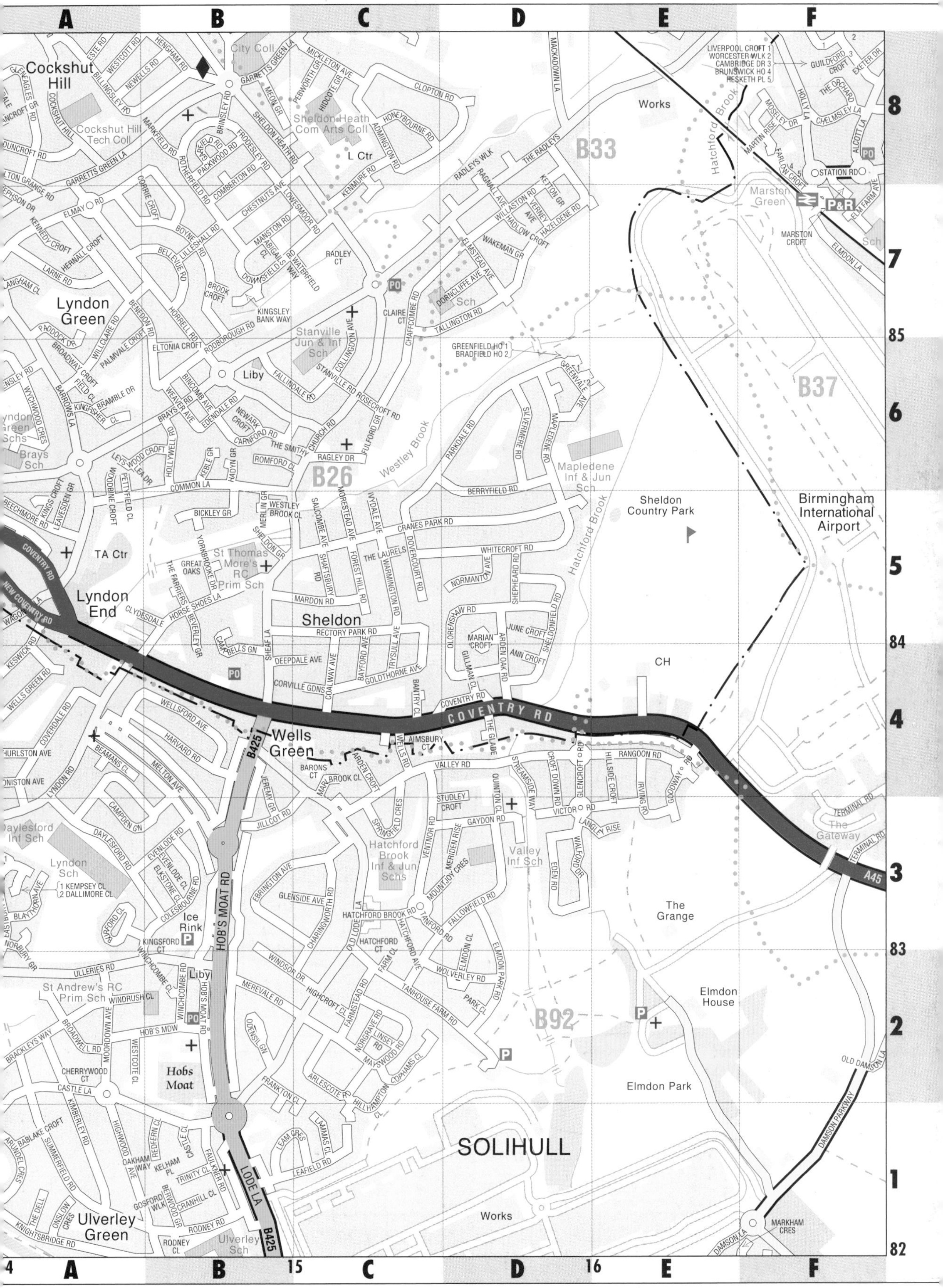
A
B
C
D
E
F
8
7
85
6
5
84
4
3
83
2
1
82
15
16
Cockshut Hill
Cockshut Hill Tech Coll
City Coll
Sheldon Heath Com Arts Coll
L Ctr
Works
B33
Hatchford Brook
Marston Green
P&R
STATION RD
ELMDON LA
Lyndon Green
Stanville Jun & Inf Sch
Liby
Sch
B37
Brays Sch
B26
Westley Brook
Mapledene Inf & Jun Sch
Sheldon Country Park
Birmingham International Airport
TA Ctr
St Thomas More's RC Prim Sch
Lyndon End
Sheldon
Hatchford Brook
COVENTRY RD
NEW COVENTRY RD
CH
Wells Green
B425
HOB'S MOAT RD
Daylesford Inf Sch
Lyndon Sch
Hatchford Brook Inf & Jun Schs
Valley Inf Sch
The Gateway
A45
The Grange
Ice Rink
Liby
St Andrew's RC Prim Sch
Elmdon House
B92
Hobs Moat
Elmdon Park
SOLIHULL
LODE LA
Works
Ulverley Green
Ulverley Sch
DAMSON PARKWAY
MARKHAM CRES
GARRETTS GREEN LA
SHELDON HEATH RD
RAGLEY DR
RECTORY PARK RD
VALLEY RD
CHURCH RD
BERRYFIELD RD
CRANES PARK RD
WHITECROFT RD
CASTLE LA
KNIGHTSBRIDGE RD
MACKADOWN LA
CLOPTON RD

89
70

A
B
C
D
E
F
8
7
85
6
5
84
4
3
83
2
1
82
17
18
19
Marston Green
Marston Green Jun & Inf Schs
Liby
Coleshill Heath
Sports Ctr
John Black Day
Pinewood Bsns Pk
Heath Farm
Birmingham Bsns Pk
B37
School Rough
Cemy
Hotel
Century Pk
Bickenhill Plantations
Elmdon Trad Est
B46
Low Brook
B40
National Exhibition Ctr (The NEC)
Birmingham International
Birmingham International Airport
Hotel
Pendigo Lake
B26
Mast
Hotels
Depot
Trinity Pk
Hotel
Wyckhams Close
CH
Dunston Farm
The Clock Inn (PH)
B92
The Jungle
Castle Hills
Grange Farm
Bickenhill
AVON PARK CVN PK
BICKENHILL GREEN CT
MOOREND AVE
1 EXETER DR
2 WELLS WLK
SYCAMORE CRES
LUDWORTH AVE
HAMAR WAY
RADLOW CRES
POPLAR AVE
ASPEN DR
CORNEL CL
ROWAN WAY
HELMSWOOD DR
BOX RD
TULIP WLK
WHITE BEAM RD
BERWICKS LA
BROOKLANDS WAY
BYFORD WAY
LEAF DR
1 NEWINGTON RD
2 FULWELL MEWS
COLESHILL RD
WAYSIDE
MALTHOUSE ROW
STATION RD
CARTERS CL
IVY LODGE CL
ELMDON CT
LAND LA
HALL DR
THE OAKLANDS
ST LEONARDS
BROOK CROFT
LYNDON CROFT
BICKENHILL RD
HEMLINGFORD CROFT
ELMDON RD
HIDCOTE GR
FARNDON AVE
SOMERTON DR
1 ROTHERBY GR
2 WOLVERTON RD
CANTERBURY DR
THE RISE
AYLESFORD DR
THE GREENWAY
ELMDON LA
NEWLANDS LA
DIGBY DR
THE FORDRIFT
COLESHILL HEATH RD
BLACKFIRS LA
BICKENHILL LA
BICKENHILL PARKWAY
STARLEY WAY
THE CRESCENT
SOLIHULL PARKWAY
THE PAVILIONS
TRIDENT CT
PARK SQ
BISHOP'S CT
KNIGHTS CT
A452
CHESTER RD
M42
B4438
A45
NORTH AVE
NORTHWAY
EXHIBITION WAY
THIRD EXHIBITION AVE
FIRST EXHIBITION AVE
PERIMETER RD
THE UNDERPASS
PENDIGO WAY
EAST CAR PARK RD
HARBET DR
RAMP
HERALD RD
TRIDENT RD
COMET RD
CONCORDE RD
AMBASSADOR RD 1
VANGUARD RD 2
STATION LINK RD 3
HERMES RD
AIRPORT WAY
HANGER RD
COMMISSARY RD
FORWARD RD
WORKS RD
ELMDON LA
EASTWAY
SOUTH WAY
FORUM RD
SOUTH CAR PARK RD
COVENTRY RD
OLD DAMSON LA
CLOCK LA
CATHERINE DE BARNES LA
PITT LA
CHURCH LA
ST PETERS LA
OLD STATION RD
6

89
108

A
B
C
D
E
F
A446 Lichfield (A38)
Warwickshire STREET ATLAS
M6 Birmingham A38(M)
M6
A446
The Bogs Farm
B37
Bannerley Rough
Depot
Todd's Rough
Mulliner's Rough
8
STONEBRIDGE RD
Nursery
B46
Nursery Farm
Ford
SCHOOL LA
Brook Farm
Foxes Den
Broadwater
Golf & Country Club
7
85
Refuse Tip
PACKINGTON LA
Fish Breeding Farm
The Ash Beds
DENBIGH CNR
Little Packington
Butler's Moors
Packington Park
Park Meadow
6
A446
FISHPOOL LA
Denbigh Spinney
Church Farm
River Blythe
Deer Park
5
Garden Spinney
CHESTER RD
84
Park Farm
MIDDLE BICKENHILL LA
Siding Wood
CV7
Packington Hall
Hall Pool
Great Pool
4
The Wilderness
Mill Shrubbery
Middle Bickenhill
B92
The Mill Farm
Little Dayhouse Wood
Beech Lodge
3
Dials Pool
EAST WAY
PH
COVENTRY RD
COVENTRY RD
BIRMINGHAM RD
Stonebridge
83
A45
Works
The National Motorcycle Mus
Pasture Farm
Geary's Heath
B4102
Mills Gorse
2
Diddington Hill
DIDDINGTON LA
Diddington Hall
KENILWORTH RD
P
CH
Shadow Brook
OLD STATION RD
SOMERS RD
1
The Somers
Mouldings Green Farm
A452
Molands Bridge
THE GROVE
B4102
82
20
A
B
21
C
D
22
E
F

91

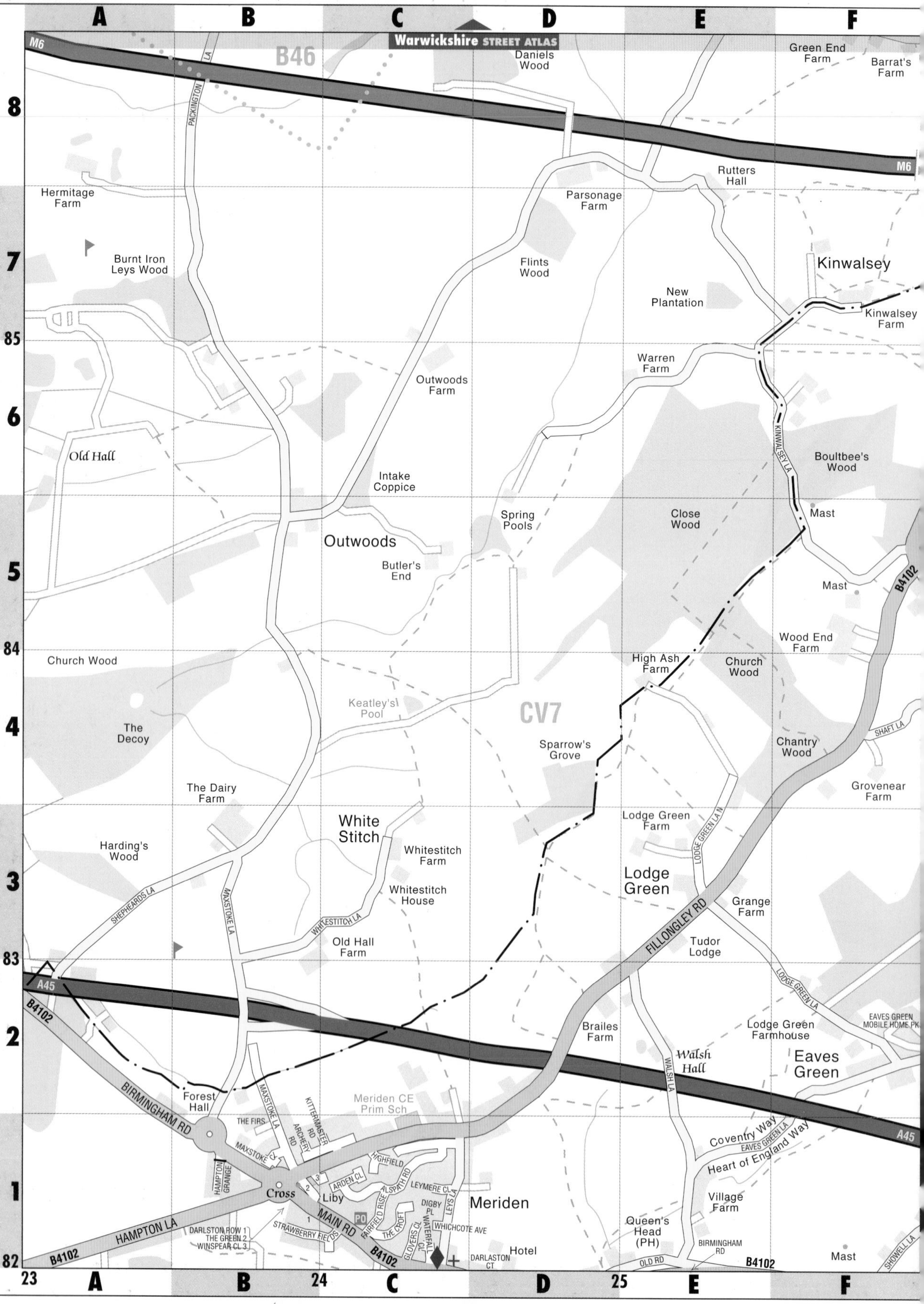
A
B
C
D
E
F
Warwickshire STREET ATLAS
M6
B46
Daniels Wood
Green End Farm
Barrat's Farm
8
PACKINGTON LA
Hermitage Farm
Rutters Hall
Parsonage Farm
M6
7
Burnt Iron Leys Wood
Flints Wood
Kinwalsey
New Plantation
Kinwalsey Farm
85
Warren Farm
Outwoods Farm
6
Old Hall
KINWALSEY LA
Boultbee's Wood
Intake Coppice
Spring Pools
Close Wood
Mast
Outwoods
5
Butler's End
Mast
B4102
Wood End Farm
84
Church Wood
High Ash Farm
Church Wood
Keatley's Pool
CV7
4
The Decoy
Sparrow's Grove
Chantry Wood
SHAFT LA
The Dairy Farm
Grovenear Farm
White Stitch
Lodge Green Farm
Harding's Wood
Whitestitch Farm
LODGE GREEN LA N
3
Lodge Green
Whitestitch House
SHEPHEARDS LA
MAXSTOKE LA
WHITESTITCH LA
FILLONGLEY RD
Grange Farm
Old Hall Farm
Tudor Lodge
83
A45
B4102
LODGE GREEN LA
EAVES GREEN MOBILE HOME PK
2
Brailes Farm
Lodge Green Farmhouse
Walsh Hall
Eaves Green
WALSH LA
Forest Hall
BIRMINGHAM RD
MAXSTOKE LA
KITTERMASTER RD
ARCHERY RD
Meriden CE Prim Sch
A45
THE FIRS
MAXSTOKE CL
HIGHFIELD
Coventry Way
EAVES GREEN LA
Heart of England Way
1
HAMPTON GRANGE
Cross
ARDEN CL
ALSPATH RD
LEYMERE CL
LEYS LA
Liby
Meriden
Village Farm
FAIRFIELD RISE
DIGBY PL
PO
MAIN RD
HAMPTON LA
THE CROFT
GLOVERS CL
WATERFALL CL
WHICHCOTE AVE
Queen's Head (PH)
DARLSTON ROW 1
THE GREEN 2
WINSPEAR CL 3
STRAWBERRY FIELDS
BIRMINGHAM RD
Hotel
B4102
DARLASTON CT
OLD RD
B4102
Mast
SHOWELL LA
82
23
24
25

91

110

94

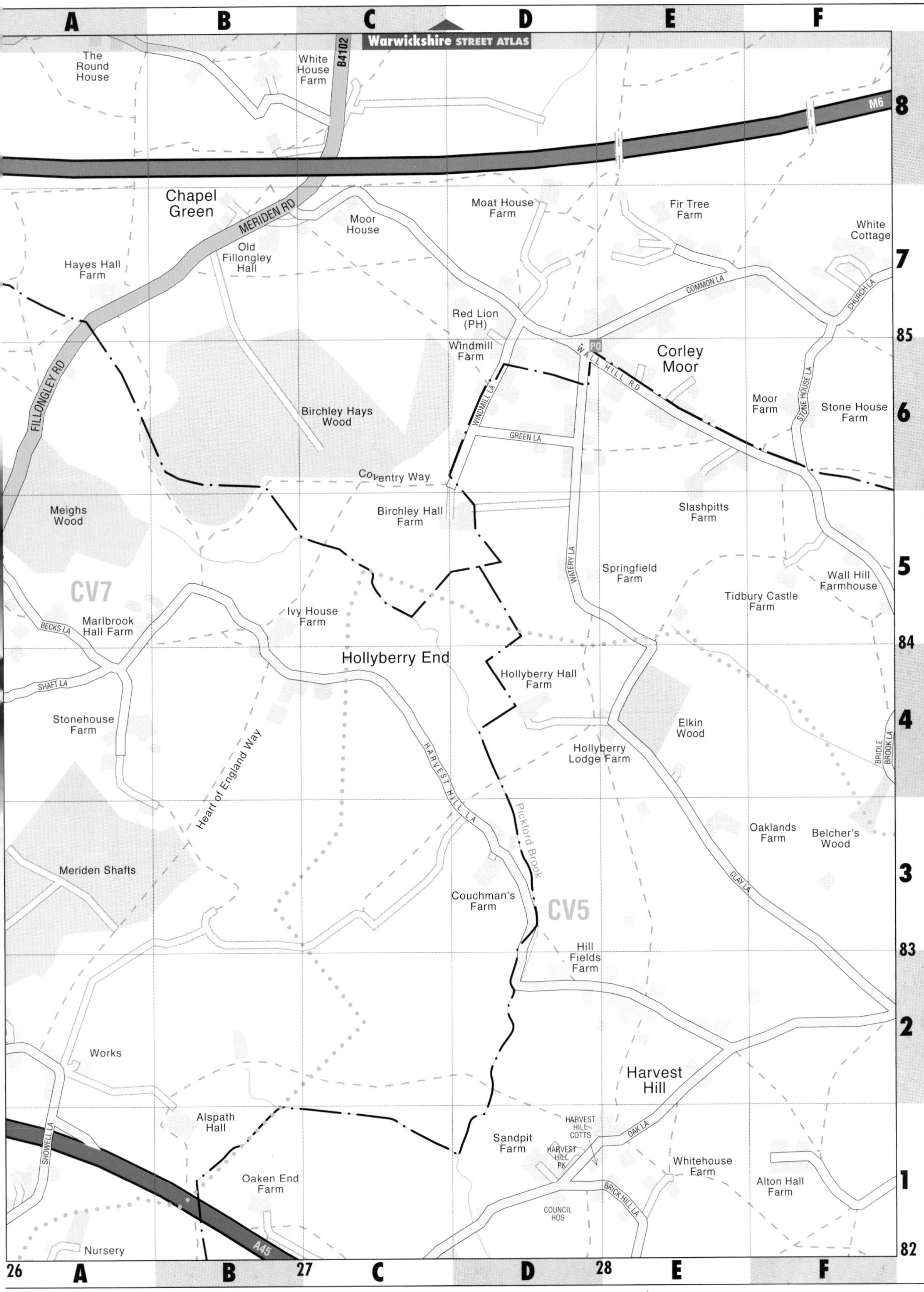
A
B
C
D
E
F
Warwickshire STREET ATLAS
The Round House
White House Farm
B4102
M6
8
Chapel Green
MERIDEN RD
Moor House
Moat House Farm
Fir Tree Farm
White Cottage
Old Fillongley Hall
Hayes Hall Farm
7
COMMON LA
CHURCH LA
Red Lion (PH)
85
Windmill Farm
PO
WALL HILL RD
Corley Moor
FILLONGLEY RD
WINDMILL LA
Birchley Hays Wood
Moor Farm
STONE HOUSE LA
Stone House Farm
6
GREEN LA
Coventry Way
Meighs Wood
Birchley Hall Farm
Slashpitts Farm
5
Springfield Farm
WATERY LA
Wall Hill Farmhouse
CV7
Tidbury Castle Farm
Ivy House Farm
Marlbrook Hall Farm
BECKS LA
84
Hollyberry End
Hollyberry Hall Farm
SHAFT LA
Stonehouse Farm
Elkin Wood
4
Hollyberry Lodge Farm
BRIDLE BROOK LA
Heart of England Way
HARVEST HILL LA
Pickford Brook
Oaklands Farm
Belcher's Wood
Meriden Shafts
3
CLAY LA
Couchman's Farm
CV5
Hill Fields Farm
83
2
Works
Harvest Hill
Alspath Hall
HARVEST HILL COTTS
Sandpit Farm
HARVEST HILL PK
OAK LA
Whitehouse Farm
SHOWELL LA
Oaken End Farm
BRICK HILL LA
Alton Hall Farm
1
COUNCIL HOS
A45
Nursery
82
26
27
28

111
94

93

A
B
C
D
E
F
M6 Birmingham
Warwickshire STREET ATLAS
M6 Coventry (A444)
Corley Ash
B4098
M6
Corley Service Area
HIGHFIELD LA
Corley Hall
CV12
TAMWORTH RD
Highfield Farm
OLD HOUSE LA
KINGSWOOD AVE
BENNETT'S ROAD N
Holly Farm
Cheshire Farm
Corley
ROCK LA
GROVE LA
Keresley Newland Prim Sch
Burrow Hill Farm
CHURCH LA
THE GLEBE
Burrow Hill
BURROW HILL LA
PH
Mast
HOWAT RD
RATHBONE CL
HILL RD
OLD WINNINGS
Corley (Coventry) Sch
THE CRESCENT
CROSS RD
SOMERS RD
Thompson's Farm
BEAUMONT
EXHALL RD
THOMPSON'S RD
Liby
CV7
Lord's Wood
Horse & Jockey (PH)
Hall Yard Wood
THOMPSON'S LA
Marslands Farm
CENTRAL BVD
Bunsons Wood
Daddley's Wood
Keresley House
Hounds Hill
Keresley
FIVEFIELD RD
BENNETT'S RD
Wall Hill Hall
Wall Hill
HOLLYFAST LA
DURHAM CL
PH
WATERY LA
QUEENSWOOD CT
Hazel Grove Farmhouse
Hollyfast Farm
The Manor
Hall Brook
WALL HILL RD
PIKERS LA
Pikers Lane Farm
BRIDLE BROOK LA
Royal Court Hotel
Grove House Farm
Golf Driving Range
AKON HO
SANDPITS LA
Hawkes End
Brownshill Green
Hillside Farm
OAK LA
TED PITTS LA
The White Lion (PH)
LONG LA
CV6
HAWKES MILL LA
The Spinney
Cardinal Newman RC Sch & Com Coll
The Old Hall (PH)
BURTON CL
CV5
WICKHAM CL
Sherbourne House Farm
Coundon Hall Park (Recn Gd)
WASHBROOK LA
KIRTON CL
CHURCH PARK CL
Keresley Grange Prim Sch
HIGH ST
River Sherbourne
BROWN'S LA
FRESHFIELD CL
COUNDON WEDGE DR
BROWNSHILL GREEN RD
WASTE LA
NEW RD
Brownshill Green Farm
CARVELL CL
NORTH BROOK RD
CHURCH CT
KERESLEY GREEN RD
B4098
The Stone House
SAUNTON CL
B4076
The Jefferys
The Grange Education Unit
BENSON RD
LOWE RD
8
7
85
6
5
84
4
3
83
2
1
82
29
30
31

93

112

77
96

A
B
C
D
E
F
8
7
85
6
5
84
4
3
83
2
1
32
33
34
Moat Farm
Bede Village
HOSPITAL LA
SWALLOW CT 1
JACKWOOD GN 2
LARKSPUR CT 3
KINGSTON HO
MOAT FARM DR
ACORN CL
NEWEY AVE
MAVOR DR
ROBINSON RD
MAYNARD AVE
JEFFREY CL
HUMPHREY-DAVY RD
NEWCOMEN RD
NEWCOMEN CL
MELROSE AVE
DARK LA
McMAHON RD
GOODYERS END LA
HENSON RD 1
CASHMORE RD 2
TOPPS DR 3
THE TEA GDN
Goodyers End Prim Sch
BOWLING GREEN LA
GARDEN GR
CONSTANCE CL
FLORENCE CL
HAYES GREEN RD
MARSHALL RD
HAYES LA
A444
St Giles Jun Sch
ROBERT RD
DAVID RD
HIGH ASH CL
DAVIS RD
STARTIN CL
BRUCE RD
HORTON CL
EXHALL GN
SCHOOL LA
Goodyers End
Field Gate
ALANDALE CT
BEDWORTH
CV12
Newland Farm
Newland Hall Farm
Breach Brook
The Royal Oak (PH)
ROYAL OAK LA
Hall Farm
TUDOR CT
Barker's Farm
NEWLAND LA
HIGH VIEW DR
ELWY CIRC
AYTON CL
CORLEY VIEW
ASH GR
VICARAGE LA
CHURCH LA
BELL DR
3
ASH GREEN MOBILE HOME PK
WINSTER CL
DE-COMPTON CL
HOPE CL
CHARITY RD
SHAFTESBURY AVE
JACKSON CL
ADDENBROOKE RD
LE HANCHE CL
ALWYNNE FREEMAN CT
SOMERS RD
COLYERE CL
BEAUMONT RD
SCHOLFIELD RD
PARKFIELD RD
SYNKERE CL
1 WOODS PIECE
2 STONE MDW
3 GARLANDS CROFT
NEW RD
Ash Green
FLUDE RD
ASH GREEN LA
Ash Green Sch
CANON DR
DEANS WAY
SHORTLANDS
ST GILES RD
River Sowe
M6
McDONNELL DR
B4113
EXHALL RD
MERCERS
MDW
Keresley Newlands
CV7
Hotel
WILSON'S LA
WEST AVE
PILGRIMS WLK
Neal's Green
Barratt's Farm
GREENODD DR
GLENMOUNT AVE
GLENMORE DR
CENTRAL BVD
Exhall Grange Sch & Science Coll
BLACKBERRY LA
WOODFORD CL
Rushton Hall Sch
Woodshires Green
Grange Farm
Wheelwright Lane Prim Sch
GLENRIDDING CL
WOODSHIRES RD
Prologis Pk
CARSAL CL
BRAMWELL GDNS
CARGILL CL
ISAMBARD DR
SILVERSTONE DR
RAYMOND CL
MAPLE WLK
OBAN RD
UNION PL
Works
BLACKBERRY LA
Gallagher Bsns Pk
BACONS BROOK DR
SYDNALL RD
WINDING HOUSE LA
NOLAN CL
BASSLEY WAY
TANNERS GR
BURBAGES LA
MALLORY WAY
OAKEY CL
COPE ARNOLDS CL
GRINDLE RD
AMY CL
COVENTRY
BLENHEIM WLK
LADYFIELDS WAY
FALLOWFIELDS
WHEELWRIGHT LA
Rowleys Green Lane Ind Est
ROWLEY'S GREEN LA
Hales Park Ind Est
LADY LANE MOBILE HOME PK
LADY LA
President Kennedy Sch & Com Coll
HEDGEROW WLK
BIRKDALE CL
1 WENTWORTH DR
2 CLOVERDALE CL
3 OATLANDS CL
HOULDSWORTH CRES
LC
MANDRAKE CL
MASSER RD
ALDER MEADOW CL
CORONEL AVE
Kwikform Bldg
MARLWOOD CL
SYDNALL FIELDS
THE CROFT
ROOKERY LA
GOSPEL OAK RD
MEADOW RD
BENTLEY CT
JOHN SHELTON DR
ORPINGTON DR
JUDDS LA
Longford
WATERY LA
NUNTS PARK AVE
BRISCOE RD
Sch
Liby
REDCAP CROFT
Ricoh Arena (Coventry City FC)
VINECOTE RD
HALL BROOK RD
ELPHIN CL
BANTAM GR
ALBERT CRES
NUNTS LA
BUTLIN RD
ORTON RD
PARKVILLE CL
DYMOND RD
HEN LA
FARNDALE AVE
GLAISDALE AVE
DOYLE DR
BLACKBURN RD
BROOKFORD AVE
FARM CL
BROOME CROFT
PARKVILLE HIGHWAY
FORGE WAY
ROLAND MOUNT
LAUDERDALE AVE
BRANSDALE AVE
LANGDALE AVE
STONEBROOK WAY
ROLAND AVE
GLENN ST
Rowley's Green
EDWARD RD
PENDEREL CL
PARKLAND CL
PARK AVE
KIRKDALE AVE
MARSHDALE AVE
ELLERMAN GDNS
Coventry Canal
LONGFORD RD
B4113
PARKGATE RD
AGATE CL
CV6
WHITMORE PARK RD
ST LUKE'S RD
SELWORTHY RD
DUNSTER PL
BRANKSOME
PHOENIX WAY
Holy Family RC Prim Sch
Parkgate Prim Sch
BERKETT RD
HALLAM RD
Holbrooks
COMPTON CT
BEACON RD
Arena Park
WINDMILL RD
PENNY PARK LA
MALMESBURY RD
CHESHOLME RD
MORLAND RD
BLENHEIM AVE
CRUMMOCK CL
LEYBURN CL
STADIUM CL
FORELAND WAY
CHARLECOTE RD
ROMFORD RD
HOLBORN AVE
WOOD HILL RISE
Midland Oak Trad Est
MARLISSA DR
BEDLAM LA
ASTLEY AVE
EVELYN AVE
DOVEDALE AVE
PAYMEAD CL
LEACREST RD
HARBOROUGH RD
ROTHERHAM RD
CHERRY CL
BRANSTREE DR
COMPTON RD
ALLIED CL
ARBURY AVE
KERESLEY BROOK RD
GLENTWORTH AVE
CANNPORE RD
DEERHURST RD
ALDERNEY DR
LADYMEAD DR
PEYTO CL
LEEDER CL
FOXGLOVE CL
FINCH CL
PEMBROOK RD
SUNNINGDALE AVE
LYTHALLS LA
BARTLETT CL
SANDOWN AVE
ACHAL CL
PARKSTONE RD
CLINTON RD
KERESLEY GUTTERIDGE AVE
LOWE AVE
HALFORD LA
HEADINGTON AVE
HALFORD LODGE
LANGLODGE RD
PAYNELL CL
LIVERPOOL RD
BRAYTOFT CL
GILES CL
LILLEY CL
HOLBROOK LA
FAIRVIEW WLK 1
ALEXANDRA TERR 2
CONGLETON CL
ELMSDALE AVE
BENTHALL RD
IVOR RD
Little Heath Ind Est
WINGFIELD WAY
DERWENT RD
GREYCOAT RD
BEAKE AVE
CHARLEWOOD RD
SHARP CL
RICHARD JOY CL
ESTERTON CL
BOOTHS FIELDS
BARTON RD
CROWN GN
GATESIDE RD
KING GEORGE'S AVE
FOLESHILL RD
COTTAGE FARM RD
CHILLATON RD
1 GREENSLEEVES CL
2 BUCKLAND RD
PENRITH CL
Monks Park
Cemy
THREE SPIRES JCT
Holbrook Prim Sch
Lythalls La Ind Est
Little Heath
TAUNTON WAY
RYLSTON AVE
1 REGIMENT CT
2 BATTALION CT
3 COTTAGE FARM LODGE
GREENS RD
Whitmore Park Prim Sch
Whitmore Park
Swallowgate Bsns Pk
JACKSON RD
NEWPORT RD
HOLBROOK WAY
COPPER BEECH CL
B4082
BENSON RD
BERWYN AVE
SWALLOW RD
Works
COLLEDGE RD
BERESFORD AVE
MEDINA RD
KITCHENER RD
LAWRENCE SAUNDERS RD
TENERIFFE RD
CARLTON RD
OLD CHURCH RD
LOCKE CL
FRASER RD
MORTON CL
SADLER RD
INSTONE RD
B4118
KINGSWOOD CL
DURBAR AVE
DELHI AVE
CHURCHILL AVE
VICTORY RD
FISHER RD
VYNTON RD
MASON RD
B4113
A444
ALBERT FEARN GDNS
SPRING RD
Schs
THE SCOTCHILL
BURNABY RD

113
96

95
78

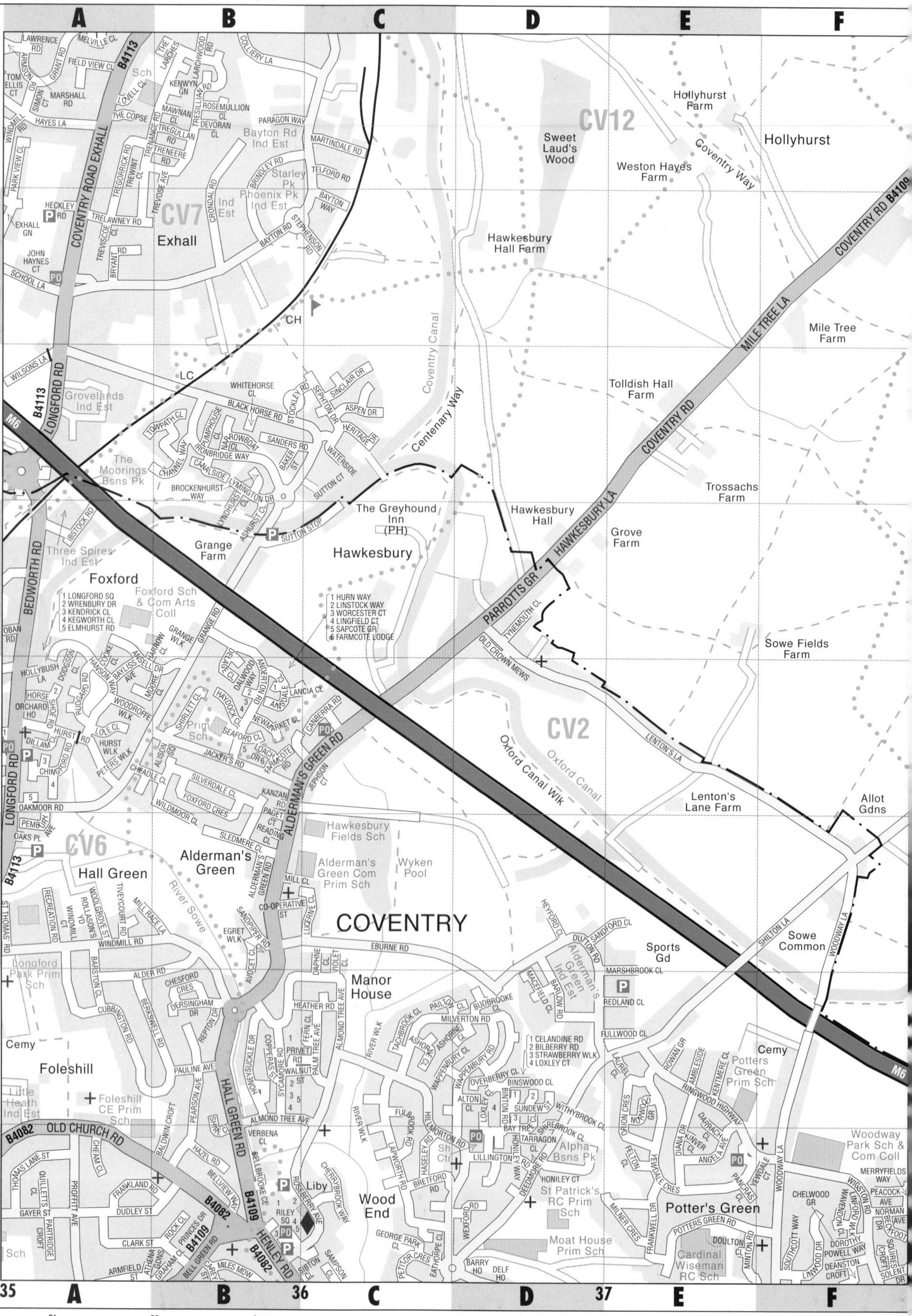
A
B
C
D
E
F
8
7
85
6
5
84
4
3
83
2
1
82
35
36
37
CV7
CV12
CV2
CV6
Exhall
Hawkesbury
Foxford
Hall Green
Alderman's Green
COVENTRY
Manor House
Foleshill
Wood End
Potter's Green
Hollyhurst
Hollyhurst Farm
Sweet Laud's Wood
Weston Hayes Farm
Coventry Way
Hawkesbury Hall Farm
Mile Tree Farm
Tolldish Hall Farm
Trossachs Farm
Hawkesbury Hall
Grove Farm
Sowe Fields Farm
Lenton's Lane Farm
Allot Gdns
Sports Gd
Sowe Common
Cemy
Coventry Canal
Centenary Way
Oxford Canal
Oxford Canal Wlk
River Sowe
The Greyhound Inn (PH)
Grange Farm
Bayton Rd Ind Est
Starley Pk
Phoenix Pk Ind Est
Ind Est
Grovelands Ind Est
The Moorings Bsns Pk
Three Spires Ind Est
Foxford Sch & Com Arts Coll
Prim Sch
Hawkesbury Fields Sch
Alderman's Green Com Prim Sch
Wyken Pool
Alderman's Green Ind Est
Longford Park Prim Sch
Little Heath Ind Est
Foleshill CE Prim Sch
Potters Green Prim Sch
Woodway Park Sch & Com Coll
Alpha Bsns Pk
St Patrick's RC Prim Sch
Moat House Prim Sch
Cardinal Wiseman RC Sch
Liby
Sh Ctr
Sch
CH
LC
M6
B4113
B4109
B4082
COVENTRY ROAD EXHALL
LONGFORD RD
BEDWORTH RD
COVENTRY RD
MILE TREE LA
HAWKESBURY LA
PARROTTS GR
ALDERMAN'S GREEN RD
HALL GREEN RD
HENLEY RD
OLD CHURCH RD
LENTON'S LA
WINDMILL RD
EBURNE RD
SHILTON LA
WOODWAY LA
1 LONGFORD SQ
2 WRENBURY DR
3 KENDRICK CL
4 KEGWORTH CL
5 ELMHURST RD
1 HURN WAY
2 LINSTOCK WAY
3 WORCESTER CT
4 LINGFIELD CT
5 SAPCOTE GR
6 FARMCOTE LODGE
1 CELANDINE RD
2 BILBERRY RD
3 STRAWBERRY WLK
4 LOXLEY CT

B1
1 ALICE ARNOLD HO
2 EMILY SMITH HO
3 JOSEPH LATHAM HO
4 DEWIS HO
5 SAMUEL HAYWARD HO

B2
1 CAMELLIA RD
2 WISTARIA CL
3 FUCHSIA CL
4 PEAR TREE CL
5 SPRUCE RD

95
114

79

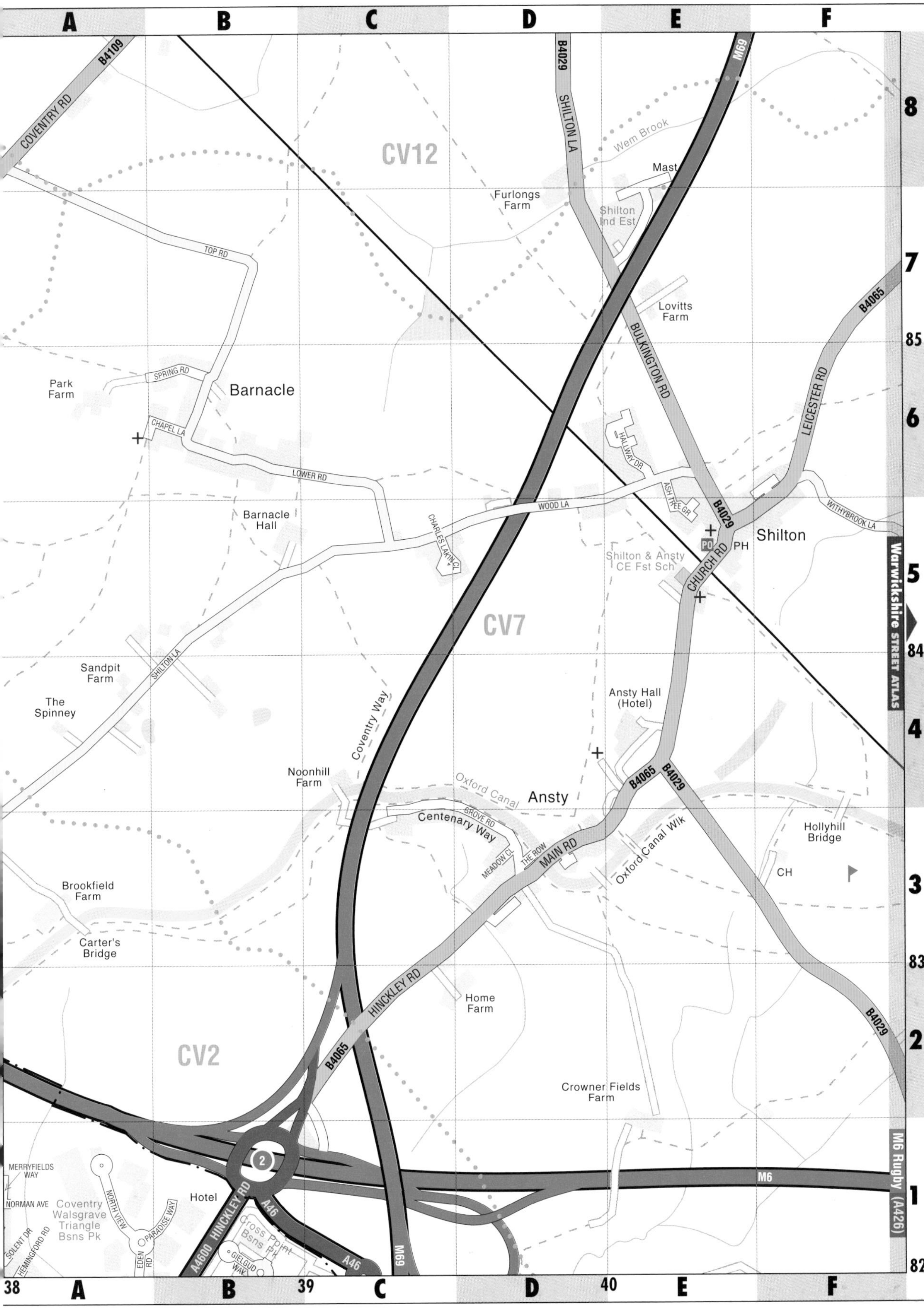
A
B
C
D
E
F
8
7
85
6
5
84
4
3
83
2
1
82
38
39
40
B4109
COVENTRY RD
B4029
SHILTON LA
M69
CV12
Wem Brook
Mast
Furlongs
Farm
Shilton
Ind Est
TOP RD
Lovitts
Farm
B4065
BULKINGTON RD
LEICESTER RD
Park
Farm
SPRING RD
Barnacle
CHAPEL LA
HALLWAY DR
LOWER RD
WOOD LA
ASH TREE GR
B4029
WITHYBROOK LA
Barnacle
Hall
CHARLES LAKIN CL
PO
CHURCH RD
PH
Shilton
Shilton & Ansty
CE Fst Sch
Warwickshire STREET ATLAS
CV7
Sandpit
Farm
SHILTON LA
The
Spinney
Coventry Way
Ansty Hall
(Hotel)
Noonhill
Farm
Oxford Canal
Ansty
B4065
B4029
GROVE RD
Centenary Way
Hollyhill
Bridge
MEADOW CL
THE ROW
MAIN RD
Oxford Canal Wlk
CH
Brookfield
Farm
Carter's
Bridge
HINCKLEY RD
Home
Farm
B4029
CV2
B4065
Crowner Fields
Farm
M6 Rugby (A426)
2
M6
MERRYFIELDS
WAY
NORMAN AVE
Coventry
Walsgrave
Triangle
Bsns Pk
NORTH VIEW
Hotel
PARADISE WAY
SOLENT DR
HEMINGFORD RD
EDEN RD
A4600 HINCKLEY RD
A46
Cross Point
Bsns Pk
GIELGUD WAY
A46
M69

115

80

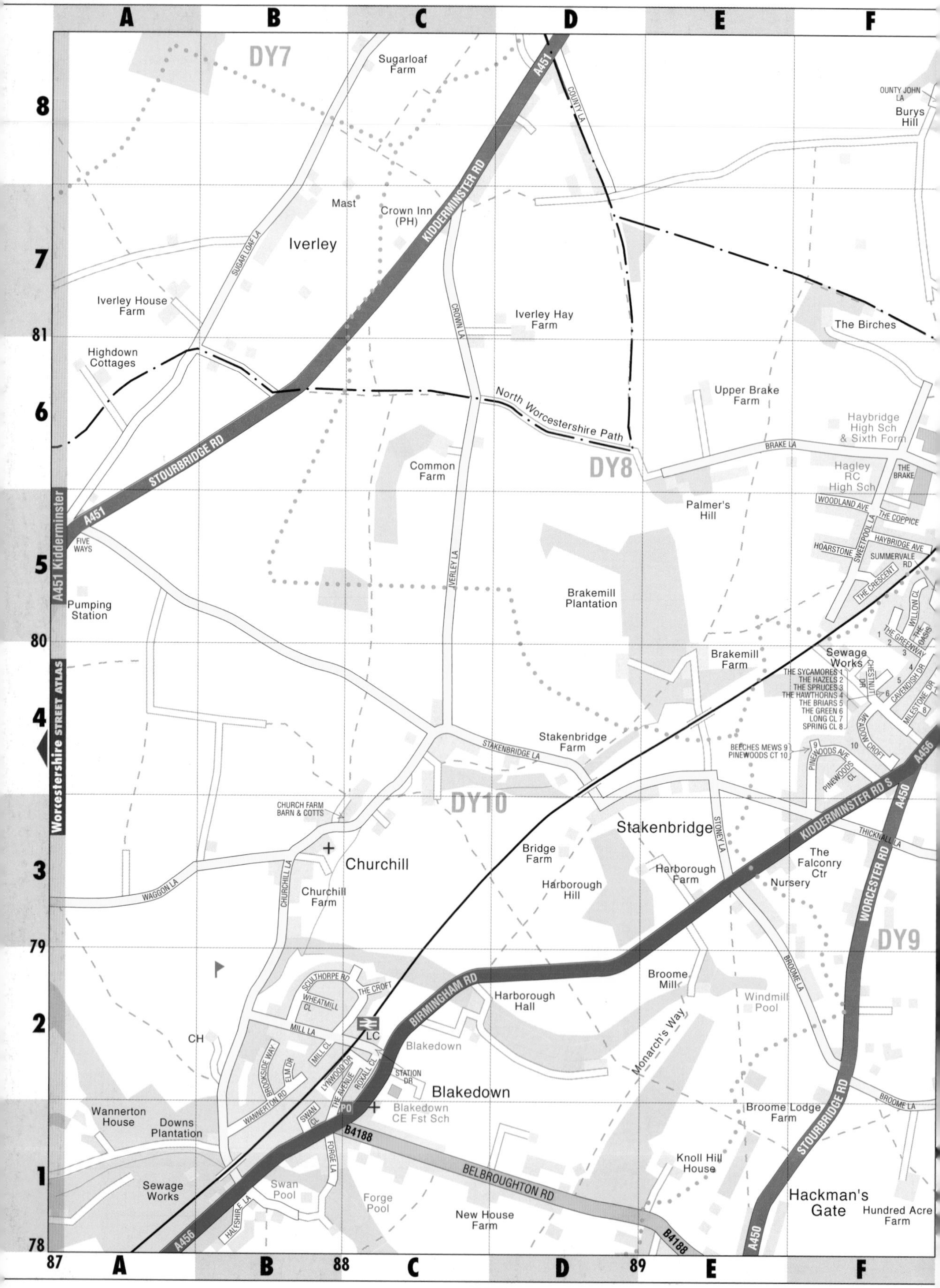
A
B
C
D
E
F
8
7
81
6
5
80
4
3
79
2
1
78
87
88
89
DY7
DY8
DY10
DY9
Sugarloaf Farm
A451
COUNTY LA
COUNTY JOHN LA
Burys Hill
KIDDERMINSTER RD
Mast
Crown Inn (PH)
Iverley
SUGAR LOAF LA
Iverley House Farm
CROWN LA
Iverley Hay Farm
The Birches
Highdown Cottages
Upper Brake Farm
North Worcestershire Path
Haybridge High Sch & Sixth Form
BRAKE LA
STOURBRIDGE RD
Common Farm
Hagley RC High Sch
THE BRAKE
WOODLAND AVE
THE COPPICE
Palmer's Hill
A451 Kidderminster
FIVE WAYS
HOARSTONE
SWEETPOOL LA
HAYBRIDGE AVE
SUMMERVALE RD
IVERLEY LA
THE CRESCENT
Pumping Station
Brakemill Plantation
WILLOW CL
THE OASIS
THE GREENWAY
Worcestershire STREET ATLAS
Brakemill Farm
Sewage Works
THE SYCAMORES 1
THE HAZELS 2
THE SPRUCES 3
THE HAWTHORNS 4
THE BRIARS 5
THE GREEN 6
LONG CL 7
SPRING CL 8
CHESTNUT DR
CAVENDISH DR
MILESTONE DR
MEADOW CROFT
Stakenbridge Farm
BEECHES MEWS 9
PINEWOODS CT 10
PINEWOODS AVE
PINEWOODS CL
STAKENBRIDGE LA
A456
CHURCH FARM BARN & COTTS
KIDDERMINSTER RD S
A450
Stakenbridge
STONEY LA
THICKNALL LA
Bridge Farm
Churchill
Harborough Farm
The Falconry Ctr
Harborough Hill
Nursery
WAGGON LA
CHURCHILL LA
Churchill Farm
WORCESTER RD
BROOME LA
Broome Mill
SCULTHORPE RD
THE CROFT
WHEATMILL CL
BIRMINGHAM RD
Harborough Hall
Windmill Pool
Monarch's Way
MILL LA
MILL CL
LC
CH
Blakedown
BROOKSIDE WAY
ELM DR
LYNWOOD DR
THE AVENUE
ROXALL CL
STATION DR
Blakedown
WANNERTON RD
SWAN CL
PO
Blakedown CE Fst Sch
Broome Lodge Farm
BROOME LA
Wannerton House
Downs Plantation
B4188
FORGE LA
STOURBRIDGE RD
Knoll Hill House
BELBROUGHTON RD
Sewage Works
Swan Pool
Forge Pool
New House Farm
Hackman's Gate
Hundred Acre Farm
HALFSHIRE LA

118

81
100

119
100

99 82

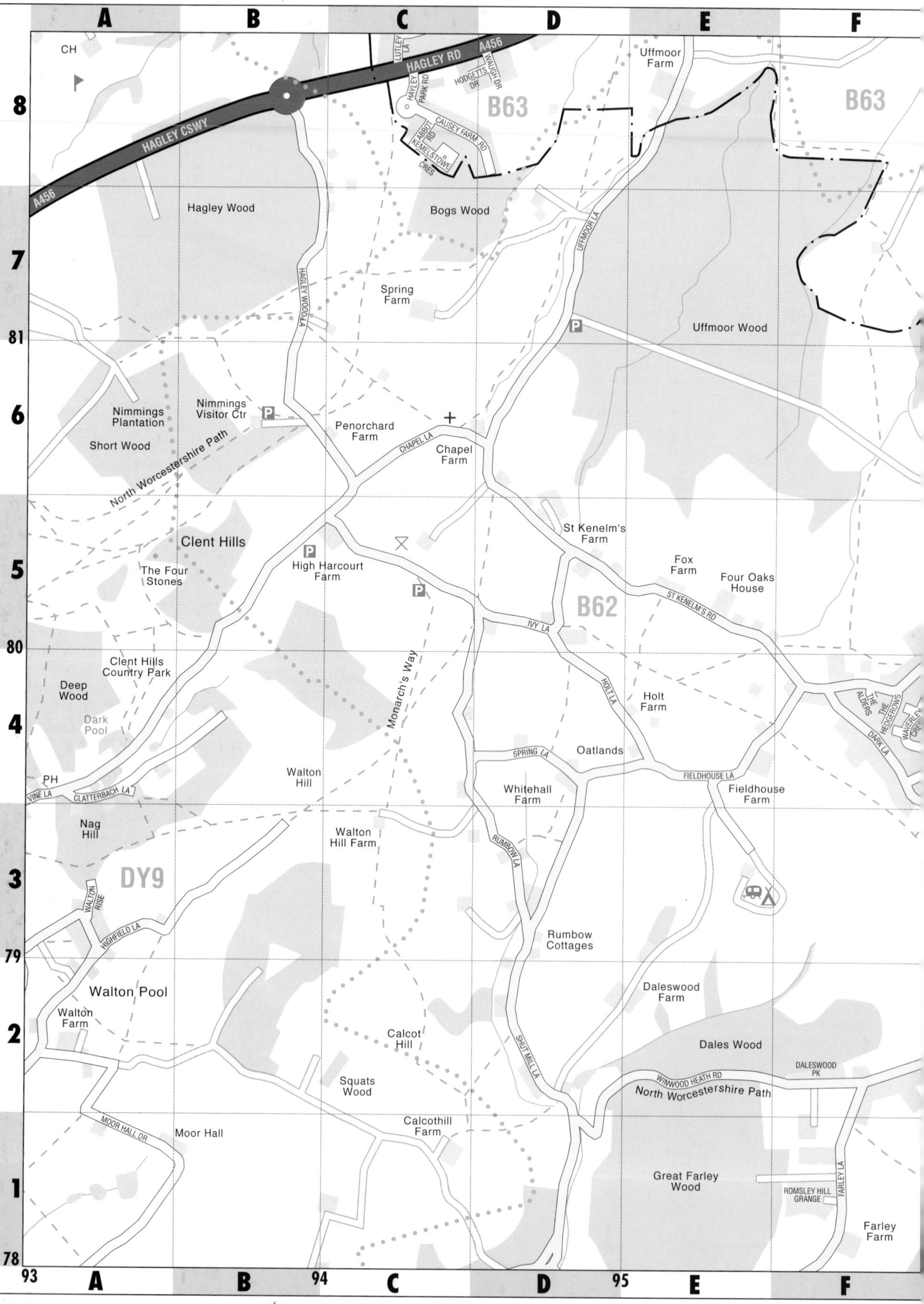
A
B
C
D
E
F
8
7
81
6
5
80
4
3
79
2
1
78
93
94
95
CH
A456
HAGLEY RD
HAGLEY CSWY
LUTLEY LA
HAYLEY PARK RD
HODGETTS DR
WAUGH DR
ABBOT RD
CAUSEY FARM RD
KEMELSTOWE CRES
B63
Uffmoor Farm
Hagley Wood
Bogs Wood
UFFMOOR LA
HAGLEY WOOD LA
Spring Farm
Uffmoor Wood
Nimmings Plantation
Nimmings Visitor Ctr
Short Wood
North Worcestershire Path
Penorchard Farm
CHAPEL LA
Chapel Farm
Clent Hills
St Kenelm's Farm
The Four Stones
High Harcourt Farm
Fox Farm
Four Oaks House
B62
ST KENELM'S RD
IVY LA
Clent Hills Country Park
Deep Wood
Dark Pool
Monarch's Way
HOLT LA
Holt Farm
THE ALDERS
THE HEDGEROWS
WAVERLEY CRES
DARK LA
Oatlands
SPRING LA
FIELDHOUSE LA
PH
VINE LA
CLATTERBACH LA
Walton Hill
Whitehall Farm
Fieldhouse Farm
Nag Hill
Walton Hill Farm
RUMBOW LA
DY9
WALTON RISE
HIGHFIELD LA
Rumbow Cottages
Walton Pool
Daleswood Farm
Walton Farm
Calcot Hill
Dales Wood
SHUT MILL LA
Squats Wood
WINWOOD HEATH RD
DALESWOOD PK
MOOR HALL DR
Moor Hall
Calcothill Farm
Great Farley Wood
ROMSLEY HILL GRANGE
FARLEY LA
Farley Farm

99 120

A
B
C
D
E
F
B63
B4551
Dovehousefields Farm
Hunnington
Goodrest Farm
Blue Bird Pk
THE CLOSE
Breach Farm
RED HILL PL
Illeybrook Farm
ILLEY LA
Innage Farm
PH
Illey
Potters Farm
Illey House Farm
Lower Illey
Warstone Farm
Frankley Service Area
M5
8
7
81
6
5
80
4
3
79
2
1
78
Twiland Wood
Kettles Wood
Raven Hays Wood
Hollies Farm
HOLLYHURST FARM CVN SITE
Hunnington Farm
Horsepool Farm
Long Kettles Wood
Brookhouse Farm
FRANKLEY GN
FRANKLEY GREEN LA
Yew Tree Farm
Porch House Farm
Monarch's Way
B32
PH
YEW TREE
ST KENELM'S RD
PO
BROMSGROVE RD
KENELM CT
EASTLEIGH DR
Romsley
B62
OXWOOD LA
Newbrook Farm
WAVERLEY CRES
HILLCREST RD
Penny Fields
WINSTON DR
Romsley, St Kenelm's CE Fst Sch
Ell Wood
Yew Tree Farm
POPLAR LA
PH
DARK LA
YEW TREE LA
Dayhouse Wood
Long Saw Croft
Round Saw Croft
Frankley Hill Farm
FRANKLEY HILL LA
POUND LA
Frankley Hill
Lower Hill Barn
Romsley Manor Farm
Newtown Farm
Sandhills Farm
Mast
FARLEY LA
NEWTOWN LA
QUEEN ELIZABETH RD
PRINCE PHILIP CL
JUBILEE RD
PRINCE ANDREW CRES
FABIAN CL
B45
NEW ST
Romsley Hill
Mast
BISHOP CL 1
PRINCE CHARLES CL 2
PRINCESS ANNE DR 3
PRINCE EDWARD DR 4
FISHER CL 5
BOURLAY CL
REGINA CL
BOLEYN RD
DORSET CL
Holly Hill Methodist & CE Inf Sch
BARLOW CL
GANNOW MANOR CRES
CORNWALL RD
NORFOLK RD
KENT RD
DEVON RD
Frankley Com High Sch
Liby
PO
P
Dayhouse Farm
PUTNEY LA
OLD HOUSE LA
Gannow Green Farm
DURANT CL
PEARMAN RD
CROMPTON RD
CANVEY CL
MULL CL
BUTE CL
Gannow Green
GANNOW GREEN LA
SHAPINSAY DR
WESTRAY CL
STRONSAY CL
ROUSAY CL
FORDWAY
HIGH TIMBERS
QUARRY HOUSE CL
Dayhouse Bank
North Worcestershire Path
DAYHOUSE BANK
FORDRAUGHT LA
ROMANY RD
SKOMER CL
LISMORE CL
Jun Sch
KINTYRE CL
ORMOND RD
CHALYBEATE CL
MITTEN AVE
GANNOW MANOR GDNS
P
Waseley Hills Visitor Ctr
Duck Pool Farm
CHAPMAN'S HILL
THURLOE CRES
WOODHAM CL
TRESCO CL
BROWNSEA CL
RAMSEY CL
OLD STONE CL
WIDE ACRES
LYALL GDNS
BRYHER WLK
NEW INNS LA
CROSS FARMS LA
RUBERY LA
Waseley Hills Country Park
B4551
96
97
98

F1
1 BROOKDALE CL
2 CHADDERSLEY CL
3 RUBERY LA S
4 HOLLY HILL
5 CALDY WLK

101
84

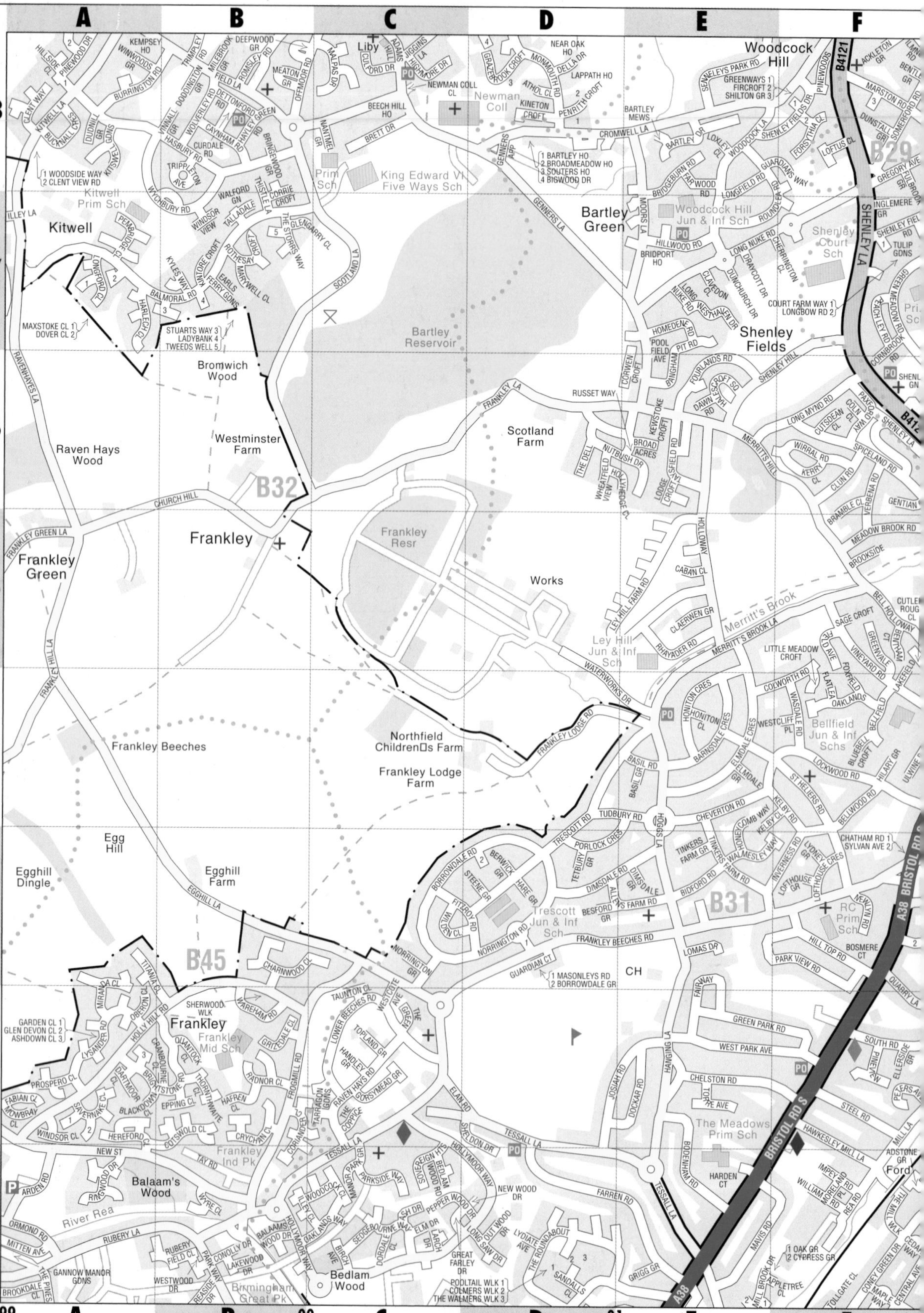

101
122

A7
1 TREDINGTON CL
2 SUMMERFIELD DR

B7
1 HAMPSHIRE CT
2 DORSET CT
3 DEVON CT
4 BATH CT
5 CHESTER CT
6 CHELSEA CT

C7
1 WARWICK CT
2 RUTLAND CT
3 DENBIGH CT
4 RICHMOND CT
5 ESSEX CT
6 NORFOLK CT
7 SUSSEX CT
8 OXFORD CT
9 LINCOLN CT
10 WILTSHIRE CT
11 ASCOT CT
12 GUILDFORD CT
13 ARUNDEL CT
14 KENDAL CT
15 BRISTOL CT
16 EPSOM CT
17 KINGSTON CT
18 SANDOWN CT
19 DOVEDALE CT
20 CROYDON CT

85
104

A1
1 CENTENARY CL
2 TENBY TOWER
3 SANDOWN TOWER
4 WELLINGTON TOWER

A4
1 CUTLERS ROUGH CL
2 SAXON WOOD CL
3 BELL HILL
4 VINEYARD RD

123

D2
1 WITLEY RD
2 GRIMLEY RD
3 HALLOW CL
4 OMBERSLEY WAY
5 AINSWORTH RD
6 ELSWORTH RD
7 ELMBRIDGE WAY

104

E1
1 BURFORD PARK RD
2 GROVEWOOD DR
3 WHITEBEAM CROFT

F1
1 WARRENS END

103
86

C3
1 BEECHWOOD CT
2 LINDSWORTH CT
3 ASHBURY COVERT
4 TAYNTON COVERT

103
124

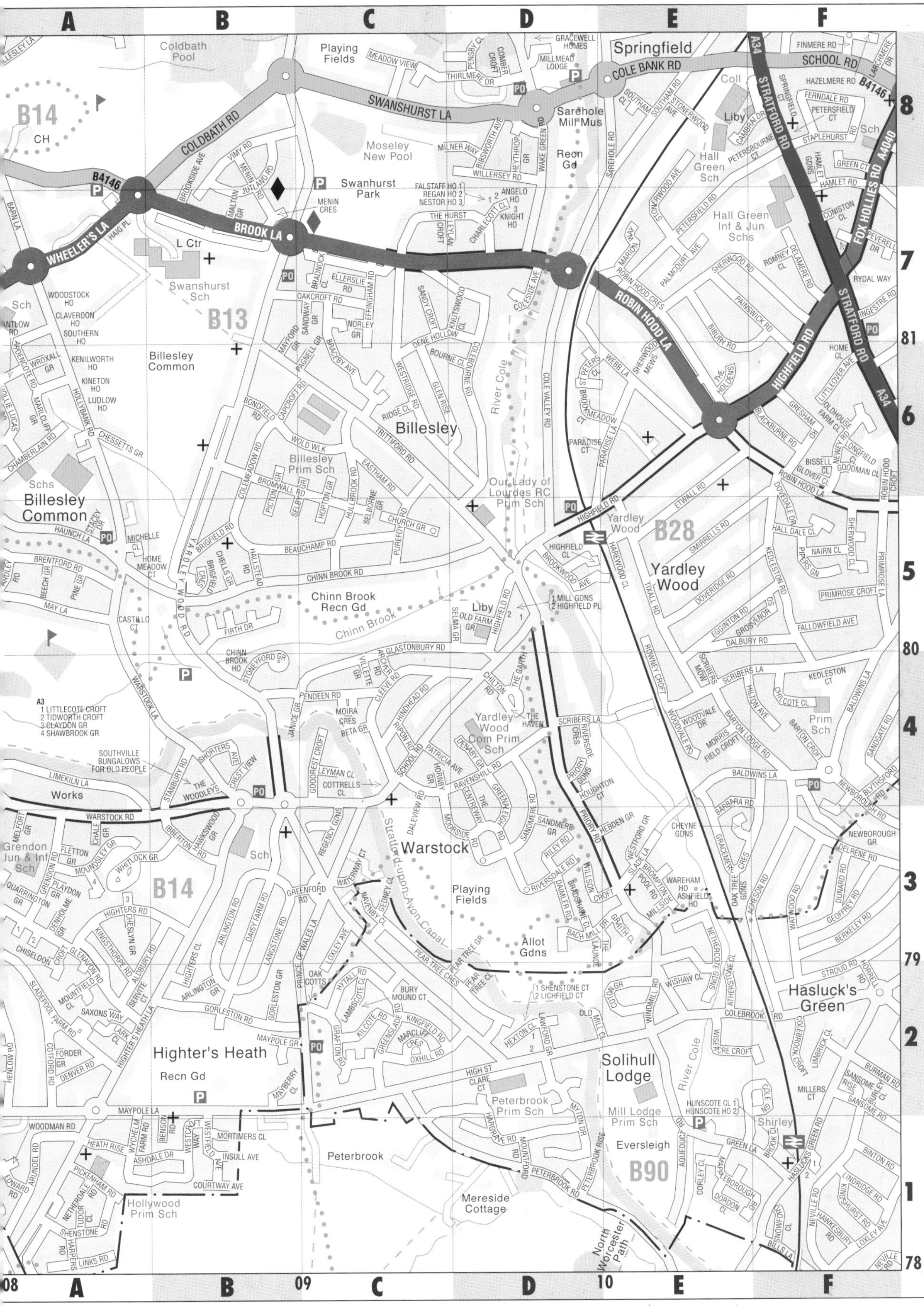
A
B
C
D
E
F
Coldbath Pool
Playing Fields
Springfield
COLE BANK RD
SCHOOL RD
SWANSHURST LA
COLDBATH RD
B14
CH
B4146
Moseley New Pool
Swanhurst Park
Sarehole Mill Mus
Recn Gd
Coll
Liby
Hall Green Sch
Hall Green Inf & Jun Schs
STRATFORD RD
A34
FOX HOLLIES RD
A4040
WHEELER'S LA
BROOK LA
L Ctr
Swanshurst Sch
B13
Billesley Common
ROBIN HOOD LA
HIGHFIELD RD
Billesley
Billesley Prim Sch
Our Lady of Lourdes RC Prim Sch
River Cole
Schs
Billesley Common
Yardley Wood
B28
Yardley Wood
CHINN BROOK RD
Chinn Brook Recn Gd
Chinn Brook
YARDLEY WOOD RD
WARSTOCK LA
Yardley Wood Com Prim Sch
Prim Sch
BALDWINS LA
Works
WARSTOCK RD
Warstock
Stratford-upon-Avon Canal
Playing Fields
Allot Gdns
Grendon Jun & Inf Sch
B14
Highter's Heath
Recn Gd
Hasluck's Green
Solihull Lodge
River Cole
Peterbrook Prim Sch
Mill Lodge Prim Sch
Eversleigh
Shirley
B90
MAYPOLE LA
Peterbrook
Hollywood Prim Sch
Mereside Cottage
North Worcester Path
8
7
81
6
5
80
4
3
79
2
1
78
08
09
10

105
88

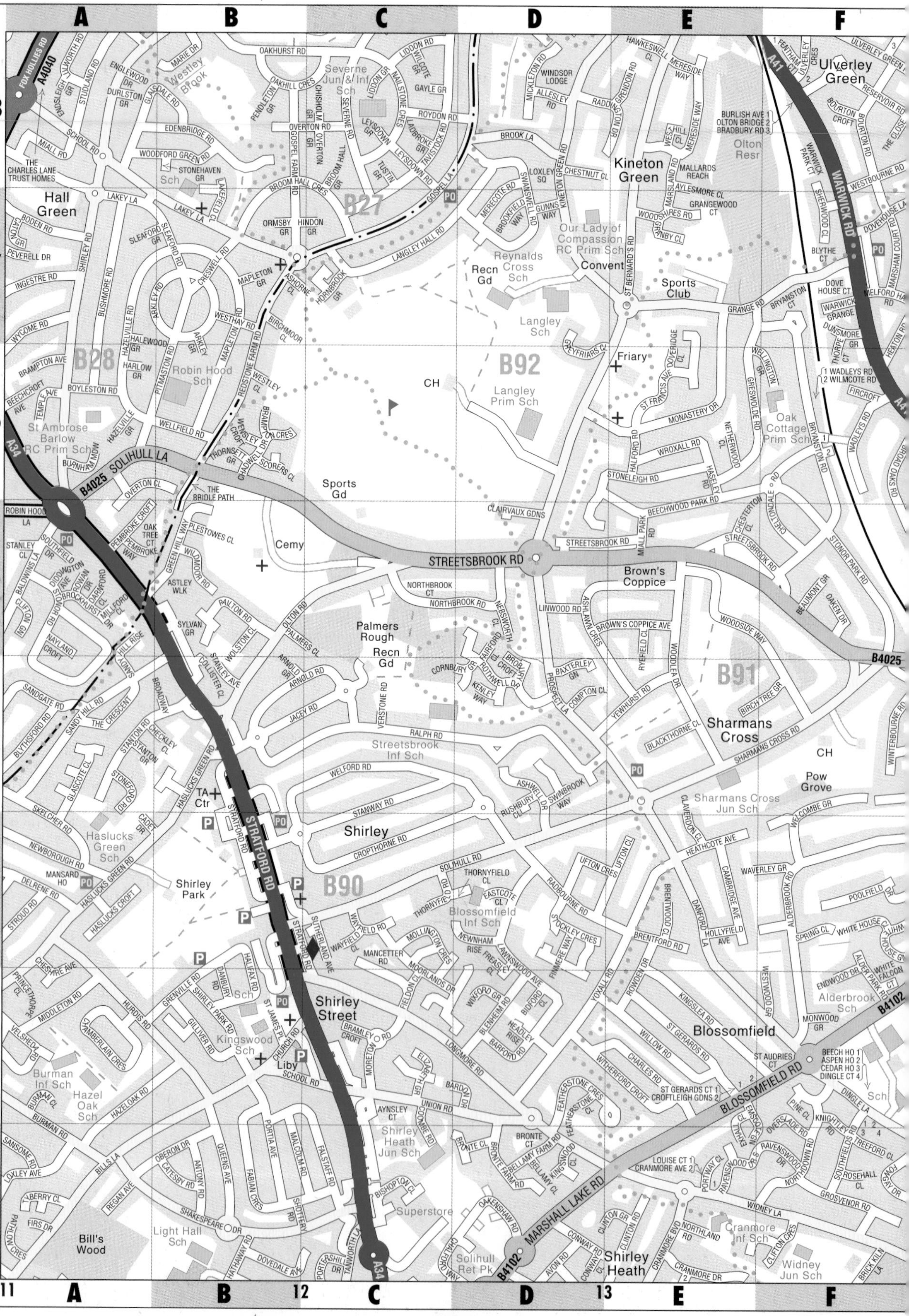
A
B
C
D
E
F
8
7
81
6
5
80
4
3
79
2
1
78
11
12
13
Hall Green
B28
Westley Brook
Severne Jun & Inf Sch
B27
Robin Hood Sch
St Ambrose Barlow RC Prim Sch
SOLIHULL LA
B4025
FOX HOLLIES RD
A4040
A34
Sports Gd
Cemy
CH
Recn Gd
Reynalds Cross Sch
Langley Sch
Langley Prim Sch
B92
Our Lady of Compassion RC Prim Sch
Convent
Kineton Green
Sports Club
Friary
Olton Resr
Ulverley Green
A41
WARWICK RD
Oak Cottage Prim Sch
STREETSBROOK RD
Brown's Coppice
Palmers Rough
Recn Gd
B91
Sharmans Cross
Streetsbrook Inf Sch
Sharmans Cross Jun Sch
Pow Grove
Shirley
STRATFORD RD
B90
TA Ctr
Haslucks Green Sch
Shirley Park
Blossomfield Inf Sch
Shirley Street
Kingswood Sch
Liby
Burman Inf Sch
Hazel Oak Sch
Shirley Heath Jun Sch
Superstore
Blossomfield
Alderbrook Sch
B4102
BLOSSOMFIELD RD
MARSHALL LAKE RD
Cranmore Inf Sch
Widney Jun Sch
Shirley Heath
Solihull Ret Pk
Light Hall Sch
Bill's Wood
THE CHARLES LANE TRUST HOMES
THE BRIDLE PATH
ROBIN HOOD LA
BURLISH AVE 1
OLTON BRIDGE 2
BRADBURY RD 3
1 WADLEYS RD
2 WILMCOTE RD
BEECH HO 1
ASPEN HO 2
CEDAR HO 3
DINGLE CT 4
ST GERARDS CT 1
CROFTLEIGH GDNS 2
LOUISE CT 1
CRANMORE AVE 2

105
126

89
108

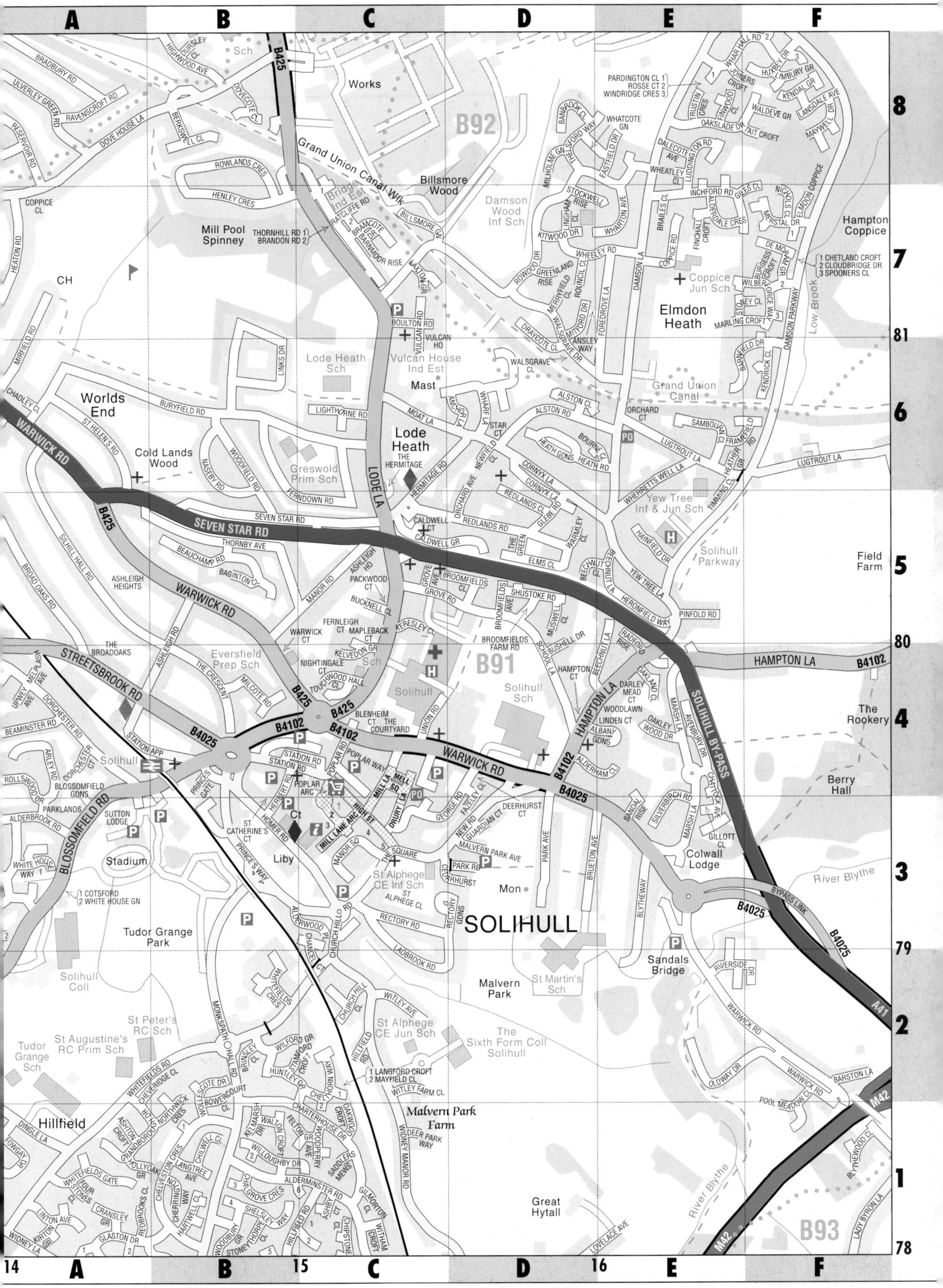
A
B
C
D
E
F
8
7
81
6
5
80
4
3
79
2
1
78
14
15
16
B92
B91
B93
Sch
Works
Grand Union Canal Wlk
Billsmore Wood
Damson Wood Inf Sch
Bridge Ind Est
Mill Pool Spinney
THORNHILL RD 1
BRANDON RD 2
CH
COPPICE CL
HEATON RD
Worlds End
Cold Lands Wood
Lode Heath Sch
Vulcan House Ind Est
Mast
Lode Heath
THE HERMITAGE
Greswold Prim Sch
LODE LA
WARWICK RD
SEVEN STAR RD
B425
ASHLEIGH HEIGHTS
THE BROADOAKS
Eversfield Prep Sch
STREETSBROOK RD
B4025
B4102
Solihull
Solihull Sch
WARWICK RD
B4025
SOLIHULL BY-PASS
HAMPTON LA
B4102
Elmdon Heath
Coppice Jun Sch
Grand Union Canal
Yew Tree Inf & Jun Sch
Solihull Parkway
Hampton Coppice
1 CHETLAND CROFT
2 CLOUDBRIDGE DR
3 SPOONERS CL
PARDINGTON CL 1
ROSSE CT 2
WINDRIDGE CRES 3
Low Brook
Field Farm
The Rookery
Berry Hall
River Blythe
Colwall Lodge
Sandals Bridge
BYPASS LINK
A41
M42
Stadium
Liby
Ct
St Alphege CE Inf Sch
Mon
SOLIHULL
Tudor Grange Park
Solihull Coll
1 COTSFORD
2 WHITE HOUSE GN
St Peter's RC Sch
St Augustine's RC Prim Sch
Tudor Grange Sch
Malvern Park
St Martin's Sch
St Alphege CE Jun Sch
The Sixth Form Coll Solihull
1 LANGFORD CROFT
2 MAYFIELD CL
Malvern Park Farm
Hillfield
Great Hytall
River Blythe
BLOSSOMFIELD RD
WARWICK RD
BARSTON LA
LOVELACE AVE
LADY BYRON LA

A1
1 BRADMORE CL
2 PINLEY WAY
B1
1 HABBERLY CROFT
2 HAZELTON CL
3 ALDERTON CL
4 BRANTHILL CROFT
5 MAYTHORN GR
6 CRANFORD GR

C1
1 HILLFIELD HALL CT
2 MALTHOUSE MDW
C3
1 Touchwood Sh Ctr
2 CRESCENT ARC
3 LIBRARY SQ
4 MANOR WLK
5 WARWICK CT

127
108

107
90

A
B
C
D
E
F
8
7
81
6
5
80
4
3
79
2
1
78
Hampton Coppice
Woodhouse Farm
Four Winds
CATHERINE DE BARNES LA
B4438
ST PETERS LA
Heath Farm
Home Farm
SHADOWBROOK LA
M42
Shadow Brook
Bunts Wood
Catherine de Barnes
Barber's Coppice
Hampton Lane Farm
SOLIHULL RD
B4102
The Limes
LUGTROUT LA
BICKENHILL LA
BARBERS LA
BRANSFORD RISE
OAKFIELDS WAY
FOXLEY DR
APPLETREE CL
PO
Asphury's Copse
B92
FIELD LA
HAMPTON LA
Boat Inn (PH)
Walford Hall Farm
B4102
Bogay Hall
Grand Union Canal Wlk
Grand Union Canal
BERRY HALL LA
Berry Hall
Brick Kiln Hole Wood
B91
CATHERINES CL
HENWOOD LA
RAVENSHAW LA
FRIDAY LA
The Woodlands
Mast
Sewage Works
EASTCOTE LA
Ford
Henwood Mill (dis)
BARSTON LA
Eastcote House
WALSAL END LA
Ravenshaw Hall
RENSHAW
Eastcote Hall
Eastcote
Wharley Hall
Eastcote Paddocks
RAVENSHAW WAY
BARSTON LA
Copt Heath Wharf
Cow Hayes
BARSTON LA
Wood Lane Farm
WOOD LA
BARSTON LA
A41
5
M42
Henwood Hall Farm
KNOWLE RD
PH
The Firs
A4141
Sports Gd
JACOBEAN LA
River Blythe
WARWICK RD
BYRON LA
LADY
Grove Farm
Copt Heath
B93
WYCHWOOD AVE
WARWICK RD A4141
HAMPTON RD
WOOD LA
17
18
19

107
128

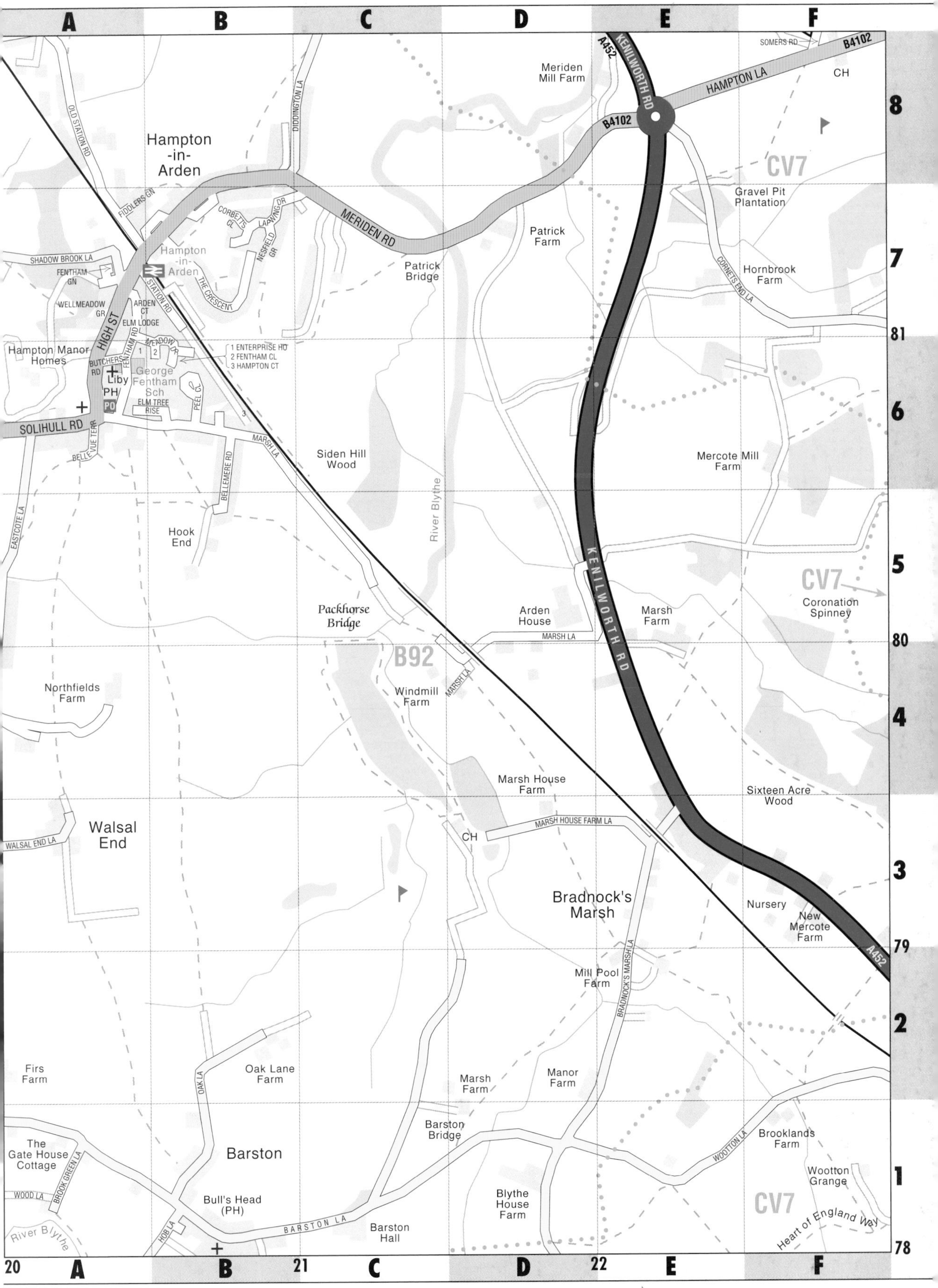
91
110
A
B
C
D
E
F
8
7
81
6
5
80
4
3
79
2
1
78
20
21
22
Hampton
-in-
Arden
Meriden
Mill Farm
KENILWORTH RD
A452
B4102
HAMPTON LA
SOMERS RD
CH
CV7
Gravel Pit
Plantation
Patrick
Farm
Hornbrook
Farm
CORNETS END LA
MERIDEN RD
DIDDINGTON LA
OLD STATION RD
FIDDLERS GN
CORBETTS CL
LAPWING DR
NESFIELD GR
THE CRESCENT
SHADOW BROOK LA
FENTHAM GN
WELLMEADOW GR
STATION RD
ARDEN CT
ELM LODGE
HIGH ST
FENTHAM RD
MEADOW DR
Patrick
Bridge
Hampton Manor
Homes
BUTCHERS RD
Liby
PH
PO
George
Fentham
Sch
ELM TREE RISE
PEEL CL
1 ENTERPRISE RD
2 FENTHAM CL
3 HAMPTON CT
SOLIHULL RD
BELLE VUE TERR
MARSH LA
BELLEMERE RD
Siden Hill
Wood
River Blythe
Mercote Mill
Farm
EASTCOTE LA
Hook
End
KENILWORTH RD
CV7
Coronation
Spinney
Packhorse
Bridge
Arden
House
Marsh
Farm
B92
Windmill
Farm
Northfields
Farm
Marsh House
Farm
Sixteen Acre
Wood
MARSH HOUSE FARM LA
CH
Walsal
End
WALSAL END LA
Bradnock's
Marsh
Nursery
New
Mercote
Farm
A452
Mill Pool
Farm
BRADNOCK'S MARSH LA
Firs
Farm
Oak Lane
Farm
OAK LA
Marsh
Farm
Manor
Farm
Barston
Bridge
Brooklands
Farm
The
Gate House
Cottage
Barston
WOOTTON LA
Wootton
Grange
WOOD LA
BROOK GREEN LA
Bull's Head
(PH)
Blythe
House
Farm
CV7
Heart of England Way
River Blythe
HOB LA
BARSTON LA
Barston
Hall
129
110

109
92

109
130

93
112

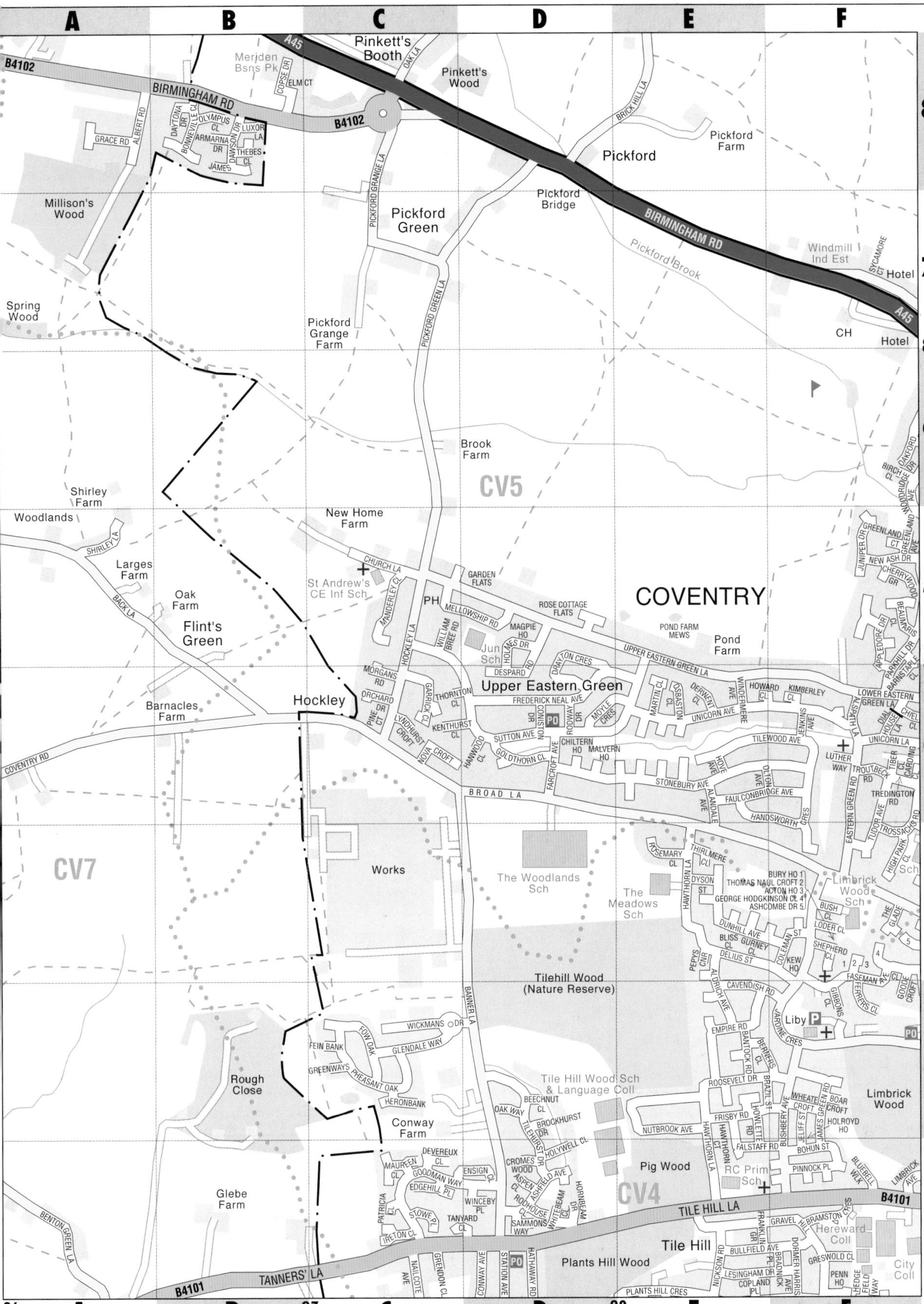

131
112

111
94

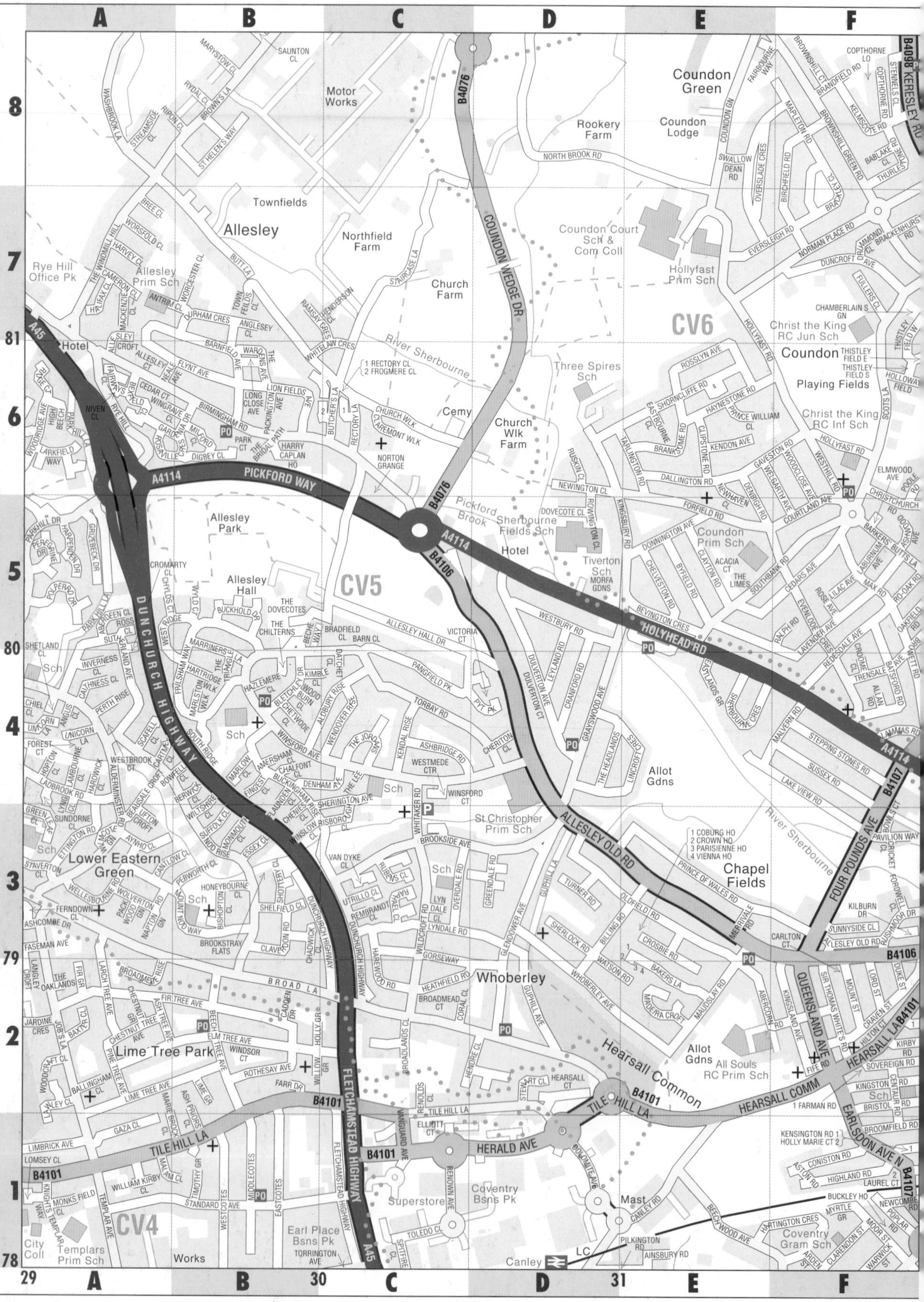

111
132

A5
1 NETHERMILL RD
2 CHILTERN CT
3 PAKE'S CROFT
4 HUMBERSTONE RD
B2
1 WELLINGTON GDNS

2 MILESTONE HO
3 TRAFALGAR HO
4 KERRY'S HO
5 GRINDLEY HO
6 GEORGE POOLE HO
7 DRINKWATER HO
8 GARDNER HO

9 GIVENS HO
10 FENNELL HO
11 WINSLOW HO
12 ST THOMAS'S HO
13 ST THOMAS'S CT

B3
1 HAWKSWORTH DR
2 COLLETT WLK
3 RIVER CT
4 COMPASS CT
5 MEADOW HO

95

114

F7
1 ADAM RD
2 WARNER ROW
3 ST NICHOLAS CT
4 PARADISE HO

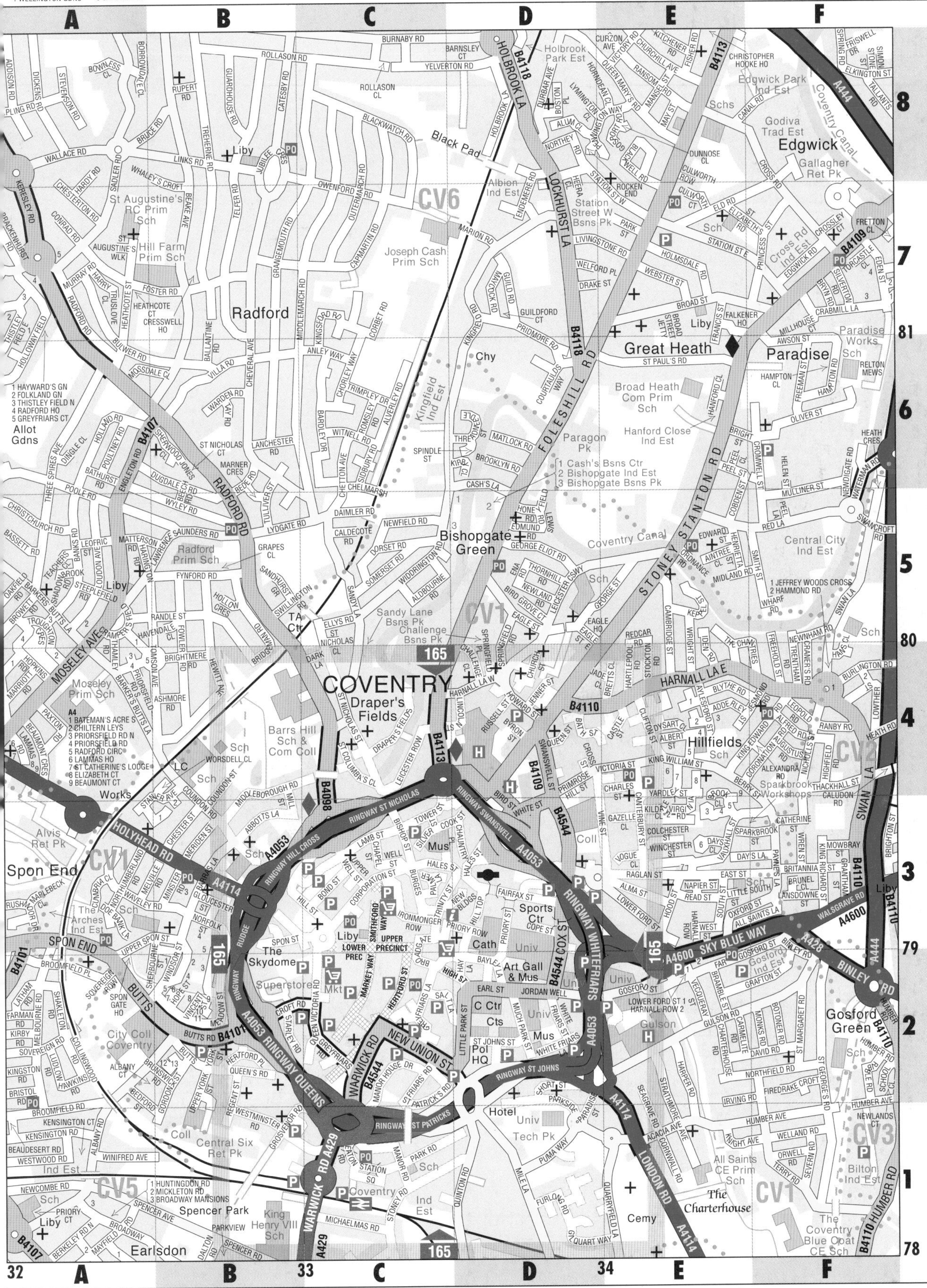

For full street detail of the highlighted area see page 165.

133

114

E3
1 HILLFIELDS HO
2 JEPHCOTT HO
3 GILBERT CL
4 VAUXHALL CL
5 VERNON CL
6 SPRING CL
7 RAGLAN CT

E4
1 CAWTHORNE CL
2 PENSILVA WAY
3 JACQUARD HO
4 LEIGH ST
5 CLARENCE ST
6 THOMAS KING HO
7 NELSON ST
8 WATERLOO ST
9 VERNON CT

113
96

D8
1 LYNE HO
2 HARRY EDWARDS HO
3 FRISWELL HO

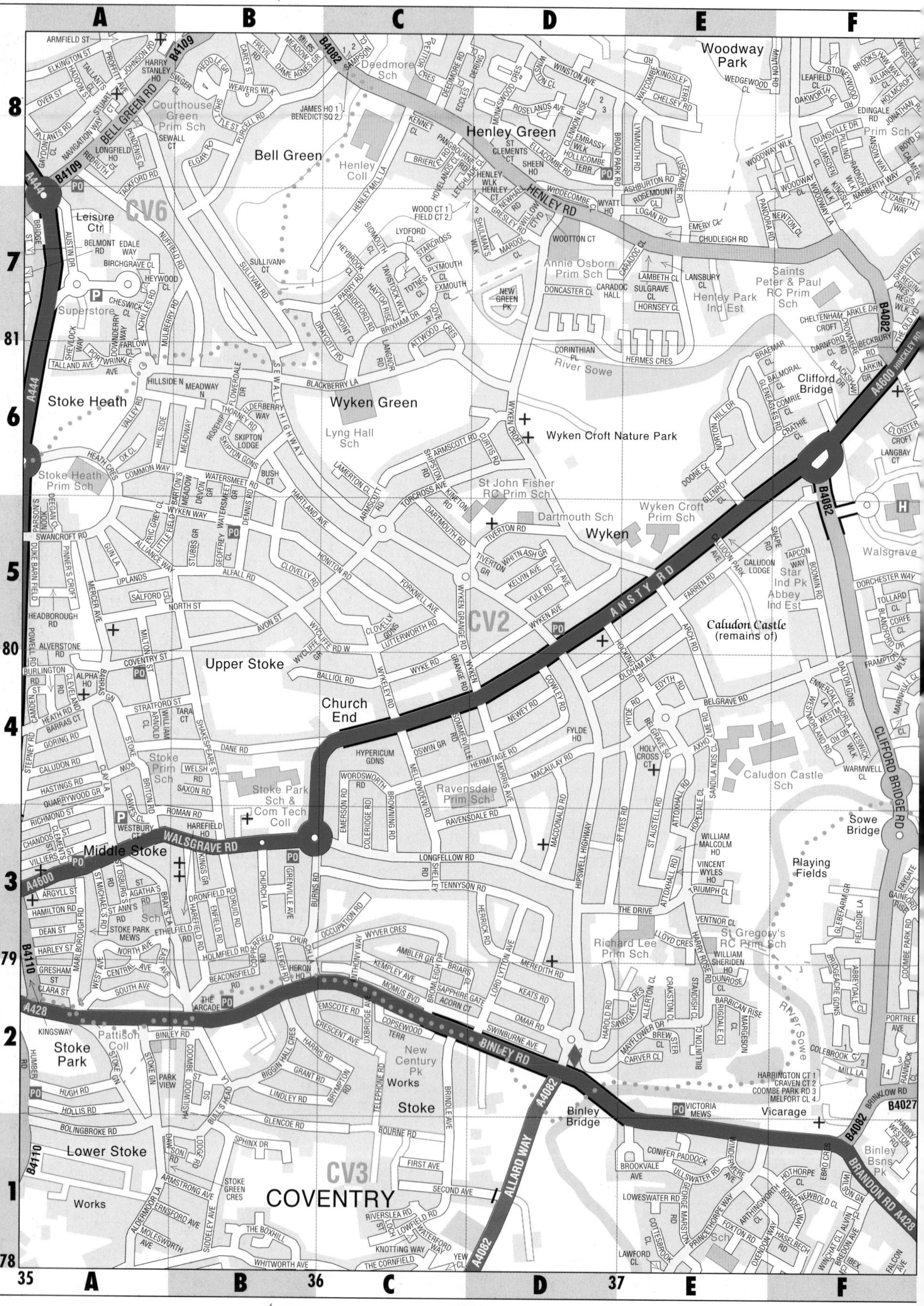

113
134

97

A
B
C
D
E
F
8
7
81
6
5
80
4
3
79
2
1
78
38
39
40
1 HEMINGFORD RD
2 DOWNTON CL
EDEN RD
A4600
Coventry Walsgrave Triangle
Cross Point Bsns Pk
OLIVIER WAY
GIELGUD WAY
A46
M69
PARKWAY
REDGRAVE CL
ASHCROFT WAY
RICHARDSON WAY
Mount Pleasant
HINCKLEY RD
3 ASHCROFT CL
4 CASPIAN WAY
5 GILLIANS WLK
6 SHARPLEY CT
Hotel
THE SQUARE
MOUNT PLEASANT COTTS
Walsgrave Ret Pk
A7
1 BRACKNELL WLK
2 STEVENAGE WLK
3 BASILDON WLK
4 REDDITCH WLK
5 WALSGRAVE GDNS
6 PETERLEE WLK
7 CUMBERNAULD WLK
8 HARLOW WLK
9 DAWLEY WLK
10 RUNCORN WLK
LISMORE CROFT
Walsgrave on Sowe
CV2
Hill Park Wood
Hotel
CV7
Works
Walsgrave CE Prim Sch
OSPREY CL
GIBBS CL
BARROW
SCHOOL HOUSE LA
FARBER RD
FITZROY CL
Walsgrave Hill Farm
PETER HALL LA
High Bridge
Hill Fields Farm
Centenary Way
Walsgrave Hill
CV2
Smite Brook
University Hospital-Walsgrave
(under construction opens summer 2006)
CRANBORNE CHASE
Little Wrautam
Pearl Hyde Com Prim Sch
Wrautam
1 SWANAGE GN
2 BRYANSTON CL
Coombe Abbey Farm
Coombe Abbey Hotel
COMBE FIELDS RD
Warwickshire STREET ATLAS
Superstore
River Sowe
Hungerley Hall Farm
Visitor Ctr
B4082
Coombe Pool
Coombe Abbey Country Park
B4027
COVENTRY RD
The Woodlands
CV3
Clifford Bridge Prim Sch
Centenary Way
SEVILLA CL
BRINKLOW RD
Oak Farm Nurseries
Birchley Wood
1 SOREDALE CROFT
2 GAULBY WLK
3 UPPERFIELD WAY
4 BULWICK CL
5 MURRAYFIELD WAY
6 DONNYBROOK DR
7 FRANKLINS GDNS
8 STRADEY CL
9 KINGSHOLM CL
10 THE STOOP
Old Pools
Old Lodge Farm
Binley Bsns Pk
The Grove
CV8
Little Rough
A428
BRANDON RD

C6
1 HABBERLEY ST
2 BENNETT ST
3 ADAMS HO
4 WOODFIELD ST
5 ST JOHN'S ST
6 ST JOHN'S CL

D6
1 MILLERS CT
2 MILLFIELD GDNS
3 RUTH CHAMBERLAIN CT
4 PATERNOSTER ROW
5 PERRETT WLK
6 ROCK COTTS
7 IDEAL BLDGS

E5
1 BRIDGE ST
2 MARLBOROUGH ST
3 WORCESTER CROSS

E6
1 BLACK HORSE LA
2 CALLOWS LA
3 FREDA EDDY CT
4 KING CHARLES SQ
5 DERICK BURCHER'S MALL
6 SIR GEORGE'S MALL
7 Swan Ctr
8 SIR WALTER'S MALL
9 Rowland Hill Ctr
10 ST GEORGES CT

F6
1 TRINITY CT
2 VICTORIA CT
3 SOUTH ST

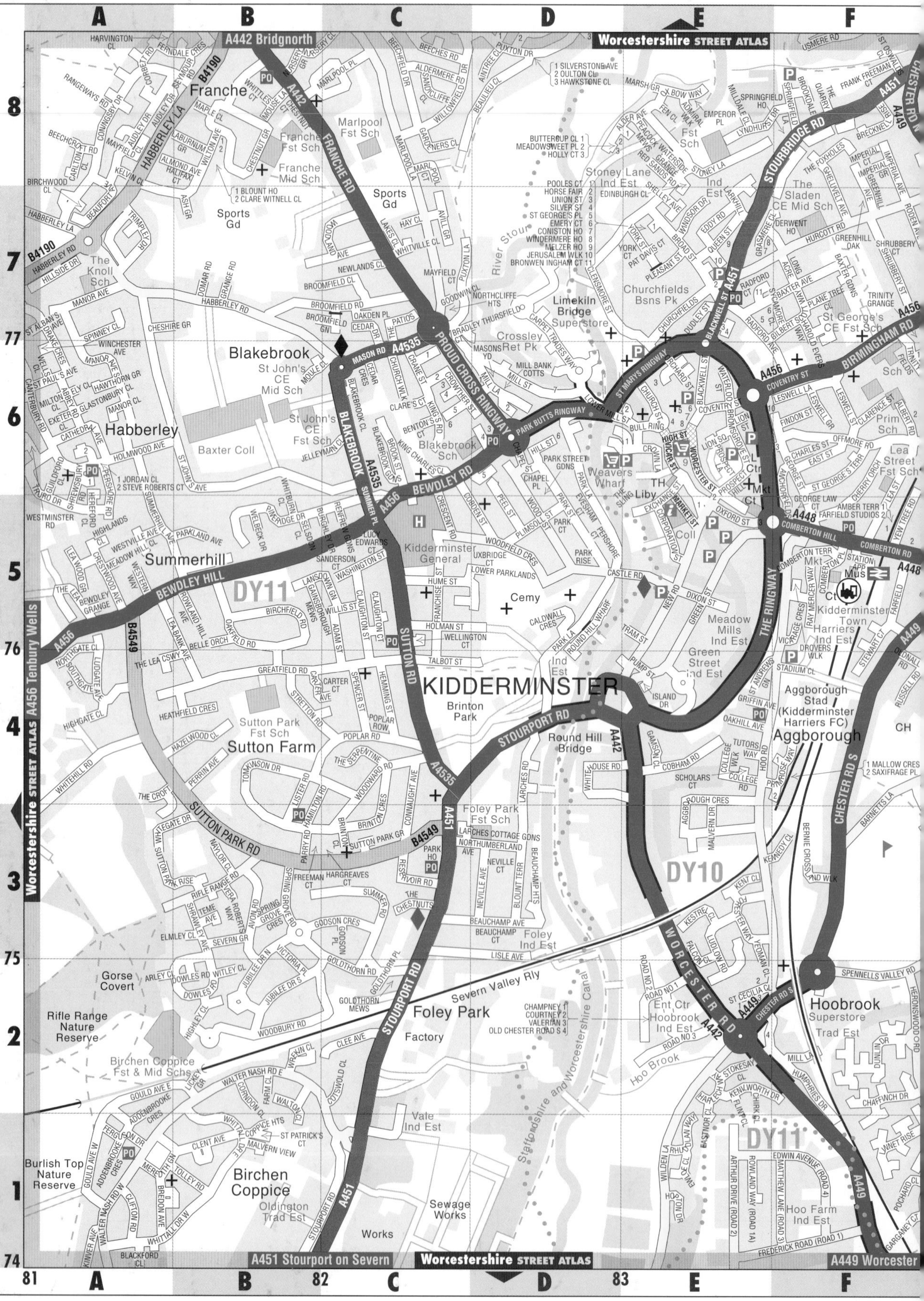

A5
1 THE HAWTHORNS
2 CHADDESLEY GDNS
3 SOMERLEYTON CT
4 COMBERTON MANS
5 COMBERTON CT

B6
1 MASEFIELD GDNS
2 GEORGE DANCE CL
3 KIPLING WLK
4 CHATTERTON WLK

118

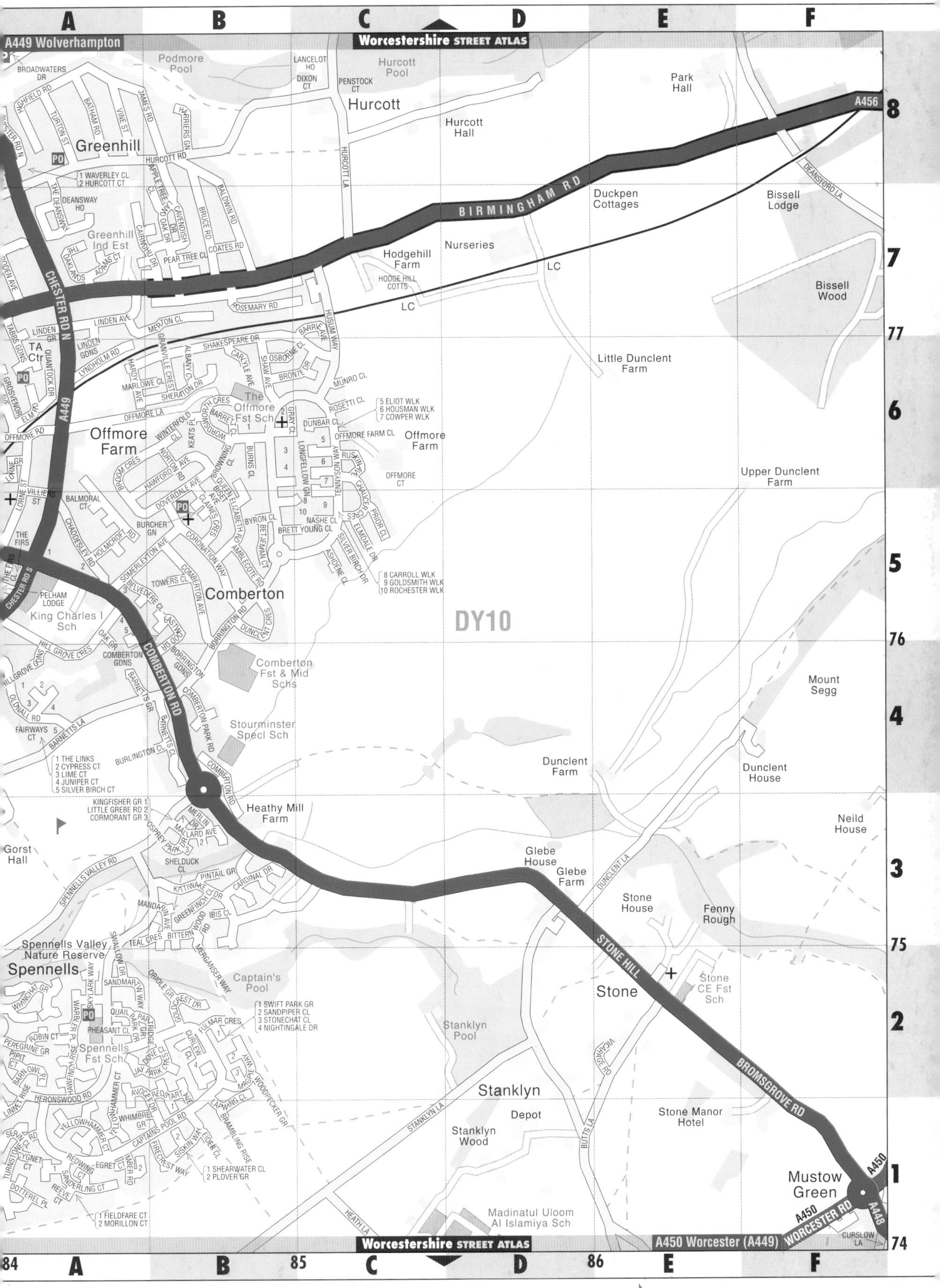

118

117
98

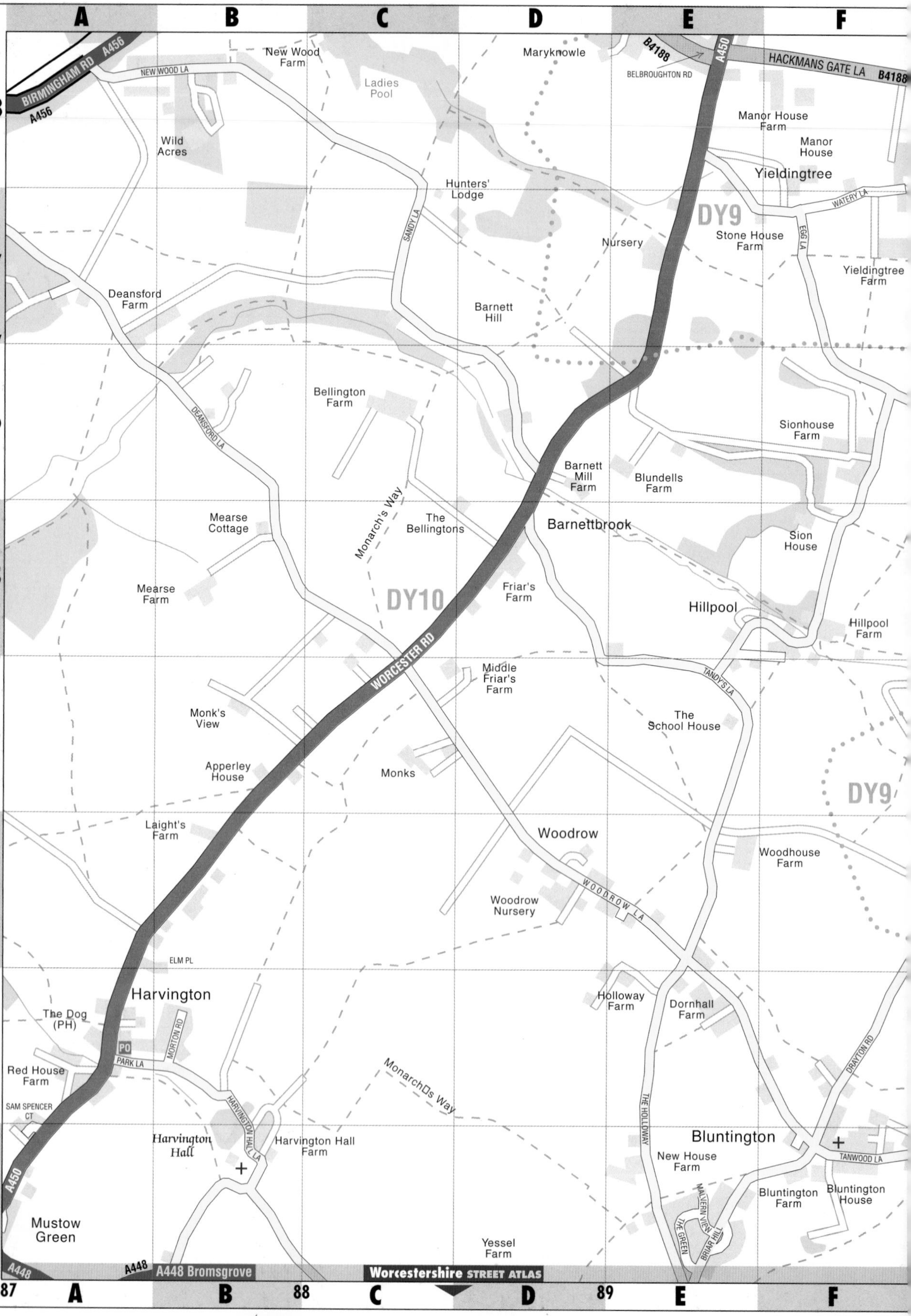
A
B
C
D
E
F
8
7
77
6
5
76
4
3
75
2
1
74
87
88
89
BIRMINGHAM RD
A456
NEW WOOD LA
New Wood Farm
Ladies Pool
Maryknowle
B4188
BELBROUGHTON RD
A450
HACKMANS GATE LA
Wild Acres
Manor House Farm
Manor House
Yieldingtree
Hunters' Lodge
WATERY LA
DY9
SANDY LA
Stone House Farm
EGG LA
Nursery
Yieldingtree Farm
Deansford Farm
Barnett Hill
Bellington Farm
Sionhouse Farm
DEANSFORD LA
Barnett Mill Farm
Blundells Farm
Monarch's Way
Mearse Cottage
The Bellingtons
Barnettbrook
Sion House
Mearse Farm
Friar's Farm
DY10
Hillpool
Hillpool Farm
WORCESTER RD
Middle Friar's Farm
TANDY'S LA
Monk's View
The School House
Apperley House
Monks
Laight's Farm
Woodrow
Woodhouse Farm
WOODROW LA
Woodrow Nursery
ELM PL
Harvington
Holloway Farm
Dornhall Farm
The Dog (PH)
MORTON RD
PO
DRAYTON RD
PARK LA
Red House Farm
MonarchOs Way
SAM SPENCER CT
HARVINGTON HALL LA
THE HOLLOWAY
Harvington Hall
Harvington Hall Farm
Bluntington
New House Farm
TANWOOD LA
MALVERN VIEW
Bluntington Farm
Bluntington House
THE GREEN
BRIAR HILL
Mustow Green
Yessel Farm
A448
A448 Bromsgrove

117

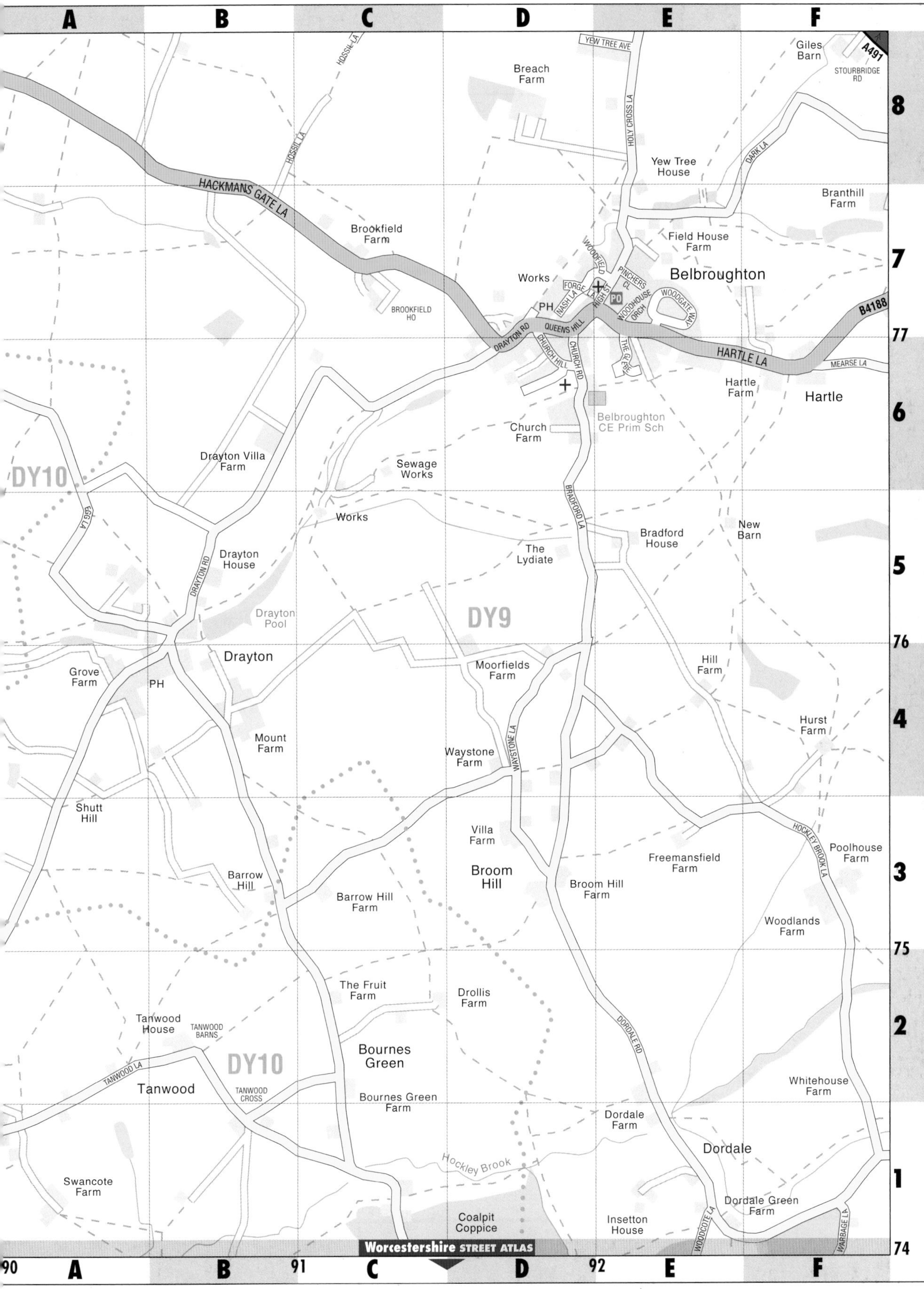
A
B
C
D
E
F
8
7
77
6
5
76
4
3
75
2
1
74
90
91
92
Giles Barn
A491
STOURBRIDGE RD
YEW TREE AVE
Breach Farm
HOSSIL LA
HOLY CROSS LA
Yew Tree House
DARK LA
Branthill Farm
HACKMANS GATE LA
Brookfield Farm
Field House Farm
Belbroughton
Works
WOODFIELD
PINCHERS CL
FORGE LA
HIGH ST
NASH LA
PO
WOODHOUSE ORCH
WOODGATE WAY
PH
BROOKFIELD HO
B4188
DRAYTON RD
QUEENS HILL
CHURCH HILL
CHURCH RD
THE GLEBE
HARTLE LA
MEARSE LA
Hartle Farm
Hartle
Church Farm
Belbroughton CE Prim Sch
Drayton Villa Farm
Sewage Works
DY10
EGG LA
BRADFORD LA
Works
New Barn
Bradford House
The Lydiate
Drayton House
DRAYTON RD
Drayton Pool
DY9
Drayton
Hill Farm
Grove Farm
PH
Moorfields Farm
Hurst Farm
Mount Farm
Waystone Farm
WAYSTONE LA
Shutt Hill
Villa Farm
HOCKLEY BROOK LA
Poolhouse Farm
Freemansfield Farm
Broom Hill
Barrow Hill
Broom Hill Farm
Barrow Hill Farm
Woodlands Farm
The Fruit Farm
Drollis Farm
Tanwood House
TANWOOD BARNS
DORDALE RD
DY10
Bournes Green
TANWOOD LA
Tanwood
TANWOOD CROSS
Whitehouse Farm
Bournes Green Farm
Dordale Farm
Dordale
Hockley Brook
Swancote Farm
Dordale Green Farm
Coalpit Coppice
Insetton House
WOODCOTE LA
WARBAGE LA

119
100

119
136

101
122

137
122

121
102

121
138

103

124

E8
1 BEECH HURST
2 CAMPION HO
3 SAFFRON HO
4 SEDGEBERROW COVERT
5 LYDBROOK COVERT
6 TARRINGTON COVERT
7 REDBROOK COVERT
F8
1 COWSLIP CL
2 MANITOBA CROFT
3 CAMPION CL
4 WILLMORE CL

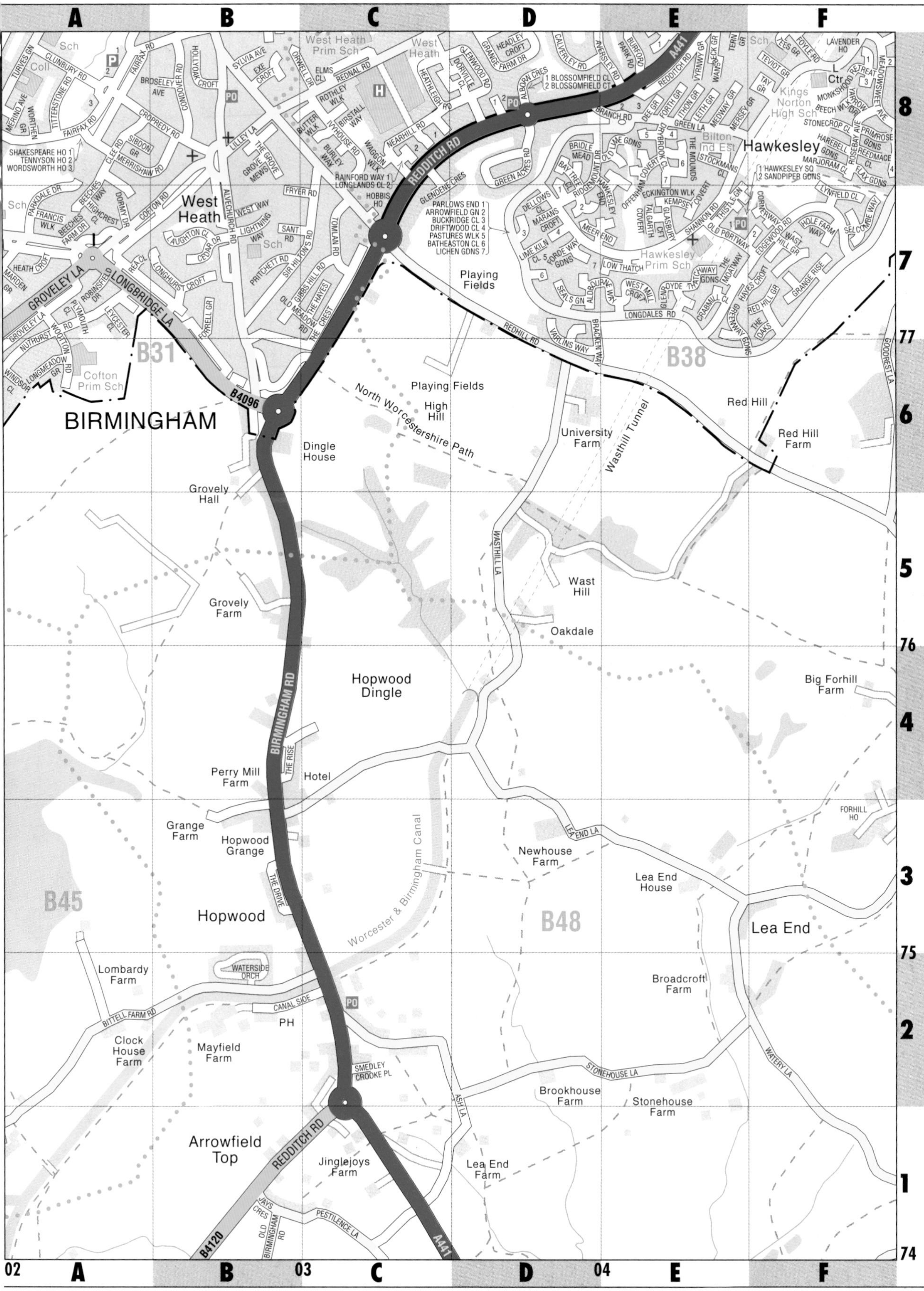

139

124

123
104

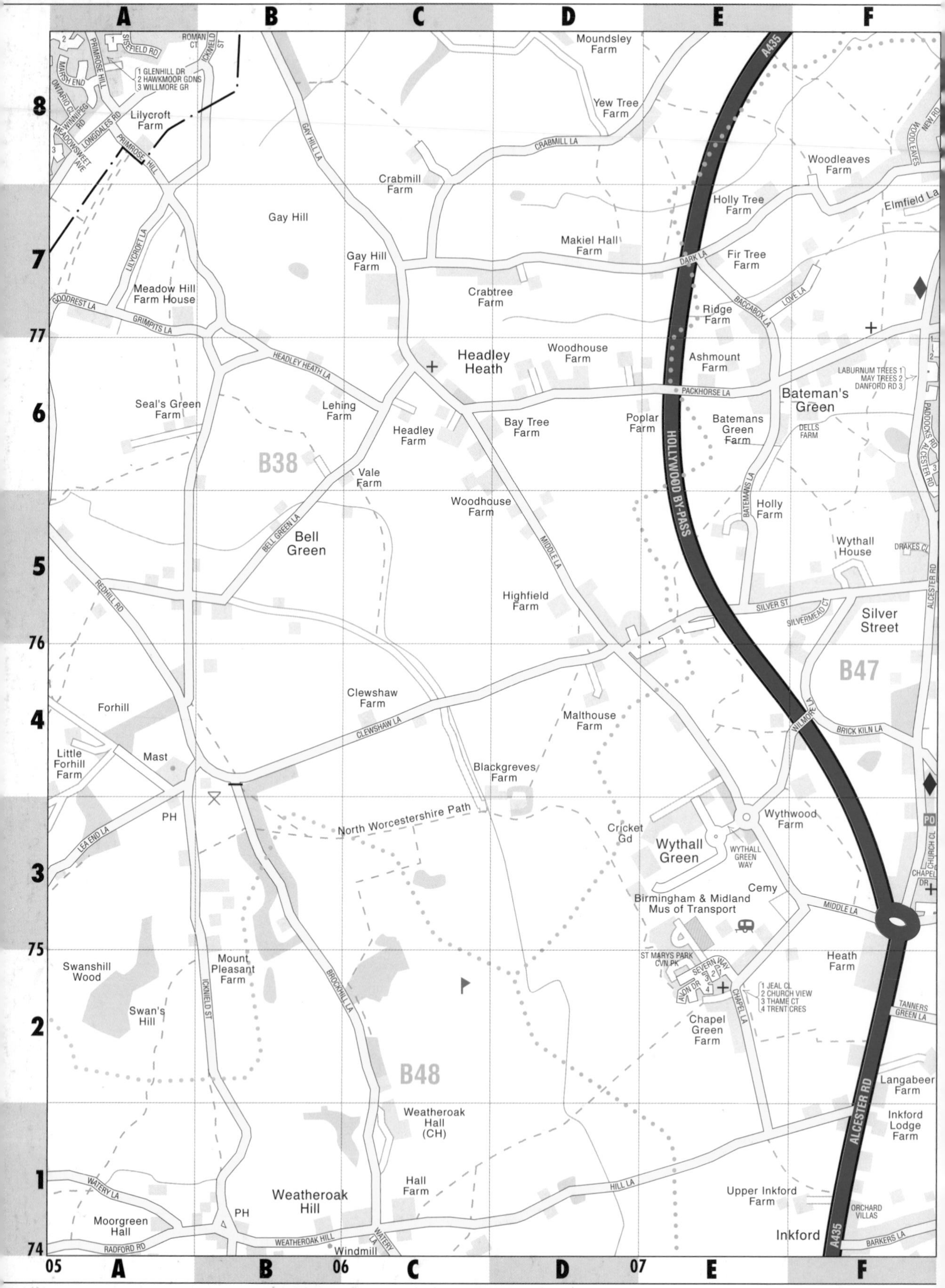
A
B
C
D
E
F
8
7
77
6
5
76
4
3
75
2
1
74
05
06
07
Moundsley Farm
Yew Tree Farm
CRABMILL LA
Crabmill Farm
Gay Hill
GAY HILL LA
Gay Hill Farm
Makiel Hall Farm
Crabtree Farm
DARK LA
Holly Tree Farm
Fir Tree Farm
Ridge Farm
BACCABOX LA
LOVE LA
Woodleaves Farm
Elmfield La
A435
PRIMROSE HILL
SISEFIELD RD
ROMAN CT
ICKNIELD ST
1 GLENHILL DR
2 HAWKMOOR GDNS
3 WILLMORE GR
MARSH END
ONTARIO CL
WINNIPEG RD
LONGDALES RD
MEADOWSWEET AVE
Lilycroft Farm
LILYCROFT LA
Meadow Hill Farm House
GOODREST LA
GRIMPITS LA
HEADLEY HEATH LA
Headley Heath
Woodhouse Farm
Ashmount Farm
PACKHORSE LA
Bateman's Green
LABURNUM TREES 1
MAY TREES 2
DANFORD RD 3
PADDOCKS
ALCESTER RD
Seal's Green Farm
Lehing Farm
Headley Farm
Bay Tree Farm
Poplar Farm
Batemans Green Farm
DELLS FARM
HOLLYWOOD BY-PASS
B38
Vale Farm
Woodhouse Farm
BATEMANS LA
Holly Farm
Bell Green
BELL GREEN LA
MIDDLE LA
Wythall House
DRAKES CL
REDHILL RD
Highfield Farm
SILVER ST
SILVERMEAD CT
Silver Street
B47
Forhill
Clewshaw Farm
CLEWSHAW LA
Malthouse Farm
WILMORE LA
BRICK KILN LA
Little Forhill Farm
Mast
Blackgreves Farm
PH
North Worcestershire Path
Cricket Gd
Wythall Green
Wythwood Farm
WYTHALL GREEN WAY
PO
CHURCH CL
CHAPEL DR
LEA END LA
Cemy
Birmingham & Midland Mus of Transport
MIDDLE LA
Swanshill Wood
Mount Pleasant Farm
ST MARYS PARK CVN PK
SEVERN WAY
AVON DR
1 JEAL CL
2 CHURCH VIEW
3 THAME CT
4 TRENT CRES
CHAPEL LA
Heath Farm
TANNERS GREEN LA
Swan's Hill
ICKNIELD ST
BROCKHILL LA
Chapel Green Farm
B48
Langabeer Farm
Weatheroak Hall (CH)
Inkford Lodge Farm
ALCESTER RD
WATERY LA
Moorgreen Hall
Weatheroak Hill
Hall Farm
HILL LA
Upper Inkford Farm
ORCHARD VILLAS
PH
Inkford
A435
BARKERS LA
RADFORD RD
WEATHEROAK HILL
WATERY LA
Windmill

105

A B C D E F

Berry Mound
Brookhouse Farm
Swing Bridge
PH
Ormen House
NEVILLE RD
BILLS LA
MALLABY CL
DRAWBRIDGE RD
B14
Hollywood
HOLLYWOOD MOTOR PK
CH
NEW RD
ALCESTER RD
ORCHARD WAY
ALFRED AVE
HOLLYWOOD GDNS
PO
DARK LA
North Worcestershire Path
Major's Green
ROWBROOK CL
PETERBROOK RD
ROLAN DR
THREE CORNER CL
LITTLEMEAD RD
NURSERY GDNS
RUSHLEIGH RD
HASLUCKS GREEN RD
FORDS RD
ROSEBRIARS
CAMBRIA CL
HOLLYWOOD DR
SIMON RD
KENWAY
LYNBROOK CL
GREEN GABLES
DOUGLAS RD
DYAS RD
FENTON RD
HOLLYWOOD LA
WINDRUSH RD
RICHMOND CL
THE FORDROUGH
Truemans Heath Farm
TRUEMANS HEATH LA
Stratford-upon-Avon Canal
B90
MILL CL
ALVESTON RD
HEATH RD
CROPTHORNE DR
FIELDWAYS CL
CHANTRY CL
THE ORCHARDS
LEE RD
CORBETT RD
SHAWHURST CROFT
COPPICE GDNS
SHAWHURST GDNS
EASTON GR
BERRYMOUND VIEW
Trueman's Heath
Blounts Hole Farm
Whitlocks End
Tyburn Farm
TYTHE BARN LA
MAY FARM CL
MAY LA
OAK TREES
ELMWOOD GR
ARDEN RD
Liby
WARMINGTON RD
BEAUDESERT CL
SHAWHURST LA
FOREST WAY
WOOD CROFT
HOLLY DR
MAYHURST RD
MAYHURST CL
WYTHWOOD RD
WYTHWOOD GR
Little Trueman's Heath Farm
Little Tyburn Coppice
77
OAKWOOD RD
BEAUDESERT RD
THE HURST
POPLAR TREES
FALSTAFF AVE
PEARMANS CROFT
The Coppice Prim Sch
HAWTHORNE DR
BEECH RD
ALDER CL
HOUNDSFIELD CL
HOUNDSFIELD LA
Cvn Site
Ford
Whitlock's End
THREE ACRES LA
6
The Woodrush Com High Sch
CHESTERWOOD
THE WILLOWS
Drakes Cross
SILVER BIRCH DR
OAK TREE LA
BRAMLEY DR
SYCAMORE DR
HAZEL DR
CHERRY WLK
ASPEN GR
Betteridges Farm
TILEHOUSE LA
BIRCHY CL
MYNORS CRES
RYE CROFT
WOODRUSH DR
BURFORD RD
YARN CL
SHAWFIELD
THE INGLE
FLAX CL
LABURNUM CL
ROWAN CL
LIME CL
Birchy Farm
BIRCHY LEASOWES LA
FISHERS DR
DRAKES CROSS PAR
SIMMS LA
HADLEY CL
HOUNDSFIELD GR
THE CLOSE
HOUNDSFIELD FARM
5
Barn Hill
LEA GREEN LA
SELSDON CL
PH
1 THE REDDINGS
2 PARK CROFT
B47
HIRDEMONSWAY
DICKENS HEATH RD
Yewtree Farm
Little Dickens' Wood
Big Dickens' Wood
76
BRAGGS FARM LA
LEA GREEN DR
Wythall
NORTON DR
Lowbrook Farm
Tidbury Green Sch
CLEOBURY LA
Grimes Hill
THREE OAKS RD
LITTLESHAW CROFT
LITTLESHAW LA
THE SPINNEY
LOWBROOK LA
Tidbury Green Farm
4
Lowbrook Bridge
Tidbury Green
Bleakhouse Farm
GORSEY LA
MANOR RD
ANN RD
Meadow Green Prim Sch
Manor Farm
River Cole
PO
NORTON LA
RUMBUSH LA
FULFORD HALL RD
Big Cleobury Farm
3
CHAPEL DR
MEADOW RD
SCHOOL DR
MEADOW CROFT
GREEN CL
STATION RD
Wythall
Rumbush
75
Nursery
Rumbush Farm
Fulford Hall
Fulford Heath
2
Little Tanners Green Farm
Mast
B94
CH
Little Fulford Farm
Kidpile Farm
Manor Farm Craft Centre
Willow Tree Farm
TANNERS GREEN LA
Tanner's Green
WOOD LA
P
STATION DR
Earlswood
BARKERS LA
MILL LA
FORSHAW HEATH RD
MASON LA
1
New Fallings Coppice
74

08 A B 09 C D 10 E F

141

126

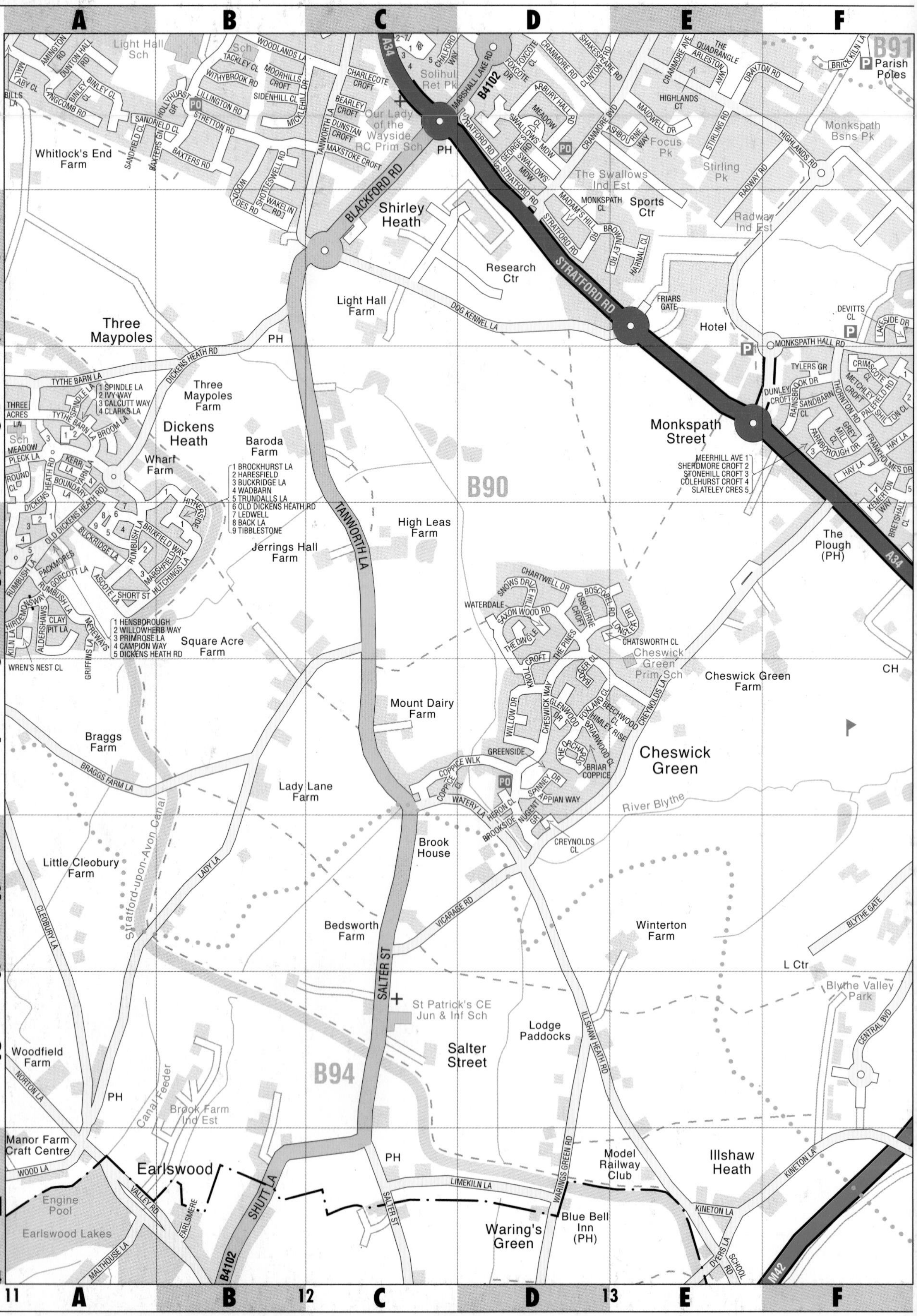
A B C D E F
8 7 6 5 4 3 2 1
77 76 75 74
11 12 13
Light Hall Sch
Whitlock's End Farm
Shirley Heath
Solihull Ret Pk
Our Lady of the Wayside RC Prim Sch
BLACKFORD RD
STRATFORD RD
B4102
A34
Research Ctr
Light Hall Farm
DOG KENNEL LA
The Swallows Ind Est
Sports Ctr
Focus Pk
Stirling Pk
Radway Ind Est
HIGHLANDS CT
Monkspath Bsns Pk
Parish Poles
B91
Hotel
FRIARS GATE
MONKSPATH HALL RD
Three Maypoles
Three Maypoles Farm
Dickens Heath
DICKENS HEATH RD
Wharf Farm
Baroda Farm
1 BROCKHURST LA
2 HARESFIELD
3 BUCKRIDGE LA
4 WADBARN
5 TRUNDALLS LA
6 OLD DICKENS HEATH RD
7 LEDWELL
8 BACK LA
9 TIBBLESTONE
1 SPINDLE LA
2 IVY WAY
3 CALCUTT WAY
4 CLARKS LA
1 HENSBOROUGH
2 WILLOWHERB WAY
3 PRIMROSE LA
4 CAMPION WAY
5 DICKENS HEATH RD
WREN'S NEST CL
B90
TANWORTH LA
High Leas Farm
Jerrings Hall Farm
Square Acre Farm
Monkspath Street
MEERHILL AVE 1
SHERDMORE CROFT 2
STONEHILL CROFT 3
COLEHURST CROFT 4
SLATELEY CRES 5
The Plough (PH)
Cheswick Green Prim Sch
Cheswick Green Farm
Cheswick Green
CHATSWORTH CL
Mount Dairy Farm
Braggs Farm
BRAGGS FARM LA
Lady Lane Farm
River Blythe
Brook House
Little Cleobury Farm
Stratford-upon-Avon Canal
Bedsworth Farm
VICARAGE RD
Winterton Farm
L Ctr
Blythe Valley Park
SALTER ST
St Patrick's CE Jun & Inf Sch
Salter Street
Lodge Paddocks
ILLSHAW HEATH RD
B94
Woodfield Farm
Canal Feeder
Brook Farm Ind Est
Manor Farm Craft Centre
Earlswood
Engine Pool
Earlswood Lakes
SHUTT LA
LIMEKILN LA
Model Railway Club
Illshaw Heath
Blue Bell Inn (PH)
Waring's Green
WARINGS GREEN RD
KINETON LA
M42
CH
PH

A6
1 HIMBLETON CROFT
2 SLIMBRIDGE CL
3 HIGHDOWN CRES
4 OLDBERROW CL
5 BELLINGTON CROFT
6 WESTGROVE AVE

B8
1 CHADBURY CROFT
2 LITTLEWOOD CL
3 HILLFIELD MEWS
4 MAYTHORN GR
5 GREYHURST CROFT
6 HUNNINGHAM GR

C8
1 CHIPSTONE CL
2 GLENFIELD CL
3 CHERRYWOOD CRES
4 LIBBARDS GATE
5 MERRINGTON CL
6 LITTLETON CROFT
7 THORNGROVE AVE

107
128

143
128

127
108

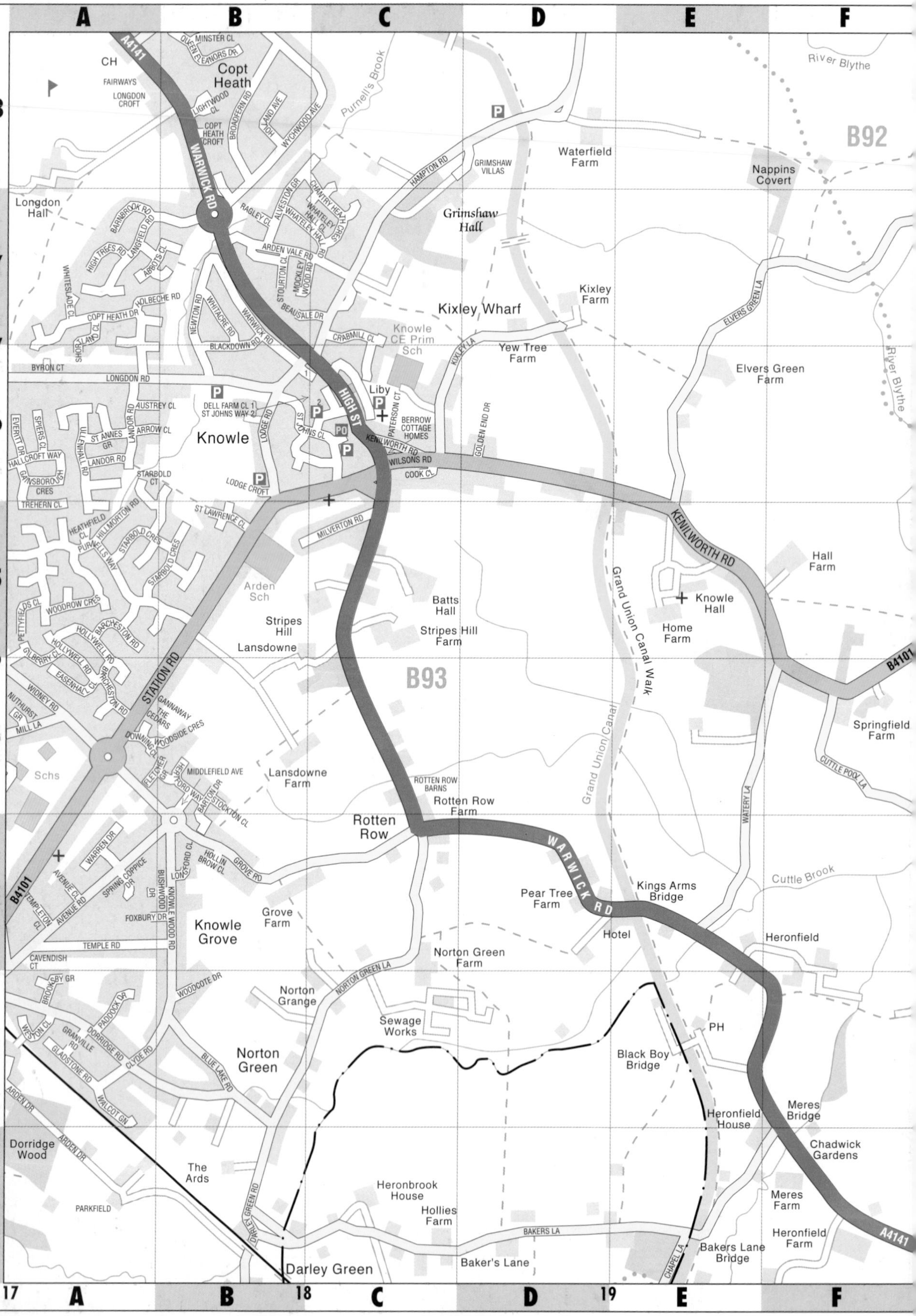

127
144

109
130

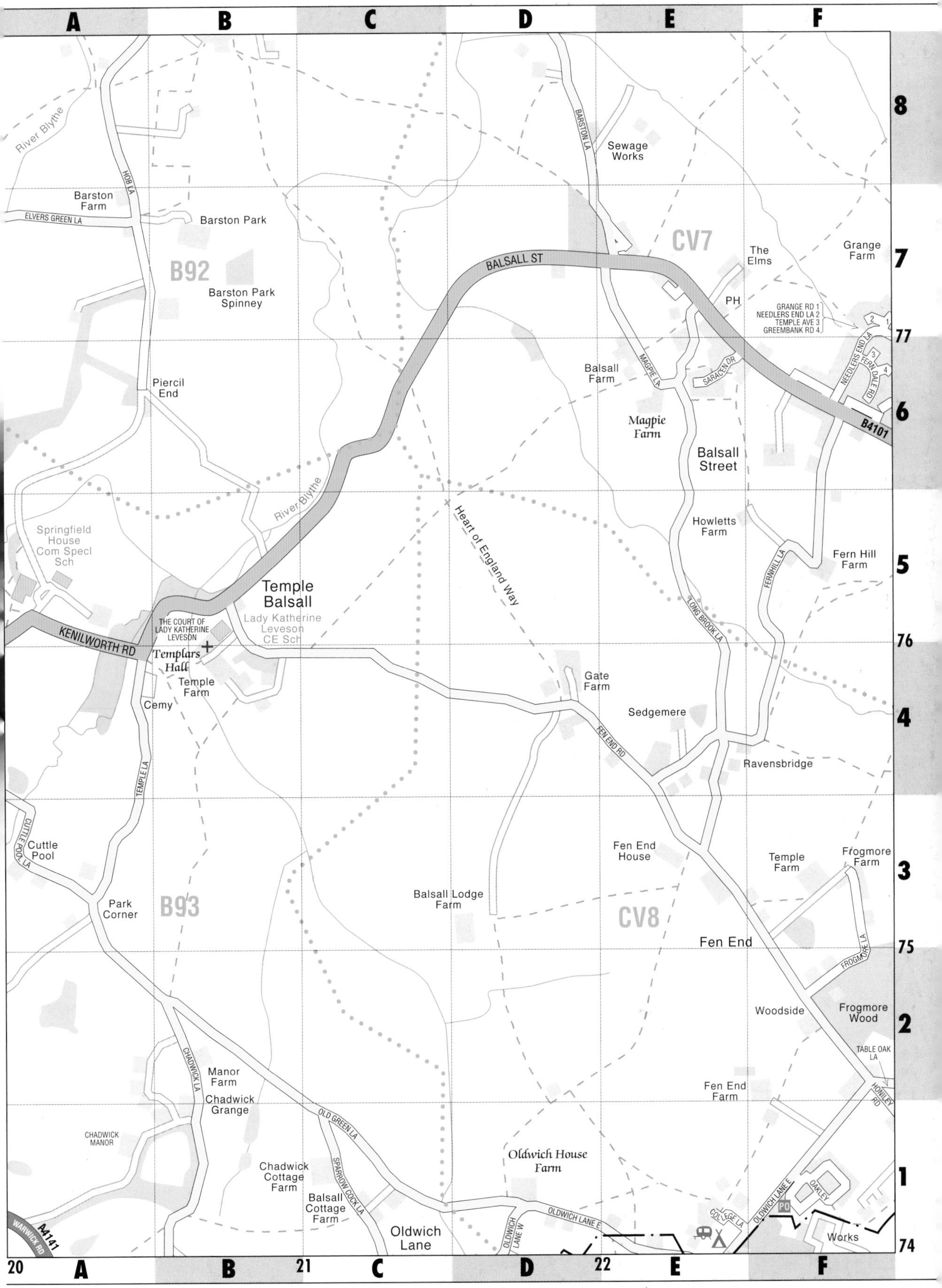

145
130

129
110

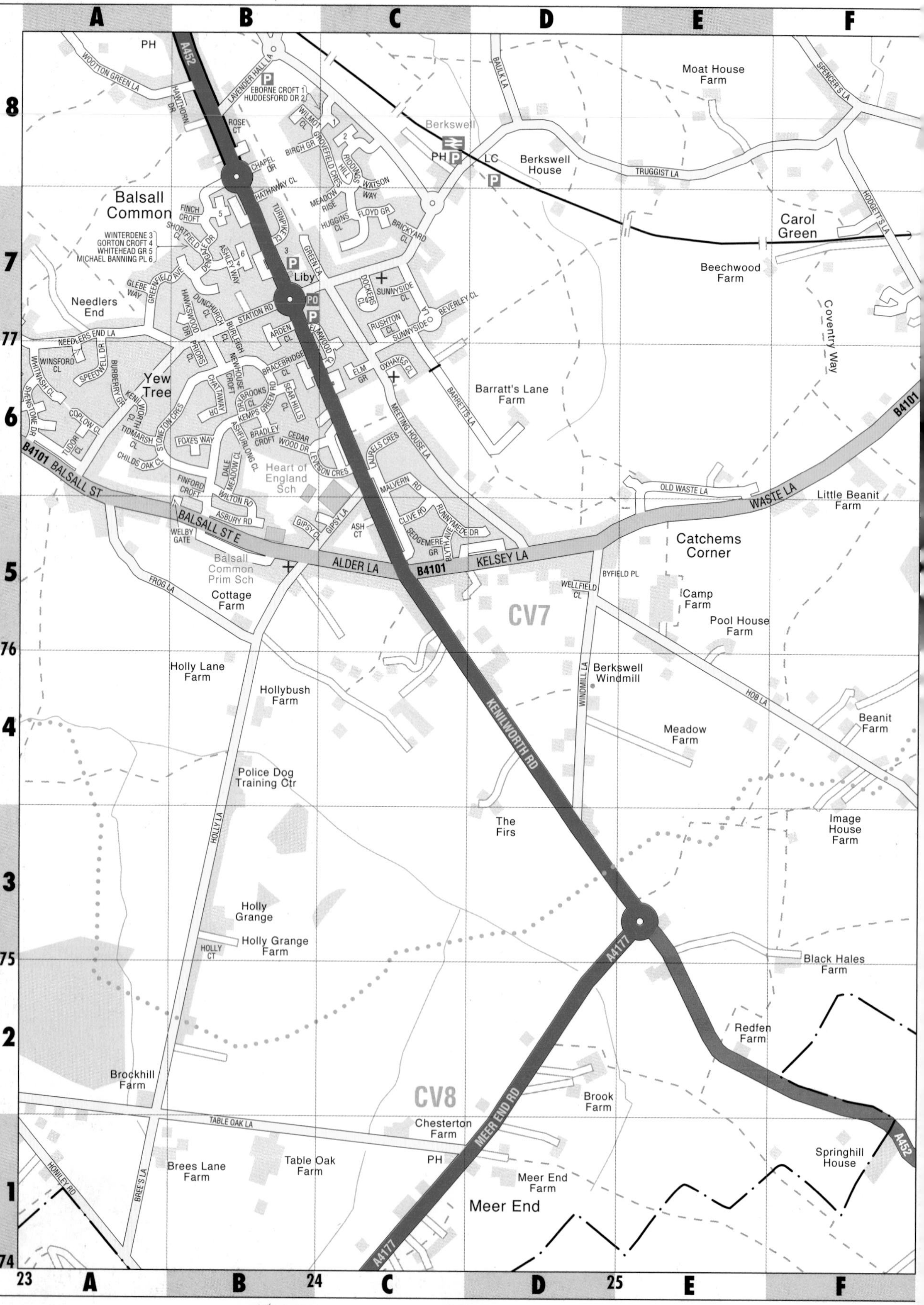

129
146

111
132

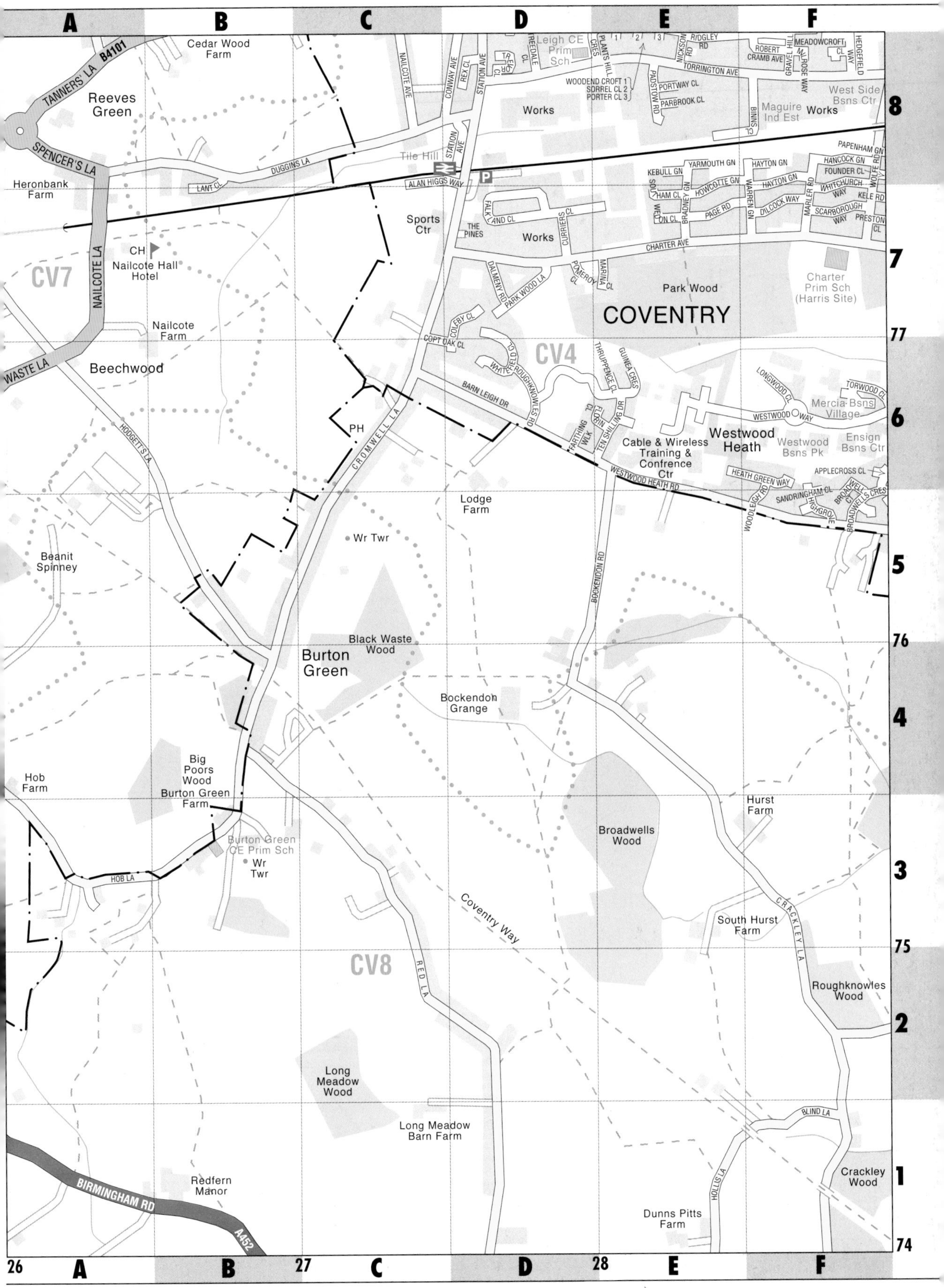

147
132

131
112

131
148

113
134

149
134

133
114

F8
1 CARDALE CROFT
2 KESTREL CROFT
3 RUTLAND CROFT
4 JIM FORREST CL
5 WILLOWHERB CL
6 WASPERTON CL
7 JOE WILLIAMS CL
8 DEERDALE TERR

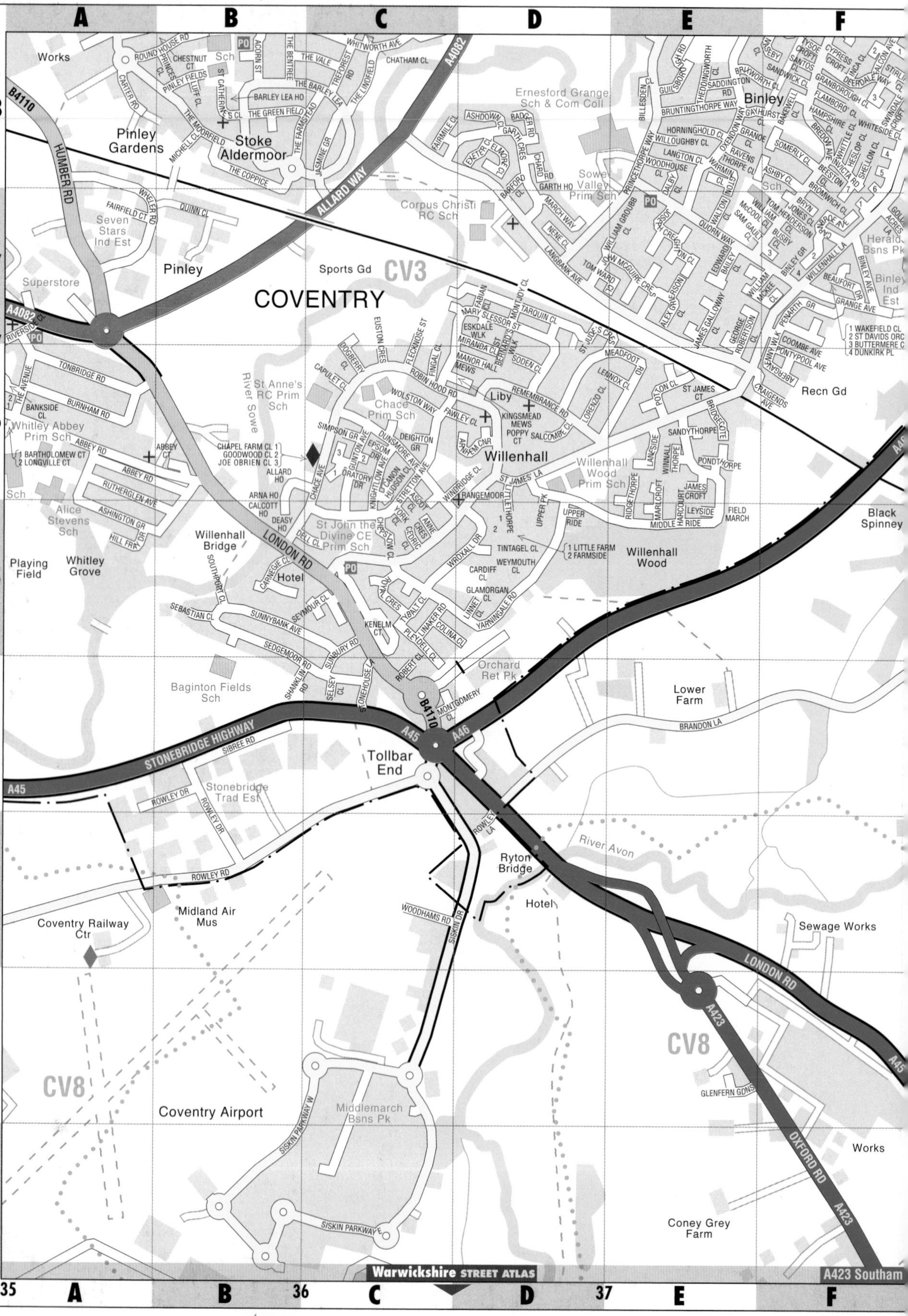

133

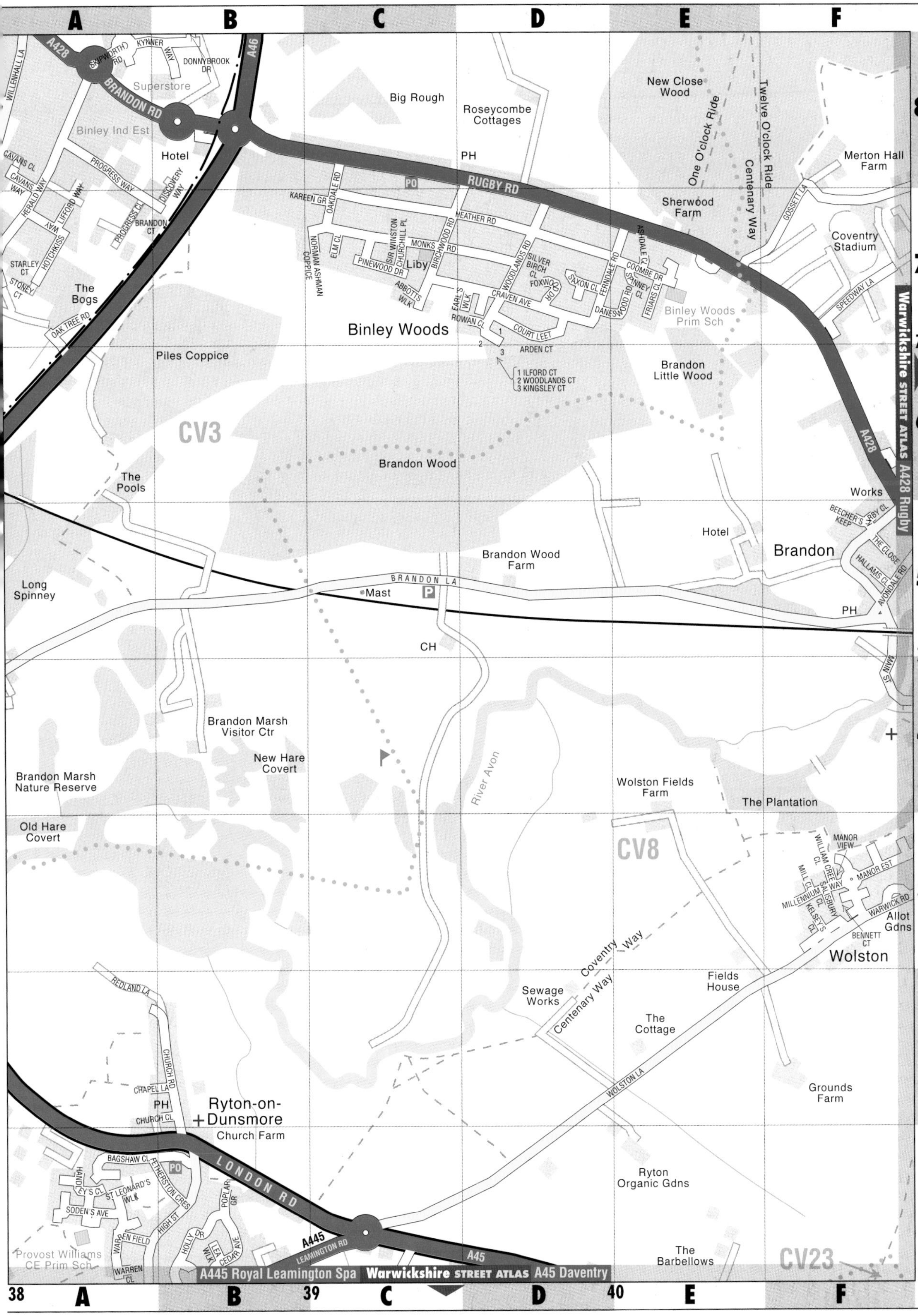
A
B
C
D
E
F
8
7
77
6
5
76
4
3
75
2
1
74
38
39
40
A428
BRANDON RD
SKIPWORTH RD
KYNNER WAY
DONNYBROOK DR
A46
Superstore
Binley Ind Est
Hotel
WILLENHALL LA
CAVANS CL
CAVANS WAY
HERALD WAY
PROGRESS WAY
DISCOVERY WAY
LIFFORD WAY
PROGRESS CL
BRANDON CT
HOTCHKISS WAY
STARLEY CT
STONEY CT
The Bogs
OAK TREE RD
Big Rough
Roseycombe Cottages
PH
PO
RUGBY RD
KAREEN GR
OAKDALE RD
HEATHER RD
NORMAN ASHMAN COPPICE
ELM CL
SIR WINSTON CHURCHILL PL
MONKS RD
BIRCHWOOD RD
PINEWOOD DR
Liby
ABBOTTS WLK
EARL'S WLK
ROWAN CL
CRAVEN AVE
WOODLANDS RD
SILVER BIRCH CL
FOXWOOD DR
SAXON CL
FERNDALE RD
DANESWOOD RD
ASHDALE CL
COOMBE DR
SPINNEY CL
FRIARS CL
COURT LEET
ARDEN CT
Binley Woods
1 ILFORD CT
2 WOODLANDS CT
3 KINGSLEY CT
Binley Woods Prim Sch
New Close Wood
One O'clock Ride
Twelve O'clock Ride
Centenary Way
Sherwood Farm
Merton Hall Farm
GOSSETT LA
Coventry Stadium
SPEEDWAY LA
Piles Coppice
CV3
Brandon Little Wood
Brandon Wood
The Pools
Works
BEECHER'S KEEP
KIRBY CL
THE CLOSE
HALLAMS CL
AVONDALE RD
Hotel
Brandon
Brandon Wood Farm
BRANDON LA
Long Spinney
Mast
P
PH
CH
MAIN ST
Brandon Marsh Visitor Ctr
New Hare Covert
Brandon Marsh Nature Reserve
River Avon
Wolston Fields Farm
The Plantation
Old Hare Covert
CV8
WILLIAM CREE WAY
MANOR VIEW
MANOR EST
MILL CL
MILLENNIUM CL
SALISBURY CT
KELSEY'S CL
WARWICK RD
Allot Gdns
BENNETT CT
Wolston
Coventry Way
Centenary Way
Sewage Works
Fields House
The Cottage
REDLAND LA
CHURCH RD
CHAPEL LA
PH
CHURCH CL
Ryton-on-Dunsmore
Church Farm
WOLSTON LA
Grounds Farm
LONDON RD
BAGSHAW CL
FETHERSTON CRES
PO
HANDLEY'S CL
ST LEONARD'S WLK
SODEN'S AVE
HIGH ST
POPLAR GR
HOLLY DR
LEA WLK
CEDAR AVE
WARREN FIELD
WARREN CL
Provost Williams CE Prim Sch
A445
LEAMINGTON RD
A45
Ryton Organic Gdns
The Barbellows
CV23

Warwickshire STREET ATLAS A428 Rugby
A445 Royal Leamington Spa Warwickshire STREET ATLAS A45 Daventry

120

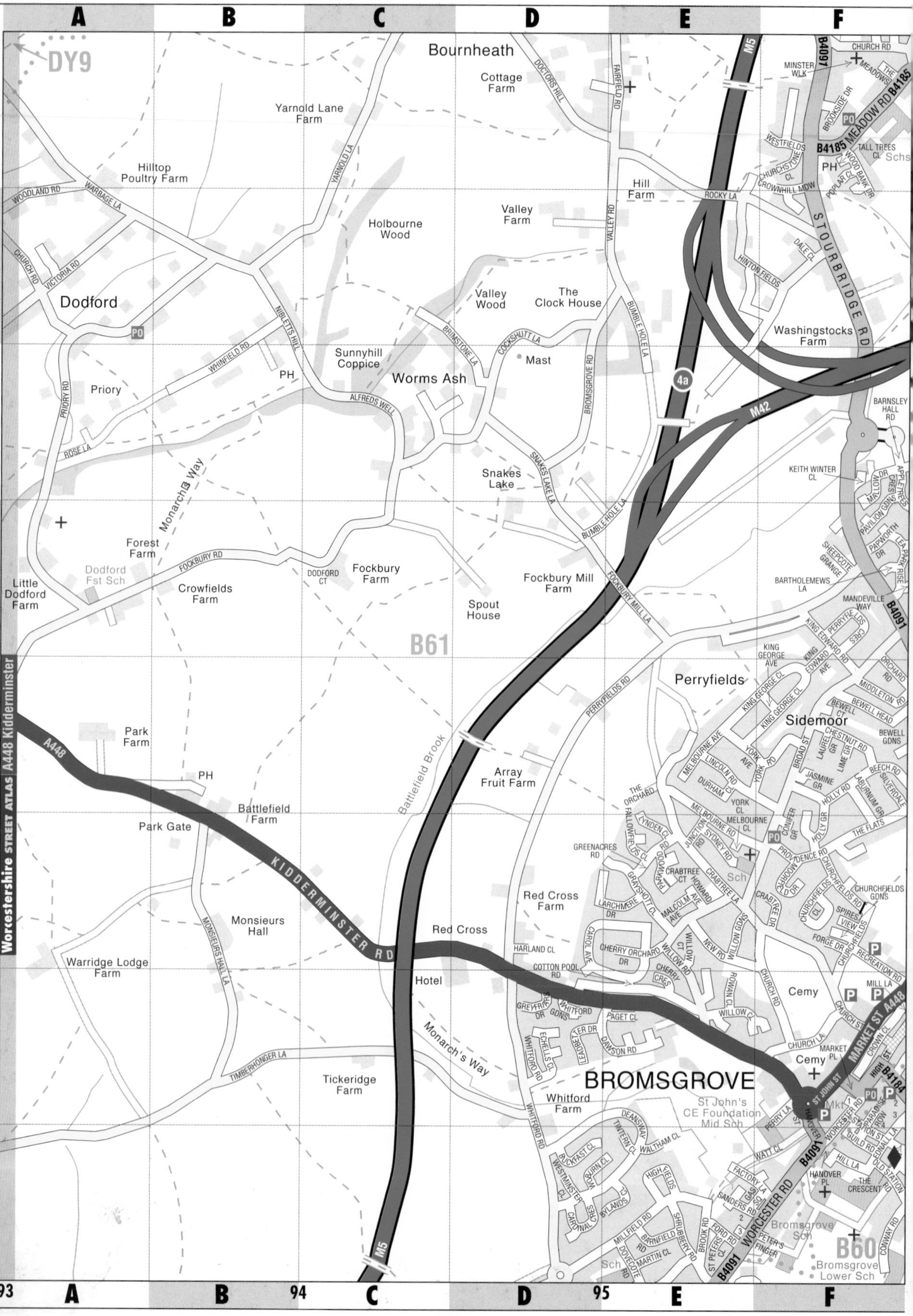

E1
1 Sanders Ind Est
2 WESTBOURNE TERR
3 WESTBOURNE CL

F2
1 GEORGE ST
2 ELGAR MEWS
3 NAILERS CT
4 GUILD CT

150

121
138

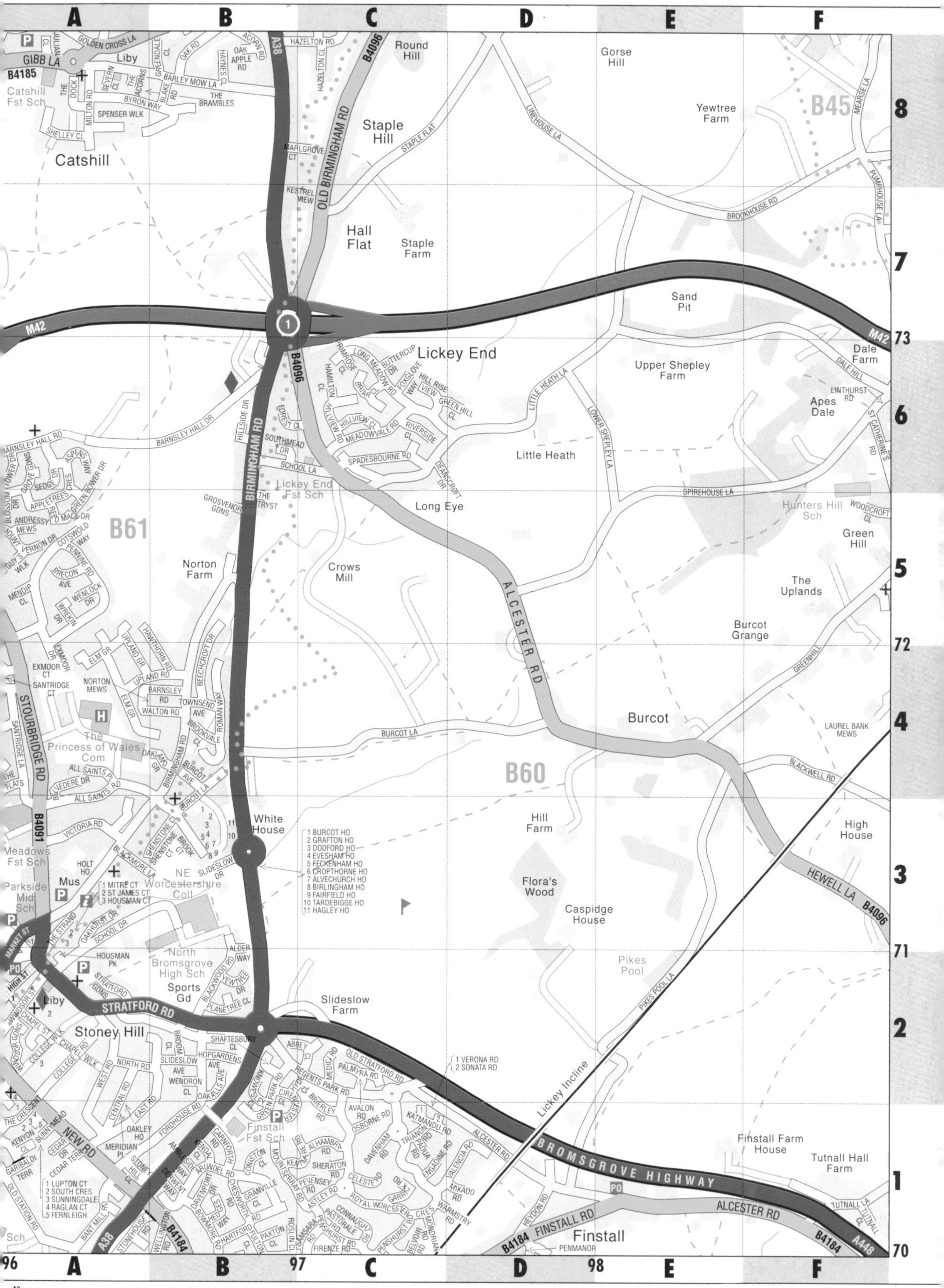

151
138

A2
1 CHAPEL STREET PREC
2 AMPHLETT CT
3 WESTMINSTER CT
4 GUARDIAN CT

137
122

137
152

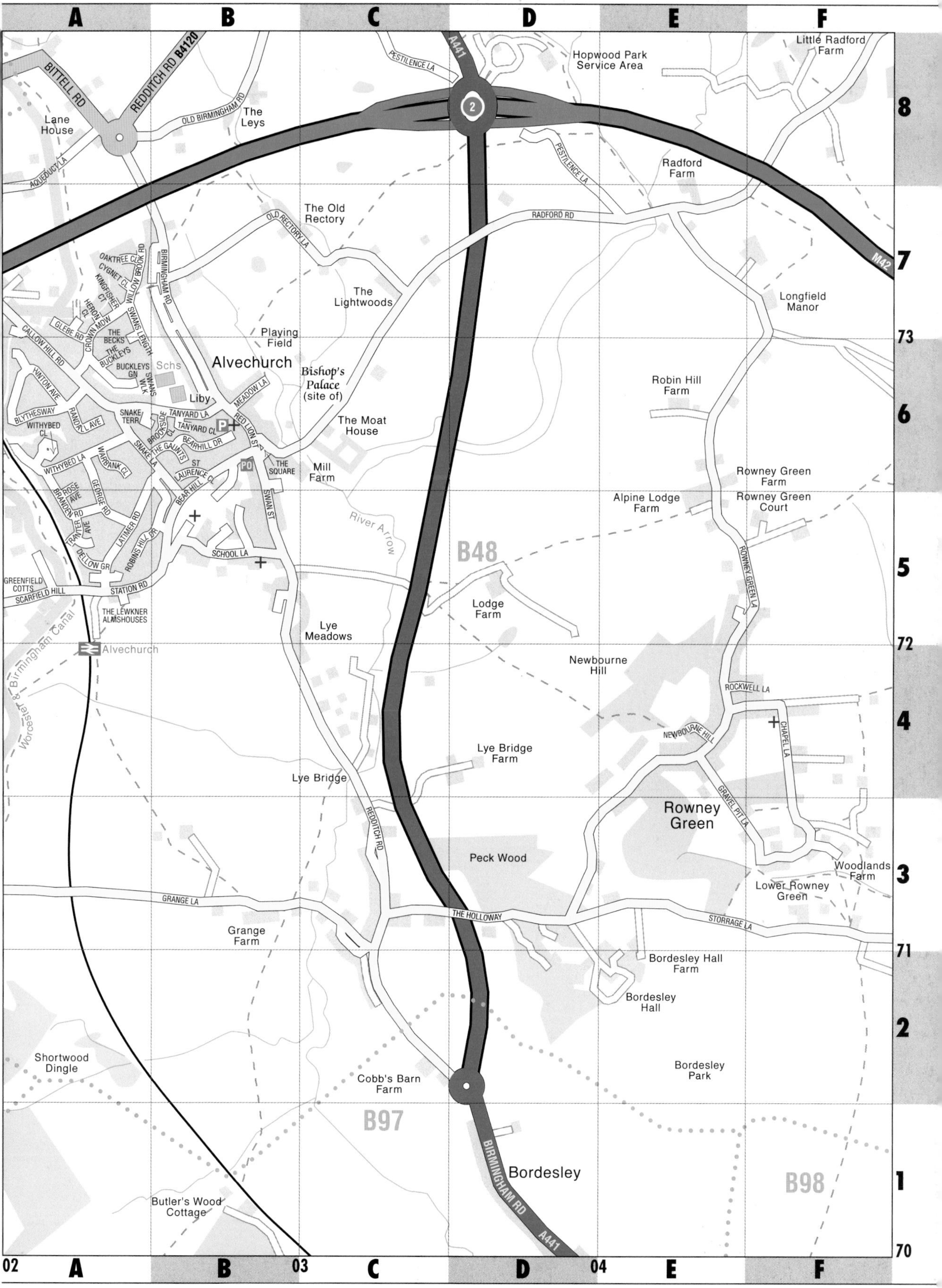
A
B
C
D
E
F
BITTELL RD
REDDITCH RD B4120
Lane House
OLD BIRMINGHAM RD
The Leys
PESTILENCE LA
A441
2
Hopwood Park Service Area
Little Radford Farm
8
AQUEDUCT LA
Radford Farm
The Old Rectory
OLD RECTORY LA
RADFORD RD
M42
7
OAKTREE CL
CYGNET CL
KINGFISHER CT
WILLOW BROOK RD
BIRMINGHAM RD
The Lightwoods
Longfield Manor
HERON CL
CROWN MDW
SWANS LENGTH
GLEBE RD
THE BECKS
THE BUCKLEYS
Playing Field
73
CALLOW HILL RD
BUCKLEYS GN
Schs
Alvechurch
Bishop's Palace (site of)
Robin Hill Farm
HINTON AVE
SWANS WLK
Liby
MEADOW LA
BLYTHESWAY
RANDALL AVE
SNAKE TERR
TANYARD LA
TANYARD CL
The Moat House
6
WITHYBED CL
BROOKSIDE CL
BEARHILL DR
RED LION ST
SNAKE LA
THE GAUNTS
WITHYBED LA
WARBANK CL
ST LAURENCE CL
PO
THE SQUARE
Mill Farm
Rowney Green Farm
BRANDEN RD
ROSE AVE
GEDGE RD
BEAR HILL DR
SWAN ST
Alpine Lodge Farm
Rowney Green Court
TRAITER RD
AVE
LATIMER RD
ROBINS HILL DR
River Arrow
B48
DELLOW GR
SCHOOL LA
5
GREENFIELD COTTS
SCARFIELD HILL
STATION RD
ROWNEY GREEN LA
Lodge Farm
THE LEWKNER ALMSHOUSES
Lye Meadows
Alvechurch
72
Worcester & Birmingham Canal
Newbourne Hill
ROCKWELL LA
4
NEWBOURNE HILL
CHAPEL LA
Lye Bridge Farm
Lye Bridge
GRAVEL PIT LA
Rowney Green
REDDITCH RD
Peck Wood
3
Woodlands Farm
Lower Rowney Green
GRANGE LA
THE HOLLOWAY
STORRAGE LA
Grange Farm
71
Bordesley Hall Farm
Bordesley Hall
2
Shortwood Dingle
Cobb's Barn Farm
Bordesley Park
B97
BIRMINGHAM RD
Bordesley
1
B98
Butler's Wood Cottage
A441
70
02
03
04

139
124

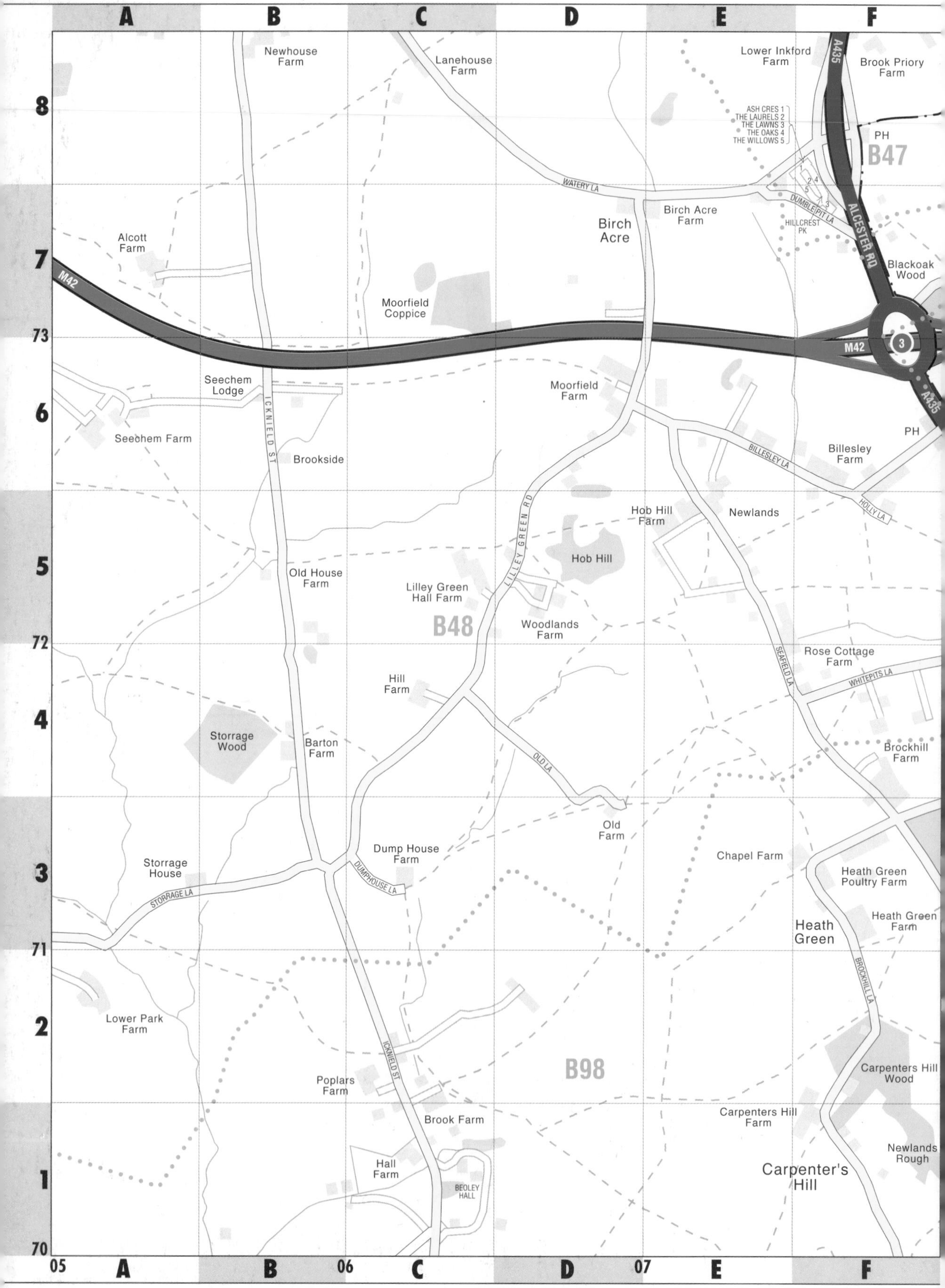
A
B
C
D
E
F
8
7
73
6
5
72
4
3
71
2
1
70
05
06
07
Newhouse Farm
Lanehouse Farm
Lower Inkford Farm
A435
Brook Priory Farm
ASH CRES 1
THE LAURELS 2
THE LAWNS 3
THE OAKS 4
THE WILLOWS 5
PH
B47
WATERY LA
Birch Acre Farm
Birch Acre
DUMBLE PIT LA
HILLCREST PK
ALCESTER RD
Alcott Farm
M42
Blackoak Wood
Moorfield Coppice
M42
3
A435
Seechem Lodge
Moorfield Farm
Seechem Farm
ICKNIELD ST
Brookside
PH
Billesley Farm
BILLESLEY LA
Newlands
Hob Hill Farm
HOLLY LA
Hob Hill
LILLEY GREEN RD
Old House Farm
Lilley Green Hall Farm
B48
Woodlands Farm
Rose Cottage Farm
SEAFIELD LA
WHITEPITS LA
Hill Farm
Storrage Wood
Barton Farm
OLD LA
Brockhill Farm
Old Farm
Dump House Farm
Chapel Farm
Storrage House
DUMPHOUSE LA
STORRAGE LA
Heath Green Poultry Farm
Heath Green Farm
Heath Green
BROCKHILL LA
Lower Park Farm
ICKNIELD ST
B98
Poplars Farm
Carpenters Hill Wood
Brook Farm
Carpenters Hill Farm
Newlands Rough
Hall Farm
Carpenter's Hill
BEOLEY HALL

139
154

A B C D E F
River Cole
B47
MILL LA
FORSHAW HEATH RD
The Poplars
Clowes Wood
Terry's Pool
Pound Close Farm
Forshaw Heath
Graves Coppice
POOLHEAD LA
CLOWESWOOD LA
The Lakes
Terry's Green
SPRINGBROOK LA
MALTHOUSE LA
White House Farm
Springbrook Farm
Glebe Farm
FORSHAW HEATH LA
JUGGINS LA
OAKTREE FARM MOBILE HOMES PK
WOODSIDE PK MOBILE HOMES PK
Checkley's Coppice
Yew Tree Farm
Forshaw Park Farm
The Plantation
The Lyndons
Small Lane Farm
SMALL LA
Earlswood Trad Est
BIDDLES HILL
Rugby Football Ground
Sewage Works
Spring Brook
M42
Tyler's Grove
Windmill Naps
B48
Portway
Pool House Farm
Ladbrookpark Coppice
B94
Poolhead Farm
WOOD END LA
Holly Farm
WHITEPITS LA
PENN LA
ALCESTER RD
Cottage Farm
Little Ladbrooke Farm
Ladbrooke Hall
Ladbrooke Hall Farm
PH
Wood End
B4101
Lion Wood
PENN LA
CH
BROCKHILL LA
Brockhill Wood
ALCESTER RD
WOODCOCK CL
Wood End
Hill Barn
RUSHBROOK LA
Rushbrook Farm
Rushbrook
High Park Farm
BROAD LA
VICARAGE HILL
Gilbert's Green
Spring Brook
Highpark Wood
B98
SEAFIELD LA
ARDEN LEYS
ASPLEY HEATH LA
Park Farm
Aspley Heath
ASPLEY HEATH
River Alne
PH
Baylis Green
BEOLEY LA
BROAD LA
Branson's Cross
BLIND LA
CHERRY PIT LA
Pinkfield Wood
Branson's Cross Farm
Aspley Farm
BATES LA
B4101
A435
Alderhanger Wood
8 73 7 6 5 72 4 3 71 2 1 70
08 09 10

141
126

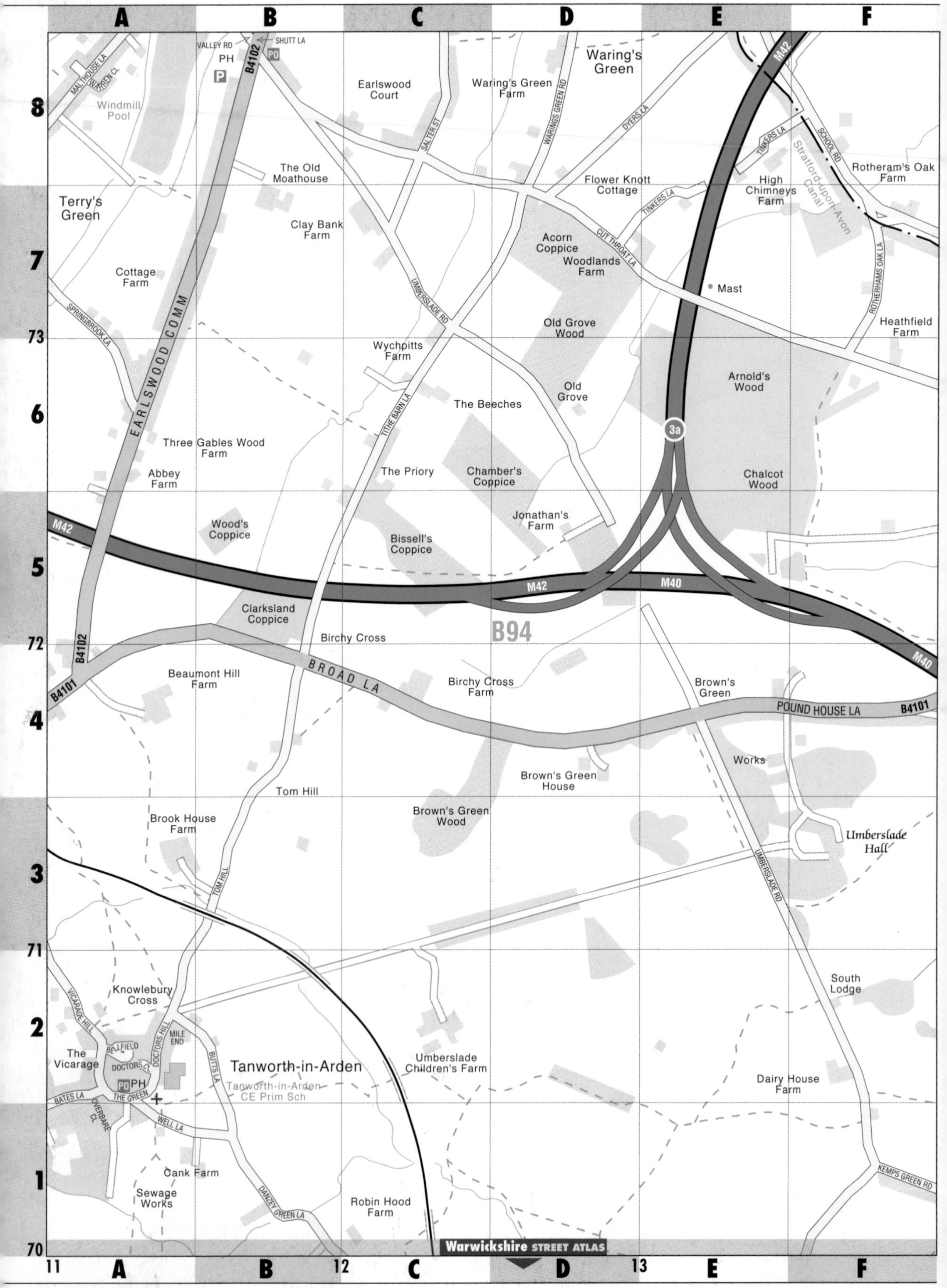
A
B
C
D
E
F
8
7
73
6
5
72
4
3
71
2
1
70
11
12
13
VALLEY RD
SHUTT LA
PH
PO
B4102
MALTHOUSE LA
WREN CL
Windmill Pool
Earlswood Court
Waring's Green Farm
Waring's Green
WARINGS GREEN RD
DYERS LA
SALTER ST
M42
TINKERS LA
SCHOOL RD
Stratford-upon-Avon Canal
Rotheram's Oak Farm
The Old Moathouse
Flower Knott Cottage
High Chimneys Farm
TINKERS LA
Terry's Green
Clay Bank Farm
CUT THROAT LA
Acorn Coppice
Woodlands Farm
Cottage Farm
Mast
ROTHERHAMS OAK LA
SPRINGBROOK LA
UMBERSLADE RD
Old Grove Wood
Heathfield Farm
EARLSWOOD COMM
Wychpitts Farm
Arnold's Wood
Old Grove
The Beeches
3a
TITHE BARN LA
Three Gables Wood Farm
Abbey Farm
The Priory
Chamber's Coppice
Chalcot Wood
Jonathan's Farm
Wood's Coppice
Bissell's Coppice
M42
M40
Clarksland Coppice
B94
Birchy Cross
B4102
Beaumont Hill Farm
BROAD LA
Birchy Cross Farm
Brown's Green
M40
B4101
POUND HOUSE LA
B4101
Works
Brown's Green House
Tom Hill
Brown's Green Wood
Brook House Farm
Umberslade Hall
UMBERSLADE RD
TOM HILL
South Lodge
Knowlebury Cross
VICARAGE HILL
DOCTORS HILL
MILE END
The Vicarage
BELLFIELD
DOCTORS CL
BUTTS LA
Tanworth-in-Arden
Umberslade Children's Farm
Dairy House Farm
PO
PH
Tanworth-in-Arden CE Prim Sch
BATES LA
OVERBARE CL
THE GREEN
WELL LA
Cank Farm
KEMPS GREEN RD
Sewage Works
DANZEY GREEN LA
Robin Hood Farm
Warwickshire STREET ATLAS

141

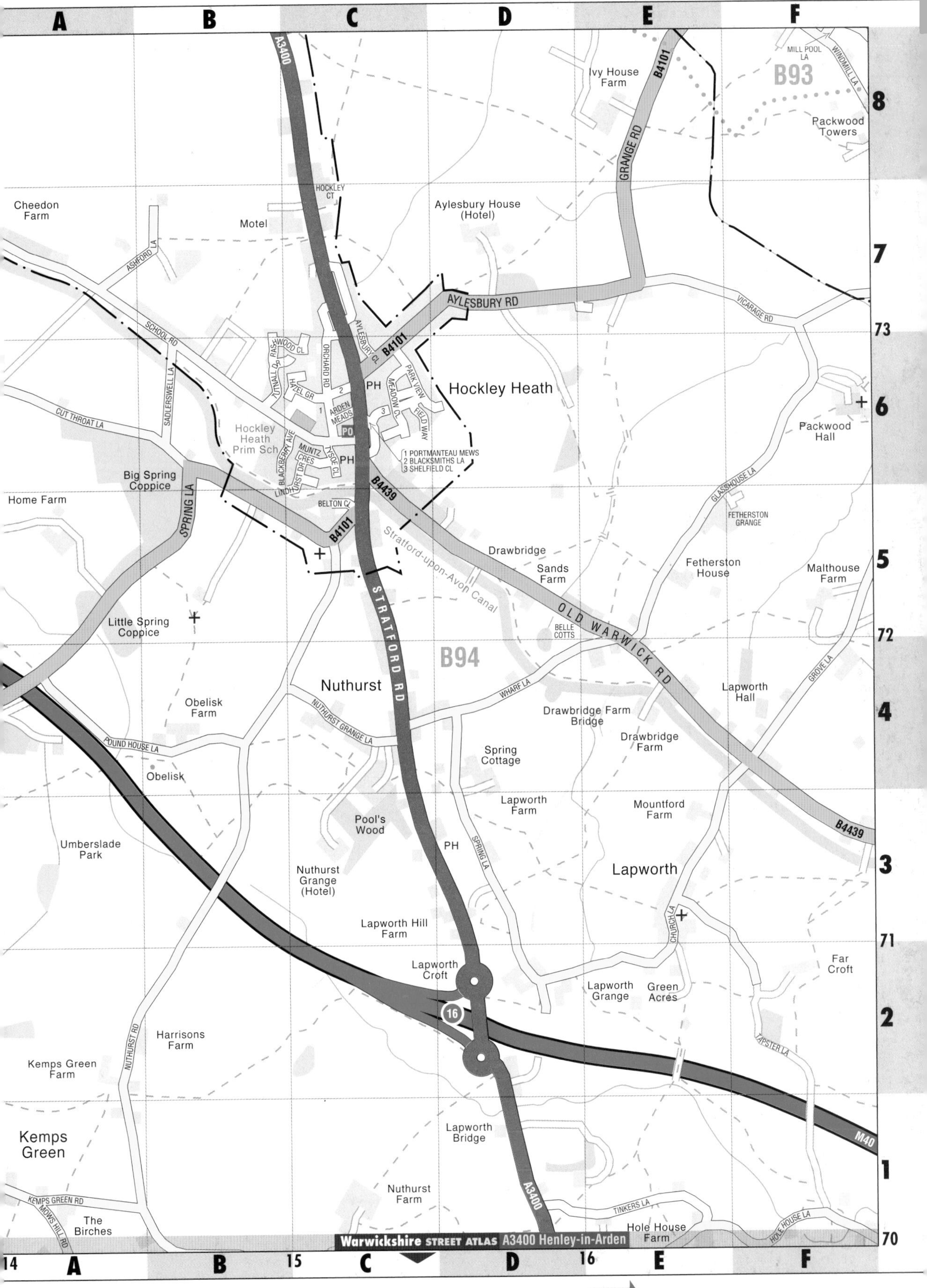
A
B
C
D
E
F
Ivy House Farm
B4101
MILL POOL LA
WINDMILL LA
B93
8
Packwood Towers
GRANGE RD
A3400
HOCKLEY CT
Cheedon Farm
Motel
Aylesbury House (Hotel)
7
ASHFORD LA
AYLESBURY RD
VICARAGE RD
73
SCHOOL RD
RASHWOOD CL
ORCHARD RD
AYLESBURY CL
B4101
PH
PARK VIEW
Hockley Heath
SADLERSWELL LA
UTNALL CL
HAZEL GR
ARDEN MEADS
MEADOW CL
FIELD WAY
6
CUT THROAT LA
Packwood Hall
PO
Hockley Heath Prim Sch
BLACKBERRY AVE
MUNTZ CRES
TYSOE CL
PH
1 PORTMANTEAU MEWS
2 BLACKSMITHS LA
3 SHELFIELD CL
Big Spring Coppice
LINDHURST DR
B4439
GLASSHOUSE LA
Home Farm
SPRING LA
BELTON CL
FETHERSTON GRANGE
B4101
Stratford-upon-Avon Canal
Drawbridge
Sands Farm
Fetherston House
Malthouse Farm
5
STRATFORD RD
OLD WARWICK RD
Little Spring Coppice
BELLE COTTS
72
B94
GROVE LA
Nuthurst
WHARF LA
Lapworth Hall
Obelisk Farm
NUTHURST GRANGE LA
Drawbridge Farm Bridge
4
Drawbridge Farm
POUND HOUSE LA
Spring Cottage
Obelisk
Lapworth Farm
Mountford Farm
Pool's Wood
B4439
Umberslade Park
PH
SPRING LA
3
Nuthurst Grange (Hotel)
Lapworth
CHURCH LA
Lapworth Hill Farm
71
Far Croft
Lapworth Croft
Lapworth Grange
Green Acres
16
2
Harrisons Farm
TAPSTER LA
NUTHURST RD
Kemps Green Farm
Kemps Green
Lapworth Bridge
M40
1
A3400
Nuthurst Farm
KEMPS GREEN RD
MOWS HILL RD
The Birches
TINKERS LA
Hole House Farm
HOLE HOUSE LA
70
14
15
16

143
128

A
B
C
D
E
F
8
7
73
6
5
72
4
3
71
2
1
70
17
18
19
MILL POOL LA
DARLEY GREEN RD
B93
Darley Green
Manor Farm
WINDMILL LA
Windmill Farm
Packwood
Windmill House
VICARAGE RD
School House
PACKWOOD RD
Corner Farm
The Homestead
Chessetts Wood Farm
CHESSETTS WOOD RD
Chessetts Wood
Fir Tree Farm
Yew Tree House
CHAPEL LA
VALLEY LA
Bon Accord Farm
Turnover Bridge
Valley Farm
Netherwood Lodge Farm
Yew Tree Farm
ARBOUR TREE LA
NETHERWOOD LA
Netherwood Heath
Netherwood Heath Farm
Packwood Farm
Cheswood Grange
B93
Uplands Farm
Netherwood
Swallowfield Stud
The Grove
GROVE LA
Two Pits Park
Gorse Wood
The Lightwoods
Priory Farm
RISING LA
Rising Bridge
The Park
Packwood House
Brick Kiln Coppice
B94
PRIORY CL
KINGSWOOD CL
Terets Farm
Pool Tail Coppice
RISING RD
PH
Kingswood Farm
Sides Coppice
The Terets
PACKWOOD LA
Pratt's Pit Wood
The Park
Gospel Oak
STATION RD
Grand Union Canal Wlk
Grand Union Canal
Fir Plantation
Baddesley Clinton
MILL LA
Lapworth
P
Kingswood House
Bear House Farm
Stratford-upon-Avon Canal
Kingswood
THE ELMS
MEADOW LA
B4439
Lapworth Court
PH
PO
Lapworth CE Prim Sch
Kingswood Brook
HARBOROUGH COTTS
CANALSIDE
LAPWORTH OAKS
STATION LA
YEW TREE CL
OLD WARWICK RD
Heart of England Way
KINGSWOOD COTTS
ST CHADS MEWS
WOODBINE COTTS
POUND CL
Pound House
CATESBY LA
Rye House
BROME HALL LA
P
PH
Clinton Farm
Kingswood Bridge
Ardenhill
Ardenhill Farm
Catesby House
LAPWORTH ST
Brome Hall Farm
CV35
Hill Park Chase
Broom Hall Bridge
Weston Hall Bridge
Hill Park House
Catesby Farmhouse
M40
APPLETREE COTTS
Weston Hall Farm
Bredon House
B4439
M40
ROWINGTON GN
THE AVENUE
FINWOOD RD
HOLE HOUSE LA
YEW TREE LA
M40 Warwick (A429)
Warwickshire STREET ATLAS

143

129
146

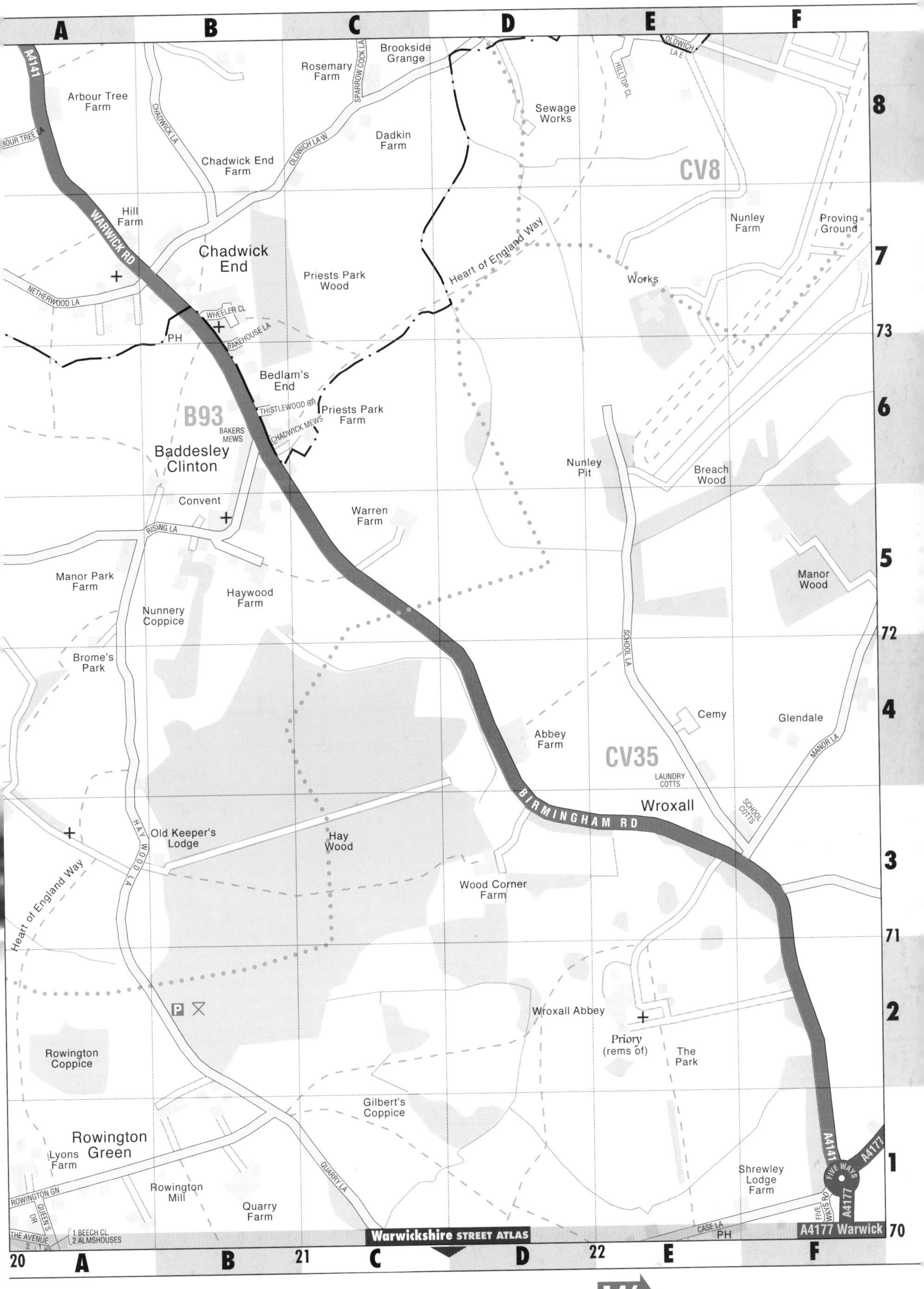
A
B
C
D
E
F
8
7
73
6
5
72
4
3
71
2
1
70
20
21
22
A4141
Arbour Tree Farm
BOUR TREE LA
CHADWICK LA
Rosemary Farm
SPARROW COCK LA
Brookside Grange
Dadkin Farm
OLDWICH LA W
Chadwick End Farm
Sewage Works
HILLTOP CL
OLDWICH LA E
CV8
Hill Farm
WARWICK RD
Chadwick End
Priests Park Wood
Heart of England Way
Nunley Farm
Proving Ground
Works
NETHERWOOD LA
WHEELER CL
BAKEHOUSE LA
PH
Bedlam's End
THISTLEWOOD GR
Priests Park Farm
CHADWICK MEWS
B93
BAKERS MEWS
Baddesley Clinton
Nunley Pit
Breach Wood
Convent
Warren Farm
RISWG LA
Manor Park Farm
Haywood Farm
Nunnery Coppice
Manor Wood
SCHOOL LA
Brome's Park
Cemy
Glendale
Abbey Farm
CV35
MANOR LA
LAUNDRY COTTS
BIRMINGHAM RD
Wroxall
SCHOOL COTTS
Old Keeper's Lodge
HAY WOOD LA
Hay Wood
Heart of England Way
Wood Corner Farm
P
Wroxall Abbey
Priory (rems of)
The Park
Rowington Coppice
Gilbert's Coppice
Rowington Green
Lyons Farm
A4141
A4177
FIVE WAYS
Shrewley Lodge Farm
Rowington Mill
QUARRY LA
Quarry Farm
ROWINGTON GN
QUEEN'S DR
THE AVENUE
1 BEECH CL
2 ALMSHOUSES
CASE LA
PH
FIVE WAYS RD
A4177 Warwick

146

145
130

A
B
C
D
E
F
8
7
73
6
5
72
4
3
71
2
1
70
HONILEY RD
A4177
MEER END RD
Proving Ground
Pear Tree Farm
Blenheim Farm
Rudfyn Manor
Runway Farm
Croft Farm
Black Hill Wood
Poors Wood
Holly Farm Bsns Pk
Wattcote Farm
Warriors Lodge Farm
CHASE LA
Chase Wood
CV8
Honiley Boot (PH)
Yew Tree Cottage
Church Farm
Honiley
Honiley Hall
Featherstons Grove
MANOR LA
Thorny Coppice
Grove Farm
Clattyland Wood
Grove Cottage
Wakefield Wood
PO
Haseley Knob
CV35
Hill Farm Cottage
Cheyneys Farm
SCHOOL CROFT
Hill Farm
Fernwood Farm
HEATH TERR
BUTLERS END
BARRACKS LA
ROUNCIL LA
The Glade
Haseleygreen Farm
Beausale
Lyon Farm
Elmwood Farm
Holly Farm
BEAUSALE LA
KITES NEST LA
Camphill Farm
23
24
25

145

131
148

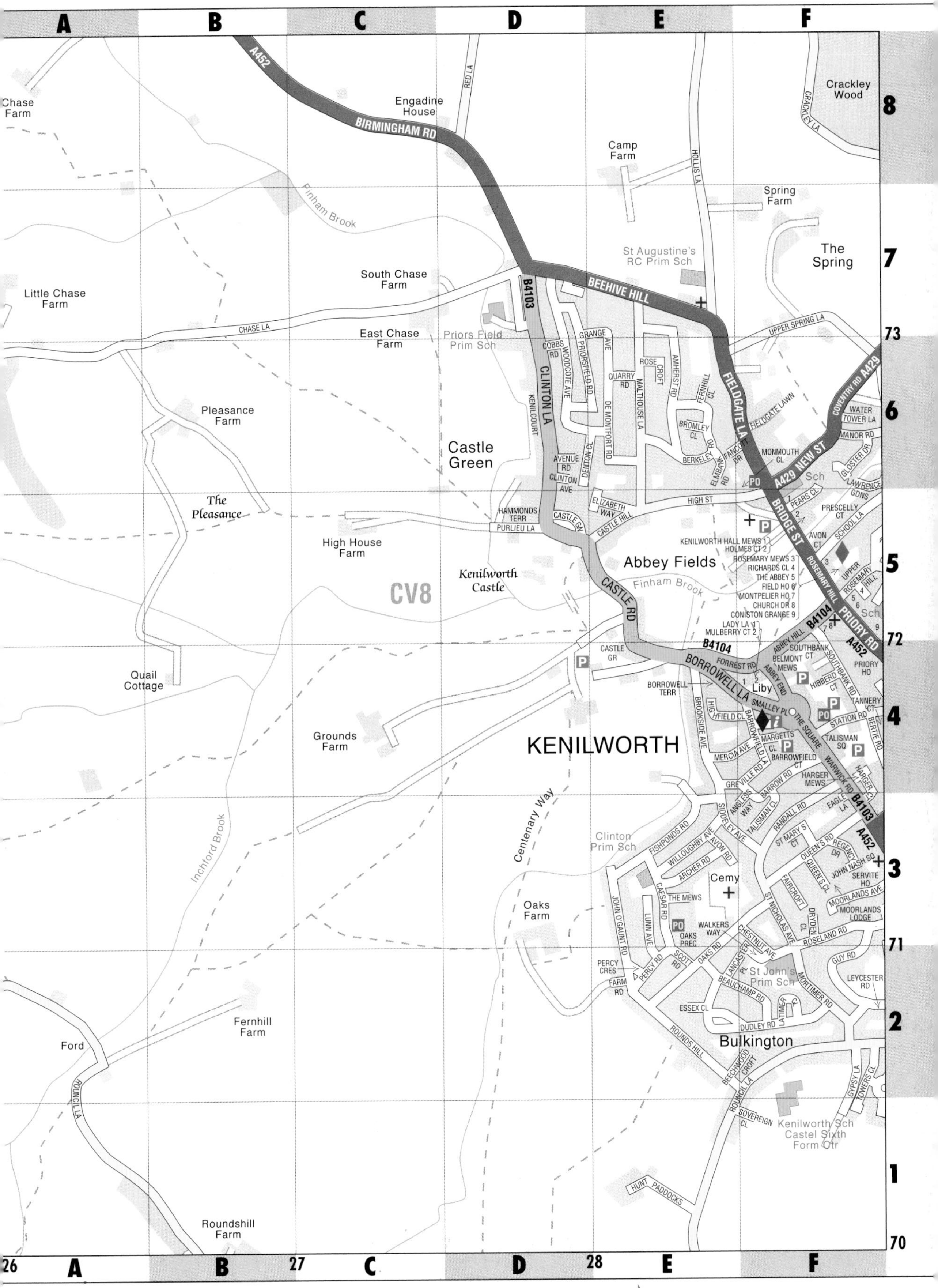
A
B
C
D
E
F
8
7
73
6
5
72
4
3
71
2
1
70
26
27
28
A452
BIRMINGHAM RD
Chase Farm
Engadine House
RED LA
Camp Farm
HOLLIS LA
Crackley Wood
CRACKLEY LA
Finham Brook
Spring Farm
St Augustine's RC Prim Sch
The Spring
Little Chase Farm
South Chase Farm
BEEHIVE HILL
B4103
CHASE LA
East Chase Farm
Priors Field Prim Sch
UPPER SPRING LA
COBBS RD
GRANGE AVE
WOODCOTE AVE
PRIORSFIELD RD
QUARRY RD
ROSE CROFT
AMHERST RD
FERNHILL CL
FIELDGATE LA
FIELDGATE LAWN
COVENTRY RD A429
WATER TOWER LA
Pleasance Farm
CLINTON LA
KENILCOURT
DE MONTFORT RD
MALTHOUSE LA
BROMLEY CL
BERKELEY RD
MANOR RD
Castle Green
AVENUE RD
DENTON CL
ELMBANK RD
FANCOTT DR
MONMOUTH CL
A429 NEW ST
GLOSTER DR
CLINTON AVE
PO
Sch
LAWRENCE GDNS
The Pleasance
HAMMONDS TERR
ELIZABETH WAY
HIGH ST
PEARS CL
BRIDGE ST
PRESCELLY CT
PURLIEU LA
CASTLE GN
CASTLE HILL
P
AVON CT
SCHOOL LA
High House Farm
KENILWORTH HALL MEWS 1
HOLMES CT 2
ROSEMARY MEWS 3
RICHARDS CL 4
THE ABBEY 5
FIELD HO 6
MONTPELIER HO 7
CHURCH DR 8
CONISTON GRANGE 9
Abbey Fields
UPPER ROSEMARY HILL
ROSEMARY HILL
Kenilworth Castle
CV8
CASTLE RD
Finham Brook
LADY LA
MULBERRY CT
B4104
PRIORY RD
A452
Quail Cottage
CASTLE GR
B4104
ABBEY HILL
SOUTHBANK
BELMONT CT
SOUTHBANK RD
PRIORY HO
FORREST RD
ABBEY END
MEWS
BORROWELL LA
BORROWELL TERR
Liby
HIBBERD CT
TANNERY CT
HIGHFIELD CL
SMALLEY PL
THE SQUARE
STATION RD
BERTIE RD
Grounds Farm
KENILWORTH
BROOKSIDE AVE
BARROWFIELD LA
MARGETTS CL
TALISMAN SQ
MERCIA AVE
BARROWFIELD CT
WARWICK RD
GREVILLE RD
HARGER MEWS
HARGER CT
ANGLESEY WAY
BARROW RD
RANDALL RD
EAGLE LA
B4103
Centenary Way
Inchford Brook
SIDDELEY AVE
TALISMAN CL
FISHPONDS RD
ST MARY'S CT
QUEEN'S RD
REGENCY DR
Clinton Prim Sch
WILLOUGHBY AVE
AVON RD
JOHN NASH SQ
ARCHER RD
QUEEN'S CL
SERVITE HO
Cemy
FAIRCROFT
MOORLANDS AVE
CAESAR RD
THE MEWS
ST NICHOLAS AVE
MOORLANDS LODGE
Oaks Farm
JOHN O'GAUNT RD
LUNN AVE
DRYDEN CL
WALKERS WAY
CHESTNUT AVE
ROSELAND RD
OAKS PREC
SCOTT RD
OAKS RD
LANCASTER PL
GUY RD
PERCY CRES
PERCY RD
St John's Prim Sch
LEYCESTER RD
FARM RD
BEAUCHAMP RD
MORTIMER RD
ESSEX CL
LATIMER CL
DUDLEY RD
Fernhill Farm
ROUNDS HILL
Bulkington
Ford
BEECHWOOD CROFT
ROUNCIL LA
GYPSY LA
TOWERS CL
SOVEREIGN CL
Kenilworth Sch Castel Sixth Form Ctr
HUNT PADDOCKS
Roundshill Farm

155
148

147
132

147
156

133

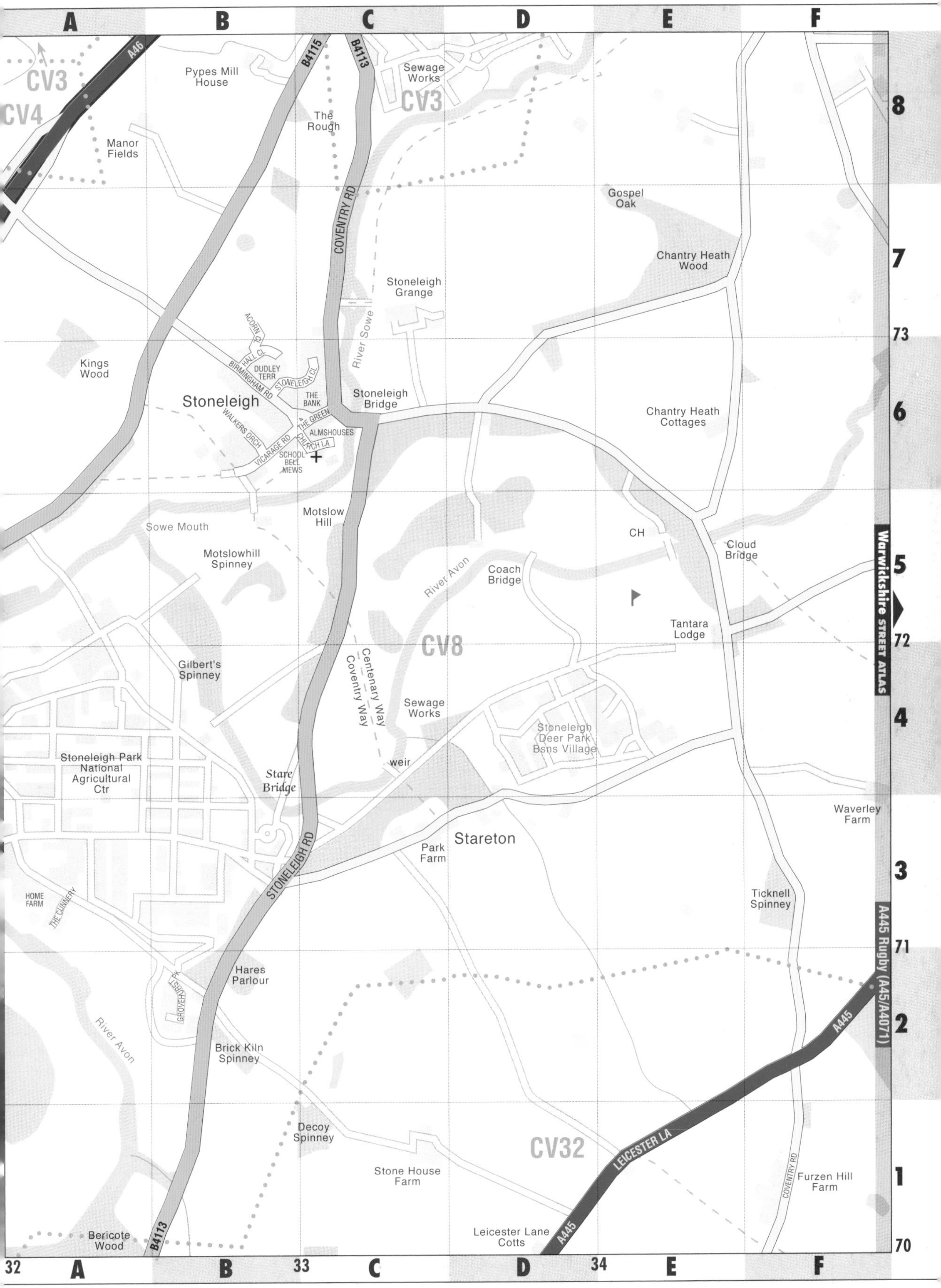
A
B
C
D
E
F
8
7
73
6
5
72
4
3
71
2
1
70
32
33
34
CV3
CV4
A46
B4115
B4113
Pypes Mill House
Sewage Works
The Rough
Manor Fields
Gospel Oak
Chantry Heath Wood
COVENTRY RD
Stoneleigh Grange
River Sowe
Kings Wood
ACORN CL
HALL CL
DUDLEY TERR
BIRMINGHAM RD
STONELEIGH CL
THE BANK
Stoneleigh
Stoneleigh Bridge
Chantry Heath Cottages
WALKERS ORCH
THE GREEN
ALMSHOUSES
CHURCH LA
VICARAGE RD
SCHOOL BELL MEWS
Motslow Hill
Sowe Mouth
CH
Cloud Bridge
Motslowhill Spinney
Coach Bridge
River Avon
Warwickshire STREET ATLAS
Tantara Lodge
CV8
Gilbert's Spinney
Centenary Way
Coventry Way
Sewage Works
Stoneleigh Deer Park Bsns Village
Stoneleigh Park National Agricultural Ctr
weir
Stare Bridge
Waverley Farm
Stareton
Park Farm
STONELEIGH RD
HOME FARM
THE GUNNERY
Ticknell Spinney
A445 Rugby (A45/A4071)
Hares Parlour
GROVEHURST PK
River Avon
A445
Brick Kiln Spinney
Decoy Spinney
CV32
LEICESTER LA
Stone House Farm
COVENTRY RD
Furzen Hill Farm
Bericote Wood
B4113
Leicester Lane Cotts
A445

157

136

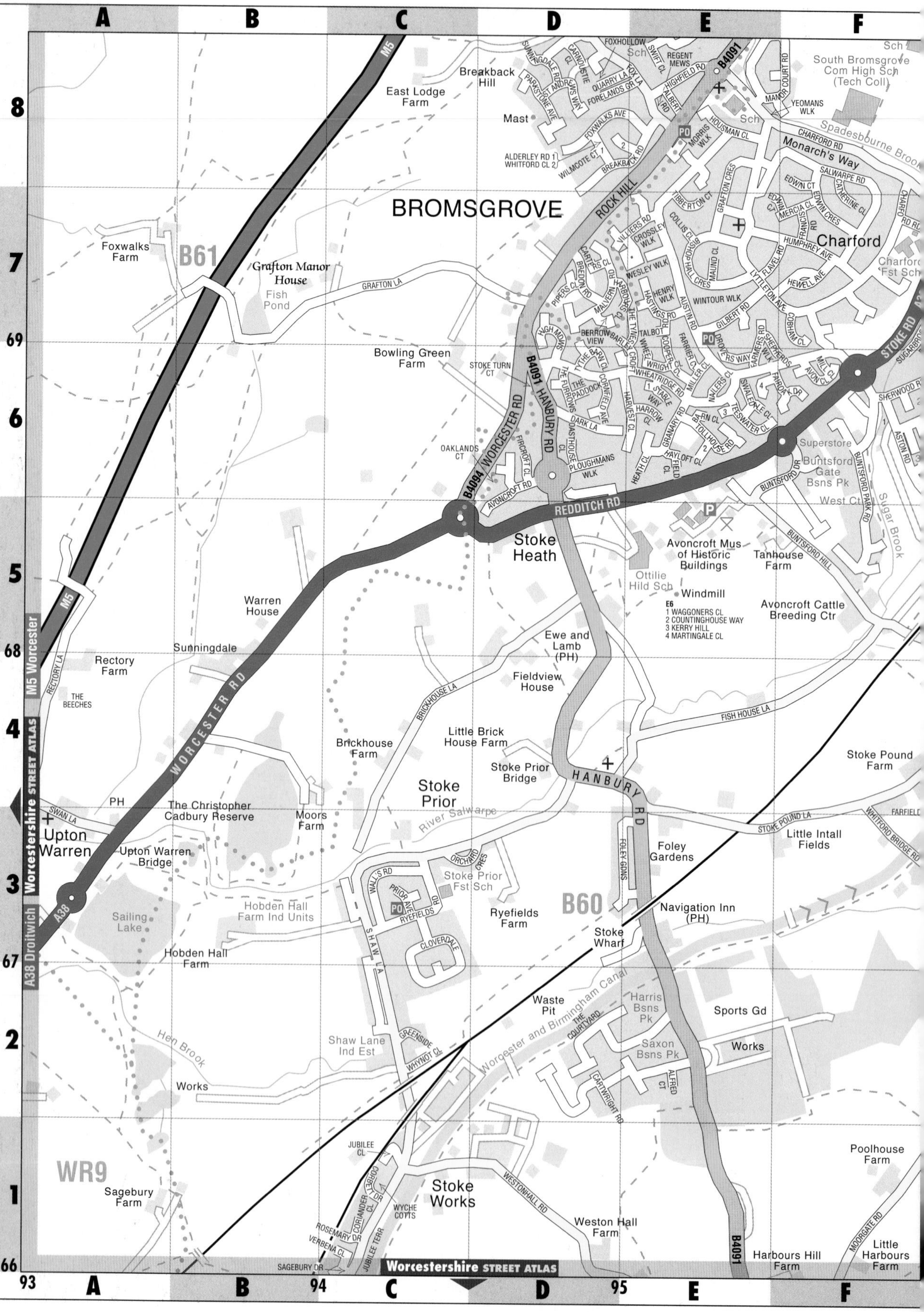
A
B
C
D
E
F
8
7
69
6
5
68
4
3
67
2
1
66
93
94
95
BROMSGROVE
Breakback Hill
East Lodge Farm
Mast
South Bromsgrove Com High Sch (Tech Coll)
Sch
FOXHOLLOW
REGENT MEWS
HIGHFIELD RD
B4091
YEOMANS WLK
MANOR COURT RD
HOUSMAN CL
MORRIS WLK
CHARFORD RD
Spadesbourne Brook
Monarch's Way
SALWARPE RD
EDWIN CT
CATHERINE CL
ALDERLEY RD 1
WHITFORD CL 2
FOXWALKS AVE
BREAKBACK RD
WILMCOTE CT
ROCK HILL
QUARRY LA
FORELANDS GR
ST ANDREWS WAY
PARKSTONE AVE
SUNNINGDALE RD
CARNOUSTIE CL
SWIFT CL
FOX LA
ALBERT RD
TIBBERTON CT
GRAFTON CRES
COLLIS CL
BISHOP HALL CRES
MAUND CL
MERCIA CL
FRANCIS RD
EDWIN CRES
HUMPHREY AVE
Charford
Charford Fst Sch
CHARFORD RD
FLAVEL RD
HEWELL AVE
LYTTLETON AVE
COBHAM CL
Foxwalks Farm
B61
Grafton Manor House
Fish Pond
GRAFTON LA
VILLIERS RD
CROSSLEY WLK
WESLEY WALK
HENRY WLK
HASTINGS RD
WINTOUR WLK
GILBERT RD
AUSTIN RD
PIPERS CL
MALVERN RD
HARBOUR CL
BERROW VIEW
TALBOT RD
COOPER CL
FARRIER CL
DROVERS WAY
FARMERS RD
SHEPHERDS CL
HIGH MDWS
THE TYNES
Bowling Green Farm
STOKE TURN CT
B4091 HANBURY RD
WORCESTER RD
THE FURROWS
THE PADDOCK
CORNFIELD AVE
DARK LA
HARVEST CL
WHEATRIDGE RD
HARROW CL
GRANARY RD
MILLER CL
NAILERS CL
SWALEDALE CL
TESWATER CL
TOLLHOUSE RD
HAYLOFT CL
HEATH CL
FIRCROFT CL
OAKLANDS CT
OASTHOUSE CL
PLOUGHMANS WLK
AVONCROFT RD
B4094
REDDITCH RD
STOKE RD
MILL CL
AVON CL
SUGARBROOK
SHERWOOD RD
ASTON RD
Superstore
Buntsford Gate Bsns Pk
BUNTSFORD DR
BUNTSFORD PARK RD
West Ct
Sugar Brook
BUNTSFORD HILL
Stoke Heath
Avoncroft Mus of Historic Buildings
Ottilie Hild Sch
Windmill
Tanhouse Farm
Avoncroft Cattle Breeding Ctr
E6
1 WAGGONERS CL
2 COUNTINGHOUSE WAY
3 KERRY HILL
4 MARTINGALE CL
Warren House
M5
M5 Worcester
Sunningdale
Rectory Farm
RECTORY LA
THE BEECHES
Ewe and Lamb (PH)
Fieldview House
BRICKHOUSE LA
FISH HOUSE LA
Little Brick House Farm
Brickhouse Farm
WORCESTER RD
Stoke Prior Bridge
HANBURY RD
Stoke Pound Farm
Stoke Prior
River Salwarpe
PH
SWAN LA
Upton Warren
The Christopher Cadbury Reserve
Moors Farm
STOKE POUND LA
Little Intall Fields
WHITFORD BRIDGE RD
FARFIELD
Foley Gardens
FOLEY GDNS
Upton Warren Bridge
WALL'S RD
ORCHARD CRES
Stoke Prior Fst Sch
PRIOR AVE
RYEFIELDS RD
Ryefields Farm
B60
Navigation Inn (PH)
Stoke Wharf
A38
A38 Droitwich
Sailing Lake
Hobden Hall Farm Ind Units
SHAW LA
CLOVERDALE
Hobden Hall Farm
Waste Pit
Worcester and Birmingham Canal
Harris Bsns Pk
THE COURTYARD
Sports Gd
Saxon Bsns Pk
Works
Hen Brook
Shaw Lane Ind Est
GREENSIDE
WHYNOT CL
CARTWRIGHT RD
ALFRED CT
Works
JUBILEE CL
Poolhouse Farm
WR9
Sagebury Farm
CORBETT DR
CORIANDER CL
WYCHE COTTS
Stoke Works
WESTONHALL RD
Weston Hall Farm
ROSEMARY DR
VERBENA CL
JUBILEE TERR
SAGEBURY DR
B4091
Harbours Hill Farm
MOORGATE RD
Little Harbours Farm
Worcestershire STREET ATLAS

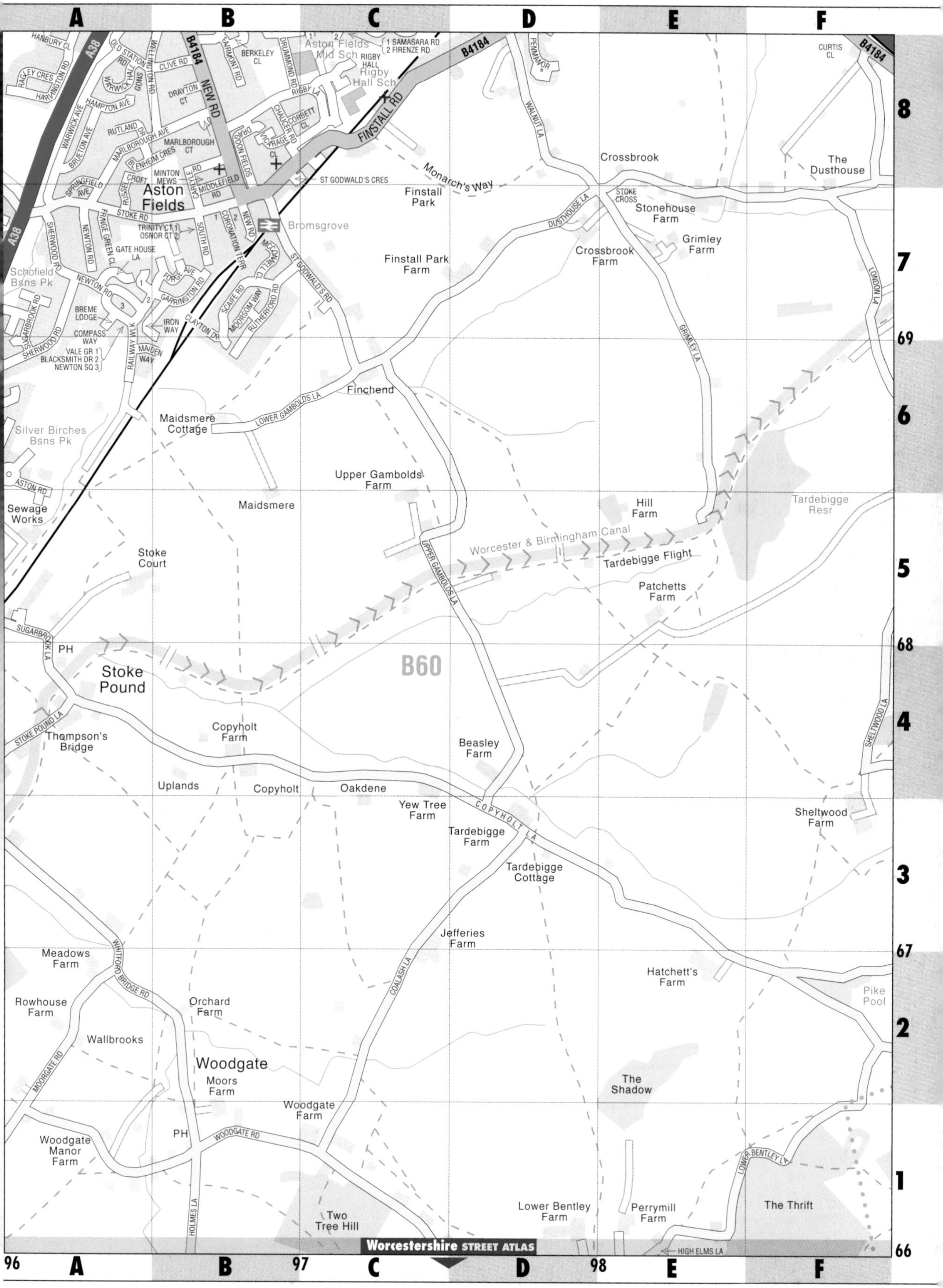
A
B
C
D
E
F
8
7
69
6
5
68
4
3
67
2
1
66
96
97
98
Aston Fields
Aston Fields Mid Sch
Rigby Hall Sch
Bromsgrove
Schofield Bsns Pk
Silver Birches Bsns Pk
Sewage Works
Finstall Park
Finstall Park Farm
Finchend
Monarch's Way
Crossbrook
Crossbrook Farm
Stonehouse Farm
Grimley Farm
The Dusthouse
Maidsmere Cottage
Maidsmere
Upper Gambolds Farm
Hill Farm
Tardebigge Resr
Worcester & Birmingham Canal
Tardebigge Flight
Patchetts Farm
Stoke Court
Stoke Pound
PH
B60
Thompson's Bridge
Copyholt Farm
Beasley Farm
Uplands
Copyholt
Oakdene
Yew Tree Farm
Tardebigge Farm
Tardebigge Cottage
Sheltwood Farm
Jefferies Farm
Meadows Farm
Hatchett's Farm
Pike Pool
Rowhouse Farm
Orchard Farm
Wallbrooks
Woodgate
Moors Farm
Woodgate Farm
The Shadow
Woodgate Manor Farm
Two Tree Hill
Lower Bentley Farm
Perrymill Farm
The Thrift
A38
B4184
NEW RD
FINSTALL RD
ST GODWALD'S CRES
STOKE RD
ST GODWALD'S RD
LOWER GAMBOLDS LA
DUSTHOUSE LA
STOKE CROSS
GRIMLEY LA
LONDON LA
WALNUT LA
UPPER GAMBOLDS LA
SUGARBROOK LA
STOKE POUND LA
COPYHOLT LA
SHELTWOOD LA
WHITFORD BRIDGE RD
COALASH LA
MOORGATE RD
WOODGATE RD
HOLMES LA
LOWER BENTLEY LA
HIGH ELMS LA
CURTIS CL
ASTON RD
1 SAMASARA RD
2 FIRENZE RD
TRINITY CT 1
OSNOR CT 2
VALE GR 1
BLACKSMITH DR 2
NEWTON SQ 3

151
138

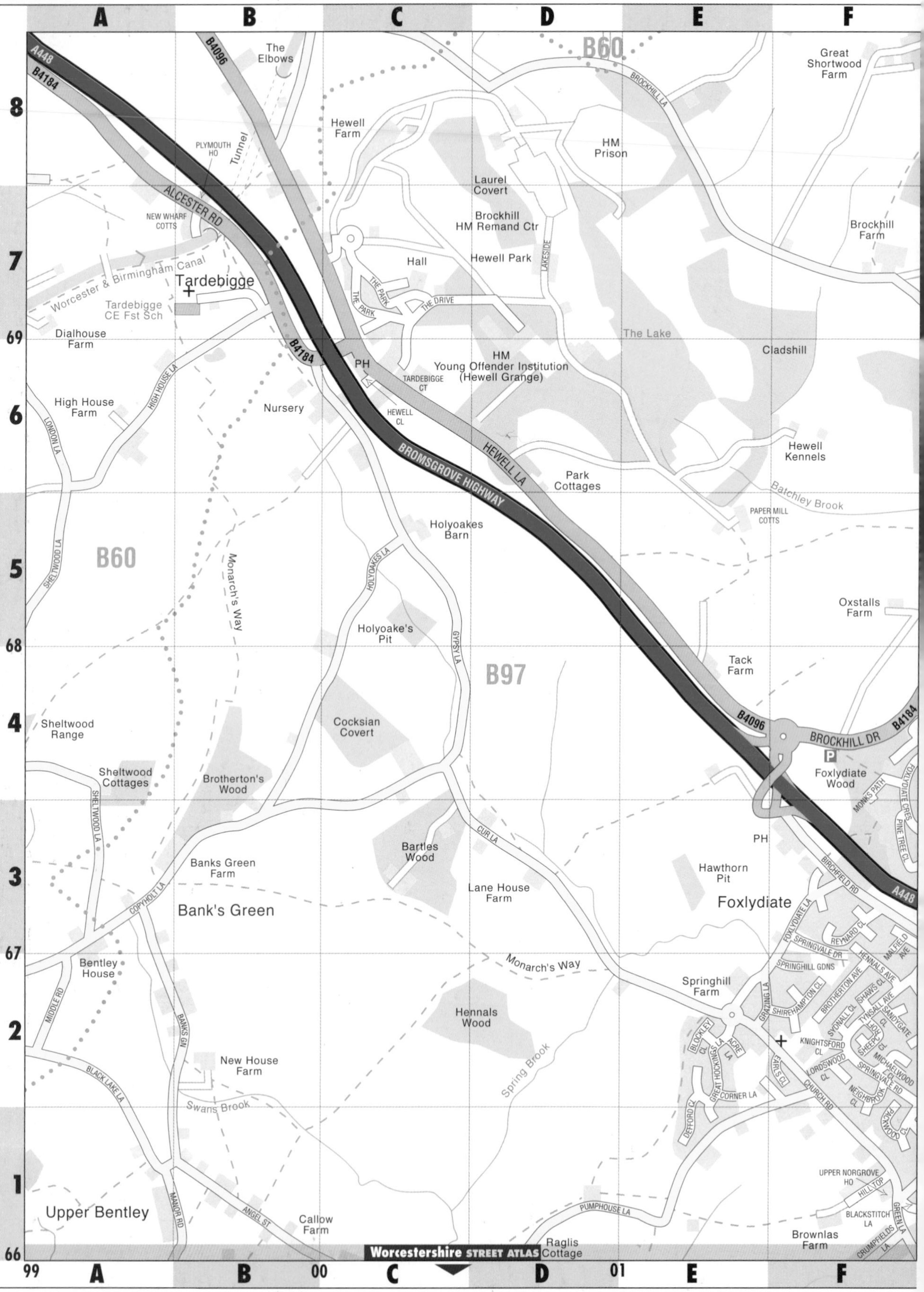
A
B
C
D
E
F
8
7
69
6
5
68
4
3
67
2
1
66
99
00
01
A448
B4184
B4096
The Elbows
B60
BROCKHILL LA
Great Shortwood Farm
Hewell Farm
HM Prison
PLYMOUTH HO
Tunnel
Laurel Covert
ALCESTER RD
NEW WHARF COTTS
Brockhill HM Remand Ctr
Brockhill Farm
Worcester & Birmingham Canal
Hall
Hewell Park
LAKESIDE
Tardebigge
THE PARK
THE DRIVE
Tardebigge CE Fst Sch
Dialhouse Farm
The Lake
Cladshill
HM Young Offender Institution (Hewell Grange)
PH
TARDEBIGGE CT
HIGH HOUSE LA
High House Farm
Nursery
HEWELL CL
LONDON LA
BROMSGROVE HIGHWAY
HEWELL LA
Hewell Kennels
Park Cottages
Batchley Brook
PAPER MILL COTTS
Holyoakes Barn
HOLYOAKES LA
SHELTWOOD LA
Monarch's Way
Oxstalls Farm
Holyoake's Pit
GYPSY LA
B97
Tack Farm
Sheltwood Range
Cocksian Covert
BROCKHILL DR
P
Foxlydiate Wood
Sheltwood Cottages
Brotherton's Wood
MONKS PATH
FOXLYDIATE CRES
PINE TREE CL
Bartles Wood
CUR LA
Banks Green Farm
Hawthorn Pit
BIRCHFIELD RD
Lane House Farm
COPYHOLT LA
Bank's Green
Foxlydiate
FOXLYDIATE LA
REYNARD CL
SPRINGVALE DR
MALFIELD AVE
HENNALS AVE
Bentley House
SPRINGHILL GDNS
BROTHERTON AVE
Springhill Farm
SHAWS CL
MIDDLE RD
GRAZING LA
SHIREHAMPTON CL
TYNSALL AVE
SANDYGATE CL
SYDNALL CL
Hennals Wood
KNIGHTSFORD CL
BANKS GN
BLOCKLEY CL
ACRE LA
SHEEPCOTE
LORDSWOOD CL
MICHAELWOOD CL
New House Farm
Spring Brook
BLACK LAKE LA
EARLS CL
HOCKINGS
SPRINGVALE RD
GREAT HOCKINGS LA
CORNER LA
NEIGHBROOK CL
CHURCH RD
Swans Brook
DEFFORD CL
PACKWOOD CL
UPPER NORGROVE HO
HILL TOP
GREEN LA
BLACKSTITCH LA
PUMPHOUSE LA
Upper Bentley
MANOR RD
ANGEL ST
Callow Farm
Raglis Cottage
Brownlas Farm
CRUMPFIELDS LA

151

139
154

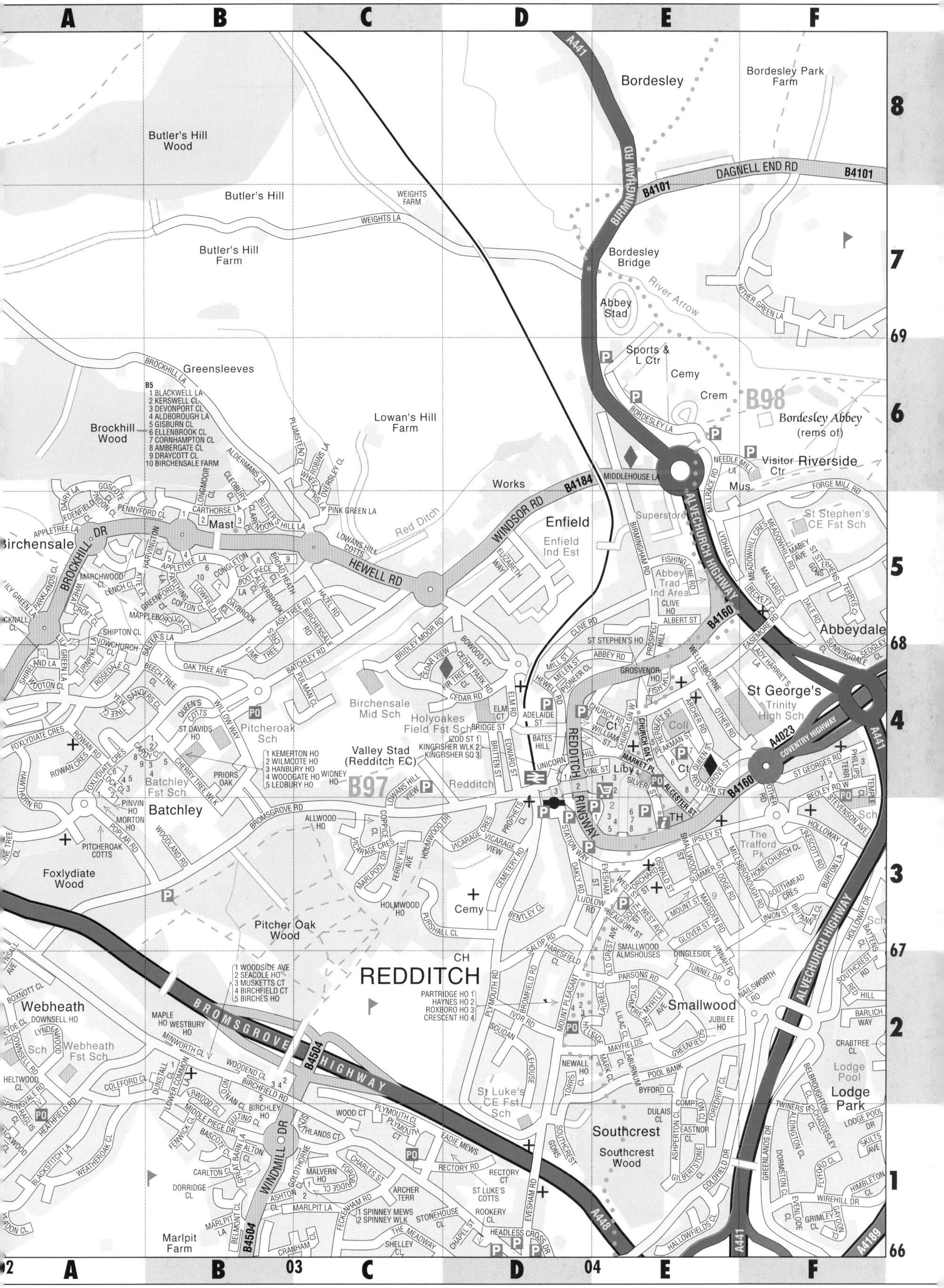

158
154

A4
1 CLADSWORTH HO
2 RADFORD HO
3 FOXLYDIATE MEWS
4 ABBERTON HO
5 HADZOR HO
6 WEETHLEY HO
7 STRETTON HO
8 RAGLEY HO
9 ELMLEY HO

E3
1 CLARKE ST
2 Kingfisher Sh Ctr
3 EVESHAM SQ
4 PARK WLK
5 GEORGE WLK
6 WALFORD WLK
7 MILWARD SQ
8 EVESHAM MEWS
9 Tudor Bsns Ctr

E4
1 WORCESTER SQ
2 EVESHAM WLK
3 NEW WLK
4 MARKET WLK
5 SMALLWOOD ARCH
6 WELLINGTON ST
7 VICTORIA ST
8 SOUTH EAST QUADRANT

F4
1 GRANGE CT
2 GRANGE RD
3 ST GEORGE'S GDNS

153
140

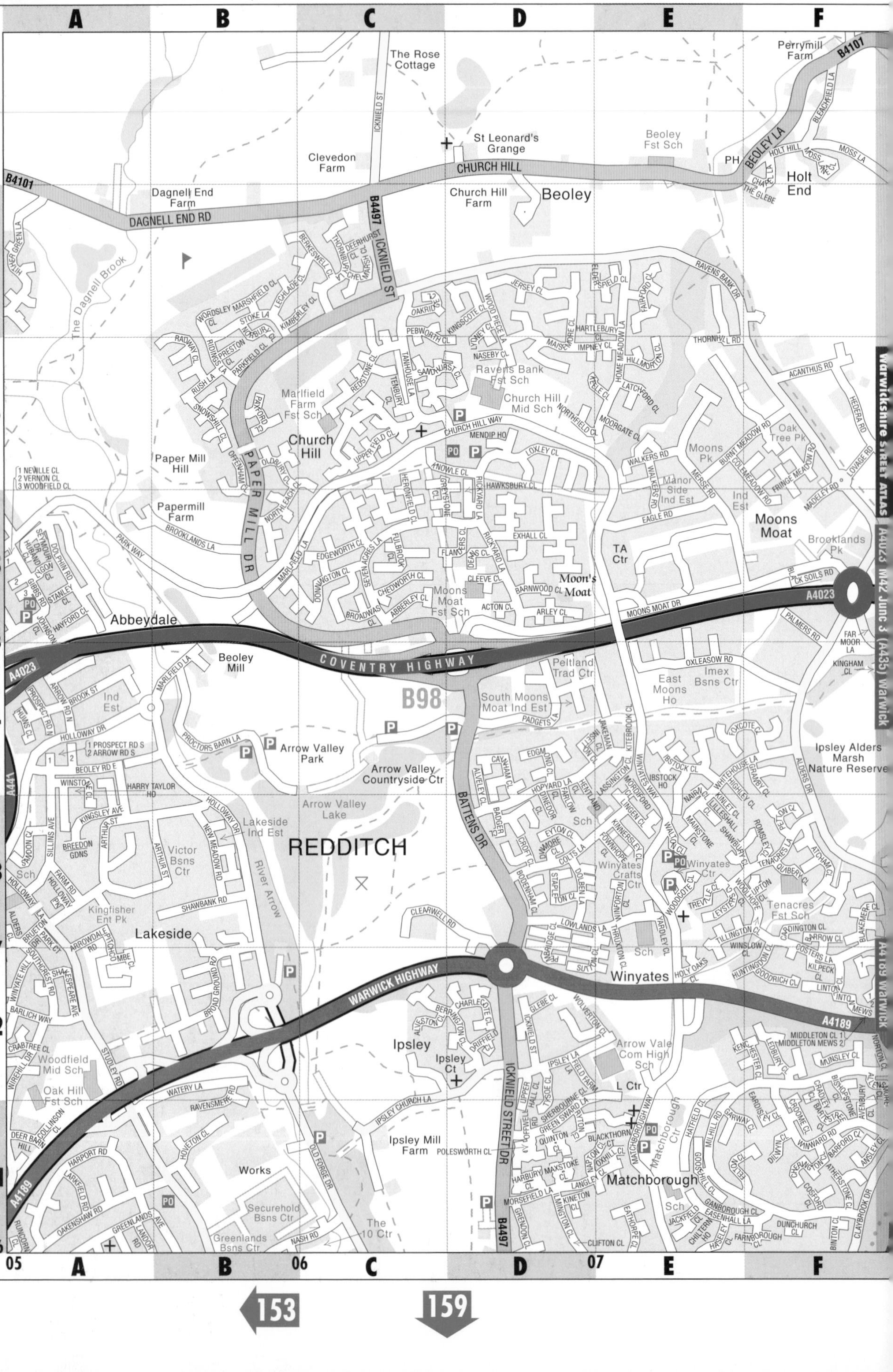

153
159

147
156

160
156

E1
1 NEWSHOLME CL
2 ADDINGHAM CL
3 WATSON CL
4 RYLSTONE WAY
5 KILDWICK WAY

F1
1 HETTON CL
2 BUCKDEN CL
3 LEYBURN CL
4 ARNCLIFFE WAY
5 HUDDISDON CL
6 PHILLIPPES RD

155
148

155
161

D1
1 THE GRANGE MEWS
2 CONISTON CT
3 GUNNERY TERR
4 CROSS RD
5 PERCY TERR

E1
1 MILVERTON CRES
2 MILVERTON LODGE
3 MILVERTON CRES W
4 HENRY TANDAY CT
5 VODENA CT
6 GULISTAN CT
7 STUART CT
8 UPPER GROVE ST
9 GROVE ST

F1
1 BEAUCHAMP CT
2 GROSVENOR CT
3 LUNN POLY HO
4 POWERS CT
5 WATERLOO PL
6 CLARENCE TERR
7 CLARENCE HO
8 KILWORTH HO
9 THE CORNER HO
10 WINDSOR PL
11 BEDFORD ST
12 GUY PL W
13 GUY PL E
14 OXFORD PL
15 CHANDOS CT
16 OXFORD ROW
17 WHITEHEADS CT
18 Royal Priors
19 ALVESTON PL
20 KENILWORTH ST
21 KIMMOND CT
22 GLADSTONE CT

F2
1 CLEVELAND CT
2 ARLINGTON CT
3 RIPLINGHAM
4 WHITE ROSE HO
5 ARLINGTON MEWS
6 WOOTTON CT
7 FININGS CT
8 PEMBROKE CT
9 BINSWOOD CT
10 ENGLAND HO
11 SAUNDERS HO
12 OAKFIELD HO
13 NORWOOD HO
14 BINSWOOD MANS
15 DORMER HO

149

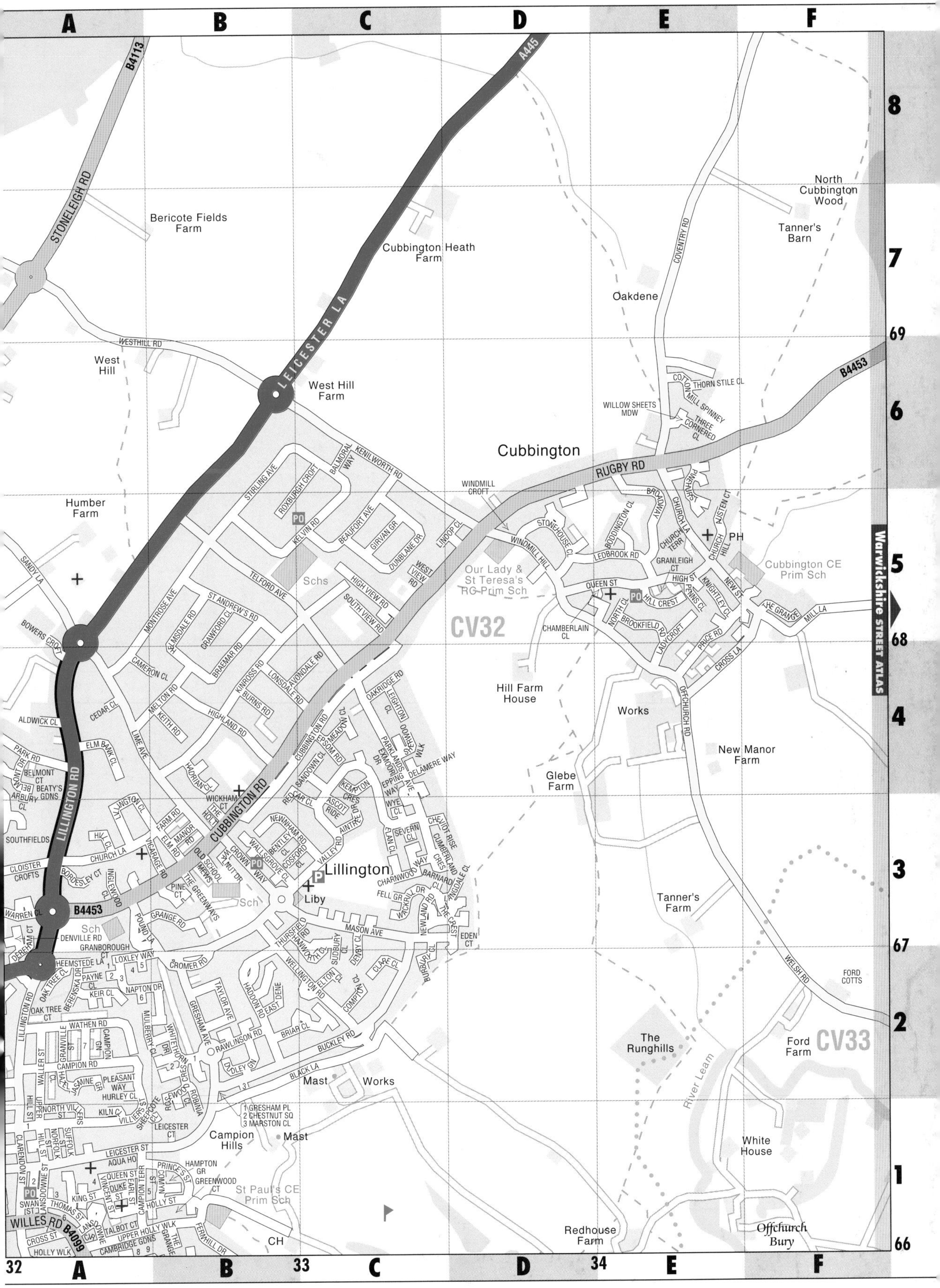

A1
1 LOWER VILLIERS ST
2 LANSDOWNE RD
3 KENNEDY SQ
4 ST PAUL'S SQ
5 MERCHANTS CT
6 LANSDOWNE CRES
7 WILLIAM THOMAS HO
8 HANOVER GDNS
9 WHITTLE CT

A2
1 ACORN CT
2 STOCKTON GR
3 WHITACRE RD
4 CHARLES WATSON CT
5 SHUCKBURGH GR
6 HELLIDON CL
7 BROWNLOW ST

162

153

A
B
C
D
E
F
REDDITCH
Downsell Wood
Morton Stanley Park
Callow Hill
Walkwood Coppice
Walkwood
Windmill La
Headless Cross
The Vaynor Fst Sch
Mid Sch
Oakenshaw Wood
Superstore
Oakenshaw
The Harry Taylor Fst Sch
Crabbs Cross
THE RAN-TAN
Hunt End Ind Est
Hunt End
St Augustine's RC High Sch
Stonepits Copse
Weavers Hill
White House
Lanehouse Farm
Lovelyne Farm
Chapel House Farm
Upper Huntend Farm
Thickwithey Brook
Monarch's Way
Slough Farm
The Moors
New Coppice
Dagtail End
Eastern Hill
Eastern Hill Farm
Foxpits
Wixon Brook
Astwood Hill Farm
The Wren's Nest Farm
Yew Tree House
Astwood Bank Fst Sch
Ridgeway Trad Est
Sambourne Lane Farm
Hole Farm
Astwood Court
Sewage Works
Doebank House
Astwood Bank
B4504
B97
B98
B96
A441
A448
A4189
B4092
BROMSGROVE HIGHWAY
WARWICK HIGHWAY
ALCESTER HIGHWAY
ROUGH HILL DR
THE SLOUGH
EVESHAM RD
WINDMILL DR
FECKENHAM RD
ASTWOOD LA
CROFTS LA
POPLARS LA
BLAZE LA
DARK LA
SAMBOURNE LA
JILL LA
DAGTAIL LA
EASTERN HILL
CHURCH RD
1 BRAMBLE HO
2 BIRCH HO
3 WILLOWBUD HO
4 MAPLE HO
5 SYCAMORE HO
6 BEECH HO
7 ALDER CARR CL
1 EASTWOOD CT
2 DEWSBURY CL
3 POST OFFICE WLK
4 NEW RD
BROOKHAMPTON CL 1
ALDERMINSTER CL 2
Worcestershire STREET ATLAS
A441 Alcester (A422)
02
03
04
62
63
64
65
1
2
3
4
5
6
7
8

154

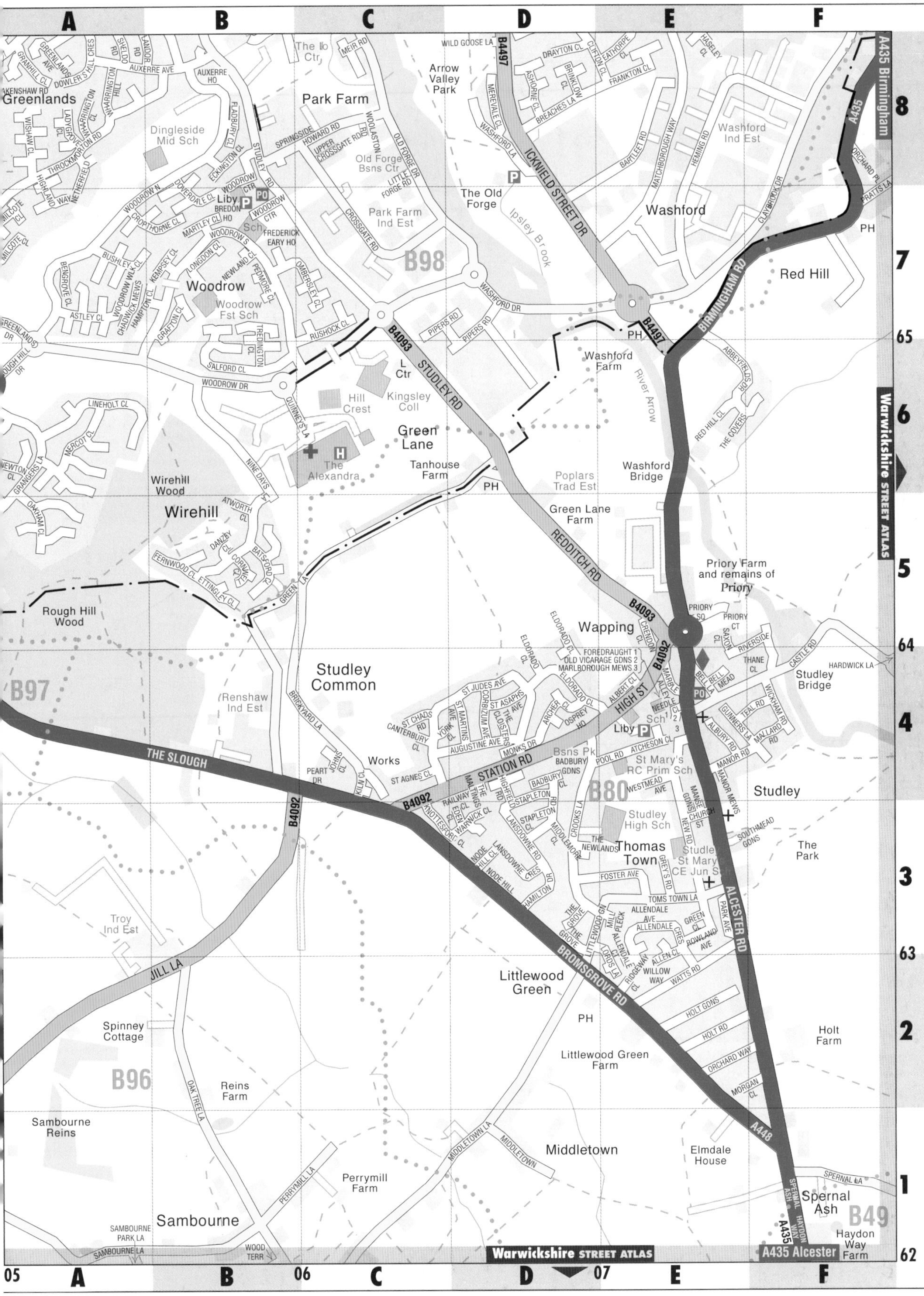
A
B
C
D
E
F
8
7
65
6
5
64
4
3
63
2
1
62
05
06
07
Greenlands
Dingleside Mid Sch
The Io Ctr
Park Farm
Arrow Valley Park
Old Forge Bsns Ctr
Park Farm Ind Est
The Old Forge
Ipsley Brook
Washford
Washford Ind Est
Red Hill
PH
A435 Birmingham
Woodrow
Woodrow Fst Sch
Liby
PO
Sch
B98
B4093
STUDLEY RD
ICKNIELD STREET DR
B4497
BIRMINGHAM RD
Washford Farm
River Arrow
L Ctr
Hill Crest
Kingsley Coll
Green Lane
The Alexandra
H
Tanhouse Farm
Poplars Trad Est
Washford Bridge
Green Lane Farm
Wirehill Wood
Wirehill
REDDITCH RD
Priory Farm and remains of Priory
Rough Hill Wood
Wapping
B4092
HIGH ST
Studley Common
Renshaw Ind Est
B97
THE SLOUGH
Works
STATION RD
Bsns Pk
St Mary's RC Prim Sch
B80
Studley High Sch
Thomas Town
Studley St Mary's CE Jun Sch
Studley
Studley Bridge
The Park
ALCESTER RD
Troy Ind Est
JILL LA
Littlewood Green
BROMSGROVE RD
PH
Littlewood Green Farm
Holt Farm
Spinney Cottage
B96
Reins Farm
Sambourne Reins
Middletown
Elmdale House
A448
Perrymill Farm
Sambourne
Sperna Ash
B49
Haydon Way Farm
A435
A435 Alcester
Warwickshire STREET ATLAS

155

E6
1 GERRARD ST
2 ALMSHOUSES
3 EASTGATE MEWS
4 EASTGATE HO
5 NEVILLE CT
6 CASTLE MEWS
7 MARKS MEWS
8 TIBBITS CT
9 THE WOOLPACK
10 WESTGATE HO
11 PUCKERINGS LA
12 LEYCESTER PL
13 LEYCESTER CT

F7
1 ALEXANDER CT
2 COACH HOUSE MEWS
3 BARTLETT CL
4 ST JOHN'S CT
5 CASTLEGATE MEWS
6 AVERY CT
7 FAIRFAX CT
8 BROOKE MEWS
9 GOODWAY CT
10 PRIORY WLK
11 CROSS ST
12 YEOMANRY CL
13 GREVILLE HO

F8
1 PEMBROKE CL
2 ARUNDEL CL
3 CORNWALL CL
4 CROSS FIELDS RD
5 MULBERRY DR
6 ROWAN DR
7 GAVESTON CL

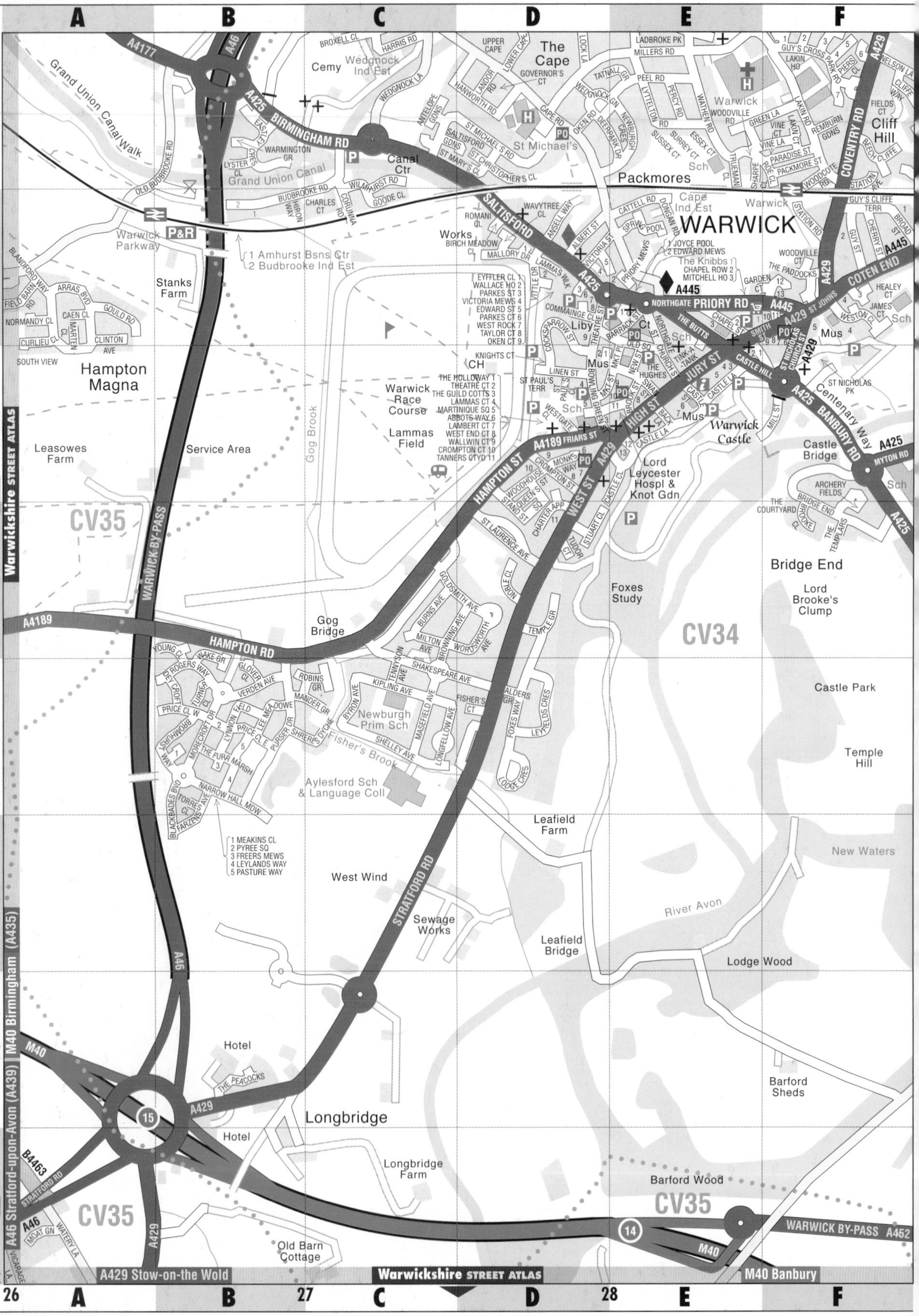

B8
1 CHARLES CT
2 ST EDITH'S HO
3 ST EDITH'S GN
4 WHITTINGTON CL
5 PACKWOOD MEWS
6 HERALDS CT

D8
1 WESTGROVE TERR
2 CROSS RD
3 THE CEDARS MEWS
4 PENDINE CT
5 GOODWAY HO
6 BEECH HO
7 OAK HO
8 BROOKLANDS HO
9 LEAM SIDE HO
10 SOUTHBANK HO
11 WILLOW HO
12 ALDER HO

E8
1 WOODBINE ST
2 WOODBINE COTTS
3 NEW BROOK ST
4 SOMERS PL
5 PORTLAND PL W
6 RIVERSDALE
7 CEDAR HO

F7
1 CHURCH WLK
2 SMITH ST
3 BATH PL
4 ABBOTTS ST
5 VICTORIA COLONNADE

156

F8
1 EUSTON SQ
2 ROSEFIELD ST
3 ROSEFIELD WLK
4 ROSEFIELD PL
5 BEDFORD PL
6 Regency Arc

162

F8
7 ST PETER'S RD
8 CARLTON HO
9 PORTLAND CT
10 PORTLAND MEWS
11 CHURCHILL HO
12 WINDSOR CT
13 CHAPEL CT
14 Royal Priors
15 SATCHWELL CT
16 SATCHWELL WLK
17 DENBY BLDGS
18 KENILWORTH ST

162

F5
1 YEW TREE CT
2 GINKGO WLK
3 CONIFER GR
4 SPRUCE GR
5 SILVER BIRCH GR
6 WYCH ELM DR
7 BONNIKSEN CL
8 LOCKHEED CL

F6
1 PHILIP CT
2 FRANCES HAVERGAL CL
3 PRINCE REGENT CT
4 FETHERSTON CT
5 TATCHBROOK CT
6 CHARLES GARDNER RD
7 MARKET CNR

A6
1 SOUTHBOROUGH TERR
2 GROVE PL
3 PRINCE REGENT CT
4 LISLE CT
5 DUGDALE CT
6 RADCLIFFE GDNS
7 AYLESFORD CT
8 BEAUMONT CT
9 CHRISTINE LEDGER SQ
10 ST GEORGE'S RD
11 CHARLES GARDNER RD
12 MAURICE MEAD CT
13 ST JOHN'S TERR

161

A6
14 CHARLES CT

A7
1 CHURCH TERR
2 CLINTON ST
3 GLOUCESTER ST
4 REGENT PL
5 CHAPEL ST
6 PACKINGTON PL

157

A7
7 RUSSELL CT
8 ASH LAWN HO
9 WARNEFORD MEWS
10 BAXTER CT
11 Victoria Bsns Ctr
12 MOSS ST
13 NEILSTON ST
14 CUMMING ST
15 Althorpe Ind Est
16 TOWER ST
17 WEST ST

B7
1 SQUIRHILL PL
2 WILLES CT
3 JEPHSON PL
4 TRAFFORD LODGE
5 CLIFTON CT
6 RICHMOND CT
7 NORTHCOTE ST
8 SOUTHLANDS
9 RUSHMORE TERR

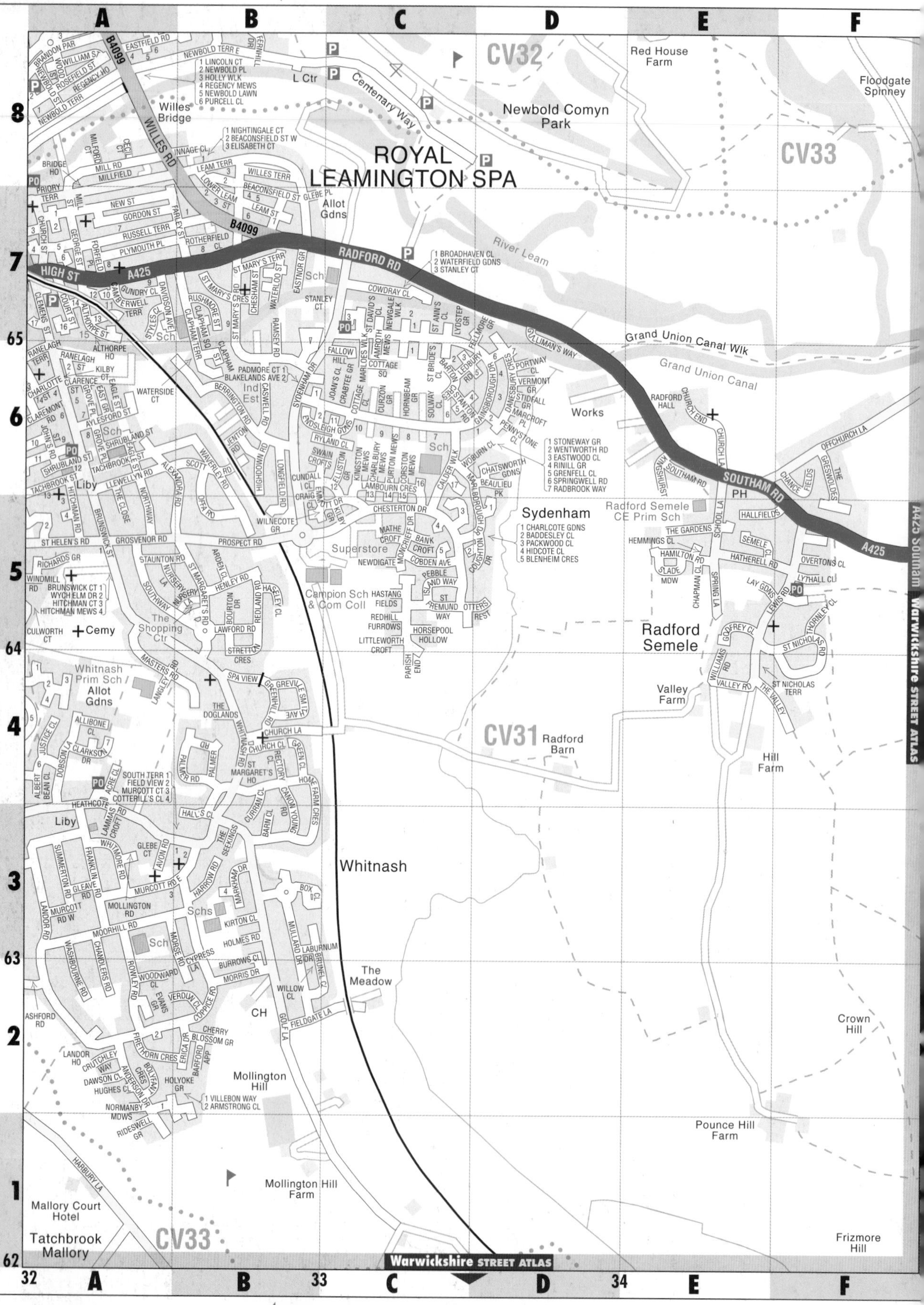
A
B
C
D
E
F
CV32
Red House Farm
Floodgate Spinney
Newbold Comyn Park
CV33
ROYAL LEAMINGTON SPA
Willes Bridge
WILLES RD
B4099
Centenary Way
L Ctr
Allot Gdns
River Leam
RADFORD RD
HIGH ST
A425
Grand Union Canal Wlk
Grand Union Canal
Works
RADFORD HALL
SOUTHAM RD
PH
OFFCHURCH LA
Radford Semele CE Prim Sch
Sydenham
Superstore
Campion Sch & Com Coll
Radford Semele
A425 Southam
Warwickshire STREET ATLAS
Valley Farm
CV31
Radford Barn
Hill Farm
Liby
Cemy
The Shopping Ctr
Whitnash Prim Sch
Allot Gdns
Whitnash
The Meadow
Crown Hill
Schs
Sch
CH
Mollington Hill
Pounce Hill Farm
HARBURY LA
Mollington Hill Farm
Mallory Court Hotel
Tatchbrook Mallory
CV33
Frizmore Hill
Warwickshire STREET ATLAS
8
7
65
6
5
64
4
3
63
2
1
62
32
33
34

A4
1 FRANCIS GIBBS GDNS
2 MONTGOMERY RD
3 COBHAM GN
4 COX'S ORCHARD
5 ANTONY GARDNER CRES
6 WEILERWIST DR
7 OSBOURNE CT

161

C6
1 FRESHWATER GR
2 ST GOVAN'S CL
3 CONINGSBY CL
4 NEWBURY CL
5 WESTON CL
6 BLADON WLK
7 HARVEST HILL CL
8 FOXDALE WLK
9 MAYFIELD CL
10 LYNWOOD WLK
11 RANDOLPH CL
12 BISSET CRES
13 BURFORD MEWS
14 STANDLAKE MEWS
15 WAVERTON MEWS
16 ALDERTON MEWS
17 LONGLEAT GR

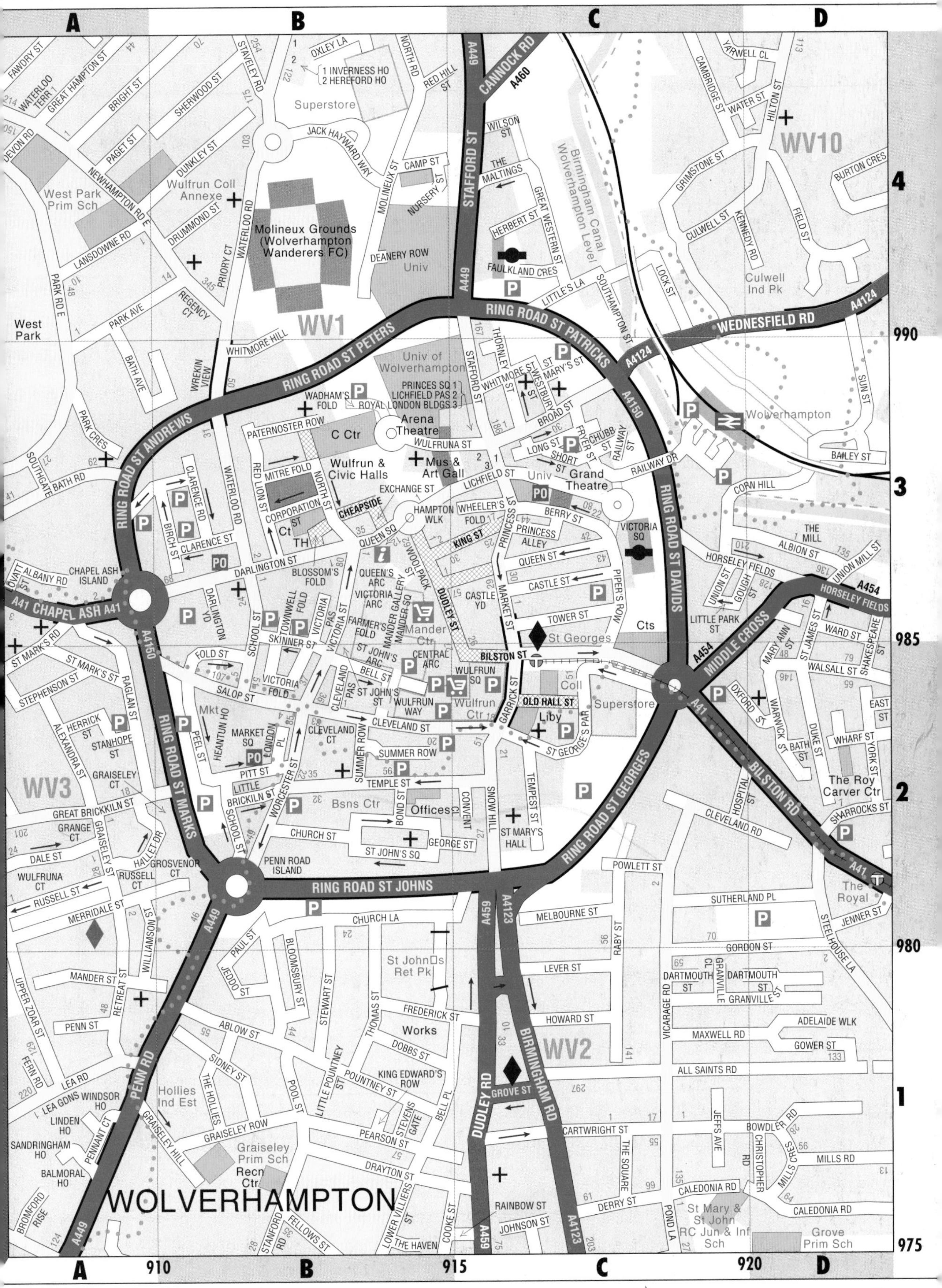
WOLVERHAMPTON
WV1
WV2
WV3
WV10
RING ROAD ST PETERS
RING ROAD ST PATRICKS
RING ROAD ST DAVIDS
RING ROAD ST GEORGES
RING ROAD ST JOHNS
RING ROAD ST MARKS
RING ROAD ST ANDREWS
Molineux Grounds (Wolverhampton Wanderers FC)
Univ of Wolverhampton
Arena Theatre
Wulfrun & Civic Halls
Mus & Art Gall
Grand Theatre
Mander Ctr
Wulfrun Ctr
St Georges
Superstore
Wolverhampton
Culwell Ind Pk
West Park Prim Sch
Wulfrun Coll Annexe
Hollies Ind Est
Graiseley Prim Sch
St John's Ret Pk
St Mary & St John RC Jun & Inf Sch
Grove Prim Sch
The Roy Carver Ctr
The Royal
Birmingham Canal Wolverhampton Level
WEDNESFIELD RD
STAFFORD ST
CANNOCK RD
PENN RD
DUDLEY RD
BIRMINGHAM RD
BILSTON RD
A41 CHAPEL ASH
HORSELEY FIELDS
MIDDLE CROSS

One-way streets

66
66

House numbers
HIGH ST

Scale: 7 inches to 1 mile
0 110 yards 220 yards
0 125 m 250 m

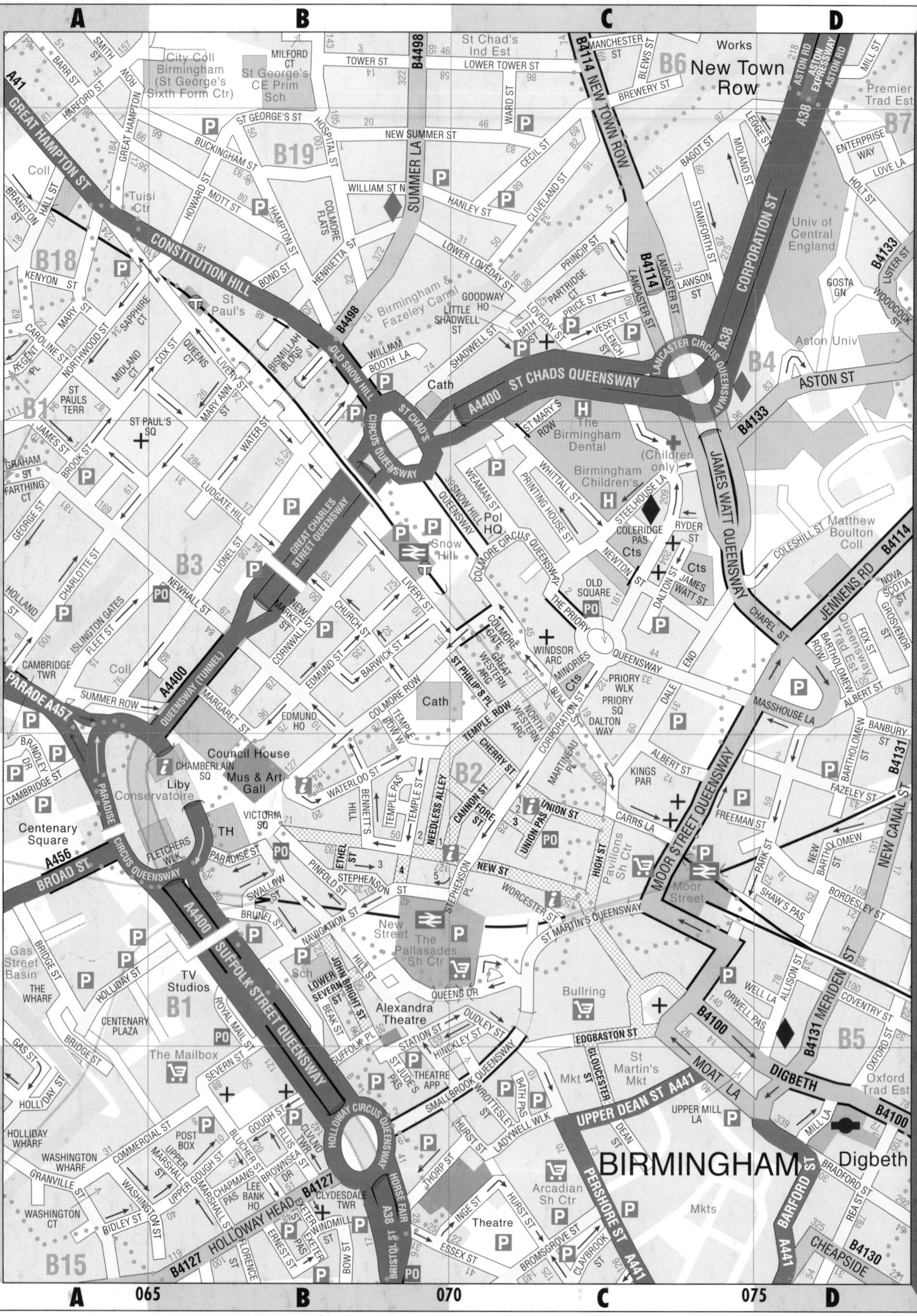

B2
1 NEWTON CHAMBERS
2 ESSEX HO
3 PICCADILLY ARC
4 LOWER TEMPLE ST
5 BURLINGTON ARC

C2
1 CITY ARC
2 VICTORIA HO
3 WARWICK PAS

Scale: 7 inches to 1 mile
110 yards 220 yards
125 m 250 m

One-way streets

113

C4
1 LITTLE CHURCH ST
2 RUSSELL ST N
3 JOSEPH HALPIN HO
4 PEARL HYDE HO

113

D4
1 SACKVILLE HO
2 WILLIAM THOMSON HO

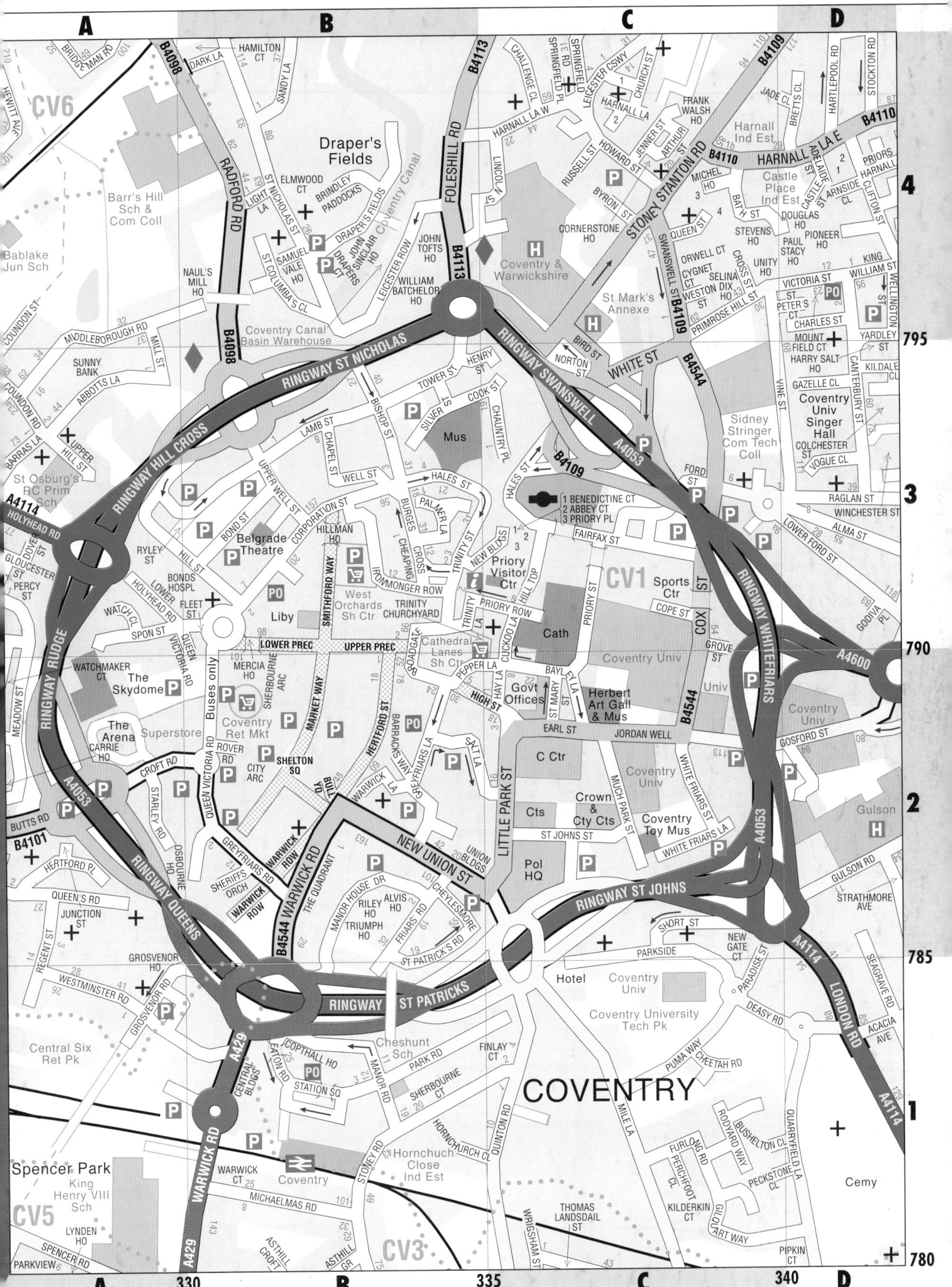

113
133
113

Index

Place name May be abbreviated on the map

Location number Present when a number indicates the place's position in a crowded area of mapping

Locality, town or village Shown when more than one place has the same name

Postcode district District for the indexed place

Page and grid square Page number and grid reference for the standard mapping

Church Rd 6 Beckenham BR2..........53 C6

Public and commercial buildings are highlighted in magenta **Places of interest** are highlighted in blue with a star★

Abbreviations used in the index

Acad	Academy	Comm	Common	Gd	Ground	L	Leisure	Prom	Promenade
App	Approach	Cott	Cottage	Gdn	Garden	La	Lane	Rd	Road
Arc	Arcade	Cres	Crescent	Gn	Green	Liby	Library	Recn	Recreation
Ave	Avenue	Cswy	Causeway	Gr	Grove	Mdw	Meadow	Ret	Retail
Bglw	Bungalow	Ct	Court	H	Hall	Meml	Memorial	Sh	Shopping
Bldg	Building	Ctr	Centre	Ho	House	Mkt	Market	Sq	Square
Bsns, Bus	Business	Ctry	Country	Hospl	Hospital	Mus	Museum	St	Street
Bvd	Boulevard	Cty	County	HQ	Headquarters	Orch	Orchard	Sta	Station
Cath	Cathedral	Dr	Drive	Hts	Heights	Pal	Palace	Terr	Terrace
Cir	Circus	Dro	Drove	Ind	Industrial	Par	Parade	TH	Town Hall
Cl	Close	Ed	Education	Inst	Institute	Pas	Passage	Univ	University
Cnr	Corner	Emb	Embankment	Int	International	Pk	Park	Wk, Wlk	Walk
Coll	College	Est	Estate	Intc	Interchange	Pl	Place	Wr	Water
Com	Community	Ex	Exhibition	Junc	Junction	Prec	Precinct	Yd	Yard

Index of localities, towns and villages

A

Abbeydale 153 F5
Abbey Fields 147 E5
Acock's Green 88 B3
Aggborough 116 F4
Alderman's Green 96 B3
Aldersley 24 F7
Aldridge 30 A6
Allen End 47 F6
Allesley 111 B7
All Saints 66 A5
Alum Rock 68 B3
Alvechurch 139 B6
Alvecote 22 D6
Amblecote 80 F7
Amington 22 B4
Ansty 97 D4
Arrowfield Top 123 B1
Ash Green 95 C6
Ashmore Lake 27 B4
Ashmore Park 27 A8
Ashow 148 E1
Aspley Heath 141 D2
Aston 67 A7
Aston Fields 151 B7
Aston Flamville 76 E6
Aston New Town 66 F6
Astwood Bank 158 F1
Attleborough 73 F2

B

Bacon's End 70 B4
Baddesley Clinton 145 B6
Baginton 133 F2
Balls Hill 42 B1
Balsall Common 130 A7
Balsall Heath 86 D6
Balsall Street 129 E6
Bank's Green 152 A3
Banners Gate 45 B4
Baptist End 62 C6
Barnacle 97 B6
Barnettbrook 118 D5
Barnt Green 138 A7
Barr Common 30 C3
Barrow Hill 61 C7
Barston 109 B1
Bartley Green 102 D7
Barwell 71 F7
Batchley 153 B3
Bateman's Green 124 F6
Batmans Hill 40 F2
Baylis Green 141 A1
Bearwood 65 A2
Beausale 146 C2
Bedworth 78 B1
Bedworth Heath 77 E1
Beech Lanes 84 E6
Beechwood 131 A6
Beechwood Gardens 132 E8
Belbroughton 119 E7
Belgrave 21 E1
Bell End 120 C7
Belle Vale 82 E5
Bell Green
 Coventry 114 B8
 Hollywood 124 B5
Bell Heath 120 E8
Bentley 27 E2
Bentley Heath 127 E5
Benton Green 110 E3
Beoley 154 D7
Berkswell 110 D3
Bermuda 78 A8
Bescot 42 C6
Bickenhill 90 D1
Bilbrook 10 C4
Billesley 105 C6
Billesley Common 105 A5
Bilston 40 D4
Binley 134 E8
Binley Woods 135 C7
Birch Acre 140 D7
Birchen Coppice 116 B1
Birchensale 153 A5
Birches Green 57 A2
Birchfield 55 E1
Birchills 28 D3
Birchmoor 36 E8
Birmingham 164 C1
Bishopgate Green 113 D5
Bitterscote 21 A4
Black Bank 78 A1
Blackdown 156 F6
Blackfords 1 E2
Blackheath 63 B2
Black Lake 53 A7
Black Patch 65 D6
Blackwell 138 A5
Blakebrook 116 B6
Blakedown 98 C2
Blakeley Green 24 F8
Blakenall Heath 28 C8
Blakenhall 39 B7
Bloomfield 51 E7
Blossomfield 106 E2
Blowers Green 62 C7
Bluntington 118 E1
Boldmere 46 A1
Bolehall 21 D4
Boley Park 9 F7
Bonehill 20 E2
Bordesley
 Birmingham 67 B2
 Redditch 139 D1
Bordesley Green 67 E2
Bordesley Green East 68 B1
Borough Park 21 C8
Borrowcop Hill 9 C6
Bournbrook 86 A2
Bournes Green 119 C2
Bournheath 136 D8
Bournville 103 E7
Bowling Green 62 E2
Box Trees 127 B1
Brades Village 52 E1
Bradley 40 E3
Bradmore 38 E8
Bradnock's Marsh 109 D3
Bramcote 79 E6
Bramford 51 A7
Brandon 135 F5
Brandwood End 104 E4
Branson's Cross 141 C2
Breedon Cross 104 B6
Bridge End 160 F5
Bridgtown 4 E6
Brierley Hill 61 E2
Brinsford 11 D7
Bristnall Fields 64 B3
Broad Green 138 B1
Brockmoor 61 C3
Bromford 57 D1
Bromley 61 B5
Bromsgrove 136 E2
Brookfields 66 B4
Broome 99 A2
Broomhill 1 E4
Broom Hill 119 D3
Brownhills 16 B6
Brown's Green 54 F4
Brownshill Green 94 C2
Buckland End 69 A7
Buckpool 60 F2
Bulkington 79 B1
Bunker's Hill 40 E7
Burbage 76 B6
Burcot 137 E4
Burnt Tree 51 F3
Burntwood 7 C5
Burntwood Green 7 D6
Burton Green 131 C4
Burton Hastings 75 A1
Bushbury 11 E2

C

Caldmore 42 E8
California 84 F2
Callow Hill 158 A7
Calthorpe Fields 86 B8
Camp Hill 72 E5
Canley 132 C7
Canley Gardens 132 E8
Cannock 1 D2
Cannon Hill 86 D4
Cape Hill 65 B4
Carol Green 130 F7
Carpenter's Hill 140 F1
Carroway Head 33 C4
Castle Bromwich 69 D8
Castlecroft 38 B8
Castle Green 147 D6
Castle Vale 58 B3
Catchems Corner 130 E5
Catherine Cross 41 C6
Catherine de Barnes 108 B6
Catshill
 Bromsgrove 137 A8
 Brownhills 16 A6
Causeway Green 63 F2
Cawney Hill 62 F8
Chadsmoor 1 F4
Chad Valley 85 F7
Chadwick End 145 B7
Chapel End 72 B7
Chapel Fields 112 E3
Chapel Green
 Coventry 93 B7
 Willenhall 27 B2
Chapman's Hill 121 B8
Charford 150 F7
Charlemont 53 D8
Chase Terrace 6 E8
Chasetown 6 F6
Chelmsley Wood 70 C2
Cheslyn Hay 4 C3
Chessetts Wood 144 D8
Chesterfield 17 E8
Chester Road 57 B6
Cheswick Green 126 E4
Cheylesmore 133 E7
Chilvers Coton 73 A1
Christ Church 9 A8
Churchbridge 4 F4
Church End 114 C4
Churchfield 53 E6
Church Hill
 Birmingham 55 B1
 Redditch 154 C6
 Wednesbury 41 E4
Churchill 98 C3
Cinder Hill 39 F1
Claregate 24 E6
Clayhanger 15 D6
Clent 99 F3
Cliff 35 C1
Cliff Hill 160 F8
Coalpit Field 78 D1
Coal Pool 28 F5
Cobley Hill 138 E4
Cockshut Hill 89 A8
Codsall 10 A3
Coft Common 122 F6
Cole End 70 E8
Colehall 69 B5
Coleshill 70 F6
Coleshill Heath 90 C8
Collycroft 78 A5
Colton Hills 39 B3
Comberton 117 B5
Compton 24 D2
Coombeswood 83 C7
Cooper's Bank 50 C1
Copt Heath 108 A1
Corley 94 B7
Corley Ash 94 A8
Corley Moor 93 E6
Cornets End 110 B6
Coseley 40 C1
Coton 20 C6
Coton Green 20 F8
Cotteridge 103 E5
Coundon 112 F6
Coundon Green 112 E8
County Bridge 27 C2
Coven Heath 11 C6
Coven Lawn 11 A8
Coventry 165 C1
Crabbs Cross 158 E6
Crackley 148 B7
Cradley 82 D6
Cradley Heath 82 D8
Cubbington 157 D6
Curborough 3 D5
Curdworth 59 B6

D

Dagtail End 158 E3
Daisy Bank 40 C2
Darby End 62 E4
Darby's Hill 63 B8
Darlaston 41 E7
Darlaston Green 41 E8

Darley Green 144 B8
Darnford 9 F6
Daw End 29 C5
Dayhouse Bank 101 A1
Deepfields 40 B2
Deritend 67 A1
Dibdale 50 F3
Dickens Heath 126 B6
Digbeth 164 D1
Dixon's Green 62 D7
Dodford 136 A7
Doe Bank 46 C7
Dordale 119 E1
Dordon 36 F6
Dorridge 127 E3
Dosthill 35 C5
Drakes Cross 125 A6
Draper's Fields 165 B4
Drayton 119 B4
Drayton Bassett 34 D5
Dudley 51 D2
Dudley Port 52 B3
Dudley's Fields 28 A8
Dudley Wood 62 C2
Dunstall Hill 25 C5

E

Eachway 121 F6
Earlsdon 113 A1
Earlswood 126 B1
Eastcote 108 E3
Eastern Hill 158 F3
Eaves Green 92 F2
Edgbaston 86 A6
Edge Hill 36 C2
Edgwick 113 F8
Edial 7 F6
Elmdon Heath 107 E7
Elmhurst 3 A5
Elston Hall 25 D8
Emscote 161 B8
Enfield 153 D5
Erdington 57 A4
Essington 12 F3
Ettingshall 40 A5
Ettingshall Park 39 D3
Eve Hill 51 B2
Exhall 96 B7

F

Fairfield 120 D3
Falcon Lodge 47 A6
Fallings Heath 41 F5
Fallings Park 25 E5
Fazeley 34 E8
Featherstone 12 C7
Fen End 129 E3
Finchfield 38 D8
Finham 133 C3
Finstall 137 D1
Fishley 14 C4
Flint's Green 111 B5
Foleshill 96 A2
Foley Park 116 C2
Footherley 17 E3
Fordbridge 70 A3
Fordhouses 11 D2
Forshaw Heath 141 C7
Four Ashes 127 D3
Four Oaks
Meriden 110 C6
Sutton Coldfield 31 F3
Four Oaks Park 46 A8
Foxford 96 A5
Foxlydiate 152 F3
Franche 116 B8
Frankley
Birmingham 102 B2
Frankley Green 102 B5
Frankley Green 102 A5
Frankley Hill 101 F3
Freasley 36 C4
Freezeland 40 B6
Friar Park 42 D2
Fulford Heath 125 D2

G

Galley Common 72 A5
Gannow Green 101 C1
Garrett's Green 69 B1
Gibbet Hill 132 E2
Gib Heath 66 A6
Gilbert's Green 141 E3
Gilbertstone 88 F6
Gillway 21 B8
Gilson 59 D1
Glascote Heath 21 F2
Glebe Farm 69 A4
Golds Green 52 E8
Goldthorn Hill 39 A5
Goldthorn Park 39 C5
Goodyers End 95 D8
Gornalwood 50 C2
Gorstey Ley 7 C7
Goscote 28 F8
Gosford Green 113 F2
Gospel End Village 50 A8
Gospel Oak 41 B1
Grace Mary Estate 63 C8
Gravelly Hill 56 E1
Great Barr 43 F2
Great Bridge 52 E6
Great Heath 113 E6
Great Wyrley 5 B3
Greenhill 117 A8
Green Lane
Coventry 133 B5
Redditch 159 C6
Green Lanes 40 C7
Greenleighs 39 C3
Greet 87 E5
Griff 78 B6
Griffin's Hill 103 D8
Grimes Hill 125 B4
Grove End 47 F3
Grove Vale 43 C1
Gunstone 10 A6
Guns Village 53 B4
Guy's Cliffe 156 A2

H

Habberley 116 A6
Hackman's Gate 98 F1
Haden Cross 83 A8
Hagley 99 D6
Halesowen 83 D4
Hall End 36 F5
Hall Flat 137 C7
Hall Green
Bilston 40 E2
Birmingham 106 A7
Coventry 96 A3
Wednesbury 42 C1
Hammerwich 7 D4
Hampton-in-Arden 109 B8
Hampton Magna 160 A6
Hamstead 54 E6
Handsworth 54 C1
Handsworth Wood 55 B3
Harborne 85 B6
Harden 28 E7
Hardwick 30 E3
Hartle 119 F6
Harts Green 85 A5
Hartshill 72 B8
Hart's Hill 61 E5
Harvest Hill 93 E2
Harvills Hawthorn 52 F7
Harvington 118 B2
Hasbury 82 E3
Haseley Knob 146 A3
Hasluck's Green 105 F2
Hateley Heath 53 C7
Hawkesbury 96 C5
Hawkes End 94 B2
Hawkesley 123 F8
Hawks Green 2 B1
Hawne 83 A6
Hayley Green 82 C1
Hay Mills 88 B6
Headless Cross 158 D8
Headley Heath 124 C6
Heathcote 161 D3
Heath End
Bloxwich 15 A1
Nuneaton 72 E2
Heath Green 140 F3
Heath Hayes 2 F1
Heath Town 26 A4
Hednesford 2 D5
Henley Green 114 D8
Highbridge 15 B6
Highfields
Burntwood 6 F4
Coseley 40 C3
Highgate 86 F7
High Heath 15 D2
Highter's Heath 105 B2
High Town 2 A5
Hill 32 A4
Hill and Cakemore 83 D7
Hillfield 107 A1
Hillfields 113 E4
Hill Hook 31 E6
Hillpool 118 E5
Hill Top
Cannock 2 C4
Nuneaton 73 C1
Oldbury 64 C3
West Bromwich 53 A7
Hill Wood 32 C5
Hill Wooton 156 C6
Hilton 17 A8
Himley 49 B3
Hinckley 75 B8
Hints 19 D3
Hobble End 14 B7
Hockley
Birmingham 66 B5
Coventry 111 C4
Tamworth 35 E5
Hockley Heath 143 D6
Hodgehill 68 D6
Holbrooks 95 C3
Holly Bank 16 B3
Hollyberry End 93 C4
Hollycroft 71 A1
Holly Hall 61 E7
Hollyhurst 96 F8
Hollywood 125 B8
Holt End 154 F8
Holy Cross 99 E2
Homer Hill 82 B6
Honiley 146 D5
Hoobrook 116 F2
Hopwas 20 B7
Hopwood 123 B3
Horeston Grange 73 F5
Horseley Heath 52 D5
Hunnington 101 B8
Hunt End 158 C5
Huntington 1 D7
Hunts Green 48 C7
Hurcott 117 C8
Hurst Green 83 F8
Hurst Hill 40 A1

I

Illey 101 E8
Illshaw Heath 126 E1
Inkford 124 F1
Ipsley 154 C2
Iverley 98 B7

K

Kate's Hill 62 E8
Kemps Green 143 A1
Kenilworth 148 D5
Keresley 94 F5
Keresley Newlands 95 B6
Kettlebrook 21 B3
Kidderminster 116 D4
Kineton Green 106 E8
King's Heath 104 F7
King's Hill 41 E4
Kingshurst 70 A5
King's Norton 103 E2
Kingstanding 45 A1
Kingswinford 60 F6
Kingswood 144 D3
King's Wood 104 D1
Kingswood Brook 144 E3
Kinwalsey 92 F7
Kitt's Green 69 C3
Kitwell 102 A7
Kixley Wharf 128 C7
Knowle 128 B6
Knowle Grove 128 B3

L

Ladyes Hills 148 A7
Ladymoor 40 D4
Ladywood 66 A2
Lady Wood 45 F8
Lakeside 154 B3
Lambert's End 53 B2
Landywood 14 A8
Lane Green 10 C3
Lane Head 27 D5
Lanesfield 39 E4
Laney Green 4 A3
Langley 64 A5
Langley Green 64 B3
Lapal 83 F3
Lapworth 143 E3
Lawns Wood 60 B2
Lea Hall 69 A2
Leamonsley 8 E7
Leamore 28 B6
Lee Bank 86 D8
Leek Wootton 155 F7
Leighswood 30 A7
Leyfields 20 F7
Ley Hill 32 B1
Lichfield 9 D5
Lickey End 137 C6
Lifford 104 B5
Lillington 157 C3
Lime Tree Park 112 A2
Linthurst 138 A6
Little Aston 31 B4
Little Bloxwich 14 E3
Little Bromwich 67 F2
Little Hay 18 C1
Little Heath 95 F1
Little London 27 A3
Little Packington 91 C6
Littlewood 4 E4
Littlewood Green 159 D2
Littleworth 2 E4
Little Wyrley 14 E8
Lode Heath 107 C6
Lodge Green 92 E3
Lodge Hill 85 B2
Lodge Park 153 F2
Londonderry 64 D4
London Fields 50 F2
Longbridge 160 C2
Longford 95 F4
Lower Bradley 41 A2
Lower Clent 99 D4
Lower Eastern Green 112 A3
Lower Gornal 50 E4
Lower Illey 101 D7
Lower Marlbrook 121 C1
Lower Penn 37 F4
Lower Stoke 114 A1
Lower Stonnall 17 A4
Low Hill 25 E7
Loxdale 41 A5
Lozells 66 C7
Lutley 82 C3
Lydiate Ash 121 C3
Lye 81 E6
Lyndon End 89 A5
Lyndon Green 89 A7

M

Madeley Heath 120 E7
Major's Green 125 D8
Maney 46 C4
Manor House 96 C2
March End 26 E5
Market End 77 D2
Marston Green 90 A8
Marston Jabbett 78 E5
Matchborough 154 E1
Mayer's Green 53 E3
Meer End 130 D1
Mere Green 32 B3
Meriden 92 D1
Merridale 24 E2
Merry Hill
Brierley Hill 61 E3
Smethwick 65 D5
Wolverhampton 38 D7
Mesty Croft 42 C2
Middle 4 A4
Middle Bickenhill 91 A3
Middle Stoke 114 A3
Middleton 34 A1
Middletown 159 D1
Mile Oak 20 D1
Mill End 148 A6
Millfields 40 C5
Mill Green
Aldridge 30 F7
Cannock 4 F8
Milverton 156 D2
Minworth 58 C5
Minworth Greaves 58 D6
Monks Park 95 C1
Monkspath 127 B5
Monkspath Street 126 E6
Monmore Green 40 A8
Moons Moat 154 F5
Moor Green 86 D1
Moor Hall 32 D1
Moseley 86 F2
Moseley Village 26 C2
Mount Pleasant
Bedworth 78 B3
Coventry 115 B8
Tamworth 21 C1
Mousesweet 62 F3
Moxley 41 B3
Muckley Corner 8 A2
Mucklow Hill 83 D6
Mushroom Green 62 B1
Mustow Green 117 F1

N

Neachells 26 D3
Neal's Green 95 D5
Nechells 67 D8
Nechells Green 67 A4
Nether Stowe 3 C3
Netherton 62 C4
Newbolds 26 A6
Newbridge 24 E3
New Cross 26 B6
New Dock 51 A1
New Invention 27 D8
New Oscott 45 D2
Newton 54 C8
Newtown 14 B6
New Town
Birmingham 66 C6
Brownhills 6 F2
Tipton 52 D4
New Town Row 164 C5
Nordley Hill 26 C6
Northfield 103 B4
Norton 80 D2
Norton Canes 5 F6
Norton East 6 A6
Norton Green 128 B2
Nuneaton 73 C6
Nurton 23 A3
Nuthurst 143 C4

O

Oakenshaw 158 E6
Oakham 63 A8
Ocker Hill 52 C8
Offmore Farm 117 A6
Oldbury 63 F6
Old Dock 62 B8
Old Fallings 25 F8
Oldfallow 1 D3
Old Hill 62 F1
Old Milverton 156 B3
Old Oscott 44 F2
Old Perton 23 B2
Old Swinford 81 A2
Oldwich Lane 129 C1
Olton 88 F1
Orton 37 F3
Outwoods 92 C5
Overend 82 E6
Over Green 47 F1
Oxbarn 38 E7
Oxley 25 B8

P

Packmores 160 E8
Packwood 144 A8
Packwood Gullet 127 E1
Palfrey 42 E7
Palmers Cross 24 D8
Paradise 113 F6
Parkes Hall 51 A6
Park Farm 159 C8
Parkfield 39 E5
Park Hill 148 C6
Park Village 25 F5
Pedmore 81 B1
Pelsall 15 B3
Pelsall Wood 14 F5
Pendeford 10 F2
Penn 38 E5
Penn Fields 38 F6
Pensett 61 C6
Pensnett 61 C6
Perry 55 E6
Perry Barr 55 B5
Perry Beeches 55 B8
Perry Common 56 C7
Perry Crofts 21 B7
Perryfields 136 E4
Perton 23 C4
Pheasey 44 C4
Piccadilly 35 F1
Pickford 111 E8
Pickford Green 111 C7
Pinkett's Booth 111 C8
Pinley 134 B7
Pinley Gdns 134 A8
Pipehill 8 C5
Pleck 42 C8
Plough Hill 72 A6
Polesworth 36 F8
Portobello 26 E1
Portway
Olbury 63 C6
Redditch 141 A5
Potter's Green 96 E1
Pouk Hill 28 A3
Priestfield 40 B7
Primrose Hill 62 C4
Princes End 51 E8
Priory 51 C3
Pype Hayes 57 D5

Q

Quarry Bank 82 A8
Quarry Hill 36 A7
Queslett 44 C2
Quinton 84 C5

R

Radford 113 B7
Radford Semele 162 E5
Reddicap Heath 46 F4
Redditch 153 C2
Rednal 122 C6
Reeves Green 131 A8
Ridgacre 84 D6
Riverside 153 F6
Romsley 101 A4
Romsley Hill 101 A2
Rood End 64 C6
Roseville 51 B8
Rotten Row 128 C3
Rotton Park 65 E3
Rough Hay 41 C7
Rough Hills 39 F6
Roughley 32 D3
Round's Green 63 E8
Rowington Green 145 A1
Rowley Regis 63 B3
Rowley's Green 95 E3
Rowney Green 139 E3
Royal Leamington Spa 156 D3
Rubery 122 B7
Ruiton 50 D5
Rumbush 125 E3
Rumer Hill 4 F7
Rushall 29 C6
Rushbrook 141 D3
Russell's Hall 61 E8
Ryecroft 28 E4
Ryton 79 D2
Ryton-on-Dunsmore 135 B2

S

St Chads 40 F7
St George's 153 F4
St Nicolas Park 74 A7
Salter Street 126 D2
Saltley 67 E4
Sambourne 159 B1
Sandfields 9 A5
Sandwell 65 A7
Sandyfields 50 B6
Scotlands 26 A7
Scott's Green 62 A7
Sedgley 50 F7
Seisdon 37 A2
Selly Hill 86 A2
Selly Oak 85 D1
Selly Park 86 A1
Shard End 69 D6
Sharmans Cross 106 E4
Sheldon 89 C5
Shelfield 15 C1
Shenley Fields 102 E7
Shenstone 18 A5
Shenstone Woodend 18 A1

Shepwell Green 27 C1
Shilton 97 F5
Shire Oak 16 A6
Shireoak Hill 16 B5
Shirley 106 C3
Shirley Heath 126 C7
Shirley Street 106 C2
Short Heath
Birmingham 56 E7
Willenhall 27 D6
Showell Green 87 B4
Shuttington 22 F7
Sidemoor 136 F4
Silver End 61 C2
Silver Street 124 F5
Sketchley 75 C6
Sketchley Hill 75 E7
Small Heath 87 D7
Smallwood 153 E2
Smethwick 65 A4
Snuff Hill 120 D1
Soho 65 C7
Solihull 107 D3
Solihull Lodge 105 E2
Southcrest 153 E1
South Yardley 88 D6
Spade Green 8 A8
Sparkbrook 87 B7
Sparkhill 87 D4
Spencer Park 165 A1
Spennells 117 A2
Spernal Ash 159 F1
Spon End 113 A3
Spring Bank 27 B3
Springfield
Bedworth 78 C2
Birmingham 105 E8
Rowley Regis 62 F5
Wolverhampton 25 E3
Springhill 16 E8
Spring Hill 38 C4
Springs Mire 62 A8
Spring Vale
Bilston 40 B4
Birmingham 67 B1
Stakenbridge 98 E3
Stambermill 81 C6
Stanklyn 117 D2
Staple Hill 137 C8
Stareton 149 D3
Stechford 68 E3
Stirchley 104 B7
Stivichall 133 D5
Stockfield 88 C5
Stockingford 72 C3
Stockland Green 56 C4
Stockwell End 24 D6
Stoke 114 C2
Stoke Aldermoor 134 B8
Stoke End 47 F7
Stoke Heath
Bromsgrove 150 D5
Coventry 114 A6
Stoke Park 114 A2
Stoke Pound 151 A4
Stoke Prior 150 C4
Stoke Works 150 C1
Stone 117 E2
Stonebridge 91 D3
Stone Cross 42 D1
Stoneleigh 149 B6
Stoney Hill 137 A2
Stonnall 16 E4
Stourbridge 80 D4
Stowe 3 C1
Stow Heath 40 B7
Stow Lawn 40 D8
Streetly 44 F8
Stubber's Green 29 E8
Studley 159 F4
Studley Common 159 C4
Summerford Place 26 F2
Summerhill 116 B5
Summer Hill 52 A8
Sutton Coldfield 46 D5
Sutton Farm 116 B4
Swan Village
Dudley 51 B6
West Bromwich 52 F4
Sydenham 162 D5

T

Tamworth 21 B3
Tanner's Green 125 B1
Tansley Hill 62 F7
Tanwood 119 B2
Tanworth-In-Arden 142 B2
Tardebigge 152 B7
Tat Bank 64 B6
Tatchbrook Mallory 162 A1
Temple Balsall 129 B5
Ten Acres 104 B8
Terry's Green 141 F7
Tettenhall 24 D5
Tettenhall Wood 24 C3
The Cape 160 D8
The Chuckery 29 A1
The Coppice 51 A7
The Delves 42 F5
The Flatts 41 E7
The Knowle 63 A4
The Leys 21 A5
The Lunt 41 A6
The Manor 27 A2
The Straits 50 A5
The Woods 42 C4
Thimble End 47 A1
Thomas Town 159 E3
Thornes 16 E3
Three Maypoles 126 A7
Tibbington 51 F7
Tidbury Green 125 E4
Tile Cross 69 E2
Tile Hill 111 E1
Tilehouse Green 127 F6
Tippity Green 63 B4
Tipton 51 F6
Tipton Green 51 D5
Titford 63 F4
Tividale 52 D3
Tollbar End 134 C4
Toll End 52 C6
Tower Hill 55 C6
Trescott 37 B7
Triangle 7 B4
Trueman's Heath 125 C7
Trysull 37 C1
Tudor Hill 46 B6
Turves Green 103 A1
Two Gates 35 D8
Tyburn 57 E3
Tyseley 88 A6

U

Uffmoor 82 E1
Ulverley Green 89 A1
Underhill 12 B2
Upper Bentley 152 A1
Upper Catshill 121 B2
Upper Eastern Green 111 D4
Upper Gornal 50 F6
Upper Landywood 13 E8
Upper Marlbrook 121 D2
Upper Stoke 114 B4
Upper Witton 56 B5
Upton Warren 150 A3

V

Vauxhall 67 B4
Vigo 15 F2

W

Wake Green 87 B1
Walker's Heath 104 B1
Walkwood 158 B6
Wall 8 D2
Wallbrook 51 D8
Wall Heath 60 B8
Wall Hill 94 A4
Wallington Heath 14 B2
Walmley 57 F8
Walsal End 109 A3
Walsall 28 B3
Walsall Wood 15 F4
Walsgrave on Sowe 115 B7
Walton Pool 100 A2
Wapping 159 E5
Ward End 68 A5
Waring's Green 142 D8
Warley Woods 84 E8
Warstock 105 C3
Warstone 13 C8
Warwick 160 E7
Washford 159 E7
Washwood Heath 67 E6
Water Orton 59 C3
Weatheroak Hill 124 B1
Weavers Hill 158 C4
Webheath 153 A2
Weddington 73 D7
Wedges Mills 4 B6
Wednesbury 41 D3
Wednesbury Oak 41 B1
Wednesfield 26 E6
Weeford 19 A4
Wellington Place 27 A4
Wells Green 89 B4
Weoley Castle 85 A1
Wergs 24 A6
West Bromwich 53 E3
West Chadsmoor 1 F5
West Coseley 51 B7
Westcroft 12 B3
West Hagley 99 A5
West Heath 123 B7
West Hill 2 B6
Weston in Arden 79 A3
West Smethwick 64 C7
Westwood Gardens 132 D8
Westwood Heath 131 E6
Whateley 35 F3
Whiteheath Gate 63 D4
Whitehouse Common 46 E7
Whitemoor 148 B5
Whitemore Park 95 C1
White Stitch 92 C3
Whitestone 79 B7
Whitlock's End 125 E6
Whitnash 162 C3
Whittleford 72 C5
Whoberley 112 D2
Wightwick 23 E1
Wildmoor 120 F4
Willenhall
Coventry 134 D6
Wolverhampton 27 B4
Wilncote 35 F8
Wilnecote 35 F8
Wimblebury 2 F3
Windmill End 62 E4
Windy Arbour 148 B3
Winson Green 65 F5
Winyates 154 E2
Wirehill 159 B5
Wishaw 48 B2
Withybed Green 138 F6
Withymoor Village 81 C8
Witton 56 A3
Wollaston 80 D6
Wollescote 81 E4
Wolston 135 F3
Wolverhampton 163 B1
Wombourne 49 B6
Woodcock Hill 102 F8
Woodcross 40 A2
Wood End
Coventry 96 C1
Tamworth 36 C1
Tanworth-in-Arden 141 F3
Wednesfield 26 D7
Woodgate
Birmingham 84 A1
Bromsgrove 151 B2
Woodgate Valley 84 C3
Wood Green 42 A5
Woodloes Park 155 D2
Woodrow
Kidderminster 118 D3
Redditch 159 B7
Woods Bank 41 B5
Woodsetton 50 E6
Woodshires Green 95 E5
Woodside 61 E6
Woodway Park 114 E8
Wootton Green 110 A1
Wordsley 60 E3
Worlds End 107 A6
World's End 84 D5
Worms Ash 136 C6
Wren's Nest 51 A4
Wroxall 145 E3
Wyken 114 D5
Wyken Green 114 C6
Wylde Green 46 C1
Wythall 125 B3
Wythall Green 124 E3

Y

Yardley 88 D8
Yardley Fields 68 D1
Yardley Wood 105 E5
Yew Tree
Balsall Common 130 A6
Wednesbury 43 B4
Yew Tree Hill 62 B4
Yieldingtree 118 F8

Index of streets, hospitals, industrial estates, railway stations, schools, shopping centres, universities and places of interest

10 Ctr The B98 154 C1
3b Bsns Village B21 65 D7

A

A1 Trad Est B66 65 A7
Aaron Ct B24 56 F3
Abberley Cl
Halesowen B63 82 F2
Redditch B98 154 C5
Abberley Ind Ctr B66 65 D5
Abberley Rd
Birmingham B68 84 B8
Dudley DY3 50 D4
Abberley St
Dudley DY2 62 C8
Smethwick B66 65 D5
Abberley B77 22 C2
Abberton Cl B63 83 C3
Abberton Ct B23 56 C2
Abberton Gr B90 127 B7
Abberton Ho 4 B97 153 A4
Abberton Way CV4 132 E3
Abbess Gr B25 68 E1
Abbey CE Inf Sch CV11 73 B5
Abbey Cl
Bromsgrove B60 137 C2
West Bromwich B71 53 C5
Abbey Cres
Halesowen B63 82 D4
Oldbury B68 64 D1
Abbey Ct
Coventry CV1 165 C3
Coventry,Pinley CV3 134 B6
Abbeydale Cl CV3 114 F2
Abbeydale Rd B31 103 A2
Abbey Dr WS3 15 A5
Abbey End CV8 147 F4
Abbeyfield Ho WV11 26 D5
Abbeyfield Rd
Birmingham B23 56 E8
Wolverhampton WV10 11 F4
Abbeyfields Dr B80 159 E6
Abbey Gate CV11 73 C4
Abbey Gate Sh Ctr CV11 73 C4
Abbey Gdns B67 64 E1
Abbey Gn CV11 73 B5
Abbey Hill CV8 147 F5
Abbey Ind Est CV2 114 F5
Abbey Inf Sch B67 64 E2
Abbey Jun Sch B67 64 E1
Abbey Mans 2 B24 57 B6
Abbey Prim Sch WS3 13 E2
Abbey RC Jun & Inf Sch The B23 57 A5
Abbey Rd
Birmingham B17 85 D5
Birmingham,Gravelly Hill B23 56 D2
Coventry CV3 134 A6
Dudley,Gornalwood DY3 50 C3
Dudley,Netherton DY2 62 D6
Halesowen B63 82 C4
Kidderminster DY11 116 A6
Redditch B97 153 E4
Smethwick B67 64 E1
Tamworth B77 21 D3
Abbey St N B18 66 A5
Abbey Sq WS3 13 E2
Abbey St
Birmingham B18 66 A5
Cannock WS12 2 B7
Dudley DY3 50 C3
Nuneaton CV11 73 B5
Abbey The CV8 147 F5
Abbey Trad Ind Area B97 153 E5
Abbey Way CV3 133 F6
Abbot Rd B63 100 C8
Abbotsbury Cl CV2 115 A4
Abbotsbury Way CV11 78 E7
Abbots Cl
Dorridge B93 128 A7
Walsall WS4 29 C6
Abbots Field WS11 1 E5
Abbotsford Ave B43 43 F2
Abbotsford Dr DY1 61 E7
Abbotsford Rd
Birmingham B11 87 C6
Lichfield WS14 9 E7
Nuneaton CV11 73 E1
Abbotsford Sch CV8 147 F6
Abbots Mews DY5 61 D1
Abbots Rd B14 104 E7
Abbots Way
Birmingham B18 66 B6
Warwick CV34 160 D6
Wolverhampton WV3 24 E1
Abbotts Gn LE10 75 F5
Abbotts La CV1 165 A3
Abbotts Pl WS3 14 D1
Abbotts Rd B24 56 F1
Abbotts St
4 Royal Leamington Spa CV31 161 F7
Walsall WS3 14 D2
Abbotts Wlk CV3 135 C7
Abdon Ave B29 103 C7
Abelia B77 21 F3
Abercorn Rd CV5 112 E2
Aberdeen Cl CV5 112 A5
Aberdeen Rd CV11 73 E1
Aberdeen St B18 65 E4
Aberford Cl WV12 27 D4
Abergavenny Wlk CV3 134 F6
Abigails Cl B26 89 B7
Abingdon Cl WV1 26 B2
Abingdon Rd
Birmingham B23 56 B7
Dudley DY2 62 D3
Walsall WS3 13 F2
Wolverhampton WV1 26 B2
Abingdon Way
Birmingham B35 58 A3
Nuneaton CV11 73 F7
Walsall WS3 13 F2
Ablewell St WS1 28 F1
Ablow St WV2 163 B1
Abnalls La WS13 8 B8
Abney Dr WV14 39 F1
Abney Gr B44 45 B2
Aboyne Cl B5 86 D6
A B Row B4 66 F3
Acacia Ave
Birmingham B37 69 F6
Coventry CV1 113 E1
Walsall WS5 43 A4
Acacia Cl
Birmingham B37 69 F6
Dudley DY1 51 A3
Tipton B69 52 B2
Acacia Cres WV8 10 B4
Acacia Ct
Coventry CV6 112 E5
Stourbridge DY8 80 E6
Acacia Dr WV14 51 B7
Acacia Gr WS12 2 F3
Acacia Rd
Birmingham B30 103 E8
Nuneaton CV10 72 E5
Royal Leamington Spa CV32 156 D1
Acanthus Rd B98 154 F6
Accord Mews WS10 41 D7
Ace Bsns Pk B33 69 D2
Acfold Rd B20 54 E5
Achal Cl CV6 95 F2
Acheson Rd B28,B90 105 F3
Achilees Cl WS6 4 F1
Achilles Cl CV34 161 F2
Achilles Rd CV6 114 A7
Ackleton Gdns WV3 38 F7
Ackleton Gr B29 84 F1
Acocks Green Prim Sch B27 88 B3
Acocks Green Sta B27 88 C4
Acorn Cl
Bedworth CV12 95 C8
Birmingham,Bournville B30 103 E8
Birmingham,Stockfield B27 88 B5
Cannock WS11 2 C2
Great Wyrley WS6 5 A1
Stoneleigh CV8 149 B7
West Bromwich B70 53 B2
Acorn Ct
1 Royal Leamington Spa CV32 157 A2
Birmingham B45 122 D7
Coventry CV2 114 C2
Acorn Ctr 1 WS1 28 F1
Acorn Gdns B30 104 A7
Acorn Gr
Birmingham B1 66 B3
Stourbridge DY8 60 E1
Acorn Rd
Catshill B61 137 B8
Halesowen B62 83 C8
Wolverhampton WV11 13 A1
Acorn Starter Units WS7 6 D7
Acorn St CV3 134 B8
Acorns The B61 137 A8
Acorn St WV13 27 C2
Acorn View WS7 7 C6
Acre Cl CV31 162 A4
Acre La B97 152 E2
Acre Rise WV12 27 B5
Acres Rd DY5 81 E8
Acres The WV3 24 C1
Acton Cl B98 154 D5
Acton Dr DY3 50 B3
Acton Gr
Bilston WV14 40 B4
Birmingham B44 45 A2
Acton Ho CV4 111 F3
Adam Ct
Cannock WS11 1 D1
Halesowen B63 82 F4
Adam Rd 1 CV6 113 F7
Adams Brook Dr B32 84 B1
Adams Cl
Smethwick B66 64 D7
Tipton DY4 40 F1
Adams Ct DY10 117 A7
Adams Hill B32 84 B1
Adam's Hill DY9 99 E4
Adams Ho 6 DY11 116 C6
Adamson Cl WS11 1 B1
Adams Rd
Brownhills WS8 16 B5
Wolverhampton WV3 38 C8
Adams St
Birmingham B7 66 F5
Adams St *continued*
Walsall WS2 28 D2
West Bromwich B70 53 B3
Adam St DY11 116 C5
Ada Rd
Birmingham B25 88 B6
Smethwick B66 65 B3
Adare Dr CV3 133 C8
Ada Wrighton Cl WV12 27 C7
Adcock Dr CV8 148 B5
Addenbrooke Cres DY11 116 A1
Addenbrooke Dr B73 46 B2
Addenbrooke Pl WS10 41 D7
Addenbrooke Rd
Keresley CV7 95 A6
Smethwick B67 64 F3
Addenbrooke St
Darlaston WS10 41 D7
Walsall WS3 28 C7
Addenbrook Ho
3 Cradley Heath B64 82 F8
Sutton Coldfield B73 46 A3
Addenbrook Way DY4 52 D8
Adderley Gdns B8 67 D5
Adderley Park Cl B8 67 E4
Adderley Park Sta B8 67 D3
Adderley Prim Sch B8 67 D4
Adderley Rd B8 67 C4
Adderley Rd S B8 67 C3
Adderley St
Birmingham B9 67 A1
Coventry CV1 113 E4
Adderley Trad Est B8 67 C4
Addingham Cl 2 CV34 155 E1
Addington Way B69 52 D3
Addison Cl
Cannock WS11 1 E5
Nuneaton CV10 72 A5
Wednesbury WS10 42 E2
Addison Croft DY3 50 A5
Addison Gr WV11 12 B1
Addison Pl
Bilston WV14 41 A7
Water Orton B46 59 B3
Addison Rd
Birmingham,King's Heath B14 104 F7
Birmingham,Nechells B7 67 C8
Brierley Hill DY5 61 B2
Coventry CV6 113 A8
Wednesbury WS10 42 E2
Wolverhampton WV3 38 F8
Addison St WS10 41 F2
Addison Terr WS10 41 F2
Adelaide Ave B70 53 A7
Adelaide Ct 3 CV12 78 A2
Adelaide Dr WS12 2 F3
Adelaide Rd CV31,CV32 161 E8
Adelaide St
Birmingham B12 86 F8
Brierley Hill DY5 61 D3
Coventry CV1 165 D4
Redditch B97 153 D4
Adelaide Twr B34 69 C5
Adelaide Wlk WV2 163 D1
Adelphi Ct 3 DY5 61 D2
Adey Rd WV11 26 F8
Adkins La B67 65 A1
Admington Rd B33 89 C8
Admiral Gdns CV8 148 C6
Admiral Parker Dr WS14 17 F5
Admiral Pl B13 86 F4
Admirals Way
Bramcote CV11 79 E6
Rowley Regis B65 63 B2
Admiral Wlk DY10 116 E8
Adonis Cl B79 21 C7
Adrian Croft B13 87 C1
Adrian Ct 1 B24 57 B6
Adria Rd B11 87 B4
Adshead Rd DY2 62 C7
Adstone Gr B31 103 A1
Advance Bsns Pk WS11 2 B3
Advanced Tech Unit CV4 132 C6
Advent Gdns B70 53 B3
Adwalton Rd WV6 23 F3
Aethelred Ct WV10 25 C6
Affleck Ave B78 20 D1
Agenoria Dr DY8 80 F5
Aggborough Cres DY10 116 E3
Aggborough Stadium (Kidderminster Harriers FC) DY10 116 F4
Agincourt Rd CV3 133 E7
Agmore La B60 138 B3
Agmore Rd B60 138 B4
Aiden Ct WS13 9 C7
Aimsbury Ct B26 89 C4
Ainsbury Rd CV5 132 E8
Ainsdale Cl
Coventry CV6 96 B4
Stourbridge DY8 80 F2
Ainsdale Gdns
Birmingham B24 57 C5
Halesowen B63 82 D2
Ainsworth Rd
5 Birmingham B31 103 D2
Wolverhampton WV10 11 E4
Aintree Cl
Bedworth CV12 78 B4
Cannock WS12 2 F6
Aintree Cl *continued*
Coventry CV6 113 E5
Kidderminster DY11 116 D8
Upper Catshill B61 121 A1
Aintree Dr CV32 157 C3
Aintree Gr B34 69 D6
Aintree Rd WV10 11 D4
Aintree Way DY1 50 F2
Aire Croft B31 103 B1
Airfield Dr WS4,WS9 29 E3
Airport Way B26 90 C3
Aitken Cl B78 21 A2
Aitken Wing B15 86 A6
Ajax Cl WS6 4 F1
Akon Ho CV6 94 F2
Akrill Cl B70 53 B5
Akrill Cottage Hos The B70 53 B5
Alamein Rd WV13 26 E1
Alan Bray Cl LE10 74 D7
Alandale Ave CV5 111 E4
Alandale Ct CV12 95 C8
Alan Higgs Way CV4 131 C8
Alasdair Ho 1 B17 85 B5
Albany Cl DY10 117 B6
Albany Cres WV14 40 C6
Albany Ct
1 Birmingham B62 84 A7
Coventry CV1 113 A2
Albany Dr WS12 2 E3
Albany Gdns B91 107 E4
Albany Gr
Kingswinford DY6 60 E7
Willenhall WV11 13 C1
Albany Ho B34 69 A7
Albany Mews WS10 41 E6
Albany Rd
Birmingham B17 85 C6
Coventry CV5 113 A1
Wolverhampton WV1 163 A3
Albany Terr CV32 156 E1
Albemarle Rd DY8 80 F2
Albermarle Rd DY6 61 A5
Albert Ave 1 B12 87 A6
Albert Bean Cl CV31 162 A4
Albert Bradbeer Inf Sch B31 122 F7
Albert Bradbeer Jun Sch B31 122 F7
Albert Clarke Dr WV12 27 C7
Albert Cl B80 159 E4
Albert Cres CV6 95 B3
Albert Davie Dr WS12 2 E4
Albert Dr B63 82 F2
Albert Fearn Gdns CV6 95 F1
Albert Ho 1 WS10 41 C6
Albert Pritchard Inf Sch WS10 42 A5
Albert Rd
Allesley CV5 111 A8
Birmingham,Aston B6 66 F8
Birmingham,Brandhall B68 84 C8
Birmingham,Gravelly Hill B23 56 D3
Birmingham,Handsworth B21 54 E1
Birmingham,Harborne B17 85 B5
Birmingham,King's Heath B14 104 F7
Birmingham,Stechford B33 68 D3
Bromsgrove B61 150 E8
Fazeley B78 35 A8
Halesowen B63 82 F3
Hinckley LE10 71 D1
Kidderminster DY10 116 F6
Tamworth B79 21 B5
Wolverhampton WV6 25 A3
Albert St E B69 64 B7
Albert Smith Pl B65 63 A4
Albert St
Birmingham B5 164 D3
Brierley Hill DY5 61 D7
Cannock,Broomhill WS11 1 E4
Cannock WS12 2 D5
Coventry CV1 113 E4
Kingswinford DY6 60 B8
Nuneaton CV10 72 E3
Oldbury B69 64 A8
Redditch B97 153 E5
Royal Leamington Spa CV32 156 C1
Stourbridge DY8 80 F5
Stourbridge,Lye DY9 81 E5
Tipton DY4 51 F8
Walsall WS1 28 E2
Warwick CV34 160 D7
Wednesbury WS10 41 F2
West Bromwich B70 53 C1
Albert Wlk 1 B17 85 C5
Albion Ave WV13 27 C2
Albion Bsns Pk B66 64 E8
Albion Cotts B46 59 B3
Albion Ct
Brierley Hill DY5 61 C6
Nuneaton CV11 73 D3
Albion Field Dr B71 53 D4
Albion Ind Est
Coventry CV6 113 D7
West Bromwich B70 52 F2
Albion Jun Sch B66 65 A7
Albion Par DY6 60 B8
Albion Pl WS11 1 E4
Albion Rd
Birmingham,Handsworth B21 54 E1
Birmingham,Sparkhill B11 87 D5
Brownhills WS8 15 E8
Albion Rdbt B70 53 B4
Albion Rd
West Bromwich B70 53 A2
West Bromwich,Sandwell B71 65 B8
Willenhall WV13 27 B2
Albion St
Bilston WV14 40 E6
Birmingham B1 66 C3
Brierley Hill DY5 61 D3
Kenilworth CV8 148 A5
Kingswinford DY6 60 B8
Oldbury B69 52 E1
Tamworth B79 21 C5
Tipton DY4 51 F5
Willenhall WV13 27 C2
Wolverhampton WV1 163 D3
Albion Terr B46 59 B3
Albion Works DY5 61 B3
Alborn Cres B38 123 D8
Albrighton Ho 4 B20 54 F3
Albrighton Rd B63 82 F3
Albrighton Wlk CV11 74 A2
Albright Rd B68 64 D4
Albury Rd B80 159 E4
Albury Wlk B11 87 A7
Albutts Rd WS11 6 B3
Alcester Dr
Sutton Coldfield B73 45 D3
Willenhall WV13 26 D1
Alcester Gdns B14 104 F7
Alcester Highway B98 158 F8
Alcester Rd
Birmingham B13 86 F3
Finstall B60 137 F1
Hollywood B47 124 F5
Lickey End B60 137 D5
Portway B47,B48 140 F7
Alcester Rd S
Birmingham,Billesley Common B14 104 E6
Birmingham,Highter's Heath B14 104 F2
Alcester Rd
Studley B80 159 E3
Tardebigge B60,B97 152 B7
Alcester St
Birmingham B12 86 F8
Redditch B98 153 E4
Alcombe Gr B33 68 E2
Alcott Cl B93 127 F2
Alcott Gr B33 69 E3
Alcott Hall Prim Sch B37 70 B1
Alcott La B37 89 F8
Alcove The WS3 14 D2
Aldborough La 4 B97 153 B5
Aldbourne Rd CV1 113 C5
Aldbourne Way B38 123 E7
Aldbury Rd B14 105 A3
Aldbury Rise CV5 112 C4
Aldeburgh Cl WS3 14 A3
Aldeford Dr DY5 81 D8
Alden Hurst WS7 6 F8
Alder Ave DY10 116 E8
Alderbrook Cl
Redditch B97 153 B5
Sedgley DY3 39 B1
Alderbrooke Dr CV11 74 A1
Alderbrook Rd B91 106 F3
Alderbrook Sch B91 106 F2
Alder Carr Cl B98 158 F8
Alder Cl
Hollywood B47 125 B6
Lichfield WS14 9 F7
Sutton Coldfield B76 57 E7
Alder Coppice Prim Sch DY3 39 C1
Alder Coppice DY3 39 C2
Alder Cres WS5 43 B4
Alder Ct B13 87 A3
Alderdale Ave DY3 39 C3
Alderdale Cres B92 107 E7
Alder Dale WV3 24 E2
Alder Dr B37 70 B1
Alderflat Pl B7 67 C5
Alderford Cl WV8 24 F8
Aldergate B79 21 B5
Alder Gr B62 83 E6
Alderham Cl B91 107 D4
Alderhithe Gr B74 31 B3
Alder Ho 12 CV34 161 D8
Alder La
Balsall Common CV7 130 C5
Birmingham B30 103 C6
Alderlea Cl DY8 81 A2
Alderley Cres WS3 28 E5
Alderley Rd B61 150 D8
Alderman Callow Sch & Com Coll CV4 132 A6
Alderman Gee Hall CV12 78 A4
Alderman's Green Com Prim Sch CV2 96 C3
Alderman's Green Ind Est CV2 96 D2

Alderman's Green Rd CV2 96 B3
Aldermans La B97 153 B6
Alderman Smith Sch CV10 72 D2
Alder Meadow Cl CV6 95 D4
Aldermere Rd DY11 116 C8
Alderminster Cl B97 158 E4
Alderminster Rd
Coventry CV5 112 A4
Solihull B91 107 C1
Aldermoor Farm Prim Sch CV3 134 B8
Aldermoor La CV3 114 A1
Aldermore Dr 1 B75 46 F6
Alderney Cl
Bramcote CV11 79 F6
Coventry CV6 95 B2
Alderney Gdns B38 103 D1
Alder Park Rd B91 106 F2
Alderpits Rd B34 69 D6
Alder Rd
Birmingham B12 87 A4
Coventry CV6 96 A2
Kingswinford DY6 60 F5
Wednesbury WS10 42 A5
Alders Cl B98 154 A3
Alders Dr B98 154 F4
Aldersea Dr B6 66 F7
Aldersgate CV11 73 C3
Alders Gr CV34 160 D4
Aldershaw Rd B26 88 E6
Aldershaws B90 126 A5
Alders La
Nuneaton CV10 72 A7
Tamworth B79 20 E6
Aldersley Ave WV6 24 E7
Aldersley Cl WV6 24 F7
Aldersley High Sch WV8 10 E1
Aldersley Rd WV6 24 F6
Aldersley Stad WV6 24 F6
Aldersmead Rd B31 103 C1
Alderson Rd B8 67 F4
Alders The
Bedworth CV12 77 E2
Romsley B62 100 F4
Alderton Cl 3 B91 107 B1
Alderton Dr WV3 38 E8
Alderton Mews 16 CV31 162 C6
Alder Way
Bromsgrove B60 137 B2
Sutton Coldfield B74 44 E8
Alderwood Pl B91 107 C3
Alderwood Prec DY3 39 C1
Alderwood Rise DY3 50 D5
Aldgate Dr DY5 81 C7
Aldgate Gr B19 66 D5
Aldin Cl B78 20 E2
Aldington Cl B98 153 F1
Aldin Way LE10 71 A3
Aldis Cl
Birmingham B28 87 E1
Walsall WS2 42 A7
Aldis Rd WS2 42 A7
Aldrich Ave CV4 111 E2
Aldridge By-Pass WS9 30 A6
Aldridge Cl
2 Stourbridge DY8 80 E8
Oldbury B68 64 C4
Polesworth B78 36 F8
Aldridge Rd
Birmingham,Brandhall B68 84 B8
Birmingham,Perry Barr B42 55 E4
Hinckley LE10 75 D6
Sutton Coldfield B74 30 D1
Sutton Coldfield,Little Aston B74, WS9 31 B6
Sutton Coldfield,Streetly B74 44 E7
Walsall WS4 29 C3
Aldridge Sch & Science Coll WS9 30 A4
Aldridge St WS10 41 D7
Aldrin Way CV4 132 D5
Aldwick Cl CV32 157 A4
Aldwych Cl WS9 30 B8
Aldwyck Dr WV3 38 A8
Aldwyn Ave B13 86 F2
Alesmore Mdw WS13 8 F6
Alesworth Dr LE10 75 F4
Alexander Cl B61 121 A1
Alexander Ct 1 CV34 160 F7
Alexander Gdns
Birmingham B42 55 D3
Hinckley LE10 71 C2
Alexander Hill DY5 81 F8
Alexander Ind Pk WV14 40 C4
Alexander Rd
Bedworth CV12 78 C3
Birmingham B27 88 C4
Codsall WV8 10 C3
Smethwick B67 64 E2
Willenhall WS2 27 F2
Alexander Stad B42 55 C6
Alexander Terr B67 64 F6
Alexander Way B9 67 F3
Alexandra Ave B21 65 D7
Alexandra Cres B71 53 E8
Alexandra Ct
Dudley DY3 50 C3
Kenilworth CV8 148 A4
Oldbury B68 63 F3
Alexandra High Sch & Sixth Form Ctr DY4 52 B6
Alexandra Hospl The B98 159 C6
Alexandra Ind Est DY4 51 F5
Alexandra Mews B79 21 C5
Alexandra Pl
Bilston WV14 40 D6
Dudley DY1 51 C4
Alexandra Rd
Birmingham,Handsworth B21 65 D7
Birmingham,Highgate B5 86 E7
Birmingham,Stirchley B30 104 A7
Coventry CV1 113 F4
Darlaston WS10 41 E6
Halesowen B63 82 F4
Royal Leamington Spa CV31 162 B6
Tipton DY4 52 A6
Walsall WS1 42 E6
Wolverhampton WV4 39 A6
Alexandra St
2 Dudley DY1 51 B1
Nuneaton CV11 73 B4
Wolverhampton WV3 163 A2
Alexandra Terr CV6 95 E2
Alexandra Theatre★ B5 164 B2
Alexandra Way
Aldridge WS9 30 B5
Tipton B69 52 A2
Alex Grierson Cl CV3 134 E7
Alex Stewart Ho CV11 73 E1
Alfall Rd CV2 114 B5
Alford Cl B45 122 C7
Alfreda Ave B47 125 A8
Alfred Ct B60 150 E2
Alfred Gunn Ho B68 64 B4
Alfred Rd
Birmingham,Handsworth B21 65 E8
Birmingham,Sparkhill B11 87 B5
Coventry CV1 113 F4
Alfred Squire Rd WV11 26 D5
Alfred St
Birmingham,Aston B6 67 B8
Birmingham,King's Heath B14 104 F7
Birmingham,Sparkbrook B12 87 B5
Darlaston WS10 41 C5
Smethwick B66 65 C7
Tamworth B79 21 A5
Walsall WS3 14 B1
West Bromwich B70 53 D3
Alfreds Well B61 136 C6
Alfreton Cl LE10 75 F5
Alfriston Rd CV3 133 C4
Alfryth Ct 4 B15 86 C8
Algate Cl CV6 95 C3
Algernon Rd B16 65 D4
Alhambra Rd B60 137 C1
Al Hira Sch B12 87 A6
Alice Arnold Ho 1 CV2 96 B1
Alice Cl CV12 77 F1
Alice St WV14 40 D6
Alice Stevens Sch CV3 134 A6
Alice Wlk WV14 40 D6
Alison Cl DY4 41 A2
Alison Dr DY8 80 E3
Alison Rd B62 83 F3
Alison Sq CV6 96 B4
Allan Cl
2 Smethwick B66 65 B5
7 Stourbridge DY8 80 F8
All Angels Wlk B68 64 B4
Allan Rd CV6 112 F4
Allard Ho CV3 134 B6
Allard B77 21 E2
Allard Way CV3 134 C7
Allbut St B64 62 D1
Allcock St
Birmingham B9 67 A1
Tipton DY4 52 C8
Allcroft Rd B11 87 F2
Allenby Cl DY6 61 A5
Allen Cl
Birmingham B43 54 E7
Studley B80 159 E3
Allendale Ave B80 159 E3
Allendale Cres B80 159 E3
Allendale Ct B80 159 E3
Allendale Gr B43 54 E8
Allendale Rd
Birmingham B25 88 B7
Sutton Coldfield B76 57 E8
Allen Dr
3 Darlaston WS10 41 C6
West Bromwich B70 53 F1
Allen Ho B43 54 E7
Allen Rd
Tipton DY4 40 F1
Wednesbury WS10 41 F5
Wolverhampton WV6 25 A3
Allens Ave
Birmingham B18 65 F6
West Bromwich B71 53 A7
Allens Cl WV12 27 B5
Allens Croft Prim Sch B14 104 C5
Allens Croft Rd B14 104 C6
Allens Farm Rd B31 102 E3
Allens La WS3 14 F2
Allensmead B77 21 C2
Allensmore Cl B98 154 F2
Allens Rd B18 65 F6
Allen St
Tamworth B77 21 C1
West Bromwich B70 53 B3
Allerdale Rd WS8 15 E6
Allerton Cl CV2 114 E2
Allerton La B71 53 C8
Allerton Rd B25 88 B7
Allesley Cl B74 46 C7
Allesley Croft CV5 112 A6
Allesley Ct CV5 112 A6
Allesley Hall Dr CV5 112 C5
Allesley Hall Prim Sch CV5 112 B4
Allesley Old Rd CV5 112 D3
Allesley Prim Sch CV5 112 A7
Allesley Rd B92 106 D8
Allesley St B6 66 E5
Alleston Rd WV10 11 D1
Alleston Wlk WV10 11 D2
Alleyne Gr B24 57 A2
Alleyne Rd B24 57 A1
Alley The DY3 50 B3
Alliance Cl CV11 73 F3
Alliance Way CV2 114 A5
Allibone Cl CV31 162 A4
Allied Cl CV6 95 D2
Allingham Gr B43 44 D4
Allington Ave 5 WS13 8 F6
Allington Cl WS5 43 D8
Allison St B5 164 D2
Allitt Gr CV8 148 B5
Allman Rd B24 57 B4
Allmyn Dr B74 45 A6
Allport Mews WS11 1 E1
Allport Rd WS11 1 E1
Allport St WS11 1 E2
All Saints CE Inf Sch CV12 78 C2
All Saints' CE Jun Sch CV34 156 A1
All Saints CE Prim Sch
Coventry CV1 113 E1
Leek Wootton CV35 156 A5
Nuneaton CV10 73 C1
West Bromwich B71 53 C6
All Saints Dr B74 32 A2
All Saints Ind Est B18 66 A5
All Saints La CV1 113 F3
All Saints Pl B61 137 A4
All Saints Rd CV12 77 F1
All Saints' Rd B18 66 B5
All Saints Rd B14 104 E7
All Saints' Rd
Bromsgrove B61 137 A3
Darlaston WS10 41 E6
All Saints Rd
Warwick CV34 161 B8
Wolverhampton WV2 163 C1
All Saints Sq CV12 78 B3
All Saints' St B18 66 A5
All Saints Way B71 53 D5
Allsops Cl B65 62 F4
All Souls RC Prim Sch CV5 112 E2
Allton Ave B78 20 D1
Allton Ct B77 21 E3
Allwell Dr B14 104 F2
Allwood Gdns B32 84 A2
Allwood Ho B97 153 C3
Alma Ave DY4 52 A7
Alma Cres B7 67 B4
Alma Ct CV11 79 F6
Alma Ind Est WS10 41 C6
Alma Pl DY2 51 C1
Alma Rd LE10 71 D1
Alma St
Birmingham B19 66 E6
Coventry CV1 165 D3
Darlaston WS10 41 C6
Halesowen B63 82 C5
Smethwick B66 65 C6
Walsall WS2 28 D4
Wednesbury WS10 42 B3
Willenhall WV13 27 B2
Wolverhampton WV10 25 F2
Alma Way B19 66 D7
Alma Wks WS10 41 D5
Almond Ave
Kidderminster DY11 116 B8
Nuneaton CV10 72 C6
Royal Leamington Spa CV32 156 F3
Walsall,Yew Tree WS5 43 A4
Willenhall WS2 27 E4
Almond Cl
Birmingham B29 103 A6
Cannock WS11 2 C2
Walsall WS3 14 F2
Almond Croft B42 54 F7
Almond Gr
Warwick CV34 156 A1
Wolverhampton WV6 25 C4
Almond Rd
Huntington WS12 1 D8
Kingswinford DY6 60 E8
Almond Tree Ave CV2 96 C2
Almshouses
2 Warwick CV34 160 E6
Rowington Green CV35 145 A1
Smethwick B67 64 F5
Stoneleigh CV8 149 C6
Alnwick Cl WS12 2 E2
Alnwick Ho B23 56 F6
Alnwick Rd WS3 14 A4
Alperton Dr DY9 81 E2
Alpha Bsns Pk CV2 96 D1
Alpha Cl B12 86 E6
Alpha Ho CV2 114 A4
Alpha Way WS6 14 A8
Alpine Ct CV8 148 A6
Alpine Dr
Cannock WS12 2 D4
Alpine Dr *continued*
Dudley DY2 62 B4
Alpine Rise CV3 133 A5
Alpine Way WV3 24 C2
Alport Croft 4 B9 67 B2
Alspath La CV5 111 F4
Alspath Rd CV7 92 C1
Alston Cl
Cannock WS12 2 E2
Solihull B91 107 D6
Sutton Coldfield B74 32 A2
Alston Gr B9 68 B2
Alston Ho B69 63 D6
Alston Prim Sch B9 68 B3
Alston Rd
Birmingham B9 68 B3
Oldbury B69 63 E7
Solihull B91 107 D6
Alston St B16 66 A2
Althorpe Dr B93 127 E3
Althorpe Ho CV31 162 A6
Althorpe Ind Est 15 CV31 162 A7
Althorpe St CV31 162 A7
Alton Ave WV12 27 B5
Alton Cl
Coventry CV2 96 D2
Redditch B97 153 B1
Wolverhampton WV10 11 E3
Alton Gr
Cannock WS11 1 B1
Dudley DY2 51 E1
West Bromwich B71 53 E7
Alton Rd B29 85 F3
Alum Cl CV6 113 D8
Alum Dr B9 68 A3
Alumhurst Ave B8 68 B4
Alum Rock Rd B8 68 B4
Alumwell Bsns & Enterprise Coll WS2 28 A1
Alumwell Cl WS2 28 B1
Alumwell Jun & Inf Schs WS2 28 B2
Alum Well Rd WS2 28 B1
Alvaston Cl WS3 14 C3
Alvechurch CE Mid Sch B48 139 B6
Alvechurch Crown Meadow Fst Sch B48 139 B6
Alvechurch Highway
Lower Marlbrook B60 121 D2
Redditch B98,B97 153 F3
Alvechurch Ho B60 137 B3
Alvechurch Rd
Birmingham B31 123 B7
Halesowen B63 82 F2
Alvechurch Sta B48 139 A4
Alvecote Cotts B79 22 D6
Alvecote La B79 22 D6
Alvecote Pools Nature Reserve★ B79 22 E6
Alveley Cl B98 154 D4
Alverley Cl DY6 60 B8
Alverley Rd CV6 113 C6
Alverstoke Cl WV9 11 A2
Alverstone Rd CV2 114 A4
Alverton Cl B77 35 C4
Alveston Cl B98 154 C2
Alveston Gr
Birmingham B9 68 B2
Knowle B93 128 B7
Alveston Pl 19 CV32 156 F1
Alveston Rd B47 125 A7
Alvin Cl
Coventry CV3 114 F1
Halesowen B62 83 F8
Alvington Cl WV12 27 D4
Alvis Cl B79 20 F7
Alvis Ho CV1 165 B2
Alvis Ret Pk CV5 113 A3
Alvis Wlk B36 58 F1
Alwen St DY8 60 F2
Alwin Rd B65 63 B2
Alwold Ct B29 84 F2
Alwold Rd B29 85 A2
Alwyn Cl WS6 5 A3
Alwynne Freeman Ct CV7 95 A6
Alwynn Wlk B23 56 C3
Alwyn B77 35 E7
Amal Way B6 55 F2
Amanda Ave WV4 38 F4
Amanda Dr B26 68 F1
Ambassador Ct CV32 156 F3
Ambassador Rd B26 90 C4
Ambell Cl B65 62 F5
Amber Bsns Village B77 22 B3
Amber Cl B77 22 B3
Amber Ct B77 22 B3
Amber Dr B69 64 A5
Ambergate Cl
8 Redditch B97 153 B5
Walsall WS3 14 C3
Ambergate Dr DY6 60 C8
Amber Gn WS11 2 C2
Amber Gr WS11 2 C2
Amberley Ave CV12 79 C2
Amberley Gn B43 54 E6
Amberley Gr B6 56 A3
Amberley Ho CV8 148 A3
Amberley Rd B92 88 F4
Amberley Way B74 30 E1
Amber Terr DY10 116 F5
Amber Way B62 83 C6
Amberwood Cl WS2 27 D3
Ambion Way LE10 71 F1
Amblecote Ave B44 44 E2
Amblecote Prim Sch DY8 80 F8
Amblecote Rd
Brierley Hill DY5 81 D8
Kidderminster DY10 117 B5
Ambler Gr CV2 114 C3
Ambleside B32 84 C1
Ambleside Cl WV14 40 E3
Ambleside CV2 96 E2
Ambleside Dr DY5 81 C8
Ambleside Gr WV11 13 B1
Ambleside Rd CV10 78 A2
Ambleside Way
Bromsgrove B60 137 B1
Kingswinford DY6 60 D6
Nuneaton CV11 73 E6
Ambrose Cl WV13 26 E2
Ambrose Cres DY6 60 D8
Ambury Way B43 54 D8
Amelas Cl 3 DY5 61 A1
Amelia Cl CV12 79 C3
Amersham Cl
Birmingham B32 84 E5
Coventry CV5 112 B4
Amesbury Rd B13 86 E3
Ames Rd WS10 41 C7
Amethyst Ct 2 B92 88 F1
Amherst Ave B20 55 A3
Amherst Rd CV8 147 E6
Amhurst Bsns Ctr CV34 160 B7
Amicombe B77 22 C1
Amington Cl B75 32 D3
Amington Hall B79 22 A8
Amington Heath Com Sch B77 22 A4
Amington Ind Est B77 22 B3
Amington Pk B77 22 A6
Amington Rd
Birmingham B25 88 B6
Solihull B90 126 A8
Tamworth B77 21 D4
Amiss Gdns B10 87 C8
Amity Cl B66 65 B5
Amos Ave
Nuneaton CV10 73 B2
Wolverhampton WV11 26 C7
Amos Jacques Rd CV12 78 A4
Amos La WV11 26 C6
Amos Rd DY9 81 F2
Amphlett Croft DY4 52 B4
Amphlett Ct 2 B60 137 A2
Amphletts Cl DY2 62 E3
Ampton Rd B15 86 B7
Amroth Cl B45 122 B7
Amroth Mews CV31 162 C6
Amwell Gr B14 104 F3
Amy Cl CV6 95 F4
Anchorage Rd
Birmingham B23 56 D3
Sutton Coldfield B74 46 B6
Anchor Cl
Birmingham B16 65 E1
Tamworth B77 21 E4
Anchor Cres B18 65 F5
Anchor Ct B77 21 C4
Anchor Dr DY4 52 A3
Anchorfields DY10 116 F6
Anchor Hill DY5 61 C1
Anchor La
Solihull B91 107 D6
Wolverhampton WV14 40 B2
Anchor Par WS9 30 B6
Anchor Rd
Aldridge WS9 30 B6
Dudley WV14 40 C2
Anchorway Rd CV3 133 B4
Andersleigh Dr WV14 51 A8
Anderson Cres B43 43 E2
Anderson Dr CV31 162 A2
Anderson Gdns DY4 52 A4
Anderson Rd
Birmingham B23 56 E6
Smethwick B66 65 A1
Tipton DY4 52 A4
Anders Sq WV6 23 E4
Anders B79 21 A6
Anderton Cl B74 46 A7
Anderton Park Prim Sch B12 87 B4
Anderton Park Rd B13 87 A3
Anderton Rd
Bedworth CV12 77 C1
Birmingham B11 87 C6
Coventry CV6 96 B4
Anderton St B1 66 B3
Andover Cres 2 DY6 60 F4
Andover Pl WS11 2 A4
Andover St B5 66 F2
Andressy Mews B61 137 A5
Andrew Cl WV12 27 D6
Andrew Ct B76 46 F3
Andrew Dr WV12 27 D6
Andrew Gdns B21 54 E1
Andrew Rd
Halesowen B63 83 A3
Wednesbury DY4 41 A1
West Bromwich B71 42 F2
Andrews Cl
Baginton CV8 133 F2
Brierley Hill DY5 81 E8
Andrews Ho WS13 9 A7
Andrews Rd WS9 16 B4
Anerley Gr B44 44 F4
Anerley Rd B44 44 F4
Angela Ave
Coventry CV2 96 E1
Rowley Regis B65 63 D4
Angela Pl WV14 40 D6
Angelica Cl 7 WS5 43 A3
Angelica B77 21 F4

Angelina St B12 ... 86 F7
Angel Mews 8 B46 ... 70 F7
Angelo Ho B13 ... 105 D7
Angel Pas DY8 ... 81 A5
Angel St
Dudley DY1 ... 62 B8
Upper Bentley B97 ... 152 B1
Anglesey Ave B36 ... 70 B6
Anglesey Bsns Pk WS12 ... 2 E4
Anglesey Cl
Allesley CV5 ... 112 B7
Burntwood WS7 ... 6 F4
Anglesey Cres
Brownhills WS8 ... 6 F2
Cannock WS12 ... 2 C5
Anglesey Mews WS12 ... 2 C5
Anglesey Prim Sch B19 ... 66 C7
Anglesey Rd
Brownhills WS8 ... 6 F2
Lichfield WS13 ... 3 B2
Anglesey St
Birmingham B19 ... 66 C7
Cannock WS12 ... 2 B5
Angless Way CV8 ... 147 F3
Anglian Rd WS9 ... 29 D6
Anglia Rd WS11 ... 1 D3
Anglo African Ind Pk B69 52 E2
Angorfa Cl WS13 ... 8 F7
Angus Cl
Coventry CV5 ... 112 A4
Kenilworth CV8 ... 148 C6
West Bromwich B71 ... 53 C6
Anita Ave DY4 ... 52 A2
Anita Croft B23 ... 56 E2
Ankadine Rd DY8 ... 81 B6
Anker Cl WS7 ... 7 D6
Ankerdine Ct B63 ... 83 A3
Ankerdrive B79 ... 21 B4
Ankermoor Cl B34 ... 69 B6
Ankermoor Ct B77 ... 21 E5
Ankermoor Prim Sch B77 21 E5
Ankerside Sh Ctr B79 ... 21 B4
Anker St CV11 ... 73 D3
Anker View B77 ... 21 C3
Anley Way CV6 ... 113 C6
Annan Ave WV10 ... 25 F7
Annandale B77 ... 22 B1
Ann Cres WS11 ... 1 E6
Ann Croft B26 ... 89 D4
Anne Cl B70 ... 52 E3
Anne Cres CV3 ... 134 C5
Anne Ct B76 ... 46 F3
Anne Gr DY4 ... 41 B1
Anne Rd
Birmingham B66 ... 65 D7
Brierley Hill DY5 ... 62 A1
Wolverhampton WV4 ... 39 B6
Annie Lennard Inf Sch
B67 ... 64 E3
Annie Osborn Prim Sch
CV2 ... 114 D7
Ann Rd B47 ... 125 A3
Annscroft B38 ... 103 D2
Ann St WV13 ... 27 B3
Ansbro Cl B18 ... 65 F5
Ansculf Rd DY5 ... 61 B1
Ansell Dr CV6 ... 96 A5
Ansell Rd
Birmingham,Gravelly Hill
B24 ... 56 F1
Birmingham,Sparkbrook
B11 ... 87 C6
Ansell Way CV34 ... 160 D7
Ansley Cl B98 ... 154 F1
Ansley Comm CV10 ... 72 A7
Ansley Rd CV10 ... 72 B3
Ansley Way B92 ... 107 D7
Anslow Gdns WV11 ... 12 F1
Anslow Rd B23 ... 56 C5
Anson Ave WS13 ... 3 A1
Anson Cl
Burntwood WS7 ... 7 C7
Great Wyrley WS6 ... 4 F1
Perton WV6 ... 23 E5
Anson Ct B78 ... 35 B8
Anson Gr B27 ... 88 D2
Anson Junc WS2 ... 27 E1
Anson Rd
Great Wyrley WS6 ... 4 F1
Walsall WS2 ... 27 E1
West Bromwich B70 ... 52 E7
Anson Way CV2 ... 114 F8
Anstey Croft B37 ... 70 A4
Anstey Ct B73 ... 57 A7
Anstey Gr B27 ... 88 B1
Anstey Rd B44 ... 55 E6
Anston Way WV11 ... 26 D7
Anstree Cl WS6 ... 4 D1
Anstruther Rd B15 ... 85 E8
Ansty Dr WS12 ... 2 D1
Ansty Rd CV2 ... 114 E5
Antelope Gdns CV34 ... 160 C8
Anthony Rd B8 ... 67 F4
Anthony Way CV2 ... 114 C2
Anton Dr B76 ... 58 A6
Antony Gardner Cres 5
CV31 ... 162 A4
Antony Rd B90 ... 106 B1
Antrim Cl CV5 ... 112 B7
Antringham Gdns B15 ... 85 D8
Antrobus Rd
Birmingham B21 ... 54 E1
Sutton Coldfield B73 ... 45 F1
Anvil Cres WV14 ... 40 C2
Anvil Dr B69 ... 63 E6
Anvil Wlk B70 ... 52 F4
Apex Bsns Pk WS11 ... 5 F4
Apex Rd WS8 ... 15 C7
Apley Rd DY8 ... 80 E7
Apollo Cl WS11 ... 2 A5
Apollo Croft B24 ... 57 D3
Apollo Rd
Oldbury B68 ... 64 C6
Stourbridge DY9 ... 82 A5
Apollo B79 ... 20 F6
Apollo Way
12 Smethwick B66 ... 65 C5
Birmingham B20 ... 55 D1
Royal Leamington Spa
CV34 ... 161 D5
Apperley Way B63 ... 82 B7
Appian Cl
Birmingham B14 ... 104 E5
Tamworth B77 ... 35 D7
Appian Way B90 ... 126 D4
Applebee Rd LE10 ... 75 D6
Applebees Mdw LE10 ... 74 E6
Applebees Wlk LE10 ... 74 F6
Appleby Cl B14 ... 104 D5
Appleby Gdns WV11 ... 13 C2
Appleby Gr B90 ... 127 B6
Appleby Ho 1 LE10 ... 71 E1
Applecross Cl CV4 ... 131 F6
Applecross B74 ... 31 F1
Appledore Cl
Cannock WS12 ... 2 E3
Great Wyrley WS6 ... 5 A3
Appledore Ct 3 WS3 ... 28 B8
Appledore Dr CV5 ... 111 F5
Appledore Rd WS5 ... 43 D8
Appledore Terr WS5 ... 43 D8
Appledorne Gdns B34 ... 69 B6
Applesham Cl B11 ... 87 D6
Appleton Ave
Birmingham B43 ... 54 E8
Stourbridge DY8 ... 81 A2
Appleton Cl B30 ... 103 E8
Appleton Cres WV4 ... 39 A5
Appleton Ct 5 B15 ... 86 B7
Apple Tree Cl B23 ... 56 B4
Appletree Cl
Birmingham B31 ... 102 F1
Catherine de B B91 ... 108 B5
Apple Tree Cl DY10 ... 117 B7
Appletree Cotts CV35 ... 144 F1
Appletree Gr
Aldridge WS9 ... 30 B5
Wolverhampton WV6 ... 25 C5
Appletree La B97 ... 153 B5
Appletrees Cres B61 ... 137 A5
Apple Wlk WS11 ... 2 C2
Applewood Gr 5 B64 ... 62 F1
Appleyard Cl CV12 ... 78 B2
Approach The CV31 ... 161 F6
April Croft B13 ... 87 B3
Apsley Cl B68 ... 84 A7
Apsley Croft B38 ... 104 B2
Apsley Gr
Birmingham B24 ... 57 A2
Dorridge B93 ... 127 F2
Apsley Ho B64 ... 62 F2
Apsley Rd B68 ... 84 A7
Aqua Ho CV32 ... 157 A1
Aqueduct La B48 ... 138 F7
Aqueduct Rd B90 ... 105 E1
Aragon Dr
Royal Leamington Spa
CV34 ... 161 D6
Sutton Coldfield B73 ... 46 B6
Aragon Ho CV3 ... 133 C8
Arbor Cl B77 ... 21 D3
Arbor Ct B71 ... 53 E6
Arboretum Rd WS1 ... 29 A3
Arboretum The CV4 ... 132 D3
Arborfields Cl CV8 ... 148 B8
Arbor Gate WS9 ... 16 B4
Arbor Way B37 ... 70 C1
Arbour Cl CV8 ... 148 C3
Arbour Mews WS11 ... 5 F6
Arbourtree Ct WV5 ... 49 B7
Arbour Tree La B93 ... 144 F7
Arbury Ave
Bedworth CV12 ... 78 A3
Coventry CV6 ... 95 F2
Arbury Cl CV32 ... 157 A4
Arbury Ct CV10 ... 72 C3
Arbury Dr DY8 ... 60 D3
Arbury Garth CV10 ... 72 C3
Arbury Hall Park & Gdns*
CV10 ... 77 D7
Arbury Hall Rd B90 ... 126 D8
Arbury Rd CV10 ... 72 D2
Arbury Wlk B76 ... 58 D5
Arcade The
Coventry CV3 ... 114 B2
Dudley DY3 ... 50 E5
Arcade WS1 ... 28 E1
Arcadian Sh Ctr B5 ... 164 C1
Arcal St DY3 ... 50 E7
Archbishop Grimshaw RC
Sch The B37 ... 69 F3
Archbishop Ilsley RC Sch
B27 ... 88 C3
Archer Cl
Oldbury B68 ... 64 B4
Studley B80 ... 159 D4
Wednesbury WS10 ... 41 E3
Archer Ct DY9 ... 81 E2
Archer Gdns B64 ... 62 C1
Archer Rd
Birmingham B14 ... 105 C4
Kenilworth CV8 ... 147 E3
Redditch B98 ... 153 E4
Walsall WS3 ... 28 E6
Archers Cl B23 ... 56 D8
Archer Terr B97 ... 153 C1
Archery Fields CV34 ... 160 F6
Archery Rd
Meriden CV7 ... 92 B1
Royal Leamington Spa
CV31 ... 161 E8
Arches Ind Est The CV5 .. 113 A3
Arch Hill St DY2 ... 62 C5
Archibald Rd B19 ... 66 C8
Arch Rd CV2 ... 114 E5
Arch The B5 ... 67 A2
Archway The 2 WS4 ... 28 F3
Arcot Rd B28 ... 87 F2
Ardath Rd B38 ... 104 A2
Ardav Rd B70 ... 52 F8
Arden Bldgs B93 ... 127 F3
Arden Cl
Balsall Common CV7 ... 130 B7
Meriden CV7 ... 92 C1
Stourbridge DY8 ... 80 E7
Stourbridge,Wordsley DY8 . 60 C3
Tamworth B77 ... 21 E5
Warwick CV34 ... 156 A1
Whitnash CV31 ... 162 B5
Ardencote Rd B13 ... 105 A6
Arden Croft
Coleshill B46 ... 59 F1
Solihull B92 ... 89 C4
Arden Ct
Binley Woods CV3 ... 135 D6
Dudley DY3 ... 50 D3
Hampton-in-A B92 ... 109 A7
Sutton Coldfield B72 ... 57 C8
Ardendale 6 B90 ... 126 C8
Arden Dr
Birmingham B26 ... 88 F7
Dorridge B93 ... 128 A1
Sutton Coldfield,Falcon Lodge
B75 ... 47 B5
Sutton Coldfield,Wylde Green
B73 ... 57 B8
Arden Forest Inf Sch
CV12 ... 79 B3
Arden Gr
8 Birmingham,Lozells
B19 ... 66 C8
Birmingham,Ladywood B16 . 66 A1
Oldbury B69 ... 64 A5
Arden Jun & Inf Sch The
B11 ... 87 C5
Ardenleigh Way B24 ... 57 A2
Arden Leys B94 ... 141 D2
Arden Meads B94 ... 143 C6
Arden Oak Rd B26 ... 89 D4
Arden Pl WV14 ... 41 B4
Arden Rd
Birmingham,Acock's Green
B27 ... 88 B4
Birmingham,Aston B6 ... 66 D8
Birmingham,Rubery B45 .. 102 A1
Birmingham,Saltley B8 ... 67 D3
Bulkington CV12 ... 79 C2
Dorridge B93 ... 127 F2
Hollywood B47 ... 125 A6
Kenilworth CV8 ... 148 B3
Nuneaton CV11 ... 74 A1
Smethwick B67 ... 65 A5
Tamworth B77 ... 35 F5
Arden Sch B93 ... 128 B5
Arden St CV5 ... 132 F8
Arden Vale Rd B93 ... 128 B7
Arderne Dr B37 ... 70 A1
Ardgay Dr WS12 ... 1 F7
Ardingley Wlk DY5 ... 81 B7
Ardley Cl DY2 ... 62 D8
Ardley Rd B14 ... 105 A5
Arena Pk CV6 ... 95 F3
Arena Studios B73 ... 57 A7
Arena Theatre* WV1 ... 163 B3
Aretha Cl DY6 ... 61 A6
Argent Ctr The B1 ... 66 C3
Argil Cl WV11 ... 26 D8
Arguile Pl LE10 ... 71 C1
Argus Cl B76 ... 46 F3
Argyle Ave B77 ... 21 D4
Argyle Cl
Stourbridge DY8 ... 60 E1
Walsall WS4 ... 29 B3
Argyle Rd
Walsall WS4 ... 29 B3
Wolverhampton WV2 ... 39 B6
Argyle St
Birmingham B7 ... 67 D8
Tamworth B77 ... 21 E4
Argyll Ct WV12 ... 13 C1
Argyll Ho 5 WV3 ... 25 C4
Argyll St CV2 ... 114 A3
Ariane B79 ... 20 E7
Arion Cl B77 ... 21 D5
Arkall Cl B79 ... 21 C7
Arkle Croft
Birmingham B36 ... 68 C8
Rowley Regis B65 ... 62 F6
Arkle Dr CV2 ... 114 F7
Arkle B77 ... 35 D4
Arklet Cl CV10 ... 72 C5
Arkley Gr B28 ... 106 B7
Arkley Rd B28 ... 106 B7
Arkwright Rd
Birmingham B32 ... 84 C5
Walsall WS2 ... 28 B5
Arlen Dr B43 ... 43 D1
Arlescote Cl B75 ... 32 C2
Arlescote Rd B92 ... 89 C2
Arless Way B17 ... 85 B3
Arleston Way B90 ... 126 E8
Arley Cl
Kidderminster DY11 ... 116 A2
Oldbury B69 ... 63 D5
Arley Cl continued
Redditch B98 ... 154 D5
Arley Ct DY2 ... 62 C6
Arley Dr DY8 ... 80 E3
Arley Gr WV4 ... 38 D5
Arley Mews CV32 ... 156 E1
Arley Rd
Birmingham B29 ... 85 F3
Birmingham,Saltley B8 ... 67 D6
Solihull B91 ... 107 A4
Arley Villas 4 B18 ... 65 D4
Arlidge Cl WV14 ... 40 D4
Arlidge Cres CV8 ... 148 C5
Arlington Ave CV32 ... 156 F2
Arlington Cl DY6 ... 60 D4
Arlington Ct
2 Royal Leamington Spa
CV32 ... 156 F2
Stourbridge DY8 ... 81 B4
Arlington Gr B14 ... 105 B2
Arlington Ho B15 ... 86 C7
Arlington Mews 5 CV32. 156 F2
Arlington Rd
Birmingham B14 ... 105 B3
West Bromwich B71 ... 53 D6
Arlington Way CV11 ... 73 F2
Arlon Ave CV10 ... 72 D7
Armada Cl B23 ... 56 D1
Armadale Cl LE10 ... 71 A1
Armarna Dr CV5 ... 111 B8
Armfield St CV6 ... 114 A8
Armitage Ho WS13 ... 3 E1
Armorial Rd CV3 ... 133 B7
Armour Cl LE10 ... 75 D5
Armoury Rd B11 ... 87 D6
Armoury Trad Est B11 ... 87 E6
Armscott Rd CV2 ... 114 C6
Armside Cl WS3 ... 15 B4
Armson Rd CV7 ... 78 A1
Armstead Rd WV9 ... 11 A3
Armstrong Ave CV3 ... 114 B1
Armstrong Cl
Stourbridge DY8 ... 81 B6
Whitnash CV31 ... 162 A2
Armstrong Dr
Birmingham B36 ... 58 F1
Walsall WS2 ... 28 A4
Wolverhampton WV6 ... 25 A5
Armstrong B79 ... 20 F6
Armstrong Way WV13 ... 41 B8
Arna Ho CV3 ... 134 B6
Arncliffe Cl CV11 ... 74 A2
Arncliffe Way 4 CV34 ... 155 F1
Arne Rd CV2 ... 115 A6
Arnhem Cl WV11 ... 26 B8
Arnhem Cnr CV3 ... 134 D6
Arnhem Rd WV13 ... 40 E8
Arnhem Way DY4 ... 52 C5
Arnold Ave CV3 ... 133 C5
Arnold Cl
Tamworth B79 ... 21 A6
Willenhall WS2 ... 27 F3
Arnold Gr
Birmingham B30 ... 103 D4
Solihull B90 ... 106 B4
Arnold Lodge Sch CV32 . 156 F2
Arnold Rd B90 ... 106 C4
Arnotdale Dr WS12 ... 1 F7
Arnside Cl CV1 ... 165 D4
Arnside Ct B23 ... 56 B4
Arnwood Cl WS2 ... 27 F2
Arosa Dr B17 ... 85 B3
Arran Cl
Birmingham B43 ... 43 E3
Cannock WS11 ... 2 A3
Nuneaton CV10 ... 73 A3
Arran Dr B77 ... 35 F7
Arran Rd B34 ... 68 F6
Arran Way
Birmingham B36 ... 70 B7
Hinckley LE10 ... 71 B1
Arras Bvd CV35 ... 160 A7
Arras Rd DY2 ... 51 E2
Arrow Cl B93 ... 128 A6
Arrowdale Rd B98 ... 154 A3
Arrowfield Gn B38 ... 123 D7
Arrow Ho 1 B68 ... 84 B8
Arrow Ind Est WV12 ... 27 D6
Arrow Rd N B98 ... 154 A4
Arrow Rd S B98 ... 154 A4
Arrow Rd WS3 ... 28 E6
Arrow Vale Com High Sch
B98 ... 154 E2
Arrow Valley Pk* B98 ... 154 C4
Arrow Wlk B38 ... 104 B1
Arsenal St B9 ... 67 C1
Artemis Dr CV34 ... 161 E5
Arthingworth Cl CV3 ... 114 E1
Arthur Alford Ho CV12 ... 77 D1
Arthur Dr (Road 2) DY11 116 E1
Arthur Greenwood Ct
WV14 ... 40 C6
Arthur Gunby Cl B75 ... 46 F7
Arthur Harris Cl B66 ... 65 C3
Arthur Pl B1 ... 66 B3
Arthur Rd
Birmingham,Edgbaston
B15 ... 86 B7
Birmingham,Erdington B24 . 57 B4
Birmingham,Handsworth
B21 ... 65 F8
Birmingham,Hay Mills B25 . 88 B6
Tipton DY4 ... 52 A7
Arthur St
Bilston WV14 ... 40 D6
Birmingham B10 ... 67 B1
Cannock,Chadsmoor WS11 .. 1 F4
Cannock WS12 ... 2 F3
Arthur St continued
Coventry CV1 ... 165 C4
Kenilworth CV8 ... 148 A5
Redditch B98 ... 154 B3
West Bromwich B70 ... 53 D1
Wolverhampton WV2 ... 39 D7
Arthur Terry Sch The B74. 32 A3
Artillery Rd CV11 ... 79 F6
Artillery St B9 ... 67 C2
Artingstall Ho B30 ... 104 B8
Arton Croft B24 ... 57 A2
Arundel Ave WS10 ... 41 F3
Arundel B17 ... 85 A6
Arundel Cl 2 CV34 ... 160 F8
Arundel Cres B92 ... 89 A1
Arundel Ct 13 B29 ... 103 C7
Arundel Dr B69 ... 62 F8
Arundel Gr WV6 ... 23 F3
Arundel Ho B23 ... 56 F6
Arundel Pl B11 ... 87 A6
Arundel Rd
Birmingham B14 ... 105 A1
Bromsgrove B60 ... 137 B1
Bulkington CV12 ... 79 C3
Coventry CV3 ... 133 D6
Stourbridge DY8 ... 60 C2
Willenhall WV12 ... 27 C7
Wolverhampton WV10 ... 11 B2
Arundel St WS1 ... 42 E7
Arundel B77 ... 35 C7
Arun Way B76 ... 47 A1
Asbury Ct B43 ... 54 C8
Asbury Rd
Balsall Common CV7 ... 130 B5
Wednesbury WS10 ... 42 E2
Ascot Cl
Bedworth CV12 ... 78 B4
Birmingham B16 ... 65 F2
Coventry CV3 ... 134 C6
Lichfield WS14 ... 9 D7
Oldbury B69 ... 63 E6
Ascot Ct 11 B29 ... 103 C7
Ascot Dr
Cannock WS11 ... 4 C8
Dudley DY1 ... 50 F2
Tamworth B77 ... 35 D4
Wolverhampton WV4 ... 39 A4
Ascote La B90 ... 126 A5
Ascot Gdns DY8 ... 60 D2
Ascot Rd B13 ... 86 F2
Ascot Ride CV32 ... 157 C3
Ascot Way B61 ... 121 B1
Ascot Wlk B69 ... 63 E6
Asfare Bsns Pk LE10 ... 75 E1
Ash Ave B12 ... 87 A5
Ashborough Dr B91 ... 127 C8
Ashbourne Cl WS11 ... 2 A4
Ashbourne Gr 3 B6 ... 66 E8
Ashbourne Rd
Birmingham B16 ... 65 D3
Walsall WS3 ... 14 C3
Wolverhampton,Heath Town
WV1 ... 26 A3
Wolverhampton,Lanesfield
WV4 ... 39 E3
Ashbourne Ridge B63 ... 82 D5
Ashbourne Way B90 ... 126 E8
Ash Bridge Ct B45 ... 122 B6
Ashbridge Rd CV5 ... 112 C4
Ashbrook Cres B91 ... 127 C8
Ashbrook Dr B45 ... 122 B8
Ashbrook Gr B30 ... 104 C8
Ashbrook Rd B30 ... 104 C8
Ashburn Gr WV13 ... 27 C2
Ashburton Cl LE10 ... 76 A6
Ashburton Rd
Birmingham B14 ... 104 D5
Coventry CV2 ... 114 E8
Ashbury Covert 3 B30 .. 104 C3
Ashby Cl
Birmingham B8 ... 68 C6
Coventry CV3 ... 134 F8
Ashby Ct
Nuneaton CV11 ... 73 D3
Solihull B91 ... 107 C1
Ashby Grange LE10 ... 71 E5
Ashby Rd
Hinckley LE9,LE10 ... 71 E5
Tamworth B79 ... 21 C8
Ash Cl WV8 ... 10 A3
Ashcombe Ave B20 ... 54 E3
Ashcombe Dr CV4 ... 111 F3
Ashcombe Gdns B24 ... 57 D3
Ashcott Cl B38 ... 103 D2
Ash Cres
Birmingham B37 ... 69 F6
Kingswinford DY6 ... 60 E6
Portway B47 ... 140 F8
Ashcroft
12 Wolverhampton WV4 ... 39 F4
4 Smethwick B66 ... 65 C5
Birmingham B15 ... 85 E5
Ashcroft Cl CV2 ... 115 A8
Ashcroft Gr B20 ... 55 D2
Ashcroft Inf Sch B79 ... 21 C7
Ashcroft La
Lichfield WS14 ... 8 E1
Shenstone WS14 ... 17 E7
Ashcroft DY4 ... 52 A2
Ashcroft Way CV2 ... 115 B8
Ash Ct
Balsall Common CV7 ... 130 C5
Oldbury B66 ... 64 C8
Stourbridge DY8 ... 81 A4

Ashdale Cl
Binley Woods CV3 . . . . 135 E7
Huntington WS12 . . . . 1 C7
Kingswinford DY6 . . . . 60 D8
Ashdale Dr B14 . . . . 105 A1
Ashdale Gr B26 . . . . 89 A8
Ashdale Rd B77 . . . . 21 D5
Ashdene Cl
Kidderminster DY10 . . . . . 117 C5
Sutton Coldfield B73 . . . . . . 46 A3
Ashdene Gdns
Kenilworth CV8 . . . . 148 B4
Stourbridge DY8 . . . . 60 C2
Ashdown Cl
Birmingham,Frankley B45 . . . . 102 A2
Birmingham,Highgate B13 . . 87 A1
Coventry CV3 . . . . 134 D8
Ashdown Dr
Nuneaton CV10 . . . . 72 F2
Stourbridge DY8 . . . . 60 E3
Ash Dr
Birmingham B31 . . . . 102 C1
Hartshill CV10 . . . . 72 A8
Kenilworth CV8 . . . . 148 A4
Lower Marlbrook B61 . . . . 121 B1
West Bromwich B71 . . . . . . 53 C6
Ashen Cl DY3 . . . . 39 C3
Ashenden Rise WV3 . . . . . . 38 A8
Ash End House Farm★ B78 . . . . 48 B8
Ashenhurst Rd DY1 . . . . . . 61 F8
Ashenhurst Wlk DY1 . . . . . 51 A1
Ashe Rd CV10 . . . . 72 B3
Ashes Rd B69 . . . . 63 F3
Ashes The
Oldbury B69 . . . . 63 F3
Wolverhampton WV11 . . . . . 26 B6
Ashfern Dr B76 . . . . 57 F7
Ashfield Ave
Birmingham B14 . . . . 86 F1
Coventry CV4 . . . . 111 D1
Ashfield Cl WS3 . . . . 28 F4
Ashfield Cres
Dudley DY2 . . . . 62 C3
Stourbridge DY9 . . . . 82 A3
Ashfield Ct B38 . . . . 103 E4
Ashfield Gdns B14 . . . . 86 F1
Ashfield Gr
Halesowen B63 . . . . 82 E2
Wolverhampton WV10 . . . . . 11 C3
Ashfield Ho B28 . . . . 105 E3
Ashfield Rd
Bilston WV14 . . . . 41 A2
Birmingham B14 . . . . 86 F1
Kenilworth CV8 . . . . 148 B4
Wolverhampton,Fordhouses WV10 . . . . 11 C3
Wolverhampton WV3 . . . . . . 24 D2
Ashford Cl B24 . . . . 57 D4
Ashford Dr
Bedworth CV12 . . . . 78 A3
Sedgley DY3 . . . . 50 E7
Sutton Coldfield B76 . . . . . . 57 F5
Ashford Gdns CV31 . . . . . 161 F3
Ashford Ind Pk WV2 . . . . . 40 A7
Ashford La B94 . . . . 143 B7
Ashford Rd
Hinckley LE10 . . . . 75 B7
Whitnash CV31 . . . . 161 F2
Ashford Twr B12 . . . . 86 F8
Ashfurlong Cl CV7 . . . . . . 130 B6
Ashfurlong Cres B75 . . . . . 46 E7
Ash Gn DY1 . . . . 51 A5
Ash Gr
11 Birmingham,Bordesley B9 . . . . 67 B2
Ash Green CV7 . . . . 95 C7
Birmingham,Balsall Heath B12 . . . . 87 A5
Cannock WS11 . . . . 1 F4
Dudley DY3 . . . . 50 C2
Ash Green La CV7 . . . . 95 D6
Ash Green Mobile Home Pk CV7 . . . . 95 C7
Ash Green Sch CV7 . . . . . . 95 D6
Ash Gr
Kidderminster DY11 . . . . . 116 B7
Lichfield WS14 . . . . 9 E8
Ashgrove WS7 . . . . 6 F5
Ashgrove Cl B60 . . . . 121 D1
Ashgrove Rd B44 . . . . 44 C2
Ash Gr
Stourbridge DY9 . . . . 81 D3
Tamworth B77 . . . . 35 F5
Ash Hill WV3 . . . . 24 D2
Ashill Rd B45 . . . . 122 B7
Ashington Gr CV3 . . . . 134 A5
Ashington Rd CV12 . . . . 77 C1
Ash La
Alvechurch B48 . . . . 123 D2
Great Wyrley WS6 . . . . 5 A3
Ashlands Cl B79 . . . . 21 C7
Ashland St
Wolverhampton WV3 . . . . . . 25 B1
Wolverhampton WV3 . . . . . . 39 B8
Ashlawn Cres B91 . . . . . . 106 D5
Ash Lawn Ho 8 CV31 . . . 162 A7
Ashlea B78 . . . . 36 F5
Ashleigh Ct 8 DY2 . . . . 62 E8
Ashleigh Dr
Birmingham B20 . . . . 55 B2
Nuneaton CV11 . . . . 73 F1
Tamworth B77 . . . . 35 E8
Ashleigh Gr B13 . . . . 87 B1
Ashleigh Ho B91 . . . . 107 C5
Ashleigh Hts B91 . . . . 107 A5
Ashleigh Mews Cotts B76 59 C6
Ashleigh Rd
Oldbury B69 . . . . 63 C8
Solihull B91 . . . . 107 B4
Ashley Cl
Birmingham B15 . . . . 86 C7
Kingswinford DY6 . . . . 60 C4
Stourbridge DY8 . . . . 80 D2
Ashley Cres CV34 . . . . 161 B6
Ashley Ct B45 . . . . 122 A1
Ashley Gdns B8 . . . . 67 D4
Ashley Ho DY2 . . . . 62 D4
Ashley Mount WV6 . . . . 24 D5
Ashley Rd
Birmingham B23 . . . . 56 E3
Walsall WS3 . . . . 13 F1
Willenhall WS3 . . . . 27 F8
Wolverhampton WV4 . . . . . . 38 E5
Ashley St WV14 . . . . 40 E6
Ashley Way CV7 . . . . 130 B7
Ashmall WS7 . . . . 7 D4
Ashmead Dr B45 . . . . 122 C4
Ashmead Gr B24 . . . . 57 A2
Ashmead Rd WS7 . . . . 7 A8
Ashmead Rise B45 . . . . . . 122 C4
Ash Mews 4 B27 . . . . 88 C5
Ashmole Ave WS7 . . . . 7 E8
Ashmole Cl WS14 . . . . 9 E6
Ashmole Rd B70 . . . . 52 F7
Ashmore Ave WV11 . . . . . . 13 A1
Ashmore Ind Est WS2 . . . . 28 E3
Ashmore Lake Rd WV12 . . 27 B4
Ashmore Lake Way WV12. 27 B4
Ashmore Rd
Birmingham B30 . . . . 103 F5
Coventry CV6 . . . . 113 B4
Ashmores Cl B97 . . . . 158 D5
Ashmore's Ind Est DY1 . . . 51 E3
Ashold Farm Rd B24 . . . . . 57 D2
Asholme Cl B36 . . . . 68 C7
Ashorne Cl
Birmingham B28 . . . . 106 B7
Coventry CV2 . . . . 96 C2
Redditch B98 . . . . 159 D8
Ashover Gr 8 B18 . . . . 65 E4
Ashover Rd B44 . . . . 44 D3
Ashow Cl CV8 . . . . 148 B4
Ash Park Ind Est WS11 . . . . . 2 B3
Ashperton Cl B98 . . . . 153 E1
Ash Priors Cl CV4 . . . . . . 112 B1
Ash Rd
Birmingham B8 . . . . 67 D4
Dudley DY1 . . . . 51 B3
Tipton DY4 . . . . 51 E4
Wednesbury WS10 . . . . 41 F5
Ashridge Cl CV11 . . . . 78 F8
Ash St
Bilston WV14 . . . . 40 E3
Cradley Heath B64 . . . . 62 F2
Ashstead Cl B76 . . . . 58 B6
Ash St
Walsall WS3 . . . . 14 D1
Wolverhampton WV3 . . . . . . 25 A1
Ashted Cir B7 . . . . 67 A4
Ashted Lock B7 . . . . 66 F4
Ashted Wlk B7 . . . . 67 B4
Ash Terr B69 . . . . 52 B1
Ashton Cl B97 . . . . 153 B1
Ashton Croft
Birmingham B16 . . . . 66 A2
Solihull B91 . . . . 107 A1
Ashton Dr WS4 . . . . 15 C2
Ashton Park Dr DY5 . . . . . . 61 C1
Ashton Rd B25 . . . . 88 C7
Ash Tree Ave CV4 . . . . 112 A2
Ashtree Cl DY5 . . . . 61 B1
Ashtree Ct WS11 . . . . 1 D4
Ash Tree Dr B26 . . . . 88 D7
Ashtree Gr WV14 . . . . 41 B3
Ash Tree Gr CV7 . . . . 97 E5
Ash Tree Rd B30 . . . . 104 A6
Ashtree Rd
Cradley Heath B64 . . . . 62 F2
Oldbury B69 . . . . 63 D8
Ash Tree Rd B97 . . . . 153 B5
Ashtree Rd WS3 . . . . 15 A3
Ashurst Cl CV6 . . . . 96 B5
Ashurst Rd B76 . . . . 57 F7
Ash View WS12 . . . . 1 D8
Ashville Ave B34 . . . . 68 F7
Ashville Dr B63 . . . . 83 A5
Ashwater Dr B14 . . . . 104 D2
Ashway B11 . . . . 87 B5
Ash Way B23 . . . . 56 C7
Ashwell Dr B90 . . . . 106 D4
Ashwells Gr WV9 . . . . 11 A2
Ashwin Rd B21 . . . . 66 A7
Ash Wlk B76 . . . . 46 F2
Ashwood Ave
Coventry CV6 . . . . 112 F5
Stourbridge DY8 . . . . 60 D2
Ashwood Cl
Oldbury B69 . . . . 63 F4
Sutton Coldfield B74 . . . . . . 44 E8
Ashwood Ct
Birmingham B13 . . . . 87 A3
Birmingham,Stechford B34 . 68 D5
Ashwood Dr B37 . . . . 70 D3
Ashwood Gr WV4 . . . . 39 A5
Ashwoodhay DY8 . . . . 60 F3
Ashwood Park Prim Sch DY8 . . . . 60 D1
Ashwood Rd CV10 . . . . 72 E5
Ashworth Ho
2 Lichfield WS13 . . . . 9 B8
Cannock WS11 . . . . 2 A4
Ashworth Rd B42 . . . . 44 B1
Askew Bridge Rd DY3 . . . . 50 B3
Askew Cl DY3 . . . . 50 E5
Aspbury Croft B36 . . . . 58 D1
Aspects Park Gate CV11 . . 73 F7
Aspen Cl
2 Lichfield WS13 . . . . 9 E8
Birmingham B27 . . . . 88 B2
Coventry CV4 . . . . 111 D1
Sutton Coldfield B76 . . . . . . 46 F2
Aspen Dr
Bedworth CV6 . . . . 96 C6
Birmingham B37 . . . . 90 C8
Aspen Gdns B20 . . . . 55 B1
Aspen Gr
Birmingham B9 . . . . 68 A3
Burntwood WS7 . . . . 6 F8
Hollywood B47 . . . . 125 B5
Willenhall WV12 . . . . 27 E7
Aspen Ho B91 . . . . 106 F2
Aspens Way B61 . . . . 137 A6
Aspen Way WV3 . . . . 25 A1
Asphodel B74 . . . . 31 F5
Asplen Ct CV8 . . . . 148 C4
Aspley Heath La B94 . . . . 141 D2
Aspley Heath B94 . . . . 141 D2
Asquith Dr
Cannock WS11 . . . . 2 C2
Oldbury B69 . . . . 52 D2
Asquith Rd B8 . . . . 68 B5
Asra Cl B66 . . . . 65 A8
Asra Ho B66 . . . . 65 A8
Astbury Ave B67 . . . . 64 F3
Astbury Cl
Walsall WS3 . . . . 14 A4
Wolverhampton WV1 . . . . . . 26 A1
Astbury Ct 1 B68 . . . . 84 B7
Aster Cl
Hinckley LE10 . . . . 75 E6
Nuneaton CV11 . . . . 74 A1
Aster Way
Hinckley LE10 . . . . 75 D6
Walsall WS5 . . . . 43 A3
Aster Wlk
Bedworth CV10 . . . . 78 A8
Wolverhampton WV9 . . . . . . 11 A3
Asthill Croft CV3 . . . . 133 C8
Asthill Gr CV3 . . . . 133 C8
Astley Ave
Coventry CV6 . . . . 95 E2
Halesowen B62 . . . . 83 F6
Astley Cl
Redditch B98 . . . . 159 A7
Royal Leamington Spa CV32 . . . . 156 D2
Tipton DY4 . . . . 52 D6
Astley Cres B62 . . . . 83 F5
Astley La
Bedworth CV12 . . . . 77 C4
Nuneaton CV10 . . . . 72 B1
Astley Rd
Birmingham B21 . . . . 54 D1
Bromsgrove B60 . . . . 137 C1
Astley Wlk B90 . . . . 106 B5
Aston Bridge B6 . . . . 66 F6
Aston Brook Gn B6 . . . . 66 F5
Aston Brook St E B6 . . . . . . 66 F5
Aston Brook St B6 . . . . 66 F6
Aston Bury B15 . . . . 85 D7
Aston Church Rd B7,B8 . . . 67 D6
Aston Cl
Darlaston WV14 . . . . 41 A4
Shenstone WS14 . . . . 17 F6
Aston Cross Bsns Village B6 . . . . 67 A6
Aston Ct B23 . . . . 56 C3
Aston Expressway B6 . . . . 66 F6
Aston Expressway (Elevated Rd) B6 . . . . 67 A8
Aston Fields Mid Sch B60 . . . . 151 C8
Aston Fields Trad Est 2 B60 . . . . 150 F6
Aston Flamville Rd LE10 . . 76 C7
Aston Hall★ B6 . . . . 66 F8
Aston Hall Rd B6 . . . . 67 B8
Aston La
Aston Flamville LE10 . . . . . . 76 D7
Birmingham B20 . . . . 55 E2
Hinckley LE10 . . . . 76 A6
Aston Manor Cl B20 . . . . . . 55 E2
Aston Manor Sch B6 . . . . . 66 F6
Aston Manor Transport Mus★ B6 . . . . 55 F1
Aston Pk Ind Est CV11 . . . . 73 B5
Aston Prim Sch B74 . . . . . . 31 C6
Aston Rd
Birmingham B6 . . . . 66 F5
Bromsgrove B60 . . . . 150 F6
Coventry CV5 . . . . 112 F1
Dudley DY2 . . . . 62 B8
Aston Rd N B6 . . . . 66 F6
Aston Rd
Nuneaton CV11 . . . . 73 B5
Oldbury B69 . . . . 52 A1
Willenhall WV13 . . . . 26 E2
Aston Science Pk B7 . . . . . 66 F4
Astons Cl DY5 . . . . 81 D7
Aston Seedbed Ctr B7 . . . . 67 A6
Astons Fold DY5 . . . . 81 D7
Aston Sta B6 . . . . 67 B8
Aston St
Birmingham B4 . . . . 164 D4
Tipton DY4 . . . . 52 C7
Wolverhampton WV3 . . . . . . 39 A8
Aston Tower Com Prim Sch B6 . . . . 66 F7
Aston Univ B5 . . . . 164 D4
Astor Dr B13 . . . . 87 C1
Astoria Cl WV12 . . . . 13 D1
Astoria Gdns WV12 . . . . . . 13 D1
Astor Rd
Kingswinford DY6 . . . . 60 F5
Sutton Coldfield B74 . . . . . . 31 A1
Astwell Prep Sch B20 . . . . 66 B8
Astwood Bank Fst Sch B96 . . . . 158 E2
Astwood La B96 . . . . 158 C2
Atcham Cl B98 . . . . 154 F3
Atcheson Cl B80 . . . . 159 E4
Athelney Ct WS3 . . . . 15 A3
Athelstan Gr WV6 . . . . 23 F5
Athelstan Way B79 . . . . 20 F7
Athena Dr CV34 . . . . 161 E5
Athena Gdns CV6 . . . . 96 A1
Atherstone Cl
Redditch B98 . . . . 154 F1
Solihull B90 . . . . 105 E2
Atherstone Rd WV1 . . . . . . 26 B2
Atherstone St B77,B78 . . . . 35 B8
Atherston Pl CV4 . . . . 132 D6
Athlone Rd WS5 . . . . 43 C8
Athol Cl B32 . . . . 102 D8
Athole St B12 . . . . 87 A7
Atholl Cres CV10 . . . . 72 E2
Atholl Ct CV10 . . . . 72 E2
Athol Rd CV2 . . . . 115 A6
Atkinson Ct WV10 . . . . 25 D6
Atkins Way LE10 . . . . 75 E7
Atlantic Ct 4 WV13 . . . . . . 27 A1
Atlantic Rd B44 . . . . 44 F1
Atlantic Way WS10 . . . . 41 E1
Atlas Croft WV10 . . . . 25 C6
Atlas Est
Birmingham,Tyseley B11 . . . 88 A5
Birmingham,Witton B6 . . . . 56 A2
Atlas Gr B70 . . . . 52 F3
Atlas Trad Est
Birmingham B11 . . . . 87 D5
Coseley WV14 . . . . 40 F2
Attenborough Cl B19 . . . . . 66 E5
Attingham Dr
Birmingham B43 . . . . 43 D2
Cannock WS11 . . . . 2 B2
Dudley DY1 . . . . 51 B2
Attleborough Fields Ind Est CV11 . . . . 73 E3
Attleborough La B46 . . . . . 59 A1
Attleborough Rd CV11 . . . . 73 D3
Attlee Cl B69 . . . . 52 D2
Attlee Cres WV14 . . . . 40 E2
Attlee Gr WS11 . . . . 2 C2
Attlee Rd WS2 . . . . 27 E3
Attoxhall Rd CV2 . . . . 114 E4
Attwell Pk WV3 . . . . 38 D7
Attwell Rd DY4 . . . . 40 F1
Attwood Bsns Ctr 2 DY9 . 81 F5
Attwood Cl B8 . . . . 67 E6
Attwood Cres CV2 . . . . . . 114 C7
Attwood Gdns WV4 . . . . 39 E5
Attwood Rd WS7 . . . . 6 C7
Attwood St
Halesowen B63 . . . . 82 F5
Stourbridge DY9 . . . . 81 F5
Atworth Cl B98 . . . . 159 B5
Aubrey Rd
Birmingham B32 . . . . 84 E7
Birmingham,Small Heath B10 . . . . 87 F8
Auchinleck Dr WS13 . . . . . . 3 C1
Auchinleck Sq 5 B15 . . . . . 66 B1
Auckland Dr B36 . . . . 70 B7
Auckland Ho B32 . . . . 84 F4
Auckland Rd
Birmingham B11 . . . . 87 A7
Kingswinford DY6 . . . . 60 E4
Smethwick B67 . . . . 64 E5
Auden Ct WV6 . . . . 23 F4
Audleigh Ho 1 B15 . . . . . . 86 C8
Audlem Wlk WV10 . . . . 26 A5
Audley Dr DY11 . . . . 116 A8
Audley Prim Sch B33 . . . . . 68 F4
Audley Rd B33 . . . . 68 F4
Audnam DY8 . . . . 60 F1
Augusta Pl CV32 . . . . 161 F8
Augusta Rd
Birmingham,Acock's Green B27 . . . . 88 C5
Birmingham,Moseley B13 . . 86 E4
Augusta Rd E B13 . . . . 86 F4
Augusta St B18 . . . . 66 C4
Augustine Ave B80 . . . . . . 159 D4
Augustine Gr
Birmingham B18 . . . . 65 F6
Sutton Coldfield B74 . . . . . . 31 F5
Augustines Wlk WS13 . . . . . 3 A3
Augustus Cl B46 . . . . 59 F1
Augustus Ct B15 . . . . 85 F8
Augustus Rd
Birmingham B15 . . . . 85 E8
Coventry CV1 . . . . 113 F4
Augustus St WS2 . . . . 28 D1
Aulton Cres LE10 . . . . 71 B1
Aulton Rd B75 . . . . 32 E2
Aulton Way LE10 . . . . 71 B1
Ault St B70 . . . . 53 D1
Austcliff Cl B97 . . . . 158 D6
Austcliff Dr B91 . . . . 127 C8
Austen Ct CV32 . . . . 157 E5
Austen Pl B15 . . . . 86 B8
Austen Wlk B71 . . . . 53 D6
Austin Cl
Birmingham B27 . . . . 88 D4
Dudley DY1 . . . . 50 F2
Austin Cote La WS14 . . . . . . 9 F7
Austin Croft B36 . . . . 58 E1
Austin Ct 4 B74 . . . . 31 E3
Austin Dr CV6 . . . . 114 A7
Austin Edwards Dr CV34. 161 B8
Austin Ho WS4 . . . . 28 F3
Austin Rd
Birmingham B21 . . . . 54 C1
Bromsgrove B60 . . . . 150 E7
Austin Rise B31 . . . . 122 F7
Austin St WV6 . . . . 25 B4
Austin Way B42 . . . . 55 A5
Austrey Cl B93 . . . . 128 A6
Austrey Gr B29 . . . . 103 A8
Austrey Rd DY6 . . . . 61 A5
Austwick Cl CV34 . . . . 155 E1
Austy Cl B36 . . . . 68 E8
Autobase Ind Est B69 . . . . 52 C3
Auto Ctr B18 . . . . 65 E5
Autumn Berry Gr DY3 . . . . 50 E6
Autumn Cl WS4 . . . . 15 C1
Autumn Dr
Dudley DY3 . . . . 50 D4
Lichfield WS13 . . . . 3 D2
Walsall WS4 . . . . 15 C2
Autumn Gr B19 . . . . 66 C6
Auxerre Ave B98 . . . . 159 B8
Auxerre Ho B98 . . . . 159 B8
Avalon Cl B24 . . . . 57 B4
Avalon Ho 2 WS11 . . . . 1 F4
Avalon Rd B60 . . . . 137 C2
Avebury Cl CV11 . . . . 73 F2
Avebury Gr B30 . . . . 104 C7
Avebury Rd B30 . . . . 104 C8
Ave Maria Cl B64 . . . . 62 E1
Avenbury Cl B98 . . . . 154 F1
Avenbury Dr B91 . . . . 107 E4
Avenue Cl
Birmingham B7 . . . . 67 A6
Dorridge B93 . . . . 128 A3
Avenue Rd
Astwood Bank B96 . . . . . . 158 E1
Birmingham,Aston B7,B6 . . . 67 A6
Birmingham,Erdington B23 . 56 F4
Birmingham,Handsworth B21 . . . . 54 D2
Birmingham,King's Heath B14 . . . . 104 D8
Cannock WS12 . . . . 2 E2
Darlaston WS10 . . . . 41 D6
Dorridge B93 . . . . 128 A3
Dudley,Woodside DY1,DY2 . . 61 F6
Kenilworth CV8 . . . . 147 D6
Nuneaton CV11 . . . . 73 D2
Rowley Regis B65 . . . . 63 D1
Royal Leamington Spa CV31 . . . . 161 F7
Tipton WV14 . . . . 51 C8
Wolverhampton WV3 . . . . . . 24 E2
Avenue The
2 Birmingham,Lozells B19 . . . . 66 C8
Birmingham,Acock's Green B27 . . . . 88 D3
Birmingham B45 . . . . 121 E7
Blackwell B60 . . . . 138 A6
Blakedown DY10 . . . . 98 B2
Coventry CV3 . . . . 134 A6
Featherstone WV10 . . . . 12 C7
Rowington Green CV35 . . . 145 A1
Rowley Regis B65 . . . . 63 A3
Sutton Coldfield B76 . . . . . . 46 F1
Wolverhampton,Castlecroft WV3 . . . . 38 B8
Wolverhampton,Park Village WV10 . . . . 25 F6
Wolverhampton,Penn WV4 . 38 E4
Averill Rd B26 . . . . 69 A1
Avern Cl DY4 . . . . 52 B6
Aversley Rd B38 . . . . 123 E8
Avery Croft B35 . . . . 57 F2
Avery Ct 6 CV34 . . . . 160 F7
Avery Dell Ind Est B30 . . 104 A6
Avery Dr B27 . . . . 88 C4
Avery Ho B16 . . . . 66 A1
Avery Myers Cl B68 . . . . . . 64 B5
Avery Rd
Smethwick B66 . . . . 65 D6
Sutton Coldfield B73 . . . . . . 45 C3
Aviary Ct B71 . . . . 53 C6
Aviemore Cl CV10 . . . . 73 A2
Aviemore Cres B43 . . . . 44 B4
Avill Gr DY11 . . . . 116 C7
Avill B77 . . . . 36 A5
Avington Cl DY3 . . . . 50 D7
Avion Cl WS1 . . . . 42 F7
Avion Ctr WV6 . . . . 25 A4
Avocet Cl
Birmingham B33 . . . . 68 E3
Coventry CV2 . . . . 96 B3
Avocet Dr DY10 . . . . 117 A2
Avonbank Cl B97 . . . . 158 C6
Avon Bsns Pk WS11 . . . . 4 C7
Avon Cl
Brierley Hill DY5 . . . . 61 B7
Bromsgrove B60 . . . . 150 F6
Bulkington CV12 . . . . 79 B6
Perton WV6 . . . . 23 F4
Avon Cres WS3 . . . . 15 A1
Avoncroft 8 WV4 . . . . 39 F4
Avoncroft Ho B37 . . . . 70 A2
Avoncroft Mus of Historic Bldgs★ B60 . . . . 150 E5
Avoncroft Rd B60 . . . . 150 D6
Avon Ct
Kenilworth CV8 . . . . 147 F5
Sutton Coldfield B73 . . . . . . 46 B5
Avondale Cl DY6 . . . . 60 E8
Avondale Rd
Birmingham B11 . . . . 87 D4

Avondale Rd *continued*
Brandon CV8 . . . . **135** F5
Coventry CV5 . . . . **133** A8
Royal Leamington Spa
CV32 . . . . **157** C4
Wolverhampton WV6 . . . . . . **24** F3
Avon Dr
Birmingham,Castle Bromwich
B36 . . . . **69** F7
Birmingham,Moseley B13 . . **87** B2
Willenhall WV13 . . . . **27** C2
Wythall B47 . . . . **124** E2
Avon Gr WS5 . . . . **43** A4
Avon Ho
[2] Dudley,Russell's Hall
DY1 . . . . **61** E8
[3] Birmingham,Brandhall
B68 . . . . **84** B8
Birmingham,Lee Bank B15 . **86** D8
Coventry CV4 . . . . **132** C6
Dudley,Dibdale DY3 . . . . **50** E3
Avonlea Rise CV32 . . . . . . **156** D2
Avon Lodge CV11 . . . . **73** A5
Avon Park Cvn Pk B92 . . . . **90** D1
Avon Rd
Burntwood WS7 . . . . **6** F5
Cannock WS11 . . . . **4** D8
Coventry CV4 . . . . **132** B6
Halesowen B63 . . . . **82** B5
Kenilworth CV8 . . . . **147** E3
Kidderminster DY11 . . . . . **116** B3
Solihull B90 . . . . **106** D1
Stourbridge DY8 . . . . **80** F3
Walsall WS3 . . . . **14** E1
Whitnash CV31 . . . . **162** A3
Avon St
Birmingham B11 . . . . **87** C5
Coventry CV2 . . . . **114** B5
Warwick CV34 . . . . **161** A7
Avon B77 . . . . **36** A5
Avon Wlk LE10 . . . . **75** A8
Avro Way B35 . . . . **58** B2
Awbridge Rd DY2 . . . . **62** C3
Awefields Cres B67 . . . . **64** E4
Awlmakers Gr WS3 . . . . . . **28** D7
Awson St CV6 . . . . **113** F6
Axcess 10 Bsns Pk WS10 . **41** E8
Axholme Rd CV2 . . . . **114** E4
Axletree Way WS10 . . . . . . **42** B5
Axminster Cl CV11 . . . . **73** F5
Ayala Croft [2] B36 . . . . **68** E8
Aylesbury Cl B94 . . . . **143** C6
Aylesbury Cres B44 . . . . . . **56** A8
Aylesbury Rd B94 . . . . **143** D7
Aylesdene Ct CV5 . . . . **132** F8
Aylesford Cl DY3 . . . . **39** C2
Aylesford Ct [7] CV31 . . . . **162** A6
Aylesford Dr
Birmingham B37 . . . . **90** A7
Sutton Coldfield B74 . . . . . . **31** E5
Aylesford Rd B21 . . . . **54** D1
Aylesford Sch & Language
Coll CV34 . . . . **160** C4
Aylesford St
Coventry CV1 . . . . **113** E4
Royal Leamington Spa
CV31 . . . . **162** A6
Aylesmore Cl
Birmingham B32 . . . . **84** C1
Solihull B92 . . . . **106** E8
Aynho Cl CV5 . . . . **112** A3
Aynsley Ct B90 . . . . **106** C2
Ayre Rd B24 . . . . **57** B4
Ayrshire Cl B36 . . . . **68** D8
Ayrton Cl WV6 . . . . **24** A4
Aysgarth Cl CV11 . . . . **74** A2
Azalea Cl
Codsall WV8 . . . . **10** B3
Hinckley LE10 . . . . **75** E5
Azalea Dr LE10 . . . . **75** E6
Azalea Gr B9 . . . . **67** F2
Azalea Wlk LE10 . . . . **75** E5
Aziz Isaac Cl B68 . . . . **64** C6

B

Babbacombe Rd CV3 . . . . **133** D5
Babington Rd B21 . . . . **65** E7
Bablake Cl CV6 . . . . **112** F8
Bablake Croft B92 . . . . **89** A1
Bablake Jun Sch CV1 . . . **165** A4
Bablake Sch CV1 . . . . **113** B4
Babors Field WV14 . . . . **40** A3
Babworth Cl WV9 . . . . **11** A2
Baccabox La B47 . . . . **124** E7
Bacchus Rd B18 . . . . **65** F6
Bache St B70 . . . . **53** D1
Bach Mill Dr B28 . . . . **105** D3
Backcester La WS13 . . . . **9** B8
Backcrofts [3] WS11 . . . . **1** E1
Backhouse La WV11 . . . . **26** C4
Back La
Aldridge WS9 . . . . **30** F8
Meriden CV7 . . . . **110** E5
Shenstone WS14 . . . . **17** E1
Solihull B90 . . . . **126** A5
Warwick CV34 . . . . **160** E6
Back Rd
Birmingham B38 . . . . **103** F2
Kingswinford DY6 . . . . **60** D7
Back St CV11 . . . . **73** C5
Badbury Cl B80 . . . . **159** D4
Badbury Gdns B80 . . . . . . **159** D4
Baddesley Clinton★ B93 . **144** F4
Baddesley Cl CV31 . . . . . . **162** C5
Baddesley Rd B92 . . . . **88** E2
Bader Rd
Perton WV6 . . . . **23** E3
Willenhall WS2 . . . . **27** F2
Bader Wlk B35 . . . . **57** F2
Badger Brook La B96 . . . **158** D1
Badger Cl
Cheswick Green B90 . . . . . **126** D4
Huntington WS12 . . . . **1** D6
Redditch B98 . . . . **154** D3
Badger Ct WV10 . . . . **25** D4
Badger Dr WV10 . . . . **25** D4
Badger Rd CV3 . . . . **134** D8
Badgers Bank Rd B74 . . . . **31** F5
Badgers Cl WS3 . . . . **15** A5
Badgers Croft B62 . . . . **83** B7
Badger St DY3 . . . . **50** E5
Badgers The B45 . . . . **122** A2
Badger St DY9 . . . . **81** E6
Badgers Way
Birmingham B34 . . . . **69** A5
Cannock WS12 . . . . **2** D1
Badger Way B60 . . . . **138** B5
Badminton Cl DY1 . . . . **50** F3
Badon Covert B14 . . . . . . **104** D2
Badsey Cl B31 . . . . **103** C4
Badsey Rd B69 . . . . **63** D5
Baggeridge Cl DY3 . . . . **50** A8
Baggeridge Ctry Pk★ DY3 **49** E6
Baggeridge Ctry Pk Visitor
Ctr★ DY3 . . . . **49** F7
Baggott St WV2 . . . . **39** C7
Baginton Cl B91 . . . . **107** B5
Baginton Fields Sch CV3 **134** B4
Baginton Rd
Birmingham B35 . . . . **58** B4
Coventry CV3 . . . . **133** C5
Bagley's Rd DY5 . . . . **81** D6
Bagley St DY9 . . . . **81** C6
Bagnall Cl B25 . . . . **88** D6
Bagnall Rd WV14 . . . . **40** C5
Bagnall St
Walsall WS3 . . . . **28** C6
Wednesbury DY4 . . . . **41** C1
West Bromwich B70 . . . . **53** E2
West Bromwich,Harvills
Hawthorn B70 . . . . **52** E7
Bagnall Wlk DY5 . . . . **61** D1
Bagnell Rd B13 . . . . **104** F7
Bagot St B4 . . . . **164** C4
Bagot Way CV34 . . . . **161** E3
Bagridge Cl WV3 . . . . **38** B8
Bagridge Rd WV3 . . . . **38** B8
Bagshaw Cl CV8 . . . . **135** A1
Bagshawe Croft B23 . . . . . **56** D7
Bagshaw Rd B33 . . . . **68** E3
Bailey Ave B77 . . . . **35** F5
Bailey Cl
Burntwood WS7 . . . . **6** D8
Cannock WS11 . . . . **2** A4
Bailey Rd WV14 . . . . **40** B7
Baileys Ct B65 . . . . **63** B3
Bailey St
West Bromwich B70 . . . . . . **53** A4
Wolverhampton WV10 . . . **163** D3
Bailye Cl WS13 . . . . **3** F1
Baines' La [1] LE10 . . . . **71** D1
Bains Dr WS13 . . . . **9** A6
Baird Ho DY6 . . . . **60** F7
Bakehouse La B93 . . . . . . **145** B6
Bakeman Ho B26 . . . . **88** D6
Baker Ave
Royal Leamington Spa
CV31 . . . . **161** F6
Wolverhampton WV14 . . . . . **39** F2
Baker Cl WS7 . . . . **6** F6
Baker House Gr B43 . . . . . . **54** D7
Baker Rd WV14 . . . . **40** E3
Baker's La
[5] Lichfield WS13 . . . . **9** B7
Aldridge WS9 . . . . **30** B6
Bakers La
Coventry CV5 . . . . **112** E2
Dorridge B93 . . . . **128** D1
Sutton Coldfield B73,B74 . . . **45** A5
Bakers Mews B93 . . . . **145** B6
Baker St
Bedworth CV6 . . . . **96** B6
Birmingham,Handsworth
B21 . . . . **65** F8
Birmingham,Small Heath
B10 . . . . **67** D1
Birmingham,Sparkhill B11 . . **87** C5
Burntwood WS7 . . . . **6** F6
Tipton DY4 . . . . **51** E4
West Bromwich B70 . . . . . . **53** B3
Bakers Way WS12 . . . . **2** B5
Bakers Wlk [1] B77 . . . . **35** F6
Bakewell Cl
Coventry CV3 . . . . **134** F8
Walsall WS3 . . . . **14** C3
Balaams Wood Dr B31 . . **102** B1
Balaclava Rd B14 . . . . **104** E8
Balcaskie Cl B15 . . . . **85** E7
Balden Rd B32 . . . . **84** F7
Baldmoor Lake Rd B23 . . . **56** F6
Bald's La DY9 . . . . **81** F5
Baldwin Cl B69 . . . . **52** D2
Baldwin Croft CV6 . . . . **96** B1
Baldwin Gr WS11 . . . . **2** C2
Baldwin Ho B19 . . . . **66** E6
Baldwin Rd
Birmingham B30 . . . . **104** A3
Kidderminster DY10 . . . . . **117** B7
Baldwins La B28 . . . . **105** F4
Baldwin St
Bilston WV14 . . . . **40** F4
Smethwick B66 . . . . **65** B6
Balfour Cl LE10 . . . . **75** E7
Balfour Cres WV6 . . . . **24** F4
Balfour Ct
[2] Wolverhampton WV6 . . . **24** F4
Sutton Coldfield B74 . . . . . . **32** A3
Balfour Dr B69 . . . . **52** D2
Balfour Ho [2] B16 . . . . **65** F1
Balfour Rd DY6 . . . . **60** E8
Balfour St B12 . . . . **86** E6
Balfour B79 . . . . **21** A4
Balham Gr B44 . . . . **45** A2
Balholm B62 . . . . **83** D5
Balking Cl WV14 . . . . **40** B3
Ballantine Rd CV6 . . . . **113** B6
Ballarat Wlk DY8 . . . . **80** F5
Ballard Cres DY2 . . . . **62** D5
Ballard Rd DY2 . . . . **62** D5
Ballard Wlk B37 . . . . **70** A6
Ball Fields DY4 . . . . **52** D5
Ball Ho [5] WS3 . . . . **28** B8
Ballingham Cl CV4 . . . . **112** A2
Balliol Bsns Pk WV9 . . . . . . **10** E3
Balliol Ho B37 . . . . **69** F2
Balliol Rd
Coventry CV2 . . . . **114** C4
Hinckley LE10 . . . . **75** F6
Ball La WV10 . . . . **11** C6
Ballot St B66 . . . . **65** B5
Balls Hill WS1 . . . . **28** F2
Balls St WS1 . . . . **28** F2
Balmain Cres WV11 . . . . **12** B1
Balmoral Cl
Coventry CV2 . . . . **114** E6
Halesowen B62 . . . . **83** B7
Lichfield WS14 . . . . **9** D6
Tamworth B79 . . . . **21** B7
Walsall WS4 . . . . **29** D7
Balmoral Ct
Birmingham B1 . . . . **66** C3
Cannock WS11 . . . . **2** A5
Kidderminster DY10 . . . . . **117** A5
Nuneaton CV10 . . . . **72** E5
Balmoral Dr
Cannock WS12 . . . . **1** F7
Willenhall WV12 . . . . **27** C7
Wombourne WV5 . . . . **38** A1
Balmoral Ho WV3 . . . . **163** A1
Balmoral Rd
Birmingham B36 . . . . **70** A7
Birmingham,Erdington B23 . **56** F5
Birmingham,Kitwell B32 . . **102** B7
Stourbridge DY8 . . . . **60** C2
Sutton Coldfield B74 . . . . . . **31** F5
Wolverhampton WV4 . . . . . . **39** A5
Balmoral View DY1 . . . . **50** E2
Balmoral Way
Rowley Regis B65 . . . . **63** D4
Royal Leamington Spa
CV32 . . . . **157** C6
Walsall WS2 . . . . **28** B4
Balsall Common Prim Sch
CV7 . . . . **130** B5
Balsall Heath Rd B12 . . . . . **86** E7
Balsall St E CV7 . . . . **130** B5
Balsall St B93,CV7 . . . . **129** D7
Balthazar Cl CV34 . . . . **161** E4
Baltic Cl WS11 . . . . **1** E2
Baltimore Rd B42 . . . . **55** A5
Balvenie Way DY1 . . . . **50** F4
Bamber Cl WV3 . . . . **38** E8
Bamburgh Gr CV32 . . . . . . **156** E3
Bamburgh B77 . . . . **35** C7
Bamford Cl WS3 . . . . **14** C3
Bamford Ho WS3 . . . . **14** C3
Bamford Rd
Walsall WS3 . . . . **14** C3
Wolverhampton WV3 . . . . . . **39** A8
Bamford St B77 . . . . **21** D3
Bampfylde Pl B42 . . . . **55** C7
Bampton Ave [4] WS7 . . . . . **7** A8
Bamville Rd B8 . . . . **68** A5
Banbrook Cl B92 . . . . **107** D8
Banbury Cl DY3 . . . . **50** E6
Banbury Croft B37 . . . . **69** F2
Banbury Ho B33 . . . . **69** E2
Banbury Rd
Cannock WS11 . . . . **4** C8
Warwick CV34 . . . . **161** A3
Banbury St B5 . . . . **66** F2
Bancroft Cl WV14 . . . . **51** B7
Bancroft B77 . . . . **21** F3
Bandywood Cres B44 . . . . . **44** F3
Bandywood Rd B44 . . . . **44** F3
Baneberry Dr WV10 . . . . . . **12** B7
Banfield Ave WS10 . . . . **41** C7
Banfield Rd WS10 . . . . **41** C4
Banford Ave B8 . . . . **68** A4
Banford Rd B8 . . . . **68** A4
Bangham Pit Rd B31 . . . . . **102** E6
Bangley La
Drayton Bassett B78 . . . . . . **33** E6
Mile Oak B78 . . . . **34** A8
Bangor Ho B37 . . . . **70** B4
Bangor Rd B9 . . . . **67** D2
Bank Cres WS7 . . . . **6** F5
Bank Croft CV31 . . . . **162** C5
Bankdale Rd B8 . . . . **68** B4
Bankes Rd B10 . . . . **67** F1
Bank Farm Cl DY9 . . . . **81** C1
Bankfield Dr CV32 . . . . . . **156** C1
Bankfield Rd
Bilston WV14 . . . . **40** D5
Tipton DY4 . . . . **52** C8
Bank Ho B27 . . . . **88** C3
Banklands Rd DY2 . . . . **62** E6
Bank Rd
Dudley,Gornalwood DY3 . . . **50** C2
Dudley,Netherton DY2 . . . . **62** D6
Banks Gn B97 . . . . **152** B2
Bankside
Birmingham,Great Barr
B43 . . . . **54** E7
Birmingham,Moseley B13 . . **87** D2
Bankside Cl CV3 . . . . **134** A6
Bankside Cres B74 . . . . **44** F7
Bankside Way WS9 . . . . **16** B2
Banks Rd CV6 . . . . **113** A5
Banks St WV13 . . . . **27** A2
Bank St
Bilston WV14 . . . . **40** E3
Birmingham B14 . . . . **86** E1
Brierley Hill DY5 . . . . **61** D3
Cannock WS12 . . . . **2** E1
Cradley Heath B64 . . . . **62** C1
Stourbridge DY9 . . . . **81** F5
Tipton WV14 . . . . **51** C8
Walsall WS1 . . . . **28** F1
West Bromwich B71 . . . . **53** D6
Wolverhampton WV10 . . . . . **25** E5
Bank The CV8 . . . . **149** C6
Bankwell St DY5 . . . . **61** D4
Banky Mdw LE10 . . . . **76** A7
Banner La CV4 . . . . **111** D2
Bannerlea Rd B37 . . . . **69** F5
Bannerley Rd B33 . . . . **69** C1
Banners Ct B73 . . . . **45** B3
Banners Gate Inf Sch B73 **45** A4
Banners Gate Jun Sch
B73 . . . . **45** A4
Banners Gate Rd B73 . . . . **45** B3
Banners Gr B23 . . . . **57** A6
Banners La
Halesowen B63 . . . . **82** D6
Redditch B97 . . . . **158** E5
Banners St B63 . . . . **82** D6
Banners Wlk B44 . . . . **45** B2
Bannington Ct WV12 . . . . . . **27** D4
Bannister Rd WS10 . . . . . . **41** D2
Bannister St B64 . . . . **62** D2
Banquo App CV34 . . . . **161** F3
Banstead Cl WV2 . . . . **39** E7
Bantam Gr CV6 . . . . **95** A3
Bantams Cl B33 . . . . **69** C2
Bant Mill Rd B60 . . . . **137** A1
Bantock Ave WV3 . . . . **38** F8
Bantock Ct WV3 . . . . **38** E8
Bantock Gdns WV3 . . . . **24** E1
Bantock House Mus★
WV3 . . . . **24** F1
Bantock Prim Sch WV3 . . . **39** A8
Bantock Rd CV4 . . . . **111** E2
Bantocks The B70 . . . . **53** A6
Bantock Way [7] B17 . . . . . . **85** D5
Banton Cl B23 . . . . **56** D8
Bantry Cl B26 . . . . **89** C4
Baptist End Rd DY2 . . . . . . **62** C6
Baptist Wlk LE10 . . . . **71** D1
Barbara Rd B28 . . . . **105** E4
Barbara St B79 . . . . **21** A5
Barbel Dr WV10 . . . . **26** B4
Barber Cl WS12 . . . . **2** E2
Barber Inst of Fine Arts The★
B15 . . . . **86** A3
Barberry Ho B38 . . . . **103** F1
Barbers La B91 . . . . **108** C6
Barbican Rise CV2 . . . . . . **114** E2
Barbourne Cl B91 . . . . **127** B7
Barbridge Cl CV12 . . . . **79** C2
Barbridge Rd CV12 . . . . **79** C3
Barbrook Dr DY5 . . . . **81** B7
Barcheston Rd
Birmingham B29 . . . . **85** A1
Dorridge B93 . . . . **128** A4
Barclay Ct WV3 . . . . **25** A2
Barclay Rd B67 . . . . **64** E1
Barcliff Ave B77 . . . . **21** E3
Barcroft Prim Sch WV13 . . **27** C2
Barcroft WV13 . . . . **27** C2
Bardell Cl WS13 . . . . **8** E6
Bardenholme Gdns DY9 . . . **81** D3
Bardfield Cl [1] B42 . . . . **55** A8
Bardley Dr CV6 . . . . **113** C6
Bardon Dr B90 . . . . **106** D2
Bardsey Cl LE10 . . . . **71** B1
Bard St B11 . . . . **87** C5
Bardwell Cl WV8 . . . . **24** F8
Barford App CV31 . . . . **162** B2
Barford Cl
Coventry CV3 . . . . **134** D8
Darlaston WS10 . . . . **41** C8
Redditch B98 . . . . **154** F1
Sutton Coldfield B76 . . . . . . **46** F4
Barford Cres [5] B38 . . . . . **104** C2
Barford Ho B5 . . . . **86** E8
Barford Prim Sch B16 . . . . **65** E3
Barford Rd
Birmingham B16 . . . . **65** F3
Kenilworth CV8 . . . . **148** B3
Solihull B90 . . . . **106** D2
Barford St B5 . . . . **86** E8
Bargate Dr WV6 . . . . **25** A4
Bargery Rd WV11 . . . . **13** A1
Barham Cl B90 . . . . **127** A5
Barker Rd B74 . . . . **46** B7
Barker's Butts La CV6 . . . **113** A4
Barkers' Butts La CV6 . . . **113** A5
Barkers La B47 . . . . **125** A1
Barker St
Birmingham B19 . . . . **66** B7
Oldbury B68 . . . . **64** C6
Bark Piece B32 . . . . **84** C3
Barlands Croft B34 . . . . **69** C6
Barle Gr B36 . . . . **70** A7
Barleston Dr LE10 . . . . **71** A1
Barley Cl
Cannock WS12 . . . . **2** B5
Dudley DY3 . . . . **50** F7
Barley Cl *continued*
Sutton Coldfield WS9 . . . . . . **30** E2
Wolverhampton WV8 . . . . . . **10** E1
Barley Croft
Perton WV6 . . . . **23** D3
Stoke Heath B60 . . . . **150** E6
Barley Ct CV32 . . . . **156** F2
Barleyfield LE10 . . . . **71** C3
Barleyfield Ho [3] WS1 . . . . **42** E8
Barleyfield Rise DY6 . . . . . . **60** A8
Barleyfield Row WS1 . . . . . **42** E8
Barley Lea Ho CV3 . . . . . . **134** B8
Barley Lea The CV3 . . . . . . **134** C8
Barley Mow La B61 . . . . . . **137** B8
Barlich Way B98 . . . . **154** A2
Barling Way CV10 . . . . **73** B1
Barlow Cl
Birmingham B45 . . . . **101** E2
Oldbury B68 . . . . **64** A3
Tamworth B77 . . . . **21** E4
Barlow Dr B70 . . . . **53** F1
Barlow Rd
Coventry CV2 . . . . **96** D2
Wednesbury WS10 . . . . **42** A5
Barlow's Rd B15 . . . . **85** E5
Barmouth Cl WV12 . . . . **27** C6
Barnabas Rd B23 . . . . **56** F4
Barnaby Sq WV10 . . . . **11** F4
Barnack Ave CV3 . . . . **133** B5
Barnack Dr CV34 . . . . **155** E1
Barnacle La CV12 . . . . **79** C1
Barnard Cl
Birmingham B37 . . . . **70** D1
Royal Leamington Spa
CV32 . . . . **157** C3
Barnard Pl WV2 . . . . **39** E6
Barnard Rd
Sutton Coldfield B75 . . . . . . **46** E7
Wolverhampton WV11 . . . . . **12** F1
Barnard Way WS11 . . . . **1** F2
Barn Ave DY3 . . . . **50** C7
Barnbridge B77 . . . . **21** C2
Barnbrook Rd B93 . . . . . . **128** A7
Barn Cl
Birmingham B30 . . . . **104** B6
Coventry CV5 . . . . **112** C5
Cradley Heath B64 . . . . **82** E6
Dordon B78 . . . . **36** F6
Halesowen B63 . . . . **82** E2
Lichfield WS13 . . . . **3** B3
Stoke Heath B60 . . . . **150** E6
Stourbridge DY9 . . . . **81** C4
Whitnash CV31 . . . . **162** B3
Barn Croft
Birmingham B32 . . . . **84** E1
Burntwood WS7 . . . . **7** A4
Great Wyrley WS6 . . . . **5** A3
Barncroft Rd B69 . . . . **63** A8
Barncroft St B70 . . . . **53** A8
Barne Cl CV11 . . . . **79** B7
Barnes Cl B37 . . . . **69** E2
Barnes Hill B29 . . . . **84** F2
Barnes Meadow Pl WV14 . **51** B8
Barnes Rd WS14 . . . . **18** A6
Barnesville Cl B10 . . . . **88** A8
Barnet Rd B23 . . . . **56** D5
Barnett Cl
Bilston WV14 . . . . **40** D4
Kingswinford DY6 . . . . **60** D4
Barnett Gn DY6 . . . . **60** D4
Barnett La DY6,DY8 . . . . . . **60** D4
Barnett Rd WV13 . . . . **26** E1
Barnetts Cl DY10 . . . . **117** B4
Barnetts Gr DY10 . . . . **117** A4
Barnetts La
Brownhills WS8 . . . . **6** F1
Kidderminster DY10 . . . . . **117** A4
Barnett St
Stourbridge DY8 . . . . **60** D3
Tipton B69 . . . . **52** A2
Tipton DY4 . . . . **52** A4
Barney Cl DY4 . . . . **51** F3
Barn Farm Cl [4] WV14 . . . **41** A7
Barnfield Ave CV5 . . . . **112** B6
Barnfield Cl WS14 . . . . **9** B6
Barnfield Dr B92 . . . . **107** F6
Barnfield Gr B20 . . . . **54** E5
Barnfield Rd
Bromsgrove B61 . . . . **136** E1
Halesowen B62 . . . . **83** D7
Tipton DY4 . . . . **51** E6
Wolverhampton WV1 . . . . . . **26** A2
Barnfield Trad Est DY4 . . . **51** E7
Barnford Cl B10 . . . . **67** C1
Barnford Cres B68 . . . . **64** B3
Barnfordhill Cl B68 . . . . . . **64** B4
Barn Gn WV3 . . . . **38** F7
Barn Ho B8 . . . . **68** D4
Barnhurst La WV8 . . . . **10** E2
Barn La
Birmingham,Handsworth
B21 . . . . **65** E7
Birmingham,King's Heath
B13 . . . . **105** A7
Solihull B92 . . . . **88** F3
Barn Leigh Dr CV4 . . . . . . **131** D6
Barn Mdw B25 . . . . **68** D1
Barnmoor Rise B91 . . . . . **107** C7
Barn Owl Dr WS3 . . . . **14** F4
Barn Owl Pl DY10 . . . . **117** A2
Barn Owl Wlk DY5 . . . . **81** C6
Barnpark Covert [9] B14 . . **104** C2
Barn Piece B32 . . . . **84** B4
Barnsbury Ave B72 . . . . **57** C6
Barns Cl WS9 . . . . **15** F4

Barns Croft B74 31 B4
Barnsdale Cres B31 102 E4
Barns La WS4 29 D7
Barnsley Ct CV6 113 D8
Barnsley Hall Dr B60 137 B6
Barnsley Hall Rd B61 137 A6
Barnsley Rd
Birmingham B17 65 A1
Bromsgrove B61 137 B4
Barnstaple Cl CV5 111 F5
Barnstaple Rd B66 65 B5
Barn St B5 66 F2
Barnswood Cl
Cannock WS11 4 B8
Halesowen B63 82 C5
Barnt Green Junc B45 138 D8
Barnt Green Rd B45 122 C3
Barn Way WS12 2 F4
Barnwood Cl B98 154 D5
Barnwood Rd
Birmingham B32 84 F4
Wolverhampton WV8 10 E1
Baron Bsns Ctr DY9 81 E5
Barons Cl B17 85 B6
Barons Court Trad Est
WS9 15 E2
Baron's Croft CV3 133 E7
Barons Croft CV10 72 C4
Barons Ct B92 89 C4
Baron's Field Rd CV3 133 E8
Barpool Rd CV10 72 F4
Barrack Cl B75 47 A6
Barrack La B63 82 B6
Barrack Cl WS3 28 E8
Barracks La
Beausale CV35 146 C2
Brownhills WS9,WS14 16 C8
Walsall WS3 28 E8
Barracks Pl WS3 28 E8
Barrack St
Birmingham B7 67 A3
Warwick CV34 160 E7
West Bromwich B70 53 A8
Barracks Way CV1 165 B2
Barra Croft B35 58 B4
Barrar Cl DY8 80 E8
Barras Ct CV2 114 A4
Barras Gn CV2 114 A4
Barras La CV1 113 B3
Barratts Croft DY5 50 C1
Barratts Ho B14 104 E2
Barratts Rd B38 104 A1
Barr Beacon Language Coll
WS9 44 B5
Barr Common Cl WS9 30 B3
Barr Common Rd WS9 30 B3
Bar Rd CV3 133 E8
Barrett Cl DY10 117 B6
Barretts La CV7 130 C6
Barrhill Cl B43 43 E2
Barrie Ave DY10 117 C7
Barrie Rd LE10 71 D3
Barrington Cl
Walsall WS5 43 A3
Wolverhampton WV10 11 C1
Barrington Rd
Birmingham B45 121 E7
Solihull B92 88 F2
Barr Lakes La
Birmingham WS9 44 A7
Walsall WS5,WS9 43 F7
Barron Rd B31 103 B3
Barrow Cl
Brownhills WS9 15 F4
Coventry CV2 115 B6
Redditch B98 154 F3
Barrowfield Ct CV8 147 F4
Barrowfield La CV8 147 F4
Barrow Hill Rd DY5 50 C1
Barrow Ho 1 B16 65 F1
Barrow Rd CV8 147 F4
Barrows La B26 89 A6
Barrows Rd B11 87 C6
Barrow Wlk B5 86 E7
Barrs Cres B64 82 F8
Barr's Hill Sch & Com Coll
CV1 165 A4
Barrs Rd B64 82 E8
Barrs St B68 64 A4
Barr St
Birmingham B19 66 C5
Dudley DY3 50 C3
Barry Ho CV2 96 D1
Barry Jackson Twr B6 66 F7
Barry Rd WS5 43 C7
Barsham Cl B5 86 C6
Barsham Dr DY5 81 C8
Barston Cl CV6 96 A2
Barston La
Balsall Common CV7 129 D8
Barston B92 109 C1
Catherine de B B91 108 B2
Eastcote B92 108 D3
Solihull B91 107 F2
Barston Rd B68 84 B7
Bartestree Cl B98 154 F1
Bartholemews La B61 136 F5
Bartholomew Ct CV3 134 A6
Bartholomew Row B5 164 D3
Bartholomew St B5 164 D2
Bartic Ave DY6 60 F4
Bartleet Rd
Redditch B98 159 E8
Smethwick B67 64 D5
Bartlett Cl
3 Warwick CV34 160 F7
Coventry CV6 95 E2
Wednesbury DY4 41 B1
Bartley Cl B92 88 F2
Bartley Dr B31 102 E8
Bartley Green Tech & Sports
Coll B32 84 C1
Bartley Ho B32 102 D8
Bartley Mews B31 102 E8
Bartley Woods B32 84 B2
Barton Cres CV31 162 C6
Barton Croft B28 105 F4
Barton Dr B93 128 B4
Barton Ind Est WV14 40 E6
Barton La DY6 60 C8
Barton Lodge Rd B28 105 E4
Barton Rd
Bedworth CV12 78 A4
Coventry CV6 95 F2
Nuneaton CV10 73 C1
Wolverhampton WV4 39 F4
Bartons Bank B6 66 E7
Barton's Mdw CV2 114 B6
Barton St B70 53 C2
Barwell Cl
Dorridge B93 127 E4
Royal Leamington Spa
CV32 156 F3
Barwell Ct 8 B9 67 B2
Barwell La LE10 71 E3
Barwell Rd B9 67 B2
Barwick St B3 164 B3
Bar Wlk WS9 16 C1
Basalt Cl WS2 28 A3
Basant Cl CV34 161 A7
Bascote Cl B97 153 B1
Baseley Way CV6 95 D4
Basford Brook Dr CV6 95 F4
Basildon Wlk 3 CV2 115 A7
Basil Gr B31 102 E4
Basil Rd B31 102 E4
Basin La B77 21 D3
Baskerville Sch B17 85 A5
Baskeyfield Cl WS14 9 D7
Baslow Cl
Birmingham B33 68 E4
Walsall WS3 14 C3
Baslow Rd WS3 14 B3
Basons La B68 64 D5
Bassano Rd 1 B65 63 C1
Bassenthwaite Ct DY6 60 D6
Bassett Cl
Sutton Coldfield B76 46 E4
Willenhall WV12 27 D4
Wolverhampton WV4 38 C6
Bassett Croft B10 87 B8
Bassett Rd
Coventry CV6 113 A5
Stourbridge B63 82 A6
Wednesbury WS10 42 D3
Bassetts Gr B37 69 E5
Bassett St WS2 28 C2
Bassnage Rd B63 82 E2
Batchcroft
Bilston WV14 40 D5
Darlaston WS10 41 D8
Batchelor Cl DY8 80 F8
Batchley Fst Sch B97 153 B4
Batchley Rd B97 153 C4
Bateman Dr B73 46 B1
Bateman Rd B46 59 F1
Bateman's Acre S 1
CV6 113 A4
Batemans La B47 124 E5
Bates Cl B76 58 B8
Bates Gr WV10 26 A4
Bates Hill B97 153 D4
Bates La B94 141 F1
Bates Rd CV5 132 E8
Bate St
3 Walsall WS2 28 E3
Wolverhampton WV4 40 A3
Batham Rd DY10 117 A8
Bath Ave WV1 163 A3
Bath Ct 4 B29 103 B7
Batheaston Cl B38 123 D7
Bath Mdw B63 82 E5
Bath Mews DY8 80 F5
Bath Pas B5 164 C1
Bath Pl 3 CV31 161 F7
Bath Rd
Brierley Hill DY5 62 A2
Cannock WS11 1 E5
Nuneaton CV11 73 C5
Stourbridge DY8 80 F5
Tipton DY4 52 A5
Walsall WS1 42 E8
Wolverhampton WV1 163 A3
Bath Row
Birmingham B15 66 C1
Oldbury B69 63 D8
Bath St
Bilston WV14 40 E5
Birmingham B4 164 C4
Coventry CV1 165 C4
Dudley DY2 62 C8
Royal Leamington Spa
CV31 161 F7
Sedgley DY3 39 E1
Walsall WS1 42 E8
Willenhall WV13 27 B1
Wolverhampton WV1 163 D2
Bathurst Rd CV6 113 A6
Bathway Rd CV3 133 A4
Bath Wlk B12 86 E5
Bath Wlk Ind Est B12 86 E5
Batmans Hill Rd WV14,
DY4 40 E1
Batsford Cl B98 159 B5
Batsford Rd CV6 112 F4
Batson Rise DY5 81 A8
Battalion Ct CV6 95 A1
Battenhall Rd B17 85 A5
Battens Cl B98 153 F3
Battens Dr B98 154 D3
Battery Way B11 87 E4
Battledown Cl LE10 71 B2
Battlefield Hill WV5 49 B7
Battlefield La WV5 49 B6
Battlefield Terr WV5 49 B6
Battling Brook Com Prim Sch
LE10 71 B2
Battling Brook Sh Ctr
LE10 71 B1
Baughan Ho B24 57 D3
Baulk La CV7 110 D1
Bavaro Gdns DY5 62 A2
Baverstock Foundation Sch
& Specialist Sports Coll
B14 104 E2
Baverstock Rd B14 104 E2
Baxter Ave DY10 116 F7
Baxter Cl CV4 112 A2
Baxter Coll DY11 116 B6
Baxter Ct
10 Royal Leamington Spa
CV31 162 A7
Birmingham B13 86 F2
Baxter Gdns DY10 116 F7
Baxterley Gn
Solihull B91 106 D4
Sutton Coldfield B76 46 F1
Baxter Rd DY5 61 C2
Baxters Gn B90 126 B8
Baxters Rd B90 126 B8
Bay Ave WV14 40 F4
Bayer St WV14 51 C8
Bayford Ave
Birmingham,Coft Common
B31 122 E6
Birmingham,Sheldon B26 89 C4
Bayley Cres WS10 41 C8
Bayley La CV1 165 C2
Bayleys La DY4 52 C8
Bayley Twr 3 B36 68 E8
Baylie Ct DY8 80 F5
Baylie St DY8 80 F4
Baylis Ave WV11 26 F8
Bayliss Ave
Coventry CV6 96 A4
Wolverhampton WV4 40 A3
Bayliss Cl
Bilston WV14 40 C7
Birmingham B31 103 B5
Bayliss Ct WV3 24 E2
Baynton Rd WV12 27 C8
Bayston Ave WV3 38 E8
Bayston Rd B14 104 E3
Bayswater Rd
Birmingham B20 55 D1
Dudley DY3 50 D2
Bayton Rd CV7 96 B7
Bayton Road Ind Est CV7 96 B8
Bayton Way CV7 96 C7
Bay Tree Cl
Birmingham B38 123 D8
Coventry CV2 96 D1
Baytree Cl WS3 14 A2
Baytree Rd WS3 14 A2
Baywell Cl B90 127 A7
Bazzard Rd CV11 79 F6
Beach Ave
Birmingham B12 87 B5
Wolverhampton WV4,WV14 40 A2
Beach Brook Cl B11 87 B5
Beachburn Way B20 55 B3
Beach Cl B31 103 C1
Beachcroft Rd DY6 49 C1
Beach Dr B63 83 A5
Beach Rd
Bilston WV14 40 D7
Birmingham B11 87 B5
Beach St B63 83 A5
Beach Trad Ctr B12 87 B5
Beachwood Ave DY6 49 C1
Beacon Cl
Birmingham,Great Barr
B43 43 F1
Birmingham,Rubery B45 122 A6
Smethwick B66 65 A7
Beacon Ct 2 B43 43 F1
Beacon Ctr for the Blind
WV4 39 D4
Beacon Ct B74 44 F8
Beacon Dr WS1 43 A8
Beaconfields 1 WS13 9 A8
Beacon Gdns WS13 3 A1
Beacon Hill
Aldridge WS9 30 C1
Birmingham,Aston B6 66 E8
Birmingham B45 121 F5
Beacon Hts WS9 44 B6
Beacon La
Birmingham B60,B45 121 E4
Sedgley DY3 39 E1
Beacon Mews
1 Birmingham B43 43 F1
5 Lichfield WS13 9 A8
Beacon Pas DY3 39 D1
Beacon Prim Sch WV12 27 D8
Beacon Rd
Aldridge WS9 30 B1
Birmingham,Pheasey WS9,
B43 44 C6
Beacon Rd *continued*
Coventry CV6 95 D3
Sutton Coldfield,Banners Gate
B44 45 A3
Sutton Coldfield,Boldmere
B73 46 A1
Walsall WS5 43 D5
Willenhall WV12 27 C8
Beacon Rise
Aldridge WS9 30 B3
Sedgley DY3 39 E1
Stourbridge DY9 81 D4
Beaconsfield Ave WV4 39 D5
Beaconsfield Cres 3 B12 86 E5
Beaconsfield Ct
Nuneaton CV11 73 D5
Walsall WS1 43 B8
Beaconsfield Dr WV4 39 D6
Beaconsfield Rd
Birmingham B12 86 E5
Coventry CV2 114 B2
Sutton Coldfield B74 46 B7
Beaconsfield St W CV31 162 B8
Beaconsfield St
Royal Leamington Spa
CV31 162 B7
West Bromwich B71 53 C5
Beaconside Prim Sch
B45 121 E6
Beacon St
Lichfield WS13 9 A8
Walsall WS1 29 A1
Wolverhampton WV14 39 F1
Beacon Trad Est WS9 30 A6
Beacon View B45 122 A6
Beacon View Dr B74 44 F5
Beaconview Ho 4 B71 42 F1
Beacon View Rd B71 42 F2
Beacon View WS2 27 F2
Beacon Way
Brownhills WS9 16 A3
Cannock WS12 2 F3
Beake Ave CV6 113 B7
Beakes Rd B67 64 F3
Beaks Farm Gdns B16 65 D2
Beaks Hill Rd B38 103 E2
Beak St B1 164 B2
Beale Cl B35 58 A2
Beale Ho B16 65 F1
Beales St B6 67 B8
Beale St DY8 80 F5
Bealeys Ave WV11 26 C8
Bealeys Cl WS3 14 A3
Bealeys Ct WV11 26 C8
Bealeys La WS3 14 A2
Beamans Cl B92 89 A4
Beaminster Rd B91 107 A4
Beamish Cl CV2 115 A6
Bean Croft B32 84 C2
Beanfield Ave CV3 132 F4
Bean Rd
Dudley,Dixon's Green DY2 62 D8
Dudley,Swan Village DY4 51 C6
Bean Road Ind Est DY4 51 C6
Beardmore Rd B72 57 C8
Bear Hill B48 139 B5
Bear Hill Dr B48 139 B6
Bearing Dr WV11 26 E4
Bearley Croft B90 126 C8
Bearmore Rd B64 62 E1
Bearnett Dr WV4 38 C2
Bearnett La WV4 38 B2
Bearsdon Cres LE10 71 B2
Bearwood Ho B66 65 A4
Bearwood Prim Sch B66 65 A2
Bearwood Rd B66 65 A3
Bearwood Sh Ctr B66 65 A1
Beasley Gr B43 44 B1
Beaton Cl WV13 26 E2
Beaton Rd B74 32 A3
Beatrice St WS3 28 C6
Beatrice Wlk B69 52 A2
Beattie Cl LE10 71 D3
Beatty Ho DY4 52 B8
Beaty's Gdns CV32 157 A4
Beaubrook Gdns DY6 60 E3
Beauchamp Ave
Birmingham B20 54 F5
Kidderminster DY11 116 D3
Royal Leamington Spa
CV32 156 F1
Beauchamp Cl
1 Birmingham B37 70 B2
Sutton Coldfield B76 58 B7
Beauchamp Ct
1 Royal Leamington Spa
CV32 156 F1
Kidderminster DY11 116 D3
Beauchamp Gdns CV34 161 B6
Beauchamp Hill CV32 156 E1
Beauchamp Hts DY11 116 D3
Beauchamp Ind Pk B77 35 D8
Beauchamp Rd
Birmingham B13 105 C5
Kenilworth CV8 147 F2
Royal Leamington Spa
CV32 156 F1
Solihull B91 107 B5
Tamworth B77 35 F5
Warwick CV34 161 B8
Beau Ct WS11 1 F1
Beaudesert Cl B47 125 A6
Beaudesert Rd
Birmingham B20 66 B8
Coventry CV5 113 A1
Hollywood B47 125 A6
Beaufell Cl CV34 155 E1
Beaufort Ave
Birmingham B34 68 D5
Kidderminster DY11 116 A7
Royal Leamington Spa
CV32 157 C5
Beaufort Cl LE10 75 E4
Beaufort Dr CV3 134 F7
Beaufort Pk B8 68 C5
Beaufort Rd
Birmingham,Gravelly Hill
B23 56 E2
Birmingham,Ladywood B16 66 A1
Beaufort Sch B34 68 D5
Beaufort St B98 153 E3
Beaufort Way WS9 30 B4
Beaulieu Ave DY6 60 F4
Beaulieu Cl DY11 116 D8
Beaulieu Pk CV31 162 D6
Beaumaris Cl
Coventry CV5 111 F5
Dudley DY1 50 F4
Beaumont Ave LE10 75 A7
Beaumont Cl
Great Wyrley WS6 4 F2
Tipton DY4 51 E6
Beaumont Cres CV6 113 A4
Beaumont Ct
8 Royal Leamington Spa
CV31 162 A6
9 Coventry CV6 113 A4
Beaumont Dr
Birmingham B17 85 B4
Brierley Hill DY5 81 B7
Beaumont Gdns B18 65 F6
Beaumont Gr B91 106 F5
Beaumont Lawns B60 121 D1
Beaumont Pk B30 103 F4
Beaumont Pl CV11 73 A4
Beaumont Rd
Birmingham B30 103 F6
Great Wyrley WS6 4 F2
Halesowen B62 83 E8
Keresley CV7 95 A6
Nuneaton CV11 73 A4
Wednesbury WS10 41 F4
Beaumont Way WS11 6 A4
Beaurevoir Way CV34 161 A8
Beausale Croft CV5 112 A3
Beausale Dr B93 128 C7
Beauty Bank B64 83 A8
Beauty Bank Cres DY8 80 F6
Beauty Bank Prim Sch
DY8 80 F6
Beaver Cl WV11 26 F5
Beaver Pk B63 82 F6
Bebington Cl WV8 24 F8
Beccles Dr WV13 40 F8
Beche Way CV5 112 B5
Beckbury Ave WV4 38 C5
Beckbury Rd
Birmingham B29 85 A1
Coventry CV2 114 F6
Beck Cl B66 65 A4
Beckenham Ave B44 45 B1
Beckensall Cl DY1 51 B1
Becket Cl B74 31 F6
Beckett Cl B98 153 F5
Beckett St WV14 40 F6
Beckfield Cl
Birmingham B14 104 E2
Walsall WS4 29 C8
Beckfoot Dr CV2 96 F1
Beckford Croft B93 127 F3
Beckford Ct B23 56 C2
Beckman Rd DY9 81 C2
Beckminster Rd WV3 38 F7
Becks La CV7 93 A5
Becks The B48 139 A7
Beconsfield Cl B93 127 F2
Becton Gr B42 55 D7
Bedale Ave LE10 71 F2
Bedcote Pl DY8 81 B5
Beddoe Cl DY4 52 D5
Beddow Ave WV14 51 C7
Beddows Rd WS3 28 E5
Bede Arc 2 CV12 78 B3
Bede Rd
Bedworth CV12 78 A4
Coventry CV6 113 B6
Nuneaton CV10 72 D3
Bedford Cl LE10 71 E3
Bedford Dr B75 46 E6
Bedford Ho
6 Wolverhampton WV3 25 C4
7 Birmingham,Erdington
B24 56 F4
Birmingham B36 70 B6
Bedford Pl
5 Royal Leamington Spa
CV32 161 F8
Cannock WS12 2 B4
Bedford Rd
Birmingham B12 87 A8
Sutton Coldfield B75 46 E7
West Bromwich B71 53 B7
Bedford St
Coventry CV1 113 A2
Royal Leamington Spa
CV32 161 F8
Tipton DY4 52 B5
Wolverhampton WV1 40 B7
Bedford Terr 4 B19 66 D8
Bedlam La CV6 95 E2
Bedlam Wood Rd B31 102 C1
Bedworth Cl CV12 79 B2
Bedworth Croft DY4 52 B4
Bedworth Gr B9 68 B2
Bedworth La CV12 77 D4

Bedworth Rd
Bedworth CV12 ... 78 F2
Bulkington CV12 ... 79 A2
Coventry CV6,CV7 ... 96 A5
Bedworth Sta CV12 ... 78 C2
Beebee Rd WS10 ... 41 F6
Beecham Bsns Pk WS9 ... 30 A8
Beecham Cl WS9 ... 30 A8
Beech Ave
5 Birmingham,Showell Green B12 ... 87 A5
Birmingham B32 ... 84 D7
Birmingham,Chelmsley Wood B37 ... 70 B1
Halesowen B62 ... 83 C8
Tamworth B77 ... 21 E3
Beech Cl CV10 ... 72 A8
Beech Cliffe CV34 ... 160 F8
Beech Cl
Rowington Green CV35 ... 145 A1
Sedgley DY3 ... 39 E1
Sutton Coldfield B75 ... 32 A4
Tamworth B79 ... 21 A8
Wolverhampton WV10 ... 25 B8
Beech Cres
Burntwood WS7 ... 6 F6
Tipton DY4 ... 52 C8
Wednesbury WS10 ... 41 F5
Beechcroft Ave B28 ... 106 A6
Beechcroft
Bedworth CV12 ... 77 F1
Birmingham B15 ... 86 A7
Beechcroft Cres B74 ... 30 D1
Beechcroft Ct B74 ... 32 A1
Beechcroft Dr B61 ... 137 B4
Beechcroft Est B63 ... 82 C6
Beechcroft Pl WV10 ... 25 C6
Beechcroft Rd
Birmingham B36 ... 69 B8
Cradley Heath B64 ... 62 F1
Kidderminster DY11 ... 116 A8
Beech Ct
Birmingham,Bournville B30 ... 103 E4
Birmingham,Great Barr B43 43 D1
Birmingham,Longbridge B45 ... 122 D7
Birmingham,Short Heath B73 ... 56 F8
Cannock WS12 ... 2 B7
Great Wyrley WS6 ... 5 A4
Oldbury B66 ... 64 C8
Royal Leamington Spa CV34 ... 161 E2
Beechdale Ave B44 ... 44 E2
Beechdale B68 ... 84 B7
Beechdale Prim Sch WS2 28 C5
Beechdale Rd WS3 ... 27 F8
Beech Dene Gr B23 ... 56 E5
Beech Dr CV8 ... 148 B5
Beechen Gr WS7 ... 6 F8
Beecher Pl B63 ... 82 D5
Beecher Rd E B63 ... 82 D5
Beecher Rd B63 ... 82 D5
Beecher's Keep CV8 ... 135 F5
Beecher St B63 ... 82 C5
Beeches Ave B27 ... 88 C4
Beeches Cl
Birmingham B45 ... 121 D8
Kingswinford DY6 ... 60 D5
Beeches Ct B45 ... 122 B7
Beeches Dr B24 ... 57 C5
Beeches Farm Dr B31 ... 123 A7
Beeches Mews DY9 ... 98 F4
Beeches Pl WS3 ... 28 D6
Beeches Rd
Birmingham B42 ... 55 C7
Kidderminster DY11 ... 116 C8
Oldbury B68 ... 64 C3
Rowley Regis B65 ... 63 C1
Walsall WS3 ... 28 D6
West Bromwich B70 ... 53 E3
Beeches The
Bedworth CV12 ... 77 E2
Birmingham B15 ... 86 C8
Sutton Coldfield B74 ... 31 D4
Sutton Coldfield,Wylde Green B73 ... 46 B1
Upton Warren B61 ... 150 A4
West Bromwich B70 ... 53 E2
Wolverhampton,Newbridge WV1 ... 25 A3
Wolverhampton WV11 ... 26 B5
Beeches View Ave B63 ... 82 C4
Beeches Way B31 ... 123 A7
Beeches Wlk B73 ... 46 B3
Beechey Cl B43 ... 44 D5
Beech Farm Croft B31 ... 103 A3
Beechfield Ave 1 B11 ... 87 B6
Beechfield Cl B62 ... 83 C8
Beechfield Dr DY11 ... 116 C8
Beechfield Gr WV14 ... 51 B7
Beechfield Rd
Birmingham B11 ... 87 B6
Smethwick B67 ... 64 F4
Beechfield Rise WS14 ... 9 D8
Beech Gate B74 ... 31 C5
Beech Gdns WS14 ... 9 C6
Beechglade B20 ... 54 F4
Beech Gn DY1 ... 51 A5
Beech Gr
Birmingham B14 ... 105 A5
Huntington WS12 ... 1 D8
Warwick CV34 ... 156 B1
Beech Hill Ct B72 ... 57 C8
Beech Hill Ho B32 ... 102 C8
Beech Hill Rd B72 ... 57 C8
Beech Ho
6 Warwick CV34 ... 161 D8
Redditch B98 ... 158 F8
Solihull B91 ... 106 F2
Sutton Coldfield B74 ... 31 B5
Beechhouse La WV5 ... 37 A1
Beech Hurst 1 B38 ... 123 E8
Beech Hurst Gdns WV5 ... 37 A2
Beech Mews B64 ... 62 E2
Beechmore Rd B26 ... 89 A5
Beechmount Dr B23 ... 57 A6
Beechnut Cl
Coventry CV4 ... 111 D2
Solihull B91 ... 107 D5
Beechnut La B91 ... 107 E4
Beech Park Dr B45 ... 138 C8
Beech Pine Cl WS12 ... 2 A8
Beech Rd
Birmingham,Bournville B30 ... 103 E6
Birmingham,Erdington B23 ... 56 F8
Bromsgrove B61 ... 136 F4
Coventry CV6 ... 113 B5
Dudley DY1 ... 51 C4
Hollywood B47 ... 125 B6
Kingswinford DY6 ... 60 E5
Oldbury B69 ... 63 A8
Stourbridge DY8 ... 80 F3
Tamworth B79 ... 21 A8
Wednesbury WS10 ... 41 F5
Willenhall WV13 ... 26 E2
Wolverhampton WV10 ... 25 B8
Beech Tree Ave
Coventry CV4 ... 112 B2
Wolverhampton WV11 ... 26 C8
Beech Tree Cl
Kingswinford DY6 ... 60 E8
Redditch B97 ... 153 B4
Beech Tree La WS11 ... 4 D8
Beech Tree Rd WS9 ... 15 F3
Beech Way B66 ... 65 B5
Beech Wlk B38 ... 123 F8
Beechwood Ave
Coventry CV5 ... 132 F8
Hinckley LE10 ... 75 D3
Wolverhampton WV11 ... 26 B8
Beechwood B20 ... 54 E3
Beechwood Bsns Pk WS11 ... 2 B3
Beechwood Cl
Cheswick Green B90 ... 126 D4
Walsall WS3 ... 14 B3
Beechwood Cres B77 ... 21 F5
Beechwood Croft
Kenilworth CV8 ... 147 F2
Sutton Coldfield B74 ... 31 D5
Beechwood Ct
1 Birmingham B30 ... 104 C3
Coventry CV5 ... 132 F8
Cradley Heath B64 ... 83 A7
Wolverhampton WV6 ... 24 C3
Beechwood Dr WV6 ... 24 A2
Beechwood Ho 10 WV3 ... 25 A2
Beechwood Park Rd B91 106 E5
Beechwood Rd
Bedworth CV12 ... 78 D4
Birmingham B67 ... 84 F8
Birmingham,Great Barr B43 43 F2
Birmingham,King's Heath B14 ... 104 F5
Dudley DY2 ... 51 E1
Nuneaton CV10 ... 72 D6
West Bromwich B70 ... 53 B3
Beecroft Ave WS13 ... 3 B1
Beecroft Ct WS11 ... 1 E2
Beecroft Hill Sch WS11 ... 1 E2
Beecroft Rd WS11 ... 1 E1
Beehive Cl B61 ... 121 A1
Beehive Hill CV8 ... 147 E7
Beehive La B76 ... 59 C6
Beehive Wlk 4 DY4 ... 51 E5
Beekes Croft B78 ... 35 A8
Bee La WV10 ... 11 D3
Beeston Cl
Birmingham B6 ... 67 A7
Brierley Hill DY5 ... 81 D8
Coventry CV3 ... 134 F8
Beeton Rd B18 ... 65 E6
Beet St B65 ... 63 C1
Beever Rd DY4 ... 52 D7
Beggars Bush La WV5 ... 49 B5
Beggars Bush B73 ... 45 D2
Begonia Cl LE10 ... 75 E5
Begonia Dr LE10 ... 75 E5
Beighton Cl B74 ... 31 F6
Beilby Rd B30 ... 104 B5
Belbroughton CE Prim Sch DY9 ... 119 E6
Belbroughton Cl B98 ... 153 F2
Belbroughton Rd
Blakedown DY10 ... 98 D1
Halesowen B63 ... 82 F2
Holy Cross DY9 ... 99 E2
Stourbridge DY8 ... 80 E3
Belchers La B8,B9 ... 68 A3
Beldray Rd WV14 ... 40 E6
Belfont Trad Est B62 ... 83 C4
Belfry Cl
Hinckley LE10 ... 75 D4
Walsall WS3 ... 14 A3
Belfry Dr DY8 ... 80 E6
Belfry The WV6 ... 23 D4
Belgrade Rd WV10 ... 11 B1
Belgrade Theatre CV1 ... 165 B3
Belgrave Ct DY6 ... 60 F4
Belgrave High Sch B77 ... 21 E1
Belgrave Middleway B5, B12 ... 86 E7
Belgrave Rd
Birmingham B12 ... 86 F6
Coventry CV2 ... 114 E4
Halesowen B62 ... 83 D8
Tamworth B77 ... 35 E8
Belgrave Sq CV2 ... 114 E4
Belgrave Terr B21 ... 66 A7
Belgrave Wlk WS2 ... 28 B3
Belgravia Cl B5 ... 86 E7
Belgravia Ct B37 ... 70 A5
Belgrove Cl B15 ... 85 E6
Belgrove Ho WS11 ... 1 D1
Belinda Cl WV13 ... 26 F3
Bellairs Ave CV12 ... 77 E1
Bellamy Cl B90 ... 106 D1
Bellamy Farm Rd B90 ... 106 D1
Bellamy La WV11 ... 26 C7
Bell Barn Rd B15 ... 86 C8
Bell Barn Sh Ctr 8 B15 ... 86 C8
Bellbrooke Cl CV6 ... 96 B1
Bell Cl
Birmingham B36 ... 70 B6
Birmingham,Bordesley Green B9 ... 67 E3
Darlaston WS10 ... 41 D7
Bellcroft 3 B16 ... 66 B2
Bell Ct CV32 ... 156 F2
Bell Dr
Ash Green CV7 ... 95 E7
Birmingham B9 ... 67 F3
Cannock WS12 ... 2 C7
Walsall WS5 ... 43 A5
Belle Cotts B94 ... 143 D5
Bellefield Ave 10 B18 ... 65 E4
Bellefield Rd B18 ... 65 E4
Belle Isle DY5 ... 61 C3
Bellemere Rd B92 ... 109 B6
Bellencroft Gdns WV3 ... 38 C7
Bell End B65 ... 63 C3
Belle Orch DY11 ... 116 B5
Belle Vale B63 ... 82 E5
Belle Vue Ave B16 ... 65 D4
Bellevue B5 ... 86 D7
Belle Vue Cl B61 ... 121 C1
Belle Vue Ct DY8 ... 60 D2
Belle Vue Dr B62 ... 83 E6
Bellevue WV14 ... 40 E2
Belle Vue Gdns B65 ... 63 C3
Belle Vue CV10 ... 72 E3
Belle Vue Prim Sch DY8 ... 60 C3
Bellevue Rd
Bilston WV14 ... 41 A2
Birmingham B26 ... 89 B7
Belle Vue Rd DY5 ... 62 A1
Belle Vue DY8 ... 60 D2
Bellevue St WV14 ... 39 F2
Belle Vue Terr B92 ... 109 A6
Belle Wlk B13 ... 87 B3
Bellfield B31 ... 102 F4
Bellfield Ho B14 ... 104 D1
Bellfield Jun & Inf Schs B31 ... 102 F4
Bellfield B94 ... 142 A2
Bellflower Cl WV10 ... 12 A7
Bellflower Dr 1 WS5 ... 42 F3
Bell Fold B68 ... 64 C6
Bell Green La B38 ... 124 B5
Bell Green Rd CV6 ... 114 A8
Bell Heather Rd WS8 ... 15 D6
Bell Heath Way B32 ... 84 B2
Bell Hill
3 Birmingham B31 ... 103 A4
Birmingham B31 ... 103 A5
Bell Holloway B31 ... 102 F5
Bellingham B77 ... 22 D1
Bellington Croft 5 B90 ... 127 A6
Bellis St B16 ... 65 F1
Bell La
Birmingham,Kitt's Green B33 ... 69 E1
Birmingham,Northfield B31 ... 103 A4
Studley B80 ... 159 E4
Walsall,Wallington Heath WS3 ... 14 B1
Walsall,Yew Tree WS5 ... 43 A5
Bellman Cl WS10 ... 41 D7
Bell Mdw DY9 ... 99 B8
Bell Meadow Way B14 ... 104 E1
Bell Mead B80 ... 159 E4
Bell Pl WV2 ... 163 B1
Bell Rd
Dudley DY2 ... 62 C5
Trysull WV5 ... 37 D1
Walsall WS5 ... 43 D6
Bell St S DY5 ... 61 D2
Bells Farm Cl B14 ... 104 C2
Bells Farm Jun & Inf Sch B14 ... 104 C2
Bell Sh Ctr The B31 ... 103 A4
Bellsize Cl WS11 ... 5 F5
Bells La
Birmingham B14 ... 104 D2
Stourbridge DY8 ... 60 D2
Bells Moor Rd B70 ... 53 A6
Bell St
Bilston WV14 ... 40 C6
Brierley Hill,Barrow Hill DY5 ... 61 D7
Brierley Hill,Silver End DY5 ... 61 D2
Darlaston WS10 ... 41 D7
Dudley WV14 ... 40 C2
Stourbridge DY8 ... 81 A5
Tipton DY4 ... 51 E5
West Bromwich B70 ... 53 D2
Wolverhampton WV1 ... 163 B2
Bell Tower Mews CV32 ... 156 F3
Bellview Way CV6 ... 96 B1
Bell Vue Rd B65 ... 63 C2
Bellwood Rd B31 ... 102 F4
Belmont Ave WS11 ... 1 C2
Belmont Cl
Aldridge WS9 ... 30 A7
Great Wyrley WS11 ... 5 A4
Redditch B97 ... 153 B1
Tipton DY4 ... 51 F6
Belmont Covert B31 ... 103 B6
Belmont Cres B31 ... 103 B6
Belmont Ct
Royal Leamington Spa CV32 ... 157 A4
Sutton Coldfield B72 ... 46 B4
Belmont Dr CV32 ... 157 A4
Belmont Gdns WV14 ... 41 A4
Belmont Mews CV8 ... 147 F4
Belmont Pas B4 ... 67 A3
Belmont Rd
Birmingham,Handsworth B21 ... 65 C8
Birmingham,Rubery B45 ... 122 A6
Brierley Hill DY5 ... 61 D6
Coventry CV6 ... 114 A7
Belmont Rd E B21 ... 65 C8
Belmont Rd
Smethwick B66 ... 65 A2
Stourbridge DY9 ... 81 F4
Tamworth B77 ... 35 E7
Wolverhampton WV4 ... 39 A5
Belmont Row B4 ... 67 A3
Belmont St WV14 ... 41 A4
Belper DY1 ... 51 B1
Belper Ent Pk B70 ... 52 F4
Belper Rd
Walsall WS3 ... 14 C3
West Bromwich B70 ... 52 F3
Belper Row DY2 ... 62 E4
Belsize B77 ... 21 E2
Belstone Cl B14 ... 104 D6
Belton Ave WV11 ... 12 B1
Belton Cl B94 ... 143 C5
Belton Gr B45 ... 122 C8
Belt Rd WS12,WS11 ... 2 A5
Belvedere Ave WV4 ... 39 B5
Belvedere Cl
Burntwood WS7 ... 6 F5
Kidderminster DY10 ... 117 A5
Kingswinford DY6 ... 60 F4
Tamworth B79 ... 21 C7
Belvedere Dr B61 ... 137 A4
Belvedere Gdns WV6 ... 24 E7
Belvedere Rd
Birmingham B24 ... 57 B2
Coventry CV5 ... 133 A8
Belvide Gr B29 ... 103 B8
Belvidere Gdns B11 ... 87 C4
Belvidere Rd WS1 ... 42 F8
Belvoir Cl DY1 ... 50 E2
Belvoir Rd B60 ... 137 C1
Belvoir B77 ... 35 C7
Belwell Dr B74 ... 32 A2
Belwell Gdns B74 ... 32 A2
Belwell La B74 ... 32 A2
Bembridge Cl WV12 ... 27 B8
Bembridge Rd B33 ... 69 A3
Benacre Dr B5 ... 66 F2
Benbeck Gr DY4 ... 51 C6
Benbow Cl LE10 ... 71 D4
Benches Cl WS7 ... 6 D6
Bencroft WV8 ... 10 B4
Bendall Rd B44 ... 45 B2
Benedictine Ct CV1 ... 165 C3
Benedictine Rd CV3 ... 133 C8
Benedict Sq CV2 ... 114 C8
Benedon Rd B26 ... 89 B7
Bengrove Cl B98 ... 159 A7
Benion Rd WS11 ... 1 F5
Benjamin Gdns 4 B20 ... 55 D1
Benmore Ave B5 ... 86 D7
Bennett Ave DY1 ... 51 B6
Bennett Ct CV8 ... 135 F3
Bennett Dr CV34 ... 161 C7
Bennett Rd B74 ... 31 D3
Bennett's Hill
Birmingham B2 ... 164 B2
Dudley DY2 ... 62 E8
Bennetts Rd B8 ... 67 D6
Bennett's Rd CV7 ... 94 F4
Bennett's Road N CV7 ... 94 E7
Bennett's Road S CV6 ... 94 F2
Bennett St
2 Kidderminster DY11 ... 116 C6
Birmingham B19 ... 66 D8
Bennetts Well Jun & Inf Sch B37 ... 69 F3
Ben Nevis Way DY8 ... 81 A6
Bennick Trad Est WS11 ... 4 E6
Bennitt Cl B70 ... 53 C1
Benn Rd CV12 ... 79 B2
Benson Ave WV4 ... 39 D5
Benson Cl
Lichfield WS13 ... 3 D1
Perton WV6 ... 23 E5
Benson Com Sch B18 ... 65 F6
Benson Ind Est B18 ... 65 F6
Benson Rd
Birmingham,Highter's Heath B14 ... 105 B1
Birmingham,Hockley B18 ... 65 F6
Coventry CV6 ... 95 A1
Benson View B79 ... 21 C8
Bent Ave B32 ... 84 D6
Benthall Rd CV6 ... 95 F2
Bentham Ct B31 ... 102 F5
Bentleybridge Island WV11 ... 26 B4
Bentleybridge Way WV11 ... 26 C4
Bentley Br L Pk WV11 ... 26 B4
Bentley Cl
Redditch B97 ... 153 D3
Royal Leamington Spa CV32 ... 157 B3
Bentley Ct
Coventry CV6 ... 95 C4
Nuneaton CV11 ... 73 A4
Sutton Coldfield B76 ... 57 F8
Bentley Drive JMI Sch WS2 ... 28 B2
Bentley Dr WS2 ... 28 B3
Bentley Farm Cl B93 ... 127 E4
Bentley Gr B29 ... 102 F8
Bentley Heath CE Prim Sch B93 ... 127 F5
Bentley Heath Cotts B93 127 F5
Bentley Lane Bsns Pk WS2 ... 28 B3
Bentley La
Walsall,Birchills WS2 ... 28 B3
Walsall,Leamore WS2 ... 28 A5
Willenhall WV12 ... 27 E5
Bentley Mill Cl WS2 ... 27 F1
Bentley Mill La WS2 ... 27 F1
Bentley Mill Way WS2 ... 27 F1
Bentley New Dr WS2 ... 28 B3
Bentley Pl WS2 ... 28 B2
Bentley Rd
Bedworth CV7 ... 78 A1
Birmingham B36 ... 69 D7
Nuneaton CV11 ... 73 A4
Bentley Rd N WS2 ... 27 E1
Bentley Rd S
Darlaston WS10 ... 41 E8
Walsall WS10 ... 27 E1
Bentley Rd WV10 ... 11 E2
Bentley Way B79 ... 20 F7
Bentley West Prim Sch WS2 ... 27 E3
Bentley Wharf WV12 ... 27 D5
Bentmead Gr B38 ... 104 A1
Benton Ave B11 ... 87 C6
Benton Cl WV12 ... 27 D4
Benton Cres WS3 ... 14 D2
Benton Green La CV7 ... 110 F2
Benton Rd B11 ... 87 C6
Benton's Ct DY11 ... 116 C6
Benton's La WS6 ... 5 A1
Bentons Mill Croft B7 ... 67 C8
Bentree The CV3 ... 134 B8
Bent St DY5 ... 61 D4
Ben Willetts Wlk 3 B65 ... 63 C1
Benyon Ctr The WS2 ... 28 A7
Beoley Cl B72 ... 46 C1
Beoley Fst Sch B98 ... 154 E8
Beoley Gr B45 ... 122 A7
Beoley Hall B98 ... 140 C1
Beoley La
Beoley B98 ... 154 F8
Portway B98 ... 141 B1
Beoley Rd E B98 ... 154 A4
Beoley Rd W B98 ... 153 F4
Berberry Cl B30 ... 103 D6
Berenska Dr CV32 ... 157 A2
Beresford Ave CV6 ... 95 E1
Beresford Cres B70 ... 53 B3
Beresford Dr B73 ... 46 A1
Beresford Rd
Oldbury B69 ... 64 C7
Walsall WS3 ... 28 E8
Berets The B75 ... 46 F6
Bericote Croft B27 ... 88 D3
Bericote Rd CV32 ... 156 E8
Berkeley Cl
Bromsgrove B60 ... 151 B8
Nuneaton CV11 ... 73 B3
Perton WV6 ... 23 F3
Willenhall WS2 ... 27 F3
Berkeley Dr DY6 ... 60 C7
Berkeley Ho
Birmingham B23 ... 56 F6
Sutton Coldfield B76 ... 57 F8
Berkeley Mews B25 ... 88 B7
Berkeley Prec B14 ... 104 F2
Berkeley Rd B25 ... 88 B7
Berkeley Rd E B25 ... 88 B7
Berkeley Rd CV8 ... 147 E6
Berkeley Rd N CV5 ... 113 A1
Berkeley Rd S CV5 ... 133 A8
Berkeley Rd B90 ... 105 F3
Berkeley St WS2 ... 42 B7
Berkeswell Cl B98 ... 154 C7
Berkett Rd CV6 ... 95 B2
Berkley Cres B13 ... 87 C1
Berkley Ct B1 ... 66 C1
Berkley St B1 ... 66 C1
Berkshire Cl
Nuneaton CV10 ... 72 E3
West Bromwich B71 ... 53 B7
Berkshire Cres WS10 ... 42 C4
Berkshire The WS3 ... 14 A3
Berkswell CE Prim Sch CV7 ... 110 C3
Berkswell Cl
Dudley DY1 ... 50 E3
Solihull B91 ... 107 B8
Sutton Coldfield B74 ... 31 E4
Berkswell Hall CV7 ... 110 C3
Berkswell Mus* CV7 ... 110 C3
Berkswell Rd
Birmingham B24 ... 57 B4
Coventry CV6 ... 96 B2
Meriden CV7 ... 110 C7
Berkswell Sta CV7 ... 130 C8

Berkswell Windmill★ CV7 130 D4
Bermuda Bsns Pk CV10 78 A7
Bermuda Cl DY1 51 B6
Bermuda Ind Est CV10 78 B8
Bermuda Rd CV10 73 A1
Bernard Pl B18 65 F5
Bernard Rd
Birmingham B17 65 B2
Oldbury B68 64 C2
Tipton DY4 52 B7
Bernard St
Walsall WS1 29 A1
West Bromwich B71 53 C4
Berners Cl CV4 111 E2
Berners St B19 66 D7
Bernhard Dr B21 65 E8
Bernie Crossland Wlk DY10 116 F3
Bernwall Cl DY8 80 F4
Berrandale Rd B36 57 F1
Berrington Cl B98 154 D2
Berrington Dr WV14 51 B8
Berrington Rd
Nuneaton CV10 72 D7
Royal Leamington Spa CV31 162 B6
Berrington Wlk B5 86 E7
Berrow Cottage Homes B93 128 C6
Berrow Dr B15 85 E7
Berrowside Rd B34 69 E6
Berrow View B61 150 D7
Berry Ave WS10 41 B5
Berrybush Gdns DY3 50 E7
Berry Cl B19 66 D6
Berry Cres WS5 43 C4
Berry Dr
Aldridge WS9 29 E5
Barnt Green B45 122 A1
Smethwick B66 65 A6
Berryfield Rd B26 89 D6
Berryfields WS9 29 E5
Berryfields Rd B76 46 F3
Berryfields WS9 16 E5
Berry Hall La B91 108 B4
Berry Hill WS12 2 C4
Berrymound View B47 125 C7
Berry Rd
Birmingham B8 67 E5
Dudley DY1 51 C5
Berry St
Birmingham B18 65 F6
Coventry CV1 113 E4
Wolverhampton WV1 163 C3
Bertha Rd B11 87 D5
Bertie Rd CV8 148 A4
Bertie Terr CV32 156 E1
Bertram Cl DY4 41 C1
Bertram Rd
5 Birmingham B10 67 D1
Smethwick B67 64 E6
Berwick Cl
Coventry CV5 112 B4
Warwick CV34 155 E2
Berwick Dr WS11 4 B8
Berwick Gr
Birmingham,Frankley B31 102 D3
Birmingham,Pheasey B43 44 B4
Berwick Ho CV8 148 A3
Berwicks La B37 70 B1
Berwood Farm Rd B72 57 C6
Berwood Gdns B24 57 C6
Berwood Gr B92 89 B1
Berwood La B24 57 E3
Berwood Pk B35 58 A2
Berwood Rd B72 57 D6
Berwyn Ave CV6 95 A1
Berwyn Gr WS6 4 F3
Berwyn Way CV10 72 C4
Beryl Ave LE10 71 A2
Besant Gr B27 88 A1
Besbury Cl B93 127 E2
Bescot Cres WS1 42 D5
Bescot Croft B42 55 B6
Bescot Dr WS2 42 B6
Bescot Ind Est The WS10 41 D4
Bescot Rd WS2 42 B6
Bescot Stadium Sta WS1 42 D5
Bescot St WS1 42 E7
Besford Gr
Birmingham B31 102 D3
Solihull B90 127 B6
Besom Way WS6 4 C2
Bessborough Rd B25 88 D8
Best Ave CV8 148 C7
Best Rd WV14 40 D7
Best St B64 62 F2
Beswick Gr B33 69 A4
Beta Gr B14 105 C4
Bethany Mews 4 WS11 1 F4
Betjeman Ct DY10 117 B5
Betjeman Pl WV10 12 A1
Betley Gr B33 69 A5
Betony Cl WS5 43 A3
Betsham Cl B44 45 B1
Bettany Glade WV10 11 E4
Betteridge Dr B76 46 E4
Bettina Cl CV10 72 B5
Bettman Cl CV3 133 E6
Betton Rd B14 104 E5
Bett Rd B20 54 F3
Betty's La WS11 6 A4
Bevan Ave WV4 39 E4
Bevan Cl
Bilston WV14 40 F6
Walsall WS4 15 C1
Bevan Ct CV3 133 D7
Bevan Lee Rd WS11 1 D3
Bevan Rd
Brierley Hill DY5 61 A2
Tipton DY4 52 B4
Bevan Way B66 64 F7
Beverley Ave CV10 72 B4
Beverley Cl
Astwood Bank B96 158 E2
Balsall Common CV7 130 C7
Sutton Coldfield B72 57 D7
Beverley Court Rd B32 84 C6
Beverley Cres WV4 39 F4
Beverley Croft B23 56 D2
Beverley Ct 1 B62 84 A6
Beverley Dr DY6 60 C7
Beverley Gr B26 89 B5
Beverley Hill WS12 2 D6
Beverley Rd
Birmingham B45 122 A7
Royal Leamington Spa CV32 156 D1
West Bromwich B71 42 D1
Beverly Dr CV4 132 D2
Beverston Rd
Perton WV6 24 A4
Wednesbury DY4 41 B2
Bevington Cres CV6 112 E5
Bevington Rd B6 66 F8
Bevin Rd WS2 27 E3
Bevis Gr B44 44 F3
Bewdley Ave 4 B12 87 A6
Bewdley Dr WV1 26 B2
Bewdley Grange DY11 116 A5
Bewdley Hill DY11 116 B5
Bewdley Rd
Birmingham B30 104 B8
Kidderminster DY11 116 C6
Bewdley Villas 3 B18 65 D4
Bewell Ct B61 136 F4
Bewell Gdns B61 136 F4
Bewell Head B61 136 F4
Bewick Ct WV6 24 C2
Bewlay Cl DY5 81 B7
Bewley Rd WV12 27 D4
Bewlys Ave B20 54 E4
Bexfield Cl CV5 112 A6
Bexhill Gr 3 B15 66 C1
Bexley Gr B71 53 E7
Bexley Rd B44 56 B8
Bexmore Dr WS13 3 F1
Beyer Cl B77 22 A2
Bhylls Acre Prim Sch WV3 38 B7
Bhylls Cres WV3 38 C7
Bhylls La WV3 38 C7
Bibbey's Gn WV10 11 F4
Bibsworth Ave B13 105 D8
Bibury Rd B28 105 E7
Bicester Sq B35 58 B4
Bickenhill Green Ct B92 90 D1
Bickenhill La
Birmingham B37 90 C6
Birmingham B40 90 D4
Catherine de B B92 108 C6
Bickenhill Park Rd B92 88 E1
Bickenhill Parkway B37 90 D6
Bickenhill Rd B37 90 B7
Bickford Rd
Birmingham B6 56 A1
Wolverhampton WV10 25 F5
Bickington Rd B32 84 D1
Bickley Ave
Birmingham B11 87 C6
Sutton Coldfield B74 31 E5
Bickley Gr B26 89 B5
Bickley Ho B74 31 E5
Bickley Rd
Bilston WV14 41 A7
Walsall WS4 29 C7
Bicknell Croft B14 104 E2
Bickton Cl B24 57 C5
Biddings La WV14 40 B2
Biddles Hill B94 141 C6
Biddlestone Pl WS10 41 B7
Biddleston Gr WS5 43 C3
Biddulph Ct 3 B73 46 A2
Bideford Dr B29 85 C1
Bideford Rd
Coventry CV2 114 C7
Smethwick B66 65 B5
Bideford Way WS11 4 B8
Bidford Cl B90 106 D2
Bidford Rd B31 102 E3
Bierton Rd B25 88 C8
Bigbury Cl CV3 133 E5
Biggin Cl
Birmingham B35 58 A3
Perton WV6 23 E5
Biggin Hall Cres CV3 114 B2
Bigwood Dr
Birmingham B32 84 D1
Sutton Coldfield B75 47 A5
Bilberry Bank WS11 1 E6
Bilberry Cres
Huntington WS12 1 C5
Sutton Coldfield B76 46 F3
Bilberry Dr B45 122 A6
Bilberry Rd
Birmingham B14 104 C6
Coventry CV2 96 D2
Bilboe Rd WV14 41 A3
Bilbrook CE Mid Sch WV8 10 B3
Bilbrook Ct WV8 10 B3
Bilbrook Gr
Birmingham B29 84 F2
Codsall WV8 10 B3
Bilbrook Rd WV8 10 B4
Bilbrook Sta WV8 10 A2
Bilbury Cl B97 158 C6
Bilhay La B70 53 A5
Bilhay St B70 53 B5
Billau Rd WV14 40 D2
Billesden Cl CV3 134 E8
Billesley La
Birmingham B13 87 A1
Portway B48 140 E6
Billesley Prim Sch B13 105 C6
Billingham Cl B91 127 B8
Billing Rd CV5 112 D3
Billingsley Rd B26 89 A8
Billinton Cl CV2 114 E2
Bills La B90 106 A1
Billsmore Gn B92 107 C7
Bills St WS10 41 E6
Billy Buns La WV5 49 B8
Billy La B45,B60 138 A7
Billy Wright Cl WV4 38 D6
Bilport La WS10 52 F8
Bilston Central Sta WV14 40 E5
Bilston CE Prim Sch WV14 40 B6
Bilston Ind Est WV14 41 A4
Bilston Key Ind Est WV14 41 A5
Bilston La WV13 41 B8
Bilston Mus & Art Gall WV14 40 E6
Bilston Rd
Darlaston WV13 41 A8
Wednesbury,Church Hill WS10 41 E3
Wednesbury,Gospel Oak DY4 41 B2
Wolverhampton WV2 39 F8
Bilston St
Darlaston WS10 41 D6
Sedgley DY3 50 E8
Willenhall WV13 27 A1
Wolverhampton WV1 163 C2
Bilton Grange Rd B26 88 F8
Bilton Ind Est
Birmingham B38 123 E8
Coventry CV3 113 F1
Binbrook Rd WV12 27 D4
Bincomb Ave B26 89 B6
Binfield St DY4 52 A4
Bingley Ave B8 68 B4
Bingley Ent Ctr WV3 39 A8
Bingley St WV3 39 A8
Binley Ave CV3 134 F7
Binley Bsns Pk CV3 115 A1
Binley Cl
Birmingham B26 88 D6
Solihull B90 126 A8
Binley Gr CV3 134 F7
Binley Ind Est CV3 135 A8
Binley Rd CV2,CV3 114 D1
Binley Woods Prim Sch CV3 135 E7
Binns Cl CV4 131 F8
Binstead Rd B44 45 A2
Binswood Ave CV32 156 F2
Binswood Cl CV2 96 D2
Binswood Ct 9 CV32 156 F2
Binswood Mans 14 CV32 156 F2
Binswood Rd B62 84 A7
Binswood St CV32 156 E1
Binton Cl B98 154 F1
Binton Croft B13 104 F8
Binton Rd
Coventry CV2 96 D2
Solihull B90 105 F1
Birbeck Ho B36 70 B6
Birbeck Pl DY5 61 B6
Birchall St B12 66 F1
Birch Ave
Birmingham B31 102 C1
Brierley Hill DY5 62 A2
Brownhills WS8 15 E8
Burntwood WS7 6 F6
Cannock WS11 4 C8
Birchbrook Ind Pk WS14 17 E6
Birch Brook La WS14 17 E6
Birch Bsns Pk WS11 4 F6
Birch Cl
Bedworth CV12 78 D4
Birmingham B30 103 E6
Coventry CV5 111 F6
Sutton Coldfield B76 46 F2
Birch Coppice DY5 62 A1
Birch Coppice Distribution Ctr B78 36 E4
Birch Coppice Gdns WV12 27 E4
Birch Cres B69 52 B1
Birchcroft 6 B66 65 C5
Birch Croft
Aldridge WS9 30 C8
Birmingham B37 70 C1
Birch Croft Rd B75 46 D7
Birch Croft B24 57 D5
Birch Ct
11 Wolverhampton WV3 25 C4
Birmingham B30 103 E4
Oldbury B66 64 D8
Royal Leamington Spa CV34 161 E2
Walsall WS4 29 A4
Birchdale Ave B23 56 E3
Birchdale WV14 40 D7
Birchdale Rd B23 56 D5
Birch Dr
Halesowen B62 63 E1
Stourbridge DY8 80 E6
Sutton Coldfield,Little Aston B74 31 D5
Sutton Coldfield,Whitehouse Common B75 46 F7
Birchen Coppice Fst Sch DY11 116 B2
Birchen Coppice Mid Sch DY11 116 B2
Birch End CV34 161 B8
Birchensale Farm 10 B97 153 B5
Birchensale Mid Sch B97 153 C4
Birchensale Rd B97 153 C5
Birches Ave WV8 10 C1
Birches Barn Ave WV3 38 F7
Birches Barn Rd WV3 38 F7
Birches Cl B13 86 F1
Birches Fst Sch WV8 10 B1
Birches Green Inf Sch B24 57 B2
Birches Green Jun Sch B24 57 B3
Birches Green Rd B24 57 B2
Birches Ho B97 153 B2
Birches La
Alvechurch B48 138 F6
Kenilworth CV8 148 B3
Birches Park Rd WV8 10 A2
Birches Rd WV8 10 B2
Birches Rise WV13 26 F1
Birches The CV12 79 B4
Birchfield Ave WV6 24 B6
Birchfield Cl
Halesowen B63 82 E2
Wood End CV9 36 C1
Birchfield Com Sch B20 55 D1
Birchfield Cres DY9 81 F3
Birchfield Ct B97 153 B2
Birchfield Gdns
8 Birmingham B6 66 D8
Walsall WS5 43 C4
Birchfield La
Oldbury,Round's Green B69 63 F6
Oldbury,Whiteheath Gate B69 63 E4
Birchfield Rd
Birmingham B20 55 D2
Coventry CV6 112 F8
Kidderminster DY11 116 B5
Redditch B97 153 B2
Stourbridge DY9 81 F3
Birchfields Dr WS12 2 D1
Birchfields Rd WV12 27 A5
Birchfield Twr 1 B20 55 D1
Birchfield Way WS5 43 C4
Birchgate DY9 81 F4
Birchglade WV3 24 D1
Birchgrave Cl CV6 114 A7
Birch Gr
Balsall Common CV7 130 B8
Birchmoor B78 36 D7
Birmingham B68 84 D7
Lichfield WS14 9 D8
Birch Hollow B15 85 F6
Birch Ho
Redditch B98 158 F8
Sutton Coldfield B74 31 B5
Birchills Canal Mus★ WS2 28 C3
Birchills CE Prim Com Sch WS2 28 D2
Birchills St WS2 28 D2
Birch La
Aldridge WS9 16 D1
Birmingham B68 84 D7
Walsall WS4 15 C1
Birchley Ho
Oldbury B69 63 D6
Redditch B97 153 B1
Birchley Ind Est B69 63 E5
Birchley Park Ave B69 63 E6
Birchley Rise B92 88 F4
Birch Meadow Cl CV34 160 D7
Birchmoor Cl B28 106 B7
Birchmoor Rd B78 36 F8
Birchover Rd WS2 28 A4
Birch Rd
Birmingham,Rubery B45 121 E6
Birmingham,Warley Woods B68 84 D7
Birmingham,Witton B6 56 A2
Birch Rd E B6 56 B2
Birch Rd
Sedgley DY3 39 F1
Wednesfield WV11 26 F8
Wolverhampton WV11 12 F1
Birch St
Oldbury B68 64 C5
Tipton DY4 51 F5
Walsall WS2 28 D3
Wolverhampton WV1 163 B3
Birch Terr DY2 62 C4
Birch Tree Gdns WS9 30 B5
Birchtree Gdns DY5 62 A1
Birch Tree Gr B91 106 F4
Birchtree Hollow WV12 27 D5
Birchtree Rd CV10 72 C6
Birchtrees Croft B26 88 D5
Birchtrees Dr B33 69 D2
Birchtrees B24 57 D4
Birchway Cl CV32 156 C1
Birch Wlk B68 84 D8
Birchwood Ave B78 36 F7
Birchwood Cl
Essington WV11 13 A3
Kidderminster DY11 116 A7
Birchwood Cres B12 87 B4
Birchwood Prim Sch B78 36 F7
Birchwood Rd
Binley Woods CV3 135 C7
Birmingham B12 87 A4
Lichfield WS14 9 F7
Wolverhampton WV4 39 A5
Birchwoods B32 84 B2
Birchwood Wlk DY6 60 E8
Birchy Cl B90 125 F6
Birchy Leasowes La B90 125 E5
Birdbrook Rd B44 55 E8
Birdcage Wlk 4 DY2 51 D1
Bird Cage Wlk B38 103 F2
Bird End B71 53 F8
Bird Grove Ct CV1 113 D5
Birdhope B77 22 C1
Birdie Cl B38 103 D1
Birdlip Gr B32 84 C6
Bird Rd CV34 161 D4
Birds Bush Prim Sch B77 35 E8
Birds Bush Rd B77 35 F8
Birds Mdw DY5 61 B7
Bird St
Coventry CV1 165 C3
Dudley DY3 50 C3
Lichfield WS13 9 B7
Birdwell Croft B13 104 F6
Birkdale Ave
Birmingham B29 85 F1
Blackwell B60 138 A5
Birkdale Cl
Coventry CV6 95 B4
Nuneaton CV11 74 A1
Stourbridge DY8 80 F2
Wolverhampton WV1 26 A2
Birkdale Dr B69 63 A7
Birkdale Gr B29 104 A8
Birkdale Rd WS3 14 A3
Birkenshaw Rd B44 55 E8
Birley Gr B63 82 C1
Birlingham Ho B60 137 B3
Birmingham Botanical Gdns★ B15 85 F7
Birmingham Bsns Pk B37 90 E8
Birmingham Children's Hospl B4 164 C3
Birmingham Christian Coll B29 85 C1
Birmingham Coll of Food, Tourism & Creative Studies B3 164 A3
Birmingham Conservatoire B1 164 B2
Birmingham Dental Hospl The B4 164 C4
Birmingham Great Pk B45 122 B8
Birmingham Heartlands Hospl B9 68 B2
Birmingham Hippodrome Theatre★ B5 164 C1
Birmingham Int Airport B40 90 B4
Birmingham Int Convention Ctr★ B1 66 C2
Birmingham Int Sta B40 90 D4
Birmingham & Midland Mus of Transport★ B47 124 E3
Birmingham Mus & Art Gal★ B3 164 B2
Birmingham Nature Ctr★ B5 86 C3
Birmingham New Rd
Dudley DY1,DY4,WV14 51 C4
Wolverhampton WV4 39 E4
Birmingham Nuffield Hospl The B15 85 F5
Birmingham Rd
Aldridge WS9 30 A4
Allesley CV5 111 E7
Alvechurch B48 139 B7
Birmingham,Buckland End B36 69 A8
Birmingham,Rubery B45, B61 121 D5
Blakedown DY10 98 C2
Burton Green CV8 131 A1
Coleshill B46 70 E5
Dudley DY1 51 E2
Hagley DY9 99 D7
Halesowen B63 83 B4
Hopwood B31,B48 123 B4
Kenilworth CV8 147 C8
Kidderminster DY10 117 D7
Lichfield WS14 9 A4
Lickey End B60,B61 137 B6
Little Packington CV7 91 E3
Lower Marlbrook B61 121 B1
Oldbury B69 64 B7
Redditch B97,B98 153 E8
Rowley Regis B65 63 C2
Shenstone WS14 18 A4
Stoneleigh CV8 149 B6
Studley B80,B98 159 E7
Sutton Coldfield B72,B73 46 B2
Walsall B43,WS1,WS5 43 D5
Warwick CV34 160 B8
Water Orton B46 59 A3
West Bromwich B71 54 A1
Wolverhampton WV2 39 D7
Wroxall B93,CV35 145 D3
Birmingham Rly Mus★ B11 87 F5

Birmingham Sch of Acting B1 164 B2
Birmingham Sch of Speech & Drama B15 86 A7
Birmingham St
Darlaston WS10 41 E6
Dudley DY2 51 D1
Halesowen B63 83 B3
Oldbury B69 64 A7
Stourbridge DY8 81 B5
Walsall WS1 28 F1
Willenhall WV13 27 C2
Birmingham Women's Hospl B15 85 D4
Birnam B15 86 A8
Birnham Cl DY4 51 D5
Birstall Way B38 123 C8
Birvell Ct CV12 78 D3
Bisell Way DY5 81 C6
Biset Ave DY10 117 B5
Bishbury Cl B15 85 E8
Bishop Asbury Cres B43 54 C8
Bishop Asbury's Cottage* B43 54 C8
Bishop Challoner RC Sch B14 104 F8
Bishop Cl
Birmingham B45 101 E1
Cannock WS11 1 D2
Dudley DY2 62 E8
Bishopgate Bsns Pk CV1 113 D5
Bishopgate Ind Est CV1 113 D5
Bishop Hall Cres B60 150 E7
Bishop Milner RC Sch DY1 51 A3
Bishop Rd WS10 42 C2
Bishops Cl B66 65 C4
Bishop's Ct
Birmingham,Coleshill Heath B37 90 E8
Birmingham,Northfield B31 103 B3
Bishops Gate B31 103 A2
Bishopsgate St B15 66 B1
Bishops Mdw B75 32 E3
Bishops Rd B73 46 B3
Bishop St
Birmingham B5 86 E8
Coventry CV1 165 B3
Bishopstone Cl B98 154 F2
Bishops Way B74 31 F6
Bishops Wlk
Coventry CV5 133 B8
Halesowen B64 83 A6
Bishopton Cl
Coventry CV5 112 B3
Solihull B90 106 C1
Bishopton Rd B67 64 F1
Bishop Ullathorne RC Sch CV3 132 F4
Bishop Vesey's Gram Sch B74 46 C6
Bishop Walsh RC Sch B72 46 D1
Bishop Wilson CE Prim Sch B37 70 C3
Bishton Gr DY2 62 D4
Bisley Gr B24 57 B2
Bismillah Bldgs B19 164 B4
Bissell Cl B28 105 F6
Bissell Dr WS10 42 B3
Bissell St
Birmingham B32 84 A6
Birmingham,Highgate B5 86 E8
Bissel St WV14 40 F5
Bisset Cres 12 CV31 162 C6
Bi Tec Ind Pk WV1 26 A1
Biton Cl B17 85 B5
Bittell Cl
Birmingham B31 122 F7
Wolverhampton WV10 11 E4
Bittell Ct B31 122 F7
Bittell Farm Rd B48 123 A2
Bittell La B45 138 E8
Bittell Rd
Alvechurch B48 139 A8
Barnt Green B45 138 E8
Bitterne Dr WV6 25 A4
Bittern Wlk DY5 81 C6
Bittern Wood Rd DY10 117 B3
Bitterscote La B78 21 A2
Blackacre Rd DY2 62 D8
Black-a-Tree Ct CV10 72 F5
Black-A-Tree Rd CV10 72 E4
Blackbades Bvd CV34 160 B4
Black Bank CV7 78 B1
Blackberry Ave
Birmingham B9 68 A3
Hockley Heath B94 143 C6
Blackberry Cl DY1 61 E8
Blackberry La
Brownhills WS9 16 B4
Coventry,Neal's Green CV7 95 C5
Coventry,Wyken Green CV2 114 C6
Halesowen B63 83 A2
Rowley Regis B65 62 F5
Sutton Coldfield B74 31 E4
Blackbird Croft B36 70 A7
Blackbrook Cl DY2 62 A3
Blackbrook Rd DY2 62 B5
Blackbrook Valley Ind Pk DY2 62 A5
Blackbrook Way WV10 11 E4
Blackburn Ave WV6 24 F7
Blackburne Rd B28 105 F6
Blackburn Rd CV6 95 F3
Blackbushe Cl B17 84 F7
Blackcat Cl B37 70 A3
Black Country Living Mus* DY1 51 D3
Black Country New Rd
Darlaston WS10 41 C4
Tipton B70,DY4 52 D6
Black Country Route
Bilston WV14 40 E5
Darlaston WV13,WS10 41 B7
Walsall WS2,WS10 27 E1
Blackdown Cl B45 102 A2
Blackdown Hall CV32 156 F6
Blackdown Rd B93 128 B6
Blackdown B77 22 C1
Blackett Ct 1 B73 46 A2
Blackfirs La B37,B46 90 D7
Blackford Cl
Halesowen B63 82 D2
Kidderminster DY11 116 A1
Blackford Rd
Birmingham B11 87 C4
Solihull B90 126 C8
Blackford St B18 65 E5
Blackfriars Cl B79 20 E5
Blackgreaves La B76 48 F1
Blackhalve La WV11 12 D1
Blackham Dr B73 57 A7
Blackham Rd WV11 26 F8
Black Haynes Rd B29 103 A6
Blackheath Mkt B65 63 C1
Blackheath Prim Sch B65 63 D2
Blackheath Trad Est B65 63 E2
Black Horse La 1 DY10 116 E6
Blackhorse La DY5 61 E1
Black Horse Rd CV6,CV7 96 B6
Black Lake La B60,B97 152 A2
Black Lake Sta B70 53 A6
Black Lake B70 53 A6
Black La CV32 157 C2
Blackley Ho B66 65 D6
Blacklow Rd CV34 156 A1
Blackmoor Croft B33 69 D2
Blackmore La B60 137 A3
Blackpit La WV4 37 E3
Black Prince Ave CV3 133 E6
Blackrock Rd B23 56 B6
Blackroot Cl WS7 7 D4
Blackroot Ho B73 45 C2
Blackroot Rd B74 46 B7
Blackshaw Dr CV2 114 F6
Blacksmith Dr
7 Sutton Coldfield B75 32 E3
Bromsgrove B60 151 A7
Blacksmiths La B94 143 C6
Blacksmith Way 3 B70 53 C2
Black Soils Rd B98 154 F5
Blackstitch La B97 153 A1
Blackthorn Ave WS7 6 F4
Blackthorn Cl
Birmingham B30 103 C6
Coventry CV4 132 D5
Blackthorn Ct B98 154 E1
Blackthorne Cl
Dudley DY1 50 F4
Solihull B91 106 E4
Blackthorne Rd
Dudley DY1 50 F5
Kenilworth CV8 148 A3
Lichfield WS14 9 D7
Smethwick B67 64 D4
Walsall WS5 42 F5
Blackthorn Gr CV11 73 F2
Blackthorn Rd
Birmingham,Bournville B30 103 D6
Birmingham,Castle Bromwich B36 69 C8
Stourbridge DY8 61 A1
Blackwatch Rd CV6 113 C8
Blackwater Cl DY5 61 A6
Blackwell La 1 B97 153 B5
Blackwell Rd
Barnt Green B45,B60 138 B5
Coventry CV6 113 E8
Sutton Coldfield B72 46 D1
Blackwell St DY10 116 E6
Blackwood Ave WV11 26 C8
Blackwood Dr B74 44 E8
Blackwood Rd
Bromsgrove B60 137 B2
Sutton Coldfield B74 30 E1
Tamworth B77 35 C7
Blackwood Sch B74 30 E1
Blades Rd B70 52 D4
Bladon Cl CV11 73 F8
Bladon Wlk 6 CV31 162 C6
Blaenwern Dr B63 82 B7
Blagdon Rd B63 83 A6
Blair Dr CV12 77 D1
Blair Gr B37 70 D1
Blakebrook Cl DY11 116 C6
Blakebrook Gdns DY11 116 C6
Blakebrook DY11 116 C6
Blakebrook Sch DY11 116 C6
Blake Cl
Cannock WS11 2 A5
Hinckley LE10 71 D4
Nuneaton CV10 72 A5
Blakedon Rd WS10 41 E3
Blakedown CE Fst Sch DY10 98 C1
Blakedown Rd B63 82 F1
Blakedown Sta DY10 98 C2
Blakedown Way 4 B69 63 E4
Blake Hall Cl DY5 81 C7
Blake Ho 2 WS2 42 C8
Blake La B9 67 F2
Blakeland Rd B44 55 E6
Blakelands Ave CV31 162 B6
Blakeland St B9 67 F2
Blakeley Ave WV6 24 F7
Blakeley Ct B72 57 C8
Blakeley Hall Gdns B69 64 B7
Blakeley Hall Rd B69 64 B7
Blakeley Heath Dr WV5 49 A5
Blakeley Heath Prim Sch WV5 49 A5
Blakeley Rise WV6 24 F7
Blakeley Wood Rd DY4 52 D8
Blakemere Ave B25 88 E8
Blakemere Cl B98 154 F3
Blakemore Cl B32 84 F3
Blakemore Dr B75 46 F6
Blakemore Rd
Brownhills WS9 16 A3
West Bromwich B70 53 A1
Blakenall Heath Jun Sch WS3 28 C8
Blakenall Heath WS3 28 D8
Blakenall La WS3 28 D8
Blakenall Row WS3 28 D8
Blakeney Ave
Birmingham B17 85 A7
Stourbridge DY8 80 D6
Blakeney Cl DY3 50 C8
Blakenhale Jun & Inf Schs B33 69 B1
Blakenhale Rd B33 69 B1
Blakenhall Gdns WV2 39 D7
Blakenhall Ind Est WV2 39 B7
Blake Pl B9 67 F2
Blake Rd B61 137 B8
Blakes Field Dr B45 122 A1
Blakesley Cl B76 57 F5
Blakesley Gr B25 68 D1
Blakesley Hall Mus* B25 68 E1
Blakesley Hall Prim Sch B25 68 D1
Blakesley Mews B25 88 D8
Blakesley Rd B25 68 D1
Blakesley Way B33 68 D2
Blake Street Sta B74 31 F6
Blake St B74 31 E6
Blake Valley Tech Coll WS12 1 F6
Blakewood Cl B34 69 C5
Blandford Ave B36 58 E1
Blandford Dr
Coventry CV2 114 F5
Stourbridge DY8 60 E3
Blandford Gdns WS7 7 C6
Blandford Rd
Birmingham B32 84 F5
Royal Leamington Spa CV32 156 C1
Blandford Way CV35 160 A7
Blanefield WV8 10 E2
Blanford Mere Prim Sch DY6 60 E8
Blanning Ct B93 127 E3
Blay Ave WS2 28 B2
Blaydon Ave B75 32 E2
Blaydon Ct 3 B17 85 D4
Blaydon Rd WV9,WV10 11 A1
Blaythorn Ave B92 89 A3
Blaze Hill Rd DY6 60 A8
Blaze La B96,B97 158 A3
Blaze Pk DY6 60 B8
Bleachfield La B98 154 F8
Bleak Hill Rd B23 56 C5
Bleak House Dr WS7 6 D8
Bleakhouse Jun Sch B68 64 C1
Bleakhouse Rd B68 64 C1
Bleak St B67 64 F6
Blenheim 5 B17 85 B6
Blenheim Ave CV6 95 C2
Blenheim Cl
Hinckley LE10 71 F4
Nuneaton CV11 73 F2
Tamworth B77 21 C4
Walsall WS4 29 D7
Blenheim Cres
Bromsgrove B60 151 A8
Royal Leamington Spa CV31 162 C5
Blenheim Ct
Birmingham B44 55 F8
Solihull B91 107 C4
Blenheim Dr
Birmingham B43 54 D8
Darlaston WS10 41 E5
Blenheim Rd
Birmingham B13 86 F1
Burntwood WS7 7 A8
Kingswinford DY6 61 A6
Norton Canes WS11 6 B4
Solihull B90 106 D2
Willenhall WV12 27 B6
Blenheim Way
Birmingham,Castle Vale B35 58 B2
Birmingham,Old Oscott B44 55 F8
Dudley DY1 50 E2
Blenheim Wlk CV6 95 B4
Bletchley Dr
Coventry CV5 112 B4
Tamworth B77 35 C8
Bletchley Rd B24 57 E4
Blewitt Cl B36 58 D2
Blewitt St
Brierley Hill DY5 61 C6
Cannock WS12 2 B7
Blews St B6 66 E5
Blick Rd CV34 161 C4
Blind La
Berkswell CV7 110 D4
Blind La *continued*
Kenilworth CV8 131 F1
Tanworth-In-A B94 141 D1
Blindpit La B76 59 B8
Bliss Cl CV4 111 E3
Blithe Cl DY8 81 A8
Blithfield Dr DY5 81 B7
Blithfield Gr B24 57 C5
Blithfield Pl WS11 2 B1
Blithfield Rd WS8 6 C2
Blockall Cl WS10 41 D7
Blockall WS10 41 D7
Blockley Cl B97 152 E2
Blockley Rd CV12 78 C4
Blockley's Yd 4 LE10 75 D8
Blondvil St CV3 133 D7
Bloomfield Cres WS13 3 B2
Bloomfield Ct 3 B42 55 A8
Bloomfield Dr WV12 13 D1
Bloomfield Pk DY4 51 D6
Bloomfield Rd
Birmingham B13 87 B3
Tipton DY4 51 E7
Bloomfield St N B63 82 F5
Bloomfield St W B63 82 F4
Bloomfield Terr DY4 51 E7
Bloomfield Way B79 20 F8
Bloomsbury Gr B14 104 C7
Bloomsbury St
Birmingham B7 67 B5
Wolverhampton WV2 163 B1
Bloomsbury Way WS14 9 E7
Bloomsbury Wlk 1 B7 67 B5
Bloor Mill Cl WV13 26 F1
Blossom Ave B29 85 F2
Blossom Dr B61 137 A5
Blossomfield Cl
Birmingham B38 123 D8
Kingswinford DY6 60 E8
Blossomfield Ct B38 123 D8
Blossomfield Gdns B91 107 A4
Blossomfield Inf Sch B90 106 D3
Blossomfield Rd B91 106 F2
Blossom Gr
Birmingham B36 68 E8
Cradley Heath B64 62 F1
Blossom Hill B24 57 A4
Blossom Rd B24 57 C4
Blossom's Fold WV1 163 B3
Blossomville Way 9 B27 88 C5
Blount Ho DY11 116 B8
Blounts Rd B23 56 D5
Blount Terr DY11 116 D3
Blowers Green Cres DY2 62 B7
Blowers Green Pl DY2 62 B7
Blowers Green Prim Sch DY2 62 B8
Blower's Green Rd DY2 62 B8
Bloxcidge St B68 64 B4
Bloxwich Bsns Pk WS2 28 A7
Bloxwich CE Prim Sch WS3 14 B1
Bloxwich Hospl WS3 28 B8
Bloxwich La WS2 28 A4
Bloxwich L Ctr WS3 28 C8
Bloxwich North Sta WS3 13 F2
Bloxwich Rd N WV12 27 D6
Bloxwich Rd S WV13 27 A3
Bloxwich Rd WS2,WS3 28 D5
Bloxwich Sta WS3 14 A1
Blucher St B1 164 B1
Blue Ball La B63 82 C7
Bluebell Cl
Cannock WS12 2 B6
Stourbridge DY8 60 C2
Bluebell Cres WV11 26 D5
Bluebell Croft
Birmingham,Northfield B31 102 F4
Birmingham,Perry Common B23 56 C7
Bluebell Dr
Bedworth CV12 77 E2
Birmingham B37 70 E2
Bluebell La WS6 5 A1
Bluebell Rd
Brownhills WS9 16 B3
Cradley Heath B64 62 E3
Dudley DY1 51 B4
Bluebell Wlk CV4 111 F1
Bluebellwood Cl B76 47 A3
Bluebird Cl WS14 9 D8
Blue Bird Pk B62 101 B7
Bluebird Trad Est WV10 25 E5
Blue Cedar Dr B74 44 F6
Blue Cedars DY8 80 C6
Blue Coat CE Comp Sch WS1 28 F1
Blue Coat CE Inf Sch WS1 28 F1
Blue Coat CE Jun Sch WS1 28 F1
Blue Coat Sch The B17 85 E6
Blue La E WS2 28 E3
Blue Lake Rd B93 128 B2
Blue La W WS2 28 D2
Blue Rock Pl B69 63 C7
Bluestone Wlk B65 63 C6
Blundell Rd B11 87 D5
Blundells The CV8 148 A5
Blyth Ave CV7 130 C5
Blyth Cl CV12 77 C1
Blyth Ct CV11 73 C3
Blythe Cl
Burntwood WS7 7 D6
Redditch B97 158 D7
Blythe Ct
Solihull B91 106 F7
Blythe Ct *continued*
Sutton Coldfield B73 46 B5
Blythefield Ave B43 43 C2
Blythe Gate B90 126 F3
Blythe Gr B44 44 F3
Blythe Rd
7 Coleshill B46 70 F7
Coventry CV1 113 E4
Blythe St B77 21 C4
Blythesway B48 139 A6
Blythe Valley Pk B90 126 F2
Blytheway B91 107 E3
Blythewood Cl B91 107 F1
Blythsford Rd B28 106 A4
Blythswood Rd B11 88 A4
Blyton Cl B16 65 F3
Boar Croft CV4 111 F2
Board School Gdns DY3 50 E6
Boar Hound Cl B18 66 A4
Boat La WS14 7 F1
Boatman's La WS9 15 E2
Bobbington Way DY2 62 E5
Bobs Coppice Wlk DY5 81 F7
Bockendon Rd CV4 131 E5
Boddington Cl CV32 157 E5
Bodenham Cl B98 154 D3
Bodenham Rd
Birmingham,Brandhall B68 84 B8
Birmingham,Frankley B31 102 E1
Boden Rd B28 106 A7
Bodens La WS9 44 B7
Bodiam Ct WV6 24 A3
Bodicote Gr B75 32 E3
Bodington Cl WS7 7 E7
Bodington Rd B75 32 B3
Bodmin Cl
Hinckley LE10 71 E4
Walsall WS5 43 D7
Bodmin Ct 16 DY5 61 D2
Bodmin Gr 2 B7 67 B5
Bodmin Rd
Coventry CV2 114 F5
Dudley DY2 62 D2
Bodmin Rise WS5 43 D7
Bodnant Way CV8 148 C6
Bodymoor Heath Rd B76 48 F5
Bognop Rd WV11 12 D4
Bohun St CV4 111 F1
Boldmere Cl B73 57 A7
Boldmere Ct B43 54 E7
Boldmere Dr B73 57 A8
Boldmere Gdns B73 57 A8
Boldmere Inf Sch B73 45 F1
Boldmere Jun Sch B73 45 F1
Boldmere Rd B73 57 A8
Bolebridge Mews B79 21 B5
Bolebridge St B79 21 C4
Bolehall Ho B77 21 C4
Boley Cl WS14 9 D7
Boley Cottage La WS14 9 E7
Boley La WS14 9 D7
Boleyn Cl
Cheslyn Hay WS6 4 D2
Warwick CV34 161 C6
Boleyn Rd B45 101 E2
Boley Park Ctr WS14 9 E7
Bolingbroke Dr CV34 161 E3
Bolingbroke Rd CV3 114 A1
Bolney Rd B32 84 E4
Bolton Cl CV3 133 E5
Bolton Ct DY4 52 C8
Bolton Rd
Birmingham B10 87 C8
Wednesfield WV11 26 D5
Bolton St B9 67 B2
Bolton Way WS3 13 F3
Bolyfant Cres CV31 162 A2
Bomers Field B45 122 C7
Bond Dr B35 58 A3
Bondfield Rd B13 105 B6
Bond Gate CV11 73 C4
Bonds Hospl CV1 165 A3
Bond Sq B18 66 A4
Bond St
Birmingham,Ladywood B19 164 B4
Birmingham,Stirchley B30 104 A7
Coventry CV1 165 B3
Dudley WV14 51 A8
Nuneaton CV11 73 C5
Rowley Regis B65 63 E3
West Bromwich B70 53 C2
Wolverhampton WV2 163 B2
Bondway WS12 1 F7
Bonehill Ind Est B78 20 F1
Bonehill Rd B78 20 E3
Bone Mill La WV1 25 D4
Boney Hay Rd WS7 7 B7
Bonfire Hill DY9 120 E6
Bonham Gr B25 68 D1
Boningale Way B93 127 E3
Bonington Dr CV12 78 A4
Bonner Dr B76 57 F5
Bonner Gr WS9 29 F5
Bonneville Cl CV5 111 B8
Bonniksen Cl 7 CV31 161 F5
Bonnington Way B43 44 D4
Bonny Stile La WV11 26 B6
Bonsall Rd B23 57 A6
Bonville Gdns WV10 11 E4
Booth Cl
Kingswinford DY6 61 A6
Lichfield WS13 3 A2
Walsall WS3 28 D8

Booth Ct 17 DY5 61 D2
Booth Ho WS4 28 F3
Booth Rd WS10 42 C2
Booths Farm Rd B42 55 B8
Booths Fields CV6 95 E2
Booth's La B42 44 B1
Booth St
Birmingham B21 65 D7
Cannock WS12 2 B6
Darlaston WS10 41 D8
Walsall WS3 28 C8
Boot Piece La B97 153 B5
Bordeaux Cl DY1 50 E3
Borden Cl WV8 24 F8
Bordesley Abbey★ B98 153 F6
Bordesley Abbey Visitor Ctr★ B98 153 F6
Bordesley Cir B10 67 B1
Bordesley Cl B9 68 A2
Bordesley Ct CV32 157 A3
Bordesley Gn B9 67 E2
Bordesley Gn E B9,B33 68 C2
Bordesley Green Girls' Sch B9 67 D2
Bordesley Green Prim Sch B9 68 A2
Bordesley Green Rd B8 67 D2
Bordesley Green Trad Est B9 67 D3
Bordesley La B98 153 E6
Bordesley Middleway B12 87 A8
Bordesley Park Rd B10 67 B1
Bordesley Sta B10 67 A1
Bordesley St B5 164 D2
Bordsley Ct 7 B9 67 B2
Bore St WS13 9 B7
Borman B79 20 F5
Borneo St WS4 28 F4
Borough Cres
Oldbury B65 63 E4
Stourbridge DY8 80 E5
Borough Ct B63 83 B4
Borough Rd B79 21 C7
Borough The LE10 75 D8
Borrington Gdns DY10 117 B4
Borrington Rd DY10 117 B5
Borrowcop Ho WS14 9 C6
Borrowcop La WS14 9 C5
Borrowdale Cl
Brierley Hill DY5 81 B8
Coventry CV6 113 A8
Borrowdale Dr CV32 156 D2
Borrowdale Gr B31 102 D3
Borrowdale Rd B31 102 C3
Borrowell La CV8 147 E4
Borrowell Terr CV8 147 E4
Borrow St WV13 27 A3
Borwick Ave B70 53 A3
Bosbury Terr B30 104 B7
Boscobel Ave DY4 51 F4
Boscobel Cl DY1 50 F3
Boscobel Cres WV1 25 C4
Boscobel Rd
Birmingham B43 43 D2
Cheswick Green B90 126 D5
Walsall WS1 43 B8
Boscombe Ave B11 87 C6
Boscombe Rd B11 87 E4
Bosmere Ct B31 102 F3
Boss Dr DY2 62 C7
Boss Gate Cl WV5 49 A5
Boston Cl WS12 2 E1
Boston Gr B44 56 B8
Boston Pl CV6 113 D8
Boston Way LE9 71 F6
Bosty La WS9 29 E5
Boswell Cl
Darlaston WS10 41 D5
Wednesbury WS10 41 C1
Boswell Dr CV2 115 A7
Boswell Gr CV34 155 D1
Boswell Rd
Bilston WV14 40 F7
Birmingham B44 55 F6
Cannock WS11 1 D4
Sutton Coldfield B74 46 C6
Bosworth Cl
Baginton CV8 133 E2
Dudley DY3 51 A6
Hinckley LE10 71 A1
Sedgley DY3 50 F7
Bosworth Dr B37 70 A2
Bosworth Ho 3 LE10 71 E1
Bosworth Rd B26 88 E4
Bosworth Wood Prim Sch
Birmingham B36 58 F1
Birmingham B36 69 F8
Botany Dr DY3 50 D6
Botany Rd WS5 43 A5
Botany Wlk 5 B16 66 A2
Botham Ho CV11 73 E1
Botha Rd B9 67 F2
Botoner Rd CV1 113 F2
Botteley Rd B70 53 A6
Bottetourt Rd B29 85 A2
Botteville Rd B27 88 C2
Bott La
Stourbridge DY9 81 E6
Walsall WS1 28 F1
Bottle Cotts B17 85 D4
Bott Rd CV5 132 D8
Bottrill St CV11 73 B5
Boughton Rd B25 88 C7
Boulevard The
Brierley Hill DY5 61 F2
Boulevard The *continued*
Sutton Coldfield B73 57 B8
Boultbee Rd B72 57 C7
Boulters La CV9 36 D1
Boulton Cir B19 66 C6
Boulton Cl WS7 7 C8
Boulton Ho 1 B70 53 D1
Boulton Ind Ctr B18 66 B5
Boulton Rd
Birmingham B21 65 E7
Smethwick B66 65 D6
Solihull B91 107 C7
West Bromwich B70 53 D1
Boulton Retreat B21 65 E7
Boultons La B97 158 D6
Boulton Sq B70 53 D1
Boulton Wlk B23 56 B4
Boundary Ave B65 63 E2
Boundary Cl WV13 26 C1
Boundary Cres DY3 50 C3
Boundary Ct B37 69 E2
Boundary Dr B13 86 D2
Boundary Farm WV6 23 F2
Boundary Hill DY3 50 C4
Boundary Ho B5 86 C5
Boundary Ind Est WV10 11 C5
Boundary La B90 126 A6
Boundary Pl B21 54 B1
Boundary Rd
Birmingham B23 56 E4
Brownhills WS9 15 F3
Sutton Coldfield B74 44 F7
Boundary Way
Wolverhampton,Penn WV4 38 C5
Wolverhampton,Tettenhall Wood WV6 23 F2
Bourlay Cl B45 101 E2
Bournbrook Ct B5 86 A3
Bournbrook Rd B29 86 A2
Bourne Ave
Fairfield B61 120 F1
Fazeley B78 20 E1
Halesowen B62 83 F4
Tipton DY4 52 C7
Bournebrook Cl DY2 62 C5
Bournebrook Cres B62 84 A4
Bourne Cl
Birmingham B13 105 D6
Cannock WS12 2 E2
Solihull B91 107 E6
Bourne Gn B32 84 E6
Bourne Hill Cl DY2 62 E3
Bourne Rd
Birmingham B6 67 B7
Coventry CV3 114 C1
Bournes Cl B63 82 F3
Bournes Cres B63 82 E4
Bournes Hill B63 82 E4
Bourne St
Dudley,Bramford DY3, WV14 51 A7
Dudley DY2,DY3 51 D1
Bourne Vale WS9 30 D3
Bourne Way Gdns B29 104 A8
Bourne Wlk B65 62 F5
Bournheath Rd B61 120 D2
Bourn Mill Dr B6 66 E6
Bournville Coll of F Ed
Birmingham B30 103 E7
Birmingham B31 103 C7
Bournville Inf Sch B30 103 E7
Bournville Jun Sch B30 103 E7
Bournville La B30 103 E6
Bournville Mews B30 103 E5
Bournville Sch of Art B30 103 E7
Bournville Sch & Sixth Form Ctr B30 103 C6
Bournville Sta B30 104 A7
Bourton Cl 1 WS5 43 A3
Bourton Croft B92 106 F8
Bourton Dr CV31 162 B5
Bourton Rd B92 106 F8
Bovey Croft B76 58 A7
Bovingdon Rd B35 58 A3
Bowater Ave B33 68 D1
Bowater Ho
2 West Bromwich B70 53 C2
Birmingham B19 66 D5
Bowater St B70 53 C2
Bowbrook Ave B90 127 A5
Bowcroft Gr B24 57 C6
Bow Ct CV5 132 D8
Bowden Rd B67 64 E6
Bowden Way CV3 114 F1
Bowdler Rd WV2 163 D1
Bowen Ave WV4 40 A3
Bowen-Cooke Ave WV6 23 E6
Bowen Ct 4 B13 87 B2
Bowen St WV4 39 E5
Bower Cl WS13 3 D2
Bowercourt Cl B91 107 B2
Bower La DY5 82 A8
Bowers Croft CV32 157 A5
Bowes Dr WS11 1 F4
Bowes Rd B45 121 E7
Bowfell Cl CV5 112 B4
Bowker St WV13 26 C1
Bowlas Ave B74 46 B8
Bowling Green Ave B77 35 F7
Bowling Green Cl
Birmingham B23 56 E7
Darlaston WS10 41 D7
Bowling Green Dr B67 64 E2
Bowling Green La
Bedworth CV7,CV12 95 E8
Birmingham B20 66 A8
Bowling Green Rd
Dudley DY2 62 E2
Hinckley LE10 71 E1
Stourbridge DY8 80 E5
Bowling Green St CV34 160 D6
Bowls Ct CV5 112 F3
Bowman Gn LE10 75 F6
Bowman Rd B42 44 B1
Bowmans Harbour Island WV10 26 B4
Bowman's Rise WV1 26 B3
Bowmore Rd B60 137 B1
Bowness Cl CV6 113 A8
Bowness Gr WV11 13 B1
Bowness Ho B65 63 D4
Bowood Cres B31 103 B2
Bowood Ct B97 153 D4
Bowood Dr WV6 24 D6
Bowood End B76 46 E3
Bowshot Cl B36 58 D1
Bow St
Bilston WV14 40 E6
Birmingham B1 164 B1
Bowstoke Rd B43 54 C8
Bow St WV13 27 A1
Bowyer Rd B8 67 E4
Bowyer St B10 67 A1
Box Cl CV31 162 B3
Boxhill Cl B6 66 F6
Boxhill The CV3 114 B1
Boxnott Cl B97 153 A2
Box Rd B37 90 C8
Box St WS1 28 F1
Box Trees Rd B93,B94 127 C1
Boyd Cl CV2 115 A8
Boyden Cl WS11 1 B1
Boyd Gr B27 88 B2
Boydon Cl WV2 40 A6
Boyleston Rd B28 106 A6
Boyne Rd B26 89 B7
Boyslade Rd LE10 75 F6
Boyslade Road E LE10 75 F5
Boyton Gr B44 44 F3
Brabazon Gr B35 57 F3
Brabham Cres B74 44 F6
Bracadale Ave B24 57 A4
Bracadale Cl CV3 115 A2
Bracebridge Cl CV7 130 B6
Bracebridge Ct 2 B17 85 D5
Bracebridge Ho
12 Sutton Coldfield,Streetly B74 31 F2
Sutton Coldfield,New Oscott B73 45 C2
Bracebridge Rd
Birmingham B24 56 F1
Sutton Coldfield B74 46 A8
Bracebridge St
Birmingham B6 66 E6
Nuneaton CV11 73 B3
Braceby Ave B13 105 C6
Braces La B60 121 C1
Brace St WS1 42 E8
Brackenbury Rd B44 56 B8
Bracken Cl
Burntwood WS7 7 C7
Cannock WS12 2 D8
Lichfield WS14 9 E6
Wolverhampton WV8 10 E1
Bracken Croft 1 B37 70 C3
Brackendale Dr
Nuneaton CV10 72 F3
Walsall WS5 43 B3
Brackendale Sh Ctr WV12 27 D4
Brackendale Way DY9 81 D4
Bracken Dr B75 47 A5
Brackenfield Rd
Birmingham B44 44 D3
Halesowen B63 82 E3
Brackenfield View DY1 61 D8
Bracken Gr B61 121 A1
Brackenhill Rd WS7 7 A8
Brackenhurst Rd CV6 113 A7
Bracken Park Gdns DY8 60 F2
Bracken Rd
Birmingham B24 57 C2
Huntington WS12 1 C5
Bracken Way
Birmingham B38 123 D6
Sutton Coldfield B74 44 F8
Brackenwood Dr WV11 26 F5
Bracken Wood WS5 43 D5
Brackleshaw Way B77 22 A6
Brackley Ave B20 55 C1
Brackley Cl CV6 112 F7
Brackleys Way B92 89 A2
Bracknell Wlk 1 CV2 115 A7
Bradbeer Ho B16 66 A1
Bradburne Way B7 67 A5
Bradburn Rd WV11 26 B8
Bradbury Cl WS8 15 F5
Bradbury Ct WS12 2 B7
Bradbury La WS12 2 B8
Bradbury Rd B92 107 A8
Braddock Cl CV3 115 A1
Brade Dr CV2 115 B7
Braden Rd WV4 38 D4
Brades Cl B63 82 B7
Brades Rd B69 63 E8
Brades Rise B69 63 D8
Bradestone Rd CV11 73 D1
Bradewell Rd B36 58 D1
Bradfield Cl CV5 112 C5
Bradfield Ho B26 89 D6
Bradfield Rd B42 55 D7
Bradford Cl B43 54 F7
Bradford Court Bsns Ctr B12 87 A8
Bradford La
Belbroughton DY9 119 D5
Walsall WS1 28 E1
Bradford Mall WS1 28 E1
Bradford Pl WS1 28 E1
Bradford Rd
Birmingham B36 69 B7
Brownhills WS8 15 E8
Dudley DY2 61 F6
Bradford St
Birmingham B12,B5 66 F1
Cannock WS11 2 A5
Tamworth B79 20 F5
Walsall WS1 28 E1
Bradgate Cl WV12 27 C6
Bradgate Dr B74 31 E5
Bradgate Pl 12 B12 87 A6
Bradgate Rd LE10 71 F2
Brading Rd CV10 73 D6
Bradley Croft CV7 130 B6
Bradley La WV14 41 A3
Bradley La Sta WV14 41 A3
Bradleymore Rd DY5 61 D3
Bradley Rd
Birmingham B34 69 D6
Stourbridge DY8 80 F6
Wolverhampton WV2 39 E7
Bradleys Cl B64 82 E7
Bradley's La DY4,WV14 51 E8
Bradley St
Bilston WV14 40 F4
Brierley Hill DY5 61 C7
Tipton DY4 51 F2
Bradley Thursfield Ct DY11 116 C7
Bradmore Cl 1 B91 107 A1
Bradmore Gr B29 103 A8
Bradmore Rd WV3 38 F8
Bradney Gn CV4 131 E7
Bradnick Pl CV4 111 F1
Bradnock Cl B13 105 C7
Bradnock's Marsh La B92 109 E2
Bradshaw Ave
Birmingham B38 103 D1
Darlaston WS10 41 C5
Bradshaw Cl
7 Birmingham B15 86 C8
Tipton DY4 52 A3
Bradshawe Cl B28 105 D3
Bradstock Rd B30 104 C4
Bradwell Croft B75 32 E3
Braeburn Cl WS13 3 D1
Braemar Ave DY8 60 C1
Braemar Cl
Coventry CV2 114 E6
Sedgley DY3 39 C1
Willenhall WV12 27 B5
Braemar Dr B23 56 B5
Braemar Gdns WS12 1 F7
Braemar Rd
Norton Canes WS11 6 B4
Royal Leamington Spa CV32 157 B4
Solihull B92 88 E1
Sutton Coldfield B73 46 A2
Braemar Way CV10 73 A2
Braeside Croft B37 70 D2
Braeside Way WS3 14 F3
Bragg Rd B20 55 D2
Braggs Farm La B90 126 A4
Braham B79 20 D6
Braid Cl B38 103 D1
Brailes Cl B92 107 E7
Brailes Dr B76 46 F3
Brailes Gr B9 68 B1
Brailsford Cl WV11 26 E8
Brailsford Dr B66 65 A5
Brain St B77 22 A2
Braithwaite Dr DY6 60 D6
Braithwaite Rd B11 87 B7
Brake La DY8 98 E6
Brakesmead CV31 161 F5
Brake The DY8 98 F6
Bramah Way DY4 52 C6
Bramber Dr WV5 49 A6
Bramber B77 21 D1
Bramber Way DY8 80 F2
Bramble Cl
6 Coleshill B46 70 F7
Birmingham,Aston B6 66 E7
Birmingham,Shenley Fields B31 102 F6
Brownhills WS8 15 E5
Cradley Heath B64 62 F4
Nuneaton CV11 73 F2
Willenhall WV12 27 C7
Bramble Dell B9 68 A3
Bramble Dr
Birmingham B26 89 A6
Cannock WS12 2 C7
Bramble Gn DY1 50 F5
Bramble Ho B98 158 F8
Bramble La WS7 7 B8
Brambleside DY8 60 F1
Bramble St CV1 113 E2
Brambles The
Catshill B61 137 A8
Lichfield WS14 9 D6
Norton Canes WS11 6 A5
Stourbridge DY9 81 D3
Sutton Coldfield B76 58 A8
Bramblewood Dr WV3 38 E8
Bramblewoods B34 69 C5
Bramblewood WV5 49 A7
Brambling Rise DY10 117 B1
Brambling B77 36 A7
Brambling Wlk
2 Birmingham B15 86 C7
Brierley Hill DY5 81 C6
Bramcote Cl
Bulkington CV12 79 D2
Hinckley LE10 71 F3
Bramcote Dr B91 107 C7
Bramcote Hospl CV11 79 E7
Bramcote Rd B32 84 C5
Bramcote Rise B75 46 C7
Bramdean Wlk WV4 38 C6
Bramdene Ave CV10 73 D8
Brame Rd LE10 71 C2
Bramerton Cl WV11 26 A6
Bramford Dr DY1 51 B6
Bramford Prim Sch DY1 51 B6
Bramley Cl
Birmingham B43 44 D3
Walsall WS5 43 D8
Bramley Croft B90 106 C2
Bramley Ct WV11 26 C6
Bramley Dr
Birmingham B20 55 B3
Hollywood B47 125 B6
Bramley Mews Ct B27 88 C4
Bramley Rd
Birmingham B27 88 C5
Walsall WS5 43 B4
Brampton Ave B28 106 A6
Brampton Cres B90 106 B6
Brampton Dr WS12 2 E2
Brampton Way CV12 79 B3
Bramshall Dr B93 127 E3
Bramshaw Cl B14 104 F2
Bramshill Ct B15 86 B8
Bramstead Ave WV6 24 B2
Bramston Cres CV4 111 F1
Bramwell Dr WS6 4 D1
Bramwell Gdns CV6 95 F5
Brancaster Cl B77 22 A5
Branchal Rd WS9 16 C1
Branch Rd B38 123 E8
Branden Rd B48 139 A5
Brandfield Rd CV6 112 F8
Brandhall Ct B68 64 A2
Brandhall La B68 64 B1
Brandhall Prim Sch B68 64 B1
Brandhall Rd B68 64 B2
Brandon Cl
Sedgley DY3 50 E7
Sutton Coldfield WS9 30 F3
West Bromwich B70 53 A2
Brandon Ct
Birmingham B31 103 B1
Coventry CV3 135 A7
Brandon Gr B31 122 F7
Brandon La CV3,CV8 135 C5
Brandon Marsh Nature Reserve★ CV3 135 A4
Brandon Marsh Visitor Ctr★ CV3 135 B4
Brandon Par CV32 162 A8
Brandon Pk WV3 38 E7
Brandon Pl B34 69 D7
Brandon Rd
Birmingham B28 87 E2
Coventry CV3 135 A8
Halesowen B62 63 E1
Hinckley LE10 75 B7
Solihull B91 107 C7
Brandon Thomas Ct B6 67 B8
Brandon Way DY5 81 E8
Brandon Way Ind Est B70 52 F3
Brandon Way B70 53 A2
Brandon Wood Farm★ CV8 135 D5
Brandwood Cres B30 104 D3
Brandwood Gr B14 104 D5
Brandwood Ho B14 104 D7
Brandwood Park Rd B14 104 C4
Brandwood Rd B14 104 D5
Branfield Cl WV14 51 A8
Branksome Ave B21 65 F8
Branksome Rd CV6 112 E6
Branscombe Cl B14 104 D5
Bransdale Ave CV6 95 D3
Bransdale Cl WV6 25 A5
Bransdale Rd WS8 15 E6
Bransford Ave CV4 132 D5
Bransford Rise B91 108 B5
Bransford Twr B12 86 F8
Branston St B18 66 C4
Branstree Dr CV6 95 D2
Brantford Rd B25 88 C8
Branthill Croft 4 B91 107 B1
Brantley Ave WV3 24 C1
Brantley Rd B6 56 A2
Branton Hill La WS9 30 C5
Brantwood Ave WS7 7 A5
Brascote Rd LE10 74 F8
Brasshouse Inf Sch B66 65 A7
Brasshouse La B66 65 A7
Brassie Cl B38 103 D1
Brassington Ave B72,B73 46 B5
Bratch Cl DY2 62 C3
Bratch Hollow WV5 49 A8
Bratch La WV5 49 A8
Brathay Cl CV3 133 D6
Bratt St B70 53 C4
Braunston Cl B76 47 A2
Brawnes Hurst B26 69 A1
Brayford Ave
Brierley Hill DY5 81 B7
Coventry CV3 133 C6
Braymoor Rd B33 69 E1
Bray's La CV2 114 A3
Brays Rd B26 89 B6
Brays Sch B26 89 A6

Bray St WV13 ... 27 B2
Braytoft Cl CV6 ... 95 C2
Brazil St CV4 ... 111 E2
Breaches La B98 ... 159 D8
Breadmarket St WS13 ... 9 B8
Breakback Rd B61 ... 150 D8
Bream Cl
Birmingham B37 ... 70 C2
Wolverhampton WV10 ... 26 B4
Breamore Cres DY1 ... 50 F3
Bream B77 ... 35 D7
Brean Ave B92 ... 88 F5
Brearley Cl B19 ... 66 E5
Brearley St
Birmingham,Handsworth B21 ... 65 D8
Birmingham,Hockley B19 ... 66 E5
Brechin Cl LE10 ... 75 A8
Brecknell Rise DY10 ... 116 F8
Brecknock Rd B71 ... 53 A6
Brecon Ave B61 ... 137 A5
Brecon Dr DY8 ... 81 B6
Brecon Rd B20 ... 66 B8
Brecon Twr 1 B16 ... 66 A2
Bredon Ave
Coventry CV3 ... 134 F8
Kidderminster DY11 ... 116 A1
Stourbridge DY9 ... 81 C5
Bredon Croft B18 ... 66 A5
Bredon Ct
Halesowen B63 ... 83 A3
Sutton Coldfield B75 ... 32 A4
Bredon Ho B98 ... 159 B7
Bredon Rd
Bromsgrove B61 ... 150 D7
Oldbury B69 ... 63 D5
Stourbridge DY8 ... 81 B6
Bredon Terr 4 B18 ... 66 A5
Bredon View B97 ... 158 D8
Breech Cl B74 ... 44 E7
Bree Cl CV5 ... 112 A7
Breeden Dr B76 ... 59 B6
Breedon Ct B30 ... 104 A5
Breedon Gdns B98 ... 154 A3
Breedon Rd B30 ... 104 A5
Breedon Way WS4 ... 15 C1
Breener Ind Est DY5 ... 61 B1
Breen Rydding Dr WV14 ... 51 B8
Bree's La CV8 ... 130 A1
Breeze Ave WS11 ... 6 B5
Brelades Cl DY1 ... 50 E3
Breme Lodge B60 ... 151 A7
Brendon B77 ... 22 B1
Brendon Way CV10 ... 72 A3
Brenfield Dr LE10 ... 75 A8
Brennand Cl B68 ... 84 C8
Brennand Rd B68 ... 84 B8
Brentford Rd
Birmingham B14 ... 105 A5
Solihull B91 ... 106 E3
Brent Ho 3 DY1 ... 61 E8
Brentmill Cl WV10 ... 11 F4
Brentnall Dr B75 ... 32 B3
Brenton Rd WV4 ... 38 F3
Brent Rd B30 ... 104 D8
Brent B77 ... 35 E7
Brentwood Ave CV3 ... 133 C3
Brentwood Cl B91 ... 106 E3
Brentwood Gdns CV3 ... 133 C3
Brentwood Gr B44 ... 55 E8
Brenwood Cl DY6 ... 60 B7
Brereton Cl DY2 ... 62 E8
Brereton Rd WV12 ... 27 D7
Brese Ave CV34 ... 155 F1
Bretby Gr B23 ... 57 A6
Bretford Rd CV2 ... 96 C1
Bretshall Cl B90 ... 126 F5
Brett Dr B32 ... 102 C8
Brettell La
Brierley Hill DY5,DY8 ... 61 B1
Stourbridge DY8 ... 80 F8
Brettell St 5 DY1 ... 62 B8
Bretton Gdns WV10 ... 25 F6
Bretton Rd B27 ... 88 D2
Bretts Cl CV1 ... 165 D4
Bretts Hall Est CV10 ... 72 A7
Brett St B71 ... 53 B5
Brett Young Cl DY10 ... 117 B5
Brevitt Rd WV2 ... 39 D6
Brewer Rd CV12 ... 79 D2
Brewers Cl CV3 ... 115 A1
Brewers Dr WS3 ... 15 A1
Brewers Terr WS3 ... 15 A2
Brewer St WS2 ... 28 E4
Brewery St
Birmingham,Handsworth B21 ... 65 D8
Birmingham,New Town Row B6 ... 164 C5
Dudley DY2 ... 51 E1
Smethwick B67 ... 64 F6
Tipton DY4 ... 51 F4
Brewins Way DY5 ... 62 A4
Brewster Cl
Coventry CV2 ... 114 E2
Fazeley B78 ... 20 E1
Brewster St DY2 ... 62 C5
Breydon Gr WV13 ... 40 F8
Brian Rd B67 ... 64 E6
Briansway CV6 ... 95 E3
Briar Ave B74 ... 31 A1
Briarbeck WS4 ... 29 C8
Briar Cl
Birmingham B24 ... 57 A4
Cannock WS12 ... 2 A8
Hinckley LE10 ... 75 F6
Lickey End B60 ... 137 C6

Briar Cl *continued*
Royal Leamington Spa CV32 ... 157 B2
Briar Coppice B90 ... 126 D4
Briar Ct
14 Brierley Hill DY5 ... 61 D2
Dudley DY2 ... 62 C6
Briardene Ave CV12 ... 78 B2
Briarfield Rd B11 ... 88 A3
Briar Hill DY10 ... 118 E1
Briar Hill Inf Sch CV31 ... 162 B3
Briarley Ho 5 B71 ... 42 F1
Briarmead LE10 ... 75 E4
Briars Cl
Brierley Hill DY5 ... 61 C4
Coventry CV2 ... 114 C2
Nuneaton CV11 ... 73 E5
Briars The
Aldridge WS9 ... 30 A7
Birmingham B23 ... 56 D6
West Hagley DY9 ... 98 F4
Briar B77 ... 22 A3
Briarwood Cl B90 ... 126 D4
Briar Wood Cl WV2 ... 40 A7
Briarwood The WV2 ... 40 A7
Brickfield Rd B25 ... 88 B6
Brickheath Rd WV1 ... 26 A3
Brickhill Dr B37 ... 70 A2
Brick Hill La CV5 ... 111 E8
Brickhouse Jun & Inf Sch B65 ... 63 A3
Brickhouse Lane S DY4 ... 52 E6
Brickhouse La
Stoke Prior B60 ... 150 C4
West Bromwich B70 ... 52 E6
Brickhouse Rd B65 ... 63 A4
Brickiln Ct 2 DY5 ... 61 D2
Brickiln St WS8 ... 15 F7
Brick Kiln La
Birmingham B44 ... 55 E6
Dudley DY3 ... 50 B3
Middleton B78 ... 48 D6
Solihull B91 ... 126 F8
Wythall B47 ... 124 F4
Brick Kiln St
Brierley Hill,Hart's Hill DY5 ... 61 E5
Brierley Hill,Quarry Bank DY5 ... 82 A8
Hinckley LE10 ... 75 C8
Tipton DY4 ... 51 F6
Brickkiln St WV13 ... 26 F1
Brick Kiln Way CV12 ... 78 D3
Brick St DY3 ... 50 D8
Brickworks Rd WS12 ... 2 E2
Brickyard Cl CV7 ... 130 C7
Brickyard La B80 ... 159 C4
Brickyard Rd
Aldridge,Leighswood WS9 ... 30 A7
Aldridge,Leighswood WS9 ... 30 A8
Aldridge,Vigo WS9 ... 15 F1
Bridal Path The CV5 ... 112 B6
Briddsland Rd B33 ... 69 E2
Bridgeacre Gdns CV3 ... 114 F2
Bridge Ave
Cheslyn Hay WS6 ... 4 E4
Tipton DY4 ... 52 C7
Bridgeburn Rd B31 ... 102 E8
Bridge Cl
Birmingham B11 ... 87 B3
Brownhills WS8 ... 15 E6
Bridgecote CV3 ... 134 E6
Bridge Croft B12 ... 86 E6
Bridge Cross Rd WS7 ... 7 A7
Bridge Ct DY8 ... 60 E2
Bridge End CV34 ... 160 F5
Bridgefield Wlk B65 ... 62 F5
Bridgefoot Wlk WV8 ... 10 F1
Bridgeford Rd B34 ... 69 B6
Bridge Ho
Royal Leamington Spa CV31 ... 162 A8
Smethwick B66 ... 65 C6
Bridge Ind Est B91 ... 107 C7
Bridgelands Way B20 ... 55 D1
Bridgeman Croft B36 ... 69 C8
Bridgeman Rd CV6 ... 113 B4
Bridgeman St WS2 ... 28 D1
Bridgemary Cl WV10 ... 11 E4
Bridge Meadow Dr B93 ... 127 F6
Bridgemeadow Ho 5 B36 ... 68 E8
Bridgend Croft DY5 ... 61 B6
Bridgenorth Ho B33 ... 69 B2
Bridge Piece B31 ... 103 B2
Bridge Rd
Birmingham B8 ... 67 E3
Hinckley LE10 ... 75 D7
Tipton DY4 ... 52 C7
Walsall WS4 ... 15 B1
Bridge St Ind Est WS10 ... 41 F1
Bridge St N B66 ... 65 B7
Bridge St S B66 ... 65 B6
Bridge St W B19 ... 66 D5
Bridge Sch The B23 ... 56 E4
Bridges Cres WS11 ... 5 F5
Bridgeside Trad Est B77 ... 21 C3
Bridges Rd WS11 ... 5 F5
Bridge St
1 Kidderminster DY10 ... 116 E5
Bilston WV14 ... 40 E5
Birmingham B1 ... 164 A2
Brownhills WS8 ... 15 E6
Cannock WS11 ... 4 E5
Coventry CV6 ... 114 A7
Halesowen B63 ... 82 C7
Kenilworth CV8 ... 147 F5
Nuneaton,Chilvers Coton CV11 ... 73 C2

Bridge St *continued*
Nuneaton CV11 ... 73 C4
Oldbury B69 ... 64 A8
Redditch B97 ... 153 D4
Stourbridge DY8 ... 60 E1
Tamworth B77 ... 21 E5
Tipton WV14 ... 51 C8
Walsall WS1 ... 28 F2
Warwick CV34 ... 161 C8
Wednesbury WS10 ... 41 F1
West Bromwich B70 ... 53 B4
Willenhall WV13 ... 26 F1
Wolverhampton WV10 ... 25 E5
Bridge The 3 WS1 ... 28 E1
Bridge Trad Ctr The B64 ... 82 D8
Bridge Trad Est The B66 ... 65 B6
Bridge View
3 Coleshill B46 ... 70 F7
Baginton CV8 ... 133 D3
Bridgewater Ave B69 ... 64 A4
Bridgewater Cres DY2 ... 51 E1
Bridgewater Dr WV14 ... 40 C2
Bridgewater St B77 ... 21 D5
Bridge Way WS8 ... 15 E6
Bridgnorth Gr WV12 ... 27 B6
Bridgnorth Rd
Himley DY3 ... 49 B3
Stourbridge DY7,DY8 ... 80 C6
Trescott WV6 ... 37 C7
Wolverhampton WV6 ... 24 B2
Bridgtown Bsns Ctr WS11 ... 4 E6
Bridgtown Prim Sch WS11 ... 4 E6
Bridgwater Cl WS9 ... 15 F3
Bridle Brook La CV5,CV7 ... 94 A3
Bridle Gr B71 ... 53 F7
Bridle La B74,WS9 ... 44 E7
Bridle Mead B38 ... 123 D8
Bridle Path The B90 ... 106 B6
Bridle Rd DY8 ... 80 D6
Bridlewood B74 ... 44 F8
Bridley Moor Rd B97 ... 153 C5
Bridport Cl CV2 ... 115 A4
Bridport Ho B31 ... 102 E7
Brierley Hill Prim Sch DY5 ... 61 D2
Brierley Hill Rd DY8 ... 60 F2
Brierley La WV14 ... 40 E2
Brierley La Cvn Site WV14 ... 40 E2
Brierley Rd
Bromsgrove B60 ... 137 C1
Coventry CV2 ... 114 C8
Brierley Trad Est The DY5 ... 61 C3
Brier Mill Rd B63 ... 83 C3
Brier Sch The DY6 ... 60 F5
Brier Specl Sch The DY5 ... 61 E2
Briery Cl B64 ... 82 F7
Briery Rd B63 ... 82 E3
Brigadoon Gdns DY9 ... 81 C2
Brigfield Cres B13 ... 105 B5
Brigfield Rd B13 ... 105 B5
Bright Cres B77 ... 21 C2
Brightmere Rd CV6 ... 113 B4
Brighton Cl WS2 ... 28 D3
Brighton Mews 8 WV3 ... 25 A2
Brighton Rd B12 ... 87 A5
Brighton St CV2 ... 113 F3
Bright Rd B68 ... 64 B5
Bright St
Coventry CV6 ... 113 E6
Darlaston WS10 ... 41 D5
Brightstone Cl WV10 ... 11 F4
Brightstone Rd B45 ... 102 B2
Bright St
Stourbridge DY8 ... 80 D6
Wolverhampton WV1 ... 163 A4
Brightwalton Rd CV3 ... 133 D7
Brightwell Cres B93 ... 127 E3
Brill Cl CV4 ... 132 C5
Brimfield Pl 1 WV6 ... 24 F4
Brimstone La B61 ... 136 D7
Brindle Ave CV3 ... 114 C2
Brindle Cl B26 ... 88 E5
Brindle Ct B23 ... 56 B3
Brindlefields Way DY4 ... 52 B2
Brindle Rd WS5 ... 43 C4
Brindley Ave WV11 ... 13 A1
Brindley Cl
1 Stourbridge DY8 ... 60 E1
Willenhall WS2 ... 27 F5
Brindley Cres WS12 ... 2 C8
Brindley Ct 5 DY4 ... 51 E5
Brindley Dr B1 ... 164 A2
Brindley Heath Rd WS12 ... 2 D8
Brindley Paddocks CV1 ... 165 B4
Brindley Pl B1 ... 66 B2
Brindley Point Apartments 7 B16 ... 66 B2
Brindley Rd
Bedworth CV7 ... 96 B8
Hinckley LE10 ... 74 E8
West Bromwich B71 ... 53 A8
Brindleys Bsns Pk WS11 ... 2 B3
Brindley Way 10 B66 ... 65 C5
Brineton Gr B29 ... 85 A1
Brineton Ind Est 1 WS2 ... 28 C1
Brineton St WS2 ... 28 C1
Bringewood Gr B32 ... 102 B8
Brinklow Cl B98 ... 159 D8
Brinklow Croft B34 ... 69 D7
Brinklow Rd
Birmingham B29 ... 84 F2
Coventry CV3 ... 115 A2
Brinklow Twr 4 B12 ... 86 F7
Brinley Way DY6 ... 60 C6
Brinsford La WV10 ... 11 D7
Brinsford Rd WV10 ... 11 C3
Brinsley Cl B91 ... 107 B2
Brinsley Rd B26 ... 89 B8

Brinton Cl DY11 ... 116 C3
Brinton Cres DY11 ... 116 C3
Brisbane Cl CV3 ... 133 E6
Brisbane Ct 2 CV12 ... 78 A2
Brisbane Rd B67 ... 64 E5
Brisbane Way WS12 ... 2 E3
Briscoe Rd CV6 ... 95 D4
Briseley Cl DY5 ... 81 D8
Bristam Cl B69 ... 63 E6
Bristnall Hall Cres B68 ... 64 C3
Bristnall Hall La B68 ... 64 D3
Bristnall Hall Rd B68 ... 64 C3
Bristnall Hall Tech Coll B68 ... 64 D3
Bristol Cl WS11 ... 2 B1
Bristol Ct 15 B29 ... 103 C7
Bristol Rd
Birmingham,Balsall Heath B5 ... 86 C5
Birmingham,Gravelly Hill B23 ... 56 E3
Coventry CV5 ... 112 F2
Dudley DY2 ... 62 D2
Bristol Rd S
Birmingham B31 ... 102 F2
Birmingham,Bournville B29,B30, B31 ... 103 C7
Birmingham,Longbridge B31, B45 ... 122 C8
Bristol St
Birmingham B15 ... 86 D8
Wolverhampton WV3 ... 39 B8
Briston Cl DY5 ... 81 C8
Britannia Cl B98 ... 153 F3
Britannia Gdns B65 ... 63 C3
Britannia Gn DY3 ... 50 E5
Britannia Rd
Bilston WV14 ... 40 F3
Hinckley LE10 ... 76 A5
Rowley Regis B65 ... 63 C2
Britannia St
Coventry CV2 ... 113 F3
Oldbury B69 ... 52 C2
Britannia Way WS13 ... 9 F8
Britannic Gdns B13 ... 86 D2
Britannic Ho B13 ... 86 D2
Britford Cl B14 ... 104 F3
Briton Rd CV2 ... 114 A4
Brittan Cl B34 ... 69 E6
Brittania Pk WS10 ... 41 D3
Brittania Rd WS1 ... 42 D5
Brittania Sh Ctr 3 LE10 ... 75 D8
Britten Cl CV11 ... 79 A7
Britten St B97 ... 153 D4
Britton Dr B72 ... 57 C8
Britwell Rd B73 ... 46 A2
Brixfield Way B90 ... 126 B5
Brixham Cl CV11 ... 73 F5
Brixham Dr CV2 ... 114 C7
Brixham Rd B16 ... 65 D4
Brixworth Cl CV3 ... 134 E8
Broad Acres B31 ... 102 E6
Broadbent Cl 1 WS13 ... 8 F6
Broadcott Ind Est B64 ... 83 A8
Broad Croft 1 DY4 ... 52 C6
Broadfern Rd B93 ... 128 B8
Broadfield Cl
Kingswinford DY6 ... 60 D5
West Bromwich B71 ... 42 F1
Broadfield House Glass Mus* DY6 ... 60 D5
Broadfields Rd B23 ... 57 B7
Broadfields DY9 ... 99 A6
Broadfield Wlk 1 B16 ... 66 B1
Broadgate CV1 ... 165 B3
Broad Ground Rd B98 ... 154 B2
Broadhaven Cl CV31 ... 162 C7
Broad Heath Cl B97 ... 153 B5
Broad Heath Com Prim Sch CV6 ... 113 E6
Broadheath Dr WS4 ... 29 D8
Broadhidley Dr B32 ... 84 B1
Broadhurst Gn WS12 ... 2 A8
Broad La
Birmingham B14 ... 104 E4
Burntwood WS7 ... 8 B5
Coventry CV5 ... 111 D4
Lichfield WS14 ... 9 D6
Broadlands Cl CV5 ... 112 C2
Broadlands Dr DY5 ... 61 E5
Broadlands Rise WS14 ... 9 D7
Broadlands WV10 ... 11 D5
Broad Lane Gdns WS3 ... 14 A2
Broad Lanes WV14 ... 40 C3
Broad La N WV12 ... 27 B7
Broad La S WV11 ... 27 A5
Broad La
Tanworth-In-A B98 ... 141 E3
Walsall,Essington WS3 ... 13 E4
Walsall WS4 ... 15 C2
Wolverhampton WV3 ... 38 E8
Broadlee B77 ... 22 C1
Broad Mdw WS9 ... 30 B8
Broadmead Ct CV5 ... 112 C2
Broadmeadow Cl B30 ... 104 B3
Broadmeadow Gn WV14 ... 40 C7
Broadmeadow Ho B32 ... 102 D8
Broadmeadow Inf Sch B30 ... 104 B2
Broadmeadow Jun Sch B30 ... 104 B2
Broadmeadow DY6 ... 60 E8
Broad Meadow La
Birmingham B30 ... 104 B3
Great Wyrley WS6 ... 5 A2
Broadmeadows Cl WV12 ... 27 E8
Broadmeadows Rd WV12 ... 27 E8
Broadmede Ho B67 ... 64 E2

Broadmere Rise CV5 ... 112 A2
Broadmoor Ave B68 ... 64 D2
Broadmoor Cl WV14 ... 40 C4
Broadmoor Rd WV14 ... 40 C3
Broadoaks Cl WS11 ... 5 F6
Broad Oaks Rd B91 ... 107 A5
Broad Oaks B76 ... 47 A1
Broadoaks The B91 ... 107 A4
Broad Park Rd CV2 ... 114 D8
Broad Rd B27 ... 88 B3
Broadsmeath B77 ... 21 C1
Broad St
Bilston WV14 ... 40 D6
Birmingham B15,B1 ... 66 C2
Brierley Hill DY5 ... 61 C6
Bromsgrove B61 ... 136 F4
Cannock WS11 ... 4 E6
Coventry CV6 ... 113 E7
Kidderminster DY10 ... 116 E7
Kingswinford DY6 ... 60 D5
Oldbury B69 ... 64 A5
Broadstone Ave
Halesowen B63 ... 82 B4
Walsall WS3 ... 28 D7
Broadstone Cl WV4 ... 39 D5
Broadstone Rd B26 ... 69 A1
Broad Street Jetty CV6 ... 113 E7
Broad St
Tipton WV14 ... 51 C8
Warwick CV34 ... 160 F7
Wolverhampton WV1 ... 163 C3
Broadsword Way LE10 ... 75 D4
Broadwalk 5 B1 ... 66 C1
Broadwalk Ret Pk WS1 ... 42 D6
Broadwas Cl B98 ... 154 C5
Broadwater CV5 ... 133 A8
Broadwaters Ave WS10 ... 41 C4
Broadwaters Dr
Kidderminster DY10 ... 117 A8
West Hagley DY9 ... 99 B4
Broadwaters Rd WS10 ... 41 C4
Broadway Ave
Birmingham B9 ... 68 A3
Halesowen B63 ... 83 A2
Broadway
Cannock WS12 ... 1 F6
Coventry CV5 ... 113 A1
Broadway Croft
Birmingham B26 ... 89 A6
Oldbury B68 ... 64 C1
Broadway CV32 ... 157 E5
Broadway Gdns WV10 ... 11 E2
Broadway Mans CV5 ... 113 A1
Broadway N WS1 ... 29 B2
Broadway B68 ... 64 C1
Broadway Plaza B16 ... 66 A1
Broadway Sch B20 ... 55 E2
Broadway Sch The (Aston Campus) B6 ... 66 E8
Broadway B90 ... 106 B4
Broadway The
Birmingham B20 ... 55 E2
Dudley DY1 ... 51 B3
Stourbridge DY8 ... 80 D3
West Bromwich B71 ... 53 B7
Wombourne WV5 ... 49 A5
Broad Way WS4 ... 15 C2
Broadway
Walsall WS5 ... 43 A6
Wolverhampton,Bushbury WV10 ... 11 E2
Wolverhampton WV3 ... 24 C2
Broadway W WS1 ... 42 D6
Broadwell Ct CV4 ... 131 F6
Broadwell Ind Pk B69 ... 53 A1
Broadwell Rd
Oldbury B69 ... 64 A8
Solihull B92 ... 89 A2
Broadwells Cres CV4 ... 132 A5
Broadyates Gr B25 ... 88 C6
Broadyates Rd B25 ... 88 C6
Brobury Croft B91 ... 106 D4
Brockenhurst Ct B73 ... 46 B1
Brockenhurst Way CV6 ... 96 B6
Brockeridge Cl WV12 ... 13 C1
Brockfield Ho WV10 ... 25 F4
Brockhall Gr B37 ... 69 F5
Brockhill Dr B97 ... 153 A5
Brockhill La
Alvechurch B48 ... 124 B2
Beoley B98 ... 140 F2
Tardebigge B97 ... 152 E8
Brockhurst Ave LE10 ... 75 D4
Brockhurst Cres WS5 ... 42 E4
Brockhurst Dr
Birmingham B28 ... 106 A5
Coventry CV4 ... 111 D2
Wolverhampton WV6 ... 25 A4
Brockhurst Ho 4 WS2 ... 28 D3
Brockhurst La
Solihull B90 ... 126 B5
Weeford B75 ... 33 B7
Brockhurst Pl WS5 ... 42 F5
Brockhurst Rd
Birmingham B36 ... 68 D6
Sutton Coldfield B75 ... 32 D1
Brockhurst St WS1 ... 42 E6
Brockley Cl DY5 ... 61 D3
Brockley Gr B13 ... 86 C1
Brockley Pl B7 ... 67 C7
Brockmoor Cl DY9 ... 81 C2
Brockmoor Prim Sch DY5 ... 61 C3
Brock Rd DY4 ... 52 C4
Brockton Rd B29 ... 85 A1
Brockwell Gr B44 ... 44 E4

Brockwell Rd B44 44 E4
Brockworth Rd B14 104 C2
Brocton Cl WV14 40 A3
Brodick Cl LE10 75 A8
Brodick Rd LE10 74 F8
Brodick Way CV10 72 F3
Brogden Cl 4 B71 53 F8
Brome Hall La B94 144 D2
Bromfield Cl B6 66 E7
Bromfield Cres WS10 42 C4
Bromfield Ct WV6 24 B3
Bromfield Rd B97 153 D2
Bromford Central B8 68 B8
Bromford Cl
Birmingham,Erdington B23 56 E5
Birmingham,Handsworth B20 55 A2
Bromford Cres B24 57 A2
Bromford Ct B8 68 B6
Bromford Dale 2 WV6 24 F3
Bromford Dell B31 103 C4
Bromford Dr B36 68 D8
Bromford Gdns B15 85 C8
Bromford Hill B20 55 C3
Bromford Ho B73 45 F2
Bromford La
Birmingham B8,B36 68 C6
West Bromwich B70 53 B2
Bromford Mere 4 B92 88 E1
Bromford Park Ho 3 B13 87 B2
Bromford Rd
Birmingham B36 68 D7
Dudley DY2 62 A6
West Bromwich B69,B70 53 A1
Bromford Rise WV3 163 A1
Bromford Road Ind Est B70 53 A1
Bromford Wlk B43 43 F1
Bromhurst Way CV34 160 B4
Bromleigh Dr CV2 114 C2
Bromleigh Villas CV8 133 F2
Bromley DY5 61 B5
Bromley Cl
Cannock WS12 2 C7
Kenilworth CV8 147 E6
Bromley Gdns WV8 10 A4
Bromley Hills Prim Sch DY6 60 F5
Bromley Ho WV4 39 A5
Bromley La DY6 60 E4
Bromley Lodge WV4 39 A5
Bromley-Pensnett Prim Sch The DY5 61 B5
Bromley Pl WV4 39 A5
Bromley St
Birmingham B9 67 A1
Stourbridge DY9 81 F6
Wolverhampton WV2 39 C7
Brompton Dr DY5 81 B7
Brompton Lawns WV6 24 A3
Brompton Pool Rd B28 105 E3
Brompton Rd B44 44 E4
Bromsgrove Highway
Bromsgrove B60 137 D1
Redditch B97 153 B2
Tardebigge B60,B97 152 C6
Bromsgrove Lower Sch B60 136 F1
Bromsgrove Mus* B61 137 A3
Bromsgrove Private Hospl B60 138 B1
Bromsgrove Rd
Clent DY9 99 D4
Dodford B61 136 D6
Halesowen B63 83 C4
Mustow Green DY10 117 F2
Redditch B97 153 B3
Romsley B62 101 A5
Studley B80 159 D2
Bromsgrove Sch B61 136 F1
Bromsgrove Sta B60 151 B7
Bromsgrove St
Birmingham B5 164 C1
Halesowen B63 83 C4
Kidderminster DY10 116 E6
Bromwall Rd B13 105 B6
Bromwich Cl CV3 134 F8
Bromwich Dr B75 46 C7
Bromwich La DY9 99 B8
Bromwich Wlk B9 68 A3
Bromwynd Cl WV2 39 B6
Bromyard Ave B76 58 A8
Bromyard Rd B11 87 E3
Bronte Cl B90 106 D1
Bronte Ct
Solihull B90 106 D1
Tamworth B79 21 A6
Bronte Dr
Cannock WS11 2 C2
Kidderminster DY10 117 C6
Bronte Farm Rd B90 106 D1
Bronte Rd WV2 39 F6
Bronwen Ingham Ct DY10 116 E7
Bronwen Rd WV14 51 C7
Bronze Cl CV11 78 E8
Brook Ave B77 36 A7
Brookbank Ave B34 69 D6
Brookbank Gdns DY3 50 B2
Brookbank Rd DY3 50 B2
Brook Cl
Birmingham B33 68 E4
Brownhills WS9 16 A3
Coventry CV1 113 E4
Brook Cl *continued*
Lichfield WS13 3 A1
Solihull B90 105 F1
Brook Cotts B25 88 A7
Brook Cres
Kingswinford DY6 60 C7
Stourbridge DY9 81 F3
West Hagley DY9 99 B5
Brook Croft
Birmingham,Lyndon Green B26 89 B7
Birmingham,Marston Green B37 90 B7
Brook Ct B60 137 B3
Brookdale Cl B45 102 A1
Brookdale Dr WV4 38 E6
Brookdale
Dudley DY3 50 C3
Hinckley LE10 75 B7
Kidderminster DY10 116 F8
Brookdale Rd CV10 73 E7
Brook Dr B32 84 D1
Brooke Cl CV34 160 F5
Brooke Mews 8 CV34 160 F7
Brook End WS7 7 A4
Brookend Dr B45 121 F7
Brook End B78 35 B8
Brooke Rd
Cannock WS12 1 F6
Kenilworth CV8 148 B4
Brookes Cl B69 52 B1
Brookes Ho 3 WS1 28 F1
Brooke St DY2 62 C8
Brook Farm Ind Est B94 126 B2
Brook Farm Wlk B37 70 D2
Brookfield Cl
Aldridge WS9 16 A1
Redditch B97 158 D4
Brookfield Dr WS11 4 E7
Brookfield Ho DY9 119 C7
Brookfield Rd
Aldridge WS9 16 A1
Birmingham B18 66 A5
Birmingham,Brandwood End B30 104 D3
Codsall WV8 10 B3
Cubbington CV32 157 E5
Hinckley LE10 75 C6
Brook Fields Cl B60 121 C1
Brookfields Prim Sch B18 66 B4
Brookfields Rd B68 64 C4
Brookfield Terr B18 66 A5
Brookfield Way
Solihull B92 106 D7
Tipton DY4 52 B6
Brookford Ave CV6 95 A3
Brook Gr WV8 10 B2
Brook Green La B92 109 A1
Brookhampton Cl B97 158 E4
Brookhill Cl WV12 13 D1
Brookhill Rd B8 68 A4
Brookhill Way WV12 13 D1
Brook Holloway DY9 81 F4
Brookhouse Cl WV10 12 B6
Brookhouse La
Featherstone WV10 12 B7
Wolverhampton WV10 11 F6
Brookhouse Rd
Blackwell B45 137 F7
Walsall WS5 43 B7
Brookhurst Ct CV32 156 D1
Brookhurst Prim Sch CV32 156 C1
Brookhus Farm Rd B76 58 A8
Brooking Cl B43 44 D4
Brook La
Birmingham B32 84 F5
Birmingham,Billesley B13 105 B7
Brownhills WS9 15 F3
Cradley Heath B64 62 E2
Great Wyrley WS6 5 A3
Brookland Gr WS9 15 F3
Brookland Rd
Brownhills WS9 15 F3
West Hagley DY9 99 A4
Brooklands Ave WS6 4 F4
Brooklands Cl B28 87 F1
Brooklands Dr B14 104 E5
Brooklands Ho 8 CV34 161 D8
Brooklands La B98 154 B5
Brooklands Par WV1 26 B2
Brooklands Pk B98 154 F5
Brooklands Rd
Birmingham B28 87 F1
Cannock WS11 2 A4
Brooklands
Stourbridge DY8 60 F1
Walsall WS5 43 B3
Brooklands Way B37 90 A8
Brook La
Nuneaton CV10 73 C6
Solihull B92 106 D8
Brooklea CV12 77 F2
Brooklea Gr B38 104 A1
Brooklime Gdns WV10 12 B7
Brooklyn Ave B6 66 F7
Brooklyn Gr
Dudley WV14 51 D8
Kingswinford DY6 60 B8
Brooklyn Rd
Burntwood WS7 7 A4
Cannock WS12 2 D1
Coventry CV1 113 D6
Brookmans Ave B32 84 D4
Brook Mdws WV8 10 B4
Brookmeadow Ct B28 105 D6
Brook Meadow Rd
Birmingham B34 69 B6
Brook Meadow Rd *continued*
Walsall WS4 29 D8
Brook Park Trad Est 4 DY9 81 F5
Brookpiece Ho B14 104 E2
Brook Piece Wlk B35 58 B3
Brook Prim Sch DY8 60 F1
Brook Rd
Birmingham,Chad Valley B15 85 E7
Birmingham,Rubery B45 121 E7
Bromsgrove B61 136 E1
Cheslyn Hay WS6 4 E4
Fairfield B61 120 C2
Oldbury B68 64 A2
Stourbridge DY8 81 B3
Willenhall WV13 26 E1
Brooksbank Dr B64 62 F4
Brooksby Gr B93 128 A2
Brooks Croft B35 58 A2
Brookshaw Way CV2 114 F8
Brookside Ave
Birmingham B13 105 B7
Coventry CV5 112 C3
Kenilworth CV8 147 E4
Brookside
Birmingham,Great Barr B43 54 D7
Birmingham,Northfield B31 102 F5
Cheswick Green B90 126 D3
Brookside Cl
Alvechurch B48 139 B6
Birmingham B23 56 C7
Halesowen B63 82 D3
Brookside Dr B61 136 F8
Brookside
Dudley DY3 50 D2
Hinckley LE10 75 E7
Brookside Ind Est WS10 42 B3
Brookside Rd B78 20 D1
Brookside Way
Blakedown DY10 98 B2
Kingswinford DY6 60 C7
Tamworth B77 36 A6
Brookside WS10 42 B3
Brooks Rd B72 57 C8
Brook St
Bedworth CV12 78 B5
Bilston WV14 40 E5
Birmingham B3 164 A3
Brierley Hill DY5 82 A8
Dudley DY3 51 A7
Dudley,Gornalwood DY3 50 C3
Kidderminster DY11 116 C6
Kingswinford DY6 49 B1
Brookstray Flats CV5 112 B3
Brook St B98 154 A4
Brook Street Bsns Ctr DY4 51 E6
Brook St
Smethwick B66 65 B6
Stourbridge,Amblecote DY8 60 F1
Stourbridge DY8 80 E5
Stourbridge,Lye DY9 81 F5
Tipton DY4 51 E6
Walsall WS2 28 D1
Warwick CV34 160 E6
West Bromwich B70 53 B3
Brook Terr WV14 40 E5
Brookthorpe Dr WV12 27 C4
Brookvale Ave CV3 114 E1
Brook Vale WS11 4 F8
Brookvale Cl B61 137 B4
Brookvale Gr B92 88 D1
Brookvale Mews B29 86 B2
Brookvale Park Rd B23 56 B4
Brookvale Prim Sch B23 56 B3
Brookvale Rd
Birmingham B23,B6 56 A3
Solihull B92 88 D1
Brookvale Trad Est B6 56 A3
Brook View Cl B19 66 C6
Brookview B67 64 F3
Brookweed B77 22 A3
Brookwillow Rd B63 82 E1
Brook Wlk B32 84 D2
Brookwood Ave B28 105 D5
Brookwood Dr B45 138 C8
Broom Cl B60 137 B2
Broom Covert Rd WS14 18 E8
Broom Cres DY10 117 A6
Broomcroft Rd B37 69 F5
Broomdene Ave B34 69 A7
Broom Dr B14 104 E4
Broome Ave B43 54 C7
Broome Cl 5 B63 83 A3
Broome Croft CV6 95 B3
Broome Ct B36 69 C8
Broome Gdns B75 46 C5
Broomehill Cl DY5 81 C7
Broome La DY9 99 B2
Broome Rd WV10 25 E7
Broomfield Ave B78 35 A8
Broomfield Cl DY11 116 C7
Broomfield Gn DY11 116 C7
Broomfield Pl CV5 113 A2
Broomfield Rd
Birmingham B23 56 D2
Coventry CV5 113 A1
Kidderminster DY11 116 C7
Wednesbury WS10 42 C3
Broomfield Rise CV10 72 F2
Broomfields Ave B91 107 D5
Broomfields Cl B91 107 D5
Broomfields Farm Rd B91 107 D5
Broomfield B67 64 F5
Broomhall Ave WV11 26 D6
Broom Hall Cres B27 106 B8
Broom Hall Gr B27 106 C8
Broomhill Bank WS11 1 E3
Broomhill Cl
Birmingham B43 54 D8
Cannock WS11 1 E4
Broomhill La B43 54 D8
Broomhill Rd B23 56 B7
Broom Ho 3 B71 42 F1
Broomhurst B15 85 E8
Broomie Cl B75 46 D4
Broom La B90 126 A6
Broomlea Cl B74 44 E8
Broom Rd
Dudley DY1 51 A5
Walsall WS5 43 B3
Broom St B12 87 A8
Broomybank CV8 148 B6
Broomy Cl B34 69 A5
Brosdale Dr LE10 71 A1
Broseley Ave B31 123 B8
Broseley Brook Cl 1 B9 67 C1
Brosil Ave B20 54 E3
Brotherton Ave B97 152 F2
Brougham St B19 66 B7
Brough Cl
Birmingham B7 67 B6
Wolverhampton WV4,WV14 39 F3
Broughton Cres B31 122 D8
Broughton Ct
2 Birmingham,Edgbaston B15 86 B7
Birmingham,Pheasey B43 44 D4
Perton WV6 24 A3
Broughton Rd
Birmingham B20 66 A8
Stourbridge DY9 81 D3
Wolverhampton WV3 24 C1
Browett Rd CV6 113 A5
Brown Ave B77 35 C8
Brownfield Rd B34 69 C7
Brownhills Com Tech Coll WS8 6 F1
Brownhills Rd
Brownhills WS8 16 A4
Norton Canes WS11 6 B4
Brownhills West Prim Sch WS8 6 C2
Brownhills West Sta* WS7 6 C3
Browning Ave CV34 160 C5
Browning Cl
Kidderminster DY10 117 B6
Nuneaton CV10 72 A5
Tamworth B79 20 F8
Willenhall WV12 27 E7
Browning Cres WV10 11 C2
Browning Dr LE10 71 C1
Browning Gr WV6 23 E4
Browning Rd
Burntwood WS7 7 C7
Coventry CV2 114 C3
Dudley DY3 50 A4
Browning St B16 66 B2
Browning Twr B31 103 C3
Brownley Rd B90 126 E7
Brown Lion St DY4 51 E7
Brownlow St 7 CV32 157 A2
Brownmead Jun & Inf Sch B34 69 B7
Brown Rd WS10 41 C7
Brown's Coppice Ave B91 106 E5
Brown's Ct 11 B13 87 B2
Browns Dr B73 56 F8
Brownsea Cl B45 101 F1
Brownsea Dr B1 164 B1
Brownsfield Rd WS13 3 D1
Browns Gn B20 54 F3
Brownshill Bsns Pk WS8 15 F5
Brownshill Ct CV6 112 F8
Brownshill Green Rd CV6 94 E1
Brownshore La WV11 13 A3
Brown's La
Brownshill Green CV5 94 C1
Dordon B78 36 F5
Browns La B93 127 E6
Brown's La B79 21 C8
Brownsover Cl B36 58 B1
Brown St WV2 39 D7
Brownswall Rd DY3 50 C7
Browsholme B79 20 D6
Broxell Cl CV34 155 C1
Broxwood Pk WV6 24 B3
Bruce Rd
Bedworth CV7 95 F7
Coventry CV6 113 B8
Kidderminster DY10 117 B7
Brueton Ave
Bromsgrove B60 151 A8
Solihull B91 107 D3
Brueton Dr
Birmingham B24 57 A3
Redditch B98 154 A3
Brueton Rd WV14 41 A7
Bruford Rd WV3 39 A8
Brunel Cl
Birmingham B12 87 A5
Burntwood WS7 7 B8
Coventry CV2 113 F3
Tamworth B79 21 B6
Whitnash CV31 162 B2
Brunel Ct
Darlaston WS10 41 F6
Tipton WV14 51 E8
Wombourne WV5 49 A7
Brunel Dr DY4 40 E1
Brunel Gr WV6 23 E5
Brunel Rd
Hinckley LE10 75 C8
Oldbury B69 63 D6
Brunel St B1 164 B2
Brunel Way WV2 40 A7
Brunel Wlk WS10 41 F6
Brunslow Cl
Willenhall WV13 27 C1
Wolverhampton WV10 11 C1
Brunswick Arc B1 66 B2
Brunswick Ct
Wednesbury WS10 42 C3
Whitnash CV31 162 A5
Brunswick Gate DY8 81 A1
Brunswick Gdns
Birmingham B21 54 F1
Wednesbury WS10 42 B4
Brunswick Ho
Birmingham,Buckland End B34 69 A7
Birmingham,Marston Green B37 89 F8
Brunswick Park Rd WS10 42 B3
Brunswick Rd
Birmingham,Handsworth B21 54 F1
Birmingham,Sparkbrook B12 87 A5
Cannock WS11 1 E2
Coventry CV1 113 B2
Brunswick St
Birmingham B1 66 B2
Royal Leamington Spa CV31 162 A5
Walsall WS2 42 C7
Brunswick Terr WS10 41 F3
Bruntingthorpe Way CV3 134 E8
Brunton Cl CV3 115 B1
Brunton Rd B10 87 F7
Brushfield Rd B42 55 D8
Brutus Dr B46 59 E1
Bryan Ave WV4 38 D4
Bryan Rd WS2 42 C6
Bryanston Cl CV2 115 A4
Bryanston Ct B91 106 F7
Bryanston Rd B91 106 F6
Bryans Way WS12 2 F4
Bryant Rd CV7 96 A7
Bryant St B18 65 E5
Bryce Rd DY5 61 B5
Bryher Wlk B45 101 E1
Brylan Croft B44 55 F6
Brymill Ind Est DY4 51 E7
Brympton Rd CV3 114 C2
Bryn Arden Rd B26 88 E5
Bryndale Ave B14 104 C4
Bryn Jones Cl CV3 134 F7
Brynmawr Rd WV4,WV14 40 A3
Bryn Rd CV6 113 F7
Brynside Cl B14 104 D2
Bryony Cl CV12 77 E1
Bryony Croft B23 56 B7
Bryony Gdns WS10 41 D7
Bryony Rd B29 103 B7
Bryony B74 31 F5
Bsns Ctr The B11 87 F6
Bubbenhall Rd CV8 133 F1
Buchanan Ave WS4 29 A3
Buchanan Cl WS4 29 A3
Buchanan Rd WS4 29 A3
Buckbury Cl DY9 81 D2
Buckbury Croft B90 127 B6
Buckden Cl 2 CV34 155 F1
Buckden B77 22 C1
Buckfast Cl
Bromsgrove B61 136 D1
Coventry CV3 133 E5
Buckhold Dr CV5 112 B5
Buckingham Cl
Hinckley LE10 71 F4
Nuneaton CV10 73 B1
Wednesbury WS10 42 D4
Buckingham Ct
Birmingham B29 85 D1
Birmingham,Griffin's Hill B29 103 D8
Buckingham Dr WV12 27 B7
Buckingham Gdns WS14 9 B6
Buckingham Gr DY6 60 C7
Buckingham Mews B73 46 A3
Buckingham Pl 3 WS12 2 C1
Buckingham Rd
Birmingham B36 69 F7
Rowley Regis B65 63 D4
Tamworth B79 20 E7
Wolverhampton WV4 39 A5
Buckingham Rise
Coventry CV5 112 B4
Dudley DY1 50 E2
Buckingham St B19 164 B4
Buckland Cl WS12 2 D1
Buckland End B34 69 A6
Buckland Ho 3 B15 86 C7
Buckland Rd CV6 95 B2
Bucklands End La B34 68 F6
Buckle Cl WS1 42 E8
Buckler's Yd 5 CV12 78 A2
Buckley Ct B14 104 F8
Buckley Ho CV5 112 F1
Buckley Rd
Royal Leamington Spa CV32 157 C2
Wolverhampton WV4 38 D5
Buckleys Gn B48 139 A6
Buckleys The B48 139 A6
Bucklow Wlk B33 68 E4
Buckminster Dr B93 127 E4

Bucknall Cres B32 . . . 102 A8
Bucknall Ct 15 B13 . . . 87 B2
Bucknall Ho B14 . . . 104 E6
Bucknall Rd WV11 . . . 13 B1
Bucknell Cl B91 . . . 107 C5
Buckridge Cl B38 . . . 123 D7
Buckridge La B90 . . . 126 A5
Bucks Hill CV10 . . . 72 C6
Buckthorn Cl WS12 . . . 1 F8
Buckton Cl B75 . . . 32 E2
Budbrooke Cl CV2 . . . 96 D2
Budbrooke Ind Est CV34 . 160 B7
Budbrooke Rd CV34 . . . 160 B7
Budbrook Gr B34 . . . 69 E6
Budden Rd WV14 . . . 51 D7
Bude Rd WS5 . . . 43 D7
Buffery Rd DY2 . . . 62 D7
Bufferys Cl B91 . . . 127 B8
Building Trade Ctr B92 . . . 88 E2
Buildwas Cl WS3 . . . 13 F2
Bulford Cl B14 . . . 104 F2
Bulger Rd WV14 . . . 40 C7
Bulkington La CV11 . . . 79 A7
Bulkington Rd
  Bedworth CV12 . . . 78 D2
  Shilton CV7 . . . 97 E6
Bullace Croft 4 B15 . . . 85 D3
Bulldog La WS13 . . . 3 B1
Buller St WV4 . . . 39 E6
Bullfield Ave CV4 . . . 111 E1
Bullfields Cl B65 . . . 62 F5
Bullfinch Cl DY1 . . . 61 E8
Bullfurlong La LE10 . . . 75 F4
Bullimore Gr CV8 . . . 148 A2
Bullivents Cl B93 . . . 127 F5
Bull La
  Darlaston WV14,WS10 . . . 41 B3
  West Bromwich B70 . . . 53 A3
  Wombourne WV5 . . . 49 B7
Bullmeadow La WV5 . . . 49 A8
Bullmoor La
  Muckley Corner WS14 . . . 8 A1
  Muckley Corner WS14 . . . 8 B1
Bullock's Row WS1 . . . 28 F1
Bullock St
  4 West Bromwich B70 . . . 53 D1
  Birmingham B7 . . . 67 A5
Bullows Rd WS8 . . . 15 C6
Bull Ring 4 B63 . . . 83 B3
Bullring B5 . . . 164 C2
Bull Ring
  Kidderminster DY10 . . . 116 E6
  Nuneaton CV10 . . . 73 B2
  Sedgley DY3 . . . 50 D8
Bull Ring Trad Est 2 B12 . 66 F1
Bull Ring WV13 . . . 27 A3
Bull's Head La CV3 . . . 114 B2
Bull's La B76 . . . 47 E1
Bull St
  Birmingham B17 . . . 85 D5
  Birmingham,Brookfields B4 . . . 164 C3
  Brierley Hill DY5 . . . 61 B1
  Darlaston WS10 . . . 41 E6
  Dudley,Gornalwood DY3 . . . 50 C2
  Dudley,Springs Mire DY1 . . . 62 A8
  Nuneaton CV11 . . . 73 D2
Bull Street Trad Est DY5 . . . 61 B2
Bull St B70 . . . 53 D3
Bull Yd CV1 . . . 165 B2
Bulrush Cl WS8 . . . 15 E7
Bulwell Cl B6 . . . 67 A7
Bulwer Rd CV6 . . . 113 A6
Bulwick Cl CV3 . . . 115 B1
Bumble Hole La B61 . . . 136 E7
Bunbury Gdns B30 . . . 103 D4
Bunbury Rd B30,B31 . . . 103 C4
Bundle Hill B63 . . . 83 A4
Bungalows The B70 . . . 52 F6
Bunker's Hill La WV14 . . . 40 E7
Bunneys Mdw LE10 . . . 74 E6
Bunn's La DY2 . . . 51 F1
Buntsford Dr B60 . . . 150 F6
Buntsford Gate Bsns Pk B60 . . . 150 F6
Buntsford Hill B60 . . . 150 F5
Buntsford Park Rd B60 . . 150 F6
Bunyan Pl WS11 . . . 1 E4
Burbage CE Inf Sch LE10 . 76 A5
Burbage Cl WV10 . . . 25 E6
Burbage Jun Sch LE10 . . . 75 F6
Burbage Rd LE10 . . . 76 A7
Burbages La CV6 . . . 95 D4
Burberry Ct 3 DY4 . . . 52 A8
Burberry Gr CV7 . . . 130 A6
Burbidge Rd B9 . . . 67 E3
Burbury Cl
  Bedworth CV12 . . . 78 C4
  Royal Leamington Spa CV32 . . . 157 C2
Burbury Ct CV34 . . . 161 B8
Burbury St S B19 . . . 66 C6
Burbury St B19 . . . 66 C7
Burcher Gn DY10 . . . 117 B5
Burcombe Twr B23 . . . 57 B6
Burcot Ave
  Bromsgrove B60 . . . 137 B4
  Wolverhampton WV1 . . . 26 A2
Burcot Ct 14 B74 . . . 31 F2
Burcote Rd B24 . . . 57 D3
Burcot Ho B60 . . . 137 B3
Burcot La
  Bromsgrove,Burcot B60 . . . 137 B3
  Bromsgrove,Stoney Hill B60 . . . 137 C4
Burdock Cl
  Cannock WS11 . . . 2 B3
  Walsall WS5 . . . 43 A3
Burdock Ho B38 . . . 103 F1
Burdock Rd B29 . . . 103 A6
Burdons Cl B34 . . . 69 A5
Bure Gr WV13 . . . 27 D1
Burfield Rd B63 . . . 82 C6
Burford Cl
  Solihull B92 . . . 89 A3
  Walsall WS5 . . . 43 A4
Burford Ct
  18 Birmingham B13 . . . 87 B2
  Stourbridge DY8 . . . 81 A4
Burford Mews 13 CV31 . . 162 C6
Burford Park Rd B38 . . . 123 E8
Burford Rd
  Birmingham B44 . . . 55 F7
  Hollywood B47 . . . 125 A6
Burgage Pl CV11 . . . 73 C4
Burgage Wlk CV11 . . . 73 C4
Burges CV1 . . . 165 B3
Burges Gr CV34 . . . 155 F1
Burgess Croft B92 . . . 107 F7
Burghley Cl CV11 . . . 73 F2
Burghley Dr
  Kidderminster DY11 . . . 116 C5
  West Bromwich B71 . . . 42 F2
Burghley Wlk DY5 . . . 81 B8
Burgh Way WS2 . . . 28 A4
Burgoyne St WS11 . . . 2 A5
Burhill Way B37 . . . 70 B5
Burke Ave B13 . . . 87 D1
Burkitt Dr DY4 . . . 52 C8
Burland Ave WV6 . . . 24 E6
Burleigh Cl
  Balsall Common CV7 . . . 130 B7
  Cannock WS12 . . . 2 A8
  Willenhall WV12 . . . 27 B6
Burleigh Croft WS7 . . . 7 A4
Burleigh Rd
  Hinckley LE10 . . . 71 C2
  Wolverhampton WV3 . . . 39 A8
Burleigh St WS1 . . . 29 A1
Burleton Rd B33 . . . 69 E2
Burley Cl B90 . . . 105 F2
Burley Way B38 . . . 123 C8
Burlington Arc 5 B2 . . . 164 B2
Burlington Ave B70 . . . 53 E1
Burlington Cl DY10 . . . 117 B4
Burlington Ct B78 . . . 35 B8
Burlington Rd
  Birmingham B10 . . . 67 F1
  Coventry CV2 . . . 113 F4
  Nuneaton CV10 . . . 78 B7
  West Bromwich B70 . . . 53 E1
Burlington St B6 . . . 66 E6
Burlish Ave 1 B92 . . . 88 F1
Burman Cl B90 . . . 106 A2
Burman Dr B46 . . . 70 F5
Burman Inf Sch B90 . . . 106 A2
Burman Rd B90 . . . 106 A1
Burmarsh Wlk WV8 . . . 24 F8
Burmese Way B65 . . . 62 F6
Burnaby Cl CV10 . . . 72 B5
Burnaby Rd CV6 . . . 95 B1
Burnaston Cres B90 . . . 127 C6
Burnaston Rd B28 . . . 87 E1
Burnbank Gr B24 . . . 57 B4
Burn Cl B66 . . . 65 A4
Burncross Way WV10 . . . 25 F6
Burnell Gdns WV3 . . . 38 E8
Burnel Rd B29 . . . 85 B2
Burnet Gr WV10 . . . 12 B8
Burnett Ho 12 B69 . . . 63 D5
Burnett Rd B74 . . . 31 B2
Burney La B8 . . . 68 C4
Burnfields Way WS9 . . . 30 A7
Burnham Ave
  Birmingham B25 . . . 88 C6
  Wolverhampton WV10 . . . 25 C8
Burnham Cl DY6 . . . 60 F4
Burnham Ct
  18 Brierley Hill DY5 . . . 61 D2
  Birmingham B23 . . . 56 C2
Burnham Gn WS11 . . . 4 B8
Burnham Mdw B28 . . . 106 A6
Burnham Rd
  Birmingham B44 . . . 55 E7
  Coventry CV3 . . . 134 A6
Burnham Rise CV11 . . . 74 A6
Burnhill Gr B29 . . . 103 A8
Burnlea Gr B31 . . . 103 C1
Burnsall Cl
  Birmingham B37 . . . 69 F2
  Wolverhampton WV9 . . . 11 A3
Burnsall Gr CV5 . . . 132 D8
Burnsall Rd CV5 . . . 132 D8
Burns Ave
  Tipton DY4 . . . 52 A7
  Warwick CV34 . . . 160 C5
  Wolverhampton WV10 . . . 11 D2
Burns Cl
  Kidderminster DY10 . . . 117 B6
  Lichfield WS14 . . . 9 B6
  Redditch B97 . . . 158 C8
  Stourbridge DY8 . . . 81 A8
Burns Dr WS7 . . . 7 C7
Burns Gr DY3 . . . 50 A4
Burnside CV3 . . . 115 A2
Burnside Ct B73 . . . 46 A1
Burnside Gdns WS5 . . . 43 D6
Burnside Way B31 . . . 122 F7
Burns Pl WS10 . . . 41 A5
Burns Rd
  Coventry CV2 . . . 114 B3
  Darlaston WS10 . . . 41 B5
  Royal Leamington Spa CV32 . . . 157 B4
  Tamworth B79 . . . 21 A6
Burns St WS11 . . . 2 A3
Burnsway LE10 . . . 71 C1
Burns Wlk CV12 . . . 78 C1
Burnthurst Cres B90 . . . 127 A7
Burnt Meadow Rd B98 . . 154 F6
Burnt Oak Dr DY8 . . . 81 B5
Burnt Tree Ind Est B69 . . . 52 B2
Burnt Tree Island DY1,DY4 51 F2
Burnt Tree Jun & Inf Sch B69 . . . 52 A2
Burnt Tree DY4 . . . 51 F2
Burntwood Bsns Pk WS7 . . 6 D7
Burntwood Rd
  Hammerwich WS7 . . . 7 D4
  Norton Canes WS11 . . . 6 A7
Burntwood Town Sh Ctr WS7 . . . 6 F7
Burrelton Way 1 B43 . . . 54 D8
Burrington Rd B32 . . . 102 A8
Burrowes St WS2 . . . 28 D3
Burrow Hill Cl B36 . . . 69 C8
Burrow Hill La CV7 . . . 94 D7
Burrows Cl CV31 . . . 162 B3
Burrows Croft WV14 . . . 40 C6
Burrows Ho 7 WS2 . . . 28 D3
Burrows Rd DY6 . . . 60 F4
Burrs Dr WS10 . . . 42 A1
Bursledon Wlk WV1 . . . 40 B8
Burslem Cl WS3 . . . 14 A3
Bursnips Rd WV11 . . . 13 C4
Burton Ave WS4 . . . 29 B8
Burton Cl
  Brownshill Green CV5 . . . 94 C2
  Tamworth B79 . . . 21 C7
Burton Cres WV10 . . . 163 D4
Burton Farm Rd WS4 . . . 29 B3
Burton Gr B64 . . . 82 E8
Burton Green CE Prim Sch CV8 . . . 131 B3
Burton La
  Bramcote CV11 . . . 79 F7
  Redditch B98 . . . 153 F3
Burton Old Rd E WS14 . . . 9 E8
Burton Old Rd
  Lichfield WS13 . . . 3 F1
  Lichfield WS14 . . . 9 F8
Burton Old Rd W WS14 . . . 9 D8
Burton Rd
  Dudley DY1 . . . 50 F4
  Lichfield WS13 . . . 3 F1
  Wolverhampton WV10 . . . 25 E3
Burton Wood Dr B20 . . . 55 D2
Burwaye Cl WS13 . . . 9 A6
Buryfield Rd B91 . . . 107 B6
Bury Hill Rd B69 . . . 63 D8
Bury Ho CV4 . . . 111 F3
Bury Mound Ct B90 . . . 105 C2
Bury Rd CV31 . . . 161 F7
Busby Cl CV3 . . . 134 F7
Bush Ave B66 . . . 65 C5
Bushbery Ave CV4 . . . 111 F2
Bushbury Croft B37 . . . 70 C3
Bushbury Hill Prim Sch WV10 . . . 11 F1
Bushbury La
  Wolverhampton,Bushbury WV10 . . . 11 E2
  Wolverhampton,Elston Hall WV10 . . . 25 D7
Bushbury Rd
  Birmingham B33 . . . 69 A5
  Wolverhampton WV10 . . . 26 A5
Bush Cl CV4 . . . 111 F3
Bush Ct CV2 . . . 114 B6
Bushell Dr B91 . . . 107 D4
Bushelton Cl CV1 . . . 165 C1
Bushey Cl B74 . . . 30 F2
Bushey Fields Hospl DY5 . 61 F8
Bushey Fields Rd DY1 . . . 61 E7
Bushfield Ct WV14 . . . 40 F5
Bush Gr
  Birmingham B21 . . . 54 C1
  Walsall WS3 . . . 15 A2
Bushley Cl B98 . . . 159 A7
Bushley Croft B91 . . . 127 B8
Bushman Way B34 . . . 69 E5
Bushmore Rd B28 . . . 106 A7
Bush Rd
  Dudley DY2 . . . 62 C2
  Tipton DY4 . . . 51 E4
Bush St WS10 . . . 41 D7
Bushway Cl DY5 . . . 61 B2
Bushwood Ct B15 . . . 86 C8
Bushwood Dr B93 . . . 128 B3
Bushwood Rd B29 . . . 85 B1
Bushy End CV34 . . . 161 E4
Busill Jones Prim Sch WS3 . . . 27 F8
Bustleholme Ave B71 . . . 42 F1
Bustleholme Cres B71 . . . 42 E1
Bustleholme La B71 . . . 42 E1
Butcher's La CV5 . . . 112 C6
Butchers La B63 . . . 82 C7
Butchers Rd B92 . . . 109 A6
Butcroft Gdns WS10 . . . 41 E6
Bute Cl
  Birmingham B45 . . . 101 E1
  Hinckley LE10 . . . 71 C1
  Willenhall WV12 . . . 27 B6
Butler Cl CV8 . . . 148 C7
Butler Rd B92 . . . 88 F3
Butlers Cl
  Birmingham,Handsworth B20 . . . 55 A3
  Birmingham,Perry Common B73 . . . 45 D1
Butlers Cres CV7 . . . 78 A1
Butlers End CV35 . . . 146 C2
Butler's Hill La B97 . . . 153 B5
Butlers Lane Sta B74 . . . 32 A3
Butlers La B74 . . . 32 A3
Butlers Prec 3 WS1 . . . 28 E2
Butler's Rd B20 . . . 55 A3
Butler St
  Astwood Bank B96 . . . 158 E1
  West Bromwich B70 . . . 53 A4
Butlin Rd CV6 . . . 95 C4
Butlin St B7 . . . 67 C7
Buttercup Cl
  6 Walsall WS5 . . . 43 A3
  Kidderminster DY10 . . . 116 E8
Buttercup Dr B60 . . . 137 C6
Buttercup Way CV12 . . . 77 D2
Butterfield Cl WV6 . . . 23 D3
Butterfield Ct DY1 . . . 51 A2
Butterfield Rd DY5 . . . 61 B7
Butterfly Way 4 B64 . . . 62 F1
Buttermere Ave CV11 . . . 74 A6
Buttermere Cl
  Brierley Hill DY5 . . . 81 B7
  Cannock WS11 . . . 2 A3
  Coventry CV3 . . . 134 F7
  Wolverhampton WV6 . . . 24 D8
Buttermere Ct WV6 . . . 23 F4
Buttermere Dr
  Birmingham B32 . . . 84 F3
  Essington WV11 . . . 13 A2
Buttermere Gr WV11 . . . 13 B1
Buttermere B77 . . . 36 B7
Butter Wlk B38 . . . 123 C8
Butterworth Cl WV14 . . . 40 A1
Butterworth Dr CV4 . . . 132 A6
Buttery Rd B67 . . . 64 E6
Butt La
  Allesley CV5 . . . 112 B7
  Hinckley LE10 . . . 71 F1
Butt Lane Cl LE10 . . . 71 E1
Buttons Farm Rd WV4 . . . 38 D3
Buttress Way B66 . . . 65 A6
Butts Cl WS11 . . . 5 E4
Butts CV1 . . . 113 A2
Butts La
  Norton Canes WS11 . . . 5 E4
  Stone DY10 . . . 117 D1
  Tanworth-In-A B94 . . . 142 B2
Butts Prim Sch WS4 . . . 28 F3
Butts Rd
  Coventry CV1 . . . 113 B2
  Walsall WS4 . . . 28 F3
  Wolverhampton WV4 . . . 38 F4
Butts St WS4 . . . 28 F3
Butts The
  Lichfield WS14 . . . 8 D2
  Walsall WS4 . . . 28 F3
  Warwick CV34 . . . 160 E7
Butts Way WS11 . . . 5 E4
Buxton Ave B78 . . . 35 B8
Buxton Cl WS3 . . . 14 C3
Buxton Rd
  Birmingham B23 . . . 56 B7
  Dudley DY2 . . . 62 A6
  Sutton Coldfield B73 . . . 57 A8
  Walsall WS3 . . . 14 C3
Byfield Cl B33 . . . 69 E1
Byfield Pl CV7 . . . 130 D5
Byfield Rd CV6 . . . 112 E5
Byfleet Cl WV14 . . . 40 A3
Byford Cl B98 . . . 153 E2
Byford Ct CV10 . . . 72 F4
Byford St CV10 . . . 72 F4
Byford Way B37 . . . 90 B8
Bylands Cl B61 . . . 136 E1
Byland B77 . . . 21 D3
Byland Way WS3 . . . 13 F2
Bypass Link B91 . . . 107 F3
By Pass Rd B77 . . . 22 A5
Byrchen Moor Gdns DY5 . 61 B7
Byrne Rd WV2 . . . 39 D7
Byron Ave
  Bedworth CV12 . . . 78 D2
  Birmingham B23 . . . 56 B3
  Lichfield WS14 . . . 9 B5
  Warwick CV34 . . . 160 C4
Byron Cl
  Birmingham B10 . . . 87 D7
  Kidderminster DY10 . . . 117 B5
Byron Cres DY1 . . . 51 B6
Byron Croft
  Dudley DY3 . . . 50 A5
  Sutton Coldfield B74 . . . 31 F6
Byron Ct
  Dorridge B93 . . . 128 A6
  Sutton Coldfield B74 . . . 32 A5
Byron Gdns B71 . . . 53 B5
Byron Pl WS11 . . . 1 F5
Byron Rd
  Birmingham B10 . . . 87 D7
  Redditch B97 . . . 158 D8
  Tamworth B79 . . . 21 A7
  Willenhall WV12 . . . 27 E7
  Wolverhampton WV10 . . . 12 A1
Byron St
  Brierley Hill DY5 . . . 61 D7
  Coventry CV1 . . . 165 C4
  West Bromwich B71 . . . 53 B5
Byron Way B61 . . . 137 A8
Bywater Cl CV3 . . . 133 B5
Bywater Ho 5 WS1 . . . 28 F1
Byways WS3 . . . 14 C3

C

Caban Cl B31 . . . 102 E5
Cable Dr WS2 . . . 28 C5
Cable St WV2 . . . 39 F8
Cabot Gr WV6 . . . 23 E4
Cadbury Dr B35 . . . 58 A2
Cadbury Ho B19 . . . 66 D5
Cadbury Rd B13 . . . 87 B4
Cadbury Sixth Form Coll B38 . . . 103 F1
Cadbury Way B17 . . . 85 B5
Cadbury World* B30 . . . 103 F7
Cadden Dr CV4 . . . 112 B2
Caddick Cres B71 . . . 53 D7
Caddick Rd B42 . . . 44 B1
Caddick St WV14 . . . 51 A8
Cadeby Cl LE10 . . . 71 B3
Cadell Ct B13 . . . 87 A1
Cadet Dr B90 . . . 106 A3
Cadgwith Gdns WV14 . . . 41 A2
Cadine Gdns B13 . . . 86 C1
Cadleigh Gdns B17 . . . 85 C3
Cadle Rd WV10 . . . 25 E7
Cadman Cl CV12 . . . 78 C3
Cadman Cres WV10 . . . 26 A7
Cadman's La WS6,WS3 . . . 14 D6
Cadnam Cl
  Birmingham B17 . . . 85 C3
  Darlaston WV13 . . . 41 B8
Cadogan Rd B77 . . . 35 D5
Caen Cl CV35 . . . 160 A7
Caernarfon Dr CV11 . . . 73 D3
Caernarvon Cl WV12 . . . 27 C7
Caernarvon Way DY1 . . . 50 E2
Caesar Rd CV8 . . . 147 E3
Caesar Way B46 . . . 59 E1
Cairndhu Dr DY10 . . . 117 B7
Cairn Dr WS2 . . . 27 F2
Cairns St WS2 . . . 28 C3
Caister Dr WV13 . . . 40 F8
Caister B77 . . . 22 A6
Caistor Cl B78 . . . 34 B8
Caithness Cl CV5 . . . 112 A4
Cakemore Rd B65 . . . 63 E2
Cala Dr B15 . . . 86 B7
Calcot Dr WV6 . . . 24 E7
Calcott Ho CV3 . . . 134 B5
Calcutt Way B90 . . . 126 A6
Caldecote Cl CV10 . . . 73 C8
Caldecote Gr B9 . . . 68 C1
Caldecote Rd CV6 . . . 113 C5
Caldeford Ave B90 . . . 127 A7
Calder Ave WS1 . . . 29 A2
Calder Cl
  Bulkington CV12 . . . 79 B2
  Coventry CV3 . . . 133 E7
Calder Dr B76 . . . 58 A7
Calderfields Cl WS4 . . . 29 A3
Calder Gr B20 . . . 54 F2
Calder Rise DY3 . . . 50 F6
Calder B77 . . . 22 B2
Calder Twr 2 B20 . . . 55 D1
Calder Wlk CV31 . . . 162 C6
Caldmore Com Prim Sch WS1 . . . 42 E8
Caldmore Gn WS1 . . . 42 E8
Caldmore Rd WS1 . . . 42 E8
Caldon Cl LE10 . . . 75 B8
Caldwall Cres DY11 . . . 116 D5
Caldwell Ct
  Nuneaton CV11 . . . 73 D1
  Solihull B91 . . . 107 C5
Caldwell Gr B91 . . . 107 C5
Caldwell Rd
  Birmingham B9 . . . 68 B3
  Nuneaton CV11 . . . 73 D1
Caldwell St B71 . . . 53 D8
Caldy Wlk 5 B45 . . . 101 F1
Cale Cl B77 . . . 21 C2
Caledonia DY5 . . . 81 D7
Caledonian Cl WS5 . . . 43 C3
Caledonian B77 . . . 21 F2
Caledonia Rd WV2 . . . 163 D1
Caledonia St WV14 . . . 40 E6
Caledon Pl WS2 . . . 42 C7
Caledon St 5 WS2 . . . 42 C7
Calewood Rd DY5 . . . 81 D7
Calgary Cl CV3 . . . 115 A2
Caliban Mews CV34 . . . 161 E3
California Ho B32 . . . 84 E2
Californian Gr WS7 . . . 6 F8
California Rd B69 . . . 63 B8
California Way B32 . . . 84 F3
Callaghan Gr 3 WS11 . . . 2 C2
Callcott Dr DY5 . . . 81 D7
Callear Rd WS10 . . . 41 D1
Callendar Cl CV11 . . . 74 A7
Calley Cl DY4 . . . 52 A3
Callis Wlk 2 B77 . . . 35 F6
Callowbridge Rd B45 . . . 121 F7
Callowbrook La B45 . . . 121 F7
Callow Hill La B97 . . . 158 B6
Callow Hill Rd B48 . . . 139 A6
Callows La 2 DY10 . . . 116 E6
Calmere Cl CV2 . . . 114 F8
Calpurnia Ave CV34 . . . 161 E2
Calshot Prim Sch B42 . . . 55 B8
Calshot Rd B42 . . . 55 A8
Calstock Rd WV12 . . . 27 D4
Calthorpe Cl WS5 . . . 43 E6
Calthorpe Mans 4 B15 . . . 66 B1
Calthorpe Rd
  Birmingham,Edgbaston B15 . . . 86 B8
  Birmingham,Handsworth Wood B20 . . . 55 C2
  Walsall WS5 . . . 43 D6
Calthorpe Sch Sports Coll B12 . . . 87 A8
Caludon Castle Sch CV2 . 114 E4

Caludon Lodge CV2 114 E5
Caludon Park Ave CV2 114 E5
Caludon Rd CV2 114 A4
Calver Cres WV11 26 F5
Calver Gr B44 44 D3
Calverley Rd B38 123 D8
Calvert Cl CV3 133 D6
Calverton Gr B43 54 E8
Calves Croft WV13 27 A3
Calvin Cl WV10 11 D3
Calving Hill WS11 1 E2
Camberley 6 B71 42 F1
Camberley Cres WV4 39 E2
Camberley Dr WV4 39 A4
Camberley Gr B23 56 E6
Camberley Rd DY6 61 A4
Camberwell Terr CV31 162 A7
Camborne Cl B6 66 E7
Camborne Dr CV11 73 F5
Camborne Rd WS5 43 D7
Cambourne Ct 4 WS5 43 D7
Cambourne Rd
Hinckley LE10 76 A6
Rowley Regis B65 63 C3
Cambrai Dr B28 105 F8
Cambria Cl B90 125 E7
Cambrian B77 22 A2
Cambria St WS11 1 D4
Cambridge Ave
Solihull B91 106 E3
Sutton Coldfield B73 57 B8
Cambridge Cl WS9 30 B8
Cambridge Cres B15 86 D7
Cambridge Dr
Birmingham B37 69 F1
Nuneaton CV10 72 E3
Cambridge Gdns CV32 157 A1
Cambridge Rd
Birmingham B13 86 F1
Dudley DY2 62 A7
Smethwick B66 65 A7
Cambridge St
Birmingham B1 164 A2
Coventry CV1 113 E5
Walsall WS1 42 E7
West Bromwich B70 53 B2
Wolverhampton WV10 163 C4
Cambridge Twr B1 164 A2
Cambridge Way B27 88 D4
Camden Cl
Birmingham B36 69 A8
Walsall WS5 43 A4
Camden Dr
Birmingham B1 66 C3
Tamworth B77 21 E3
Camden St
Birmingham B18,B1 66 B4
Brownhills WS9 15 F4
Coventry CV2 114 A4
Walsall WS1 42 E8
Camden Way DY6 49 D1
Camel Cotts DY9 99 E2
Camellia Gdns
Stourbridge DY8 60 E2
Wolverhampton WV9 10 F3
Camellia Rd 1 CV2 96 B2
Camelot Cl WS11 1 F4
Camelot Gr CV8 148 C5
Camelot Way B10 87 C8
Cameo Dr DY8 80 F8
Cameron Cl
Allesley CV5 112 A7
Royal Leamington Spa CV32 157 A4
Cameron Rd WS4 29 B3
Camford Gr B14 104 F3
Cam Gdns DY5 61 B6
Cam Ho 7 DY1 61 E8
Camhouses B77 22 B1
Camino Rd B32 84 F3
Camomile Cl 5 WS5 43 A3
Campbell Cl
Nuneaton CV10 72 A4
Tamworth B79 20 F8
Walsall WS4 29 A3
Campbells Gn B26 89 B4
Campbell St DY5 61 C4
Campden Cl B97 158 D6
Campden Gn B92 89 A3
Camp Hill B12 87 A8
Camp Hill Cir B12 87 A8
Camp Hill Dr CV10 72 D7
Camp Hill Ind Est B12 87 A7
Camphill La WS10 41 F2
Camp Hill Middleway B12 87 A7
Camp Hill Prim Sch CV10 72 E6
Camp Hill Rd CV10 72 C7
Camp Hill DY8 60 E1
Campian's Ave WS6 4 D2
Campion Cl
3 Birmingham B38 123 F8
Coventry CV3 133 D6
Walsall WS5 43 A3
Campion Ct 2 DY4 51 E5
Campion Dr
Featherstone WV10 12 A7
Tamworth B77 21 C3
Campion Gn CV32 157 A2
Campion Gr B63 82 D3
Campion Ho
2 Birmingham B38 123 E8
Wolverhampton WV10 25 F4
Campion Rd CV32 157 A2
Campion Sch & Com Coll CV31 162 C5
Campion B74 31 F5
Campion Terr CV32 157 A1
Campion Way
3 Bedworth CV12 77 D2
Solihull B90 126 A5
Camp La
Birmingham,Handsworth B21 54 C2
Birmingham,King's Norton B38 103 F3
Camplea Croft B37 70 A2
Camplin Cres B20 54 E5
Campling Cl CV12 79 B2
Camp Rd B75 32 D6
Campriano Dr CV34 161 A8
Camp St
Birmingham B9 67 C1
Wednesbury WS10 41 F2
Wolverhampton WV1 163 B4
Campton Cl LE10 75 E7
Campville Cres B71 42 E1
Campville Gr B37 69 F5
Camp Wood Cl B30 103 F8
Camrose Croft
Birmingham,Balsall Heath B12 86 F5
Birmingham,Castle Bromwich B34 69 B6
Camrose Gdns WV9 11 A3
Camrose Twr B7 67 B6
Camsey La WS7 7 E8
Camville CV3 115 A2
Canal La B24 57 A1
Canal Rd CV6 113 F8
Canalside CV6 96 B6
Canalside Cl
Walsall WS3 14 F1
Wednesbury WS10 42 E2
Canal Side
Dudley DY2 62 E4
Hopwood B48 123 B2
Canal Side Ind Est DY5 61 C1
Canalside B94 144 D3
Canal St
Brierley Hill DY5 61 E5
Dudley DY1 51 D4
Oldbury B69 64 A7
Stourbridge DY8 80 F6
Tipton WV14 51 C8
Canal View Ind Est DY5 61 B1
Canal Way LE10 74 F7
Canary Gr B19 66 C8
Canberra Ct 2 CV12 77 F2
Canberra Ho B34 69 E6
Canberra Rd
Coventry CV2 96 C4
Walsall WS5 43 C6
Canberra Way
4 Birmingham B12 86 F8
Hinckley LE10 75 E4
Canford Cl
Birmingham B12 86 F7
Coventry CV3 133 C3
Canley Ford CV4,CV5 132 E7
Canley Rd CV5 132 D8
Canley Sta CV5 112 D1
Cannel Rd WS7 6 D6
Cannes Ct CV4 132 D6
Canning Cl WS5 43 D6
Canning Gdns B18 65 E4
Canning Rd
Tamworth B77 21 F4
Walsall WS5 43 D6
Canning St LE10 71 C1
Cannock Chase High Sch WS11 1 E2
Cannock Chase Tech Coll
Cannock,Blackfords WS11 1 D1
Cannock,Bridgtown WS11 4 E7
Cannock Com Hospl WS11 1 E2
Cannock Ind Ctr WS11 4 D5
Cannock Motor Village WS11 2 B3
Cannock Rd
Burntwood,Chase Terrace WS7 6 D7
Burntwood,Gorstey Ley WS7 7 B7
Cannock,Heath Hayes WS12 5 C8
Cannock WS12,WS11 2 A5
Featherstone WV10 12 C7
Willenhall WV12 27 C7
Cannock Sh Ctr WS11 1 E1
Cannocks La CV4 132 D6
Cannock Sta WS11 4 F8
Cannon Cl CV4 132 F6
Cannon Dr WV14 40 D2
Cannon Hill Gr 2 B12 86 E5
Cannon Hill Pl 1 B12 86 E5
Cannon Hill Rd
Birmingham B12 86 E5
Coventry CV4 132 D5
Cannon Park District Ctr CV4 132 C6
Cannon Park Prim Sch CV4 132 D5
Cannon Park Rd CV4 132 E5
Cannon Rd WV5 49 A7
Cannon St N WS2 28 E4
Cannon St
Birmingham B2 164 C2
Walsall WS2 28 E4
Willenhall WV13 27 B2
Canon Bsns Pk WV14 40 C1
Canon Dr CV7 95 D6
Canon Evans CE Inf Sch CV12 78 A2
Canon Hudson Cl CV3 134 C6
Canon Maggs CE Jun Sch CV12 78 B2
Canon Young Rd CV31 162 B3
Canterbury Ave WV13 27 D2
Canterbury Cl
9 Rowley Regis B65 63 E4
Birmingham B23 56 D2
Kenilworth CV8 148 C3
Lichfield WS13 3 C3
Studley B80 159 C4
Tamworth B77 21 D3
Walsall WS3 15 A4
West Bromwich B71 53 E8
Canterbury Cross Prim Sch B20 55 D1
Canterbury Dr
Birmingham B37 90 A7
Burntwood WS7 7 E7
Perton WV6 23 E4
Canterbury Rd
Birmingham B20 55 D1
Kidderminster DY11 116 A6
West Bromwich B71 53 D8
Wolverhampton WV4 38 E5
Canterbury St CV1 165 D3
Canterbury Twr 1 B1 66 B3
Canterbury Way
Cannock WS12 2 B1
Nuneaton CV11 74 A8
Cantlow Cl CV5 112 A3
Cantlow Ho 2 B12 86 F7
Cantlow Rd B13 105 A6
Canton Ho LE10 71 C4
Canute Cl WS1 42 F7
Canvey Cl B45 101 E1
Canwell Ave B37 69 F5
Canwell Dr B75 33 B5
Canwell Gate B75 32 E4
Canwell Gdns WV14 40 C4
Capcroft Rd B13 105 B6
Cape Cl WS8 16 A6
Cape Hill Ret Ctr B66 65 C4
Cape Hill B66 65 C4
Cape Ind Est CV34 160 E7
Capener Rd B43 44 A2
Cape Prim Sch B66 65 C4
Cape Rd CV34 160 D8
Capern Gr B32 84 F5
Cape St
Birmingham B18 65 D4
West Bromwich B70 52 E4
Capethorn Rd B66 65 A3
Capilano Rd B23 56 C7
Capmartin Rd CV6 113 C7
Cappers La WS13,WS14 9 F8
Capponfield Cl WV14 40 B3
Capstone Ave
Birmingham B18 66 A4
Wolverhampton WV10 25 C8
Captain's Cl WV3 24 D2
Captains Pool Rd DY10 117 A1
Captain's Pool Rd DY10 117 B2
Capulet Cl CV3 134 C6
Capulet Dr CV34 161 E3
Caradoc Cl CV2 114 D7
Caradoc Hall CV2 114 D7
Caradoc B77 22 A2
Carcroft Rd B25 88 D8
Cardale Croft 1 CV3 134 F8
Cardale St B65 63 D1
Carden Cl B70 52 F4
Carder Cres WV14 40 D4
Carder Dr DY5 61 C2
Cardiff Cl CV3 134 D5
Cardiff St WV3 39 B8
Cardigan Cl B71 53 C7
Cardigan Dr WV12 27 B6
Cardigan Ho WS12 2 C5
Cardigan Pl WS12 2 C5
Cardigan Rd CV12 77 C1
Cardigan St B4 66 F3
Cardinal Cres B61 136 D1
Cardinal Dr DY10 117 B3
Cardinal Griffin RC High Sch WS11 1 D2
Cardinal Newman RC Sch B17 65 A2
Cardinal Newman RC Sch & Com Coll CV6 94 F2
Cardinal Way WS11 1 D2
Cardinal Wiseman RC Sch CV2 96 E1
Cardinal Wiseman Tech Coll B44 44 F2
Carding Cl CV5 111 F4
Cardington Ave B42 44 B1
Cardington Cl B98 154 F3
Cardoness Pl DY1 50 F2
Cardy Cl B97 153 B4
Careless Gn DY9 81 F4
Carey St CV6 114 B8
Carey B77 36 A5
Carfax WS11 4 E8
Cargill Cl CV6 95 F5
Carhampton Rd B75 47 A5
Carillon Gdns B65 63 C3
Carisbrooke Ave B37 70 C2
Carisbrooke Cl WS10 42 E2
Carisbrooke Cres WS10 42 E3
Carisbrooke Dr B62 83 D3
Carisbrooke Gdns WV10 11 E3
Carisbrooke Rd
Birmingham B17 65 B1
Perton WV6 24 A3
Wednesbury WS10 42 E2
Wolverhampton WV10 11 E3
Carisbrooke B77 22 A2
Carisbrook Rd CV10 73 D6
Carlcroft B77 22 B2
Carless Ave B17 85 B7
Carless St WS1 42 E8
Carl Eynon Ct 2 WS3 28 B8
Carlisle Rd WS11 4 B7
Carlisle St B18 65 F5
Carlson Pk 2 B17 85 B5
Carl St WS2 28 D5
Carlton Ave
Bilston WV14 40 F7
Birmingham B21 54 E1
Stourbridge DY9 81 E3
Sutton Coldfield B74 31 A2
Wolverhampton WV11 26 A7
Carlton Cl
Bulkington CV12 79 B3
Cannock WS12 2 D1
Dudley DY1 51 C6
Kidderminster DY11 116 A8
Redditch B97 153 B1
Sutton Coldfield B75 46 E7
Carlton Cres
Burntwood WS7 7 A8
Tamworth B79 20 F8
Carlton Croft B74 31 A2
Carlton Ct CV5 112 F2
Carlton Gdns CV5 133 A8
Carlton Ho
8 Royal Leamington Spa CV32 161 F8
Sutton Coldfield B75 32 B2
Carlton Mews B36 69 D7
Carlton Mews Flats B36 69 D7
Carlton Rd
Birmingham B9 67 D1
Coventry CV6 95 F1
Smethwick B66 65 B8
Wolverhampton WV3 39 A7
Carlyle Ave DY10 117 B6
Carlyle Bsns Pk B70 52 F5
Carlyle Gr WV10 26 A8
Carlyle Rd
Birmingham,Edgbaston B16 65 E1
Birmingham,Lozells B19 66 C8
Bromsgrove B60 151 B8
Rowley Regis B65 63 C2
Wolverhampton WV10 26 A8
Carmel Cl WS12 2 C5
Carmel Gr B32 84 B1
Carmelite Rd CV1 113 E2
Carmichael Cl WS14 9 D7
Carmodale Ave B42 55 B5
Carnation Way CV10 78 A8
Carnbroe Ave CV3 134 F7
Carnegie Ave DY4 52 B4
Carnegie Cl CV3 134 B5
Carnegie Dr WS10 42 A3
Carnegie Rd B65 63 B2
Carnford Rd B26 89 B6
Carnforth Cl DY6 60 B7
Carnforth Rd B60 137 B1
Carnoustie Cl
Bromsgrove B61 150 D8
Nuneaton CV11 79 C8
Sutton Coldfield B75 46 C8
Walsall WS3 14 A3
Carnoustie B77 22 C5
Carnwath Rd B73 45 E2
Carol Ave B61 136 D3
Carol Cres
Halesowen B63 82 F5
Wednesfield WV11 26 E6
Carol Gdns DY8 80 F8
Caroline Cl CV11 78 F7
Caroline Pl B13 86 F3
Caroline Rd B13 86 F4
Caroline St
Birmingham B3 164 A4
Dudley DY2 51 E1
West Bromwich B70 53 B2
Carousel Pk LE9 71 F8
Carpathian Ct 4 B18 66 C4
Carpathian The 5 B18 66 C4
Carpenter Glade B63 82 D5
Carpenter Pl 7 B12 87 A6
Carpenter Rd B15 86 B7
Carpenters Cl LE10 75 F5
Carpenters Ct B12 86 F8
Carpenter's Rd B19 66 C7
Carpet Trades Way DY11 116 D7
Carrick Cl WS3 15 A5
Carrie Ho CV1 165 A2
Carriers Cl WS2 27 F1
Carriers Fold WV5 49 B7
Carrington Rd WS10 42 D2
Carroll Wlk DY10 117 C5
Carroway Head Hill B78 33 D4
Carrs La B4 164 C2
Carsal Cl CV7 95 D5
Carshalton Gr WV2 39 E7
Carshalton Rd B44 45 A2
Cartbridge Cres WS3 28 F6
Cartbridge La S WS4 29 A5
Cartbridge La WS4 29 A6
Cartbridge Wlk WS3 29 A6
Carter Ave
Codsall WV8 10 B3
Kidderminster DY11 116 B4
Carter Ct DY11 116 C4
Carter Rd
Birmingham B43 43 F2
Coventry CV3 134 A8
Wolverhampton WV6 25 B5
Carters Cl
Birmingham B37 90 A7
Bromsgrove B61 150 D7
Carters Cl *continued*
Sutton Coldfield B76 46 F3
Cartersfield La WS9 16 E6
Carter's Gn B70 53 B4
Carters Hurst B33 69 B1
Carter's La
Birmingham B62 84 A3
Halesowen B62 83 F4
Carthorse La B97 153 B5
Carthusian Rd CV3 133 C7
Cartland Rd
Birmingham,Sparkbrook B11 87 C6
Birmingham,Stirchley B14, B30 104 C7
Cartmel Cl CV5 112 A4
Cartmel Ct B23 56 B4
Cartway The WV6 23 D4
Cartwright Gdns B69 52 C2
Cartwright Ho WS3 14 B1
Cartwright Rd
Stoke Prior B60 150 D2
Sutton Coldfield B75 32 C3
Cartwright St WV2 163 C1
Carvell Cl CV5 94 B1
Carver Cl CV2 114 E2
Carver Ct
Sutton Coldfield B24 57 C6
Wednesbury DY4 41 A1
Carver Gdns DY8 80 E2
Carver St B1 66 B4
Casa Mia Ct WS12 2 C5
Cascade Cl CV3 133 E6
Case La CV35 145 E1
Casern View B75 47 A6
Casewell Rd DY6 60 C8
Casey Ave B23 56 D8
Cash Joynson Ave WS10 41 C8
Cashmore Ave CV31 161 F5
Cashmore Rd
Bedworth CV12 77 E1
Kenilworth CV8 148 C4
Cash's Bsns Ctr CV1 113 D5
Cash's La CV1 113 D6
Casita Gr CV8 148 C4
Caslon Cres DY8 80 D4
Caslon Flats B63 82 C4
Caslon Prim Sch B63 82 C4
Caslon Rd B63 82 C6
Caspian Way CV2 115 A8
Cassandra Cl
Coventry CV4 132 D3
Dudley DY5 50 C1
Cassandra Gr CV34 161 D4
Cassowary Rd 2 B20 54 F3
Castello Dr B36 58 D1
Castillo Ct B14 105 A5
Castings The WV14 40 D2
Castlebridge Gdns WV11 26 F7
Castlebridge Rd WV11 27 A6
Castle Bromwich Bsns Pk B35 58 A1
Castle Bromwich Hall Gdns* B36 69 A8
Castle Bromwich Inf Sch B36 69 E8
Castle Bromwich Jun Sch B36 69 E7
Castle Cl
Brownhills WS8 6 F2
Coventry CV3 133 D6
Cradley Heath B64 63 B1
Solihull B92 89 B1
Tamworth B77 21 E4
Warwick CV34 160 E6
Castle Cres B36 69 C8
Castlecroft Ave WV3 38 A8
Castle Croft B68 84 D8
Castlecroft Gdns WV3 38 C8
Castlecroft Ho WV3 38 A8
Castlecroft La WV6 23 F1
Castlecroft WS11 5 E5
Castlecroft Prim Sch WV3 38 B8
Castlecroft Rd
Bilston WV14 40 F7
Wolverhampton WV3 38 B8
Castle Ct
5 Darlaston WS10 41 D6
Hinckley LE10 75 D6
Kenilworth CV8 148 A6
Castleditch La B98 158 E7
Castle Dr
Coleshill B46 70 F5
Willenhall WV12 27 B5
Castle Dyke 6 WS13 9 B7
Castleford Gr B11 87 C4
Castleford Rd B11 87 C4
Castlefort Jun Mix & Inf Sch WS9 16 B3
Castlefort Rd WS9 16 A3
Castlegate Dr DY1 51 E2
Castle Gate Island DY2 51 E2
Castlegate Mews 5 CV34 160 F7
Castlegate Way DY1 51 E2
Castle Gn CV8 147 D5
Castle Gr
Kenilworth CV8 147 E4
Stourbridge DY8 81 B3
Castlehall B77 22 A2
Castle High Sch DY1 51 B2
Castle Hill
Dudley DY1 51 D2
Kenilworth CV8 147 E5
Castlehill Rd WS9 16 C3
Castlehills Dr B36 69 A8
Castle Hill CV34 160 E6

Castle Ho B33 69 B2
Castle Hts B64 83 B8
Castle La
Solihull B92 89 A2
Warwick CV34 160 E6
Castlemaine Dr LE10 71 E3
Castle Mews 6 CV34 160 E6
Castle Mill DY1 51 D4
Castle Mill Rd DY1 51 C4
Castle Place Ind Est CV1 165 D4
Castle Rd
Birmingham B29 85 B1
Birmingham,Kings Norton B30 103 F4
Brownhills WS9 16 A2
Castle Rd E B68 84 D8
Castle Rd
Kenilworth CV8 147 E5
Kidderminster DY11 116 E5
Nuneaton CV10 73 C7
Studley B80 159 F4
Tamworth B77 35 F5
Tipton DY4 51 D4
Castle Rd W B68 84 C8
Castlereagh Ct WV10 25 C6
Castle Specl Sch WS3 28 B7
Castle Sq B29 85 A1
Castle St
Astwood Bank B96 158 E2
Brownhills WS8 6 F2
Coventry CV1 165 D4
Darlaston WS10 41 D8
Dudley DY1 51 D1
Hinckley LE10 75 D8
Sedgley DY3 50 D8
Tipton DY4 51 E5
Warwick CV34 160 E6
West Bromwich B70 53 A8
Wolverhampton WV1 163 C3
Castle The DY8 81 B3
Castleton Ct 1 B15 86 B7
Castleton Rd
Birmingham B42 55 D7
Walsall WS3 14 C3
Castleton St DY2 62 C4
Castle Vale Ent Pk B76 58 C4
Castle Vale Ind Est B76 58 A5
Castle Vale Ret Pk B35 57 F3
Castle Vale Sch B35 58 B3
Castle View Cl WS10 41 A4
Castle View DY1 51 B2
Castle View Rd WV14, WS10 41 B4
Castle View B77 21 C3
Castle Yd WV1 163 C3
Caswell Rd
Royal Leamington Spa CV31 162 B6
Sedgley DY3 50 C8
Caterbanck Way 2 WS13 8 F6
Cater Dr B76 46 F2
Caterham Dr DY6 60 F3
Catesby Dr DY6 60 D8
Catesby Ho B37 69 F4
Catesby La B94 144 B2
Catesby Pk
Birmingham B38 103 E3
Birmingham B38 103 E3
Catesby Rd
Coventry CV6 113 B8
Solihull B90 106 B1
Cateswell Rd B11,B28 87 F2
Cathcart Rd DY8 80 E5
Cathedral Ave DY11 116 A6
Cathedral Cl DY4 51 E5
Cathedral Ct 4 WS13 9 B8
Cathedral Lanes Sh Ctr CV1 165 B3
Cathedral Rise WS13 9 A8
Cathel Dr B42 55 A7
Catherine Cl B60 150 F8
Catherine Ct B24 57 C4
Catherine de Barnes La
Bickenhill B92 90 D1
Catherine de B B92 108 C7
Catherine Dr B73 46 A6
Catherine Rd WV14 40 A1
Catherines Cl B91 108 B4
Catherine St
Birmingham B6 67 A7
Coventry CV2 113 F3
Catherine Ward Hall CV12 78 B5
Catherton Cl DY4 41 C1
Catholic La DY3 50 D7
Catisfield Cres WV8 10 F1
Cat & Kittens La WV10 11 E6
Cat La B34 69 B7
Caton Gr B28 106 A7
Cato St N B7 67 C5
Cato St B7 67 B5
Catshill Fst Sch B61 137 A8
Catshill Mid Sch B61 136 F8
Catshill Rd WS8 16 A7
Cattell Dr B75 47 B5
Cattell Rd
Birmingham B9 67 C1
Warwick CV34 160 E7
Cattells Gr B7 67 C6
Cattermole Gr B43 44 C3
Cattock Hurst Dr B72 57 D7
Causeway Green Prim Sch B68 63 F3
Causeway Green Rd B68 64 A4
Causeway Rd WV14 51 D8
Causeway B65 63 C2
Causeway The B25 88 D7
Causey Farm Rd B63 100 C8
Cavalier Cir WV10 11 E4
Cavalier Cl CV11 73 E2
Cavalier Dr B63 83 A3
Cavandale Ave B44 44 E1
Cavan's Cl WS11 1 E4
Cavans Cl CV3 135 A8
Cavans Way CV3 135 A8
Cavans Wood Park Home Est WS12 1 D5
Cavell Cl 1 WS2 28 D2
Cavell Rd
Burntwood WS7 7 E8
Dudley DY2 51 F1
Cavendish Cl
Birmingham B38 104 B1
Kingswinford DY6 60 D4
Lower Marlbrook B60 121 C1
Cavendish Ct
Birmingham B17 85 B8
Dorridge B93 128 A3
Cavendish Dr
Kidderminster DY10 117 B7
West Hagley DY9 98 F4
Cavendish Gdns
Walsall WS2 28 A4
Wolverhampton WV1 26 C1
Cavendish Rd
Birmingham B16 65 D4
Coventry CV4 111 E2
Halesowen B62 83 F4
Walsall WS2 28 B5
Wolverhampton WV1 26 B1
Cavendish B79 20 E7
Cavendish Way WS9 30 B5
Cavendish Wlk CV11 79 C8
Caversham Cl CV11 74 A7
Caversham Pl B73 46 B4
Caversham Rd B44 45 A2
Cawdon Gr B93 127 F3
Cawdor Cres B16 65 F1
Cawnpore Rd CV6 95 B2
Cawthorne Cl 1 CV1 113 E4
Caxton Ct 4 WS11 4 E8
Caxton Gr B44 45 C1
Caxton St WS11 4 E8
Caynham Cl B98 154 D4
Caynham Rd B32 102 B8
Cayton Gr B23 56 F6
Cearl Ct B27 88 C2
Cecil Ct CV31 162 A8
Cecil Dr B69 52 D2
Cecil Leonard Knox Cres CV11 79 F6
Cecil Rd
Birmingham,Gravelly Hill B24 56 F3
Birmingham,Selly Park B13 86 C1
Cecil St
Birmingham B19 164 C4
Cannock WS11 1 F4
Stourbridge DY8 80 F5
Walsall WS4 28 F3
Cecily Rd CV3 133 E7
Cedar Ave
Birmingham B36 69 C8
Brownhills WS8 16 A8
Dudley WV14 51 B7
Ryton-on-D CV8 135 B1
Cedar Bridge Croft B74 46 B8
Cedar Cl
Birmingham,Bournville B30 103 E6
Birmingham,Brandhall B68 84 C8
Burntwood WS7 7 A6
Cannock WS11 2 A8
Lichfield WS14 9 F7
Royal Leamington Spa CV32 157 A4
Stourbridge DY8 80 D2
Walsall WS5 43 B4
Cedar Cres DY11 116 C6
Cedar Ct
Allesley CV5 112 A6
Birmingham B43 54 B8
Hinckley LE10 76 A6
Tamworth B77 35 E6
Cedar Dr
Birmingham,Pype Hayes B24 57 C5
Birmingham,West Heath B31 123 B7
Bromsgrove B60 137 A1
Kidderminster DY11 116 C7
Sutton Coldfield B74 30 E1
Tamworth B79 21 A8
Cedar Gr
Bilston WV14 40 F7
Codsall WV8 10 B3
Great Wyrley WS6 5 B4
Warwick CV34 156 A1
West Hagley DY9 99 A6
Wolverhampton WV3 38 F7
Cedarhill Dr WS11 1 F3
Cedar Ho
7 Royal Leamington Spa CV32 161 E8
Birmingham B36 68 F8
Solihull B91 106 F1
Sutton Coldfield B74 31 B5
Cedarhurst
Birmingham B32 85 A5
Solihull B91 107 C3
Cedar Park Rd
Redditch B97 153 D4
Willenhall WV12 13 C1
Cedar Rd
Birmingham B30 103 E6
Burntwood WS7 7 A7
Dudley DY1 51 B3
Cedar Rd *continued*
Nuneaton CV10 72 D6
Redditch B97 153 D4
Tipton DY4 51 D5
Wednesbury WS10 42 A2
Willenhall WV13 26 E2
Cedars Ave
Birmingham B27 88 C4
Coventry CV6 112 F5
Kingswinford DY6 60 D4
Wombourne WV5 49 A5
Cedars Bsns Ctr The WS11 4 C7
Cedars Hort Unit The WV3 24 D2
Cedars Mews The 3 CV32 161 D8
Cedars Rd CV7 78 B1
Cedars The
5 Wolverhampton,Newbridge WV6 24 F3
Birmingham B25 68 E1
Dorridge B93 128 A4
Wolverhampton,Tettenhall WV6 24 D5
Cedar Terr B60 137 A1
Cedar View B97 153 C4
Cedar Way
Birmingham B31 102 F1
Wolverhampton WV11 26 C7
Cedar Wlk 6 B37 70 B2
Cedarwood Croft B42 54 F8
Cedar Wood Dr CV7 130 B6
Cedar Wood Rd DY3 50 D5
Cedarwood B74 46 B8
Cedric Cl CV3 134 C5
Celandine Cl DY6 60 C4
Celandine Rd
Coventry CV2 96 D2
Dudley DY1 51 A4
Celandine
Sutton Coldfield B74 31 F5
Tamworth B77 21 C3
Celandine Way CV12 77 E2
Celbury Way B43 54 D8
Celeste Rd B60 137 C1
Celtic Rd WS11 1 E3
Celts Cl B65 63 C4
Cemetery La B18 66 B5
Cemetery Rd
Cannock WS11 1 E4
Darlaston WS10 41 F8
Oldbury B68 64 C6
Redditch B97 153 D3
Smethwick B67 64 F4
Stourbridge DY9 81 E5
Sutton Coldfield B75 46 D6
Willenhall WV13 27 A2
Cemetery St
Bilston WV14 40 C6
Cheslyn Hay WS6 4 C2
Cemetery Way WS3 14 B1
Centaur Rd CV5 112 F2
Centenary Bsns Ctr CV11 73 E3
Centenary Cl 1 B31 103 A1
Centenary Dr B21 54 E1
Centenary Plaza B1 164 A2
Centenary Rd CV4 132 D7
Centenary Sq B1 164 A2
Central Arc WV1 163 B2
Central Ave
13 Wolverhampton WV4 39 F4
Bilston WV14 40 E7
Birmingham B31 122 F8
Cannock WS11 1 F5
Coventry CV2 114 A2
Cradley Heath B64 82 D7
Nuneaton CV11 73 B5
Rowley Regis B65 63 C2
Royal Leamington Spa CV31 161 F6
Stourbridge DY9 81 E3
Tipton DY4 51 F7
Central Bldgs CV3 165 B1
Central Bsns Pk B33 69 D1
Central Bvd
Cheswick Green B90 127 A3
Coventry CV6,CV7 95 A5
Central City Ind Est CV6 113 F5
Central Cl WS3 14 A1
Central Dr
Dudley,Gornalwood DY3 50 D2
Dudley,West Coseley WV14 51 D7
Walsall WS3 14 A1
Central Gr B27 88 C2
Central Park Dr B18 65 F5
Central Park Ind Est DY2 62 E3
Central Rd B60 137 A2
Central Six Ret Pk CV1 165 A1
Central Sq B23 57 A4
Central Trad Est
Darlaston WS10 41 E6
Wolverhampton WV2 39 F8
Central Way DY5 61 F3
Centre Ct B63 83 B3
Centre La B63 83 B3
Centre Link Ind Est B7 67 B6
Centreway The B14 105 D4
Centrovell Ind Est CV11 73 C2
Centurion Cl B46 59 F1
Centurion Pk B77 36 B6
Centurion Way B77 36 B6
Century Ho B69 63 D6
Century Ind Est B44 44 E3
Century Mews B64 62 F2
Century Pk
Birmingham,Bordesley Green B9 67 C2
Century Pk *continued*
Birmingham,Marston Green B26 90 C6
Century Rd B69 64 A8
Century Twr B5 86 C5
Ceolmund Cres B37 70 B2
CE Prim Sch of St Edmund & St John The DY2 51 E1
Chace Ave CV3 134 C6
Chaceley Cl CV2 115 A8
Chaceley Ct B97 158 D8
Chaceley Gr B23 56 E7
Chace Prim Sch CV3 134 C6
Chadbrook Crest B15 85 E7
Chadbury Croft 1 B91 127 B8
Chadbury Rd B63 83 C3
Chadcote Way B61 120 F1
Chaddersley Cl 2 B45 101 F1
Chaddesley Cl
Oldbury B69 63 D5
Redditch B98 153 F1
Chaddesley Dr DY9 81 B1
Chaddesley Gdns 2 DY10 117 A5
Chaddesley Rd
Birmingham B31 103 D2
Halesowen B63 82 F2
Kidderminster DY10 117 A5
Chadley Cl B91 107 A6
Chad Rd
Birmingham B15 85 F8
Dudley DY1,WV14 51 B7
Chadsgrove Sch B61 136 F8
Chadshunt Cl B36 58 D2
Chadsmead Prim Sch WS13 3 A1
Chadsmoor CE Jun Sch WS11 2 A3
Chadsmoor Inf Sch WS11 2 A4
Chadsmoor Terr B7 67 B6
Chad Sq B15 85 E8
Chadstone Cl B90 127 B6
Chadswell Hts WS13 3 D2
Chad Vale Prim Sch B15 85 D7
Chad Valley Cl B17 85 D6
Chadwell Dr B90 106 B6
Chadwich La DY9 120 F7
Chadwick Ave B45 122 B6
Chadwick Cl
Coventry CV5 112 B3
Wolverhampton WV4 38 D6
Chadwick Ct B42 54 E8
Chadwick La
Chadwick End B93 145 B8
Temple Balsall B93 129 B2
Chadwick Manor B93 129 A1
Chadwick Mews
Chadwick End B93 145 B6
Redditch B98 159 A7
Chadwick Rd B75 46 F5
Chadworth Ave B93 127 E3
Chaffcombe Rd B26 89 C7
Chaffinch Cl
Cannock WS12 2 B4
Sedgley DY3 39 C3
Chaffinch Dr
Birmingham B36 70 B7
Kidderminster DY10 116 F2
Chaffinch Rd DY9 81 D3
Chainmakers Cl WV14 40 D2
Chainshop Mus* DY2 62 B1
Chain Wlk B19 66 D7
Chalcot Dr WS12 2 A7
Chalcot Gr B20 54 E5
Chaldon Cl WV9 11 A1
Chale Gr B14 105 A3
Chalfield B79 20 D6
Chalfont Ave WS11 4 C7
Chalfont Cl
Bedworth CV12 78 A4
Coventry CV5 112 B4
Chalfont Ct WS11 4 C7
Chalfont Pl DY9 81 E2
Chalfont Rd B20 55 C1
Chalford Rd B23 56 C8
Chalford Way B90 106 C1
Chalgrove Ave B38 103 E1
Chalgrove Cres B91 107 B1
Challenge Bsns Pk CV1 113 D5
Challenge Cl CV1 165 C4
Challenge Way WV10 25 E5
Challenor Ave WV13 26 D1
Chalybeate Cl B45 101 F1
Chamberlain Cl
Cubbington CV32 157 E5
Oldbury B69 52 D2
Chamberlain Cres B90 106 A2
Chamberlain Ct
3 Birmingham,Hockley B18 66 C4
Birmingham,King's Heath B14 86 E1
Chamberlaine St CV12 78 B3
Chamberlain Ho B16 66 A1
Chamberlain Rd B13 105 A6
Chamberlain's Gn CV6 112 F7
Chamberlain's La WV4 38 E3
Chamberlain Sq B3 164 B2
Chamberlain Wlk
10 Coleshill B46 70 F7
1 Smethwick B66 65 B5
Champney DY10 116 E2
Chance Croft B68 84 B8
Chance Fields CV31 162 F6
Chancel Ct B91 107 C2
Chancel Ind Est
Darlaston WS10 41 D5
Kingswinford DY6 49 E1
Chancel Ind Est The WV1 26 A1
Chancel Ind Est WV13 27 B2
Chancellor's Cl B15 85 E8
Chancellors Cl CV4 132 D4
Chancel Way
Birmingham B6 55 F5
Halesowen B62 83 C6
Chancery Ct CV10 72 A7
Chancery Dr WS12 2 C7
Chancery La CV10 72 B7
Chancery Way DY5 61 F2
Chanders Rd CV34 155 D1
Chandler Dr WV4 38 D3
Chandler Ho B65 63 D4
Chandlers Cl
Birmingham B18 65 F5
Redditch B97 158 D7
Wolverhampton WV9 11 A1
Chandlers Dr B77 22 B5
Chandlers Keep WS8 16 A6
Chandlers Rd CV31 162 A2
Chandlers CV31 161 D7
Chandos Ave B13 86 F3
Chandos Ct 15 CV32 156 F1
Chandos Prim Sch B12 86 E8
Chandos St
Coventry CV2 114 A3
Nuneaton CV11 73 A4
Royal Leamington Spa CV32 156 F1
Change Brook Cl CV11 73 F8
Channel Way CV6 96 B6
Channon Dr DY5 81 D8
Chanston Ave B14 104 E4
Chanterelle Ct WV4 39 B4
Chanterelle Gdns WV4 39 B4
Chantrey Cres
Bilston WV14 40 F7
Birmingham B43 44 D4
Chantries The CV1 113 E5
Chantry Ave WS3 28 D8
Chantry Cl B47 125 A7
Chantry Ct B13 86 F3
Chantry Dr B62 84 A6
Chantry Heath Cres B93 128 C7
Chantry Ind Est B76 59 B7
Chantry Rd
Birmingham,Handsworth B21 65 F8
Birmingham,Moseley B13 86 E4
Stourbridge DY7 80 C7
Chantry The CV34 156 A1
Chapel Ash Island WV1 163 A3
Chapel Ash WV3 25 B2
Chapel Ave WS8 6 E2
Chapel Cl B64 83 B8
Chapel Ct
13 Royal Leamington Spa CV32 161 F8
4 Brierley Hill,Silver End DY5 61 D2
Astwood Bank B96 158 E1
Brierley Hill,Barrow Hill DY5 61 C7
Chapel Dr
Balsall Common CV7 130 B8
Brownhills WS8 6 E2
Mile Oak B78 20 C1
Wythall B47 124 F3
Chapel Farm Cl CV3 134 C6
Chapelfield Mews
Birmingham B45 121 F6
Stourbridge DY8 81 A4
Chapelfield Rd B45 122 A7
Chapel Fields Jun Sch B92 88 F3
Chapel Fields Rd B92 88 F2
Chapel Gn WV13 27 B2
Chapel House La B63 82 C6
Chapelhouse Rd B37 69 F1
Chapel House St 1 B12 66 F1
Chapel La
Barnacle CV7 97 B6
Beoley B98 154 F8
Birmingham B29 85 E2
Birmingham,Great Barr B43, WS9 44 A5
Kingswood B94 144 D7
Lichfield WS14 9 B6
Madeley Heath DY9 120 D7
Romsley B62 100 C6
Rowney Green B48 139 F4
Ryton-on-D CV8 135 B2
Walsall B43 43 F4
Wythall B47 124 E2
Chapel Mews B77 22 A5
Chapel Mill Apartments B62 83 C8
Chapelon B77 22 A2
Chapel Pl DY11 116 D6
Chapel Rd B96 158 E1
Chapel Row CV34 160 E7
Chapel Sq WS6 4 D3
Chapel St
5 Royal Leamington Spa CV31 162 A7
Astwood Bank B96 158 E1
Bedworth CV12 78 C3
Bilston WV14 40 F4
Birmingham B5 164 D3
Birmingham,Handsworth B21 65 D7
Brierley Hill,Barrow Hill DY5 61 C6

Chapel St *continued*
Brierley Hill,Quarry Bank DY5 61 F1
Brierley Hill,Silver End DY5 61 D2
Bromsgrove B60 137 A2
Brownhills WS8 6 E2
Burntwood WS7 6 E8
Cannock WS12 2 E1
Coventry CV1 165 B3
Dudley DY2 62 D4
Halesowen B63 83 A3
Kidderminster DY11 116 D6
Kingswinford DY6 60 B8
Norton Canes WS11 5 F5
Nuneaton CV11 73 C4
Redditch B97 153 D1
Chapel Street Prec 1 B60 137 A2
Chapel St
Stourbridge,Lye DY9 81 E5
Stourbridge,Wollaston DY8 81 A4
Stourbridge,Wordsley DY8 60 D3
Tipton DY4 51 E5
Walsall,Blakenall Heath WS3 28 D8
Walsall WS3 15 A3
Warwick CV34 160 E7
Wednesbury WS10 41 E3
West Bromwich B70 53 B5
West Hagley DY9 99 A5
Wolverhampton WV2 39 D7
Chapel View B67 64 F4
Chapel Wlk
Birmingham B30 104 A2
Bromsgrove B60 137 A2
Dudley DY3 50 C2
Chapelwood Gr B42 55 D5
Chaplain Rd WS12 2 E2
Chapman Cl CV31 162 E5
Chapman Ct CV34 161 C8
Chapman Rd B10 87 C8
Chapman's Hill B62 101 B1
Chapmans Pas B1 164 B1
Chapman St B70 53 B3
Chapter Ho B70 53 A5
Chard Rd CV3 134 D8
Charfield Cl B30 103 D7
Charford Fst Sch B60 150 F7
Charford Rd B60 150 F8
Charingworth Rd B92 89 C3
Charity Bick Way 7 B70 53 C2
Charity Rd CV7 95 A7
Charlbury Ave B37 69 F2
Charlbury Cres B26 88 F8
Charlbury Mews CV31 162 C6
Charlbury Twr 2 B5 86 E8
Charlecote Cl B98 154 D2
Charlecote Croft B90 126 C8
Charlecote Dr
Birmingham B23 56 E7
Dudley DY1 50 E3
Charlecote Gdns
Royal Leamington Spa CV31 162 D5
Sutton Coldfield B73 57 A8
Charlecote Rd CV6 95 A2
Charlecote Rise 1 WV13 40 F8
Charlecote Wlk CV11 78 F8
Charlecott Cl B13 105 D7
Charlemont Ave B71 53 E8
Charlemont Cl WS5 43 C6
Charlemont Cres B71 42 E1
Charlemont Cl WS12 2 D3
Charlemont Gdns WS5 43 C6
Charlemont Jun & Inf Sch B71 53 E8
Charlemont Rd
Walsall WS5 43 C6
West Bromwich B71 53 F8
Charles Ave
Essington WV11 12 F4
Rowley Regis B65 63 C4
Wolverhampton WV4 39 B5
Charles Burns Sch B13 86 E1
Charles Cl
Birmingham B8 67 D4
Cheslyn Hay WS6 4 D1
Charles Cres WS3 15 A5
Charles Ct
14 Royal Leamington Spa CV31 162 A6
1 Warwick,Emscote CV34 161 B8
8 Birmingham B13 87 B2
Sutton Coldfield B76 46 F3
Warwick CV34 160 C7
Charlesdale Dr WS9 30 B4
Charles Dr B7 67 B6
Charles Eaton Rd CV12 77 F3
Charles Edward Rd B26 88 D6
Charles Foster St WS10 41 C6
Charles Gardner Rd 6 CV31 161 F6
Charles Hayward Bglws WV4 39 D3
Charles Henry St B12 86 F8
Charles Holland St 2 WV13 27 B2
Charles Lakin Cl CV7 97 C5
Charles Lane Trust Homes The B28 106 A8
Charles Pearson Ct B66 65 B5
Charles Rd
Birmingham,Aston B6 56 A1

Charles Rd *continued*
Birmingham,Bordesley Green B9, B10 67 E1
Birmingham,Handsworth B20 55 C1
Brierley Hill DY5 62 B1
Halesowen B63 82 F4
Solihull B91 106 E2
Stourbridge DY8 80 E4
Tipton DY4 52 A7
Charles St
Coventry CV1 165 D4
Hinckley LE10 71 E1
Kidderminster DY10 116 F6
Nuneaton CV11 73 A5
Redditch B97 153 C1
Smethwick B66 65 C7
Walsall WS2 28 D2
Warwick CV34 161 A8
West Bromwich B70 52 E5
Willenhall WV13 27 C3
Charles Watson Ct 4 CV32 157 A2
Charles Wesley Ct WV3 39 A7
Charles Wlk B65 63 C5
Charlesworth Ave B90 127 B6
Charleville Rd B19 66 B7
Charlewood Rd CV6 95 B2
Charlock Gr WS11 2 C3
Charlotte Cl
Nuneaton CV10 72 C6
Tipton B69 52 A2
Charlotte Rd
Birmingham,Edgbaston B15 86 C7
Birmingham,Stirchley B30 104 A6
Wednesbury WS10 41 C2
Charlotte St
15 Dudley DY1 51 B1
Birmingham B3 164 A3
Royal Leamington Spa CV31 161 F6
Walsall WS1 29 A2
Charlton Dr B64 82 D7
Charlton Pl B8 67 D5
Charlton Rd B44 56 A8
Charlton St
4 Dudley DY1 51 B1
Brierley Hill DY5 61 A3
Charminster Ave B25 88 D8
Charminster Dr CV3 133 D4
Charnley Dr B75 32 E2
Charnwood Ave
Nuneaton CV10 72 E2
Sedgley DY3 39 D2
Charnwood Bsns Pk WV14 40 C5
Charnwood Cl
Birmingham B45 102 B3
Brierley Hill DY5 81 B8
Cannock WS12 2 C3
Darlaston WV14 41 B3
Hinckley LE10 71 E2
Lichfield WS13 3 C1
Charnwood Ct DY9 81 E2
Charnwood Ho WS13 3 B2
Charnwood Prim Sch WS13 3 C2
Charnwood Rd
Birmingham B42 54 F7
Hinckley LE10 71 D2
Walsall WS5 43 A4
Charnwood Way CV32 157 C3
Charter App CV34 160 D5
Charter Ave CV4 132 B7
Charter Cl WS11 5 E4
Charter Cres B64 83 B8
Charterfield Dr
Cannock WS12 2 C1
Kingswinford DY6 60 D8
Charterfields Sh Ctr DY6 60 D8
Charter Ho CV4 132 A7
Charterhouse Dr B91 107 C1
Charterhouse Rd CV1 113 E2
Charter Prim Sch (Harris Site) CV4 131 F7
Charter Prim Sch (Parkes Site) CV4 132 C8
Charter Rd DY4 41 C1
Charters Ave WV8 10 B1
Charter St DY5 61 E5
Charters The WS13 3 B1
Chartist Rd B8 67 D6
Chartley Cl
Dorridge B93 127 E3
Perton WV6 23 F4
Chartley Rd
Birmingham B23 56 D1
West Bromwich B71 53 D6
Chartway The WS3 15 B4
Chartwell Cl
Dudley DY1 51 B6
Nuneaton CV11 73 F1
Chartwell Ct B72 57 C8
Chartwell Dr
Cheswick Green B90 126 D5
Sutton Coldfield B74 31 D4
Wolverhampton WV10 11 E1
Chartwell Grange B64 83 A7
Chartwell B79 20 D7
Chase Acad WS11 4 E8
Chase Ave WS6 4 E3
Chase Cl CV11 73 E6
Chase Gr B24 57 D6
Chase La CV8 147 B7
Chaselands WS7 6 D7
Chase L Ctr WS11 1 D2
Chaseley Ave WS11 1 C2

Chaseley Croft WS11 1 C2
Chaseley Gdns WS7 7 C7
Chase Park Ind Est WS7 6 D7
Chase Rd
Brownhills WS8 7 A1
Burntwood WS7 7 B6
Dudley DY3,DY5 50 C1
Walsall WS3 28 A8
Chaseside Dr WS11 2 B3
Chaseside Ind Est WS11 2 B3
Chase Terrace Prim Sch WS7 6 F7
Chase Terrace Tech Coll WS7 7 A7
Chase The
Sutton Coldfield B76 57 D7
Wolverhampton WV6 25 B6
Chasetown Com Sch WS7 6 E5
Chasetown Ind Est WS7 6 E7
Chasetown Specialist Sports Coll WS7 6 E4
Chasetown Sta★ WS7 6 D5
Chase Vale WS7 6 E6
Chase View WV4 39 E2
Chasewater★ WS7 6 C4
Chasewater Country Pk★ WS7 6 C5
Chasewater Heaths Sta★ WS7 6 D6
Chasewater Rly★ WS11 6 B5
Chasewater Way WS11 5 F5
Chase Wlk WS12 1 C4
Chasewood Park Bsns Ctr WS12 2 E1
Chater Dr B76 47 A1
Chaters Cl DY4 51 E5
Chatham Cl CV3 134 C8
Chatham Rd B31 103 A3
Chatillon Cl CV34 161 E3
Chatsworth Ave B43 43 C1
Chatsworth Cl
Cheswick Green B90 126 E5
Hinckley LE10 75 F6
Sutton Coldfield B72 57 D7
Willenhall WV12 27 B5
Chatsworth Cres WS4 29 D7
Chatsworth Dr
Cannock WS11 2 A4
Nuneaton CV11 73 F2
Chatsworth Gdns
Royal Leamington Spa CV31 162 D6
Wolverhampton WV6 24 A7
Chatsworth Gr CV8 148 C5
Chatsworth Rd B62 83 A7
Chatsworth Rise CV3 133 E6
Chatsworth B79 20 C7
Chattaway Dr CV7 130 B6
Chattaway St B7 67 C7
Chatterton Ave WS13 8 E6
Chatterton Wlk 4 DY10 117 B6
Chattle Hill B46 59 E2
Chattock Ave B91 107 E3
Chattock Cl B36 68 E7
Chatwell Gr B29 85 B2
Chatwin Pl WV14 40 E3
Chatwin St B66 64 F7
Chatwins Wharf DY4 51 F5
Chaucer Ave
Dudley DY3 50 A5
Tipton DY4 52 B8
Willenhall WV12 27 E8
Chaucer Cl
Birmingham B23 56 B3
Dudley WV14 51 D8
Lichfield WS14 9 B6
Stourbridge DY8 81 A8
Tamworth B79 21 A6
Chaucer Cres DY10 117 C5
Chaucer Dr CV10 72 A4
Chaucer Gr B27 88 B2
Chaucer Ho B63 82 B5
Chaucer Rd
Bromsgrove B60 151 B8
Walsall WS3 28 E8
Chauntry Pl CV1 165 C3
Chauson Gr B91 127 A8
Chavasse Rd B72 46 D3
Chawnhill Cl DY9 81 C3
Chawn Hill DY9 81 C3
Chawn Park Dr DY9 81 C3
Chaynes Gr B33 69 D2
Chaytor Dr CV10 72 B6
Cheadle Cl CV2 96 A4
Cheadle Dr B23 56 D8
Cheam Cl CV6 96 A1
Cheam Gdns WV6 24 E8
Cheapside
3 Willenhall WV13 27 A1
Birmingham B5,B12 164 D1
Cheapside Ind Est 3 B12 66 F1
Cheapside WV1 163 B3
Cheatham St B7 67 C6
Cheatle Ct B77 35 D5
Checketts St WS2 28 C2
Checkley Cl B90 106 B4
Checkley Croft B76 57 F8
Cheddar Rd B12 86 E6
Chedworth Cl
Birmingham B29 103 B6
Redditch B98 154 C5
Cheedon Cl B93 127 E2
Cheetah Rd CV1 165 C1
Chelford Cres DY6 61 A3
Chells Gr B13 105 B5
Chelmar Cl B36 69 F8
Chelmar Dr DY5 61 A6
Chelmarsh Ave WV3 38 B8

Chelmarsh Cl B98 154 C7
Chelmarsh CV6 113 C6
Chelmorton Rd B42 55 D7
Chelmscote Rd B92 88 F1
Chelmsley Ave B46 70 F6
Chelmsley Circ B37 70 B2
Chelmsley Gr B33 69 E3
Chelmsley La B37 90 A8
Chelmsley Rd B37 70 C2
Chelmsley Wood Ind Est B37 70 B4
Chelney Wlk CV3 115 A1
Chelsea B37 69 F5
Chelsea Cl
Birmingham B32 84 F4
Nuneaton CV11 73 F7
Chelsea Ct 6 B29 103 B7
Chelsea Dr B74 31 F4
Chelsea Trad Est B7 67 A6
Chelsea Way DY6 60 C6
Chelsey Rd CV2 114 E8
Chelston Dr WV6 24 E4
Chelston Rd B31 102 E2
Cheltenham Ave B61 121 B1
Cheltenham Cl
Bedworth CV12 78 B4
Wolverhampton WV6 25 B5
Cheltenham Croft CV2 114 F7
Cheltenham Dr
Birmingham B36 68 D8
Kingswinford DY6 60 B6
Chelthorn Way B91 107 C2
Cheltondale 3 B90 126 C8
Cheltondale Rd B91 106 F6
Chelveston Cres B91 107 B1
Chelveston Rd CV6 112 E5
Chelwood Gdns WV14 40 B5
Chelwood Gr CV2 96 F1
Chelworth Rd B38 104 B2
Chem Rd WV14 40 C5
Chenet Way WS11 1 E2
Chenies Cl CV5 112 B3
Cheniston Rd WV12 27 C7
Chepstow Cl
Coventry CV3 134 C5
Perton WV6 23 F4
Chepstow Dr B61 121 B1
Chepstow Gr B45 122 B6
Chepstow Rd
Walsall WS3 13 F1
Wolverhampton WV10 11 D5
Chepstow Villas 5 B12 87 B5
Chepstow Way WS3 13 F1
Chequerfield Dr WV4 39 A6
Chequers Ave WV5 38 A1
Chequers Ct WS11 6 A5
Chequer St CV12 79 C2
Chequers The 3 WS13 9 C8
Chequer St WV3 39 A6
Cherhill Covert 7 B14 104 C2
Cherington Cl B98 154 F1
Cherington Rd B29 104 A8
Cheriton Cl CV5 112 D4
Cheriton Gr WV6 23 E3
Cheriton Wlk B23 56 B3
Cherrington Cl B31 102 F7
Cherrington Dr WS6 4 F4
Cherrington Gdns
Stourbridge DY9 99 C7
Wolverhampton WV6 24 B2
Cherrington Way B91 107 B1
Cherry Bank WS12 2 C6
Cherry Blossom Gr CV31 162 B2
Cherrybrook Way CV2 96 C1
Cherry Cl
Burntwood WS7 6 F6
Coventry CV6 95 D2
Cherry Cres
Birmingham B24 56 F3
Bromsgrove B61 136 E2
Cherrydale Ct DY1 50 F2
Cherry Dr
1 Cradley Heath B64 62 F1
Birmingham B9 67 B1
Cherry Gn DY1 50 F4
Cherry Gr
Barnt Green B45 138 C8
Smethwick B66 65 C5
Stourbridge DY8 80 E4
Wolverhampton WV11 26 C7
Cherry Hill Ave B45 138 C8
Cherry Hill Dr B45 138 C8
Cherry Hill Rd B45 138 C8
Cherry Hill Wlk DY1 62 A8
Cherry La
Himley DY3 49 C3
Sutton Coldfield B73 57 A7
Wednesbury WS10 42 A2
Cherry Lea B34 69 B6
Cherryl Ho 3 B74 31 E3
Cherry Oak Sch B29 85 D2
Cherry Orchard Ave B63 82 F5
Cherry Orchard Cres B63 82 F6
Cherry Orchard Dr B61 136 E3
Cherry Orchard Prim Sch B20 55 A3
Cherry Orchard Rd B20 55 A4
Cherry Orch
Cradley Heath B64 62 F1
Kenilworth CV8 148 A5
Kidderminster DY10 116 F6
Lichfield WS14 9 C7
Cherry Pit La B98 141 A1
Cherry Rd DY4 51 F7
Cherry St
Birmingham B2 164 C2
Halesowen B63 82 F5
Stourbridge DY8 80 E4

Cherry St *continued*
Tamworth B79 21 B5
Warwick CV34 160 F7
Wolverhampton WV3 25 B1
Cherry Tree Ave
Nuneaton CV10 72 E6
Walsall WS5 43 A5
Cherry Tree Croft 5 B27 88 C5
Cherrytree Ct DY9 81 E3
Cherry Tree Gdns WV8 10 B3
Cherry Tree La
Codsall WV8 10 B3
Halesowen B63 82 D1
Cherry Tree Rd
Huntington WS12 1 D8
Kingswinford DY6 60 E8
Norton Canes WS11 6 B5
Cherry Tree Wlk
Redditch B97 153 B4
Tamworth B79 21 A8
Cherry Way CV8 148 A5
Cherry Wlk B47 125 B5
Cherrywood Cl WV14 40 C1
Cherrywood Cres 3 B91 127 C8
Cherrywood Ct B92 89 A2
Cherrywood Gn WV14 40 D8
Cherrywood Gr CV5 111 F5
Cherrywood Ind Est B9 67 D3
Cherrywood Rd
Birmingham B9 67 E2
Sutton Coldfield B74 30 D1
Sutton Coldfield B74 44 D8
Cherrywood Way B74 31 D4
Chervil Cl B42 55 C7
Chervil Rise WV10 25 F3
Cherwell Cl LE10 75 A8
Cherwell Ct B73 46 B5
Cherwell Dr
Birmingham B36 69 F8
Brownhills WS8 6 C2
Cherwell Gdns 7 B6 66 D8
Cherwell B77 21 D1
Chesford Cres
Coventry CV6 96 B2
Warwick CV34 156 B1
Chesham St CV31 162 B7
Cheshire Ave B90 106 A2
Cheshire Cl
Burntwood WS7 7 F8
Stourbridge DY8 80 D8
Cheshire Gr
Kidderminster DY11 116 A7
Perton WV6 23 E4
Cheshire Ho 8 B66 65 B5
Cheshire Rd
Birmingham B6 56 A2
Smethwick B67 65 A4
Willenhall WS2 27 F2
Chesholme Rd CV6 95 B2
Cheshunt Ho 3 B37 70 B2
Cheshunt Sch CV1 165 B1
Chesils The CV3 133 D6
Cheslyn Dr WS6 4 D2
Cheslyn Gr B14 105 A3
Cheslyn Hay High Sch WS6 4 C3
Cheslyn Hay Prim Sch WS6 4 C3
Chessetts Gr B13 105 A6
Chessetts Wood Rd B94 144 C7
Chessher St LE10 71 C1
Chester Ave WV6 24 F7
Chester Cl
Birmingham B37 70 A2
Cannock WS11 2 B1
Lichfield WS13 3 C3
Willenhall WV13 27 D2
Chester Ct
4 Birmingham,Chelmsley Wood B37 70 D2
5 Birmingham,Weoley Castle B29 103 B7
Birmingham,Chester Road B73 57 A7
Chesterfield Cl B31 103 B2
Chesterfield Ct
Birmingham B38 103 E4
Brownhills WS9 15 F4
Chesterfield Rd WS14 9 A5
Chestergate Croft B24 57 D4
Chester Gdns B73 45 E1
Chester Hayes Ct B24 57 C5
Chester Pl WS2 28 B1
Chester Rd
Aldridge B74 30 E4
Birmingham,Castle Bromwich B36 69 E7
Birmingham,Chelmsley Wood B37 90 F8
Cradley Heath B64 82 C8
Dudley DY2 62 D2
Hampton-in-A B46,B92,CV7 91 B5
Chester Rd N
Kidderminster DY10 117 A7
Sutton Coldfield B73 45 B4
Sutton Coldfield B74 30 F2
Chester Rd S DY10 116 F4
Chester Rd
Stonnall WS9 16 D3
Sutton Coldfield B23,B24,B35, B73 57 E4
West Bromwich B71 42 B1
Chester Rise B68 84 B8
Chester Road N WS8 6 D1
Chester Road Sta B73 57 A7
Chester St
Birmingham B6 67 A6
Coventry CV1 113 B3

Chester St *continued*
Wolverhampton WV6 ...... 25 B4
Chesterton Ave B12 ...... 87 B5
Chesterton Cl
Redditch B97 .... 158 D4
Solihull B91 .... 106 E5
Chesterton Ct B13 .... 86 F1
Chesterton Dr
Nuneaton CV10 .... 72 A5
Royal Leamington Spa
CV31 .... 162 C5
Chesterton Rd
Birmingham B12 .... 87 B5
Coventry CV6 .... 113 A7
Wolverhampton WV10 ..... 26 A8
Chesterton Way B79 ..... 21 A7
Chesterwood Gdns B20 .. 55 D2
Chesterwood B47 .... 125 A6
Chesterwood Rd B13 .... 104 F6
Chester Wood WS9 ...... 30 F2
Chestnut Ave
Dudley DY1 .... 51 C3
Kenilworth CV8 .... 147 F3
Tamworth B79 .... 21 B7
Tipton DY4 .... 51 F7
Chestnut Cl
Birmingham B27 .... 88 C4
Cannock WS11 .... 2 C2
Solihull B92 .... 106 D8
Stourbridge DY8 .... 80 D3
Sutton Coldfield B74 ...... 31 A3
Chestnut Cres CV10 ...... 72 E6
Chestnut Ct
Birmingham B36 .... 69 E7
Burntwood WS7 .... 6 F4
Coventry CV3 .... 134 B8
Kidderminster DY11 ..... 116 B8
Royal Leamington Spa
CV34 .... 161 E2
Chestnut Dr
Birmingham,Buckland End
B36 .... 69 B7
Birmingham,Erdington B24 . 57 C4
Birmingham,Rednal B45 .. 122 D4
Cheslyn Hay WS6 .... 4 D3
Great Wyrley WS6 .... 4 F3
Nuneaton CV11 .... 73 E3
Shenstone WS14 .... 17 F5
Walsall WS4 .... 29 B8
West Hagley DY9 .... 98 F4
Wombourne WV5 .... 49 A5
Chestnut Gr
4 Birmingham B17 .... 85 D5
Coventry CV4 .... 112 A2
Kidderminster DY11 ..... 116 B8
Kingswinford DY6 .... 60 F6
Tamworth B77 .... 21 C3
Wolverhampton WV11 ..... 26 C7
Chestnut Pl
Birmingham B14 .... 104 E8
Walsall WS3 .... 28 D6
Chestnut Rd
Astwood Bank B96 ...... 158 E1
Bedworth CV12 .... 78 D4
Birmingham,Brandhall B68 . 84 C7
Birmingham,Showell Green
B13 .... 87 A4
Bromsgrove B61 .... 136 F4
Walsall WS3 .... 28 E6
Wednesbury WS10 .... 42 A2
Chestnuts Ave B26 .... 89 B7
Chestnut Sq CV32 .... 157 B2
Chestnuts The
Bedworth CV12 .... 77 E2
Kidderminster DY11 ..... 116 C3
Wolverhampton WV11 ..... 26 B6
Chestnut Tree Ave CV4 .. 112 A2
Chestnut Way WV3 .... 38 D8
Chestnut Wlk 2 B37 ...... 70 B2
Chestom Rd WV14 .... 40 B5
Cheston Ind Est B7 ...... 67 B7
Cheston Rd B7 .... 67 B6
Cheswell Cl WV6 .... 24 B2
Cheswick Cl
Coventry CV6 .... 114 A7
Willenhall WV13 .... 40 F8
Cheswick Green Prim Sch
B90 .... 126 E4
Cheswick Way B90 ...... 126 D4
Cheswood Dr B76 .... 58 B6
Chesworth Rd B60 ...... 137 B1
Chetland Croft B92 ..... 107 F7
Chettle Rd WV14 .... 40 F3
Chetton Ave CV6 .... 113 C6
Chetton Gn WV10 .... 11 B3
Chetwode Cl CV5 .... 112 B4
Chetwood Cl WV6 .... 25 A5
Chetwynd Cl WS2 .... 27 D3
Chetwynd Dr CV11 .... 79 B7
Chetwynd Gdns WS11 ...... 1 D3
Chetwynd Jun Sch CV11 .. 79 A7
Chetwynd Rd
Birmingham B8 .... 68 B5
Wolverhampton WV2 ...... 39 B6
Cheveley Ave B45 .... 122 B7
Chevening Cl DY3 .... 50 E7
Cheveral Ave CV6 .... 113 B6
Cheveral Rd CV12 .... 78 A3
Cheverel Pl CV11 .... 73 B2
Cheverel St CV11 .... 73 B3
Cheveridge Cl B91 ...... 107 A2
Cheverton Rd B31 ...... 102 E4
Cheviot Cl CV10 .... 72 B3
Cheviot Ct B75 .... 32 A4
Cheviot Rd
Stourbridge DY8 .... 81 A6
Wolverhampton WV2 ...... 39 F7
Cheviot Rise
Cannock WS12 .... 2 C5
Royal Leamington Spa
CV32 .... 157 C3
Cheviot B77 .... 22 C1
Cheviot The CV4 .... 132 D6
Cheviot Way B63 .... 82 D2
Cheylesmore Cl B73 ..... 46 B4
Cheylesmore CV1 .... 165 B2
Cheyne Ct 3 B17 .... 85 D5
Cheyne Gdns B28 .... 105 E3
Cheyne Pl B17 .... 85 D5
Cheyne Wlk DY5 .... 81 C7
Cheyney Cl WV6 .... 25 A5
Chichester Ave DY2 ...... 62 D5
Chichester Cl CV11 ...... 74 A7
Chichester Ct B73 .... 46 B5
Chichester Dr
Birmingham B32 .... 84 A5
Cannock WS12 .... 2 C1
Chichester Gr B37 .... 70 B1
Chideock Hill CV3 ...... 133 A6
Chiel Cl CV5 .... 111 F4
Chigwell Cl B35 .... 58 A3
Chilcote Cl B28 .... 105 F4
Chilcote Prim Sch B28 .. 105 F4
Childs Ave WV14 .... 40 A2
Childs Oak Cl CV7 ...... 130 A6
Chilgrove Gdns WV6 ..... 24 C5
Chilham Dr B37 .... 70 C2
Chillaton Rd CV6 .... 95 B2
Chillenden Ct WV13 ...... 27 C2
Chillingham B77 .... 35 C7
Chillinghome Rd B36 .... 68 D8
Chillinghome Twr B36 .... 57 F1
Chillington Cl WS6 .... 4 F1
Chillington Dr
Codsall WV8 .... 10 A4
Dudley DY1 .... 50 F3
Chillington Fields WV1 ... 26 A1
Chillington Ho WV6 ...... 24 E5
Chillington Pl WV14 ...... 40 C5
Chillington Rd DY4 .... 41 C1
Chillington St WV1 .... 25 F1
Chillington Wlk B65 ..... 63 D3
Chillington Works Ind Est
WV1 .... 25 F1
Chiltern Cl
Cheslyn Hay WS6 .... 4 D1
Dudley DY3 .... 50 D3
Halesowen B63 .... 82 D1
Chiltern Ct
2 Coventry CV6 .... 113 A5
Sutton Coldfield B75 ...... 32 A4
Chiltern Dr WV13 .... 26 D1
Chiltern Ho
Coventry CV5 .... 111 D4
Redditch B98 .... 154 E1
Chiltern Leys 2 CV6 .... 113 A4
Chiltern Rd
Stourbridge DY8 .... 81 B6
Tamworth B77 .... 22 C1
Chilterns The
Coventry CV5 .... 112 B4
Oldbury B69 .... 63 E5
Chilton Ct B23 .... 56 C2
Chilton Rd B14 .... 105 D4
Chilvers Coton Com Inf Sch
CV11 .... 73 B3
Chilvers Coton Craft Ctr
CV11 .... 73 C2
Chilvers Ct CV11 .... 73 C3
Chilvers Gr B37 .... 69 F5
Chilwell Cl B91 .... 107 B1
Chilwell Croft B19 .... 66 E6
Chilworth Ave WV11 ..... 26 F7
Chilworth Cl
4 Birmingham B6 .... 66 F6
Nuneaton CV11 .... 78 E8
Chimes Cl B33 .... 69 E1
Chimney Rd DY4 .... 52 D6
Chines The CV10 .... 73 D7
Chingford Cl DY8 .... 60 C4
Chingford Rd
Birmingham B44 .... 56 A8
Coventry CV6 .... 96 A4
Chinley Gr B44 .... 45 C1
Chinn Brook Ho B14 ..... 105 B4
Chinn Brook Rd B13 .... 105 C5
Chip Cl B38 .... 103 D2
Chipperfield Rd B36 ..... 68 E8
Chipstead Rd B23 .... 56 E7
Chipstone Cl B91 .... 107 C1
Chirbury Gr B31 .... 103 B1
Chirk Cl DY10 .... 116 E2
Chirton Gr B14 .... 104 D6
Chiseldon Croft B14 .... 105 A3
Chisholm Gr B27 .... 106 C8
Chiswell Rd B18 .... 65 E4
Chiswick Ct 1 B23 .... 56 E2
Chiswick Ho 2 B15 .... 86 C8
Chiswick Wlk B37 .... 70 E2
Chivenor Ho B35 .... 58 A2
Chivenor Jun & Inf Sch
B35 .... 58 A2
Chivington Cl B90 ...... 127 B6
Chorley Ave B34 .... 68 F6
Chorley Gdns WV14 ...... 40 B5
Chorley Way CV6 .... 113 C6
Christ Church CE Inf Sch
Wolverhampton,Dunstall Hill
WV6 .... 25 B4
Wolverhampton WV6 ...... 24 B3
Christ Church CE Jun Sch
WV6 .... 24 C4
Christ Church CE Prim Sch
Birmingham B11 .... 87 B7
Dudley WV14 .... 40 D1
Christ Church CE Prim Sch
continued
Lichfield WS13 .... 8 F7
Oldbury B69 .... 64 A8
Walsall WS3 .... 28 D7
Christchurch Cl
Birmingham B15 .... 85 E8
Nuneaton CV10 .... 72 F1
Christ Church Gdns WS13 .. 8 F7
Christ Church Gr WS1 .... 43 A7
Christchurch La WS13 ...... 8 F7
Christchurch Rd CV6 .... 113 A5
Christina Ct 5 B71 ...... 53 D4
Christine Cl DY4 .... 41 C2
Christine Ledger Sq 9
CV31 .... 162 A6
Christopher Cadbury Reserve
The★ B61 .... 150 B3
Christopher Hooke Ho
CV6 .... 113 E8
Christopher Rd
Birmingham B29 .... 85 C2
Halesowen B62 .... 83 E3
Wolverhampton WV2 ..... 163 D1
Christopher Wlk WS13 .... 3 A3
Christ the King RC Inf Sch
CV6 .... 112 F6
Christ the King RC Jun Sch
CV6 .... 112 F7
Christ The King RC Prim Sch
B44 .... 56 A8
Chubb St WV1 .... 163 C3
Chub B77 .... 35 D7
Chuckery Prim Sch WS1 .. 29 A1
Chuckery Rd WS1 .... 29 A1
Chudleigh Gr B43 .... 54 D8
Chudleigh Rd
Birmingham B23 .... 56 E4
Coventry CV2 .... 114 E7
Churchacre B23 .... 56 C8
Church Ave
Birmingham,Handsworth
B20 .... 55 C1
Birmingham,Moseley B13 .. 86 F3
Clent DY9 .... 99 F3
Stourbridge DY8 .... 81 A7
Water Orton B46 .... 59 B3
Churchbridge B69 .... 63 F6
Churchbridge Pk WS11 ..... 4 E5
Church Cl
Birmingham B37 .... 70 A6
Drayton Bassett B78 ...... 34 E5
Hartshill CV10 .... 72 B8
Hinckley LE10 .... 76 A5
Ryton-on-D CV8 .... 135 B2
Shenstone WS14 .... 18 A5
Whitnash CV31 .... 162 B4
Wood End CV9 .... 36 C1
Wythall B47 .... 124 F3
Church Cres WV11 .... 12 F3
Church Croft
Birmingham B17 .... 85 B4
Halesowen B63 .... 83 A4
Church Cross View DY1 .. 61 D8
Church Ct
3 Cradley Heath B64 ..... 62 E1
Astwood Bank B96 ...... 158 E2
Coventry CV6 .... 94 F1
Stourbridge DY8 .... 81 A5
Walsall WS1 .... 28 F1
Churchdale Cl CV10 ...... 72 C4
Churchdale Rd B44 .... 44 D3
Church Down Cl B97 .... 158 D6
Churchdown Ct B23 ...... 56 C2
Church Dr
Birmingham B30 .... 104 B7
Hopwas B78 .... 20 B7
Kenilworth CV8 .... 147 F5
Church End CV31 .... 162 E6
Church Farm Barn & Cotts
DY10 .... 98 B3
Churchfield Ave DY4 ..... 51 F8
Churchfield Cl B7 .... 67 C6
Churchfield Ind Est DY2 .. 62 C8
Churchfield Rd WV10 .... 25 B8
Churchfields
Birmingham B43 .... 44 D4
Bromsgrove B61 .... 136 F3
Churchfields Bsns Pk
DY10 .... 116 E7
Churchfields Cl B61 ..... 136 F3
Churchfields Gdns B61 .. 136 F3
Churchfields DY10 .... 116 E7
Churchfields Rd
Bromsgrove B61 .... 136 F3
Wednesbury WS10 .... 42 A4
Churchfield St DY2 .... 62 C8
Church Gdns
Smethwick B67 .... 65 A4
Wolverhampton WV10 ..... 26 A4
Church Gn
Bilston WV14 .... 40 D8
Birmingham B20 .... 55 A2
Church Gn E B98 .... 153 E4
Church Gn W B97 .... 153 E4
Church Gr B13 .... 105 C5
Church Hill
6 Wednesbury WS10 ..... 41 F3
8 Walsall WS1 .... 28 F1
Belbroughton DY9 .... 119 D6
Beoley B98 .... 154 D8
Birmingham,Northfield
B31 .... 103 B3
Brierley Hill DY5 .... 61 D2
Cannock WS12 .... 2 D4
Church Hill Cl B91 ...... 107 C2
Church Hill Ct 1 WS10 ... 41 F3
Church Hill CV32 .... 157 E5
Church Hill Dr WV6 ...... 24 E5
Church Hill B32 .... 102 B6
Church Hill Mid Sch
B98 .... 154 D6
Church Hill Rd
Birmingham B20 .... 55 C1
Solihull B91 .... 107 C3
Wolverhampton WV6 ...... 24 D5
Church Hill CV32 .... 161 E8
Church Hill St B67 .... 64 F6
Church Hill Way B98 .... 154 D6
Church Hill WV4 .... 38 E4
Church Ho
Brierley Hill DY5 .... 61 C2
Walsall WS2 .... 42 C7
Churchill Ave
Coventry CV6 .... 113 E8
Kenilworth CV8 .... 148 A6
Churchill Cl B69 .... 52 C2
Churchill Dr
Rowley Regis B65 .... 63 B2
Stourbridge DY8 .... 81 A7
Churchill Gdns DY3 ...... 50 C7
Churchill Ho 11 CV32 .... 161 F8
Churchill La DY10 .... 98 B3
Churchill Par B75 .... 47 A5
Churchill Pl B33 .... 69 B1
Churchill Rd
Birmingham B9 .... 67 F3
Halesowen B63 .... 82 F2
Shenstone WS14 .... 18 A5
Sutton Coldfield,Falcon Lodge
B75 .... 47 A5
Sutton Coldfield,New Oscott
B73 .... 45 C3
Upper Catshill B61 ...... 121 A1
Walsall WS2 .... 27 E3
Churchill Sh Ctr 3 DY2 .. 51 D1
Churchill Wlk 5 DY4 ..... 52 A8
Church La
Ash Green CV7 .... 95 E7
Aston Flamville LE10 ...... 76 F1
Berkswell CV7 .... 110 C3
Bickenhill B92 .... 90 E2
Birmingham,Aston B6 ..... 67 A8
Birmingham,Handsworth
B20 .... 55 A2
Birmingham,Kitt's Green
B33 .... 69 A3
Bromsgrove B61 .... 136 F2
Corley CV7 .... 94 B7
Coventry,Middle Stoke
CV2 .... 114 B3
Coventry,Upper Eastern Green
CV5 .... 111 C5
Cubbington CV32 .... 157 E5
Curdworth B76 .... 59 B6
Halesowen B63 .... 83 B4
Hammerwich WS7 .... 7 D3
Lapworth B94 .... 143 E3
Leek Wootton CV35 ...... 155 F6
Meriden CV7 .... 110 E8
Middleton B78 .... 34 C1
Church Lane Ind Est B71 . 53 C6
Church La
Nuneaton CV10 .... 73 C7
Radford Semele CV31 .... 162 E6
Royal Leamington Spa
CV32 .... 157 A3
Shuttington B79 .... 22 E7
Stoneleigh CV8 .... 149 C6
Stonnall WS9 .... 16 E4
Tamworth B79 .... 21 B5
Trysull WV5 .... 37 B2
West Bromwich B71 ...... 53 C6
Whitnash CV31 .... 162 B4
Wishaw B76 .... 48 A2
Wolverhampton WV2 ..... 163 B2
Church Mews
Tipton DY4 .... 51 E8
Walsall WS3 .... 28 B8
Church Moat Way 1 WS3 28 B8
Church of the Ascension CE
Prim Sch DY6 .... 60 C8
Churchover Cl B76 .... 57 D6
Church Park Cl CV6 ...... 94 F1
Church Pl
Birmingham B12 .... 86 F5
Walsall WS3 .... 28 D8
Church Rd
Astwood Bank B96 ...... 158 E2
Baginton CV8 .... 133 F2
Belbroughton DY9 .... 119 D6
Birmingham,Aston B6 ..... 67 B7
Birmingham,Edgbaston B15 86 A7
Birmingham,Erdington B24 . 57 A4
Birmingham,Moseley B13 .. 87 A3
Birmingham,Northfield
B31 .... 103 A4
Birmingham,Perry Barr B42 55 D5
Birmingham,Sheldon B26 .. 89 C6
Birmingham,South Yardley
B25 .... 88 E8
Birmingham,Stechford B33 . 68 F2
Bromsgrove B61 .... 136 F2
Brownhills WS8 .... 15 F7
Burntwood WS7 .... 7 D7
Catshill B61 .... 136 F8
Coseley,Daisy Bank WV14 .. 40 D1
Dodford B61 .... 136 A7
Dudley,Netherton DY2 ..... 62 C4
Halesowen B63 .... 82 C7
Hartshill CV10 .... 72 B8
Huntington WS11 .... 1 A2
Norton Canes WS11 .... 5 E4
Nuneaton,Stockingford
CV10 .... 72 C3
Perton WV6 .... 23 E4
Church Rd *continued*
Redditch,St George's B97 . 153 E4
Redditch,Webheath B97 .. 152 F2
Rowley Regis B65 .... 63 C3
Ryton-on-D CV8 .... 135 B2
Shenstone WS14 .... 17 F5
Shilton CV7 .... 97 E5
Smethwick B67 .... 65 A4
Solihull B90 .... 106 B2
Stonnall WS9 .... 16 E3
Stourbridge DY8 .... 60 E2
Stourbridge,Lye DY9 ...... 81 E5
Stourbridge,Old Swinford
DY8 .... 81 B3
Sutton Coldfield B73 ...... 56 F8
Sutton Coldfield,Maney B72,
B73 .... 46 B3
Tamworth B77 .... 35 C4
Walsall WS3 .... 15 A3
Willenhall WV12 .... 27 D6
Wolverhampton,Oxbarn
WV3 .... 38 F7
Wolverhampton,Oxley
WV10 .... 11 C1
Wolverhampton,Tettenhall Wood
WV6 .... 24 B3
Wolverhampton,Tettenhall
WV6 .... 24 E5
Wombourne WV5 .... 49 B7
Church Row Cotts DY9 ... 99 F3
Church Row B78 .... 34 B1
Churchside Way WS9 .... 16 B2
Church Sq 4 B69 .... 64 A7
Church St
Bilston WV14 .... 40 D5
Birmingham B3 .... 164 B3
Birmingham,Lozells B19 ... 66 C7
Brierley Hill,Barrow Hill
DY5 .... 61 D7
Brierley Hill,Quarry Bank
DY5 .... 61 F1
Brierley Hill,Silver End DY5 . 61 C2
Bromsgrove B61 .... 136 F2
Brownhills WS8 .... 15 E6
Bulkington CV12 .... 79 C2
Burntwood WS7 .... 6 E5
Cannock,Bridgtown WS11 ... 4 D6
Cannock,Chadsmoor WS11 .. 2 A4
Cannock WS11 .... 1 E1
Coventry CV1 .... 165 C4
Cradley Heath B64 .... 62 E1
Darlaston,Woods Bank
WS10 .... 41 C4
Darlaston WS10 .... 41 D6
Dudley,Gornalwood DY3 ... 50 D3
Dudley,Kate's Hill DY2 ..... 62 C8
Halesowen B62 .... 63 D1
Hinckley LE10 .... 76 A5
Kidderminster DY10 ..... 116 E6
Lichfield WS13,WS14 .... 9 C8
Nuneaton CV11 .... 73 C4
Oldbury B69 .... 64 A8
Churchstone Cl B61 ..... 136 F8
Church St
Royal Leamington Spa
CV31 .... 162 A7
Stourbridge DY8 .... 81 A5
Studley B80 .... 159 E3
Tamworth B79 .... 21 B5
Tipton DY4 .... 52 A2
Walsall,Blakenall Green
WS3 .... 28 B8
Walsall WS1 .... 28 F1
Warwick CV34 .... 160 E6
Wednesfield WV11 .... 26 C5
West Bromwich B70 ...... 53 C4
West Hagley DY9 .... 99 A5
Willenhall WV13 .... 27 B2
Wolverhampton,Heath Town
WV10 .... 26 A4
Wolverhampton WV2 ..... 163 B2
Church Terr
1 Royal Leamington Spa
CV31 .... 162 A7
Cubbington CV32 .... 157 E5
Sutton Coldfield B75 ...... 32 C3
Church Vale B20 .... 55 B1
Church Vale Mews B71 ... 53 D5
Church Vale
Norton Canes WS11 .... 5 E4
West Bromwich B71 ...... 53 D5
Church View
Aldridge WS9 .... 30 B6
Birmingham B11 .... 87 C6
Brownhills WS9 .... 15 F3
Church View Cl WS3 ..... 28 D8
Church View Dr B64 ...... 62 F1
Church View
Dudley DY3 .... 50 D3
Tamworth B77 .... 35 F7
Wythall B47 .... 124 E2
Churchward Cl DY8 .... 81 B6
Churchward Gr WV5 ...... 49 A8
Church Way
Bedworth CV12 .... 78 B2
Walsall WS4 .... 15 C2
Churchwell Ct
Halesowen B63 .... 83 B2
Wombourne WV5 .... 49 A6
Churchwell Gdns B71 .... 53 E6
Church Wlk
1 Royal Leamington Spa
CV31 .... 161 F7
Allesley CV5 .... 112 C6
Birmingham B8 .... 68 A6

Church Wlk continued
Hinckley LE10 75 D8
Kidderminster DY11 116 C6
Rowley Regis B65 63 C4
Wolverhampton,Oxbarn WV3 38 F7
Wolverhampton,Tettenhall WV6 24 E5
Churchyard Rd DY4 52 B5
Churnet Gr WV6 23 F4
Churn Hill Rd WS9 30 B4
Churns Hill La DY3 49 B3
Churston Cl WS3 14 A3
Chylds Ct CV5 112 A5
Cicero App CV34 161 E2
Cider Ave DY5 81 E8
Cinder Bank DY2 62 C6
Cinder Bank Island DY2 62 B7
Cinder Rd
Burntwood WS7 6 E7
Dudley DY3 50 B2
Cinder Way 2 WS10 41 E3
Cinquefoil Leasow 5 DY4 52 C6
Circle The
Birmingham B17 85 C6
Nuneaton CV10 72 F4
Circuit Cl WV13 27 B3
Circular Rd B27 88 C2
Circus Ave B37 70 C2
Cirencester Cl B60 137 B2
City Arc
1 Birmingham B2 164 C2
1 Lichfield WS13 9 B7
Coventry CV1 165 B2
City Coll
Birmingham B33 89 B8
Birmingham,Sparkbrook B11 87 A7
Birmingham,Sparkhill B11 87 D5
City Coll Birmingham (St George's Sixth Form Ctr) B19 164 B5
City Coll Coventry (Butts Ctr) CV1 113 A2
City Coll Coventry (Maxwell Ctr) CV1 113 B1
City College Coventry (Tile Hill Ctr) CV4 111 F1
City Coll (Handsworth Campus) B21 65 F8
City Est B64 82 D8
City Hospl B18 65 F4
City of Wolverhampton Coll (Bilston Campus) WV14 40 B7
City of Wolverhampton Coll (Metro One Campus) WV1 163 C2
City Rd
Birmingham B16 65 C2
Oldbury B69 63 C8
City Road Prim Sch B16 65 D3
City Tech Coll The B37 70 A4
City Trad Est B16 66 A3
City View
Birmingham,Saltley B8 67 D4
Birmingham,Stockland Green B23 56 D3
Civic Cl B1 66 C2
Civic Hall★ WV1 163 B3
Cladsworth Ho 1 B97 153 A4
Claerwen Gr B31 102 E5
Claines Cres DY10 117 B5
Claines Rd
Birmingham B31 103 C4
Halesowen B63 82 D5
Claire Ct B26 89 C7
Clairvaux Gdns B91 106 D5
Clandon Cl B14 104 C2
Clanfield Ave WV11 26 F7
Clapgate Gdns WV14 40 A3
Clapgate La B32 84 C2
Clapham Sq CV31 162 B7
Clapham St CV31 162 B6
Clapham Terrace Com Prim Sch CV31 162 B7
Clapham Terr CV31 162 B7
Clapton Gr B44 45 B1
Clarage Ho B62 83 D8
Clara St CV2 114 A2
Clare Ave WV11 12 F1
Clare Cl CV32 157 C2
Clare Cres WV14 39 F2
Clare Ct B90 105 D2
Clare Dr B15 85 F8
Claregate Prim Sch WV6 24 F7
Clarel Ave B8 67 C3
Claremont Cl CV12 79 B4
Claremont Cotts DY3 50 E8
Claremont Ct 2 B64 62 E1
Claremont Mews WV3 39 A7
Claremont Pl 1 B18 66 A5
Claremont Rd
Birmingham,Hockley B18 66 B6
Birmingham,Sparkbrook B11 87 B7
Royal Leamington Spa CV31 161 F6
Sedgley DY3 50 E8
Smethwick B66 65 B4
Tamworth B79 21 A8
Wolverhampton WV3 39 B7
Claremont St
Bilston WV14 40 C6
Cradley Heath B64 62 E1
Claremont Way B63 83 A3
Claremont Wlk CV5 112 C6
Clarence Ave B21 65 C8
Clarence Ct
5 Hinckley LE10 75 E8
Oldbury B68 64 C2
Clarence Gdns B74 31 F3
Clarence Ho 7 CV32 156 F1
Clarence Mews 1 B17 85 D6
Clarence Rd
Bilston WV14 40 F7
Birmingham B17 85 D6
Birmingham,Gravelly Hill B23 56 D3
Birmingham,Handsworth B21 65 C8
Birmingham,King's Heath B13 87 A1
Birmingham,Sparkhill B11 87 D4
Dudley DY2 62 D6
Hinckley LE10 75 E8
Sutton Coldfield B74 31 F4
Wolverhampton WV1 163 B3
Clarence St
5 Coventry CV1 113 E4
Dudley DY3 50 E5
Kidderminster DY10 116 F6
Nuneaton CV11 73 A4
Royal Leamington Spa CV31 162 A6
Wolverhampton WV1 163 B3
Clarence Terr 6 CV32 156 F1
Clarenden Pl B17 85 C5
Clarendon Ave CV32 156 F1
Clarendon Cl B97 153 B5
Clarendon Cres CV32 156 E1
Clarendon Dr DY4 52 D8
Clarendon Gdns 3 B20 55 D1
Clarendon Ho LE10 75 B7
Clarendon Pl
Birmingham B62 84 A6
Royal Leamington Spa CV32 156 E1
Walsall WS3 14 F3
Clarendon Rd
Birmingham B16 65 E1
Hinckley LE10 75 C7
Kenilworth CV8 148 A3
Smethwick B67 64 F4
Sutton Coldfield B75 32 C3
Walsall WS4 15 C2
Clarendon Sq CV32 156 F1
Clarendon St
Coventry CV5 112 F1
Royal Leamington Spa CV32 157 A1
Walsall WS3 14 B1
Wolverhampton WV3 25 A2
Clare Rd
Walsall WS3 29 A6
Wolverhampton WV10 25 E7
Clare's Ct DY11 116 C6
Clarewell Ave B91 127 B8
Clare Witnell Cl DY11 116 B8
Clarion Way WS11 1 E5
Clarke Ho WS3 14 B1
Clarke's Ave CV8 148 A3
Clarkes Gr DY4 52 C6
Clarkes Ind Est B73 46 A2
Clarke's La B71 53 C7
Clarkes La WV13 27 C3
Clarke St 1 B97 153 E3
Clark Rd WV3 24 F2
Clarksland Gr B37 90 A8
Clarks La B90 126 A6
Clarkson Dr CV31 162 A4
Clarkson Place Ind Est DY5 81 E7
Clarkson Rd WS10 42 A3
Clark St
Birmingham B16 65 F2
Coventry CV6 96 A1
Stourbridge DY8 80 E4
Clarry Dr B74 45 F8
Clary Gr WS5 43 A3
Clatterbach La DY9 100 A4
Claughton Ct DY11 116 C5
Claughton Rd DY2 51 D1
Claughton Road N 8 DY2 51 D1
Claughton St DY11 116 C5
Clausen Cl B43 44 E4
Clavedon Cl B31 102 E7
Claverdon Cl
Brownhills WS8 16 A8
Redditch B97 158 D4
Solihull B91 106 E3
Claverdon Dr
Birmingham B43 54 D7
Sutton Coldfield B74 31 B4
Claverdon Gdns B27 88 B5
Claverdon Ho
Birmingham B13 105 A7
Warwick CV34 161 B8
Claverdon Rd CV5 112 B3
Claverley Ct 6 DY1 51 B1
Claverley Dr WV4 38 D5
Clay Ave CV11 73 F7
Claybrook Dr B98 159 F7
Claybrook St B5 164 C1
Claycroft Pl DY9 81 E5
Claycroft Terr DY1 51 B6
Claydon Gr 3 B14 105 A3
Claydon Rd DY6 49 C1
Clay Dr B32 84 A5
Claygate Rd WS12 2 E3
Clayhanger La WS8 15 D6
Clayhanger Rd WS8 15 F6
Clay La
Birmingham B26 88 E5
Coventry CV2 114 A4
Harvest Hill CV5 93 E3
Oldbury B69 64 A4
Claymore B77 35 E7
Claypit Cl B70 53 A3
Claypit La B61 120 E1
Clay Pit La
Lichfield WS14 8 F3
Solihull B90 126 A5
Claypit La B70 53 A4
Clayton Cl WV2 39 C7
Clayton Dr
Birmingham B36 69 C7
Bromsgrove B60 151 B7
Clayton Gdns B45 122 A2
Clayton Ho 3 B16 65 F1
Clayton Rd
Birmingham B8 67 D5
Coventry CV6 112 E5
Dudley WV14 51 B7
Clayton Wlk B35 58 A2
Clear View DY6 60 B6
Clearwater Ind Est WV2 40 A7
Clearwell Gdns DY1 50 F3
Clearwell Rd B98 154 C3
Cleasby B77 22 C1
Cleaveland Mews 2 WS13 3 A1
Cleaver Gdns CV10 73 C6
Clee Ave DY11 116 C2
Clee Hill Dr WV3 24 A1
Clee Hill Rd DY3 50 D4
Clee Rd
Birmingham B31 123 A8
Dudley DY2 62 A7
Oldbury B68 64 C4
Stourbridge DY8 81 A6
Cleeton St WS12 2 D1
Cleeve Cl B98 154 D5
Cleeve Dr B74 31 F6
Cleeve Ho B24 57 A2
Cleeve Rd
Birmingham B14 105 C4
Walsall WS3 13 F3
Cleeves Ave CV34 161 D6
Cleeve B77 21 D3
Cleeve Way WS3 13 F3
Clee View Mdw DY3 39 D2
Clegg Rd WS7 7 E7
Clematis Dr WV9 10 F3
Clematis B77 21 F3
Clem Attlee Ct WV13 40 D8
Clemens St CV31 162 A7
Clement Ho CV8 148 A5
Clement Pl WV14 40 D7
Clement Rd
Bilston WV14 40 D7
Halesowen B62 63 D1
Clements Cl
Kenilworth CV8 148 A5
Oldbury B69 63 F4
Clements Rd B25 88 D8
Clements St CV2 114 A3
Clement St
Birmingham B1 66 B3
Nuneaton CV11 73 B3
Walsall WS2 28 D1
Clemson St WV13 27 A2
Clennon Rise CV2 114 D8
Clensmore St DY10 116 D7
Clent Ave
Kidderminster DY11 116 B1
Redditch B97 158 D7
Clent Cott DY9 99 F3
Clent Ct 5 DY1 51 B1
Clent Dr
Hagley DY9 99 D6
Nuneaton CV10 72 B3
Clent Hill Dr B65 63 A5
Clent Hills Ctry Pk★ DY9 100 A4
Clent Ho B63 83 A2
Clent Prim Sch DY9 99 F2
Clent Rd
Birmingham B45 121 E8
Birmingham,Handsworth B21 54 D1
Oldbury B68 64 C1
Stourbridge DY8 81 A6
Clent View Rd
Birmingham B32 84 A1
Halesowen B63 82 C5
Stourbridge DY8 80 C2
Clent View B66 65 B3
Clent Villas B12 87 B4
Clent Way B32 102 A8
Cleobury Cl B97 153 B5
Cleobury La B94 126 A3
Cleopatra Gr CV34 161 E4
Cleton Street Bsns Pk DY4 52 B3
Cleton St DY4 52 B3
Clevedon Ave B36 69 E8
Clevedon Rd B12 86 E6
Cleveland Cl
Willenhall WV13 26 D1
Wolverhampton WV11 12 F1
Cleveland Ct
16 Birmingham B13 87 B2
1 Royal Leamington Spa CV32 156 F2
Wolverhampton WV2 163 B2
Cleveland Dr
Barnt Green B45 122 A2
Cannock WS11 2 B4
Cleveland Pas WV1 163 B2
Cleveland Rd
Bulkington CV12 79 B3
Cleveland Rd continued
Coventry CV2 114 A4
Hinckley LE10 75 C8
Wolverhampton WV2 163 C2
Cleveland St
14 Dudley,New Dock DY1 51 B1
4 Dudley,Old Dock DY1 62 B8
Stourbridge DY8 80 E4
Wolverhampton WV1 163 B2
Cleveland Twr B1 164 B1
Cleveley Dr CV10 72 D7
Cleves Cres WS6 4 D1
Cleves Dr B45 121 E7
Cleves Rd B45 121 E8
Clewley Dr WV9 11 B3
Clewley Gr B32 84 B5
Clews Cl WS1 42 E7
Clewshaw La B38 124 C4
Clews Rd B98 158 F7
Cley Cl B5 86 D6
Clifden Gr CV8 148 C6
Cliffe Ct CV32 156 D1
Cliffe Dr B33 69 C3
Cliffe Rd CV32 156 D1
Cliffe Way CV34 161 A8
Cliff Hall La B78 35 C1
Clifford Bridge Prim Sch CV3 115 A3
Clifford Bridge Rd CV3 114 F4
Clifford Cl B77 21 F3
Clifford Rd
Bentley Heath B93 127 F4
Smethwick B67 64 F1
West Bromwich B70 53 B2
Clifford St
3 Dudley DY1 62 B8
Birmingham B19 66 D7
Tamworth B77 21 E3
Wolverhampton WV6 25 A3
Clifford Wlk B19 66 D7
Cliff Rock Rd B45 122 B7
Clift Cl WV12 27 C6
Clifton Ave
Aldridge WS9 16 C1
Brownhills WS8 15 D7
Cannock WS11 4 C7
Tamworth B79 21 A7
Clifton Cl
Birmingham B6 66 F7
Oldbury B69 64 A4
Redditch B98 159 E8
Clifton Cres B91 106 F1
Clifton Ct
5 Royal Leamington Spa CV31 162 B7
Hinckley LE10 71 B1
Clifton Dr B73 46 B6
Clifton Gdns WV8 10 C3
Clifton Gn B28 106 A5
Clifton La B71 53 E8
Clifton Prim Sch B12 87 A5
Clifton Rd
Birmingham,Aston B6 66 F7
Birmingham,Balsall Heath B12 87 A5
Birmingham,Castle Bromwich B36 69 E8
Halesowen B62 83 E8
Kidderminster DY11 116 A1
Nuneaton CV10 72 F4
Smethwick B67 64 F4
Sutton Coldfield B73 46 B5
Wolverhampton WV6 24 D5
Clifton Road Ind Est B12 86 F5
Clifton St
Coventry CV1 165 D4
Cradley Heath B64 62 F1
Dudley WV14 51 A8
Sedgley WV14 39 F1
Stourbridge DY8 80 F4
Wolverhampton WV3 25 B2
Clifton Terr B23 56 F4
Clifton Way LE10 71 A1
Clinic Dr
Nuneaton CV11 73 C3
Stourbridge DY9 81 E5
Clinton Ave
Hampton Magna CV35 160 A7
Kenilworth CV8 147 D6
Clinton Cres WS7 7 B8
Clinton Gr B90 106 E1
Clinton La CV8 147 D6
Clinton Prim Sch CV8 147 E3
Clinton Rd
Bilston WV14 41 A7
Coleshill B46 70 F6
Coventry CV6 95 F2
Solihull B90 106 E1
Clinton St
2 Royal Leamington Spa CV31 162 A7
Birmingham B18 65 E5
Clipper View B16 65 E1
Clipstone Rd CV6 112 E6
Clipston Rd B8 67 F4
Clissold Cl B12 86 E7
Clissold Pas B18 66 A4
Clissold St B18 66 A4
Clive Cl B75 32 D2
Cliveden Ave
Aldridge WS9 16 B1
Birmingham B42 55 D4
Cliveden Coppice B74 31 F1
Cliveden Wlk CV11 78 E8
Clivedon Way B62 83 B7
Cliveland St B19 164 C4
Clive Rd
Balsall Common CV7 130 C5
Clive Rd continued
Birmingham B32 84 D7
Bromsgrove B60 151 B8
Burntwood WS7 7 A7
Redditch B97 153 D5
Clive St B71 53 C5
Clivesway LE10 71 C2
Clockfields Dr DY5 61 A1
Clock La B92 90 D2
Clockmill Ave WS3 14 E3
Clockmill Pl WS3 14 F3
Clockmill Rd WS3 14 E3
Clodeshall Rd B8 67 E4
Cloister Croft CV2 114 F6
Cloister Crofts CV32 156 F3
Cloister Dr B62 83 D3
Cloisters The
Royal Leamington Spa CV32 156 F3
Studley B80 159 D4
Walsall WS4 28 F3
Cloister Way CV32 156 F3
Clonmel Rd B30 104 A6
Clopton Cres B37 70 C4
Clopton Rd B33 89 C8
Closers Bsns Ctr CV11 73 D2
Close The
Birmingham B17 84 F7
Birmingham,Griffin's Hill B29 103 D8
Brandon CV8 135 F5
Dudley DY3 50 C4
Halesowen B63 82 D6
Hollywood B47 125 A5
Hunnington B62 101 A7
Kenilworth CV8 148 A6
Lichfield WS13 9 B8
Solihull B92 106 F8
Wednesbury WS10 41 E3
Whitnash CV31 162 A5
Clothier Gdns WV13 27 A3
Clothier Street Prim Sch WV13 27 A3
Clothier St WV13 27 A3
Cloudbridge Dr B92 107 F7
Cloud Gn CV4 132 D5
Cloudsley Gr B92 88 F3
Clovelly Gdns CV2 114 C5
Clovelly Rd CV2 114 B5
Clovelly Way CV11 73 E5
Clover Ave B37 70 D2
Clover Ct B38 103 D2
Cloverdale Cl CV6 95 B4
Cloverdale
Perton WV6 23 D4
Stoke Prior B60 150 C3
Clover Dr B32 84 D2
Cloverfield LE10 71 C3
Clover Hill WS5 43 E8
Clover La DY6 60 B7
Clover Lea Sq B8 68 A6
Clover Ley WV10 25 F3
Clover Mdws WS12 2 C1
Clover Piece 6 DY4 52 C6
Clover Pk Trad Est LE10 71 B3
Clover Rd B29 103 A7
Clover Ridge WS6 4 C3
Clover Way CV12 77 D2
Cloweswood La B94 141 F8
Club Cotts WV10 11 C6
Club La WV10 11 C6
Club Row DY3 50 E5
Club View B38 103 D2
Clunbury Croft B34 69 B5
Clunbury Rd B31 123 A8
Clun Cl B69 52 A1
Clunes Ave CV11 73 E6
Clun Rd B31 102 F6
Clusters The DY9 81 E5
Clyde Ave B62 83 E8
Clyde Ct B73 46 B5
Clyde Mews DY5 61 B6
Clyde Rd
Bulkington CV12 79 A2
Dorridge B93 128 A2
Clydesdale B26 89 B5
Clydesdale Rd
Birmingham B32 84 B6
Brownhills WS8 15 E6
Clydesdale Twr B1 164 B1
Clyde St
Birmingham B12 67 A1
Cradley Heath B64 62 E1
Clyde Twr 3 B19 66 D7
Coach Cotts B45 138 D8
Coach House Mews 2 CV34 160 F7
Coach House Rise B77 35 F7
Coalash La B60 151 C2
Coalbourne Gdns B63 82 C5
Coalbourn La DY8 80 F7
Coalbourn Way DY5 61 A3
Coal Haulage Rd WS12 5 F8
Coalheath La WS4 29 C8
Coalmeadow Cl WS3 13 F3
Coalpit Fields Rd CV12 78 C1
Coal Pool La WS3 28 F5
Coalpool Pl WS3 28 F6
Coalport Rd WV1 26 A1
Coalway Ave
Birmingham B26 89 C4
Wolverhampton WV3 39 A6
Coalway Gdns WV3 38 D7
Coalway Rd
Walsall WS3 28 A8
Wolverhampton WV3 38 E6
Coates Rd DY10 117 B7

Coat Of Arms Bridge Rd
CV3 133 A6
Coatsgate Wlk WV8 10 F1
Cobbett Rd WS7 6 D7
Cobbles The B72 57 C7
Cobble Wlk B18 66 A5
Cobbs Rd CV8 147 D6
Cobbs Wlk B65 62 F5
Cobden Ave CV31 162 C5
Cobden Cl
Cannock WS12 2 C7
Darlaston WS10 41 F6
Tipton DY4 51 F8
Cobden Gdns B12 86 E6
Cobden St
Coventry CV6 113 E5
Darlaston WS10 41 F6
Kidderminster DY11 116 D5
Stourbridge DY8 80 E5
Walsall WS1 42 D7
Cobham Bsns Ctr B9 67 D2
Cobham Cl
Birmingham B35 57 F3
Bromsgrove B60 150 F7
Cobham Court Mews DY9 99 D6
Cobham Gn 3 CV31 162 A4
Cobham Rd
Birmingham B9 67 D2
Halesowen B63 83 B4
Kidderminster DY10 116 E4
Stourbridge DY8 81 B2
Wednesbury WS10 42 E2
Cobia B77 35 D7
Cob La B30 103 C6
Cobley Hill B48 138 E4
Cobnall Rd B61 121 A2
Cobs Field B30 103 C6
Coburg Croft 4 DY4 52 C6
Coburg Ho CV5 112 E3
Coburn Dr B75 32 D2
Cochrane Cl
2 Tipton DY4 52 C6
Stourbridge DY9 99 C8
Cochrane Rd DY2 61 F5
Cockermouth Cl CV32 156 D2
Cock Hill La B45 121 F8
Cocksheds La B62 83 C8
Cockshut Hill B26 89 A8
Cockshut Hill Tech Coll
B26 89 A8
Cockshutt La B61 136 D7
Cockshutts La WV2 39 D7
Cocksmead Croft B14 104 D5
Cocksmoor Ho B14 104 D7
Cocksparrow La WS12,
WS19 1 B5
Cocksparrow St CV34 160 D7
Cockspur St B78 36 E7
Cockthorpe Cl B17 84 F7
Cocton Cl WV6 23 E5
Codsall Com High Sch
WV8 10 A4
Codsall Mid Sch WV8 10 A3
Codsall Rd
Codsall WV8 10 C1
Cradley Heath B64 82 E8
Wolverhampton WV6 24 D7
Cofield Rd B73 45 F1
Cofton Church La B45 122 D3
Cofton Cl B97 153 B5
Cofton Ct B45 122 D7
Cofton Gr B31 122 E6
Cofton Lake Rd B45 122 C3
Cofton Prim Sch B31 123 A6
Cofton Rd B31 123 B7
Cokeland Pl B64 82 D8
Colaton Cl WV10 25 E4
Colbourne Ct B33 68 D3
Colbourne Gr CV32 156 D2
Colbourne Rd
Tamworth B78 21 A2
Tipton DY4 52 A4
Colbrand Gr B15 86 D8
Colbrook B77 21 D1
Coldbath Rd B13 105 B8
Coldfield Dr B98 158 E7
Coldridge Cl WV8 10 F1
Coldstream Cl LE10 71 A1
Coldstream Dr DY8 60 E3
Coldstream Rd B76 57 E8
Cole Bank Rd B28 105 E8
Colebourne Prim Sch B33 68 E5
Colebourne Rd B13 105 D6
Colebridge Cres B46 70 F8
Colebrook Cl CV3 114 F2
Colebrook Croft B90 105 F2
Colebrook Rd
Birmingham B11 87 D5
Solihull B90 105 F2
Coleby Cl CV4 131 D7
Cole Ct B37 70 B2
Coleford Cl
Redditch B97 153 A2
Stourbridge DY8 60 C2
Coleford Dr B37 70 A2
Cole Gn B90 105 F2
Cole Hall La B34 69 A5
Colehill B79 21 B5
Colehurst Croft B90 126 F6
Coleman Rd WS10 42 A5
Coleman St
Coventry CV4 111 F3
Wolverhampton WV6 24 F4
Colemeadow Rd
Birmingham B13 105 B6
Coleshill B46 70 F7
Redditch B98 154 F6
Colenso Rd B16 65 D4
Coleraine Rd B42 55 A6
Coleridge Cl
Redditch B97 158 C8
Tamworth B79 21 A6
Walsall WS3 15 A5
Willenhall WV12 27 E7
Coleridge Dr WV6 23 E4
Coleridge Pas B4 164 C3
Coleridge Rd
Birmingham B43 54 E7
Coventry CV2 114 C3
Coleridge Rise DY3 50 A4
Colesbourne Ave B14 104 C2
Colesbourne Rd B92 89 B3
Coles Cres B71 53 B7
Colesden Wlk WV4 38 C6
Coleshill CE Prim Sch
B46 70 F6
Coleshill Cl B97 158 C5
Coleshill Heath Rd
Birmingham B37 90 C7
Coleshill B37,B46 70 E2
Coleshill Heath Sch B37 70 C1
Coleshill Ind Est B46 59 F2
Coleshill Rd
Birmingham,Hodgehill B34,
B36 68 E6
Birmingham,Marston Green
B37 90 B8
Curdworth B76 59 C5
Fazeley B78 35 A7
Hartshill CV10 72 A7
Sutton Coldfield B75 46 D5
Water Orton B46 59 B2
Coleshill St
Birmingham B5 164 D3
Fazeley B78 35 A8
Sutton Coldfield B72 46 C5
Coleside Ave B13 105 D7
Coles La
Sutton Coldfield B72 46 C3
West Bromwich B71 53 B7
Cole St DY2 62 E4
Cole Valley Rd B28 105 D6
Coleview Cres B33 69 E3
Coleville Rd B76 58 B6
Coley Cl LE10 75 D7
Coleys La B31 103 A2
Colgreave Ave B13 87 D2
Colina Cl CV3 134 C5
Colindale Rd B44 45 A3
Colinwood Cl WS6 4 F1
Colledge Rd CV6 95 D1
Colleen Ave B30 104 B3
College Cl WS10 42 A1
College Ct WV6 24 D4
College Dr
Birmingham B20 54 F2
Royal Leamington Spa
CV32 156 F2
College Farm Dr B73 45 D1
College Gate B8 67 E4
College High Sch The
B44 56 B6
College Hill B73 46 B4
College La
Balsall Common CV8 129 E1
Hinckley LE10 71 E1
Tamworth B79 21 B5
College of Law The B18 164 A4
College Rd
Birmingham,Alum Rock B8 67 E4
Birmingham B32 84 A6
Birmingham,Handsworth
B20 54 E2
Birmingham,Moseley B13 87 C2
Birmingham,Perry Common
B44 56 B7
Bromsgrove B60 137 A2
Kidderminster DY10 116 E4
Stourbridge DY8 81 A4
Wolverhampton WV6 24 D4
College St
Birmingham B18 66 A4
Nuneaton CV10 73 C1
College View WV6 24 D3
College Wlk
Birmingham B29 103 D8
Bromsgrove B60 137 A2
Kidderminster DY10 116 E4
Collet Rd WV6 23 E5
Collets Brook B75 33 A2
Collett Cl DY8 81 A6
Colletts Gr B37 69 F4
Collett B77 22 A1
Collett Wlk 2 CV1 113 B3
Colley Ave WV10 25 F7
Colley Gate B63 82 C6
Colley La B63 82 C6
Colley Lane Prim Sch
B63 82 C6
Colley Orch B63 82 C6
Colley St B70 53 D4
Collier Cl
Cheslyn Hay WS6 4 D2
Walsall WS8 15 C7
Colliers Cl WV12 27 B6
Colliers Fold DY5 61 B5
Colliery Dr WS3 13 F3
Colliery La CV7 78 B1
Colliery La N CV7 78 B1
Colliery Rd
Smethwick B71 65 A8
West Bromwich B71 54 A1
Wolverhampton WV1 25 F2
Collindale Ct DY6 49 D1
Collingbourne Ave B36 68 E8
Collingdon Ave B26 89 C6
Collings Ho B16 66 A1
Colling Wlk B37 70 A5
Collingwood Dr B43 44 D3
Collingwood Ho B43 44 D3
Collingwood Rd
Birmingham,Brandwood End
B30 104 D3
Coventry CV5 113 A2
Wolverhampton WV10 11 E2
Collins Cl B32 84 A5
Collins Dr 3 WS13 8 F6
Collins Gr CV4 132 D5
Collins Hill WS13 3 A2
Collinson Cl B98 154 A1
Collins Rd
Brownhills WS8 16 A5
Royal Leamington Spa
CV34 161 D5
Wednesbury WS10 42 C3
Collins St
Walsall WS1 42 E7
West Bromwich B70 52 E3
Collis Cl B60 150 E7
Collis St DY8 80 F8
Collister Cl B90 106 B4
Colly Croft B37 69 F5
Collycroft Pl B27 88 B5
Colman Ave WV11 26 F6
Colman Cres B68 64 C2
Colman Hill Ave B63 82 D6
Colman Hill B63 82 D5
Colmers Farm Inf Sch
B45 122 B8
Colmers Farm Jun Sch
B45 122 B8
Colmers Sch & Sports Coll
B45 122 B8
Colmers Wlk B31 102 D1
Colmore Ave B14 104 D7
Colmore Circus Queensway
B4 164 C3
Colmore Cres B13 87 B1
Colmore Dr B75 47 A5
Colmore Flats B19 164 B4
Colmore Gate B2 164 C3
Colmore Inf Sch B14 104 D7
Colmore Jun Sch B14 104 D7
Colmore Rd B14 104 D7
Colmore Row B3 164 B3
Coln Cl B31 102 F6
Colonial Ind Pk B64 82 D7
Colonial Rd B9 67 F2
Colshaw Rd DY8 80 E4
Colston Rd B24 57 B2
Colt Cl B74 44 E7
Coltham Rd WV12 27 D7
Coltishall Cl B35 57 F2
Coltman Cl WS14 9 D7
Colton Hills Com Sch
WV4 39 B4
Colts Cl LE10 75 D4
Coltsfoot Cl WV11 26 E5
Coltsfoot View WS6 4 E2
Colts La B98 154 D3
Columbia Cl B5 86 D7
Columbia Gdns CV12 78 E2
Columbian Cres WS7 6 F8
Columbian Dr WS11 1 F3
Columbian Way WS11 1 F3
Columbine Cl 4 WS5 42 F3
Columbine Way CV12 77 E1
Columbus Ave DY5 61 F3
Colville Cl DY4 52 D8
Colville Rd B12 87 B5
Colville Wlk B12 87 B5
Colwall Rd DY3 50 D4
Colwall Wlk B27 88 D4
Colworth Rd B31 102 F4
Colyere Cl CV7 95 A6
Colyns Gr B33 68 F5
Combe Fields Rd CV3 115 F4
Comber Croft B13 105 D8
Comber Dr DY5 61 B6
Comberford Ct 5 WS10 42 A3
Comberford Dr WS10 42 D4
Comberford Rd B79 21 A7
Comberton Ave DY10 117 B5
Comberton Ct 5 DY10 117 A5
Comberton Fst Sch
DY10 117 B4
Comberton Gdns DY10 117 B5
Comberton Hill DY10 116 F5
Comberton Mans 4
DY10 117 A5
Comberton Mid Sch
DY10 117 B4
Comberton Park Rd
DY10 117 B4
Comberton Pl DY10 116 F5
Comberton Rd
Birmingham B26 89 B8
Kidderminster DY10 117 B4
Comberton Terr DY10 116 F5
Combine Cl B75 32 D4
Combrook Gn B34 69 D6
Comet Rd B26 90 C4
Commainge Cl CV34 160 D7
Commercial Rd
Walsall WS2 28 A7
Wolverhampton WV1 25 E1
Commercial St B1 164 A1
Commissary Rd B26 90 A3
Commonfield Croft B8 67 D5
Common La
Birmingham,Sheldon B26 89 B6
Birmingham,Washwood Heath
B8 67 F6
Cannock WS11 2 A3
Common La *continued*
Corley Moor CV7 93 E7
Kenilworth CV8 148 B7
Tamworth B79 21 B4
Common Rd WV5 49 A6
Commonside
Brierley Hill DY5 61 C6
Brownhills WS8 16 A6
Walsall WS3 15 A2
Common View WS12 2 B7
Common Way CV2 114 A6
Common Wlk WS12 1 C5
Communication Row B15 66 C1
Compass Ct 4 CV1 113 B3
Compass Way B60 151 A7
Compton Cl
Redditch B98 153 E2
Royal Leamington Spa
CV32 157 C2
Solihull B91 106 D4
Compton Croft B37 70 D1
Compton Ct
1 Sutton Coldfield B74 31 F3
7 Wolverhampton WV3 25 A2
Coventry CV6 95 D2
Dudley DY2 62 C6
Compton Dr
Dudley DY2 62 F8
Kingswinford DY6 60 D5
Sutton Coldfield B74 44 E7
Compton Grange B64 82 C8
Compton Gr
Halesowen B63 82 C4
Kingswinford DY6 60 D5
Compton Hill Dr WV3 24 D2
Compton Ho B33 69 B2
Compton Pk WV6 24 E3
Compton Rd
Birmingham B24 56 E1
Coventry CV6 95 D2
Cradley Heath B64 62 C1
Halesowen B62 83 F5
Stourbridge DY9 81 D2
Tamworth B79 20 F7
Wolverhampton WV3 24 F2
Compton Rd W WV3 24 D2
Comrie Cl CV2 114 F6
Comsey Rd B43 44 B3
Comwall Cl WS3 28 C7
Comyn St CV32 157 B1
Conchar Cl B72 46 C2
Conchar Rd B72 46 C2
Concorde Dr B35 57 F2
Concorde Rd B26 90 C4
Condor Gr WS12 2 C1
Condover Cl WS2 27 D3
Condover Rd B31 123 B8
Conduit Rd WS11 6 A4
Conduit St WS13 9 B8
Coneybury Wlk B76 58 D5
Coneyford Rd B34 69 C6
Coney Gn DY8 81 B5
Coneygre Bsns Pk DY4 51 F3
Coneygree Ind Est DY4 52 A3
Coney Green Dr B31 122 F8
Coneygree Rd DY4 52 A3
Coneygre Ind Est DY4 51 F2
Congleton Cl
Coventry CV6 95 E2
Redditch B97 153 B5
Congreve Cl CV34 155 F2
Congreve Wlk 3 CV12 78 B3
Conifer Cl
Bedworth CV12 78 C4
Brierley Hill DY5 81 C8
Cannock WS12 2 A8
Conifer Ct B13 86 E2
Conifer Dr
Birmingham,Handsworth
B21 65 E7
Birmingham,Northfield
B31 103 B3
Conifer Gr
3 Royal Leamington Spa
CV31 161 F5
Bromsgrove B61 136 F3
Conifer Paddock
Coventry CV3 114 E1
Halesowen B62 83 E8
Conifer Rd B74 44 E8
Conifers The CV8 148 B3
Coningsby Cl 3 CV31 162 C6
Coningsby Dr DY11 116 A8
Conington Gr B17 85 A5
Coniston Ave B92 88 F4
Coniston Cl
Birmingham B28 105 F7
Bromsgrove B60 137 B1
Bulkington CV12 79 C3
Coniston Cres B43 54 F7
Coniston Ct
2 Royal Leamington Spa
CV32 156 D1
Nuneaton CV11 73 F7
Coniston Dr
Coventry CV5 111 D4
Kingswinford DY6 60 B7
Coniston Grange CV8 147 F5
Coniston Ho
10 Birmingham B17 85 D5
7 Oldbury B69 63 D5
Kidderminster DY10 116 E7
Coniston Rd
Birmingham B23 56 D4
Coventry CV5 112 F1
Royal Leamington Spa
CV32 156 D1
Sutton Coldfield B74 30 F3
Coniston Rd *continued*
Wolverhampton WV6 24 D8
Coniston B77 36 B7
Coniston Way
Cannock WS11 1 E1
Nuneaton CV11 73 F7
Connaught Ave
Kidderminster DY11 116 C4
Wednesbury WS10 42 C3
Connaught Cl WS5 43 C7
Connaught Dr WV5 38 A1
Connaught Gdns B5 86 E6
Connaught Ho 1 WV3 25 A2
Connaught Rd
Bilston WV14 40 F7
Bromsgrove B60 137 C1
Wolverhampton WV1 25 A2
Connops Way DY9 81 E5
Connor Rd B71 53 E8
Conolly Dr B45 102 B1
Conrad Cl B11 87 A7
Conrad Rd CV6 113 A7
Consort Cres DY5 61 C6
Consort Dr WS10 41 C8
Consort Pl B79 21 C5
Consort Rd B30 104 A3
Constable Cl
Bedworth CV12 78 A5
Birmingham B43 44 D3
Constables The B68 64 B2
Constance Ave B70 53 D1
Constance Cl CV12 95 F8
Constance Rd B5 86 D5
Constantine La B46 59 F1
Constantine Way WV14 41 A2
Constitution Hill
1 Dudley DY2 62 D8
Birmingham B19 164 B4
Constitution Hill E DY2 62 D8
Consul Ho 6 LE10 71 D1
Convent Cl
Cannock WS11 4 D8
Kenilworth CV8 148 A7
Wolverhampton WV1 163 C2
Conway Ave
Birmingham B32 84 B6
Coventry CV4 131 D8
Oldbury B68 64 B2
West Bromwich B71 42 B1
Conway Cl
Dudley DY1 51 C6
Kingswinford DY6 60 F4
Solihull B90 106 D1
Conway Cres WV12 27 C7
Conway Gr B43 54 D7
Conway Ho WS3 28 D6
Conway Prim Sch B11 87 C6
Conway Rd
Birmingham B37 70 B3
Birmingham,Sparkbrook
B11 87 C6
Bromsgrove B60 136 F1
Cannock WS11 4 B8
Perton WV6 23 F3
Royal Leamington Spa
CV32 161 D8
Solihull B90 106 D1
Conwy Cl
Nuneaton CV11 73 D3
Walsall WS2 28 A4
Conybere St B12 86 F7
Conyworth Cl B27 88 D4
Cook Ave DY2 62 D7
Cook Cl
Knowle B93 128 C6
Perton WV6 23 E4
Cooke Cl
Coventry CV6 96 A4
Warwick CV34 155 F2
Cookes Croft B31 103 B2
Cookesley Cl B43 44 D4
Cooke St WV2 163 B1
Cookley Cl B63 82 F2
Cookley Way B69 63 E5
Cookley Wharf Ind Est
DY5 61 B4
Cooknell Dr DY8 60 E2
Cook Rd WS3 14 D2
Cooksey La B44 44 F4
Cooksey Rd B10 87 C8
Cooks La B37 70 A4
Cookspiece Wlk B33 68 F3
Cook St
Birmingham B7 67 C7
Coventry CV1 165 B3
Darlaston WS10 41 F6
Coombe Abbey Ctry Pk★
CV3 115 E3
Coombe Abbey Visitor Ctr★
CV3 115 E4
Coombe Ave CV3 134 F7
Coombe Croft WV9 11 A3
Coombe Ct CV3 115 A2
Coombe Dr
Binley Woods CV3 135 E7
Nuneaton CV10 72 B4
Coombe Hill B64 83 B8
Coombe Park Rd CV3 114 F2
Coombe Pk B74 45 F7
Coombe Rd
Birmingham B20 55 E1
Solihull B90 106 C2
Coombes La B31 122 F7
Coombes Rd B62 83 B7
Coombe St CV3 114 B2

Coombs Rd B62 83 B7
Coombswood Way B65 83 B8
Co-Operative St CV2 96 B3
Cooper Ave DY5 61 A2
Cooper Cl
Bromsgrove B60 150 E6
West Bromwich B70 53 E2
Cooper & Jordan CE Prim Sch WS9 30 C6
Cooper's Bank Rd DY5 50 C1
Coopers Hill B48 138 E6
Cooper's La B67 65 A5
Coopers Rd B20 55 A4
Cooper St
Nuneaton CV11 73 D4
West Bromwich B70 53 D3
Wolverhampton WV2 39 F8
Cope Arnolds Cl CV6 95 F4
Copeley Hill B23 56 D1
Copenhagen Mews B73 45 F1
Copes Cres WV10 26 A7
Cope's Dr B79 21 B7
Cope St
Birmingham B18 66 A3
Coventry CV1 165 C3
Darlaston WS10 41 E6
Walsall WS3 28 C6
Cophall St DY4 52 D5
Cophams Cl B92 89 C2
Copland Pl CV4 111 E1
Coplow Cl CV7 130 A6
Coplow Cotts B16 65 F3
Coplow St B16 65 F3
Coplow Terr B16 65 F3
Copnor Gr B26 88 E6
Coppenhall Gr B33 69 A3
Copperas St CV2 96 B2
Copperbeach Dr 2 B12 87 A5
Copperbeech Cl B32 84 F5
Copper Beech Cl CV6 95 E1
Copper Beech Dr
Kingswinford DY6 49 D1
Wombourne WV5 49 B6
Copper Beech Gdns B20 55 A2
Copperfield Rd CV2 114 B3
Copperfields WS14 9 D7
Copperkins Rd WS12 2 E4
Coppermill Cl WS12 1 F7
Coppice Ash Croft B19 66 D8
Coppice Ave DY9 81 F3
Coppice Cl
1 Birmingham,Erdington B24 56 F3
Birmingham B45 121 F7
Brierley Hill DY5 61 F1
Burntwood WS7 6 F8
Cheslyn Hay WS6 4 D4
Cheswick Green B90 126 C4
Hinckley LE10 71 F3
Redditch B97 153 C3
Sedgley DY3 50 C7
Solihull B92 107 A7
Wolverhampton WV11 13 A1
Coppice Cres WS8 15 D7
Coppice Ct WS11 4 B7
Coppice Dr
Birmingham B27 88 B2
Polesworth B78 36 F7
Coppice Farm Way
Walsall WV11 13 B1
Willenhall WV12 27 B8
Coppice Gdns B47 125 A7
Coppice Gr WS14 9 F7
Coppice Ho
Birmingham,Acock's Green B27 88 A2
Birmingham,Handsworth B66 65 D6
Coppice Hollow B32 84 B1
Coppice Ho WV12 27 C7
Coppice Hts DY11 116 B1
Coppice Jun Sch B92 107 E7
Coppice La
Aldridge WS9 15 F1
Brierley Hill DY5 62 A2
Brownhills WS8 15 D8
Cheslyn Hay WS6 4 D4
Middleton B78 33 D2
Muckley Corner WS7,WS14 8 A3
Willenhall WV12 27 C6
Wolverhampton WV6 24 B6
Coppice Oaks B13 87 A3
Coppice Performing Arts Sch WV11 27 A8
Coppice Prim Sch B75 32 B1
Coppice Prim Sch The B47 125 A6
Coppice Rd
Birmingham B13 87 A3
Brownhills WS8,WS9 15 F4
Cradley Heath B64 82 E7
Dudley WV14 51 A8
Solihull B92 107 E7
Whitnash CV31 162 B2
Wolverhampton WV3 38 D8
Coppice Rise DY5 62 A2
Coppice Side WS8 15 D7
Coppice Side Ind Est WS8 15 C8
Coppice St
Dudley DY1 51 D4
Tipton DY4 51 E5
West Bromwich B70 53 A4
Coppice The
Birmingham,Frankley B31 102 C2
Birmingham,Handsworth Wood B20 55 A2
Cannock WS12 2 E1
Coventry CV3 134 B8
Hinckley LE10 75 F8
Nuneaton CV10 73 C7
Wednesbury DY4 41 C1
West Hagley DY8 98 F5
Willenhall WV12 27 C6
Coppice View Rd B73 45 A4
Coppice Way 7 B37 70 B2
Coppice Wlk
Cheswick Green B90 126 D4
Hinckley LE10 71 F3
Copplestone Cl B34 69 B6
Copps Rd CV32 161 D8
Coppy Hall Gr WS9 16 B1
Coppy Nook La WS7 7 C5
Copse Cl B31 103 A2
Copse Cres WS3 15 A4
Copse Dr CV5 111 B8
Copsehill Ct B75 46 E4
Copse Rd DY2 62 B3
Copse The
Bedworth CV7 96 A8
Sutton Coldfield B74 31 F1
Copsewood Ave CV11 79 B7
Copsewood Terr CV3 114 C2
Copson Cl B70 53 A3
Copstone Dr B93 127 F3
Copston Gr B29 103 B8
Copthall Ho CV1 165 B1
Copthall Rd B21 54 C2
Copt Heath Croft B93 128 B8
Copt Heath Dr B93 128 A7
Copthorne Ave WS7 6 F4
Copthorne Lo CV6 112 F8
Copthorne Rd
Birmingham B44 44 E3
Coventry CV6 112 F8
Wolverhampton WV3 39 A7
Copt Oak Cl CV4 131 C6
Copyholt La
Stoke Prior B60 151 D3
Upper Bentley B60,B97 152 A3
Coral Cl
Coventry CV5 112 C2
Hinckley LE10 75 F4
Coralin Cl B37 70 C2
Corbet Rd CV6 113 C7
Corbett Cl B60 151 B8
Corbett Cres DY8 81 A7
Corbett Dr B60 150 C1
Corbett Ho 8 DY8 80 F8
Corbett Hospl DY8 80 F7
Corbett Ind Est DY2 62 C6
Corbett Rd
Brierley Hill DY5 61 E1
Hollywood B47 125 A7
Kidderminster DY11 116 A8
Corbetts Cl B92 109 B7
Corbett St B66 65 B4
Corbin Rd B78 36 F6
Corbison Cl CV34 155 D1
Corbizum Ave B80 159 D4
Corbridge Ave B44 44 F1
Corbridge Rd B73 45 F2
Corbyn Rd
Birmingham B9 68 B3
Dudley DY1 61 F8
Corbyns Cl DY5 61 B7
Corbyns Hall La DY5 61 B7
Corbyns Hall Rd DY5 61 B7
Cordelia Gn CV34 161 D4
Cordley St B70 53 B4
Corfe Cl
Birmingham B32 84 F5
Coventry CV2 114 F5
Perton WV6 23 F3
Corfe Dr B69 63 A8
Corfe Rd WV14 51 A8
Corfton Dr WV6 24 C3
Coriander Cl
Birmingham B45 102 B2
Stoke Prior B60 150 C1
Corinne Cl B45 122 A6
Corinne Croft B37 70 A4
Corinthian Pl CV2 114 D6
Coriolanus Sq CV34 161 F3
Corisande Rd B29 85 C2
Corley Ave B31 103 B3
Corley Cl B90 105 E1
Corley (Coventry) Sch CV7 94 B6
Corley View CV7 95 C6
Cormorant Gr DY10 117 B3
Cornbow Ctr B63 83 B3
Cornbrook Rd B29 102 F7
Cornbury Gr B91 106 D4
Corncrake Cl B72 46 D2
Corncrake Dr B36 70 A7
Corncrake Rd DY1,DY3 50 E3
Corndon Cl DY11 116 B2
Cornel Cl B37 90 C8
Cornelius St CV3 133 D8
Cornel B77 21 F4
Corner Ho B66 65 D6
Corner Ho The 9 CV32 156 F1
Corner La B97 152 E2
Corner Pl The 3 B17 85 D6
Cornerstone B13 86 F3
Cornerstone Ho CV1 165 C4
Cornerway B38 123 F7
Cornet's End La CV7 110 B6
Cornets End La CV7 109 E7
Corn Exchange The 5 WS13 9 B8
Cornfield Ave B60 150 D6
Cornfield Cl DY6 60 A8
Cornfield Croft
Birmingham B37 70 D3
Sutton Coldfield B76 46 F3
Cornfield Dr WS14 9 E7
Cornfield LE10 71 C4
Cornfield Pl B65 62 F4
Cornfield Rd
Birmingham B31 103 B4
Rowley Regis B65 62 F4
Sutton Coldfield B76 46 F2
Cornfield The CV3 114 C1
Cornfield WV8 10 F2
Cornflower Cl WV10 12 A7
Cornflower Cres DY2 62 F8
Cornflower Rd WS8 15 D6
Corngreaves Jun & Inf Sch B64 62 D1
Corngreaves Rd B64 82 E7
Corngreaves The B34 69 B6
Corngreaves Trad Est B64 82 D7
Corngreaves Wlk B64 82 E7
Cornhampton Cl 7 B97 153 B5
Cornhill WS11 1 E5
Cornhill Gr
Birmingham B30 104 C7
Kenilworth CV8 148 C5
Corn Hill
Walsall WS5 43 E8
Wolverhampton WV10 163 D3
Cornish Cres CV10 73 A2
Corn Mdws CV12 78 C2
Corn Mill Cl
Birmingham B32 84 E1
Sutton Coldfield B76 46 F1
Cornmill Cl WS1 42 D7
Cornmill Gdns B60 138 A5
Cornmill Gr WV6 23 D3
Cornovian Cl WV6 23 E5
Corns Ho WS10 41 E6
Cornwall Ave
Birmingham B68 84 B8
Tamworth B78 21 A1
Cornwall Cl
3 Warwick CV34 160 F8
Aldridge WS9 16 A1
Kingswinford DY6 60 D8
Wednesbury WS10 42 D3
Cornwall Gate WV12 27 B5
Cornwall Ho CV32 156 D1
Cornwall Ind Est
Birmingham B8 67 C4
Smethwick B66 65 C7
Cornwallis Rd B70 53 A1
Cornwall Pl
Royal Leamington Spa CV32 156 D1
Walsall WS2 27 E3
Cornwall Rd
Birmingham,Handsworth B20 54 F2
Birmingham,Rubery B45 101 E1
Cannock WS12 2 B5
Coventry CV1 113 E1
Smethwick B66 65 C7
Stourbridge DY8 80 D8
Walsall WS5 43 B7
Wolverhampton WV6 24 C4
Cornwall St B3 164 B3
Cornwall Twr B18 66 B5
Cornwall Way LE10 71 E4
Cornwell Cl
Redditch B98 159 B5
Tipton DY4 52 A5
Cornyx La B91 107 D6
Coronation Ave
Mile Oak B78 20 D1
Willenhall WV13 27 D2
Coronation Cres B79 22 F7
Coronation Ct CV11 73 B4
Coronation Rd
Bilston WV14 40 C6
Birmingham B29 85 F2
Birmingham,Great Barr B43 43 E4
Birmingham,Washwood Heath B8 67 F6
Brownhills WS9 16 A3
Coventry CV1 113 F4
Tipton DY4 52 B8
Walsall WS4 15 B2
Wednesbury WS10 42 C4
Wolverhampton WV10 26 A5
Coronation St B79 21 A5
Coronation Terr B60 151 B7
Coronation Way DY10 117 B5
Coronel Ave CV6 95 E4
Corporation Rd DY2 51 F1
Corporation St W WS1 42 D8
Corporation St
Birmingham B2 164 C3
Birmingham,New Town Row B4 164 D4
Coventry CV1 165 B3
Kidderminster DY10 116 E5
Nuneaton CV11 73 B5
Tamworth B79 21 B5
Walsall WS1 42 E8
Wednesbury WS10 42 A2
Wolverhampton WV1 163 B3
Corpus Christi RC Prim Sch
Birmingham B33 68 D2
Wednesfield WV11 27 A8
Corpus Christi RC Sch CV3 134 D7
Correen B77 22 C1
Corrie Croft
Birmingham,Bartley Green B32 102 B7
Birmingham,Lyndon Green B26 89 B7
Corrie Roy Cotts B78 21 A4
Corrin Gr DY6 60 C8
Corron Hill B63 83 B4
Corser St
Dudley DY1 51 A2
Stourbridge DY8 81 A3
Wolverhampton WV1 25 F1
Corsican Cl
Burntwood WS7 7 A8
Willenhall WV12 27 E7
Corsican Dr WS12 2 A8
Corston Mews CV31 162 C6
Cort Dr WS7 7 B8
Corunna Rd CV34 160 C7
Corvedale Rd B29 103 A6
Corve Gdns WV6 24 E5
Corve View DY3 39 C1
Corville Gdns B26 89 C4
Corville Rd B62 83 F6
Corwen Croft B31 102 E6
Cory Croft DY4 52 A5
Coseley Hall 1 WV14 51 C8
Coseley Rd WV14 40 C4
Coseley Road Island WV14 40 C4
Coseley Sch The WV14 40 B1
Coseley Sta WV14 40 C1
Cosford Cl
Redditch B98 154 F1
Royal Leamington Spa CV32 157 B3
Cosford Cres B35 58 A3
Cosford Ct WV6 23 E5
Cosford Dr DY2 62 E5
Cosgrove Wlk WV8 10 F1
Cossington Rd B23 56 E7
Costard Ave CV34 161 E3
Costers La B98 154 F2
Costock Cl B37 90 B8
Coten End Prim Sch CV34 160 F7
Coten End CV34 160 F7
Cotes Rd LE10 75 F5
Cotford Rd B14 105 A2
Cotheridge Cl B90 127 C6
Cot La DY6,DY8 60 C5
Cotleigh Gr B43 44 D3
Cotman Cl
Bedworth CV12 78 A4
Birmingham B43 44 C3
Cotman Dr LE10 71 A3
Coton Green Prec B79 20 F7
Coton Green Prim Sch B79 20 F8
Coton Gr B90 105 E2
Coton La
Birmingham B23 56 F4
Tamworth B79 20 E8
Coton Rd
Nuneaton CV11 73 C3
Wolverhampton WV4 39 B5
Cotsdale Rd WV4 38 E3
Cotsford B91 107 A3
Cotswold Ave WS6 4 F3
Cotswold Cl
Aldridge WS9 16 C1
Birmingham B45 102 B2
Cannock WS12 2 A8
Kidderminster DY11 116 C2
Oldbury B69 63 E5
Cotswold Cres CV10 72 B3
Cotswold Croft B63 82 C1
Cotswold Ct
Sutton Coldfield B75 32 A4
Wolverhampton WV3 39 B6
Cotswold Dr CV3 133 C3
Cotswold Gr WV12 13 B1
Cotswold Rd
Cannock WS12 2 A8
Stourbridge DY8 81 B6
Wolverhampton WV2 39 F7
Cotswold Way B61 137 A5
Cottage Cl
Burntwood WS7 6 F5
Cannock WS12 2 D5
Nuneaton CV11 73 D4
Royal Leamington Spa CV31 162 C6
Wolverhampton WV11 26 C6
Cottage Ct WS7 6 F5
Cottage Dr B60 121 D1
Cottage Farm La B60 121 C1
Cottage Farm Lodge CV6 95 A1
Cottage Farm Rd
Coventry CV6 95 A2
Tamworth B77 35 D7
Cottage Gdns B45 121 F6
Cottage La
Burntwood WS7 6 F5
Lower Marlbrook B60 121 C1
Minworth B76 58 D6
Wolverhampton WV10 11 D3
Cottage Mews WS9 30 E4
Cottage Sq CV31 162 C6
Cottage St DY5 61 D3
Cottages The
Birmingham B24 67 F8
Cradley Heath B63 82 E6
Cottage St DY6 60 D7
Cottage View WV8 10 B4
Cottage Wlk
4 Tamworth B77 35 F6
Cottage Wlk *continued*
West Bromwich B70 53 D2
Cotterell Ct 3 WS4 28 F3
Cotteridge Jun & Inf Sch B30 104 A5
Cotteridge Rd B30 104 A4
Cotterills Ave B8 68 C4
Cotterill's Cl CV31 162 B3
Cotterills La B8 68 C4
Cotterills Rd DY4 52 B7
Cottesbrook Cl CV3 114 E1
Cottesbrook Inf Sch B27 88 C4
Cottesbrook Jun Sch B27 88 C4
Cottesbrook Rd B27 88 D4
Cottesfield Cl B8 68 B4
Cottesmore Cl B71 53 F8
Cottesmore Ho 7 B20 54 F3
Cottle Cl WS2 27 F3
Cotton Dr CV8 148 C6
Cotton La B13 87 A2
Cotton Mill Spinney CV32 157 E6
Cotton Pool Rd B61 136 E2
Cottrells Cl B14 105 C4
Cottrells Mews B46 59 B2
Cottrell St B71 53 D4
Cottsmeadow Dr B8 68 C4
Cotwall End Countryside & Craft Ctr* DY3 50 C6
Cotwall End Ho DY3 50 C7
Cotwall End Prim Sch DY3 50 D7
Cotwall End Rd DY3 50 C5
Cotysmore Rd B75 46 D7
Couchman Rd B8 67 E4
Coughton Dr CV31 162 D5
Coulter Gr WV6 23 D4
Coulter La WS7 7 E8
Council Cres WS12 27 C4
Council Ho* B3 164 B2
Council Hos CV5 93 D1
Council Rd 3 LE10 71 D1
Coundon Court Sch & Com Coll CV6 112 E7
Coundon Gn CV6 112 E8
Coundon Prim Sch CV6 112 E5
Coundon Rd CV1 113 B3
Coundon St CV1 165 A4
Coundon Wedge Dr CV5, CV6 112 D7
Counterfield Dr B65 62 F5
Countess Dr WS4 29 D7
Countess Rd CV11 73 A4
Countess's Croft The CV3 133 D7
Countess St WS1 42 D7
Countinghouse Way 2 B60 150 E6
County Bridge Prim Sch WS2 27 E1
County Cl
Birmingham B32 84 D3
Birmingham,Stirchley B30 104 C6
County Dr B78 21 A2
County La DY8 98 D8
County Park Ave B62 83 D3
Courtaulds Way CV6 113 D6
Court Cres DY6 60 C5
Court Dr WS14 17 F4
Courtenay Gdns B43 43 E2
Courtenay Rd B44 55 E8
Court Farm Prim Sch B23 56 E6
Court Farm Rd B23 56 E6
Court Farm Way B29 102 F7
Courthouse Croft CV8 148 C4
Courthouse Green Prim Sch CV6 114 A8
Court La B23 56 E7
Courtland Ave CV6 112 F5
Courtland Rd DY6 60 E8
Courtlands Cl B5 86 C6
Courtlands The WV6 24 E4
Court Leet CV3 135 D7
Court Leet Rd CV3 133 E7
Courtney Cl CV11 73 F7
Courtney DY10 116 E2
Court Oak Rd B17 85 A6
Court of Lady Katherine Leveson The B93 129 B5
Court Par WS9 30 B6
Court Pas DY1 51 C1
Court Rd
Birmingham,Balsall Heath B12 86 E6
Birmingham,Sparkhill B11 87 C4
Wolverhampton WV6 24 F4
Woodcross WV4 40 A3
Court St
2 Cradley Heath B64 62 F1
9 Stourbridge DY8 81 A5
Royal Leamington Spa CV31 162 A7
Courtway Ave B14 105 B1
Court Way WS2 28 E2
Courtyard The
Coleshill B46 59 F2
Solihull B91 107 C4
Stoke Prior B60 150 D2
Warwick CV34 160 F5
West Bromwich B70 53 A3
Cousins St WV2 39 D7
Coveley Gr B18 66 A5
Coven Cl WS3 15 A5
Coven Gr B29 85 B2
Coven St WV10 25 D4
Coventry Airport CV8 134 B2
Coventry Blue Coat CE Sch The CV1 113 F1

Coventry Bsns Pk CV5 112 D1
Coventry Canal Basin Warehouse CV1 165 B4
Coventry Cath Church of St Michael★ CV1 165 C3
Coventry Gram Sch CV5 112 F1
Coventry Highway B98 154 C4
Coventry Muslim Sch CV6 113 E8
Coventry Prep Sch CV3 133 B8
Coventry Railway Ctr CV8 134 A3
Coventry Rd
Aston Flamville LE10 76 F1
Baginton CV8 133 F2
Barnacle CV7,CV12 97 A8
Bedworth CV12 78 B2
Bedworth,Hawkesbury CV2 96 E6
Berkswell CV7 110 E3
Bickenhill B26,B92 90 C2
Birmingham B10,B25,B26 88 C6
Bulkington CV12 79 B1
Coventry CV3 115 F3
Cubbington CV32 157 E7
Hampton-in-A B92 91 B3
Hinckley LE10 75 B7
Hinckley,Sketchley Hill LE10 75 F5
Kenilworth CV8 148 A7
Nuneaton CV10 78 C7
Stoneleigh CV8,CV3 149 C7
Warwick CV34 160 F8
Coventry Ret Mkt CV1 165 B2
Coventry Road Exhall CV7 96 A8
Coventry Sta CV1 165 B1
Coventry St
Birmingham B5 164 D2
Coventry CV2 114 A4
Kidderminster DY10 116 F6
Nuneaton CV11 73 C4
Stourbridge DY8 81 A5
Wolverhampton WV1 26 A2
Coventry Toy Mus★ CV1 165 C2
Coventry Univ CV1 165 C2
Coventry University Tech Pk CV1 165 C1
Coventry Walsgrave Triangle Bsns Pk CV2 97 A1
Coventry & Warwickshire Hospl CV1 165 C4
Cove Pl CV2 114 C7
Cover Croft B76 47 A1
Coverdale Rd B92 89 A4
Covers The B80 159 E6
Covert La DY8 80 D2
Covert The WV8 10 E1
Covey Cl WS13 3 D1
Cowdray Cl CV31 162 C7
Cow La B78 35 F3
Cowles Croft B25 68 E1
Cowley Cl B36 58 F1
Cowley Dr
Birmingham B27 88 D4
Dudley DY1 50 F2
Cowley Gn WS12 1 F8
Cowley Gr B11 87 E5
Cowley Rd
Birmingham B11 87 E5
Coventry CV2 114 D4
Cowley B77 21 E2
Cowper Cl
Warwick CV34 155 E1
Willenhall WV12 27 E7
Cowper Rd LE10 75 D6
Cowper Wlk DY10 117 C6
Cowslip Cl
1 Birmingham,Hawkesley B38 123 F8
Birmingham,Selly Oak B29 103 A7
Cowslip Wlk DY5 81 C6
Coxcroft Ave DY5 81 F8
Coxmoor Cl WS3 13 F3
Cox Rd WV14 40 E1
Cox's Cl CV10 73 B3
Cox's La B64 62 F2
Cox's Orch 4 CV31 162 A4
Cox St
Birmingham B3 164 B4
Coventry CV1 165 C3
Coxwell Ave WV10 25 C5
Coxwell Gdns B16 65 F2
Coyne Cl DY4 51 D5
Coyne Rd B70 53 B2
Cozens Cl CV12 78 A4
Crabbe St DY9 81 F5
Crabbs Cross La B97 158 E5
Crab La
Cannock WS11 2 A3
Willenhall WV12 13 D1
Crabmill Cl
Birmingham B38 123 E7
Knowle B93 128 C7
Crabmill La
Birmingham B38 124 D8
Coventry CV6 113 F7
Crabourne Rd DY2 62 B2
Crabtree Cl
Birmingham B31 103 C2
Redditch B98 154 A2
West Bromwich B71 53 F8
West Hagley DY9 99 B6
Crabtree Ct B61 136 E3
Crabtree Dr
Birmingham B37 69 F2
Bromsgrove B61 136 F3
Crabtree Gr CV31 162 C6
Crab Tree Ho B33 68 E3
Crabtree La B61 136 E3
Crabtree Rd
Barwell LE9 71 F5
Birmingham B18 66 A5
Walsall WS1 29 A2
Crackley Cotts CV8 148 B8
Crackley Cres CV8 148 B8
Crackley Hall Sch CV8 148 B7
Crackley La
Coventry CV4 131 F3
Kenilworth CV8 148 A7
Crackley Way DY2 62 A6
Craddock Ct CV10 72 C7
Craddock Dr CV10 72 C7
Craddock Rd B67 64 E6
Craddock St WV6 25 B4
Cradley CE Prim Sch B63 82 C7
Cradley Cl B98 154 F2
Cradley Croft B21 54 C3
Cradley Fields B63 82 D5
Cradley Forge DY5 82 A8
Cradley Heath Factory Ctr B64 82 B8
Cradley Heath Sta B64 82 B8
Cradley High Sch B63 82 B6
Cradley Park Rd DY2 62 D2
Cradley Rd
Cradley Heath B64 82 C8
Dudley DY2 62 D3
Cradock Rd B8 67 E5
Craig Cl CV31 162 B6
Craig Croft B37 70 D2
Craigends Ave CV3 134 E6
Crail Gr B43 44 B4
Crakston Cl CV2 114 E2
Cramlington Rd B42 55 A8
Crammond Cl LE10 75 B8
Cramnore Cl DY4 52 A8
Cramper's Field CV6 113 A5
Cramp Hill WS10 41 D6
Cranborne Chase CV2 115 A5
Cranbourne Ave WV4 39 E3
Cranbourne Cl B45 102 B2
Cranbourne Gr B44 56 A8
Cranbourne Pl B71 53 D4
Cranbourne Rd
Birmingham B44 45 A1
Stourbridge DY8 81 B4
Cranbrook Ct WV13 27 C2
Cranbrook Gr WV6 23 F3
Cranbrook Rd B21 54 C2
Cranby St B8 67 C5
Craneberry Rd B37 69 E3
Cranebrook Hill B78 33 E5
Cranebrook La WS14 16 F7
Crane Cl CV34 155 D1
Crane Ct WS1 29 A3
Crane Dr WS7 7 A4
Crane Field WS13 3 B1
Cranehouse Rd B44 45 A2
Cranemoor Cl B7 67 C6
Crane Rd WV14 40 F3
Craner's Rd CV1 113 F4
Cranesbill Cl WV10 12 C7
Cranesbill Rd B29 103 A6
Cranes Park Rd B26 89 C5
Crane St DY11 116 C6
Crane Terr WV6 24 E5
Cranfield Gr B26 88 F8
Cranfield Pl WS5 42 F5
Cranfield Rd WS7 7 A7
Cranford Gr 6 B91 107 B1
Cranford Pl WS11 1 F1
Cranford Rd
Coventry CV5 112 D4
Wolverhampton WV3 38 D8
Cranford St B66 65 C5
Cranford Way B66 65 C5
Cranham Cl B97 153 B1
Cranham Dr DY6 60 E5
Cranhill Cl B92 89 B1
Crankhall La WS10 42 C3
Cranleigh Cl
Aldridge WS9 30 B5
Willenhall WV12 13 C1
Cranleigh Ho B23 56 F6
Cranleigh Pl B44 55 E5
Cranleigh Way WS14 9 F7
Cranmer Ave WV12 27 D7
Cranmer Cl WS6 4 D1
Cranmere Ave WV6 24 A6
Cranmere Ct WV6 24 A6
Cranmer Gr
Royal Leamington Spa CV34 161 D3
Sutton Coldfield B74 31 F6
Cranmoor Cres B63 83 A5
Cranmore Ave
Birmingham B21 65 D7
Solihull B90 126 E8
Cranmore Bvd B90 126 D8
Cranmore Dr B90 106 E1
Cranmore Inf Sch B91 106 E1
Cranmore Rd
Birmingham B36 58 E1
Solihull B90 126 D8
Wolverhampton WV3 24 F3
Cransley Gr B91 107 A1
Crantock Cl WV11 13 C1
Crantock Rd B42 55 C4
Crantock Way CV11 73 F4
Cranwell Gr B24 57 D3
Cranwell Rise B78 20 C1
Cranwell Way B35 58 A3
Crathie Cl CV2 114 F6
Crathorne Ave WV10 11 C1
Craufurd Ct DY8 81 A3
Craufurd St DY8 81 A3
Craven Ave CV3 135 D7
Craven Ct CV3 114 F2
Craven St
Coventry CV5 112 F2
Wolverhampton WV2 39 F6
Craven B77 22 B1
Crawford Ave
Darlaston WS10 41 C7
Smethwick B67 64 F4
Wolverhampton WV4 39 F3
Crawford Cl CV32 157 B5
Crawford Rd
Sutton Coldfield B76 57 F8
Wolverhampton WV3 25 A2
Crawford St B8 67 C5
Crawley Wlk 1 B64 62 D1
Crawshaws Rd B36 58 C1
Crayford Rd B44 45 A1
Craythorne Ave B20 54 E4
Crecy Cl B76 46 E4
Crecy Rd CV3 133 E7
Credenda Rd B70 53 A1
Crediton Cl CV11 73 F5
Cregoe St B15 86 C8
Cremore Ave B8 67 E5
Cremorne Rd B75 32 B2
Cremorne Wlk B75 32 B2
Crendon Cl B80 159 E5
Crendon Rd B65 63 A6
Crescent Arc 2 B91 107 C3
Crescent Ave
Birmingham B18 66 B6
Brierley Hill DY5 61 C1
Coventry CV3 114 C2
Crescent Grange Rd The DY9 81 C4
Crescent Ho B97 153 D2
Crescent Ind Pk DY2 62 B7
Crescent Rd
Darlaston WS10 41 D6
Dudley DY2 62 B5
Kidderminster DY11 116 C5
Willenhall WV13 27 C2
Crescent Sta The WV14 40 D6
Crescent The
Bilston WV14 40 D6
Birmingham,Coleshill Heath B37 90 E8
Birmingham,Great Barr B43 44 A1
Birmingham,Hockley B18 66 B6
Birmingham,Sparkbrook B12 87 B5
Bromsgrove B60 136 F1
Cradley Heath B64 83 A7
Dudley DY1 51 E4
Great Wyrley WS6 5 A2
Hampton-in-A B92 109 B7
Keresley CV7 94 F6
Rowley Regis B65 63 C2
Solihull,Lode Heath B91 107 B4
Solihull,Shirley B90 106 A4
Walsall WS1 43 A8
Wednesbury WS10 42 A4
West Hagley DY8 98 F5
Willenhall WS10,WV13 27 C1
Wolverhampton WV6 24 B3
Crescent Twr B1 66 C2
Cressage Ave B31 103 A1
Cressage Rd CV2 115 A6
Cressett Ave DY5 61 C4
Cressett La DY5 61 C4
Cressida Cl CV34 161 F3
Cressington Dr B74 32 A1
Cresswell Cl CV10 73 C8
Cresswell Cres WS3 13 F2
Cresswell Ct WV10 11 A3
Cresswell Gr B24 57 D4
Cresswell Ho CV6 113 B7
Crest The
Birmingham B31 123 C7
Royal Leamington Spa CV32 157 D3
Crest View
Birmingham B14 105 B4
Sutton Coldfield B74 44 F8
Crestwood Ave DY11 116 A5
Crestwood Dr B44 55 E7
Crestwood Glen WV6 24 E7
Crestwood Park Prim Sch DY6 61 A5
Crestwood Sch The DY6 60 F5
Crestwood B77 22 A5
Creswell Rd B28 106 B7
Creswick Gr B45 122 C7
Crewe Dr DY4 52 A2
Crew La CV8 148 E6
Crew Rd WS10 42 A4
Creynolds Cl B90 126 D3
Creynolds La B90 126 E4
Cricket Cl
Coventry CV5 112 F3
Walsall WS5 43 B7
Cricketers Mdw B64 82 F7
Cricket La WS14 9 C5
Cricket Mdw
Dudley DY3 50 E5
Wolverhampton WV10 11 D4
Crick La B20 66 A8
Cricklewood Dr B62 83 D3
Crigdon B77 22 C1
Crimmond Rise B63 82 E5
Crimscote Cl B90 126 F6
Cringlebrook B77 21 D1
Cripps Rd WS2 27 E3
Crocketts Ave B21 65 D7
Crocketts Lane Prim Sch B66 65 B5
Crockett's La B66 65 A6
Crocketts Rd B21 65 D8
Crockett St DY1 51 A2
Crockford Dr B75 32 B3
Crockford Rd B71 42 C1
Crockington La WV5 37 A1
Crocus Cres WV9 11 A3
Croft Apartments 2 WV13 27 A2
Croft Ave B79 21 B6
Croft Cl
Birmingham B25 88 E8
Redditch B98 154 D3
Warwick CV34 161 C7
Croft Cres WS8 15 D7
Croft Ct B36 69 B8
Croftdown Rd B17 85 A7
Croft Down Rd B92 89 D4
Crofters Cl DY8 81 B4
Crofters Ct B15 85 E6
Crofters La B75 32 E3
Crofters Wlk WV8 10 E1
Croft Fields CV12 78 B2
Croft Gdns WS7 7 A8
Croft Ho 2 WS1 28 F1
Croft Ind Est B37 70 D2
Croft Jun Sch CV10 72 F3
Croft La WV10 26 A7
Croftleigh Gdns B91 106 E2
Croft Mews CV10 73 A4
Croft Par WS9 30 B6
Croft Pool CV12 77 F2
Croft Rd
Bedworth CV12 77 F2
Birmingham B26 88 E8
Coventry CV1 165 A2
Leek Wootton CV35 156 A7
Nuneaton CV10 72 F3
Crofts La B96 158 B2
Crofts The B76 58 A8
Croft Street JMI Sch WS2 28 D3
Croft St
Tamworth B79 21 B6
Walsall WS2 28 D3
Willenhall WV13 27 A2
Croft The
Birmingham B31 103 B2
Blakedown DY10 98 C2
Bulkington CV12 79 B2
Cheslyn Hay WS6 4 E2
Coventry CV6 95 F4
Dudley DY2 61 F6
Kidderminster DY11 116 A4
Meriden CV7 92 C1
Sedgley DY3 39 E1
Walsall WS5 43 E8
Croftway The B20 54 E6
Croftwood Rd DY9 81 D4
Cromane Sq B43 54 E7
Cromarty Cl CV5 112 A5
Cromdale Cl CV10 72 A3
Cromdale Dr B63 82 D3
Cromdale B77 22 C1
Crome Rd B43 44 D3
Cromer Gdns WV6 24 F5
Cromer Rd
Birmingham B12 86 F5
Royal Leamington Spa CV32 157 B2
Cromes Wood CV4 111 D1
Crompton Ave B20 55 C1
Crompton Cl WS2 28 A5
Crompton Ct
Codsall WV8 10 B4
Warwick CV34 160 D6
Crompton Rd
Birmingham,Handsworth B20 55 C1
Birmingham,Nechells B7 67 C8
Birmingham,Rubery B45 101 D1
Tipton DY4 52 A4
Crompton St CV34 160 D6
Cromwell Cl
Rowley Regis B65 63 A5
Willenhall WS2 27 E4
Cromwell Ct WS6 5 A1
Cromwell Dr DY2 62 F8
Cromwell Jun & Inf Sch B7 67 B6
Cromwell La
Birmingham B31 102 E8
Coventry CV4,CV8 131 C6
Cromwell Rd
Cannock WS12 2 E1
Tamworth B79 20 E8
Wolverhampton WV10 11 E4
Cromwells Mdw WS14 9 C5
Cromwell St
Birmingham B7 67 B5
Coventry CV6 113 F6
Dudley DY2 62 E8
West Bromwich B71 53 C4
Crondal Pl B15 86 B7
Crondal Rd CV7 96 B7
Cronehills Jun & Inf Sch B70 53 D4
Cronehills Linkway B70 53 D3
Cronehills St B70 53 D4
Crookham Cl B17 84 F7
Crookhay La B71 53 B8
Crook La
Aldridge WS9 30 B1
Birmingham WS9 44 A7
Crooks La B80 159 D3
Croome Cl
Birmingham B11 87 B3
Coventry CV6 112 F4
Redditch B98 154 F1
Cropredy Rd B31 123 B8
Cropthorne Cl B98 159 B7
Cropthorne Dr B47 125 B7
Cropthorne Ho B60 137 B3
Cropthorne Rd B90 106 C3
Crosbie Rd
Birmingham B17 85 B6
Coventry CV5 112 E3
Crosby Cl
Birmingham B1 66 B3
Wolverhampton WV6 24 F5
Cross Cheaping CV1 165 B3
Cross Cl B64 62 F2
Cross Farm Rd B17 85 D4
Cross Farms La B45 101 F1
Crossfell B77 22 B1
Crossfield Rd B33 69 A3
Crossfield Rd Ind Est WS13 9 E8
Crossfield Rd WS13 9 E8
Cross Fields Rd 4 CV34 160 F8
Crossfield Way WV14 40 E5
Crossgate Rd
Dudley DY2 61 F6
Redditch B98 159 C7
Cross Ho WV2 39 C7
Crossings Ind Est The 4 WS3 28 B8
Crossings The 5 WS14 9 E8
Crosskey Cl B33 69 E2
Cross Keys Island WS12 2 C3
Cross Keys WS13 9 B8
Cross La
Birmingham B43 43 E1
Cubbington CV32 157 E4
Lichfield WS14 9 D6
Crossland Cres WV6 24 F7
Crossland Row LE10 76 A6
Cross La DY3 39 E1
Crossley Ct CV6 113 F7
Crossley Ret Pk DY11 116 D6
Crossley St DY2 62 D4
Crossley Wlk B60 150 E7
Cross Pl DY3 39 E1
Cross Point Bsns Pk CV2 115 B8
Cross Rd
4 Royal Leamington Spa CV32 156 D1
Coventry CV6 113 F8
Keresley CV7 94 F6
Cross Road Ind Est CV6 113 F7
Cross St N WV1 25 D4
Cross St S WV2 39 C7
Cross St
11 Warwick CV34 160 F7
2 Willenhall WV13 27 A1
4 Rowley Regis B65 63 C1
4 Stourbridge,Wordsley DY6 60 D3
Bilston WV14 40 F2
Birmingham B21 65 C8
Burntwood WS7 6 E8
Cannock,Bridgtown WS11 4 E5
Cannock WS12 2 E1
Cheslyn Hay WS6 4 D2
Coventry CV1 165 C4
Dudley DY1 51 C1
Halesowen B63 83 A3
Kingswinford DY6 60 D6
Kingswinford,Wall Heath DY6 60 B8
Nuneaton CV10 72 D3
Oldbury B68 64 A4
Royal Leamington Spa CV32 157 A1
Smethwick B66 65 A6
Stourbridge DY8 80 E5
Tamworth B79 21 B5
Tamworth,Kettlebrook B77 21 C3
Walsall WS3 15 A1
Wednesbury WS10 41 E3
Wolverhampton WV1 25 F1
Cross The
Kingswinford DY6 60 D6
Stourbridge DY9 81 E6
Crossway La B44 55 F6
Crossway Rd CV3 133 B4
Crossways Ct B44 56 B7
Crossways Gn B44 56 B7
Crossways LE10 75 F5
Crossways Sh Ctr WV10 26 A3
Crosswells Rd B68 64 B5
Cross Wlk B69 63 C8
Cross Wlks DY9 81 E5
Crowberry Cl WS8 15 D6
Crowberry La B78 48 C8
Crowden Rd B77 22 A1
Crowesbridge Mews WV14 51 B8
Crowhill Rd CV11 74 A1
Crowhurst Rd B31 122 E7
Crowland Ave WV6 23 E4
Crowle Dr DY9 81 C5
Crowmere Rd CV2 114 F7
Crown Cl
Bromsgrove B61 136 F2
Rowley Regis B65 63 D4
Sedgley DY3 39 D1
Crown Ct
10 Hinckley LE10 71 D1
1 Sutton Coldfield B74 31 E3
Darlaston WS10 41 C8
Crown Ctr The 3 DY8 81 A5
Crown Gn CV6 95 E2
Crownhill Mdw B61 136 F7
Crownhill Rd LE10 75 D4
Crown Ho CV5 112 E3

Crown La
Iverley DY8 . . . . . 98 C7
Kidderminster DY10 . . . . . 116 E6
Stourbridge DY8 . . . . . 80 F5
Sutton Coldfield B74 . . . . . 31 E3
Crown Mdw B48 . . . . . 139 A7
Crownmeadow Dr DY4 . . . 52 D7
Crown Rd
Birmingham,Bordesley Green B9 . . . . . 67 D2
Birmingham,King's Norton B30 . . . . . 104 A4
Crown St WV1 . . . . . 25 D4
Crown Terr CV31 . . . . . 161 F7
Crown Way CV32 . . . . . 157 B3
Crown Wharf Sh Pk WS2 . 28 D2
Crown Wlk DY4 . . . . . 52 A2
Crows Nest Cl B76 . . . . . 46 F3
Crowther Gdns B63 . . . . . 82 C7
Crowther Gr WV6 . . . . . 24 F4
Crowther Rd
Birmingham B23 . . . . . 56 D5
Wolverhampton WV6 . . . . . 24 F5
Crowther St
Kidderminster DY11 . . . . . 116 C6
Wolverhampton WV10 . . . . . 25 E4
Croxall Way B66 . . . . . 65 B5
Croxdene Ave WS3 . . . . . 14 A1
Croxhall St CV12 . . . . . 78 C3
Croxley Dr WS12 . . . . . 2 C3
Croxley Gdns WV13 . . . . . 40 F8
Croxstalls Ave WS3 . . . . . 28 A8
Croxstalls Cl WS3 . . . . . 14 A1
Croxstalls Pl WS3 . . . . . 28 A8
Croxstalls Rd WS3 . . . . . 28 A8
Croxton Gr B33 . . . . . 69 A4
Croyde Ave B42 . . . . . 55 A8
Croydon Cl CV3 . . . . . 133 E6
Croydon Ct 20 B29 . . . . . 103 C7
Croydon Rd
Birmingham B29 . . . . . 85 F3
Birmingham,Erdington B24 . 57 A2
Croy Dr B35 . . . . . 58 B4
Crucible The WV14 . . . . . 40 D2
Crummock Cl CV6 . . . . . 95 D3
Crumpfields La B97 . . . . . 152 F1
Crump Ho WS1 . . . . . 28 F1
Crusader Cl B69 . . . . . 63 E5
Crutchley Ave B78 . . . . . 21 A2
Crutchley Way CV31 . . . . . 162 A2
Crychan Cl B45 . . . . . 102 B2
Cryersoak Cl B90 . . . . . 127 B7
Cryfield Grange Rd CV4, CV8 . . . . . 132 C2
Cryfield Hts CV4 . . . . . 132 D2
Cryfield Village CV4 . . . . . 132 B4
Crystal Ave DY8 . . . . . 60 F1
Crystal Dr B66 . . . . . 64 C8
Crystal Ho B66 . . . . . 65 C6
Cubbington CE Prim Sch CV32 . . . . . 157 F5
Cubbington Rd
Coventry CV6 . . . . . 96 A2
Royal Leamington Spa CV32 . . . . . 157 B3
Cubley Rd B28 . . . . . 87 E1
Cuckoo Cl WS11 . . . . . 2 C2
Cuckoo La CV1 . . . . . 165 C3
Cuckoo Rd B7 . . . . . 67 D8
Cuin Rd B66 . . . . . 65 C5
Cuin Wlk 11 B66 . . . . . 65 C5
Culey Gr B33 . . . . . 69 D2
Culey Wlk B37 . . . . . 70 D2
Culford Dr B32 . . . . . 102 C8
Culham Cl B27 . . . . . 88 D2
Cullwick St WV1 . . . . . 40 A8
Culmington Rd B31 . . . . . 122 F8
Culmore Cl WV12 . . . . . 27 D4
Culmore Rd B62 . . . . . 63 E1
Culpepper Cl CV10 . . . . . 72 E4
Culverhouse Dr DY5 . . . . . 61 A1
Culverley Cres B93 . . . . . 127 F6
Culvert Way B66 . . . . . 64 D7
Culwell Ind Pk WV10 . . . 163 D4
Culwell St WV10 . . . . . 163 C4
Culwell Trad Est WV10 . . . . 25 F4
Culworth Cl CV31 . . . . . 161 F5
Culworth Ct
Coventry CV6 . . . . . 113 E7
Whitnash CV31 . . . . . 162 A5
Culworth Row CV6 . . . . . 113 E8
Cumberford Ave B33 . . . . . 69 E1
Cumberland Ave 3 B5 . . . 86 E7
Cumberland Cl DY6 . . . . . 60 E4
Cumberland Cres
Burntwood WS7 . . . . . 7 A8
Royal Leamington Spa CV32 . . . . . 157 C3
Cumberland Dr
Nuneaton CV10 . . . . . 72 E3
Tamworth B78 . . . . . 21 A1
Cumberland Ho 7 WV3 . . 25 C4
Cumberland Rd
Bilston WV14 . . . . . 40 D7
Birmingham B68 . . . . . 84 B7
Cannock WS11 . . . . . 2 A4
West Bromwich B71 . . . . . 53 D7
Willenhall WV13 . . . . . 27 D2
Cumberland St B1 . . . . . 66 B2
Cumberland Wlk B75 . . . . . 47 B5
Cumbernauld Wlk 7 CV2 . . . . . 115 A7
Cumbrae Dr LE10 . . . . . 71 B2
Cumbria Cl CV1 . . . . . 113 A3
Cumbrian Croft B63 . . . . . 82 D2
Cumbria Way B8 . . . . . 67 D6
Cumming St 14 CV31 . . . . 162 A7
Cundall Cl CV31 . . . . . 162 B6
Cunnery The CV8 . . . . . 149 A3
Cunningham Rd
Perton WV6 . . . . . 23 E4
Walsall WS2 . . . . . 27 E2
Cupfields Ave DY4 . . . . . 52 C8
Cupfields Cres DY4 . . . . . 52 C7
Curbar Rd B42 . . . . . 55 C6
Curborough Rd WS13 . . . . . 3 B2
Curdale Rd B32 . . . . . 102 B8
Curdworth La B76 . . . . . 59 A8
Curdworth Prim Sch B76 . 59 C6
Cur La B97 . . . . . 152 D3
Curlew Cl
Kidderminster DY10 . . . . . 117 B2
Lichfield WS14 . . . . . 9 E7
Curlew Dr WS8 . . . . . 15 E7
Curlew Hill WS11 . . . . . 2 A3
Curlews Cl B23 . . . . . 56 C8
Curlew B77 . . . . . 36 A7
Curlieu Cl CV35 . . . . . 160 A7
Curral Rd B65 . . . . . 63 C3
Curran Cl CV31 . . . . . 162 B4
Curriers Cl CV4 . . . . . 131 D7
Curslow La DY10 . . . . . 117 F1
Curtin Dr WS10 . . . . . 41 B4
Curtis Cl
Finstall B60 . . . . . 151 F8
Smethwick B66 . . . . . 65 C4
Curtis Rd CV2 . . . . . 114 D6
Curzon Ave CV6 . . . . . 113 E8
Curzon Cl LE10 . . . . . 75 F7
Curzon Gr CV31 . . . . . 162 C6
Curzon St
Birmingham B4 . . . . . 67 A3
Wolverhampton WV2 . . . . . 39 D7
Cuthbert Rd B18 . . . . . 65 E4
Cutlers Rough Cl B31 . . . 102 F5
Cutler St B66 . . . . . 65 B6
Cutsdean Cl B31 . . . . . 102 F6
Cutshill Cl B36 . . . . . 69 C8
Cut Throat La B94 . . . . . 142 D7
Cutting The WS4 . . . . . 28 F4
Cuttle Mill La B76 . . . . . 48 D3
Cuttle Pool La B93 . . . . . 128 F4
Cutworth Cl B76 . . . . . 47 A3
Cwerne Ct DY3 . . . . . 50 C3
Cygnet Cl
Alvechurch B48 . . . . . 139 A7
Cannock WS12 . . . . . 2 C7
Wolverhampton WV6 . . . . . 24 C2
Cygnet Ct
Coventry CV1 . . . . . 165 C4
Kidderminster DY10 . . . . . 117 A1
Cygnet Dr
Brownhills WS8 . . . . . 15 E7
Tamworth B79 . . . . . 20 F5
Cygnet Gr B23 . . . . . 56 B6
Cygnet La DY5 . . . . . 61 C7
Cygnet Rd B70 . . . . . 53 A5
Cygnus Way B70 . . . . . 52 F5
Cymbeline Way CV34 . . . . 161 E4
Cypress Ave DY3 . . . . . 50 D5
Cypress Croft CV3 . . . . . 134 F8
Cypress Ct DY10 . . . . . 117 A4
Cypress Gdns
Kingswinford DY6 . . . . . 60 D4
Sutton Coldfield B74 . . . . . 46 A7
Walsall WS5 . . . . . 43 C4
Cypress Gr B31 . . . . . 102 E1
Cypress La CV31 . . . . . 162 B3
Cypress Rd
Dudley DY2 . . . . . 51 F1
Walsall WS5 . . . . . 43 C4
Cypress Sq 2 B27 . . . . . 88 C5
Cypress Way
Birmingham B31 . . . . . 122 F8
Nuneaton CV10 . . . . . 72 D6
Cyprus Ave B96 . . . . . 158 D2
Cyprus Cl B29 . . . . . 103 A7
Cyprus St
Oldbury B69 . . . . . 64 A8
Wolverhampton WV2 . . . . . 39 C6
Cyril Gr 5 B10 . . . . . 87 C8
Cyril Rd B10 . . . . . 87 D8

D

Dacer Cl B30 . . . . . 104 B5
Dace Rd WV10 . . . . . 26 B4
Dace B77 . . . . . 35 D7
Dadford View DY5 . . . . . 61 B2
Dad's La B13 . . . . . 86 C1
Daffern Rd CV7 . . . . . 78 A1
Daffodil Cl DY3 . . . . . 50 E7
Daffodil Dr 4 CV12 . . . . . 77 D2
Daffodil Pl WS5 . . . . . 43 D8
Daffodil Rd WS5 . . . . . 43 D8
Daffodil Way B31 . . . . . 122 E8
Dagger La B71 . . . . . 53 E4
Dagnall Rd B27 . . . . . 88 D3
Dagnell End Rd B98 . . . . . 154 B7
Dagtail La B97 . . . . . 158 D3
Dahlia Cl
Hinckley LE10 . . . . . 75 E6
Wolverhampton WV1 . . . . . 26 C1
Dahlia Wlk CV10 . . . . . 78 A8
Daimler Cl B36 . . . . . 58 F1
Daimler Rd
Birmingham B14 . . . . . 105 D3
Coventry CV6 . . . . . 113 C5
Dainton Gr B32 . . . . . 84 C1
Daintree Croft CV3 . . . . . 133 C7
Daintry Dr B78 . . . . . 20 B7
Dairy Cl DY4 . . . . . 52 B5
Dairy Ct B68 . . . . . 84 D7
Dairy La B97 . . . . . 153 A5
Daisy Bank WS12 . . . . . 1 F8
Daisy Bank Cl WS3 . . . . . 15 B2
Daisy Bank Cres WS5 . . . . 43 D8
Daisy Croft CV12 . . . . . 77 D2
Daisy Dr B23 . . . . . 56 A5
Daisy Farm Rd B14 . . . . . 105 B3
Daisy Mdw DY4 . . . . . 52 C6
Daisy Rd B16 . . . . . 65 F2
Daisy St
Dudley WV14 . . . . . 40 D2
Wolverhampton WV6 . . . . . 25 A4
Daisy Wlk WV9 . . . . . 11 A3
Dakota Apartments B16 . . 66 B1
Dalbeg Cl WV8 . . . . . 24 E8
Dalbury Rd B28 . . . . . 105 E5
Dalby Cl CV3 . . . . . 134 E8
Dalby Rd WS3 . . . . . 28 F6
Dale Cl
Birmingham B43 . . . . . 43 D1
Catshill B61 . . . . . 136 F7
Smethwick B66 . . . . . 65 A3
Tipton DY4 . . . . . 52 D5
Warwick CV34 . . . . . 161 A8
Dalecote Ave B92 . . . . . 107 E8
Dale Ct WV1 . . . . . 25 A3
Dale Dr WS7 . . . . . 7 B7
Dale End B4 . . . . . 164 C3
Dale End Cl LE10 . . . . . 75 A7
Dale End
Darlaston WS10 . . . . . 41 D6
Nuneaton CV10 . . . . . 72 E5
Dale Hill B60 . . . . . 137 F6
Dalehouse Flats CV8 . . . . 148 B6
Dalehouse La CV8 . . . . . 148 D7
Dale Meadow Cl CV7 . . . . 130 B6
Dale Rd
Birmingham B29 . . . . . 85 E3
Halesowen B62 . . . . . 83 F8
Redditch B98 . . . . . 153 F5
Stourbridge DY8 . . . . . 80 F2
Dales Cl WV6 . . . . . 25 B6
Dales Com Jun Sch B77 . . 36 B8
Dales Inf Sch The B77 . . . 36 B8
Dalesman Cl DY6 . . . . . 60 B7
Dale St
Bilston WV14 . . . . . 41 A5
Royal Leamington Spa CV32 . . . . . 161 E8
Smethwick B66 . . . . . 65 A3
Walsall WS1 . . . . . 42 E7
Wednesbury WS10 . . . . . 41 E3
Wolverhampton WV3 . . . . . 163 A2
Daleswood Pk B62 . . . . . 100 F2
Dale Terr B69 . . . . . 63 C8
Daleview Rd B14 . . . . . 105 C4
Daleway Rd CV3 . . . . . 133 B4
Dale Wlk B25 . . . . . 88 B7
Dalewood Croft B26 . . . . . 88 F6
Dalewood Rd B37 . . . . . 69 F5
Daley Cl B1 . . . . . 66 B3
Daley Rd WV14 . . . . . 40 F2
Dalkeith Rd B73 . . . . . 45 E2
Dalkeith St WS2 . . . . . 28 C3
Dallas Rd B23 . . . . . 56 D5
Dallimore Cl B92 . . . . . 89 A3
Dallington Rd CV6 . . . . . 112 E6
Dalloway Cl B5 . . . . . 86 D6
Dalmahoy Cl CV11 . . . . . 79 C8
Dalmeny Rd CV4 . . . . . 131 D7
Dalston Cl DY2 . . . . . 62 D6
Dalston Rd B27 . . . . . 88 C4
Dalton Ct B23 . . . . . 56 B3
Dalton Gdns CV2 . . . . . 114 F4
Dalton Rd
Bedworth CV12 . . . . . 78 A2
Coventry CV5 . . . . . 113 B1
Walsall WS2 . . . . . 28 A3
Dalton St
Birmingham B4 . . . . . 164 C3
Wolverhampton WV3 . . . . . 39 B8
Dalton Way B4 . . . . . 164 C3
Dalvine Rd DY2 . . . . . 62 B2
Dalwood Cl WV14 . . . . . 51 B7
Dalwood Way CV6 . . . . . 96 B4
Damar Croft B14 . . . . . 104 D4
Dama Rd B78 . . . . . 34 F8
Dame Agnes Gr CV6 . . . . . 114 B8
Dame Elizabeth Cadbury Tech Coll B30 . . . . . 103 D7
Dame Ellen Pinsent Sch B13 . . . . . 105 A7
Damien Cl B67 . . . . . 64 F5
Damson Cl
Redditch B97 . . . . . 158 C6
Wednesfield WV12 . . . . . 27 A6
Damson Ct LE10 . . . . . 75 B7
Damson La B91,B92 . . . . . 107 E7
Damson Parkway B91, B92 . . . . . 107 F7
Damson Wharf DY4 . . . . . 52 A3
Damson Wood Inf Sch B92 . . . . . 107 D7
Dam St WS13 . . . . . 9 B8
Danbury Cl B76 . . . . . 47 A2
Danbury Gdns WV10 . . . . . 11 C2
Danbury Rd B90 . . . . . 106 B2
Danby Gr B24 . . . . . 57 B2
Dando Rd DY2 . . . . . 62 D8
Dandy Bank Rd DY6 . . . . . 61 A8
Dandy's Wlk WS1 . . . . . 42 F8
Dane Gr B13 . . . . . 104 D8
Danehill Wlk WV8 . . . . . 24 F8
Danehurst Ctr WV1 . . . . . 26 A3
Danelagh Cl B79 . . . . . 20 F7
Dane Rd CV2 . . . . . 114 B4
Danesbury Cres
Birmingham B44 . . . . . 56 A8
Royal Leamington Spa CV31 . . . . . 162 D6
Danes Cl WV11 . . . . . 12 F4
Danescourt Rd WV6 . . . . . 24 C6
Danesmoor Ho B26 . . . . . 88 E7
Danesmore Park Jun & Inf Sch WV11 . . . . . 13 A1
Daneswood Dr WS9 . . . . . 15 F3
Daneswood Rd CV3 . . . . . 135 E7
Dane Terr B65 . . . . . 63 C5
Daneways Cl B74 . . . . . 45 A8
Danford Cl DY8 . . . . . 81 A4
Danford Gdns B10 . . . . . 87 C8
Danford La B91 . . . . . 106 E3
Danford Rd B47 . . . . . 124 F6
Danford Way B43 . . . . . 54 D8
Dangerfield Ho B70 . . . . . 53 E1
Dangerfield La WS10 . . . . 41 C4
Daniel Ave CV10 . . . . . 72 C3
Daniels La WS9 . . . . . 30 C5
Daniels Rd B9 . . . . . 68 A2
Danilo Rd WS11 . . . . . 1 D1
Danks St DY4 . . . . . 52 A2
Danzey Cl B98 . . . . . 159 B5
Danzey Gr B14 . . . . . 104 C3
Danzey Green La B94 . . . 142 B1
Danzey Green Rd B36 . . . . 58 B1
Daphne Cl CV2 . . . . . 96 C3
Darby Cl WV14 . . . . . 40 A2
Darby End Rd DY2 . . . . . 62 E4
Darby Ho 2 WS2 . . . . . 42 C7
Darby Rd
Oldbury B68 . . . . . 64 C5
Wednesbury WS10 . . . . . 42 B4
Darbys Hill Rd B69 . . . . . 63 B7
Darby St B65 . . . . . 63 C1
Darbys Way DY4 . . . . . 52 B5
Darell Croft B76 . . . . . 46 E3
Daren Cl B36 . . . . . 69 F8
Dare Rd B23 . . . . . 56 E4
Dare's Wlk LE10 . . . . . 71 D1
Darfield Wlk 2 B12 . . . . . 86 F8
Darges La WS6 . . . . . 4 F4
Darkhouse La WV14 . . . . . 40 C2
Dark La
Astwood Bank B96 . . . . . 158 D1
Bedworth CV12 . . . . . 77 D1
Belbroughton DY9 . . . . . 119 F8
Birchmoor B78 . . . . . 36 E8
Brinsford WV10 . . . . . 11 D8
Coventry CV1 . . . . . 165 B4
Featherstone WV10 . . . . . 12 D7
Great Wyrley WS6 . . . . . 5 C1
Hollywood B38,B47 . . . . . 124 E7
Romsley B62 . . . . . 100 F4
Stoke Heath B60 . . . . . 150 D6
Darlaston Com Science Coll WS10 . . . . . 41 B6
Darlaston Ct CV7 . . . . . 92 D1
Darlaston La WV14 . . . . . 41 A7
Darlaston Rd
Walsall WS2 . . . . . 42 A8
Wednesbury WS10 . . . . . 41 E4
Darlaston Road Ind Est WS10 . . . . . 41 D5
Darley Ave B34 . . . . . 68 F6
Darleydale Ave B44 . . . . . 44 E1
Darley Dr WV6 . . . . . 25 B5
Darley Green Rd B93 . . . . 128 B1
Darley Ho B69 . . . . . 63 D6
Darley Mead Ct B91 . . . . . 107 E4
Darley Rd LE10 . . . . . 75 E6
Darley Way B74 . . . . . 45 A7
Darlington St
Darlaston WS10 . . . . . 41 D5
Wolverhampton WV1 . . . . . 163 B3
Darlington Yd WV1 . . . . . 163 B3
Darlston Row CV7 . . . . . 92 B1
Darnbrook B77 . . . . . 22 C1
Darnel Croft 3 B10 . . . . . 67 B1
Darnel Hurst Rd B75 . . . . . 32 D3
Darnford Cl
Birmingham B28 . . . . . 106 A5
Coventry CV2 . . . . . 114 F7
Sutton Coldfield B72 . . . . . 57 D7
Darnford La WS14 . . . . . 9 F6
Darnford Moors WS14 . . . . . 9 E6
Darnford View WS13 . . . . . 3 E1
Darnick Rd B73 . . . . . 45 D2
Darnley Rd 3 B16 . . . . . 66 A2
Darrach Cl CV2 . . . . . 96 E1
Darris Rd B29 . . . . . 104 A8
Dart Cl LE10 . . . . . 75 A8
Dartford Rd WS3 . . . . . 13 F1
Dartington Way CV11 . . . . 78 F8
Dartmoor Cl B45 . . . . . 102 A2
Dartmouth Ave
Cannock WS11 . . . . . 4 C8
Stourbridge DY8 . . . . . 60 D3
Walsall WS3 . . . . . 28 E6
Willenhall WV13 . . . . . 27 A2
Dartmouth Cir B6 . . . . . 66 F5
Dartmouth Cl WS3 . . . . . 28 E5
Dartmouth Cres 2 WV14 . 41 A7
Dartmouth Dr WS9 . . . . . 30 A5
Dartmouth High Sch B43 . 43 D3
Dartmouth Ho 2 WS3 . . . . 28 F6
Dartmouth Middleway B7 66 F4
Dartmouth Pl WS3 . . . . . 28 F6
Dartmouth Rd
Birmingham B29 . . . . . 85 F2
Cannock WS11 . . . . . 1 D1
Coventry CV2 . . . . . 114 C5
Smethwick B66 . . . . . 64 F8
Dartmouth Sch CV2 . . . . . 114 D5
Dartmouth Sq B70 . . . . . 53 D2
Dartmouth Street Sta B70 53 B3
Dartmouth St
West Bromwich B70 . . . . . 53 B3
Wolverhampton WV2 . . . . . 163 C1
Wolverhampton WV2 . . . . . 163 D1
Dart St B9 . . . . . 67 B1
Dart B77 . . . . . 36 A5
Darvel Mews WV12 . . . . . 27 D4
Darvel Rd WV12 . . . . . 27 D4
Darwall St WS1 . . . . . 28 E2
Darwell Pk B77 . . . . . 22 B2
Darwin Cl
Burntwood WS7 . . . . . 7 B7
Cannock WS12 . . . . . 2 E2
Coventry CV2 . . . . . 115 A6
Hinckley LE10 . . . . . 71 E3
Lichfield WS13 . . . . . 9 A8
Darwin Ct
1 Bedworth CV12 . . . . . 78 A2
Perton WV6 . . . . . 23 E4
Darwin Ho
3 Birmingham,Chelmsley Wood B37 . . . . . 70 C1
3 Birmingham,Showell Green B13 . . . . . 87 A2
Kingswinford DY6 . . . . . 60 F7
Darwin Pl WS2 . . . . . 28 B6
Darwin Rd WS2 . . . . . 28 B6
Darwin St B12 . . . . . 86 F8
Dassett Gr B9 . . . . . 68 C2
Dassett Rd B93 . . . . . 127 F4
Datchet Cl CV5 . . . . . 112 C4
Datteln Rd WS11 . . . . . 2 A4
D'aubeny Rd CV4 . . . . . 132 C8
Dauntsey Covert B14 . . . . 104 D2
Davena Dr B29 . . . . . 84 E2
Davena Gr WV14 . . . . . 40 D3
Davenham Rd B60 . . . . . 137 C1
Davenport Dr
Birmingham B35 . . . . . 58 C3
Bromsgrove B60 . . . . . 137 B1
Davenport Lodge Sch CV5 . . . . . 133 B8
Davenport Rd
Coventry CV5 . . . . . 133 B8
Wednesfield WV11 . . . . . 26 E6
Wolverhampton WV6 . . . . . 24 B5
Davenport Terr LE10 . . . . . 75 E8
Daventry Gr B32 . . . . . 84 D6
Daventry Rd CV3 . . . . . 133 D7
Davey Cl WS7 . . . . . 6 F4
Davey Rd
Birmingham B20 . . . . . 55 E1
West Bromwich B70 . . . . . 53 A5
David Cox Ct 1 B17 . . . . . 85 D5
David Garrick Gdns WS13 . . 3 B2
David Harman Dr B71 . . . . 53 F7
David Peacock Cl DY4 . . . . 52 A5
David Rd
Bedworth CV7 . . . . . 95 F8
Birmingham B20 . . . . . 55 B2
Coventry CV1 . . . . . 113 F2
Tipton DY4 . . . . . 52 A7
Davidson Ave CV31 . . . . . 162 A7
Davidson Rd WS14 . . . . . 9 B7
Davids The B31 . . . . . 103 C5
Davies Ave WV14 . . . . . 40 D3
Davies Ho
7 Oldbury B69 . . . . . 64 A7
Walsall WS3 . . . . . 14 B1
Davies Rd CV7 . . . . . 95 F7
Davis Ave DY4 . . . . . 51 E4
Davis Cl CV32 . . . . . 156 D2
Davis Gr B25 . . . . . 88 D6
Davison Rd B67 . . . . . 64 F3
Davis Rd
Tamworth B77 . . . . . 21 F4
Willenhall WV12 . . . . . 27 D8
Davy Rd WS2 . . . . . 28 A5
Dawberry Cl B14 . . . . . 104 D5
Dawberry Fields Rd B14 104 D5
Dawberry Rd B14 . . . . . 104 C6
Daw End La WS4 . . . . . 29 C6
Daw End Sch WS4 . . . . . 29 C6
Daw End WS4,WS9 . . . . . 29 C6
Dawes Ave B70 . . . . . 53 C1
Dawes Cl CV2 . . . . . 114 A3
Dawes La WS8 . . . . . 7 A1
Dawley Brook Prim Sch DY6 . . . . . 60 C7
Dawley Brook Rd DY6 . . . . 60 D7
Dawley Cl 1 WS2 . . . . . 42 B7
Dawley Cres B37 . . . . . 70 B1
Dawley Rd DY6 . . . . . 60 C8
Dawley Trad Est DY6 . . . . . 60 D8
Dawley Wlk 9 CV2 . . . . . 115 A7
Dawlish Cl CV11 . . . . . 73 E5
Dawlish Dr CV3 . . . . . 133 D5
Dawlish Rd
Birmingham B29 . . . . . 85 F2
Dudley DY1 . . . . . 51 C5
Smethwick B66 . . . . . 65 B5
Dawn Dr DY4 . . . . . 41 C2
Dawney Dr B75 . . . . . 32 A4
Dawn Rd B31 . . . . . 102 E6
Dawson Ave WV14 . . . . . 39 F2
Dawson Cl CV31 . . . . . 162 A2
Dawson Ct B24 . . . . . 56 F4
Dawson Rd
Birmingham B21 . . . . . 65 F8
Bromsgrove B61 . . . . . 136 E2
Coventry CV3 . . . . . 114 A1
Dawson Sq WV14 . . . . . 40 C5
Dawson St
Smethwick B66 . . . . . 65 A3
Walsall WS3 . . . . . 28 D8
Day Ave WV11 . . . . . 26 E7
Daybrook Cl B97 . . . . . 153 B5

Day Ho DY4 52 C8
Dayhouse Bank B62 101 B1
Daylesford Inf Sch B92 89 A3
Daylesford Rd B92 89 A3
Days Cl CV1 113 E3
Day's La CV1 113 F3
Day St WS2 28 E3
Daytona Dr CV5 111 B8
Deacon St CV11 73 C3
Deakin Ave WS8 6 F1
Deakin Rd
Birmingham B24 57 A3
Sutton Coldfield B75 46 E7
Deakins Rd B25 88 B7
Deal Ave WS7 7 A8
Deal Dr B69 52 A1
Deal Gr B31 103 A3
Deanbrook Cl B90 127 A6
Dean Cl
Birmingham B44 56 B8
Hinckley LE10 71 E2
Stourbridge DY8 81 B6
Sutton Coldfield B72 57 B7
Dean Ct
5 Brierley Hill DY5 61 D2
Perton WV6 23 E6
Deanery CE Prim Sch The B76 57 F8
Deanery Row WV1 163 B4
Dean Rd
Birmingham B23 56 F5
Hinckley LE10 71 E2
Walsall WS4 29 C7
Dean Rd W LE10 71 E2
Deans Cl B98 154 D5
Deanscroft Dr B60 137 C6
Deans Croft WS14 9 C8
Deansfield High Sch WV1 26 C2
Deansfield Rd WV1 26 A2
Deansford La DY10 118 B6
Deans Pl WS3 28 F6
Dean's Rd WV1 26 B2
Deans Slade Dr WS14 9 A5
Dean St
Birmingham B5 164 C1
Coventry CV2 114 A3
Deanston Croft CV2 96 F1
Dean St DY3 50 D8
Deansway B61 136 E2
Deans Way CV7 95 D6
Deansway Ho DY10 117 A7
Deansway The DY10 117 A7
Deansway CV34 155 E1
Dearman Rd B11 87 B7
Dearmont Rd B31 122 E7
Dearne Ct DY3 51 A6
Deasy Ho CV3 134 B5
Deasy Rd CV1 165 C1
Deavall Way WS11 2 B2
Debden Cl B93 127 E2
Debenham Cres B25 68 D1
Debenham Rd B25 68 D1
Deblen Dr B16 65 D1
Deborah Cl WV4 39 C6
De-Compton Cl CV7 95 A7
Deedmore Rd CV2 96 D1
Deedmore Sch CV2 114 C8
Deegan Cl CV2 114 A5
Dee Gr
Birmingham B38 123 E8
Cannock WS11 4 D8
Dee Ho 8 DY1 61 E8
Deelands Rd B45 121 F8
Deeley Cl
Birmingham B15 86 C7
Cradley Heath B64 82 E7
Deeley Dr 3 DY4 52 C6
Deeley Pl WS3 28 B8
Deeley St
Brierley Hill DY5 61 E1
Walsall WS3 28 B8
Deeley B77 22 A1
Deepdale Ave B26 89 B4
Deepdale La DY3 50 E3
Deepdale B77 22 D2
Deeplow Cl 2 B72 46 C4
Deepmoor Rd B33 68 F3
Deepmore Ave WS2 28 B2
Deepwood Cl WS4 29 B8
Deepwood Gr B32 102 B8
Deer Barn Hill B98 154 A1
Deer Cl
Huntington WS12 1 C6
Norton Canes WS11 6 B7
Walsall WS3 14 C1
Deerdale Terr 8 CV3 134 F8
Deerdale Way CV3 134 F8
Dee Rd WS3 14 E1
Deerfold Cres WS7 7 B7
Deerham Cl B23 56 D7
Deerhill B77 22 C1
Deerhurst Cl B98 154 C7
Deerhurst Ct B91 107 D4
Deerhurst Rd
Birmingham B20 54 F5
Coventry CV6 95 B2
Deerhurst Rise WS12 2 F6
Deer Leap The CV8 148 B6
Deerpark Dr CV34 160 E8
Deer Park Rd B78 20 E1
Deer Park Way B91 107 C1
Deer Wlk WV8 10 F2
Dee Wlk
Birmingham B36 70 A7
Birmingham B36 70 A8
Defford Ave WS4 15 C1
Defford Cl B97 152 E1
Defford Dr B68 64 B4
Dehavilland Cl CV11 73 B5
De Havilland Dr B35 58 A2
De Havilland Way LE10 75 E4
Deighton Gr CV3 134 C6
Deighton Rd WS5 43 B4
De-La-Bere Cres LE10 76 A6
Delage Cl CV6 96 B4
Delamere Cl B36 58 D1
Delamere Dr WS5 43 C3
Delamere Rd
Bedworth CV12 77 F2
Birmingham B28 105 F7
Willenhall WV12 27 C7
Delamere Way CV32 157 C4
Delancey Keep B75 47 A5
Delaware Rd CV3 133 C5
Delf Ho CV2 96 D1
Delhi Ave CV6 95 D1
Delhurst Ave WV4 39 E3
Delhurst Rd B44 44 D1
Delingpole Wlk 2 B64 82 E8
Delius St CV4 111 E3
Della Dr B32 102 D8
Dell Cl CV3 134 C5
Dell Farm Cl B93 128 B6
Dellow Gr B48 139 A5
Dellows Cl B38 123 D7
Dell Rd
Birmingham B30 104 A5
Brierley Hill DY5 61 B5
Dells Farm B47 124 F6
Dell The
Birmingham,Edgbaston B16 65 F2
Birmingham,Shenley Fields B31 102 D6
Cannock WS12 2 F4
Lichfield WS13 8 F7
Solihull B92 89 A1
Stourbridge DY8 80 E6
Tamworth B79 21 B6
Dellway Ct DY8 80 E5
Delmore Way B76 58 B6
Delph Dr DY5 81 E7
Delphinium Cl B9 67 F3
Delph La DY5 81 D8
Delphl Cl CV34 161 E4
Delph Rd DY5 61 D1
Delph Road Ind Est DY5 61 C1
Delrene Rd B28,B90 105 F3
Delta Trad Est WV2 39 F8
Delta Way Bsns Ctr WS11 4 D6
Delta Way WS11 4 D7
Deltic La B77 35 F8
Deltic B77 22 A1
Delves Cres
Walsall WS5 43 A5
Wood End CV9 36 C1
Delves Green Rd WS5 43 A5
Delves Inf Sch WS5 43 A5
Delves Jun Sch WS5 43 A5
Delves Rd WS1 42 F7
Delville Cl WS10 41 F4
Delville Rd WS10 41 F4
Delville Terr WS10 41 F3
De Marnham Cl B70 53 E1
De Montfort Ho B37 69 F5
De Montfort Rd
Hinckley LE10 71 E1
Kenilworth CV8 147 E6
De Montfort Way CV4 132 D5
De Moram Gr B92 107 F7
Dempster Ct CV11 73 C4
Dempster Rd CV12 78 A4
Demuth Way B69 63 F6
Denaby Gr B14 105 D4
Denbigh Cl DY1 50 F2
Denbigh Cnr B46 91 A6
Denbigh Cres B71 53 B6
Denbigh Ct 3 B29 103 C7
Denbigh Dr
Wednesbury WS10 42 D4
West Bromwich B71 53 B6
Denbigh Rd
Coventry CV6 112 E5
Tipton DY4 52 C4
Denbigh St B9 67 D2
Denbury Cl WS12 2 D1
Denby Bldgs 17 CV32 161 F8
Denby Cl
Birmingham B7 67 B5
Royal Leamington Spa CV32 157 C3
Denby Croft B90 127 B6
Dencer Cl B45 122 A8
Dencer Dr CV8 148 C4
Dencil Cl B63 82 D5
Dene Ave DY6 60 C4
Dene Court Rd B92 88 F1
Dene Croft WS3 14 A1
Denegate Cl B76 58 B6
Dene Hollow B13 105 C7
Denehurst Cl B45 122 A1
Denehurst Way CV10 72 F3
Denemoor Ct CV8 148 B5
Dene Rd
Lower Penn WV4 37 F4
Stourbridge DY8 80 F3
Denewood Ave B20 55 B2
Denewood Way CV8 148 C6
Denford Gr B14 104 D5
Dengate Dr CV7 130 B7
Denham Ave CV5 112 C4
Denham Ct B23 56 C2
Denham Gdns WV3 38 B8
Denham Rd B27 88 C5
Denholme Gr B14 105 A3
Denholm Rd B73 45 D2
Denise Dr
Birmingham B17 85 C4
Birmingham,Kingshurst B37 69 F4
Dudley WV14 51 B8
Denis Rd LE10 75 D5
Denleigh Rd DY6 60 F4
Denmark Cl WV6 25 A4
Denmark Rise WS12 2 D7
Denmark Villas WS13 8 C5
Denmead Dr WV11 26 F8
Denmore Gdns WV1 26 C2
Dennett Cl CV34 155 F2
Dennfield Dr WS6 4 C2
Dennis Hall 9 DY8 80 F8
Dennis Hall Rd DY8 81 A8
Dennis Rd
Birmingham B12 87 B4
Coventry CV2 114 B6
Dennis St DY8 80 F8
Dennis B77 21 E2
Denshaw Croft CV2 115 A8
Denshaw Rd B14 104 D6
Denston Ct 6 B74 31 F2
Denstone Gdns WV10 11 F3
Denton Cl CV8 147 D6
Denton Croft B93 127 D3
Denton Gr
Birmingham,Great Barr B43 54 D7
Birmingham,Stechford B33 68 D2
Denton Rd DY9 82 A4
Dent St B79 21 C5
Denver Rd B14 105 A2
Denville Cl WV14 40 E7
Denville Cres B9 68 B3
Denville Rd CV32 157 A3
Derby Ave WV6 24 F7
Derby Dr B37 70 B2
Derby Rd LE10 71 D1
Derby St
Birmingham B9 67 A2
Walsall WS2 28 E4
Dereham Cl B8 67 C4
Dereham Ct CV32 157 A2
Dereham Wlk WV14 40 E2
Dereton Cl DY1 61 E8
Derick Burcher's Mall 5 DY10 116 E6
Dering Cl CV2 114 D8
Deronda Cl CV12 78 A3
Derron Ave B26 88 E5
Derry Cl B17 85 A3
Derrydown Cl B23 56 E3
Derrydown Rd B42 55 B5
Derry St
Brierley Hill DY5 61 D2
Wolverhampton WV2 163 C1
Dersingham Dr CV6 96 B2
Derwent Cl
Brierley Hill DY5 61 B6
Coventry CV5 111 E4
Royal Leamington Spa CV32 156 D1
Sutton Coldfield WS9 30 F3
Willenhall WV13 27 C2
Derwent Ct B73 46 B5
Derwent Gr
Birmingham B13 86 C1
Burntwood WS7 7 D6
Cannock WS11 4 D8
Derwent Ho
5 Oldbury B69 63 D5
8 Birmingham B17 85 D5
Kidderminster DY10 116 F7
Derwent Rd
Bedworth CV12 78 A2
Birmingham B30 104 C8
Coventry CV6 95 A2
Wolverhampton WV6 24 E8
Derwent B77 21 D1
Derwent Way
Bromsgrove B60 137 B1
Nuneaton CV11 73 F6
Desdemona Ave CV34 161 E4
Desford Ave B42 55 C7
De Somerley Ho 1 B69 64 A7
Despard Rd CV5 111 D4
Dettonford Rd B32 102 B8
Devereux Cl
Birmingham B36 69 C8
Coventry CV4 111 C1
Devereux Ho B79 21 A4
Devereux Rd
Sutton Coldfield B75 32 C1
West Bromwich B70 53 E1
Deveron Ct LE10 71 B1
Deveron Way LE10 71 B1
Devey Dr DY4 52 D6
Devine Croft DY4 52 A5
Devitts Cl B90 126 F7
Devon Cl
Birmingham B20 54 F2
Nuneaton CV10 72 F3
Devon Cres
Aldridge WS9 16 A1
Dudley DY2 61 F7
West Bromwich B71 53 C6
Devon Ct
3 Birmingham B29 103 B7
Cannock WS11 4 C8
Devon Gn WS11 4 F8
Devon Gr CV2 114 B6
Devon Ho 4 DY8 80 F8
Devonport Cl 3 B97 153 B5
Devon Rd
Birmingham B45 101 F1
Cannock WS11 4 F8
Smethwick B67 84 E7
Devon Rd *continued*
Stourbridge DY8 80 E7
Wednesbury WS10 42 C4
Willenhall WV13 27 D1
Wolverhampton WV1 163 A4
Devonshire Ave B18 65 F6
Devonshire Ct B74 32 A2
Devonshire Dr
Tamworth B78 21 A1
West Bromwich B71 53 E3
Devonshire Inf Sch B67 64 E5
Devonshire Jun Sch B67 64 E5
Devonshire Rd
Birmingham B20 54 F2
Smethwick B67 64 E6
Devonshire St B18 66 A6
Devonshire Villas B10 87 D8
Devon St B7 67 C5
Devoran Cl
Bedworth CV7 96 B8
Wolverhampton WV6 25 B4
Dewberry Dr WS5 43 A3
Dewberry Rd 3 DY8 60 F1
Dewhurst Croft B33 69 B3
Dewis Ho 4 CV2 96 B1
Dewsbury Ave CV3 133 B5
Dewsbury Cl
Astwood Bank B96 158 E1
Stourbridge DY8 60 E3
Dewsbury Dr
Burntwood WS7 7 C6
Wolverhampton WV4 39 A4
Dewsbury Gr B42 55 C5
Dexter Ho B67 64 F6
Dexter Way B78 36 F8
Dey Croft CV34 160 B4
Deykin Ave B6 56 B2
Deykin Avenue Jun & Inf Sch B6 56 B2
Deykin Rd WS13 9 A6
D'Eyncourt Prim Sch WV11 26 B7
D'Eyncourt Rd WV10 26 A7
Dial Cl B14 104 E2
Dial House La CV5 111 F4
Dial La
Stourbridge DY8 80 E8
West Bromwich B70 52 F6
Diamond Ct 3 B64 62 D1
Diamond Gr WS11 2 C3
Diamond Park Dr 3 DY8 60 E1
Diana Cl WS9 16 B3
Diana Dr CV2 96 E1
Diane Cl DY4 41 B2
Dibble Cl WV12 27 D5
Dibble Rd B67 64 F6
Dibdale Ct DY3 50 D3
Dibdale Rd DY1 50 F3
Dibdale Rd W DY1 50 E3
Dibdale St DY1 51 A2
Dice Pleck B31 103 C2
Dickens Cl
Dudley DY3 50 B5
Nuneaton CV10 72 A4
Dickens Heath Prim Com Sch B90 126 A6
Dickens Heath Rd
Solihull B90 126 A5
Solihull B90 126 A6
Solihull B90 126 B6
Dickens Rd
Coventry CV6 113 A8
Dudley WV14 40 D2
Wolverhampton WV10 12 A1
Dickinson Ave WV10 25 F8
Dickinson Dr
Sutton Coldfield B76 46 E4
Walsall WS2 42 C6
Dickinson Rd WV5 49 A4
Dickins Rd CV34 156 B1
Dick Sheppard Ave DY4 52 B8
Didcot Cl B97 158 C5
Diddington Ave B28 106 A5
Diddington La B92,CV7 91 C1
Didgley Gr B37 70 A5
Didsbury Rd CV7 78 A1
Digbeth
Birmingham B5 164 D1
Walsall WS1 28 E1
Digbey Cl CV5 112 B6
Digby Cres B46 59 B3
Digby Ct 3 B27 88 C3
Digby Dr B37 90 B6
Digby Ho B37 69 F4
Digby Pl CV7 92 C1
Digby Rd
Coleshill B46 70 F6
Kingswinford DY6 60 D8
Sutton Coldfield B73 46 B4
Dilcock Way CV4 131 F7
Dilke Rd WS9 29 F5
Dillam Cl CV6 96 A4
Dilliars Wlk B70 53 A5
Dillington Ho 8 B37 70 B2
Dillon Ct CV11 73 B5
Dillotford Ave CV3 133 D6
Dilloways La WV13 40 F8
Dilwyn Cl B98 154 F1
Dimbles Hill WS13 3 B1
Dimbles La WS13 3 A2
Dimmingsdale Bank B32 84 C4
Dimmingsdale Rd WV4 37 E5
Dimminsdale WV13 27 A1
Dimmocks Ave WV14 51 D8
Dimmock St WV4 39 E5
Dimsdale Gr B31 102 E3
Dimsdale Rd B31 102 D3
Dinedor Cl B98 154 D3
Dingle Ave B64 82 E8
Dingle Cl
Birmingham B30 103 D7
Coventry CV6 113 A6
Dudley DY2 62 E7
Dingle Com Prim Sch DY6 61 A4
Dingle Ct B91 106 F1
Dingle Hollow B69 63 D8
Dingle La
Solihull B91 106 F2
Willenhall WV13 27 A4
Dingle Mead B14 104 C4
Dingle Rd
Brownhills WS8 15 E6
Dudley DY2 62 E7
Kingswinford DY6 61 A4
Stourbridge DY9 81 C2
Dingleside Mid Sch B98 159 B8
Dingleside B98 153 E2
Dingle St B69 63 E8
Dingle The
Birmingham B29 85 E2
Cheswick Green B90 126 D5
Nuneaton CV10 72 E6
Oldbury B69 63 D8
Wolverhampton WV3 24 D1
Dingle View DY3 50 C7
Dingley Rd
Bulkington CV12 79 B2
Wednesbury WS10 42 A5
Dinham Gdns DY1 50 E3
Dinmore Ave B31 103 B4
Dinmore Cl B98 154 D3
Dinsdale Wlk WV6 25 A5
Dippons Dr WV6 24 A3
Dippons Ho WV6 24 A3
Dippons Mill Cl WV6 24 A3
Dirtyfoot La WV4 38 A5
Discovery Cl DY4 52 C5
Discovery Way CV3 135 B7
District Ctr WS12 2 C2
Ditchford Cl B97 158 D4
Ditch The WS1 28 F1
Ditton Gr B31 122 F6
Dixon Cl
Birmingham B35 58 A2
Tipton DY4 52 C6
Dixon Ct DY10 117 C8
Dixon Ho B16 66 A1
Dixon Rd B10 87 B8
Dixons Green Ct 7 DY2 62 E8
Dixon's Green Rd DY2 62 E8
Dixon St
Kidderminster DY10 116 E5
Wolverhampton WV2 39 E7
Doal Trad Est B66 65 B6
Dobbins Oak Rd DY9 81 E1
Dobbs Mill Cl B29 86 B2
Dobbs St WV2 163 B1
Dobson La CV31 162 A4
Dockar Rd B31 102 E2
Dockers Cl CV7 130 C7
Dock La 10 DY1 51 B1
Dock Lane Ind Est 13 DY1 51 B1
Dock Mdw Dr Ind Est WV4 40 B4
Dock Meadow Dr WV4 40 A4
Dock Rd DY8 60 F2
Dock The
Catshill B61 137 A8
Stourbridge DY9 81 F5
Doctors Cl B94 142 A2
Doctors Hill
Bournheath B61 136 D8
Stourbridge DY9 81 C3
Tanworth-In-A B94 142 A2
Doctors La
Kingswinford DY6 60 A4
Shenstone WS14 18 A6
Doctor's Piece WV13 27 B2
Dodd Ave CV34 161 C7
Doddington Gr B32 102 B8
Dodford Cl B45 121 F7
Dodford Ct B61 136 C6
Dodford Fst Sch B61 136 A5
Dodford Ho B60 137 B3
Dodford Rd B61 120 D1
Dodgson Cl CV6 96 A4
Dodwells Bridge Ind Est LE10 74 E8
Dodwells Rd LE10 74 E8
Doe Bank Ct B74 46 B8
Doe Bank La
Birmingham B43,WS9 44 D5
Coventry CV1 113 A3
Doe Bank Rd DY4 41 C1
Dogberry Cl CV3 134 C6
Dogberry Way CV34 161 F2
Dogge Lane Croft B27 88 B2
Dog Kennel La 3 WS1 28 F2
Dogkennel La
Halesowen B63 83 B3
Oldbury B68 64 C5
Dog Kennel La B90 126 D7
Doglands The CV31 162 B4
Dog La
Tamworth B77 22 B6
Weeford WS14 19 A4
Dogpool La B30 86 B1
Doidge Rd B23 56 D3
Dolben La B98 154 D3
Dollery Dr B5 86 C5
Dollis Gr B44 44 F3
Dollman St B7 67 B4

Dolman Rd B6 66 E8
Dolobran Rd B11 87 D7
Dolomite Ave CV4 112 D1
Dolphin Cl WS3 14 F1
Dolphin Ct WV12 27 D8
Dolphin La B27 88 C1
Dolphin Rd
Birmingham B11 87 D5
Redditch B98 154 A5
Dolton Way DY4 51 E6
Domar Rd DY11 116 B7
Dominic Dr B30 103 D4
Donalbain Cl CV34 161 F3
Doncaster Cl CV2 114 D7
Doncaster Way B36 68 C8
Don Cl B15 85 D8
Donegal Cl CV4 132 A7
Donegal Rd B74 44 F5
Dongan Rd CV34 160 E7
Don Gr WS11 4 D7
Donibristle Croft B35 58 A4
Donnington Ave CV6 112 E5
Donnington Cl B98 154 C5
Donnington Ho B33 69 B2
Donnithorne Ave CV10, CV11 73 D1
Donovan Dr B73 46 A6
Dooley Cl WV13 26 E2
Doone Cl CV2 114 E6
Dorado B77 35 D7
Dora Herbert Ct B12 86 E5
Doran Cl B63 82 D1
Doranda Way B71 53 F1
Dora Rd
Birmingham B10 87 E8
Birmingham,Handsworth B21 65 E7
West Bromwich B70 53 C1
Dora St WS2 42 B7
Dorcas Cl CV11 79 C8
Dorchester Cl WV12 27 C8
Dorchester Ct B91 107 A4
Dorchester Dr B17 85 B4
Dorchester Rd
Cannock WS11 1 B1
Hinckley LE10 76 B7
Solihull B91 107 A4
Stourbridge DY9 81 D2
Willenhall WV12 13 C1
Dorchester Way
Coventry CV2 115 A4
Nuneaton CV11 74 A7
Dordale Cl B31 102 C1
Dordale Rd DY9 119 E2
Dordon Cl B90 105 E1
Dordon Rd B78 36 F8
Doreen Gr B24 57 B2
Doris Rd
Birmingham B11 87 B4
Birmingham,Bordesley Green B9 67 D2
Coleshill B46 70 F8
Dorlcote Rd B8 68 A4
Dorlecote Ct CV10 73 C1
Dorlecote Pl CV10 78 C8
Dorlecote Rd CV10 78 C8
Dormer Ave B77 21 D5
Dormer Harris Ave CV4 111 F1
Dormer Ho 15 CV32 156 F2
Dormer Pl CV32 161 F8
Dormie Cl B38 103 D1
Dormington Rd B44 44 F3
Dormston Cl
Redditch B98 153 F1
Solihull B91 127 C8
Dormston Dr
Birmingham B29 84 F2
Sedgley DY3 50 E8
Dormston Sch The DY3 50 E8
Dormston Trad Est DY1 50 F4
Dormy Dr B31 123 A7
Dorncliffe Ave B33 89 D7
Dorney Cl CV5 132 E8
Dornie Dr B38 103 F1
Dornton Rd B30 104 C8
Dorothy Adams Cl 3 B64 82 E8
Dorothy Gdns B20 55 A2
Dorothy Goodman Specl Sch LE10 71 D2
Dorothy Pattison Hospl WS2 28 B1
Dorothy Powell Way CV2 96 F1
Dorothy Rd
Birmingham B11 88 B5
Smethwick B67 65 A4
Dorothy St WS1 42 D7
Dorridge Cl B97 153 B1
Dorridge Croft B93 127 F2
Dorridge Jun & Inf Schs B93 128 A4
Dorridge Rd B93 128 A2
Dorridge Sta B93 127 F2
Dorrington Gn B42 55 A5
Dorrington Prim Sch B42 55 A5
Dorrington Rd B42 55 A5
Dorset Cl
Birmingham B45 101 F2
Nuneaton CV10 72 F3
Tamworth B78 21 A1
Dorset Cotts B30 104 A6
Dorset Ct 2 B29 103 B7
Dorset Dr WS9 16 B1
Dorset Pl WS3 28 C7
Dorset Rd
Birmingham B8 67 C6

Dorset Rd *continued*
Cannock WS12 2 E1
Coventry CV1 113 C5
Smethwick B17 65 B3
Stourbridge DY8 80 D8
Dorsett Rd
Darlaston WS10 41 C6
Wednesbury WS10 42 D2
Dorsett Road Terr WS10 41 C6
Dorset Twr B18 66 B4
Dorsheath Gdns B23 56 F4
Dorsington Rd B27 88 D1
Dorstone Covert B14 104 C2
Dorville Cl B38 123 D8
Dosthill Prim Sch B77 35 D5
Dosthill Rd (Two Gates) B77 35 D7
Dotterel Pl DY10 117 A1
Douay Rd B24 57 B6
Double Row DY2 62 E4
Doughty St DY4 52 C5
Douglas Ave
Birmingham B36 68 D6
Oldbury B68 64 D5
Douglas Davies Cl WV12 27 C4
Douglas Ho CV1 165 D4
Douglas Pl WV10 25 C6
Douglas Rd
Birmingham B27 88 C4
Birmingham,Handsworth B21 65 F8
Dudley WV14 51 D8
Halesowen B62 63 E1
Hollywood B47 125 A7
Oldbury B68 64 D4
Sutton Coldfield B72 46 C3
Douglass Rd DY2 62 D8
Doulton Cl
Birmingham B32 84 F3
Coventry CV2 96 E1
Doulton Dr B66 65 A6
Doulton Rd B64,B65 62 F4
Doulton Trad Est B65 62 F3
Douper Hall B29 85 F3
Dovebridge Cl B76 46 F4
Dove Cl
Bedworth CV12 77 E3
Birmingham B25 88 E8
Burntwood WS7 7 D6
Hinckley LE10 75 A8
Kidderminster DY10 117 B2
Walsall WS1 29 A1
Wednesbury WS10 42 B4
Dovecote Cl
Coventry CV6 112 D5
Solihull B91 107 B8
Tipton DY4 52 C5
Wolverhampton WV6 24 C4
Dovecote Rd B61 136 E1
Dovecotes Prim Sch WV8 10 F1
Dovecotes The
Coventry CV5 112 B5
Sutton Coldfield B75 32 B3
Dovedale Ave
Coventry CV6 95 F2
Solihull B90 106 B1
Walsall WS3 15 B5
Willenhall WV12 27 B4
Dovedale WS11 2 A5
Dovedale Ct
19 Birmingham B29 103 C7
Wolverhampton WV4 39 F2
Dovedale Dr B28 105 F5
Dovedale Rd
Birmingham B23 56 C7
Kingswinford DY6 60 E8
Wolverhampton WV4 39 E3
Dove Dr DY8 81 A8
Dove Gdns B38 104 B2
Dove Hollow
Cannock WS12 2 E4
Great Wyrley WS6 4 F1
Dove House Ct B91 106 F7
Dovehouse Fields WS14 9 B6
Dovehouse La B91 106 F7
Dove House La B91 107 A8
Dovehouse Pool Rd 1 B6 66 E8
Dover Cl B32 102 A7
Dovercourt Rd B26 89 C5
Doverdale Ave DY10 117 B5
Doverdale Cl
Halesowen B63 82 E5
Redditch B98 159 B7
Dover Farm Cl B77 36 B8
Dover Ho WS3 28 C7
Doveridge Cl B91 106 E6
Doveridge Pl WS1 42 F8
Doveridge Rd B28 105 E5
Dove Ridge DY8 81 A7
Doversley Rd B14 104 C5
Dover St
Bilston WV14 40 D6
Birmingham B18 66 A6
Coventry CV1 165 A3
Dovestone B77 22 D1
Doveton Ho DY8 81 A3
Dove Way B36 69 F8
Dovey Dr B76 58 A7
Dovey Rd
Birmingham B13 87 D2
Oldbury B69 63 D8
Dowar Rd B45 122 C7
Dowells Cl B13 86 F2
Dowells Gdns DY8 60 D3
Doweries The B45 121 F8
Dower Rd B75 32 B1
Dowler's Hill Cres B98 159 A8
Dowles Cl B29 103 B6

Dowles Rd DY11 116 B2
Dowley Croft CV3 115 B1
Downcroft Ave B38 103 E2
Downderry Way CV6 114 A6
Downend Cl WV10 11 F4
Downes Ct 7 DY4 51 E5
Downesway WS11 1 C2
Downey Cl B11 87 B7
Downfield Cl WS3 14 A4
Downfield Dr DY3 50 E6
Downham Cl WS5 29 E1
Downham Pl WV3 38 F8
Downham Wood WS5 43 E8
Downie Rd WV8 10 C3
Downing Cl
6 Rowley Regis B65 63 C1
Dorridge B93 128 A4
Wednesfield WV11 27 A7
Downing Cres CV12 78 C4
Downing Ct 2 B68 84 B7
Downing Dr B79 20 E5
Downing Ho B37 70 B1
Downing St
Halesowen B63 83 A5
Smethwick B66 65 C7
Downland Cl B38 103 F1
Downsell Ho B97 153 A2
Downsell Rd B97 153 A2
Downsfield Rd B26 89 B7
Downside Rd B24 56 E1
Downs Rd WV13 41 C8
Downs The
Sutton Coldfield WS9 30 E2
Wolverhampton WV10 25 C6
Downton Cl CV2 115 A8
Downton Cres B33 69 E3
Dowty Ave CV12 77 D1
Dowty Way WV9 11 A3
Doyle Dr CV6 95 F3
Dragoon Fields B60 151 B8
Drake Cl WS3 14 B1
Drake Cres DY11 116 A7
Drake Croft 4 WS13 9 C8
Drake Ct WS3 14 B1
Drake Rd
Birmingham B23 56 C3
Smethwick B66 64 E7
Walsall WS3 14 C1
Drakes Cl
Redditch B97 158 C6
Wythall B47 124 F4
Drakes Cross Par B47 125 A5
Drake's Gn WV14 40 F3
Drakes Hill Cl DY8 80 C4
Drake St
Coventry CV6 113 D7
West Bromwich B71 53 C5
Drake Way LE10 71 D4
Drancy Ave WV12 27 D6
Draper Cl CV8 148 C4
Drapers Ct CV1 165 B4
Draper's Fields CV1 165 B4
Drawbridge Rd B90 125 E8
Draycote Cl B92 107 D6
Draycott Ave B23 56 D4
Draycott Cl
9 Redditch B97 153 B5
Wolverhampton WV4 38 C5
Draycott Cres B77 21 D1
Draycott Dr B31 102 E7
Draycott Rd
Coventry CV2 114 C7
Smethwick B66 64 E7
Drayman Cl WS1 42 F8
Drayton Cl
Hartshill CV10 72 A8
Redditch B98 159 D8
Sutton Coldfield B75 32 B3
Drayton Cres CV5 111 D5
Drayton Ct
Bromsgrove B60 151 B8
Warwick CV34 155 E2
Drayton La B78 34 C5
Drayton Manor Dr
Drayton Bassett B78 34 F7
Fazeley B78 34 F8
Drayton Manor Pk★ B78 34 E7
Drayton Rd
Bedworth CV12 78 D2
Belbroughton DY9 119 B5
Birmingham B14 104 F8
Smethwick B66 65 A1
Solihull B90 126 E8
Drayton St
Walsall WS2 28 C2
Wolverhampton WV2 163 B1
Drayton Way CV10 72 C7
Dreadnought Rd DY5 61 B8
Dreamwell Ind Est B11 88 A6
Dreel The B15 85 E7
Dreghorn Rd B36 68 F8
Drem Croft B35 58 A2
Dresden Cl WV4 40 A4
Drew Cres
Kenilworth CV8 148 A4
Stourbridge DY9 81 D2
Drew Rd DY9 81 D3
Drews Ho B14 104 D1
Drews Holloway B63 82 D5
Drews Holloway S B63 82 D5
Drews La B8 68 A7
Drews Meadow Cl 1 B14 104 C2
Driffield Cl B98 154 D2
Driffold B73 46 B3
Driftwood Cl B38 123 D7
Drinkwater Ho 7 CV1 113 B2
Drive Fields WV4 38 B6

Drive Sch (Tettenhall Coll) The WV6 24 D4
Drive The
Birmingham,Gravelly Hill B23 56 E2
Birmingham,Handsworth B20 55 B2
Brierley Hill DY5 61 C5
Coventry CV2 114 E3
Halesowen,Cradley B63 82 D5
Halesowen,Hasbury B63 83 A3
Hopwood B48 123 B3
Redditch B97 152 C7
Shenstone WS14 18 E8
Walsall,Pelsall WS3 14 E2
Walsall WS4 15 C1
Wolverhampton WV6 24 C5
Droicon Trad Est B65 63 C5
Dronfield Rd CV2 114 B3
Drovers Way B60 150 E6
Drovers Wlk DY10 116 F5
Droveway The WV9 10 F2
Droxford Wlk WV8 10 E1
Droylsdon Park Rd CV3 133 B3
Dr Phillips Sh Ctr The CV2 96 D1
Druid Park Rd WV12 13 C1
Druid Rd CV2 114 B3
Druids Ave
Aldridge WS9 30 C8
Rowley Regis B65 63 D4
Druids La B14 104 D1
Druid St LE10 71 D1
Druids Wlk WS9 16 A3
Drummond Cl
Coventry CV6 112 F7
Wolverhampton WV11 13 A2
Drummond Gr B43 44 C3
Drummond Rd
Birmingham B9 68 A2
Bromsgrove B60 151 B8
Stourbridge DY9 81 F4
Drummond St WV1 163 B4
Drummond Way B37 70 C2
Drury La
Solihull B91 107 C3
Stourbridge DY8 81 A5
Drybrook Cl B38 123 E8
Drybrooks Cl CV7 130 B6
Dryden Cl
Kenilworth CV8 147 F3
Tipton DY4 52 A7
Willenhall WV12 27 E8
Dryden Gr B27 88 B2
Dryden Pl WS3 28 E7
Dryden Rd
Tamworth B79 21 A6
Walsall WS3 28 E7
Wolverhampton WV10 11 F1
Drylea Gr B36 68 F8
Dual Way WS12 1 D8
Dubarry Ave DY6 60 C7
Duchess Pl B16 66 A1
Duchess Rd
Birmingham B16 66 A1
Walsall WS1 42 D5
Duckhouse Rd WV11 26 D7
Duck La WV8 10 B3
Duddeston Dr B8 67 D4
Duddeston Manor Rd B7 67 A4
Duddeston Mill Rd B7,B8 67 C4
Duddeston Mill Trad Est B8 67 C4
Duddeston Sta B7 67 B4
Dudding Rd WV4 39 D5
Dudhill Rd B65 63 A3
Dudhill Wlk B65 63 A3
Dudley Castle★ DY1 51 D2
Dudley Central Trad Est DY2 62 C8
Dudley Cl B65 63 A5
Dudley Coll (Castle View Campus) DY1 51 B2
Dudley Coll (International Glass Ctr) DY5 61 D3
Dudley Coll of Tech (Broadway Campus) DY1 51 C2
Dudley Coll of Tech (Mons Hill Campus) DY1 51 B5
Dudley Coll of Tech (Wolverhampton St Campus) DY1 51 B1
Dudley Cres WV11 26 E6
Dudley Gn CV32 157 B2
Dudley Gr 6 B18 65 E4
Dudley Innovation Ctr DY6 60 F7
Dudley L Ctr DY1 51 B1
Dudley Mus & Art Gall★ DY1 51 C1
Dudley Park Rd B27 88 C3
Dudley Port Sta DY4 52 B4
Dudley Port DY4 52 A3
Dudley Rd
Birmingham B18 65 E4
Brierley Hill DY5,DY6 61 D4
Dudley DY3 50 E6
Halesowen B63 83 B5
Himley DY3 49 D3
Kenilworth CV8 147 F2
Kingswinford DY6 60 F7
Kingswinford,Wall Heath DY6 60 C8
Oldbury B69 63 F8
Rowley Regis B65 63 A5
Stourbridge DY9 81 E6
Tipton DY4 51 E5

Dudley Rd *continued*
Wolverhampton WV2 39 D7
Dudley Rise LE10 75 D6
Dudley Road E B69 52 D1
Dudley Road W B69 52 B2
Dudley Row DY2 51 D1
Dudley Southern Bypass DY2 62 C7
Dudley St
Bilston WV14 40 D4
Birmingham B5 164 C2
Coventry CV6 96 A1
Kidderminster DY10 116 E7
Dudley Street,Guns Village Sta B70 53 B4
Dudley St
Sedgley DY3 50 D8
Walsall WS1 28 E1
Wednesbury WS10 41 E2
West Bromwich B70 53 A5
Wolverhampton WV1 163 B3
Dudley Terr CV8 149 B6
Dudley Wlk WV4 39 C5
Dudley Wood Ave DY2 62 C2
Dudley Wood Prim Sch DY2 62 C2
Dudley Wood Rd DY2 62 C2
Dudley Zoo★ DY1 51 D2
Dudmaston Way DY1 50 E3
Dudnill Gr B32 102 A8
Duffield Cl WV8 10 F1
Dufton Rd B32 84 E4
Dugdale Cl WS12 2 F3
Dugdale Cres B75 32 C3
Dugdale Ct 5 CV31 162 A6
Dugdale Ho CV11 73 C3
Dugdale Rd CV6 113 B6
Dugdale St
Nuneaton CV11 73 C4
Smethwick B18 65 D4
Duggins La CV4,CV7 131 B8
Duke Barn Field CV2 114 A5
Dukes Rd
Birmingham B30 104 A3
Dordon B78 36 F6
Duke St
Coventry CV5 112 F2
Dudley DY3 50 D5
Nuneaton CV11 73 B4
Rowley Regis B65 63 B2
Royal Leamington Spa CV32 157 A1
Stourbridge DY8 81 A6
Sutton Coldfield B72 46 B4
Wednesfield WV11 26 D5
West Bromwich B70 53 B4
Wolverhampton,Springfield WV1 163 D2
Wolverhampton WV3 39 A7
Dulais Cl B98 153 E1
Dulvern Gr B14 104 D5
Dulverton Ave CV5 112 D4
Dulverton Cl CV5 112 D4
Dulverton Rd B6 56 B1
Dulwich Gr B44 56 B8
Dulwich Rd B44 56 A8
Dumbleberry Ave DY3 50 C7
Dumblederry Ct WS9 29 F5
Dumblederry La
Aldridge WS9 29 F6
Walsall WS9 29 E7
Dumble Pit La B47,B48 140 F7
Dumolo's La B77 21 F3
Dumphouse La B48 140 C3
Dunard Rd B90 105 F3
Dunbar Cl
Birmingham B32 84 D1
Kidderminster DY10 117 C6
Dunbar Gr B43 44 B4
Dunblane Dr CV32 157 C5
Dunblane Way LE10 71 A2
Duncalfe Dr B75 32 B3
Duncan Edwards Cl DY1 62 A8
Duncan Ho B73 46 B1
Duncan St WV2 39 C7
Dunchurch Cl
Balsall Common CV7 130 B7
Redditch B98 154 F1
Dunchurch Cres B73 45 C3
Dunchurch Dr B31 102 E7
Dunchurch Highway CV5 112 A4
Dunchurch Ho 4 B5 86 E8
Dunclent Cres DY10 117 B5
Dunclent La DY10 117 E3
Duncombe Gn 12 B46 70 F7
Duncombe Gr B17 85 A7
Duncombe St DY8 80 D5
Duncroft Ave CV6 112 F7
Duncroft Rd B26 89 A8
Duncroft Wlk DY1 51 B6
Duncumb Rd B75 47 A5
Dundalk La WS6 4 D2
Dundas Ave DY2 62 F8
Dunedin Dr B45 122 B1
Dunedin Ho B32 84 F4
Dunedin Rd B44 44 F3
Dunedin B77 22 A1
Dunham Croft B93 127 D3
Dunhill Ave CV4 111 E3
Dunkirk Ave B70 52 E3
Dunkirk Pl CV3 134 F7
Dunkley St WV1 163 B4
Dunley Croft B90 126 F6
Dunley Ct B23 56 C2
Dunlin Cl
Birmingham B23 56 C2
Kingswinford DY6 61 A6

Dunlin Dr
Featherstone WV10 12 B7
Kidderminster DY10 116 F2
Dunlop Rd B97 158 D5
Dunlop Way B35 57 F2
Dunnerdale Rd WS8 15 D6
Dunnigan Rd B32 84 F3
Dunnose Cl CV6 113 E8
Dunns Bank DY5 81 F7
Dunrose Cl CV2 114 E2
Dunsfold Cl WV14 40 A3
Dunsfold Croft 3 B6 66 F6
Dunsford Cl DY5 81 B7
Dunsford Rd B66 65 A2
Dunsink Rd B6 55 F1
Dunslade Cres DY5 81 F8
Dunslade Rd B23 56 E7
Dunsley Dr DY8 60 E3
Dunsley Gr WV4 39 A4
Dunsley Rd DY8 80 C4
Dunsmore Ave CV3 134 C6
Dunsmore Dr DY5 81 F8
Dunsmore Gr B91 106 F7
Dunsmore Rd B28 87 E2
Dunstall Ave WV6 25 C4
Dunstall Cl B97 153 B2
Dunstall Gr B29 102 F8
Dunstall Hill Jun & Inf Sch WV6 25 C4
Dunstall Hill Trad Est WV6 25 C5
Dunstall Hill WV6 25 C5
Dunstall La
Hopwas B78 20 D4
Wolverhampton WV6 25 B5
Dunstall Rd
Halesowen B63 82 D3
Wolverhampton WV6 25 B4
Dunstan Croft B90 126 C8
Dunstan Ct 3 B15 86 B7
Dunster Cl B30 104 C4
Dunster Gr WV6 23 F3
Dunster Pl CV6 95 D3
Dunster Rd B37 70 D2
Dunster B77 35 C7
Dunston Cl
Great Wyrley WS6 13 E8
Kingswinford DY6 60 D7
Dunston Dr WS7 7 A8
Dunsville Dr CV2 114 F8
Dunton Cl B75 32 A4
Dunton Hall Rd B90 126 A8
Dunton La B76 48 C1
Dunton Pk B76 59 C7
Dunton Rd B37 69 F5
Dunton Trad Est B7 67 D7
Dunvegan Cl
Coventry CV3 115 A2
Kenilworth CV8 148 C4
Dunvegan Rd B24 57 A4
Duport Rd LE10 75 F7
Durant Cl B45 101 D1
Durban Rd B66 65 C4
Durbar Ave CV6 113 D8
D'Urberville Cl WV2 39 F6
D'Urberville Rd WV2 39 F6
D'Urberville Wlk 1 WS11 2 A2
Durham Ave WV13 27 D3
Durham Cl
Bromsgrove B61 136 E4
Keresley CV7 94 F4
Tamworth B78 21 A2
Durham Cres CV5 112 B7
Durham Croft B37 70 B2
Durham Dr B71 53 D7
Durham Ho 1 WV3 25 C4
Durham Pl WS2 28 B1
Durham Rd
Birmingham B11 87 B4
Dudley DY2 62 D2
Rowley Regis B65 63 E4
Stourbridge DY8 80 D8
Walsall WS2 42 B8
Wednesbury WS10 42 D4
Durham Twr 3 B1 66 B3
Durley Dean Rd B29 85 C2
Durley Dr B73 45 C3
Durley Rd B25 88 C6
Durlston Cl B77 21 F5
Durlston Gr B28 106 A8
Durnford Croft B14 104 E1
Dursley Cl
Solihull B92 107 B8
Willenhall WV12 27 D4
Dursley Dr WS11 1 B2
Dursley Rd WS7 7 A7
Dusthouse La B60 151 D7
Dutton Rd CV2 96 D3
Dutton's La B75 32 E4
Duxford Cl B97 158 B8
Duxford Rd B42 55 B7
Dwarris Wlk CV34 155 E2
Dwellings La B32 84 B5
Dyas Ave B42 55 A7
Dyas Rd
Birmingham B44 44 E1
Hollywood B47 125 A7
Dyce Cl B35 58 A4
Dyers La B94 142 D8
Dyers Rd CV11 79 F6
Dymoke St B12 86 F8
Dymond Rd CV6 95 D3
Dynes Wlk B67 65 A5
Dyott Rd B13 87 A1
Dysart Cl CV1 113 E4
Dyson Cl WS2 27 F3
Dysons Gdns B8 67 E5
Dyson St CV4 111 E3

E

Eachelhurst Rd B24,B76 57 F5
Eachus Rd WV14 51 D8
Eachway B45 121 F6
Eachway Farm Cl B45 122 A6
Eachway La B45 122 A6
Eacott Cl CV6 95 A3
Eadgar Ct B43 54 D7
Eadie Mews B97 153 D1
Eadie St CV10 72 D4
Eagle Cl
Cheslyn Hay WS6 4 D2
Dudley DY1 50 F1
Nuneaton CV11 79 B8
Rowley Regis B65 63 A4
Eagle Croft B14 104 E2
Eagle Ct
Wolverhampton,Pendeford WV10 11 B3
Wolverhampton WV3 39 A7
Eagle Dr B77 22 C4
Eagle Gdns B24 57 A2
Eagle Gr
Birmingham B36 70 A8
Cannock WS12 2 C1
Eagle Ho CV1 113 D5
Eagle Ind Est DY4 52 E7
Eagle La
Kenilworth CV8 147 F3
Tipton DY4 52 D6
Eagle Rd B98 154 E5
Eagle St E CV1 113 D5
Eagle St
Coventry CV1 113 D5
Royal Leamington Spa CV31 162 A6
Tipton DY4 52 C6
Wolverhampton,Penn Fields WV3 39 A7
Wolverhampton WV2 39 E8
Eagle Trad Est B63 83 A4
Eales Yd 9 LE10 71 D1
Ealing Gr B44 45 A1
Ealingham B77 22 B1
Eanwulf Ct B15 86 C8
Eardisley Cl B98 154 F1
Earl Place Bsns Pk CV4 112 B1
Earlsbury Gdns B20 55 D1
Earls Cl B97 152 F2
Earls Court Rd B17 85 A6
Earl's Croft The CV3 133 D7
Earlsdon Ave CV5 133 A8
Earlsdon Ave N CV5 112 F1
Earlsdon Ave S CV5 133 A8
Earlsdon Ho CV5 133 A8
Earlsdon Prim Sch CV5 113 A1
Earlsdon St CV5 132 F8
Earls Ferry Gdns B32 102 B7
Earls High Sch The B63 83 B4
Earlsmead Rd B21 65 C7
Earlsmere B94 126 B1
Earls Rd
Nuneaton CV11 73 A5
Walsall WS4 29 D7
Earls Rivers Ave CV34 161 D3
Earl St
Bedworth CV12 78 C2
Bilston WV14 40 D5
Coventry CV1 165 C2
Dudley WV14 51 D8
Kingswinford DY6 60 D4
Earlston Way B43 54 D8
Earl St
Royal Leamington Spa CV32 157 A1
Walsall WS1 42 D7
West Bromwich B70 53 B4
Earls Way B63 83 B4
Earl's Wlk CV3 135 D7
Earlswood Comm B94 142 A6
Earlswood Cres WV9 11 A3
Earlswood Ct B20 55 A2
Earlswood Dr B74 46 C7
Earlswood Ho 1 B5 86 E7
Earlswood Rd
Birmingham,Brandwood End B30 104 D3
Dorridge B93 127 D2
Kingswinford DY6 60 E8
Earlswood Sta B94 125 D1
Earlswood Trad Est B94 141 C6
Easby Way
Birmingham B8 67 E5
Walsall WS3 13 F2
Easedale Cl
Coventry CV3 133 B6
Nuneaton CV11 74 A6
Easemore Rd B98 153 F5
Easenhall Cl B93 128 A4
Easenhall La B98 154 E1
Easmore Cl B14 104 D2
Eastacre WV13 27 A1
East Ave
Bedworth CV12 78 D2
Coventry CV2 114 A2
Oldbury B69 63 C7
Wolverhampton WV11 26 C6
East Birmingham Coll Bordesley Green Campus B9 68 A2
Eastboro Ct CV11 73 E2
Eastboro Fields CV11 74 A4
Eastboro Way CV11 73 F2
Eastbourne Ave B34 68 E6
Eastbourne Cl CV6 112 E6
Eastbourne House Sch B27 88 C4
Eastbourne St WS4 28 F3
Eastbrook Cl B76 46 D4
Eastbury Dr B92 89 A3
East Cannock Rd WS12 2 C4
East Car Park Rd B40 90 F4
East Cl LE10 75 D7
Eastcote Cl B90 106 D3
Eastcote Cres WS7 7 A5
Eastcote La B92 108 F4
Eastcote Rd
Birmingham B27 88 A1
Wolverhampton WV10 25 F5
Eastcotes CV4 112 B1
East Croft Rd WV4 38 C5
Eastdean Cl B23 56 D6
East Dene CV32 157 B2
East Dr B5 86 C4
Eastern Ave
Brierley Hill DY5 61 B2
Lichfield WS13 3 C2
Eastern Green Jun Sch CV5 111 D5
Eastern Green Rd CV5 111 F4
Eastern Hill B96 158 F2
Eastern Rd
Birmingham B29 86 B3
Sutton Coldfield B73 46 B1
Eastern Way WS11 2 A2
Easterton Croft B14 104 E2
East Farm Croft B10 87 D8
Eastfield Cl WS9 30 A6
Eastfield Dr B92 107 E8
Eastfield Gr WV1 25 F2
Eastfield Jun & Inf Sch WV1 25 F2
Eastfield Rd
Birmingham B9 68 C3
Nuneaton CV10 73 D6
Royal Leamington Spa CV32 162 A8
Tipton DY4 52 A8
Wolverhampton WV1 25 F2
Eastfield Retreat WV1 25 F2
East Gate B16 65 E3
Eastgate Ct WS14 9 C6
Eastgate Ho 4 CV34 160 E6
Eastgate Mews 3 CV34 160 E6
Eastgate St WS7 6 E8
East Gn WV4 38 D6
East Gr CV31 162 A6
Eastham Rd B13 105 C6
East Holme B9 67 C2
Easthope Rd B33 69 A4
Eastlake Cl B43 44 D3
Eastlands Gr CV5 112 E4
Eastlands Rd B13 87 A1
Eastleigh Ave CV5 132 F7
Eastleigh Croft B76 58 A7
Eastleigh Dr B62 101 A4
Eastleigh Gr B25 88 D8
Eastleigh DY3 50 C8
Eastley Cres CV34 160 B8
East Meadway B33 69 E3
East Mews B44 44 D2
East Moons Ho B98 154 E4
Eastmoor Cl B74 31 B2
Eastney Cres WV8 24 F8
Eastnor Cl
Kidderminster DY10 116 E2
Redditch B98 153 E1
Eastnor Gr CV31 162 B7
Easton Gdns WV11 26 F5
Easton Gr
Birmingham B27 88 C1
Hollywood B47 125 B7
East Park Inf Sch WV1 26 B1
East Park Jun Sch WV1 40 B8
East Park Trad Est WV1 40 A8
East Park Way WV1 26 A1
East Pathway B17 85 C6
East Rd
Bromsgrove B60 137 A1
Featherstone WV10 12 A7
Tipton DY4 52 B8
Wolverhampton WV4 39 F4
Eastridge Croft WS14 18 A5
East Rise B75 46 D6
East St
Brierley Hill DY5 82 A8
Cannock WS11 4 E6
Coventry CV1 113 E3
Dudley,Gornalwood DY3 50 D3
Dudley,Kate's Hill DY2 62 E8
Kidderminster DY10 116 F6
Tamworth B77 35 D5
Wolverhampton WV1 163 D2
East View Rd B72 46 D2
East View
Shuttington B79 22 F7
Tamworth B77 21 E3
Eastville B31 103 B3
Eastward Glen WV8 10 C1
Eastway B17 85 C6
East Way B92 91 B3
Eastway B40 90 F3
Eastwood Ave WS7 7 A8
Eastwood Cl CV31 162 D6
Eastwood Ct B96 158 E1
Eastwood Dr DY10 117 B5
Eastwood Rd
Birmingham,Balsall Heath B12 86 D5
Birmingham,Great Barr B43 54 F8
Dudley DY2 62 E6
Eastwoods Rd LE10 71 F2
Eatesbrook Rd B33 69 C3
Eathorpe Cl
Birmingham B34 69 D6
Coventry CV2 96 C1
Redditch B98 154 E1
Eaton Ave B70 53 A4
Eaton Cl CV32 156 D2
Eaton Cres DY3 50 B3
Eaton Ct
Royal Leamington Spa CV32 156 D1
Sutton Coldfield B74 46 B7
Eaton Pl DY6 60 E5
Eaton Rd CV1 165 B1
Eaton Rise WV12 27 B6
Eaton Wood Dr B26 88 D5
Eaton Wood B24 57 D4
Eaves Court Dr DY3 39 C1
Eaves Green Gdns B27 88 B5
Eaves Green La CV7 92 E1
Eaves Green Mobile Home Pk CV7 92 F2
Ebbw Vale Terr CV3 133 D7
Ebenezer St
Cannock WS12 2 A7
Tipton WV14 51 C8
West Bromwich B70 52 F6
Ebley Rd B20 55 A4
Ebmore Dr B14 104 D2
Eborall Cl CV34 155 E2
Eborne Croft CV7 130 C8
Ebourne Cl CV8 148 A4
Ebrington Ave B92 89 B3
Ebrington Cl B14 104 D4
Ebrington Rd B71 53 D6
Ebro Cres CV3 114 F1
Ebrook Rd B72 46 C4
Ebstree Mdw WV5 37 A2
Ebstree Rd
Seisdon WV5 37 A2
Seisdon WV5 37 C4
Eburne Rd CV2 96 C3
Ebury Rd B30 104 B4
Eccles Cl CV2 114 C8
Eccleshall Ave WV10 25 C8
Eccleston Cl B75 46 F5
Ecclestone Rd WV11 27 A8
Eccleston Sch B17 85 B5
Echells Cl B61 136 D2
Echo Way WV4 40 A4
Eckersall Rd B38 103 E3
Eckington Cl B98 159 B8
Eckington Wlk B38 123 E7
Eclipse Ind Est 1 DY4 51 E5
Edale Cl
Kingswinford DY6 60 B7
Wolverhampton WV4 39 E3
Edale Gn LE10 75 F6
Edale Rd B42 55 C7
Edale B77 22 B1
Edale Way CV6 114 A7
Eddens Wood Cl B78 34 E5
Eddie Miller Ct CV12 78 B2
Eddish Rd B33 69 B3
Eddy Rd DY10 116 E7
Edelweiss Cl WS5 43 B3
Edenbridge Rd B28 106 B8
Edenbridge View DY1 50 E3
Eden Cl
Birmingham B31 122 E8
Cannock WS12 2 E2
Oldbury B69 52 D2
Studley B80 159 D3
Edencroft B15 86 C8
Eden Croft CV8 148 B3
Eden Ct
Featherstone WV10 11 F8
Nuneaton CV10 72 C7
Royal Leamington Spa CV32 157 D3
Edendale Dr LE10 71 E4
Edendale Rd B26 89 B6
Edenfield Cl B97 153 A5
Edenfield Pl B77 22 B1
Eden Gdns
Rowley Regis B65 63 B2
Sedgley DY3 50 E8
Eden Gr
Birmingham B37 70 D1
West Bromwich B71 53 D5
Edenhall Rd B32 84 B6
Eden Ho 2 DY8 81 A5
Edenhurst Rd B31 122 F7
Eden Rd
Coventry CV2 115 A8
Solihull B92 89 D3
Edensor Cl WV10 25 E4
Eden St CV6 113 F7
Edgar Cl B79 20 F7
Edgar Stammers Jun & Inf Schs WS3 28 F6
Edgbaston High Sch for Girls
Birmingham B15 85 F7
Birmingham,Calthorpe Fields B15 86 B8
Edgbaston Park Rd B15 86 A5
Edgbaston Rd B12 86 D5
Edgbaston Rd E B12 86 F5
Edgbaston Rd B66 65 A4
Edgbaston Sh Ctr B16 86 A8
Edgbaston St B5 164 C2
Edgbaston (Warwickshire Cty Cricket Club) B5 86 D5
Edgcombe Rd B28 87 F1
Edgefield Rd CV2 115 A8
Edge Hill Ave WV10 12 B1
Edge Hill Dr
Perton WV6 23 E3
Sedgley DY3 39 C2
Edgehill Pl CV4 111 C1
Edgehill Rd B31 103 B1
Edge Hill Rd B74 31 E4
Edge Hill CV9 36 B2
Edgemond Ave B24 57 F4
Edgemoor Mdw WS12 2 C1
Edge St WV14 51 D8
Edgewick Com Prim Sch CV6 113 E8
Edgewood Cl 2 B64 82 F8
Edgewood Dr B45 122 B1
Edgewood Rd
Birmingham,King's Norton B38 123 F7
Birmingham,Rednal B45 122 B6
Edgeworth Cl
Redditch B98 154 C5
Willenhall WV12 27 C4
Edgeworth Ho WS13 3 A2
Edgmond Cl B98 154 D4
Edgware Rd B23 56 D5
Edgwick Park Ind Est CV6 113 F8
Edgwick Rd CV6 113 F7
Edgwood Ct 4 B16 65 F1
Edinburgh Ave WS2 27 F3
Edinburgh Cl DY10 116 E8
Edinburgh Cres
Royal Leamington Spa CV31 161 F6
Stourbridge DY8 60 C1
Edinburgh Ct B24 57 D4
Edinburgh Dr
Walsall WS4 29 D7
Willenhall WV12 27 B6
Edinburgh La WS2 28 A4
Edinburgh Rd
Bilston WV14 40 F3
Birmingham B68 84 B8
Dudley DY2 62 D6
Nuneaton CV10 72 D6
Walsall WS5 43 B8
Edinburgh Villas CV8 133 F2
Edingale Rd CV2 114 F8
Edison Cl WS12 2 C7
Edison Ct WV12 27 D7
Edison Gr B32 84 D5
Edison Rd
Curdworth B46,B76 59 F4
Walsall WS2 28 B5
Edison Wlk WS2 28 B5
Edith Rd B66 65 C3
Edith St B70 53 B3
Edmondes Cl CV34 155 F1
Edmonds Cl B33 69 B2
Edmondscote Rd CV32 161 D8
Edmonds Ct
Birmingham,Gilbertstone B26 88 F7
Birmingham,Small Heath B10 87 D7
Edmonds Rd B68 64 C2
Edmonton Ave B44 45 B1
Edmonton Cl WS11 2 B2
Edmonton Ho B5 86 D7
Edmoor Cl WV12 27 C6
Edmund Ho B3 164 B3
Edmund Rd
Birmingham B8 67 D4
Coventry CV1 113 D5
Dudley DY3 50 E6
Edmund St B3 164 B3
Ednall La B60 136 F1
Ednam Cl 3 B71 53 F8
Ednam Gr WV5 38 A1
Ednam Rd
Dudley DY1 51 C2
Wolverhampton WV4 39 C5
Edsome Way B36 68 F8
Edstone Cl B93 127 F4
Edstone Mews B36 68 F8
Education Ctr The DY5 61 D7
Edward Ave WS9 30 A7
Edward Bailey Cl CV3 134 E7
Edward Cl WV14 40 E3
Edward Ct
Birmingham B16 65 C1
Nuneaton CV11 73 C3
Sutton Coldfield B76 46 F3
Tamworth B77 21 F4
Walsall WS1 43 A8
Edward Fisher Dr DY4 52 A5
Edward Mews CV34 160 E7
Edward Rd
Bedworth CV12 78 C3
Birmingham B68 84 C8
Birmingham,Balsall Heath B12 86 E5
Birmingham,Highter's Heath B14 105 A1
Coventry CV6 95 A3
Halesowen B63 82 F4
Perton WV6 23 E5
Smethwick B67 65 A4
Tipton DY4 52 A7
Water Orton B46 59 C3
Edwards Ctr 7 LE10 75 D8
Edwards Gr CV8 148 C5
Edwards Rd
Birmingham B24 57 A4
Burntwood WS7 6 F5
Dudley DY2 62 C4
Sutton Coldfield B75 32 D3
Edward St
3 Dudley DY1 51 B1

Edward St *continued*
Birmingham B1 .... 66 C3
Cannock WS11 .... 1 E4
Coventry CV6 .... 113 E5
Darlaston WS10 .... 41 E6
Hinckley LE10 .... 71 C2
Nuneaton CV11 .... 73 C3
Oldbury B68 .... 64 A4
Redditch B97 .... 153 D4
Edward Street Hospl B70. 53 C3
Edward St
Royal Leamington Spa CV32 .... 156 C1
Tamworth B79 .... 21 A5
Walsall WS2 .... 28 C3
Warwick CV34 .... 160 D7
West Bromwich B70 .... 53 C3
Wolverhampton WV4 .... 39 F5
Edward Tyler Rd CV7 .... 78 A1
Edwin Ave (Road 4) DY10 .... 116 F1
Edwin Cres B60 .... 150 F7
Edwin Ct
Bromsgrove B60 .... 150 F7
Bromsgrove B60 .... 150 F8
Edwin Phillips Dr B71 .... 53 B8
Edwin Rd B30 .... 104 B7
Edyth Rd CV2 .... 114 E4
Edyvean Walker Ct CV11 . 73 B5
Eel St B69 .... 63 F7
Effingham Rd B13 .... 105 C7
Egbert Cl B6 .... 67 B8
Egelwin Cl WV6 .... 23 E5
Egerton Ct [4] B15 .... 86 B7
Egerton Rd
Birmingham B24 .... 57 E3
Sutton Coldfield B74 .... 30 F1
Wolverhampton WV10 .... 11 E3
Egghill La B31,B45 .... 102 B3
Eggington Rd DY8 .... 80 D6
Egginton Rd B28 .... 105 E5
Egg La DY9,DY10 .... 119 A5
Eglamour Way CV34 .... 161 F3
Egmont Gdns WV11 .... 26 F5
Egret Ct DY10 .... 117 A1
Egret Wlk CV2 .... 96 B3
Eider Cl DY10 .... 117 B1
Eights Croft WS7 .... 6 D8
Eileen Gdns B37 .... 69 F4
Eileen Rd B11 .... 87 C3
Elan Cl
Dudley DY3 .... 50 D3
Royal Leamington Spa CV32 .... 157 C3
Elan Rd
Birmingham B31 .... 102 C2
Sedgley DY3 .... 50 C8
Elbow St B64 .... 62 F2
Elbury Croft B93 .... 127 F5
Elcock Dr B42 .... 55 D5
Eldalade Way WS10 .... 42 D2
Elderberry Cl
[3] Walsall WS5 .... 42 F3
Stourbridge DY8 .... 80 C3
Elderberry Way CV2 .... 114 B6
Elder Cl WS11 .... 2 C2
Elderfield Rd B30 .... 104 B3
Elder La WS7 .... 7 C7
Eldersfield Cl B98 .... 154 E7
Eldersfield Gr B91 .... 127 B7
Elderside Cl WS8 .... 15 F8
Elder Way B23 .... 56 E2
Eldon Ct WS1 .... 28 F1
Eldon Dr B76 .... 57 E7
Eldon Rd
Birmingham B32 .... 84 A3
Birmingham,Edgbaston B16 65 F2
Halesowen B62 .... 83 F3
Eldon St
Darlaston WS10 .... 41 D7
Walsall WS1 .... 28 F1
Eldorado Cl B80 .... 159 D4
Eld Rd CV6 .... 113 E7
Eldridge Cl WV9 .... 10 F2
Eleanor Rd WV14 .... 40 D6
Electra Park Ind Pk B6 .... 56 B1
Electric Ave B6 .... 56 B1
Elford Cl
Birmingham B14 .... 104 E5
Sutton Coldfield B74 .... 31 A2
Elford Gr
Bilston WV14 .... 40 C4
Birmingham B37 .... 70 B1
Elford Rd
Birmingham B17,B29 .... 85 B3
West Bromwich B71 .... 42 E2
Elgar Cl
Cannock WS11 .... 1 E5
Lichfield WS13 .... 3 B2
Nuneaton CV11 .... 79 A7
Redditch B97 .... 158 C8
Elgar Cres DY5 .... 61 D7
Elgar Ct B15 .... 86 A7
Elgar Mews [2] B60 .... 136 F2
Elgar Rd CV6 .... 114 B8
Elgin Cl
Sedgley DY3 .... 39 E1
Stourbridge DY8 .... 81 A7
Elgin Ct WV6 .... 23 E4
Elgin Gr B25 .... 88 C7
Elgin Rd WS3 .... 14 A4
Elias Cl WS14 .... 9 E6
Eliot Cl
Tamworth B79 .... 21 A7
Warwick CV34 .... 155 E2
Eliot Croft WV14 .... 40 D2
Eliot St B7 .... 67 C8
Eliot Way CV10 .... 73 B2
Eliot Wlk DY10 .... 117 C6
Elisabeth Ct
Royal Leamington Spa CV31 .... 162 B8
Sutton Coldfield B74 .... 32 B3
Elizabeth Ave
Bilston WV14 .... 40 F3
Wednesbury WS10 .... 42 C3
Wolverhampton WV4 .... 39 B5
Elizabeth Cres B68 .... 64 D2
Elizabeth Ct
[1] Birmingham B17 .... 85 D4
[2] Birmingham,Acock's Green B27 .... 88 C2
[8] Coventry CV6 .... 113 A4
Warwick CV34 .... 161 B6
Elizabeth Dr B79 .... 21 A6
Elizabeth Gr
Dudley DY2 .... 62 F7
Solihull B90 .... 106 C2
Elizabeth Ho
[1] Walsall WS5 .... 43 D7
Stourbridge DY9 .... 81 E5
Sutton Coldfield B76 .... 46 F3
Elizabeth Mews B69 .... 52 A2
Elizabeth Prout Gdns B65 63 B1
Elizabeth Rd
Birmingham,Moseley B13 .. 86 C2
Birmingham,New Oscott B73 .... 45 D1
Birmingham,Stechford B33 . 68 D3
Cannock WS11 .... 1 E6
Halesowen B63 .... 82 F3
Hinckley LE10 .... 71 D2
Royal Leamington Spa CV31 .... 161 F6
Walsall WS5 .... 43 C7
West Bromwich B70 .... 52 D4
Elizabeth Way
Coventry CV2 .... 114 F7
Kenilworth CV8 .... 147 E5
Redditch B97 .... 153 D5
Elizabeth Wlk DY4 .... 41 A2
Eliza Gdns B61 .... 121 B1
Elkington Croft B90 .... 127 A5
Elkington St
Birmingham B6 .... 66 E5
Coventry CV6 .... 113 F8
Elkstone Cl B92 .... 89 B3
Elkstone Covert B14 .... 104 C2
Ellacombe Rd CV2 .... 114 D8
Elland Gr B27 .... 88 D2
Ellards Dr WV11 .... 26 F5
Ellenbrook Cl [6] B97 .... 153 B5
Ellen St B18 .... 66 B4
Ellenvale Cl WV14 .... 51 A8
Ellerbeck B77 .... 22 B1
Ellerby Gr B24 .... 57 E4
Ellerdene Cl B98 .... 158 D8
Ellerman Gdns CV6 .... 95 F3
Ellerside Gr B31 .... 102 F2
Ellerslie Cl DY5 .... 81 D8
Ellerslie Rd B13 .... 105 C7
Ellerton Rd B44 .... 45 B1
Ellerton Wlk WV10 .... 25 F5
Ellesboro' Rd B17 .... 85 B7
Ellesmere Rd
Bedworth CV12 .... 78 A2
Birmingham B8 .... 67 D4
Cannock WS11 .... 4 B8
Ellice Dr B36 .... 70 B7
Elliot Ct [1] WV4 .... 39 F4
Elliot Gdns B45 .... 122 B5
Elliott Cl WS11 .... 1 F5
Elliott Ct CV5 .... 112 C1
Elliott Rd B29 .... 85 E1
Elliotts La WV8 .... 10 A3
Elliott's Rd DY4 .... 51 E5
Elliott Way B6 .... 55 F3
Ellis Ave DY5 .... 61 A2
Ellison St B70 .... 53 C1
Ellis Park Dr CV3 .... 115 B1
Ellis St B1 .... 164 B1
Elliston Ave B44 .... 55 E8
Elliston Gr CV31 .... 162 C6
Ellis Wlk WS11 .... 4 F8
Ellowes Hall Sch The DY3 50 C5
Ellowes Rd DY3 .... 50 C4
Ellsmore Mdw WS13 .... 9 A6
Ellys Rd CV1 .... 113 C5
Elm Ave
Bilston WV14 .... 40 D6
Birmingham B12 .... 87 A5
Wednesbury WS10 .... 41 F4
Wolverhampton WV11 .... 26 B8
Elmay Rd B26 .... 89 A7
Elm Bank B13 .... 87 A3
Elm Bank Cl CV32 .... 157 A4
Elmbank Gr B20 .... 54 E5
Elmbank Rd
Kenilworth CV8 .... 147 E6
Walsall WS5 .... 43 C4
Elmbridge Cl B63 .... 82 D5
Elmbridge Dr B90 .... 127 B6
Elmbridge Rd B44 .... 55 E6
Elmbridge Way
[7] Birmingham B31 .... 103 D2
Sedgley DY3 .... 50 E6
Elm Cl
Binley Woods CV3 .... 135 C7
Dudley DY3 .... 50 B2
Stourbridge DY8 .... 80 D2
Elmcroft [5] B66 .... 65 C5
Elmcroft Ave B32 .... 84 A1
Elm Croft B68 .... 84 C7
Elmcroft Gdns WV10 .... 11 E3
Elmcroft Rd B26 .... 88 F7
Elm Ct
Allesley CV5 .... 111 B8
Birmingham B13 .... 86 F4
Oldbury B66 .... 64 C8
Redditch B97 .... 153 D4
Walsall WS1 .... 43 A8
Elmdale B62 .... 84 A7
Elmdale Cres B31 .... 102 E4
Elmdale Dr
Aldridge WS9 .... 30 C8
Kidderminster DY10 .... 117 C5
Elmdale Gr B31 .... 102 E4
Elmdale Rd WV14 .... 51 A7
Elm Dale Rd WV4 .... 39 A5
Elmdene Rd CV8 .... 148 B4
Elmdon Cl
Solihull B92 .... 89 D2
Wolverhampton WV10 .... 11 A1
Elmdon Coppice B92 .... 107 F7
Elmdon Ct B37 .... 90 A7
Elmdon La
Birmingham B37 .... 90 A6
Solihull B26 .... 90 A3
Elmdon Park Rd B92 .... 89 D2
Elmdon Rd
Birmingham,Acock's Green B27 .... 88 D4
Birmingham,Marston Green B37 .... 90 A7
Birmingham,Selly Park B29. 86 A2
Wolverhampton WV10 .... 11 A1
Elmdon Trad Est B37 .... 90 C5
Elm Dr
Birmingham,Frankley B31 .... 102 C1
Birmingham,Grove Vale B43 43 D1
Blakedown DY10 .... 98 B2
Halesowen B62 .... 63 E1
Elm Farm Ave B37 .... 89 F7
Elm Farm Rd WV2 .... 39 D7
Elmfield Ave B24 .... 57 F4
Elmfield Cres B13 .... 86 F2
Elmfield Rd
Birmingham B36 .... 69 F7
Nuneaton CV10 .... 73 C7
Elmfield Rudolf Steiner Sch Ltd DY8 .... 81 A3
Elmfield View DY1 .... 51 A3
Elm Gdns WS14 .... 9 C7
Elm Gn DY1 .... 51 A5
Elm Gr
Balsall Common CV7 .... 130 C6
Birmingham B37 .... 69 F6
Bromsgrove B61 .... 137 A4
Codsall WV8 .... 10 A3
Huntington WS12 .... 1 D8
Elmhurst Ave B65 .... 63 C3
Elmhurst B15 .... 85 D8
Elmhurst Cl B97 .... 158 D4
Elmhurst Dr
Burntwood WS7 .... 7 A4
Kingswinford DY6 .... 60 F4
Elmhurst Rd
Birmingham B21 .... 54 E1
Coventry CV6 .... 96 A4
Elmhurst Sch B5 .... 86 B5
Elmley Cl
Dudley WV14 .... 51 B7
Kidderminster DY11 .... 116 B3
Elmley Ct B23 .... 56 C2
Elmley Gr
Birmingham B30 .... 104 B2
Perton WV6 .... 23 F3
Elmley Ho [9] B97 .... 153 A4
Elm Lodge B92 .... 109 A7
Elmore Cl
Birmingham B37 .... 70 A4
Coventry CV3 .... 134 D8
Elmore Green Cl WS3 .... 28 B8
Elmore Green Prim Sch WS3 .... 14 B1
Elmore Green Rd WS3 .... 14 B1
Elmore Rd B33 .... 69 A3
Elmore Row WS3 .... 14 B1
Elm Pl DY10 .... 118 B3
Elm Rd
Birmingham B15 .... 85 F5
Birmingham,Bournville B30 .... 103 F8
Dudley DY1 .... 51 C4
Kidderminster DY10 .... 117 A6
Kingswinford DY6 .... 60 E6
Norton Canes WS11 .... 6 B5
Redditch B97 .... 153 D4
Royal Leamington Spa CV32 .... 157 B3
Sutton Coldfield B76 .... 46 F2
Walsall WS3 .... 28 D6
Elms Cl
Birmingham B38 .... 123 C8
Solihull B91 .... 107 D5
Elmsdale Ave CV6 .... 95 F2
Elmsdale Ct [6] WS1 .... 42 F8
Elmsdale WV6 .... 24 A2
Elms Dr WS11 .... 1 C1
Elms Farm Prim Sch B33. 89 D7
Elms Rd B72 .... 46 C3
Elmstead Ave B33 .... 89 D7
Elmstead Cl WS5 .... 29 E1
Elmstead Twr [2] B5 .... 86 E7
Elmstead Wood WS5 .... 29 E1
Elms The
Bedworth CV12 .... 77 E2
Birmingham B16 .... 65 F3
Kingswood B94 .... 144 D3
Leek Wootton CV35 .... 155 F6
Elms The *continued*
Wolverhampton WV11 .... 26 B5
Elmstone Cl
Dudley DY3 .... 50 F4
Redditch B97 .... 158 C5
Elm St
Willenhall WV13 .... 27 C2
Wolverhampton WV3 .... 25 A1
Elm Terr B69 .... 52 B1
Elm Tree Ave CV4 .... 112 B2
Elm Tree Dr LE10 .... 75 F8
Elm Tree Gr B63 .... 82 D6
Elm Tree Rd
Birmingham B17 .... 85 A7
Birmingham,Stirchley B30 104 A6
Bulkington CV12 .... 79 D2
Elmtree Rd
Sutton Coldfield B74 .... 30 D1
Sutton Coldfield B74 .... 44 D8
Elm Tree Rise B92 .... 109 B6
Elm Tree Way B64 .... 62 F1
Elm Tree Wlk B79 .... 20 F8
Elm Way CV10 .... 72 A8
Elmwood Ave
Coventry CV6 .... 112 F5
Essington WV11 .... 13 A3
Elmwood Cl
Balsall Common CV7 .... 130 C7
Cannock WS11 .... 2 A3
Elmwood Ct
Birmingham B5 .... 86 D6
Coventry CV1 .... 165 B4
Sutton Coldfield B74 .... 45 A5
Elmwood Gdns B20 .... 55 B2
Elmwood Gr B47 .... 125 A6
Elmwood Rd
Birmingham B24 .... 57 C2
Stourbridge DY8 .... 60 C2
Sutton Coldfield B74 .... 45 A5
Elmwood Rise DY3 .... 39 B1
Elmwoods B32 .... 84 B2
Elphin Cl CV6 .... 95 A4
Elphinstone End B24 .... 57 C6
Elsma Rd B68 .... 84 C8
Elston Hall La WV10 .... 11 D1
Elston Hall Prim Sch WV10 .... 11 D2
Elstree Rd B23 .... 56 D5
Elswick Gr B44 .... 56 B8
Elswick Rd B44 .... 45 B1
Elsworth Gr B25 .... 88 C6
Elsworth Rd [6] B31 .... 103 D2
Eltham Gr B44 .... 45 B1
Eltham Rd CV3 .... 133 E7
Elton Cl
Royal Leamington Spa CV32 .... 157 C2
Wolverhampton WV10 .... 11 E4
Elton Croft B93 .... 127 F4
Elton Gr B27 .... 88 A2
Eltonia Croft B26 .... 89 B6
Elunda Gr WS7 .... 6 E5
Elva Croft B36 .... 58 F1
Elvers Green La B92,B93 . 128 E7
Elvetham Rd B15 .... 86 C8
Elviron Dr WV6 .... 24 B5
Elwell Cres DY1 .... 50 F6
Elwells Cl WV14 .... 40 A3
Elwell St
Wednesbury WS10 .... 42 B3
West Bromwich B70 .... 52 E5
Elwy Circ CV7 .... 95 C6
Elwyn Rd B73 .... 46 A3
Ely Cl
Birmingham B37 .... 70 B2
Cannock WS11 .... 2 B1
Coventry CV2 .... 115 A6
Kidderminster DY11 .... 116 A6
Rowley Regis B65 .... 63 E4
Ely Cres B71 .... 53 B7
Ely Gr B32 .... 84 F4
Ely Pl WS2 .... 28 B1
Ely Rd WS2 .... 28 B1
Emay Cl B70 .... 52 F8
Embankment The DY5 .... 61 E3
Embassy Dr
Birmingham B15 .... 86 B8
Oldbury B69 .... 63 E8
Embassy Ind Est [1] DY9 .. 81 F5
Embassy Rd B69 .... 63 E8
Embassy Wlk CV2 .... 114 D8
Emberton Way B77 .... 21 F5
Embleton Cl LE10 .... 71 B1
Embleton Gr B34 .... 69 A6
Emerald Ct
[5] Solihull B92 .... 88 F1
Birmingham B8 .... 68 C5
Emerald Way CV31 .... 161 F5
Emerson Cl DY3 .... 50 A4
Emerson Gr WV10 .... 25 F8
Emerson Rd
Birmingham B17 .... 85 C6
Coventry CV2 .... 114 C3
Wolverhampton WV10 .... 25 E8
Emery Cl
Birmingham B23 .... 56 D1
Coventry CV2 .... 114 E7
Walsall WS1 .... 42 F8
Emery Ct DY10 .... 116 E7
Emery St WS1 .... 42 F8
Emily Gdns B16 .... 65 F3
Emily Rd B26 .... 88 D6
Emily Smith Ho [2] CV2 .. 96 B1
Emily St
Birmingham B12 .... 86 F7
West Bromwich B70 .... 53 B2
Emmanuel Rd
Burntwood WS7 .... 7 B7
Emmanuel Rd *continued*
Sutton Coldfield B73 .... 57 B8
Emmeline St B9 .... 67 B1
Emmott Dr CV31 .... 162 B5
Emperor Pl DY10 .... 116 E8
Empire Cl WS9 .... 29 F8
Empire Ind Est WS9 .... 15 F1
Empire Ind Pk WS9 .... 29 F8
Empire Rd CV4 .... 111 E2
Empress Way WS10 .... 41 D8
Emscote Dr B73 .... 57 B7
Emscote Gn B91 .... 106 E2
Emscote Inf Sch CV34 .. 161 B8
Emscote Rd
Birmingham B6 .... 55 F1
Coventry CV3 .... 114 C2
Warwick CV34 .... 161 B8
Emsworth Cres WV9 .... 11 A2
Emsworth Gr B14 .... 104 D6
Ena Rd CV1 .... 113 D5
Endemere Rd CV6 .... 113 D7
Enderby Cl B93 .... 127 F4
Enderby Dr WV4 .... 39 A5
Enderby Gr [9] B18 .... 65 E4
Enderby Rd B23 .... 56 C7
Enderley Cl WS3 .... 14 B3
Enderley Dr WS3 .... 14 B3
End Hall Rd WV6 .... 24 A3
Endhill Rd B44 .... 45 A3
Endicott Rd B6 .... 55 F1
Endmoor Gr B23 .... 56 D6
Endsleigh Gdns CV31 .... 162 B6
Endsleigh Gr B28 .... 106 A8
Endwood Court Rd B20 .. 55 A2
Endwood Ct
Birmingham B11 .... 87 D4
Birmingham,Handsworth Wood B20 .... 55 A2
Endwood Dr
Solihull B91 .... 106 F2
Sutton Coldfield B74 .... 31 C4
Enfield Cl B23 .... 56 F6
Enfield Ind Est B97 .... 153 D5
Enfield Rd
Birmingham B15 .... 86 B8
Coventry CV2 .... 114 B3
Redditch B97 .... 158 D5
Rowley Regis B65 .... 63 D3
Enford Cl B34 .... 69 D6
Engadine Rd B60 .... 137 C1
Engine La
Brierley Hill DY5 .... 61 F4
Darlaston WS10 .... 41 A4
Stourbridge DY9 .... 81 D6
Tamworth B77 .... 22 A2
Walsall WS8 .... 15 C8
Engine St
Oldbury B69 .... 64 B6
Smethwick B66 .... 65 B6
England Cres CV31 .... 161 E7
England Ho [10] CV32 .... 156 F2
Englestede Cl B20 .... 54 F3
Engleton Rd CV6 .... 113 A6
Englewood Dr B28 .... 106 A8
English Martyrs CE Prim Sch B11 .... 87 C4
Ennerdale Cl
Brownhills WS8 .... 15 E7
Royal Leamington Spa CV32 .... 156 D2
Ennerdale Cres CV11 .... 73 F6
Ennerdale Dr
Halesowen B63 .... 82 D2
Perton WV6 .... 23 F4
Ennerdale La CV2 .... 114 F4
Ennerdale Rd
Birmingham B43 .... 54 F6
Wolverhampton WV6 .... 24 D8
Ennersdale Bglws B46 .... 59 F1
Ennersdale Cl B46 .... 59 F1
Ennersdale Rd B46 .... 59 F1
Enright Cl CV32 .... 156 E2
Ensall Dr DY8 .... 60 E1
Ensbury Cl WV12 .... 27 D4
Ensdale Row WV13 .... 27 A1
Ensdon Gr B44 .... 45 B1
Ensford Cl B74 .... 31 E5
Ensign Bsns Ctr CV4 .... 131 F6
Ensign Cl CV4 .... 111 D1
Ensor Cl CV11 .... 74 A6
Ensor Dr B78 .... 22 F1
Enstone Rd
Birmingham B23 .... 57 A7
Dudley DY1 .... 61 F8
Enterprise Dr
Stourbridge DY9 .... 81 F6
Sutton Coldfield B74 .... 44 F7
Enterprise Gr WS3 .... 15 B5
Enterprise Ho B92 .... 109 A6
Enterprise Ind Pk WS13 .... 9 F8
Enterprise Trad Est DY5 .. 61 F3
Enterprise Way B7 .... 164 D4
Enterprise Workshops DY6 .... 61 A7
Enville Cl
Birmingham B37 .... 70 B1
Walsall WS3 .... 14 A3
Enville Gr B11 .... 87 D5
Enville Pl DY8 .... 80 E5
Enville Rd
Dudley DY3 .... 50 D4
Kingswinford DY6 .... 60 B8
Wolverhampton WV4 .... 38 C4
Enville St DY8 .... 80 F5
Epperston Ct CV31 .... 161 F7
Epping Cl
Birmingham B45 .... 102 B2
Walsall WS3 .... 28 F6

Epping Gr B44 ... 56 A7
Epping Way CV32 ... 157 C4
Epsom Cl
Bedworth CV12 ... 78 B4
Lichfield WS14 ... 9 D7
Perton WV6 ... 23 F4
Redditch B97 ... 158 C8
Tamworth B77 ... 35 C4
Epsom Ct 16 B29 ... 103 C7
Epsom Dr CV3 ... 134 C6
Epsom Gr B44 ... 56 B8
Epsom Rd
Royal Leamington Spa CV32 ... 157 C4
Upper Catshill B61 ... 121 A1
Epwell Gr B44 ... 55 F6
Epwell Rd B44 ... 55 F6
Epworth Ct DY5 ... 61 B5
Erasmus Rd B11 ... 87 A7
Erasmus Way WS13 ... 9 A8
Ercall Cl B23 ... 56 A6
Erdington Hall Prim Sch B24 ... 56 F1
Erdington Hall Rd B24 ... 56 F2
Erdington Ind Pk B24 ... 57 F4
Erdington Rd WS9 ... 30 C3
Erdington Sta B23 ... 56 F5
Erica Ave CV12 ... 77 F2
Erica Cl B29 ... 103 A8
Erica Dr CV31 ... 162 B2
Erica Rd WS5 ... 43 B3
Eric Grey Cl CV2 ... 114 A5
Eringden B77 ... 22 B1
Erithway Rd CV3 ... 133 B4
Ermington Cres B36 ... 68 E7
Ermington Rd WV4 ... 39 D4
Ernesford Grange Prim Sch CV3 ... 114 E1
Ernesford Grange Sch & Com Coll CV3 ... 134 D8
Ernest Clarke Cl WV12 ... 27 C4
Ernest Ct B38 ... 104 A1
Ernest Rd
Birmingham B12 ... 87 B4
Dudley DY2 ... 51 F1
Smethwick B67 ... 64 E6
Ernest Richards Rd CV12 ... 78 B4
Ernest St B1 ... 164 B1
Ernsford Ave CV3 ... 114 B1
Ernsford Cl B93 ... 127 F2
Erskine Cl LE10 ... 71 A2
Erskine St B7 ... 67 B3
Erwood Cl B97 ... 153 B2
Esher Dr CV3 ... 133 E7
Esher Rd
Birmingham B44 ... 44 F4
West Bromwich B71 ... 53 D6
Eskdale Cl WV1 ... 26 A2
Eskdale Rd LE10 ... 75 A7
Eskdale Wlk
Brierley Hill DY5 ... 81 B8
Coventry CV3 ... 134 D7
Esk Ho 1 DY1 ... 61 E8
Eskrett St WS12 ... 2 C5
Esme Rd B11 ... 87 B4
Esmond Cl B30 ... 103 D5
Essendon Gr B8 ... 68 B4
Essendon Rd B8 ... 68 B4
Essendon Wlk B8 ... 68 B4
Essex Ave
Kingswinford DY6 ... 60 B5
Wednesbury WS10 ... 42 C4
West Bromwich B71 ... 53 D7
Essex Cl
Coventry CV5 ... 112 B3
Kenilworth CV8 ... 147 E2
Essex Ct
5 Birmingham B29 ... 103 C7
Warwick CV34 ... 160 E8
Essex Dr WS12 ... 2 B4
Essex Gdns DY8 ... 80 D7
Essex Ho
2 Birmingham B2 ... 164 B2
2 Wolverhampton WV3 ... 25 C4
Essex Rd
Dudley DY2 ... 62 A6
Sutton Coldfield B75 ... 32 D2
Essex St
Birmingham B5 ... 164 C1
Walsall WS2 ... 28 E5
Essington Cl
Lichfield WS14 ... 9 A5
Shenstone WS14 ... 18 A7
Stourbridge DY8 ... 60 E1
Essington Ind Est WV11 ... 12 F4
Essington Rd WV12 ... 13 B1
Essington St B16 ... 66 B1
Essington Way WV1 ... 26 B1
Este Rd B26 ... 69 A1
Esterton Cl CV6 ... 95 C2
Estone Wlk B6 ... 66 F7
Estria Rd B15 ... 86 B7
Estridge La WS6 ... 5 A2
Etchell Rd B78 ... 20 F3
Ethelfield Rd CV2 ... 114 B3
Ethelfleda Rd B77 ... 35 F5
Ethelfleda Terr WS10 ... 41 F3
Ethel Rd B17 ... 85 D5
Ethelred Cl B74 ... 32 A3
Ethel St
Birmingham B2 ... 164 B2
Oldbury B68 ... 64 A4
Smethwick B67 ... 64 F2
Etheridge Rd WV14 ... 40 D7
Eton Cl DY3 ... 50 F6
Eton Ct
1 Sutton Coldfield B74 ... 31 F2
Lichfield WS14 ... 9 B6
Eton Dr DY8 ... 81 A3
Etone Com Sch CV11 ... 73 D5
Etone Ct CV11 ... 73 B5
Eton Rd B12 ... 87 B4
Eton Wlk DY9 ... 99 A6
Etruria Way WV14 ... 40 E7
Etta Gr B44 ... 44 F4
Ettingley Cl B98 ... 159 B5
Ettingshall Park Farm La WV4 ... 39 E4
Ettingshall Prim Sch WV14 ... 40 B6
Ettingshall Rd
Bilston WV14 ... 40 A2
Wolverhampton WV2 ... 40 A7
Ettington Cl B93 ... 127 D2
Ettington Rd
Birmingham B6 ... 66 E8
Coventry CV5 ... 112 A3
Ettymore Cl DY3 ... 50 D8
Ettymore Rd DY3 ... 50 D8
Ettymore Rd W DY3 ... 50 C8
Etwall Rd B28 ... 105 E6
Euan Cl B17 ... 85 C8
Eunal Ct B97 ... 158 E5
Euro Bsns Pk B69 ... 52 D1
Euro Ct B13 ... 87 B2
Europa Ave B70 ... 53 F2
Europa Way
Lichfield WS13 ... 9 F8
Royal Leamington Spa CV34 ... 161 D5
European Bsns Pk B69 ... 63 E7
Eustace Rd CV12 ... 79 D1
Euston Cres CV3 ... 134 C6
Euston Pl CV32 ... 161 F8
Euston Sq 1 CV32 ... 161 F8
Evans Cl
Bedworth CV12 ... 78 C3
Dudley DY4 ... 51 C5
Evans Croft B78 ... 21 A1
Evans Gdns B29 ... 85 D1
Evans Gr CV31 ... 162 A2
Evans Pl WV14 ... 40 E7
Evans St
Willenhall WV13 ... 26 D1
Wolverhampton,Dunstall Hill WV6 ... 25 B4
Wolverhampton WV4,WV14 ... 39 F1
Eva Rd
Birmingham B18 ... 65 D6
Oldbury B68 ... 64 D3
Evason Ct B6 ... 55 E1
Eve La DY1 ... 50 F5
Evelyn Ave CV6 ... 95 F2
Evelyn Croft B73 ... 57 A8
Evelyn Rd B11 ... 87 D4
Evenlode Cl
Redditch B98 ... 153 F1
Solihull B92 ... 89 B3
Evenlode Cres CV6 ... 112 F5
Evenlode Gr WV13 ... 27 D1
Evenlode Rd B92 ... 89 B3
Everard Ct CV11 ... 73 E2
Everdon Rd CV6 ... 95 B2
Everene Ho 1 B27 ... 88 C3
Everest Cl B66 ... 64 F8
Everest Rd
Birmingham B20 ... 55 A3
Willenhall WS2 ... 27 F3
Everglade Rd CV9 ... 36 C2
Evergreen Cl WV14 ... 51 B8
Evergreen Hts WS12 ... 2 A8
Evergreens The CV10 ... 72 F6
Everitt Dr B93 ... 128 A6
Eversfield Prep Sch B91 ... 107 B4
Eversleigh Rd CV6 ... 112 E7
Eversley Dale B24 ... 57 A2
Eversley Gr
Sedgley DY3 ... 39 C2
Wolverhampton WV11 ... 26 C6
Eversley Rd 2 B9 ... 67 D1
Evers St DY5 ... 82 A8
Everton Rd B8 ... 68 C4
Eves Croft B32 ... 84 C1
Evesham Cres WS3 ... 13 F3
Evesham Ct DY11 ... 116 D5
Evesham Ho B60 ... 137 B3
Evesham Mews 8 B97 ... 153 E3
Evesham Rd B96,B97 ... 158 E3
Evesham Rise DY2 ... 62 D3
Evesham Sq 3 B97 ... 153 E3
Evesham St B97 ... 153 E3
Evesham Wlk
2 Redditch B97 ... 153 E4
Coventry CV4 ... 132 D5
Eveson Rd DY8 ... 80 E2
Ewart Rd WS2 ... 27 E3
Ewell Rd B24 ... 57 B4
Ewhurst Ave B29 ... 85 F1
Ewhurst Cl WV13 ... 40 F8
Ewloe Cl DY10 ... 116 E1
Exbury Cl WV9 ... 10 F2
Exbury Way CV11 ... 78 E8
Excelsior Gr WS3 ... 15 B5
Exchange Ind Est The WS11 ... 4 E5
Exchange St
Brierley Hill DY5 ... 61 D4
Kidderminster DY10 ... 116 E6
Wolverhampton WV1 ... 163 B3
Exchange The WS3 ... 14 B1
Exe Croft B31 ... 123 B8
Exeter Cl
Coventry CV3 ... 134 D8
Kidderminster DY11 ... 116 A6
Exeter Dr
Birmingham B37 ... 89 F8
Exeter Dr *continued*
Tamworth B79 ... 20 E5
Exeter Ho 8 B24 ... 56 F4
Exeter Pas B1 ... 164 B1
Exeter Pl WS2 ... 28 B1
Exeter Rd
Birmingham B29 ... 85 F2
Cannock WS11 ... 4 B8
Dudley DY2 ... 62 D2
Smethwick B66 ... 65 B5
Exeter St B1 ... 164 B1
Exford Cl DY5 ... 81 B7
Exhall Cedars Inf Sch CV7 96 A8
Exhall Cl
Redditch B98 ... 154 D5
Solihull B91 ... 106 E2
Exhall Ct B23 ... 56 C2
Exhall Gn CV7 ... 95 F7
Exhall Grange Sch & Science Coll CV7 ... 95 C5
Exhall Rd CV7 ... 95 A6
Exham Cl CV34 ... 155 E1
Exhibition Way B40 ... 90 D4
Exis Ct CV11 ... 73 E2
Exley B77 ... 21 D1
Exminster Rd CV3 ... 133 E5
Exmoor Ct B61 ... 137 A4
Exmoor Dr
Bromsgrove B61 ... 137 A4
Royal Leamington Spa CV32 ... 157 C4
Exmoor Gn WV11 ... 26 C7
Exmouth Cl CV2 ... 114 C7
Exonbury Wlk 5 WS11 ... 1 F2
Exon Ct DY4 ... 51 F6
Expressway The B70 ... 53 C4
Exton Cl
Ash Green CV7 ... 95 C6
Wednesfield WV11 ... 26 F8
Exton Way B8 ... 67 D5
Eyffler Cl CV34 ... 160 D7
Eyland Gr WS1 ... 28 F2
Eymore Cl B29 ... 103 B6
Eynsham Ct WV6 ... 24 E5
Eyre St B18 ... 66 A3
Eyston Ave DY4 ... 52 D8
Eyton Cl B98 ... 154 D3
Eyton Croft B12 ... 86 F7
Ezekiel La WV12 ... 27 C6

F

Fabian Cl
Birmingham B45 ... 102 A2
Coventry CV3 ... 134 D7
Fabian Cres B90 ... 106 B1
Fabius Cl LE10 ... 75 C7
Facet Rd B38 ... 104 A2
Factory La B61 ... 136 F1
Factory Rd
Birmingham B18 ... 66 A6
Hinckley LE10 ... 71 D1
Tipton DY4 ... 51 E6
Factory St WS10 ... 41 C6
Fairbanks Cl CV2 ... 115 A7
Fairbourne Ave
Birmingham B44 ... 44 E2
Rowley Regis B65 ... 63 E4
Fairbourne Gdns B97 ... 158 C7
Fairbourne Twr B23 ... 57 A6
Fairbourne Way CV6 ... 112 E8
Fairburn Cres WS3 ... 15 B5
Faircroft Ave B76 ... 57 F6
Faircroft CV8 ... 147 F3
Faircroft Rd B36 ... 58 D1
Fairdene Way 3 B43 ... 54 D8
Fairfax Ct 7 CV34 ... 160 F7
Fairfax Rd
Birmingham B31 ... 123 A8
Sutton Coldfield B75 ... 46 F5
Wolverhampton WV10 ... 11 E3
Fairfax Sch B75 ... 46 F5
Fairfax St CV1 ... 165 C3
Fairfield Cl WS12 ... 2 D1
Fairfield Ct CV3 ... 134 A7
Fairfield Dr
Halesowen B62 ... 63 E1
Walsall WS3 ... 15 B4
Fairfield Fst Sch B61 ... 120 D3
Fairfield Gr B62 ... 63 E1
Fairfield Ho B60 ... 137 B3
Fairfield Mount WS1 ... 42 F8
Fairfield Park Ind Est B62 63 E1
Fairfield Rd
Birmingham B14 ... 104 E8
Dudley DY2 ... 62 D7
Fairfield B61 ... 120 D1
Halesowen B63 ... 83 A2
Halesowen,Hurst Green B62 63 E1
Stourbridge DY8 ... 60 F2
Fairfield Rise
Meriden CV7 ... 92 C1
Stourbridge DY8 ... 80 D5
Fairfields Hill B78 ... 36 F8
Fairford Cl
Redditch B98 ... 154 E7
Solihull B91 ... 106 D5
Fairford Gdns
Burntwood WS7 ... 7 C6
Stourbridge DY8 ... 60 E3
Fairford Rd B44 ... 55 F6
Fairgreen Gdns DY5 ... 61 C5
Fairgreen Way
Birmingham B29 ... 85 F1
Sutton Coldfield B74 ... 31 A1
Fairground Way WS1 ... 42 D8
Fairhaven Croft B62 ... 63 E1
Fairhaven Prim Sch DY8 ... 60 D3
Fairhills DY3 ... 50 D8
Fairhill Way B11 ... 87 C7
Fairholme Rd B36 ... 68 B7
Fairhurst Dr CV32 ... 156 E3
Fair Isle Dr CV10 ... 72 F2
Fair Lady Dr WS7 ... 6 D8
Fairlands Pk CV4 ... 132 E5
Fairlawn B15 ... 86 A7
Fairlawn Cl
Royal Leamington Spa CV32 ... 156 D1
Willenhall WV12 ... 13 C1
Fairlawn Dr DY6 ... 60 D4
Fairlawns
Birmingham B26 ... 69 A1
Sutton Coldfield B76 ... 58 A8
Fairlawn Way WV12 ... 13 C1
Fairlie Cres B38 ... 103 D1
Fairlight Dr B45 ... 122 A1
Fairmead Rise B38 ... 103 E1
Fairmile Cl CV3 ... 134 C8
Fairmile Rd B63 ... 83 A6
Fairmont Rd B60 ... 151 B8
Fairmount Dr 5 WS11 ... 4 E8
Fairoak Dr
Bromsgrove B60 ... 150 F6
Wolverhampton WV6 ... 24 B3
Fair Oaks Dr WS6 ... 14 A8
Fairview Ave B42 ... 55 B6
Fairview Cl
Cheslyn Hay WS6 ... 4 D2
Tamworth B77 ... 21 F5
Wolverhampton WV11 ... 26 B7
Fairview Cres
Kingswinford DY6 ... 60 F6
Wolverhampton WV11 ... 26 B7
Fairview Ct WS2 ... 27 D2
Fairview Gr WV11 ... 26 B7
Fairview Ind Est B76 ... 59 B7
Fairview Mews 9 B46 ... 70 F7
Fairview Rd
Dudley DY1 ... 51 A3
Wolverhampton,Scotlands WV11 ... 26 B7
Wolverhampton,Spring Hill WV4 ... 38 C4
Fairview Wlk CV6 ... 95 E2
Fairway Ave B69 ... 63 A8
Fairway
Birmingham B31 ... 102 E3
Cannock WS11 ... 4 D6
Fairway Ct B77 ... 22 B3
Fairway Dr B45 ... 121 F6
Fairway Gn WV14 ... 40 D8
Fairway CV11 ... 79 B8
Fairway Prim Sch B38 ... 103 D1
Fairway Rd B68 ... 63 F2
Fairway Rise CV8 ... 148 C6
Fairways Ave DY8 ... 80 E2
Fairways Cl
Coventry CV5 ... 112 A6
Stourbridge DY8 ... 80 E2
Fairways B93 ... 128 A8
Fairways Dr B60 ... 138 B5
Fairways The CV32 ... 156 D2
Fairway B77 ... 35 F5
Fairway The
Birmingham B38 ... 103 D2
Hinckley LE10 ... 75 F7
Fairway WS4 ... 15 D1
Fairyfield Ave B43 ... 43 D1
Fairyfield Ct B43 ... 43 D1
Fakenham Croft B17 ... 84 F7
Falcon Ave CV3 ... 134 F8
Falcon Cl
Cannock WS11 ... 1 C2
Cheslyn Hay WS6 ... 4 C2
Kidderminster DY10 ... 116 E2
Nuneaton CV11 ... 79 B8
Falcon Cres WV14 ... 39 F2
Falcondale Rd WV12 ... 13 C1
Falconers Gn LE10 ... 75 F6
Falconhurst Rd B29 ... 85 C2
Falcon Lodge Cres B75 ... 47 A6
Falcon Pk B77 ... 35 E7
Falcon Pl B69 ... 63 C7
Falcon Rd B68 ... 63 F2
Falcon Rise DY8 ... 80 C6
Falconry Ctr The* DY9 ... 98 F3
Falcons The B75 ... 47 B5
Falcon B77 ... 36 A6
Falcon View B30 ... 104 A4
Falcon Way DY1 ... 50 F1
Falfield Cl B65 ... 63 D6
Falfield Gr B31 ... 122 E7
Falkener Ho CV6 ... 113 E7
Falkland Cl CV4 ... 131 D7
Falkland Croft B30 ... 104 B6
Falkland Way B36 ... 70 B5
Falkwood Gr B93 ... 127 F6
Fallindale Rd B26 ... 89 B6
Fallings Heath Cl WS10 ... 41 F7
Fallings Park Ind Est WV10 ... 25 F5
Fallings Park Prim Sch WV10 ... 26 A8
Fallowfield Ave B28 ... 105 F5
Fallowfield B15 ... 85 E8
Fallow Field
Cannock WS11 ... 1 E3
Lichfield WS13 ... 3 C3
Fallowfield WV6 ... 23 D4
Fallowfield Rd
Halesowen B63 ... 82 D3
Rowley Regis B65 ... 63 A3
Solihull B92 ... 89 D3
Walsall WS5 ... 43 E8
Fallowfields Cl B61 ... 136 E3
Fallowfields CV6 ... 95 C4
Fallow Field B74 ... 31 B3
Fallowfield WV8 ... 10 E2
Fallow Hill CV31 ... 162 C6
Fallow Rd B78 ... 20 F1
Fallows Ho B19 ... 66 E5
Fallows Rd B11 ... 87 C6
Fallow Wlk B32 ... 84 A2
Falmouth Cl CV11 ... 74 A5
Falmouth Dr
Hinckley LE10 ... 71 E4
Tamworth B77 ... 21 F5
Falmouth Rd
Birmingham B34 ... 68 F6
Walsall WS5 ... 43 D7
Falna Cres B79 ... 20 F7
Falstaff Ave B47 ... 125 A6
Falstaff Cl
Nuneaton CV11 ... 74 A1
Sutton Coldfield B76 ... 58 B7
Falstaff Ct B75 ... 47 C5
Falstaff Gr CV34 ... 161 E3
Falstaff Ho B13 ... 105 D7
Falstaff Rd
Coventry CV4 ... 111 E1
Solihull B90 ... 106 C1
Falstone Rd B73 ... 45 D2
Fanad Ho B23 ... 56 E3
Fancott Dr CV8 ... 147 F6
Fancott Rd B31 ... 103 A5
Fancourt Ave WV4 ... 38 D4
Fane Rd WV11 ... 13 B2
Fanshawe Rd B27 ... 88 C1
Faraday Ave
Birmingham B32 ... 84 D5
Curdworth B46,B76 ... 59 F5
Faraday Ct B32 ... 84 D5
Faraday Ho 5 B15 ... 86 C8
Faraday Rd
Hinckley LE10 ... 74 E7
Walsall WS2 ... 28 B6
Farber Rd CV2 ... 115 A6
Farbrook Way WV12 ... 27 B6
Farclose Ho B15 ... 86 C7
Farcroft Ave
Birmingham B21 ... 65 D8
Coventry CV5 ... 111 D4
Farcroft Gr B21 ... 54 D1
Farcroft Rd B21 ... 54 D1
Fardon Way B23 ... 56 D8
Fareham Cres WV4 ... 38 C6
Farewell La WS7 ... 7 E6
Farfield Cl B31 ... 103 B2
Farfield
Kidderminster DY10 ... 116 F5
Stoke Prior B60 ... 150 F4
Farfield Studios DY10 ... 116 F5
Far Gosford St CV1 ... 113 E2
Far High Dr 6 DY4 ... 52 B5
Far Highfield B76 ... 46 E4
Far Hill Cl B71 ... 53 F8
Faringdon B77 ... 21 F1
Farlands Dr DY8 ... 81 A3
Farlands Gr B43 ... 54 F7
Farlands Rd DY8 ... 81 A3
Far Lash LE10 ... 75 F7
Farleigh Dr WV3 ... 38 A8
Farleigh Rd WV6 ... 24 A3
Farley Ctr The B70 ... 53 D2
Farley La B62 ... 100 F1
Farley Rd B23 ... 56 B4
Farley St
Royal Leamington Spa CV31 ... 162 B7
Tipton DY4 ... 52 D5
Farlow Cl
Coventry CV6 ... 114 A6
Redditch B98 ... 154 D3
Farlow Croft B37 ... 89 F8
Farlow Rd B31 ... 103 C3
Farmacre B9 ... 67 B2
Farman Rd CV5 ... 113 A2
Farm Ave B68 ... 64 A3
Farmbridge Cl WS2 ... 27 D3
Farmbridge Rd WS2 ... 27 D3
Farmbridge Way WS2 ... 27 D3
Farmbrook Ave WV10 ... 11 D3
Farm Cl
Birmingham B33 ... 68 F3
Cannock WS12 ... 2 C3
Codsall WV8 ... 10 B2
Coventry CV6 ... 95 B3
Kidderminster DY11 ... 116 B2
Sedgley DY3 ... 50 B7
Solihull B92 ... 89 C2
Tamworth B79 ... 21 C7
Farmcote Cl B97 ... 158 D4
Farmcote Lodge CV2 ... 96 B4
Farmcote Rd
Birmingham B33 ... 69 A4
Coventry CV2 ... 96 B4
Farm Croft B19 ... 66 C6
Farmcroft Rd DY9 ... 81 E2
Farmdale Gr B45 ... 122 A6
Farmer Rd B10 ... 88 A7
Farmers Cl B76 ... 46 E4
Farmers Ct B63 ... 82 F4
Farmer's Fold WV1 ... 163 B3
Farmers Rd B60 ... 150 E7
Farmers Wlk B21 ... 65 D7
Farmer Ward Rd CV8 ... 148 A3
Farmer Way DY4 ... 41 C1
Farm House La 6 B75 ... 32 E3
Farmhouse Rd WV12 ... 27 D5

Farm House Way B43 43 E4
Farmhouse Way
Solihull B90 127 B7
Willenhall WV12 27 D5
Farmoor Gr B34 69 E6
Far Moor La B98 154 F5
Farmoor Way WV10 11 E4
Farm Rd
Birmingham B11 87 B7
Brierley Hill DY5 61 E1
Dudley DY2 62 A4
Hinckley LE10 75 E6
Kenilworth CV8 147 E2
Oldbury B68 64 A3
Redditch B98 154 A3
Rowley Regis B65 63 A4
Royal Leamington Spa CV32 157 B3
Smethwick B67 64 E3
Tipton DY4 52 B7
Wolverhampton WV3 38 C8
Farmside Cl DY9 82 A3
Farmside CV3 134 D5
Farmside Gn WV9 10 F2
Farm St B19 66 C6
Farmstead Cl WS1 42 E5
Farmstead Rd B92 89 C2
Farmstead The CV3 134 B8
Farm St
Walsall WS2 28 E4
West Bromwich B70 53 C1
Farnborough Cl B98 154 F1
Farnborough Ct B75 32 C2
Farnborough Dr B90 126 F6
Farnborough Rd B35 58 B3
Farnbury Croft B38 104 B2
Farncote Dr B74 31 F3
Farndale Ave
Coventry CV6 95 D3
Wolverhampton WV6 24 F5
Farndale Cl DY5 81 B6
Farndon Ave B37 90 B7
Farndon Cl CV12 79 B3
Farndon Rd B8 67 F4
Farneway LE10 71 B1
Farnham Cl B43 54 F8
Farnham Rd B21 54 E2
Farnhurst Rd B36 68 B7
Farnol Rd B26 68 F1
Farnworth Gr B36 58 E1
Farquhar Rd
Birmingham B15 85 F6
Birmingham,Moseley B13 86 F3
Farquhar Rd E B15 85 F6
Farran Way B43 54 E7
Farr Dr CV4 112 B2
Farren Rd
Birmingham B31 102 D1
Coventry CV2 114 E5
Farrier Cl
Bromsgrove B60 150 E6
Sutton Coldfield B76 57 F8
Farrier Rd B43 44 D3
Farriers Mill WS3 14 E4
Farriers The B26 89 B5
Farriers Way
Hinckley LE10 75 F6
Nuneaton CV11 73 F2
Farrier Way DY6 60 A7
Farringdon Ho 5 WS2 28 D3
Farringdon St WS2 28 D3
Farrington Rd
Birmingham B23 56 B5
Wolverhampton WV4 39 E3
Farrow Rd B44 44 E3
Farthing Ct 8 B1 66 C3
Farthing La
Curdworth B76 59 C6
Redditch B97 153 B5
Sutton Coldfield B72 46 B4
Farthing Pools Cl 1 B72 46 C4
Farthings La DY2 62 A7
Farthings Lodge 7 DY1 51 B1
Farthings The
Birmingham B17 85 D6
Shenstone WS14 17 F5
Farthing Wlk CV4 131 D6
Farvale Rd B76 58 C6
Far View WS9 16 B2
Far Wood Rd B31 102 E8
Farzens Ave CV34 160 B3
Faseman Ave CV4 111 F3
Fashoda Rd B29 86 B1
Fasson Cl B77 35 C8
Fastlea Rd B32 84 D1
Fastmoor Oval B33 69 E1
Fast Pits Rd B25 88 C7
Fatherless Barn Cres B63 82 D5
Faulconbridge Ave CV5 111 E4
Faulconbridge Way CV34 161 E3
Faulkland Cres WV1 163 C4
Faulkner Cl DY8 80 F4
Faulkner Rd B92 89 B1
Faulkners Farm Dr B23 56 B6
Faulknor Dr DY5 61 B7
Faultlands Cl CV11 78 F8
Faversham Cl
Willenhall WS2 27 D3
Wolverhampton WV8 24 E8
Fawdry Cl B73 46 B5
Fawdry St
Birmingham B9 67 A2
Smethwick B66 65 C5
Wolverhampton WV1 163 A4
Fawley Cl
Coventry CV3 134 C6
Willenhall WV13 26 F1
Fawley Gr B14 104 B5
Fawn Cl WS12 1 C6
Faygate Cl CV3 114 F3
Fazeley Cl B91 107 D4
Fazeley Ind Est B5 67 A2
Fazeley Rd
Tamworth B78 21 A4
Tamworth,Fazeley B78 21 B2
Fazeley St B5 66 F2
Fearnings Cotts B97 158 D5
Fearon Pl 4 B66 65 A5
Featherbed La
Coventry CV4 132 A5
Redditch B97 158 C5
Featherston Dr LE10 75 E6
Featherstone Cl
Nuneaton CV10 73 C2
Solihull B90 106 D2
Featherstone Cres B90 106 D2
Featherstone La WV10 12 B8
Featherstone Prim Sch B23 56 E4
Featherstone Rd B14 104 E6
Featherston Rd B74 31 A2
Feckenham Ho B60 137 B3
Feckenham Rd
Astwood Bank B96 158 E2
Redditch,Headless Cross B97 158 C8
Redditch,Hunt End B97 158 C4
Fecknam Way WS13 3 C1
Feilding Cl CV2 115 A6
Feilding Way CV10 72 A5
Fein Bank CV4 111 C2
Felbrigg Cl DY5 81 D8
Feldings The B24 57 C4
Feldon La B62 83 E7
Felgate Cl B90 127 A6
Fellbrook Cl B33 68 F4
Fell Gr
Birmingham B21 54 C2
Royal Leamington Spa CV32 157 C3
Fellmeadow Rd B33 69 A2
Fellmeadow Way DY3 50 E7
Fellmore Gr CV31 162 D7
Fellows Ave DY6 60 C8
Fellows La B17 85 A5
Fellows Park Gdns WS2 42 B6
Fellows Rd WV14 40 D7
Fellows St WV2 163 B1
Felspar Rd B77 22 B3
Felstead Cl B77 35 C4
Felsted Way B7 67 A4
Felstone Rd B44 44 E1
Feltham Cl B33 69 E1
Felton Cl
Coventry CV2 96 E1
Redditch B98 154 E1
Felton Croft B33 69 A3
Felton Gr B91 107 C1
Fenbourne Cl WS4 29 C8
Fenchurch Cl WS2 28 D4
Fen Cl DY10 116 E8
Fencote Ave B37 70 A4
Fen End Rd CV8 129 E4
Fenmere Cl WV4 39 D5
Fennel Cl WS6 4 D3
Fennel Croft B34 69 B7
Fennell Ho 10 CV1 113 B2
Fennel Rd DY5 81 C7
Fennis Cl B93 127 F3
Fenn Rise
Stourbridge DY8 60 D3
Willenhall WV12 27 B5
Fenn St B77 21 E1
Fennyland La CV8 148 B7
Fens Cres DY5 61 C5
Fenside Ave CV3 133 D4
Fens Pool Ave DY5 61 D5
Fensway The B34 69 A5
Fenter Cl B13 86 F5
Fentham Cl B92 109 B6
Fentham Ct B92 106 F8
Fentham Gn B92 109 A7
Fentham Rd
Birmingham,Aston B6 66 E8
Birmingham,Gravelly Hill B23 56 E3
Hampton-in-A B92 109 A6
Fenton Rd
Birmingham B27 88 B5
Hollywood B47 125 A7
Fenton St
Brierley Hill DY5 61 D3
Smethwick B66 64 E7
Fenton Way B27 88 B5
Fenwick Cl B97 153 B1
Fereday Rd WS9 16 B3
Fereday's Croft DY3 50 D7
Fereday St DY4 51 F8
Ferguson Dr
Kidderminster DY11 116 A1
Tipton DY4 52 B6
Ferguson Rd B68 64 D5
Ferguson St WV11 13 A1
Fern Ave DY4 51 F7
Fernbank Cl B63 82 E2
Fernbank Cres WS5 43 C4
Fernbank Rd B8 68 A4
Fern Cl
Coventry CV2 96 C2
Dudley WV14 51 B8
Ferncliffe Rd B17 85 B4
Fern Cl WS4 15 D1
Ferndale Ave B43 54 F7
Ferndale Cl
Burntwood WS7 7 B6
Nuneaton CV11 73 E5
Upper Catshill B61 121 A1
West Hagley DY9 99 A5
Ferndale Cres
Birmingham B12 87 A8
Kidderminster DY11 116 B8
Ferndale Ct 2 B17 85 D4
Ferndale Dr CV8 148 A2
Ferndale Gr LE10 75 A7
Ferndale Pk DY9 99 C8
Ferndale Prim Sch B43 54 E8
Fern Dale Rd CV7 129 F6
Ferndale Rd
Binley Woods CV3 135 D7
Birmingham B28 105 F8
Essington WV11 13 B3
Oldbury B68 64 A2
Sutton Coldfield B74 44 F8
Fern Dell Cl WS11 1 C2
Ferndene Rd B11 88 A3
Ferndown Ave DY3 50 C7
Ferndown Cl
Birmingham B26 69 A1
Coventry CV4 112 A3
Walsall WS3 14 B4
Ferndown Gdns WV11 26 F5
Ferndown Rd B91 107 C5
Fern Dr WS6 5 A4
Ferneley Ave LE10 71 A3
Ferness Cl LE10 71 B2
Ferness Rd LE10 71 B2
Ferney Hill Ave B97 153 C3
Fern Gr CV12 77 E2
Fernhill Cl CV8 147 E6
Fernhill Ct B23 56 C2
Fernhill Dr CV32 157 B1
Fernhill Gr B44 44 F3
Fernhill La CV7,CV8 129 F5
Fernhill Rd B92 88 E2
Fernhurst Dr DY5 61 B7
Fernhurst Rd B8 68 A3
Fernleigh Ave WS7 7 A8
Fernleigh B60 137 A1
Fernleigh Ct B91 107 C5
Fernleigh Gdns DY8 60 C3
Fernleigh Rd WS4 29 B3
Fernley Ave B29 86 B2
Fernley Rd B11 87 C4
Fern Leys WV3 24 D1
Fern Rd
Birmingham B24 57 A4
Dudley DY1 51 C4
Huntington WS12 1 D5
Wolverhampton WV3 163 A1
Fernside Gdns B13 87 B3
Fernside Rd WV13 26 D3
Fernwood Cl
Redditch B98 159 B5
Sutton Coldfield B73 45 E1
Fernwood Croft
Birmingham B14 104 E6
Tipton DY4 51 F4
Fernwood Rd B73 56 E8
Fernwoods B32 84 B2
Ferrers Cl
Coventry CV4 111 F2
Sutton Coldfield B75 32 D2
Ferrers Rd B77 21 D4
Ferrie Gr WS8 15 E8
Ferris Gr B27 88 A1
Festival Ave WS10 41 C4
Festival Ct
Cannock WS11 1 E5
Dudley DY2 62 C5
Lichfield WS13 9 A7
Festival Mews WS12 1 F6
Festival Way WV6 25 B5
Fetherston Cres CV8 135 B1
Fetherston Ct 4 CV31 161 F6
Fetherston Grange B94 143 F5
Ffernfail Ct B23 56 E5
Fibbersley Bank WV13 26 F4
Fibbersley WV13,WV11 26 F4
Fiddlers Gn B92 109 A7
Field Ave B31 102 F5
Field Barn Rd CV35 160 A7
Field Cl
Birmingham B26 89 A6
Bromsgrove B60 150 E6
Hinckley LE10 71 F3
Kenilworth CV8 148 B5
Stourbridge DY8 61 A2
Tamworth B77 21 C2
Walsall,Blakenall Heath WS3 28 C8
Walsall WS4 15 B2
Warwick CV34 161 B7
Field Cottage Dr DY8 81 B3
Field Ct
Coventry CV2 114 D7
Walsall WS4 15 B2
Fieldfare Cl B64 62 F4
Fieldfare Croft B36 70 A8
Fieldfare Ct DY10 117 A1
Fieldfare WS7 7 D5
Fieldfare Rd DY9 81 D4
Field Farm La B98 154 D2
Field Farm Rd B77 21 D1
Fieldgate La
Kenilworth CV8 147 F6
Whitnash CV31 162 B2
Fieldgate Lawn CV8 147 F6
Fieldgate Trad Est WS1 28 F1
Field Head La CV34 161 B6
Field Head Pl WV6 24 B4
Fieldhead Rd B11 88 A3
Field Ho CV8 147 F5
Fieldhouse La B62 100 E4
Fieldhouse Rd
Birmingham B25 88 C8
Burntwood WS7 7 A7
Cannock WS12 1 F7
Wolverhampton WV4 39 E4
Field La
Birmingham B32 102 B8
Catherine de B B91 108 A5
Clent DY9 99 D4
Great Wyrley WS6 4 F3
Stourbridge DY8 81 A3
Walsall WS4 15 B2
Field Maple Rd B74 44 F6
Field March CV3 134 E5
Field Mews DY2 62 E2
Fieldon Cl B90 106 C2
Field Rd DY2 51 E2
Field Rd Ind Est WS3 28 C8
Field Rd
Lichfield WS13 3 B3
Tipton DY4 52 A8
Walsall WS3 14 C1
Fields Ct CV34 160 F8
Fieldside La CV3 114 F3
Fieldside Wlk WV14 40 D8
Field St
Bilston WV14 40 E3
Cannock WS11 1 F3
Fields The WV8 10 B4
Fieldstone View DY3 50 D4
Field St
Willenhall WV13 27 A2
Wolverhampton WV10 163 D4
Field View Cl CV7 96 A8
Fieldview Cl WV14 40 E2
Field View Dr B65 63 F3
Field View CV31 162 B3
Field Way B94 143 C6
Fieldways Cl B47 125 A7
Field Wlk WS9 30 B7
Fiery Hill Dr B45 138 C8
Fiery Hill Rd B45 138 C8
Fife Rd CV5 112 F2
Fife St CV11 73 A4
Fifield Cl CV11 73 D2
Fifield Gr B33 68 F3
Fifth Ave
Birmingham B9 67 F2
Wolverhampton WV10 25 E7
Filey Cl WS11 4 C8
Filey Rd WV10 11 B2
Filey B77 21 F6
Fillingham Cl B37 70 D1
Fillongley Rd CV7 92 E3
Filton Ave WS7 7 A8
Filton Croft B35 58 A4
Fimbrell Cl DY5 81 A8
Finbury Cl B92 88 F1
Finchall Croft B92 107 E7
Fincham Cl WV9 11 A3
Finch Cl
Coventry CV6 95 C2
Rowley Regis B65 62 F4
Finch Croft CV7 130 B7
Finchdene Gr WV3 24 D1
Finch Dr B74 45 A5
Finches End B34 69 C5
Finchfield Cl DY8 80 C4
Finchfield Gdns WV3 24 E1
Finchfield Hill WV3 24 C1
Finchfield La WV3 38 C8
Finchfield Rd WV3 24 E1
Finchfield Rd W WV3 24 D1
Finchley Ave 1 B19 66 C8
Finchley Cl DY3 50 D2
Finchley Rd B44 45 B1
Finchmead Rd B33 69 E2
Finchpath Rd B70 53 A6
Finch Rd B19 66 C8
Findlay Rd B14 86 E1
Findon Cl
Bulkington CV12 79 C3
Redditch B97 153 A5
Findon Rd B8 68 B6
Findon St DY10 116 F6
Finford Croft CV7 130 B6
Fingal Cl CV3 134 C6
Finger Post Dr WS3 15 A5
Fingest Cl CV5 112 B4
Finham Cres CV8 148 B6
Finham Flats CV8 148 B6
Finham Gr CV3 133 C3
Finham Green Rd CV3 133 B3
Finham Park Sch CV3 133 A4
Finham Prim Sch CV3 133 B3
Finham Rd CV8 148 B6
Finings Ct 7 CV32 156 F2
Finlarigg Dr B15 85 F6
Finlay Ct CV1 165 C1
Finmere Rd B28 105 F8
Finmere Way B90 106 D3
Finnemore Cl CV3 133 B5
Finnemore Rd B9 68 A2
Finney Well Cl WV14 40 B3
Finsbury Dr DY5 81 C7
Finsbury Gr B23 56 D6
Finstall Cl
Birmingham B7 67 A4
Sutton Coldfield B72 46 C1
Finstall Fst Sch B60 137 B1
Finstall Rd
Bromsgrove B60 151 C8
Finstall B60 137 D1
Finwood Cl B92 107 E8
Finwood Rd CV35 144 F1
Fir Ave B12 87 A5
Firbank Cl B30 103 E7
Firbank Way WS3 14 F2
Firbarn Cl B76 46 D3
Firbeck Gr B44 45 A1
Firbeck Rd B44 45 A1
Fir Cl WS12 1 D8
Fircroft
9 Wolverhampton WV4 39 F4
Birmingham B31 102 F8
Fir Croft DY5 81 C8
Fircroft Cl
3 Cannock WS11 2 A3
Stoke Heath B60 150 D6
Fircroft Coll B29 103 D8
Fircroft WV14 41 A3
Fircroft Ho B37 70 A2
Fircroft B91 106 F6
Firecrest Cl
Birmingham B23 56 B7
Cannock WS11 2 C2
Firecrest Way DY10 117 B1
Firedrake Croft CV1 113 F2
Firenze Rd B60 137 C1
Fire Sta B44 56 A7
Fire Station Flats B30 103 F4
Firethorn Cres CV31 162 A2
Fir Gr
Birmingham B14 104 F5
Coventry CV4 112 A2
Stourbridge DY8 80 D6
Wolverhampton WV3 25 A1
Firhill Croft B14 104 D2
Firleigh Dr CV12 79 D2
Firmstone Ct DY8 80 E7
Firmstone St DY8 80 E7
Firsbrook Cl WV6 25 A5
Firsbrook Ho WV6 25 A5
Firsby Rd B32 84 E5
Firs Cl
Lower Marlbrook B60 121 D1
Smethwick B67 65 A5
Firs Cl The DY10 117 A5
Firs Dr B90 106 A1
Firs Farm Dr B36 68 F7
Firs Ho B36 68 F8
Firsholm Cl B73 57 A7
Firs La B67 65 A5
Firs Mobile Home Pk The 4 WS11 2 A2
Firs Prim Sch B36 68 F8
Firs Rd DY6 60 E6
Firs St DY2 51 D1
First Ave
Birmingham,Bordesley Green B9 67 E1
Birmingham,Selly Oak B29 86 B3
Birmingham,Tyburn B35 58 A5
Birmingham,Witton B6 55 F2
Brownhills WS8 16 A8
Coventry CV3 114 C1
Kingswinford DY6 50 A1
Wolverhampton WV10 25 E6
First Exhibition Ave B40 90 D4
Fir St DY3 49 F7
Firs The
Bedworth CV12 77 E2
Birmingham B11 87 C6
Coventry CV5 133 B8
Kidderminster DY10 117 A5
Meriden CV7 92 B1
Wolverhampton WV11 26 B5
First Meadow Piece B32 84 E4
Firsvale Rd WV11 26 F5
Firsway WV6 24 A2
Firswood Rd B33 69 C1
Firth Dr
Birmingham B14 105 B5
Halesowen B62 83 E8
Firth Park Cres B62 83 E8
Fir Tree Ave CV4 112 B2
Fir Tree Cl
Birmingham B44 55 E7
Redditch B97 153 D4
Tamworth B79 20 E7
Fir Tree Dr
Dudley DY3 50 E7
Walsall WS5 43 B4
Fir Tree Gr
Nuneaton CV11 78 D8
Sutton Coldfield B73 45 F1
Fir Tree Prim Sch WS5 43 A4
Firtree Rd B24 57 B2
Fir Tree Rd WV3 38 D8
Fisher Cl B45 101 E2
Fisher Rd
Coventry CV6 113 E8
Oldbury B69 64 C7
Walsall WS3 13 F2
Fisher's Ct CV34 160 D4
Fishers Dr B90 125 F5
Fisher St
Brierley Hill DY5 61 B2
Cannock WS12 1 F8
Dudley DY2 51 D1
Tipton,Burnt Tree DY4 52 A3
Tipton,Great Bridge DY4 52 D5
Willenhall WV13 27 C2
Wolverhampton WV3 39 B8
Fish Hill B97 153 E4
Fish House La B60 150 E4
Fishing Line Rd B97 153 E5
Fishley Cl WS3 14 C4
Fishley La WS3 14 D5
Fishponds Rd CV8 147 E3
Fishpool Cl B36 68 C8
Fishpool La CV7 91 B5
Fistral Gdns WV3 38 F7

Fitchet's Bank WS7 7 F6
Fithern Cl DY3 50 E5
Fitters Mill Cl B5 86 E6
Fitton Ave DY6 61 A5
Fitton St CV11 73 B3
Fitzgerald Pl DY5 81 B6
Fitzguy Cl B70 53 E1
Fitzmaurice Rd WV11 27 A7
Fitz Roy Ave B17 84 F7
Fitzroy Cl CV2 115 B6
Fitzroy Rd B31 102 D3
Fivefield Rd CV7 94 E5
Five Fields Rd WV12 27 A5
Five Oaks Rd WV13 40 E8
Fives Gr WS7 6 C8
Five Ways
Birmingham B33 68 D2
Birmingham,Bordesley Green B9 67 D2
Birmingham,Ladywood B16 66 B1
Churchill DY10 98 A5
Cradley Heath B64 82 C8
Dudley DY3 50 D3
Five Ways Prim Sch WS12 2 D2
Five Ways Rd CV35 145 F1
Five Ways Sta B15 86 B8
Five Ways
Wolverhampton,Dunstall Hill WV3 25 C4
Wolverhampton WV3 38 C7
Wroxall CV35 145 F1
Flackwell Rd B23 56 E7
Fladbury Cl
Dudley DY2 62 D3
Redditch B98 159 B8
Fladbury Cres B29 85 D1
Fladbury Gdns B20 66 C8
Fladbury Pl 3 B19 66 C7
Flamboro' Cl CV3 134 F8
Flamborough Cl B34 69 A7
Flamborough Way WV14 51 B7
Flamville Rd LE10 76 B5
Flanders Cl B98 154 D5
Flanders Dr DY6 60 D8
Flash La WV4 37 E2
Flash Rd B69 64 A7
Flatlea B31 102 F4
Flats La WS14 19 A6
Flats The B61 136 F3
Flatts The WS10 41 E7
Flaunden Cl CV5 112 B4
Flavel Cres CV31 161 F7
Flavell Ave WV14 40 D1
Flavell Cl B32 84 B1
Flavells La
Birmingham B25 88 C8
Dudley DY3 50 B2
Flavell St DY1 51 B6
Flavel Rd B60 150 E7
Flax Cl B47 125 A5
Flax Gdns B38 123 F8
Flaxhall St WS2 42 B8
Flax Hill Jun Sch B79 21 B7
Flaxley Cl B33 68 F3
Flaxley Parkway B33 68 E4
Flaxley Rd B33 68 E4
Flaxton Gr B33 69 A4
Flaxton Wlk WV6 25 A5
Flecknoe Cl B36 58 C1
Flecknose St CV3 134 C6
Fledburgh Dr B76 46 D4
Fleet St
Birmingham B3 164 A3
Coventry CV1 165 B3
Fleetwood Gr B26 69 A1
Fleetwood Ho 3 B13 86 F4
Fleming Pl WS2 28 A6
Fleming Rd
Birmingham B32 84 D5
Hinckley LE10 74 F7
Walsall WS2 28 A6
Fletchamstead Highway CV5 132 D7
Fletcher Gr B93 128 B4
Fletcher Rd
Hinckley LE10 75 E7
Walsall WV12 13 D1
Willenhall WV12 27 D8
Fletcher's La WV13 27 C2
Fletcher St DY9 81 F5
Fletchers Wlk B3 164 B2
Fletchworth Gate CV5 132 D8
Fletchworth Gate Ind Est CV4 132 D8
Fletton Gr B14 105 A3
Fleur de-lys Ct CV34 161 B8
Flinkford Cl WS5 43 D6
Flinn Cl WS14 9 D7
Flint Cl DY10 116 E2
Flint Green Rd B27 88 B3
Flintham Cl B92 88 E3
Flint Ho 3 WV3 25 C4
Flintway The B33 68 E4
Floodgate St B5 66 F1
Flood St DY2 51 D1
Flood Street Island DY2 62 D8
Flora Cl B79 21 C7
Flora Rd B25 88 B7
Florence Ave
5 Sutton Coldfield B73 57 B7
Birmingham B11 87 C5
Wolverhampton WV4 40 A4
Florence Bldgs 3 B29 85 F2
Florence Cl CV12 95 F8
Florence Dr 4 B73 57 B7
Florence Gr
2 Birmingham B18 65 E4
West Bromwich B71 42 E1
Florence Pl 10 B12 87 A6
Florence Rd
Birmingham,Acock's Green B27 88 D4
Birmingham,Handsworth B21 65 D8
Birmingham,King's Heath B14 104 F8
Codsall WV8 10 C3
Coventry CV3 115 A2
Oldbury B69 63 E7
Smethwick B66 65 B4
Sutton Coldfield B73 57 B7
Tipton DY4 52 A7
West Bromwich B70 53 E1
Florence St
Birmingham B1 164 B1
Cannock WS12 2 B7
Walsall WS1 29 A1
Florence Villas B11 87 C7
Florendine Com Prim Sch B77 21 F5
Florendine St B77 21 F5
Florian Gr WS10 41 E7
Florian Way LE10 71 A1
Florida Way DY6 61 A6
Florin Cl CV4 131 E6
Flowerdale Cl WV14 51 B8
Flowerdale Dr CV2 114 B6
Floyd Gr CV7 130 C7
Floyds La WS4 29 C6
Floyer Rd B10 67 F1
Flude Rd CV7 95 C6
Flyford Cl B98 153 F1
Flyford Croft B29 84 F2
Flynt Ave CV5 112 B6
Fockbury Mill La B61 136 E5
Fockbury Rd B61 136 B5
Focus Pk B90 126 E8
Foden Cl WS14 17 F6
Foden Rd B42 55 A7
Foinavon Cl B65 62 F6
Fold St WV1 163 B2
Fold The
Birmingham B38 104 A1
Darlaston WS10 41 D6
Wolverhampton WV4 38 F4
Foldyard Cl B76 58 A8
Foleshill CE Prim Sch CV6 96 A2
Foleshill Rd CV1,CV6 113 D6
Foley Ave WV6 24 C3
Foley Church Cl B74 31 A2
Foley Ct B74 30 F1
Foley Dr WV6 24 C3
Foley Gdns B60 150 E3
Foley Ind Est DY11 116 D3
Foley Park Fst Sch DY11 116 D3
Foley Rd B8 68 B5
Foley Rd E B74 31 A2
Foley Rd DY9 81 C2
Foley Rd W B74 30 E1
Foley St WS10 42 A3
Foley Wood Cl B74 30 E1
Foliot Fields B25 88 D8
Folkes Rd DY9 82 A6
Folkestone Croft B36 68 E8
Folkland Gn CV6 113 A7
Folliott Rd B33 69 B3
Follyhouse Cl WS1 42 F7
Follyhouse La WS1 42 F7
Folly The B97 158 D8
Fontenaye Rd B79 20 F7
Fontley Cl B26 69 A2
Fontmell Cl CV2 115 A4
Fontwell Rd WV10 11 D4
Footherley La WS14 17 C4
Footherley Rd WS14 17 F5
Fordbridge Cl B97 153 C1
Fordbridge Inf Sch B37 70 A5
Fordbridge Rd B37 70 A5
Ford Brook La WS3 15 B2
Ford Cotts CV33 157 F2
Forder Gr B14 105 A2
Forde Way Gdns B38 123 D7
Fordfield Rd B33 69 C4
Fordham Gr WV9 11 A3
Fordhouse La B30 104 B6
Fordhouse Rd B60 137 B1
Fordhouse Rd Ind Est WV10 11 D1
Fordhouse Rd WV10 11 D1
Fordhouse Road Ind Est WV10 25 D8
Fordraught La B62 101 B1
Ford Rd B61 136 E1
Fordrift The B37 90 A6
Fordrough Ave B9 67 E3
Fordrough B25 87 F7
Fordrough La B9 67 E2
Fordrough The
Birmingham B31 103 C1
Hollywood B90 125 C7
Sutton Coldfield B74 32 A1
Fords Rd B90 125 E7
Ford St
Birmingham B18 66 B5
Coventry CV1 165 C3
Nuneaton CV10 72 E4
Smethwick B67 64 F6
Walsall WS2 42 C7
Fordwater Rd B74 44 F6
Fordwell Cl CV5 112 F3
Foredraft Cl B32 84 C2
Foredraft St B63 82 D5
Foredraught B80 159 E4
Foredrift Cl B98 153 E2
Foredrove La B92 107 E7
Foregate St B96 158 E1
Forelands Gr B61 150 D8
Foreland Way CV6 95 A3
Forest Ave WS3 28 D7
Fore St B2 164 C2
Forest Cl
Lickey End B60 137 B6
Smethwick B66 64 E7
Sutton Coldfield B74 44 E7
Forest Ct
Birmingham B13 87 A3
Coventry CV5 112 A4
Dorridge B93 127 F3
Willenhall WV12 27 C8
Forest Dale B45 122 B6
Forest Dr
Birmingham B17 85 D6
Cradley Heath B64 62 F3
Forester's Rd CV3 133 E6
Forester Way DY10 116 E3
Forest Gate WV12 27 D8
Forest Glade WS6 4 F2
Forest Hill Rd B26 89 C5
Forest La WS2 28 D5
Forest Lawns B74 31 C3
Forest Oak Sch B36 58 E1
Forest Pk B76 46 E4
Forest Pl WS3 28 E6
Forest Rd
Birmingham B68 84 C7
Birmingham,Moseley B13 87 A3
Birmingham,South Yardley B25 88 C6
Dorridge B93 127 F3
Dudley DY1 51 C4
Hinckley LE10 75 F8
Forest View B97 158 E6
Forest Way
Great Wyrley WS6 5 A1
Hollywood B47 125 B6
Nuneaton CV10 72 E2
Forfar Wlk B38 103 D2
Forfield Pl CV31 162 A7
Forfield Rd CV6 112 E5
Forge Ave B60 151 B7
Forge Cl
Hammerwich WS7 7 D5
Wolverhampton WV8 10 E1
Forge Croft B76 58 B6
Forge Dr B61 136 F3
Forge La
Aldridge,Leighswood WS9 30 A5
Aldridge,Mill Green WS9 30 F7
Belbroughton DY9 119 D7
Blakedown DY10 98 B1
Burntwood WS7 7 F6
Cradley Heath B64 82 B8
Halesowen B62 83 C5
Kingswinford DY6 60 A8
Lichfield WS13 3 A1
Shenstone B74,WS14 31 C7
Sutton Coldfield B76 58 B5
West Bromwich B71 54 A6
Forge Mill Farm* B71 54 B6
Forge Mill Needle Mus* B98 153 F6
Forge Mill Rd B98 153 F6
Forge Rd
Darlaston WS10 41 C6
Kenilworth CV8 148 A6
Stourbridge DY8 80 F6
Walsall WS3 14 F5
Willenhall WV12 27 C4
Forge St
Cannock WS12 2 C4
Wednesbury WS10 41 E4
Forge The B63 82 B8
Forge Trad Est B62 83 C5
Forge Way
Coventry CV6 95 C3
Oldbury B69 63 E6
Forhill Ho B38 123 F3
Forknell Ave CV2 114 C5
Formans Rd B11 87 E3
Formans Trad Est B11 87 D3
Formby Ave WV6 23 D4
Formby Way WS3 14 A3
Forrell Gr B31 123 B7
Forrest Ave
Cannock WS11 4 E8
Essington WV11 13 A4
Forrest Ct 9 WS13 9 B7
Forresters Cl LE10 75 F6
Forresters Rd LE10 75 F6
Forrester Street Prec 3 WS2 28 C2
Forrester St WS2 28 C2
Forrest Rd CV8 147 E4
Forryan Rd LE10 75 F7
Forshaw Heath La B94 141 A7
Forshaw Heath Rd B94 125 C1
Forster St
Birmingham B7 67 A3
Smethwick B67 64 E7
Forsythia Cl B31 102 F8
Forsythia Gr WV8 10 A3
Fort Cres WS9 16 A3
Forth Dr B37 70 B4
Forth Gr B38 123 E8
Forth Way B62 83 E8
Forties B77 35 E7
Fort Ind Pk The B35 57 F1
Fortnum Cl B33 69 D2
Forton Cl WV6 24 B2
Fort Parkway B24,B35,B36 57 D1
Fort Sh Pk The B24 57 C1
Forum Rd B40 90 E3
Forum The 5 WS11 1 E1
Forward Cotts B48 138 F6
Forward Rd B26 90 A3
Fosberry Cl CV34 161 B8
Fosbrooke Rd B10 88 A8
Fossdale Rd B77 36 A8
Fosse Cl LE10 76 A5
Fosseway Dr B23 56 E8
Fosseway La WS13,WS14 8 E4
Fosseway WS14 9 A5
Fosseway Rd CV3 133 B4
Fossil Dr B45 122 A7
Foster Ave
Cannock WS12 1 F6
Studley B80 159 E3
Wolverhampton WV14 40 B1
Foster Gdns B18 65 F6
Foster Gn WV6 23 E3
Foster Pl DY8 80 E6
Foster Rd
Coventry CV6 113 B7
Wolverhampton WV10 25 E7
Foster St E DY8 81 A5
Foster St
8 Stourbridge DY8 81 A5
Darlaston WS10 41 D7
Walsall WS3 28 D8
Foster Way B5 86 C5
Fotherley Brook Rd WS9 30 F5
Founder Cl CV4 131 F7
Foundry La
Smethwick B66 65 D6
Walsall WS3 14 E3
Foundry Prim Sch B18 65 E6
Foundry Rd
Birmingham B18 65 E5
Kingswinford DY6 60 C8
Foundry St
Dudley WV14 40 C1
Kingswinford DY6 60 C8
Tipton DY4 51 E8
Fountain Arc 4 DY1 51 C1
Fountain Cl B31 122 E6
Fountain La
Tipton DY4,WV14 51 E8
West Bromwich B69 53 A1
Fountain Rd B17 65 C1
Fountains Rd WS3 13 E2
Fountains Way WS3 13 E2
Four Acres B32 84 C4
Four Ashes Rd B93 127 E4
Four Crosses Rd WS4 15 C1
Four Dwellings High Sch B32 84 B5
Fourlands Ave B72 57 D7
Fourlands Rd B31 102 E6
Four Oaks Cl B98 158 D8
Four Oaks Common Rd B74 31 F3
Four Oaks Ct B74 32 B1
Four Oaks Dr B61 121 B1
Four Oaks Inf Sch B74 31 E4
Four Oaks Jun Sch B74 31 E4
Four Oaks Rd B74 32 A1
Four Oaks Sta B74 46 B8
Four Pounds Ave CV5 112 F3
Four Stones Cl B91 107 A1
Four Stones Gr B5 86 D6
Fourth Ave
Birmingham,Bordesley Green B9 67 F2
Birmingham,Selly Oak B29 86 C3
Brownhills WS8 7 A1
Wolverhampton WV10 25 E6
Four Winds Rd DY2 62 E6
Fowey Cl B76 58 A7
Fowey Rd B34 68 F6
Fowgay Dr B91 106 F1
Fowler Cl
Perton WV6 23 E6
Smethwick B66 65 A8
Fowler Rd
Coventry CV6 113 B4
Sutton Coldfield B75 47 B5
Fowler St
Birmingham B7 67 B6
Wolverhampton WV2 39 C6
Fowlmere Rd B42 55 B8
Fownhope Cl B98 154 E3
Fow Oak CV4 111 C2
Fox Ave
Nuneaton CV10 73 D7
Willenhall WV13 27 A2
Foxbury Dr B93 128 B3
Fox Cl
Sutton Coldfield B75 46 F7
Tamworth B77 35 C8
Foxcote Ave B21 65 E7
Foxcote Cl
Redditch B98 154 F4
Solihull B90 126 D8
Foxcote Dr B90 126 D8
Foxcote La B63,DY9 82 B4
Fox Covert DY8 80 E5
Fox Cres B11 87 D4
Foxcroft Cl WS7 7 B5
Foxdale Dr DY5 61 B3
Foxdale Gr B33 69 C3
Foxdale Wlk 8 CV31 162 C6
Foxes Cl B60 138 B5
Foxes Mdw
Birmingham B30 103 F4
Sutton Coldfield B76 58 A8
Foxes Rake WS11 1 E3
Foxes Ridge B64 82 E8
Foxes Way
Balsall Common CV7 130 B6
Warwick CV34 160 D4
Foxfield B31 102 F4
Foxfield Dr DY8 81 A3
Foxfields Way WS12 1 C7
Fox Foot Dr DY5 61 C4
Foxford Cl
Birmingham B36 58 D1
Sutton Coldfield B72 57 D7
Foxford Cres CV2 96 B4
Foxford Sch & Com Arts Coll CV6 96 A5
Foxglove Cl
Bedworth CV12 77 E1
Birmingham B27 88 B1
Coventry CV6 95 C2
Featherstone WV10 12 B7
Lichfield WS14 9 A5
Walsall WS3 15 A5
Wednesfield WV11 26 E5
Foxglove Cres B37 69 E3
Foxglove Rd DY1 51 A4
Foxglove B77 22 A4
Foxglove Way B21 65 D7
Fox Glove Way B23 56 B7
Foxglove Way B60 137 C6
Foxglove Wlk WS12 2 C7
Fox & Goose Sh Ctr B8 68 C5
Fox Gr B27 88 A2
Fox Green Cres B27 88 A2
Foxhill Barns B48 138 E5
Fox Hill B29 103 C8
Fox Hill Cl B29 103 C8
Foxhill Cl WS12 2 D2
Foxhill La B48 138 E5
Fox Hill Rd B75 32 F2
Foxhill's Cl WS7 7 A5
Foxhills Cl CV11 74 C1
Foxhills Pk DY2 62 C4
Foxhills Rd
Stourbridge DY8 60 D1
Wolverhampton WV4 38 C4
Foxholes La B97 158 A6
Foxholes The DY10 116 F8
Foxhollies Dr B63 82 E4
Fox Hollies L Ctr B27 88 B1
Fox Hollies Rd
Birmingham B27,B28 88 A1
Sutton Coldfield B76 47 B2
Fox Hollies Sch
Birmingham,Acock's Green B27 88 A1
Birmingham,Moseley B13 86 E2
Foxhollow B61 150 D8
Fox Hollow Cl B45 122 C7
Fox Hollow WV6 24 C2
Foxhope Cl B38 104 B2
Foxhunt Rd B63 82 E2
Fox La
Bromsgrove B61 150 E8
Lichfield WS13 3 A5
Foxland Ave
Birmingham B45 122 C7
Great Wyrley WS6 5 A3
Foxland Cl
Birmingham B37 70 D2
Cheswick Green B90 126 D4
Foxlands Ave WV4 38 D3
Foxlands Cres WV4 38 C3
Foxlands Dr
Dudley DY3 50 D5
Gospel End Village WV4 38 D3
Sutton Coldfield B72 57 D7
Foxlea Rd B63 82 D1
Foxley Dr B91 108 B5
Foxlydiate Cres B97 153 A4
Foxlydiate La B97 152 F3
Foxlydiate Mews 3 B97 153 A4
Foxmeadow Cl DY3 50 E7
Fox Mill Est B11 87 D3
Foxoak Ent Ctr B64 62 D1
Foxoak St B64 62 C1
Fox's La WV6 25 C4
Fox St
Birmingham B5 164 D3
Dudley DY1 51 C6
Foxtail Way WS12 2 E4
Foxton Ct LE10 75 B7
Foxton Man B74 32 A1
Foxton Rd
Birmingham B8 67 F4
Coventry CV3 114 E1
Foxwalks Ave B61 150 D8
Foxwell Gr B9 68 C3
Foxwell Rd B9 68 C3
Fox Wlk WS9 16 B3
Foxwood Ave B43 44 B2
Foxwood Dr CV3 135 D7
Foxwood Gr B37 69 F5
Foxwood Rd B78 36 F8
Foxyards Cl DY4 51 D5
Foxyards Prim Sch DY4 51 C5
Foxyards Rd DY4 51 D5
Foyle Rd B38 103 F1
Fozdar Cres WV14 40 B1
Fradley Cl B30 103 D4
Framefield Dr B91 107 F6
Framlingham Gr
Kenilworth CV8 148 C6
Perton WV6 24 A3
Frampton Cl
Birmingham,Bournville B30 103 D7
Birmingham,Chelmsley Wood B37 70 D3
Frampton Way B43 44 D5
Frampton Wlk CV2 114 F4
Frances Ave CV34 161 A7

Frances Cres CV12 78 A3
Frances Dr WS3 14 B2
Frances Havergal Cl 2 CV31 161 F6
Frances Rd
Baginton CV8 133 F3
Birmingham,King's Norton B30 104 A5
Birmingham,Lozells B19 66 C8
Birmingham,Stockland Green B23 56 D3
Franche Fst Sch DY11 116 B8
Franche Mid Sch DY11 116 B8
Franche Rd DY11 116 C8
Franchise Gdns WS10 41 F6
Franchise St
Birmingham B42 55 E2
Darlaston WS10 41 F6
Kidderminster DY11 116 C5
Franciscan Rd CV3 133 D8
Francis Cl
1 Kingswinford DY6 60 D8
Sutton Coldfield B74 44 F8
Francis Gibbs Gdns 1 CV31 162 A4
Francis Rd
Birmingham,Acock's Green B27 88 D5
Birmingham,Edgbaston B16 66 A1
Birmingham,South Yardley B25 88 A6
Birmingham,Stechford B33 68 D2
Bromsgrove B60 150 F7
Lichfield WS13 3 A2
Smethwick B67 64 D4
Stourbridge DY8 80 C5
Francis St
Birmingham B7 67 A4
Coventry CV6 113 E7
West Bromwich B70 53 D1
Wolverhampton WV1 25 C4
Francis Ward Cl B71 53 A8
Francis Wlk B31 123 A7
Frankburn Rd B74 44 F8
Frank F Harrison Comp Sch WS2 27 F7
Frank Fisher Way B70 53 C2
Frankfort St B19 66 D6
Frank Freeman Ct DY10 116 F8
Frankholmes Dr B90 127 A6
Frankland Rd CV6 96 A1
Frankley Ave B62 83 F5
Frankley Beeches Rd B31 102 D3
Frankley Com High Sch B45 101 F1
Frankley Gn B32 101 D5
Frankley Green La B32 101 E5
Frankley Hill La B32 102 A4
Frankley Ind Pk B45 102 B1
Frankley La B31,B32 102 D6
Frankley Lodge Rd B31 102 D4
Frankley Mid Sch B45 102 B2
Frankley Rd B68 84 B8
Frankley Terr B17 85 B5
Franklin Ct CV11 73 D1
Franklin Dr WS7 7 B7
Franklin Gr CV4 111 E1
Franklin Rd
Birmingham B30 103 F5
Nuneaton CV11 73 D1
Whitnash CV31 162 A3
Franklins Gdns CV3 115 B1
Franklin St B18 65 E5
Franklin Way B30 103 F6
Franklyn Cl WV6 23 E5
Frankpledge Rd CV3 133 E7
Frank Rd B67 64 E6
Frank St
Birmingham B12 86 F7
Nuneaton CV11 73 B3
Franks Way B33 68 E2
Frank Tommey Cl 5 B65 63 C1
Frankton Ave CV3 133 C5
Frankton Cl
Redditch B98 159 E8
Solihull B92 89 B2
Frankton Gr B9 68 B2
Frank Walsh Ho CV1 165 C4
Frankwell Dr CV2 96 E1
Fraser Cl CV10 72 B6
Fraser Rd
Birmingham B11 87 D5
Coventry CV6 95 A1
Fraser St WV14 40 E6
Frayne Ave DY6 60 C7
Freasley Cl B90 106 D3
Freasley Rd B34 69 E6
Freda Eddy Ct 3 DY10 116 E6
Freda Rd B70 53 D1
Freda Rise B69 63 D8
Fredas Gr B17 85 A4
Frederick Ave LE10 71 B2
Frederick Bird Prim Sch CV2 113 F5
Frederick Ct B77 21 E3
Frederick Eary Ho B98 159 B7
Frederick Neal Ave CV5 111 D4
Frederick Rd
Birmingham,Aston B6 66 F8
Birmingham,Beech Lanes B68 84 D7
Birmingham,Edgbaston B15 86 B8
Birmingham,Gravelly Hill B23 56 E2
Frederick Rd *continued*
Birmingham,Selly Oak B29 85 D2
Birmingham,Sparkhill B11 87 C4
Birmingham,Stechford B33 68 D3
Frederick Rd (Road 1) DY10 116 F1
Frederick Rd
Sutton Coldfield B73 46 A2
Wolverhampton WV11 26 C5
Fredericks Cl DY8 80 E4
Frederick St
Birmingham B1 66 C4
Walsall WS2 28 D1
West Bromwich B70 53 C4
Wolverhampton WV2 163 B1
Frederick William St 1 WV13 27 B2
Fred Lee Gr CV3 133 D4
Fred Smith Cl WS10 42 B5
Freeburn Cswy CV4 132 C7
Freeford Gdns WS14 9 E6
Freehold St CV1 113 F4
Freeland Gr 3 DY6 60 F4
Freeman Cl CV10 72 D4
Freeman Ct DY11 116 B3
Freeman Dr B76 46 F4
Freeman Pl WV14 40 E8
Freeman Rd
Birmingham B7 67 B6
Wednesbury WS10 42 D3
Freemans Cl CV32 156 E2
Freeman's La LE10 76 A5
Freeman St
Birmingham B5 164 C2
Coventry CV6 113 F6
Wolverhampton WV10 25 F2
Freemantle Ct B37 69 F5
Freemantle Ho B24 57 D3
Freemount Sq B43 54 E7
Freer Dr WS7 7 E7
Freer Rd B6 66 E8
Freers Mews CV34 160 B4
Freer St
Nuneaton CV11 73 E2
Walsall WS1 28 F2
Freesland Rise CV10 72 B6
Freeth Rd WS8 7 A1
Freeth St
Birmingham B16 65 F2
Oldbury B69 63 F8
Freezeland St WV14 40 B6
Fremantle Dr WS12 2 F2
Fremantle Ho B34 69 E6
Fremont Dr DY1 50 E3
French Ave B78 20 C1
French Rd DY2 51 F1
Frensham Cl
Birmingham B37 70 C2
Cheslyn Hay WS6 4 E4
Frensham Dr CV10 72 B5
Frensham Way B17 85 C6
Frenshaw Gr B44 55 F7
Freshfield Cl CV5 94 C1
Freshwater Dr DY5 81 B8
Freshwater Gr 1 CV31 162 C6
Fretton Cl CV6 113 F7
Freville Cl B79 21 A5
Frevill Rd CV6 114 B8
Friardale Cl WS10 42 D3
Friar Park Rd WS10 42 D3
Friar's Alley WS13 9 B7
Friars Cl
Binley Woods CV3 135 E7
Stourbridge DY8 60 C3
Friars Gate B90 126 E7
Friars Gorse DY7 80 C8
Friars' Rd CV1 165 B2
Friars St CV34 160 D6
Friar St WS10 42 B3
Friars Wlk
Birmingham B37 70 D2
Tamworth B77 21 C3
Friary Ave
Lichfield WS13 9 A6
Solihull B90 127 A6
Friary Cl
Birmingham B20 54 F3
Hinckley LE10 71 E1
Friary Cres WS4 29 C6
Friary Dr B74 31 F3
Friary Gdns
Birmingham B21 54 D2
Lichfield WS13 9 A7
Friary Rd
Birmingham B20 54 E3
Lichfield WS13 9 A7
Friary St CV11 73 B5
Friary The WS13 9 A7
Friday Acre WS13 3 A2
Friday Bridge 6 B1 66 C1
Friday La B92 108 D4
Friesland Dr WV1 26 B3
Friezeland Rd WS2 28 B2
Friezland La WS8 16 A5
Friezland Way WS8 16 A5
Frilsham Way CV5 112 B4
Fringe Green Cl B60 151 A7
Fringe Meadow Rd B98 154 F6
Frinton Gr B21 65 C7
Frisby Ct CV11 73 E2
Frisby Rd CV4 111 E2
Friston Ave B16 66 B1
Friswell Dr CV6 113 F8
Friswell Ho 3 CV2 114 D8
Frith Way LE10 71 A3
Frobisher Cl
Great Wyrley WS6 4 F1
Hinckley LE10 71 D4
Frobisher Rd CV3 133 C5
Frobisher Way B66 64 D7
Frodesley Rd B26 89 B8
Froggatt Rd WV14 40 D7
Froggatts Ride B76 46 F3
Frog La
Balsall Common CV7 130 A5
Lichfield WS13 9 B7
Frogmere Cl CV5 112 C6
Frogmill Rd B45 102 B2
Frogmoor Ho B26 88 E7
Frogmore La CV8 129 F2
Frome Cl DY3 50 D2
Frome Dr WV11 26 C5
Frome Ho 4 DY1 61 E8
Frome Way B14 104 D6
Front Cotts B48 138 F6
Frost St WV2 40 A6
Froxmere Cl B91 127 C8
Froyle Cl WV6 24 C5
Froysell St WV13 27 B2
Fryer Ave CV32 156 E3
Fryer Rd B31 123 B7
Fryers Cl WS3 28 B7
Fryers Rd WS2,WS3 28 A7
Fryer St WV1 163 C3
Frythe Cl CV8 148 C6
Fuchsia Cl 3 CV2 96 B2
Fuchsia Dr WV9 10 F3
Fugelmere Cl B17 84 F7
Fulbrook Cl B98 154 C5
Fulbrook Gr B29 102 F8
Fulbrook Rd
Coventry CV2 96 C2
Dudley DY1 51 A1
Fulfen Prim Sch WS7 7 D7
Fulford Dr B76 58 B5
Fulford Gr B26 89 C6
Fulford Hall Rd B90,B94 125 D3
Fulham Rd B11 87 B5
Fullbrook Cl B90 127 A5
Fullbrook Rd WS5 42 E5
Fullelove Rd WS8 16 A7
Fullers Cl CV6 112 F7
Fullerton Cl WV8 10 E1
Fullwood Cl CV2 96 E2
Fullwood Cres DY1,DY2 61 F6
Fullwoods End WV14 40 C1
Fulmar Cres DY10 117 B2
Fulmer Wlk B18 66 A3
Fulton Cl B60 137 B1
Fulwell Gr B44 56 A8
Fulwell Mews B37 90 B8
Fulwood Ave B62 83 F8
Furber Pl DY6 60 F6
Furlong Ct B63 82 C6
Furlong La B63 82 D6
Furlong Mdw B31 103 C2
Furlong Rd CV1 165 C1
Furlongs Rd DY3 50 D6
Furlongs The
Stourbridge DY8 81 B3
Wolverhampton WV11 26 B5
Furlong The WS10 41 E5
Furlong Wlk DY3 50 D4
Furnace Cl CV12 78 D3
Furnace Hill B63 83 B5
Furnace La B63 83 B5
Furnace Par DY4 51 E6
Furnace Rd
Bedworth CV12 78 D4
Dudley DY2 62 C8
Furness Cl WS3 13 F3
Furness B77 21 D3
Furnivall Cres WS13 3 D1
Furr Marsh The CV34 160 B4
Furrows The B60 150 D6
Furst St WS8 16 A8
Furzebank Way WV12 27 E4
Furze Way WS5 43 E8
Fylde Ho CV2 114 D4
Fynford Rd CV6 113 B5

G

Gable Croft WS14 9 F6
Gables The
Kingswinford DY6 60 B8
Sutton Coldfield B24 57 D4
Gaddesby Rd B14 104 F8
Gadds Dr B65 63 D4
Gadsby Ave WV11 27 A7
Gadsby Ct CV11 73 E3
Gadsby St CV11 73 E3
Gads Gn DY2 62 E5
Gads Green Cres DY2 62 E6
Gadshill CV34 161 E4
Gads La
Dudley DY1 51 C1
West Bromwich B70 53 A3
Gadwall Croft B23 56 B3
Gaelic Rd WS11 1 D4
Gagarin B79 20 F5
Gaiafields Rd WS13 3 B1
Gaia La WS13 9 B8
Gaialands Cres WS13 3 B1
Gaia Stowe WS13 3 B1
Gail Cl WS9 16 B4
Gailey Croft B44 44 E3
Gail Pk WV3 38 D7
Gainford Cl WV8 10 F1
Gainford Rd B44 45 C1
Gainford Rise CV3 115 A3
Gainsborough Ave LE10 71 A3
Gainsborough Cres
Birmingham B43 44 D4
Dorridge B93 128 A6
Gainsborough Dr
Bedworth CV12 78 A4
Mile Oak B78 34 B8
Perton WV6 24 A4
Royal Leamington Spa CV31 162 D6
Gainsborough Hill DY8 81 A3
Gainsborough Mews DY11 116 B5
Gainsborough Pl DY1 50 E2
Gainsborough Rd B42 55 B6
Gainsborough Trad Est DY9 81 C4
Gainsbrook Cres WS11 5 F5
Gainsford Dr B62 83 B6
Gains La WS3,WS11 5 D2
Gairloch Rd WV11 13 B1
Gaitskell Terr B69 52 D2
Gaitskell Way B66 64 F7
Galahad Way WS10 42 A2
Galbraith Cl WV14 51 D8
Galena Cl B77 22 B2
Galena Way B6 66 E6
Gale Wlk B65 62 F5
Galey's Rd CV3 133 D8
Gallagher Bsns Pk CV6 95 E5
Gallagher Ct 14 B13 87 B2
Gallagher Rd CV12 78 A2
Gallagher Ret Pk CV6 113 F8
Gallery Sq 1 WS1 28 E2
Gallery The WV4 39 A6
Galliards The CV4 132 D4
Galliers Cl B77 35 F5
Galloway Ave B34 68 F6
Galloway Cl LE9 71 F7
Gallows Hill CV34 161 B4
Gallus Dr LE10 71 A1
Galmington Dr CV3 133 B6
Galton Cl
Sutton Coldfield B24 57 F4
Tipton DY4 52 C6
Galton Dr DY2 62 B6
Galton Ho B67 64 F2
Galton Rd B67 64 F1
Galtons La DY9 120 A7
Galton Twr B1 66 C2
Galway Rd WS7 7 A7
Gamesfield Gn WV3 24 F1
Gammage St DY2 62 B8
Gamson Cl DY10 116 E4
Ganborough Cl B98 154 E1
Gandy Rd WV12 27 A7
Gannahs Farm Cl B76 46 F3
Gannaway B93 128 A4
Gannow Green La B45 101 D1
Gannow Manor Cres B45 101 E2
Gannow Manor Gdns B45 101 F1
Gannow Rd B45 121 E7
Gannow Wlk B45 121 E7
Ganton Rd WS3 14 A3
Ganton Wlk WV8 24 F8
Garage Cl B77 21 D5
Garden Cl
Birmingham,Frankley B45 102 A2
Birmingham,Ward End B8 68 A5
Hinckley LE10 75 D6
Knowle B93 127 F6
Garden Cres WS3 14 F3
Garden Croft WS9 30 B7
Garden Ct
3 Birmingham B16 66 B1
Warwick,Emscote CV34 161 C8
Warwick,Packmores CV34 160 E7
Gardeners Cl DY11 116 C8
Garden Flats CV5 111 D5
Garden Gr
Bedworth CV12 95 F8
Birmingham B20 54 E6
Gardenia Dr CV5 112 B6
Garden Rd LE10 71 D1
Gardens The
Birmingham,Chester Road B73 57 B8
Birmingham,Stockland Green B23 56 E3
Kenilworth CV8 148 A3
Radford Semele CV31 162 E5
Sutton Coldfield B72 46 B1
Garden St WS2 28 E3
Garden Wlk
Bilston WV14 40 F6
Dudley DY3 50 C2
Gardner Ho 8 CV1 113 B2
Gardner Way CV8 148 A2
Garfield Rd B26 89 B8
Garganey Ct DY10 116 F1
Garibaldi Terr B60 137 A1
Garland Cres B62 83 E8
Garlands Croft CV7 95 A6
Garland St B9 67 C3
Garlands The WV11 26 C7
Garland Way B31 103 C4
Garlick Dr CV8 148 C6
Garman Cl B43 43 E2
Garner Cl WV14 40 D3
Garnet Ave B43 44 B3
Garnet Cl WS9 16 E4
Garnet Ct 4 B92 88 F1
Garnett Dr B75 46 E6
Garnette Cl CV10 72 B5
Garrard Gdns B73 46 B5
Garrat St DY5 61 E5
Garratt Cl B68 64 C4
Garratt's La B65 63 A2
Garratt St B71 53 B5
Garratts Wlk B14 104 E1
Garret Cl DY6 60 D8
Garretts Green La B26,B33 89 A8
Garrett St CV11 73 E2
Garrick Cl
Coventry CV5 111 C4
Dudley DY1 50 F3
Garrick Rd
Bromsgrove B60 137 C1
Cannock WS11 1 D4
Garrick Rise WS7 7 B7
Garrick St WV1 163 C2
Garrigill B77 22 B1
Garrington Rd B60 151 B7
Garrington St WS10 41 C7
Garrison Ct 9 B9 67 B2
Garrison La B9 67 C2
Garrison St B9 67 B3
Garston Way 4 B43 54 D8
Garth Cres CV3 134 D8
Garth Ho CV3 134 D8
Garth The
Birmingham B14 105 D4
Lichfield WS13 3 B2
Garway Cl
Redditch B98 154 E1
Royal Leamington Spa CV32 156 F4
Garway Gr B25 88 C6
Garwood Rd B26 68 F2
Gas Sq B61 136 F1
Gas St B1 66 C2
Gas Street Basin* B1 164 A2
Gas St CV31 161 F7
Gatacre St DY3 50 D3
Gatcombe Cl WV10 11 F4
Gatcombe Rd DY1 50 E2
Gatehouse Fold 5 DY2 51 D1
Gatehouse La CV12 78 A2
Gate House La B60 151 A7
Gatehouse CV31 161 D7
Gatehouse Trad Est WS8 7 B1
Gate La
Dorridge B93,B94 127 C3
Sutton Coldfield B73 45 F2
Gateley Rd B68 84 D7
Gateside Rd CV6 95 E2
Gate St
Birmingham B8 67 D5
Sedgley DY3 50 E7
Tipton DY4 52 A2
Gateway The B26 89 F3
Gatis St WV6 25 A5
Gatwick Rd B35 58 B4
Gauden Rd DY9 81 D2
Gaulby Wlk CV3 115 A1
Gaunts The B48 139 B6
Gaveston Cl 7 CV34 160 F8
Gaveston Rd
Coventry CV6 112 F6
Royal Leamington Spa CV32 156 E1
Gavin Way B6 55 F4
Gawne La B64 62 F3
Gawsworth B79 20 D7
Gaydon Cl
Coventry CV6 114 A8
Perton WV6 23 E5
Redditch B98 153 F1
Gaydon Gr B29 85 A2
Gaydon Pl B73 46 B4
Gaydon Rd
Aldridge WS9 30 A4
Solihull B92 89 D3
Gayer St CV6 96 A1
Gayfield Ave DY5 61 E1
Gay Hill La B38 124 B8
Gayhurst Cl CV3 134 E8
Gayhurst Dr B25 88 E8
Gayle Gr B27 106 C8
Gayle B77 22 A1
Gayton Rd B71 53 D6
Gaywood Croft B15 86 C8
Gaza Cl CV4 112 A1
Gazelle Cl CV1 165 D3
Geach St B19 66 D6
Geach Twr B19 66 D5
Gedney Cl B90 105 C3
Geeson Cl B35 58 B4
Gee St B19 66 D6
Gemini Dr WS11 4 F6
Gendle Ct B77 21 D4
Geneva Rd DY4 51 D5
Genge Ave WV4 39 E4
Genners App B31 102 D8
Genners La B31 102 D7
Genthorn Cl 11 WV4 39 F4
Gentian Cl B31 102 F6
Gentian B74 31 F4
Geoffrey Cl
Coventry CV2 114 B5
Sutton Coldfield B76 58 B7
Geoffrey Pl B11 87 C3
Geoffrey Rd
Birmingham B11 87 C3
Solihull B90 105 F3
George Arthur Rd B8 67 D5
George Ave
Mile Oak B78 20 C1
Rowley Regis B65 63 D2
George Betts Prim Sch B66 64 C7
George Bird Cl B66 65 A6
George Cl DY2 62 E8
George Dance Cl 2 DY10 117 B6

George Dixon Int Sch & Sixth Form Ctr B17 65 C2
George Dixon Jun & Inf Sch B17 65 C2
George Eliot Ave CV12 78 D2
George Eliot Com Sch
Nuneaton CV11 73 D1
Nuneaton CV11 78 D8
George Eliot Hospl CV10 73 B2
George Eliot Rd CV1 113 D5
George Eliot St CV11 73 C2
George Fentham Endowed Sch B92 109 B6
George Frederick Rd B73 45 A4
George Henry Rd DY4 52 E6
George Hodgkinson Cl CV4 111 F3
George La WS13 9 C8
George Law Ct DY10 116 F5
George Marston Rd CV3 114 E1
George Park Cl CV2 96 C1
George Poole Ho 6 CV1 113 B2
George Rd
Alvechurch B48 139 A5
Birmingham B29 85 E3
Birmingham,Edgbaston B15 86 B8
Birmingham,Great Barr B43 43 F2
Birmingham,South Yardley B25 88 A6
Birmingham,Stockland Green B23 56 C3
Coseley,Daisy Bank WV14 40 D1
Dudley,Tipton Green DY4 51 D6
Halesowen B63 82 F4
Oldbury B68 64 C2
Solihull B91 107 D3
Sutton Coldfield B73 45 D1
Warwick CV34 161 A8
Water Orton B46 59 C3
George Robertson Cl CV3 134 E7
George Rose Gdns WS10 41 C6
George St W B18 66 A4
George Salter High Sch B70 53 A4
George St
1 Bromsgrove B61 136 F2
Birmingham,Balsall Heath B12 86 F5
Birmingham,Brookfields B3 164 A3
Birmingham,Handsworth B21 65 C8
Birmingham,Lozells B19 66 B7
Cannock WS12 2 C4
Coventry CV1 113 E5
Dudley DY1 51 B6
Hinckley LE10 75 D8
Kidderminster DY10 116 F6
Nuneaton CV11 73 E2
George Street Ringway CV12 78 B3
George St
Royal Leamington Spa CV31 162 A7
Stourbridge DY8 60 F1
Stow Heath WV2 40 A7
Tamworth B79 21 B4
Walsall WS1 28 E1
West Bromwich B70 53 D2
Willenhall WV13 27 A4
Wolverhampton WV2 163 C2
George Wlk 5 B97 153 E3
Georgian Gdns 2 WS10 41 F3
Georgian Pl WS11 1 E2
Georgina Ave WV14 40 D3
Geraghty Ct DY4 41 A2
Geraldine Rd B25 88 B7
Gerald Rd DY8 80 E7
Geranium Gr B9 67 F3
Geranium Rd DY2 62 F8
Gerard Ave CV4 132 B8
Gerardsfield Rd B33 69 E2
Gerard B79 20 E7
Germander Dr WS5 43 A3
Germander B74 31 F5
Gerrard Cl B19 66 D7
Gerrard Rd WV13 26 E1
Gerrard St
1 Warwick CV34 160 E6
Birmingham B19 66 C7
Gertrude Pl B18 66 A5
Gervase Dr DY1 51 C3
Geston Rd DY1 61 F8
Gettings Cl WS7 7 F7
Gheluvelt Ave DY10 116 F7
Gibbet Hill Rd CV4 132 B3
Gibbet La DY7 80 B4
Gibbins Rd B29 85 D2
Gibb La B61 137 A8
Gibbons Cl CV4 111 F2
Gibbons Gr WV6 24 F4
Gibbons Hill Rd DY3 39 D2
Gibbons Ind Pk DY6 61 A7
Gibbons La DY5 61 A7
Gibbons Rd
Sutton Coldfield B75 32 B3
Wolverhampton WV6 24 F4
Gibbs Cl CV2 115 B6
Gibbs Hill Rd B31 123 C7
Gibb Sq B12 67 A1
Gibbs Rd
Redditch B98 154 A5
Stourbridge DY9 82 A5
Gibbs St WV6 25 A4
Gibb St B9 66 F1
Gibson Cres CV12 78 A1
Gibson Dr
Birmingham B20 66 B8
Smethwick B66 65 A6
Gibson Rd
Birmingham B20 66 B8
Perton WV6 23 E3
Gideon Cl B25 88 D6
Gideons Cl DY3 50 D5
Gielgud Way CV2 115 B8
Giffard RC Prim Sch The WV6 24 F5
Giffard Rd
Bilston WV1 40 B7
Wolverhampton WV10 11 F3
Giffard Way CV34 155 E1
Gifford Ct 13 DY5 61 D2
Giffords Croft WS13 3 A1
Gigg La B76 48 B3
Gig Mill Prim Sch DY8 80 E4
Gigmill Way DY8 80 E4
Gilbanks Rd DY8 80 D7
Gilberry Cl B93 128 A4
Gilbert Ave B69 63 B7
Gilbert Cl
3 Coventry CV1 113 E3
Bedworth CV12 78 B2
Wednesfield WV11 27 A7
Gilbert Ent Pk WV12 27 B4
Gilbert La WV5 49 B7
Gilbert Rd
Bromsgrove B60 150 E7
Lichfield WS13 3 C2
Smethwick B66 65 B3
Gilbert Scott Way DY10 116 F7
Gilberts Ct WS4 29 A4
Gilbertstone Ave B26 88 E5
Gilbertstone Cl B98 153 E1
Gilbertstone Prim Sch B26 88 E5
Gilbert St DY4 52 A2
Gilbert Wlk WS13 3 C2
Gilbeys Cl 5 DY8 60 E1
Gilby Rd B16 66 A1
Gilchrist Dr B15 85 E8
Gildas Ave B38 104 A1
Giles Cl
Birmingham B33 68 E3
Coventry CV6 95 C2
Giles Close Ho B33 68 E3
Giles Cl B92 107 F7
Giles Rd
Lichfield WS13 3 A3
Oldbury B68 64 B5
Gilfil Rd CV10 73 B1
Gilldown Pl B15 86 B7
Gillespie Croft B6 66 F7
Gillet Cl CV11 73 B3
Gillhurst Rd B17 85 C7
Gillians Wlk CV2 115 A8
Gilling Gr B34 69 A6
Gillingham Cl WS10 42 D4
Gillity Ave WS5 43 C8
Gillity Cl WS5 43 C8
Gillity Ct 3 WS5 43 D7
Gilliver Rd B90 106 B2
Gillman Cl B26 89 D4
Gillott Cl B91 107 E3
Gillott Rd B16 65 D2
Gillows Croft B90 127 A7
Gillscroft Rd B33 69 A3
Gill St
Dudley DY2 62 E4
West Bromwich B70 53 C1
Gillway B79 21 B8
Gilmorton Cl
Birmingham B17 85 B7
Solihull B91 107 C1
Gilpin Cl B8 68 C7
Gilpin Cres WS3 15 A4
Gilpins Croft WS6 4 D1
Gilquart Way CV1 165 C1
Gilson Dr B46 70 D8
Gilson Rd B46 70 E8
Gilson St DY4 52 C8
Gilson Way B37 70 A5
Gilwell Rd B34 69 E6
Gimble Wlk 2 B17 84 F7
Ginkgo Wlk 2 CV31 161 F5
Gipsy Cl CV7 130 B5
Gipsy La
Balsall Common CV7 130 C5
Birmingham B23 56 B5
Nuneaton CV10,CV11 78 D7
Willenhall WV13 27 B1
Girdlers Cl CV3 133 B5
Girtin Cl CV12 78 A4
Girton Ho B36 69 F8
Girton Rd WS11 4 F8
Girvan Gr CV32 157 C5
Gisborn Cl B10 87 B8
Gisburn Cl
5 Redditch B97 153 B5
Warwick CV34 155 F1
Givens Ho 9 CV1 113 B2
GK Davies Trad Est DY9 82 A6
Gladeside Cl WS4 29 D8
Glades The WS9 30 B7
Glade The
Birmingham B26 89 D4
Cannock WS11 1 C2
Coventry CV5 111 F3
Stourbridge DY9 81 E5
Sutton Coldfield B74 30 E1
Wolverhampton WV8 10 E1
Gladman Bsns Quarter WV9 10 F3
Gladstone Cl LE10 71 E4
Gladstone Ct 22 CV32 156 F1
Gladstone Dr
Oldbury B69 52 D3
Stourbridge DY8 80 D6
Gladstone Gr 3 DY6 60 D8
Gladstone Rd
Birmingham,Gravelly Hill B23 56 D3
Birmingham,South Yardley B26 88 D6
Birmingham,Sparkbrook B11 87 B6
Cannock WS12 2 E1
Dorridge B93 128 A2
Stourbridge DY8 80 D6
Gladstone St
Birmingham B6 67 B8
Darlaston WS10 41 E6
Walsall WS2 28 D4
West Bromwich B71 53 C5
Gladstone Terr LE10 75 E8
Gladys Rd
Birmingham B25 88 B7
Smethwick B67 64 F2
Gladys Terr B67 65 A2
Glaisdale Ave CV6 95 E3
Glaisdale Gdns WV6 25 A5
Glaisdale Rd B28 106 B8
Glaisedale Gr WV13 27 C2
Glaisher Dr WV10 25 C6
Glamis Rd WV12 27 B7
Glamorgan Cl CV3 134 D5
Glanville Dr B75 32 A4
Glasbury Croft B38 123 E7
Glascote Cl B90 106 A4
Glascote Ct B77 21 E4
Glascote Gr B34 69 C6
Glascote Heath Prim Sch B77 22 A2
Glascote La B77 35 F8
Glascote Rd
Tamworth B77 22 B2
Tamworth,Glascote Heath B77 21 E3
Glasscroft Cotts WS7 7 F7
Glassford Dr WV6 24 E6
Glasshouse Coll DY8 80 F7
Glasshouse Hill DY8 81 B3
Glasshouse La
Hockley Heath B94 143 F6
Kenilworth CV8 148 D4
Glastonbury Cl DY11 116 A6
Glastonbury Cres WS3 13 E2
Glastonbury Rd
Birmingham B14 105 C5
West Bromwich B71 42 D1
Glastonbury Way WS3 13 E1
Glaston Dr B91 107 A1
Gleads Croft B62 84 A3
Gleaston Wlk WV1 26 C1
Gleave Rd
Birmingham B29 85 E1
Whitnash CV31 162 A3
Glebe Ave CV12 77 E1
Glebe Cl
Coventry CV4 132 A7
Redditch B98 154 D2
Glebe Cres CV8 148 A3
Glebe Ct CV31 162 A3
Glebe Dr B73 56 F8
Glebefarm Gr CV3 114 F3
Glebe Farm Rd B33 69 A5
Glebe Fields B76 59 B6
Glebefields Prim Sch DY4 52 A8
Glebefields Rd DY4 52 A7
Glebeland Cl B16 66 B1
Glebe La
Nuneaton CV11 73 F6
Stourbridge DY8 80 E4
Glebe Pl
Darlaston WS10 41 B6
Royal Leamington Spa CV31 162 B7
Glebe Rd
Alvechurch B48 139 A7
Hinckley LE10 71 F1
Nuneaton CV11 73 D4
Solihull B91 107 D5
Willenhall WV13 40 F8
Glebe St WS1 42 E8
Glebe The
Belbroughton DY9 119 E6
Beoley B98 154 F7
Corley CV7 94 C7
Glebe Way CV7 130 A7
Gledhill Pk WS14 9 C5
Gleeson Dr CV34 155 E1
Glenavon Rd B14 105 A3
Glen Bank LE10 71 E1
Glenbarr Cl LE10 75 A8
Glenbarr Dr LE10 75 A8
Glen Cl
Cannock WS11 1 E5
Walsall WS4 29 A3
Glencoe Dr WS11 2 A4
Glencoe Rd
Birmingham B16 65 C4
Coventry CV3 114 B1
Glencroft Rd B92 89 D4
Glen Ct
Codsall WV8 10 A4
Wolverhampton WV6 24 E2
Glendale Ave CV8 148 A6
Glendale Cl
Halesowen B63 83 B4
Wolverhampton WV3 38 C8
Glendale Ct B77 36 B6
Glendale Dr
Birmingham B33 68 F3
Glendale Dr *continued*
Wombourne WV5 49 A6
Glendale Gdns WS11 2 A4
Glendale Inf Sch CV10 72 F2
Glendale Twr 5 B23 57 B6
Glendale Way CV4 111 C2
Glendawn Cl 1 WS11 2 A3
Glendene Cres B38 123 C7
Glendene Dr 2 B43 54 D8
Glendene Rd WS12 2 D6
Glen Devon Cl B45 102 A2
Glendon Gdns CV12 79 C3
Glendon Rd B23 56 D6
Glendon Way B93 127 E3
Glendower App CV34 161 E3
Glendower Ave CV5 112 D3
Glendower Rd
Aldridge WS9 16 B1
Birmingham B42 55 D4
Gleneagles Cl
Hinckley LE10 75 D4
Nuneaton CV11 74 C1
Gleneagles Dr
Birmingham B43 43 E3
Blackwell B60 138 A5
Oldbury B69 63 A7
Sutton Coldfield B75 46 D8
Gleneagles Rd
Birmingham B26 89 A8
Coventry CV2 114 E6
Perton WV6 23 D5
Walsall WS3 13 F3
Gleneagles B77 22 B5
Glenelg Dr DY8 81 B2
Glenelg Mews WS5 43 D5
Glenfern Gdns CV8 134 E2
Glenfern Rd WV14 51 A8
Glenfield Ave CV10 73 D7
Glenfield Cl
2 Solihull B91 127 C8
Redditch B97 158 D6
Sutton Coldfield B76 46 E3
Glenfield Gr B29 86 A1
Glenfield
Tamworth B77 21 C1
Wolverhampton WV8 10 E2
Glengarry Cl B32 102 B7
Glengarry Gdns WV3 24 F1
Glenhill Dr B38 124 A8
Glen Ho DY1 61 D8
Glenhurst Cl WS2 27 D3
Glenmead Prim Sch B44 55 D8
Glenmead Rd B44 55 D8
Glenmore Ave WS7 7 A6
Glenmore Cl WV3 38 E7
Glenmore Dr
Birmingham B38 103 D2
Coventry CV6 95 F5
Glenmount Ave CV6 95 F5
Glenn St CV6 95 D3
Glenpark Rd B8 67 F5
Glen Park Rd DY3 50 D2
Glen Rd
Dudley DY3 50 E6
Stourbridge DY8 80 F3
Glenridding Cl CV6 95 F5
Glen Rise B13 105 C6
Glenrosa Wlk CV4 132 A7
Glenroy Cl CV2 114 E6
Glenroyde B38 123 E7
Glenside Ave B92 89 C3
Glen Side B32 84 D2
Glen The B60 138 A5
Glenthorne Dr WS6 4 E3
Glenthorne Ho WS6 4 D2
Glenthorne Prim Sch WS6 4 E3
Glenthorne Rd B24 57 A2
Glentworth Ave CV6 95 A2
Glentworth Gdns WV6 25 B5
Glentworth B76 47 A2
Glenville Ave CV9 36 C1
Glenville Dr B23 56 E5
Glenwood Cl DY5 81 D8
Glenwood Dr B90 126 D4
Glenwood Gdns
Bedworth CV12 78 A5
Tamworth B77 36 B6
Glenwood Rd B38 123 D8
Glenwood Rise WS9 16 D3
Globe St WS10 41 F1
Gloster Dr CV8 147 F6
Gloucester Cl
Lichfield WS13 3 B3
Nuneaton CV11 74 A7
Gloucester Ho
4 Birmingham B24 56 F4
4 Wolverhampton WV3 25 C4
Gloucester Pl WV13 27 D2
Gloucester Rd
Dudley DY2 62 D2
Walsall WS5 43 C8
Wednesbury WS10 42 C3
Gloucester St
3 Royal Leamington Spa CV31 162 A7
Birmingham B5 164 C1
Coventry CV1 113 B3
Wolverhampton WV6 25 B4
Gloucester Way
Birmingham B37 70 A1
Cannock WS11 2 B1
Glover Cl
Birmingham B28 105 F6
Warwick CV34 160 B4
Glover Rd B75 47 A5
Glovers Cl CV7 92 C1
Glovers Croft B37 69 F3
Glovers Field Dr B7 67 C7
Glovers Rd B10 87 D8
Glover St
Birmingham B9 67 A2
Cannock WS12 2 F3
Coventry CV3 133 D8
Redditch B98 153 E3
Glover's Trust Homes B73 56 F7
Glover St B70 53 D1
Glyde Ct B27 88 B2
Glyme Dr WV6 24 E5
Glyn Ave WV14 41 B3
Glyndebourne B79 20 D7
Glyn Dr WV14 41 B3
Glyne Ct B73 46 B5
Glyn Farm Rd B32 84 C6
Glynn Cres B63 82 B7
Glynne Ave DY6 60 D5
Glynne Prim Sch DY6 60 C4
Glyn Rd B32 84 D6
Glynside Ave B32 84 D6
Godfrey Cl CV31 162 E5
Godiva Pl CV1 165 D3
Godiva Trad Est CV6 113 F8
Godolphin B79 20 D7
Godrich Ho B13 87 B3
Godson Cres DY11 116 C3
Godson Pl DY11 116 C3
Goffs Cl B32 84 F3
Gofton B77 36 A8
Goldacre Cl CV31 161 F4
Goldborough Cl WV14 40 D3
Goldby Dr WS10 41 E4
Gold Cl CV11 78 E8
Goldcrest Cl DY2 62 D2
Goldcrest Croft B36 70 A8
Goldcrest Dr DY10 117 B2
Goldcrest B77 36 A6
Golden Acres La CV3 134 F7
Goldencrest Dr B69 63 E8
Golden Croft B20 54 F1
Golden Cross La B61 121 B1
Goldencross Way DY5 61 B1
Golden End Dr B93 128 D6
Golden Hillock Rd
Birmingham B11 87 D6
Dudley DY2 62 C3
Golden Hillock Sch & Specialist Sports Coll B11 87 D5
Goldfinch Cl B30 103 D8
Goldfinch Rd DY9 81 C3
Goldicroft Rd WS10 42 A4
Goldieslie Cl B73 46 B2
Goldieslie Rd B73 46 B2
Goldsborough B77 22 A1
Golds Hill Gdns B21 65 F7
Golds Hill Rd B21 65 F8
Golds Hill Way DY4 52 D7
Goldsmith Ave CV34 160 C5
Goldsmith Pl B79 21 A7
Goldsmith Rd
Birmingham B14 104 F8
Walsall WS3 28 E7
Goldsmith Wlk DY10 117 C5
Goldstar Way B33 69 C2
Goldtel Ind Est WV4 40 A5
Goldthorn Ave WV4 39 B6
Goldthorn Cl CV5 111 D4
Goldthorn Cres WV4 39 A6
Goldthorne Ave
Birmingham B26 89 C4
Cannock WS11 1 F2
Goldthorne Cl B97 153 C1
Goldthorne Wlk DY5 81 D8
Goldthorn Hill WV2,WV4 39 C6
Goldthorn Mews DY11 116 C2
Goldthorn Park Prim Sch WV4 39 D5
Goldthorn Pl DY11 116 C2
Goldthorn Rd
Kidderminster DY11 116 C2
Wolverhampton WV2,WV3 39 B6
Golf Dr CV11 74 B1
Golf La
Bilston WV14 40 D7
Whitnash CV31 162 B2
Golson Cl B75 46 F6
Gomeldon Ave B14 104 A5
Gomer St W WV13 27 A2
Gomer St WV13 27 A2
Gonville Ho B36 69 F8
Gooch Cl DY8 81 B6
Gooch St N B5 86 E8
Gooch St B5 86 E8
Goodall Gr B43 44 E5
Goodall St WS1 28 F1
Goodby Rd B13 86 D3
Goode Ave B18 66 A5
Goode Cl
Oldbury B68 64 C4
Warwick CV34 160 C7
Goode Croft CV4 111 F2
Goodeve Wlk B75 47 B5
Goodfellow St CV32 156 C1
Good Hope Hospl B75 46 D6
Goodison Gdns B24 57 B5
Goodleigh Ave B45 122 E6
Goodman Cl B28 105 F6
Goodman St B1 66 B3
Goodman Way CV4 111 C1
Goodrest Ave B62 84 A5
Goodrest Croft B14 105 C4
Goodrest La B38 123 F6
Goodrich Ave WV6 24 A3
Goodrich Cl B98 154 F2

Goodrich Covert 10 B14 104 C2
Goodrick Way B7 67 B6
Good Shepherd RC Sch CV6 95 F1
Goodway Ct 9 CV34 160 F7
Goodway Ho
5 Royal Leamington Spa CV32 161 D8
Birmingham B4 164 C4
Kenilworth CV8 148 A5
Goodway Rd
Birmingham B44 55 F8
Solihull B92 89 E4
Goodwin Cl DY11 116 C7
Goodwood Cl
Birmingham B36 68 D8
Coventry CV3 134 C6
Lichfield WS14 9 D7
Goodwood Dr B74 44 F7
Goodwood Rd B61 121 B1
Goodwyn Ave B68 84 C7
Goodyear Ave WV10 25 E7
Goodyear Rd B67 64 E2
Goodyers End La CV12 95 D8
Goodyers End Prim Sch CV12 95 E8
Goosehill Cl B98 154 E1
Goosehills Rd LE10 75 E5
Goosemoor La B23 56 F7
Goostry Cl B77 21 D5
Goostry Rd B77 21 D5
Gopsall Rd LE10 71 D2
Gopsal St B4 67 A3
Gorcott La B90 126 A5
Gordon Ave
Birmingham B19 66 D7
West Bromwich B71 53 C8
Wolverhampton WV4 39 F3
Gordon Cl
Bedworth CV12 78 C4
Oldbury B69 52 D2
Gordon Cres DY5 61 E5
Gordon Ct B33 68 D3
Gordon Dr DY4 52 C6
Gordon Pl WV14 40 C5
Gordon Rd
Birmingham B17 85 D6
Birmingham,Lozells B19 66 C8
Gordon St
5 Birmingham B9 67 B2
Coventry CV1 113 B2
Darlaston WS10 41 E6
Royal Leamington Spa CV31 162 A7
Wolverhampton WV2 163 C2
Gorey Cl WV12 27 B8
Gorge Rd
Sedgley DY3 50 E8
Wolverhampton WV14,DY3 39 F1
Goring Rd CV2 114 A4
Gorleston Gr B14 105 B2
Gorleston Rd B14 105 B2
Gorsebrook Rd WV6 25 B5
Gorse Cl
Birmingham,Fordbridge B37 69 F2
Birmingham,Selly Oak B29 103 A8
Gorse Dr WS12 1 D5
Gorse Farm Rd
Birmingham B43 54 E8
Nuneaton CV11 79 B8
Gorsefield Rd B34 69 C5
Gorse Green La DY9 120 C8
Gorse La WS14 9 E6
Gorse Meadow Dr B45 138 B8
Gorsemoor Prim Sch WS12 2 D1
Gorsemoor Rd WS12 2 D1
Gorsemoor Way WV11 13 B3
Gorse Rd
Dudley DY1 51 A4
Wednesfield WV11 27 A8
Gorseway WS7 7 B5
Gorse Way WS12 2 C8
Gorseway CV5 112 C3
Gorsey La
Cannock WS11 1 C1
Coleshill B46 59 F2
Great Wyrley WS6 4 F1
Norton Canes WS3 5 E1
Wythall B47 125 A3
Gorsey Way
Aldridge WS9 29 E5
Coleshill B46 59 E2
Gorsly Piece B32 84 C4
Gorstey Lea WS7 7 C7
Gorstie Croft B43 54 E8
Gorsty Ave DY5 61 C3
Gorsty Bank WS14 9 E8
Gorsty Cl 2 B71 53 F8
Gorsty Hill Rd B65 83 B8
Gorsy Bank Rd B77 35 F5
Gorsymead Gr B31 102 C2
Gorsy Rd B32 84 D5
Gorsy Way CV10 72 D5
Gorton Croft CV7 130 B7
Gorway Cl WS1 42 F7
Gorway Gdns WS1 43 A7
Gorway Rd WS1 43 A7
Goscote Cl
Redditch B97 153 A5
Walsall WS3 28 F7
Goscote Hospl WS3 28 F8
Goscote Ind Est WS3 14 E1
Goscote La WS3 28 F8
Goscote Lodge Cres WS3 29 A7
Goscote Pl WS3 29 A7
Goscote Rd WS3 15 A1
Gosford Dr LE10 71 A1
Gosford Ind Est CV1 113 F2
Gosford Park Prim Sch CV1 113 F2
Gosford St
Birmingham B12 86 F6
Coventry CV1 165 D2
Gosford Wlk B92 89 B1
Gosmoor Ho B26 88 E7
Gospel End Rd DY3 50 B8
Gospel End St DY3 50 D8
Gospel Farm Rd B27 106 B8
Gospel La B27 106 C8
Gospel Oak Rd
Coventry CV6 95 B4
Wednesbury DY4 41 B1
Gosport Cl WV1 40 B7
Gosport Rd CV6 113 E8
Goss Croft B29 85 D1
Gossett La CV8 135 F7
Gossey La B33 69 C2
Gossey Lane Jun & Inf Sch B33 69 C2
Goss The DY5 61 D1
Gosta Gn B4 164 D4
Gotham Rd B26 88 E6
Goths Cl B65 63 C4
Gough Ave WV11 26 B8
Gough Rd
Birmingham,Edgbaston B15 86 C7
Birmingham,Sparkhill B11 87 D5
Dudley WV14 40 C1
Gough St
Birmingham B1 164 B1
Willenhall WV13 27 C2
Wolverhampton WV1 163 C3
Gould Ave E DY11 116 A2
Gould Ave W DY11 116 A1
Gould Firm La WS9 30 E6
Gould Rd CV35 160 A7
Governor's Ct CV34 160 D8
Gowan Rd B8 67 E4
Gower Ave DY6 60 F4
Gower Ho B62 83 F6
Gower Rd
Halesowen B62 83 F6
Sedgley DY3 50 B8
Gower St
Birmingham B19 66 D7
Walsall WS2 42 B7
Willenhall WV13 27 A2
Wolverhampton WV2 163 D1
Gowland Dr WS11 1 B1
Gowrie Cl LE10 71 B2
Goya Cl WS11 2 D2
Gozzard St WV14 40 E5
Gracechurch Sh Ctr B72 46 B5
Grace Mary Prim Sch B69 63 C7
Gracemere Cres B28 105 E3
Grace Moore Ct WS11 1 F4
Grace Rd
Allesley CV5 111 A8
Birmingham B11 87 C7
Oldbury B69 63 C8
Tipton DY4 52 A7
Gracewell Homes B13 105 D8
Gracewell Rd B13 87 D1
Grafton Cl B98 159 B7
Grafton Cres B60 150 E8
Grafton Ct
4 Wolverhampton WV6 24 F4
Birmingham B23 56 C2
Coventry CV4 132 B7
Grafton Dr WV13 26 D1
Grafton Gdns DY3 50 B3
Grafton Gr 1 B19 66 C7
Grafton Ho
Bromsgrove B60 137 B3
Wolverhampton WV4 39 E5
Grafton La B61 150 C7
Grafton Pl WV14 40 E7
Grafton Rd
Birmingham,Handsworth B21 54 D1
Birmingham,Sparkbrook B11 87 B7
Oldbury B68 63 F2
Solihull B90 105 C2
West Bromwich B71 53 D4
Grafton St CV1 113 F2
Graham Cl
Coventry CV6 96 B1
Wednesbury DY4 41 B1
Graham Cres B45 122 A7
Graham Ho B74 30 F2
Graham Rd
Birmingham,Saltley B9 67 F3
Birmingham,South Yardley B25 88 C6
Halesowen B62 83 C8
Kingswinford DY6,DY8 60 D4
West Bromwich B71 53 D4
Graham St
Birmingham,Hockley B1 66 C3
Birmingham,Lozells B19 66 C7
Nuneaton CV11 73 C5
Grainger Cl DY4 52 D6
Grainger Ct WS11 1 D2
Grainger's La B64 82 D8
Grainger St DY2 62 D7
Graiseley Ct WV3 163 B2
Graiseley Hill WV2 163 B1
Graiseley La WV11 26 C5
Graiseley Prim Sch WV2 163 B1
Graiseley Row WV2 163 B1
Graiseley St WV3 163 A2
Graith Cl B28 105 E3
Grammar School La B63 83 A4
Grampian Rd DY8 81 A6
Granada Trad Est B69 63 F6
Granary Cl
Cannock WS12 2 B5
Kingswinford DY6 60 A8
Granary La B76 46 F3
Granary Rd
Stoke Heath B60 150 E6
Wolverhampton WV8 10 E1
Granary The WS9 30 B6
Granborough Cl CV3 134 F8
Granborough Ct CV32 157 A3
Granbourne Rd WS2 27 D4
Granby Ave B33 69 C1
Granby Bsns Pk B33 69 D1
Granby Cl
Hinckley LE10 75 C7
Redditch B98 154 F4
Solihull B92 106 E7
Granby Rd
Hinckley LE10 75 C7
Nuneaton CV10 72 F3
Grandborough Dr B91 107 A1
Grand Cl B66 65 B3
Grand Depot Rd CV11 79 F6
Grand Junction Way WS1 42 D5
Grand Theatre★ WV1 163 C3
Grandys Croft B37 69 F2
Granefield Ct 4 B9 67 D1
Grange Ave
Aldridge WS9 16 A1
Birmingham B8 68 B6
Burntwood WS7 7 B7
Coventry,Binley CV3 134 F7
Coventry,Finham CV3 133 C3
Kenilworth CV8 147 E7
Sutton Coldfield B75 32 C3
Grange Cl
Nuneaton CV10 72 C7
Tamworth B77 35 C8
Warwick CV34 161 C8
Grange Cres
Birmingham B45 121 F8
Halesowen B63 83 B3
Walsall WS4 29 B8
Grange Ct
1 Dudley DY1 51 B1
1 Redditch B98 153 F4
Stourbridge DY9 81 C3
Willenhall WS2 27 D2
Wolverhampton WV3 163 A2
Grange Dr
Cannock WS11 1 F2
Hinckley LE10 75 E5
Grange Education Unit The CV6 94 E1
Grange Farm Dr B38 123 D8
Grange Farm Prim Sch CV3 133 B5
Grangefield Cl WV8 10 F1
Grange Hill B62 83 C2
Grange Hill Rd B38 103 E1
Grangehurst Prim Sch CV6 96 B4
Grange La
4 Kingswinford DY6 60 F4
Alvechurch B48 139 B3
Stourbridge DY9 81 D4
Sutton Coldfield B75 32 C3
Grange Mews The 1 CV32 156 D1
Grangemouth Rd CV6 113 B7
Grange Pk DY1 51 A1
Grange Rd
2 Redditch B98 153 F4
Balsall Common CV7 129 F7
Birmingham,Aston B6 66 E8
Birmingham B29 85 F3
Birmingham,Bordesley Green B10 67 D1
Birmingham,Erdington B24 57 C5
Birmingham,King's Heath B14 104 E8
Burntwood WS7 7 A5
Coventry CV6 96 B5
Cradley Heath B64 83 B8
Dorridge B93 127 E2
Dudley,New Dock DY1 51 B1
Dudley,Roseville WV14 51 B7
Halesowen B63 83 C3
Hockley Heath B94 143 E8
Kidderminster DY11 116 B7
Norton Canes WS11 6 B6
Royal Leamington Spa CV32 157 B3
Smethwick B66 65 A3
Solihull B91 106 E7
Stourbridge DY9 81 C4
West Bromwich B70 53 B3
Wolverhampton,Blakenall WV2 39 B6
Wolverhampton,Tettenhall Wood WV6 24 C4
Grange Rise B38 123 F7
Grangers La B98 158 F5
Grange St
Dudley DY1 51 B1
Walsall WS1 42 F7
Grange The
Birmingham B20 54 F4
Cubbington CV32 157 F5
Halesowen B62 83 F6
Royal Leamington Spa CV32 157 B1
Grange The *continued*
Warwick CV34 161 C7
Wombourne WV5 49 A7
Grange Wlk CV6 96 B5
Grangewood Ct
Solihull B92 106 E7
Sutton Coldfield B73 57 A7
Granhill Cl B98 159 A8
Granleigh Ct CV32 157 E5
Granoe Cl CV3 134 E8
Granshaw Cl B38 103 F1
Grant Cl
Kingswinford DY6 60 D8
West Bromwich B71 53 C5
Grant Ct B30 104 A5
Grantham Rd
Birmingham B11 87 B6
Smethwick B66 65 B3
Grantham St CV2 113 F3
Grantley Cres DY6 60 C7
Grantley Dr B37 70 B3
Granton Cl B14 104 D5
Granton Rd B14 104 D5
Grantown Gr WS3 14 A4
Grant Rd
Bedworth CV7 78 A1
Coventry CV3 114 B2
Grant St
Birmingham B15 86 D8
Walsall WS3 28 B8
Granville Cl
Bromsgrove B60 137 B1
Wolverhampton WV2 163 C1
Granville Crest DY10 117 B6
Granville Dr DY6 60 F5
Granville Gdns LE10 75 C8
Granville Rd
Cradley Heath B64 83 B8
Dorridge B93 128 A2
Hinckley LE10 75 C8
Granville Sq B1 66 C1
Granville St
Birmingham B1 164 A1
Royal Leamington Spa CV32 157 A2
Willenhall WV13 27 A3
Wolverhampton WV2 163 C1
Granville B77 21 F1
Grapes Cl CV6 113 B5
Grasdene Gr B17 85 C4
Grasmere Ave
Coventry CV3 132 F6
Perton WV6 23 F4
Sutton Coldfield B74 31 A2
Grasmere Cl
Birmingham B43 54 F7
Kidderminster DY10 116 E7
Kingswinford DY6 60 B7
Wolverhampton,Palmers Cross WV6 24 E8
Wolverhampton WV11 26 C7
Grasmere Cres CV11 73 F7
Grasmere Ho 13 B69 63 D5
Grasmere Pl WS11 1 E5
Grasmere Rd
Bedworth CV12 78 B2
Birmingham B21 65 F7
Grasscroft Dr CV3 133 E6
Grassholme B77 36 A8
Grassington Ave CV34 155 F1
Grassington Dr
Birmingham B37 69 F1
Nuneaton CV11 74 A2
Grassmere Ct WS6 4 D3
Grassmere Dr DY8 80 F3
Grassmoor Rd B38 103 E2
Grassy La WV10,WV11 12 B2
Graston Cl B16 66 A2
Gratham Cl DY5 81 B7
Gratley Croft WS12 1 C4
Grattidge Rd B27 88 D2
Gratton Ct CV3 132 F6
Gravel Bank B32 84 D2
Gravel Hill
Coventry CV4 111 F1
Wombourne WV5 49 B6
Gravel La WS12 1 C5
Gravelly Ct 4 B23 56 E2
Gravelly Hill B23 56 E2
Gravelly Hill N B23 56 E3
Gravelly Hill Sta B23 56 E2
Gravelly Ind Pk B24 67 F8
Gravelly La
Birmingham B23 56 F5
Stonnall WS9 16 F3
Gravel Pit La B48 139 E3
Gravel The B76 48 B2
Gray Cl DY10 117 B6
Graydon Ct B74 46 B7
Grayfield Ave B13 87 A3
Grayland Cl B27 88 B2
Graylands The CV3 133 C4
Grayling Cl WS10 41 B3
Grayling Rd DY9 81 C6
Grayling B77 35 D6
Grayling Wlk
Birmingham B37 70 C3
Wolverhampton WV10 26 B4
Gray Rd WS12 1 F6
Grayshott Cl
Birmingham B23 56 E5
Bromsgrove B61 136 E3
Grays Rd B17 85 D6
Gray St B9 67 B2
Grayston Ave B77 21 E4
Grayswood Ave CV5 112 D4
Grayswood Park Rd B32 84 C6
Grayswood Rd B31 122 F7
Grazebrook Croft B32 102 D8
Grazebrook Ind Pk DY2 62 B6
Grazebrook Rd DY2 62 C7
Grazewood Cl WV12 27 B7
Grazier Ave B77 35 C8
Grazing La B97 152 F2
Greadier St WV12 27 C5
Great Arthur St B66 64 F7
Great Barn La B97 153 B1
Great Barr Bsns Pk B42 55 A5
Great Barr Prim Sch B44 44 D1
Great Barr Sch B44 44 D1
Great Barr St B9 67 A2
Great Brickkiln St WV3 25 B1
Great Bridge Ind Est DY4 52 C7
Great Bridge Prim Sch DY4 52 C6
Great Bridge Rd WV14 41 B3
Great Bridge St B70 52 E5
Great Bridge DY4 52 D5
Great Brook St B7 67 A4
Great Charles St WS8 15 F8
Great Charles Street Queensway B3 164 B3
Great Colmore St B15 86 D8
Great Cornbow 5 B63 83 B3
Great Croft Ho 2 WS10 41 D6
Great Farley Dr B31 102 C1
Greatfield Rd DY11 116 B4
Great Francis St B7 67 B4
Great Hampton Row B19 164 A4
Great Hampton St
Birmingham B18 164 A4
Wolverhampton WV1 25 B4
Greatheed Rd CV32 156 E2
Great Hockings La B97 152 E2
Great King St N B19 66 C6
Great King St B19 66 C5
Great Lister St B7 67 A4
Great Mdw DY4 52 B5
Greatmead B77 21 C1
Great Moor Rd WV6 23 A3
Great Oaks B26 89 B5
Greatorex Ct B71 53 B8
Great Stone Rd B31 103 A3
Great Tindal St B16 66 A2
Great Western Arc B2 164 C3
Great Western Cl B18 65 E6
Great Western Ct B27 88 C4
Great Western Dr B64 63 A1
Great Western St
Wednesbury WS10 41 E2
Wolverhampton WV1 163 C4
Great Western Way DY4 52 D6
Great Wood Rd B10 67 C1
Great Wyrley High Sch WS6 4 F3
Greaves Ave WS5 43 C8
Greaves Cl
Walsall WS5 43 C8
Warwick CV34 161 C7
Greaves Cres WV12 27 C8
Greaves Rd DY2 62 D5
Greaves Sq B38 104 B1
Greaves The B76 58 F6
Grebe Cl B23 56 B3
Greenacre Cl B77 22 B5
Greenacre Dr WV8 10 B2
Greenacre Rd DY4 41 B1
Greenacres Ave WV10 12 B2
Green Acres B27 88 B2
Greenacres B32 84 E2
Greenacres Cl WS9 30 E2
Green Acres Prim Sch WV14 40 F6
Greenacres Prim Sch B77 22 B5
Green Acres Rd B38 123 D8
Greenacres Rd B61 136 E3
Greenacres
Sedgley DY3 39 B1
Sutton Coldfield B76 58 A8
Wolverhampton WV6 24 B5
Greenaleigh Rd B14 105 D3
Green Ave B28 87 E1
Greenaway Cl B43 44 C3
Greenaway Ct WV10 12 C7
Green Bank Ave B28 87 E1
Greenbank B45 138 D8
Greenbank Gdns DY8 60 E2
Greenbank Rd CV7 129 F6
Green Barns La WS14 32 C8
Green Bower Dr B61 137 A5
Greenbush Dr B63 83 A5
Green Cl
Studley B80 159 E3
Whitnash CV31 162 B4
Wythall B47 125 A3
Greencroft WV14 40 D6
Green Croft B9 68 A3
Greencroft
Kingswinford DY6 60 D4
Lichfield WS13 3 A2
Green Ct
8 Lichfield WS13 9 B7
Birmingham,Gravelly Hill B23 56 E2
Birmingham,Hall Green B28 105 F8
Greendale Cl B61 137 B8
Greendale Rd CV5 112 D3
Green Dr
Birmingham B32 84 C1
Wolverhampton WV10 25 C7
Greenend Rd B13 86 F2
Greenfels Rise DY2 62 F8
Greenfield Ave
Balsall Common CV7 130 A7

Greenfield Ave *continued*
Cradley Heath B64 ... 62 B1
Lower Marlbrook B60 ... 121 D1
Stourbridge DY8 ... 80 F5
Greenfield Bldgs WV5 ... 49 A7
Greenfield Cotts B48 ... 139 A5
Greenfield Cres B15 ... 86 A8
Greenfield Croft WV14 ... 40 D2
Greenfield Ho B26 ... 89 D6
Greenfield La WV10 ... 11 E5
Greenfield Prim Sch
Stourbridge DY8 ... 80 F5
Walsall WS4 ... 29 C8
Greenfield Rd
Birmingham B17 ... 85 D5
Birmingham,Newton B43 ... 54 D7
Smethwick B67 ... 64 E4
Greenfields
Aldridge WS9 ... 30 B7
Cannock WS11 ... 1 E2
Greenfields Rd
Kingswinford DY6 ... 60 E6
Walsall WS4 ... 15 D2
Wombourne WV5 ... 49 A5
Greenfields B98 ... 153 E2
Green Field The CV3 ... 134 B8
Greenfield View DY3 ... 50 B7
Greenfinch Cl
Birmingham B36 ... 70 A7
Kidderminster DY10 ... 117 B3
Greenfinch Rd
Birmingham B36 ... 70 A7
Stourbridge DY9 ... 81 D3
Greenford Cl B97 ... 153 B5
Greenford Ho
7 West Bromwich B70 ... 53 D1
Birmingham B23 ... 56 B6
Greenford Rd B14 ... 105 C3
Green Gables
Hollywood B47 ... 125 A7
Sutton Coldfield B74 ... 46 B7
Greenheart B77 ... 22 A4
Green Heath Rd WS12 ... 2 A7
Greenhill Ave DY10 ... 116 F7
Greenhill B60 ... 137 F4
Green Hill Cl B60 ... 137 D6
Greenhill Cl
Tamworth B77 ... 35 C5
Willenhall WV12 ... 27 B5
Greenhill Ct
Halesowen B62 ... 83 E7
Sutton Coldfield B72 ... 57 C8
Wombourne WV5 ... 49 B5
Greenhill Dr B29 ... 85 C1
Greenhill Gdns
Birmingham B43 ... 43 E2
Halesowen B62 ... 83 D6
Wombourne WV5 ... 49 B5
Greenhill Ind Est DY10 ... 117 A7
Greenhill WS13 ... 9 C8
Greenhill Mews WS13 ... 9 C8
Greenhill Oak DY10 ... 116 F7
Greenhill Rd
Birmingham,Handsworth
B21 ... 54 E2
Birmingham,Moseley B13 ... 87 A1
Dudley DY3 ... 50 E5
Halesowen B62 ... 83 D7
Sutton Coldfield B72 ... 57 C8
Whitnash CV31 ... 162 B4
Greenhill Way WS9 ... 16 B1
Green Hill Way B90 ... 106 B5
Greenhill WV5 ... 49 B6
Greenholm Prim Sch B44 55 E7
Greenholm Rd B44 ... 55 E7
Greenhough Rd WS13 ... 9 A8
Greenhurst Dr B45 ... 122 A1
Greening Dr B15 ... 86 B7
Green La
Aldridge WS9 ... 30 E5
Balsall Common CV7 ... 130 B7
Birchmoor B77,B78 ... 36 D7
Birmingham B32 ... 84 C6
Birmingham,Bordesley Green
B9 ... 67 E1
Birmingham,Castle Bromwich
B36 ... 69 E8
Birmingham,Great Barr B43 43 D1
Birmingham,Handsworth
B21 ... 65 C8
Birmingham,Hawkesley
B38 ... 123 E8
Birmingham,Newton B43 ... 54 D8
Brownhills WS8 ... 7 B2
Cannock WS11 ... 4 E6
Coleshill B46 ... 70 F5
Corley Moor CV7 ... 93 D6
Coventry CV3 ... 133 B4
Dudley DY3 ... 50 F5
Halesowen B62 ... 63 D1
Kingswinford DY6 ... 60 D7
Lichfield WS14 ... 8 D2
Middleton B78 ... 48 B6
Greenland Ave CV5 ... 111 F5
Greenland Cl DY6 ... 60 E8
Greenland Ct
Birmingham B8 ... 67 E6
Coventry CV5 ... 111 F5
Greenland Rd B29 ... 86 B1
Greenland Rise B92 ... 107 D7
Greenlands Ave B98 ... 154 A1
Greenlands Bsns Ctr
B98 ... 154 B2
Greenlands Dr B98 ... 158 F8
Greenlands Rd B37 ... 70 C1
Green Lane Ind Est B9 ... 67 E1
Green Lanes WV14 ... 40 C7
Green Lanes Prim Sch
B36 ... 69 F8
Green Lanes B73 ... 57 B8
Green Lane Venture Ctr
WS11 ... 4 E6
Green La
Nuneaton CV10 ... 72 C7
Redditch B97 ... 158 A7
Solihull B90 ... 105 E1
Stourbridge DY9 ... 81 E5
Studley B80 ... 159 B5
Tamworth B77 ... 36 C6
Upper Catshill B61 ... 121 A1
Walsall,Birchills WS2,WS3 . 28 C5
Walsall,High Heath WS4,
WS9 ... 15 D3
Walsall,Pelsall WS3 ... 15 A4
Warwick CV34 ... 160 F8
Greenlawns DY4 ... 52 B8
Green La WV6 ... 24 F7
Greenleaf Cl CV5 ... 112 A3
Greenleas Gdns B63 ... 83 C3
Greenlea B77 ... 36 A8
Green Leigh B23 ... 56 F8
Greenleighs DY3 ... 39 D3
Greenly Rd WV4 ... 39 D5
Green Mdws 2 WS12 ... 2 C1
Green Mdw
Stourbridge DY9 ... 99 B7
Wednesfield WV11 ... 26 E5
Green Meadow Prim Sch
B29 ... 102 F7
Green Meadow Rd
Birmingham B29 ... 103 A7
Willenhall WV12 ... 27 B7
Greenmoor Rd
Hinckley LE10 ... 75 D5
Nuneaton CV10 ... 73 A3
Greenoak Cres
Birmingham B30 ... 104 C8
Dudley WV14 ... 51 A7
Green Oak Rd WV8 ... 10 B2
Greenodd Dr CV6 ... 95 F5
Green Park Ave WV14 ... 40 C8
Green Park Dr WV14 ... 40 C8
Green Park Rd
Birmingham B31 ... 102 E2
Bromsgrove B60 ... 137 B2
Dudley DY2 ... 62 F8
Green Park Sch WV14 ... 40 B8
Green Rd
Birmingham B28 ... 87 E1
Dudley DY2 ... 62 D7
Greenridge Rd B20 ... 54 E5
Green Rock La WS3 ... 14 D1
Green Rock Prim Sch
WS3 ... 14 E1
Greenroyde DY9 ... 81 B1
Greensand Dr WV14 ... 40 D2
Greenside
Birmingham B17 ... 85 C5
Cheswick Green B90 ... 126 D4
Greenside Cl CV11 ... 74 C1
Greenside Rd B24 ... 57 C5
Greenside B60 ... 150 C2
Greenside Way WS5 ... 43 A4
Greensill Ave DY4 ... 51 F8
Greens Ind Est WS12 ... 2 C7
Green Slade Cres B60 ... 121 C1
Greenslade Croft B31 ... 103 A2
Green Slade Gr WS12 ... 2 C7
Greenslade Rd
Sedgley DY3 ... 39 B2
Solihull B90 ... 105 C2
Walsall WS5 ... 43 C7
Greensleeves Cl CV6 ... 95 B2
Greensleeves B74 ... 31 F1
Greens Rd CV6 ... 95 A1
Green St B12 ... 66 F1
Greenstead Rd B13 ... 87 D1
Greens The WV6 ... 23 E3
Green St
Kidderminster DY10 ... 116 E5
Oldbury B69 ... 64 A7
Green Street Ind Est
DY10 ... 116 E4
Green St
Smethwick B67 ... 64 F5
Stourbridge DY8 ... 80 F5
Tipton WV14 ... 51 C8
Walsall WS2 ... 28 C3
West Bromwich B70 ... 64 E8
Greensward Cl CV8 ... 148 B6
Green Sward La B98 ... 154 D1
Greensward The CV3 ... 115 A2
Greensway WV11 ... 26 B8
Greens Yd CV12 ... 78 C3
Green The
4 Birmingham,Quinton
B32 ... 84 A6
Aldridge WS9 ... 30 C6
Birmingham,Castle Bromwich
B36 ... 69 B7
Birmingham,Erdington B23 . 57 A4
Birmingham,Frankley B31 102 C2
Birmingham,King's Norton
B38 ... 103 F2
Bluntington DY10 ... 118 E1
Darlaston WS10 ... 41 D7
Fazeley B78 ... 20 E2
Freasley B78 ... 36 C4
Meriden CV7 ... 92 B1
Nuneaton CV11 ... 73 E2
Oldbury B68 ... 64 B1
Solihull B91 ... 107 D5
Stoneleigh CV8 ... 149 C6
Stourbridge DY8 ... 60 D2
Sutton Coldfield B72 ... 46 D1
Green The *continued*
Tamworth B77 ... 22 B5
Tanworth-In-A B94 ... 142 A2
Walsall WS3 ... 14 B1
West Hagley DY9 ... 98 F4
Greenvale Ave B26 ... 89 D6
Greenvale B31 ... 102 F5
Green Way WS9 ... 16 B2
Greenway Ave 2 DY8 ... 60 E1
Greenway B20 ... 54 F6
Greenway Dr B73 ... 45 C3
Greenway Gdns
Birmingham B38 ... 123 E7
Sedgley DY3 ... 39 E1
Greenway CV11 ... 79 B8
Greenway Rd WV14 ... 40 E4
Greenways
Birmingham B31 ... 102 F8
Coventry CV4 ... 111 C2
Greenway DY3 ... 39 E1
Greenways
Halesowen B63 ... 82 C6
Stourbridge DY8 ... 60 C1
Greenway St B9 ... 67 C1
Greenways The CV32 ... 157 B3
Greenway The
Birmingham,Marston Green
B37 ... 90 A6
Sutton Coldfield,New Oscott
B73 ... 45 B3
West Hagley DY9 ... 98 F5
Greenway CV34 ... 155 E1
Greenway Wlk B33 ... 69 E1
Green Wickets B13 ... 104 E6
Green Wlk 4 B17 ... 84 F7
Greenwood Ave
Birmingham B27 ... 88 B1
Oldbury B68 ... 64 C5
Rowley Regis B65 ... 63 D3
Greenwood B25 ... 88 D8
Greenwood Cl B14 ... 104 E5
Greenwood Cotts DY1 ... 51 A5
Greenwood Ct
Nuneaton CV11 ... 73 E3
Royal Leamington Spa
CV32 ... 157 B1
Greenwood Dr WS14 ... 9 B6
Greenwood Pk
Aldridge WS9 ... 16 C2
Cannock WS12 ... 2 B8
Greenwood Pl B44 ... 45 B1
Greenwood Rd
Aldridge WS9 ... 16 B2
West Bromwich B71 ... 53 B8
Wolverhampton WV10 ... 25 C7
Greenwood Sq 5 B37 ... 70 B2
Greenwoods The DY8 ... 80 E5
Greenwood Way B37 ... 70 B2
Greethurst Dr B13 ... 87 C2
Greet Prim Sch B11 ... 87 D4
Greets Green Ind Est B70. 52 F4
Greets Green Rd B70 ... 52 F3
Greetville Cl B34 ... 69 A5
Gregory Ave
Birmingham B29 ... 103 A8
Coventry CV3 ... 133 A6
Gregory Cl 3 WS10 ... 41 F2
Gregory Ct WV11 ... 26 E5
Gregory Dr DY1 ... 51 A2
Gregory Hood Rd CV3 ... 133 E4
Gregory Rd
Burntwood WS7 ... 7 E7
Stourbridge DY8 ... 80 D5
Gregston Ind Est B69 ... 64 B8
Greig Ct WS11 ... 2 C2
Grendon Cl
Coventry CV4 ... 111 C1
Redditch B98 ... 154 D1
Grendon Dr B73 ... 45 D3
Grendon Gdns WV3 ... 38 D6
Grendon Jun & Inf Sch
B14 ... 105 A3
Grendon Rd
Birmingham B14 ... 105 A3
Solihull B92 ... 106 E8
Grenfell Cl CV31 ... 162 D6
Grenfell Ct B73 ... 46 B1
Grenfell Dr B15 ... 85 F8
Grenfell Rd WS3 ... 14 D3
Grenville Ave CV2 ... 114 B3
Grenville Cl WS2 ... 27 D3
Grenville Dr
Birmingham B23 ... 56 B3
Smethwick B66 ... 64 D8
Grenville Pl B70 ... 52 E3
Grenville Rd
Dudley DY1 ... 50 E1
Solihull B90 ... 106 B2
Gresham Ave CV32 ... 157 B2
Gresham Pl CV32 ... 157 B2
Gresham Rd
Birmingham B28 ... 105 F6
Cannock WS11 ... 1 F3
Nuneaton CV10 ... 78 B8
Oldbury B68 ... 64 C6
Gresham St CV2 ... 114 A2
Gresham Twr B12 ... 86 F8
Gresley Cl B74 ... 32 A4
Gresley Gr B23 ... 56 C1
Gresley Rd CV2 ... 114 D7
Gresley Row WS13 ... 9 C8
Gresley B77 ... 21 F1
Gressel La B33 ... 69 D3
Grestone Ave B20 ... 54 E3
Grestone Prim Sch B20 ... 54 E4
Greswold Cl CV4 ... 111 F1
Greswolde Dr B24 ... 57 B4
Greswolde Park Rd B27 ... 88 B4
Greswolde Rd
Birmingham B11 ... 87 D3
Solihull B91 ... 106 E6
Greswoldes The CV31 ... 162 F6
Greswold Gdns B34 ... 69 A5
Greswold Prim Sch B91 107 C6
Greswold St B71 ... 53 B5
Gretna Rd CV3 ... 132 F4
Gretton Cres WS9 ... 29 E5
Gretton Rd
Aldridge WS9 ... 29 F5
Birmingham B23 ... 56 D7
Greville Dr B15 ... 86 C6
Greville Ho 13 CV34 ... 160 F7
Greville Rd
Kenilworth CV8 ... 147 F4
Warwick CV34 ... 156 B1
Greville Smith Ave CV31. 162 B4
Grevis Cl B13 ... 86 F4
Grevis Rd B25 ... 68 E1
Greycoat Rd CV6 ... 95 A2
Greyfort Cres B92 ... 88 F1
Greyfriars Cl
Dudley DY1 ... 50 E3
Solihull B92 ... 106 D6
Greyfriars Ct CV6 ... 113 A7
Greyfriars Dr
Bromsgrove B61 ... 136 D2
Tamworth B79 ... 20 E6
Greyfriars La CV1 ... 165 B2
Greyfriars Rd CV1 ... 165 B2
Greyhound La
Lower Penn WV4 ... 37 E5
Stourbridge DY8 ... 80 D2
Greyhurst Croft 5 B91 ... 127 B8
Grey Mill Cl B90 ... 126 F6
Greysbrooke Prim Sch
WS14 ... 18 A6
Greysbrooke WS14 ... 18 A5
Grey's Rd B80 ... 159 E3
Greystoke Ave B36 ... 68 D7
Greystoke Dr DY6 ... 60 D6
Greystone Cl B98 ... 154 C5
Greystone Pas 16 DY1 ... 51 B1
Grey Tree Cres B93 ... 127 E3
Grice St B70 ... 64 D8
Griffin Ave DY10 ... 116 E4
Griffin Bsns Pk B37 ... 70 C3
Griffin Cl
Birmingham B31 ... 103 B6
Burntwood WS7 ... 6 E8
Griffin Ct B5 ... 86 C5
Griffin Gdns B17 ... 85 D4
Griffin Ho B16 ... 65 E1
Griffin Ind Est B65 ... 63 F3
Griffin Rd
Birmingham B23 ... 56 C5
Warwick CV34 ... 161 C7
Griffins Brook Cl B30 ... 103 D7
Griffins Brook La B30 ... 103 D6
Griffins La B90 ... 126 A5
Griffin St
Dudley DY2 ... 62 C4
West Bromwich B70 ... 53 D3
Wolverhampton WV1 ... 25 F1
Griffiths Dr
Wolverhampton WV11 ... 13 A1
Wombourne WV5 ... 49 A5
Griffiths Rd
Dudley DY1 ... 51 A6
West Bromwich B71 ... 42 C1
Willenhall WV12 ... 27 D8
Griffiths St DY4 ... 51 E5
Griff La
Nuneaton CV10 ... 78 A6
Nuneaton CV10 ... 78 B6
Grigg Gr B31 ... 102 E1
Grimley Cl B98 ... 153 F1
Grimley La B60 ... 151 E6
Grimley Rd 2 B31 ... 103 D2
Grimley Way WS11 ... 1 F4
Grimpits La B38 ... 124 A7
Grimshaw Rd B27 ... 88 A1
Grimshaw Villas B93 ... 128 D8
Grimston Cl CV3 ... 115 A2
Grimstone St WV10 ... 163 C4
Grindleford Rd B42 ... 55 D7
Grindle Rd CV6 ... 95 F4
Grindley Ho 5 CV1 ... 113 B2
Grindsbrook B77 ... 36 A8
Gristhorpe Rd B29 ... 104 A8
Grizebeck Dr CV5 ... 112 A5
Grizedale Cl B45 ... 102 B2
Grocott Rd WS10 ... 41 B4
Grosmont Ave 8 B12 ... 87 A6
Grosvenor Ave
Birmingham B20 ... 55 C2
Kidderminster DY10 ... 117 A6
Sutton Coldfield B74 ... 30 F1
Grosvenor Cl
Lichfield WS14 ... 9 D6
Sutton Coldfield B75 ... 32 C1
Wolverhampton WV10 ... 11 D2
Grosvenor Cres
Hinckley LE10 ... 76 A6
Wolverhampton WV10 ... 11 D2
Grosvenor Ct
2 Royal Leamington Spa
CV32 ... 156 F1
Birmingham,Handsworth
B20 ... 55 C2
Dudley DY3 ... 50 D2
Shenstone WS14 ... 17 F6
Stourbridge DY9 ... 81 B1
Wednesfield WV11 ... 26 E5
Wolverhampton,Tettenhall Wood
WV6 ... 24 A3
Wolverhampton WV3 ... 163 B2
Grosvenor Gdns B61 ... 137 B5
Grosvenor Ho
Birmingham,Erdington
B23 ... 57 A5
Coventry CV1 ... 165 A2
Redditch B97 ... 153 E4
Grosvenor Pk WV4 ... 38 F5
Grosvenor Rd
Birmingham,Aston B6 ... 67 B8
Birmingham B17 ... 85 A6
Birmingham,Handsworth
B20 ... 55 C2
Coventry CV1 ... 165 A1
Dudley DY3 ... 50 D2
Oldbury B68 ... 64 A3
Solihull B91 ... 106 F1
Whitnash CV31 ... 162 A5
Wolverhampton,Bushbury
WV10 ... 11 D2
Wolverhampton WV4 ... 39 E3
Grosvenor Road S DY3 ... 50 D2
Grosvenor St W B16 ... 66 B1
Grosvenor Sh Ctr B31 ... 103 A4
Grosvenor Sq B28 ... 105 F5
Grosvenor St
Birmingham B5 ... 164 D3
Wolverhampton WV10 ... 25 F3
Grosvenor Way DY5 ... 81 E7
Grotto La WV6 ... 24 E5
Groucutt St 6 WV14 ... 51 C8
Grounds Dr B74 ... 31 F3
Grounds Rd B74 ... 31 F3
Grout St B70 ... 52 E4
Grove Ave
Birmingham B27 ... 88 B3
Birmingham,Handsworth
B21 ... 65 F8
Birmingham,Moseley B13 .. 87 A2
Halesowen B63 ... 82 F3
Solihull B91 ... 107 C5
Grove Cl WS11 ... 5 F5
Grove Cottage Rd B9 ... 67 D2
Grove Cres
Brierley Hill DY5 ... 61 C5
Walsall WS3 ... 14 F3
Grove Ct
Birmingham B43 ... 54 F6
Coventry CV5 ... 133 B8
Nuneaton CV11 ... 73 E2
Grove Farm Dr B75 ... 46 F5
Grovefield Cres CV7 ... 130 C8
Grove Fields CV10 ... 73 D8
Grove Gdns
Birmingham B20 ... 54 F2
Bromsgrove B61 ... 137 A6
Grove Hill Rd B21 ... 54 F1
Grove Hill WS5 ... 29 E1
Grovehurst Pk CV8 ... 149 B2
Grove La
Birmingham B17 ... 85 C4
Birmingham,Handsworth
B20 ... 54 F1
Keresley CV7 ... 94 F7
Lapworth B94 ... 143 F4
Groveland Rd DY4 ... 52 B3
Grovelands Cres WV10 ... 11 D3
Grovelands Ind Est CV7 .. 96 A6
Grove La
Norton Canes WS3 ... 5 E1
Smethwick B66 ... 65 C5
Wishaw B76 ... 47 F2
Wolverhampton WV6 ... 24 B2
Groveley La B31,B45 ... 122 E5
Grove Mews B31 ... 123 B8
Grove Pk
Hinckley LE10 ... 76 A6
Kingswinford DY6 ... 60 C8
Grove Pl
2 Royal Leamington Spa
CV31 ... 162 A6
Nuneaton CV10 ... 72 D3
Grove Prim Sch WV2 ... 163 D1
Grove Rd
Ansty CV7 ... 97 D3
Birmingham,King's Heath
B14 ... 104 D6
Birmingham,Sparkhill B11 .. 87 C2
Dorridge B93 ... 128 B3
Hinckley LE10 ... 76 A6
Nuneaton CV10 ... 72 D3
Oldbury B68 ... 64 D1
Solihull B91 ... 107 C5
Stourbridge DY9 ... 81 F3
Grove Sch B21 ... 65 F8
Groveside Way WS3 ... 15 A5
Grove St
Coventry CV1 ... 165 C3
Dudley DY2 ... 62 E8
Redditch B98 ... 153 E4
Royal Leamington Spa
CV32 ... 161 E8
Smethwick B66 ... 65 D4
Wolverhampton,Springfield
WV10 ... 25 F3
Wolverhampton WV2 ... 163 C1
Grove Terr WS1 ... 28 F1
Grove The
Bedworth CV12 ... 78 C3
Birmingham,Edgbaston B16 65 F2
Birmingham,Great Barr B43 43 E4
Birmingham,Lozells B19 ... 66 B7
Birmingham,Rednal B45 .. 122 D4
Birmingham,Saltley B8 ... 67 C4
Birmingham,West Heath
B31 ... 123 B8

Grove The *continued*
Brierley Hill DY5 .... **61** C1
Burntwood WS7 .... **6** D8
Coleshill B46 .... **70** F4
Hampton-in-A B92 .... **91** A1
Hinckley LE10 .... **75** C8
Rowley Regis B65 .... **63** C2
Studley B80 .... **159** D3
Sutton Coldfield B74 ..... **31** D6
Walsall WS5 .... **43** B3
Wolverhampton,New Cross WV11 .... **26** B6
Wolverhampton,Parkfield WV4 .... **39** E5
Grove Vale Ave B43 ...... **43** C1
Grove Vale Prim Sch B43 . **43** D1
Grove Villas B64 .... **82** D7
Grove Way B74 .... **44** F7
Grovewood Dr 2 B38 ... **103** E1
Guardhouse Rd CV6 ..... **113** B8
Guardian Angels RC Prim Sch B34 .... **69** E6
Guardian Ct
4 Bromsgrove B60 ..... **137** A2
Birmingham,Frankley B31 **102** D3
Birmingham,Gilbertstone B26 .... **88** F7
Solihull B91 .... **107** D3
Guardian Ho B68 .... **84** C7
Guardians Way B31 ..... **102** E8
Guernsey Dr B36 .... **70** B6
Guest Ave WV11 .... **26** C8
Guest Gr B19 .... **66** C6
Guest Hospl DY1 .... **51** E3
Guild Ave WS3 .... **28** D8
Guild Cl B16 .... **66** A2
Guild Cotts The CV34 .... **160** D6
Guild Croft B19 .... **66** D6
Guild Ct 4 B60 .... **136** F2
Guildford Cl DY11 .... **116** A6
Guildford Croft B37 ...... **89** F8
Guildford Ct
12 Birmingham B29 ...... **103** C7
Coventry CV6 .... **113** D7
Guildford Dr B19 .... **66** D6
Guildford St 4 B19 ...... **66** D7
Guildhall Mews The 7 WS1 .... **28** F1
Guild Rd
Bromsgrove B60 .... **136** F1
Coventry CV6 .... **113** D7
Guillemard Ct B37 .... **70** B1
Guilsborough Rd CV3 ... **134** E8
Guinea Cres CV4 .... **131** E6
Guinness Cl B98 .... **158** D8
Guiting Cl B97 .... **153** B1
Guiting Rd B29 .... **103** A7
Gulistan Ct 6 CV32 ..... **156** E1
Gulistan Rd CV32 .... **156** E1
Gullane Cl B38 .... **103** D1
Gullet The B78 .... **22** F1
Gullick Way WS7 .... **6** D8
Gulliman's Way CV31 .... **162** D7
Gullswood Cl B14 .... **104** D2
Gulson Hospl CV1 .... **165** D2
Gulson Rd CV1 .... **113** E2
Gumbleberrys Cl B8 ..... **68** C4
Gun Barrel Ind Ctr B63 ... **82** F6
Gundry Cl CV31 .... **162** A7
Gun La CV2 .... **114** A5
Gunmakers Wlk B19 ..... **66** D7
Gunner Gr B75 .... **47** A6
Gunner La B45 .... **121** D7
Gunners La B80 .... **159** E4
Gunnery Terr 3 CV32 ... **156** D1
Gunns Way B92 .... **106** D7
Guns La B70 .... **53** B4
Gunstock Cl B74 .... **44** E7
Guns Village Prim Sch B70 .... **53** A3
Gunter Prim Sch B24 .... **57** E3
Gunter Rd B24 .... **57** E3
Gunton Ave CV3 .... **134** C6
Guphill Ave CV5 .... **112** D2
Guphill La CV5 .... **112** D3
Gupta Trad Est B69 .... **52** F1
Gurnard Cl WV12 .... **13** B1
Gurnard B77 .... **35** D6
Gurney Cl CV4 .... **111** E3
Gurney Pl WS2 .... **28** A5
Gurney Rd WS2 .... **28** A5
Guthrie Cl B19 .... **66** D6
Guthrum Cl
Birmingham B23 .... **56** E8
Perton WV6 .... **23** F5
Gutteridge Ave CV6 ..... **95** A2
Gutter The DY9 .... **120** E7
Guy Ave WV10 .... **25** E6
Guy Pl E 13 CV32 .... **156** F1
Guy Pl W 12 CV32 .... **156** F1
Guy Rd CV8 .... **147** F2
Guy's Almshouses B79 ... **21** B5
Guy's Cliffe Ave CV32 ... **156** D2
Guys Cliffe Ave B76 ...... **46** F1
Guy's Cliffe Rd CV32 .... **161** E8
Guy's Cliffe Terr CV34 ... **160** F7
Guys Cl B79 .... **20** F7
Guy's Cl CV34 .... **161** A8
Guy's Cross Park Rd CV34 .... **160** F8
Guy's La DY3 .... **50** B2
Guys Motors Ind Pk WV10 **25** F5
Guy St
Royal Leamington Spa CV32 .... **156** F1
Guy St *continued*
Warwick CV34 .... **160** F7
Guy's Wlk B61 .... **137** A5
Gwalia Gr B23 .... **56** F4
Gwendoline Ave LE10 .... **71** A2
Gwendoline Way WS9 .... **16** B4
GWS Ind Est WS10 .... **41** D1
Gypsy La
Kenilworth CV8 .... **147** F2
Redditch B97 .... **152** C5
Water Orton B46 .... **59** D2

H

Habberley La DY11 ...... **116** A8
Habberley Rd
Kidderminster DY11 ..... **116** B7
Rowley Regis B65 .... **63** D2
Habberley St 1 DY11 ... **116** C6
Habberly Croft 1 B91 ... **107** B1
Habitat Ct B76 .... **46** F3
Hackett Cl WV14 .... **39** F1
Hackett Ct 2 B69 .... **64** A7
Hackett Dr B66 .... **64** D7
Hackett Rd B65 .... **63** E3
Hackett St DY4 .... **52** C7
Hackford Rd WV4 .... **39** F4
Hackmans Gate La DY9 .. **119** B7
Hack St B9 .... **67** A1
Hackwood Ho 10 B69 .... **63** D5
Hackwood Rd WS10 ...... **42** B2
Hadcroft Grange DY9 .... **81** D4
Hadcroft Rd DY9 .... **81** C4
Haddock Rd WV14 .... **40** C7
Haddon Cres WV12 ...... **27** C7
Haddon Croft B63 .... **82** C1
Haddon End CV3 .... **133** E6
Haddon Rd
Birmingham B42 .... **55** D6
Royal Leamington Spa CV32 .... **157** B2
Haddon St CV6 .... **114** A8
Haddon Twr 1 B15 ...... **86** D8
Haden Arch Ct B64 ...... **83** A7
Haden Cl
Cradley Heath B64 .... **83** A7
Stourbridge DY8 .... **60** D2
Haden Cres WV11 .... **26** F6
Haden Cross Dr B64 ..... **83** A7
Haden Ct 5 WV3 .... **25** A2
Hadendale B64 .... **83** A7
Haden Hill Rd B63 .... **83** B6
Haden Hill WV3 .... **25** A2
Haden Park Rd B64 ...... **82** F7
Haden Rd
Cradley Heath B64 .... **62** E2
Wednesbury DY4 .... **41** A1
Haden St B12 .... **86** F6
Haden Way B12 .... **86** F6
Haden Wlk 2 B65 .... **63** C3
Hadfield Cl B24 .... **57** E3
Hadfield Croft B19 ...... **66** C5
Hadfield Way B37 .... **70** A4
Hadland Rd B33 .... **69** B1
Hadleigh Croft B76 ...... **58** A6
Hadleigh Rd CV3 .... **133** C4
Hadley Cl
Dudley DY2 .... **62** E4
Hollywood B47 .... **125** A5
Hadley Croft B66 .... **65** A7
Hadley Ct B16 .... **65** D1
Hadley Mews CV11 ...... **73** D1
Hadley Pl WV14 .... **40** C7
Hadley Rd
Bilston WV14 .... **40** C7
Willenhall WS2 .... **27** F6
Hadley St B68 .... **64** A4
Hadley Way WS2 .... **28** A6
Hadlow Croft B33 .... **89** D7
Hadrian Cl CV32 .... **157** B4
Hadrian Dr B46 .... **59** F1
Hadrians Cl B77 .... **35** D8
Hadyn Gr B26 .... **89** B6
Hadzor Ho 5 B97 .... **153** A4
Hadzor Rd B68 .... **84** D8
Hafren Cl B45 .... **102** B2
Hafton Gr B9 .... **67** D1
Haggar St WV2 .... **39** C6
Haglay Ct N DY5 .... **61** E4
Haglay Ct S DY5 .... **61** E4
Hagley Cl DY9 .... **99** C6
Hagley Cswy DY9 .... **100** B8
Hagley Ct DY3 .... **50** D3
Hagley Hall Gdns DY9 .... **99** D6
Hagley Hall* DY9 .... **99** D6
Hagley Hill DY9 .... **99** E7
Hagley Ho B60 .... **137** B3
Hagley Mews DY9 .... **99** D6
Hagley Park Dr B45 ..... **122** A6
Hagley Prim Sch DY9 .... **99** B5
Hagley RC High Sch DY8 . **98** F6
Hagley Rd
Birmingham B16 .... **65** C1
Halesowen B63 .... **82** E2
Stourbridge DY8 .... **81** B3
Hagley Rd W B32,B68 .... **84** D7
Hagley St 3 B63 .... **83** B3
Hagley Sta DY9 .... **99** A6
Hagley View Rd DY2 ..... **62** C8
Hagley Villas B12 .... **87** B4
Hagley Wood La DY9,B62 **100** B7
Haig Cl
Cannock WS11 .... **2** A5
Sutton Coldfield B75 ...... **46** C7
Haig Pl B13 .... **105** A7
Haig Rd DY2 .... **51** F1
Haig St B71 .... **53** C5
Hailes Park Cl WV2 ...... **39** E6
Hailsham Rd B23 .... **56** F5
Hailstone Cl B65 .... **63** A5
Haines Cl DY4 .... **52** B4
Haines St B70 .... **53** D2
Hainfield Dr B91 .... **107** E5
Hainge Rd B69 .... **52** C1
Hainult Cl DY8 .... **60** D4
Halas Ct B64 .... **62** E2
Halas Ind Est B62 .... **83** C5
Halberd Cl LE10 .... **75** D5
Halberton St B66 .... **65** D4
Haldane Ct B33 .... **69** B2
Haldon Gr B31 .... **122** E7
Halecroft Ave WV11 ..... **26** D5
Hale Gr B24 .... **57** D4
Halesbury Ct B63 .... **82** F2
Halesbury Sch B62 .... **83** E7
Hales Cres B67 .... **64** E4
Halescroft Sq B31 ...... **102** E6
Hales Gdns B23 .... **56** C8
Hales La B67 .... **64** E4
Halesmere Way B63 ..... **83** C3
Halesowen CE Prim Sch B63 .... **83** B4
Halesowen Coll (E-Business Ctr) B62 .... **83** C8
Halesowen Coll (Whittingham main campus) B63 .... **83** B5
Halesowen Ind Pk B62 ... **83** B6
Halesowen Rd
Dudley BY2,B64 .... **62** D4
Halesowen B62 .... **83** F6
Lower Marlbrook B61 .... **121** C3
Halesowen St
Oldbury B69 .... **63** F7
Rowley Regis B65 .... **63** C1
Hales Park Ind Est CV6 ... **95** E4
Hales Rd
Halesowen B63 .... **83** A4
Wednesbury WS10 .... **42** A5
Hales St CV1 .... **165** C3
Hales Way B69 .... **63** F7
Halesworth Rd WV9 ..... **10** F2
Hale Trad Est DY4 .... **52** B6
Halewood Gr B28 .... **106** A7
Haley St WV12 .... **27** C5
Halfcot Ave DY9 .... **81** C3
Halford Cres WS3 .... **28** F5
Halford Gr B24 .... **57** E4
Halford La CV6 .... **95** A2
Halford Lodge CV6 ...... **95** A2
Halford Rd B91 .... **106** E6
Halford's La B66 .... **65** A8
Halfords Pk B66 .... **65** A8
Halford St B79 .... **21** A5
Halfpenny Field Wlk B35 . **58** A3
Halfshire La DY10 .... **98** B1
Halfway Cl B44 .... **55** E6
Halifax Cl CV5 .... **112** A7
Halifax Ct DY11 .... **116** B8
Halifax Gr 7 B18 .... **65** E4
Halifax Ho B5 .... **86** D7
Halifax Rd B90 .... **106** B2
Haliscombe Gr 4 B6 ..... **66** E8
Halkett Glade B33 .... **68** D3
Halladale B38 .... **103** F1
Hallam Cl B71 .... **53** E5
Hallam Cres WV10 .... **25** E6
Hallam Ct B71 .... **53** E5
Hallam Dr B71 .... **53** E5
Hallam Rd CV6 .... **95** B2
Hallams Cl CV8 .... **135** F5
Hallam St
Birmingham B12 .... **86** E5
West Bromwich B71 ...... **53** D5
Hallbridge Cl WS3 .... **14** F2
Hallbridge Way B69 ..... **52** B2
Hall Brook Rd CV6 ...... **95** A4
Hallchurch Rd DY2 ...... **61** F6
Hall Cl CV8 .... **149** B6
Hallcourt Cl 3 WS11 ...... **4** E8
Hallcourt Cres 2 WS11 .... **4** E8
Hallcourt La WS11 .... **4** E8
Hall Cres B71 .... **53** C6
Hallcroft Cl B72 .... **57** C7
Hallcroft Way
Aldridge WS9 .... **30** C5
Dorridge B93 .... **128** A6
Hall Dale Cl B28 .... **105** F5
Hall Dr
Baginton CV8 .... **133** E3
Birmingham B37 .... **90** A7
Hagley DY9 .... **99** D6
Hall End CV11 .... **73** D2
Hall End Pl CV11 .... **73** D2
Hall End WS10 .... **41** F3
Hallens Dr WS10 .... **41** D2
Hallet Dr WV3 .... **163** A2
Hallewell Rd B16 .... **65** D3
Hallfield Sch B15 .... **86** A7
Hallfields CV31 .... **162** E5
Hall Green Inf Sch B28 .. **105** F7
Hall Green Jun Sch B28 . **105** F7
Hall Green Prim Sch B71 . **42** D1
Hall Green Rd
Coventry CV2,CV6 .... **96** B2
West Bromwich B71 ...... **42** D1
Hall Green Sch B28 ..... **105** E8
Hall Green Sta B28 .... **87** F1
Hallgreen St WV14 ...... **40** E2
Hall Gr WV14 .... **51** C8
Hall Hays Rd B34 .... **69** E7
Hall La
Brownhills WS9 .... **15** E3
Coventry CV2 .... **114** F6
Dudley DY2 .... **62** C6
Hall La *continued*
Great Wyrley WS6 .... **5** A3
Hagley DY9 .... **99** D6
Hammerwich WS7 .... **7** E4
Muckley Corner WS7,WS14 .. **7** F2
Tipton DY4 .... **52** B8
Walsall WS3 .... **14** F3
Wolverhampton WV14 ..... **39** F1
Hall Mdw
Hagley DY9 .... **99** D7
Wedges Mills WS11 .... **4** B6
Hallmoor Rd B33 .... **69** B3
Hallmoor Sch B33 .... **69** B3
Hallot Cl B23 .... **56** D8
Halloughton Rd B74 ..... **46** A7
Hallow Cl 3 B31 .... **103** D2
Hallowfields Cl B98 ..... **153** E1
Hall Park St WV14 .... **40** B7
Hall Rd
Birmingham,Castle Bromwich B36 .... **69** A8
Birmingham,Handsworth B20 .... **66** A8
Birmingham,Saltley B8 .... **67** D4
Hinckley LE10 .... **75** D5
Royal Leamington Spa CV32 .... **156** F1
Smethwick B67 .... **64** E4
Hall St E WS10 .... **41** C7
Hall St S B70 .... **64** D8
Hall's Cl CV31 .... **162** B3
Hall St
Bilston WV14 .... **40** E5
Birmingham B18 .... **164** A4
Cradley Heath B64 .... **62** F2
Darlaston WS10 .... **41** B7
Dudley DY2 .... **51** D1
Hallstead Rd B13 .... **105** B5
Hall St
Oldbury B68 .... **64** B5
Sedgley DY3 .... **50** D8
Stourbridge DY8 .... **81** A3
Tipton DY4 .... **51** E5
Walsall WS2 .... **28** D3
West Bromwich B70 ...... **53** C2
Willenhall WV13 .... **27** B1
Wolverhampton WV11 ..... **26** C5
Hallswelle Gr B43 .... **44** E4
Hallway Dr CV7 .... **97** E6
Hall Wlk B46 .... **70** F4
Halsbury Gr B44 .... **56** B8
Halstead Gr B91 .... **127** A8
Halston Rd WS7 .... **7** B8
Haltonlea B77 .... **36** A8
Halton Rd B73 .... **45** E2
Halton St DY2 .... **62** C5
Hamar Way B37 .... **70** B1
Hamberley Ct B18 .... **65** D5
Hamble Cl DY5 .... **61** A6
Hamble Ct B73 .... **46** B5
Hambledon Cl WV9 ...... **11** A2
Hamble Gr WV6 .... **23** E4
Hamble Rd
Birmingham B42 .... **43** F1
Wolverhampton WV4 ..... **38** C6
Hamble B77 .... **21** D2
Hambleton Rd B63 .... **82** D2
Hambletts Rd B70 .... **53** A3
Hambrook Cl WV6 .... **25** A5
Hambury Dr B14 .... **104** D7
Ham Dingle Prim Sch DY9 .... **81** C2
Hamelin St WS11 .... **1** E3
Hamilton Ave
Birmingham B17 .... **85** A7
Halesowen B62 .... **83** C3
Stourbridge DY8 .... **80** D6
Hamilton Cl
Bedworth CV12 .... **77** C1
Cannock WS12 .... **2** F4
Hinckley LE10 .... **71** A2
Lickey End B60 .... **137** C6
Sedgley DY3 .... **50** C8
Stourbridge DY8 .... **60** C2
Hamilton Ct
1 Birmingham,Moseley B13 .... **86** F4
Birmingham,Showell Green B13 .... **87** B3
Coventry CV1 .... **165** B4
Nuneaton CV10 .... **72** D4
Hamilton Dr
Birmingham B29 .... **103** D8
Oldbury B69 .... **52** C2
Stourbridge DY8 .... **60** C2
Studley B80 .... **159** D3
Hamilton Gdns WV10 .... **11** F3
Hamilton Ho WS3 .... **14** C1
Hamilton Lea WS11 .... **6** A6
Hamilton Rd
Birmingham B21 .... **65** D8
Coventry CV2 .... **114** A3
Kidderminster DY11 .... **116** B3
Radford Semele CV31 .... **162** E5
Redditch B97 .... **158** C8
Smethwick B67 .... **64** E2
Tipton DY4 .... **52** C6
Hamilton Sch B21 .... **65** D8
Hamilton St WS3 .... **14** D1
Hamilton Terr CV32 ..... **161** F8
Ham La
Kingswinford DY6 .... **49** E1
Stourbridge DY9 .... **81** C2
Hamlet Cl CV11 .... **74** B1
Hamlet Gdns B28 .... **105** F8
Hamlet Rd B28 .... **105** F8
Hamlet The
Leek Wootton CV35 ...... **156** A7
Hamlet The *continued*
Norton Canes WS11 .... **5** E5
Hammer Bank DY5 .... **82** A8
Hammersley Cl B63 ...... **82** C7
Hammersley St CV12 ..... **77** E1
Hammerwich Hospl WS7 ... **7** B5
Hammerwich La WS7 ...... **7** F3
Hammerwich Rd WS7 ..... **7** D5
Hammond Ave WV10 ..... **25** E8
Hammond Bsns Ctr CV11 . **73** E3
Hammond Cl CV11 .... **73** E3
Hammond Dr B23 .... **56** F5
Hammond Rd CV2 ...... **113** F4
Hammonds Terr CV8 .... **147** D5
Hammond Way DY8 ...... **81** A7
Hampden Cl 3 DY5 ...... **82** A8
Hampden Retreat B12 .... **86** E6
Hamps Cl WS7 .... **7** D7
Hampshire Cl
Coventry CV3 .... **134** F8
Tamworth B78 .... **20** F2
Hampshire Ct 1 B29 .... **103** E7
Hampshire Dr B15 .... **85** E8
Hampshire Rd B71 .... **42** A1
Hampson Cl B11 .... **87** B6
Hampstead Glade B63 .... **83** C2
Hampton Ave
Bromsgrove B60 .... **151** A8
Nuneaton CV10 .... **72** B4
Hampton Cl
Coventry CV6 .... **113** F6
Redditch B98 .... **159** B7
Sutton Coldfield B73 ..... **45** C2
Tamworth B79 .... **21** C7
Hampton Court Rd B17 ... **85** A6
Hampton Ct
Birmingham B15 .... **86** B8
Hampton-in-A B92 ...... **109** B6
Solihull B91 .... **107** D4
Wednesbury B71 .... **42** C1
Wolverhampton WV10 ..... **12** B2
Hampton Dr B74 .... **46** B8
Hampton Gdns DY9 ...... **81** D3
Hampton Gn WS11 .... **4** E7
Hampton Grange CV7 .... **92** B1
Hampton Gr
Royal Leamington Spa CV32 .... **157** B1
Walsall WS3 .... **15** A4
Hampton-in-Arden Sta B92 .... **109** B7
Hampton La
Catherine de B B91 ..... **108** B5
Meriden CV7 .... **109** E8
Hampton Pl WS10 .... **41** C8
Hampton Rd
Birmingham,Aston B6 ..... **66** D8
Birmingham,Stockland Green B23 .... **56** D4
Coventry CV6 .... **113** F6
Knowle B93 .... **128** C8
Warwick CV34 .... **160** B5
Wolverhampton WV10 ..... **11** B1
Hampton St
Birmingham B19 .... **164** B4
Cannock WS11 .... **4** D7
Dudley,Netherton DY2 ..... **62** C5
Dudley WV14 .... **51** B8
Warwick CV34 .... **160** D6
Hampton View WV10 ..... **25** F3
Hampton Wlk WV1 ...... **163** B3
Hams La B76 .... **59** F6
Hams Rd B8 .... **67** D4
Hamstead Cl WV11 ...... **26** D6
Hamstead Ct B19 .... **66** B7
Hamstead Hall Ave B20 .. **54** E5
Hamstead Hall Rd B20 ... **54** F4
Hamstead Hall Sch B20 .. **54** E6
Hamstead Hill B20 .... **54** F4
Hamstead Ho B43 .... **54** F7
Hamstead Jun & Inf Sch B43 .... **54** D7
Hamstead Rd
Birmingham,Hamstead B43 .... **54** D7
Birmingham,Lozells B19,B20 **66** B7
Hamstead Sta B42 .... **54** F6
Hamstead Terr WS10 ..... **42** A2
Hanam Cl B75 .... **46** F6
Hanbury Cl
Bromsgrove B60 .... **151** A8
Halesowen B63 .... **82** F2
Hanbury Cres WV4 .... **38** E6
Hanbury Croft B27 .... **88** E3
Hanbury Ct DY8 .... **81** A4
Hanbury Hill DY8 .... **81** A4
Hanbury Ho B97 .... **153** B4
Hanbury Rd
Bedworth CV12 .... **78** C4
Brownhills WS8 .... **6** F2
Dorridge B93 .... **127** F4
Norton Canes WS11 .... **5** F5
Stoke Heath B60 .... **150** D4
Tamworth B77 .... **21** F4
West Bromwich B70 ...... **53** A3
Hanbury's Farm Com Prim Sch B77 .... **21** D1
Hanch Pl WS1 .... **42** F8
Hancock Gn CV4 .... **131** F8
Hancock Rd B8 .... **67** F4
Hancox St B68 .... **64** B2
Handcross Gr CV3 ...... **133** A5
Handel Ct WS11 .... **2** C2
Handel Wlk WS13 .... **3** C2
Handley Gr
Birmingham B31 .... **102** C2
Warwick CV34 .... **155** D1
Handley's Cl CV8 .... **135** A1

Handley St WS10 42 A4
Handsworth, Booth Street Sta B21 65 C7
Handsworth Cl B21 65 D7
Handsworth Coll B6 66 E8
Handsworth Cres CV5 111 E4
Handsworth Dr B43 44 A3
Handsworth Gram Sch B21 65 F8
Handsworth New Rd B18 65 E6
Handsworth Wood Girls' Sch B20 54 F2
Handsworth Wood Rd B20 55 A2
Hanford Cl CV6 113 E6
Hanford Close Ind Est CV6 113 E6
Hanger Rd B26 90 A3
Hanging La B31 102 E2
Hangleton Dr B11 87 D6
Hangman's La LE10 71 E3
Hanley Cl B63 82 E4
Hanley Ct B23 56 C2
Hanley St B19 164 C4
Hanley Villas 1 B12 87 B5
Hanlith B77 36 A8
Hannaford Way WS11 1 F2
Hannafore Rd B16 65 D3
Hannah Rd WV14 41 A3
Hanney Hay Rd WS7,WS8 7 B3
Hannon Rd B14 104 E5
Hanover Cl B6 66 E7
Hanover Ct
Hinckley LE10 75 E6
Redditch B97 158 D8
Tamworth B79 20 E7
Walsall WS2 27 E1
Wolverhampton WV6 24 C4
Hanover Dr B24 67 F8
Hanover Gdns 8 CV32 157 A1
Hanover Glebe CV11 73 C2
Hanover Ho 6 DY8 80 F8
Hanover Pl
Bromsgrove B60 136 F1
Cannock WS11 1 E2
Hanover Rd B65 63 C4
Hanover St B61 136 F1
Hans Cl CV2 113 F4
Hansell Dr B93 127 E2
Hansom Ct 2 LE10 75 D8
Hansom Rd
Birmingham B32 84 C5
Hinckley LE10 71 F2
Hanson Gr B92 88 F5
Hanson Man B74 32 A1
Hanson's Bridge Rd B24 57 F5
Hanson Way CV6 96 A4
Hanwell Cl B76 58 B7
Hanwood Cl
Birmingham B12 86 F8
Coventry CV5 111 D4
Hanwood Ho 1 B12 86 F8
Hanworth Cl CV32 157 C2
Hanworth Rd CV34 160 D8
Harald Cl WV6 23 E5
Harbeck Ave B44 55 F8
Harberrow Cl DY9 99 A6
Harbet Dr B40 90 E4
Harbinger Rd B38 104 B2
Harborne Ct B17 85 C4
Harborne Hill Sch B15 85 E6
Harborne Ho B17 85 A4
Harborne La B17 85 D3
Harborne Park Rd B17 85 C4
Harborne Prim Sch B17 85 C6
Harborne Rd
Birmingham,Chad Valley B15 85 E7
Birmingham,Warley Woods B68 84 E8
Harborough Cotts B94 144 D3
Harborough Ct B74 32 A2
Harborough Dr
Aldridge WS9 30 B5
Birmingham B36 58 D1
Harborough Rd CV6 95 B2
Harborough Wlk DY9 81 B2
Harbourne Cl CV8 148 A5
Harbours Cl B61 150 D7
Harbours Hill DY9 120 E6
Harbury Cl
Redditch B98 154 D1
Sutton Coldfield B76 58 B6
Harbury La CV33,CV34 161 E2
Harbury Rd B12 86 D5
Harby Cl B37 90 B8
Harcourt CV3 134 E5
Harcourt Dr
Dudley DY3 50 D2
Sutton Coldfield B74 31 F4
Harcourt Gdns CV11 73 C3
Harcourt Ho B79 21 A4
Harcourt Rd
Birmingham B23 56 E6
Cradley Heath B64 82 F8
Wednesbury WS10 41 F4
Harden Cl WS3 28 E7
Harden Ct B31 102 E1
Harden Gr WS3 28 E7
Harden Keep B66 65 A4
Harden Manor Ct B63 83 C3
Harden Prim Sch WS3 28 E7
Harden Rd WS3 28 E7
Harden Vale B63 82 E5
Hardie Ct 2 WV4 39 F4
Hardie Gn WS11 1 F3
Harding St WV14 40 D2
Hardon Rd WV4 39 F5
Hardware St B70 53 D4
Hardwick Cl CV5 112 A4
Hardwick Ct
Stourbridge DY9 81 D5
Sutton Coldfield B74 30 F2
Tamworth B79 21 C5
Hardwick Dr B62 83 A7
Hardwicke Way DY9 81 D5
Hardwick La B80 159 F4
Hardwick Rd
Solihull B92 88 E4
Sutton Coldfield B74 31 A2
Hardwike Wlk B14 104 D2
Hardwyn Cl CV3 115 A1
Hardy Ave DY10 117 A6
Hardy Cl
Hinckley LE10 71 D4
Nuneaton CV10 72 A4
Hardy Ct 4 B13 86 F4
Hardy Rd
Coventry CV6 113 A8
Walsall WS3 28 E8
Wednesbury WS10 42 A3
Hardy Sq WV2 39 F6
Harebell Cl
Cannock WS12 2 D2
Featherstone WV10 12 A7
Walsall WS5 43 A3
Harebell Cres DY1 51 A4
Harebell Gdns B38 123 F8
Harebell B77 22 A4
Harebell Wlk 1 B37 70 D2
Harefield Ho CV2 114 B3
Harefield La CV12 77 F8
Harefield Rd
Coventry CV2 114 B3
Nuneaton CV11 73 C4
Hare Gr B31 102 D3
Hare & Hounds La CV10 73 A2
Haresfield Cl B97 153 D3
Haresfield B90 126 A5
Hare St WV14 40 F5
Harewell Dr B75 32 C1
Harewood 6 B17 85 B6
Harewood Ave
Birmingham B43 43 C2
Wednesbury WS10 42 C3
Harewood Cl B28 105 E5
Harewood Rd CV5 112 C2
Harford St B18,B19 164 A5
Hargate La B71 53 D4
Hargate Prim Sch B71 53 C4
Harger Ct CV8 147 F4
Harger Mews CV8 147 F4
Hargrave Cl
Coventry CV3 115 A1
Water Orton B46 59 B3
Hargrave Rd B90 105 D1
Hargreave Cl B76 57 F8
Hargreaves Ct DY11 116 C3
Hargreaves St WV1 40 A7
Harington Rd CV6 113 A5
Harland Cl B61 136 D3
Harland Rd B74 32 A3
Harlech Cl
Birmingham B32 102 A7
Kenilworth CV8 148 C5
Oldbury B69 52 A1
Harlech Ho 2 WS3 28 C6
Harlech Rd WV12 27 C6
Harlech Twr B23 57 A6
Harlech Way
Dudley DY1 50 F2
Kidderminster DY10 116 E2
Harlequin Dr B13 86 E2
Harlestones Ho DY8 80 F7
Harleston Rd B44 55 F8
Harley Cl WS8 16 A6
Harley Dr WV14 40 B4
Harley Grange 6 DY2 62 E8
Harley St CV2 114 A3
Harlow Gr B28 106 A6
Harlow Wlk 8 CV2 115 A7
Harlstones Cl DY8 81 A8
Harlyn Cl WV14 41 A2
Harman Dr WS13 8 F6
Harman Rd B72 57 B6
Harmar Cl CV34 155 D1
Harmer Cl CV2 115 A7
Harmer St B18 66 A5
Harmon Rd DY8 80 C5
Harmony Ct CV10 73 B2
Harmony Ho 3 B12 67 C1
Harnall Cl B90 126 E7
Harnall Ind Est CV1 165 C4
Harnall La CV1 165 C4
Harnall La E CV1 113 E4
Harnall La W CV1 165 C4
Harnall Row
Coventry CV1 113 E2
Coventry CV1 113 E3
Harness Cl WS5 42 F4
Harold Evers Way DY10 116 F7
Harold Rd
Birmingham B16 65 F1
Coventry CV2 114 D2
Smethwick B67 64 E3
Harold St CV11 73 C3
Harpenden Dr CV5 112 A5
Harper Ave WV11 26 C7
Harper Bell Sch The B12 87 A8
Harper Rd
Bilston WV14 40 D6
Coventry CV1 113 E2
Harpers Rd
Birmingham,Highter's Heath B14 105 A1
Harpers Rd *continued*
Birmingham,Northfield B31 103 A2
Harper St WV13 27 A2
Harport Rd B98 154 A1
Harpur Cl WS4 29 A4
Harpur Rd WS4 29 A4
Harrier Rd B27 88 D2
Harriers Gn DY10 117 B8
Harriers Ind Est DY10 116 F5
Harriet Cl DY5 61 B5
Harringay Dr DY8 80 E3
Harringay Rd B44 45 A2
Harrington Croft B71 53 F7
Harrington Ct CV3 114 F2
Harrington Way CV10 78 A7
Harrington Wlk WS13 8 F8
Harringworth Ct WS4 29 C8
Harriott Dr CV34 161 D4
Harris Bsns Pk B60 150 E2
Harris Cl B98 158 F8
Harris Ct B18 66 A6
Harris Dr
2 Birmingham B42 55 A8
Smethwick B66 65 B3
Harrison Cl
Cheslyn Hay WS6 4 D1
Walsall WS3 14 C1
Harrison Cres CV12 78 A2
Harrison Ct DY8 61 A1
Harrison Ho B14 104 F3
Harrison Rd
Birmingham B24 56 F4
Cannock WS11 4 E7
Redditch B97 158 C8
Stourbridge DY8 61 A1
Sutton Coldfield B74 31 E5
Walsall WS4 15 C2
Harrison's Fold DY2 62 C5
Harrisons Gn B15 85 E6
Harrisons Pleck B13 86 F3
Harrison's Rd B15 85 E6
Harrison St WS3 14 C1
Harrison Way CV31 161 F5
Harris Rd
Coventry CV3 114 B2
Warwick CV34 160 C8
Harrold Ave B65 63 E3
Harrold Rd B65 63 E3
Harrold St DY4 52 C7
Harrold Terr B19 66 C8
Harrop Way DY8 80 E8
Harrowbrook Ind Est LE10 74 E7
Harrowbrook Rd LE10 74 E7
Harrowby Ct WV10 11 B3
Harrowby Dr DY4 52 A4
Harrowby Pl WV13 27 D1
Harrowby Rd
Darlaston WV14 41 A4
Wolverhampton WV10 11 C2
Harrow Cl
Coventry CV6 96 A4
Stoke Heath B60 150 E6
West Hagley DY9 99 A6
Harrow Ct 5 B74 31 F2
Harrowfield Rd B33 68 E4
Harrow Rd
Birmingham B29 85 F3
Kingswinford DY6 49 D1
Whitnash CV31 162 B3
Harrow St WV1 25 B4
Harry Caplan Ho CV5 112 B6
Harry Edwards Ho 2 CV2 114 D8
Harry Perks St WV13 27 A3
Harry Price Ho 9 B69 63 D5
Harry Rose Rd CV2 114 E3
Harry Salt Ho CV1 165 D3
Harry Stanley Ho CV6 114 A8
Harry Taylor Fst Sch The B97 158 E6
Harry Taylor Ho B98 154 A4
Harry Truslove Cl CV6 113 A7
Harry Weston Rd CV3 115 A1
Hart Dr B73 57 A8
Hartfield Cres B27 88 B2
Hartfields Way B65 62 F5
Hartford Cl B17 85 A7
Hartford Rd B60 137 B1
Hartill Rd WV4 38 D3
Hartill St WV13 41 B8
Hartington Cl B93 127 E3
Hartington Cres CV5 112 F1
Hartington Gn LE10 75 E6
Hartington Rd B19 66 D7
Hartland Ave
Coventry CV2 114 B5
Dudley WV14 51 A8
Hartland Rd
Birmingham B31 122 E6
Tipton DY4 51 D5
West Bromwich B71 53 F8
Hartland St DY5 61 D7
Hartlebury Cl
Cannock WS11 2 C2
Dorridge B93 127 F3
Redditch B98 154 E7
Hartlebury Rd
Halesowen B63 82 F2
Oldbury B69 63 D5
Hartledon Rd B17 85 B5
Hartle La DY9 119 F6
Hartlepool Rd CV1 165 D4
Hartleyburn B77 36 A8
Hartley Dr WS9 30 B4
Hartley Gr B44 45 B3
Hartley Pl B15 85 F8
Hartley Rd B44 45 B3
Hartley St WV3 25 A2
Harton Way B14 104 C5
Hartopp Rd
Birmingham B8 67 E4
Sutton Coldfield B74 45 F8
Hart Rd
Birmingham B24 57 A5
Willenhall WV11 26 D4
Hartridge Wlk CV5 112 B4
Hartsbourne Dr B62 83 D4
Harts Cl B17 85 D6
Harts Green Rd B17 85 A5
Hartshill Cl B34 69 A6
Hartshill Ho B27 88 E2
Hartshill Rd
Birmingham B34 69 A6
Solihull B27 88 D2
Hartshill Sch CV10 72 B8
Hartshorn St WV14 40 D5
Hartside Cl B63 82 D2
Hartslade WS14 9 E6
Harts Rd B8 67 E5
Hart St WS1 42 E8
Hartswell Dr B13 104 F6
Hartwell Cl B91 107 B1
Hartwell La WS6 5 A3
Hartwell Rd B24 57 B2
Hartwood Cres WV3 38 F5
Harvard Cl DY1 50 F4
Harvard Rd B92 89 B4
Harvest Cl
Birmingham B30 104 B6
Dudley DY3 50 E5
Stoke Heath B60 150 E6
Harvesters Cl
Coventry CV3 115 A2
Sutton Coldfield WS9 30 E2
Harvesters Rd WV12 27 D5
Harvesters Way WV12 27 D5
Harvesters Wlk WV8 10 E1
Harvester Way DY6 60 A8
Harvest Fields Way
Sutton Coldfield B75 32 D4
Sutton Coldfield B75 32 E3
Harvest Gdns B68 64 A4
Harvest Hill Cl 7 CV31 162 C6
Harvest Hill Cotts CV5 93 D1
Harvest Hill La CV5,CV7 93 C4
Harvest Hill Pk CV5 93 D1
Harvest Rd
Rowley Regis B65 63 A3
Smethwick B67 64 D3
Harvest Wlk B65 63 A3
Harvey Cl CV5 112 A7
Harvey Ct B33 69 D3
Harvey Dr B75 32 C2
Harvey Mews B30 103 D7
Harvey Rd
Birmingham B26 88 D7
Walsall WS2 28 B5
Harveys Terr DY2 62 D4
Harvey Works Ind Est B63 82 F6
Harvills Hawthorn Prim Sch B70 52 F7
Harvills Hawthorn B70 52 F7
Harvine Wlk DY8 80 E3
Harvington Cl
Kidderminster DY11 116 A8
Redditch B97 153 B5
Harvington Dr B90 127 B6
Harvington Hall* DY10 118 B1
Harvington Hall La DY10 118 B1
Harvington Rd
Birmingham,Brandhall B68 84 A8
Birmingham,Weoley Castle B29 103 A8
Bromsgrove B60 151 A8
Dudley WV14 40 B1
Halesowen B63 82 F2
Harvington Way B76 58 A8
Harvington Wlk 5 B65 63 C3
Harwell Cl B79 21 C7
Harwin Cl WV6 24 F7
Harwood Dr
Hinckley LE10 71 F4
Tamworth B77 35 D4
Harwood Gr 1 B90 126 C8
Harwood Rd WS13 3 B3
Harwood St B70 53 B3
Hasbury CE Prim Sch B63 82 F2
Hasbury Cl B63 82 E2
Hasbury Rd B32 102 B8
Haselbech Rd CV3 114 F1
Haselbury Cnr CV10 72 F1
Haseley Cl
Redditch B98 154 E1
Whitnash CV31 162 B5
Haseley Rd
Birmingham B21 65 E7
Coventry CV2 96 C1
Solihull B91 106 E6
Haselor Rd B73 45 E1
Haselour Rd B37 69 F5
Haselwell Dr B30 104 D3
Hasilwood Sq CV3 114 B2
Haskell St WS1 42 F7
Haslucks Croft B90 106 A3
Haslucks Green Rd
Solihull,Major's Green B90 125 E7
Solihull,Shirley B90 106 B4
Haslucks Green Sch B90 106 A3
Hassop Rd B42 55 D7
Hastang Fields CV31 162 C5
Hastings Cl B77 35 F6
Hastings Ct DY1 50 E2
Hastings High Sch LE10 75 F7
Hastings Rd
Birmingham B23 56 B7
Bromsgrove B60 150 E7
Coventry CV2 114 A4
Hastingwood Ind Pk B24 57 B1
Haswell Rd B63 82 D4
Hatcham Rd B44 45 C2
Hatchford Ave B92 89 C3
Hatchford Brook Inf Sch B92 89 C3
Hatchford Brook Jun Sch B92 89 C3
Hatchford Brook Rd B92 89 C3
Hatchford Com Prim Sch B37 69 F2
Hatchford Ct B92 89 C3
Hatchford Wlk B37 70 B1
Hateley Dr WV4 39 E4
Hateley Heath Prim Sch B71 53 B7
Hatfield Cl
Birmingham B23 56 D8
Redditch B98 154 E1
Hatfield Rd
Birmingham B19 66 D8
Stourbridge DY9 81 C4
Hathaway Cl
Balsall Common CV7 130 B7
Willenhall WV13 40 F8
Hathaway Dr
Nuneaton CV11 74 A1
Warwick CV34 155 E2
Hathaway Mews DY8 60 C3
Hathaway Rd
Coventry CV4 111 D1
Solihull B90 106 B1
Sutton Coldfield B74 32 A4
Hatherden Dr B76 47 A2
Hatherell Rd CV31 162 E5
Hathersage Rd B42 55 D7
Hatherton Croft WS11 1 C1
Hatherton Gdns WV10 11 E2
Hatherton Gr B29 84 F1
Hatherton Pl WS9 30 A7
Hatherton Prim Sch WS2 28 A6
Hatherton Rd
Bilston WV14 40 F6
Cannock WS11 1 C1
Walsall WS1 28 E2
Hatherton St
Cheslyn Hay WS6 4 C2
Walsall WS1,WS4 28 E3
Hatters Ct CV12 78 D2
Hattersley Gr B11 88 A3
Hatton Cres WV10 26 A7
Hatton Gdns B42 55 B7
Hatton Rd
Cannock WS11 1 A1
Wolverhampton WV6 24 F3
Hattons Gr WV8 10 B2
Hatton St WV14 40 E4
Haughton Rd B20 55 D1
Haunch La B13 105 A5
Haunchwood Dr B76 57 F7
Haunchwood Rd CV10 72 D4
Havacre La WV14 40 C1
Havefield Ave WS14 9 E7
Havelock Cl WV3 38 F8
Havelock Rd
Birmingham,Handsworth B20 55 C1
Birmingham,Saltley B8 67 D5
Birmingham,Sparkhill B11 87 E4
Haven Croft B43 54 D8
Havendale Cl CV6 113 B5
Haven Dr B27 88 B3
Haven The
Barnt Green B45 138 A8
Birmingham B14 105 D4
Stourbridge DY8 60 D2
Wolverhampton WV2 163 B1
Haverford Dr B45 122 B6
Havergal Wlk B63 82 B4
Haverhill Cl WS3 14 A3
Hawbridge Cl B90 127 B6
Hawbush Gdns DY5 61 A1
Hawbush Prim Sch DY5 61 B2
Hawbush Rd
Brierley Hill DY5 61 A2
Walsall WS3 28 E6
Hawcroft Gr B34 69 C6
Hawes Cl WS1 42 F6
Hawes La B65 63 B3
Hawes Rd WS1 42 F6
Haweswater Dr DY6 60 D6
Hawfield Cl B69 63 C7
Hawfield Gr B72 57 C7
Hawfield Rd B69 63 C7
Hawfinch Rise DY10 117 A2
Hawfinch B77 36 A6
Hawford Ave DY10 117 B6
Hawk Cl CV11 79 B8
Hawker Dr B35 57 F2
Hawkesbury Fields Sch CV2 96 C3
Hawkesbury La CV2 96 D5
Hawkesbury Rd B90 105 F1
Hawkes Cl B30 104 A7
Hawkes Dr CV34 161 D4
Hawkesford Cl
Birmingham B36 69 A8
Sutton Coldfield B74 32 B1
Hawkesford Rd B33 69 D3
Hawkes La B70 53 A7

Hawkesley CE & Methodist Prim Sch B38 123 E7
Hawkesley Cres B31 103 A1
Hawkesley Dr B31 122 F8
Hawkesley End B38 123 E7
Hawkesley Mill La B31 102 F2
Hawkesley Rd DY1 61 F8
Hawkesley Sq B38 123 E7
Hawkes Mill La CV5 94 B2
Hawkesmoor Dr WS14 9 D8
Hawkes St B10 87 D8
Hawkestone Cres B70 53 A6
Hawkestone Rd B29 103 A7
Hawkesville Dr 7 WS11 1 F2
Hawkeswell Cl B92 106 E8
Hawkeswell Dr 4 DY6 60 D8
Hawkesworth Dr CV8 148 A6
Hawkesyard Rd B24 56 E1
Hawkhurst Rd B14 104 F2
Hawkinge Dr B35 58 A4
Hawkins Cl
Birmingham B5 86 E6
Hinckley LE10 71 D4
Lichfield WS13 3 B2
Hawkins Croft DY4 52 A3
Hawkins Dr WS11 4 C4
Hawkin's Pl WV14 40 F3
Hawkins Rd CV5 113 A2
Hawkins St B70 53 A8
Hawkley Cl WV1 26 B2
Hawkley Rd WV1 26 B2
Hawkmoor Gdns B38 124 A8
Hawksbury Cl B98 154 D5
Hawks Cl WS6 4 D2
Hawksford Cres WV10 25 E7
Hawks Green La WS11 2 A1
Hawkshead Dr B93 127 F6
Hawkside B77 36 B8
Hawksmill Ind Est B9 67 C1
Hawksmoor Dr WV6 23 D3
Hawkstone Cl DY11 116 D8
Hawkstone Ct WV6 23 D5
Hawkswell Ave WV5 49 A5
Hawkswell Dr WV13 40 F8
Hawkswood Dr
Balsall Common CV7 130 B7
Darlaston WS10 41 B3
Hawkswood Gr B14 105 B3
Hawksworth Cres B37 70 D3
Hawksworth Dr 1 CV1 113 B3
Hawksworth B77 21 F2
Hawkyard Ct WS11 2 A4
Hawley Cl WS4 28 F4
Hawley Ct B43 43 E1
Hawley Rd LE10 75 D7
Hawnby Gr B76 47 A2
Hawne Cl B63 82 E6
Hawne La B63 82 F6
Hawnelands The B63 82 F5
Hawskford Cres WV10 25 D7
Hawthorn Ave WS6 5 A1
Hawthorn Brook Way B23 56 E8
Hawthorn Cl
Birmingham,Erdington B23 56 F7
Birmingham,Spring Vale B9 67 B1
Lichfield WS14 9 D8
Hawthorn Coppice DY9 99 A6
Hawthorn Cres LE10 75 E4
Hawthorn Croft B68 84 D7
Hawthorn Ct CV4 111 E1
Hawthornden Ct B76 57 D7
Hawthorn Dr
Balsall Common CV7 130 B8
Birmingham B29 85 C1
Hawthorne Ave B79 21 B8
Hawthorne Cres WS7 7 A6
Hawthorne Croft B30 103 D5
Hawthorne Dr B47 125 B6
Hawthorne Gr DY3 50 D2
Hawthorne Ho WV10 25 F3
Hawthorne Rd
Birmingham B15 85 E7
Birmingham,Castle Bromwich B36 69 F7
Birmingham,King's Norton B30 103 D5
Cannock WS12 2 F3
Cheslyn Hay WS6 4 E4
Dudley DY1 51 C4
Essington WV11 13 A3
Halesowen B63 82 E2
Huntington WS12 1 D8
Wednesfield WV11 27 A5
Willenhall WV12 27 D7
Wolverhampton WV2 39 D6
Hawthorne Terr CV10 72 F5
Hawthorn Gr
9 Birmingham B19 66 C8
Kidderminster DY11 116 A6
Hawthorn La CV4 111 E1
Hawthorn Park Dr 1 B20 54 F3
Hawthorn Pk B20 54 E3
Hawthorn Pl WS2 27 E3
Hawthorn Prim Sch B44 56 A7
Hawthorn Rd
Bilston WV1 40 B8
Birmingham B44 56 A7
Brierley Hill DY5 81 E8
Bromsgrove B61 137 B4
Redditch B97 153 A4
Royal Leamington Spa CV31 161 F6
Sutton Coldfield,Streetly B74 31 A1
Hawthorn Rd *continued*
Sutton Coldfield,Wylde Green B72 46 C1
Tipton DY4 52 B8
Walsall,Bescot WS5 42 F5
Walsall,Shelfield WS4 29 B8
Walsall WS4 15 B1
Wednesbury WS10 41 F4
Hawthorns Sta The B71 65 A8
Hawthorns The
1 Kidderminster DY10 117 A5
Birmingham,Showell Green B13 86 F3
Birmingham,Warley Woods B68 84 D7
Hawthorns The (West Bromwich Albion FC) B21 54 B1
Hawthorns The
West Hagley DY9 98 F4
Wolverhampton WV11 26 B6
Hawthorn Terr WS10 41 F4
Hawthorn Way CV10 72 A8
Haxby Ave B34 69 A6
Haybarn The B76 58 A8
Haybridge Ave DY8 98 F5
Haybridge High Sch & Sixth Form DY8 98 F6
Hay Brook Dr B11 87 F4
Hay Cl DY11 116 C7
Haycock Pl WS10 41 C8
Haycroft Ave B8 67 E5
Haycroft Dr B74 32 A4
Haydn Sanders Sq 7 WS1 42 E8
Haydock Cl
Birmingham B36 68 C8
Coventry CV6 96 B4
Tamworth B77 35 D4
Wolverhampton WV6 25 B5
Haydock Rd B61 121 B1
Haydon Cl B93 127 F2
Haydon Croft B33 69 A3
Haydon Way B49 159 F1
Haye House Gr B36 68 E7
Hayes Cres B68 64 D5
Hayes Croft B38 123 F7
Hayes Dr B24 57 D5
Hayes Green Rd CV12 95 F8
Hayes Gr B24 57 D6
Hayes La
Bedworth CV7 96 A8
Stourbridge DY9 82 A6
Hayes Mdw B72 57 D7
Hayes Rd
Hartshill CV10 72 A8
Oldbury B68 64 D5
Hayes St B70 53 A4
Hayes The
Birmingham B31 123 C7
Leek Wootton CV35 155 F5
Stourbridge DY9 82 A5
Willenhall WV12 27 B6
Hayes Trad Est DY9 82 A6
Hayes View Dr WS6 4 E4
Hayes Way WS12 2 C1
Hayfield Ct B13 87 B2
Hayfield Gdns B13 87 C2
Hayfield Rd B13 87 B2
Hayford Cl B98 154 A5
Hay Gn DY9 81 D5
Hay Gr WS8 15 F8
Hay Green Cl B30 103 D6
Hay Green La B30 103 D6
Hay Hall Rd B11 87 F5
Hayhead Wood Nature Reserve* WS4 29 E2
Hay Hill WS5 43 E8
Hay La CV1 165 C2
Hayland Rd B23 56 E6
Hay La B90 127 A6
Hayle Ave CV34 155 F1
Hayle Cl
Birmingham B38 104 B2
Nuneaton CV11 74 A5
Hayle B77 21 D2
Hayley Ct
Kingswinford DY6 60 D6
Sutton Coldfield B24 57 C6
Hayley Green Rd B32 102 B8
Hayley Park Rd B63 100 C8
Hayling Cl B45 101 F1
Hayling Ct WS4 15 D1
Hayling Gr WV2 39 B6
Hayloft Cl B60 150 E6
Haylofts The B63 82 C1
Haymaker Way WS12 2 F4
Haymarket The WV8 10 E1
Haymoor WS14 9 E7
Haynes Cl B61 137 B8
Haynes Ho B97 153 D2
Haynes La WS5 43 B4
Haynestone Rd CV6 112 E6
Haypits Cl B71 53 E7
Hay Pk B5 86 D6
Hay Rd B25 88 A7
Hayrick Dr DY6 60 B7
Hayseech B64 83 A7
Hayseech Rd B63 82 F6
Hays Kent's Moat The B26 69 A1
Hays La LE10 75 B7
Hayton Gn CV4 131 F8
Haytor Ave B14 104 D5
Haytor Rise CV2 114 C7
Haywain Cl WV9 10 F2
Hayward Rd B75 46 C7
Haywards Cl
Birmingham B23 56 E5
Walsall WS3 14 F3
Hayward's Gn CV6 113 A7
Hayward St WV14 51 B8
Haywharf Rd DY5 61 B5
Haywood Dr
Halesowen B62 83 C8
Wolverhampton WV6 24 D4
Hay Wood La B93,CV35 145 A3
Haywood Rd B33 69 E2
Haywood's Farm B71 42 F2
Hayworth Cl B79 20 F8
Hayworth Rd WS13 3 C2
Hazel Ave
Birmingham B73 45 C1
Wednesbury WS10 42 A4
Hazelbank B38 103 E2
Hazelbeach Rd B8 67 F5
Hazelbeech Rd B70 53 B3
Hazel Cl
Hartshill CV10 72 A8
Royal Leamington Spa CV32 157 A2
Hazel Croft
Birmingham,Chelmsley Wood B37 70 B1
Birmingham,Northfield B31 103 A3
Hazeldene Gr 5 B6 66 E8
Hazeldene Rd
Birmingham B33 89 D7
Halesowen B63 82 E2
Hazel Dr B47 125 B5
Hazeley Cl B17 85 A7
Hazelgarth B77 36 B8
Hazel Gdns
Birmingham B27 88 C5
Codsall WV8 10 A4
Hazel Gr
Bedworth CV12 78 D3
Bilston WV14 40 E7
Hockley Heath B94 143 C6
Lichfield WS14 9 C7
Stourbridge DY8 80 C3
West Bromwich B70 53 C1
Wolverhampton WV11 26 C7
Wombourne WV5 49 A7
Hazelhurst Rd
Birmingham,Castle Bromwich B36 69 E7
Birmingham,King's Heath B14 104 E7
Hazel La WS6 5 B2
Hazell Way CV10 73 A1
Hazelmead Ct B73 57 A7
Hazelmere Dr
Burntwood WS7 6 F4
Wolverhampton WV3 24 A1
Hazelmere Rd B28 105 F8
Hazeloak Rd B90 106 A2
Hazel Oak Sch B90 106 A2
Hazel Rd
Birmingham B45 121 F6
Coventry CV6 96 B1
Dudley DY1 51 C2
Kingswinford DY6 60 E5
Nuneaton CV10 72 D5
Redditch B97 153 C5
Wednesbury DY4 41 D1
Wolverhampton WV3 38 E7
Hazelslade Ho WS12 2 F6
Hazels The DY9 98 F5
Hazelton Cl
2 Solihull B91 107 B1
Catshill B61 137 C8
Hazelton Rd B61 121 C1
Hazeltree Croft B27 88 B2
Hazeltree Gr B93 127 E3
Hazelville Gr B28 106 A6
Hazelville Rd B28 106 A7
Hazelwell Cres B30 104 B6
Hazelwell Dr B14 104 D6
Hazelwell Fordrough B30 104 B6
Hazelwell La B30 104 B7
Hazelwell Rd B30 104 A6
Hazelwell St B30 104 A7
Hazelwood Cl
Cheslyn Hay WS6 4 D2
Kidderminster DY11 116 B4
Hazelwood Dr WV11 26 A5
Hazelwood Gr
Cannock WS11 4 C8
Willenhall WV12 27 D5
Hazelwood Rd
Birmingham B27 88 B2
Dudley DY1 50 F5
Sutton Coldfield B74 30 D1
Hazlemere Cl CV5 112 B4
Hazlemere Dr B74 32 B1
Hazlemere Gr WS11 4 B8
Hazlitt Gr B30 103 D4
Headborough Rd CV2 114 A5
Headborough Wlk WS9 16 B1
Headingley Rd B21 54 E2
Headington Ave CV6 95 A2
Headland Dr B8 67 D5
Headland Rd WV3 24 A1
Headlands The
Coventry CV5 112 D4
Sutton Coldfield B74 31 C3
Headless Cross Dr B97 153 D1
Headley Croft B38 123 D8
Headley Ct B97 158 D8
Headley Heath La B38 124 B6
Headley Rise B90 106 D2
Headway Rd WV10 11 C3
Heale Cl B63 82 A7
Healey Ct CV34 160 F7
Healey B77 21 E2
Health Centre Rd CV4 132 C4
Heanor Croft B6 67 B8
Heantun Croft WV10 26 A5
Heantun Ct WV3 25 B1
Heantun Ho WV3 163 B2
Heantun Lodge WV14 40 C6
Heantun Mill Ct WS10 41 D1
Heantun Rise WV3 25 C4
Heantun Row WV11 13 B2
Hearsall Comm CV5 112 F2
Hearsall Com Prim Sch CV5 112 F2
Hearsall Ct CV4 112 D2
Hearsall La CV5 112 F2
Heartland Mews B65 63 B2
Heartlands High Sch B7 67 B4
Heartlands Parkway B7 67 D7
Heartlands Pl B8 67 E4
Heart of England Sch CV7 130 C6
Heart of England Way CV11 73 F3
Heart Of The Country Ctr* WS14 18 E8
Heath Acres WS10 41 C4
Heath Ave CV12 77 E1
Heathbank Dr WS12 1 C6
Heath Bridge Cl WS4 29 A8
Heathbrook Ave DY6 60 B7
Heath Cl
Birmingham B30 103 D5
Bromsgrove B60 150 E6
Heathcliff Rd
Birmingham B11 87 F4
Dudley DY2 62 F7
Heath Cl
Stonnall WS14 16 E5
Sutton Coldfield B75 46 F7
Tipton DY4 52 B5
Heathcote Ave B91 106 E3
Heathcote Cl B77 36 B7
Heathcote Ct CV6 113 A7
Heathcote Dr B78 20 C1
Heathcote Ho B17 85 C5
Heathcote Ind Est CV34 161 D4
Heathcote La
Royal Leamington Spa CV34 161 D4
Warwick CV34 161 A5
Heathcote Rd
Birmingham B30 104 A5
Whitnash CV31 162 A4
Heathcote St CV6 113 A7
Heathcote Way CV34 161 D4
Heathcot Pl WS13 8 F5
Heath Cres CV2 114 A6
Heath Croft B31 123 A7
Heath Croft Rd B75 32 D1
Heath Ct 2 B12 86 F5
Heath Cvn Pk WV10 11 C6
Heath End Rd
Madeley Heath DY9 120 D7
Nuneaton CV10 72 F2
Heather Ave WS5 43 B4
Heather Cl
Birmingham B36 70 A8
Lichfield WS13 3 D1
Nuneaton CV10 72 F3
Walsall WS3 28 A8
Wednesfield WV11 26 E5
Heather Court Gdns B74 46 A8
Heather Croft B44 44 F1
Heather Ct B13 86 D3
Heather Dale B13 86 C2
Heather Dr
Bedworth CV12 77 E2
Birmingham B45 121 F6
Huntington WS12 1 D5
Heather Gr
Solihull B91 107 E6
Willenhall WV12 27 E4
Heather Ho B38 103 F1
Heatherleigh Rd B36 69 F8
Heather Mews WS12 2 A8
Heather Rd
Binley Woods CV3 135 D7
Birmingham,Great Barr B43 54 D8
Birmingham,Small Heath B10 87 F8
Cannock WS12 2 A8
Coventry CV2 96 C2
Dudley DY1 51 C4
Smethwick B67 64 E6
Walsall WS3 28 A8
Heather Valley WS12 2 D6
Heath Farm Rd
Codsall WV8 10 B2
Stourbridge DY8 80 E3
Heathfield Ave B20 66 B8
Heathfield Cl
Cradley Heath B64 62 F2
Dorridge B93 128 A5
Heathfield Cres DY11 116 B4
Heathfield Ct 1 B19 66 B7
Heathfield Dr WS3 14 B2
Heathfield Foundation Technology Coll The B64 62 F2
Heathfield Gdns DY8 80 F4
Heathfield La WS10 41 C6
Heathfield La W WS10 41 B6
Heathfield Prim Sch B19 66 C8
Heathfield Rd
Birmingham,King's Heath B14 104 F8
Heathfield Rd *continued*
Birmingham,Lozells B19 66 C8
Coventry CV5 112 C2
Halesowen B63 82 E3
Redditch B97 153 A1
Sutton Coldfield B74 31 F3
Heathfields WV8 23 E8
Heathfields Inf Sch B77 35 F6
Heathfield Way B64 62 F1
Heath Gap Rd WS11 1 F3
Heath Gdns B91 107 D6
Heath Gn DY1 50 F5
Heath Gr WV8 10 B3
Heathgreen Cl B37 70 D3
Heath Green Gr 4 B18 65 E4
Heath Green Rd B18 65 E4
Heath Green Way CV4 131 F6
Heath Hayes Prim Sch WS12 2 F2
Heath Hill Rd WV6 23 E1
Heath Ho B14 104 F2
Heath House La WV8 23 E8
Heath La DY10 117 C1
Heathland Ave B34 69 A7
Heathland Cl WS12 2 D2
Heathlands Cl DY6 60 E8
Heathlands Cres B73 45 F1
Heathlands Gr B31 103 A1
Heathlands Prim Sch B34 68 F7
Heathlands Rd B73 45 F1
Heathlands The
2 Rowley Regis B65 63 C1
Stourbridge DY8 81 B4
Heath Lane Hospl B71 53 D7
Heath La
Stourbridge DY8 81 A4
West Bromwich B71 53 D7
Heathleigh Rd B38 123 C8
Heathley La B78 34 E5
Heathmere Ave B25 88 D8
Heathmere Dr B37 69 F2
Heath Mill La B9 67 A1
Heath Mount Prim Sch B12 86 F6
Heath Park Bsns & Ent Coll WV11 26 A5
Heath Rd
Bedworth CV12 77 F1
Birmingham B30 103 D5
Coventry CV2 114 A4
Darlaston WS10 41 E8
Dudley DY2 62 C2
Hollywood B47 125 A7
Heath Rd S B31 103 B4
Heath Rd
Solihull B91 107 D6
Willenhall WV12 13 D1
Heath Rise B14 105 A1
Heath St S B18 65 F4
Heathside Dr
Birmingham B38 104 B2
Walsall WS3 15 A4
Heath St
Birmingham B18 65 E4
Cannock WS12 2 B7
Rowley Regis B65 63 C1
Tamworth B79 21 C5
Heath Terr
Beausale CV35 146 C2
Royal Leamington Spa CV32 156 E1
Heath Trad Pk B66 65 D5
Heath View
Cannock WS12 5 E8
Willenhall WS2 27 F3
Heath Way
Birmingham B34 69 B6
Cannock WS11 2 B2
Heathway Cl B34 69 A7
Heathy Farm Cl B32 84 B1
Heathy Rise B32 84 A2
Heaton Cl WV10 11 E5
Heaton Dr
Birmingham B15 85 E8
Sutton Coldfield B73 45 F8
Heaton Rd B91 107 A7
Heaton St B18 66 B5
Hebden Ave CV34 155 F1
Hebden Gr
Birmingham B28 105 E3
Willenhall WV11 13 B1
Hebden B77 36 B8
Hebden Way CV11 74 A2
Heckley Rd CV7 96 A7
Heddle Gr CV6 114 B8
Heddon Pl B7 67 A3
Hedera Cl WS5 43 B3
Hedera Rd B98 154 F6
Hedgefield Gr B63 82 C4
Hedgefield Way CV4 131 F8
Hedgerow Cl WS12 1 F7
Hedgerow Dr DY6 49 D1
Hedgerows The
Lichfield WS14 9 B5
Nuneaton CV10 72 F6
Romsley B62 100 F4
Tamworth B77 35 F8
Hedgerow Wlk
Coventry CV6 95 B4
Wolverhampton WV8 10 E1
Hedges Way B60 137 B1
Hedgetree Croft B37 70 C2
Hedge Way CV10 72 C7
Hedging Lane Ind Est B77 35 E5
Hedging La B77 35 E5
Hedgings The B34 69 B6
Hedgley Gr B33 69 A4
Hedingham Gr B37 70 D2

Hedley Croft B35 . . . . 58 B4
Hednesford Hills Common Nature Reserve★ WS12 . . 2 E5
Hednesford Rd
Brownhills WS8 . . . . 6 C2
Cannock,Blackfords WS11 . . . . 1 F2
Cannock WS12 . . . . 2 E1
Norton Canes WS11 . . . . 5 F6
Hednesford Sta WS12 . . . . . . 2 B5
Hednesford St WS11 . . . . 1 E1
Heeley Rd B29 . . . . 85 F1
Heemstede La CV32 . . . . . . 157 A2
Heera Cl CV6 . . . . 113 D8
Hefford Dr B66 . . . . 65 A6
Helena Cl CV10 . . . . 72 F3
Helena St 2 B1 . . . . 66 C3
Helen Dixon Ct 8 B13 . . . 86 F4
Helenny Cl WV11 . . . . 26 A5
Helen St CV6 . . . . 113 F6
Hele Rd CV3 . . . . 133 D6
Helford Cl DY4 . . . . 51 D4
Heligan Pl WS12 . . . . 2 E2
Hellaby Cl 3 B72 . . . . 46 C4
Hellaby Ct B73 . . . . 57 A7
Hellaby Ho B74 . . . . 31 F3
Hellidon Cl 6 CV32 . . . . . 157 A2
Hellier Ave DY4 . . . . 52 B4
Hellier Rd WV10 . . . . 11 E2
Hellier St DY2 . . . . 62 C8
Helming Dr WV1 . . . . 26 B3
Helmingham B79 . . . . 20 D7
Helmsdale Rd CV32 . . . . . 157 B5
Helmsdale Way DY3 . . . . . . 51 A7
Helmsley Cl DY5 . . . . 81 C8
Helmsley Rd WV11 . . . . 26 C8
Helmswood Dr B37 . . . . . . 90 C8
Helston Cl
Nuneaton CV11 . . . . 74 A5
Stourbridge DY8 . . . . 60 C2
Tamworth B79 . . . . 21 C8
Walsall WS5 . . . . 43 D7
Helstone Gr B11 . . . . 88 A3
Helston Rd WS5 . . . . 43 D7
Hembs Cres B43 . . . . 54 C8
Hemdale Bsns Pk CV11 . . . . 74 A4
Hemdale CV11 . . . . 74 A4
Hemingford Rd CV2 . . . . . 115 A8
Heming Rd B98 . . . . 159 E8
Hemlingford Croft B37 . . . 90 A7
Hemlingford Rd
Birmingham B37 . . . . 69 F6
Sutton Coldfield B76 . . . . . . 58 A6
Hemlock Bsns Ctr WS11 . . . . 2 B2
Hemlock Pk WS11 . . . . 2 B2
Hemlock Way WS11 . . . . 2 B3
Hemmings Cl
Radford Semele CV31 . . . . 162 E5
Stourbridge DY8 . . . . 80 F5
Wolverhampton WV10 . . . . . 25 E3
Hemmings St WS10 . . . . . . 41 C8
Hemming St DY11 . . . . . . 116 C4
Hemmings Yd DY6 . . . . 61 A8
Hemplands Rd DY8 . . . . . . 80 F5
Hempole La DY4 . . . . 52 D6
Hemsby Cl CV4 . . . . 132 A7
Hemsworth Dr CV12 . . . . . 79 B2
Hemyock Rd B29 . . . . 103 B8
Henbury Rd B27 . . . . 88 D3
Henderson Cl
Allesley CV5 . . . . 112 C7
Lichfield WS14 . . . . 9 D7
Henderson Ct 7 B68 . . . . . 84 B8
Henderson Way B65 . . . . . 63 C1
Henderson Wlk DY4 . . . . . . 52 B8
Hendon Cl
Dudley DY3 . . . . 50 D2
Wolverhampton WV10 . . . . . 25 E7
Hendon Rd B11 . . . . 87 B5
Hendre Cl CV5 . . . . 112 D2
Heneage Pl 6 B7 . . . . 67 A4
Heneage St W B7 . . . . 66 F4
Heneage St B7 . . . . 67 A4
Henfield Cl WV11 . . . . 26 D7
Hengham Rd B26 . . . . 69 A1
Hen La CV6 . . . . 95 D3
Henley Cl
Burntwood WS7 . . . . 7 B5
Nuneaton CV11 . . . . 73 F8
Sutton Coldfield B73 . . . . . . 57 B8
Tamworth B79 . . . . 21 C6
Tipton DY4 . . . . 52 D5
Walsall WS3 . . . . 14 E1
Henley Coll CV2 . . . . 114 C8
Henley Cres B91 . . . . 107 B7
Henley Ct
Coventry CV2 . . . . 114 D7
Lichfield WS14 . . . . 9 B6
Henleydale 4 B90 . . . . . . 126 C8
Henley Dr B74 . . . . 32 A3
Henley Mill La CV2 . . . . . . 114 C7
Henley Park Ind Est CV2 114 E7
Henley Rd
Coventry CV2 . . . . 114 D7
Whitnash CV31 . . . . 162 B5
Wolverhampton WV10 . . . . . 11 B1
Henley St B11 . . . . 87 B7
Henley Wlk CV2 . . . . 114 D8
Henlow Cl DY4 . . . . 51 D5
Henlow Rd B14 . . . . 105 A2
Hennalls The B36 . . . . 68 F7
Hennals Ave B97 . . . . 152 F2
Henn Dr DY4 . . . . 40 E1
Henne Dr WV14 . . . . 40 C1
Henn St DY4 . . . . 52 A8
Henrietta St
Birmingham B19 . . . . 164 B4
Coventry CV6 . . . . 113 E5
Henry Boteler Rd CV4 . . . 132 B7
Henry Boys' Almshouses WS1 . . . . 42 D8
Henry Ct DY1 . . . . 51 B1
Henry Lloyd Ind Est WS10 41 C7
Henry Rd B25 . . . . 88 C7
Henry St
Coventry CV1 . . . . 165 B3
Hinckley LE10 . . . . 71 A2
Kenilworth CV8 . . . . 148 A5
Nuneaton CV11 . . . . 73 C2
Walsall WS2 . . . . 28 D1
Henry Tanday Ct 4 CV32 . . . . 156 E1
Henry Wlk B60 . . . . 150 E7
Hensborough B90 . . . . . . 126 A5
Hensel Dr WV3 . . . . 38 C8
Henshaw Gr
6 Birmingham,Small Heath B10 . . . . 87 C8
Birmingham,Yardley B25 . . . 88 C7
Henshaw Rd B10 . . . . 87 D8
Henson Rd CV12 . . . . 77 E1
Henstead St B5 . . . . 86 D8
Hentland Cl B98 . . . . 154 D4
Henwood Cl WV6 . . . . 24 C3
Henwood La B91 . . . . 108 B4
Henwood Rd WV6 . . . . 24 D3
Hepburn Cl WS9 . . . . 30 A4
Hepburn Edge B24 . . . . 57 B4
Hepworth Cl WV6 . . . . 23 F4
Hepworth Rd CV3 . . . . 115 B1
Herald Ave CV5 . . . . 112 D1
Herald Bsns Pk CV3 . . . . . 134 F7
Herald Ct 2 DY1 . . . . 51 C1
Herald Rd B26 . . . . 90 C4
Heralds Ct 6 CV34 . . . . . . 161 B8
Herald Way
Coventry CV3 . . . . 135 A7
Hinckley LE10 . . . . 75 D4
Herbert Art Gall & Mus★ CV1 . . . . 165 C2
Herbert Austin Dr B60 . . 121 E1
Herbert Rd
Aldridge WS9 . . . . 16 A1
Birmingham,Handsworth B21 . . . . 54 F1
Birmingham,Small Heath B10 . . . . 87 C8
Smethwick B67 . . . . 65 A1
Solihull B91 . . . . 107 B4
Herbert's La CV8 . . . . 148 A5
Herberts Park Rd WS10 . . 41 B6
Herbert St
Bilston WV14 . . . . 40 B6
Nuneaton CV10 . . . . 72 E3
Redditch B98 . . . . 153 E4
West Bromwich B70 . . . . 53 D3
Wolverhampton WV1 . . . . . 163 C4
Herbhill Cl WV4 . . . . 39 D4
Hereford Ave 5 B12 . . . . . 87 A6
Hereford Cl
Aldridge WS9 . . . . 30 A8
Barwell LE9 . . . . 71 F6
Birmingham B45 . . . . 102 A2
Kidderminster DY11 . . . . . 116 A5
Nuneaton CV10 . . . . 72 E4
Hereford Ho WV1 . . . . 163 B4
Hereford Pl B71 . . . . 53 B7
Hereford Rd
Birmingham B68 . . . . 84 B7
Bramcote CV11 . . . . 79 F6
Cannock WS12 . . . . 2 B4
Dudley DY2 . . . . 62 E3
Hereford Sq B8 . . . . 67 C5
Hereford St WS2 . . . . 28 E4
Hereford Way B78 . . . . 21 A2
Hereford Wlk B37 . . . . 69 F1
Hereward Coll CV4 . . . . . . 111 F1
Hereward Rise B62 . . . . 83 C5
Herford Way LE10 . . . . 75 F6
Heritage Cl B68 . . . . 64 C4
Heritage Ct
Birmingham B18 . . . . 66 C4
Coventry CV4 . . . . 132 D3
Kenilworth CV8 . . . . 148 B7
Lichfield WS14 . . . . 9 D6
Heritage Dr CV6 . . . . 96 C6
Heritage The 7 WS1 . . . . . 28 E1
Heritage Way
Birmingham B33 . . . . 69 D3
Tipton DY4 . . . . 52 B5
Hermes Cl CV34 . . . . 161 E5
Hermes Cres CV2 . . . . 114 E6
Hermes Ct
Royal Leamington Spa CV34 . . . . 161 E5
Sutton Coldfield B74 . . . . . . 31 F3
Hermes Rd
Birmingham B26 . . . . 90 C4
Lichfield WS13 . . . . 3 D1
Hermione Cl CV34 . . . . . . 161 F3
Hermitage Cl B78 . . . . 22 F1
Hermitage Dr B76 . . . . 47 A4
Hermitage Rd
Birmingham B15 . . . . 85 C8
Birmingham,Gravelly Hill B23 . . . . 56 E3
Coventry CV2 . . . . 114 D4
Solihull B91 . . . . 107 C6
Hermitage The B91 . . . . . 107 C6
Hermitage Way CV8 . . . . . 148 A3
Hermit's Croft CV3 . . . . . 133 D8
Hermit St DY3 . . . . 50 D5
Hernall Croft B26 . . . . 89 A7
Herne Cl B18 . . . . 66 A4
Hernefield Rd B34 . . . . 69 A7
Hernehurst B32 . . . . 84 C6
Hern Rd DY5 . . . . 81 C6
Heronbank CV4 . . . . 111 C2
Heron Cl
Alvechurch B48 . . . . 139 A7
Brownhills WS8 . . . . 15 E7
Cheswick Green B90 . . . . . 126 D4
Heron Ct 3 B73 . . . . 57 B7
Herondale WS12 . . . . 2 B4
Herondale Cres DY8 . . . . . 80 C4
Herondale Rd
Birmingham B26 . . . . 88 F6
Stourbridge DY8 . . . . 80 C4
Heronfield Cl B98 . . . . 154 C5
Heronfield Dr B31 . . . . . . 122 F6
Heronfield Way B91 . . . . . 107 E5
Heron Ho CV3 . . . . 114 B2
Heron Mill WS3 . . . . 14 E3
Heron Rd B68 . . . . 64 A2
Heronry The WV6 . . . . 23 F2
Herons Ct LE10 . . . . 75 A7
Heronsville Ho DY4 . . . . . . 52 B3
Herons Way B29 . . . . 85 C3
Heronswood Dr DY5 . . . . . 61 D1
Heronswood Rd
Birmingham B45 . . . . 122 B6
Kidderminster DY10 . . . . . 117 A2
Heronville Dr B70 . . . . 53 A7
Heronville Rd B70 . . . . 53 A6
Heron Way B45 . . . . 121 F7
Herrick Rd
Birmingham B8 . . . . 67 E5
Coventry CV2 . . . . 114 D3
Herrick St WV3 . . . . 163 A2
Herringshaw Croft B76 . . . 46 E3
Hertford Pl CV1 . . . . 165 A2
Hertford St
Birmingham B12 . . . . 87 A5
Coventry CV1 . . . . 165 B2
Hertford Way B93 . . . . 128 B4
Hervey Gr B24 . . . . 57 D6
Hesket Ave B68 . . . . 64 C1
Hesketh Cres B23 . . . . 56 C5
Hesketh Pl B37 . . . . 89 F8
Hesleden B77 . . . . 36 B8
Heslop Cl CV3 . . . . 134 F8
Hessian Cl WV14 . . . . 40 B2
Hestia Dr B29 . . . . 103 E8
Heston Ave B42 . . . . 55 B8
Hetton Cl 1 CV34 . . . . 155 F1
Hever Ave B44 . . . . 45 A1
Hever Cl DY1 . . . . 50 E3
Hewell Ave B60 . . . . 150 F7
Hewell Cl
Birmingham B31 . . . . 122 F7
Kingswinford DY6 . . . . 49 D1
Redditch B97 . . . . 152 C6
Hewell La
Barnt Green B45 . . . . 138 D8
Redditch B60,B97 . . . . 152 D6
Hewell Rd
Barnt Green B45 . . . . 138 D8
Redditch B97 . . . . 153 D4
Hewitson Gdns B67 . . . . . . 64 F2
Hewitt Ave CV6 . . . . 113 B4
Hewitt Cl WS13 . . . . 3 A2
Hewitt St WS10 . . . . 41 C5
Hewston Croft WS12 . . . . . . 2 D4
Hexby Cl CV2 . . . . 115 A6
Hexham Way DY1 . . . . 50 F2
Hexton Cl B90 . . . . 105 D2
Hexworthy Ave CV3 . . . . . 133 B5
Heybarnes Cir B10 . . . . 87 F7
Heybarnes Rd B10 . . . . 88 A8
Heybrook Cl CV2 . . . . 114 C7
Heycott Gr B38 . . . . 104 C2
Heycroft CV4 . . . . 132 D4
Heydon Rd
Brierley Hill DY5 . . . . 61 B6
Finstall B60 . . . . 137 D1
Heyford Cl CV2 . . . . 96 D3
Heyford Gr B91 . . . . 127 C8
Heyford Way B35 . . . . 58 B5
Heygate Way WS9 . . . . 16 B1
Heyland Cnr B10 . . . . 67 F1
Heynesfield Rd B33 . . . . . . 69 C3
Heythrop Gr B13 . . . . 105 D8
Heyville Croft CV8 . . . . . . 148 C3
Heywood Cl CV6 . . . . 114 A7
Hibberd Ct CV8 . . . . 147 F4
Hickman Ave WV1,WV2 . . . 40 A8
Hickman Gdns B16 . . . . 65 F1
Hickman Rd
Bilston WV14 . . . . 40 C5
Birmingham B11 . . . . 87 B6
Brierley Hill DY5 . . . . 61 C4
Tipton DY4 . . . . 51 F8
Hickman's Ave B64 . . . . . . 62 E2
Hickmans Cl 2 B62 . . . . . . 84 A6
Hickman St DY9 . . . . 81 C6
Hickmerelands La DY3 . . . 39 C1
Hickory Ct WS11 . . . . 2 C2
Hickory Dr B17 . . . . 65 A2
Hicks Cl CV34 . . . . 155 E2
Hidcote Ave B76 . . . . 58 A8
Hidcote Cl
Nuneaton CV11 . . . . 78 F8
Royal Leamington Spa CV31 . . . . 162 C5
Hidcote Gr
Birmingham,Garret's Green B33 . . . . 89 C8
Birmingham,Marston Green B37 . . . . 90 A7
Hidcote Rd CV8 . . . . 148 C6
Hidson Rd B23 . . . . 56 C5
Higgins Ave WV14 . . . . 40 D2
Higgins La B32 . . . . 84 C5
Higgins Wlk B66 . . . . 65 B6
Higgs Field Cres B64 . . . . . 63 B1
Higgs Rd WV11 . . . . 13 A1
Higham Lane Sch CV10 . . . 73 D6
Higham La CV11 . . . . 73 E7
Higham's Cl B65 . . . . 63 B3
Higham Way LE10 . . . . 75 E7
Higham Way Ho LE10 . . . . . 75 E7
Higham Way WV10 . . . . 25 E6
High Arcal Dr DY3 . . . . 50 F7
High Arcal Rd DY3 . . . . 49 F4
High Arcal Sch The DY3 . . . 50 F6
High Ash Cl CV7 . . . . 95 F7
High Ave B64 . . . . 82 F8
High Bank WS11 . . . . 4 E8
High Beech CV5 . . . . 112 A6
High Beeches B43 . . . . 43 D1
Highbridge Rd
Dudley DY2 . . . . 62 B3
Sutton Coldfield B73 . . . . . . 46 A1
High Brink Rd B46 . . . . 70 F7
Highbrook Cl WV9 . . . . 11 A2
High Broome Ct B78 . . . . . 21 A3
High Brow B17 . . . . 85 B7
High Bullen WS10 . . . . 41 F3
Highbury Ave
Birmingham B21 . . . . 65 F8
Rowley Regis B65 . . . . 63 D3
Highbury Cl B65 . . . . 63 D3
Highbury Ct B13 . . . . 104 E7
Highbury Gn CV10 . . . . 72 C7
Highbury Rd
Birmingham B14 . . . . 104 D8
Oldbury B68 . . . . 64 B5
Smethwick B66 . . . . 64 D7
Sutton Coldfield B74 . . . . . . 31 C3
Highclare Sch B23 . . . . 57 A5
Highclare Sch St Paul's B74 . . . . 46 C7
Highclare Woodfield Sch B72 . . . . 46 C1
High Clere B64 . . . . 83 A7
Highcliffe Rd B77 . . . . 35 D8
Highcrest Cl B31 . . . . 123 A7
High Croft WS9 . . . . 16 B2
Highcroft Ave DY8 . . . . 60 C3
High Croft B43 . . . . 43 C1
Highcroft Cl B92 . . . . 89 C2
High Croft Cres WS14 . . . . . 9 C7
Highcroft Cres CV32 . . . . 156 C1
Highcroft Dr B74 . . . . 31 E3
Highcroft Hospl B23 . . . . . 56 D3
Highcroft Rd B23 . . . . 56 E3
Highcroft WS3 . . . . 15 B6
Highdown Cres 3 B90 . . . 127 A6
Highdown Rd CV31 . . . . . . 162 B6
High Elms La B60 . . . . 151 E1
High Ercal Ave DY5 . . . . . . 61 C2
High Farm Rd
Halesowen,Hasbury B63 . . . 82 F3
Halesowen,Hurst Green B62 83 F8
Highfield Ave
Bilston WV14 . . . . 40 E4
Burntwood WS7 . . . . 7 B7
Redditch B97 . . . . 158 D8
Tamworth B77 . . . . 22 A5
Walsall WS4 . . . . 29 C8
Wolverhampton WV10 . . . . . 12 A2
Highfield Cl
Birmingham B28 . . . . 105 D5
Burntwood WS7 . . . . 7 B7
Kenilworth CV8 . . . . 147 E4
Highfield Cres
Halesowen B63 . . . . 82 D6
Rowley Regis B65 . . . . 63 B1
Wolverhampton WV11 . . . . . 26 B6
Highfield Ct
Cannock WS11 . . . . 2 B5
Sutton Coldfield B73 . . . . . . 46 B1
Highfield Dr B73 . . . . 56 F7
Highfield Gdns WS14 . . . . . . 9 E6
Highfield Inf & Jun Sch B8 . . . . 67 E5
Highfield La
1 Halesowen B63 . . . . 83 A3
Birmingham B32 . . . . 84 B4
Clent DY9 . . . . 100 A3
Corley CV7 . . . . 94 D8
Highfield CV7 . . . . 92 C1
Highfield Mews B63 . . . . . . 82 D6
Highfield Pl B14 . . . . 105 D5
Highfield Rd
Birmingham,Edgbaston B15 . . . . 86 A8
Birmingham,Moseley B13 . . 87 B3
Birmingham,Newton B43 . . . 54 C7
Birmingham,Saltley B8 . . . . 67 E5
Birmingham,Yardley Wood B14, B28 . . . . 105 D5
Bromsgrove B61 . . . . 150 E8
Burntwood WS7 . . . . 7 C7
Cannock WS12 . . . . 2 E1
Coventry CV2 . . . . 113 F4
Dudley DY2 . . . . 51 E1
Halesowen B63 . . . . 82 D5
Kidderminster DY10 . . . . . 117 A8
Nuneaton CV11 . . . . 73 E2
Highfield Rd N WS3 . . . . . . 14 F5
Highfield Rd
Redditch B97 . . . . 158 D8
Rowley Regis B65 . . . . 63 B1
Sedgley DY3 . . . . 39 D1
Smethwick B67 . . . . 65 A5
Stourbridge DY8 . . . . 61 A2
Studley B80 . . . . 159 D4
Tipton DY4 . . . . 52 B8
Walsall WS3 . . . . 15 A4
Highfields
Bromsgrove B61 . . . . 136 E1
Burntwood WS7 . . . . 7 B7
Highfields Ct WV4 . . . . 38 D6
Highfields Dr
Dudley WV14 . . . . 40 D3
Wombourne WV5 . . . . 49 A5
Highfields Grange WS6 . . . 4 D1
Highfields Pk WS6 . . . . 4 D1
Highfields Prim Sch
Burntwood WS7 . . . . 7 C7
Cradley Heath B65 . . . . 83 C8
Dudley WV14 . . . . 40 C2
Highfields Rd
Burntwood WS7 . . . . 6 F4
Dudley WV14 . . . . 40 D3
Hinckley LE10 . . . . 71 E1
Highfields Science Specialist Sch WV4 . . . . 38 C5
Highfields The WV6 . . . . . . 24 A3
Highfield Terr
Birmingham B18 . . . . 66 A5
Royal Leamington Spa CV32 . . . . 156 D1
Highfield Way WS9 . . . . . . 16 B2
Highgate Ave
Walsall WS1 . . . . 42 F8
Wolverhampton WV4 . . . . . . 38 D6
Highgate Bsns Ctr B12 . . . 87 B6
Highgate Cl
Birmingham B12 . . . . 86 F7
Kidderminster DY11 . . . . . 116 A4
Walsall WS1 . . . . 42 F7
Highgate Ct 4 WS1 . . . . . . 42 F8
Highgate Dr WS1 . . . . 42 F7
Highgate DY3 . . . . 50 E5
Highgate Ho 1 B5 . . . . 86 E8
Highgate Middleway B12 . 86 F7
Highgate Pl B12 . . . . 87 A7
Highgate Prim Sch DY2 . . 61 F6
Highgate Rd
Birmingham B12 . . . . 87 A6
Dudley DY1,DY2 . . . . 61 F6
Walsall WS1 . . . . 42 F7
Highgate Ret Pk B11 . . . . . 87 A7
Highgate Sq B12 . . . . 86 F7
Highgate Sq Craft Ctr 9 B12 . . . . 86 F7
Highgate St
Birmingham B12 . . . . 86 F7
Cradley Heath B64 . . . . 62 F2
Highgate B74 . . . . 31 A1
High Gn WS11 . . . . 1 D1
High Grange WS11 . . . . 2 A5
High Green Ct WS11 . . . . . . 1 D1
Highgrove Cl
Tamworth B79 . . . . 21 B7
Willenhall WV12 . . . . 27 B7
Highgrove CV4 . . . . 131 F5
Highgrove Pl DY1 . . . . 50 F2
Highgrove WV6 . . . . 24 C3
High Haden Cres B64 . . . . 83 A8
High Haden Rd B64 . . . . . . 83 A8
High Heath Cl B30 . . . . . . 103 D5
High Hill WV11 . . . . 13 A2
High Holborn DY3 . . . . 50 D7
High House Dr B45 . . . . . 121 F3
High House La B60 . . . . . . 152 A6
Highland Ho B62 . . . . 83 C8
Highland Mews WV14 . . . . 40 D1
Highland Rd
Birmingham,Erdington B23 . . . . 56 F5
Birmingham,Great Barr B43 43 E3
High Land Rd WS9 . . . . 16 B3
Highland Rd
Cannock WS12 . . . . 1 C4
Coventry CV5 . . . . 112 F1
Cradley Heath B64 . . . . 62 E2
Dudley DY1 . . . . 51 A3
Kenilworth CV8 . . . . 148 C7
Royal Leamington Spa CV32 . . . . 157 B4
Highland Ridge B62 . . . . . . 83 E5
Highlands Cl
Kidderminster DY11 . . . . . 116 A5
Warwick CV34 . . . . 161 A8
Highlands Ct B90 . . . . 126 E8
Highlands Rd
Solihull B90 . . . . 126 F8
Wolverhampton WV3 . . . . . . 38 D8
Highland Way B98 . . . . . . 159 A7
High Leasowes B63 . . . . . . 83 A4
Highley Cl
Kidderminster DY11 . . . . . 116 B2
Redditch B98 . . . . 154 E4
High Mdws
Bromsgrove B60 . . . . 150 D7
Wolverhampton WV6 . . . . . . 24 C3
Wombourne WV5 . . . . 49 B6
High Meadow Inf Sch B46 70 F8
High Meadow Rd B38 . . . 104 A2
Highmoor Cl
Dudley WV14 . . . . 40 D3
Willenhall WV12 . . . . 27 B7
Highmoor Rd B65 . . . . 63 B3
Highmore Dr B32 . . . . 102 C8
High Mount St WS12 . . . . . . 2 B6
High Oak DY5 . . . . 61 C7
Highover Dr B75 . . . . 32 A4
Highpark Ave DY8 . . . . 80 D5
High Park Cl
Coventry CV5 . . . . 111 F3
Sedgley DY3 . . . . 50 D8
Smethwick B66 . . . . 65 B5
High Park Cnr B7 . . . . 67 B6
High Park Cres DY3 . . . . . . 39 D1
High Park Rd B63 . . . . 82 C5

High Park St B7 .... 67 B6
High Point B15 .... 85 E6
High Rd WV12 .... 27 C5
High Ridge WS9 .... 29 F5
High Ridge Cl
Aldridge WS9 .... 29 E5
Darlaston WS10 .... 41 A4
High St Duchess Par B70 .. 53 D3
High St Princess Par B70 .. 53 D3
High St
1 Halesowen B63 .... 83 B3
7 Dudley,Old Dock DY1 ... 62 B8
Aldridge WS9 .... 30 B6
Astwood Bank B96 ...... 158 E1
Bedworth CV12 .... 78 B2
Belbroughton DY9 ...... 119 E7
Bilston WV14 .... 40 D5
Birmingham,Aston B6,B19 .. 66 E7
Birmingham B4 .... 164 C2
Birmingham,Castle Vale B35 58 B4
Birmingham,Erdington B23 . 56 F4
Birmingham,Harborne B17 . 85 D6
Birmingham,King's Heath B14 .... 104 E8
Birmingham,Quinton B32 ... 84 A6
Birmingham,Saltley B8 .... 67 D5
Brierley Hill,Barrow Hill DY5 .... 61 C7
Brierley Hill,Brockmoor DY5 61 C4
Brierley Hill,Quarry Bank DY5 .... 82 A8
Bromsgrove B61 .... 137 A2
Brownhills,Clayhanger WS8 15 E6
Brownhills,Vigo WS9 ...... 15 F3
Brownhills WS8 .... 15 F8
Burntwood,Chasetown WS7 .. 6 F6
Cheslyn Hay WS6 .... 4 D2
Coleshill B46 .... 70 F7
Coventry CV1 .... 165 C2
Coventry,Keresley CV6 .... 94 F1
Cradley Heath B64 .... 62 D1
Cubbington CV32 .... 157 E5
Darlaston WS10 .... 41 A4
Dudley DY1 .... 51 C1
Hampton-in-A B92 .... 109 A7
Kenilworth CV8 .... 147 E5
Kidderminster DY10 ...... 116 E6
Kingswinford DY6 .... 60 E6
Kingswinford,Wall Heath DY6 .... 60 C8
Knowle B93 .... 128 C6
Norton Canes WS11 ...... 6 B5
Nuneaton CV11 .... 73 B4
High Street Bordesley B12 .... 67 A1
High Street Deritend B12 . 66 F1
High St
Rowley Regis B65 .... 63 C1
Royal Leamington Spa CV31 .... 162 A7
Ryton-on-D CV8 .... 135 B1
Sedgley DY3 .... 50 D8
Smethwick B66 .... 65 A5
Solihull B91 .... 107 C3
Solihull,Shirley B90 ...... 105 D2
Stourbridge,Amblecote DY8 80 F7
Stourbridge DY8 .... 81 A5
Stourbridge,Lye DY9 ...... 81 E5
Stourbridge,Wollaston DY8 . 80 E7
Stourbridge,Wordsley DY8 . 60 E2
Studley B80 .... 159 E4
Sutton Coldfield B72 ...... 46 C5
Tamworth B77 .... 35 C5
Tipton,Princes End DY4 .... 51 F8
Tipton,Tipton Green DY4 ... 51 E5
Walsall,Pelsall WS3 ...... 15 A4
Walsall,Wallington Heath WS3 .... 14 B1
Walsall WS1 .... 28 E1
Warwick CV34 .... 160 E6
Wednesfield WV11 ...... 26 D5
West Bromwich B70 ...... 53 C3
Wolverhampton WV6 ...... 24 D4
Wombourne WV5 .... 49 B7
Highters Cl B14 .... 105 B2
Highter's Heath La B14 .. 105 A2
Highters Heath Prim Sch B14 .... 105 B3
Highters Rd B14 .... 105 A3
High Timbers B45 .... 101 F1
Hightown B63 .... 82 C6
Hightree Cl B32 .... 84 B1
High Trees B20 .... 54 F3
High Trees Cl B98 .... 158 E7
High Trees Ho B69 .... 63 F3
High Trees Rd B93 ...... 128 A7
Highview 9 WS1 .... 42 F8
High View Dr CV7 .... 95 C7
Highview Dr DY6 .... 60 F4
High View Rd CV32 ...... 157 C5
Highview St DY2 .... 51 E1
High View WV14 .... 39 F1
Highwaymans Croft CV4 132 D5
Highwood Ave B92 .... 89 A1
High Wood Cl DY6 .... 60 C6
Highwood Croft B38 .... 103 D1
Hiker Gr 3 B37 .... 70 D2
Hilary Cres DY1 .... 51 B6
Hilary Dr
Aldridge WS9 .... 30 A5
Sutton Coldfield B76 ...... 47 A3
Wolverhampton WV3 ...... 38 D7
Hilary Gr B31 .... 102 F4
Hilary Rd
Coventry CV4 .... 132 E6
Hilary Rd *continued*
Nuneaton CV10 .... 72 F5
Hilden Rd B7 .... 67 B4
Hilderic Cres DY1 .... 61 F7
Hilderstone Rd B25 ...... 88 C6
Hildicks Cres WS3 .... 28 F7
Hildicks Pl WS3 .... 29 A7
Hilditch Way CV11 ...... 73 E2
Hillaire Cl B38 .... 104 C2
Hillaries Rd B23 .... 56 D2
Hillary Ave WS10 .... 42 C3
Hillary Crest DY3 .... 50 E5
Hillary Prim Sch WS2 .... 42 C7
Hillary St WS2 .... 42 C7
Hill Avenue Prim Sch WV4 .... 39 F3
Hill Ave WV4 .... 39 F3
Hill Bank Dr B33 .... 68 D4
Hillbank B69 .... 63 D8
Hill Bank Rd
Birmingham B38 .... 104 A2
Halesowen B63 .... 82 D6
Hill Bank DY9 .... 81 F5
Hillborough Rd B27 ...... 88 D2
Hillbrook Gr B33 .... 68 F3
Hillbrow Cres B62 .... 83 F8
Hillbury Dr WV12 .... 27 B8
Hill Cl
Birmingham B31 .... 103 C1
Royal Leamington Spa CV32 .... 157 A3
Sedgley DY3 .... 39 E1
Hillcrest Ave B43 .... 43 E2
Hill Crest Ave DY5 ...... 61 C2
Hillcrest Ave
Halesowen B63 .... 82 B7
Wolverhampton WV10 .... 11 E1
Hillcrest Bsns Pk DY2 .... 62 C7
Hillcrest Cl
Dudley DY2 .... 62 C5
Tamworth B79 .... 21 B6
Hill Crest CV32 .... 157 E5
Hill Crest Dr WS13 .... 3 A1
Hill Crest DY3 .... 50 C4
Hillcrest Gdns WV12 ...... 27 D5
Hill Crest Gr B44 .... 56 A7
Hill Crest Hosp B98 ...... 159 C6
Hillcrest Ind Est B64 ...... 82 D8
Hillcrest Pk B47 .... 140 F8
Hill Crest Rd B13 .... 86 E2
Hillcrest Rd
Birmingham B43 .... 43 E2
Dudley DY2 .... 51 E1
Nuneaton CV10 .... 72 E5
Polesworth B78 .... 36 F7
Romsley B62 .... 101 A4
Sutton Coldfield B72 ...... 46 C1
Hillcrest Rise WS7 .... 7 B4
Hillcrest Sch & Com Coll The DY2 .... 62 C5
Hillcrest Sch & Sixth Form Ctr B32 .... 84 E3
Hillcroft Ho B14 .... 104 F2
Hill Croft Rd B14 .... 104 C6
Hillcroft Rd DY6 .... 60 E7
Hillcross Wlk B36 .... 68 F8
Hilldene Rd DY6 .... 60 C4
Hilldrop Gr 1 B17 .... 85 D3
Hilleys Croft B37 .... 69 F2
Hill Farm Ave CV11 .... 74 B1
Hill Farm Prim Sch CV6 . 113 B7
Hillfield Hall Ct 1 B91 .. 107 C1
Hillfield Mews 3 B91 .. 127 B8
Hillfield Rd
Birmingham B11 .... 87 D3
Solihull B91 .... 107 C2
Solihull,Hillfield B91 ...... 107 B1
Hillfields Ho 1 CV1 ...... 113 E3
Hillfields Rd DY5 .... 81 B7
Hillfields B67 .... 64 D3
Hillfield Wlk B65 .... 62 F5
Hill Fray Dr CV3 .... 134 A5
Hill Gr B20 .... 55 C2
Hill Grove Cres DY10 .... 117 A4
Hillgrove Gdns DY10 .... 117 A4
Hillhampton Cl B92 ...... 89 C1
Hill Hook Ho B74 .... 31 E5
Hill Hook Rd B74 .... 31 F5
Hill Ho B66 .... 65 C6
Hill House La B33 .... 68 F3
Hillhurst Gr B36 .... 58 D1
Hillhurst Rd B73 .... 45 C3
Hilliard Cl CV12 .... 78 B4
Hilliards Croft B42 ...... 55 A8
Hillingford Ave B43 ...... 44 D3
Hill La
Alvechurch B47,B48 ...... 124 D1
Birmingham B43 .... 43 E2
Bromsgrove B60 .... 136 F1
Clent DY9 .... 99 E4
Middleton B75 .... 33 B2
Hillman Dr DY2 .... 62 E7
Hillman Gr B36 .... 58 F1
Hillman Ho CV1 .... 165 B3
Hillman B77 .... 21 E2
Hillmeads Dr DY2 .... 62 F7
Hillmeads Rd B38 .... 104 A1
Hillmorton Cl B98 .... 154 E6
Hillmorton Rd
Coventry CV2 .... 96 C1
Dorridge B93 .... 128 A5
Sutton Coldfield B74 ...... 31 F4
Hillmorton B74 .... 31 F3
Hillmount Cl B28 .... 87 E2
Hill Pas B64 .... 62 E2
Hill Pk WS9 .... 16 A4
Hill Pl WV11 .... 13 A1
Hill Rd
Keresley CV7 .... 94 F6
Tipton B69 .... 52 A2
Willenhall WV13 .... 26 E1
Hillrise LE10 .... 75 F8
Hill Rise View B60 ...... 137 C6
Hillsborough Ho B27 ..... 88 E2
Hillside Ave
Brierley Hill DY5 .... 82 A8
Cradley Heath B65 .... 83 B8
Halesowen B63 .... 82 D6
Hillside WS8 .... 16 A6
Hillside Cl
Birmingham B32 .... 102 A8
Brownhills WS8 .... 16 A6
Burntwood WS7 .... 6 E5
Cannock WS12 .... 2 A7
Kidderminster DY11 ...... 116 A7
Hill Side CV2 .... 114 A6
Hillside Cres WS3 .... 14 F3
Hillside Croft B92 .... 89 E4
Hillside Ct B43 .... 43 E2
Hillside Dr
Birmingham,Great Barr B42 .... 55 A6
Birmingham,Kingshurst B37 69 F4
Kidderminster DY11 ...... 116 A7
Lickey End B61 .... 137 B6
Nuneaton CV10 .... 72 C7
Sutton Coldfield B74 ...... 44 F7
Hill Side DY3 .... 50 C4
Hillside Gdns
Birmingham B37 .... 69 F4
Wolverhampton WV1 ...... 26 A3
Hillside
Hartshill CV10 .... 72 A8
Lichfield WS14 .... 9 D6
Hillside N CV2 .... 114 A6
Hillside Rd
Birmingham,Gravelly Hill B23 .... 56 D2
Birmingham,Great Barr B43 43 D2
Dudley DY1 .... 51 A5
Hinckley LE10 .... 75 D6
Sutton Coldfield B74 ...... 32 A4
Hillside B98 .... 153 D2
Hill St
Bedworth CV12 .... 78 B5
Bilston WV14 .... 40 E3
Birmingham B5 .... 164 B2
Brierley Hill,Quarry Bank DY5 .... 82 A8
Brierley Hill,Silver End DY5 . 61 D2
Burntwood WS7 .... 6 E5
Cannock WS12 .... 2 C3
Cheslyn Hay WS6 .... 4 C2
Coventry CV1 .... 165 B3
Darlaston WS10 .... 41 E6
Dudley,Netherton DY2 ..... 62 C5
Dudley,Upper Gornal DY3 .. 50 D5
Essington WV11 .... 12 F3
Halesowen B63 .... 83 A3
Hinckley LE10 .... 75 E8
Kidderminster DY11 ...... 116 D6
Norton Canes WS11 .... 5 F6
Nuneaton CV10 .... 72 D4
Hillstone Gdns WV10 ..... 25 F8
Hillstone Prim Sch B34 .. 69 D5
Hillstone Rd B34 .... 69 D5
Hill St
Royal Leamington Spa CV32 .... 157 A1
Smethwick B66 .... 65 A6
Stourbridge,Amblecote DY8 80 F8
Stourbridge DY8 .... 80 F4
Stourbridge,Lye DY9 ...... 81 F5
Tipton DY4 .... 51 F4
Walsall WS1 .... 28 F1
Warwick CV34 .... 161 B8
Hill The B32 .... 84 E2
Hill Top Ave
Halesowen B62 .... 83 E7
Tamworth B79 .... 21 B8
Hill Top Cl B44 .... 55 E6
Hilltop Cl CV8 .... 145 E8
Hill Top CV1 .... 165 C3
Hill Top Ct DY3 .... 50 E3
Hilltop Dr B36 .... 68 D7
Hill Top Ind Est B70 ...... 52 F8
Hill Top Rd B31 .... 102 F3
Hilltop Rd DY2 .... 62 E8
Hill Top Rd B68 .... 64 C2
Hill Top B97 .... 152 F1
Hilltop DY9 .... 81 F3
Hill Top B70 .... 53 A7
Hill Top Wlk WS9 .... 16 C1
Hill View WS9 .... 16 B2
Hillview Cl
Halesowen B63 .... 82 E6
Lickey End B60 .... 137 C6
Hillview Rd
Birmingham B45 .... 121 E8
Lickey End B60 .... 137 C6
Hill Village Rd B75 ...... 32 A4
Hillville Gdns DY8 .... 81 B3
Hill West Prim Sch B74 .. 31 F4
Hillwood Ave B90 .... 127 A6
Hillwood Cl DY6 .... 60 C4
Hillwood Common Rd B75 .... 32 B6
Hillwood Rd
Birmingham B31 .... 102 E7
Halesowen B62 .... 83 C7
Sutton Coldfield B75 ...... 32 C5
Hill Wood WS3 .... 14 F2
Hill Wootton Rd CV32, CV35 .... 156 C6
Hillyfields Rd B23 .... 56 C4
Hilly Rd WV14 .... 40 E2
Hilmore Way B77 .... 35 E8
Hilsea Cl WV8 .... 10 F1
Hilston Ave
Halesowen B63 .... 82 F4
Wolverhampton WV4 ...... 38 C4
Hilton Ave
Birmingham B28 .... 105 F4
Nuneaton CV10 .... 72 B6
Hilton Cl WS3 .... 14 A2
Hilton Cross Bsns Pk WV10 .... 12 B5
Hilton Cross WV10 .... 12 B5
Hilton Ct
Coventry CV5 .... 112 F2
Sutton Coldfield B72 ...... 57 C8
Hilton Dr B72 .... 57 C8
Hilton La
Featherstone WV10,WV11 . 12 E8
Great Wyrley,Warstone WV11 .... 13 B7
Great Wyrley WS6 .... 5 A2
Hilton Main Ind Est WV11 12 C5
Hilton Park Service Area WV11 .... 13 B7
Hilton Pl WV14 .... 40 F5
Hilton Rd
Burntwood WS7 .... 6 C8
Featherstone WV10 ...... 12 C7
Oldbury B69 .... 63 C8
Willenhall WV12 .... 13 C1
Wolverhampton WV4 ...... 39 F4
Hilton St
West Bromwich B70 ...... 53 A3
Wolverhampton WV10 .... 163 D4
Hilton Trad Est WV4 ...... 39 F4
Hilton Way WV12 .... 27 C8
Himbleton Cl B98 .... 153 F1
Himbleton Croft 1 B90 . 127 A6
Himley Ave DY1 .... 50 F2
Himley Cl
Birmingham B43 .... 43 C2
Willenhall WV12 .... 27 B5
Himley Cres WV4 .... 39 B5
Himley Ct DY3 .... 50 E3
Himley Gdns DY3 .... 49 F4
Himley Gr B45 .... 122 B6
Himley Hall★ DY3 .... 49 D4
Himley Rd
2 Bedworth CV12 .... 77 D2
Dudley DY1,DY3 .... 50 C2
Himley Rise B90 .... 126 E4
Himley St DY1 .... 51 A1
Hinbrook Rd DY1 .... 50 E1
Hinchliffe Ave WV14 ...... 40 B2
Hinchwick Ct B93 .... 127 F3
Hinckes Rd WV6 .... 24 B5
Hinckley Bsns Pk LE10 ... 74 F8
Hinckley Coll LE10 .... 71 F1
Hinckley & District Hospl LE10 .... 75 D8
Hinckley & District Mus★ LE10 .... 71 D1
Hinckley Rd
Ansty CV2,CV7 .... 97 C2
Aston Flamville LE10 ...... 76 E6
Barwell LE9 .... 71 E5
Burbage LE9 .... 76 D8
Burton Hastings CV11 ...... 75 A1
Burton Hastings CV11,LE10. 75 D1
Burton Hastings LE10 ...... 75 E1
Coventry CV2 .... 115 A8
Hinckley LE10 .... 76 A6
Nuneaton CV11 .... 73 E5
Hinckley Sta LE10 .... 75 D7
Hinckley St B5 .... 164 C2
Hincks St WV2 .... 40 A7
Hind Cl CV34 .... 155 F2
Hindhead Rd B14 .... 105 C4
Hindlip Cl B63 .... 82 F2
Hindlow Cl B7 .... 67 B4
Hindon Gr B27 .... 106 C7
Hindon Sq B15 .... 85 F8
Hindon Wlk B32 .... 84 C2
Hingeston St B18 .... 66 B4
Hingley Croft WS9 .... 30 F3
Hingley Ind Pk B64 .... 62 C1
Hingley Rd DY9 .... 82 A6
Hingley St B64 .... 62 D1
Hinsford Cl DY6 .... 60 E8
Hinstock Cl WV4 .... 39 A4
Hinstock Rd B20 .... 54 F1
Hintlesham Ave B15 ...... 85 D5
Hinton Ave B48 .... 139 A6
Hinton Fields B61 .... 136 E7
Hinton Gr WV11 .... 26 F5
Hintons Coppice B93 .... 127 E6
Hints Ct B78 .... 19 D2
Hints La
Hopwas B78 .... 20 B5
Weeford B78 .... 19 F4
Hints Rd
Hopwas B78 .... 20 B6
Mile Oak B78 .... 20 C2
Hipkins St DY4 .... 51 E7
Hiplands Rd B62 .... 83 F4
Hipsley Cl B36 .... 58 C1
Hipsmoor Cl B37 .... 69 F3
Hipswell Highway CV2 .. 114 D3
Hirdemonsway B90 ...... 126 A5
Hiron Croft CV3 .... 133 C8
Hiron The CV3 .... 133 C8
Hiron Way CV34 .... 160 B7
Histons Hill WV8 .... 10 A3
Hitchcock Cl B67 .... 64 D5
Hitches La B15 .... 86 B7
Hitchman Ct CV31 .... 162 A5
Hitchman Rd CV31 .... 162 A5
Hither Green La B98 .... 153 F7
Hitherside B90 .... 126 B5
Hive Ind Ctr The B18 ...... 66 A6
HM Young Offender Inst (Swinfen Hall) WS14 ...... 9 E1
Hoarestone Ave CV11 .... 79 A7
Hoarstone DY8 .... 98 F5
Hobacre Cl B45 .... 122 A8
Hobart Croft 1 B7 .... 67 A4
Hobart Ct B74 .... 32 A3
Hobart Dr WS5 .... 43 C6
Hobart Rd
Cannock WS12 .... 2 E2
Tipton DY4 .... 40 E1
Hobbis Ho B38 .... 123 C7
Hobble End La WS6 .... 14 B7
Hobden Hall Farm Ind Units B60 .... 150 B3
Hobgate Cl WV10 .... 25 F4
Hobgate Rd WV10 .... 25 F4
Hob Green Prim Sch DY9 . 81 E2
Hob Green Rd DY9 .... 81 E2
Hobhouse Cl B43 .... 54 F7
Hob La
Balsall Common CV7 ...... 130 E4
Burton Green CV8 .... 131 A3
Temple Balsall B92 ...... 129 A8
Hobley St WV13 .... 27 C2
Hobmoor Croft B25 .... 88 D7
Hobmoor Prim Sch B25 .. 88 D8
Hob Moor Rd B10,B25 .... 88 C8
Hobnock Rd WV11 .... 13 B5
Hobs Hole La WS9 .... 30 D7
Hob's Mdw B92 .... 89 B2
Hob's Moat Rd B92 ...... 89 B3
Hobson Cl B18 .... 66 A5
Hobson Rd B29 .... 86 B1
Hob's Rd WS13 .... 3 E1
Hobs Rd WS10 .... 42 A4
Hockett St CV3 .... 133 D8
Hocking Rd CV2 .... 114 E4
Hockley Brook Cl B18 .... 66 A5
Hockley Brook La DY9 ... 119 F3
Hockley Brook Trad Est B18 .... 66 A6
Hockley Cir B18 .... 66 B6
Hockley Cl B19 .... 66 D6
Hockley Ct B94 .... 143 C7
Hockley Ctr 1 B18 .... 66 C4
Hockley Heath Prim Sch B94 .... 143 C6
Hockley Hill B18 .... 66 B5
Hockley La
Coventry CV5 .... 111 C5
Dudley DY2 .... 62 C4
Hockley Pool Cl B18 ...... 66 B5
Hockley Rd
Birmingham B23 .... 56 D4
Dudley WV14 .... 51 A7
Tamworth B77 .... 35 F5
Hockley St B19 .... 66 C5
Hodder Gr B71 .... 53 F7
Hodge Hill Ave DY9 ...... 81 F3
Hodge Hill Comm B36 .... 68 E7
Hodge Hill Cotts DY10 ... 117 C7
Hodgehill Ct B36 .... 68 E7
Hodge Hill Girls Sch B36 . 68 C7
Hodge Hill Prim Sch B36 . 68 D7
Hodge Hill Rd B34 .... 68 E6
Hodge Hill Sch B36 .... 68 C7
Hodge La B77 .... 22 B6
Hodges Dr B69 .... 63 B8
Hodgetts Cl B67 .... 64 D3
Hodgetts Dr B63 .... 100 C8
Hodgett's La
Balsall Common CV7 ...... 130 F7
Coventry CV7,CV8 .... 131 A6
Hodgkins Cl WS8 .... 16 A6
Hodgkiss Cl WS10 .... 41 E4
Hodgson Twr B19 .... 66 D6
Hodnell Cl B36 .... 58 C1
Hodnet Cl
Bilston WV14 .... 40 B5
Kenilworth CV8 .... 148 B5
Hodnet Dr DY5 .... 61 C6
Hodnet Gr B5 .... 86 E8
Hodnet Pl WS11 .... 2 B2
Hodson Ave WV13 .... 27 C1
Hodson Cl WV11 .... 26 F8
Hodson Way WS11 .... 2 B2
Hoff Beck Ct 6 B9 .... 67 B2
Hogarth Cl
Bedworth CV12 .... 78 A4
Birmingham B43 .... 44 D5
Hinckley LE10 .... 71 A3
Willenhall WV13 .... 26 E2
Hogarth Dr LE10 .... 71 A3
Hogarth Ho 6 B15 .... 86 C8
Hoggs La B31 .... 102 E4
Holbeache La DY6 .... 49 D1
Holbeache Rd DY6 .... 60 C8
Holbeach Rd B33 .... 69 B2
Holbeche Rd
Dorridge B93 .... 128 A7
Sutton Coldfield B75 ...... 47 B5
Holbein Cl CV12 .... 78 A4
Holberg Gr WV11 .... 26 F5
Holborn Ave CV6 .... 95 C2
Holborn Hill B6,B7 .... 67 C7
Holborn Sh Ctr The DY3 .. 50 D7
Holbrook Gr B37 .... 70 A1
Holbrook La CV6 .... 95 D2
Holbrook Park Est CV6 .. 113 D8
Holbrook Prim Sch CV6 .. 95 E1
Holbrook Twr B36 .... 68 D8
Holbrook Way CV6 .... 95 D1
Holbury Cl WV9 .... 11 A2
Holcombe Rd B11 .... 88 A3

Holcroft Rd
Halesowen B63 82 C5
Kingswinford DY6 49 C1
Stourbridge DY9 81 C4
Holcroft St
Tipton DY4 52 A2
Wolverhampton WV2 40 A7
Holden Cl B23 56 E2
Holden Cres WS3 28 F5
Holden Croft DY4 52 A3
Holden Pl WS3 28 E5
Holden Rd
Wednesbury WS10 42 A2
Wolverhampton WV4 38 D3
Holdens The B28 105 E6
Holder Dr WS11 1 B2
Holder Rd
Birmingham,South Yardley B25 88 C7
Birmingham,Sparkbrook B11 87 C6
Holders Gdns B13 86 C2
Holders La B13 86 C2
Holdford Rd B6 55 F2
Holdgate Rd B29 103 C7
Hole Farm Rd B31 103 C5
Hole Farm Way B38 123 F7
Hole House La B94 143 F1
Hole La B31 103 C5
Holford Ave WS2 42 C6
Holford Dr B42,B6 55 F4
Holford Way B6 55 F3
Holifast Rd B72 57 C7
Holioak Dr CV34 161 B6
Holland Ave
Knowle B93 128 B8
Oldbury B68 64 D4
Holland Ho B19 66 D5
Holland House Inf Sch B72 46 C4
Holland Ind Pk WS10 41 D8
Holland Rd
Bilston WV14 40 E7
Birmingham B43 54 D7
Coventry CV6 113 A6
Sutton Coldfield B72 46 C4
Holland Rd W 6 B6 66 F6
Hollands Pl WS3 14 D1
Hollands Rd WS3 14 D1
Holland St
1 Dudley DY1 62 B8
Birmingham B3 164 A3
Sutton Coldfield B72 46 C4
Tipton DY4 52 C7
Holland's Way WS3 14 F4
Hollaway Ct B63 82 D5
Hollemeadow Ave WS3 28 D7
Holliars Gr B37 69 F5
Hollicombe Terr CV2 114 D8
Holliday Rd
Birmingham,Erdington B24 57 A4
Birmingham,Handsworth B21 65 F7
Holliday St
Birmingham B1 164 A2
Birmingham B1 66 C1
Holliday Wharf B1 164 A1
Hollie Lucas Rd B13 104 F7
Holliers Walk Prim Sch LE10 71 D1
Hollier's Wlk LE10 71 D1
Hollies Ave WS11 1 F1
Hollies Croft B5 86 C5
Hollies Ct WS11 1 F1
Hollies Dr
Halesowen B62 83 E6
Wednesbury WS10 41 F3
Hollies Ind Est WV2 163 B1
Hollies La WV6 23 A4
Hollies Park Rd WS11 1 F1
Hollies Rd B69 63 B8
Hollies Rise B64 82 F8
Hollies St DY5 61 D7
Hollies The
Barnt Green B45 122 A1
Birmingham,Aston B6 67 B8
Birmingham,Winson Green B16 65 F3
Smethwick B66 65 C4
Wolverhampton,New Cross WV11 26 B5
Wolverhampton WV2 163 B1
Hollin Brow Cl B93 128 B3
Hollingberry La B76 46 F3
Hollings Gr B91 127 B8
Hollington Cres B33 69 A4
Hollington Rd WV1 26 B1
Hollington Way B90 127 C7
Hollinwell Cl
Nuneaton CV11 79 C8
Walsall WS3 14 A3
Hollis La CV8 147 E8
Hollis Rd CV3 114 A2
Hollister Dr B32 84 F3
Holloway Bank Trad Est WS10 41 F1
Holloway Bank
Wednesbury WS10 41 F1
West Bromwich B70,B71 53 A8
Holloway B31 102 E5
Holloway Circus Queensway B1 164 B1
Holloway Dr B98 154 B3
Holloway Field CV6 113 A6
Holloway Head B1 164 B1
Holloway La B98 153 F3
Holloway Pk B98 154 A3
Holloway St W DY3 50 D4
Holloway St
Dudley DY3 50 D4
Wolverhampton WV1 40 A7
Holloway B79 21 B4
Holloway The
Alvechurch B48 139 D3
Bluntington DY10 118 E2
Seisdon WV5 37 A3
Stourbridge DY8 80 F7
Warwick CV34 160 D6
Wolverhampton WV6 24 C2
Hollow Cres CV6 113 B5
Hollow Croft B31 103 B3
Hollow Croft Rd WV12 27 B7
Hollowmeadow Ho B36 68 D8
Hollows The CV11 73 F1
Hollow The B13 86 E4
Hollowtree La B60 138 A3
Holly Ave
Birmingham,Balsall Heath B12 87 A5
Birmingham,Selly Oak B29 86 B1
Hollybank Ave WV11 13 A3
Hollybank Cl WS3 14 A2
Holly Bank CV5 133 A8
Hollybank Gr B63 82 D1
Hollybank Rd B13 105 A6
Hollyberry Ave B91 127 A8
Hollyberry Cl 8 B63 83 A3
Hollyberry Croft B34 69 C6
Hollybrow B29 103 B7
Holly Bush Gr B32 84 D7
Hollybush La
Coventry CV6 96 A4
Stourbridge DY8 80 F7
Wolverhampton WV4 38 D4
Hollybush Wlk 2 B64 62 D1
Holly Cl
Hinckley LE10 75 E5
Sutton Coldfield B76 46 F2
Tamworth B79 21 B7
Willenhall WV12 27 C6
Hollycot Gdns B12 86 F6
Hollycroft Cres LE10 71 C1
Hollycroft Gdns WV6 24 B6
Hollycroft LE10 71 C1
Hollycroft Rd B21 54 D1
Holly Ct
Balsall Common CV7 130 B3
Birmingham B23 57 A5
Kidderminster DY10 116 D8
Walsall WS5 43 A4
Hollydale Rd
Birmingham B24 57 C3
Rowley Regis B65 63 D2
Holly Dell B38 104 B2
Holly Dr
Birmingham B27 88 B2
Hollywood B47 125 B7
Ryton-on-D CV8 135 B1
Holly Farm Bsns Pk CV8 146 B7
Hollyfaste Rd B33 69 B1
Hollyfast La CV7 94 C4
Hollyfast Prim Sch CV6 112 F7
Hollyfast Rd CV6 112 E6
Hollyfield Ave B91 106 E3
Hollyfield Cres B75 46 E4
Hollyfield Ct B75 46 E5
Hollyfield Dr
Barnt Green B45 122 A1
Sutton Coldfield B75 46 E5
Hollyfield Prim Sch B75 46 F5
Hollyfield Rd S B76 46 F4
Hollyfield Rd B75 46 E5
Holly Gr 4 B29 85 F2
Holly Grange B66 64 D7
Holly Gr
Birmingham,Bournville B30 103 F8
Birmingham,Lozells B19 66 B8
Bromsgrove B61 136 F3
Coventry CV4 112 B2
Stourbridge DY8 80 F5
Wolverhampton WV3 38 F7
Holly Hall Maths & Computing Coll DY1 61 F8
Holly Hall Rd DY2 62 A7
Hollyhedge Cl
Birmingham B31 102 D6
Walsall WS2 28 C2
Hollyhedge La WS2 28 C2
Hollyhedge Prim Sch B71 53 E8
Hollyhedge Rd B71 53 E7
Holly Hill
4 Birmingham B45 101 F1
Great Wyrley WS6 13 E8
Hollyhill La WS14 17 E5
Holly Hill Meth & CE Inf Sch B45 101 F2
Holly Hill Rd
Birmingham B45 102 A2
Shenstone WS14 17 F5
Hollyhock Rd
Birmingham B27 88 A2
Dudley DY2 51 F1
Hollyhurst CV12 77 F1
Hollyhurst Dr DY6 60 E3
Hollyhurst Farm Cvn Site B62 101 B6
Hollyhurst Gr
Birmingham B26 88 E6
Solihull B90 126 B8
Hollyhurst Rd B73 45 B3
Hollyhurst B46 59 C2
Holly La
Aldridge WS9 30 F8
Balsall Common CV7 130 B3
Holly La *continued*
Birmingham,Erdington B24 57 C4
Birmingham,Marston Green B37 89 F8
Brownhills WS9 16 A4
Great Wyrley WS6 13 F8
Huntington WS12 1 C7
Portway B48 140 F5
Smethwick B66 64 E6
Sutton Coldfield B74 32 A3
Wishaw B76 47 D4
Holly Lodge High Sch Coll of Science B67 64 D6
Holly Lodge Wlk B37 69 F2
Holly Marie Ct CV5 112 F1
Hollymoor Way
Birmingham B31 102 B1
Birmingham B31 102 D1
Holly Mount 7 B15 65 D1
Hollymount B62 84 A7
Hollyoak Croft B31 123 B8
Hollyoake Cl B68 64 A2
Hollyoak Gr B91 107 A1
Hollyoak Rd B74 44 F6
Hollyoak St B71 53 D4
Hollyoak Way WS11 1 F1
Holly Park Dr B24 57 C4
Holly Park Ind Est B24 57 C2
Hollypiece Ho B27 88 A2
Holly Pl B29 86 B2
Holly Rd
Birmingham B68 84 C8
Birmingham,Edgbaston B16 65 D1
Birmingham,Handsworth B20 66 A8
Birmingham,King's Norton B30 104 A4
Bromsgrove B61 136 F4
Dudley DY1 51 A3
Rowley Regis B65 63 B1
Wednesbury WS10 41 F5
West Bromwich B71 53 E8
Holly St
Cannock WS12 1 F6
Dudley DY1 61 E6
Hollystitches Rd CV10 72 E6
Holly St
Royal Leamington Spa CV32 157 B1
Smethwick B67 64 F5
Holly View WV11 13 A3
Hollywell Rd
Birmingham B26 89 B6
Dorridge B93 128 A5
Hollywell St WV14 40 A1
Holly Wlk
Baginton CV8 133 E2
Nuneaton CV11 73 F2
Royal Leamington Spa CV32 157 A1
Holly Wood B43 44 A1
Hollywood By-Pass
Birmingham B47 104 F1
Hollywood B38,B47 124 E6
Hollywood Croft B42 54 F8
Hollywood Gdns B47 125 A8
Hollywood La B47 125 B7
Hollywood Motor Pk B47 125 A8
Hollywood Prim Sch B14 105 A1
Hollyword Dr B47 125 A8
Holman Cl WV13 26 E2
Holman Rd WV13 26 E2
Holman St DY11 116 C5
Holman Way
Nuneaton CV11 73 D3
Willenhall WV13 26 E2
Holmbridge Gr WS4 15 D2
Holmcroft
10 Wolverhampton WV4 39 F4
Coventry CV2 114 F8
Holmcroft Rd DY10 117 A5
Holme Mill WV10 11 D4
Holmes Ct CV8 147 F5
Holmes Dr
Birmingham B45 121 F6
Coventry CV5 111 D5
Holmesfield Rd B42 55 C7
Holmes La B60 151 B1
Holmes Rd
Whitnash CV31 162 B3
Willenhall WV12 27 D6
Holmes The WV10 11 D3
Holme Way WS4 29 B7
Holmewood Cl CV8 148 B5
Holmewood Ct CV8 148 B5
Holmfield Rd CV2 114 B3
Holmsdale Rd CV6 113 E7
Holm View Cl WS14 17 F6
Holmwood Ave DY11 116 A6
Holmwood Dr B97 153 C3
Holmwood Ho B97 153 C3
Holmwood Rd 3 B10 67 D1
Holroyd Ho CV4 111 F2
Holston Cl WS12 2 F1
Holsworth Cl B77 21 D1
Holsworthy Cl CV11 73 E5
Holt & Bracebridge Almshouses B24 57 A4
Holt Cres WS11 2 B2
Holt Ct B7 66 F4
Holte Dr B75 32 D2
Holte Rd
Birmingham,Aston B6 56 A1
Birmingham,Sparkhill B11 87 D5
Holte Sch B19 66 D7
Holtes Wlk B6 67 B8
Holt Farm Prim Sch B62 63 E1
Holt Gdns B80 159 E2
Holt Hill B98 154 F8
Holt Ho B61 137 A3
Holt La B62 100 D4
Holton Ct WV13 27 C2
Holt Rd
Halesowen B62 63 E1
Hinckley LE10 75 E6
Studley B80 159 E2
Holtshill La WS1 28 F2
Holt St B7 164 D4
Holt The CV32 157 B3
Holwick B77 36 B8
Holy Cross Ct CV2 114 E4
Holy Cross Gn DY9 99 E2
Holy Cross La DY9 119 E8
Holy Cross RC Prim Sch B76 47 A3
Holy Family RC Prim Sch
Birmingham B10 87 F7
Coventry CV6 95 B3
Holyhead L Ctr B21 65 D8
Holyhead Prim Sch WS10 41 E3
Holyhead Rd
Birmingham B21 65 D8
Codsall WV8 23 E7
Coventry CV5 112 E5
Darlaston WS10 41 C4
Wednesbury WS10 41 E3
Holyhead Road Ind Est WS10 41 D3
Holyhead Sch B21 65 D8
Holyhead Way B21 65 D8
Holy Name RC Prim Sch B43 43 E1
Holyoak Cl
3 Birmingham B6 55 F1
Bedworth CV12 77 F1
Holyoakes Field Fst Sch B97 153 D4
Holyoakes La B97 152 C5
Holy Oaks Cl B98 154 E2
Holyoke Gr CV31 162 B2
Holyrood Ct CV10 72 D5
Holyrood Gr 2 B6 66 E8
Holy Rosary RC Prim Sch WV1 26 A1
Holy Souls RC Prim Sch B27 88 C3
Holy Trinity CE Prim Sch
Birmingham B20 55 C2
Brownhills WS8 15 E6
West Bromwich B70 53 D1
Holy Trinity RC Prim Sch WV14 40 E6
Holy Trinity RC Sch B10 87 C8
Holy Trinity Sch DY10 116 F6
Holy Well Cl B16 66 A2
Holywell Cl CV4 111 D1
Holywell La B45 121 D6
Holywell Prim Sch B45 121 D7
Holywell Rise WS14 9 D6
Home Cl B28 105 F6
Homecroft Rd B26 88 E8
Homedene Rd B31 102 E7
Home Farm Cres CV31 162 B4
Home Farm
Leek Wootton CV35 155 F6
Stoneleigh CV8 149 A3
Homefield Rd WV8 10 C3
Homelands B42 55 B7
Homelands Park The WV10 11 C6
Homelea Rd B25 88 D8
Homelodge Ho 7 WS13 9 B7
Homemead Gr B45 121 F7
Home Meadow Ct B13 105 A5
Home Meadow Ho B27 88 A2
Home Meadow La B98 154 E6
Home Park Rd CV11 73 C3
Home Peal Ho B14 104 E6
Homer Cl CV34 161 E5
Homer Hill Rd B63 82 C7
Homer Rd
Solihull B91 107 B3
Sutton Coldfield B75 32 D2
Homers Fold WV14 40 D5
Homer St B12 86 F5
Homerton Rd B44 45 B1
Homestead Cl DY3 50 E5
Homestead Dr B75 32 C3
Homestead Rd B33 69 B1
Homeward Way CV3 115 A1
Homewood Cl B76 46 E3
Honesty Cl WS8 15 D6
Honeswode Cl B20 66 A8
Honeyborne Rd B75 46 D7
Honeybourne Cl
3 Halesowen B63 83 A3
Coventry CV5 112 B3
Honeybourne Rd
Birmingham B33 89 C8
Halesowen B63 83 C3
Honeybourne Sch B28 105 F8
Honeybourne B77 21 D2
Honeybourne Way WV13 27 C2
Honeychurch Cl B98 153 F3
Honeycomb Way B31 102 E3
Honeyfield Rd CV1 113 D5
Honeysuckle Ave DY6 60 E7
Honeysuckle Cl B32 84 B5
Honeysuckle Dr
Coventry CV2 96 B2
Featherstone WV10 12 C7
Walsall WS5 43 A3
Honeysuckle Gr 8 B27 88 C5
Honeysuckle Way WS6 5 B4
Honeytree Cl DY6 60 F3
Honiley Ct CV2 96 D1
Honiley Dr B73 45 C2
Honiley Rd
Birmingham B33 69 A2
Honiley CV8 146 B6
Meer End CV8 130 A1
Honiley Way CV2 96 D1
Honister Cl DY5 61 F1
Honiton Cl B31 102 E4
Honiton Cres B31 102 E4
Honiton Rd CV2 114 C5
Honiton Way WS9 29 F5
Honiton Wlk 7 B66 65 B5
Honnington Ct 2 B29 84 F1
Honor Ave WV4 39 C5
Hoobrook Ent Ctr DY10 116 E2
Hoobrook Ind Est DY10 116 E2
Hood Gr B30 103 D4
Hood St CV1 113 E3
Hoo Farm Ind Est DY10 116 F1
Hook Dr B74 31 F4
Hook La WS14 17 C3
Hoopers La B96 158 E1
Hooper St B18 65 F4
Hoo Rd DY10 116 E4
Hoosen Cl B62 84 A6
Hope Aldridge Bsns Ctr CV10 73 C6
Hope Cl CV7 95 A7
Hopedale Cl CV2 114 E3
Hopedale Rd B32 84 C5
Hope Pl 10 B29 85 F2
Hope Rd DY4 52 C6
Hope St
Birmingham B5 86 E8
Coventry CV1 113 B2
Dudley DY2 62 C8
Halesowen B62 83 D8
Stourbridge DY8 60 D3
Walsall WS1 42 E8
West Bromwich B70 53 E2
Hope Terr DY2 62 C5
Hopgardens Ave B60 137 B2
Hopkins Ct 4 WS10 42 A3
Hopkins Dr B71 53 E7
Hopkins Rd CV6 113 A4
Hopkins St DY4 52 A2
Hopleys Cl B77 21 E4
Hopstone Gdns WV4 38 F4
Hopstone Rd B29 85 A1
Hopton Cl
Coventry CV5 112 A4
Perton WV6 23 F3
Wednesbury DY4 41 C2
Hopton Cres WV11 26 E6
Hopton Crofts CV32 156 C2
Hopton Dr DY10 116 E1
Hopton Gdns DY1 51 A3
Hopton Gr B13 105 C5
Hopton Mdw WS12 2 C1
Hopwas Gr B37 69 F5
Hopwas Hill B78 20 A6
Hopwood Cl B63 83 A2
Hopwood Gr B31 122 E6
Hopyard Cl DY3 50 B3
Hopyard Gdns WV14 40 B3
Hopyard La
Dudley DY3 50 B3
Redditch B98 154 D4
Hopyard Rd WS2 27 E2
Horace Partridge Rd WS10 41 A5
Horace St WV14 51 A8
Horatio Dr B13 86 F4
Hordern Cl WV6 24 F5
Hordern Cres DY5 81 D8
Hordern Gr WV6 24 F5
Hordern Rd WV6 24 F5
Horeston Grange Sh Ctr CV11 74 A5
Hornbeam Cl B29 103 B7
Hornbeam Dr CV4 111 D1
Hornbeam Gr CV31 162 C6
Hornbeam B77 22 A4
Hornbeam Wlk WV3 25 A1
Hornbrook Gr B92 106 C7
Hornby Gr B14 105 C4
Hornby Rd WV4 39 C5
Hornchuch Close Ind Est CV1 165 B1
Hornchurch Cl CV1 165 B1
Horndean Cl CV6 113 E8
Horner Way B62 63 C1
Horne Way B34 69 E5
Horning Dr WV14 40 C3
Horninghold Cl CV3 134 E8
Hornsey Cl CV2 114 E7
Hornsey Gr B44 45 A2
Hornsey Rd B44 45 A2
Hornton Cl B74 31 D5
Horrell Rd
Birmingham B26 89 B7
Solihull B90 105 F2
Horsecroft Dr B71 54 A8
Horse Fair
Birmingham B1 164 B1
Kidderminster DY10 116 E7
Horsefair The 8 LE10 75 D8
Horsehills Dr WV3 24 E2
Horselea Croft B8 68 C4
Horseley Fields WV1 163 D3
Horseley Heath DY4 52 C5
Horseley Rd
Tipton DY4 52 C5

Horseley Rd *continued*
Tipton DY4 52 C6
Horsepool LE10 76 A5
Horsepool Hollow CV31 162 C5
Horseshoe Cl 2 WS2 42 B7
Horseshoe Dr WS12 2 F4
Horse Shoe Rd CV6 96 A4
Horse Shoes La B26 89 B5
Horseshoe The B68 64 C2
Horseshoe Wlk 6 DY4 51 E5
Horsfall Rd B75 47 A5
Horsford Rd CV3 133 E6
Horsham Ave DY8 60 C3
Horsley La WS14 17 D8
Horsley Rd
Birmingham B43 44 D4
Sutton Coldfield B74 31 B2
Horton Cl
3 Cannock WS11 1 F4
Bedworth CV7 95 F7
Darlaston WS10 41 D7
Sedgley DY3 50 C8
Horton Gr B90 127 A5
Horton Pl WS10 41 D7
Horton Sq B12 86 E7
Horton St
Darlaston WS10 41 D7
Tipton DY4 52 D5
West Bromwich B70 53 C2
Hosiery St CV12 78 C2
Hospital Dr B15 85 E4
Hospital La
Bedworth CV12 77 B1
Cheslyn Hay WS6 4 B2
Dudley WV14 51 B7
Hospital Rd WS7 7 B5
Hospital St
Birmingham B19 164 B4
Birmingham,Newtown B19 66 D6
Birmingham,Stockland Green B23 56 E4
Tamworth B79 21 B5
Walsall WS2 28 D4
Wolverhampton WV2 163 C2
Hossil La
Belbroughton DY9 119 C8
Clent DY9 99 D1
Hotchkiss Way CV3 135 A7
Hotel Bldgs WS14 8 A2
Hothersall Dr B73 56 F8
Hothorpe Cl CV3 114 F1
Hotspur Rd B44 44 F1
Hough Pl WS2 42 B7
Hough Rd
Birmingham B14 104 D6
Walsall WS2 42 A7
Houghton Ct B28 105 D4
Houghton St
Oldbury B69 63 F6
West Bromwich B70 64 D8
Houlbrooke Ho 1 WS14 9 C8
Houldey Rd B31 103 B1
Houldsworth Cres CV6 95 C4
Houliston Cl WS10 42 B5
Houndsfield Cl B47 125 C6
Houndsfield Farm B47 125 B5
Houndsfield Gr B47 125 A5
Houndsfield La B47 125 C6
Housman Cl B60 150 E8
Housman Ct B60 137 A3
Housman Pk B60 137 A2
Housman Wlk DY10 117 C6
Houting B77 35 D5
Houx The DY8 80 E8
Hove Ave CV5 111 E4
Hovelands Cl CV2 114 C8
Hove Rd B27 88 C1
Hoveton Cl B98 154 B2
Howard Ave B61 136 E3
Howard Cl CV5 111 E4
Howard Cres WS12 2 C7
Howard Ct B16 65 E1
Howard Rd
Bilston WV14 40 F3
Birmingham,Handsworth B20 55 B2
Birmingham,King's Heath B14 104 E7
Birmingham,Newton B43 54 C8
Birmingham,South Yardley B25 88 C7
Howard Rd E B13 104 F7
Howard Rd
Nuneaton CV10 73 A3
Redditch B98 159 C8
Solihull B92 88 E3
Wednesfield WV11 26 F8
Howard St
Birmingham B19 164 B4
Coventry CV1 165 C4
Howard Street Ind Est B70 52 F8
Howard St
Tipton DY4 52 B5
West Bromwich B70 52 F7
Wolverhampton WV2 163 C1
Howard Wlk CV31 161 D6
Howarth Way B6 67 A7
Howat Rd CV7 94 F7
Howcotte Gn CV4 131 E8
Howden Pl B33 69 A5
Howdle's La WS8 6 F2
Howe Cres WV12 27 C6
Howell Rd WV2 39 E7
Howells Cl CV12 77 D1
Howes Com Prim Sch CV3 133 E5
Howes Croft B35 58 A2
Howes La CV3 133 D3
Howe St B4 66 F3
Howfield Ct B16 65 C1
Howford Gr B7 67 B4
Howland Cl WV9 10 F2
Howlette Rd CV4 111 E2
Howley Ave B44 44 E1
Howley Grange Prim Sch B62 83 F5
Howley Grange Rd B62 84 A4
Howl Pl DY4 51 F5
Hoylake Cl
Nuneaton CV11 74 B1
Walsall WS3 14 B4
Hoylake Dr B69 63 A7
Hoylake Rd WV6 23 D5
Hoylake B77 22 B4
Hoyland Way B30 103 E8
HRS Bsns Pk B33 69 C1
Huband Cl B98 154 A5
Hubert Croft B29 85 F2
Hubert Rd B29 85 F2
Hubert St B6 66 F5
Hucker Cl WS2 42 A7
Hucker Rd WS2 42 A7
Huddesford Dr CV7 130 C8
Huddisdon Cl 5 CV34 155 F1
Huddlestone Cl WV10 12 B6
Huddleston Way B29 85 C1
Huddocks View WS3 14 F5
Hudson Ave B46 70 F6
Hudson Cl WS11 2 B2
Hudson Dr WS7 7 C6
Hudson Gr WV6 23 E5
Hudson Rd
Birmingham B20 55 A4
Tipton DY4 52 C4
Hudson's Dr B30 104 A4
Hudswell Dr DY5 81 D8
Huggins Cl CV7 130 C7
Hughes Ave WV3 38 F8
Hughes Cl
Warwick CV34 155 D2
Whitnash CV31 162 A2
Hughes Pl WV14 40 D7
Hughes Rd
Bilston WV14 40 D7
Darlaston WS10 41 A5
Hughes The CV34 160 E6
Hugh Gaitskill Ct WV14 40 C8
Hugh Porter Way WV6 24 F6
Hugh Rd
Birmingham B10 67 E1
Coventry CV3 114 A2
Smethwick B67 64 E5
Hugh Villas B10 67 E1
Huins Cl B98 154 A4
Hulbert Dr DY2 62 B6
Hulbert Ind Est DY2 62 B6
Hulland Pl DY5 61 C3
Hullbrook Rd B13 105 C6
Hulme Cl CV3 115 B1
Humara Ghar 9 WS1 42 E8
Humber Ave
Coventry CV1 113 F1
Sutton Coldfield B76 58 A7
Humber Gdns B63 82 C5
Humber Gr B36 58 F1
Humber Ho DY1 61 D8
Humber Rd
Coventry CV3 134 A8
Wolverhampton WV3 25 A1
Humberstone Rd
4 Coventry CV6 113 A5
Sutton Coldfield B24 57 E4
Humber Twr 2 B7 67 A4
Hume St
Kidderminster DY11 116 C5
Smethwick B66 65 B4
Humpage Rd B9 67 E2
Humphrey Ave B60 150 F7
Humphrey Burton's Rd CV3 133 C8
Humphrey-Davy Rd CV12 95 D8
Humphrey Middlemore Dr B17 85 D4
Humphrey St DY3 50 D3
Humphries Cres WV14 40 F2
Humphries Dr DY10 116 F2
Humphries Ho WS8 15 F7
Humphries Rd WV10 25 D6
Humphris St CV34 161 B8
Hundred Acre Rd B74 44 F7
Hungary Cl DY9 81 C5
Hungary Hill DY9 81 C5
Hungerfield Rd B36 58 C1
Hungerford Rd DY8 80 E2
Hungry La WS14 18 F5
Hunningham Gr 6 B91 127 B8
Hunnington Cl B32 84 A1
Hunnington Cres B63 83 B2
Hunscote Cl B90 105 F1
Hunscote Ho B90 105 F1
Hunslet Cl B32 84 F4
Hunslet Rd
Birmingham B32 84 F4
Burntwood WS7 7 B8
Hunstanton Ave B17 84 F8
Hunstanton Cl DY5 81 C7
Hunt End Ind Est B97 158 C5
Hunt End La B97 158 C5
Hunter Ave WS7 7 B7
Hunter Cl WS14 9 D6
Hunter Cres WS3 28 F7
Hunter Ct B5 86 D5
Hunter Rd WS11 4 E8
Hunters Cl
Bilston WV14 41 A7
Coventry CV3 115 A2
Hunters Hill Sch B60 137 F6
Hunters Rd B19 66 B7
Hunter's Ride DY7 60 B2
Hunters Rise B63 82 D1
Hunter St WV6 25 A4
Hunters Vale B19 66 C6
Hunters Wlk B23 56 C8
Hunter Terr CV5 132 D8
Huntingdon Cl
Redditch B98 154 F2
Tamworth B78 20 F2
Huntingdon Rd
Coventry CV5 133 A8
West Bromwich B71 53 B7
Huntingdon Way CV10 72 E3
Huntington Ho B23 56 B6
Huntington Ind Est WS12 1 B6
Huntington Prim Sch WS12 1 C8
Huntington Rd WV12 27 D8
Huntington Terrace Rd WS11 1 F4
Huntingtree Prim Sch B63 82 E3
Huntingtree Rd B63 82 E3
Huntlands Rd B63 82 F2
Huntley Dr B91 107 B2
Huntly Rd B16 66 A1
Hunton Ct 2 B23 56 E2
Hunton Hill B23 56 E2
Hunton Rd B23 56 E3
Hunt Paddocks CV8 147 E1
Hunt's La WV12 27 D6
Huntsman Cl WV14 40 D2
Huntsmans Gate WS7 7 B8
Huntsmans Rise WS12 1 C8
Hunts Mill Dr DY5 50 C1
Hunts Rd B30 104 B7
Hunt Terr CV4 132 B7
Hurcott Ct DY10 117 A8
Hurcott La DY10 117 C8
Hurcott Rd DY10 117 B8
Hurdis Rd B90 106 A2
Hurdlow Ave B18 66 B5
Hurlbutt Rd CV34 161 C4
Hurley Cl
Royal Leamington Spa CV32 157 A2
Sutton Coldfield B72 46 C2
Walsall WS5 43 D6
Hurley Gr B37 69 F5
Hurleys Fold DY2 62 C5
Hurlingham Rd B44 45 A1
Hurn Way CV6 96 B4
Huron Cl WS11 2 B2
Hurricane Pk B24 68 A8
Hurricane Way B35 58 A2
Hursey Dr DY4 52 A6
Hurstbourne Cres WV1 26 B1
Hurst Bsns Pk DY6 62 A4
Hurst Cl B36 69 E7
Hurstcroft Rd B33 69 B3
Hurst Ct DY9 81 F5
Hurst Green Prim Sch B62 83 E8
Hurst Green Rd
Bentley Heath B93 127 F4
Halesowen B62 83 F8
Minworth B76 58 D6
Hurst Hill Ct WV14 51 A8
Hurst Hill Prim Sch WV14 51 A8
Hurst La
Birmingham B34 69 E6
Brierley Hill DY5 61 F3
Hurst Lane N B36 69 E7
Hurst La DY4 51 D6
Hurst Rd
Bedworth CV12 78 B3
Coventry CV6 96 A4
Dudley WV14 40 A1
Hinckley LE10 75 D8
Sedgley WV14 39 F1
Smethwick B67 64 D2
Hurst St B5 164 C1
Hurst The
Birmingham B13 105 D7
Hollywood B47 125 A6
Hurstway The B23 56 C8
Hurst Wlk CV6 96 A4
Hurstwood Rd B23 56 C8
Huskison Cl B69 52 B1
Huskisson Ct WV10 25 C6
Hussey Rd
Brownhills WS8 15 E8
Norton Canes WS11 5 F5
Husum Way DY10 117 C7
Hutchings La B90 126 B5
Hut Hill La WS6 5 A4
Hutton Ave B8 67 D5
Hutton Rd
Birmingham,Handsworth B20 55 C1
Birmingham,Saltley B8 67 D5
Huxbey Dr B92 107 F8
Huxley Cl WV9 11 A3
Hyacinth Cl 9 WS5 43 A3
Hyacinth Way LE10 75 D5
Hyatt Sq DY5 81 C7
Hyatts Wlk B65 62 F5
Hyde Cl B60 137 B2
Hyde Pl CV32 161 E8
Hyde Rd
Coventry CV2 114 E4
Kenilworth CV8 148 A5
Hyde Rd *continued*
Wednesfield WV11 26 E6
Hydes La LE10 74 E4
Hydes Rd
Wednesbury WS10 42 B2
West Bromwich B71 42 C1
Hydesville Tower Sch WS1 29 A2
Hyde The DY9 81 D2
Hyett Way WV14 41 B2
Hylda Rd B20 55 B1
Hylstone Cres WV11 26 D6
Hylton St B18 66 C5
Hypericum Gdns CV2 114 C4
Hyperion Dr WV4 39 A3
Hyperion Rd
Stourbridge DY7 80 C7
Sutton Coldfield B36 57 F1
Hyron Hall Rd B27 88 C2
Hyssop Cl
Birmingham B7 67 A5
Cannock WS11 2 B3
Hytall Rd B90 105 C2
Hythe Gr B25 88 D8

I

Ibberton Rd B14 105 B3
Ibex Cl CV3 114 F1
Ibis Cl DY10 117 B3
Ibis Gdns DY6 61 A6
Ibstock Cl B98 154 E4
Ibstock Dr DY8 81 A4
Ibstock Ho B98 154 E4
Ibstock Rd CV6 96 A5
Icknield Cl B74 31 A1
Icknield Fst Sch B98 154 D1
Icknield Port Rd B16 65 F3
Icknield Sq B16 66 A3
Icknield St
Alvechurch B38 124 B2
Beoley B48,B98 140 C2
Birmingham B18 66 B4
Redditch,Church Hill B98 154 C7
Redditch,Ipsley B98 154 D2
Icknield Street Dr B98 159 D7
Icknield St B48 140 B6
Ida Rd
Walsall WS2 28 C1
West Bromwich B70 53 D1
Idbury Rd B44 56 A7
Ideal Bldgs 7 DY11 116 D6
Ideal Wks DY9 82 A6
Iden Rd CV1 113 E4
Idmiston Croft B14 104 F2
Idonia Rd WV6 23 F5
Ilam Pk CV8 148 C5
Ilex Ct CV34 161 A7
Ilford Cl CV12 78 A3
Ilford Ct CV3 135 D7
Ilford Dr CV3 133 B5
Ilford Rd B23 56 D6
Ilfracombe Gr CV3 133 A5
Iliffe Ho LE10 75 B7
Iliffe Way B17 85 D4
Ilkley Gr B37 69 F2
Illeybrook Sq B32 84 D2
Illey Cl B31 102 C1
Illey La
Birmingham B32 102 A7
Halesowen B62 101 E8
Illshaw Heath Rd B90, B94 126 D2
Illshaw WV9 11 A3
Ilmington Cl
Coventry CV3 133 B5
Redditch B98 154 D1
Ilmington Dr B73 45 C3
Ilmington Rd B29 84 F1
Ilminster Cl LE10 76 B7
Ilsham Gr B31 122 E6
Ilsley Rd B23 56 E4
Image Bsns Pk WS11 2 B3
I-Max Bsns Pk B11 88 A6
Imber Rd DY10 117 A1
Imex Auto Ctr DY4 52 A3
Imex Bsns Ctr
Bilston WV14 40 E4
Redditch B98 154 E4
Wolverhampton WV13 26 C3
Imex Bsns Pk
Birmingham,Bordesley Green B9 67 D2
Birmingham,Stechford B33 68 E4
Tipton DY4 52 A3
Wolverhampton WV2 39 C7
Imex Ho WV2 39 B7
Imogen Gdns CV34 161 E3
Imperial Ave DY10 116 F8
Imperial Ct DY10 116 F8
Imperial Gr DY10 116 F8
Imperial Rd B9 67 E1
Imperial Rise B46 59 E2
Impey Rd B31 102 F1
Impney Cl B98 154 E6
Impsley Cl B36 69 B8
Inca Cl CV3 134 F8
Ince Rd WS10 41 C7
Incestre Dr B43 43 D1
Inchbrook Rd CV8 148 C7
Inchcape Ave B20 55 A3
Inchford Ave CV34 155 E2
Inchford Cl CV11 73 F1
Inchford Rd B92 107 E7
Inchlaggan Rd WV10 25 F6
Infantry Pl B75 47 A6
Ingatestone Dr DY8 60 C3
Inge St B5 164 C1
Ingestre Cl
Cannock WS11 2 B1
Walsall WS3 13 F3
Ingestre Dr B43 43 C1
Ingestre Ho WV6 24 E5
Ingestre Rd
Birmingham B28 106 A7
Wolverhampton WV10 11 C1
Ingeva Dr B45 122 A1
Ingham Way B17 85 A8
Ingleby Gdns WV6 25 A5
Ingle Ct CV31 161 E7
Ingledew Cl WS2 27 D3
Inglefield Rd B33 68 F3
Inglemere Gr B29 102 F7
Inglenook Dr B20 55 B2
Ingleside Villas 3 B11 87 C5
Ingleton Cl CV11 74 A2
Ingleton Rd B8 68 A7
Inglewood Ave WV3 38 F8
Inglewood Cl
Kingswinford DY6 60 D5
Royal Leamington Spa CV32 157 A3
Inglewood Gr B74 30 F2
Inglewood Rd B11 87 C5
Ingoldsby Ct 17 B13 87 B2
Ingoldsby Rd B31 103 C3
Ingot Cl WS2 28 B6
Ingram Gr B27 88 A2
Ingram Pit La B77 22 A5
Ingram Pl WS3 14 D1
Ingram Rd
Coventry CV5 132 D8
Walsall WS3 14 D1
Inhedge St DY3 50 E5
Inhedge The DY1 51 C1
Inkberrow Cl 1 B65 63 E4
Inkberrow Rd B63 82 F2
Inkerman Gr WV10 25 F2
Inkerman Ho B19 66 E6
Inkerman St
Birmingham B7 67 B4
Wolverhampton WV10 25 F3
Inland Rd B24 57 B2
Innage Cl CV31 162 B8
Innage Rd B31 103 B4
Innage The B47 125 A5
Innis Rd CV5 132 E8
Innsworth Dr B35 58 A4
Insetton Cl B98 154 D4
Inshaw Cl B33 68 E3
Institute Rd B14 104 F8
Instone Rd
Coventry CV6 95 A1
Halesowen B63 83 A3
Instow Cl WV12 27 B8
Insull Ave B14 105 B1
Intended St B63 82 C7
International Ho B43 54 F6
Intersection Ho B70 53 F1
Intown Row WS1 28 F2
Intown WS1 28 F2
Int Sch & Com Coll The B33 69 D3
Inveraray Cl CV8 148 C4
Inverclyde Rd B20 55 A3
Inverness Cl CV5 112 A4
Inverness Ho WV1 163 B4
Inverness Rd B31 102 F3
Invicta Rd CV3 134 F8
Inworth WV9 11 B3
Io Ctr The B98 159 C8
Ipsley Alders Marsh Nature Reserve* B98 154 F4
Ipsley CE Mid Sch B98 154 E3
Ipsley Church La B98 154 C1
Ipsley Gr B23 56 A5
Ipsley La B98 154 D2
Ipsley St B98 153 E3
Ipstones Ave B33 68 F4
Ipswich Cres B42 55 B7
Ipswich Wlk B37 70 B2
Ireland Green Rd B70 53 B2
Ireton Cl CV4 111 C1
Ireton Rd
Birmingham B20 55 A4
Wolverhampton WV10 11 E3
Iris Cl
Birmingham B29 103 B8
Dudley DY2 51 F1
Hinckley LE10 75 E5
Tamworth B79 21 C6
Iris Dr B14 104 D3
Irnham Rd B74 32 B1
Ironbridge Way CV6 96 B6
Iron Bridge Wlk DY9 99 B8
Iron La B33 68 D4
Ironmonger Row CV1 165 B3
Ironstone Rd WS7 6 E8
Iron Way B60 151 B7
Irvan Ave B70 52 F5
Irvine Cl WS3 28 B7
Irvine Rd WS3 28 B7
Irving Cl DY3 50 A4
Irving Rd
Coventry CV1 113 E2
Solihull B92 89 E3
Wednesbury DY4 41 A1
Irving St B1 66 D1
Irwell B77 21 E2
Irwin Ave B45 122 C7
Isaac Walton Pl B70 52 E7
Isambard Dr CV6 95 F5
Isbourne Way 1 B9 67 B2
Isis Ct B73 46 B5

Isis Gr
Birmingham B36 . . . . 69 F8
Willenhall WV13 . . . . 27 C2
Isis Ho DY1 . . . . 61 D8
Island Cl LE10 . . . . 71 E2
Island Dr DY10 . . . . 116 E4
Island Rd B21 . . . . 54 C1
Island The B78 . . . . 20 C1
Islington Cres CV9 . . . . 36 C1
Islington Gates B3 . . . . . . 164 A3
Islington B63 . . . . 83 A4
Islington Row B15 . . . . 66 B1
Islington Row Middleway
B15 . . . . 86 C8
Ismere Rd B24 . . . . 57 B2
Itchen Gr WV6 . . . . 23 E4
Ithon Gr B38 . . . . 123 E8
Ivanhoe Ave CV11 . . . . 73 E1
Ivanhoe Rd
Birmingham B43 . . . . 44 C3
Lichfield WS14 . . . . 9 B6
Wolverhampton WV2 . . . . . . 40 A6
Ivanhoe St DY2 . . . . 62 A7
Ivatt Cl WS4 . . . . 29 B7
Ivatt B77 . . . . 21 F2
Iverley La DY10,DY8 . . . . . . 98 C5
Iverley Rd B63 . . . . 83 C4
Iverley Wlk DY9 . . . . 81 C2
Ivor Rd
Birmingham B11 . . . . 87 B4
Coventry CV6 . . . . 95 F2
Redditch B97 . . . . 153 D2
Ivy Ave
3 Birmingham B12 . . . . 87 B5
Birmingham B12 . . . . 87 A5
Ivybridge Gr B42 . . . . 55 C3
Ivybridge Rd CV3 . . . . 133 D6
Ivy Cl WS11 . . . . 4 D8
Ivy Croft WV9 . . . . 10 F3
Ivydale Ave B26 . . . . 89 C5
Ivy Farm La CV4 . . . . 132 D6
Ivyfield Rd B23 . . . . 56 B5
Ivy Gdns WS11 . . . . 6 A5
Ivy Gr
Brownhills WS8 . . . . 16 A4
Nuneaton CV10 . . . . 72 D6
Ivy Ho WS9 . . . . 16 A4
Ivyhouse La WV14 . . . . 51 B8
Ivyhouse Rd B38 . . . . 123 C8
Ivy House Rd B69 . . . . 63 D6
Ivyhouse Wlk 6 B77 . . . . . 35 F6
Ivy La
Birmingham B9 . . . . 67 A2
Romsley B62 . . . . 100 D5
Ivy Lodge Cl B37 . . . . 90 A7
Ivy Rd
Birmingham,Handsworth
B21 . . . . 66 A7
Birmingham,Stirchley B30 104 A6
Dudley DY1 . . . . 51 A4
Sutton Coldfield B73 . . . . . . 45 F1
Tipton DY4 . . . . 51 F7
Ivy Way B90 . . . . 126 A6
Izod St B97 . . . . 153 D4
Izons Ind Est B70 . . . . 53 A1
Izons Lane Ind Est B70 . . . 53 A1
Izons La B70 . . . . 53 A1
Izons Rd B70 . . . . 53 C3

J

Jacey Rd
Birmingham B16 . . . . 65 D2
Solihull B90 . . . . 106 B4
Jack Cade Way CV34 . . . . . 161 E4
Jack David Ho DY4 . . . . 52 D5
Jackdaw Cl DY3 . . . . 39 C2
Jackdaw Dr B36 . . . . 70 A8
Jacker's Rd CV2 . . . . 96 B4
Jackfield Cl B98 . . . . 154 E1
Jack Hayward Way WV1. 163 B4
Jack Holden Ave WV14 . . . 40 A2
Jacklin Dr CV3 . . . . 133 C4
Jacknell Rd LE10 . . . . 74 D8
Jack Newell Ct 3 WV14 . . 51 C8
Jack O'Watton Bsns Pk
B46 . . . . 59 D3
Jackson Ave B8 . . . . 67 F4
Jackson Cl
Birmingham B11 . . . . 87 B7
Featherstone WV10 . . . . 12 A6
Keresley CV7 . . . . 95 A7
Norton Canes WS11 . . . . 5 E4
Oldbury B68 . . . . 64 B5
Wednesbury DY4 . . . . 41 B1
Jackson Ct
Brierley Hill DY5 . . . . 61 F1
Oldbury B69 . . . . 63 F4
Jackson Dr B67 . . . . 64 D5
Jackson Gr CV8 . . . . 148 C4
Jackson Ho 9 B69 . . . . 64 A7
Jackson Rd
Birmingham B8 . . . . 67 F4
Coventry CV6 . . . . 95 D1
Lichfield WS13 . . . . 3 B3
Jackson St
Oldbury B68 . . . . 64 B4
Stourbridge DY9 . . . . 81 E6
Wolverhampton WV6 . . . . . . 25 B4
Jackson Way B32 . . . . 84 A5
Jackson Wlk B35 . . . . 58 A2
Jackwood Gn CV12 . . . . 95 C8
Jacmar Cres B67 . . . . 64 E6
Jacob Dr CV4 . . . . 132 D6
Jacobean La B93 . . . . 108 B1
Jacob's Hall La WS6 . . . . 5 B1
Jacoby Pl B5 . . . . 86 C5
Jacox Cres CV8 . . . . 148 C5
Jacquard Cl CV3 . . . . 133 D4
Jacquard Ho 3 CV1 . . . . 113 E4
Jade Cl CV1 . . . . 165 D4
Jade Gr WS11 . . . . 2 C2
Jaffray Cres B24 . . . . 56 F3
Jaffray Ct B23 . . . . 56 E3
Jaffray Rd B24 . . . . 56 F3
Jaguar B77 . . . . 21 E2
Jakeman Cl B98 . . . . 154 E4
Jakeman Rd B12 . . . . 86 E5
James Beattie Ho WV6 . . . 24 C4
James Bridge Cl WS2 . . . . 42 B7
James Brindley Sch
(Parkway Ctr) B15 . . . . . . 86 C8
James Brindley Sch (Willow
Ctr) B13 . . . . 86 E1
James Cl WS10 . . . . 41 F7
James Clift Ho 3 B69 . . . . 63 D5
James Cl B67 . . . . 65 A5
Jamescroft CV3 . . . . 134 E6
James Ct
13 Birmingham,Moseley
B13 . . . . 87 B2
Birmingham,King's Norton
B38 . . . . 103 F2
Warwick CV34 . . . . 160 F7
James Dawson Dr CV5 . . 111 B8
James Dee Cl DY5 . . . . 62 A1
James Diskin Ct CV11 . . . . 73 E2
James Eaton Cl B71 . . . . . . 53 C5
James Galloway Cl CV3 . 134 E7
James Green Rd CV4 . . . . 111 F2
James Greenway WS13 . . . . 3 A2
James Ho
Birmingham B19 . . . . 66 C6
Coventry CV2 . . . . 114 C8
James Hutchens Ct WS7 . . . 6 F5
James Lloyd Trust Flats
B30 . . . . 103 C5
James Meml Homes The 4
B7 . . . . 67 C7
Jameson Rd B6 . . . . 67 C8
Jameson St WV6 . . . . 25 B4
James Rd
Birmingham,Great Barr
B43 . . . . 54 E7
Birmingham,Tyseley B11 . . . 87 F6
Coleshill B46 . . . . 70 F8
Kidderminster DY10 . . . . . 117 A8
James Samuel Pl 7 B12 . 86 F7
James Scott Rd B63 . . . . . . 82 A6
James St
Bilston WV14 . . . . 40 E6
Birmingham B3 . . . . 164 A3
Cannock WS11 . . . . 1 F5
Nuneaton CV11 . . . . 73 A5
Willenhall WV13 . . . . 27 A3
James Turner St B18 . . . . . 65 E6
James Watt Dr B19 . . . . . . 66 C8
James Watt Ho B66 . . . . . . 65 B6
James Watt Prim Sch
B21 . . . . 65 E7
James Watt Queensway
B4 . . . . 164 C3
James Watt St
Birmingham B4 . . . . 164 C3
West Bromwich B71 . . . . . . 53 B8
Jane Lane Cl WS2 . . . . 27 F4
Jane Lane Sch WS2 . . . . 27 F3
Janice Gr B14 . . . . 105 B4
Janie Ct B13 . . . . 87 C2
Janine Ave WV11 . . . . 26 E7
Jaques Cl B46 . . . . 59 B2
Jardine Cres CV4 . . . . 111 F2
Jardine Rd B6 . . . . 55 F1
Jarvis Cl LE10 . . . . 71 D4
Jarvis Cres B69 . . . . 64 A4
Jarvis Rd B23 . . . . 56 F6
Jarvis Way B24 . . . . 67 E8
JAS Ind Pk B65 . . . . 63 E4
Jasmin Croft B14 . . . . 104 E3
Jasmine Cl WV9 . . . . 11 A3
Jasmine Gr
Bromsgrove B61 . . . . 136 F4
Codsall WV8 . . . . 10 B3
Coventry CV3 . . . . 134 C8
Royal Leamington Spa
CV32 . . . . 157 A2
Jasmine Rd
Dudley DY2 . . . . 51 F1
Tamworth B77 . . . . 22 A4
Jasmine Way WS10 . . . . 41 D7
Jason Cl B77 . . . . 21 D5
Jason Rd DY9 . . . . 81 F4
Javelin Ave B35 . . . . 58 B2
Javelin Way WS10 . . . . 41 D2
Jayne Cl
Wednesfield WV11 . . . . 26 D7
West Bromwich B71 . . . . . . 42 E1
Jay Park Cres DY10 . . . . . 117 B2
Jay Rd DY6 . . . . 60 D8
Jays Ave DY4 . . . . 52 B4
Jays Cres B48 . . . . 123 B1
Jayshaw Ave B43 . . . . 54 E8
Jeal Cl B47 . . . . 124 E2
Jean Dr DY4 . . . . 52 D6
Jeavons Pl WV14 . . . . 40 C5
Jedburgh Ave WV6 . . . . . . 23 E4
Jedburgh Gr CV3 . . . . 133 A4
Jeddo St WV2 . . . . 163 B1
Jeffcock Rd WV3 . . . . 39 A7
Jefferies Cl LE10 . . . . 71 E2
Jefferson Cl B71 . . . . 53 B8
Jeffrey Ave WV4 . . . . 39 F5
Jeffrey Cl CV12 . . . . 95 D8
Jeffrey Rd B65 . . . . 63 E3
Jeffrey Woods Cross
CV1 . . . . 113 F4
Jeffries Ho 11 B69 . . . . 64 A7
Jeffs Ave WV2 . . . . 163 C1
Jeliff St CV4 . . . . 111 F2
Jelleyman Cl DY11 . . . . . . 116 C6
Jellicoe Ho 9 DY4 . . . . 52 A8
Jellicoe Way LE10 . . . . 71 D3
Jenkins Ave CV5 . . . . 111 F4
Jenkins Cl WV14 . . . . 40 C5
Jenkinson Rd WS10 . . . . . . 41 D1
Jenkins St B10 . . . . 87 C8
Jenks Ave WV10 . . . . 25 E8
Jennens Rd B4 . . . . 66 F3
Jenner Cl WS2 . . . . 28 A6
Jenner Ho WS2 . . . . 27 F6
Jenner Rd WS2 . . . . 28 A6
Jenner St
Coventry CV1 . . . . 165 C4
Wolverhampton WV2 . . . . . 163 D2
Jennifer Wlk B25 . . . . 88 E8
Jennings St B64 . . . . 62 F2
Jenny Cl WV14 . . . . 40 E1
Jennyns Ct 3 WS10 . . . . . . 42 A3
Jenny Walkers La WV6 . . . 23 D1
Jensen B77 . . . . 21 E2
Jenton Rd CV31 . . . . 162 B6
Jephcott Gr B8 . . . . 68 A4
Jephcott Ho 2 CV1 . . . . . 113 E3
Jephcott Rd B8 . . . . 68 A4
Jephson Ct CV2 . . . . 96 C4
Jephson Dr B26 . . . . 88 F7
Jephson Pl 3 CV31 . . . . . 162 B7
Jeremy Gr B92 . . . . 89 B3
Jeremy Rd WV4 . . . . 39 C5
Jerome Ct B74 . . . . 30 F1
Jerome Dr WS11 . . . . 6 A5
Jerome K Jerome Mus★
WS1 . . . . 28 E1
Jerome Prim Sch WS11 . . . . 5 F5
Jerome Rd
Norton Canes WS11 . . . . 6 A5
Sutton Coldfield B72 . . . . . . 46 D4
Walsall WS2 . . . . 28 B1
Jerome Way WS7 . . . . 7 C7
Jerrard Dr B75 . . . . 46 C6
Jerrard Mews B75 . . . . 46 C5
Jerry's La
Birmingham B23 . . . . 56 E6
Weeford WS14 . . . . 19 B8
Jersey Cl B98 . . . . 154 D7
Jersey Croft B36 . . . . 70 B6
Jersey Rd B8 . . . . 67 D4
Jerusalem Wlk DY10 . . . . 116 E7
Jervis Cl DY5 . . . . 61 C7
Jervis Cres B74 . . . . 31 D3
Jervis Ct 2 WS1 . . . . 28 F2
Jervis Pk B74 . . . . 31 C4
Jervis Rd B77 . . . . 35 F5
Jervis Terr B21 . . . . 65 D8
Jervoise Dr B31 . . . . 103 B5
Jervoise Jun & Inf Sch
B29 . . . . 85 A1
Jervoise La B71 . . . . 42 E1
Jervoise Rd B29 . . . . 85 A2
Jervoise St B70 . . . . 53 A4
Jesmond Gr B24 . . . . 57 E4
Jesmond Rd CV1 . . . . 113 F4
Jessel Rd WS2 . . . . 28 C2
Jessie Rd WS9 . . . . 16 B1
Jesson Cl WS1 . . . . 43 A7
Jesson Ct WS1 . . . . 43 A8
Jesson Rd
Dudley DY3 . . . . 51 A6
Sutton Coldfield B75 . . . . . . 47 A5
Walsall WS1 . . . . 43 A8
Jesson's CE Prim Sch
DY1 . . . . 51 B1
Jesson St B70 . . . . 53 E2
Jessop Dr B77 . . . . 21 E5
Jevons Dr 7 DY4 . . . . 52 B5
Jevons Rd B73 . . . . 45 C3
Jevon St WV14 . . . . 51 B8
Jewellery Quarter Sta
B18 . . . . 66 B4
Jew's La DY3 . . . . 50 E4
Jiggins La B32 . . . . 84 D1
Jill Ave B43 . . . . 43 C1
Jillcot Rd B92 . . . . 89 B3
Jill La B96 . . . . 159 B2
Jim Forrest Cl 4 CV3 . . . 134 F8
Jinnah Cl B12 . . . . 86 F8
Jinnah Rd B98 . . . . 153 E2
Joanna Dr CV3 . . . . 133 C3
Joan of Arc Ho CV3 . . . . . 133 E6
Joan's Cl CV31 . . . . 162 C6
Joan St WV2 . . . . 39 E6
Joan Ward St CV3 . . . . . . 133 D8
Job's La CV4 . . . . 112 A2
Jockey Field DY3 . . . . 50 E6
Jockey La WS10 . . . . 42 A4
Jockey Rd B73 . . . . 46 A2
Jodrell St CV11 . . . . 73 B6
Joe Jones Ct DY3 . . . . 39 D1
Joe OBrien Cl CV3 . . . . . . 134 C6
Joe Williams Cl 7 CV3 . . 134 F8
Joeys La WV8 . . . . 10 C3
John Black Day Hospl
B37 . . . . 90 C8
John Bosco Cl B71 . . . . 53 B7
John Bright Cl DY4 . . . . 51 F8
John Bright St B1 . . . . 164 B2
John Cleveland Coll LE10 71 F1
Johndory B77 . . . . 35 D6
John F Kennedy Wlk 4
DY4 . . . . 52 A8
John Fletcher Cl WS10 . . . 42 B4
John Grace St CV3 . . . . . . 133 D8
John Gulson Prim Sch
CV1 . . . . 113 D5
John Harper St WV13 . . . . 27 B2
John Haynes Ct CV7 . . . . . 96 A7
John Ho DY1 . . . . 61 D8
John Howell Dr DY4 . . . . . 52 A5
John Kempe Way B12 . . . . 87 A7
John Knight Rd CV12 . . . . . 78 B5
John McGuire Cres CV3 . 134 E7
John Nash Sq CV8 . . . . . . 147 F3
John Nichols St LE10 . . . . . 75 B7
John of Gaunt Ho CV3 . . . 133 E6
John O'Gaunt Rd CV8 . . . 147 E3
John Rd B62 . . . . 83 F3
John Riley Dr WV12 . . . . . . 27 C8
John Rous Ave CV4 . . . . . 132 B7
John's Cl LE10 . . . . 75 D5
Johns Cl B80 . . . . 159 C4
Johns Gr B43 . . . . 54 C8
John Shelton Com Prim Sch
CV6 . . . . 95 D4
John Shelton Dr CV6 . . . . . 95 D4
John Sinclair Ho CV1 . . . 165 B4
Johns La WS6 . . . . 5 A3
John's La
Oldbury B69 . . . . 52 C3
Tipton DY4 . . . . 52 B4
John Smith Ho 3 B1 . . . . . 66 C3
Johnson Ave WV11 . . . . 26 F7
Johnson Cl
Birmingham,Sparkhill B11 . . 87 C5
Birmingham,Ward End B8 . . 68 C6
Darlaston WS10 . . . . 41 D5
Lichfield WS13 . . . . 3 C1
Redditch B98 . . . . 154 A5
Johnson Dr B35 . . . . 57 F3
Johnson Pl 3 WV14 . . . . . . 41 A7
Johnson Rd
Bedworth CV12 . . . . 78 C3
Birmingham B23 . . . . 57 A6
Burntwood WS7 . . . . 6 F8
Cannock WS11 . . . . 1 D4
Coventry CV6 . . . . 114 A8
Darlaston WS10 . . . . 41 D5
Wednesbury WS10 . . . . 42 C2
Willenhall WV12 . . . . 27 D7
Johnsons Bridge Rd B71 . 53 C6
Johnsons Gr B68 . . . . 84 D8
Johnson St
Birmingham B7 . . . . 67 C6
Wolverhampton,Cinder Hill
WV14 . . . . 39 F1
Wolverhampton WV2 . . . . . . 39 D7
Wood End CV9 . . . . 36 C1
John St
Bedworth CV12 . . . . 78 A2
Birmingham B19 . . . . 66 B7
Brierley Hill DY5 . . . . 61 D4
Cannock,Chadsmoor WS11 . . 2 A4
Cannock,Wimblebury WS12 . . 2 F3
Hinckley LE10 . . . . 71 E1
Nuneaton,Coton CV11 . . . . . 73 C2
Nuneaton,Stockingford
CV10 . . . . 72 E3
Oldbury B69 . . . . 64 A7
Johnstone St B19 . . . . 66 D8
Johnston St B70 . . . . 53 D1
John Street N B71 . . . . 53 B5
John St
Rowley Regis B65 . . . . 63 C1
Royal Leamington Spa
CV32 . . . . 161 F8
Stourbridge DY8 . . . . 60 F1
Tamworth B77 . . . . 21 E4
Walsall WS2 . . . . 28 E3
West Bromwich,Great Bridge
B70 . . . . 52 F5
West Bromwich,Guns Village
B70 . . . . 53 B4
Willenhall WV13 . . . . 27 A1
Wolverhampton WV2 . . . . . . 40 A6
John Tofts Ho CV1 . . . . . . 165 B4
John Wesley Way WS10 . . 42 A1
John Willmott Sch B76 . . . . 46 F4
John Wooton Ho 3
WS10 . . . . 41 D6
Joiners Croft B92 . . . . 107 E8
Joinings Bank B68 . . . . 64 B4
Jonathan Rd CV2 . . . . 114 F8
Jon Baker Ct LE10 . . . . 75 E8
Jonesfield Cres WV1 . . . . . 26 B2
Jones Ho WS2 . . . . 28 D3
Jones La
Burntwood WS7 . . . . 7 F7
Great Wyrley WS6 . . . . 5 B1
Jones Rd
Bedworth CV7 . . . . 78 A1
Walsall WV12 . . . . 13 D1
Willenhall WV12 . . . . 27 D8
Wolverhampton WV10 . . . . . 25 C6
Jones Wood Cl B76 . . . . . . 58 A7
Jonfield Gdns B43 . . . . 43 F1
Jonkel Ave B77 . . . . 36 A5
Jonquil Cl B23 . . . . 56 C7
Jordan Cl
4 Lichfield WS13 . . . . 9 A8
Kenilworth CV8 . . . . 148 B2
Kidderminster DY11 . . . . . 116 A6
Smethwick B66 . . . . 65 B5
Sutton Coldfield B75 . . . . . . 32 B1
Jordan Ho B36 . . . . 68 E8
Jordan Leys 2 DY4 . . . . . . 52 B5
Jordan Pl WV14 . . . . 40 E3
Jordan Rd B75 . . . . 32 C2
Jordans Cl B97 . . . . 158 D6
Jordans The CV5 . . . . 112 C4
Jordan Way WS9 . . . . 16 B1
Jordan Well CV1 . . . . 165 C2
Joseph Cash Prim Sch
CV6 . . . . 113 C7
Joseph Chamberlain Coll
B12 . . . . 86 F6
Joseph Creighton Cl
CV3 . . . . 134 E7
Joseph Dewsbury Cl WS7 . . 6 F8
Joseph Halpin Ho 3
CV1 . . . . 165 C4
Joseph Latham Ho 3
CV2 . . . . 96 B1
Joseph Leckie Com Tech
Coll WS5 . . . . 42 E5
Joseph Luckman Rd CV12 78 B4
Joseph St B69 . . . . 63 F6
Joseph Turner Prim Sch
DY4 . . . . 52 B7
Josiah Mason Coll B23 . . . 56 C4
Josiah Rd B31 . . . . 102 D2
Jourdain Pk CV34 . . . . 161 E3
Jovian Dr LE10 . . . . 71 A1
Jowett's La B71 . . . . 53 B8
Jowett B77 . . . . 21 E2
Joyberry Dr DY8 . . . . 81 A3
Joyce Pool CV34 . . . . 160 E7
Joynson St WS10 . . . . 41 E5
Jubilee Ave
Redditch B97 . . . . 158 D7
West Bromwich B71 . . . . . . 53 B7
Jubilee Bldgs WS10 . . . . . . 41 D7
Jubilee Bsns Pk DY9 . . . . . 82 A5
Jubilee Cl
Great Wyrley WS6 . . . . 4 F2
Stoke Prior B60 . . . . 150 C1
Walsall WS3 . . . . 28 E6
Jubilee Cres CV6 . . . . 113 B7
Jubilee Ct
Birmingham,Acock's Green
B27 . . . . 88 C2
Birmingham,Turves Green
B31 . . . . 103 B1
Jubilee Dr N DY11 . . . . . . 116 B2
Jubilee Dr S DY11 . . . . . . 116 B2
Jubilee Gdns B23 . . . . 56 B7
Jubilee Ho B98 . . . . 153 E2
Jubilee Park Prim Sch
DY4 . . . . 52 B8
Jubilee Rd
Birmingham B45 . . . . 101 E2
Darlaston WV14 . . . . 41 A4
Tipton DY4 . . . . 52 B8
Jubilee St B71 . . . . 53 D8
Jubilee Terr
Bedworth CV12 . . . . 78 B4
Stoke Prior B60 . . . . 150 C1
Jubilee Trad Ctr B5 . . . . . . 66 E1
Judd Cl CV12 . . . . 77 F3
Judds La CV6 . . . . 95 E4
Judge Cl B69 . . . . 64 A7
Judge Rd DY5 . . . . 81 F7
Juggins La B94 . . . . 141 B7
Julia Ave B24 . . . . 57 F4
Julia Gdns B71 . . . . 53 F8
Julian Cl
Catshill B61 . . . . 137 A8
Coventry CV2 . . . . 114 F8
Great Wyrley WS6 . . . . 5 A3
Wolverhampton WV1 . . . . . . 26 B2
Julian Rd WV1 . . . . 26 B2
Julie Croft WV14 . . . . 40 E1
Juliet Cl CV11 . . . . 74 A1
Juliet Dr CV34 . . . . 161 F3
Juliet Rd B62 . . . . 83 F3
Julius Dr B46 . . . . 59 F1
Junction 2 Ind Est B69 . . . 63 F5
Junction 6 Ind Pk B6 . . . . . 56 B2
Junction Rd
Birmingham B21 . . . . 65 C8
Bromsgrove B61 . . . . 136 E3
Stourbridge,Amblecote DY8 60 E1
Stourbridge DY8 . . . . 81 B4
Wolverhampton WV2 . . . . . . 40 B7
Junction St S B69 . . . . 64 A5
Junction St
Coventry CV1 . . . . 165 A2
Dudley DY2 . . . . 62 B8
Oldbury B69 . . . . 52 E1
Walsall WS1 . . . . 42 D7
Junction The 1 DY8 . . . . . 80 E8
June Cres B77 . . . . 21 E5
June Croft B26 . . . . 89 D5
Juniper Cl
Bedworth CV12 . . . . 77 E2
Birmingham B27 . . . . 88 B5
Burntwood WS7 . . . . 7 A6
Sutton Coldfield B76 . . . . . . 46 F3
Juniper Ct DY10 . . . . 117 A4
Juniper Dr
Coventry CV5 . . . . 111 F5
Sutton Coldfield B76 . . . . . . 58 A7
Walsall WS5 . . . . 43 B4
Juniper Ho B36 . . . . 68 F7
Juniper Rise B63 . . . . 82 C5
Juniper B77 . . . . 22 A4
Juno Dr CV31 . . . . 161 F5
Jurist Ho 5 LE10 . . . . 71 D1
Jury Rd DY5 . . . . 81 F7
Jury St CV34 . . . . 160 E6
Justice Cl CV31 . . . . 162 A4
Jutland Rd B13 . . . . 105 B8

K

Kanzan Rd CV2 . . . . 96 B4

Kareen Gr CV3 135 C7
Karen Cl CV10 72 E7
Karen Way DY5 81 D8
Karlingford Cl CV5 132 D8
Kate's Hill Prim Sch DY2 62 E8
Katherine Ho 3 B17 85 B5
Katherine Rd B67 64 F2
Kathleen Ave CV12 77 E1
Kathleen Rd
Birmingham B25 88 C7
Sutton Coldfield B72 46 C4
Katie Rd B29 85 E1
Katmandu Rd B60 137 C1
Katrine Cl CV10 72 C5
Kayne Cl DY6 60 C7
Keanscott Dr B68 64 C4
Keasden Gr WV13 27 C3
Keating Gdns B75 32 A4
Keatley Ave B33 69 E2
Keats Ave
Birmingham B10 87 D7
Cannock WS11 1 E5
Keats Cl
Dudley DY3 50 A5
Nuneaton CV10 72 A4
Stourbridge DY8 81 A8
Sutton Coldfield B74 31 F6
Tamworth B79 20 F8
Keats Dr WV14 40 D2
Keats Gr
Birmingham B27 88 B1
Wolverhampton WV10 26 A8
Keats Ho
2 Oldbury B68 64 C4
Redditch B97 158 C8
Keats Pl DY10 117 B6
Keats Rd
Coventry CV2 114 D2
Walsall WS3 28 E7
Willenhall WV12 27 E7
Wolverhampton WV10 12 A1
Keble Cl
Burntwood WS7 7 C7
Cannock WS11 4 E8
Keble Gr
Birmingham B26 89 B6
Walsall WS1 43 A7
Keble Ho B37 70 A2
Keble Wlk B79 21 A6
Kebull Gn CV4 131 E8
Kedleston Cl WS3 14 A3
Kedleston Ct B28 105 F4
Kedleston Rd B28 105 F5
Keegan Wlk WS2 27 F4
Keel Dr B13 87 D1
Keele Cl B98 154 E6
Keele Ho B37 70 B4
Keeley St B9 67 B2
Keeling Dr WS11 1 B1
Keelinge St DY4 52 B5
Keeling Rd CV8 148 B5
Keenan Dr CV12 77 D1
Keen St B66 65 D5
Keepers Cl
Birmingham B18 65 F5
Brownhills WS9 15 F3
Keeper's Cl WS7 7 A6
Keepers Cl
Kingswinford DY6 60 B8
Lichfield WS14 9 E7
Keepers Gate Cl B74 46 C7
Keepers Ho B73 45 C2
Keepers La WV6,WV8 10 A1
Keepers Rd B74 31 C5
Keepers Wlk CV12 77 D1
Keer Ct B9 67 B2
Kegworth Cl CV6 96 A4
Kegworth Rd B23 56 C2
Keir Cl CV32 157 A2
Keir Hardie Wlk B69 52 D2
Keir Pl DY8 80 E8
Keir Rd WS10 42 D2
Keith Rd CV32 157 B4
Keith Winter Cl B61 136 F6
Kelby Cl B31 102 E4
Kelby Rd B31 102 F4
Keldy Cl WV6 24 F5
Kele Rd CV4 132 A7
Kelfield Ave B17 85 B4
Kelham Pl B92 89 B1
Kelia Dr B67 64 F6
Kellett Rd B7 67 A4
Kelling Cl DY5 81 C8
Kellington Cl B8 67 F4
Kelmarsh Dr B91 107 B1
Kelmscote Rd CV6 112 F8
Kelmscott Rd B17 85 B7
Kelsall Cl WV1 26 B2
Kelsall Croft B1 66 B3
Kelsey Cl
Birmingham B7 67 B4
Nuneaton CV11 73 E3
Kelsey La CV7 130 D5
Kelsey's Cl CV8 135 F3
Kelso Gdns WV6 23 D4
Kelsull Croft B37 70 A2
Kelton Ct B15 86 A7
Kelvedon Gr B91 107 C4
Kelverdale Gr B14 104 C4
Kelverley Gr B71 43 A1
Kelvestone Ho WS11 1 D1
Kelvin Ave CV2 114 D5
Kelvin Cl DY11 116 A8
Kelvin Dr WS11 2 A3
Kelvin Pl WS2 28 B6
Kelvin Rd
Birmingham B31 103 B1
Royal Leamington Spa CV32 157 C5
Walsall WS2 28 B6
Kelvin Way Trad Est B70 53 B1
Kelvin Way B70 53 C1
Kelway Ave B43 44 B3
Kelway CV3 115 A2
Kelwood Dr B63 83 A5
Kelynmead Rd B33 69 A2
Kemberton Cl WV3 24 C1
Kemberton Rd
Birmingham B29 85 B2
Wolverhampton WV3 24 C1
Kemble Cl WV12 27 D3
Kemble Croft B5 86 E7
Kemble Dr B35 58 A3
Kemelstowe Cres B63 100 C8
Kemerton Ho B97 153 B4
Kemerton Way B90 126 F6
Kemp Cl CV34 161 A7
Kempe Rd B33 69 A4
Kempley Ave CV2 114 C2
Kempsey Cl
Halesowen B63 82 E4
Oldbury B69 63 E4
Redditch B98 159 B7
Solihull B92 89 A3
Kempsey Covert B38 123 E7
Kempsey Ho B32 102 A8
Kempsford Cl B98 158 F6
Kemps Green Rd
Balsall Common CV7 130 B6
Kemps Green B94 143 A1
Kempson Ave
Sutton Coldfield B72 46 C1
West Bromwich B71 53 B5
Kempson Rd B36 68 F8
Kempsons Gr WV14 40 B3
Kempthorne Ave
Wolverhampton WV10 11 E1
Wolverhampton WV10 25 E8
Kempthorne Gdns WS3 14 A2
Kempthorne Rd WV14 40 F6
Kempton Cres CV32 157 C4
Kempton Ct B61 121 A1
Kempton Dr
Great Wyrley WS6 4 F2
Tamworth B77 35 D4
Kempton Park Rd B36 68 D8
Kempton Way DY8 80 E3
Kemsey Dr WV14 40 F3
Kemshead Ave B31 122 E8
Kemsley Rd B14 104 F2
Kem St CV11 73 E2
Kenchester Cl B98 154 F2
Kendal Ave
Birmingham B45 122 B7
Coleshill B46 70 F7
Royal Leamington Spa CV32 156 C2
Kendal Cl
Bromsgrove B60 137 B1
Nuneaton CV11 74 A6
Wolverhampton WV6 24 F6
Kendal Ct
14 Birmingham,Selly Oak B29 103 C7
Birmingham,Stockland Green B23 56 B3
Brownhills WS9 15 F4
Cannock WS11 4 B8
Kendal Dr B45 122 D1
Kendal End Rd B45 122 D1
Kendal Gr B92 107 F8
Kendall Ho 15 B69 63 D5
Kendall Rise DY6 60 F5
Kendal Rd B11 87 B7
Kendal Rise
Coventry CV5 112 C4
Oldbury B68 64 B3
Kendal Rise Rd B45 122 B7
Kendal Rise WV6 24 F6
Kendal Twr 5 B17 85 D5
Kenderdine Montessori Sch CV5 133 A8
Kendon Ave CV6 112 E6
Kendrick Ave B34 69 E5
Kendrick Cl
Coventry CV6 96 A4
Solihull B92 107 F6
Kendrick Pl WV14 41 A4
Kendrick Rd
Darlaston WV14 41 A4
Sutton Coldfield B76 57 F5
Wolverhampton WV10 25 E6
Kendricks Rd WS10 41 F7
Kendrick St WS10 42 A3
Kenelm Cl
Coventry CV3 134 C5
Romsley B62 101 A4
Sutton Coldfield B73 46 B4
Kenelm Rd
Birmingham B10 87 E8
Dudley WV14 40 C1
Oldbury B68 64 A3
Sutton Coldfield B73 46 B4
Kenilcourt CV8 147 D6
Kenilworth Castle★ CV8 147 D5
Kenilworth Cl
Balsall Common CV7 130 A6
Redditch B97 158 D6
Stourbridge DY8 60 D2
Sutton Coldfield B74 46 A8
Tipton DY4 51 D4
Kenilworth Cres
Walsall WS2 28 A4
Kenilworth Cres *continued*
Wolverhampton WV4 39 E4
Kenilworth Ct
2 Cannock WS11 1 E1
Birmingham B15 85 F8
Birmingham,Gravelly Hill B24 56 E2
Coventry CV3 133 C8
Dudley DY1 61 F8
Kenilworth Dr
Cannock WS11 1 D4
Kidderminster DY10 116 E2
Nuneaton CV11 73 B3
Kenilworth Hall Mews CV8 147 F5
Kenilworth Ho
3 Walsall WS3 28 C6
Birmingham B13 105 A6
Kenilworth Rd
Balsall Common CV7, CV8 130 D4
Birmingham,Birchfield B20 55 E2
Birmingham,Warley Woods B68 84 D7
Blackdown CV32 156 E5
Bradnock's Marsh B92 109 E5
Coventry CV4 132 E3
Kenilworth CV8 148 C8
Knowle B93 128 E5
Lichfield WS14 9 B6
Meriden CV7 91 D1
Perton WV6 23 F4
Royal Leamington Spa CV32 157 C6
Tamworth B77 21 E4
Kenilworth Sch Castle Hall Sixth Form CV8 147 F2
Kenilworth Sch CV8 148 C5
Kenilworth St 20 CV32 156 F1
Kenley Gr B30 104 B3
Kenley Way B91 106 D4
Kenmare Way WV11 26 C4
Kenmore Ave WS12 1 F7
Kenmore Dr LE10 71 B2
Kenmure Rd B33 89 C8
Kennan Ave CV31 161 F6
Kennedy Cl
Kidderminster DY10 116 F3
Sutton Coldfield B72 46 C4
Tamworth B77 21 C1
Kennedy Cres
Darlaston WS10 41 C7
Dudley DY3 50 D4
Kennedy Croft B26 89 A7
Kennedy Ct DY8 80 F5
Kennedy Gr B30 104 B6
Kennedy Rd WV10 163 D4
Kennedy Sq 3 CV32 157 A1
Kenneggy Mews B29 85 F2
Kennerley Rd B25 88 D6
Kennet Cl
Brownhills WS8 6 C2
Coventry CV2 114 C8
Kennet Gr B36 69 F8
Kenneth Gr B23 56 B5
Kennet Ho 5 DY1 61 E8
Kenneth Vincent Cl B97 158 E4
Kennet B77 21 D1
Kennford Cl B65 63 C6
Kennington Rd WV10 25 F5
Kenpas Highway CV3 133 A5
Kenrick Croft B35 57 F2
Kenrick Ho
Birmingham B16 66 A1
West Bromwich B70 53 E1
Kenrick Park Sta B70 53 E1
Kenrick Way B70 64 E8
Kensington Ave B12 87 A4
Kensington Ct
Coventry CV5 113 A1
Nuneaton CV10 72 C6
Kensington Dr
Sutton Coldfield B74 31 F5
Tamworth B79 21 B7
Kensington Gdns
Cannock WS11 1 C2
Stourbridge DY8 60 C1
Kensington Pl
Birmingham B8 67 E5
Cannock WS12 5 C8
Kensington Rd
Birmingham B29 86 B2
Coventry CV5 113 A1
Willenhall WV12 27 B7
Kensington St B19 66 D6
Kenswick Dr B63 83 A2
Kent Ave
Fazeley B78 20 F2
Walsall WS2 28 B3
Kent Cl
Aldridge WS9 16 B1
Coventry CV3 133 E6
Kidderminster DY10 116 E3
Kent Close Jun & Inf Sch B71 53 B7
Kent Cl
Walsall WS2 28 E5
West Bromwich B71 53 C7
Kent Dr LE10 71 F4
Kenthurst Cl CV5 111 C4
Kentish Rd B21 65 C8
Kentmere Cl CV2 96 E2
Kentmere Rd B60 137 C1
Kentmere Twr 4 B23 57 B6
Kenton Ave WV6 24 F4
Kenton Wlk 7 B29 85 F2
Kent Pl
Cannock WS12 2 F1
Kent Pl *continued*
Dudley DY2 62 A6
Kent Rd
Birmingham B45 101 F1
Halesowen B62 83 F5
Stourbridge DY8 80 D7
Wednesbury WS10 42 D4
Willenhall WS2 27 F3
Wolverhampton WV2 39 E7
Kent St N B18 65 F5
Kent's Cl B92 88 F3
Kents Ho B33 69 B2
Kent St
Birmingham B5 66 E1
Dudley DY3 50 E5
Walsall WS2 28 E5
Kentwell B79 20 D7
Kenward Croft B17 84 F7
Kenway B47 125 A7
Kenwick Rd B17 85 B4
Kenwood Rd B9 68 B3
Kenwyn Gn CV7 96 B8
Kenyon Cl
Bromsgrove B60 137 A1
Stourbridge DY8 81 A7
Kenyon St B18 164 A4
Kepler B79 20 E7
Keppel St CV1 113 E5
Kerby Rd B23 56 D4
Kererwin Cl B64 63 A1
Keresley Brook Rd CV6 95 A2
Keresley Cl
Coventry CV6 95 A2
Solihull B91 107 C5
Keresley Grange Prim Sch CV6 94 F1
Keresley Gr B29 84 F2
Keresley Green Rd CV6 94 F1
Keresley Newland Prim Sch CV7 94 F7
Keresley Rd CV6 113 A8
Kernthorpe Rd B14 104 D4
Kerr Dr DY4 51 E8
Kerria Ct 3 B15 86 D8
Kerria Ctr B77 22 A4
Kerria Rd B77 22 B4
Kerridge Cl WV9 11 A2
Kerris Way CV3 115 A1
Kerr La B90 126 A6
Kerry Cl
Barwell LE9 71 F7
Birmingham B31 102 F6
Brierley Hill DY5 61 C4
Kerry Croft Cl B97 158 E5
Kerry Ct WS1 43 A8
Kerry Hill 3 B60 150 E6
Kerry's Ho 4 CV1 113 B2
Kersley Gdns WV11 26 F5
Kerswell Cl 2 B97 153 B5
Kerswell Dr B90 127 A5
Kesterton Rd B74 31 E5
Kesteven Cl B15 86 B6
Kesteven Rd B71 53 C7
Keston Rd B44 44 F4
Kestrel Ave B25 88 C8
Kestrel Cl
Birmingham,Castle Vale B35 58 B3
Birmingham,Short Heath B23 56 D6
Hinckley LE10 75 F6
Kidderminster DY10 116 E3
Kestrel Croft 2 CV3 134 F8
Kestrel Ct WS7 7 F8
Kestrel Dr B74 31 F5
Kestrel Gr
Birmingham B30 103 D8
Cannock WS12 2 C1
Willenhall WV12 27 C8
Kestrel Rd
Dudley DY1 51 A1
Halesowen B63 82 B7
Oldbury B68 63 F2
Kestrel Rise WV6 24 F7
Kestrel B77 36 A6
Kestrel View B60 137 C7
Kestrel Way WS6 4 C2
Keswick Cl CV11 74 A6
Keswick Dr DY6 60 D6
Keswick Gn CV32 156 D1
Keswick Gr B74 30 F2
Keswick Ho 14 B69 63 D5
Keswick Rd B92 89 A4
Keswick Wlk CV2 114 F4
Ketley Croft B12 86 F7
Ketley Fields DY6 61 A5
Ketley Hill Rd DY1 61 F8
Ketley Rd
Kingswinford DY6 60 F6
Kingswinford DY6 60 F7
Kettlebrook Rd
Solihull B90 127 C6
Tamworth B77 21 C3
Kettlehouse Rd B44 44 F3
Kettlesbank Rd DY3 50 B2
Kettles Wood Dr B32 84 C2
Kettlewell Cl CV34 155 E1
Kettlewell Way B37 69 F1
Ketton Gr B33 89 D7
Keviliok St CV3 133 D6
Kew Cl
Birmingham B37 69 F3
Kenilworth CV8 148 C5
Kew Dr DY1 51 A2
Kew Gdns B33 68 E1
Kew Ho CV4 111 F3
Kewstoke Cl WV12 13 B1
Kewstoke Croft B31 102 E6
Kewstoke Rd WV12 13 C1
Key Bsns Pk B24 57 D3
Keyes Dr DY6 49 D1
Key Hill B18 66 B5
Key Hill Dr B18 66 B5
Key Ind Pk WV13 26 D3
Keynell Covert B30 104 C2
Keynes Dr WV14 40 E6
Keys Cl WS12 2 C3
Keys Cres B71 53 C6
Keyse Rd B75 46 F7
Keysmith Cl WV13 27 C1
Keys Park Rd WS12 2 E3
Keyte Cl DY4 52 A5
Keyway Jct WV13 41 B8
Keyway Ret Pk WV13 41 B8
Keyway The WV13 41 A8
Keyworth Cl DY4 52 B5
Khyber Cl WS10 41 C8
Kidd Croft DY4 41 C2
Kidderminster Coll DY10 116 E5
Kidderminster General Hospl DY11 116 C5
Kidderminster Railway Mus★ DY10 116 F5
Kidderminster Rd
Bromsgrove B61 136 C3
Iverley DY8 98 C7
Kingswinford DY6 60 B7
Kidderminster Rd S DY9 98 F3
Kidderminster Rd DY9 99 B5
Kidderminster Sta DY10 116 F5
Kidderminster Town Sta★ DY10 116 F5
Kidson Eventide Homes WV6 24 F5
Kielder Cl
Cannock WS12 2 E2
Walsall WS5 43 C3
Kielder Dr CV10 72 E2
Kielder Gdns DY9 81 B1
Kier's Bridge Cl DY4 52 B3
Kilberry Cl LE10 71 A1
Kilburn Dr
Coventry CV5 112 F3
Kingswinford DY6 49 E1
Kilburn Gr B44 44 F3
Kilburn Pl DY2 62 D6
Kilburn Rd B44 44 F3
Kilby Ave B16 66 A2
Kilby Ct CV31 162 A6
Kilbye Cl B77 35 F5
Kilby Gn LE10 75 F6
Kilby Gr CV31 162 C5
Kilbys Gr B20 54 F2
Kilcote Rd B90 105 C2
Kildale Cl CV1 165 D3
Kilderkin Ct CV1 165 C1
Kildwick Way 5 CV34 155 E1
Kilmarie Cl LE10 71 A1
Kilmet Wlk 1 B67 65 A5
Kilmore Croft B36 68 E8
Kilmorie Rd
Birmingham B27 88 C5
Cannock WS11 1 C2
Kiln Cl
Nuneaton CV10 72 E3
Royal Leamington Spa CV32 157 A1
Studley B80 159 C4
Kiln Croft B65 63 A4
Kiln La
Birmingham B11 88 B6
Solihull B90 126 A5
Kilnsey Gr CV34 155 E1
Kiln Way B78 22 F1
Kilpeck Cl B98 154 F2
Kilsall Ct 12 WV3 25 C4
Kilsby Gr B91 127 C8
Kilvert Rd WS10 42 B2
Kilworth Ho 8 CV32 156 F1
Kimberley Ave B8 67 E5
Kimberley Cl
Coventry CV5 111 F4
Redditch B98 154 B7
Sutton Coldfield B74 31 A2
Kimberley Pl WV14 51 B7
Kimberley Rd
Baginton CV8 133 F2
Bedworth CV12 78 C4
Smethwick B66 65 A7
Solihull B92 89 A1
Kimberley St WV3 25 A1
Kimberley B77 35 F7
Kimberley Wlk B76 58 D6
Kimble Cl CV5 112 B4
Kimble Gr B24 57 D3
Kimbley Rise B71 53 A7
Kimbolton Dr B60 138 A5
Kimmond Ct 21 CV32 156 F1
Kimpton Cl B14 104 E2
Kimsan Croft B74 45 A7
Kinchford Cl B91 127 B8
Kineton Cl B98 154 D1
Kineton Croft B32 102 D8
Kineton Green Prim Sch B92 88 D1
Kineton Green Rd B92 106 D8
Kineton Ho B13 105 A6
Kineton La B90,B94 127 A1
Kineton Rd
Birmingham B45 121 E7
Coventry CV2 114 C6
Kenilworth CV8 148 C4
Sutton Coldfield B73 45 E1
Kineton Rise DY3 39 C2
Kinfare Dr WV6 24 B4
Kinfare Rise DY3 50 E4

King Charles Ave WS2 ... 27 E2
King Charles Cl DY11 ... 116 C6
King Charles Ct B44 ... 45 B2
King Charles I Sch DY10 117 A5
King Charles Prim Sch
WS2 ... 27 F2
King Charles Rd B62 ... 83 F4
King Charles Sq 4 DY10 116 E6
King David Jun & Inf Sch
B13 ... 86 F2
King Edmund St 1 DY1 .. 51 B2
King Edward Ave B61 ... 136 F5
King Edward Rd
Birmingham B13 ... 86 F3
Bromsgrove B61 ... 136 F5
Coventry CV1 ... 113 F4
Nuneaton CV11 ... 73 D4
King Edwards Cl B20 ... 66 B8
King Edwards Gdns B20 .. 66 B7
King Edwards Rd B1 ... 66 B2
King Edward's Row WV2 163 B1
King Edward's Sch B15 .. 86 A4
King Edward's Sq B73 ... 46 B5
King Edward St WS10 ... 41 D6
King Edwards Wharf B16 . 66 B2
King Edward VI Aston Sch
B6 ... 66 F8
King Edward VI Camp Hill
Sch For Boys B14 ... 104 D7
King Edward VI Camp Hill
Sch For Girls B14 ... 104 D7
King Edward VI Coll
Nuneaton CV11 ... 73 D4
Stourbridge DY8 ... 81 A6
King Edward VI Five Ways
Sch B32 ... 102 C8
King Edward VI Handsworth
Sch B21 ... 66 A7
King Edward VI High Sch for
Girls B15 ... 86 A4
King Edward VI Sch WS14 . 9 C6
Kingfield Ind Est CV1 ... 113 C6
Kingfield Rd
Coventry CV1,CV6 ... 113 D7
Solihull B90 ... 105 C2
Kingfisher Ave CV10 ... 72 C5
Kingfisher Cl
Birmingham B26 ... 89 A6
Brownhills WS8 ... 15 E7
Sedgley DY3 ... 39 C2
Kingfisher Ct
Alvechurch B48 ... 139 A7
Burntwood WS7 ... 7 E8
Hinckley LE10 ... 74 F6
Kingfisher Dr
Birmingham B36 ... 70 A8
Cannock WS12 ... 2 C5
Stourbridge DY8 ... 80 C4
Kingfisher Ent Pk B98 ... 154 A3
Kingfisher Gr
Kidderminster DY10 ... 117 B3
Willenhall WV12 ... 27 C8
Kingfisher Ind Est B70 ... 52 F4
Kingfisher Prim Sch B36 . 70 A8
Kingfisher Rd B23 ... 56 C7
Kingfisher Sh Ctr 2 B97 153 E3
Kingfisher Sq B97 ... 153 D4
Kingfisher B77 ... 36 A6
Kingfisher View B34 ... 69 A5
Kingfisher Way B30 ... 103 D8
Kingfisher Wlk B97 ... 153 D4
King George Ave B61 ... 136 F4
King George Cl B61 ... 136 F4
King George Cres WS4 ... 29 B6
King George Pl WS4 ... 29 B6
King George's Ave
Bedworth CV12 ... 78 B5
Coventry CV6 ... 95 F2
King George's Way LE10 .. 75 B7
King George VI Ave WS5 . 29 C1
King George V Prim Sch
B70 ... 53 D3
Kingham Cl
Dudley DY3 ... 50 C2
Redditch B98 ... 154 F4
Kingham Covert B14 ... 104 D2
King Henry VIII Sch CV3 165 A1
Kingland Dr CV32 ... 156 C1
Kingmead Ho B14 ... 104 D4
King Richard Rd LE10 ... 71 C2
King Richard St CV2 ... 113 F3
Kings Ave WS12 ... 2 C4
King's Ave B69 ... 52 B2
Kingsbridge Ho B23 ... 56 B6
Kingsbridge Rd
Birmingham B32 ... 84 D1
Nuneaton CV10 ... 73 D6
Kingsbridge Wlk 6 B66 .. 65 B5
Kingsbrook Dr B91 ... 127 B8
Kings Bsns Pk B44 ... 44 E3
Kingsbury Ave B24 ... 57 D3
Kingsbury Bsns Pk B76 ... 58 E6
Kingsbury Cl
Minworth B76 ... 58 D5
Walsall WS4 ... 29 B4
Kingsbury Rd
2 Tipton DY4 ... 52 A8
Birmingham B35,B76 ... 58 B5
Birmingham,Birches Green
B24 ... 57 B3
Birmingham,Tyburn B24,B35 57 E3
Coventry CV6 ... 112 E5
Curdworth B76 ... 59 B6
Minworth B76 ... 58 D5
Kingsbury Sch & Sports Coll
B24 ... 57 A2
King's CE Sch The WV6 ... 24 B5
Kings Cl B14 ... 104 C6
Kingsclere Wlk WV4 ... 38 C6
Kingscliff Rd B10 ... 88 A8
Kingscote Cl B98 ... 154 D7
Kingscote Gr CV3 ... 133 A4
Kingscote Rd
Birmingham B15 ... 85 E6
Dorridge B93 ... 127 E2
Kings Croft
Birmingham,Castle Bromwich
B36 ... 69 F7
Birmingham,Sheldon B26 .. 89 A5
Cannock WS12 ... 2 E4
Kingscroft Cl B74 ... 45 A8
Kingscroft Rd B74 ... 45 A8
King's Ct CV11 ... 73 B4
Kings Ctr B23 ... 56 E3
Kings Ct
Stourbridge DY8 ... 80 E5
Sutton Coldfield B75 ... 32 B3
Tipton DY4 ... 52 A4
Kingsdene Ave DY6 ... 60 C4
Kingsdown Ave B42 ... 55 A6
Kingsdown Rd B31 ... 84 F1
Kingsfield Rd B14 ... 104 E8
Kingsford Cl B36 ... 58 D1
Kingsford Ct B92 ... 89 B3
Kingsford Nouveau DY6 .. 61 A5
Kingsford Rd CV6 ... 113 C7
Kingsgate Ho B37 ... 70 A2
Kings Gdn B30 ... 103 E4
Kings Gdns CV12 ... 78 C2
Kings Gr CV2 ... 114 B3
Kings Green Ave B38 ... 103 F2
Kings Hall 2 B13 ... 87 A2
Kingshayes Rd WS9 ... 16 B1
Kings Heath Boys
Mathematics & Computing
Coll B13 ... 105 A6
Kings Heath Jun Sch B14 86 F1
King's High Sch for Girls The
CV34 ... 160 E7
Kings Hill Cl WS10 ... 41 E5
King's Hill Day Hospl
WS10 ... 41 E5
Kingshill Dr B38 ... 103 F2
King's Hill Field WS10 ... 41 E5
King's Hill La CV3 ... 133 B2
Kings Hill Mews WS10 ... 41 D5
Kings Hill Pk Ind Est
WS10 ... 41 E4
King's Hill Prim Sch
WS10 ... 41 E5
King's Hill Rd WS14 ... 9 C6
Kings Ho B24 ... 57 A4
Kingsholm Cl CV3 ... 115 B1
Kingshurst Ho B37 ... 69 F5
Kingshurst Inf Sch B37 .. 70 A6
Kingshurst Jun Sch B37 .. 70 A6
Kingshurst CV31 ... 162 E6
Kingshurst Rd
Birmingham B31 ... 103 A3
Solihull B90 ... 105 F1
Kingshurst Way B37 ... 69 F5
Kingsland Ave CV5 ... 112 F2
Kingsland Dr B93 ... 127 E4
Kingsland Prim Sch B44 . 44 F4
Kingsland Rd
Birmingham B44 ... 44 F4
Wolverhampton WV1 ... 25 B3
Kingslea Rd B91 ... 106 E2
Kingslea B73 ... 45 F1
Kingsleigh Croft B75 ... 32 B2
Kingsleigh Dr B36 ... 69 A8
Kingsleigh Rd B20 ... 55 B2
Kingsley Ave
Cannock WS12 ... 2 C7
Redditch B98 ... 154 A3
Wolverhampton WV6 ... 24 B4
Kingsley Bank Way B26 .. 89 B7
Kingsley Cl B79 ... 21 A6
Kingsley Coll B98 ... 159 C6
Kingsley Cres CV12 ... 79 B3
Kingsley Ct
Binley Woods CV3 ... 135 D6
Birmingham B25 ... 88 E8
Kingsley Gr DY3 ... 50 A5
Kingsley Prep Sch B93 .. 128 A4
Kingsley Rd
Birmingham,Balsall Heath
B12 ... 87 A6
Birmingham,King's Norton
B30 ... 103 D4
Kingswinford DY6 ... 60 C5
Kingsley Sch The CV32 .. 156 F1
Kingsley St
Dudley DY2 ... 62 C5
Walsall WS2 ... 42 B7
Kingsley Terr CV2 ... 114 E8
Kingsley Wlk CV2 ... 114 F7
Kingslow Ave WV4 ... 38 D6
King's Mdw DY9 ... 99 E3
Kings Mdw CV10 ... 72 A3
Kingsmead Mews CV3 ... 134 D6
Kingsmead Tech Coll
WS12 ... 2 C4
Kingsmere Cl B24 ... 56 F2
Kings Mews WS14 ... 9 B5
King's Norton Boys Sch
B30 ... 103 E4
Kings Norton Bsns Ctr
B30 ... 104 A4
King's Norton Girls Sch
B30 ... 103 F5
Kings Norton High Sch
B38 ... 123 F8
King's Norton Prim Sch
B30 ... 104 A2
King's Norton Sta B30 ... 103 F4
Kingsoak Gdns DY2 ... 62 E7
Kings Par B4 ... 164 C2
Kings Park Dr CV3 ... 115 B1
Kingspiece Ho 6 B36 ... 68 E8
King's Rd B44 ... 44 E3
Kings Rd
Birmingham,Stirchley
B14 ... 104 C6
Birmingham,Stockland Green
B23 ... 56 D4
Birmingham,Tyseley B11 ... 88 A6
King's Rd DY11 ... 116 C6
Kings Rd
Sedgley DY3 ... 50 E8
Sutton Coldfield B44,B73 .. 45 B2
Walsall WS4 ... 29 C7
King's Rise Com Prim Sch
B44 ... 45 A2
Kings Road Ind Est B25 .. 88 A6
Kings Sq WV14 ... 51 A8
King St
2 Hinckley LE10 ... 71 D1
6 Willenhall WV13 ... 27 B2
Kingstanding Ctr B44 ... 44 F3
Kingstanding Rd B44 ... 55 F7
Kingstanding Sch B44 ... 44 E1
King St
Bedworth CV12 ... 78 C2
Bilston WV14 ... 40 E3
Birmingham B11 ... 87 A7
Brierley Hill DY5 ... 82 A8
Brownhills WS9 ... 15 F2
Burntwood WS7 ... 6 F5
Cradley Heath B64 ... 62 F1
Darlaston WS10 ... 41 D6
Dudley DY2 ... 51 C1
Dudley,The Coppice WV14 .. 51 A8
Kings Terr B14 ... 104 D6
King St B63 ... 83 A4
Kingsthorne Prim Sch
B44 ... 45 A1
Kingsthorpe Rd B14 ... 105 A3
Kingston Arc WS11 ... 1 E1
Kingston Cl B79 ... 21 C7
Kingston Ct 17 B29 ... 103 C7
Kingston Ctr PRU WV6 ... 24 F5
Kingston Ct B74 ... 46 B7
Kingston Dr LE10 ... 71 E4
Kingston Ho CV12 ... 95 C8
Kingston Ind Est B9 ... 67 B1
Kingston Mews CV31 ... 162 C6
Kingston Rd
Birmingham B9 ... 67 B1
Coventry CV5 ... 112 F2
Sutton Coldfield B75 ... 46 F6
Kingston Row B1 ... 66 C2
Kingston Way DY6 ... 60 C7
King Street Pas
2 Dudley DY2 ... 51 D1
Brierley Hill DY5 ... 82 A8
King St
Royal Leamington Spa
CV32 ... 157 A1
Smethwick B66 ... 65 B7
Stourbridge DY8 ... 80 E6
Stourbridge,Lye DY9 ... 81 F5
Tamworth B79 ... 21 B5
Walsall WS1 ... 42 D7
Wednesbury WS10 ... 41 E3
Wolverhampton WV1 ... 163 C3
Kingsway Ave 8 DY4 ... 52 A8
Kingsway
Birmingham B68 ... 84 B7
Cannock WS11 ... 2 A4
Kingsway Com Prim Sch
CV31 ... 161 F6
Kingsway CV2 ... 114 A3
Kingsway Dr B38 ... 103 F2
Kingsway WV11 ... 13 A4
Kingsway Ho CV12 ... 78 C2
Kingsway CV11 ... 73 B4
Kingsway Rd WV10 ... 26 A6
Kingsway
Royal Leamington Spa
CV31 ... 161 F6
Stourbridge DY8 ... 80 E8
Wolverhampton WV10 ... 26 A6
Kingswear Ave WV6 ... 23 F3
Kingswinford Rd DY1 ... 61 F7
Kingswinford Sch The
DY6 ... 60 D7
Kingswood Ave
Cannock WS11 ... 4 C7
Corley CV7 ... 94 B8
Kingswood Cl
Coventry CV6 ... 95 D1
Kingswood B94 ... 144 E5
Solihull B90 ... 106 D1
Kingswood Colliery Cvn Site
WS6 ... 5 A4
Kingswood Cotts B94 ... 144 D3
Kingswood Croft B7 ... 67 C7
Kingswood Dr
Birmingham B30 ... 104 C3
Great Wyrley WS6 ... 5 A4
Norton Canes WS11 ... 5 F5
Sutton Coldfield B74 ... 44 F5
Kingswood Gdns
Nuneaton CV10 ... 72 B4
Wolverhampton WV4 ... 38 F6
Kingswood Ho B14 ... 104 E2
Kingswood Rd
Birmingham,Coft Common
B31 ... 122 F7
Birmingham,Moseley B13 .. 87 A4
Kingswinford DY6 ... 60 C4
Nuneaton CV10 ... 72 B4
Kingswood Sch B90 ... 106 B2
Kington Cl WV12 ... 27 B8
Kington Gdns B37 ... 69 F2
Kington Way B33 ... 68 E1
King William St
Coventry CV1 ... 113 E4
Stourbridge DY8 ... 80 F8
Kiniths Cres B71 ... 53 E5
Kiniths Way
Halesowen B62 ... 63 E1
West Bromwich B71 ... 53 E4
Kinlet Cl
Redditch B98 ... 154 E3
Wolverhampton WV3 ... 38 A8
Kinlet Gr B31 ... 103 C2
Kinloch Dr DY1 ... 50 F3
Kinnerley St WS1 ... 29 A1
Kinnersley Cl B98 ... 154 E3
Kinnersley Cres B69 ... 63 D5
Kinnerton Cres B29 ... 84 F2
Kinross Ave WS12 ... 1 F7
Kinross Cl CV10 ... 72 F2
Kinross Cres B43 ... 44 B4
Kinross Rd CV32 ... 157 B4
Kinross Way LE10 ... 71 A1
Kinsall Gn B77 ... 36 C6
Kinsey Gr B14 ... 104 F4
Kinsham Dr B91 ... 127 B8
Kintore Croft B32 ... 102 B7
Kintyre Cl
Birmingham B45 ... 101 E1
Hinckley LE10 ... 71 B1
Kintyre The CV2 ... 115 B7
Kinver Ave
Kidderminster DY11 ... 116 A1
Willenhall WV12 ... 27 B5
Kinver Cl CV2 ... 96 E1
Kinver Cres WS9 ... 16 C1
Kinver Croft
Birmingham B12 ... 86 E7
Sutton Coldfield B76 ... 58 A8
Kinver Ct B11 ... 87 D4
Kinver Dr
Hagley DY9 ... 99 C7
Wolverhampton WV4 ... 38 C5
Kinver Rd B31 ... 103 D2
Kinver St DY8 ... 60 E1
Kinwalsey La CV7 ... 92 F6
Kinwarton Cl B26 ... 88 D6
Kipling Ave
Dudley WV14 ... 40 B1
Warwick CV34 ... 160 C4
Kipling Cl
Nuneaton CV10 ... 72 A5
Tipton DY4 ... 52 A8
Kipling Rd
Birmingham B30 ... 103 C4
Coventry CV6 ... 113 A8
Dudley DY3 ... 50 A5
Willenhall WV12 ... 27 E8
Wolverhampton WV10 ... 11 D2
Kipling Rise B79 ... 20 F8
Kipling Wlk 3 DY10 ... 117 B6
Kirby Ave CV34 ... 155 F1
Kirby Cl
Bilston WV14 ... 40 E3
Brandon CV8 ... 135 F5
Coventry CV1 ... 113 D6
Kirby Cnr CV4 ... 132 B5
Kirby Corner Rd CV4 ... 132 B6
Kirby Dr DY1 ... 50 E3
Kirby Rd
Birmingham B18 ... 65 E6
Coventry CV5 ... 112 F2
Kirfield Dr LE10 ... 71 F3
Kirkby Gn B73 ... 46 B3
Kirkdale Ave CV6 ... 95 D3
Kirkham Gdns DY5 ... 61 C6
Kirkham Gr B33 ... 68 F4
Kirkham Way DY4 ... 52 A5
Kirkland Way B78 ... 34 B8
Kirkside Gr WS8 ... 15 F7
Kirkstall Cl WS3 ... 13 F2
Kirkstall Cres WS3 ... 13 F2
Kirkstone Cres
Birmingham B43 ... 54 F6
Wombourne WV5 ... 49 A6
Kirkstone Ct DY5 ... 81 B8
Kirkstone Rd CV12 ... 78 A2
Kirkstone Way DY5 ... 81 B8
Kirkstone Wlk CV11 ... 74 A6
Kirkwall Rd B32 ... 84 D1
Kirkwood Ave B23 ... 56 F7
Kirmond Wlk WV6 ... 25 C5
Kirstead Gdns WV6 ... 24 B3
Kirtley B77 ... 21 E2
Kirton Cl
Coventry CV6 ... 94 F1
Whitnash CV31 ... 162 B3
Kirton Gr
Birmingham B33 ... 69 A4
Solihull B91 ... 107 A1
Wolverhampton WV6 ... 24 C4
Kitchener Rd
Birmingham B29 ... 86 B1
Coventry CV6 ... 113 E8
Dudley DY2 ... 51 F1
Kitchener St B66 ... 65 D6
Kitchen La
Wednesfield WV11 ... 26 F8
Wolverhampton WV11 ... 12 F1
Kitebrook Cl
Redditch B98 ... 154 E4
Solihull B90 ... 127 A7
Kite La B97 ... 153 A5
Kites Cl CV34 ... 155 E2
Kites Nest La CV35 ... 146 C1
Kitsland Rd B34 ... 69 E6
Kitswell Gdns B32 ... 102 A8
Kittermaster Rd CV7 ... 92 C1
Kittiwake Dr
Brierley Hill DY5 ... 81 D7
Kidderminster DY10 ... 117 B3
Kittoe Rd B74 ... 32 A3
Kitt's Green Rd B33 ... 69 B3
Kitwell La B32 ... 102 A8
Kitwell Prim Sch B32 ... 102 A7
Kitwood Ave B78 ... 36 F6
Kitwood Dr B92 ... 107 D7
Kixley La B93 ... 128 C6
Klaxon Ind Est B11 ... 87 F4
Klevedon Cl CV11 ... 74 A1
Knapton Cl LE10 ... 71 A3
Knaresdale Cl DY5 ... 81 C8
Knaves Castle Ave WS8 ... 6 F2
Knebley Cres CV10 ... 73 C1
Knebworth Cl B44 ... 55 E8
Knibbs The CV34 ... 160 E7
Knight Ave CV1 ... 113 E1
Knightcote Dr
Royal Leamington Spa
CV32 ... 161 E8
Solihull B91 ... 127 B8
Knight Ct B75 ... 47 C5
Knight Ho B13 ... 105 D7
Knightley Cl CV32 ... 157 E5
Knightley Rd B91 ... 106 F2
Knightlow Ave CV3 ... 134 C6
Knightlow Cl CV8 ... 148 C3
Knightlow Rd B17 ... 85 B8
Knighton Cl B74 ... 31 F3
Knighton Ct B23 ... 56 C2
Knighton Dr B74 ... 31 F3
Knighton Rd
Birmingham B31 ... 103 C4
Cannock WS12 ... 2 E3
Dudley DY2 ... 62 D4
Sutton Coldfield B74 ... 31 D5
Knights Ave WV6 ... 24 E6
Knightsbridge Ave CV12 .. 78 C4
Knightsbridge Cl B74 ... 31 F4
Knightsbridge Ct B37 ... 69 F5
Knightsbridge La WV12 .. 27 C6
Knightsbridge Rd B92 ... 89 A1
Knights Cl
3 Willenhall WV13 ... 27 B2
Birmingham B23 ... 56 E2
Hinckley LE10 ... 75 D4
Knights Cres WV6 ... 24 E7
Knights Ct
Birmingham B37 ... 90 E8
Hinckley LE10 ... 74 E8
Norton Canes WS11 ... 6 A4
Warwick CV34 ... 160 D6
Knightsfield Cl B73 ... 45 C3
Knightsford Cl B97 ... 152 F2
Knights Hill WS9 ... 30 B3
Knights Rd B11 ... 88 A4
Knights Templar Way
CV4 ... 112 A1
Knightstone Ave B18 ... 66 A4
Knights Wood Cl B75 ... 46 D7
Knightwick Cres B23 ... 56 C5
Knipersley Rd B73 ... 57 A7
Knoll Cl WS7 ... 7 A5
Knollcroft 4 B16 ... 66 A2
Knoll Croft
Aldridge WS9 ... 16 C1
Cheswick Green B90 ... 126 D4
Coventry CV3 ... 133 C6
Knoll Dr
Coventry CV3 ... 133 C6
Warwick CV34 ... 155 E1
Knoll Sch The DY11 ... 116 A7
Knoll The
Birmingham B32 ... 84 C1
Kingswinford DY6 ... 60 E5
Knott Ct 11 DY5 ... 61 D2
Knottesford Cl B80 ... 159 C3
Knotting Way CV3 ... 114 C1
Knottsall La B68 ... 64 B3
Knotts Farm Rd DY6 ... 61 A4
Knowesley Cl B60 ... 137 B2
Knowlands Rd B90 ... 127 A7
Knowle CE Prim Sch
B93 ... 128 C6
Knowle Cl
Birmingham B45 ... 122 D7
Redditch B98 ... 154 C6
Knowle Hill CV8 ... 148 C6
Knowle Hill Rd DY2 ... 62 B4
Knowle La WS14 ... 9 B3
Knowle Rd
Birmingham B11 ... 87 D3
Eastcote B92 ... 108 E2
Rowley Regis B65 ... 63 A4
Knowles Ave CV10 ... 72 C4
Knowles Dr B74 ... 46 A7
Knowles Rd WV1 ... 25 F1
Knowles St WS10 ... 42 A3
Knowle Wood Rd B93 ... 128 B3
Knox Cres CV11 ... 73 F8
Knox Rd WV2 ... 39 D6
Knox's Grave La WS14,B78 19 D7
Knoyle Ct 1 DY8 ... 80 F6
Knutswood Cl B13 ... 105 D7
Kohima Dr DY8 ... 80 E5
Kossuth Rd WV14 ... 40 A1
Kurtus B77 ... 35 D6
Kwikform Bldg CV6 ... 95 E4
Kyle Cl WV10 ... 11 B1
Kyles Way B32 ... 102 B7
Kynaston Cres WV8 ... 10 B2
Kynaston Ho B71 ... 53 C8

Kyngsford Rd B33 69 D3
Kynner Way CV3 135 B8
Kynoch Wks B6 55 F3
Kyotts Lake Rd B11 87 B7
Kyotts Lake Unit Factory B11 87 B7
Kyrwicks La B11 87 A7
Kyter La B36 69 B8

L

Laburnham Ct WS14 9 C5
Laburnham Rd DY6 60 E6
Laburnum Ave
Birmingham B37 69 F6
Cannock WS11 4 E7
Coventry CV6 112 F5
Kenilworth CV8 148 A4
Smethwick B67 64 E4
Tamworth B79 21 B8
Laburnum Cl
Bedworth CV12 77 E2
Birmingham B37 69 F6
Cannock WS11 4 E7
Hollywood B47 125 A5
Redditch B98 153 E2
Stourbridge DY8 80 E7
Walsall WS3 15 A2
Laburnum Cotts B21 65 E8
Laburnum Croft B69 52 B2
Laburnum Dr
Sutton Coldfield B76 47 A3
Whitnash CV31 162 B3
Laburnum Gr
Birmingham B13 86 F3
Bromsgrove B61 136 F4
Burntwood WS7 6 F6
Kidderminster DY11 116 B8
Nuneaton CV10 72 D6
Warwick CV34 156 B1
Willenhall WS2 27 F3
Laburnum Ho WS4 15 D1
Laburnum Rd
Bilston WV1 40 B8
Birmingham B30 103 F8
Brownhills WS9 16 A3
Dudley DY1 51 C4
Tipton DY4 51 F7
Walsall WS5 43 C4
Wednesbury WS10 42 B4
Wolverhampton WV4 39 F3
Laburnum St
Stourbridge DY8 80 E7
Wolverhampton WV3 25 B1
Laburnum Trees B47 124 F7
Laburnum Villas 2 B11 87 C5
Laburnum Way B31 103 A1
Laceby Gr B13 87 D1
Lacell Cl CV34 155 E1
Ladbroke Dr B76 46 F2
Ladbroke Gr B27 106 C8
Ladbroke Pk CV34 155 E1
Ladbrook Cl B98 158 E7
Ladbrook Gr DY3 50 B3
Ladbrook Rd
Coventry CV5 112 A4
Solihull B91 107 C2
Ladbury Gr WS5 43 A4
Ladbury Rd WS5 43 A3
Ladeler Gr B33 69 E2
Ladies Wlk DY3 50 D8
Lady Bank
Birmingham B32 102 B7
Tamworth B79 21 B4
Lady Bracknell Mews B31 103 C4
Lady Brades Ho 5 B69 64 A7
Lady Byron La B93 127 F8
Ladycroft
5 Birmingham B16 66 B2
Cubbington CV32 157 E5
Ladyfields Way CV6 95 B4
Lady Grey Ave CV34 161 E3
Lady Grey's Wlk DY8 80 D5
Ladygrove Cl B98 159 A8
Lady Harriet's La B98 153 F4
Lady Katherine Leveson CE Sch B93 129 B5
Lady La
Coventry CV6 95 F4
Earlswood B90,B94 126 B3
Kenilworth CV8 147 F4
Lady Lane Mobile Home Pk CV6 95 F4
Ladymead Dr CV6 95 B2
Lady Meadow Cl B78 21 A3
Ladymoor Rd WV14 40 C3
Ladypool Ave 3 B11 87 B6
Ladypool Cl
Halesowen B62 83 C4
Walsall WS4 29 A5
Ladypool Rd B11,B12 87 A5
Ladypool Sch B11 87 B6
Ladysmith Rd B63 82 C6
Lady Warwick Ave CV12 78 D2
Ladywell Cl WV5 49 A8
Ladywell Wlk B5 164 C1
Ladywood Cl DY5 61 F2
Ladywood Middleway B16 66 A2
Ladywood Rd
Birmingham B16 66 A1
Sutton Coldfield B74 46 A8
Laertes Gr CV34 161 F2
Laggan Cl CV10 72 C5
Lagonda B77 21 E3
Lagrange B79 20 E6
Laing Ho 2 B69 63 D5
Lair The B78 36 F8
Lake Ave WS5 43 C7
Lake Cl WS5 43 C7
Lakedown Cl B14 104 E1
Lakefield B31 102 F4
Lakefield Cl B28 106 B7
Lakefield Rd WV11 26 E5
Lakehouse Ct B23 56 E8
Lakehouse Gr B38 103 D3
Lakehouse Rd B73 56 F8
Lakeland Dr B77 36 B7
Lakeland Ho CV34 161 A7
Lakenheath B79 21 C7
Laker Cl DY8 81 A7
Lakes Cl DY11 116 C7
Lakeside CV12 78 A2
Lakeside Cl WV13 26 E3
Lakeside Ct
Birmingham B20 55 A4
Brierley Hill DY5 81 B8
Lakeside Dr
Birmingham B23 56 B6
Norton Canes WS11 6 B6
Solihull B90 126 F7
Lakeside Ind Est B98 154 B3
Lakeside Pk B78 20 F1
Lakeside Prim Sch
Tamworth B77 21 E2
Willenhall WV13 26 E3
Lakeside Rd B70 53 A6
Lakeside
Redditch B97 152 D7
Sutton Coldfield B74 31 B5
Lakeside Wlk B23 56 C3
Lakes Rd B23 56 A6
Lake St DY3 50 D3
Lakes The B94 141 F8
Lakeview Cl B43 44 B2
Lake View Rd CV5 112 F4
Lakewood Dr B45 102 B1
Lakey La B28 106 B7
Lakey Lane Jun & Inf Sch B28 106 B7
Lakin Ct CV34 160 F8
Lakin Ho CV34 160 F8
Lakin Rd CV34 160 F8
Lambah Cl WV14 40 F7
Lamb Cl B34 69 E5
Lambert Cl B23 56 D6
Lambert Ct
Kingswinford DY6 60 D8
Warwick CV34 160 D6
Lambert Dr WS7 7 A8
Lambert End B70 53 B3
Lambert Fold 4 DY2 62 E8
Lambert Rd WV10 25 F6
Lambert St B70 53 B3
Lambeth Cl
Birmingham B37 70 B4
Coventry CV2 114 E7
Lambeth Rd
Bilston WV14 40 B7
Birmingham B44 44 E3
Lambourn Cl WS3 14 C2
Lambourn Cres CV31 162 C6
Lambourne Cl
4 Lichfield WS14 9 E8
Coventry CV5 112 A4
Great Wyrley WS6 4 F3
Lambourne Gr B37 69 E2
Lambourne Way
Brierley Hill DY5 81 B8
Norton Canes WS11 6 A5
Lambourn Rd
Birmingham B23 56 D4
Willenhall WV13 27 D1
Lambscote Cl B90 105 C2
Lamb St CV1 165 B3
Lamerton Cl CV2 114 C6
Lamford Cl LE10 71 B1
Lamintone Dr CV32 156 D2
Lammas Cl B92 89 C1
Lammas Croft CV31 162 A3
Lammas Ct CV34 160 D6
Lammas Ho 6 CV6 113 A4
Lammas Rd
Coventry CV6 112 F4
Stourbridge DY8 60 C3
Lammas Wlk CV34 160 D7
Lammermoor Ave B43 43 F2
Lamont Ave B32 84 F3
Lamorna Cl
Nuneaton CV11 73 F4
Wolverhampton WV3 38 B8
Lamprey B77 35 D6
Lanark Cl DY6 60 F5
Lanark Croft B35 57 F3
Lancaster Ave
Aldridge WS9 30 B8
Birmingham B45 122 A8
Wednesbury WS10 42 C3
Lancaster Circus Queensway B4 164 C4
Lancaster Cl B30 104 A6
Lancaster Dr B35 58 B2
Lancaster Gdns WV4 38 E5
Lancaster Ho
5 Stourbridge DY8 80 F8
7 Rowley Regis B65 63 E4
Cannock WS12 2 D1
Lancaster Pl
Kenilworth CV8 147 E2
Walsall WS3 14 C2
Lancaster Rd
Brierley Hill DY5 61 C2
Hinckley LE10 75 D8
Lancaster St B4 164 C4
Lance Cl LE10 75 D5
Lancelot Cl B8 67 E3
Lancelot Ho DY10 117 C8
Lancelot Pl B70 52 E4
Lanchester Cl B79 20 E7
Lanchester Rd
Birmingham B38 104 A1
Coventry CV6 113 B6
Lanchester Way B36 58 F1
Lancia Cl CV6 96 B4
Lancing Rd CV12 79 C2
Lander Cl B45 122 A6
Landgate Rd B21 54 C2
Land La B37 90 A7
Land Oak Dr DY10 117 B7
Landor Ho CV31 162 A2
Landor Rd
Dorridge B93 128 A6
Redditch B98 154 A1
Warwick CV34 160 D8
Whitnash CV31 162 A3
Landor St B8 67 B3
Landport Rd WV2 39 F8
Landrail Wlk B36 70 A8
Landrake Rd DY6 61 A5
Landsberg B79 20 F6
Landsdown Pl 2 B18 66 A5
Landseer Dr LE10 71 B3
Landseer Gr B43 44 D4
Landsgate DY8 81 A1
Landswood Cl B44 45 A1
Landswood Rd B68 64 C4
Landywood Ent Pk WS6 13 F8
Landywood Gn WS6 4 E2
Landywood La WS6 4 E2
Landywood Prim Sch WS6 13 F8
Landywood Sta WS6 4 F2
Lane Ave WS2 28 B3
Lane Cl WS2 28 B3
Lane Croft B76 58 A8
Lane Ct 8 WV3 25 C4
Lane Green Ave WV8 10 C1
Lane Green Ct WV8 10 B3
Lane Green Fst Sch WV8 10 B4
Lane Green Rd WV8 10 C2
Lane Green Rd Masionettes WV8 10 B3
Lane Green Sh Par WV8 10 B3
Lane Rd WV4 40 A3
Lanesfield Drive Ind Est WV4 40 A4
Lanesfield Dr WV4 40 A4
Lanesfield Jun & Inf Sch WV4 40 A4
Laneside Ave B74 44 F7
Laneside CV3 134 E6
Laneside Dr LE10 71 F3
Laneside Gdns WS2 28 B2
Lanes Sh Ctr The 1 B73 57 B7
Lane St WV14 40 D3
Lanfear Ct LE10 75 C7
Langbank Ave CV3 134 D7
Langbay Ct CV2 114 F6
Langcliffe Ave CV34 155 F1
Langcomb Rd B90 126 A8
Langdale Ave CV6 95 D3
Langdale Cl
Brownhills WS8 15 E6
Royal Leamington Spa CV32 157 D3
Langdale Croft B21 65 E7
Langdale Ct B77 22 A6
Langdale Dr
Bilston WV14 40 D7
Cannock WS11 4 C7
Nuneaton CV11 74 A6
Langdale Gn WS11 4 C7
Langdale Rd
Birmingham B43 54 F7
Hinckley LE10 75 A8
Langdale Way DY9 81 D4
Langdon St B9 67 B2
Langdon Wlk B27 88 E4
Langfield Rd B93 128 A7
Langford Ave B43 54 E8
Langford Cl WS1 29 A1
Langford Croft B91 107 C2
Langford Gr B17 85 C3
Langham Cl B26 89 A7
Langham Gn B74 30 F1
Langholm Dr
Birmingham B44 45 D1
Cannock WS12 2 E2
Langland Dr DY3 50 C8
Langley Ave WV14 51 C8
Langley Cl
Brownhills WS9 16 A3
Redditch B98 154 D1
Langley Cres B68 64 B4
Langley Croft CV4 112 A2
Langley Dr B35 58 A1
Langley Gdns
Oldbury B68 64 B4
Wolverhampton WV3 38 D7
Langley Gr B10 87 D8
Langley Green Rd B69 64 A4
Langley Green Sta B68 64 B5
Langley Hall Dr B75 47 B5
Langley Hall Rd
Solihull B92 106 C7
Sutton Coldfield B75 47 B5
Langley Heath Dr B76 47 A3
Langley High Sch B68 64 C4
Langley High St B69 64 A5
Langley Mede B68 64 B5
Langley Park Way B75 46 F6
Langley Prim Sch
Oldbury B69 64 A5
Solihull B92 106 D6
Langley Rd
Birmingham B10 87 D8
Oldbury B68 64 B4
Whitnash CV31 162 A4
Wolverhampton WV3,WV4 38 B7
Langley Rise B92 89 D3
Langley Sch B92 106 D7
Langley Specl Sch B75 47 A6
Langleys Rd B29 85 E1
Langley Wlk B37 70 D2
Langlodge Rd CV6 95 B2
Langmead Cl WS2 27 D3
Langnor Rd CV2 114 C6
Langsett Rd WV10 25 E4
Langstone Rd
Birmingham B14 105 B3
Dudley DY1 50 F1
Langton Cl
Birmingham B36 70 B6
Coventry CV3 134 E8
Langton Ct 1 WS13 3 A1
Langton Pl WV14 41 A6
Langton Rd B8 67 E4
Langtree Ave B91 107 B1
Langtree Cl WS12 2 D1
Langwood Cl CV4 132 B7
Langwood Ct B36 69 B8
Langworth Ave B27 88 C5
Lannacombe Rd B31 122 E6
Lansbury Ave WS10 41 C4
Lansbury Cl CV2 114 E7
Lansbury Dr WS11 1 E4
Lansbury Gn B64 83 B8
Lansbury Rd B64 83 B8
Lansbury Wlk 6 DY4 52 A8
Lansdale Ave B92 107 F8
Lansdowne Cir CV32 157 A1
Lansdowne Cl
Bedworth CV12 78 A3
Dudley,West Coseley WV14 51 A7
Rowley Regis DY2 62 F6
Lansdowne Cres
6 Royal Leamington Spa CV32 157 A1
Studley B80 159 D3
Tamworth B77 35 D8
Lansdowne Ct DY9 81 C1
Lansdowne Rd
2 Royal Leamington Spa CV32 157 A1
Bilston WV14 40 E7
Birmingham,Erdington B24 56 F3
Birmingham,Handsworth B21 66 A8
Halesowen,Hasbury B63 82 D2
Halesowen,Hurst Green B62 63 F1
Studley B80 159 D3
Wolverhampton WV1 163 A4
Lansdowne St
Birmingham B18 65 F4
Coventry CV2 113 F3
Royal Leamington Spa CV32 157 A1
Lansdown Gn DY11 116 C5
Lansdown Ho B15 86 D8
Lant Cl CV7 131 B7
Lantern Rd DY2 62 C2
Lanthorn Cl WS13 9 A7
Lapal La B62 84 A2
Lapal La N B62 83 E3
Lapal La S B32,B62 83 F2
Lapal Prim Sch B62 83 F4
Lapley Cl WV1 26 B2
Lappath Ho B32 102 D8
Lapper Ave WV4 39 F2
Lapwing Cl
Brownhills WS8 15 E7
Cheslyn Hay WS6 4 C1
Kidderminster DY10 117 B1
Lapwing Croft B23 56 C7
Lapwing Dr B92 109 B7
Lapwing B77 36 A6
Lapwood Ave DY6 61 A5
Lapworth CE Prim Sch B94 144 D3
Lapworth Cl B98 158 F7
Lapworth Dr B73 45 C3
Lapworth Gr B12 86 F6
Lapworth Oaks B94 144 D3
Lapworth Rd CV2 96 C1
Lapworth Sta B94 144 D4
Lapworth St B94 144 B2
Lara Cl B17 85 B8
Lara Gr DY4 52 A2
Larch Ave B21 54 D2
Larch Cl WS14 9 E7
Larch Croft
Birmingham B37 70 B2
Tipton B69 52 B2
Larch Dr B31 102 C1
Larches Cottage Gdns DY11 116 C3
Larches La WV3 25 A2
Larches Rd DY11 116 D4
Larches St B11 87 B6
Larches The
Bedworth CV7 96 B8
Wolverhampton WV11 26 B5
Larchfield Cl B20 55 B3
Larch Gdns WV14 40 F4
Larch Gr
Sedgley DY3 50 E7
Larch Gr *continued*
Warwick CV34 156 A1
Larch Ho
Birmingham B36 68 F8
Stourbridge DY8 80 C6
Larchmere Dr
Birmingham B28 105 F8
Bromsgrove B61 136 E3
Essington WV11 13 B3
Larch Rd DY6 60 E7
Larch Tree Ave CV4 112 A2
Larch Wlk B25 88 B8
Larchwood Cres B74 44 E8
Larchwood Dr WS11 2 A4
Larchwood Gn WS5 43 B4
Larchwood Rd
Bedworth CV7 78 B1
Walsall WS5 43 A4
Larcombe Dr WV4 39 D5
Large Ave WS10 41 C4
Lark Cl B14 105 A2
Larkfield Ave B36 69 B8
Larkfield Rd B98 154 A1
Larkfield Way CV5 112 A6
Lark Hall Com Inf Sch B79 21 A8
Larkhill DY10 116 E7
Larkhill Rd DY8 80 C4
Larkhill Wlk B14 104 D1
Larkin Cl
Bulkington CV12 79 B3
Wolverhampton WV10 12 A1
Larkin Gr CV2 114 F6
Lark Meadow Dr B37 69 F3
Larksfield Mews DY5 81 C7
Larksfield B66 65 B4
Larks Mill WS3 14 E4
Larkspur Ave WS7 7 A5
Larkspur Croft B36 68 D8
Larkspur Ct
Bedworth CV12 95 C8
Halesowen B62 83 F7
Larkspur Dr WV10 12 B7
Larkspur Gr 5 CV12 77 D2
Larkspur Rd DY2 62 F8
Larkspur B77 35 D4
Larkspur Way WS8 15 D6
Larkswood Dr
Sedgley DY3 50 D7
Wolverhampton WV4 38 C3
Larne Rd B26 89 A7
Lashbrooke Ho B45 121 F7
Lassington Cl B98 154 E4
Latches Cl WS10 41 E6
Latchford Cl B98 154 E6
Latelow Rd B33 69 A2
Latham Ave B43 54 E7
Latham Cres DY4 52 A3
Latham Rd CV5 113 A2
Lath La B66 64 D8
Lathom Gr B33 68 F5
Latimer Cl CV8 147 F2
Latimer Gdns B15 86 D7
Latimer Pl B18 65 E6
Latimer Rd B48 139 A5
Latimer St WV13 27 B3
Latymer Cl B76 58 A7
Lauder Cl
Sedgley DY3 39 C1
Willenhall WV13 26 D1
Lauderdale Ave CV6 95 D3
Lauderdale Cl WS8 15 E6
Lauderdale Gdns WV10 11 E3
Laughton Cl B31 123 B7
Launce Gr CV34 161 F2
Launceston Cl
Tamworth B77 21 D2
Walsall WS5 43 D7
Launceston Dr CV11 73 F4
Launceston Rd WS5 43 D7
Launde The B28 105 E3
Laundry Cotts CV35 145 E4
Laundry Rd B66 65 C3
Laureates Wlk B74 46 A8
Laurel Ave B12 87 A5
Laurel Bank Mews B60 137 F4
Laurel Bank B79 21 B6
Laurel Cl
Coventry CV2 96 E2
Dudley DY1 51 A3
Lichfield WS14 9 D8
Redditch B98 153 E2
Laurel Ct
Birmingham B13 87 A2
Coventry CV5 112 F1
Laurel Dr
Burntwood WS7 7 C7
Cannock WS12 2 E4
Hartshill CV10 72 A7
Smethwick B66 65 A8
Sutton Coldfield B74 44 E8
Laurel Gdns
3 Birmingham,Stockfield B27 88 C5
Barnt Green B45 138 E8
Birmingham B21 54 E1
Laurel Gr
Birmingham B30 103 E6
Bromsgrove B61 136 F4
Darlaston WV14 41 A4
Wolverhampton WV4 38 E6
Laurel La B63 83 B3
Laurel Rd
Birmingham,Handsworth B21 54 F1
Birmingham,King's Norton B30 104 A4
Dudley DY1 51 A3

Laurel Rd *continued*
Tipton DY4 51 F7
Walsall WS5 43 B4
Laurels Cres CV7 130 C6
Laurels The
Bedworth CV12 77 E2
Birmingham B68 84 B6
Birmingham,Ladywood B16 65 F3
Birmingham,Sheldon B26 89 C5
Coventry CV4 132 F6
Portway B47 140 F8
Smethwick B66 65 C4
Sutton Coldfield B73 46 B1
Laurence Ct B31 103 B5
Laurence Gr WV6 24 E7
Lauriston Cl DY1 50 F3
Lavender Ave CV6 112 F5
Lavender Cl
2 Walsall WS5 42 F3
Bedworth CV12 77 E1
Wolverhampton WV9 10 F3
Lavender Gdns 1 B23 56 B7
Lavender Gr
Bilston WV14 40 F6
Walsall WS3 28 E5
Lavender Hall La CV7 110 C2
Lavender Ho B38 123 F8
Lavender La DY8 80 D3
Lavender Rd
Dudley DY1 51 B3
Tamworth B77 21 F4
Lavendon Rd B42 55 B5
Lavenham Cl CV11 79 C8
Lavinia Rd B62 83 E3
Law Cliff Rd B42 55 B6
Law Cl B69 52 D2
Lawden Rd B10 87 B8
Lawford Ave WS14 9 E7
Lawford Cl
Birmingham B7 67 A3
Coventry CV3 114 E1
Lawford Gr
Birmingham B5 86 E8
Solihull B90 105 D2
Lawford Rd CV31 162 B5
Lawfred Ave WV11 26 D5
Lawley Cl
Coventry CV4 112 A2
Walsall WS4 15 B1
Lawley Middleway B4 67 A3
Lawley Rd WV14 40 B6
Lawley St
Dudley DY1 51 A1
West Bromwich B70 52 F3
Lawley The B63 82 D1
Lawn Ave DY8 80 E4
Lawn La WV9 11 A7
Lawnoaks Cl WS8 6 D2
Lawn Rd WV2 39 F6
Lawns Bsns Ctr The LE10 75 E8
Lawnsdale Cl B46 70 F7
Lawnsdown Rd DY5 81 F6
Lawnsfield Gr B23 56 D7
Lawnside Gn WV14 40 D8
Lawns The
Bedworth CV12 77 C2
Hinckley LE10 75 E8
Portway B47 140 F7
Lawn St DY8 80 E4
Lawnswood Ave
Burntwood WS7 6 F5
Solihull B90 106 D3
Stourbridge DY8 60 C3
Wolverhampton,Parkfield WV4 39 E4
Wolverhampton WV6 24 E8
Lawnswood Cl 2 WS12 2 D1
Lawnswood Dr
Brownhills WS9 16 A3
Stourbridge DY7 60 A2
Lawnswood Gr B21 54 C1
Lawnswood LE10 75 A8
Lawnswood Rd
Dudley DY3 50 D5
Stourbridge DY8 60 D3
Lawnswood Rise WV6 24 F8
Lawnswood
Stourbridge DY7 60 A2
Sutton Coldfield B76 58 A8
Lawnwood Rd DY2 62 C2
Lawrence Ave
Wednesfield WV11 26 F6
Wolverhampton WV10 26 A4
Lawrence Ct
6 Birmingham B68 84 B8
Tamworth B79 21 A6
Lawrence Dr B76 58 D6
Lawrence Gdns CV8 148 A6
Lawrence La B64 62 E1
Lawrence Rd CV7 96 A8
Lawrence Saunders Rd CV6 113 B5
Lawrence St
Stourbridge DY9 81 C6
Willenhall WV13 27 A3
Lawrence Way WS13 8 F5
Lawrence Wlk B43 44 D4
Lawson Cl WS9 30 B4
Lawson St B4 164 C4
Law St B71 53 C5
Lawton Ave B29 86 B2
Lawton Cl
Hinckley LE10 74 F8
Rowley Regis B65 63 D6
Lawton Ct WV3 25 B1
Laxey Rd B16 65 D3
Laxford Cl B12 86 E6
Laxton Cl DY6 61 A5
Laxton Gr
Birmingham B25 68 D1
Solihull B91 107 C7
Lay Gdns CV31 162 E5
Lazy Hill B38 104 B2
Lazy Hill Rd WS9 16 C1
Lazy Hill WS9 16 D2
Lea Ave WS10 41 D1
Lea Bank Ave DY11 116 B5
Lea Bank Rd DY2 62 C3
Leabon Gr B17 85 C4
Leabrook B26 88 F8
Leabrook Rd N WS10 41 D2
Leabrook Rd DY4,WS14 41 D1
Leach Green La B45 122 B6
Leach Heath La B45 122 A7
Leacliffe Way WS9 30 F3
Leacote Dr WV6 24 C4
Leacrest Rd CV6 95 A2
Leacroft Ave WV10 25 E8
Leacroft Cl WS9 16 B1
Leacroft Gr B71 53 B7
Leacroft La WS11 4 F5
Leacroft Rd DY6 60 E8
Lea Croft Rd B97 158 D5
Leacroft WV12 27 C7
Lea Cswy The DY11 116 A4
Leadbeater Ho 6 WS3 28 B8
Leadbetter Dr B61 136 D2
Lea Dr B26 89 A6
Lea End La B48 123 D3
Leaf Ct CV3 133 D4
Leafdown Cl WS12 2 D3
Leafenden Ave WS7 7 A6
Leafield Cl CV2 114 F8
Leafield Cres B33 69 A5
Leafield Gdns B62 83 D8
Leafield Rd B92 89 C1
Leaf La CV3 133 E5
Lea Ford Rd B33 69 C4
Leaford Way DY6 60 F5
Leafy Glade B74 31 A3
Leafy Rise DY3 50 D4
Lea Gdns WV3 163 A1
Leagh Cl CV8 148 B7
Lea Green Ave DY4 51 D5
Lea Green Dr B47 125 C4
Lea Green La B47 125 C5
Lea Hall Rd B33 69 A2
Lea Hall Sta B33 69 B2
Leahill Croft B37 69 F2
Lea Hill Rd B20 55 C2
Lea Ho 6 DY1 61 E8
Leaholme Gdns DY9 81 B2
Leahouse Gdns B68 64 A3
Lea House Rd B30 104 A7
Leahouse Rd B68 64 A3
Leahurst Cres B17 85 C4
Lea La WS6 5 A3
Lealholme Ct CV5 132 F8
Lea Manor Dr WV4 38 E4
Leam Cl CV11 73 F1
Leam Cres B92 89 B1
Leam Dr WS7 7 D7
Leam Gn CV4 132 D5
Leamington Cl WS11 4 C7
Leamington Rd
Birmingham B12 87 B5
Coventry CV3 133 C6
Kenilworth CV8 148 B2
Ryton-on-D CV8 135 B1
Leamington Spa Art Gallery & Mus* CV32 161 F8
Leamington Spa Sta CV31 161 F7
Leamore Cl WS2 28 A7
Leamore Ind Est WS2 28 C6
Leamore La WS2 28 B6
Leamore Prim Sch WS3 28 C7
Leamount Dr B44 45 C2
Leam Rd CV31 161 D7
Leam Side Ho 9 CV34 161 D8
Leam St CV31 162 B7
Leam Terr CV31 162 B8
Leander Cl WS6 4 F1
Leander Gdns B14 104 F5
Leander Rd DY9 81 F4
Leandor Dr B74 45 A7
Lea Park Rise B61 136 F5
Lea Rd
Birmingham B11 87 D4
Wolverhampton WV3 39 B8
Lear Gr CV34 161 E4
Lear Rd WV5 49 B8
Leas Cl CV12 78 A3
Leason La WV10 26 A7
Leasow Dr B15 85 D3
Leasowe Rd
Birmingham B45 121 F8
Tipton DY4 51 E4
Leasowe's Ave CV3 132 F4
Leasowes Com Coll B62 83 E6
Leasowes Ct B63 82 F3
Leasowes Dr
Perton WV6 23 D4
Wolverhampton WV4 38 D6
Leasowes La B62 83 D4
Leasowes Rd B14 86 F1
Leasowes The DY4 52 C5
Leasowe The WS13 3 A1
Leasow The WS9 29 E5
Leas The WV10 12 C7
Lea St DY10 116 F6
Lea Street Fst Sch DY10 116 F6
Lea The
Birmingham B33 69 A2
Kidderminster DY11 116 A5
Leatherhead Cl 5 B6 66 F6
Lea Vale Rd DY8 80 F3
Leavesden Gr B26 89 A5
Lea View
Aldridge WS9 29 E5
Wednesfield WV12 27 A5
Lea Village B33 69 B3
Leaward Cl CV10 72 E2
Lea Wlk
Birmingham B45 121 F8
Ryton-on-D CV8 135 B1
Lea Wood Gr DY11 116 A5
Lea Yield Cl B30 104 A7
Lebanon Gr WS7 6 F8
Lechlade Cl B98 154 B7
Lechlade Rd B43 54 E8
Leckie Rd WS2 28 E4
Ledbrook Rd CV32 157 E5
Ledbury Cl
Aldridge WS9 16 C1
Birmingham B16 66 A2
Redditch B98 154 F2
Ledbury Dr WV1 26 B1
Ledbury Ho
Birmingham B33 69 E2
Redditch B97 153 B4
Ledbury Rd CV31 162 C6
Ledbury Way B76 58 A8
Ledsam Gr B32 84 F6
Ledsam St B16 66 A2
Ledwell B93 126 A5
Lee Bank Ho B1 164 B1
Lee Bank Middleway B15 86 C8
Leebank Rd B63 82 E2
Leech St DY4 52 C5
Lee Cl CV34 155 E2
Lee Cres B15 86 C8
Lee Ct WS9 15 F3
Leeder Cl CV6 95 C2
Leedham Ave B77 21 D5
Lee Gdns B67 64 E5
Lee Meadowe CV34 160 B4
Leeming Cl CV4 132 C6
Lee Mount B15 86 C8
Lee Rd
Cradley Heath B64 82 F8
Hollywood B47 125 A7
Royal Leamington Spa CV31 161 E6
Leeson Wlk 9 B17 85 D5
Lees Rd WV14 40 F3
Lees St B18 65 F6
Lees Terr WV14 40 F3
Lee St B70 53 A8
Lee The CV5 112 C4
Lee Wlk WS11 2 B4
Legg Bros Ind Est WV4 40 A5
Legge La
Birmingham B1 66 C3
Dudley WV14 40 D1
Legge St
Birmingham B4 164 D4
West Bromwich B70 53 E3
Wolverhampton WV2 39 E6
Legion Cl WS11 6 A6
Legion Rd B45 121 E7
Legs La WV10 11 F3
Le Hanche Cl CV7 95 A7
Leicester Cl B67 64 E1
Leicester Cswy CV1 113 D5
Leicester Ct CV12 79 C2
Leicester La
Cubbington CV32 149 E1
Royal Leamington Spa CV32 157 C6
Leicester Pl B71 53 C7
Leicester Rd
Bedworth CV12 78 B4
Hinckley LE10 71 F2
Nuneaton CV11 73 D5
Shilton CV7 97 F6
Leicester Row CV1 165 B4
Leicester St
Bedworth CV12 78 B3
Bulkington CV12 79 C2
Royal Leamington Spa CV32 157 A1
Walsall WS1 28 E2
Wolverhampton WV6 25 B4
Leigham Dr B17 85 A7
Leigh Ave
Burntwood WS7 7 B7
Coventry CV3 133 C3
Leigh CE Prim Sch CV4 131 D8
Leigh Cl WS4 29 A4
Leigh Ct
Birmingham B23 56 C2
Walsall WS4 29 A3
Leigh Jun &Inf Sch B8 67 E6
Leigh Rd
Birmingham B8 67 E6
Sutton Coldfield B75 47 B5
Walsall WS4 29 A4
Leighs Cl WS4 15 C1
Leighs Rd WS4 15 C1
Leigh St 4 CV1 113 E4
Leighswood Ave WS9 30 B7
Leighswood Cl WS11 5 F5
Leighswood Ct WS9 30 B6
Leighswood Gr WS9 30 A7
Leighswood Ind Est WS9 30 A8
Leighswood Rd WS9 30 A6
Leighswood Sch WS9 30 B8
Leighton Cl
Birmingham B43 44 C3
Coventry CV4 132 D2
Dudley DY1 50 E2
Royal Leamington Spa CV32 157 C4
Leighton Rd
Birmingham B13 86 F2
Darlaston WV14 41 A4
Wolverhampton WV4 38 F6
Leisure Wlk 7 B77 35 F6
Leith Gr B38 123 E8
Lelant Gr B17 85 A5
Lellow St B71 53 C8
Lemar Ind Est B30 86 B1
Le More B74 32 A2
Lemox Rd B70 53 A8
Lench Cl
Halesowen B62 63 C1
Redditch B97 153 A5
Lench's Cl B13 87 A3
Lenchs Gn B5 86 E7
Lench St B4 164 C4
Lench's Trust Almshouses
3 Birmingham,Edgbaston B12 87 A8
3 Birmingham,Highgate B12 86 F7
Lenchs Trust B32 84 E6
Len Davis Rd WV12 27 B7
Lennox Cl CV3 134 E6
Lennox Gdns WV3 39 A8
Lennox Gr B73 57 A7
Lennox St B19 66 D6
Lenton Croft B26 88 E4
Lenton's La CV2 96 E4
Lenwade Rd B68 84 D8
Leofric Ct 3 B15 86 C8
Leofric St CV6 113 A5
Leomansley Cl WS13 8 F7
Leomansley Ct WS13 8 E7
Leomansley Rd WS13 8 F7
Leomansley View WS13 8 E7
Leominster Ct B45 121 F8
Leominster Ho B33 69 E2
Leominster Rd B11 87 E3
Leominster Wlk B45 121 F8
Leona Ind Est B62 63 D1
Leonard Ave 5 B19 66 D8
Leonard Gr 6 B19 66 D8
Leonard Parkins Ho CV12 79 D2
Leonard Rd
Birmingham B19 66 D8
Stourbridge DY8 80 C5
Leontes Mdws CV34 161 E3
Leopold Ave B20 54 F5
Leopold Rd CV1 113 F4
Leopold St B12 86 F8
Lepid Gr B29 85 D2
Lerryn Cl DY6 60 F5
Lerwick Cl DY6 60 F5
Lesingham Dr CV4 111 E1
Lesley Bentley Ho 4 B1 66 C3
Lesley Dr DY6 60 E4
Leslie Dr DY4 41 B1
Leslie Rd
Birmingham,Edgbaston B16 65 F2
Birmingham,Handsworth B20 55 D2
Sutton Coldfield B74 31 B2
Wolverhampton WV10 25 F4
Leslie Rise B69 63 C8
Lesscroft Cl WV9 11 A3
Lester Gr WS9 30 E2
Lester St WV14 40 F5
Leswell Gr DY10 116 F6
Leswell La DY10 116 F6
Leswell St DY10 116 F6
Letchlade Cl CV2 114 C8
Levante Gdns B33 68 D2
Leve La WV13 27 B1
Level St DY5 61 E3
Leven Cl LE10 75 B8
Leven Croft B76 58 A7
Leven Dr WV11 13 B1
Leven Way CV2 115 A8
Levenwick Way DY6 61 A5
Leverretts The B21 54 C3
Lever St WV2 163 C1
Leverton Rise WV10 25 C6
Leveson Ave WS6 4 E2
Leveson Cl DY2 62 E8
Leveson Cres CV7 130 B6
Leveson Ct
1 Willenhall WV13 27 A2
Wolverhampton WV6 25 A4
Leveson Dr DY4 51 E6
Leveson Rd
Wednesfield WV11 26 F8
Wolverhampton WV11 12 F1
Leveson St WV13 27 A2
Leveson Wlk 5 DY2 62 E8
Levett Rd B77 22 B5
Levetts Fields WS14 9 C7
Levetts Hollow WS12 2 D3
Levetts Sq 4 WS13 9 B7
Levington Cl WV6 23 F5
Leviss Trad Est B33 68 D4
Lewis Ave WV1 26 B2
Lewis Cl
Lichfield WS14 9 E7
Willenhall WV12 27 D5
Lewis Gr WV11 26 D6
Lewisham Ind Est B66 65 A7
Lewisham Rd
Smethwick B66 65 A7
Wolverhampton WV10 11 B2
Lewisham St B71 53 D4
Lewis Rd
Birmingham,Brandhall B68 84 B7
Birmingham,Stirchley B30 104 C7
Coventry CV1 113 D5
Lewis Rd *continued*
Radford Semele CV31 162 F5
Stourbridge DY9 81 D5
Lewis St
Bilston WV14 40 E6
Tipton DY4 52 D5
Walsall WS2 28 D3
Lewkner Almshouses The B48 139 A5
Lewthorn Rise WV4 39 D4
Lexington Ct CV11 73 B5
Lexington Gn DY5 81 C7
Leybourne Cres WV9 10 F2
Leybourne Gr B25 88 C6
Leybrook Rd B45 122 B8
Leyburn Cl
3 Warwick CV34 155 F1
Coventry CV6 95 E2
Nuneaton CV11 74 A2
Willenhall WS2 27 D3
Leyburn Rd B16 66 A1
Leycester Cl B31 123 A7
Leycester Ct 13 CV34 160 E6
Leycester Pl 12 CV34 160 E6
Leycester Rd CV8 148 A2
Leycroft Ave B33 69 D3
Leydon Croft B38 104 B2
Leyes La CV8 148 C5
Leyfields Cres CV34 160 D4
Leyfields WS13 3 B2
Ley Hill Farm Rd B31 102 E5
Ley Hill Jun & Inf Sch B31 102 E5
Ley Hill Rd B75 32 C1
Leylan Croft B13 105 D7
Leyland Ave WV3 24 F1
Leyland Croft WS3 14 F4
Leyland Rd
Bulkington CV12 79 B2
Coventry CV5 112 D4
Nuneaton CV11 73 E1
Tamworth B77 21 E3
Leylands Way CV34 160 B4
Leyman Cl B14 105 C4
Leymere Cl CV7 92 C1
Ley Rise DY3 39 C1
Leys Cl DY9 81 C2
Leys Cres DY5 61 B3
Leysdown Gr B27 106 C8
Leysdown Rd B27 106 C8
Leyside CV3 134 E5
Leys Ind Est DY5 61 A3
Leys La CV7 92 C1
Leys Rd DY5 61 B3
Leysters Cl B98 154 E3
Leys The
1 Darlaston WS10 41 D6
Birmingham B31 103 B5
Hinckley LE10 76 A6
Leys Wood Croft B26 89 B6
Leyton Cl DY5 81 D8
Leyton Gr B44 45 A1
Leyton Rd B21 65 F8
Libbards Gate 4 B91 127 C8
Libbards Way B91 127 B8
Liberty Ct WS6 4 D3
Liberty Pl 1 B16 66 B2
Liberty Rd B77 35 F5
Liberty Way CV11 73 F3
Libra Cl B79 20 F7
Library Cl LE10 76 A5
Library Rd CV4 132 B5
Library Sq 3 B91 107 C3
Library Way B45 121 F7
Lich Ave WV11 26 E7
Lichen Cl WS12 1 C6
Lichen Gdns B38 123 D7
Lichen Gn CV4 132 D5
Lichfield Bsns Ctr WS13 3 D1
Lichfield Cathedral Sch WS13 9 B8
Lichfield Cath* WS13 9 B8
Lichfield City Sta WS14 9 B7
Lichfield Cl CV11 74 A7
Lichfield Cres B78 20 B7
Lichfield Ct
Solihull B90 105 D2
Sutton Coldfield B75 46 C5
Walsall WS4 29 A4
Lichfield Pas WV1 163 C3
Lichfield Rd
Birmingham B6 67 B8
Brownhills,Shireoak Hill WS8, WS9 16 B5
Brownhills WS8,WS14 16 A8
Burntwood WS7 7 D6
Cannock WS11 5 B8
Coventry CV3 133 D8
Lichfield SW7,SW13 8 B6
Sutton Coldfield B74 32 A3
Tamworth B78,B79 20 E6
Walsall,Highbridge WS3 15 B5
Walsall,New Invention WS3,WS4, WS8,WS9 13 E1
Walsall,Rushall WS4 29 B6
Walsall,Shelfield WS4 15 C1
Walsall,Wallington Heath WS3 14 C2
Water Orton B46,B76 59 D4
Wednesfield WV11 26 E6
Willenhall WV12 27 D8
Wishaw B76,B78 48 B3
Lichfield Road Ind Est B79 20 E6

Lichfield St
Bilston WV14 40 E5
Fazeley B78 20 F1
Tamworth B79 21 A5
Tipton DY4 51 F8
Walsall WS1 28 F2
Wolverhampton WV1 163 C3
Lichfield Trent Valley Sta WS13 9 F8
Lichwood Rd WV11 26 F7
Lickey Coppice B45 122 C4
Lickey End Fst Sch B60 137 C6
Lickey Grange Dr B60 121 E1
Lickey Gr DY11 116 B2
Lickey Hills Country Pk & Visitor Ctr★ B45 122 B3
Lickey Hills Prim Sch B45 121 F3
Lickey Rd
Birmingham B45 122 C6
Stourbridge DY8 81 B6
Lickey Rock B60 121 D1
Lickey Sq B45 122 A2
Liddiard Ct DY8 80 E6
Liddon Gr B27 106 C8
Liddon Rd B27 106 C8
Lifford Cl B14 104 C4
Lifford La B30 104 B4
Lifford Way CV3 135 A7
Lifton Croft DY6 60 F5
Lightfields Wlk B65 63 A5
Light Hall Sch B90 126 B8
Lighthorne Ave B16 66 B2
Lighthorne Rd B91 107 C6
Light La CV1 165 B4
Lightning Way B31 123 B7
Lightoak Cl B97 158 C6
Lightwood Cl B93 128 B8
Lightwood Rd DY1 51 A3
Lightwoods Hill B67 84 E8
Lightwoods Jun & Inf Sch B68 84 D8
Lightwoods Rd
Smethwick B67 65 A1
Stourbridge DY9 81 C1
Lilac Ave
1 Birmingham,Balsall Heath B12 87 A5
Birmingham,Perry B44 55 E7
Cannock WS11 4 D7
Coventry CV6 112 F5
Sutton Coldfield B74 44 E8
Tipton DY4 51 E7
Walsall WS5 43 A4
Lilac Cl
Hinckley LE10 75 E6
Redditch B98 153 E2
Lilac Gr
Burntwood WS7 6 F7
Walsall WS2 27 E3
Warwick CV34 156 A1
Wednesbury WS10 42 A2
Lilac Ho WS4 15 D1
Lilac La WS6 14 A8
Lilac Rd
Bedworth CV12 78 D5
Bilston WV1 40 B8
Dudley DY1 51 C4
Tamworth B79 21 A8
Willenhall WV12 27 E7
Lilacvale Way CV4 132 D5
Lilac Way B62 83 F8
Lilian Gr WV14 40 E1
Lilleburne Dr CV10 72 B7
Lilleshall Cl B98 154 E3
Lilleshall Cres WV2 39 D7
Lilleshall Rd B26 89 B7
Lilley Cl CV6 95 C2
Lilley Green Rd B48 140 D5
Lilley La B31 123 B8
Lillington Ave CV32 156 F2
Lillington Cl
2 Lichfield WS13 9 A8
Royal Leamington Spa CV32 157 A3
Sutton Coldfield B75 47 A4
Lillington Gr B34 69 D5
Lillington Prim Sch CV32 157 B3
Lillington Rd
Coventry CV2 96 D1
Royal Leamington Spa CV32 157 A3
Solihull B90 126 B8
Lilycroft La B38 124 A7
Lily Green La B97 153 A4
Lily Rd B26 88 D7
Lily St B71 53 C5
Limberlost Cl B20 55 A3
Limbrick Ave CV4 112 A1
Limbrick Cl B90 105 F2
Limbrick Wood Prim Sch CV4 111 F3
Limbury Gr B92 107 F8
Lime Ave
8 Birmingham B29 85 F2
Royal Leamington Spa CV32 157 A4
Walsall WS2 27 E3
Lime Cl
Great Wyrley WS6 4 F4
Hollywood B47 125 A5
Tipton DY4 51 E5
Walsall WS2 27 E3
West Bromwich B70 53 A4
Lime Ct
Birmingham B11 87 C4
Kidderminster DY10 117 A4
Lime Gr
Bilston WV14 40 C7
Birmingham B25,B26 88 D6
Birmingham,Balsall Heath B12 86 F5
Birmingham,Chemsley Wood B37 70 B1
Birmingham,Lozells B19 66 C8
Birmingham,Small Heath B10 87 D8
Bromsgrove B61 136 F4
Burntwood WS7 7 C6
Coventry CV4 112 B2
Kenilworth CV8 148 A4
Lichfield WS14 9 D8
Nuneaton CV10 72 E5
Smethwick B66 65 B3
Smethwick B66 65 B4
Sutton Coldfield B73 57 B7
Walsall WS4 29 C6
Limehurst Ave WV3 24 C1
Limehurst Rd WS4 29 C6
Lime Kiln Cl B38 123 D7
Limekiln La
Birmingham B14 105 A4
Earlswood B94 126 D1
Lime La
Norton Canes WS3 6 A1
Walsall WS3 15 A7
Limepit La
Dudley DY1 51 A3
Huntington WS11,WS12 1 D6
Lime Rd
Huntington WS12 1 D8
Sedgley DY3 39 F1
Wednesbury WS10 41 F4
Limes Ave
Brierley Hill DY5 61 C5
Rowley Regis B65 63 C2
Limescroft Cl WS4 29 B7
Limes Ct WV6 24 D5
Limes Rd
Dudley DY1 51 B3
Wolverhampton WV6 24 D4
Lime St WV14 51 A8
Limes The
Bedworth CV12 77 E2
Birmingham,Gravelly Hill B24 56 F3
Birmingham,Ladywood B16 65 F2
Birmingham,Rotton Park B16 65 F3
Birmingham,Sparkbrook B11 87 C6
Coventry CV6 112 E5
Himley DY3 49 B3
Walsall WS1 29 A2
Wolverhampton WV11 26 B5
Lime St
Walsall WS1 29 A1
Wolverhampton WV3 39 B8
Limes View DY3 50 D7
Lime Tree Ave
Coventry CV4 112 A2
Wolverhampton WV6 24 A3
Lime Tree Cres B97 153 B4
Lime Tree Gdns WV8 10 B3
Lime Tree Gr B31 103 C2
Lime Tree Rd
Birmingham,Acock's Green B27 88 C5
Birmingham,Saltley B8 67 F6
Codsall WV8 10 B4
Limetree Rd B74 30 D1
Lime Tree Rd WS5 43 A4
Linacre Ho B37 69 F2
Linaker Rd CV3 134 C5
Linchmere Rd B21 54 C2
Lincoln Ave
Nuneaton CV10 72 B7
Tamworth B79 20 E6
Willenhall WV13 27 D2
Lincoln Cl
Birmingham B27 88 E3
Lichfield WS13 3 C3
Warwick CV34 155 E1
Lincoln Croft WS14 17 F6
Lincoln Ct
9 Birmingham B29 103 C7
Royal Leamington Spa CV32 162 A8
Lincoln Dr WS11 4 F8
Lincoln Gn WV10 11 D2
Lincoln Gr B37 70 A1
Lincoln Ho WV10 25 E3
Lincoln Rd
Birmingham B27 88 D2
Bromsgrove B61 136 E4
Dudley DY2 62 D2
Lincoln Rd N B27 88 E3
Lincoln Rd
Smethwick B67 64 E2
Walsall WS1 29 A1
West Bromwich B71 42 D1
Lincoln St
Birmingham B12 86 E6
Coventry CV1 165 C4
Wolverhampton WV10 25 E3
Lincoln Twr B16 66 A1
Lincroft Cres CV5 112 E4
Lindale Ave B36 68 C6
Lindale Cres DY5 81 B6
Linden Ave
Birmingham B43 54 D8
Burntwood WS7 7 A8
Linden Ave *continued*
Halesowen B62 83 E7
Kidderminster DY10 117 A7
Oldbury B69 63 D8
Linden Cl
Tamworth B77 21 F4
Warwick CV34 155 E2
Willenhall WS2 27 D2
Linden Ct B91 107 E4
Linden Dr DY8 81 A3
Linden Gdns DY10 117 A6
Linden Glade B63 83 A4
Linden Gr DY10 117 A7
Linden Ho WV3 163 A1
Linden La WV12 27 E6
Linden Lea
Bedworth CV12 78 B3
Wolverhampton WV3 24 D1
Linden Rd
Birmingham B30 103 E7
Dudley DY1 51 B3
Hinckley LE10 71 C1
Smethwick B66 65 A2
Lindens Dr B74 44 F5
Lindens Prim Sch B74 44 F6
Lindens The
Birmingham B32 84 E7
Birmingham,Edgbaston B16 65 D1
Wolverhampton WV6 24 E3
Linden View WS12 2 B4
Lindenwood B73 46 B6
Lindera B77 22 A4
Lindfield The CV3 134 C8
Lindford Way B38 104 B2
Lindhurst Dr B94 143 C6
Lindisfarne Dr CV8 148 C4
Lindisfarne B77 21 D3
Lindley Ave DY4 51 F4
Lindley Rd
Bedworth CV12 77 D2
Coventry CV3 114 B2
Lindon Cl WS8 16 A6
Lindon Dr WS8 15 F7
Lindon Rd WS8 15 F5
Lindon View WS8 16 A5
Lindop Cl CV32 157 D5
Lindrick Cl WS3 13 F3
Lindridge Dr B76 58 D6
Lindridge Rd
Birmingham B23 56 C5
Solihull B90 105 F1
Sutton Coldfield B75,B76 47 B6
Lindrosa Rd B74 30 F3
Lindsay Rd B42 44 B1
Lindsey Ave B31 103 C4
Lindsey Cres CV8 148 A1
Lindsey Pl DY5 61 C3
Lindsey Rd B71 53 C7
Lindsworth App B30 104 C3
Lindsworth Ct 2 B30 104 C3
Lindsworth Rd B30 104 C3
Lindsworth Sch (North) B23 57 A6
Lindsworth Sch (South) B30 104 C3
Lineholt Cl B98 159 A6
Linehouse La
Catshill B60 137 D8
Lower Marlbrook B60 121 D1
Linen St CV34 160 D6
Linfield Gdns DY3 39 C1
Linford Gr B25 68 D1
Linford Wlk CV2 96 F1
Linforth Dr B74 45 A7
Lingard Cl B7 67 B5
Lingard Ho B76 57 F8
Lingard Rd B75 47 A5
Lingen Cl B98 154 E3
Lingfield Ave
Birmingham B44 44 F1
Wolverhampton WV10 11 D5
Lingfield Cl WS6 4 F2
Lingfield Ct
Birmingham B43 54 D7
Coventry CV6 96 B4
Lingfield Dr WS6 4 F2
Lingfield Gdns B34 69 B6
Lingfield Gr WV6 23 F4
Lingfield Rd WS11 6 A5
Lingfield Way DY6 61 A5
Lingfield Wlk B61 121 B1
Lingham Cl B92 107 D7
Ling Ho WV10 25 F3
Lingmoor Gr WS9 30 A7
Ling Rd WS12 1 C5
Lingwood Dr CV10 72 F3
Linhope Dr DY6 61 A5
Link One Ind Pk DY4 52 E6
Link Rd
Birmingham B16 65 E3
Brownhills WS9 16 B3
Wombourne WV5 49 A7
Links Ave WV6 24 D7
Links Cres B68 84 B8
Links Dr
Birmingham B45 122 A5
Solihull B91 107 B6
Stourbridge DY8 80 E2
Links Rd
Birmingham,Brandhall B68 84 B8
Birmingham,Highter's Heath B14 105 A1
Coventry CV6 113 B8
Wolverhampton WV4 39 A3
Links Side Way WS9 30 C8
Links The DY10 117 A4
Links View
Halesowen B62 83 D4
Sutton Coldfield B74 31 B1
Linkswood Cl B13 87 B1
Link The B27 88 A1
Linkway Ret Pk WS11 4 B6
Linkway CV31 161 E6
Linkwood Ind Est DY8 80 F6
Linley Cl WS9 29 E5
Linley Dr WV10 11 E1
Linley Gr
Birmingham B14 104 C6
Dudley DY3 50 B2
Linley Lodge Ind Est WS9 29 E6
Linley Rd WS4 29 D7
Linley Wood Rd WS9 29 E5
Linnet Cl
Birmingham B30 103 E8
Coventry CV3 134 D5
Halesowen B62 83 B6
Huntington WS12 1 D7
Linnet Gr
Birmingham B23 56 B6
Willenhall WV12 27 C8
Linnet Rise DY10 116 F1
Linpole Wlk B14 104 D2
Linsey Rd B92 89 C2
Linslade Cl WV4 39 D4
Linstock Way CV6 96 B4
Linthouse La WV11 26 E8
Linthouse Wlk 3 B77 35 F6
Linthurst Fst Sch B60 138 A6
Linthurst Newtown B60 138 B5
Linthurst Rd B45,B60 138 A7
Lintly B77 22 B1
Linton Ave B91 107 A1
Linton Cl
Halesowen B63 82 D5
Redditch B98 154 F2
Linton Croft WV14 40 D5
Linton Mews B98 154 F2
Linton Rd
Birmingham,Acock's Green B11 88 A4
Birmingham,Great Barr B43 44 C3
Cradley Heath B64 62 F3
Wolverhampton WV4 38 E5
Linton Wlk B23 56 C3
Linwood Cl LE10 71 B2
Linwood Ct B15 86 D7
Linwood Dr
Cannock WS12 1 F7
Coventry CV2 96 F1
Linwood Rd
Birmingham B21 65 E8
Dudley DY1 51 B5
Solihull B91 106 D5
Lionel St B3 164 B3
Lion Fields Ave CV5 112 B6
Lion Ind Est WS9 30 A8
Lion Pas DY8 80 F5
Lion's Den WS7,WS14 7 E2
Lion Sq DY10 116 E6
Lion St
Kidderminster DY10 116 E6
Stourbridge DY8 80 F5
Liskeard Cl CV11 74 A5
Liskeard Rd WS5 43 D7
Lisko Cl DY5 81 A8
Lisle Ave DY11 116 D3
Lisle Ct 4 CV31 162 A6
Lismore Cl B45 101 E1
Lismore Croft CV2 115 B7
Lismore Dr
Birmingham B17 85 A3
Hinckley LE10 71 C1
Lissimore Dr DY4 52 B2
Lisson Gr B44 44 F4
Listelow Cl B36 69 B8
Lister Cl
Tipton DY4 52 A4
Walsall WS2 28 B5
Lister Rd
Dudley DY2 62 D7
Kidderminster DY11 116 B4
Walsall WS2 28 B5
Lister St
Birmingham B7 66 F4
Nuneaton CV11 73 D3
Willenhall WV13 27 B1
Listowel Rd B14 104 D6
Lisures Dr B76 46 D4
Little Acre B97 158 D6
Little Albert St WS2 28 E2
Little Ann St B5 66 F2
Little Aston Hall Dr B74 31 B5
Little Aston Hall B74 31 B5
Little Aston Hospl B74 31 B5
Little Aston La B74 31 D6
Little Aston Park Rd B74 31 A3
Little Aston Rd WS9 30 D6
Little Bloxwich Wlk 3 WS13 3 A1
Little Barr St B9 67 A2
Little Birches WV3 38 F8
Little Bloxwich CE Prim Sch WS3 14 D3
Little Brickiln St WV3 163 B2
Little Bromwich Rd B9 68 C2
Little Broom St B12 87 A8
Little Caldmore 6 WS1 42 E8
Little Church La B79 21 B5
Little Church St 1 CV1 165 C4
Little Clothier St WV13 27 A3
Little Clover Cl 3 B7 67 C7
Little Comm WS3 15 A4
Little Cornbow B63 83 B3
Littlecote Croft 1 B14 105 A3
Littlecote Dr B23 56 F7
Littlecote B79 20 D7
Little Cottage St DY5 61 D2
Little Croft B43 43 C1
Little Cross St WS10 41 D7
Little Cryfield CV4 132 C2
Little Duke St CV11 73 B4
Little Edward St B9 67 A2
Little Farm CV3 134 D5
Little Field CV2 114 A5
Little Fields Way B69 63 F7
Little Forge Rd B98 159 C8
Little Francis Gr 3 B7 67 B5
Little Gorway WS1 42 F7
Little Grebe Rd DY10 117 B3
Little Green La B9 67 C1
Little Green Lanes B73 57 B7
Little Hall Rd B7 67 B5
Little Hardwick Rd WS9 30 D2
Little Hay La WS14 18 C3
Little Heath Croft B34 69 B7
Little Heath Ind Est CV6 96 A2
Little Heath La B60 137 D6
Little Heath Prim Sch CV6 95 F1
Little Hill Gr B38 104 A1
Little Hill Way B32 84 D2
Little Hill WS10 41 F3
Little Johnson's La
Aldridge WS9 30 B1
Walsall WS9 44 B8
Little John St DY5 61 D4
Little La
West Bromwich B71 53 D5
Willenhall WV12 27 D7
Little Lawns Cl WS9 16 A4
Little London Ho 1 WS1 42 F7
Little London JMI Sch WV13 27 A2
Little London WS1 42 F8
Littlemead Ave B31 103 C1
Little Meadow Croft B31 102 F4
Little Meadow Wlk B33 68 F3
Littlemead Rd B90 125 E8
Little Moor Hill B67 64 F5
Little Newport St 5 WS1 28 E1
Little Oaks Dr DY7 60 A2
Little Oaks Rd B6 66 E8
Littleover Ave B28 105 F6
Little Park St
Coventry CV1 165 C2
Wolverhampton WV1 163 C3
Little Pitts Cl B24 57 D5
Little Pk B32 84 B4
Little Potter St DY5 61 D2
Little Pountney St WV2 163 B1
Little Shadwell St B4 164 C4
Littleshaw Croft B47 125 C4
Littleshaw La B47 125 C4
Little's La WV1 163 C4
Little South St CV1 113 E3
Little Station St WS2 28 E2
Little St DY2 51 D1
Little Sutton La B75 46 C8
Little Sutton Prim Sch B75 32 D3
Little Sutton Rd B75 32 D2
Littlethorpe CV3 134 D6
Littleton Bsns Pk WS12 1 C7
Littleton Cl
Kenilworth CV8 148 A7
Sutton Coldfield B76 47 A2
Littleton Croft 6 B91 127 C8
Littleton Dr WS12 1 C7
Littleton Rd WV12 27 D7
Littleton St E WS1 28 F3
Littleton St W WS1 28 E2
Littlewood Cl 2 B91 127 B8
Littlewood Gn B80 159 D3
Littlewood La WS6 4 E4
Littlewood Rd WS6 4 E4
Little Woods B97 158 E6
Little Wood St WV13 27 A2
Littleworth Ave DY1 51 B6
Littleworth Croft CV31 162 C5
Littleworth Gr B76 46 F4
Littleworth Hill WS12 2 D4
Littleworth Rd WS12 2 E4
Litton B77 22 C1
Liveridge Cl B93 127 F6
Liverpool Croft B37 89 F8
Liverpool St B9 67 A2
Livery St
Birmingham B3 164 B3
Birmingham B3 164 B4
Royal Leamington Spa CV32 161 F8
Livingstone Ave WV6 23 E5
Livingstone Rd
Bilston WV14 40 B5
Birmingham,Handsworth B20 55 D1
Birmingham,King's Heath B14 104 E6
Coventry CV6 113 E7
Walsall WS3 14 E2
West Bromwich B70 53 B1
Lizafield Ct B66 64 E7
Llewellyn Rd CV31 162 A6
Lloyd Cl CV11 73 D2
Lloyd Cres CV2 114 E3
Lloyd Dr WV4 38 C2
Lloyd George Gr WS11 2 C2
Lloyd Hill WV4 38 C3
Lloyd Ho B19 66 C6
Lloyd Rd
Birmingham B20 55 A4
Wolverhampton WV6 24 D5
Lloyd Roberts Bldgs WV4 38 F1
Lloyds Rd B62 83 C8

Lloyd St
Birmingham B10 .... 87 D8
Cannock WS11.............. 1 D1
Dudley DY2 .... 62 D8
Wednesbury WS10 .... 41 E3
West Bromwich B71 .... 53 E4
Wolverhampton WV6...... 24 F4
Loach Dr CV2............. 96 B4
Lobelia Cl LE10 .... 75 E5
Locarno Rd DY4 .... 52 A6
Lochalsh Gr WV11 .... 13 B1
Lochmore Cl LE10.......... 75 A8
Lochmore Dr LE10 .... 75 A8
Lochmore Way LE10 ...... 75 A8
Lochranza Croft B43 ..... 43 E2
Lochsong Cl B77........... 35 D4
Loch St CV3 .... 114 C1
Lock Cl B97 .... 153 A4
Lock Dr B33 .... 68 D3
Locke Cl CV6 .... 95 A1
Locket Cl WS2 .... 27 F4
Locketts Ct WS11 .... 1 F5
Lockfield Cl DY8 .... 60 F2
Lockhart Cl CV8 .... 148 A4
Lockhart Dr B75 .... 32 C1
Lockheed Cl 8 CV31 .... 161 F5
Lockhurst La CV6 .... 113 D7
Locking Croft B35 .... 58 B3
Lockington Croft B62 .... 83 F6
Lock Keepers Cl WS11 ..... 5 F4
Lock Keepers Reach
B48 .... 138 F6
Lock La CV34 .... 160 D8
Lockley Cl WV10.......... 25 F4
Lock Mus The★ WV13 .... 27 A1
Lockside WS9 .... 29 F7
Lockside Cl DY5 .... 61 D1
Locksmith Cl WV13 .... 27 B2
Locks The CV31........... 161 D7
Lock St WV1............... 163 C4
Locks View DY8........... 60 E1
Lockton Rd B30........... 104 C8
Lockwood Rd B31......... 102 F4
Lode Heath Sch B91 .... 107 C6
Lode La B91 .... 107 C6
Loder Cl CV4 .... 111 F3
Lodge Cl
Halesowen B62 .... 83 E3
Hinckley LE10 .... 76 A5
Walsall WS5 .... 43 D6
Lodge Cres
Dudley DY2 .... 62 A4
Warwick CV34........... 160 D4
West Hagley DY9.......... 99 B5
Lodge Croft
Birmingham B31 .... 102 E6
Knowle B93 .... 128 B6
Lodge Dr B26............. 88 F8
Lodge Farm Cl B76 ...... 46 F3
Lodge Farm JMI Sch
WV12 .... 27 E4
Lodgefield Rd B62 .... 83 B7
Lodge Forge Trad Est
B64........................ 82 C7
Lodge Gr WS9 .... 30 A5
Lodge Green La CV7 ..... 92 F2
Lodge Green La N CV7 ... 92 E3
Lodge Hill Rd B29......... 85 D1
Lodge La
Cheslyn Hay WS11......... 4 C5
Kingswinford DY6 .... 60 B6
Lodgepool Cl B44.......... 55 E6
Lodge Pool Dr B98...... 153 F1
Lodge Prim Sch B70 ..... 53 B3
Lodge Rd
Bilston WV14 .... 40 F4
Birmingham B18 .... 65 F5
Coventry CV3............ 114 B1
Darlaston WS10........... 41 D5
Knowle B93 .... 128 B6
Redditch B98............. 153 E3
Smethwick B67 .... 64 E7
Walsall,The Chuckery WS5 . 43 D6
Walsall WS4 .... 15 B1
West Bromwich B70 ...... 53 C3
Lodge Rd/ West Bromwich
TH Sta B70............... 53 C3
Lodge Rd WV10............ 25 B8
Lodge St
Oldbury B69............... 64 A7
Willenhall WV12 .... 27 C5
Lodge The B15 .... 65 D1
Lodge View WS6........... 4 C3
Loeless Rd B33 .... 69 A3
Lofthouse Cres B31 ..... 102 F3
Lofthouse Gr B31 .... 102 F3
Lofthouse Rd B20.......... 54 F3
Loftus Cl B29............. 102 F8
Loftus Ct WS7 .... 7 A5
Logan Cl WV10 .... 25 C6
Logan Rd CV2 .... 114 E7
Lole Cl CV6 .... 96 A4
Lollard Croft CV3 .... 133 D8
Lomaine Dr B30 .... 103 E4
Lomas Dr B31 .... 102 E3
Lomas St WV1 .... 25 C4
Lomax Cl WS13 .... 3 A1
Lomax Rd WS12 .... 2 B7
Lombard Ave DY2.......... 62 D3
Lombard Gdns 1 WS13 ....9 B8
Lombard St W B70 .... 53 C3
Lombard St
Birmingham B12 .... 86 F8
Lichfield WS13............. 9 B8
West Bromwich B70 ...... 53 C3
Lombardy Croft 3 B62.... 84 A6
Lombardy Gdns WV12.... 27 E7
Lombardy Gr WS7 .... 6 F8
Lomita Cres B77......... 35 D8
Lomond Cl
Birmingham B34 .... 69 E6
Hinckley LE10 .... 75 B8
Tamworth B79 .... 20 F8
Lomond Rd DY3 .... 39 C1
Lomond Way CV10 .... 72 C5
Lomsey Cl CV4........... 112 A1
Londonderry Gr B67 ..... 64 F5
Londonderry La B67 ..... 64 E4
Londonderry Rd B68 ..... 64 D4
London Hts DY1 .... 51 A2
London La
Bromsgrove B60 .... 151 F7
Tardebigge B60......... 152 A6
London Pl WV2 .... 163 B2
London Rd
Birmingham B20 .... 55 E2
Coventry,Cheylesmore
CV3..................... 133 E8
Coventry,Willenhall CV3... 134 B5
Hinckley LE10 .... 75 E8
Lichfield WS14............. 9 C5
Middleton B75,B78 .... 47 D7
Ryton-on-D CV8 .... 135 B1
Shenstone B75,WS14 ..... 32 F7
Sutton Coldfield B75 ..... 33 A4
Weeford WS14 .... 18 F3
London St B66............ 65 C5
Lones Rd B71.............. 65 B8
Long Acre B7.............. 67 C7
Longacre WS10........... 41 A8
Longacre Ind Est B7 ..... 67 C7
Long Acre DY10.......... 116 F7
Longacres
Cannock WS12.............. 2 F5
Sutton Coldfield B74 ..... 31 C4
Long Acre St WS2........ 28 D3
Long Acre Trad Est B7 ... 67 B7
Longbank Rd B69 .... 63 C8
Longboat La DY8.......... 60 E1
Longboat Quay DY2....... 62 D4
Longborough Cl B97 .... 158 B6
Longbow Rd B29.......... 102 F7
Longbridge La B31....... 122 E8
Long Bridge Rd WS14 ..... 9 C5
Longbridge Sta B31...... 122 E8
Long Brook La CV7,CV8 .. 129 E5
Long Close Ave CV5..... 112 B6
Long Close Wlk B35...... 58 A3
Long Cl DY9 .... 99 A4
Long Compton Dr DY9 ... 99 A6
Longcroft Ave 1 WS10... 42 A3
Long Croft WS12........... 1 C4
Longcroft Cl B35.......... 58 A3
Longcroft The
Halesowen B63 .... 82 E4
Walsall WS4 .... 29 C7
Longdales Rd B38......... 123 E7
Longdon Ave WV4 .... 39 D5
Longdon Cl B98.......... 159 B7
Longdon Croft B93....... 128 A8
Longdon Dr B74 .... 31 E4
Longdon Rd B93 .... 128 A6
Longfellow Ave CV34.... 160 C4
Longfellow Cl B97 ...... 158 C7
Longfellow Gn DY10 .... 117 C6
Longfellow Pl WS11........ 1 E4
Longfellow Rd
Birmingham B30 .... 103 D4
Coventry CV2............ 114 C3
Dudley DY3 .... 50 B5
Longfellow Wlk B79....... 20 F8
Longfield Cl
Birmingham B28 .... 105 F6
Tamworth B77 .... 21 E4
Longfield Dr B74 .... 31 D4
Longfield Ho
Coventry CV6............ 114 A8
Wolverhampton WV10...... 25 F3
Longfield Rd
Birmingham B31 .... 102 E8
Royal Leamington Spa
CV31 .... 162 B6
Stourbridge DY9 .... 81 D5
Longford Cl
Birmingham B32 .... 102 A7
Dorridge B93............ 128 B3
Longford Ct WS11 .... 4 B8
Longford Gn WS11......... 4 C7
Longford Gr B44.......... 45 A3
Longford Ind Est WS11 .... 4 D6
Longford Park Prim Sch
CV6........................ 96 A3
Longford Prim Sch WS11.. 4 C8
Longford Rd
Bedworth CV7 .... 96 A6
Birmingham B44 .... 45 A2
Cannock WS11............. 4 D7
Coventry CV6.............. 96 A4
Wolverhampton WV10...... 26 A4
Longford Sq CV6.......... 96 A4
Long Furrow WV8.......... 10 E1
Longham Croft B32 ...... 84 F4
Longhurst Croft B31 ..... 123 B7
Long Hyde Rd B67 .... 64 F1
Long Innage B63.......... 82 B6
Long Knowle La WV11.... 26 B8
Long Knowle Prim Sch
WV11 .... 26 C8
Long La
Brownshill Green CV5,
CV7 .... 94 D2
Great Wyrley WS6 .... 13 E6
Halesowen B62 .... 83 E8
Longlake Ave WV6 .... 24 B3
Longlands Cl B38 .... 123 C8
Longlands Dr B77......... 21 F4
Longlands Rd B62 .... 83 E3
Longlands The
Barnt Green B45 .... 138 D7
Wombourne WV5........... 49 A6
Long La Trad Est B62..... 83 D8
Long Leasow B29 .... 103 B7
Longleat Ave 2 B15 ..... 66 C1
Longleat B43 .... 43 C2
Longleat Dr
Cheswick Green B90..... 126 E5
Dudley DY1 .... 50 E2
Longleat Gr 17 CV31 .... 162 C6
Longleat Rd WS9 .... 16 A1
Longleat B79 .... 20 D7
Longley Ave B76.......... 58 D5
Longley Cres B26 .... 88 E4
Long Leys Croft B46 ..... 59 B2
Long Leys Ct B46 .... 59 B2
Longley Wlk B37.......... 70 C2
Long Ley WV10 .... 25 F3
Long Mdw B65............ 63 C3
Longmeadow Cl B75 ..... 46 F5
Longmeadow Cres B34... 69 E6
Long Meadow Dr
Hinckley LE10 .... 74 F7
Sedgley DY3.............. 39 B2
Longmeadow Gr B31.... 123 A6
Long Meadow Rd B60... 137 C6
Longmeadow Rd WS5.... 43 E8
Long Mill Ave WV11...... 26 B7
Long Mill N WV11......... 26 B7
Long Mill S WV11 .... 26 B7
Longmoor Cl
Redditch B97 .... 153 B5
Wednesfield WV11 .... 26 F5
Longmoor Ho 13 B74..... 31 F2
Longmoor Rd
Halesowen B63 .... 82 E3
Sutton Coldfield B73 ..... 45 B3
Longmoor Sch B73 .... 45 A4
Longmore Ave WS2 ...... 27 F1
Longmore Cl B73 .... 45 A5
Longmore Ho B73 .... 45 C3
Longmore Rd B90....... 106 D2
Longmore St
Birmingham B12 .... 86 E7
Wednesbury WS10 .... 41 F3
Long Mynd Cl WV11....... 13 B1
Long Mynd B63........... 82 D1
Long Mynd Rd B31...... 102 F6
Long Nuke Rd B31 ...... 102 E7
Long Saw Dr B31 .... 102 D1
Longshaw Gr B34 .... 69 D6
Long Shoot The CV11 .... 74 C6
Long St
Birmingham B11 .... 87 A6
Bulkington CV12 .... 79 D2
Longstone Cl B90 .... 127 B6
Longstone Rd B42 .... 55 C7
Long St
Walsall WS2 .... 28 D1
Wolverhampton WV1..... 163 C3
Longville Ct CV3 .... 134 A6
Longwill Prim Sch For Deaf
Children B31 .... 103 A5
Long Wood B30.......... 103 E5
Longwood Cl CV4......... 131 F6
Longwood La WS5,WS4... 29 E2
Longwood Path B78 ..... 20 D1
Longwood Prim Sch B78 . 20 D1
Longwood Rd
Aldridge WS9.............. 30 B2
Birmingham B45 .... 122 A7
Longwood Rise WV12 .... 27 D5
Lonicera Cl WS5 .... 43 B3
Lonscale Dr CV3 .... 133 B5
Lonsdale Cl
Birmingham B33 .... 68 D2
Willenhall WV12 .... 27 B5
Lonsdale Ct B17 .... 85 C6
Lonsdale Rd
Bilston WV14.............. 40 F6
Birmingham B17 .... 85 B6
Royal Leamington Spa
CV32 .... 157 B4
Smethwick B66 .... 64 D7
Walsall WS5 .... 43 C6
Wolverhampton WV3...... 39 B7
Lord Austin Dr B60....... 121 E1
Lord Cromwell Ct WS11 ... 2 A5
Lord Leycester Hospl & Knot
Gdn★ CV34............... 160 E6
Lord Lytton Ave CV2 .... 114 D2
Lord St W WV14 .... 40 E3
Lord's Dr WS2 .... 28 E3
Lords La B80 .... 159 E2
Lordsmore Cl WV14....... 40 D1
Lord St
Bilston WV14.............. 40 E3
Birmingham B7 .... 66 F5
Coventry CV5............ 112 F2
Walsall WS1 .... 42 E6
Wolverhampton WV3...... 25 B1
Lordswood Boys Sch B17. 65 A1
Lordswood Cl B97 .... 152 F2
Lordswood Girls Sch & Sixth
Form Ctr B17 .... 85 A8
Lordswood Rd B17........ 85 A7
Lordswood Sq B17........ 85 B7
Lorenzo Cl CV3 .... 134 D6
Lorimer Way B43 .... 44 D5
Loriners Gr WS1 .... 29 B1
Lorne Gr DY10 .... 117 A6
Lorne St
Burntwood WS7............ 6 E8
Kidderminster DY10 ..... 117 A5
Tipton DY4................ 51 F8
Lorrainer Ave DY5 .... 81 A8
Lorton B79 .... 20 D7
Lothersdale B77 .... 36 C8
Lothians Rd
Walsall WS3 .... 15 A5
Wolverhampton WV6...... 24 E6
Lottie Rd B29............. 85 E1
Lotus Croft B67.......... 64 F4
Lotus Ct B16.............. 65 E1
Lotus Dr
Cannock WS11............. 1 E5
Cradley Heath B64 .... 62 F2
Lotus B77 .... 21 E3
Lotus Way B65............ 63 A4
Loudon Ave CV6 .... 113 A5
Loudon Gate CV11 .... 73 F1
Loughshaw B77........... 22 C1
Loughton Gr B63 .... 82 F4
Louisa Pl 3 B18 .... 66 A5
Louisa St 1 B1 .... 66 C3
Louis Ct B67.............. 64 F5
Louise Croft B14........ 104 E2
Louise Ct
2 Birmingham B27 .... 88 C3
Solihull B91 .... 106 E1
Louise Ho DY5............ 61 D7
Louise Lorne Rd B13 ..... 86 F4
Louise Rd B21 .... 65 F7
Louise St DY3............. 50 C3
Lount Wlk B19............ 66 E5
Lovage Rd B98........... 154 F6
Lovatt Cl DY4 .... 41 C1
Lovatt Pl WS11 .... 1 E5
Lovatt St WV1 .... 163 A3
Loveday Dr CV32 .... 156 E2
Loveday Ho B70 .... 53 D3
Loveday St B4 .... 164 C4
Love La B7 .... 164 D4
Lovelace Ave B91 .... 127 D8
Love La
Great Wyrley WS6 .... 5 B3
Hinckley LE10 .... 76 A6
Hollywood B47............ 124 F7
Stourbridge,Lye DY9 ..... 81 F5
Stourbridge,Old Swinford
DY8...................... 81 A3
Walsall WS1 .... 42 E7
Wolverhampton WV6...... 24 D6
Lovell Cl
Bedworth CV7 .... 96 A8
Birmingham B29 .... 103 B6
Lovell Rd CV12............ 78 A3
Lovell B79................ 20 F6
Love Lyne B97 .... 158 B5
Lover's Wlk 5 WS10...... 41 F3
Lovett Ave B69 .... 63 D5
Lovetts Cl LE10 .... 74 F8
Lowans Hill Cotts B97... 153 C5
Lowans Hill View B97 ... 153 C4
Low Ave B43 .... 43 F2
Lowbridge Cl WV12 ...... 27 C5
Lowbrook La B90........ 125 D4
Lowcroft Gdns WV10...... 25 E8
Lowden Croft B26........ 88 E4
Lowdham B77 .... 22 C1
Lowe Ave WS10........... 41 C7
Lowe Dr
Kingswinford DY6 .... 60 E4
Sutton Coldfield B73 ..... 45 C3
Lower Ave CV31 .... 161 F7
Lower Beeches Rd B31.. 102 C2
Lower Bentley La B60.... 151 F1
Lower Bond St LE10....... 71 D1
Lower Cape CV34 .... 160 D8
Lower Chapel St B69...... 52 C2
Lower Church La DY4 .... 52 B5
Lower City Rd B69 .... 52 D1
Lower Common La B97.. 153 B2
Lowercroft Way B74 ..... 31 E6
Lower Dartmouth St B9.. 67 B2
Lower Darwin St B12...... 86 F8
Lowe Rd CV6 .... 95 A2
Lower Derry St DY5 ...... 61 D2
Lower Eastern Green La
CV5 .... 111 F4
Lower Essex St B5 .... 66 E1
Lower Farm Prim Sch
WS3 .... 14 C3
Lower Farm WS9 .... 16 E4
Lower Ford St CV1...... 165 D3
Lower Forster St WS1..... 28 F2
Lower Gambolds La B60. 151 B6
Lower Gn
Tipton DY4................ 51 E5
Wolverhampton WV6...... 24 E5
Lower Grinsty La B97 ... 158 A8
Lower Ground Cl 1 B6... 55 F1
Lower Gungate B79...... 21 B5
Lower Hall La WS1....... 28 E1
Lower Hall St WV13 ...... 27 B1
Lower High St
Cradley Heath B64 .... 82 C8
Stourbridge DY8 .... 80 F6
Wednesbury WS10 .... 41 F2
Lower Higley Cl B32 ..... 84 E4
Lower Holyhead Rd CV1. 165 A3
Lower Horseley Fields
WV1 .... 25 F2
Lower House La CV9 ..... 36 F2
Lower Keys Bsns Pk WS12. 2 D3
Lower Ladyes Hills CV8 . 148 A6
Lower Leam St CV31...... 162 B7
Lower Lichfield St WV13 . 27 B2
Lower Loveday St B19... 164 C4
Lower Mill St DY11....... 116 D6
Lower Moor B30......... 103 E8
Lower North St WS4 ..... 28 E3
Lower Parklands DY11 .. 116 C5
Lowerpark B77 .... 21 C1
Lower Par The B72 ...... 46 C5
Lower Prec CV1 .... 165 B3
Lower Prestwood Rd
WV11..................... 26 C7
Lower Queen St B72 ..... 46 C4
Lower Rd
Barnacle CV7.............. 97 C6
Cannock WS12............. 2 C3
Lower Reddicroft B73.... 46 C5
Lower Rushall St WS1.... 28 F2
Lower Sandford St WS13 .. 9 A7
Lower Severn St B1..... 164 B2
Lower Shepley La B60... 137 E6
Lowerstack Croft B37 .... 69 F3
Lower St WV6 .... 24 E5
Lower Temple St 4 B2.. 164 B2
Lower Tower St B19 .... 164 C5
Lower Trinity St B9 ...... 67 A1
Lower Valley Rd DY5..... 61 A2
Lower Vauxhall WV1 ..... 25 A3
Lower Villiers St
1 Royal Leamington Spa
CV32..................... 157 A1
Wolverhampton WV2...... 39 C7
Lower Walsall St WV1.... 25 F1
Lower White Rd B32 ..... 84 D5
Lowes Ave CV34 .... 155 E1
Lowesmoor Rd B26 ...... 89 C7
Lowe St
Birmingham B12 .... 87 A8
Wolverhampton WV6...... 25 B4
Loweswater Cl CV11 ..... 74 A6
Loweswater Dr DY3...... 50 D3
Loweswater Ho B38..... 104 B1
Loweswater Rd CV3..... 114 E1
Lowfield Cl B62........... 84 A3
Lowfield La B97 .... 153 B5
Lowfield Rd CV3 .... 114 C1
Lowforce B77 .... 22 C1
Low Hill Cres WV10 ...... 25 E8
Lowhill La B45........... 122 D6
Lowland Cl B64............ 62 F1
Lowland Rd WS12.......... 1 C5
Lowlands Ave
Sutton Coldfield B74 ..... 44 E8
Wolverhampton WV6...... 24 E6
Lowlands Ct WV6 .... 24 E6
Lowlands La B98........ 154 D3
Lowndes Rd DY8.......... 80 E6
Lowrey Ct B68............ 64 C3
Lowry Cl
Bedworth CV12 .... 78 A4
Perton WV6............... 23 F4
Smethwick B67 .... 64 F6
Willenhall WV13 .... 26 E2
Low St WS6 .... 4 D3
Low Thatch B38 .... 123 E7
Lowther Ct 10 DY5 .... 61 D2
Lowther St CV2.......... 113 F4
Low Town 6 B69 .... 64 A7
Low Wood Rd B23 .... 56 E5
Loxdale Park Ind Est
WV14 .... 40 E4
Loxdale Prim Sch WV14 .. 40 F4
Loxdale Sidings WV14.... 40 F4
Loxdale Sta WV14......... 40 F4
Loxdale St
Bilston WV14.............. 40 F4
Wednesbury WS10 .... 41 E2
Loxley Ave
Birmingham B14 .... 105 C3
Solihull B90 .... 105 F1
Loxley Cl
Birmingham B31 .... 102 E8
Coventry CV2............. 96 D2
Redditch B98............ 154 D6
Loxley Ct CV2............. 96 D2
Loxley Rd
Smethwick B67 .... 64 F1
Sutton Coldfield B75 ..... 32 D3
Loxley Sq B92 .... 106 D8
Loxley Way CV32........ 157 A2
Loxton Cl B74 .... 31 D5
Loynells Rd B45 .... 122 B7
Loyns Cl B37 .... 69 E3
Lozells Inf & Jun Sch B19 66 D7
Lozells Rd B19............ 66 C7
Lozells St B19 .... 66 C7
Lozells Wood Cl 2 B19 .. 66 B7
Luanne Cl B64 .... 63 A1
Lucas Ct CV32 .... 161 D8
Lucas Ho CV32........... 156 F2
Lucas Rd LE10 .... 75 D6
Luce Cl B35 .... 58 B4
Luce Rd WV10 .... 25 E6
Lucerne Cl CV2 .... 96 C3
Lucerne Ct B23 .... 56 D6
Lucian Cl CV2............ 115 B7
Lucknow Rd WV12 .... 27 B5
Lucy Edwards Ct DY11... 116 C5
Luddington Rd B92 ..... 107 E8
Ludford Cl B75 .... 46 E7
Ludford Rd
Birmingham B32 .... 84 A1
Nuneaton CV10 .... 72 C6
Ludgate Ave DY11 ...... 116 A4
Ludgate Cl
Oldbury B69............... 63 B8
Water Orton B46.......... 59 B3
Ludgate Ct 2 WS5........ 43 D7
Ludgate Hill B3.......... 164 B3
Ludgate Ho B13 .... 86 F4
Ludgate St 11 DY1 .... 51 B1
Ludgate B79............... 21 A5
Lud La B79 .... 21 A5

Ludlow Cl
Birmingham B37 70 C2
Cannock WS11 2 C2
Willenhall WV12 27 B6
Ludlow Ct B11 87 B6
Ludlow Ho
1 Walsall WS3 28 C6
Birmingham B13 105 A6
Ludlow La WS2 28 A4
Ludlow Rd
Birmingham B8 67 F4
Coventry CV5 113 A2
Kidderminster DY10 116 E3
Redditch B97 153 E3
Ludlow Way DY1 50 E2
Ludmer Way B20 55 C2
Ludstone Ave WV4 38 D5
Ludstone Rd B29 84 F1
Ludworth Ave B37 90 B8
Luff Cl CV3 134 B8
Lugtrout La
Catherine de B B91 108 A6
Solihull B91 107 F6
Lukes The B64 62 C1
Lukes Wlk WS13 3 A2
Lulworth Cl B63 82 C6
Lulworth Pk CV8 148 C6
Lulworth Rd
Birmingham B28 88 A1
Burntwood WS7 7 A7
Lulworth Wlk WV4 38 C6
Lumley Gr B37 70 D2
Lumley Rd WS1 29 A1
Lumsden Cl CV2 114 F8
Lunar Cl CV4 132 D5
Lundy Cl LE10 71 B1
Lundy View B36 70 B6
Lunn Ave CV8 147 E3
Lunn Poly Ho 3 CV32 156 F1
Lunns Croft WS13 9 C8
Lunt Gr B32 84 D5
Lunt Jct The WV14 41 A6
Lunt Pl WV14 41 A6
Lunt Rd WV14 40 F6
Lunt The* CV8 133 E3
Lupin Cl LE10 75 D5
Lupin Gr
Birmingham B9 67 F3
Walsall WS5 43 B4
Lupin Rd DY2 51 F1
Lupton Ave CV3 133 C7
Lupton Ct B60 137 A1
Lusbridge Cl B63 82 B4
Luscombe Rd CV2 114 E8
Luther Way CV5 111 F4
Lutley Ave B63 82 E4
Lutley Cl WV3 38 E7
Lutley Dr DY9 81 C3
Lutley Gr B32 84 B1
Lutley La B63 82 C2
Lutley Mill Rd B63 82 E4
Lutley Prim Sch B63 82 D1
Luton Rd B29 85 F3
Lutterworth Rd
Coventry CV2 114 C5
Hinckley LE10 76 C3
Nuneaton CV11 79 C8
Luttrell Rd B74 32 A1
Luxor La CV5 111 B8
Lyall Gdns B45 101 E1
Lyall Gr B27 88 A2
Lychgate Ave DY9 81 C1
Lychgate Cl LE10 76 A5
Lychgate La LE10 76 C5
Lydate Rd B62 83 F4
Lydbrook Covert 5 B38 123 E8
Lydbury Gr B33 69 A4
Lyd Cl WV11 26 B5
Lydd Croft B35 58 B4
Lyddington Dr B62 83 B7
Lyde Gn B63 82 B7
Lydford Cl CV2 114 C7
Lydford Gr B24 57 A1
Lydford Rd WS3 14 B3
Lydgate Ct
Bedworth CV12 78 A4
Nuneaton CV11 73 C3
Lydgate Rd
Coventry CV6 113 B5
Kingswinford DY6 60 F6
Lydget Gr B23 56 D7
Lydham Cl
Bilston WV14 40 B4
Birmingham B44 56 A6
Redditch B98 153 E5
Lydia Croft B74 31 E6
Lydian Cl WV6 25 B4
Lydiate Ash Rd B60 121 C3
Lydiate Ave B31 102 D1
Lydiates Cl DY3 50 B7
Lydney Cl
Redditch B98 154 D7
Willenhall WV12 27 D4
Lydney Gr B31 102 F3
Lydstep Gr CV31 162 C7
Lye Ave B32 84 A2
Lye Bsns Ctr DY9 81 F6
Lye By-Pass DY9 81 E6
Lye Close La B32 84 A2
Lyecroft Ave B37 70 D2
Lye Cross Rd B69 63 B7
Lye Sta DY9 81 E6
Lye Valley Ind Est DY9 81 F6
Lygon Cl B98 154 A5
Lygon Gr B32 84 E4
Lymedene Rd B42 55 B5
Lyme Green Rd B33 68 F4
Lymer Rd WV10 11 C1
Lymesy St CV3 133 D7
Lymington Cl CV6 113 D8
Lymington Ct B73 46 B1
Lymington Dr CV6 96 B6
Lymington Rd WV13 27 D2
Lymore Croft CV2 115 A8
Lymsey Croft DY8 60 C3
Lynbrook Cl
Dudley DY2 62 D5
Hollywood B47 125 A7
Lynbrook Rd CV5 132 D8
Lynchgate Ct CV4 132 C6
Lynchgate Ho CV4 132 C6
Lynchgate Rd CV4 132 C6
Lynch The
Nuneaton CV11 73 D2
Polesworth B78 22 F1
Lyncourt Gr B32 84 B6
Lyncroft Rd B11 87 F2
Lyndale Cl CV5 112 C3
Lyndale Dr WV11 26 E6
Lyndale Rd
Coventry CV5 112 C3
Dudley DY2 62 E6
Sedgley DY3 39 B2
Lyndale B77 35 F6
Lynden Cl B61 136 E3
Lynden Ho CV5 133 B8
Lyndenwood B97 153 A2
Lyndholm Rd DY10 117 A6
Lyndhurst Cl
Bedworth CV6 96 B6
Hinckley LE10 76 A7
Lyndhurst Croft CV5 111 C4
Lyndhurst Dr
Kidderminster DY10 116 E8
Stourbridge DY8 60 F1
Lyndhurst Rd
Birmingham B24 56 F2
Cannock WS12 2 E1
West Bromwich B71 53 E7
Wolverhampton WV3 39 A7
Lyndon Cl
Birmingham,Castle Bromwich B36 69 C8
Birmingham,Handsworth B20 55 C2
Halesowen B63 82 F4
Sedgley DY3 39 E1
Lyndon Croft B37 90 B7
Lyndon Ct CV32 161 E8
Lyndon Green Inf Sch B26 89 A6
Lyndon Green Jun Sch B26 89 A6
Lyndon Gr
Kingswinford DY6 60 B8
West Bromwich B71 53 D4
Lyndon Ho B31 103 B3
Lyndon Rd
Birmingham,Rubery B45 121 E7
Birmingham,Stechford B33 68 E3
Solihull B92 88 F2
Sutton Coldfield B73 46 B5
Lyndon Sch B92 89 A3
Lyndon B71 53 D5
Lyndworth Rd B30 104 C8
Lyneham Cl
Hinckley LE10 71 A1
Tamworth B79 21 C8
Lyneham Gdns B76 58 B6
Lyneham Way B35 57 F3
Lyne Ho 1 CV2 114 D8
Lynfield Cl B38 123 F7
Lyng Cl CV5 112 A4
Lyng Hall Sch CV2 114 C6
Lyng La B70 53 C2
Lyng Prim Sch B70 53 C1
Lynmouth Cl
Aldridge WS9 30 A5
Nuneaton CV11 73 E5
Lynmouth Rd CV2 114 E8
Lynn Gr B29 85 C3
Lynn La WS14 17 D6
Lynnon Field CV34 160 B4
Lynton Ave
Smethwick B66 65 A6
West Bromwich B71 53 C7
Wolverhampton WV6 24 F6
Lynton Cl CV34 155 E1
Lynton Ho B23 56 B6
Lynton Rd
Birmingham B6 67 B7
Coventry CV6 95 F1
Lynval Rd DY5 81 F7
Lynwood Ave DY6 60 B7
Lynwood Cl
Walsall WV12 13 E1
Willenhall WV12 27 E8
Lynwood Dr DY10 98 C2
Lynwood Way B45 122 A3
Lynwood Wlk
10 Royal Leamington Spa CV31 162 C6
Birmingham B17 85 D4
Lyon Ct B72 46 C5
Lyons Gr B11 87 C3
Lysander Cl LE10 75 E4
Lysander Rd B45 102 A2
Lysander Way
Birmingham B35 58 B2
Cannock WS11 1 E3
Lyster Cl CV34 160 B8
Lysway Ct 3 WS1 42 F8
Lysways St WS1 42 F8
Lythall Cl CV31 162 F5
Lythalls La CV6 95 E2
Lythalls Lane Ind Est CV6 95 E1
Lytham Cl
Stourbridge DY8 80 F2
Sutton Coldfield B76 58 B6
Lytham Croft B15 86 D8
Lytham Gr WS3 14 A4
Lytham Rd WV6 23 D4
Lytham B77 22 C5
Lythwood Dr DY5 81 C8
Lyttelton Pl DY9 99 C6
Lyttelton Rd
Birmingham,Edgbaston B16 65 D1
Birmingham,Stechford B33 68 D3
Stourbridge DY8 80 D5
Warwick CV34 160 E8
Lyttleton Ave
Bromsgrove B60 150 E7
Halesowen B62 83 E7
Lyttleton Cl
Coventry CV3 115 A1
Dudley DY2 62 C4
Lyttleton Ho B63 83 A2
Lyttleton St B70 53 C2
Lytton Ave WV4 38 E4
Lytton Gr B27 88 B1
Lytton La B32 84 F3

M

Maas Rd B31 103 A4
Mabey Ave B98 153 F5
MacAdam Cl WS7 7 B8
MacArthur Rd B64 82 C8
MacAulay Ho 5 B70 53 D1
MacAulay Rd CV2 114 D4
McBean Rd WV6 24 F4
Macbeth App CV34 161 D4
McCalla Ho WV3 25 B1
McConnell Cl B60 151 B7
MacDonald Cl B69 52 D2
MacDonald Rd CV2 114 D3
MacDonald St B5 86 E8
McDonnell Dr CV6,CV7 95 F6
McDougall Rd WS10 42 C3
Macefield Cl CV2 96 D2
Mace St B64 62 E1
McGeough Wlk WS11 2 B5
McGhie St WS12 2 B6
McGregor Cl 4 B6 55 F1
MacGregor Cres B77 21 F3
MacGregor Tithe B79 21 B5
Machin Rd B23 56 F4
Mackadown B33 69 D2
Mackay Rd WS3 14 D2
McKean Rd
Oldbury B69 64 A8
West Bromwich B70 53 C1
Mcken Ct B70 53 C1
Mackenzie Cl CV5 112 A7
Mackenzie Rd B11 87 C2
Mackmillan Rd B65 63 C2
McLean Rd WV10 11 C1
McMahon Rd CV12 95 E8
Macmillan Cl B69 52 C2
Macrome Rd WV6 24 E8
Madam's Hill Rd B90 126 D7
Maddocke Wlk 4 WS13 8 F6
Maddocks Hill B72 46 C2
Madehurst Rd B23 56 E6
Madeira Ave WV8 10 A2
Madeira Croft CV5 112 E2
Madeira Ct DY8 60 F1
Madeley Rd
Birmingham B11 87 C5
Kingswinford DY6 61 A4
Madeley Heath DY9 120 D6
Redditch B98 154 F5
Madinatul Uloom Al Islamiya Sch DY10 117 D1
Madin Rd DY4 51 E4
Madison Ave
Birmingham B36 68 D6
Brierley Hill DY5 61 F3
Walsall WS2 28 B2
Madley Cl B45 121 E8
Madox Cl B79 20 E8
Madresfield Dr B63 83 B2
Madrona B77 22 B4
Maer Cl B65 63 C3
Mafeking Rd B66 65 A7
Mafeking Villas B62 83 B7
Magdala St B18 65 E5
Magdalen Cl DY1 51 A2
Magdalen Ct B16 65 E1
Magdalene Rd WS1 43 A7
Magee Cl LE10 71 C2
Magna Cl WS6 4 E3
Magness Cres WV12 27 C5
Magnet Wlk B23 56 C3
Magnolia Cl
Birmingham B29 103 A7
Coventry CV3 133 B5
Magnolia Dr 1 WS5 42 F4
Magnolia Gr
Codsall WV8 10 B3
Willenhall WV12 27 B4
Magnolia B77 22 A4
Magnolia Way 1 DY8 60 F1
Magnum Cl B74 44 F7
Magnus B77 35 E6
Magpie Cl DY2 62 E3
Magpie Ho CV5 111 D5
Magpie La CV7 129 E6
Magpie Way DY10 117 B2
Maguire Ind Est CV4 131 F8
Magyar Cres CV11 79 A8
Maidavale Cres CV3 133 C4
Maiden Cl WV13 27 C2
Maidendale Rd DY6 60 B7
Maidensbridge Dr DY6 60 C8
Maidensbridge Gdns DY6 49 B1
Maidensbridge Prim Sch DY6 49 B1
Maidensbridge Rd DY6 49 B1
Maiden Way B60 151 A6
Maidstone Dr
Burntwood WS7 7 D6
Stourbridge DY8 60 E3
Maidstone Rd B20 55 E1
Maidwell Dr B90 126 E8
Mailbox The B1 164 B1
Main Rd
Ansty CV7 97 D3
Meriden CV7 110 D8
Tamworth B79 21 B8
Main St
Birmingham B11 87 A7
Brandon CV8 135 F4
Mainstone Cl B98 154 E3
Mainstream Forty Seven Ind Pk B7 67 C5
Mainstream Way B7 67 C5
Main St
Shenstone WS14 17 F6
Stonnall WS9 16 D4
Main Terr B11 87 A7
Mainwaring Dr B75 32 E2
Maisemore Cl B98 154 D6
Maitland Rd
Birmingham B8 67 F4
Dudley DY1 50 E1
Maitland B77 21 F2
Maizefield LE10 71 C4
Majestic Way B65 63 D4
Major Ct 6 B13 87 B2
Major St WV2 39 E7
Majuba Rd B16 65 C4
Makepeace Ave CV34 155 F1
Malam Cl CV4 112 A1
Malcolm Ave
Birmingham B24 57 C5
Bromsgrove B61 136 E3
Malcolm Ct WV1 25 A3
Malcolm Gr B45 122 A7
Malcolm Rd B90 106 B1
Malcolmson Cl B15 85 F8
Maldale B77 22 C1
Malfield Ave B97 152 F3
Malfield Dr B27 88 E3
Malham Cl CV11 74 A2
Malham Rd
Tamworth B77 36 C8
Warwick CV34 155 F1
Malhay Gdns 4 B42 55 A8
Malin Ct B23 56 B8
Malins Rd
Birmingham B17 85 D5
Wolverhampton WV4 39 E5
Malins The CV34 161 B6
Malkit Cl WS2 27 F4
Mallaby Cl B90 126 A8
Mallard Ave
Kidderminster DY10 117 B3
Nuneaton CV10 72 C6
Mallard Cl
Birmingham B27 88 C3
Brierley Hill DY5 81 C7
Redditch B98 153 F5
Walsall WS3 15 A5
Mallard Croft 5 WS13 9 C8
Mallard Dr
Birmingham B23 56 B3
Hinckley LE10 75 A7
Oldbury B69 63 F4
Mallard Rd B80 159 F4
Mallards Reach B92 106 E8
Mallender Dr B93 127 F6
Mallen Dr B69 52 B1
Mallerin Croft CV10 72 B5
Mallicot Cl WS13 3 D1
Mallin Gdns DY1 61 E8
Mallin St B66 64 D7
Mallory Cres WS3 14 D2
Mallory Dr
Kidderminster DY11 116 D8
Warwick CV34 160 D7
Mallory Rd WV6 23 E3
Mallory Rise B13 87 C1
Mallory Way CV6 95 E4
Mallow Cl 8 WS5 43 A3
Mallow Cres DY10 116 F4
Mallow Croft CV12 77 E2
Mallow Ct WV6 25 B5
Mallow Dr B61 136 F6
Mallow Rise 2 B23 56 B7
Mallows Cl WS10 41 D6
Malmesbury Pk B15 85 E7
Malmesbury Rd
Birmingham B10 87 E7
Coventry CV6 95 A3
Malpas Dr B32 102 C8
Malpass Rd DY5 81 F7
Malpas Wlk WV10 26 A4
Malt Cl B17 85 D6
Malthouse Croft B6 66 E8
Malthouse Dr DY1 51 A2
Malthouse Gdns B19 66 D7
Malthouse Gr B25 68 E1
Malthouse La
Birmingham B8 67 E6
Birmingham,Great Barr B42 55 D8
Earlswood B94 141 E7
Malthouse La *continued*
Kenilworth CV8 147 E6
Wolverhampton WV6 24 E6
Malthouse Mdw 2 B91 107 C1
Malthouse Rd DY4 51 E5
Malthouse Row B37 90 A8
Maltings Ct B17 65 A1
Maltings The
Aldridge WS9 30 C6
Nuneaton CV11 73 E5
Royal Leamington Spa CV32 156 F2
Studley B80 159 D4
Wolverhampton WV1 163 C4
Malt Mill La B62 83 D8
Malt Mill Lane Trad Est B62 83 D8
Malton Ave B65 63 D6
Malton Gr B13 105 B7
Malvern Ave
Nuneaton CV10 72 B3
Stourbridge DY9 81 C5
Malvern Cl
Birmingham B15 85 C8
West Bromwich B71 53 D5
Willenhall WV12 27 B4
Malvern Cres DY2 61 F6
Malvern Ct
8 Sutton Coldfield B74 31 F2
Birmingham,Stockfield B27 88 C4
Birmingham,Stockland Green B23 56 C2
Wolverhampton WV10 25 D8
Malvern Dr
Aldridge WS9 30 C8
Kidderminster DY10 116 E3
Sutton Coldfield B76 58 A8
Wolverhampton WV1 26 B1
Malvern Hill Rd B7 67 C7
Malvern Ho
7 Halesowen B63 83 A3
Coventry CV5 111 D4
Redditch B97 153 C1
Malvern Park Ave B91 107 D3
Malvern Rd
Balsall Common CV7 130 C6
Barnt Green B45 122 A2
Birmingham,Acock's Green B27 88 D4
Birmingham B68 84 B8
Birmingham,Handsworth B21 54 C1
Bromsgrove B61 150 D7
Coventry CV5 112 F4
Redditch B97 158 D8
Malvern St B12 87 A5
Malvern View
Bluntington DY10 118 E1
Kidderminster DY11 116 B1
Malvern View Rd DY3 50 D4
Mamble Rd DY8 80 E5
Mammoth Dr WV10 25 D6
Manby Cl WV6 25 A4
Manby Rd B35 58 A4
Manby St DY4 51 F8
Mancetter Rd
Nuneaton CV10 72 D7
Solihull B90 106 C3
Manchester St
Birmingham B6 164 C5
Oldbury B69 64 B7
Mancroft Cl DY6 60 B7
Mancroft Gdns WV6 24 C5
Mancroft Rd WV6 24 C5
Mandale Rd WV10 25 F6
Mandarin Ave DY10 117 B3
Mandarin Cl LE10 75 A6
Mander Ctr WV1 163 B3
Mander Gallery WV1 163 B3
Mander Gr CV34 160 C4
Manderley Cl
Coventry CV5 111 C5
Sedgley DY3 39 C2
Manders Ind Est WV1 26 A3
Mander Sq WV1 163 B3
Manderston Cl DY1 50 E3
Mander St WV3 163 A1
Manderville Gdns DY6 60 C6
Mandeville Gdns WS1 42 F8
Mandeville Way B61 136 F5
Mandrake Cl CV6 95 D4
Maney Cnr B72 46 B4
Maney Hill Prim Sch B72 46 D2
Maney Hill Rd B72 46 C2
Manfield Ave CV2 115 A7
Manfield Rd WV13 26 C3
Manifold Cl WS7 7 D6
Manifoldia Grange B70 53 B2
Manifold Way WS10 42 E3
Manilla Rd B29 86 B1
Manitoba Croft 2 B38 123 F8
Manley Cl B70 53 A3
Manley Rd WS13 3 D1
Manlove St WV3 39 A8
Manningford Ct B14 104 F3
Manningford Rd B14 104 E3
Manor Abbey Rd B62 83 E4
Manor Ave
Cannock WS11 1 D1
Great Wyrley WS6 5 A4
Kidderminster DY11 116 A7
Manor Ave S DY11 116 A6
Manor Cl
Birmingham B16 65 D1
Codsall WV8 10 B4
Hinckley LE10 75 C5
Kidderminster DY11 116 A6
Willenhall WV13 26 F3

Manor Cl *continued*
Wolverhampton WV4 . . . 38 F4
Manor Cotts WS14 . . . 8 E2
Manor Court Ave CV11 . . . 73 B5
Manor Court Mews CV11 . 73 A5
Manor Court Rd
Bromsgrove B60 . . . 150 F8
Nuneaton CV11 . . . 73 A5
Manor Ct
5 Birmingham,Hurst Green B62 . . . 84 A7
Birmingham,King's Norton B30 . . . 104 A2
Dorridge B93 . . . 127 F2
Dudley DY2 . . . 62 C5
Kenilworth CV8 . . . 148 A6
Mile Oak B78 . . . 20 D1
Royal Leamington Spa CV31 . . . 161 F7
Walsall WS2 . . . 28 C1
Manor Dr
Dudley DY3 . . . 50 B3
Sutton Coldfield B73 . . . 46 B4
Manor Est CV8 . . . 135 F3
Manor Farm Craft Ctr* B94 . . . 125 F2
Manor Farm Dr WV12 . . . 27 D5
Manor Farm Rd B11 . . . 87 E4
Manor Flats DY3 . . . 50 D8
Manorford Ave B71 . . . 43 A1
Manor Gdns
Birmingham B33 . . . 68 D2
Wednesbury WS10 . . . 41 F4
Wombourne WV5 . . . 49 B7
Manor Hall Mews CV3 . . . 134 D6
Manor High Sch WS10 . . . 42 D3
Manor Hill B73 . . . 46 B4
Manor Hospl WS2 . . . 28 C1
Manor Ho The CV31 . . . 161 F7
Manor House Cl
Aston Flamville LE10 . . . 76 E6
Birmingham B29 . . . 84 F1
Manor House Dr
Birmingham B29 . . . 103 B7
Coventry CV1 . . . 165 B2
Manor House La
Astwood Bank B96 . . . 158 E3
Birmingham B26 . . . 88 F6
Water Orton B46 . . . 59 B3
Manor House Pk WV8 . . . 10 B4
Manor House Rd WS10 . . . 41 F4
Manor Ho WV6 . . . 24 D5
Manorial Rd B75 . . . 32 E3
Manor Ind Est WS2 . . . 28 C1
Manor Jun & Inf Sch WV14 . . . 40 B2
Manor La
Halesowen B62 . . . 83 E4
Honiley CV8,CV35 . . . 146 A5
Lower Marlbrook B61 . . . 121 C4
Stourbridge DY8 . . . 80 D3
Wroxall CV35 . . . 145 F4
Manor Mews B80 . . . 159 E4
Manor Park Cl B13 . . . 87 A2
Manor Park Com Sch CV11 . . . 73 A5
Manor Park Gr B31 . . . 102 C1
Manor Park Prim Sch
Birmingham B6 . . . 67 A8
Coventry CV3 . . . 133 D7
Manor Park Rd
Birmingham B36 . . . 69 D8
Nuneaton CV11 . . . 73 A5
Manor Pk DY6 . . . 60 D6
Manor Pl LE10 . . . 71 D1
Manor Prim Sch
Drayton Bassett B78 . . . 34 E5
Sutton Coldfield B74 . . . 31 A1
Manor Rd
Birmingham,Birchfield B6 . . 55 F1
Birmingham,Edgbaston B16 65 D1
Birmingham,Stechford B33 . 68 E3
Coventry CV1 . . . 165 B1
Dorridge B93 . . . 127 F3
Ettingshall WV4 . . . 40 A5
Kenilworth CV8 . . . 147 F6
Mile Oak B78 . . . 20 D1
Manor Rd N B16 . . . 65 D1
Manor Rd
Royal Leamington Spa CV32 . . . 157 B3
Smethwick B67 . . . 64 E4
Solihull B91 . . . 107 C5
Stourbridge DY8 . . . 60 E2
Studley B80 . . . 159 E4
Sutton Coldfield B74 . . . 31 A1
Sutton Coldfield,Maney B73 46 B4
Sutton Coldfield,Streetly B74 . . . 45 A8
Tamworth B77 . . . 21 D4
Tipton DY4 . . . 51 F4
Upper Bentley B97 . . . 152 B1
Walsall WS2 . . . 28 C2
Wednesbury WS10 . . . 42 D2
Wolverhampton,Oxley WV10 . . . 25 C7
Wolverhampton WV4 . . . 38 F4
Wythall B47 . . . 125 A3
Manor Rise
Burntwood WS7 . . . 7 A5
Lichfield WS14 . . . 9 C7
Manor Road Prec 2 WS2 28 C2
Manor Side Ind Est B98 . 154 E6
Manor Sq B91 . . . 107 C3
Manor St
Hinckley LE10 . . . 71 C1
Wolverhampton WV6 . . . 24 D5
Manor Terr CV8 . . . 148 A6
Manor View CV8 . . . 135 F3
Manor Way
Halesowen B62,B63 . . . 83 D3
Hinckley LE10 . . . 75 D5
Manor Way Prim Sch B63 83 C3
Manor Wlk
4 Solihull B91 . . . 107 C3
Sutton Coldfield B73 . . . 46 B4
Mansard Cl
Wolverhampton,Bradmore WV3 . . . 38 F8
Wolverhampton,Scotlands WV10 . . . 26 B8
Mansard Ho B90 . . . 106 A3
Manse Cl CV7 . . . 78 A1
Manse Gdns B80 . . . 159 E3
Mansell Cl B63 . . . 82 B7
Mansell Rd
Redditch B97 . . . 158 D7
Tipton DY4 . . . 52 A8
Mansel Rd B10 . . . 87 E8
Mansel St CV6 . . . 113 E8
Mansfield Cl B79 . . . 20 E6
Mansfield Green Com Sch B6 . . . 66 E8
Mansfield Ho B37 . . . 70 D3
Mansfield Rd
Birmingham,Aston B6 . . . 66 E8
Birmingham,South Yardley B25 . . . 88 C5
Mansion Cl DY1 . . . 51 A3
Mansion Cres B67 . . . 64 E4
Mansion Ct B62 . . . 83 E7
Mansion Dr
Hammerwich WS7 . . . 7 D4
Tipton DY4 . . . 52 C5
Mansion St 1 LE10 . . . 75 D8
Manson Ct WV4 . . . 38 D5
Manson Dr B64 . . . 63 A1
Manston Dr WV6 . . . 23 E5
Manston Rd B26 . . . 89 B7
Manston View B79 . . . 21 C8
Manta Rd B77 . . . 35 D6
Mantilla Dr CV3 . . . 133 A5
Manton Croft B93 . . . 127 E3
Manton Ho B19 . . . 66 E7
Manway Cl B20 . . . 54 F4
Manwoods Cl B20 . . . 55 B2
Maple Ave
Bedworth CV7 . . . 78 B1
Wednesbury WS10 . . . 42 C4
Mapleback Ct B91 . . . 107 C5
Maple Bank B15 . . . 86 A7
Maplebeck Cl CV5 . . . 113 A3
Maple Bsns Pk B7 . . . 67 B6
Maple Cl
Birmingham B21 . . . 54 E1
Burntwood WS7 . . . 6 F7
Dudley WV14 . . . 51 A7
Hinckley LE10 . . . 75 E5
Kidderminster DY11 . . . 116 B8
Stourbridge DY8 . . . 80 D2
Maple Cres WS11 . . . 1 C1
Maple Croft B13 . . . 104 F5
Maple Ct
1 Birmingham,Harborne B17 . . . 85 B6
2 Birmingham,Erdington B24 . . . 56 F3
Bilston WV14 . . . 40 F2
Lichfield WS14 . . . 9 C5
Oldbury B66 . . . 64 D8
Maple Ctr The WS10 . . . 41 B3
Mapledene B13 . . . 87 B2
Mapledene Inf Sch B26 . . 89 D6
Mapledene Jun Sch B26 . 89 D6
Mapledene Rd B26 . . . 89 D6
Maple Dr
Birmingham B44 . . . 56 C8
Dudley DY3 . . . 50 B2
Huntington WS12 . . . 1 D8
Walsall,Shelfield WS4 . . . 29 B8
Walsall,Yew Tree WS5 . . . 43 B4
Maple Gn DY1 . . . 51 A5
Maple Gr
Bilston WV14 . . . 40 F4
Birmingham,Aston B19 . . . 66 D8
Birmingham,Kingshurst B37 69 F6
Kingswinford DY6 . . . 60 E6
Lichfield WS14 . . . 9 F7
Warwick CV34 . . . 156 A1
Wolverhampton WV3 . . . 24 C2
Maple Hayes Hall Sch WS13 . . . 8 D8
Maple Ho
Redditch,Greenlands B98 . . . 158 F8
Redditch,Webheath B97 . . 153 B2
Sutton Coldfield B74 . . . 31 B5
Walsall WS4 . . . 15 D1
Maple Leaf Dr B37 . . . 90 B8
Maple Leaf Ind Est WS2 . . 28 A3
Maple Leaf Rd WS10 . . . 41 C1
Maple Rd
Birmingham B45 . . . 121 F6
Birmingham,Selly Oak B30 103 E8
Dudley DY1 . . . 51 C3
Halesowen B62 . . . 83 D8
Nuneaton CV10 . . . 72 E5
Royal Leamington Spa CV31 . . . 161 F6
Sutton Coldfield B72 . . . 46 C3
Walsall WS3 . . . 14 F2
Wolverhampton WV3 . . . 38 E8
Maple Rise
Oldbury B68 . . . 64 C2
Tamworth B77 . . . 22 A4
Maple Row 1 DY5 . . . 61 D2
Maples The
Bedworth CV12 . . . 77 E2
Wolverhampton WV11 . . . 26 B5
Maple St WS3 . . . 14 D2
Mapleton Gr B28 . . . 106 B7
Mapleton Rd
Birmingham B28 . . . 106 B7
Coventry CV6 . . . 112 F8
Maple Tree La B63 . . . 82 C6
Maple Way B31 . . . 102 F1
Maple Wlk
4 Birmingham B37 . . . 70 B2
Coventry CV6 . . . 95 F5
Maplewood B76 . . . 58 A8
Mapperley Cl CV2 . . . 115 A8
Mapperley Gdns B13 . . . 86 C3
Mappleborough Cl B97 . . 153 B5
Mappleborough Rd B90 . 105 E1
Mapps Cl B63 . . . 82 C6
Marans Croft B38 . . . 123 D7
Marble Alley B80 . . . 159 E4
Marbury Cl B38 . . . 103 D2
Marbury Dr WV14 . . . 41 A6
Marbury Mews DY5 . . . 61 D1
Marchant Rd
Bilston WV14 . . . 40 D7
Hinckley LE10 . . . 75 C8
Wolverhampton WV6 . . . 24 F2
March Cl WS6 . . . 4 D1
March End Rd WV11 . . . 26 D5
Marchfont Cl CV11 . . . 74 A1
Marchmont Rd B9 . . . 68 A2
Marchmount Rd B72 . . . 57 C8
March Way
Aldridge WS9 . . . 16 C1
Coventry CV3 . . . 134 D7
Marchwood Cl B97 . . . 153 A5
Marcliff Cres B90 . . . 105 C2
Marconi Pl WS12 . . . 2 C7
Marcos Dr B36 . . . 58 F1
Marcot Rd B92 . . . 88 F5
Marcroft Pl CV31 . . . 162 D6
Marden Cl WV13 . . . 26 F1
Marden Gr B31 . . . 123 A7
Marden Wlk B23 . . . 56 C3
Mardol Cl CV2 . . . 114 D7
Mardon Rd B26 . . . 89 C5
Maree Gr WV11 . . . 13 B1
Maret Ct 2 WS1 . . . 42 F8
Marfield Cl B76 . . . 58 A6
Margam Cres WS3 . . . 13 F2
Margam Terr WS3 . . . 13 F2
Margam Way WS3 . . . 13 F2
Margaret Ave
Bedworth CV12 . . . 78 B3
Halesowen B63 . . . 82 F4
Margaret Cl DY5 . . . 81 E8
Margaret Dr
Cannock WS11 . . . 1 E6
Stourbridge DY8 . . . 81 B4
Margaret Gdns B67 . . . 64 E5
Margaret Gr B17 . . . 85 C7
Margaret Ho B76 . . . 46 F3
Margaret Rd
Birmingham,Harborne B17 . . . 85 C5
Birmingham,New Oscott B73 . . . 45 D1
Darlaston WS10 . . . 41 C4
Walsall WS2 . . . 27 E3
Margaret St
Birmingham B3 . . . 164 B3
West Bromwich B70 . . . 53 B2
Margaret Vale DY4 . . . 41 C1
Margaret Vine Ct B62 . . . 63 F1
Margeson Cl CV2 . . . 114 E2
Margesson Dr B45 . . . 122 D1
Margetts Cl CV8 . . . 147 F4
Margreal Ind Est B16 . . . 65 F3
Marholm Cl WV9 . . . 10 F2
Marian Croft B26 . . . 89 D5
Maria St B70 . . . 64 E8
Marie Brock Cl CV4 . . . 112 B1
Marie Dr B27 . . . 106 B8
Marigold Cl WS11 . . . 2 C3
Marigold Cres DY1 . . . 51 A4
Marigold Dr LE10 . . . 75 E5
Marigold Wlk CV10 . . . 78 A8
Marina Cl CV4 . . . 131 E7
Marina Cres WS12 . . . 2 A5
Marine Cres DY8 . . . 60 E1
Marine Dr B44 . . . 55 E6
Marine Gdns DY8 . . . 60 E1
Mariner Ave B16 . . . 65 E1
Mariner B79 . . . 20 E6
Marion Cl DY5 . . . 61 F2
Marion Rd
Coventry CV6 . . . 113 D7
Smethwick B67 . . . 64 E5
Marion Way B28 . . . 105 E7
Marita Cl DY2 . . . 62 E3
Marjoram Cl B38 . . . 123 F8
Marjorie Ave B30 . . . 104 B3
Mark Antony Dr CV34 . . . 161 D4
Mark Ave WS10 . . . 41 E3
Markby Rd B18 . . . 65 E6
Mark Cl B98 . . . 153 E2
Mark Ct WS1 . . . 29 A3
Market Cnr
7 Royal Leamington Spa CV31 . . . 161 F6
Baginton CV8 . . . 133 F2
Market End Cl CV12 . . . 77 C2
Market Hall St WS11 . . . 1 E1
Market La
Lichfield WS14 . . . 8 E2
Lower Penn WV4 . . . 37 F5
Market Pl
4 Cannock WS11 . . . 1 E1
Bromsgrove B61 . . . 136 F2
Dudley DY1 . . . 51 D1
Hinckley LE10 . . . 75 D8
Nuneaton CV11 . . . 73 C4
Redditch B98 . . . 153 E4
Rowley Regis B65 . . . 63 C1
Tamworth B79 . . . 21 B4
Tipton DY4 . . . 52 D5
Walsall WS3 . . . 14 B1
Warwick CV34 . . . 160 E6
Wednesbury WS10 . . . 41 F2
Willenhall WV13 . . . 27 A1
Market Sq
Cradley Heath B64 . . . 82 C8
Wolverhampton WV3 . . . 163 B2
Market St
Bromsgrove B61 . . . 136 F2
Cannock WS12 . . . 2 C5
Kidderminster DY10 . . . 116 E5
Kingswinford DY6 . . . 60 D6
Lichfield WS13 . . . 9 B8
Oldbury B69 . . . 64 A8
Stourbridge DY8 . . . 81 A5
Tamworth B79 . . . 21 B4
Warwick CV34 . . . 160 D6
Wolverhampton WV1 . . . 163 C3
Market Way
Bilston WV14 . . . 40 D5
Coventry CV1 . . . 165 B2
Hagley DY9 . . . 99 C6
Market Wlk 4 B97 . . . 153 E4
Markfield Rd B26 . . . 89 B8
Markford Wlk B19 . . . 66 D6
Markham Cres B92 . . . 89 F1
Markham Croft WV9 . . . 11 A2
Markham Dr
Kingswinford DY6 . . . 60 E4
Whitnash CV31 . . . 162 B3
Markham Rd B73 . . . 45 C3
Mark Ho B13 . . . 87 A2
Marklew Cl WS8 . . . 16 A5
Marklin Ave WV10 . . . 11 D1
Mark Rd WS10 . . . 41 E3
Marksbury Cl WV6 . . . 25 A5
Marks Mews 7 CV34 . . . 160 E6
Marks Wlk WS13 . . . 3 A2
Marlbank Rd DY8 . . . 61 A1
Marlborough Ave B60 . . . 151 A8
Marlborough Cl
Hinckley LE10 . . . 76 B7
Sutton Coldfield B74 . . . 31 E6
Marlborough Ct
3 Sutton Coldfield B74 . . . 31 F2
Bromsgrove B60 . . . 151 B8
Lichfield WS13 . . . 9 B7
Sutton Coldfield,Falcon Lodge B75 . . . 47 A6
Marlborough Dr
Royal Leamington Spa CV31 . . . 162 D5
Stourbridge DY8 . . . 81 A3
Marlborough Gdns
Stourbridge DY8 . . . 60 D2
Wolverhampton WV6 . . . 24 E4
Marlborough Gr B25 . . . 68 D1
Marlborough Ind Est WV2 . . . 39 D7
Marlborough Inf Sch B10 67 E1
Marlborough Jun Sch B10 . . . 67 E1
Marlborough Mews B80 . 159 E4
Marlborough Rd
Birmingham,Castle Bromwich B36 . . . 69 D8
Birmingham,Small Heath B10 . . . 67 E1
Coventry CV2 . . . 114 A3
Dudley DY3 . . . 50 F6
Nuneaton CV11 . . . 73 B3
Smethwick B66 . . . 65 A3
Marlborough St
2 Kidderminster DY10 . . . 116 E5
Walsall WS3 . . . 14 B1
Marlborough Way B77 . . . 21 F2
Marlbrook Cl B92 . . . 89 C4
Marlbrook Dr WV4 . . . 39 B6
Marlbrook Gdns B61 . . . 121 B1
Marlbrook La B60 . . . 121 D2
Marlcliff Gr B13 . . . 105 A6
Marlcroft CV3 . . . 134 E5
Marldon Rd B14 . . . 104 E6
Marlene Croft B37 . . . 70 C1
Marler Rd CV4 . . . 131 F7
Marley Hts B27 . . . 88 D4
Marley Rd DY6 . . . 61 A4
Marlfield Farm Fst Sch B98 . . . 154 C6
Marlfield La
Redditch,Abbeydale B98 . . 154 B4
Redditch,Church Hill B98 . . 154 B5
Marlgrove Ct B61 . . . 137 B8
Marling Croft B92 . . . 107 F7
Marlin B77 . . . 35 D6
Marlissa Dr CV6 . . . 95 E2
Marloes Wlk CV31 . . . 162 C6
Marlow Cl
Coventry CV5 . . . 112 B4
Dudley DY2 . . . 62 E3
Marlowe Cl DY10 . . . 117 B6
Marlowe Dr WV12 . . . 27 A7
Marlow Rd
Birmingham B23 . . . 56 D5
Tamworth B77 . . . 21 D5
Marlow St
Rowley Regis B65 . . . 63 B1
Walsall WS2 . . . 28 E3
Marlpit La
Redditch B97 . . . 153 C1
Sutton Coldfield B75 . . . 32 D3
Marlpit Rise 1 B75 . . . 32 E3
Marlpool Ct DY11 . . . 116 C8
Marlpool Dr
Redditch B97 . . . 153 C3
Walsall WS3 . . . 15 A1
Marlpool Fst Sch DY11 . . 116 C8
Marlpool La DY11 . . . 116 C8
Marlpool Pl DY11 . . . 116 C8
Marl Rd DY2 . . . 62 B4
Marlston Wlk CV5 . . . 112 B4
Marl Top B38 . . . 103 F2
Marlwood Cl CV6 . . . 95 F4
Marmion Dr B43 . . . 43 F2
Marmion Gr DY1 . . . 62 A8
Marmion Ho B70 . . . 52 F6
Marmion Pk B79 . . . 21 B6
Marmion St B79 . . . 21 B5
Marmion Way B70 . . . 52 F6
Marne Cl CV34 . . . 161 A8
Marnel Dr WV3 . . . 38 E7
Marner Cres CV6 . . . 113 B5
Marner Rd
Bedworth CV12 . . . 78 A3
Nuneaton CV10 . . . 73 B1
Marnhull Cl CV2 . . . 114 F4
Marquis Dr B62 . . . 83 A7
Marrick B77 . . . 22 C1
Marriners La CV5 . . . 112 B5
Marriott Rd
Bedworth CV12 . . . 77 D2
Coventry CV6 . . . 113 A4
Dudley DY2 . . . 62 C4
Smethwick B66 . . . 64 D7
Marroway St B16 . . . 65 F3
Marrowfat La B21 . . . 65 F7
Mars Cl WV14 . . . 40 A1
Marsdale Dr CV10 . . . 72 E3
Marsden Cl B92 . . . 88 E1
Marsden Rd B98 . . . 153 E3
Marsett B77 . . . 36 C8
Marshall Cl WS9 . . . 30 B4
Marshall Gr B44 . . . 55 F7
Marshall Ho 4 WS2 . . . 42 C8
Marshall Lake Rd B90 . . . 106 D1
Marshall Rd
Bedworth CV7 . . . 95 F8
Oldbury B68 . . . 64 C1
Willenhall WV13 . . . 26 D1
Marshalls Ind Est WV2 . . . 39 C7
Marshall St
Birmingham B1 . . . 164 B1
Smethwick B67 . . . 64 D7
Tamworth B77 . . . 21 E5
Marsham Cl CV34 . . . 161 B8
Marsham Court Rd B91 . 106 F7
Marsham Rd B14 . . . 104 F3
Marshbrook Cl
Coventry CV2 . . . 96 E3
Sutton Coldfield B24 . . . 57 E4
Marshbrook Rd B24 . . . 57 D4
Marsh Cl B23 . . . 56 F5
Marsh Cres DY8 . . . 60 D3
Marshdale Ave CV6 . . . 95 E3
Marsh End B38 . . . 124 A8
Marshfield Cl B98 . . . 154 B7
Marshfield Dr CV4 . . . 132 D2
Marshfield Gdns B24 . . . 56 F2
Marshfield B90 . . . 126 B5
Marsh Gr DY10 . . . 116 E8
Marsh Hill B23 . . . 56 C4
Marsh Hill Jun & Inf Sch B23 . . . 56 C4
Marsh Ho CV2 . . . 115 A7
Marsh House Farm La B92 . . . 109 D3
Marsh La
Birmingham B23 . . . 56 E5
Bradnock's Marsh B92 . . 109 D5
Curdworth B76 . . . 59 D5
Hampton-in-A B92 . . . 109 B6
Lichfield WS14 . . . 9 C5
Marshland Way WS2 . . . 27 E1
Marsh Lane Par WV10 . . . 11 C2
Marsh La
Solihull B91 . . . 107 E3
Walsall WS2 . . . 28 E2
Water Orton B46 . . . 59 C3
West Bromwich B71 . . . 53 D8
Wolverhampton WV10 . . . 11 B2
Marshmont Way B23 . . . 56 D8
Marsh St WS2 . . . 28 E2
Marsh The WS10 . . . 41 E3
Marsh Way B61 . . . 120 F1
Marshwood Cl 2 WS11 . . . 2 A2
Marshwood Croft B62 . . . 84 A3
Marsland Cl B17 . . . 65 C1
Marsland Rd B92 . . . 106 E8
Marston Ave WS10 . . . 41 C6
Marston Cl
Royal Leamington Spa CV32 . . . 157 B2
Stourbridge DY8 . . . 80 D4
Marston Croft B37 . . . 89 F7
Marston Dr B37 . . . 70 A5
Marston Gr B43 . . . 54 C8
Marston Green Inf Sch B37 . . . 90 A7
Marston Green Jun Sch B37 . . . 90 A7
Marston Green Sta B37 . . . 89 F7
Marston Ind Est WV2 . . . 39 C7

Marston La
Bedworth CV12 78 D5
Nuneaton CV11 78 E8
Wishaw B76 48 E1
Marston Pk B78 20 F4
Marston Rd
Birmingham B29 102 F8
Cannock WS12 1 F6
Dudley DY1 61 E8
Sutton Coldfield B73 57 A7
Wolverhampton WV2 39 C7
Marston St WV13 27 C2
Marten Cl CV35 160 A7
Martham Dr WV6 24 B2
Martin Cl
Birmingham B26 88 D6
Bromsgrove B61 136 E1
Coventry CV5 111 E4
Dudley WV14 51 D7
Martin Croft WS13 3 A1
Martindale WS11 2 A2
Martindale Rd CV7 96 C8
Martindale Trad Est WS11 2 A2
Martindale Wlk DY5 81 B6
Martin Dr WV12 27 C5
Martineau Pl B2 164 C2
Martineau Twr B19 66 D5
Martingale Cl
4 Bromsgrove B60 150 E6
Walsall WS5 42 F4
Martin Hill St DY2 62 C8
Martinique Sq CV34 160 D6
Martin Rd
Bilston WV14 40 F3
Tipton DY4 52 A4
Walsall WS5 43 C8
Martin Rise B37 89 F8
Martins Rd CV12 77 E1
Martin St WV4 39 F5
Martlesham Sq B35 58 A4
Martley Cl B98 159 B7
Martley Croft
Birmingham B32 84 E4
Solihull B91 127 B8
Martley Dr DY9 81 C4
Martley Rd
Oldbury B69 63 D5
Walsall WS4 15 C2
Marton Ave WS7 7 A8
Marton Cl B7 67 B6
Martyrs' Cl The CV3 133 D8
Marwood Cl CV11 78 E7
Marwood Croft B74 31 A2
Mary Ann St
Birmingham B3 164 B4
Wolverhampton WV1 163 D2
Mary Elliot Specl Sch
WS2 28 E4
Mary Herbert St CV3 133 D7
Maryland Ave B34 68 F5
Maryland Cl LE9 71 F6
Maryland Dr B31 103 B5
Maryland Rd DY5 81 F7
Marylebone Cl DY8 81 A7
Mary Macarthur Dr B64 62 C1
Mary Rd
Birmingham,Handsworth
B21 65 E7
Birmingham,Stechford B33 68 D3
Oldbury B69 63 C8
West Bromwich B70 53 D1
Mary Rose Cl WS6 4 D1
Mary Slessor St CV3 134 D7
Mary St
Birmingham,Balsall Heath
B12 86 E5
Birmingham,Brookfields
B3 164 A4
Cannock WS12 2 B7
Marystow Cl CV5 112 B8
Mary St WS2 28 D3
Maryvale Ct
2 Walsall WS1 42 E8
Lichfield WS14 9 D7
Maryvale RC Prim Sch
B44 44 E1
Mary Vale Rd B30 103 F6
Marywell Cl B32 102 B7
Masefield Ave
Dudley DY1 51 C7
Warwick CV34 160 C4
Masefield Cl
Bilston WV14 40 F2
Lichfield WS14 9 B6
Masefield Dr B79 21 A7
Masefield Gdns 1 DY10 117 B6
Masefield Gr WS11 1 E4
Masefield Mews WV10 12 A1
Masefield Rd
Dudley DY3 50 A4
Walsall WS3 28 E7
Wolverhampton WV10 12 A1
Masefield Rise B62 83 D3
Masefield Sq B31 103 C4
Masham Cl B33 68 E3
Mashie Gdns B38 103 D1
Maslen Pl B63 83 B3
Maslin Dr WV14 40 A1
Mason Ave CV32 157 C3
Mason Cl B97 158 D7
Mason Cotts B24 57 B5
Mason Cres WV4 38 E5
Mason Ct LE10 75 B8
Mason Gr CV8 148 B5
Mason La B94 125 F1
Masonleys Rd B31 102 D3
Mason Rd
Birmingham B24 57 A4
Coventry CV6 95 F1
Kidderminster DY11 116 C6
Redditch B97 158 D8
Walsall WS2 28 B5
Masons Cl B63 82 C6
Mason St
Dudley WV14 51 B7
West Bromwich B70 53 B4
Wolverhampton WV2 39 C7
Masons View B24 57 A2
Mason's Way B92 88 E2
Masons Yd DY11 116 D6
Massbrook Gr WV10 25 F6
Massbrook Rd WV10 25 F6
Masser Rd CV6 95 D4
Masshouse La
Birmingham,Digbeth B5 164 D3
Birmingham,King's Norton
B38 103 F1
Masters La B62 63 E1
Masters Rd CV31 162 A4
Matchborough Ctr B98 154 E1
Matchborough Fst Sch
B98 154 E1
Matchborough Way B98 154 E1
Matchlock Cl B74 44 E7
Matfen Ave B73 45 F2
Mathe Croft CV31 162 C5
Math Mdw B32 84 F5
Matlock Cl
Dudley DY2 62 D3
Walsall WS3 14 C3
Matlock Dr WS11 2 A4
Matlock Rd
Birmingham B11 87 F3
Coventry CV1 113 D6
Walsall WS3 14 C3
Matlock Villas 2 B12 87 B5
Matterson Rd CV6 113 A5
Matthew Boulton Coll
Birmingham B5 164 D3
Birmingham,Lee Bank B15 86 D8
Matthew Boulton Com Prim
Sch B21 65 E7
Matthew La (Road 3)
DY10 116 F1
Matthews Cl B65 63 B1
Matthews Wlk WS13 3 A2
Mattox Rd WV11 26 D6
Matty Rd B68 64 C4
Maud Rd
Water Orton B46 59 D3
West Bromwich B70 53 C1
Maudslay Rd CV5 112 E2
Maughan St
Brierley Hill DY5 82 A8
Dudley DY1 51 B1
Maund Cl B60 150 E7
Maureen Cl CV4 111 C1
Maurice Gr WV10 26 A6
Maurice Mead Ct 12
CV31 162 A6
Maurice Rd
Birmingham B14 104 E5
Smethwick B67 64 E2
Mavis Gdns B68 84 B8
Mavis Rd
Birmingham B31 102 E1
Cannock WS12 2 B7
Mavor Dr CV12 77 D1
Mawgan Dr WS14 9 D6
Mawnan Cl CV7 96 B8
Maw St WS1 42 F6
Maxholm Rd B74 44 E8
Max Rd
Birmingham B32 84 D5
Coventry CV6 112 F5
Maxstoke Cl
Birmingham B32 102 A7
Meriden CV7 92 B1
Redditch B98 154 D1
Sutton Coldfield B73 45 E2
Tamworth B77 35 C4
Walsall WS3 14 A3
Maxstoke Croft B90 126 C8
Maxstoke Gdns CV31 161 F6
Maxstoke La
Meriden CV7 92 B2
White Stitch CV7 92 B3
Maxstoke Rd B73 45 E1
Maxstoke St B9 67 B2
Maxted Rd B23 56 C7
Maxtock Ave WS13 9 A6
Maxwell Ave B20 55 B1
Maxwell Cl WS14 9 C7
Maxwell Ct B33 68 F3
Maxwell Rd WV2 163 C1
Mayall Dr B75 32 D4
Mayama Rd B78 34 F8
May Ave 3 B12 87 A5
Maybank B9 67 F3
Maybank Cl WS14 9 E8
Maybank Pl B44 55 E6
Maybank Rd DY2 62 C3
Mayberry Cl B14 105 B2
Maybridge Dr B91 127 B8
Maybrook Ind Est WS8 15 F5
Maybrook Rd
Brownhills WS8 15 F5
Sutton Coldfield B76 58 A5
Maybush Gdns WV10 11 C1
Maycock Rd CV6 113 D7
Maycroft Cl WS12 1 F7
Maydene Croft B12 86 F6
Mayfair B37 69 F5
Mayfair Cl
Birmingham B44 56 B7
Dudley DY1 51 A2
Mayfair Dr
Fazeley B78 35 A7
Kingswinford DY6 60 C7
Mayfair Gdns
Tipton DY4 52 A4
Wolverhampton WV3 24 D2
Mayfair DY9 81 D2
May Farm Cl B47 125 A6
Mayfield Ave B29 86 B2
Mayfield Cl
9 Royal Leamington Spa
CV31 162 C6
Bedworth CV12 78 B3
Fairfield B61 120 F1
Kidderminster DY11 116 A8
Solihull B91 107 C1
Mayfield Cres B65 63 A3
Mayfield Ct
Birmingham B13 87 A2
Kidderminster DY11 116 C7
Mayfield Dr CV8 148 C4
Mayfield Prep Sch WS1 43 A8
Mayfield Rd
Birmingham,Acock's Green
B11 88 A3
Birmingham,Lozells B19 66 C8
Birmingham,Moseley B13 87 A3
Birmingham,Stirchley B30 104 A6
Coventry CV5 113 A1
Dudley DY1 51 C4
Halesowen B62 63 F1
Halesowen,Hasbury B63 82 E2
Nuneaton CV11 73 E2
Sutton Coldfield,Boldmere
B73 46 A2
Sutton Coldfield,Streetly
B74 44 F8
Wolverhampton WV1 26 B1
Mayfield Sch B19 66 C8
Mayfields Dr WS8 6 B2
Mayfields B98 153 E2
Mayfield B77 36 C8
Mayfield The WV1 26 B1
Mayflower Cl B19 66 D6
Mayflower Dr
Brierley Hill DY5 61 A7
Coventry CV2 114 E2
Mayford Gr B13 105 B6
Maygrove Rd DY6 60 C7
Mayhurst Cl
Hollywood B47 125 C6
Tipton DY4 52 A8
Mayhurst Rd B47 125 B6
May La
Birmingham B14 104 F5
Hollywood B47 125 A7
Mayland Dr B74 45 A5
Mayland Rd B16 65 C2
Maynard Ave
Bedworth CV12 95 D8
Stourbridge DY8 80 D3
Warwick CV34 161 A7
Mayo Dr CV8 148 A4
Mayor's Croft CV4 132 B7
Mayou Ct WS3 15 A4
Maypole Cl B64 82 B8
Maypole Ct WV5 49 A6
Maypole Dr DY8 80 E5
Maypole Fields B63 82 A7
Maypole Gr B14 105 B2
Maypole Hill B63 82 A7
Maypole La B14 105 A2
Maypole Rd B68 64 B1
Maypole St WV5 49 B7
May St
Coventry CV6 113 E8
Walsall WS3 28 D6
Mayswood Dr WV6 23 F1
Mayswood Gr B32 84 D4
Mayswood Rd B92 89 C2
Maythorn Ave B76 58 A6
Maythorn Gdns
Codsall WV8 10 A4
Wolverhampton WV6 24 C3
Maythorn Gr 4 B91 127 B8
Maytree Cl B37 70 A2
May Tree Gr B20 54 F3
May Trees B47 124 F6
Maywell Dr B92 107 F8
Maywood Cl DY6 60 B6
Meaburn Cl B29 103 A7
Mead Cl WS9 30 B6
Mead Cres B9 68 B3
Meadfoot Ave B14 104 F3
Meadfoot Dr DY6 60 B7
Meadfoot Rd CV3 134 E6
Meadow Ave B71 53 F8
Meadowbank Dr B46 59 D1
Meadowbank Grange WS6 4 E4
Meadow Bank B78 21 B1
Meadowbrook Gdns WV8 10 B4
Meadow Brook Rd B31 102 F5
Meadowbrook Rd
Halesowen B63 82 E3
Lichfield WS13 3 B3
Meadow Cl
Ansty CV7 97 D3
Birmingham B17 65 B1
Hockley Heath B94 143 C6
Royal Leamington Spa
CV32 157 C4
Solihull B90 126 D8
Sutton Coldfield B74 30 F2
Sutton Coldfield B76 46 F1
Walsall WS4 29 C8
Meadow Croft WS12 1 C4
Meadowcroft Cl CV4 131 F8
Meadow Croft
Perton WV6 23 D3
West Hagley DY9 98 F4
Wythall B47 125 A3
Meadow Ct
Birmingham B17 65 B1
Nuneaton CV11 73 B4
Meadow Dr
Hampton-in-A B92 109 B7
Hinckley LE10 76 A7
Meadowfield Rd B45 122 A6
Meadowfields Cl DY8 60 E2
Meadow Grange Dr WV12 27 B7
Meadow Green Prim Sch
B47 125 A3
Meadow Gr
Great Wyrley WS6 5 A2
Solihull B92 88 D1
Meadow Hill Cl DY11 116 A5
Meadowhill Cres B98 153 F5
Meadow Hill Dr 5 WS11 2 A3
Meadowhill Dr DY8 60 E2
Meadow Hill Rd B38 103 E2
Meadowhill Rd B98 153 F5
Meadow Ho 5 CV1 113 B3
Meadow La
Alvechurch B48 139 B6
Coven Heath WV10 11 C6
Kingswood B94 144 D3
Meadowlands Dr WS4 15 D1
Meadow Lark Cl WS12 2 B4
Meadow La
Wednesfield WV12 27 A5
Wolverhampton WV14 40 B2
Wombourne WV5 49 B8
Meadow Mills Ind Est
DY10 116 E5
Meadowpark Rd DY8 80 D8
Meadow Pk B79 20 F5
Meadow Pleck La B90 126 A6
Meadow Rd
Aldridge WS9 30 A4
Birmingham B32 84 A6
Birmingham,Harborne B17 65 B1
Catshill B61 136 F8
Coventry CV6 95 B4
Dudley DY1 51 B3
Halesowen B62 83 C8
Hartshill CV10 72 A8
Oldbury B68 64 B3
Smethwick B67 65 A4
Tamworth B78 20 E3
Warwick CV34 161 A7
Wolverhampton WV3 38 D8
Wythall B47 125 A3
Meadow Rise
Balsall Common CV7 130 C7
Birmingham B30 103 E7
Meadows Fst Sch B61 137 A3
Meadows Gr WV8 10 A4
Meadowside Cl B43 43 E1
Meadowside CV11 79 B8
Meadowside Rd B74 31 F3
Meadows Prim Sch The
B31 102 E1
Meadows Sch The
Coventry CV4 111 E3
Oldbury B69 52 E1
Meadow St
1 Wolverhampton WV1 25 B2
5 Cradley Heath B64 82 F8
Coventry CV1 165 A2
Meadows The
Aldridge WS9 29 E5
Catshill B61 136 F8
Hinckley LE10 76 A7
Leek Wootton CV35 156 A7
Stourbridge DY9 99 B7
Meadow St
Nuneaton CV11 73 B5
Tamworth B77 21 C3
Walsall WS1 42 D8
Meadowsweet Ave B38 123 F8
Meadowsweet Pl DY10 116 D8
Meadowsweet Way
Cannock WS12 2 E4
Kingswinford DY6 61 A6
Meadow Vale WV8 10 B2
Meadowvale Rd B60 137 C6
Meadow View
Birmingham B13 105 C8
Burntwood WS7 7 D6
Meadow View Cvn Pk
WV10 11 C6
Meadow View JMI Sch
B43 44 D5
Meadow View DY3 39 C1
Meadow View Terr WV6 24 E4
Meadow Way
Cannock WS12 2 C1
Stourbridge DY8 60 C2
Meadow Wlk
Birmingham B14 104 E1
Cradley Heath B64 82 D8
Mead Rise B15 85 F6
Mead The DY3 50 B8
Meadthorpe Rd B44 55 D8
Meadvale Rd B45 122 B6
Meadway B33 69 B2
Meadway Cl WS12 2 C3
Meadway CV2 114 B6
Meadway N CV2 114 B6
Meadway St WS7 7 A5
Meadway The
Hinckley LE10 75 F7
Redditch B97 153 C1
Meadway The *continued*
Wolverhampton WV6 24 A5
Meadwood Ind Est WV14 40 E5
Meakins Cl CV34 160 B4
Mears Cl B23 56 D8
Mears Coppice DY5 81 E6
Mears Dr B33 68 D4
Mearse Cl B18 66 A5
Mearse La
Barnt Green B45 122 A1
Madeley Heath DY9 120 B6
Mease Ave WS7 7 D6
Mease Croft 2 B9 67 B2
Measham Gr B26 88 E5
Measham Way WV11 26 E7
Meaton Gr B32 102 B8
Medcroft Ave B20 54 E4
Medici Rd B60 137 C2
Medina Cl WV10 11 F4
Medina Rd
Birmingham B11 87 E4
Coventry CV6 95 E1
Medina B77 21 E1
Medina Way DY6 60 C6
Medland Ave CV3 132 F5
Medley Gdns DY4 52 E4
Medley Gr CV31 161 F3
Medley Rd B11 87 D5
Medlicott Rd B11 87 C6
Medway Cl DY5 61 A6
Medway Croft B36 69 F7
Medway Ct B73 46 B5
Medway Gr B38 123 E8
Medway Rd WS8 6 C2
Medway B77 21 E1
Medway Twr B7 67 B5
Medway Wlk WS8 6 C2
Medwin Gr B23 56 D7
Meerash La WS7 7 C3
Meer End B38 123 D7
Meer End Rd CV8 130 D1
Meerhill Ave B90 127 A6
Meeting Ho The 3 WS10 41 E3
Meeting House La
Balsall Common CV7 130 C6
Birmingham B31 103 A4
Meeting La DY5 61 B1
Meeting Lane Ind Est DY5 61 B1
Meeting St
Dudley DY2 62 C5
Tipton DY4 52 D5
Wednesbury WS10 41 E3
Meg La WS7 7 C8
Meir Rd B98 159 C8
Melbourne Ave
Birmingham,Newtown
B19 66 C6
Birmingham,Selly Oak B66 65 B7
Bromsgrove B61 136 E4
Melbourne Cl
Bromsgrove B61 136 E3
Kingswinford DY6 60 E4
Nuneaton CV11 78 E8
West Bromwich B70 53 A7
Melbourne Cres WS12 2 F2
Melbourne Ct 3 CV12 77 F2
Melbourne Gdns WS5 43 B6
Melbourne Rd
Bromsgrove B61 136 E3
Cannock WS12 2 F2
Coventry CV5 113 A2
Halesowen B63 83 B5
Smethwick B66 65 B7
Melbourne St WV2 163 C2
Melbury Cl WV3 25 A1
Melbury Gr B14 104 E5
Melbury Way 1 WS11 1 F2
Melchester Wlk 2 WS11 1 F2
Melchett Rd B30 104 A4
Melcote Gr B44 55 E8
Meldon Dr WV14 41 A2
Meldrum Rd CV10 72 D4
Melen St B97 153 D4
Melford Cl DY3 39 C2
Melford Hall Rd B91 106 F7
Melford B79 20 E6
Melfort Cl
Coventry CV3 114 F2
Nuneaton CV10 72 C5
Melfort Gr B14 105 A3
Melksham Sq B35 58 A3
Mellis Gr B23 56 A5
Mellish Ct WS4 29 A3
Mellish Dr WS4 29 B3
Mellish Rd WS4 29 B3
Mellor Dr B74 31 E3
Mellors Cl B17 85 B3
Mellowdew Rd
Coventry CV2 114 C4
Stourbridge DY8 60 C3
Mellowship Rd CV5 111 D5
Mell Sq B91 107 C4
Mellwaters B77 36 C8
Melmerby B77 36 C8
Melplash Ave B91 107 A4
Melrose Ave
Bedworth CV12 95 D8
Birmingham,Sparkbrook
B12 87 A6
Birmingham,Sparkhill B11 87 C6
Stourbridge DY8 81 A2
Sutton Coldfield B73 45 E2
West Bromwich B71 42 D1
Melrose Cl
Birmingham B38 103 F1
Hinckley LE10 75 B8
Melrose Ct WS4 29 A3

Melrose Dr
Cannock WS12 ... 1 F7
Perton WV6 ... 23 E4
Melrose Gr B19 ... 66 B7
Melrose Pl B66 ... 64 D8
Melrose Rd B20 ... 55 E1
Melstock Cl DY4 ... 51 D5
Melstock Rd B14 ... 104 D7
Melton Ave B92 ... 89 B4
Melton Dr B15 ... 86 B7
Melton Rd
Birmingham B14 ... 104 F8
Royal Leamington Spa CV32 ... 157 B4
Melverley Gr B44 ... 55 F7
Melverton Ave WV10 ... 25 E8
Melville Cl CV7 ... 96 A8
Melville Hall 1 B16 ... 65 D1
Melville Rd
Birmingham B16 ... 65 D1
Coventry CV1 ... 113 A3
Melvina Rd B7 ... 67 B5
Melzer Ho DY10 ... 116 E7
Membury Rd B8 ... 67 D6
Memorial Cl WV13 ... 27 A2
Memory La
Darlaston WS10 ... 41 D8
Wolverhampton WV11 ... 26 B5
Menai Cl WV12 ... 27 C6
Menai Wlk B37 ... 70 B4
Mendip Ave B8 ... 67 E5
Mendip Cl
Bromsgrove B61 ... 137 A5
Dudley DY3 ... 50 D3
Wolverhampton WV2 ... 39 F7
Mendip Dr CV10 ... 72 B3
Mendip Ho B98 ... 154 D6
Mendip Rd
Birmingham B8 ... 67 E5
Halesowen B63 ... 82 D1
Stourbridge DY8 ... 81 B6
Mendip Way B77 ... 22 C1
Menin Cres B13 ... 105 B7
Menin Rd
Birmingham B13 ... 105 B8
Tipton DY4 ... 51 D5
Mentone Ct B20 ... 54 E3
Menzies High Sch B71 ... 53 C8
Meon Gr
Birmingham B33 ... 89 B8
Perton WV6 ... 23 F4
Meon Rise DY9 ... 81 C3
Meon Way WV11 ... 26 F7
Meranti Cl WV12 ... 27 C8
Mercer Ave
Coventry CV2 ... 114 A5
Water Orton B46 ... 59 A3
Mercer Gr WV11 ... 26 D7
Mercers Mdw CV7 ... 95 A6
Merchants Ct 5 CV32 ... 157 A1
Merchants Pk WS9 ... 30 A7
Merchants Way WS9 ... 30 A7
Mercia Ave CV8 ... 147 F4
Mercia Bsns Village CV4 ... 131 F6
Mercia Cl
Bromsgrove B60 ... 150 F7
Tamworth B79 ... 20 E7
Mercia Dr
Birmingham B14 ... 104 D6
Perton WV6 ... 23 E5
Mercia Ho CV1 ... 165 B3
Mercian Ct WS14 ... 9 C7
Mercian Pk B77 ... 22 A3
Mercian Way B77 ... 22 B3
Mercia Way CV34 ... 161 B7
Mercot Cl B98 ... 159 A6
Mercury Pk B77 ... 22 B3
Mercury Rd WS11 ... 2 A5
Mere Ave B35 ... 58 B3
Mere Cl WV12 ... 27 A5
Merecote Rd B92 ... 106 D7
Mere Croft WS11 ... 5 F4
Meredith Gn DY11 ... 116 A1
Meredith Pool Cl B18 ... 65 F6
Meredith Rd
Coventry CV2 ... 114 D2
Dudley DY3 ... 50 A5
Wolverhampton WV11 ... 26 C8
Meredith St B64 ... 62 D1
Mere Dr B75 ... 32 B2
Mere Green Cl B75 ... 32 C2
Mere Green Comb Sch B75 ... 32 B2
Mere Green Rd B75 ... 32 C2
Mere Oak Rd WV6 ... 23 E5
Mere Pool Rd B75 ... 32 E2
Mere Rd
Birmingham B23 ... 56 D3
Stourbridge DY8 ... 80 E3
Mereside Way B92 ... 106 E8
Meres Rd B63 ... 82 C5
Mere St B23 ... 56 E3
Merevale Ave
Hinckley LE10 ... 75 C7
Nuneaton CV11 ... 73 A4
Merevale Cl
Hinckley LE10 ... 75 C7
Redditch B98 ... 159 D8
Merevale Ct CV11 ... 73 A4
Merevale Rd B92 ... 89 B2
Mere View WS4 ... 29 C8
Mereways B90 ... 126 A5
Merganser B77 ... 36 A6
Merganser Way DY10 ... 117 B3
Meriden Ave DY8 ... 80 D6
Meriden Bsns Pk CV5 ... 111 B8
Meriden CE Prim Sch CV7 ... 92 C1
Meriden Cl
Birmingham B25 ... 88 B7
Cannock WS11 ... 4 B8
Stourbridge DY8 ... 80 D6
Meriden Cross★ CV7 ... 92 B1
Meriden Ct 3 WV4 ... 39 F4
Meriden Dr B37 ... 70 A6
Meriden Hill CV7 ... 110 E8
Meriden Park Homes CV7 ... 110 C8
Meriden Rd
Berkswell CV7 ... 110 C4
Chapel Green CV7 ... 93 B7
Hampton-in-A B92 ... 109 C7
Wolverhampton WV10 ... 25 A8
Meriden Rise B92 ... 89 D3
Meriden St
Birmingham B5 ... 164 D2
Coventry CV1 ... 113 B3
Meridian Pl B60 ... 137 A1
Merino Ave B31 ... 123 A8
Merlin Ave CV10 ... 72 B6
Merlin Cl
Birmingham B35 ... 58 A3
Cannock WS11 ... 1 C2
Dudley DY1 ... 61 F8
Tamworth B77 ... 36 A6
Merlin Ct WS7 ... 7 F8
Merlin Dr DY10 ... 117 B3
Merlin Gr B26 ... 89 B5
Merrick Cl B63 ... 82 D2
Merrick Ct LE10 ... 75 F5
Merrick Rd WV11 ... 27 A6
Merridale Ave WV3 ... 24 F2
Merridale Cres WV3 ... 25 A2
Merridale Ct WV3 ... 24 F1
Merridale Gdns WV3 ... 25 A1
Merridale Gr WV3 ... 24 E1
Merridale Jun & Inf Sch WV3 ... 25 A1
Merridale La WV3 ... 25 A2
Merridale Rd WV3 ... 25 A1
Merridale St W WV3 ... 39 A8
Merridale St WV3 ... 163 A2
Merriemont Dr B45 ... 122 A1
Merrifield Gdns LE10 ... 75 E5
Merrill Cl WS6 ... 4 E2
Merrill Gdns B60 ... 121 D2
Merrills Hall Island WV11 ... 26 D4
Merrills Hall La WV11 ... 26 E4
Merrington Cl 5 B91 ... 127 C8
Merrion's Cl B43 ... 43 E4
Merrishaw Rd B31 ... 123 A8
Merritts Brook Cl B29 ... 103 A5
Merritt's Brook La B31 ... 102 E5
Merritts Hill B31 ... 102 E6
Merrivale Rd
Coventry CV5 ... 112 E3
Halesowen B62 ... 83 F8
Smethwick B66 ... 65 A2
Merryfield Cl B92 ... 107 D7
Merryfield Gr B17 ... 85 C4
Merryfield Rd DY1 ... 50 E1
Merryfields Way CV2 ... 96 F1
Merry Hill DY5 ... 61 F2
Merry Hill Ctr DY5 ... 61 F3
Merryhill Dr B18 ... 65 F6
Merryhills Ent Pk WV10 ... 25 F5
Merry Husrt Pl LE10 ... 74 E7
Merse Rd B98 ... 154 E6
Mersey Gr B38 ... 123 E8
Mersey Rd
Bulkington CV12 ... 79 A3
Walsall WS3 ... 14 E1
Merstal Dr B92 ... 107 F7
Merstone Cl WV14 ... 40 C6
Merstone Sch B37 ... 70 A1
Merstowe Cl B27 ... 88 B3
Merton Cl
Kidderminster DY10 ... 117 B7
Oldbury B68 ... 64 B2
Merton Ct WS7 ... 6 F5
Merton Ho B37 ... 69 F2
Merton Rd B13 ... 87 B3
Mervyn Pl WV14 ... 41 A3
Mervyn Rd
Bilston WV14 ... 41 A3
Birmingham B21 ... 54 E1
Meryhurst Rd WS10 ... 42 B5
Merynton Ave CV4 ... 132 E5
Meschines St CV3 ... 133 D6
Mesnes Gn WS14 ... 9 C7
Messenger La B70,B71 ... 53 D3
Messenger Rd B66 ... 65 B6
Mesty Croft Prim Sch WS10 ... 42 B3
Metalloys Ind Est B76 ... 58 B5
Metcalf Cl WS7 ... 7 C8
Metcalfe Cl WS12 ... 2 C6
Metchley Abbey 11 B17 ... 85 D5
Metchley Croft B90 ... 126 F6
Metchley Ct B17 ... 85 D4
Metchley Dr B17 ... 85 D5
Metchley Ho 6 B17 ... 85 D5
Metchley La B17 ... 85 D5
Metchley Park Rd B15 ... 85 E4
Metfield Cl B79 ... 21 C8
Metfield Croft
Birmingham B17 ... 85 D4
Kingswinford DY6 ... 60 F6
Metlin Gr B33 ... 69 E3
Metric Wlk 2 B67 ... 65 A5
Metro Way B66 ... 65 C7
Mews Rd CV32 ... 161 D8
Mews The
Bedworth CV12 ... 78 B2
Birmingham B27 ... 88 B3
Cannock WS11 ... 1 D1
Mews The *continued*
Kenilworth CV8 ... 147 E3
Rowley Regis B65 ... 63 B2
Mey Coppice B36 ... 69 F7
Meynell Ho 5 B20 ... 54 F3
Meyrick Rd B70 ... 53 A6
Meyrick Wlk B16 ... 65 F1
Miall Park Rd B91 ... 106 E5
Miall Rd B28 ... 106 A8
Mica Cl B77 ... 22 B2
Michael Banning Pl CV7 ... 130 B7
Michael Blanning Gdns B93 ... 127 E3
Michael Blanning Ho 10 B13 ... 87 B2
Michael Ct B5 ... 86 D6
Michael Drayton Jun Sch CV10 ... 72 B8
Michael Dr B15 ... 86 C6
Michaelmas Rd CV3 ... 165 B1
Michael Rd
Darlaston WS10 ... 41 B7
Smethwick B67 ... 64 E6
Michaelwood Cl B97 ... 152 F2
Michel Ho CV1 ... 165 C4
Michell Cl CV3 ... 134 B8
Michelle Cl B13 ... 105 A5
Michigan Cl WS11 ... 2 B2
Micklehill Dr B90 ... 126 B8
Mickle Mdw B46 ... 59 B3
Mickleover Rd B8 ... 68 C5
Mickleton Ave B33 ... 89 C8
Mickleton Cl B98 ... 158 E7
Mickleton Rd
Coventry CV5 ... 133 A8
Solihull B92 ... 106 D8
Mickleton B77 ... 36 C8
Mickley Ave WV10 ... 25 E5
Midacre WV13 ... 27 A1
Middelburg Cl CV11 ... 74 A1
Middle Acre Rd B32 ... 84 E2
Middle Ave WV13 ... 40 E8
Middle Bickenhill La B92 ... 91 A4
Middleborough Rd CV1 ... 165 A4
Middlecotes CV4 ... 112 B1
Middle Cres WS3 ... 29 A7
Middle Cross WV1 ... 163 D3
Middle Dr B45 ... 122 D4
Middle Entry B79 ... 21 B4
Middlefield Ave
Dorridge B93 ... 128 B4
Halesowen B62 ... 63 F1
Middlefield Cl
Halesowen B62 ... 63 F1
Hinckley LE10 ... 71 D2
Middlefield Ct LE10 ... 71 D2
Middlefield Dr CV3 ... 115 B1
Middlefield Gdns B62 ... 83 F8
Middlefield Ho B14 ... 104 F3
Middlefield La
Hinckley LE10 ... 71 D3
West Hagley DY9 ... 99 B6
Middlefield Pl LE10 ... 71 D3
Middle Field Rd B31 ... 103 D2
Middlefield Rd
Bromsgrove B60 ... 151 B7
Oldbury B69 ... 63 A8
Middlefield WV8 ... 10 E2
Middlefleld Dr CV3 ... 115 A1
Middle Gdns WV13 ... 27 B2
Middlehill Rise B32 ... 84 D3
Middle House Dr B60 ... 121 D1
Middlehouse La B97 ... 153 E6
Middle La
Wolverhampton WV9 ... 11 A5
Wythall B38 ... 124 D5
Middle Leaford B34 ... 69 A5
Middle Leasowe B32 ... 84 D4
Middlemarch Bsns Pk CV3 ... 134 C2
Middlemarch Rd
Coventry CV6 ... 113 C7
Nuneaton CV10 ... 73 C1
Middlemarch Sch CV10 ... 73 B1
Middle Mdw DY4 ... 52 B5
Middle Meadow Ave B32 ... 84 C5
Middlemist Gr B43 ... 54 F6
Middlemore Bsns Pk WS9 ... 29 E6
Middlemore Cl B80 ... 159 D3
Middlemore Ind Est B66 ... 65 B8
Middlemore La WS9 ... 30 A6
Middlemore La W WS9 ... 29 E6
Middlemore Rd
Birmingham B31 ... 103 B3
Smethwick B66 ... 65 B8
Middle Park Cl B29 ... 103 B8
Middlepark Dr B31 ... 103 B6
Middle Park Rd B29 ... 103 C8
Middlepark Rd DY1 ... 61 F8
Middle Piece Dr B97 ... 153 B1
Middle Rd
Fairfield B61 ... 120 F4
Upper Bentley B60 ... 152 A2
Middle Ride CV3 ... 134 E5
Middlesmoor B77 ... 36 C8
Middleton Cl
Hammerwich WS7 ... 7 D4
Redditch B98 ... 154 F2
Walsall WS5 ... 42 F5
Middleton Gdns B30 ... 103 D4
Middleton Grange B31 ... 103 C4
Middleton Hall
Birmingham B30 ... 103 E4
Middleton B78 ... 34 E1
Middleton Hall Rd B30 ... 103 E4
Middleton La B78 ... 47 F6
Middleton Mews B98 ... 154 F2
Middleton Rd
Birmingham B14 ... 104 F7
Bromsgrove B61 ... 136 F4
Brownhills WS8 ... 7 A1
Solihull B90 ... 106 A2
Sutton Coldfield B74 ... 31 A1
Middleton Trad Est WV13 ... 26 E1
Middletown La B96,B80 ... 159 D1
Middletown B80 ... 159 D1
Middletree Rd B63 ... 82 C7
Middle Vauxhall 4 WV1 ... 25 A2
Middleway Ave DY8 ... 60 C3
Middleway Gn WV14 ... 40 C8
Middleway Rd WV14 ... 40 C7
Middleway View B18 ... 66 A3
Midford Gr B15 ... 86 C8
Midgley Dr B74 ... 32 A2
Midhill Dr B65 ... 63 C6
Midhurst Dr WS12 ... 2 C7
Midhurst Gr WV6 ... 24 C5
Midhurst Rd B30 ... 104 B3
Midland Air Mus★ CV8 ... 134 B3
Midland Cl B21 ... 66 A7
Midland Croft B33 ... 69 D3
Midland Ct B3 ... 164 A4
Midland Dr B72 ... 46 C5
Midland Oak Trad Est CV6 ... 95 E2
Midland Rd
Birmingham B30 ... 103 F5
Coventry CV6 ... 113 E5
Darlaston WS10 ... 41 C8
Huntington WS12 ... 1 C5
Nuneaton CV11 ... 73 A5
Sutton Coldfield B74 ... 46 A6
Walsall WS1 ... 28 E1
Midland St B9 ... 67 C3
Midpoint Ctr WV6 ... 24 F5
Midpoint Park Ind Est B76 ... 58 C5
Midvale Dr B14 ... 104 D2
Mikado Rd B60 ... 137 D1
Milburn Hill Rd CV4 ... 132 B6
Milburn Rd B44 ... 45 A3
Milburn B77 ... 36 C8
Milby Ct CV11 ... 73 C2
Milby Dr CV11 ... 74 A7
Milby Prim Sch CV11 ... 73 F8
Milcote Cl B98 ... 159 A7
Milcote Dr
Sutton Coldfield B73 ... 45 C3
Willenhall WV13 ... 26 D1
Milcote Rd
Birmingham B29 ... 103 A8
Smethwick B67 ... 64 F1
Solihull B91 ... 107 B4
Milcote Way DY6 ... 60 B7
Mildenhall Rd B42 ... 44 A1
Mildenhall B79 ... 21 C8
Mildred Rd B64 ... 62 E2
Mildred Way B65 ... 63 C6
Milebrook Gr B32 ... 102 B8
Mile End B94 ... 142 A2
Mile Flat DY6 ... 60 A7
Mile La CV1 ... 165 C1
Mile Oak Cross Rds B78 ... 20 C2
Miles Ave B36 ... 58 D1
Miles Gr DY2 ... 62 F7
Miles Mdw CV6 ... 96 B1
Miles Meadow Cl WV12 ... 27 C8
Milestone Ct WV6 ... 24 A3
Milestone Dr DY9 ... 98 F4
Milestone Ho 2 CV1 ... 113 B2
Milestone La B21 ... 65 D8
Milestone Way WV12 ... 27 C8
Mile Tree La CV2 ... 96 F7
Milfoil Cl LE10 ... 74 F7
Milford Ave
3 Birmingham B12 ... 87 A6
Willenhall WV12 ... 27 A5
Milford Cl
Allesley CV5 ... 112 B6
Redditch B97 ... 158 C6
Stourbridge DY8 ... 60 E3
Milford Copse B17 ... 85 B5
Milford Croft B65 ... 62 F6
Milford Ct
Birmingham B19 ... 164 B5
Royal Leamington Spa CV31 ... 162 A8
Milford Gr B90 ... 127 C7
Milford Pl B14 ... 104 E8
Milford Rd
Birmingham B17 ... 85 B5
Wolverhampton WV2 ... 39 C7
Milford St CV10 ... 73 B2
Milhill Rd B98 ... 154 E1
Milholme Gn B92 ... 107 D8
Milking Bank DY1 ... 50 E2
Milking Bank Prim Sch DY1 ... 50 E2
Milk St B5 ... 66 F1
Millais Cl CV12 ... 78 A4
Millais Rd LE10 ... 71 A3
Millard Ind Est B70 ... 53 A1
Millard Rd WV14 ... 40 B1
Mill Bank Cotts DY11 ... 116 D6
Millbank Gr B23 ... 56 B6
Mill Bank Mews CV8 ... 148 B6
Mill Bank DY3 ... 50 D8
Millbank St WV11 ... 12 F1
Millbank CV34 ... 156 B1
Millbrook Cl 4 WS11 ... 1 F2
Millbrook Ct B62 ... 83 A7
Mill Brook Dr B31 ... 122 E8
Millbrook Dr WS14 ... 17 F6
Millbrook Rd B14 ... 104 C4
Millbrook Way DY5 ... 81 B8
Mill Burn Way 3 B9 ... 67 B2
Mill Cl
Blakedown DY10 ... 98 B2
Bromsgrove B60 ... 150 F6
Coventry CV2 ... 96 B3
Dudley DY3 ... 50 D6
Hollywood B47 ... 125 A7
Nuneaton CV11 ... 73 F1
Wolston CV8 ... 135 F3
Mill Cres WS11 ... 2 B2
Mill Croft WV14 ... 40 E6
Millcroft Cl B32 ... 84 E2
Millcroft Rd B74 ... 45 A8
Mill Ct WS14 ... 18 A6
Milldale Cl DY10 ... 116 E8
Milldale Cres WV10 ... 11 D3
Milldale Rd WV10 ... 11 D4
Mill Dr B66 ... 65 B5
Mill End CV8 ... 148 A6
Millenium Pk B70 ... 53 A5
Millennium Cl WS3 ... 15 A4
Millennium Forge DY4 ... 51 D5
Millennium Gdns B64 ... 62 F2
Millennium Way
Codsall WV8 ... 10 B4
Wolston CV8 ... 135 F3
Miller Cl
Bromsgrove B60 ... 150 E6
Lichfield WS13 ... 3 B2
Miller Cres WV14 ... 40 A1
Millers Cl WS2 ... 27 F1
Millers Ct
1 Kidderminster DY11 ... 116 D6
Solihull B90 ... 105 F2
Millersdale Dr B71 ... 42 F2
Millers Gn LE10 ... 75 F6
Millers Green Dr DY6 ... 60 A8
Millers Rd CV34 ... 160 E8
Miller St B6 ... 66 E5
Millers Vale WS12 ... 2 D1
Millers Wharf B78 ... 22 F1
Millers Wlk WS3 ... 14 E3
Mill Farm Pk CV12 ... 79 B6
Mill Farm Rd B17 ... 85 C3
Millfield Ave
Walsall,Little Bloxwich WS3 ... 14 D3
Walsall WS4 ... 15 B1
Millfield B31 ... 103 A4
Millfield Gdns 2 DY11 ... 116 D6
Millfield Prim Sch
Brownhills WS8 ... 16 A7
Fazeley B78 ... 35 A8
Millfield Rd
Birmingham B20 ... 54 F5
Bromsgrove B61 ... 136 E1
Brownhills WS8 ... 16 A7
Millfield CV31 ... 162 A8
Millfields B33 ... 69 E3
Millfields Cl B71 ... 42 B1
Millfields Fst Sch B61 ... 136 E1
Millfields Rd
Bilston WV14,WV4 ... 40 B5
West Bromwich B71 ... 42 B1
Millfield View B63 ... 82 E4
Millford Cl B28 ... 106 A5
Mill Gdns
Birmingham B14 ... 105 D5
Smethwick B67 ... 64 F3
Mill Gn WV10 ... 11 D4
Mill Gr WV8 ... 10 C3
Mill Green Nature Pk★ WS11 ... 1 F1
Millhaven Ave B30 ... 104 B6
Mill Hill CV8 ... 133 D3
Mill Hill Rd LE10 ... 71 C1
Mill Hill B67 ... 64 F3
Mill Ho B8 ... 68 D4
Mill House Cl CV32 ... 161 C8
Millhouse Ct CV6 ... 113 F7
Mill House Dr CV32 ... 161 C8
Millhouse Rd B25 ... 88 C8
Mill House Terr CV32 ... 161 C8
Millicent Cl WS12 ... 2 B6
Millicent Pl 11 B12 ... 87 A6
Millichip Rd WV13 ... 26 E1
Millington Rd
Birmingham B36 ... 68 E7
Tipton DY4 ... 40 F1
Wolverhampton WV10 ... 25 E6
Millison Gr B90 ... 127 A7
Mill La WS9 ... 31 A7
Mill La Arc B91 ... 107 C3
Mill La
Bentley Heath B93 ... 127 F4
Birmingham B32 ... 84 E2
Birmingham,Digbeth B5 ... 164 D1
Birmingham,Northfield B31 ... 103 A2
Blakedown DY10 ... 98 B2
Bramcote CV11 ... 79 F8
Bromsgrove B61 ... 136 F2
Bulkington CV12 ... 79 A3
Coventry CV3 ... 114 F2
Cubbington CV32 ... 157 F5
Earlswood B94 ... 141 B8
Fairfield B61 ... 120 F3
Fazeley B78 ... 35 A8
Halesowen B63 ... 83 C4
Hammerwich WS7 ... 7 D3
Kidderminster,Blakebrook DY11 ... 116 D6
Kidderminster,Hoobrook DY10 ... 116 F2
Kingswood B94 ... 144 C4

Mill La *continued*
Oldbury B69 64 A5
Shenstone WS14 18 A6
Solihull B91 107 C4
Stonnall WS9,WS14 17 A4
Tamworth B79 21 C5
Walsall WS3,WS4 28 F4
Willenhall WV12 27 C5
Wolverhampton,Scotlands WV11 26 B7
Wolverhampton,Tettenhall Wood WV6 24 A3
Wombourne WV5 49 B6
Wythall B47,B94 125 B1
Mill Lodge Prim Sch B90 105 E2
Millmead Lodge B13 105 D8
Millmead Rd B32 84 E1
Mill Park Ind Est WS11 2 A1
Mill Pk WS11 2 A2
Mill Pleck B80 159 E3
Mill Pl WS3 28 E4
Mill Pond The WS13 3 C2
Mill Pool Cl DY9 99 A4
Millpool Gdns B14 104 F3
Millpool Hill B14 104 F4
Mill Pool La B93 144 A8
Mill Pool Rd WS12 2 B6
Millpool Way B66 65 A4
Mill Race La
Coventry CV6 96 B3
Stourbridge DY8 81 A6
Millrace Rd B98 153 E5
Mill Rd
Brownhills WS8 16 A7
Cradley Heath B64 82 E7
Royal Leamington Spa CV31 162 A8
Walsall WS4 15 C1
Mills Ave B76 46 E4
Millsborough Rd B98 153 F3
Mills Cl WV11 26 B8
Mills Cres WV2 163 D1
Millside B28 105 E3
Mills Rd WV2 163 D1
Mill St
Barwell LE9 71 F5
Bedworth CV12 78 B3
Bilston WV14 40 C5
Birmingham B6 164 D5
Brierley Hill DY5 61 E2
Cannock WS11 1 E1
Coventry CV1 165 A3
Darlaston WS10 41 C6
Halesowen B63 82 C7
Kidderminster DY11 116 D6
Nuneaton CV11 73 C4
Millstone Cl B76 46 F1
Mill Stream Cl WV8 10 B4
Mill St
Redditch B97 153 D4
Royal Leamington Spa CV31 162 A7
Stourbridge DY8 60 F2
Sutton Coldfield B72 46 C5
Tipton DY4 52 D5
Walsall WS2 28 E3
Warwick CV34 160 F6
West Bromwich B70 53 C4
Willenhall WV13 27 C2
Millsum Ho 6 WS1 28 F1
Mills Wlk DY4 51 F7
Mill Terr CV12 78 B5
Mill The WV1 163 D3
Millthorpe Cl B8 67 F5
Mill View
Birmingham B33 69 C4
Hinckley LE10 71 E1
Millwalk Dr WV9 11 A3
Millward St
Birmingham B9 67 C1
West Bromwich B70 53 A3
Mill Wlk CV11 73 C4
Mill Wlk The B31 102 F1
Millwright Cl 4 DY4 52 B5
Milner Cl CV12 79 D2
Milner Cres CV2 96 E1
Milner Dr B79 22 E7
Milner Rd B29 86 A1
Milner Way B13 105 D8
Milnes Walker Ct B44 44 E1
Milo Cres B78 21 A2
Milrose Way CV4 131 F8
Milsom Gr B34 69 D6
Milstead Rd B26 69 A1
Milston Cl B14 104 E1
Milton Ave
2 Birmingham B12 87 A6
Tamworth B79 21 A7
Warwick CV34 160 C5
Milton Cl
Bedworth CV12 78 D1
Bentley Heath B93 127 F4
Hinckley LE10 71 C1
Kidderminster DY11 116 A6
Redditch B97 158 C8
Stourbridge DY8 81 A7
Walsall WS1 42 D6
Willenhall WV12 27 E7
Milton Cres
Birmingham B25 88 D7
Dudley DY3 50 A5
Milton Ct WV6 23 E4
Milton Dr DY9 99 D7
Milton Gr
Birmingham,Edgbaston B29 85 F3
Birmingham,Handsworth B21 65 C8
Milton Ho B63 82 B5
Milton Pl WS1 42 D6
Milton Rd
Bentley Heath B93 127 F4
Cannock WS11 1 E4
Catshill B61 137 A8
Dudley WV14 51 D8
Smethwick B67 64 E5
Wolverhampton WV10 26 A5
Milton St
Birmingham B19 66 E6
Brierley Hill DY5 61 D7
Coventry CV2 114 A4
Walsall WS1 42 D7
West Bromwich B71 53 B5
Milverton Cl
Halesowen B63 83 A6
Sutton Coldfield B76 57 F7
Milverton Cres 1 CV32 156 E1
Milverton Cres W 3 CV32 156 E1
Milverton Ct
3 Birmingham B62 84 A7
Royal Leamington Spa CV32 161 E8
Milverton Hill CV32 161 E8
Milverton House Prep Sch CV11 73 D3
Milverton Lodge 2 CV32 156 E1
Milverton Prim Sch CV32 156 E1
Milverton Rd
Birmingham B23 56 E4
Coventry CV2 96 D2
Knowle B93 128 C5
Milverton Terr CV32 161 E8
Milward Sq 7 B97 153 E3
Mimosa Cl B29 103 B7
Mimosa Wlk DY6 60 E8
Mincing La B65 63 D3
Mindelsohn Way B15 85 D4
Minden Gr B29 85 B1
Minehead Rd
Dudley DY1 61 D8
Wolverhampton WV10 11 B2
Miner St WS2 28 C3
Miners Way WS7 6 C7
Miners Wlk B78 22 F1
Minerva Cl
Tamworth B77 21 D5
Willenhall WV12 27 E4
Minerva La WV1 25 E1
Minewood Cl WS3 13 F3
Minith Rd WV14 51 D8
Miniva Dr B76 47 A2
Minivet Dr B12 86 E6
Minley Ave B17 84 F7
Minories B4 164 C3
Minories The 1 DY2 51 D1
Minors Hill WS14 9 D6
Minstead Rd B24 56 D1
Minster Cl
Knowle B93 128 B8
Rowley Regis B65 63 E3
Minster Dr B10 87 D7
Minsterley Cl WV3 38 E8
Minsterpool Wlk WS13 9 B8
Minster Rd CV1 113 B3
Minster The WV3 39 A7
Minster Wlk B61 136 F8
Mintern Rd B25 88 C8
Minton Cl WV1 26 A1
Minton Ho 3 B12 86 F5
Minton Mews B60 151 B8
Minton Rd
Birmingham B32 84 F4
Coventry CV2 96 E1
Minworth Cl B97 153 B2
Minworth Ind Pk B76 58 B5
Minworth Jun & Inf Sch B76 58 D5
Minworth Rd B46 59 A3
Miranda Cl
Birmingham B45 102 A2
Coventry CV3 134 D7
Miranda Dr CV34 161 E2
Miras Bsns Est WS12 2 D3
Mirfield Cl WV9 11 A3
Mirfield Rd
Birmingham B33 69 B2
Solihull B91 107 A6
Mission Cl B64 63 A1
Mission Dr DY4 52 A3
Mistletoe Dr WS5 43 B3
Mistral Cl LE10 75 F8
Mitcham Cl WS12 1 F7
Mitcham Gr B44 45 B1
Mitcheldean Cl B98 158 E7
Mitcheldean Covert B14 104 D2
Mitchell Ave
Coventry CV4 132 A7
Dudley WV14 40 B1
Mitchell Ho
Coventry CV4 132 A7
Warwick CV34 160 E7
Mitchell Rd CV12 78 C2
Mitchell's Ct B79 21 B5
Mitchel Rd DY6 60 F4
Mitford Dr B92 107 D7
Mitre Cl
Essington WV11 13 A3
Willenhall WV12 27 D7
Mitre Ct
Bromsgrove B61 137 A3
Sutton Coldfield B74 46 C6
Mitre Fold WV1 163 B3
Mitre Rd
Cheslyn Hay WS6 4 D2
Stourbridge DY9 81 E5
Mitten Ave B45 102 A1
Mitton Rd B20 54 E2
Moat Ave CV3 132 F5
Moat Coppice B62 84 A1
Moat Croft
Birmingham B37 70 A2
Sutton Coldfield B76 58 B7
Moat Dr
Drayton Bassett B78 34 E5
Halesowen B62 63 F1
Moat Farm Dr
Bedworth CV12 95 C8
Birmingham B32 84 A1
Moat Farm Inf Sch B68 64 C3
Moat Farm Jun Sch B68 64 C3
Moat Farm Way WS3 15 A5
Moatfield Terr 2 WS10 42 A3
Moat Gn CV35 160 A1
Moat Green Ave WV11 26 E7
Moat Hall Prim Sch WS6 4 F3
Moat House La CV4 132 C7
Moathouse La E WV11 26 E7
Moathouse La W WV11 26 D7
Moat House Prim Sch
Coventry CV2 96 D1
Wednesfield WV11 26 F7
Moat House Rd B8 68 A4
Moat La
Birmingham,Digbeth B5 164 C1
Birmingham,South Yardley B26 88 E7
Great Wyrley WS6 5 A2
Solihull B91 107 C6
Moat Mdws B32 84 E4
Moatmead Wlk B36 68 E8
Moat Rd
Oldbury B68 64 B3
Tipton DY4 52 A7
Walsall WS2 28 C2
Moatside Cl WS3 15 A5
Moat St WV13 27 A2
Moat Way LE9 71 F6
Moatway The B38 123 E7
Mobberley Rd WV14 40 A1
Mob La WS4 15 C3
Mockley Wood Rd B93 128 B7
Modbury Ave B32 84 D1
Modbury Cl CV3 133 D5
Moden Cl DY3 50 D6
Moden Hill DY3 50 D6
Mogul La B63 82 A7
Moillett St B18 65 D4
Moilliett Ct B66 65 C6
Moira Cres B14 105 C4
Moises Hall Rd WV5 49 B7
Moland St B4 164 C4
Mole St B11 87 B6
Molesworth Ave CV3 114 A1
Molineux Grounds (Wolverhampton Wanderers FC) WV1 163 B4
Molineux St WV1 163 B4
Mollington Cres B90 106 C3
Mollington Rd CV31 162 A3
Molyneux Rd DY2 62 E2
Momus Bvd CV2 114 C2
Monarch Dr DY4 52 C6
Monarch Ho B68 64 B2
Monarch Ind Est B11 88 A5
Monarch Way DY2 62 C4
Monarch Works 7 DY9 81 F5
Mona Rd B23 56 F5
Monastery Dr B91 106 E6
Monckton Rd B68 84 A7
Moncrieff Dr CV31 162 C5
Moncrieffe Cl DY2 62 E8
Moncrieffe St WS1 29 A1
Mondrian Rd B60 137 C1
Money La B61 121 A7
Monica Rd B10 87 F8
Monins Ave DY4 52 A2
Monk Cl DY4 52 B3
Monkgate Dr B71 53 C6
Monk Rd B8 68 B5
Monk's Croft The CV3 133 C7
Monks Dr B80 159 D4
Monkseaton Rd B72 46 B2
Monksfield Ave B43 43 D1
Monks Field Cl CV4 112 A1
Monkshood Mews B23 56 B7
Monkshood Retreat B38 123 F8
Monks Kirby Rd B76 46 F3
Monkspath Bsns Pk B90 126 F8
Monkspath Cl B90 126 D7
Monkspath Hall Rd B90, B91 127 B7
Monkspath Jun & Inf Sch B90 127 B6
Monks Path B97 152 F4
Monkspath
Solihull B90 127 A6
Sutton Coldfield B76 46 F1
Monks Rd
Binley Woods CV3 135 C7
Coventry CV1 113 F2
Monksway B38 104 B1
Monks Way
Tamworth B77 21 F5
Warwick CV34 160 D6
Monkswell Cl
Birmingham B10 87 D7
Monkswell Cl *continued*
Brierley Hill DY5 61 D1
Monkswood Cres CV2 114 D8
Monkswood Rd B31 103 C2
Monkton Rd B29 85 A2
Monmer Close Ind Est WV13 27 B3
Monmer Cl WV13 27 B3
Monmer Ct WV12 27 B5
Monmer La WV12,WV13 27 B4
Monmore Bsns Pk WV2 39 F7
Monmore Park Ind Est WV2 40 A6
Monmore Rd WV1 40 A7
Monmouth Cl
Coventry CV5 112 B3
Kenilworth CV8 147 F6
Monmouth Dr
Sutton Coldfield B73 45 D3
West Bromwich B71 53 B7
Monmouth Gdns CV10 72 E3
Monmouth Ho B33 69 E2
Monmouth Rd
Birmingham,Bartley Green B32 102 D8
Birmingham,Warley Woods B67 84 E8
Walsall WS2 27 E3
Monnington Ho CV8 148 B7
Monsal Ave WV10 25 E4
Monsaldale Cl WS8 15 D7
Monsal Rd B42 55 C7
Monsieurs Hall La B61 136 B3
Mons Rd DY2 51 F1
Montague Ho
Birmingham B16 65 E1
Warwick CV34 161 A8
Montague Rd
Birmingham,Birches Green B24 57 A1
Birmingham,Edgbaston B16 65 E1
Birmingham,Handsworth B21 65 F8
Smethwick B66 65 C3
Warwick CV34 161 A8
Montague St
Birmingham,Aston B6 67 B8
Birmingham,Bordesley B9 67 A2
Montalt Rd CV3 133 E7
Montana Ave B42 55 A5
Montana Wlk CV10 72 E3
Monteagle Dr DY6 49 D1
Montford Gr DY3 50 D7
Montfort Rd
Coleshill B46 70 F5
Walsall WS2 42 B6
Montfort Wlk B32 84 A2
Montgomery Cl
Coventry CV3 134 C4
Upper Catshill B61 121 A1
Montgomery Cres DY5 81 F7
Montgomery Croft B11 87 C7
Montgomery Prim Sch B11 87 C7
Montgomery Rd
Walsall WS2 27 E2
Whitnash CV31 161 F4
Montgomery St Bsns Ctr B11 87 D7
Montgomery St B11 87 C7
Montgomery Way B8 68 A4
Montgomery Wlk 1 B71 53 D4
Montjoy Cl CV3 134 D7
Montley B77 36 C8
Montpelier Ho CV8 147 F5
Montpelier Rd B24 57 A1
Montpellier Cl CV3 133 C6
Montpellier Gdns DY1 50 E2
Montpellier St B12 87 A6
Montreal Ho B5 86 D7
Montrose Ave CV32 157 B5
Montrose Cl WS11 1 F5
Montrose Dr
Birmingham B35 58 A4
Dudley DY1 62 A8
Nuneaton CV10 72 F3
Montsford Cl B93 127 F6
Monument Ave DY9 81 E4
Monument Dr WV10 12 C8
Monument Ho 6 B16 65 F1
Monument La
Birmingham B45 121 F4
Hagley DY9 99 D7
Sedgley DY3 39 E1
Monument Rd B16 65 F2
Monway Bldgs 1 WS10 41 E3
Monway Ind Est WS10 41 E3
Monway Terr WS10 41 E3
Monwood Gr B91 106 F2
Monyhull Hall Rd B30 104 C3
Moodyscroft Rd B33 69 C3
Moon's La WS6 4 D1
Moons Moat Dr B98 154 E5
Moons Moat Fst Sch B98 154 D5
Moons Pk B98 154 E6
Moorbrooke CV10 72 A7
Moor Cl WS7 7 B7
Moorcroft Cl
Nuneaton CV11 74 B1
Redditch B97 158 B6
Moorcroft Dr WS10 41 C2
Moorcroft Gdns B97 158 B6
Moorcroft Pl 5 B7 67 A4
Moorcroft Rd B13 86 E3
Moorcroft Wood Prim Sch WV14 41 B3
Moor Ct B24 56 F3
Moor Ctr The DY5 61 D3
Moordown Ave B92 89 A2
Moore Cl
Coventry CV6 96 A5
Perton WV6 23 F4
Sutton Coldfield B74 31 F6
Warwick CV34 155 E2
Moore Cres B68 64 C3
Moorend Ave B37 70 B2
Moor End Ct B24 57 B4
Moor End La B24 57 B4
Moore Rd WV12 27 D8
Moore's Row B5 66 F1
Moore St
Cannock WS12 2 C7
Wolverhampton WV1 25 F1
Moore Wlk CV34 161 C7
Moorfield Ave B93 127 F6
Moorfield Dr
Bromsgrove B61 136 F3
Halesowen B63 83 A5
Sutton Coldfield B73 57 A8
Moorfield Rd
Birmingham B34 69 B6
Wolverhampton WV2 39 C7
Moorfields Cl WS9 30 A7
Moorfield The CV3 134 B8
Moorfoot Ave B63 82 C1
Moorgate Cl B98 154 E6
Moorgate Com Prim Sch B79 21 A5
Moorgate Rd B60 151 A2
Moorgate B79 21 A5
Moor Green Inf Sch B13 86 C1
Moor Green Jun Sch B13 86 C1
Moor Green La B13 86 D2
Moor Hall Dr
Clent DY9 100 A1
Sutton Coldfield B75 32 D1
Moor Hall Prim Sch B75 32 D2
Moorhen Cl WS8 15 E7
Moorhill Prim Sch
Cannock WS11 1 E4
Cannock WS11 1 E5
Moorhill Rd CV31 162 A3
Moorhills Croft B90 126 B8
Moor Ho B14 104 C2
Moorings Bsns Pk The CV6 96 A6
Moorings The
Birmingham B18 65 F5
Brierley Hill DY5 62 A4
Oldbury B69 63 E8
Royal Leamington Spa CV31 161 D7
Wolverhampton WV9 10 F2
Moor La B6 56 A4
Moorland Ave WV10 25 C6
Moorland Ct B16 65 D1
Moorland Rd
Birmingham B16 65 D1
Cannock WS11 1 E5
Walsall WS3 28 A8
Moorlands Ave CV8 147 F3
Moorlands Cl 6 B75 46 F6
Moorlands Ct B65 63 D4
Moorlands Dr B90 106 C2
Moorlands Lodge CV8 147 F3
Moorlands Prim Sch B71 53 B8
Moorlands Rd B71 42 C1
Moorlands The B74 45 F8
Moor Lane Ind Est B6 55 F5
Moor La
Rowley Regis B65 63 B3
Shenstone WS14 17 E2
Tamworth B77 22 A6
Tamworth,Bolehall B77 21 D5
Moor Leasow B31 103 C2
Moor Meadow Rd B75 46 D7
Moorpark Cl CV11 79 C8
Moorpark Rd B31 103 A1
Moor Pk
Perton WV6 23 D5
Walsall WS3 14 B3
Moor Pool Ave B17 85 C6
Moor Rd CV10 72 A8
Moor St S WV2 39 C7
Moors Croft B32 84 B1
Moorside Gdns WS2 28 B3
Moorside Rd B14 105 D3
Moors La B31 102 E7
Moors Mill La DY4 52 D7
Moorsom St B6 66 E5
Moorsom Way B60 151 B7
Moor St
Brierley Hill DY5 61 C3
Coventry CV5 112 F1
Moors The B36 68 F8
Moor Street Ind Est DY5 61 C3
Moor Street Queensway B5 164 C2
Moor Street Sta B5 164 C2
Moor St
Tamworth B79 21 A5
Wednesbury WS10 42 B2
West Bromwich B70 53 C2
Moor The B76 58 A8
Moorville Wlk B11 87 A7
Moorwood Cres CV10 72 A8
Moorwood La
Hartshill CV10 72 A7
Hartshill CV10 72 A8
Morar Cl B35 58 C4
Moray Cl
Halesowen B62 83 E8
Hinckley LE10 75 A8
Morcom Rd B11 87 E5
Morcroft WV14 41 A3

Mordaunt Dr B75 . . . . 32 E2
Morden Rd B33. . . . . 68 D3
Mordern Mobile Home Pk
WV10. . . . . 11 C6
Mordiford Cl B98 . . . . 154 E4
Moreall Mdws CV4. . . . . . 132 D3
Morecroft Dr CV34. . . . . . 160 B4
Moreland Croft B76. . . . . . 58 B6
Moreland Pl B31. . . . . 102 F1
Morelands The B31 . . . . . 103 B1
Morestead Ave B26 . . . . . . 89 C5
Moreton Ave
Birmingham B43 . . . . 44 C3
Wolverhampton WV4. . . . . . 39 E4
Moreton Cl
Birmingham,Queen's Park
B32. . . . . 84 F5
Birmingham,Yardley B25 . . . 88 B7
Wednesbury DY4. . . . . 41 B2
Moreton Com Sch WV10. . 11 F1
Moreton Rd
Solihull B90 . . . . 106 C2
Wolverhampton WV10. . . . . 11 D1
Moreton St
Birmingham B1 . . . . 66 B4
Cannock WS11. . . . . 1 F4
Morfa Gdns CV6 . . . . 112 D5
Morford Rd WS9. . . . . 30 A7
Morgan Cl
1 Cradley Heath B64. . . . . 82 E8
Oldbury B69. . . . . 63 D8
Studley B80 . . . . 159 F2
Willenhall WV12 . . . . 27 B4
Morgan Ct B24 . . . . 57 C6
Morgan Gr B36 . . . . 58 F1
Morgan Rd B78. . . . . 21 A2
Morgans Rd CV5. . . . . 111 C4
Morgrove Ave B93 . . . . . . 127 F6
Morillon Ct DY10. . . . . 117 A1
Morjon Dr B43. . . . . 43 F2
Morland Cl CV12. . . . . 79 D2
Morland Dr LE10. . . . . 71 B3
Morland Rd
Birmingham B43 . . . . 44 C4
Coventry CV6. . . . . 95 C2
Morley Gr WV6 . . . . 25 C4
Morley Rd
Birmingham B8 . . . . 68 B6
Burntwood WS7. . . . . 7 B7
Morley Road Sh Ctr WS7 . . .7 B7
Morlich Rise DY5 . . . . 81 B8
Morlings Dr WS7 . . . . 7 B8
Morning Pines DY8 . . . . . . 80 E4
Morningside
Coventry CV5. . . . . 133 B8
Sutton Coldfield B73 . . . . . 46 B6
Mornington Rd B66 . . . . . . 65 B7
Morpeth B77 . . . . 35 C7
Morrell St CV32. . . . . 156 F1
Morris Ave
Coventry CV2. . . . . 114 D4
Walsall WS2 . . . . 27 E2
Morris Cl B27. . . . . 88 D4
Morris Croft B36. . . . . 58 F1
Morris Ct
4 Wolverhampton WV4 . . . 39 F4
Brierley Hill DY5 . . . . 61 B1
Morris Dr
Nuneaton CV11 . . . . 73 D1
Whitnash CV31 . . . . 162 B2
Morris Field Croft B28 . . 105 E4
Morris Hill B78 . . . . 36 F7
Morrison Ave WV10. . . . . . . 25 D8
Morrison Rd DY4 . . . . 52 C4
Morris Rd B8 . . . . 68 C6
Morris St B70. . . . . 53 C1
Morris Wlk B60. . . . . 150 E8
Morsefield La B98 . . . . . . 154 D1
Morse Rd CV31 . . . . 162 B3
Morston B77 . . . . 35 D4
Mortimer Rd CV8 . . . . 147 F2
Mortimers Cl B14 . . . . 105 B1
Morton Cl CV6. . . . . 95 A1
Morton Ho B97 . . . . 153 A3
Morton La B97. . . . . 158 B7
Morton Rd
Brierley Hill DY5 . . . . 81 D7
Harvington DY10 . . . . 118 B2
Morton St CV32. . . . . 156 F1
Morvale Ct DY9. . . . . 81 E5
Morvale Gdns DY9 . . . . 81 E5
Morvale St DY9 . . . . 81 E5
Morven Rd B73 . . . . 46 A3
Morville Cl B93 . . . . 127 D3
Morville Croft WV14 . . . . . 40 B5
Morville Rd DY2 . . . . 62 E4
Morville St B16 . . . . 66 B2
Mosborough Cres B19 . . . 66 C5
Mosedale Dr WV11. . . . . . . 26 F5
Moseley Ave CV6 . . . . 113 A4
Moseley CE Prim Sch B13 86 F2
Moseley Ct
19 Birmingham B13. . . . . . . 87 B2
Essington WV11. . . . . 12 F3
Willenhall WV13 . . . . 26 D1
Moseley Dr B37. . . . . 89 F8
Moseley Gate B13. . . . . 86 F3
Moseley Hall Hospl B13 . . 86 E3
Moseley Old Hall★ WV10 . 12 A5
Moseley Old Hall La
WV10. . . . . 12 A5
Moseley Park Sch WV14. . 40 E8
Moseley Prim Sch CV6 . . 113 A4
Moseley Rd
Bilston WV14. . . . . 40 E8
Birmingham B12 . . . . 86 F6
Kenilworth CV8 . . . . 148 B3
Willenhall WV14,WV13 . . . . 26 D1
Moseley Rd *continued*
Wolverhampton WV10. . . . 12 A4
Moseley Sch B13 . . . . 87 C2
Moseley St
Birmingham B12 . . . . 86 F8
Tipton DY4. . . . . 52 C7
Wolverhampton WV6. . . . . . 25 C4
Mossbank Ave WS7 . . . . 7 A6
Moss Cl
Aldridge WS9. . . . . 30 A5
Walsall WS4 . . . . 29 A3
Moss Cres WS12. . . . . 1 C5
Mossdale Cl CV6. . . . . 113 B6
Mossdale Cres CV10 . . . . . 72 F2
Mossdale B77 . . . . 36 C8
Mossdale Way DY3. . . . . . . 50 E7
Moss Dr B72. . . . . 46 C3
Mossfield Rd B14 . . . . 104 F7
Moss Gdns WV14 . . . . 40 B3
Moss Gr
Birmingham B14 . . . . 104 D6
Kenilworth CV8 . . . . 148 B7
Kingswinford DY6 . . . . 60 D7
Moss House Cl B15 . . . . . . 66 B1
Moss La B98. . . . . 154 F8
Moss Lane Cl B98. . . . . . . 154 F8
Mossley Cl WS3. . . . . 13 F1
Mossley La WS3 . . . . 13 F2
Mossley Prim Sch WS3. . . 13 F2
Mosspaul Cl CV32. . . . . . . 156 D2
Moss Rd WS11. . . . . 2 A3
Moss St
12 Royal Leamington Spa
CV31. . . . . 162 A7
Cannock WS11. . . . . 2 A4
Mossvale Cl B64. . . . . 62 F1
Mossvale Gr B8. . . . . 67 F5
Moss Way B74. . . . . 44 F7
Mosswood St WS11 . . . . 4 D7
Mostyn Cres B71. . . . . 53 A7
Mostyn Rd
Birmingham,Edgbaston
B16. . . . . 65 F2
Birmingham,Handsworth
B21. . . . . 65 F8
Mostyn St WV1 . . . . 25 B4
Mother Teresa Ho B70 . . . 53 B3
Mott Cl DY4 . . . . 52 C8
Mottistone Cl CV3 . . . . . . 133 D6
Mottram Cl B70. . . . . 53 B2
Mottrams Cl B72. . . . . 46 C2
Mott St B19 . . . . 164 B4
Moule Cl DY11. . . . . 116 C6
Moundsley Gr B14 . . . . . . 105 A3
Moundsley Ho B14. . . . . . 104 F2
Mounds The B38. . . . . 123 E8
Mountain Ash Dr DY9 . . . . 81 C2
Mountain Ash Rd WS8 . . . 15 E5
Mountain Pine Cl WS12 . . . 2 A8
Mount Ave
Brierley Hill DY5 . . . . 61 C4
Cannock WS12. . . . . 2 B7
Mountbatten Ave CV8 . . . 148 C3
Mountbatten Cl B70. . . . . . 53 F2
Mountbatten Rd WS2 . . . . 27 F2
Mount Cl
Birmingham B13 . . . . 86 F4
Cheslyn Hay WS6. . . . . 4 E2
Dudley DY3 . . . . 50 C2
Wombourne WV5. . . . . 49 A7
Mount Ct WV6 . . . . 24 B2
Mount Dr
Bedworth CV12 . . . . 78 A3
Wombourne WV5. . . . . 49 A7
Mountfield Cl B14 . . . . . . 105 A2
Mount Field Ct CV1 . . . . . 165 D4
Mountford Cl 1 B65 . . . . . 63 C3
Mountford Cres WS9. . . . . 30 C8
Mountford Dr B75 . . . . 46 B8
Mountford Ho B70 . . . . 53 E1
Mountford La WV14. . . . . . . 40 D6
Mountford Rd B90 . . . . . . 105 D1
Mountford St B11. . . . . 87 D5
Mount Gdns CV5. . . . . 133 B8
Mount Grace High Sch
LE10 . . . . 71 E1
Mountjoy Cres B92. . . . . . . 89 C3
Mount La
Clent DY9. . . . . 99 E4
Dudley DY3 . . . . 50 C2
Mount Nod Prim Sch
CV5. . . . . 112 A3
Mount Nod Way CV5 . . . . 112 B3
Mount Pleasant Ave B21 . 54 E1
Mount Pleasant
Bilston WV14. . . . . 40 E6
Birmingham,King's Heath
B14. . . . . 86 F1
Birmingham,Small Heath
B10. . . . . 67 B1
Brierley Hill DY5 . . . . 61 E1
Cheslyn Hay WS6. . . . . 4 E2
Mount Pleasant Cotts
CV2 . . . . 115 A7
Mount Pleasant Ct 1 B10 67 B1
Mount Pleasant DY6 . . . . . 60 C4
Mount Pleasant Mobile
Home Pk B77 . . . . 21 C1
Mount Pleasant Prim Sch
DY5. . . . . 61 E1
Mount Pleasant Rd CV12 . 78 A3
Mount Pleasant B97 . . . . 153 D2
Mount Pleasant St
Dudley WV14 . . . . 51 B8
West Bromwich B70 . . . . . . 53 C2
Mount Pleasant B77 . . . . . 35 C8
Mount Pleasant Terr
CV10 . . . . 72 F6
Mountrath St WS1. . . . . . . 28 E1
Mount Rd
Birmingham B21 . . . . 65 D7
Burntwood WS7. . . . . 7 B6
Fairfield B61 . . . . 120 E2
Hinckley LE10 . . . . 75 D8
Oldbury B69. . . . . 63 C8
Rowley Regis B65 . . . . 63 E3
Stourbridge,Stambermill
DY8. . . . . 81 B5
Stourbridge,Wordsley DY8 . 60 E2
Walsall WS3 . . . . 15 A4
Willenhall WV13 . . . . 40 E8
Wolverhampton,Goldthorn Hill
WV4 . . . . 39 A4
Wolverhampton,Tettenhall Wood
WV6 . . . . 24 A3
Wolverhampton,Woodcross
WV4 . . . . 39 F2
Wombourne WV5. . . . . 49 A7
Mount Road Ind Est WS7 . . 7 B6
Mountserrat Rd B60 . . . . 137 B1
Mount Side St WS12 . . . . . . 2 C7
Mounts Rd WS10. . . . . 41 F2
Mount St
Birmingham B7 . . . . 67 C7
Cannock WS12. . . . . 2 B7
Coventry CV5. . . . . 112 F2
Halesowen B63 . . . . 83 A3
Nuneaton CV11 . . . . 73 B4
Redditch B98. . . . . 153 E3
Mount Street Bsns Ctr B7 67 C6
Mount Street Ind Est B7 . 67 D7
Mount Street Pas CV11. . . 73 B4
Mount St
Stourbridge DY8 . . . . 81 B5
Tipton DY4. . . . . 52 C6
Walsall WS1 . . . . 42 E8
Mounts Way B7. . . . . 67 C7
Mount The
Birmingham B23 . . . . 56 D1
Coventry CV3. . . . . 133 E8
Cradley Heath B64 . . . . 63 A1
Curdworth B76 . . . . 59 C6
Mount Vernon Dr B61. . . . 137 A5
Mount View B75 . . . . 46 E4
Mountwood Covert WV6 . 24 B3
Mousehall Farm Rd DY5. . 81 D7
Mouse Hill WS3. . . . . 14 F3
Mouse La DY11 . . . . 116 B8
Mousesweet Cl DY2. . . . . . 62 E4
Mousesweet La DY2. . . . . . 62 E3
Mousesweet Wlk B64 . . . . 82 B8
Mowbray Cl B45 . . . . 102 A2
Mowbray St
Birmingham B5 . . . . 86 E8
Coventry CV2. . . . . 113 F3
Mowe Croft B37 . . . . 90 B7
Mows Hill Rd B94. . . . . . . 143 A1
Moxhull Cl WV12. . . . . 13 C1
Moxhull Dr B76. . . . . 57 E7
Moxhull Gdns WV12. . . . . . 13 C1
Moxhull Rd B37. . . . . 70 A5
Moxley Ind Ctr WS10 . . . . . 41 C4
Moxley Jct WS10. . . . . 41 B4
Moxley Rd WS10. . . . . 41 C5
Moyle Cres CV5. . . . . 111 D4
Moyle Dr B63. . . . . 82 B7
Moyses Croft B66. . . . . 65 A8
Mozart Ct WS11. . . . . 2 C2
Muchall Rd WV4 . . . . 39 A5
Much Park St CV1. . . . . . . 165 C2
Mucklow Hill B62. . . . . 83 D5
Mucklow Hill Trad Est
B62. . . . . 83 C5
Muirfield Cl WS3 . . . . 14 A3
Muirfield Cres B69. . . . . . . 63 B7
Muirfield Gdns B38 . . . . . 103 D1
Muirfields Cl CV11 . . . . . . 79 C8
Muirfield B77. . . . . 22 C5
Muirville Cl 1 DY8. . . . . . . 60 D3
Mulberry Cl CV32 . . . . 157 A2
Mulberry Ct CV8 . . . . 147 F4
Mulberry Dr
3 Lichfield WS13. . . . . 9 E8
5 Warwick CV34 . . . . 160 F8
Birmingham B13 . . . . 87 B1
Mulberry Gn DY1 . . . . 50 F5
Mulberry Pl WS3. . . . . 13 F1
Mulberry Rd
Birmingham B30 . . . . 103 C5
Cannock WS11. . . . . 1 E3
Coventry CV6. . . . . 114 A7
Walsall WS3 . . . . 14 A1
Mulberry Way CV10 . . . . . 72 A8
Mulberry Wlk B74 . . . . 44 E8
Muldoon Cl WS11. . . . . 2 B4
Mullard Dr CV31 . . . . 162 B3
Mull Cl B45. . . . . 101 E1
Mull Croft B36. . . . . 70 B7
Mullein B74 . . . . 31 F5
Mullensgrove Rd B37 . . . . 70 A5
Mullett Rd WV11. . . . . 26 B7
Mullett St DY5. . . . . 61 B5
Mulliners Cl 2 B37 . . . . . . 70 D2
Mulliner St CV6. . . . . 113 F5
Mullion Croft B38. . . . . . . 103 E1
Mulroy Rd B74. . . . . 46 B6
Mulwych Rd B33. . . . . 69 E3
Munches La B62 . . . . 120 C8
Munnings Dr LE10 . . . . 71 A3
Munro Cl DY10. . . . . 117 C6
Munsley Cl B98 . . . . 154 F2
Munslow Gr B31. . . . . 122 F8
Muntz Cres B94. . . . . 143 C6
Muntz Ho B16 . . . . 66 A1
Muntz St B10. . . . . 87 D8
Murcott Ct CV31 . . . . 162 A3
Murcott Rd E CV31. . . . . . 162 A3
Murcott Rd W CV31 . . . . . 162 A3
Murcroft Rd DY9. . . . . 81 E1
Murdoch Dr DY6. . . . . 60 C7
Murdoch Rd WV14. . . . . 41 A6
Murdock Ct WV12. . . . . 27 D7
Murdock Gr B21 . . . . 65 E7
Murdock Rd
Birmingham B21 . . . . 65 E8
Smethwick B66 . . . . 65 D6
Murdock Way 1 WS2 . . . . 28 A5
Murray Ct
Birmingham B20 . . . . 55 A2
Sutton Coldfield B73 . . . . . . 46 A3
Murrayfield Way CV3. . . . 115 B1
Murray Ho WV14. . . . . 40 D5
Murray Rd CV6 . . . . 113 A7
Murrell Cl B5. . . . . 86 D7
Murton B77 . . . . 36 C8
Musborough Cl B36. . . . . . 58 C1
Muscott Gr B17. . . . . 85 B5
Muscovy Rd B23. . . . . 56 C3
Musgrave Cl B76. . . . . 46 E3
Musgrave Rd B18. . . . . 65 F6
Mushroom Hall Rd B68. . . 64 B5
Musketts Ct B97 . . . . 153 B2
Musk La DY3 . . . . 50 B3
Musk La W DY3. . . . . 50 B3
Mus of British Road
Transport★ CV1 . . . . 165 B3
Mus of Cannock Chase★
WS12 . . . . 2 D6
Mus of the Jewellery
Quarter★ B19 . . . . 66 C5
Muswell Cl B91 . . . . 107 D5
Muxloe Cl WS3 . . . . 14 A3
Myatt Ave
Aldridge WS9. . . . . 29 F5
Burntwood WS7. . . . . 7 A7
Wolverhampton WV2. . . . . . 39 E6
Myatt Cl WV2. . . . . 39 E6
Myatt Way WS9. . . . . 29 F5
Myddleton St B18. . . . . 66 A4
Myles Ct DY5 . . . . 61 D4
Mylgrove CV3. . . . . 133 D3
Mynors Cres B47 . . . . 125 A6
Myring Dr B75. . . . . 46 F5
Myrtle Ave
4 Birmingham,Balsall Heath
B12. . . . . 87 A5
Birmingham,Highter's Heath
B14. . . . . 104 F2
Redditch B98. . . . . 153 E2
Myrtle Cl WV12 . . . . 27 E7
Myrtle Gr
10 Birmingham B19. . . . . . . 66 C8
Coventry CV5. . . . . 112 F1
Wolverhampton WV3. . . . . . 38 E6
Myrtle Pl B29. . . . . 86 B2
Myrtle Rd DY1 . . . . 51 B3
Myrtle St WV2 . . . . 39 F6
Myrtle Terr DY4. . . . . 41 B2
Myton Cres CV34. . . . . 161 C6
Myton Crofts CV31 . . . . . . 161 D7
Myton Dr B90. . . . . 105 D1
Myton Gdns CV34 . . . . 161 A6
Myton La CV34. . . . . 161 C6
Myton Rd CV31,CV34. . . . . 161 B6
Myton Sch CV34 . . . . 161 B6
Mytton Cl DY2 . . . . 51 E1
Mytton Gr DY4. . . . . 51 E5
Mytton Rd
Birmingham B30 . . . . 103 C5
Water Orton B46. . . . . 58 F3
Myvod Rd WS10 . . . . 42 A5

N

Naden Ho WS12 . . . . 1 C5
Naden Rd B19 . . . . 66 B6
Nadin Rd B73. . . . . 57 A8
Naesby Rd WV6. . . . . 23 F3
Nafford Gr B14 . . . . 104 F2
Nagersfield Rd DY5 . . . . . . 61 A2
Nailcote Ave CV4 . . . . 131 C8
Nailcote La CV7. . . . . 131 A7
Nailers Cl
Birmingham B32 . . . . 83 F2
Stoke Heath B60 . . . . 150 E6
Nailers Ct 3 B60 . . . . 136 F2
Nailers Dr WS7 . . . . 7 D6
Nailors Fold WV14 . . . . 40 D2
Nailstone Cres B27 . . . . . 106 C8
Nailsworth Rd
Dorridge B93. . . . . 127 D2
Redditch B98. . . . . 153 F2
Nairn Cl
Birmingham B28 . . . . 105 F5
Nuneaton CV10 . . . . 73 A2
Redditch B98. . . . . 154 E4
Nairn Rd WS3 . . . . 14 A4
Nally Dr WV14 . . . . 40 A2
Nanaimo Way DY6 . . . . 61 A4
Nansen Prim Sch B8. . . . . 67 F5
Nansen Rd
Birmingham B8 . . . . 67 F5
Birmingham,Sparkhill B11. . 87 C3
Nantmel Gr B32 . . . . 102 C8
Naomi Way WS9. . . . . 16 B4
Napier Dr DY4 . . . . 52 C6
Napier Rd
Walsall WS2 . . . . 28 A5
Wolverhampton WV2. . . . . . 39 D7
Napier St CV1 . . . . 113 E3
Napier B77 . . . . 21 E3
Napton Cl B98 . . . . 154 D1
Napton Dr CV32. . . . . 157 A2
Napton Gn CV5 . . . . 112 A3
Napton Gr B29. . . . . 84 F2
Narberth Way CV2 . . . . . . 114 F8
Narraway Gr DY4 . . . . 52 D8
Narrowboat Cl CV6 . . . . . . 96 B6
Narrowboat Way DY5,DY2. 62 A5
Narrow Hall Mdw CV34. . 160 B4
Narrow La
Brownhills WS8. . . . . 15 F8
Halesowen B62 . . . . 83 E8
Walsall WS2 . . . . 42 B7
Narrows The 1 LE10. . . . . 75 E8
Naseby Cl
Coventry CV3. . . . . 134 F8
Redditch B98. . . . . 154 D6
Naseby Dr B63. . . . . 82 D2
Naseby Rd
Birmingham B8 . . . . 67 F5
Solihull B91 . . . . 107 B6
Nash Ave WV6. . . . . 23 E3
Nash Cl B65 . . . . 63 C1
Nash Croft B37 . . . . 90 B8
Nashe Cl DY10 . . . . 117 C5
Nash Ho B15 . . . . 86 D8
Nash La
Belbroughton DY9 . . . . . . 119 D7
Lichfield WS13. . . . . 3 A5
Nash Rd B98. . . . . 154 B1
Nash Sq B42. . . . . 55 D4
Nash Wlk 8 B66. . . . . 65 C5
Nately Gr B29. . . . . 85 C3
Nathan Cl B75 . . . . 46 C8
Nathaniel Newton Inf Sch
CV10. . . . . 72 B8
National Ex Ctr B40. . . . . . 90 E4
National Indoor Arena★
B1. . . . . 66 B2
National Motorcycle Mus
The★ B92. . . . . 91 A2
National Sea Life Ctr★ B1 66 B2
Naul's Mill Ho CV1 . . . . . . 165 B4
Naunton Cl B29. . . . . 103 A7
Naunton Rd WS2. . . . . 28 A3
Navenby Cl B90. . . . . 105 C3
Navigation Dr DY5 . . . . 62 A4
Navigation La B71 . . . . 42 F2
Navigation Rdbt DY4 . . . . . 52 E6
Navigation St
Birmingham B2 . . . . 164 B2
Walsall WS2 . . . . 28 D1
Wolverhampton WV1. . . . . . 25 E1
Navigation Way
Birmingham B18 . . . . 65 F5
Cannock WS11. . . . . 2 A2
Coventry CV6. . . . . 114 A8
West Bromwich B70 . . . . . . 52 F2
Nayland Croft B28 . . . . . . 106 A5
Naylor Cl DY11. . . . . 116 B3
Naylors Gr DY3 . . . . 50 E4
Neachells Ct WV13. . . . . . . 26 E1
Neachells Lane Ind Est
WV11 . . . . 26 D4
Neachells Lane Island
WV11. . . . . 26 D4
Neachells La
Wednesfield WV11 . . . . 26 D5
Willenhall WV13 . . . . 26 D3
Neachless Ave WV5. . . . . . . 49 A5
Neachley Gr B33. . . . . 68 F4
Neal Ct CV2 . . . . 115 A8
Neale Ave CV5. . . . . 112 A6
Neale Cl CV12 . . . . 79 C1
Neale Ho
6 West Bromwich B70. . . . 53 D1
Wolverhampton WV2. . . . . . 39 C7
Neale St WS2. . . . . 28 C2
Neander B79 . . . . 20 F6
Near High Dr 5 DY4 . . . . . 52 B5
Nearhill Rd B38. . . . . 123 C8
Near Lands Cl B32 . . . . 84 B4
Nearmoor Rd B34. . . . . 69 D6
Near Oak Ho B32 . . . . 102 D8
Neasden Gr B44 . . . . 56 B8
Neath Rd WS3 . . . . 13 F2
Neath Way
Dudley DY3 . . . . 51 A6
Walsall WS3 . . . . 13 F2
Nebsworth Cl B90. . . . . . . 106 D5
Nechells Jun & Inf Sch
B7. . . . . 67 C8
Nechells Park Rd B7 . . . . . 67 C7
Nechells Parkway B7 . . . . 67 A5
Nechells Pl B7. . . . . 67 C5
Needham St B7. . . . . 67 C7
Needhill Cl B93 . . . . 127 F6
Needle Cl B80 . . . . 159 E4
Needle Mill La B98. . . . . . 153 E6
Needlers End La CV7. . . . 130 A7
Needless Alley B2 . . . . . . 164 B2
Needwood Cl WV2. . . . . 39 B6
Needwood Dr WV4. . . . . 39 F4
Needwood Gr B71 . . . . 42 E1
Needwood Hill WS13. . . . . . 3 A2
Needwood Ho B27 . . . . 88 D3
Neighbrook Cl B97. . . . . . 152 F2
Neilston St 13 CV31 . . . . . 162 A7
Nelson Ave
Bilston WV14. . . . . 40 C7
Warwick CV34 . . . . 161 A8
Nelson Ct 5 B13 . . . . 86 F4
Nelson Dr
Cannock WS12. . . . . 2 F4
Hinckley LE10 . . . . 71 D4
Nelson Ho DY4 . . . . 52 A7
Nelson La CV34 . . . . 161 A8

Nelson Mandela Sch B12 87 B5
Nelson Prim Sch B1 66 B3
Nelson Rd
Birmingham B6 55 F1
Dudley DY1 51 B1
Nelson St
[7] Coventry CV1 113 E4
Birmingham B1 66 B3
Oldbury B69 64 B6
West Bromwich B71 53 C5
Willenhall WV13 27 B3
Nemesia B77 22 B4
Nene Cl
Coventry CV3 134 D7
Stourbridge DY8 81 A5
Nene Way B36 69 F8
Neptune Ind Est WV13 41 B8
Neptune St DY4 51 E5
Nesbit Gr B9 68 B3
Nesfield Cl B38 103 C1
Nesfield Gr B92 109 B7
Nesscliffe Gr B23 56 D7
Nest Comm WS3 14 F5
Neston Gr B33 68 C2
Nestor Ho B13 105 D7
Netheravon Cl B14 104 D1
Nether Beacon WS13 3 A1
Netherbridge Ave WS14 9 E7
Netherbrook Prim Sch DY2 62 D2
Netherby Rd DY3 50 C8
Nethercote Gdns B90 105 E3
Netherdale Cl B72 57 C7
Netherdale Rd B14 105 A1
Netherend Cl B63 82 A7
Netherend La B63 82 B7
Netherend Sq B63 82 A7
Netherfield Gdns B27 88 B3
Netherfield B98 159 A8
Nethergate DY3 50 F5
Nether La WS7 7 D8
Netherley Ct LE10 71 D3
Netherley Rd LE10 71 D3
Nethermill Rd [1] CV6 113 A5
Netherstone Gr B74 31 F5
Nether Stowe High Sch WS13 3 B1
Netherstowe La WS13 3 D2
Netherstowe WS13 3 C2
Netherton Bsns Pk DY2 62 E3
Netherton CE Prim Sch DY2 62 B4
Netherton Gr B33 69 C3
Netherwood Cl B91 106 E6
Netherwood La B93 145 A7
Nethy Dr WV6 24 B5
Netley Gr B11 87 F3
Netley Ho B32 84 F5
Netley Rd WS3 13 E2
Netley Way WS3 13 E2
Network Pk B7 67 C4
Nevada Way B37 70 C1
Neve Ave WV10 25 F8
Nevill Cl CV31 161 F6
Neville Ave
Kidderminster DY11 116 D3
Wolverhampton WV4 39 D5
Neville Cl B98 154 A5
Neville Ct
[5] Warwick CV34 160 E6
Birmingham B13 104 F6
Kidderminster DY11 116 D3
Neville Gr CV34 155 F1
Neville Ho DY3 50 D7
Neville Rd
Birmingham,Castle Bromwich B36 58 E1
Birmingham,Stockland Green B23 56 C3
Solihull B90 105 F1
Neville St B77 21 E3
Neville Wlk B35 58 A2
Nevill St B79 21 A5
Nevin Gr B42 55 C5
Nevis Ct WV6 24 E2
Nevis Gr WV12 13 B1
Nevison Gr B43 44 B4
Newall Ho B97 153 D2
Newark Croft B26 89 B6
Newark Rd
Dudley DY2 62 D2
Willenhall WV12 27 C7
New Art Gall The★ WS2 28 E2
New Ash Dr CV5 111 F5
Newbank Gr B9 68 A3
New Barns La WS14 17 B3
New Bartholomew St B5 164 D2
New Birmingham Rd B69, DY2 52 B1
New Bldgs
Coventry CV1 165 C3
Darlaston WS10 41 E6
Hinckley LE10 71 D1
Newbold Cl
Bentley Heath B93 127 F5
Coventry CV3 114 F1
Lichfield WS13 9 A5
Newbold Comyn Pk★ CV32 162 D8
Newbold Croft B7 67 B5
Newbold Ct B63 83 B3
Newbold Lawn CV32 162 A8
Newbold Pl CV32 162 A8
Newbolds Rd WV10 26 A6
Newbold St CV32 162 A8
Newbold Terr E CV32 162 B8
Newbold Terr CV32 162 A8
Newbolt Rd WV14 40 E6
Newbolt St WS5 42 E5
New Bond St
[2] Dudley DY2 62 D8
Birmingham B9 67 B1
Newborough Gr B28,B90 105 F3
Newborough Rd
Birmingham B28 105 F4
Solihull B90 106 A3
Newbourne Hill B48 139 E4
Newbridge Ave WV6 24 E3
Newbridge Cres WV6 24 E4
Newbridge Dr WV6 24 E4
Newbridge Gdns WV6 24 E4
Newbridge Mews [3] WV6 24 F4
Newbridge Prep Sch WV6 24 E4
Newbridge Rd
Birmingham B9 68 B1
Kingswinford DY6 60 C8
Newbridge St WV6 24 F4
Newbrook Farm★ B32 101 D4
New Brook St [3] CV32 161 E8
Newburgh Cres CV34 160 E8
Newburgh Prim Sch CV34 160 C4
Newburn Croft B32 84 B5
Newbury Cl
[4] Royal Leamington Spa CV31 162 C6
Great Wyrley WS6 4 F2
Halesowen B62 83 D3
Lower Marlbrook B61 121 B1
Newbury Ho [1] B69 63 D5
Newbury La B69 63 D6
Newbury Rd
Birmingham B19 66 E7
Norton Canes WS11 6 A5
Stourbridge DY8 60 D1
Wolverhampton WV10 11 C2
Newbury Wlk B65 63 C6
Newby Cl CV3 133 E6
Newby Gr B37 70 B5
New Canal St B5 164 D2
Newcastle Croft B35 58 C3
New Century Pk CV3 114 C2
New Century Way CV11 73 B4
Newchurch Gdns [6] B24 56 E2
New Church Rd B73 57 A8
New Cole Hall La B33,B34 69 B5
New College Cl WS1 43 A7
Newcombe Rd
Birmingham B21 54 D2
Coventry CV5 113 A1
Newcome Ct B24 57 D4
Newcomen Cl
Bedworth CV12 95 D8
Burntwood WS7 7 C8
Newcomen Ct WS4 29 B7
Newcomen Dr DY4 51 F3
Newcomen Rd CV12 77 D1
New Coppice Ct B97 158 E6
Newcott Cl WV9 10 F2
New Coventry Rd B26 89 A5
New Croft B19 66 E7
Newcroft Gr B26 88 E7
New Cross Ave WV10 26 B4
New Cross Hospl WV11 26 B5
New Cross Ind Est WV1 26 A3
New Cross Junc WV10 26 B4
New Cross St
Darlaston WS10 41 D5
Tipton DY4 51 E5
New Ct [7] DY5 61 D2
Newdegate Cl CV12 78 A4
Newdegate Pl CV11 73 C4
Newdegate Rd CV12 78 A3
Newdegate St CV11 73 C4
Newdigate Prim Sch CV12 77 C1
Newdigate Rd
Coventry CV6 113 F6
Sutton Coldfield B75 47 A5
Newdigate CV31 162 C5
New Dudley Rd DY6 60 C8
Newells Dr DY4 52 D7
Newells Rd B26 89 B8
New England Cl B69 52 E1
New England B62 83 E7
Newent Cl WV12 27 D3
Newent Rd B31 103 C4
New Ent Workshops B18 66 A5
Newey Ave CV12 95 D8
Newey Cl B45 122 A6
Newey Dr CV8 148 A2
Newey Rd
Birmingham B28 105 F6
Coventry CV2 114 D4
Wednesfield WV11 27 A8
Newey St DY1 51 A2
New Farm Rd DY9 81 C4
Newfield Ave CV8 148 B3
Newfield Cl
Solihull B91 107 D6
Walsall WS2 28 C5
Newfield Cres B63 83 A5
Newfield Dr DY6 60 E4
Newfield Gdns DY9 99 A4
Newfield La B63 83 B5
Newfield Park Prim Sch B63 83 A5
Newfield Pl DY9 99 A4
Newfield Rd
Coventry CV1 113 C5
Oldbury B69 63 F8
West Hagley DY9 99 A4
New Forest Rd WS3 28 F6
Newgale Wlk CV31 162 C7
New Gas St B70 53 A5
New Gate Ct CV1 165 C2
Newgate St WS7 7 A5
New Gdns WS7 6 F5
New Green Pk CV2 114 D7
Newhall Cres WS11 2 B3
Newhall Ct [9] B3 66 C3
New Hall Dr
Sutton Coldfield,Maney B75 46 D4
Sutton Coldfield,Wylde Green B76 46 E2
Newhall Farm Cl B76 46 D4
Newhall Gdns WS11 1 F2
Newhall Hill B1 66 C3
Newhall Ho [5] WS1 42 E8
New Hall Inf Sch B75 47 B5
New Hall Jun Sch B75 47 B5
Newhall Pl B1 66 C3
New Hall Pl WS10 42 A3
Newhall Rd
Coventry CV2 114 D7
Rowley Regis B65 63 C3
Newhall St
Birmingham B3 164 B3
Cannock WS11 1 D1
Tipton DY4 51 E8
Walsall WS1 42 E8
West Bromwich B70 53 C2
New Hall St WV13 27 B2
Newhall Wlk B72 46 C4
Newham Gn CV10 72 C7
Newhampton Rd E WV1 163 A4
New Hampton Rd W WV6 24 F4
Newhaven Cl
Birmingham B7 67 A5
Coventry CV6 112 E6
Newhay Croft B19 66 C7
New Heath Cl WV11 26 B5
New Henry St B68 64 B4
Newhope Cl [2] B15 86 D8
New Hope Rd B66 65 C4
New Horse Rd WS6 4 E3
Newhouse Croft CV7 130 B6
Newhouse Farm Cl B76 46 F3
New House Farm Dr B31 103 C6
Newick Ave B74 31 B3
Newick Gr B14 104 C4
Newick St DY2 62 C4
Newington Cl CV6 112 D6
Newington Rd B37 90 B8
New Inn Rd [2] B19 66 D8
New Inns Cl B21 65 D8
New Inns La B45 101 E1
New Invention Inf & Jun Schs WV12 27 C7
New John St W B19 66 D5
New John St
Birmingham B6 66 E5
Halesowen B62 83 C8
New King St [7] DY1 51 C1
Newland Cl
Redditch B98 159 B7
Walsall WS4 15 C2
Newland Ct B23 56 C3
Newland Gdns B64 82 E7
Newland Gr DY2 61 F7
Newland La CV7 95 B7
Newland Rd
Birmingham B9 67 F1
Coventry CV1 113 D5
Royal Leamington Spa CV32 157 C3
Newlands Cl
Kidderminster DY11 116 C7
Willenhall WV13 27 A1
Newlands Ct
Cannock WS12 5 E8
Coventry CV3 113 F2
Newlands Dr B62 83 E7
Newlands Gn B66 65 A4
Newlands La
Birmingham B37 90 A6
Norton Canes WS12 5 D8
Newlands Rd
Bentley Heath B93 127 F4
Birmingham B30 104 C7
Newlands The
Birmingham B34 69 C7
Studley B80 159 D3
New Landywood La WS6 13 E7
New Leasow B76 58 A7
Newlyn Cl
Lichfield WS14 9 D7
Nuneaton CV11 73 F4
Newlyn Rd
Birmingham B31 102 F3
Cradley Heath B64 82 D8
Newman Ave WV4 39 F4
Newman Cl CV12 78 B4
Newman College Cl B32 102 C8
Newman Coll of Higher Ed B32 102 C8
Newman Pl WV14 40 F7
Newman Rd
Birmingham B24 56 F4
Wednesbury DY4 41 C1
Wolverhampton WV10 12 A1
Newmans Cl B66 65 C4
Newman Way B45 122 A6
Newmarket Cl
Coventry CV6 96 B4
Wolverhampton WV6 25 A5
Newmarket Rd WS11 6 B4
New Market St B3 164 B3
Newmarket Way B36 68 B7
Newmarsh Rd B76 58 A6
New Meadow Cl B31 103 B2
New Meadow Rd B98 154 B3
New Meeting St B69 64 A8
New Mill La B78 35 A7
New Mills St WS1 42 D7
New Mill St DY2 51 C1
Newmore Gdns WS5 43 C5
New Moseley Rd B12 87 A8
Newnham Gr B23 56 E6
Newnham Ho B36 70 B5
Newnham Rd
Birmingham B16 65 C2
Coventry CV1 113 F5
Royal Leamington Spa CV32 157 B3
Newnham Rise B90 106 D3
New Oscott Prim Sch B73 45 C3
New Park Sch WV6 24 F5
New Penkridge Rd WS11 1 C1
New Plant La WS7 6 C8
New Pool Rd B64 82 B8
Newport Cl B97 158 B6
Newport Rd
Birmingham,Balsall Heath B12 87 A4
Birmingham,Buckland End B36 68 F8
Coventry CV6 95 D1
Newport St
[4] Walsall WS1 28 E1
Wolverhampton WV10 25 E4
Newport B77 21 F5
Newquay Cl
Hinckley LE10 71 E4
Nuneaton CV11 73 F5
Walsall WS5 43 E7
Newquay Rd WS5 43 D7
New Railway St WV13 27 B2
New Rd
Aldridge WS9 30 A5
Ash Green CV7 95 B6
Astwood Bank B96 158 E1
Birmingham B45 121 F7
Bromsgrove B60 137 A1
Bromsgrove,Sidemoor B61 136 E3
Brownhills WS8 15 F7
Burntwood WS7 7 B6
Coventry CV6 94 F1
Dudley DY2 62 C7
Fairfield B61 120 E2
Halesowen B63 83 B4
Hinckley LE10 76 A6
Hollywood B47 125 A8
Kidderminster DY10 116 E5
Shenstone WS14 17 F6
Shuttington B79 22 E8
Solihull B91 107 D3
Stourbridge DY8 81 A5
Studley B80 159 E3
Tamworth B77 35 F7
Tipton DY4 52 D6
Water Orton B46 59 B3
Willenhall WV13 27 A1
Wolverhampton,Newbridge WV6 24 E4
Wolverhampton,Scotlands WV10 26 B8
New Row B78 34 E5
New Rowley Rd DY2 62 E7
New Shipton Cl B76 46 F1
Newshire Ind Est B11 87 D6
Newsholme Cl [1] CV34 155 E1
New Spring St N B18 66 A4
New Spring St B18 66 A4
New St
[6] Cannock,Mill Green WS11 4 E8
Bedworth CV12 78 C2
Birchmoor B78 36 E7
Birmingham B23 57 A4
Birmingham,Castle Bromwich B36 69 B8
Birmingham,Digbeth B2 164 C2
Birmingham,Erdington B23 56 F5
Birmingham,Frankley B45 102 A1
Brierley Hill DY5 82 A8
Bulkington CV12 79 D2
Burntwood,Chase Terrace WS7 6 E8
Burntwood,Chasetown WS7 6 E5
Cannock,Bridgtown WS11 4 D6
Cannock WS12 2 C4
Cubbington CV32 157 E5
Darlaston WS10 41 D6
Dudley,Eve Hill DY1 51 D1
Dudley,Gornalwood DY3 50 C3
Newstead Ave LE10 75 D4
Newstead Cl CV11 73 F2
Newstead Rd B44 45 B3
Newstead B79 20 D6
Newstead Way CV3 115 B1
New St
Essington WV11 13 A3
Ettingshall WV2 40 A6
Fazeley B78 35 B8
Great Wyrley WS6 5 A1
Hinckley LE10 71 D1
Kenilworth CV8 147 F6
Kingswinford DY6 60 D4
Kingswinford,Wall Heath DY6 60 C8
New Street N B71 53 D3
New Street Sta B2 164 B2
New St
Royal Leamington Spa CV31 162 A7
New St *continued*
Smethwick B66 65 B6
Stourbridge DY8 80 F5
Stourbridge,Wordsley DY8 60 D2
Tamworth,Bolehall B77 21 E4
Tamworth,Mount Pleasant B77 21 C1
Tipton DY4 51 F5
Walsall,Rushall WS4 29 B7
Walsall,The Chuckery WS1 28 F1
Walsall,Wallington Heath WS3 14 B1
Walsall WS4 15 D1
Warwick CV34 160 E6
Wednesbury WS10 41 F1
West Bromwich,Hill Top B70 53 A7
West Bromwich,Mayer's Green B70 53 D3
Willenhall WV13 26 E1
Wolverhampton,Merry Hill WV3 38 D7
Wolverhampton,Parkfield WV4 39 E6
New Summer St B19 164 B4
New Swan La B70 53 A5
New Swinford Hall DY9 81 C4
Newton Chambers [1] B2 164 B2
Newton Cl
Birmingham B43 43 C1
Coventry CV2 114 F7
Redditch B98 159 A6
Newton Gdns B43 54 B8
Newton Gr [5] B29 85 F2
Newton Ind Est B9 67 D2
Newton Manor Cl B43 54 D8
Newton Pl
Birmingham B18 66 A7
Walsall WS2 28 B6
Newton Rd
Birmingham,Balsall Heath B11 87 B5
Birmingham,Newton B43 54 B8
Bromsgrove B60 151 A7
Hinckley LE10 74 E7
Knowle B93 128 B7
Walsall WS2 28 B5
West Bromwich B71 53 F6
Newton's Coll WS13 9 B8
Newton Sq
Birmingham B43 43 E1
Bromsgrove B60 151 A7
Newton St
Birmingham B4 164 C3
West Bromwich B71 53 E7
Newton Works B60 151 A6
Newtown Bldgs CV12 78 B3
New Town DY5 61 C4
Newtown Dr B19 66 C6
New Town DY2 62 D1
Newtown La
Cradley Heath B64 62 D1
Madeley Heath B62 120 D8
Romsley B62 101 D2
Newtown Middleway B6 66 E5
Newtown Prim Sch B70 52 D3
Newtown Rd
Bedworth CV12 78 A2
Nuneaton CV11 73 C5
New Town Row B6 66 E5
Newtown Sh Ctr B19 66 E6
Newtown St B64 62 D2
New Union St CV1 165 B2
New Village DY2 62 C2
New Wharf Cotts B60 152 B7
New Wlk [3] B97 153 E4
New Wood Cl DY7 80 C8
New Wood Dr B31 102 D1
New Wood Gr WS9 16 A3
New Wood La DY10 118 B8
Ney Ct DY4 51 F2
Niall Cl B15 85 E8
Nibletts Hill B61 136 B7
Nicholas Chamberlaine Tec Coll CV12 78 D3
Nicholas Cl CV12 78 C3
Nicholas Rd B74 44 E8
Nicholds Cl WV14 40 B1
Nicholls Fold WV11 26 D5
Nicholls Rd DY4 40 E1
Nicholls St
Coventry CV2 113 F4
West Bromwich B70 53 E2
Nicholls Way WS12 2 F1
Nichols Cl B92 107 F7
Nicholson Cl CV34 155 F1
Nickson Rd CV4 111 E1
Nigel Ave B31 103 A5
Nigel Ct B16 65 E1
Nigel Rd
Birmingham B8 67 E6
Dudley DY1 51 A2
Nightingale Ave B36 70 A8
Nightingale Cl
Birmingham B23 56 C7
Huntington WS12 1 C7
Nightingale Cres
Brierley Hill DY5 81 D7
Willenhall WV12 27 C8
Nightingale Ct
Burntwood WS7 7 F8
Royal Leamington Spa CV31 162 B8
Solihull B91 107 C4
Nightingale Dr
Kidderminster DY10 117 B2
Tipton DY4 52 C5

Nightingale La CV5 132 E7
Nightingale Pl WV14 40 D7
Nightingale B77 36 A6
Nightingale Wlk
1 Birmingham B15 86 C7
Burntwood WS7 7 F8
Nightjar Gr B23 56 C6
Nighwood Dr B74 44 F7
Nijon Cl B21 54 D1
Nimbus B77 35 D4
Nimmings Cl B31 122 F6
Nimmings Rd B62 63 D1
Nimmings Visitor Ctr★ B62 100 B6
Nineacres Dr B37 70 A3
Nine Days La B98 159 B6
Nine Elms La WV10 25 E4
Ninefoot La
Tamworth,Belgrave B77 35 E8
Tamworth,Wilnecote B77 35 F7
Nine Leasowes B66 64 E7
Nine Locks Ridge DY5 61 D2
Nine Pails Wlk 2 B70 53 D1
Ninestiles Sch (Tech Coll) B27 88 B1
Nineveh Ave B21 65 F7
Nineveh Rd B21 65 F7
Ninfield Rd B27 88 A4
Ninian Pk B77 35 D6
Ninian Way B77 35 E6
Nirvana Cl WS11 1 C2
Nith Pl DY1 51 B3
Niton Rd CV10 73 D6
Niven Cl CV5 112 A6
Noakes Ct WS10 41 F7
Noble Cl CV34 160 D5
Nocke Rd WV11 12 F1
Nock St DY4 52 C7
Noddy Park Rd WS9 30 B7
Noddy Pk WS9 30 B7
Node Hill Cl B80 159 D3
Node Hill B80 159 D3
Nod Rise CV5 112 B3
Noel Ave B12 87 A6
Noel Ct B97 158 C8
Noele Gordon Gdns 10 WS1 42 E8
Noel Rd B16 65 F1
Nolan Cl CV6 95 D4
Nolton Cl B43 54 D8
No Name Rd WS7 6 E7
Nonsuch Prim Sch B32 84 D2
Nooklands Croft B33 69 A2
Nook The
Brierley Hill DY5 61 B5
Cheslyn Hay WS6 4 C1
Nuneaton CV11 73 E2
Noonan Cl B97 153 B2
Noose Cres WV13 26 E2
Noose La WV13 26 E3
Nora Rd B11 87 C3
Norbiton Rd B44 56 A8
Norbreck Cl B43 43 D1
Norbury Ave WS3 15 A3
Norbury Cl B98 154 B7
Norbury Cres WV4 40 A4
Norbury Dr DY5 61 D1
Norbury Gr B92 89 A3
Norbury Rd
Bilston WV14 40 F6
Birmingham B44 44 F3
West Bromwich B70 53 A7
Wolverhampton WV10 25 F6
Norcombe Gr B90 127 A5
Nordic Drift CV2 115 A6
Nordley Rd WV11 26 C5
Norfolk Ave B71 53 D7
Norfolk Cl
Birmingham B30 104 B6
Hinckley LE10 75 D4
Norfolk Cres
Aldridge WS9 30 B8
Nuneaton CV10 72 E4
Norfolk Ct
6 Birmingham,Selly Oak B29 103 C7
Birmingham B16 65 D1
Norfolk Dr
Tamworth B78 21 A1
Wednesbury WS10 42 D4
Norfolk Gdns B75 46 B7
Norfolk Gr WS6 4 F1
Norfolk Ho
Birmingham,Short Heath B23 56 F5
Birmingham,Walker's Heath B30 104 A3
Norfolk House Sch B15 85 D8
Norfolk New Rd WS2 28 A4
Norfolk Pl WS2 28 D5
Norfolk Rd
Birmingham,Brandhall B68 84 B7
Birmingham,Chad Valley B15 85 D8
Birmingham,Erdington B23 56 F5
Birmingham,Frankley B45 101 F2
Dudley DY2 62 A7
Stourbridge DY8 80 D8
Sutton Coldfield B75 46 C7
Wolverhampton WV3 39 A8
Norfolk St
Coventry CV1 113 B3
Royal Leamington Spa CV32 157 A1
Norfolk Twr B18 66 B5
Norgrave Rd B92 89 C2
Norlan Dr B14 104 F3
Norland Rd B27 88 C1
Norley Gr B13 105 C7
Norman Ashman Coppice CV3 135 C7
Norman Ave
Birmingham B32 84 E7
Coventry CV2 96 F1
Nuneaton CV11 73 B4
Normanby Mdws CV31 162 A2
Norman Cl B79 20 E7
Normandy Cl CV35 160 A7
Normandy Rd B20 55 E1
Normandy Way LE10 71 C3
Norman Place Rd CV6 112 F7
Norman Rd
Birmingham B31 103 B3
Smethwick B67 64 E2
Walsall WS5 43 D7
Normansell Twr B6 67 B8
Norman St
Birmingham B18 65 E5
Dudley DY2 62 E7
Norman Terr B65 63 C4
Normanton Ave B26 89 D5
Normanton Twr B23 57 A6
Normid Ct B13 87 A4
Norrington Gr B31 102 C3
Norrington Rd B31 102 D3
Norris Dr B33 68 E3
Norris Rd B6 55 F1
Norris Way B75 46 D5
Northampton St B18 66 C4
Northam Wlk WV6 25 B4
Northanger Rd B27 88 B2
North Ave
Bedworth CV12 78 D2
Birmingham B40 90 F5
Coventry CV2 114 A3
Wolverhampton WV11 26 C6
Northbourne Dr CV11 78 F7
North Bromsgrove High Sch B60 137 B3
Northbrook Ct B90 106 C5
North Brook Rd CV6 112 D8
Northbrook Rd B90 106 D5
Northbrook St B16 65 F4
North Cl
Cubbington CV32 157 E5
Hinckley LE10 75 E6
Northcliffe Hts DY11 116 C7
Northcote Rd B33 68 D4
Northcote St
7 Royal Leamington Spa CV31 162 B7
Walsall WS2 28 D4
Northcott Rd
Bilston WV14 40 F4
Dudley DY2 62 D4
North Cres WV10 12 C7
Northdale WV6 24 B4
Northdown Rd B91 106 F1
North Dr
Birmingham,Balsall Heath B5 86 C5
Birmingham,Lozells B20 66 B8
Sutton Coldfield B75 46 C6
North East Worcestershire Coll (Bromsgrove Campus) B60 137 B3
North East Worcestershire Coll (Redditch Campus) B98 153 E4
Northey Rd CV6 113 D8
Northfield Children's Farm★ B31 102 C4
Northfield Cl B98 154 D6
Northfield Gr WV3 38 C7
Northfield Manor Prim Sch B29 103 B7
Northfield Rd
Birmingham B17,B32 85 A3
Birmingham,King's Norton B30 103 E4
Coventry CV1 113 F2
Dudley DY2 62 D4
Hinckley LE10 75 C7
Northfield Road Prim Sch DY2 62 D5
Northfield Sta B31 103 A2
Northfields Way WS8 15 D7
Northfolk Terr CV4 132 B7
Northgate WS9 30 A7
North Gate B17 85 C7
Northgate Cl
2 Dudley DY1 51 B2
Kidderminster DY11 116 A4
Northgate B64 82 D8
Northgate St CV34 160 E7
Northgate CV34 160 E7
Northgate Way WS9 30 A8
North Gn WV4 38 D6
North Holme B9 67 C2
Northicote Recn Ctr WV10 11 E3
Northicote Sch The WV10 11 E3
Northland Rd B90 106 E1
Northlands Rd B13 87 A1
Northleach Ave B14 104 D2
Northleach Cl B98 154 B5
North Leamington Com Sch & Arts Coll CV32 156 F4
North Leamington Com Sch & Arts Coll (Sixth Form) CV32 156 F2
Northleigh Rd B8 68 A6
Northmead B33 69 A2
Northolt Dr B35 58 A4
Northolt Gr B42 43 F1
North Oval DY3 50 E5
Northover Cl WV9 11 A2
North Park Rd B23 56 B3
North Pathway B17 85 B7
North Rd
Birmingham,Edgbaston B29 85 F3
Birmingham,Handsworth B20 55 E2
Birmingham,Harborne B17 85 D6
Bromsgrove B60 137 A2
Tipton DY4 52 B8
Wolverhampton,Dunstall Hill WV1 25 C4
Wolverhampton,Parkfield WV4 39 F5
North Roundhay B33 69 A4
Northside Cl B98 158 E7
Northside Dr B74 44 F8
North Springfield DY3 39 E1
North St
Brierley Hill DY5 61 C2
Cannock WS11 4 E6
Coventry CV2 114 B5
Dudley DY2 51 D1
Nuneaton CV10 72 F3
North Street Ind Est DY5 61 C2
North St
Smethwick B67 64 F5
Walsall WS2,WS4 28 E3
Wednesbury WS10 41 F3
Wolverhampton WV1 163 B3
Northumberland Ave
Kidderminster DY11 116 D3
Nuneaton CV10 72 F3
Northumberland Cl B78 21 A1
Northumberland Lodge CV32 156 F3
Northumberland Mews CV32 156 F3
Northumberland Pk CV32 156 F3
Northumberland Rd
Coventry CV1 113 A3
Royal Leamington Spa CV32 156 E2
Northumberland St B7 67 A3
Northvale Cl CV8 148 B6
North View CV2 97 A1
North View Dr DY5 61 E5
North Villiers St CV32 157 A1
North Walsall Prim Sch WS2 28 E4
North Warwickshire & Hinckley Coll LE10 71 E1
North Warwickshire & Hinkley Coll
Hinckley LE10 75 F8
Nuneaton CV11 73 E6
North Warwick St 1 B9 67 D1
Northway
Birmingham B40 90 F5
Sedgley DY3 39 C2
Whitnash CV31 162 A5
North Western Arc B2 164 C3
North Western Rd B66 65 A6
North Western Terr B18 65 F7
Northwick Cres B91 107 B1
North Wlk B31 103 C1
Northwood Ct 9 DY5 61 D2
Northwood Park Cl WV10 11 E3
Northwood Park Prim Sch WV10 11 E1
Northwood Park Rd WV10 11 E3
Northwood St B3 164 A4
Northwood Way DY5 81 B8
Northycote Farm & Ctry Pk★ WV10 11 F3
Northycote La WV10 11 F4
Norton Canes High Sch WS11 6 A7
Norton Canes Prim Sch WS11 6 A6
Norton Cl
Birmingham B31 103 A3
Redditch B98 154 F2
Smethwick B66 65 C5
Tamworth B79 21 C7
Wolverhampton WV4 38 C3
Norton Cres
Bilston WV14 40 D1
Birmingham B9 68 B3
Dudley DY2 62 E3
Norton Dr
Warwick CV34 155 E2
Wythall B47 125 C4
Norton East Rd WS11 6 B6
Norton Gate B38 103 F1
Norton Grange CV5 112 C6
Norton Grange Cres WS11 5 F4
Norton Grange WS11 5 F4
Norton Green La
Dorridge B93 128 C2
Norton Canes WS11 5 F4
Norton Hall La WS11 5 D4
Norton Hill Dr CV2 114 E6
Norton La
Burntwood WS7 7 C6
Great Wyrley WS6 5 A4
Norton Lakeside Sta★ WS11 6 C6
Norton La
Norton Canes WS12 5 B7
Tidbury Green B47,B90, B94 125 E3
Norton Mews B61 137 A4
Norton Rd
Coleshill B46 70 F8
Norton Rd *continued*
Kidderminster DY10 117 B6
Norton Canes WS11,WS12 5 F8
Stourbridge DY8 80 E2
Walsall WS3 15 A5
Norton Springs WS11 5 F5
Norton St
Birmingham B18 66 A6
Coventry CV1 165 C3
Norton Terr
Birmingham B30 104 B6
Norton Canes WS11 5 F6
Norton Twr B1 66 C2
Norton View B14 104 D7
Norton Wlk B23 56 C3
Nortune Cl B38 103 D2
Norwich Cl
Lichfield WS13 3 C3
Nuneaton CV11 74 A8
Norwich Croft B37 69 F1
Norwich Dr
Birmingham B17 84 F8
Coventry CV3 133 B5
Norwich Rd
Dudley DY2 62 D2
Walsall WS2 28 B1
Norwood Ave B64 82 E7
Norwood Cl LE10 71 E3
Norwood Gr
Birmingham B19 66 B7
Coventry CV2 96 E2
Norwood Ho 13 CV32 156 F2
Norwood Rd
Birmingham B9 67 E2
Brierley Hill DY5 61 C3
Norwood Villas B16 65 F1
Nottingham Dr WV12 27 C7
Nottingham New Rd WS2 28 A5
Nottingham Way DY5 61 F2
Nova Croft CV5 111 C4
Nova Ct B43 44 B1
Nova Lodge CV32 156 E3
Nova Scotia St B4 164 D3
Nowell St WS10 41 E5
Nuffield Ho B36 70 A8
Nuffield Hospl WV6 24 C4
Nuffield Rd
Coventry CV6 114 A7
Hinckley LE10 74 E7
Nugent Cl B6 66 E7
Nugent Gr B90 126 D3
Nuneaton Borough Football Club CV11 73 A4
Nuneaton Mus & Art Gal★ CV11 73 C3
Nuneaton Rd
Bedworth CV12 78 B4
Bulkington CV12 79 B4
Nuneaton CV10 72 D8
Nuneaton Trent Valley Sta CV11 73 C5
Nunts La CV6 95 B3
Nunts Park Ave CV6 95 B4
Nursery Ave
Aldridge WS9 30 B5
Birmingham B12 86 F5
Nursery Cl
Birmingham B30 103 F5
Kidderminster DY11 116 B8
West Hagley DY9 99 A4
Nursery Dr B30 103 F5
Nursery Gdns
Solihull B90 125 E8
Stourbridge DY8 60 F1
Nursery Gr DY11 116 B8
Nursery La
Hopwas B78 20 B6
Sutton Coldfield B74 32 A2
Whitnash CV31 162 A5
Nursery Rd
Birmingham,Cotteridge B30 103 E5
Birmingham,Harborne B15 85 D7
Birmingham,Lozells B19 66 C6
Walsall WS3 28 B7
Nursery St WV1 163 B4
Nursery View Cl WS9 30 E2
Nursery Wlk WV6 24 D4
Nurton Bank WV6 23 A3
Nutbrook Ave CV4 111 E2
Nutbush Dr B31 102 D6
Nutfield Wlk B32 84 F5
Nutgrove Cl B14 104 F7
Nuthatch Dr DY5 81 C7
Nuthurst Dr WS11 4 F4
Nuthurst Grange Rd B94 143 C4
Nuthurst Gr
Birmingham B14 104 F2
Dorridge B93 128 A4
Nuthurst Rd
Birmingham B31 122 F6
Kemps Green B94 143 A2
Nuthurst B75 47 B4
Nutley Dr DY4 52 D8
Nutmeg Gr WS1 29 A2
Nuttall Gr B21 65 C7
Nutt's La LE10 75 A7
Nymet B77 35 E8

O

Oakalls Ave B60 137 B2
Oak Apple Rd B61 137 B8
Oak Ave
Birmingham B12 87 A5
Great Wyrley WS6 5 A1
Huntington WS12 1 D8
Oak Ave *continued*
Walsall WS2 27 E3
West Bromwich B70 53 B3
Oak Bank B18 66 A6
Oak Barn Rd B62 83 E8
Oak Cl
Baginton CV8 133 F2
Bedworth CV12 78 C4
Birmingham B17 85 A6
Hinckley LE10 75 E5
Wednesbury DY4 41 A1
Oak Cottage Prim Sch B91 106 F6
Oak Cotts B14 105 C2
Oak Cres
Oldbury B69 52 B1
Walsall WS3 28 D6
Oak Croft B37 69 E3
Oakcroft Rd B13 105 C7
Oak Ct
Coventry CV3 133 F7
Halesowen B63 82 F2
Oldbury B66 64 C8
Royal Leamington Spa CV34 161 E2
Stourbridge DY8 81 A4
Sutton Coldfield B74 31 E5
Walsall WS5 43 A4
Oakdale Cl
Brierley Hill DY5 61 A7
Oldbury B68 64 A2
Oakdale Rd
Binley Woods CV3 135 C7
Birmingham B36 68 E7
Oldbury B68 64 A2
Oakdale B74 31 A1
Oakdale Trad Est DY6 49 E1
Oakdene Cl WS6 4 D2
Oakdene Cres CV10 73 D7
Oakdene Dr B45 138 C8
Oakdene Rd WS7 7 A6
Oakden Pl DY11 116 C7
Oak Dr
Birmingham B23 56 C7
Hartshill CV10 72 A8
Mile Oak B78 20 C1
Oaken Dr
Solihull B91 106 F5
Willenhall WV12 27 E7
Oakenfield WS13 3 A2
Oaken Gdns WS7 7 A8
Oaken Grange WS6 4 F1
Oakenhayes Cres
Brownhills WS8 6 F1
Minworth B76 58 C5
Oakenhayes Dr WS8 6 F1
Oaken Pk WV8 10 A2
Oakenshaw Rd
Redditch B98 154 A1
Solihull B90 106 D1
Oakeswell St WS10 42 A3
Oakey Cl CV6 95 F4
Oakeywell St DY2 51 D1
Oak Farm Cl B76 58 A7
Oak Farm Craft Ctr★ B78 34 B5
Oak Farm Rd B30 103 E5
Oakfield Ave
9 Birmingham,Balsall Heath B12 87 A6
Birmingham,Sparkbrook B11 87 C6
Dudley DY1 51 B6
Kingswinford DY6 60 E5
Oakfield Cl
Smethwick B66 65 C6
Stourbridge DY8 60 F1
Oakfield Ct 6 DY5 61 D2
Oakfield Dr
Birmingham B45 122 D4
Walsall WS3 15 B5
Oakfield Ho
12 Royal Leamington Spa CV32 156 F2
Coventry CV3 115 A1
Oakfield Rd
Birmingham,Balsall Heath B12 86 E5
Birmingham,Erdington B24 56 F3
Birmingham,Selly Oak B29 86 B3
Codsall WV8 10 C2
Coventry CV6 112 F5
Kidderminster DY11 116 B5
Smethwick B66 65 C6
Stourbridge DY8 61 A1
Stourbridge,Wollescote DY9 81 F2
Oakfields Way B91 108 B5
Oakford Dr CV5 111 F6
Oak Gn
Dudley DY1 51 A5
Wolverhampton WV6 24 B3
Oak Gr B31 102 E1
Oak Green Way B68 64 A4
Oak Gr
Kidderminster DY10 117 A5
Wolverhampton WV11 26 B7
Oakhall Dr B93 127 F4
Oakham Ave DY2 62 E7
Oakham Cl B98 159 A5
Oakham Cres
Bulkington CV12 79 D2
Dudley DY2 62 E7
Oakham Ct 9 DY2 62 E8
Oakham Dr DY2 62 F8
Oakham Prim Sch B69 63 B7

Oakham Rd
Birmingham B17 ... 85 B7
Dudley DY2 ... 62 F7
Oldbury B69 ... 63 A7
Oakham Way B92 ... 89 A1
Oakhill Ave DY10 ... 116 E4
Oakhill Cl B17 ... 85 B8
Oakhill Cres B27 ... 106 B8
Oak Hill Dr B15 ... 85 E7
Oakhill Dr DY5 ... 81 B7
Oak Hill Fst Sch B98 ... 154 A2
Oakhill Prim Sch B77 ... 21 F2
Oakhill Rd WS11 ... 1 F2
Oak Hill WV3 ... 24 C1
Oak Ho
7 Warwick CV34 ... 161 D8
Great Wyrley WS6 ... 5 A1
Sutton Coldfield B74 ... 31 B5
Oak House Mus* B70 ... 53 B2
Oakhurst Ct B72 ... 57 C8
Oakhurst Dr B60 ... 137 A3
Oakhurst WS14 ... 9 C7
Oakhurst Rd
Birmingham B27 ... 106 B8
Sutton Coldfield B72 ... 57 C8
Oak Ind Pk The DY6 ... 49 E1
Oakington Dr B35 ... 58 A3
Oak La
Barston B92 ... 109 B2
Harvest Hill CV5 ... 93 E1
Kingswinford DY6 ... 50 A1
Oakland Cl B91 ... 107 E4
Oakland Ct B79 ... 21 A5
Oakland Dr DY3 ... 50 B2
Oakland Gr B61 ... 137 B4
Oakland Ho B74 ... 32 A4
Oakland Rd
Birmingham,Handsworth B21 ... 65 E8
Birmingham,Moseley B13 ... 87 A3
Walsall WS3 ... 28 E7
Oaklands Ave B17 ... 85 B5
Oaklands
Birmingham B62 ... 84 A4
Birmingham,Moseley B13 ... 87 A3
Birmingham,Northfield B31 ... 102 F4
Oaklands Cl WS12 ... 1 C6
Oaklands Croft B76 ... 58 B7
Oaklands Ct
Bromsgrove B61 ... 150 D6
Kenilworth CV8 ... 148 A2
Oaklands B76 ... 59 B6
Oaklands Dr B20 ... 54 F2
Oaklands Gn WV14 ... 40 D8
Oaklands Ind Est WS12 ... 2 B3
Oaklands Prim Sch The B27 ... 88 C2
Oaklands Rd
Sutton Coldfield B74 ... 46 B8
Wolverhampton WV3 ... 39 B8
Oaklands The
Birmingham B37 ... 90 A7
Coventry CV4 ... 112 A2
Halesowen B62 ... 83 F6
Kidderminster DY10 ... 117 A7
Oaklands Way
Birmingham B31 ... 102 C1
Walsall WS3 ... 15 B3
Oaklands WV3 ... 39 B8
Oak La B70 ... 53 B3
Oaklea Dr B64 ... 62 F2
Oakleaf Cl B32 ... 84 C2
Oak Leaf Dr B13 ... 87 A3
Oak Leasow B32 ... 84 B4
Oakleigh B31 ... 103 C2
Oakleigh Ct 3 WV3 ... 25 B2
Oakleigh Dr
Codsall WV8 ... 10 A3
Sedgley DY3 ... 50 C7
Oakleigh Rd DY8 ... 81 B2
Oakleighs DY8 ... 60 C1
Oakleigh Trad Est WV14 ... 40 B2
Oakleigh Wlk DY6 ... 60 E8
Oakley Ave
Aldridge WS9 ... 30 A5
Tipton DY4 ... 52 A6
Oakley CV8 ... 129 F1
Oakley Cl WS13 ... 3 B2
Oakley Ct
Bedworth CV12 ... 77 D1
Birmingham B15 ... 85 E5
Oakley Gr WV4 ... 38 D5
Oakley Ho
Bromsgrove B60 ... 137 A1
Smethwick B66 ... 65 C6
Oakley Rd
Birmingham,Sparkbrook B10 ... 87 C7
Birmingham,Stirchley B30 ... 104 B5
Wolverhampton WV4 ... 38 D5
Oak Leys WV3 ... 24 C1
Oakley Wood Dr B91 ... 107 E4
Oakley Wood Rd CV33 ... 161 F1
Oakly Rd B97 ... 153 D3
Oakmeadow Ave B24 ... 57 D3
Oakmeadow Cl
Birmingham,Acock's Green B26, B27 ... 88 D4
Birmingham,Tile Cross B33 ... 69 D3
Oak Meadow Jun & Inf Sch WV11 ... 27 A7
Oakmeadow Way B24 ... 57 D3
Oakmoor Pl WS9 ... 30 F2
Oakmoor Rd CV6 ... 96 A4
Oakmount Cl WS3 ... 14 F3
Oakmount Rd B74 ... 45 A7
Oak Park Ct
5 Sutton Coldfield B74 ... 31 E3
Stourbridge DY8 ... 60 F1
Oak Park Rd DY8 ... 60 F1
Oak Rd
Birmingham B68 ... 84 C7
Brownhills WS9 ... 16 A3
Catshill B61 ... 137 B8
Dudley DY1 ... 51 C3
Tipton DY4 ... 51 E6
Walsall,Pelsall Wood WS3 ... 14 F5
Walsall WS4 ... 15 C1
West Bromwich B70 ... 53 B2
Willenhall WV13 ... 26 E2
Oakridge Cl
Redditch B98 ... 154 C7
Willenhall WV12 ... 27 C4
Oakridge Dr
Cheslyn Hay WS6 ... 4 E2
Willenhall WV12 ... 27 C4
Oakridge Rd
Birmingham B31 ... 103 D2
Royal Leamington Spa CV32 ... 157 C4
Oak Rise B46 ... 70 F5
Oakroyd Cres CV10 ... 72 D7
Oaks Cres WV3 ... 25 A1
Oaks Dr
Cannock WS11 ... 1 C1
Featherstone WV10 ... 11 F8
Wolverhampton WV3 ... 25 B2
Wombourne WV5 ... 49 A5
Oakslade Dr B92 ... 107 E8
Oaks Pl CV6 ... 96 A3
Oaks Prec CV8 ... 147 E3
Oaks Prim Sch The B14 ... 104 D2
Oaks Rd CV8 ... 147 E2
Oak St
Brierley Hill DY5 ... 61 F1
Cradley Heath B64 ... 62 D1
Dudley,Darby End DY2 ... 62 E4
Dudley,West Coseley DY1, WV14 ... 51 B7
Oaks The
Bedworth CV12 ... 77 F2
Birmingham B34 ... 69 B7
Birmingham,Hawkesley B38 ... 123 F7
Portway B47 ... 140 F8
Redditch B98 ... 158 F7
Royal Leamington Spa CV32 ... 161 D8
Smethwick B67 ... 64 F5
Sutton Coldfield B76 ... 47 A3
Walsall WS3 ... 14 A1
Wolverhampton,Merridale WV3 ... 25 A2
Wolverhampton WV11 ... 26 B5
Oak St DY6 ... 60 D6
Oakstreet Ent Ctr B64 ... 62 D1
Oak Street Trad Est DY5 ... 61 F1
Oak St WV3 ... 25 A1
Oakthorpe Dr B37 ... 69 F5
Oakthorpe Gdns B69 ... 52 A2
Oak Tree Ave
Coventry CV3 ... 133 A6
Redditch B97 ... 153 B4
Oaktree Cl B48 ... 139 A7
Oak Tree Cl
Bentley Heath B93 ... 127 E4
Royal Leamington Spa CV32 ... 157 A2
Oak Tree Cres B62 ... 83 F6
Oak Tree Ct
Birmingham B28 ... 106 A5
Royal Leamington Spa CV32 ... 157 A2
Oaktree Farm Mobile Homes Pk B94 ... 141 B7
Oak Tree Gdns
2 Stourbridge DY8 ... 61 A1
Birmingham B28 ... 105 E3
Oak Tree Ho B30 ... 103 E7
Oak Tree La
Birmingham B29 ... 85 E1
Hollywood B47 ... 125 B6
Sambourne B96 ... 159 B2
Oak Tree Pk B98 ... 154 F6
Oak Tree Rd
Birmingham B8 ... 67 D6
Coventry CV3 ... 135 A7
Oaktree Rd WS10 ... 42 B3
Oak Trees B47 ... 125 A7
Oak Tree Wlk B79 ... 20 F7
Oak View WS2 ... 27 E3
Oak Way
Coventry CV4 ... 111 D2
Sutton Coldfield B76 ... 46 F2
Oak Wlk The B31 ... 103 A1
Oakwood Cl
Brownhills WS9 ... 15 E4
Essington WV11 ... 13 B3
Shenstone WS14 ... 18 A6
Oakwood Cres DY2 ... 61 F6
Oakwood Croft B91 ... 107 C1
Oakwood Ct B63 ... 83 A4
Oakwood Dr
Birmingham B14 ... 104 D4
Sutton Coldfield B74 ... 44 E8
Oakwood Gr CV34 ... 156 A1
Oakwood Rd
Birmingham B11 ... 87 C3
Hollywood B47 ... 125 A6
Smethwick B67 ... 64 F4
Sutton Coldfield B73 ... 45 E1
Walsall WS3 ... 28 E7
Oakwoods WS11 ... 4 D8
Oakwood Specl Sch WS9 ... 16 A3
Oakwood St B70 ... 53 B5
Oakworth Cl CV2 ... 114 F8
Oasis The DY9 ... 98 F5
Oast Ho B8 ... 68 D4
Oasthouse Cl
Kingswinford DY6 ... 60 A7
Stoke Heath B60 ... 150 D6
Oaston Rd
Birmingham B36 ... 69 D8
Nuneaton CV11 ... 73 D4
Oatfield Cl WS7 ... 7 A4
Oatlands Cl CV6 ... 95 C4
Oatlands Way WV6 ... 23 D3
Oatlands Wlk 3 B14 ... 104 C2
Oatmill Cl WS10 ... 41 E5
Oban Dr CV10 ... 73 A2
Oban Rd
Coventry CV6 ... 95 F5
Hinckley LE10 ... 75 A7
Solihull B92 ... 88 F1
Oberon Cl
Birmingham B45 ... 102 A2
Nuneaton CV11 ... 74 A1
Royal Leamington Spa CV34 ... 161 E4
Oberon Dr B90 ... 106 B1
Occupation Rd
Brownhills WS8 ... 16 A4
Coventry CV2 ... 114 C3
Occupation St DY1 ... 51 A2
Ocean Dr WS10 ... 41 E1
Ockam Croft B31 ... 103 C2
Ocker Hill Inf Sch DY4 ... 52 C8
Ocker Hill Jun Sch DY4 ... 41 C1
Ocker Hill Rd DY4 ... 52 C8
O'Connor Dr DY4 ... 41 C1
Oddicombe Croft CV3 ... 133 D5
Oddingley Ct B23 ... 56 C3
Oddingley Rd B31 ... 103 C2
Odell Cres WS3 ... 28 C7
Odell Pl B5 ... 86 C5
Odell Rd WS3 ... 28 B7
Odell Way WS3 ... 28 B7
Odensil Gn B92 ... 89 B2
Odiham Cl B79 ... 21 C7
Odin Cl WS11 ... 2 A5
Odnall La DY9 ... 99 F3
Odstone Dr LE10 ... 74 F8
Offadrive B79 ... 21 B5
Offa Dr CV8 ... 148 A4
Offa Rd CV31 ... 162 B5
Offa's Dr WV6 ... 23 E5
Offa St B79 ... 21 B5
Offchurch La CV31 ... 162 F6
Offchurch Rd CV32 ... 157 E4
Offenham Cl B98 ... 154 B6
Offenham Covert B38 ... 123 E8
Offini Cl B70 ... 53 F2
Offmoor Rd B32 ... 102 B8
Offmore Ct DY10 ... 117 C6
Offmore Farm Cl DY10 ... 117 C6
Offmore Fst Sch The DY10 ... 117 B6
Offmore La DY10 ... 117 A6
Offmore Rd DY10 ... 116 F6
Offwell Rd B98 ... 154 D1
Ogbury Cl B14 ... 104 C2
Ogley Cres WS8 ... 16 A7
Ogley Dr B75 ... 47 A5
Ogley Hay Rd
Burntwood,Gorstey Ley WS7 ... 7 B8
Burntwood,Triangle WS7, WS8 ... 7 A3
Ogley Rd WS8 ... 16 A7
Ogley Vale WS7 ... 7 B8
O'Hare Ho WS4 ... 28 F3
O'keeffe Cl B11 ... 87 B6
Okeford Way CV10 ... 73 A1
Okehampton Dr B71 ... 53 C6
Okehampton Rd CV3 ... 133 E5
Okement Dr WV11 ... 26 C5
Oken Ct CV34 ... 160 D7
Oken Rd CV34 ... 160 D8
Olaf Pl CV2 ... 115 A7
Old Abbey Gdns B17 ... 85 D4
Oldacre Cl B76 ... 57 D6
Old Acre Dr B21 ... 65 E7
Oldacre Rd B68 ... 84 A7
Oldany Way CV10 ... 72 F2
Old Bakery Ct DY9 ... 99 A5
Old Bank Pl B72 ... 46 C5
Old Bank Top B31 ... 103 B2
Old Barn Rd
Birmingham B30 ... 103 D6
Stourbridge DY8 ... 61 A1
Old Beeches B23 ... 56 C8
Old Bell Rd B23 ... 57 B6
Oldberrow Cl 4 B90 ... 127 A6
Old Birchills WS2 ... 28 C3
Old Birmingham Rd
Alvechurch B48 ... 139 B8
Catshill B60 ... 137 C8
Lower Marlbrook B60,B45 ... 121 E1
Old Bridge St B19 ... 66 C6
Old Bridge Wlk B65 ... 62 F5
Old Bromford La B8 ... 68 C6
Old Brookside B33 ... 68 E2
Old Budbrooke Rd CV35 ... 160 A8
Oldbury Bsns Ctr B68 ... 64 A2
Oldbury Cl B98 ... 154 B6
Oldbury Ct B79 ... 21 B5
Oldbury Green Ret Pk B69 ... 63 F8
Oldbury Rd
Hartshill CV10 ... 72 A8
Oldbury Rd *continued*
Rowley Regis B65 ... 63 D2
Smethwick B66 ... 64 D7
West Bromwich B70 ... 52 F2
Oldbury Ringway B69 ... 63 F8
Oldbury Road Ind Est
Smethwick B66 ... 64 D7
West Bromwich B70 ... 52 F2
Oldbury St WS10 ... 42 B3
Old Bush St DY5 ... 61 E3
Old Bush Trad Est DY5 ... 61 E3
Old Camp Hill B12 ... 87 A8
Old Canal Wlk 1 DY4 ... 52 B5
Old Castle Gr WS8 ... 6 F2
Old Chapel Rd B67 ... 64 F3
Old Chapel Wlk B68 ... 64 A4
Old Chester Rd S DY10 ... 116 E2
Old Church CE Prim Sch WS10 ... 41 C6
Old Church Ct 4 B17 ... 85 B5
Old Church Gn B33 ... 68 E2
Old Church Rd
Birmingham B17 ... 85 B4
Coventry CV6 ... 96 A1
Water Orton B46 ... 59 B3
Old Crescent Ct 8 B68 ... 84 B8
Old Crest Ave B98 ... 153 E2
Old Croft La
Birmingham B34 ... 69 C7
Birmingham,Castle Bromwich B36 ... 69 B7
Old Cross St DY4 ... 51 E5
Old Crown Cl B32 ... 84 B1
Old Crown Mews CV2 ... 96 D5
Old Damson La B92 ... 90 A2
Old Dickens Heath Rd B90 ... 126 A5
Old Dominion Wks WV1 ... 40 A7
Olde Hall La WS6 ... 4 F3
Olde Hall Rd WV10 ... 12 C7
Old End La WV14 ... 51 C7
Old Fallings Cres WV10 ... 25 F6
Old Fallings La WV10 ... 25 F8
Old Fallow Ave WS11 ... 1 E3
Old Fallow Rd WS11 ... 1 E3
Old Falls Cl WS6 ... 4 D3
Old Farm Dr WV8 ... 10 A4
Old Farm Gr B14 ... 105 D5
Old Farm Mdw WV3 ... 38 C8
Old Farm Rd B33 ... 68 E4
Oldfield Dr DY8 ... 81 A3
Oldfield Rd
Birmingham B12 ... 87 A6
Coventry CV5 ... 112 E3
Dudley WV14 ... 51 A8
Oldfields
Cradley Heath B64 ... 82 D8
West Hagley DY9 ... 99 B6
Oldfield Trad Est B64 ... 82 D8
Old Fire Sta The B17 ... 85 D6
Old Flour Mills 6 B70 ... 53 C2
Old Fordrove B76 ... 46 D3
Old Forest Way B34 ... 69 B6
Old Forge Bsns Ctr B98 ... 159 C8
Old Forge Cl WS1 ... 42 F8
Old Forge Dr B98 ... 159 C8
Old Forge Trad Est DY9 ... 81 E6
Old Grange Rd B11 ... 87 C4
Old Green La CV8 ... 129 C1
Old Grove Gdns DY9 ... 81 D3
Old Hall Cl DY8 ... 81 A8
Old Hall Ct WS9 ... 44 A5
Old Hall Ind Est WS3 ... 28 C8
Old Hall La
Norton Canes WS11,WS12 ... 5 B7
Walsall WS9 ... 44 B5
Old Hall Sch WS2 ... 27 E5
Old Hall St WV1 ... 163 C2
Oldham Ave CV2 ... 114 E4
Old Ham La DY9 ... 81 D2
Old Hampton La WV11 ... 12 C2
Old Hawne La B63 ... 83 A5
Old Heath Cres WV1 ... 26 A1
Old Heath Rd WV1 ... 26 A2
Old Hedging La B77 ... 35 D5
Old Hednesford Rd WS11 ... 2 A3
Old High St DY5 ... 61 F1
Old Hill Prim Sch B64 ... 62 F1
Old Hill Sta B64 ... 83 A8
Old Hill WV6 ... 24 D5
Old Hinckley Rd CV10 ... 73 D5
Old Hobicus La B68 ... 64 B5
Old Horns Cres B43,B44 ... 44 C2
Oldhouse Farm Cl B28 ... 105 F6
Old House La
Hawkes End CV7 ... 94 A7
Romsley B62 ... 101 B1
Oldington Gr B91 ... 127 B8
Oldington Trad Est DY11 ... 116 B1
Old Kingsbury Rd B76 ... 58 C5
Old Know Ct B10 ... 87 E7
Oldknow Jun Sch B10 ... 87 E7
Oldknow Rd B10 ... 87 E7
Old La WV10 ... 12 C7
Old Landywood La WS6 ... 13 D7
Old Langley Hall B75 ... 47 C4
Old La
Rowney Green B48 ... 140 D4
Walsall WS3 ... 28 C8
Wolverhampton WV6 ... 23 F2
Old Level Way DY2 ... 62 D4
Old Lime Gdns B38 ... 123 E8
Old Lindens Cl B74 ... 44 E7
Old Lode La B92 ... 89 C3
Old London Rd WS14 ... 9 D1
Old Manor Cl B78 ... 34 E5
Old Manor Flats WV6 ... 24 D5
Old Masters Cl WS1 ... 29 A1
Old Meadow Rd B31 ... 123 C7
Old Meeting Rd WV14 ... 51 C8
Old Meeting St B70 ... 53 B5
Old Meeting Yd 1 CV12 ... 78 B3
Old Mill Ave CV4 ... 132 D5
Old Mill Cl B90 ... 105 D2
Old Mill Gdns
Birmingham B33 ... 68 E2
Walsall WS4 ... 15 C2
Old Mill Gr B20 ... 55 C2
Old Mill House Cl WS4 ... 15 B1
Old Mill Rd B46 ... 70 F7
Old Milverton La CV32 ... 156 E5
Old Milverton CV32 ... 156 C3
Old Milverton Rd CV32 ... 156 C2
Old Moat Dr B31 ... 103 B3
Old Moat Way B8 ... 68 B6
Oldnall Cl DY9 ... 81 F4
Oldnall Rd
Kidderminster DY10 ... 117 A4
Stourbridge B63,DY9 ... 82 A4
Old Oak Cl WS9 ... 30 B8
Old Oak Rd B38 ... 104 A2
Old Oscott Hill B44 ... 44 F2
Old Oscott La B44 ... 55 E8
Old Park Cl B6 ... 66 E7
Old Park La B69 ... 64 A5
Old Park Prim Sch WS10 ... 41 E5
Old Park Rd
Darlaston WS10 ... 41 E5
Dudley DY1 ... 51 A5
Old Park Special Sch DY1 ... 61 F8
Old Park Trad Est WS10 ... 41 E4
Old Park Wlk B6 ... 66 E7
Old Penkridge Mews WS11 ... 1 D1
Old Penkridge Rd WS11 ... 1 C2
Old Penns La B46 ... 70 F7
Old Penn's Yd 4 CV12 ... 78 A2
Old Pk B29 ... 103 A5
Old Pleck Rd WS2 ... 42 C7
Old Pl WS3 ... 28 C8
Old Port Cl DY4 ... 52 B2
Old Portway B38 ... 123 E7
Old Postway B19 ... 66 D7
Old Quarry Cl B45 ... 121 F8
Old Quarry Dr DY3 ... 50 D5
Old Rd CV7 ... 92 E1
Old Rectory Gdns WS9 ... 30 C6
Old Rectory La B48 ... 139 B7
Old School Cl WV13 ... 27 A2
Old School Dr 2 B65 ... 63 C3
Old School Mews CV32 ... 157 B3
Old School Wlk B79 ... 21 B6
Old School Yd The B77 ... 22 A5
Old Scott Cl B33 ... 69 C2
Old Smithy Pl B18 ... 66 A5
Old Snow Hill B3 ... 164 B4
Old Sq B4 ... 164 C3
Old Sq The 1 WS1 ... 28 E1
Old Sq CV34 ... 160 E6
Old Stables Wlk 2 B7 ... 67 C7
Old Stafford Rd WV10 ... 11 C8
Old Station Rd
Birmingham B33 ... 68 D4
Bromsgrove B60 ... 137 A1
Hampton-in-A B92 ... 109 A8
Old Stone Cl B45 ... 101 F1
Old Stone Yd CV32 ... 156 E1
Old Stowheath La WV1 ... 26 C1
Old Stratford Rd B60 ... 137 C2
Oldswinford CE Prim Sch DY8 ... 81 A3
Old Swinford Hospl DY8 ... 81 A4
Old Tokengate 2 B17 ... 85 D6
Old Town Cl B38 ... 103 F2
Old Town La WS3 ... 14 F3
Old Union Mill B16 ... 66 B2
Old Vicarage Cl
Walsall WS3 ... 15 A2
Wombourne WV5 ... 49 B7
Old Vicarage Gdns B80 ... 159 E4
Old Walsall Rd B42 ... 54 F7
Old Warstone La WV11 ... 13 B8
Old Warwick Ct 1 B92 ... 88 E1
Old Warwick Rd
Kingswood B94,CV35 ... 144 D3
Royal Leamington Spa CV31 ... 161 E7
Solihull B92 ... 88 E1
Old Waste La CV7 ... 130 E6
Oldway Dr B91 ... 107 E2
Old Well Cl WS4 ... 29 B7
Old Wharf Rd DY8 ... 80 F6
Oldwich La E
Balsall Common CV8 ... 129 D1
Honiley CV8 ... 145 E8
Oldwich La W B93 ... 145 C8
Old Winnings Rd CV7 ... 94 F6
Old Woodyard The DY9 ... 99 D6
Old Yd The CV2 ... 114 F7
Olga Dr DY4 ... 41 B1
Olinthus Ave WV11 ... 26 E7
Olive Ave
Coventry CV2 ... 114 D5
Wolverhampton WV4 ... 39 E5
Olive Dr B62 ... 83 C8
Olive Hill Prim Sch B62 ... 83 D7
Olive Hill Rd B62 ... 83 D8
Olive La B62 ... 83 D8
Olive Mount B69 ... 63 D8
Olive Pl B14 ... 104 E7
Oliver Cl 1 DY2 ... 62 E8
Oliver Cres WV14 ... 40 F2
Oliver Ct B65 ... 63 B2
Oliver Rd
Birmingham,Erdington B23 ... 56 F6
Birmingham,Ladywood B16 ... 65 F2

Oliver Rd *continued*
Smethwick B66 65 C3
Oliver St
Birmingham B7 67 B5
Coventry CV6 113 F6
Olivier Way CV2 115 B8
Ollerton Rd B26 88 F7
Ollison Dr B74 30 F2
Olliver Cl B62 84 A3
Olorenshaw Rd B26 89 D5
Olton Ave CV5 111 E4
Olton Bridge B92 106 F8
Olton Bvd E B27 88 C2
Olton Bvd W B11 87 F3
Olton Croft B27 88 D2
Olton Mere B92 88 E1
Olton Pl CV11 72 F4
Olton Rd B90 106 B5
Olton Sta B92 88 E1
Olton Wharf B92 88 E2
Olympus Ave CV34 161 D5
Olympus Cl CV5 111 B8
Olympus Dr DY4 52 D6
Omar Rd CV2 114 D2
Ombersley Cl
Oldbury B69 63 D5
Redditch B98 159 C7
Ombersley Rd
Birmingham B12 87 A6
Halesowen B63 82 F2
Ombersley Way 4 B31 103 D2
One Stop Sh Ctr B42 55 D3
Onibury Rd B21 54 D1
Onley Terr CV4 132 C7
Onslow Cres B92 89 A1
Onslow Croft CV32 156 F2
Onslow Rd B11 88 A4
Ontario Cl B38 124 A8
Oozells St N B1 66 B2
Oozells Sq B1 66 B2
Oozells St B1 66 C2
Open Field Cl B31 103 C2
Openfield Croft B46 59 C2
Ophelia Dr CV34 161 E3
Orangery The DY9 99 D7
Oratory Dr CV3 134 C6
Oratory RC Prim Sch The B16 65 F2
Orbital Way WS11 4 F6
Orchard Ave
Cannock WS11 1 C2
Solihull B91 107 D5
Orchard Cl
Birmingham B21 54 F1
Cheslyn Hay WS6 4 E3
Coleshill B46 70 F7
Curdworth B76 59 B7
Halesowen B63 82 C6
Hartshill CV10 72 B7
Hinckley LE10 76 A5
Rowley Regis B65 63 A3
Sutton Coldfield B73 57 A8
Tamworth B77 35 C5
Walsall WS4 29 C5
West Hagley DY9 99 B4
Willenhall WV13 27 B1
Orchard Cres
Coventry CV3 133 C8
Stoke Prior B60 150 C3
Wolverhampton WV3 38 B7
Orchard Croft B45 138 D8
Orchard Ct
Birmingham,Erdington B23 57 A5
Birmingham,Stockland Green B23 56 B4
Coventry CV3 115 A1
Kingswinford DY6 60 D6
Rowley Regis B65 63 B3
Orchard Ctr PRU WV3 25 B1
Orchard Ct
Solihull B91 107 E6
Wolverhampton WV3 38 B7
Orchard Dr
Birmingham B31 122 F7
Coventry CV5 111 C4
Orchard Gdns WS12 1 F6
Orchard Gr
Aldridge WS9 30 B4
Dudley DY3 50 B3
Sutton Coldfield B74 31 F3
Wolverhampton WV4 39 A4
Orchard Ho CV6 96 A4
Orchard La
Codsall WV8 10 B3
Kenilworth CV8 148 C3
Orchard Leigh B13 87 A3
Orchard Meadow Wlk B35 58 B3
Orchard Pl B80 159 F8
Orchard Rd
Birmingham B24 57 B5
Bromsgrove B61 136 F4
Dudley DY2 62 C2
Hockley Heath B94 143 C6
Walsall WS5 43 B3
Willenhall WV13 27 B1
Wolverhampton WV11 26 C7
Orchard Ret Pk CV3 134 D4
Orchard Rise B26 88 F7
Orchard Sch The B67 65 A5
Orchard St
Bedworth CV12 78 B4
Brierley Hill DY5 61 D4
Orchards The
Astwood Bank B96 158 D1
Cheswick Green B90 126 D4
Hollywood B47 125 A7
Orchards The *continued*
Sutton Coldfield B74 46 A8
Orchard St
Hinckley LE10 75 E8
Kidderminster DY10 116 E6
Nuneaton CV11 73 D4
Redditch B98 153 E3
Tamworth,Kettlebrook B77 21 C3
Tamworth,The Leys B79 21 B5
Tipton DY4 51 F2
Orchard The
Bilston WV14 40 E5
Birmingham B37 89 F8
Bromsgrove B61 136 E4
Burntwood WS7 7 B7
Oldbury B68 64 C4
Walsall WS3 14 D2
Wolverhampton WV6 24 E6
Orchard Villas
Fairfield B61 120 D2
Wythall B47 124 F1
Orchard Way
Birmingham,Acock's Green B27 88 B4
Birmingham,Balsall B12 86 E6
Birmingham,Great Barr B43 43 F1
Hollywood B47 125 A8
Nuneaton CV10 72 C6
Studley B80 159 E2
Orcheston Wlk B14 104 D2
Orchid Cl
Bedworth CV12 77 E2
Smethwick B66 64 D7
Orchid Dr B19 66 D6
Ordnance Rd CV6 113 E5
Oregon Cl DY6 60 F6
Oregon Dr WV12 27 E7
Oregon Gdns WS7 6 F8
Orford Gr B21 65 C8
Oriel Cl
Cannock WS11 4 E8
Dudley DY1 50 E2
Oriel Dr WV10 11 D3
Oriel Ho B37 70 A3
Oriel Villas 4 B11 87 C5
Oriole Gr DY10 117 B2
Orion Cl
Birmingham B8 68 B4
Great Wyrley WS6 4 F1
Orion Cres CV2 96 E2
Orion Way WS11 1 F5
Orkney Ave B34 68 F7
Orkney Cl
Hinckley LE10 71 C1
Nuneaton CV10 73 A2
Orkney Croft B36 70 B7
Orkney Dr B77 35 F7
Orlando Cl WS1 42 E8
Orlando Ho 4 WS1 42 E8
Orlescote Rd CV4 132 E6
Ormande Cl B63 82 B7
Orme Cl DY5 81 B8
Ormes La WV6 24 C3
Ormond Pl WV14 40 F6
Ormond Rd B45 101 F1
Ormonds Cl WS13 8 E6
Ormsby Gr B27 106 B7
Ormscliffe Rd B45 122 B6
Orphanage Rd B24 57 B6
Orpington Dr CV6 95 D4
Orpington Rd B44 44 E3
Orpwood Rd B33 69 B2
Orsino Cl CV34 161 E2
Orslow Wlk WV10 26 A5
Orton Ave B76 58 A6
Orton Cl B46 59 A3
Orton Gr WV4 38 D4
Orton La WV4,WV5 38 A2
Orton Rd CV6 95 D4
Orton Way B35 58 A1
Orwell Cl
Nuneaton CV10 72 A5
Stourbridge DY8 80 D4
Wednesfield WV11 26 F5
Orwell Ct CV1 165 C4
Orwell Dr
Birmingham B38 123 C8
West Bromwich B71 53 D6
Orwell Pas B5 164 C2
Orwell Rd
Coventry CV1 113 F1
Walsall WS1 43 B8
Osbaston Cl
Coventry CV5 111 E4
Hinckley LE10 71 F3
Osberton Dr DY1 50 F2
Osborn Ct B73 46 B1
Osborne Cl
Birmingham B6 67 A7
Brierley Hill DY5 81 F8
Kidderminster DY10 117 B6
Osborne Ct 7 CV31 162 A4
Osborne Dr WS10 41 D8
Osborne Gr B19 66 C7
Osborne Prim Sch B23 57 A5
Osborne Rd
Birmingham,Erdington B23 56 F5
Birmingham,Handsworth B21 65 F8
Bromsgrove B60 137 C1
Coventry CV5 133 A8
Osborne Rd S 1 B23 56 F4
Osborne Rd
West Bromwich B70 53 C3
Wolverhampton WV4 38 F5
Osborne B79 20 D7
Osborne Twr B6 67 A8
Osborn Rd B11 87 C6
Osbourne Croft B90 126 D5
Osbourne Ho CV1 165 A2
Oscott Cir B6 55 F3
Oscott Coll B73 45 D1
Oscott Gdns B42 55 E3
Oscott Rd B6,B42 55 E3
Oscott School La B44 44 E2
Osier Gr B23 56 B6
Osier Pl WV1 25 F2
Osier St WV1 25 F2
Osler St B16 65 F2
Oslo Gdns CV2 115 A7
Osmaston Rd
Birmingham B17 85 B3
Stourbridge DY8 80 F2
Osmington Gr B63 82 D6
Osnor Ct B60 151 B7
Osprey Cl
Coventry CV2 115 B6
Nuneaton CV11 79 B8
Osprey Ct WS7 7 F8
Osprey Dr DY1 50 F1
Osprey Gr WS12 2 C1
Osprey Ho B80 159 D4
Osprey Park Dr DY10 117 B3
Osprey Rd
Birmingham,Acock's Green B27 88 D2
Birmingham,Perry Common B23 56 C6
Osprey B77 36 A6
Ostler Cl DY6 60 B7
Oswald Rd CV32 161 D8
Oswald St B98 153 E3
Oswestry Cl B97 158 C7
Oswestry Ct B11 87 B6
Oswin Gr CV2 114 C4
Oswin Pl WS3 28 F5
Oswin Rd WS3 28 F5
Othello Ave CV34 161 F3
Other Rd B98 153 E4
Otley Gr B9 68 C3
Ottawa Twr 2 B5 86 D7
Otterburn Cl WS12 2 E2
Otter Croft B34 69 D5
Otters Rest CV31 162 C5
Otterstone Cl DY3 39 C2
Ottery B77 36 B5
Ottilie Hild Sch B60 150 E5
Oughton Rd B12 87 A7
Oulsnam Ct 12 B13 87 B2
Oulton Cl DY11 116 D8
Oundle Ct 7 B74 31 F2
Oundle Rd B44 55 F7
Ounsdale Cres WV5 49 A7
Ounsdale Dr DY2 62 C4
Ounty John La DY8 81 A1
Our Lady & Kenelm RC Sch B63 83 A4
Our Lady of Compassion RC Prim Sch B92 106 D7
Our Lady of Fatima RC Prim Sch B17 84 F7
Our Lady of Lourdes RC Prim Sch B13 105 D5
Our Lady of Mount Carmel RC Fst Sch B97 153 A2
Our Lady of the Angels RC Inf Sch CV11 73 C3
Our Lady of the Assumption RC Prim Sch CV4 111 E1
Our Lady Of the Wayside RC Prim Sch B90 126 C8
Our Lady & St Chad's RC Sch WV10 25 F7
Our Lady & St Rose of Lima RC Prim Sch B29 85 B1
Our Lady & St Teresa's RC Prim Sch CV32 157 D5
Our Lady's RC Prim Sch B33 69 D2
Outermarch Rd CV6 113 C7
Outfields B13 104 E6
Outlands Dr LE10 71 B2
Outmore Rd B33 69 B1
Outwood Cl B98 158 E7
Out Wood Dr B31 102 D1
Outwoods The LE10 75 F8
Oval Prim Sch The B33 68 F2
Oval Rd
Birmingham B24 56 E1
Tipton DY4 51 F6
Oval The
Dudley DY1 61 E8
Smethwick B67 64 D2
Wednesbury WS10 41 F4
Overbare Cl B94 142 A1
Overberry Cl CV2 96 D2
Overbrook Cl DY3 50 C2
Over Brunton Cl B31 103 B2
Overbury Cl
Birmingham B31 103 C3
Halesowen B63 83 B2
Overbury Rd B31 103 C3
Overdale B96 158 E1
Overdale Ave B76 57 F5
Overdale Cl WS2 27 C3
Overdale Ct B13 86 F4
Overdale Dr WS2 27 D3
Overdale Rd
Birmingham B32 84 E5
Coventry CV5 112 C3
Overell Gr CV32 156 D2
Overend Rd B63,B64 82 D7
Overend St B70 53 D2
Overfield Dr WV14 40 A3
Overfield Rd
Birmingham B32 84 F1
Dudley DY1 61 E8
Over Green Dr B37 69 F5
Overhill Rd WS7 7 B5
Overlea Ave B27 88 B3
Over Mill Dr B29 86 B2
Overmoor Cl B19 66 C7
Over Pool Rd B8 68 A6
Overseal Rd WV11 26 E8
Overslade Cres CV6 112 E8
Overslade Rd B91 106 F2
Oversley Cl B97 153 C5
Oversley Rd B76 58 A6
Over St CV6 114 A8
Overstrand WV9 10 F3
Overton Cl B28 106 A6
Overton Dr B46 59 C3
Overton Gr B27 106 C8
Overton La WS7 7 C4
Overton Pl
Birmingham B7 67 A3
West Bromwich B71 53 D6
Overton Rd B27 106 C8
Overtons Cl CV31 162 F5
Overton Wlk WV4 38 C6
Overwood Croft B8 67 E3
Overwoods Rd B77 36 A4
Owenford Rd CV6 113 C7
Owen Pl WV14 40 D6
Owen Rd
Bilston WV14 40 D6
Darlaston WV13 41 C8
Wolverhampton WV3 39 A8
Owen Road Ind Est WV13 27 C1
Owens Croft B38 104 A1
Owen St
Darlaston WS10 41 D7
Dudley DY2 62 E8
Tipton DY4 51 E5
Owens Way B64 63 A1
Ownall Rd B34 69 C6
Oxbarn Ave WV3 38 E7
Ox Bow Way DY10 116 E8
Oxbridge Way B79 20 E6
Ox Cl CV2 114 A6
Oxendon Way CV3 134 E8
Oxenton Croft B63 82 D2
Oxford Cl
Birmingham B8 68 B5
Great Wyrley WS6 4 F3
Nuneaton CV11 73 F8
Oxford Ct 8 B29 103 C7
Oxford Dr
Birmingham B27 88 D4
Stourbridge DY8 80 F4
Oxford Gn WS11 4 F8
Oxford Pl 14 CV32 156 F1
Oxford Rd
Birmingham,Acock's Green B27 88 C3
Birmingham,Erdington B23 56 F4
Birmingham,Moseley B13 87 A2
Cannock WS11 4 F8
Ryton-on-D CV8 134 F1
Smethwick B66 65 A7
West Bromwich B70 53 B3
Oxford Row 16 CV32 156 F1
Oxford St
Bilston WV14 40 F5
Birmingham,Digbeth B5 164 D2
Birmingham,Stirchley B30 104 A7
Coventry CV1 113 E3
Dudley DY1 51 B1
Kidderminster DY10 116 E5
Oxford Street Ind Pk WV14 40 F5
Oxford Street Island WV14 40 E5
Oxford St
Royal Leamington Spa CV32 156 F1
Walsall WS2 42 C7
Wednesbury WS10 42 B3
Wolverhampton WV1 163 D2
Oxford Terr WS10 42 B2
Oxford Trad Est B5 164 D1
Oxford Way DY4 51 D5
Oxhayes Cl CV7 130 C6
Oxhill Cl B98 154 E1
Oxhill Rd
Birmingham B21 54 E2
Solihull B90 105 C2
Ox Leasow B32 84 C2
Oxleasow Rd B98 154 E4
Oxley Ave WV10 25 C6
Oxley Cl
Dudley DY2 62 B2
Great Wyrley WS6 4 F1
Oxley Court Cvn Pk WV10 25 A8
Oxley Dr CV3 133 C3
Oxley Gr B29 103 A8
Oxley La WV1 163 B4
Oxley Links Rd WV10 25 B8
Oxley Moor Rd WV9,WV10 25 A8
Oxley Prim Sch WV10 25 C7
Ox Leys Rd B75,B76 47 D3
Oxley St WV1 25 C4
Oxlip Cl WS5 43 A3
Oxpiece Dr B36 68 D8
Oxstall Cl B76 58 D5
Ox St DY3 50 D5
Oxted Cl WV11 26 F5
Oxted Croft B23 56 E3
Oxwood La B32 101 D4

P

Pace Cres WV14 41 A2
Pacific Ave WS10 41 D1
Packenham Dr B76 57 F8
Packhorse La B38,B47 124 E6
Packington Ave
Allesley CV5 112 B6
Birmingham B34 69 D5
Packington Ct B74 31 E4
Packington La
Little Packington CV7 91 C6
Outwoods B46,CV7 92 B8
Weeford B78 19 F5
Packington Pl 6 CV31 162 A7
Packmores B90 126 A5
Packmore St CV34 160 F8
Packwood Cl
Bentley Heath B93 127 E4
Birmingham B20 55 A2
Nuneaton CV11 78 F8
Redditch B97 152 F1
Royal Leamington Spa CV31 162 C5
Willenhall WV13 40 F8
Packwood Cotts B93 127 F1
Packwood Ct
1 Birmingham B29 84 F1
Solihull B91 107 C5
Packwood Dr B43 43 D1
Packwood Gn CV5 112 A3
Packwood Ho
Birmingham B15 86 C8
Lapworth B94 144 A5
Sutton Coldfield B73 46 A3
Packwood La B94 144 A4
Packwood Mews 5 CV34 161 B8
Packwood Rd
Birmingham B26 89 B8
Lapworth B94 144 A7
Oldbury B69 52 A1
Padarn Cl DY3 39 C1
Padbury Ho B31 102 D5
Padbury WV9 11 B3
Paddiford Pl CV10 72 C3
Paddington Rd B21 54 C1
Paddington Wlk WS2 27 F4
Paddock Dr
Birmingham B26 89 A7
Dorridge B93 128 A2
Paddock La
Aldridge WS9 30 A5
Great Wyrley WS6 5 A3
Redditch B98 158 E7
Walsall WS1 28 F1
Paddocks Cl B78 22 F1
Paddocks Gn B18 66 A5
Paddocks Rd B47 124 F6
Paddocks The
Bulkington CV12 79 B3
Kenilworth CV8 148 B5
Warwick CV34 160 F7
Paddock The
Bilston WV14 40 D1
Birmingham B31 103 C4
Dudley DY3 50 E5
Lichfield WS14 9 C5
Perton WV6 23 D4
Stoke Heath B60 150 D6
Stourbridge DY9 99 C8
Sutton Coldfield B76 47 A4
Paddock View WV6 25 B5
Paddock Way LE10 74 E6
Paddys Wide Water Est DY5 61 C5
Padgate Cl B35 58 B3
Padgets La B98 154 D4
Padmore Ct CV31 162 B6
Padstow Cl CV11 73 F5
Padstow Rd
Birmingham B24 57 D4
Coventry CV4 131 E8
Padstow B77 21 F5
Padua Rd B60 137 C1
Paganal Dr B70 53 E1
Paganel Dr DY1 51 C3
Paganel Prim Sch B29 85 A2
Paganel Rd B29 85 A2
Pageant Ct B12 86 E5
Page Rd CV4 131 E7
Pages Cl B75 46 C5
Pages Ct B43 43 E1
Pages La B43 43 E1
Paget Cl
Bromsgrove B61 136 E2
Dudley WV14 51 B8
Lichfield WS13 3 B2
Paget Ct CV2 96 B3
Paget Ho DY4 52 B3
Paget Mews B76 46 F2
Paget Prim Sch B24 57 C4
Paget Rd
Birmingham B24 57 D4
Wolverhampton WV3,WV6 24 F3
Paget St WV1 163 A4
Pagham Cl WV9 10 F2
Pagnell Gr B13 105 C6
Paignton Rd B16 65 D3
Pailton Cl CV2 96 C2
Pailton Gr B29 85 B1
Pailton Rd B90 106 B5

Painswick Cl
Redditch B98 158 E6
Walsall WS5 43 B3
Painswick Rd B28 105 F7
Paint Cup Row DY2 62 C2
Painters Cnr 7 B66 65 C5
Painters Croft WV14 40 E1
Pakefield Rd B30 104 C3
Pakenham Cl B76 57 F8
Pakenham Ho B76 57 F8
Pakenham Rd B15 86 C7
Pakenham Village B15 86 C7
Pake's Croft 3 CV6 113 A5
Pakfield Wlk B6 66 F8
Palace Cl B65 63 D4
Palace Dr B66 64 D8
Palace Rd B9 67 E1
Palefield Rd B90 126 F6
Pale La B17 84 F8
Palermo Ave CV3 133 E6
Pale St DY3 50 E5
Palethorpe Rd DY4 52 A8
Palfrey Inf Sch WS1 42 D7
Palfrey Jun Sch WS1 42 D7
Palfrey Rd DY8 80 D5
Pallasades Sh Ctr The
B2 164 B2
Pallett Dr CV11 73 F7
Palmcourt Ave B28 105 E7
Palm Croft DY5 81 C8
Palmer Cl WV11 12 F1
Palmer La CV1 165 B3
Palmer Rd
Hinckley LE10 71 B2
Whitnash CV31 162 B4
Palmers Cl
Codsall WV8 10 C1
Solihull B90 106 B5
Palmers Cross Prim Sch
WV6 24 D8
Palmers Gr B36 68 E8
Palmers Rd B98 154 F5
Palmer St B9 67 A2
Palmerston Ave B77 35 E6
Palmerston Ct B77 35 F6
Palmerston Dr B69 52 D2
Palmerston Rd
Birmingham B11 87 B6
Coventry CV5 132 F8
Palmers Way WV8 10 C1
Palm Tree Ave CV2 96 C2
Palmvale Croft B26 89 A6
Palmyra Rd B60 137 C2
Palomino Pl B16 65 F2
Pamela Rd B31 103 A3
Pancras Cl CV2 96 E1
Pan Croft B36 68 C7
Pandora Rd CV2 114 E7
Pangbourne Cl CV11 73 F8
Pangbourne Rd CV2 114 C8
Pangfield Pk CV5 112 C4
Panjab Gdns B67 64 F6
Pannel Croft B19 66 D6
Panther Croft B34 69 D5
Papenham Gn CV4 132 A8
Paper Mill Cotts B97 152 E5
Paper Mill Dr B98 154 B5
Paper Mill End B44 55 D6
Paper Mill End Ind Est
B42 55 D6
Papworth Dr B61 136 F5
Papyrus Way B36 57 F1
Parade
Birmingham B1 164 A3
Royal Leamington Spa
CV32 161 F8
Parade The
6 Hinckley LE10 75 D8
Birmingham B37 70 A5
Brownhills WS8 6 E1
Cradley Heath B64 82 E8
Dudley DY1 51 B2
Kingswinford DY6 60 B7
Nuneaton CV11 73 C3
Sutton Coldfield B72 46 C5
Parade View WS8 15 E8
Paradise Circus Queensway
B1,B3 164 A2
Paradise Ct B28 105 D6
Paradise DY2 62 D8
Paradise Gr WS3 14 F3
Paradise Ho 4 CV6 113 F7
Paradise La
Birmingham B28 105 E6
Walsall WS3 14 F3
Wolverhampton WV10 11 E8
Paradise Row B60 136 F2
Paradise St
Birmingham B3 164 B2
Coventry CV1 165 C1
Warwick CV34 160 F8
Paradise Way CV2 97 B1
Paradise Works CV6 113 F7
Paragon Pk CV1 113 D6
Paragon Way CV7 96 B8
Parbrook Cl CV4 131 E8
Parbury B77 35 D5
Parchments The WS13 3 B1
Pardington Cl B92 107 E8
Pargeter Ct 1 WS2 28 C2
Pargeter Rd B67 64 F2
Pargeter St
Stourbridge DY8 80 F4
Walsall WS2 28 C3
Par Gn B38 103 D1
Parish End CV31 162 C4
Parish Gdns DY9 81 C1
Parish Hill B61 120 D1
Parisienne Ho CV5 112 E2
Park App B23 56 C2
Park Ave
1 Birmingham,Balsall Heath
B12 86 F5
Birmingham,Hockley B18 66 A6
Birmingham,King's Norton
B30 104 A5
Burntwood WS7 7 B5
Coleshill B46 70 F6
Coventry CV6 95 C3
Norton Canes WS11 6 A5
Nuneaton CV11 73 E3
Oldbury B68 64 B3
Rowley Regis B65 63 C3
Smethwick B67 64 F4
Solihull B91 107 D3
Studley B80 159 E3
Tipton DY4 51 E5
Willenhall WV13 26 F2
Wolverhampton,Goldthorn Park
WV4 39 C5
Wolverhampton WV1 163 A4
Wombourne WV5 49 A5
Park Bldgs DY3 50 C4
Parkbrook Ind Est 5 DY9 81 F5
Park Butts Ringway
DY11 116 D6
Park Cir B6 66 F7
Park Cl
Brownhills WS8 15 F8
Cheslyn Hay WS6 4 E3
Dudley DY1 51 B7
Kenilworth CV8 148 B5
Oldbury B69 63 C7
Solihull B92 89 D2
Sutton Coldfield B24 57 D5
Park Cres
West Bromwich B71 53 D4
Wolverhampton WV1 163 A3
Park Croft
Burntwood WS7 6 C8
Hollywood B47 125 A5
Park Ct
Allesley CV5 112 B6
Kidderminster DY11 116 D5
Redditch B98 154 A3
Rowley Regis B65 63 C3
Sutton Coldfield B73 45 F1
Parkdale Ave WS10 42 A4
Parkdale Cl B24 56 F2
Parkdale Ct WS10 42 A4
Park Dale Ct WV1 25 A3
Parkdale Dr B31 123 A7
Park Dale E WV1 25 A3
Parkdale Rd B26 89 D6
Parkdale DY3 50 D8
Park Dale W WV1 25 A3
Park Dr
17 Sutton Coldfield,Four Oaks
B74 31 F2
Royal Leamington Spa
CV31 161 E7
Sutton Coldfield,Streetly
B74 31 C4
Wolverhampton WV4 39 C5
Park Edge B17 85 C7
Park End Dr B32 84 D1
Park End WS14 9 E7
Parker Ho B14 104 F3
Parker Paul Ind Est WV2 39 C7
Parker Rd WV11 12 F1
Parker St
Birmingham B16 65 F1
Walsall WS3 14 A1
Parkes Ave WV8 10 B2
Parkes Ct CV34 160 D7
Parkes Fold DY4 51 F8
Parkes Hall Rd DY1 51 A6
Parkes Ho 8 B69 64 A7
Parkes La
Dudley DY3 51 A7
Tipton DY4 51 F8
Parkes St
Brierley Hill DY5 61 D3
Smethwick B67 64 F4
Warwick CV34 160 D7
Willenhall WV13 27 B1
Parkeston Cres B44 45 C1
Park Farm Ind Est B98 159 C7
Park Farm Rd
Birmingham B43 44 B3
Tamworth B77 21 C1
Parkfield Ave B77 21 C1
Parkfield B32 84 A2
Parkfield Chalet Pk WV2 39 D6
Parkfield Cl
Birmingham,Lee Bank B15 86 C7
Birmingham,Quinton B62 84 A5
Redditch B98 154 B6
Tamworth B77 35 C8
Parkfield Colliery WV4 39 F5
Parkfield Cres
Tamworth B77 35 C8
Wolverhampton WV2 39 E6
Parkfield Ct 11 B46 70 F7
Parkfield B93 128 A1
Parkfield Dr
Birmingham B36 58 C1
Kenilworth CV8 148 B5
Parkfield Gr WV2 39 E6
Parkfield High Sch WV4 39 E5
Parkfield Jun & Inf Sch
B8 67 E3
Parkfield Prim Sch WV4 39 E5
Parkfield Rd
Birmingham B8 67 E4
Coleshill B46 70 F6
Dudley DY2 62 E6
Keresley CV7 95 A6
Oldbury B68 64 A3
Stourbridge DY8 81 B5
Wolverhampton WV2,WV4 39 E6
Parkgate Prim Sch CV6 95 B3
Parkgate Rd CV6 95 C3
Park Gr
Birmingham B10 87 D8
Water Orton B46 59 C2
Park Hall Cl WS5 43 C6
Park Hall Cres B36 69 C8
Parkhall Croft B34 69 C7
Park Hall Inf Sch WS5 43 C7
Park Hall Jun Sch WS5 43 C7
Park Hall Rd
Walsall WS5 43 D6
Wolverhampton WV4 39 D5
Park Hall Sch B36 58 E1
Park Head Cres DY2 62 B8
Park Head Rd DY2 62 B8
Park Hill B13 86 E4
Park Hill Dr B20 54 F4
Parkhill Dr CV5 112 A5
Park Hill Jun Sch CV8 148 C5
Park Hill CV8 148 B5
Park Hill La
Allesley CV5 112 A6
Coventry CV5 112 A5
Park Hill Prim Sch
Birmingham B13 86 F4
Coventry CV5 112 A4
Wednesbury WS10 42 C4
Park Hill Rd B17 85 C6
Parkhill Rd WS7 7 A8
Park Hill Rd B67 65 A5
Parkhill Rd B76 57 F6
Park Hill B65 63 B1
Park Hill St DY2 62 E8
Park Hill WS10 42 C4
Park Ho
1 Smethwick B66 65 C5
Essington WV11 13 A3
Kidderminster DY11 116 C3
Parkhouse Ave WV11 26 B6
Parkhouse Dr B23 56 B5
Parkhouse Gdns DY3 50 C4
Park Inn DY4 52 A4
Park La
Berkswell CV7 110 B2
Birmingham,Aston B6 66 F7
Birmingham,Castle Vale
B35 58 C4
Birmingham,Handsworth
B21 54 B3
Fazeley B78 20 E2
Great Wyrley WS6 5 A3
Halesowen B63 82 B6
Harvington DY10 118 A2
Kidderminster DY11 116 D6
Kingswinford DY6 60 E7
Parkland Ave DY11 116 B5
Parkland Cl CV6 95 C3
Parklands Ave CV32 157 C4
Parklands Cl B97 153 A5
Parklands Ct B17 85 A6
Parklands Dr B74 45 F8
Parklands Gdns WS1 43 A8
Parklands Rd
Bilston WV14 40 D3
Darlaston WS10 41 E5
Wolverhampton WV1 26 A1
Parklands B91 107 A3
Parklands The
Birmingham B23 56 D6
Kingswinford DY6 60 D6
Stourbridge DY9 81 D3
Wolverhampton WV3 24 D1
Park Lane E DY4 52 B4
Park Lane Ind Est
West Bromwich B21 54 B1
Wolverhampton WV10 25 E5
Park Lane Trad Est B69 64 A6
Park Lea
Nuneaton CV10 72 A3
Oldbury B69 64 A6
Shenstone WS14 18 B4
Wednesbury WS10 42 A5
Wolverhampton WV10 25 E6
Park La W DY4 51 F4
Park Lime Dr WS4 29 B4
Park Lime Pits Ctry Pk*
WS4 29 C4
Park Mall WS1 28 E2
Park Meadow Ave WV14 40 C8
Park Mews B29 85 B1
Park Paling The CV3 133 E7
Park Pl B7 67 C7
Park Rd
Bedworth CV12 78 B2
Bilston WV14 40 C5
Birmingham,Aston B6 67 A7
Birmingham,Hockley B18 66 A6
Birmingham,Moseley B13 86 F4
Birmingham,Sparkhill B11 87 C3
Birmingham,Stockland Green
B23 56 C2
Brierley Hill DY5 81 F8
Burntwood,Chase Terrace
WS7 6 F8
Burntwood,Triangle WS7 7 B5
Cannock WS11 1 D1
Coleshill B46 70 F6
Coventry CV1 165 B1
Darlaston WS10 41 C6
Park Rd *continued*
Dudley,Lower Gornal DY3 50 C4
Dudley,Netherton DY2 62 C6
Dudley,West Coseley DY1 51 B7
Park Rd E WV1 163 A4
Park Rd
Featherstone WV10 12 D8
Halesowen B63 82 B5
Hinckley LE10 75 E8
Kenilworth CV8 148 A6
Park Rd N B6 67 A7
Park Rd
Norton Canes WS11 6 A5
Oldbury B69 63 C8
Royal Leamington Spa
CV32 157 A4
Park Rd S B18 66 B5
Park Rd
Smethwick B67 64 F1
Solihull B91 107 D3
Stourbridge DY8 80 D5
Sutton Coldfield B73 46 B5
Tamworth B77 35 C5
Walsall,Daw End WS4 29 C5
Walsall,The Chuckery WS5 43 D5
Walsall,Wallington Heath
WS3 14 B1
West Hagley DY9 99 B6
Willenhall WV13 26 F3
Park Rd W
Stourbridge DY8 80 D5
Wolverhampton WV1 25 A3
Park Retreat B66 65 B5
Park Ridge Dr B63 82 B6
Park Ridge B74 46 A7
Park Rise
Kidderminster DY11 116 D5
Wolverhampton WV3 24 E2
Parkrose Ind Est B66 65 B7
Park St Arc 4 WS1 28 E2
Park St S WV2 39 C6
Park Sch B79 21 A7
Parks Cres WV11 13 A3
Parkside Ave WV13 26 E2
Parkside B32 84 C2
Parkside Cl WS10 42 B3
Parkside CV1 165 C2
Parkside Ct LE10 75 E8
Parkside Ind Est WV1 25 F1
Parkside La WS11 1 A2
Parkside Mid Sch B61 137 A3
Parkside Rd
Birmingham B20 54 E6
Halesowen B63 82 D5
Parkside B77 21 E1
Parkside Way
Birmingham B31 102 C1
Sutton Coldfield B74 31 A1
Park Sq B37 90 D8
Park St
Birmingham,Aston B6 67 A7
Birmingham,Digbeth B5 164 D2
Cannock WS11 4 E6
Cheslyn Hay WS6 4 E3
Coventry CV6 113 E7
Cradley Heath B64 62 E2
Darlaston WS10 41 C5
Kidderminster DY11 116 D5
Kingswinford DY6 60 D6
Nuneaton CV11 73 D3
Oldbury B69 63 F6
Parkstone Ave B61 150 D8
Parkstone Cl WS4 15 C1
Parkstone Rd CV6 95 F2
Park Street Gdns DY11 116 D6
Park St
Rowley Regis B65 63 D1
Royal Leamington Spa
CV32 156 F1
Stourbridge DY8 80 F8
Stourbridge,Lye DY9 81 F5
Stourbridge,Stambermill
DY8 81 A5
Tamworth B79 21 A5
Tipton DY4 52 A5
Walsall WS1 28 E2
Wednesbury WS10 41 F3
West Bromwich B70 53 D3
Park Terr
Birmingham B21 65 E8
Darlaston WS10 41 B6
Park The B97 152 C7
Park Trad Est B18 66 A6
Parktree Wlk B24 57 D4
Park Venture Ctr WS11 4 E6
Park View
Birmingham,Rotton Park
B18 65 E4
Birmingham,Small Heath
B10 87 D7
Burntwood WS7 6 E8
Park View Cl CV7 96 A8
Park View CV3 114 A2
Parkview CV5 165 A1
Parkview Cres WS2 28 A4
Park View Ct WS11 1 D1
Parkview Ct DY6 60 B8
Park View WS10 41 C6
Parkview Dr
Birmingham B8 68 A6
Brownhills WS8 6 F2
Park View B94 143 C6
Parkview Rd WV14 40 C8
Park View Rd
Birmingham B31 102 F3
Stourbridge DY9 81 F4
Sutton Coldfield B74 31 D3
Park View Sch B8 67 F5
Park View B73 46 A6
Parkview Trad Est B38 103 F3
Park Villas 10 B9 67 B2
Parkville Ave B17 85 B3
Parkville Cl CV6 95 C3
Parkville Highway CV6 95 B3
Park Way B45 122 B8
Parkway
Birmingham B8 68 A5
Coventry CV2 115 B8
Parkway Ind Ctr B7 67 A4
Parkway Rdbt WS10 41 E1
Parkway Rd DY1 51 A2
Park Way B98 154 A5
Parkway The
Perton WV6 23 F4
Walsall WS4 29 C8
Park Way WV11 13 A1
Park Wlk
4 Redditch B97 153 E3
Brierley Hill DY5 81 F8
Parkwood Cl WS8 16 A5
Parkwood Croft B43 44 B1
Park Wood Ct 11 B74 31 F2
Parkwood Ct CV8 148 B5
Parkwood Dr B73 45 C2
Park Wood La CV4 131 D7
Parkwood Rd B61 136 E3
Parkyn St WV2 163 D1
Parliament St
Birmingham,Aston B6 66 F6
Birmingham,Small Heath
B10 87 C8
West Bromwich B70 53 D1
Parlows End B38 123 D7
Parmington Cl B97 158 B6
Parmiter Ho CV32 156 F2
Parnell Ave WS13 9 A6
Parolles Cl CV34 161 E3
Parr Cl CV34 161 D6
Parrotts Gr CV2 96 D5
Parry Rd
Coventry CV2 114 C7
Kidderminster DY11 116 B3
Wednesfield WV11 27 A8
Parsonage Dr
Birmingham B45 122 D4
Halesowen B63 82 A7
Parsonage St
Oldbury B69 64 B7
West Bromwich B71 53 D6
Parson's Hill B30 104 B2
Parsons Hill B68 64 B2
Parsons Hollow B77 35 E7
Parson's La LE10 75 F8
Parson's Nook CV2 114 A5
Parsons Rd B98 153 E2
Parsons St DY1 51 C1
Parson St B77 35 E7
Parsons Way WS2 27 F6
Partons Rd B14 104 D6
Partridge Ave WS10 41 B6
Partridge Cl
Birmingham B37 70 D3
Cannock WS11 2 A1
Huntington WS12 1 D7
Partridge Croft
Coventry CV6 96 A1
Lichfield WS13 9 C8
Partridge Ct
4 Wednesbury WS10 41 F3
Birmingham B4 164 C4
Partridge Gr DY10 117 A2
Partridge Ho B97 153 D2
Partridge La B97 158 A7
Partridge Mill WS3 14 E3
Partridge Rd
Birmingham B26 69 A1
Stourbridge DY8 80 C4
Passey Rd B13 87 D2
Passfield Ave WS12 2 C7
Passfield Rd B33 69 A3
Pastorale Rd B60 137 C1
Pasture Gate WS11 1 C2
Pastures The WV6 23 D4
Pastures Wlk B38 123 D7
Pasture View WS3 14 F2
Pasture Way CV34 160 B4
Patch La B98 158 F6
Pat Davis Ct DY10 116 E7
Patent Dr WS10 41 D3
Patent Shaft Rdbt WS10 41 D3
Paternoster Row
4 Kidderminster DY11 116 D6
Wolverhampton WV1 163 B3
Paterson Ct B93 128 C6
Paterson Pl WS8 16 B5
Pathlow Cres B90 106 A1
Pathway The B14 104 C5
Patience Gr CV34 161 F3
Patios The DY11 116 C7
Patman Gdns B15 65 C1
Paton Gr B13 86 F2
Patricia Ave
Birmingham B14 105 C4
Wolverhampton WV4 39 D5
Patricia Cl CV4 111 C1
Patricia Cres DY1 51 B7
Patricia Dr DY4 52 A2
Patrick Gregory Rd WV11 26 F7
Patrick Ho 2 WS11 2 A3
Patrick Rd B26 88 E7
Patriot Cl WS1 42 D5
Patshull Ave WV10 11 B3
Patshull Cl B43 43 D1
Patshull Ct WV10 11 B3
Patshull Gr WV10 11 B3
Patshull Ho WV6 24 E5

Patshull Pl 7 B19 . . . . 66 C7
Pattens Rd CV34 . . . . 156 B1
Patterdale Rd
Birmingham B23 . . . . 56 D4
Cannock WS11 . . . . 2 A4
Patterdale Way DY5 . . . . . . 81 B8
Patterton Dr B76 . . . . 58 A7
Pattingham Rd WV6 . . . . . . 23 C2
Pattison Coll CV3 . . . . 114 A2
Pattison Gdns B23 . . . . 56 D2
Pattison St WS5 . . . . 42 E5
Paul Byrne Ct B20 . . . . 55 B1
Pauline Ave CV6 . . . . 96 B2
Paul Pursehouse Rd
WV14 . . . . 40 D3
Pauls Coppice WS8 . . . . . . 16 A5
Paul Stacy Ho CV1 . . . . . . 165 D4
Paul St
Dudley WV14 . . . . 40 A1
Wednesbury WS10 . . . . 42 B2
Wolverhampton WV2 . . . . 163 B2
Pauls Wlk WS13 . . . . 3 A3
Paul Vale DY4 . . . . 52 B5
Pavenham Dr B5 . . . . 86 C4
Pavilion Ave B67 . . . . 64 D3
Pavilion Dr B6 . . . . 55 F3
Pavilion Gdns
Bromsgrove B61 . . . . 136 F5
Dudley DY2 . . . . 62 C2
Pavilions Sh Ctr B4 . . . . . 164 C2
Pavilions The B37 . . . . 90 E8
Pavilion The B77 . . . . 22 B3
Pavilion Way CV5 . . . . 112 F3
Pavillion Cl WS9 . . . . 30 C7
Pavior's Rd WS7 . . . . 6 E4
Paxford Cl B98 . . . . 154 B6
Paxford Way B31 . . . . 102 F6
Paxmead Cl CV6 . . . . 95 A2
Paxton Ave WV6 . . . . 23 E3
Paxton Cl B60 . . . . 137 B1
Paxton Rd
Birmingham B18 . . . . 66 A5
Coventry CV6 . . . . 113 A4
Stourbridge DY9 . . . . 82 A4
Payne Cl CV32 . . . . 157 A2
Paynell Cl CV6 . . . . 95 B2
Payne's La CV1 . . . . 113 F3
Payne St B65 . . . . 63 C1
Payton Cl B69 . . . . 52 E1
Payton Rd B21 . . . . 65 D8
PDH Ind Est
Wednesbury WS10 . . . . 41 C3
Willenhall WV13 . . . . 26 D3
Peace Cl WS6 . . . . 4 E3
Peace Wlk B37 . . . . 70 B1
Peach Ave WS10 . . . . 41 C6
Peachley Cl 8 B63 . . . . 83 A3
Peach Ley Rd B29 . . . . 102 F7
Peach Rd WV12 . . . . 27 A6
Peacock Ave
Coventry CV2 . . . . 96 F1
Wednesfield WV11 . . . . 27 A7
Peacock Cl DY4 . . . . 52 B4
Peacock Mews DY10 . . . . 116 E8
Peacock Rd
Birmingham B13 . . . . 104 F6
Darlaston WS10 . . . . 41 B7
Peacocks Est B64 . . . . 62 C1
Peacocks The CV34 . . . . . 160 B2
Peak Croft B36 . . . . 68 D8
Peak Dr DY3 . . . . 50 E3
Peake Ave CV11 . . . . 73 E7
Peake Cres WS8 . . . . 15 F5
Peake Dr DY4 . . . . 52 B4
Peake Rd WS8 . . . . 16 A5
Peak House Rd B43 . . . . . . 43 E4
Peakman Cl B45 . . . . 122 A6
Peakman St B98 . . . . 153 E4
Peak Rd DY8 . . . . 81 B6
Peaks L Ctr B79 . . . . 21 B3
Peal St WS1 . . . . 28 F1
Pearce Cl DY1 . . . . 61 E8
Pearl Gr
3 Birmingham,Rotton Park
B18 . . . . 65 E4
Birmingham,Acock's Green
B27 . . . . 88 B3
Pearl Hyde Com Prim Sch
CV2 . . . . 115 A5
Pearl Hyde Ho 4 CV1 . . . 165 C4
Pearman Rd
Birmingham B45 . . . . 101 D1
Smethwick B66 . . . . 65 A3
Pearmans Croft B47 . . . . 125 A6
Pearsall Dr B69 . . . . 63 E8
Pears Cl CV8 . . . . 147 F5
Pearson Ave CV6 . . . . 96 B2
Pearson Ct WV12 . . . . 27 D4
Pearson St
Brierley Hill DY5 . . . . 61 D3
Cradley Heath B64 . . . . 62 E1
Stourbridge DY9 . . . . 81 F4
West Bromwich B70 . . . . . . 53 B4
Wolverhampton WV2 . . . . . 163 B1
Peart Dr B80 . . . . 159 C4
Pear Tree Ave
Nuneaton CV10 . . . . 72 E6
Tipton DY4 . . . . 51 F5
Peartree Ave WV13 . . . . . . 27 B1
Pear Tree Cl
4 Coventry CV2 . . . . 96 B2
Birmingham,Grove Vale B43 43 B1
Birmingham,Stechford B33 . 68 D2
Huntington WS12 . . . . 1 C7
Kidderminster DY10 . . . . . 117 B7
Shuttington B79 . . . . 22 E7
Solihull B90 . . . . 105 D2
Pear Tree Cres B90 . . . . . 105 C2
Pear Tree Ct
Birmingham B43 . . . . 54 C8
Rowley Regis B65 . . . . 63 D3
Pear Tree Dr
Birmingham B43 . . . . 43 C1
Rowley Regis B65 . . . . 63 D3
Peartree Dr DY8 . . . . 81 A2
Pear Tree Gr B90 . . . . 105 D2
Peartree Ind Est DY2 . . . . . 62 A6
Pear Tree La WS8 . . . . 6 C2
Peartree La
Cradley Heath B64 . . . . 62 E1
Dudley DY2 . . . . 62 A6
Pear Tree La
Dudley WV14 . . . . 51 D8
Wolverhampton WV11 . . . . . 26 B8
Pear Tree Rd
Birmingham B34 . . . . 69 C6
Birmingham,Grove Vale B43 43 B1
Smethwick B67 . . . . 64 E4
Peascroft La WV14 . . . . 40 E6
Peasefield Cl B21 . . . . 65 C8
Pebblebrook Way CV12 . . 78 C1
Pebble Cl
Stourbridge DY8 . . . . 81 B5
Tamworth B77 . . . . 22 B3
Pebble Island Way CV31 . 162 C5
Pebble Mill Cl WS11 . . . . 1 F2
Pebble Mill Dr WS11 . . . . . . 2 A2
Pebble Mill Rd B5 . . . . 86 C4
Pebworth Ave B90 . . . . . . 127 B6
Pebworth Cl
Birmingham B29 . . . . 86 B2
Coventry CV5 . . . . 112 B3
Redditch B98 . . . . 154 C7
Pebworth Gr
Birmingham B33 . . . . 89 C8
Dudley DY1 . . . . 51 B3
Peckham Rd B44 . . . . 45 A2
Peckingham St 2 B63 . . . . . 83 B3
Peckover Cl B65 . . . . 63 C1
Peckstone Cl CV1 . . . . 165 C1
Peddimore La B76 . . . . 58 C7
Pedmore CE Prim Sch
DY9 . . . . 81 C1
Pedmore Cl B98 . . . . 159 B7
Pedmore Court Rd DY8 . . . 81 B1
Pedmore Gr B44 . . . . 44 F2
Pedmore Hall La DY9 . . . . 99 C8
Pedmore La
Hagley DY9 . . . . 99 F8
Stourbridge DY9 . . . . 81 E1
Pedmore Rd
Brierley Hill DY5,DY2 . . . . . 61 F4
Stourbridge DY9 . . . . 81 E5
Pedmore Road Ind Est
DY5 . . . . 61 F4
Pedmore Tech Coll & Com
Sch DY9 . . . . 81 D4
Pedmore Wlk B69 . . . . 63 D5
Peel Cl
Coventry CV6 . . . . 113 E6
Darlaston WS10 . . . . 41 D8
Drayton Bassett B78 . . . . . . 34 E5
Hampton-in-A B92 . . . . . . 109 B6
Willenhall WV13 . . . . 27 A1
Peel Ct
Fazeley B78 . . . . 35 B8
Tamworth B77 . . . . 35 F6
Peel Dr
Cannock WS12 . . . . 1 F8
Tamworth B77 . . . . 35 F6
Peelers Way B77 . . . . 21 C1
Peel Ho B79 . . . . 21 A4
Peel La CV6 . . . . 113 F5
Peel Rd CV34 . . . . 160 E8
Peel St
Birmingham B18 . . . . 65 E5
Coventry CV6 . . . . 113 E6
Dudley DY2 . . . . 62 E8
Kidderminster DY11 . . . . . 116 D5
Tipton DY4 . . . . 52 A4
West Bromwich B71 . . . . . . 53 C5
Willenhall WV13 . . . . 27 A1
Wolverhampton WV3 . . . . . 163 B2
Peel Way B69 . . . . 52 D2
Peel Wlk 3 B17 . . . . 84 F7
Pegasus Ct
Halesowen B62 . . . . 83 F5
Sutton Coldfield B74 . . . . . . 32 A3
Pegasus Prim Sch B35 . . . 58 B3
Pegasus Wlk
Birmingham B29 . . . . 85 D1
Tamworth B79 . . . . 20 F7
Pegleg Wlk 2 B14 . . . . 104 C2
Pegmill Cl CV3 . . . . 133 F8
Pelham Dr DY1 . . . . 51 A2
Pelham Lodge DY10 . . . . . 117 A5
Pelham Rd B8 . . . . 68 B4
Pelham St WV3 . . . . 25 B1
Pelsall La
Walsall,Little Bloxwich
WS3 . . . . 14 D3
Walsall,Shelfield WS4 . . . . . 29 B8
Walsall WS3,WS4 . . . . 15 A1
Pelsall Rd WS8 . . . . 15 D7
Pelsall Village Sch WS3 . . 14 F4
Peltland Trad Ctr B98 . . . 154 D4
Pemberley Rd B27 . . . . 88 A2
Pemberton Cl B66 . . . . 65 B3
Pemberton Cres WS10 . . . 42 D5
Pemberton Rd
Dudley WV14 . . . . 40 D1
West Bromwich B70 . . . . . . 53 A6
Pemberton St B18 . . . . 66 B4
Pembridge Cl
Birmingham B32 . . . . 102 A7
Brierley Hill DY5 . . . . 61 F1
Pembridge Cl continued
Redditch B98 . . . . 154 D2
Pembridge Rd B93 . . . . . . 127 E3
Pembroke Ave WV2 . . . . . . 40 A7
Pembroke Cl
1 Warwick CV34 . . . . 160 F8
Bedworth CV12 . . . . 77 C1
Tamworth B79 . . . . 20 D6
West Bromwich B71 . . . . . . 42 B1
Willenhall WV12 . . . . 27 B6
Pembroke Croft B28 . . . . 106 A5
Pembroke Ct 8 CV32 . . . . 156 F2
Pembroke Gdns DY8 . . . . . 60 C2
Pembroke Ho 4 WS3 . . . . 28 C6
Pembroke Rd
Birmingham B12 . . . . 87 A4
West Bromwich B71 . . . . . . 42 B1
Pembroke Way
Birmingham,Vauxhall B8 . . . 67 C5
Birmingham,Yardley Wood
B28 . . . . 106 A5
Nuneaton CV11 . . . . 73 D3
West Bromwich B71 . . . . . . 53 B7
Pembrook Rd CV6 . . . . 95 C2
Pembury Ave CV6 . . . . 96 A3
Pembury Cl B74 . . . . 44 F6
Pembury Croft B44 . . . . . . 45 A1
Penarth Gr CV3 . . . . 134 F7
Pencombe Dr WV4 . . . . 39 D5
Pencraig Cl CV8 . . . . 148 C5
Pencroft Rd B34 . . . . 69 C7
Penda Ct B20 . . . . 66 A8
Penda Gr WV6 . . . . 23 F5
Pendeen Rd B14 . . . . 105 C4
Pendeford Ave WV6 . . . . . . 24 E8
Pendeford Bsns Pk WV9 . . 10 F3
Pendeford Cl WV6 . . . . 24 E8
Pendeford Hall La WV9 . . 10 D5
Pendeford High Sch
WV10 . . . . 11 B2
Pendeford La WV9 . . . . 11 A3
Pendeford Mill La WV8 . . . 10 C3
Pendeford Mill Nature
Reserve* WV9 . . . . 10 E4
Pendene Ct WV4 . . . . 39 A5
Pendenis Cl CV6 . . . . 114 A8
Pendennis Cl B30 . . . . 103 D5
Pendennis Dr B69 . . . . 63 A8
Penderel Ct CV6 . . . . 95 C3
Penderell Cl WV10 . . . . 12 A6
Penderel St WS3 . . . . 14 C1
Pendigo Way
Birmingham B40 . . . . 90 E3
Birmingham B40 . . . . 90 F4
Pendinas Dr WV8 . . . . 10 B3
Pendine Ct 4 CV32 . . . . . 161 D8
Pendle Hill WS12 . . . . 2 C4
Pendleton Gr B27 . . . . 106 B8
Pendock Ct B23 . . . . 56 C3
Pendragon Rd B42 . . . . 55 C4
Pendrel Cl WS6 . . . . 13 F8
Pendrell Cl
Birmingham B37 . . . . 70 A3
Codsall WV8 . . . . 10 A3
Pendrill Rd WV10 . . . . 11 E3
Penfields Rd DY8 . . . . 81 B6
Penge Gr B44 . . . . 44 E3
Penhallow Dr WV4 . . . . 39 E5
Penhurst Ave B20 . . . . 55 D1
Penk Dr WS7 . . . . 7 D6
Penkridge Cl WS2 . . . . 28 D3
Penkridge Ct WS11 . . . . 1 D1
Penkridge Gr B33 . . . . 68 F4
Penkridge St WS2 . . . . 28 D3
Penk Rise WV6 . . . . 24 B4
Penley Gr B8 . . . . 68 B6
Penmakers Ct B67 . . . . 65 B4
Penmanor B60 . . . . 151 D8
Pennant Ct
Rowley Regis B65 . . . . 63 B3
Wolverhampton WV3 . . . . . 163 A1
Pennant Gr B29 . . . . 85 A2
Pennant Rd
Cradley Heath B64 . . . . 62 D1
Hinckley LE10 . . . . 75 D5
Rowley Regis B65 . . . . 63 B3
Pennard Gr B32 . . . . 84 F4
Penn Cl WS3 . . . . 14 C1
Penn Common Rd WV4 . . . 38 F1
Penncricket Ct B68 . . . . 63 F3
Penncricket La B65,B68 . . . 63 E3
Penn Croft La WV4 . . . . 39 A1
Penncroft WV4 . . . . 38 E4
Penndale Cl B24 . . . . 57 C6
Penn Fields Sch WV3 . . . . 38 F7
Penn Gr B29 . . . . 85 B2
Penn Hall Sch WV4 . . . . . . 38 E3
Penn Ho CV4 . . . . 111 F1
Penn Hospl WV4 . . . . 38 E4
Pennhouse Ave WV4 . . . . . 38 F5
Penn Ind Est B64 . . . . 62 D1
Pennine Dr
Cannock WS11 . . . . 1 E2
Dudley DY3 . . . . 50 D3
Pennine Rd B61 . . . . 137 A5
Pennine Way
Birmingham B8 . . . . 67 D6
Nuneaton CV10 . . . . 72 B3
Stourbridge DY8 . . . . 81 A6
Tamworth B77 . . . . 36 C8
Willenhall WV12 . . . . 27 D4
Pennington Cl B70 . . . . 53 A2
Pennington Way CV6 . . . . 113 E8
Penn La B94 . . . . 141 C4
Penn Rd
Gospel End Village DY3 . . . . 49 F8
Rowley Regis B65 . . . . 63 E3
Penn Rd continued
Wolverhampton WV2,WV3,
WV4 . . . . 39 A6
Penn Road Island WV2 . . 163 B2
Penns Cl CV32 . . . . 157 E5
Penns Ct B76 . . . . 57 F7
Penns Lake Rd B76 . . . . 57 E7
Penns La B72,B76 . . . . 57 D7
Penns Prim Sch B72 . . . . . 57 D6
Penn St
6 Cradley Heath B64 . . . . . 82 F8
Birmingham B4 . . . . 67 A3
Wolverhampton WV3 . . . . . 163 A1
Penns Wood Cl DY3 . . . . . . 39 C2
Penns Wood Dr B76 . . . . . . 57 D7
Pennwood Ct WV4 . . . . 38 D6
Pennwood La WV4 . . . . 38 F3
Pennyacre Rd B14 . . . . . . 104 D2
Pennycress Gdns WV10 . . 12 C7
Penny Cress Gn WS11 . . . . . 5 F4
Pennycroft Ho B33 . . . . 68 E3
Penny Ct
Great Wyrley WS6 . . . . 13 F8
Tamworth B79 . . . . 21 B5
Penny Farthing Arc DY3 . . 50 D8
Pennyfield Croft B33 . . . . . 68 E3
Pennyford Cl B97 . . . . 153 A5
Pennyhill La B71 . . . . 53 F7
Pennymoor Rd B77 . . . . 36 B7
Penny Park La CV6 . . . . 95 A3
Penny Royal Cl DY3 . . . . . . 50 D2
Pennyroyal Cl WS5 . . . . 43 B3
Pennys Croft WS13 . . . . 3 E1
Pennystone Cl CV31 . . . . . 162 D6
Penrice Dr B69 . . . . 52 A1
Penrith Cl
Brierley Hill DY5 . . . . 81 B8
Coventry CV6 . . . . 95 C2
Royal Leamington Spa
CV32 . . . . 156 C2
Penrith Croft B32 . . . . 102 D8
Penrith Gr B37 . . . . 70 C2
Penrose Cl CV4 . . . . 132 A7
Penryhn Cl CV8 . . . . 148 C5
Penryn Cl
Nuneaton CV11 . . . . 74 A4
Walsall WS5 . . . . 43 D7
Penryn Rd WS5 . . . . 43 D7
Pensby Cl B13 . . . . 105 D8
Pensett Trad Est The DY6 . 50 A1
Pensford Rd B31 . . . . 103 C3
Pensham Croft B90 . . . . . . 127 A6
Penshaw Cl WV9 . . . . 11 A2
Penshaw Gr B13 . . . . 87 D1
Penshurst Rd B60 . . . . 137 C1
Penshurst Way CV11 . . . . . 78 F8
Pensilva Way 2 CV1 . . . . . 113 E4
Pens Meadow Sch DY8 . . . 60 E3
Pensnett Rd
Brierley Hill DY5 . . . . 61 C4
Dudley DY1 . . . . 61 F7
Pensnett Sch of Tech
DY5 . . . . 61 B6
Pensnett Trad Est The
DY6 . . . . 60 F8
Penstock Ct DY10 . . . . 117 C8
Penstock Dr B69 . . . . 64 A4
Penstone La WV4 . . . . 37 E4
Pentire Cl CV11 . . . . 73 F5
Pentire Rd WS14 . . . . 9 D6
Pentland Cl LE10 . . . . 71 B1
Pentland Croft B12 . . . . 86 F7
Pentland Gdns WV6 . . . . . . 24 E2
Pentos Dr B11 . . . . 87 D3
Pentridge Cl B76 . . . . 57 F5
Penwood Gdns WV14 . . . . . 51 C8
Penzance Cl LE10 . . . . 71 E4
Penzance Way CV11 . . . . . . 74 A5
Penzer Dr B45 . . . . 138 D8
Penzer St DY6 . . . . 60 D7
Peolsford Rd WS3 . . . . 15 A4
Peony Wlk B23 . . . . 56 B3
Peplins Way B30 . . . . 104 B3
Peplow Rd B33 . . . . 69 A4
Pepperbox Dr DY4 . . . . 52 A5
Peppercorn Pl B70 . . . . 53 C4
Pepper Hill DY8 . . . . 81 A4
Pepper La CV1 . . . . 165 B2
Pepperwood Cl B61 . . . . . . 120 C3
Pepper Wood Dr B31 . . . . 102 C1
Pepys Cnr CV4 . . . . 111 E3
Pepys Ct B43 . . . . 54 E7
Perch Ave B37 . . . . 70 A3
Perch Cl WV10 . . . . 26 B4
Perchfoot Cl CV1 . . . . 165 C1
Perch Rd WS2 . . . . 28 A4
Percival Rd B16 . . . . 65 C1
Percy Bsns Pk B69 . . . . 63 F7
Percy Cres CV8 . . . . 147 E2
Percy Rd
Birmingham B11 . . . . 87 D4
Kenilworth CV8 . . . . 147 E2
Warwick CV34 . . . . 160 E8
Percy Shurmer Prim Sch
B12 . . . . 86 E7
Percy St CV1 . . . . 165 A3
Percy Terr 5 CV32 . . . . . . 156 D1
Peregrine Cl DY1 . . . . 50 F1
Peregrine Dr CV5 . . . . 112 A5
Peregrine Gr DY10 . . . . . . 117 A2
Pereira Rd B17 . . . . 85 C7
Pericles Cl CV34 . . . . 161 E3
Perimeter Rd
Birmingham B40 . . . . 90 D4
Birmingham B40 . . . . 90 E4
Perivale Gr
Bilston WV14 . . . . 40 D1
Dudley WV14 . . . . 51 D8
Perivale Way DY8 . . . . 81 A8
Periwinkle Cl WS8 . . . . 15 D6
Perkins Cl DY1 . . . . 51 C6
Perks Rd WV11 . . . . 13 A1
Perott Dr B75 . . . . 32 D2
Perrett Wlk 5 DY11 . . . . . 116 D6
Perrin Ave DY11 . . . . 116 B4
Perrins Gr B8 . . . . 68 A6
Perrins La DY9 . . . . 81 F4
Perrins Rise DY9 . . . . 81 F4
Perrott Gdns DY5 . . . . 61 B1
Perrott St B18 . . . . 65 E6
Perry Ave
Birmingham B42 . . . . 55 C5
Wolverhampton WV10 . . . . . 25 F8
Perry Barr Sta B20 . . . . 55 D2
Perry Barr Stad (Greyhound)
B42 . . . . 55 D3
Perry Beeches Inf Sch
B42 . . . . 55 C8
Perry Beeches Jun Sch
B42 . . . . 55 C8
Perry Beeches Sch B42 . . . 55 C8
Perry Cl
Dudley DY2 . . . . 62 D8
Tamworth B79 . . . . 21 B6
Perry Common Jun & Inf Sch
B23 . . . . 56 B7
Perry Common Rd B23 . . . . 56 C6
Perrycrofts Cres B79 . . . . . 21 C7
Perry Ct B68 . . . . 84 B7
Perryfields Cl B98 . . . . . . 158 F6
Perryfields Cres B61 . . . . 136 F5
Perryfields High Sch B68 . 84 A8
Perryfields Prim Sch B68 84 A7
Perryfields Rd B61 . . . . . . 136 D4
Perryford Dr B91 . . . . 127 C8
Perry Green Ho B42 . . . . . . 55 D5
Perry Hall Dr WV12 . . . . . . 27 B5
Perry Hall Prim Sch WV11 26 F6
Perry Hall Rd WV11 . . . . . . 26 F6
Perry Hill Cres B68 . . . . . . 84 B7
Perry Hill Ho B68 . . . . 84 C8
Perry Hill La B68 . . . . 84 B7
Perry Hill Rd B68 . . . . 84 B7
Perry La B61 . . . . 136 F2
Perrymill La B96 . . . . 159 B1
Perry Park Cres B42 . . . . . 55 C6
Perry Park Rd B64 . . . . 63 B1
Perry St
Bilston WV14 . . . . 40 E3
Darlaston WS10 . . . . 41 D8
Smethwick B66 . . . . 65 A7
Tipton DY4 . . . . 52 A4
Wednesbury WS10 . . . . 41 F2
Perry Trad Est WV14 . . . . . 40 E3
Perry Villa Dr B42 . . . . 55 D5
Perrywell Rd A4 . . . . 56 A4
Perry Wood Rd B42 . . . . . . 55 A8
Persehouse St WS1 . . . . . . 28 F2
Pershore Ave B29 . . . . 86 B2
Pershore Cl WS3 . . . . 13 F2
Pershore Ct DY11 . . . . 116 D5
Pershore Pl CV4 . . . . 132 E6
Pershore Rd
Birmingham,Balsall Heath
B5 . . . . 86 C4
Birmingham,Breedon Cross
B30 . . . . 104 A5
Birmingham,Ten Acres
B30 . . . . 104 B8
Halesowen B63 . . . . 83 A2
Kidderminster DY11 . . . . . 116 A6
Pershore Rd S B30 . . . . . . 103 F3
Pershore Rd WS3 . . . . 13 F2
Pershore St B5 . . . . 164 C1
Pershore Way WS3 . . . . 13 F2
Perth Rd WV12 . . . . 27 B6
Perth Rise CV5 . . . . 112 A4
Perton Brook Vale WV6 . . 23 F2
Perton Fst Sch WV6 . . . . . . 23 E5
Perton Gr
Birmingham B29 . . . . 103 A8
Wolverhampton WV6 . . . . . . 23 F2
Perton Mid Sch WV6 . . . . . 24 A5
Perton Rd WV6 . . . . 23 F2
Perton Sandown Fst Sch
WV6 . . . . 23 F4
Pestilence La
Alvechurch,Arrowfield Top
B48 . . . . 139 C8
Alvechurch B48 . . . . 139 D8
Petard Cl B77 . . . . 35 C8
Petchells Cl DY5 . . . . 61 B5
Peter Ave WV14 . . . . 40 F2
Peterborough Dr WS12 . . . . 2 C1
Peterbrook Cl B98 . . . . . . 158 F7
Peterbrook Prim Sch
B90 . . . . 105 D2
Peterbrook Rd B90 . . . . . . 105 D1
Peterbrook Rise B90 . . . . . 105 D1
Peterdale Dr WV4 . . . . 38 F3
Peter Hall La CV7 . . . . 115 F6
Peterhead B77 . . . . 21 F5
Peterhouse Mews 1 B13 . . 87 A2
Peterlee Wlk 6 CV2 . . . . . 115 A7
Peters Ave B31 . . . . 102 F2
Petersbourne Ct B28 . . . . 105 F8
Petersfield WS11 . . . . 1 F4
Petersfield Ct B28 . . . . . . 105 F8
Petersfield Dr B65 . . . . 63 E3
Petersfield Rd B28 . . . . . . 105 E7
Peter's Finger B60 . . . . . . 136 F1
Petersham Pl B15 . . . . 85 E6
Petersham Rd B44 . . . . 45 C1

Peter's Hill Prim Sch DY5 81 C7
Peter's Hill Rd DY5 81 C6
Petershouse Dr B74 31 F5
Peter's La WS7 8 A5
Peters St B70 53 A7
Peters Wlk
Coventry CV6 96 A4
Lichfield WS13 3 A2
Petford St B64 62 E1
Petitor Cres CV2 96 C1
Peto Gr CV34 161 F2
Pettitt Cl B14 104 E2
Petton Cl B98 154 F3
Pettyfield Cl B26 89 A6
Pettyfields Cl B93 128 A5
Petunia Cl CV10 78 A8
Petworth Cl 3 WV13 40 F8
Petworth Gr B26 88 E6
Pevensey Cl B69 62 F8
Pevensey Rd B60 137 C1
Peverell Dr B28 105 F7
Peveril Dr CV3 133 B5
Peveril Gr B76 46 E4
Peverill Rd
Perton WV6 23 F4
Wolverhampton WV4 39 E3
Pevril Way B43 43 F2
Peyto Cl CV6 95 C2
Pheasant Cl
Bedworth CV12 77 D1
Kidderminster DY10 117 A2
Pheasant Croft B36 70 A8
Pheasant La B98 158 F7
Pheasant Oak CV4 111 C2
Pheasant Rd B67 64 D1
Pheasant St DY5 61 C3
Pheasant Way WS11 2 A1
Pheasey Park Farm Prim Sch B43 44 C4
Philip Ct
1 Royal Leamington Spa CV31 161 F6
Sutton Coldfield B76 46 F3
Philip Gr WS11 1 E6
Philip Rd
Halesowen B63 82 F3
Tipton DY4 52 D5
Philip Sidney Rd B11 87 C3
Philip St WV14 40 D1
Philip Victor Rd B20 54 F1
Phillimore Rd B8 67 D5
Phillip Docker Ct CV12 79 B2
Phillippes Rd 6 CV34 155 F1
Phillip Rd WS2 42 C6
Phillips Ave WV11 12 F1
Phillips St B6 66 E6
Phillips Street Ind Est B6 66 F6
Phillips Terr B98 153 F4
Phipson Rd B11 87 B3
Phoebe Cl CV34 161 E3
Phoenix Bsns Pk
Birmingham B7 67 A6
Hinckley LE10 74 E8
Phoenix Ct
Birmingham,Castle Vale B35 58 A3
Birmingham,Edgbaston B5 86 C5
Phoenix Ctr WS11 4 E6
Phoenix Gn B15 85 E7
Phoenix Ind Est
Bilston WV14 40 F4
Willenhall WV11 26 D3
Phoenix International Ind Est B70 52 F5
Phoenix Pk Ind Est CV7 96 B7
Phoenix Pk B62 63 E2
Phoenix Rd
Cannock WS11 2 A2
Tipton DY4 51 F6
Willenhall WV11 26 D3
Phoenix Rise
Birmingham B23 56 B7
Wednesbury WS10 41 E4
Wolverhampton WV2 39 C6
Phoenix St
West Bromwich B70 52 F4
Wolverhampton WV2 39 D6
Phoenix Way CV6 95 E3
Picasso Cl WS11 2 D2
Piccadilly Arc 3 B2 164 B2
Piccadilly Cl B37 70 C1
Piccadilly Cres B78 35 F1
Piccadilly B78 35 F1
Pickard St CV34 161 A7
Pickenham Rd B14 105 A1
Pickering Croft B32 84 D1
Pickering Rd WV11 26 D5
Pickersleigh Cl 6 B63 83 A3
Pickford Cl CV11 74 A1
Pickford Grange La CV5 111 C7
Pickford Green La CV5 111 C7
Pickford St B5 66 F2
Pickford Way CV5 112 B6
Pickrell Rd WV14 40 B1
Pickwick Cl B13 87 B2
Pickwick Gr B13 87 C2
Pickwick Pl WV14 40 E4
Picton Croft 6 B37 70 D2
Picton Gr B13 105 B6
Picturedrome Way 4 WS10 41 D6
Piddock Rd B66 65 A5
Pierce Ave B92 88 E3
Piercy St B70 53 A3
Piers Cl CV34 160 F8
Piers Rd B21 66 A7
Pier St WS8 15 F7
Piggots Croft B37 69 F3
Pike Cl
Birmingham B20 54 F1
Hinckley LE10 75 D5
Pike Dr B37 70 C3
Pikehelve St B70 52 E7
Pike Hill B60 138 A7
Pikehorne Croft B36 58 D2
Pike Rd WS2 28 A4
Pikers La CV7 94 A3
Pikes Pool La B60 137 E2
Pikes The B45 121 F8
Pikewater Rd B9 67 D2
Pilgrims Gate LE10 76 A6
Pilgrims Wlk CV6,CV7 95 B6
Pilkington Ave B72 46 C2
Pilkington Rd CV5 132 D8
Pillaton Dr WS12 1 C6
Pilling Cl CV2 114 F8
Pilson Cl B36 68 F8
Pimbury Rd WV12 27 D7
Pimlico Ct DY3 50 D3
Pimpernel Dr WS5 43 A3
Pinbury Croft B37 70 B1
Pinchers Cl DY9 119 E7
Pineapple Cl B14 104 C6
Pineapple Gr B30 104 C8
Pineapple Pl B14 104 D6
Pineapple Rd B30 104 C7
Pine Ave
Smethwick B66 64 E7
Wednesbury WS10 41 F4
Pine Cl
Great Wyrley WS6 4 F4
Kingswinford DY6 60 D5
Solihull B91 106 F2
Tamworth B79 21 B8
Wolverhampton WV3 25 A1
Pine Ct
Coventry CV5 111 C4
Royal Leamington Spa CV32 157 B3
Stourbridge DY9 81 B1
Wolverhampton WV11 26 C6
Pine Gn DY1 51 A5
Pine Gr
Birmingham B14 105 A5
Burntwood WS7 6 F5
Lower Marlbrook B45 121 F2
Pine Ho B36 68 F8
Pinehurst CV32 157 E6
Pinehurst Dr B38 103 F3
Pine Leigh B74 32 B1
Pineneedle Croft WV12 27 E4
Pine Rd
Dudley DY1 51 C4
Oldbury B69 63 A8
Pineridge Dr DY11 116 B5
Pines Park Home Est The WS12 1 D5
Pine Sq B37 70 B2
Pines Specl Sch The B36 68 F8
Pines The
Bedworth CV12 77 E2
Birmingham B45 102 A1
Cheswick Green B90 126 D5
Coventry CV4 131 D7
Lichfield WS14 9 F7
Walsall WS1 42 F8
Wolverhampton WV3 24 D1
Pine St WS3 14 D2
Pine Tree Ave CV4 112 A2
Pine Tree Cl B97 152 F3
Pine Tree Ct CV12 78 C4
Pinetree Dr B74 30 D1
Pine Tree Rd CV12 78 D4
Pineview B31 102 F2
Pinewall Ave B38 104 A1
Pineways Dr WV6 24 E4
Pineways
Stourbridge DY8 60 C2
Sutton Coldfield B74 31 C3
Pineways The B69 63 C5
Pine Wlk
Birmingham B31 103 B3
Stourbridge DY9 81 D3
Pinewood Ave
Cannock WS11 1 D4
Wood End CV9 36 C1
Pinewood Bsns Pk B37 90 B8
Pinewood Cl
Birmingham B45 121 D8
Birmingham,Great Barr B44 55 E7
Brownhills WS8 6 E2
Walsall WS5 43 B4
Willenhall WV12 27 E7
Wolverhampton WV3 38 A8
Wombourne WV5 49 A6
Pinewood Dr
Binley Woods CV3 135 C7
Birmingham B32 84 A1
Pinewood Gr CV5 133 B8
Pinewoods Ave DY9 98 F4
Pine Woods B32 84 A2
Pinewoods
Birmingham,Hurst Green B62 84 A7
Birmingham,Woodcock Hill B31 102 F8
Pinewoods Cl DY9 98 F4
Pinewoods Ct DY9 98 F4
Pinewood Wlk DY6 60 E8
Pinfield Dr B45 122 B1
Pinfold Cl LE10 74 F7
Pinfold Cres WV4 38 D6
Pinfold Ct WS10 41 C5
Pinfold Gdns WV11 26 D5
Pinfold Gr WV4 38 D6
Pinfold Hill WS14 17 F6
Pinfold Ind Est WS3 28 C8
Pinfold La
Cheslyn Hay WS6 4 C2
Norton Canes WS11 5 E4
Walsall WS9 44 B6
Wolverhampton WV4 38 E5
Pinfold Rd B91 107 E5
Pinfold St
Bilston WV14 40 D5
Birmingham B2 164 B2
Darlaston WS10 41 D5
Oldbury B69 64 A8
Pinfold Street Extension WS10 41 C5
Pinfold Street JMI Sch WS10 41 C5
Pinfold WS3 28 C8
Pingle Cl B71 42 F1
Pingle Ct CV11 73 D2
Pingle La WS7 7 D5
Pink Green La B97 153 C5
Pinkney Pl B68 64 C3
Pinley Fields CV3 134 B8
Pinley Gr B43 44 C3
Pinley Way 2 B91 107 A1
Pinnacle Ho B97 158 E5
Pinner Ct B17 85 C6
Pinner Gr B32 84 E4
Pinner's Croft CV2 114 A5
Pinnock Pl CV4 111 F1
Pinson Gdns WV13 26 F1
Pinson Rd WV13 26 F2
Pintail Dr B23 56 C2
Pintail Gr DY10 117 B3
Pinto Cl B16 65 F2
Pinvin Ho B97 153 A3
Pinza Croft B36 68 D8
Pioli Pl WS2 28 D5
Pioneer Cl B97 153 D4
Pioneer Ho CV1 165 D4
Pioneer Way B35 58 B2
Pipe Hall Farm Nature Reserve★ WS13 8 A8
Piper Cl WV6 23 F4
Piper Pl DY8 80 F8
Piper Rd WV3 38 C8
Pipers Cl B61 150 D7
Pipers Croft WS13 3 A2
Pipers Ct CV3 132 F4
Pipers Gn B28 105 F5
Piper's La CV8 148 A5
Pipers Rd B98 159 D7
Piper's Row WV1 163 C3
Pipes Mdw WV14 40 E5
Pipit Ct DY10 117 A2
Pipkin Ct CV1 165 D1
Pippin Ave B63 82 B7
Pirbright Cl WV14 40 E3
Pirrey Cl WV14 40 E1
Pitcairn Cl B30 104 B6
Pitcairn Dr B62 83 B5
Pitcairn Ho B67 64 E2
Pitcairn Rd B67 64 D2
Pitchcombe Cl B98 154 A2
Pitcheroak Cotts B97 153 A3
Pitcheroak Sch B97 153 B4
Pitclose Rd B31 103 B1
Pitfield Rd B33 69 E1
Pitfield Row 17 DY1 51 B1
Pitfields Cl B68 84 A8
Pitfields Rd B68 84 A8
Pitfield St 5 DY1 51 C1
Pithall Rd B34 69 D5
Pit Leasow Cl B30 104 B8
Pitman Rd B32 84 C5
Pitmaston Ct B13 86 D3
Pitmaston Rd B28 106 B6
Pitmeadow Ho B14 104 E2
Pitsford St B18 66 B4
Pitt La B92 90 D2
Pitts Farm Rd B24 57 C6
Pitt St
Birmingham B4 67 A3
Wolverhampton WV3 163 B2
Pixall Dr B15 86 B6
Pixhall Wlk B35 58 B3
Plainview Cl WS9 30 E2
Plaistow Ave B36 68 C7
Plane Cl CV10 72 E7
Plane Gr B37 70 B1
Planetary Ind Est WV13 26 C4
Planetary Rd WV13 26 C3
Planet Rd DY5 61 D4
Planetree Cl B60 137 B2
Plane Tree Cl DY10 116 F7
Planetree Rd B74 44 D8
Plane Tree Rd WS5 43 C4
Plank La B46 59 A2
Planks La WV5 49 A7
Plantagenet Pk CV34 161 E3
Plantation Dr B75 46 F6
Plantation La
Himley DY3 49 B3
Hopwas B78 20 B4
Plantation Rd WS5 43 A4
Plantation The DY5 61 B7
Plant Ct 19 DY5 61 D2
Plant La WS7 6 E7
Plants Brook Rd B76 57 F6
Plantsbrook Sch B72 46 C4
Plants Cl
Great Wyrley WS6 14 A8
Sutton Coldfield B73 45 D1
Plants Gr B24 57 D5
Plants Hill Cres CV4 111 E1
Plants Hollow DY5 61 D1
Plant St
Cradley Heath B64 62 D1
Stourbridge DY8 60 E2
Plant Way WS3 14 F4
Plascom Rd WV1 26 A1
Plato Cl CV34 161 E5
Platts Cres DY8 80 E8
Platts Dr DY8 80 F8
Platts Rd DY8 80 E8
Platt St
Cannock WS11 2 A5
Darlaston WS10 41 D5
Playdon Gr B14 105 A3
Pleasant Cl DY6 60 C4
Pleasant St
Kidderminster DY10 116 E7
West Bromwich,Hill Top B70 53 A8
West Bromwich,Lambert's End B70 53 C2
Pleasant View DY3 50 D2
Pleasant Way CV32 157 A2
Pleck Bsns Pk WS2 28 C1
Pleck Ho B14 104 C1
Pleck Ind Est WS2 42 C8
Pleck Rd WS2 28 C1
Pleck Wlk B38 104 A1
Plestowes Cl B90 106 B5
Pleydell Cl CV3 134 C5
Plimsoll Gr B32 84 C5
Plimsoll St DY11 116 D5
Plough Ave B32 84 C2
Plough & Harrow Rd B16 65 F1
Plough Hill Rd CV10 72 A6
Ploughmans Pl B75 32 D4
Ploughmans Wlk
Kingswinford DY6 60 A7
Lichfield WS13 3 C3
Stoke Heath B60 150 D6
Wolverhampton WV8 10 F1
Plover Cl WV10 12 B7
Ploverdale Cres DY6 61 A6
Plover Gr DY10 117 B1
Plowden Rd B33 68 F4
Plume St B6 67 C8
Plumstead Cl B97 153 C6
Plumstead Rd B44 56 B8
Plym Cl WV11 26 C5
Plymouth Cl
Birmingham B31 123 A7
Coventry CV2 114 C7
Redditch B97 153 C1
Plymouth Ct B97 153 C1
Plymouth Dr B45 138 A8
Plymouth Ho B60 152 B7
Plymouth Pl CV31 162 A7
Plymouth Rd
Barnt Green B45 138 A8
Birmingham B30 104 B7
Redditch B97 153 D2
Plympton Mews B71 53 C6
Pochard Cl DY10 116 F1
Poets Cnr B10 87 D7
Poins Cl CV34 161 F3
Pointon Cl WV14 40 A2
Poitiers Rd CV3 133 D6
Polden Cl B63 82 C1
Polesworth Cl B98 154 D1
Polesworth Gr B34 69 B6
Polesworth High Sch B78 36 F7
Pollard Rd B27 88 C1
Pollards The B23 56 E8
Polly Brooks Yd DY9 81 E5
Polo Fields DY9 81 B1
Polperro Dr CV5 112 A5
Pomeroy Cl CV4 131 D7
Pomeroy Rd
Birmingham B32 84 C1
Birmingham,Pheasey B43 44 D4
Pommel Cl WS5 42 F4
Pond Cres WV2 39 E7
Pond Farm Mews CV5 111 E5
Pond Gr WV2 39 E7
Pond La WV2 39 D7
Pondthorpe CV3 134 E6
Ponesfield Rd WS13 3 B2
Ponesgreen WS13 3 B2
Pontypool Ave CV3 134 F6
Pool Ave WS11 6 B5
Pool Bank B98 153 E2
Pool Bank St CV11 73 B4
Poole Cres
Birmingham B17 85 C3
Brownhills WS8 6 D2
Dudley WV14 40 D2
Poolehouse Rd B43 43 E3
Pool End Cl B93 127 F6
Poole Rd CV6 113 A6
Pooles Ct DY10 116 E7
Pooles La WV12 27 D8
Poole St
Stourbridge DY8 80 E4
Wolverhampton WV10 25 E4
Poole's Way WS7 7 C7
Pooley La B78 22 F2
Pool Farm Rd B27 88 C1
Pool Field Ave B31 102 E7
Poolfield Dr B91 106 F3
Poolfield Rd WS13 8 E6
Pool Furlong DY9 99 E1
Pool Gn WS9 30 A5
Pool Green Terr WS9 30 A5
Pool Hall Cres WV3 38 A8
Pool Hall Rd WV3 38 A8
Pool Hayes Com Sch WV12 27 B5
Pool Hayes La WV12 27 B5
Pool Hayes Prim Sch WV12 27 B6
Poolhead La
Earlswood B94 141 C7
Tanworth-In-A B94 141 E5
Pool La B69 63 F3
Pool Mdw
Cheslyn Hay WS6 4 D1
Sutton Coldfield B76 58 A8
Pool Meadow Cl
Birmingham B13 87 C1
Solihull B91 107 F2
Pool Rd
Brownhills WS7 6 E3
Burntwood WS7 6 E4
Halesowen B63 83 B3
Nuneaton CV10 72 F5
Smethwick B66 65 B5
Studley B80 159 E4
Wednesfield WV11 27 A6
Pool Road Bsns Ctr CV10 72 F5
Poolside Gdns CV3 133 A5
Pool St
Birmingham B6 66 F6
Dudley DY1 51 A6
Walsall WS1 28 F1
Wolverhampton WV2 163 B1
Pooltail Wlk B31 102 D1
Pool View
Great Wyrley WS6 5 A4
Walsall WS4 29 D7
Pool Way B33 69 A1
Pope Gr WS12 1 F6
Pope Rd WV10 12 B1
Popes La
Astwood Bank B96 158 E2
Birmingham B30,B31,B38 103 D3
Pope's La B69 64 B7
Popes La WV6 24 A6
Pope St
Birmingham B1 66 B3
Smethwick B66 65 B7
Poplar Arc B91 107 C4
Poplar Ave
2 Birmingham,Erdington B23 56 F4
6 Birmingham,Lozells B19 66 C8
Bedworth CV12 78 D2
Birmingham,Balsall Heath B12 87 A5
Birmingham,Coleshill Heath B37 90 C8
Birmingham,Edgbaston B17 65 B2
Birmingham,King's Heath B14 104 F8
Brownhills WS8 16 A8
Burntwood WS7 6 F6
Cannock WS11 1 F4
Oldbury,Grace Mary Estate B69 63 C8
Oldbury,Langley B69 64 A4
Sutton Coldfield B75 46 F7
Tipton DY4 51 D5
Walsall,Yew Tree WS5 43 A4
West Bromwich B70 53 E2
Willenhall WS2 27 E4
Wolverhampton WV11 26 B7
Poplar Cl
Catshill B61 136 F8
Oldbury B69 52 C1
Willenhall WS2 27 E4
Wombourne WV5 49 B6
Poplar Cres
Dudley DY1 51 B3
Stourbridge DY8 80 D3
Poplar Dr
Barnt Green B45 138 D8
Birmingham,Washwood Heath B8 67 D6
Birmingham,Witton B6 55 F5
Poplar Gn DY1 51 A6
Poplar Gr
7 Birmingham B19 66 C8
Ryton-on-D CV8 135 B1
Smethwick B66 65 B3
West Bromwich B70 53 E1
Poplar Ho CV12 78 D2
Poplar La
Cannock WS11 1 B1
Romsley B62 101 A4
Poplar Rd
Bilston WV14 40 F7
Birmingham,Moseley B14 86 E1
Birmingham,Sparkhill B11 87 C5
Brownhills WS8 16 A8
Coventry CV5 112 F1
Dorridge B93 127 F3
Great Wyrley WS6 5 A1
Kidderminster DY11 116 C4
Kingswinford DY6 60 E5
Oldbury B69 64 A8
Redditch B97 153 A3
Smethwick B66 65 A1
Solihull B91 107 C4
Stourbridge DY8 80 E3
Wednesbury WS10 42 A5
Wolverhampton WV3 39 A6
Poplar Rise
Birmingham B42 55 B7
Oldbury B69 63 C8
Sutton Coldfield B74 31 D6
Poplar Row DY11 116 C4
Poplars Dr B36 69 B8
Poplars La B96 158 A1
Poplars The
Birmingham,Rotton Park B16 65 F3
Birmingham,Sparkhill B11 87 C6

Poplars The *continued*
Brierley Hill DY5 . . . . 61 B7
Cannock WS11. . . . . 1 E4
Nuneaton CV10 . . . . 72 D3
Smethwick B66 . . . . 65 C4
Stourbridge DY8 . . . . 60 F2
Poplar St WS11. . . . . 6 A6
Poplars Trad Est B80 . . . . 159 D6
Poplar St
Smethwick B66 . . . . 65 C5
Wolverhampton WV2. . . . . . 39 D6
Poplar Trad Est B6. . . . . . . 55 F5
Poplar Trees B47 . . . . 125 A6
Poplar Way B91 . . . . 107 C4
Poplarwoods B32. . . . . 84 B2
Poppy Cl CV10. . . . . 78 A8
Poppy Ct CV3. . . . . 134 D6
Poppy Dr 3 WS5 . . . . 43 A3
Poppyfield Ct CV4 . . . . . . 132 D3
Poppy Gr B8. . . . . 67 F4
Poppy La B24. . . . . 57 C5
Poppymead B23 . . . . 56 B8
Porchester Cl
Brownhills WS9. . . . . 16 A2
Coventry CV3. . . . . 115 A2
Porchester Dr B19 . . . . 66 D6
Porchester St B19 . . . . 66 D6
Porlock Cl CV3 . . . . 133 E5
Porlock Cres B31 . . . . 102 D3
Porlock Rd DY8. . . . . 81 A6
Portal Rd WS2. . . . . 27 F2
Portchester Dr WV11. . . . . 26 D5
Porter Cl
Coventry CV4. . . . . 131 E8
Sutton Coldfield B72 . . . . . 57 B7
Porters Croft B17. . . . . 85 A8
Porters Field 6 DY2 . . . . . 51 D1
Portersfield Ind Est B64. . 82 D8
Portersfield Rd B64. . . . . . 82 C8
Portershill Dr B90 . . . . . . 106 C1
Porter St DY2. . . . . 51 D1
Porter Street S 9 DY2 . . . 51 D1
Porters Way B9. . . . . 67 E2
Portfield Dr DY4 . . . . 52 A3
Portfield Gr B23 . . . . 57 A6
Porthkerry Gr DY3 . . . . 50 B7
Port Hope Rd B11. . . . . 87 A7
Porthouse Gr WV14 . . . . . . 40 B3
Portia Ave B90. . . . . 106 B1
Portia Cl CV11 . . . . 74 A1
Portia Way CV34 . . . . 161 E3
Portland Ave
Aldridge WS9. . . . . 30 B5
Tamworth B79 . . . . 20 F8
Portland Cres DY9 . . . . 81 B1
Portland Ct
9 Royal Leamington Spa
CV32. . . . . 161 F8
Aldridge WS9. . . . . 30 B6
Portland Dr
Hinckley LE10 . . . . 71 E4
Nuneaton CV10 . . . . 72 C4
Oldbury B69. . . . . 52 D3
Stourbridge DY9 . . . . 81 B1
Portland Mews 10 CV32 . 161 F8
Portland Pl
Cannock WS11. . . . . 4 C7
Dudley WV14 . . . . 51 B7
Portland Pl E CV32. . . . . . 161 F8
Portland Pl W 5 CV32 . . 161 E8
Portland Rd
Aldridge WS9. . . . . 30 B6
Birmingham B16 . . . . 65 D1
Portland St
Birmingham B6 . . . . 67 A7
Royal Leamington Spa
CV32. . . . . 161 F8
Walsall WS2 . . . . 28 E3
Portland Terr 6 B18. . . . . 66 A5
Portleys La B78. . . . . 34 D4
Portman Rd B13 . . . . 104 F7
Portmanteau Mews B94. 143 C6
Portobello Cl WV13 . . . . . . 26 D1
Portobello Rd B70 . . . . 53 A8
Portreath Dr CV11 . . . . 74 A5
Portree Ave CV3 . . . . 114 F2
Portrush Ave B38 . . . . 103 D1
Portrush Rd WV6 . . . . 23 D4
Portsdown Cl WV10 . . . . . . 25 F7
Portsdown Rd B63 . . . . 82 D2
Portsea Cl CV3 . . . . 133 D6
Portsea St WS3. . . . . 28 C6
Portswood Cl WV9 . . . . 10 F1
Portway Cl
Coventry CV4. . . . . 131 E8
Kingswinford DY6 . . . . 60 E5
Royal Leamington Spa
CV31. . . . . 162 D6
Solihull B91 . . . . 106 E1
Portway Hill B65. . . . . 63 C6
Portway Rd
Bilston WV14. . . . . 40 E7
Oldbury B69. . . . . 63 F7
Rowley Regis B65 . . . . 63 B5
Wednesbury WS10 . . . . 41 E2
Portway The DY6 . . . . 60 E5
Portway Wlk B65 . . . . 63 C6
Portwrinkle Ave CV6 . . . . 114 A6
Poseidon Way CV34. . . . . 161 F4
Posey Cl B21 . . . . 54 C3
Post Box B1 . . . . 164 B1
Postbridge Rd CV3. . . . . . 133 D5
Post Office Wlk B96. . . . . 158 E1
Poston Croft B14 . . . . 104 D3
Potter Cl B23. . . . . 56 D8
Potter Ct 8 DY5 . . . . 61 D2
Potters Brook 8 DY4 . . . . 52 B5
Potters Green Prim Sch
CV2. . . . . 96 E2
Potters Green Rd CV2 . . . . 96 E1
Potters La
Birmingham B6 . . . . 66 E7
Wednesbury WS10 . . . . 41 F2
Potters Rd CV12 . . . . 77 E1
Potterton Way B66. . . . . . . 64 F8
Pottery Rd B68 . . . . 64 D1
Potton Cl CV3 . . . . 134 E6
Potts Cl CV8. . . . . 148 C4
Pouk Hill Cl WS2. . . . . 28 A3
Pouk La WS14 . . . . 16 F7
Poultney Rd CV6. . . . . 113 A6
Poultney St B70 . . . . 52 F7
Poulton Cl B13 . . . . 87 A2
Pound Cl
Berkswell CV7 . . . . 110 D3
Lapworth B94 . . . . 144 B3
Oldbury B68. . . . . 63 F3
Pound Gn B8 . . . . 67 F6
Pound House La
Nuthurst B94. . . . . 143 A4
Tanworth-in-A B94. . . . . . . 142 F4
Pound La
Birmingham B32 . . . . 101 F3
Royal Leamington Spa
CV32. . . . . 157 A3
Poundley Cl B36 . . . . 69 C8
Pound Rd
Birmingham B14 . . . . 104 E2
Oldbury B68. . . . . 64 A2
Wednesbury WS10 . . . . 42 A3
Pountney St WV2 . . . . 163 B1
Pourbaix Ho WS13 . . . . 9 B6
Poverty B96 . . . . 158 E2
Powell Ave B32. . . . . 84 A6
Powell Pl
Bilston WV14. . . . . 40 E3
Tipton DY4. . . . . 52 C5
Powell Rd CV2. . . . . 114 A4
Powells Cl B72 . . . . 46 C2
Powells Ho B73. . . . . 45 C2
Powell St
7 Halesowen B63 . . . . 83 B3
Birmingham B1 . . . . 66 B3
Wolverhampton WV10. . . . . 25 F4
Powell Way CV11 . . . . 73 C4
Power Cres B16 . . . . 66 A2
Powers Ct 4 CV32 . . . . . . 156 F1
Powers Rd LE9 . . . . 71 F5
Power Way DY4. . . . . 52 D8
Powick Rd B23 . . . . 56 D1
Powis Ave DY4. . . . . 52 B7
Powis Gr CV8. . . . . 148 C5
Powke La B65 . . . . 63 A2
Powke Lane Ind Est B65. . 63 A2
Powlers Cl DY9 . . . . 81 E2
Powlett St WV2. . . . . 163 C2
Poxon Rd WS9. . . . . 16 A3
Poynings The WV6. . . . . . . 24 C5
Poyser Rd CV10. . . . . 78 C8
Praetor Ho 8 LE10 . . . . . . 71 D1
Pratts La B80. . . . . 159 F7
Precinct The
Tamworth B79. . . . . 21 B5
Willenhall WV12 . . . . 27 B5
Premier Bsns Ctr 3 DY9 . 81 F5
Premier Bsns Pk WS2. . . . 28 D1
Premier Ct B30 . . . . 104 C3
Premier Partnership Ind Est
DY5. . . . . 61 A3
Premier St B7 . . . . 67 D8
Premier Trad Est B7 . . . . . 66 F5
Prescelly Cl CV10 . . . . 72 B3
Prescelly Ct CV8 . . . . 147 F5
Prescot Rd DY9 . . . . 81 C3
President Kennedy Sch &
Com Coll CV6. . . . . 95 B4
Prestbury Rd B6 . . . . 66 E8
Presthope Rd B29 . . . . 103 B7
Prestley Smith Sch B42 . . 55 C8
Preston Ave B76. . . . . 46 E3
Preston Cl
Coventry CV4. . . . . 131 F7
Redditch B98. . . . . 154 B6
Preston Ho 4 WS1 . . . . . . 28 F1
Preston Rd
Birmingham,Hockley B18. . . 65 E6
Birmingham,South Yardley
B26 . . . . 88 D7
Hinckley LE10 . . . . 71 B2
Prestons Row WV14. . . . . . 40 A3
Prestwick Cl B75 . . . . 46 C7
Prestwick Rd
Birmingham B35 . . . . 58 B4
Kingswinford DY6 . . . . 60 C6
Prestwood Ave WV11 . . . . 26 D7
Prestwood Dr DY7 . . . . 80 B7
Prestwood Rd
Birmingham B29 . . . . 103 B8
Wolverhampton WV11. . . . . 26 A5
Prestwood Rd W WV11. . . 26 B7
Pretoria Rd B9 . . . . 67 E3
Priam Cir CV34 . . . . 161 F3
Priam Gr WS3 . . . . 15 B5
Price Ave B78 . . . . 20 D1
Price Cl E CV34 . . . . 160 B4
Price Cl W CV34 . . . . 160 B4
Price Cres WV14. . . . . 40 D7
Price Rd
Cubbington CV32. . . . . 157 E5
Stourbridge DY9 . . . . 82 A6
Wednesbury WS10 . . . . 42 C3
Prices Rd DY3 . . . . 50 C3
Price St
Bilston WV14. . . . . 40 F5
Birmingham B4 . . . . 164 C4
Price St *continued*
Cannock WS11. . . . . 1 E1
Dudley DY2 . . . . 51 E1
Smethwick B66 . . . . 65 B5
West Bromwich B70 . . . . . . 53 C3
Pridmore Rd CV6 . . . . 113 D7
Priestfield Cl B44. . . . . 44 D2
Priestfield Rd B97 . . . . . . 158 E5
Priestfield Sta WV2 . . . . . . 40 A7
Priestfield St WV14 . . . . . . 40 B6
Priesthills Rd LE10. . . . . . . 75 D8
Priestland Rd B34 . . . . 69 B7
Priestley Cl
Birmingham B20 . . . . 55 A2
Halesowen B63 . . . . 82 B6
Priestley Rd
Birmingham B11 . . . . 87 A7
Walsall WS2 . . . . 28 A5
Priest Meadow Cl B96. . . 158 D1
Priest St B64 . . . . 62 F1
Primley Ave
Birmingham B36 . . . . 68 D7
Tamworth B77 . . . . 35 F5
Walsall WS2 . . . . 28 B2
Primley Cl WS2. . . . . 28 B2
Primrose Ave
Birmingham B11 . . . . 87 C5
Tipton DY4. . . . . 52 C8
Wolverhampton WV10. . . . . 11 D3
Primrose Bank B68 . . . . . . 64 B4
Primrose Cl
Cradley Heath B64 . . . . 82 B8
Lickey End B60 . . . . 137 C6
Walsall WS3 . . . . 15 A5
Primrose Cres DY1. . . . . . . 51 C4
Primrose Croft
Birmingham,Perry Common
B23. . . . . 56 C7
Birmingham,Yardley Wood
B28. . . . . 105 F5
Primrose Dr
Bedworth CV12 . . . . 77 E1
Hinckley LE10 . . . . 75 E5
Primrose Gdns
Birmingham B38 . . . . 123 F8
Codsall WV8 . . . . 10 A3
Featherstone WV10. . . . . . . 12 B7
Primrose Hill B38. . . . . . . 124 A8
Primrose Hill Com Sch
B38. . . . . 123 F8
Primrose Hill B67. . . . . 64 D4
Primrose Hill St CV1 . . . . 165 C4
Primrose Hill DY8. . . . . 60 E1
Primrose Hill Trad Est
DY2. . . . . 62 D4
Primrose Hill CV34. . . . . . 155 E2
Primrose La
Birmingham B28 . . . . 105 F5
Solihull B90. . . . . 126 A5
Wolverhampton WV10. . . . . 26 A8
Primrose Mdw 1 WS11 . . . 2 C2
Primrose Pk DY5 . . . . 61 C7
Primrose Rd DY2 . . . . 62 C4
Primroses The WS5. . . . . . 43 B4
Primrose Way DY10. . . . . . 116 F4
Primrose Woods B32. . . . . 84 B2
Primsland Cl B90 . . . . 127 C7
Prince Albert Inf & Jun Sch
B6. 66 E8
Prince Albert St B9 . . . . . . 67 D1
Prince Andrew Cres B45 101 E2
Prince Charles Cl B45. . . . 101 E2
Prince Charles Rd WV14. . 40 F3
Prince Edward Dr B45 . . 101 E2
Prince George Rd WS10. . 42 A5
Prince Of Wales La B14 . 105 C3
Prince Of Wales Rd CV5 . 112 E3
Prince of Wales Wlk 3
B66 . . . . 65 C5
Princep Cl B43 . . . . 44 D4
Prince Philip Cl B45 . . . . 101 E2
Prince Rd B30 . . . . 104 A3
Prince Regent Ct 3
CV31 . . . . 161 F6
Prince Rupert Mews WS13 9 A8
Prince Rupert's Way WS13 9 A8
Prince's Ave
Nuneaton CV11 . . . . 73 B3
Walsall WS1 . . . . 29 B1
Princes Ave WS1. . . . . 43 A8
Princes Cl CV3. . . . . 134 B8
Princes Dr
Codsall WV8 . . . . 10 A2
Coventry CV6. . . . . 96 B1
Kenilworth CV8 . . . . 148 B7
Prince's Dr CV31. . . . . 161 D7
Princes End Ind Pk DY4 . . 40 E1
Princes Gate
Solihull B91. . . . . 107 B4
West Bromwich B70 . . . . . . 53 E2
Princes Gdns WV8 . . . . 10 A2
Princes Rd DY8. . . . . 80 D3
Prince's Rd B69 . . . . 52 B2
Princess Alice Dr B73 . . . . 45 D2
Princess Alley WV1 . . . . . 163 C3
Princess Anne Dr B45. . . . 101 E2
Princess Anne Rd
Bilston WV14. . . . . 40 F3
Willenhall WS2 . . . . 27 F3
Princess Cl WS7 . . . . 6 E7
Princess Cres B63 . . . . 82 E6
Princess Ct WV10 . . . . 26 A6
Princess Gr B71 . . . . 53 D8
Princess of Wales Com Hospl
The B61. . . . . 137 A4
Princes Sq WV1 . . . . 163 C3
Princess Rd
Birmingham B5 . . . . 86 E7
Princess Rd *continued*
Hinckley LE10 . . . . 75 E8
Oldbury B68. . . . . 64 D2
Princess Sq WV14. . . . . 40 F3
Princess St
Burntwood WS7. . . . . 6 E8
Cannock WS11. . . . . 1 F5
Coventry CV6. . . . . 113 F7
Wolverhampton WV1. . . . . 163 C3
Prince's St
Nuneaton CV11 . . . . 73 C3
Royal Leamington Spa
CV32. . . . . 157 B1
Princess Way WS10 . . . . . . 41 C8
Prince St
Brownhills WS9 . . . . 15 F2
Cannock WS12. . . . . 1 E6
Cradley Heath B64 . . . . 82 D8
Dudley DY2 . . . . 62 C6
Walsall WS2 . . . . 42 C8
Prince's Way B91 . . . . 107 B3
Princethorpe Cl
Birmingham B34 . . . . 69 D7
Solihull B90. . . . . 106 A2
Princethorpe Inf Sch B29 85 A1
Princethorpe Jun Sch
B29. . . . . 85 A1
Princethorpe Rd B29. . . . . 85 A1
Prince Thorpe Rd WV13 . . 41 B8
Princethorpe Way CV3 . . 134 E8
Princeton Gdns WV9 . . . . . 10 F2
Prince William Cl
Birmingham B23 . . . . 56 D2
Coventry CV6. . . . . 112 E6
Principal Ct B67 . . . . 65 A5
Princip St B4. . . . . 164 C4
Printing House St B4 . . . 164 C3
Prior Ave B60. . . . . 150 C3
Prior Cl DY10. . . . . 117 C5
Prior Deram Wlk CV4 . . . 132 C7
Priors Cl CV7 . . . . 130 B6
Priors Field Prim Sch
CV8. . . . . 147 D7
Priorsfield Rd
4 Coventry CV6 . . . . 113 A4
Kenilworth CV8 . . . . 147 D6
Priorsfield Rd N 3 CV6 . 113 A4
Priorsfield Rd S CV6 . . . . 113 A4
Priors Harnall CV1 . . . . . . 165 D4
Priors Mill DY3 . . . . 50 E5
Priors Oak B97 . . . . 153 B4
Priors The CV12 . . . . 78 C2
Priors Way B23 . . . . 56 C8
Priory Ave B29. . . . . 86 B2
Priory Cl
Dudley DY1 . . . . 51 B2
Kingswood B94 . . . . 144 D5
Smethwick B66 . . . . 65 C4
Stourbridge DY8 . . . . 81 B3
Tamworth B79 . . . . 20 F7
West Bromwich B70 . . . . . . 53 F2
Priory Croft CV8 . . . . 148 A4
Priory Ct
3 Dudley DY1. . . . . 51 C1
Brownhills WS9 . . . . 16 A4
Coventry CV5. . . . . 113 A1
Nuneaton CV11 . . . . 73 A4
Solihull B90. . . . . 127 B7
Priory Cts The B2. . . . . . . 164 C3
Priory Ct
Stourbridge DY8 . . . . 81 B3
Studley B80 . . . . 159 E5
Wolverhampton WV1. . . . . 163 B4
Priory Dr B68. . . . . 64 C5
Priory Field Cl WV14 . . . . . 39 F1
Priorygate Way B9. . . . . . . 67 E3
Priory Gdns B28 . . . . 105 D4
Priory Green Prim Sch
WV9 . . . . 11 A2
Priory Ho
Halesowen B63 . . . . 82 F5
Kenilworth CV8 . . . . 147 F4
Priory Hospl The B5 . . . . . 86 C5
Priory La DY3. . . . . 50 D7
Priory Mews CV34 . . . . . . 160 E7
Priory New Way Ind Est
B6. 66 F5
Priory Pl CV1 . . . . 165 C3
Priory Prim Sch DY1 . . . . . 51 B3
Priory Prim Sch The
WS10 . . . . 42 D2
Priory Queensway The
B4 . . . . 164 C3
Priory Rd
Birmingham,Aston B6 . . . . . 67 B8
Birmingham,Edgbaston B5,
B15. . . . . 86 B5
Birmingham,Stirchley B14 104 C7
Birmingham,Warstock B28 105 D3
Cannock WS12. . . . . 2 D4
Dodford B61 . . . . 136 A6
Dudley DY1 . . . . 51 C3
Halesowen B62 . . . . 83 F4
Kenilworth CV8 . . . . 148 A4
Stourbridge DY8 . . . . 81 B3
Warwick CV34. . . . . 160 E7
Priory Row CV1 . . . . 165 C3
Priory Sch B15 . . . . 86 B6
Priory Sq
Birmingham B4 . . . . 164 C3
Studley B80 . . . . 159 E5
Priory St
Coventry CV1. . . . . 165 C3
Dudley DY1 . . . . 51 C1
Nuneaton CV10 . . . . 72 D3
Royal Leamington Spa
CV31. . . . . 161 F6
Priory Terr CV31. . . . . 162 A7
Priory The DY3 . . . . 50 D8
Priory Visitors Ctr* CV1 165 C3
Priory Wlk
10 Warwick CV34 . . . . 160 F7
Birmingham B4 . . . . 164 C3
Hinckley LE10 . . . . 71 E1
Sutton Coldfield B72 . . . . . 57 C7
Pritchard Ave WV11. . . . . . 26 E6
Pritchard Cl B66. . . . . 65 B5
Pritchard St
Brierley Hill DY5 . . . . 61 B3
Wednesbury WS10 . . . . 42 A3
Pritchatts Rd B15 . . . . 85 F5
Pritchett Ave WV4 . . . . 39 F3
Pritchett Rd B31 . . . . 123 B7
Pritchett St B6 . . . . 66 E5
Pritchett Twr 4 B10 . . . . . 67 B1
Private Way B45 . . . . 122 C4
Privet Cl B44 . . . . 44 E3
Privet Rd CV2. . . . . 96 B2
Probert Rd WV10 . . . . 11 B1
Proctors Barn La B98 . . . 154 B4
Proctor St B7. . . . . 67 A5
Proffitt Ave CV6 . . . . 96 A1
Proffitt Cl
Brownhills WS8 . . . . 16 A5
Walsall WS2 . . . . 28 E4
Proffitt St WS2 . . . . 28 E4
Progress Cl CV3 . . . . 135 A7
Progress Dr WS11 . . . . 4 F6
Progress Ind Ctr WS11 . . . . . 4 F7
Progress Way CV3 . . . . . . 135 A8
Prole St WV10 . . . . 25 E4
Prologis Pk CV6 . . . . 95 B5
Promenade The DY5 . . . . . 61 D2
Prophets Cl B97 . . . . 153 D3
Prospect Rd WS13 . . . . 9 F8
Prospect Gdns DY8 . . . . . . 81 A4
Prospect Hill
Kidderminster DY10 . . . . . 116 E6
Redditch B97. . . . . 153 E4
Stourbridge DY8 . . . . 81 A4
Prospect La
Kidderminster DY10 . . . . . 116 E6
Solihull B91. . . . . 106 D4
Prospect Manor Ct WS12. . 2 C3
Prospect Pk WS11 . . . . 4 D7
Prospect Pl B12 . . . . 86 F5
Prospect Rd
Birmingham B13 . . . . 86 F1
Burntwood WS7. . . . . 7 B6
Dudley DY3 . . . . 50 C2
Halesowen B62 . . . . 83 C5
Prospect Rd N B98. . . . . . 154 A4
Prospect Rd S B98. . . . . . 154 A4
Prospect Rd CV31. . . . . . . 162 B5
Prospect Row
Dudley DY2 . . . . 62 D8
Stourbridge DY8 . . . . 81 A3
Prospect St
Bilston WV14. . . . . 40 E6
Tamworth B79 . . . . 21 A5
Wednesbury DY4 . . . . 41 C1
Prosper Mdw DY6. . . . . 60 F7
Prospero Cl B45 . . . . 102 A2
Prospero Dr CV34. . . . . . . 161 E3
Prosser St
Bilston WV14. . . . . 40 D5
Wolverhampton WV10. . . . . 25 E5
Prossers Wlk B46. . . . . 70 F7
Proud Cross Ringway
DY11 . . . . 116 C6
Proud's La WV14. . . . . 40 D7
Provence Cl WV10 . . . . 25 F4
Providence Cl WS3 . . . . 28 C7
Providence Ct B64. . . . . 82 C8
Providence Dr DY9. . . . . . . 81 E6
Providence Ind Est DY9 . . 81 E6
Providence La WS3 . . . . 28 C6
Providence Rd B61 . . . . . . 136 F3
Providence Row WV14 . . . . 51 B8
Providence St
Coventry CV5. . . . . 132 F8
Cradley Heath B64 . . . . 62 D1
Stourbridge DY9 . . . . 81 F6
Tipton DY4. . . . . 52 C5
Providence Terr WS10 . . . 41 E6
Provost Williams CE Prim
Sch CV8. . . . . 135 A1
Pruden Ave WV4. . . . . 39 F3
Pryor Rd B68 . . . . 64 C4
Ptarmigan Pl CV11 . . . . 73 F3
Puckering's La 11 CV34 . 160 E6
Pudsey Dr B75. . . . . 32 C3
Pugh Cres WS2 . . . . 27 E2
Pughe's Cl LE10 . . . . 76 A6
Pugh Rd
Bilston WV14. . . . . 40 E3
Birmingham B6 . . . . 67 A8
Wolverhampton WV4,WV14. 39 F2
Pugin Cl WV6. . . . . 23 D3
Pugin Gdns B23 . . . . 56 D8
Pullman Cl B77 . . . . 22 A2
Pulman Cl B97. . . . . 153 C4
Puma Way CV1 . . . . 165 C1
Pumphouse Cl CV6. . . . . . . 96 B6
Pumphouse La
Blackwell B45,B60. . . . . . . 137 F7
Redditch B97 . . . . 152 D1
Pumphouse Way 2 B69. . . 63 F4
Pump St
Kidderminster DY10 . . . . . 116 E4
Wolverhampton WV2. . . . . . 40 A7
Puppy Gn DY4 . . . . 52 B5
Purbeck Cl B63 . . . . 82 D1

Purbeck Croft B32 84 F4
Purbrook Rd WV1 40 A8
Purbrook B77 35 E8
Purcell Ave
Lichfield WS13 3 C2
Nuneaton CV11 79 A7
Purcell Cl CV32 162 A8
Purcell Rd
Coventry CV6 114 B8
Wolverhampton WV10 25 D8
Purdy Rd WV14 40 E2
Purefoy Rd
Birmingham B13 105 C5
Coventry CV3 133 D8
Purley Gr B23 56 A5
Purlieu La CV8 147 D5
Purnells Way B93 128 A5
Purser Dr CV34 160 B4
Purshall Cl B97 153 C3
Purslet Rd WV1 26 A2
Purslow Gr B31 103 A1
Purton Mews CV31 162 C6
Putney Ave B20 55 C1
Putney La B62 101 B1
Putney Rd B20 55 C1
Putney Wlk B37 70 B3
Puxton Dr DY11 116 D8
Puxton La DY11 116 C7
Pye Green Rd WS11 1 E4
Pye Green Valley Prim Sch WS12 2 A7
Pyeharps Rd LE10 75 E5
Pype Hayes Cl B24 57 D4
Pype Hayes Rd B24 57 D4
Pyree Sq CV34 160 B4
Pytchley Ho 6 B20 54 F3
Pytman Dr B76 58 A7
Pyt Pk CV5 112 D4

Q

Quadrangle The B90 126 E8
Quadrant Ho B32 84 E7
Quadrant The
Coventry CV1 165 B2
Nuneaton CV11 73 E3
Sedgley DY3 39 D1
Quadrille Lawns WV9 10 F2
Quail Gn WV6 23 F2
Quail Park Dr DY10 117 A2
Qualcast Rd WV1,WV10 25 F2
Quantock Cl
Birmingham B45 102 B2
Brownhills WS8 16 A4
Halesowen B63 82 D2
Quantock Dr
Kidderminster DY10 117 A6
Nuneaton CV10 72 B3
Quantock Rd DY8 81 B6
Quantry La DY9 120 F8
Quarrington Gr B14 105 A3
Quarry Bank Prim Sch DY5 62 A1
Quarry Brow DY3 50 E6
Quarry Cl
Cheslyn Hay WS6 4 E3
Leek Wootton CV35 155 F7
Quarryfield La CV1 165 D1
Quarry Fields CV35 155 F7
Quarry Hill B63 82 F2
Quarry Hills La WS14 9 D6
Quarry House Cl B45 101 F1
Quarry La
Birmingham B31 103 A2
Bromsgrove B61 150 D8
Halesowen B63 83 A2
Nuneaton CV11 73 F1
Rowington Green CV35 145 C1
Quarry Lodge WS14 9 D5
Quarry Park Rd DY8 99 A8
Quarry Rd
Birmingham B29 103 A8
Dudley DY2 62 B1
Kenilworth CV8 147 E6
Quarry Rise B69 63 B8
Quarry St CV32 161 C8
Quarry The DY10 116 F8
Quarry Wlk B45 122 A7
Quarrywood Gr CV2 114 A4
Quarry Yd CV10 72 C4
Quasar Ctr 2 WS1 28 E2
Quatford Gdns WV10 25 E5
Quayle Gr 2 DY8 60 D3
Quayside B18 66 A5
Quayside Cl B69 63 E8
Quayside Dr WS2 42 C8
Queen Alexandra Coll B17 85 A6
Queen Eleanors Dr B93 128 B8
Queen Elizabeth Ave WS2 27 F2
Queen Elizabeth Ct B19 66 B6
Queen Elizabeth Hospl B15 85 E4
Queen Elizabeth Psychiatric Hospl B15 85 E4
Queen Elizabeth Rd
Birmingham B45 101 E2
Kidderminster DY10 117 B5
Nuneaton CV10 72 D5
Queen Elizabeth's Mercian Sch B79 21 C6
Queen Isabel's Ave CV3 133 D8
Queen Margaret's Rd CV4 132 C8
Queen Mary's Gram Sch WS1 43 A8
Queen Mary's High Sch WS4 28 F3
Queen Mary's Rd
Bedworth CV12 78 C5
Coventry CV6 113 E8
Queen Mary St WS1 42 D6
Queen Philippa St CV3 133 D6
Queens Arc CV11 73 C4
Queen's Arc WV1 163 B3
Queens Ave B14 104 E8
Queen's Ave B69 52 A1
Queens Ave B90 106 B1
Queensbridge Rd B13 86 E2
Queensbridge Sch B13 86 E2
Queensbury Sch B24 56 F2
Queens CE Jun Sch CV11 73 A4
Queens Cl B24 56 F2
Queen's Cl CV8 147 F3
Queens Cl B67 65 A5
Queen's Coll The B15 85 F5
Queen's Cotts B97 153 B4
Queens Court Trad Est B70 52 F3
Queens Cres WV14 40 A1
Queen's Cres DY8 81 A7
Queen's Croft Com Sch WS13 9 B7
Queen's Cross DY1 62 B8
Queens Ct
Birmingham B3 164 B4
Brierley Hill DY5 61 C6
Nuneaton CV11 73 A4
Queen's Ct WV10 26 A6
Queens Dr
Birmingham B5 164 C2
Birmingham,Lifford B30 104 A4
Burntwood WS7 6 F5
Queen's Dr CV35 145 A1
Queens Dr B65 63 D4
Queens Dr The B62 83 C5
Queens Gdns
4 Birmingham B23 56 B7
Bilston WV14 40 D7
Dudley DY2 62 C4
Queens Head Rd B21 65 E7
Queens Hill DY9 119 D7
Queens Hospital Cl B15 66 C1
Queensland Ave CV5 112 F2
Queensland Gdns 4 CV12 77 F2
Queen's Lea WV12 27 C5
Queen's Own Hussars Mus The* CV34 160 E6
Queen's Park Ct 3 LE10 75 E8
Queen's Park Flats 2 LE10 75 E8
Queen's Park Rd B32 84 F6
Queen's Park Terr 4 LE10 75 E8
Queens Par WS3 14 B1
Queen Sq WV1 163 B3
Queens Rd B6 67 A8
Queen's Rd B23 56 C3
Queens Rd B26 68 F1
Queen's Rd
Coventry CV1 165 A2
Hinckley LE10 75 E8
Kenilworth CV8 147 F3
Nuneaton CV11 73 B4
Oldbury B68 64 D5
Queens Rd DY3 50 E8
Queen's Rd
Smethwick B67 64 D4
Stourbridge DY8 80 F6
Tipton DY4 51 F5
Queens Rd WS4 29 C7
Queen's Rd WS5 43 B6
Queen's Ride B12 86 D4
Queens Sq WS11 1 E1
Queen's Sq CV34 160 D5
Queen St
Astwood Bank B96 158 E1
Bedworth CV12 78 C2
Bilston,Bunker's Hill WV14 40 E5
Birmingham B12 87 B5
Brierley Hill,Pensnett DY5 61 C6
Brierley Hill,Quarry Bank DY5 82 A8
Brownhills WS9 15 F2
Burntwood WS7 6 F5
Cannock,Blackfords WS11 1 D1
Cannock WS11 2 A5
Cheslyn Hay WS6 4 D3
Coventry CV1 165 C4
Cradley Heath B64 62 D1
Cubbington CV32 157 E5
Darlaston,Darlaston Green WS10 41 D8
Darlaston,Moxley WS10 41 B4
Halesowen B63 83 A4
Kidderminster DY10 116 E7
Kingswinford DY6 60 D7
Lichfield WS13 9 A7
Oldbury B69 64 A8
Redditch B98 153 E4
Queen Street Pas 1 DY5 82 A8
Queen St
Royal Leamington Spa CV32 157 A1
Stourbridge DY8 80 F6
Stourbridge,Wordsley DY8 60 E3
Sutton Coldfield B72 46 C4
Tipton DY4 51 F8
Walsall WS2 28 D1
Wednesbury WS10 41 E3
West Bromwich B70 53 D3
Wolverhampton WV1 163 C3
Queensway B6 55 F2
Queensway Cl B68 64 B1
Queens Way B78 36 F6
Queensway
Halesowen B63 83 B3
Nuneaton CV10 73 E6
Oldbury B68 64 B1
Royal Leamington Spa CV31 161 E6
Stourbridge DY9 81 E2
Sutton Coldfield B74 45 A8
Tamworth B79 21 A8
Queensway Trad Est
Birmingham B5 164 D3
Royal Leamington Spa CV31 161 E6
Queensway (Tunnel) B3 164 B3
Queenswood Ct CV7 94 D4
Queens Wood Ho B14 104 D4
Queenswood Rd
Birmingham B13 87 A4
Sutton Coldfield B75 32 B1
Queen Victoria Ct 4 LE10 71 D1
Queen Victoria Prim Sch DY3 50 E8
Queen Victoria Rd
Coventry CV1 165 B2
Coventry CV1 165 B3
Quenby Dr DY1 51 A3
Quentin Dr DY1 61 F8
Queslade Cl B43 44 A1
Queslett Rd B43 44 C2
Queslett Rd E B74,B43 44 F5
Quibery Cl B98 154 F3
Quicksand La WS9 29 F4
Quigley Ave B9 67 B2
Quillets Rd DY8 60 C3
Quilletts Cl CV6 96 A1
Quilter Cl
Dudley WV14 51 A8
Willenhall WS2 27 F3
Quilter Rd B24 57 B2
Quince B77 22 B3
Quince Tree Sch B77 22 A3
Quincey Dr B24 57 C3
Quincy Rise DY5 81 C7
Quinn Cl CV3 134 B7
Quinneys La B98 159 B6
Quinton Ave WS6 4 F3
Quinton Bsns Pk B32 84 A4
Quinton Church Prim Sch B32 84 A6
Quinton Cl
Redditch B98 154 D1
Solihull B92 89 D3
Quintondale 5 B90 126 C8
Quinton Expressway B32 84 B4
Quinton Flats CV3 133 D7
Quinton La B32 84 D6
Quinton Par CV3 133 D7
Quinton Pk CV3 133 D7
Quinton Pl WS11 6 A4
Quinton Rd
Birmingham B17 85 C3
Coventry CV1 165 C1
Quinton Rd W B32 84 D4
Quonians La WS13 9 B8
Quorn Cres DY8 60 C3
Quorn Gr B24 57 B2
Quorn Ho 3 B20 54 F3
Quorn Way CV3 134 E7

R

Rabbit La WV10 12 A8
Rabone La B66 65 C6
Raby Cl B69 62 F8
Raby St WV2 163 C2
Racecourse La DY8 80 F1
Racecourse Rd WV6 25 A5
Race Leys Inf Sch CV12 78 B3
Race Leys Jun Sch CV12 78 B4
Racemeadow Cres B64 62 C1
Rachael Gdns WS10 42 C4
Rachel Cl DY4 41 C1
Rachel Gdns B29 85 D2
Radbourn Dr B74 46 C6
Radbourne Dr B63 82 A7
Radbourne Rd B90 106 D3
Radbrook Way CV31 162 D6
Radcliffe Dr B62 83 E6
Radcliffe Gdns 6 CV31 162 A6
Radcliffe Rd CV5 132 F8
Radcliffe Twr 3 B12 86 F8
Radclyffe Ho B16 86 A8
Raddens Rd B62 83 F3
Raddington Dr B92 106 E8
Raddlebarn Ct B29 86 A1
Raddlebarn Farm Dr B29 103 F8
Raddlebarn Prim Sch B29 85 F1
Raddlebarn Rd B29 103 F8
Radford Ave DY10 116 E7
Radford Circ 5 CV6 113 A4
Radford Cl WS5 43 A3
Radford Ct DY10 116 E7
Radford Dr WS4 15 C2
Radford Hall CV31 162 E6
Radford Ho
2 Redditch B97 153 A4
Coventry CV6 113 A7
Radford La WV3,WV4 37 F7
Radford Prim Sch CV6 113 B5
Radford Rd
Alvechurch B48 139 D7
Birmingham B29 103 A6
Radford Rd *continued*
Coventry CV1,CV6 113 B5
Royal Leamington Spa CV31 162 C7
Radford Rise B91 107 E5
Radford Semele CE Prim Sch CV31 162 E5
Radley Ct B26 89 C7
Radley Dr CV10 73 A1
Radley Gr B29 85 A2
Radley Rd
Stourbridge DY9 81 F4
Walsall WS4 29 C7
Radleys Prim Sch The WS4 29 D7
Radleys The B33 89 D8
Radleys Wlk B33 89 D8
Radlow Cres B37 90 B8
Radmore Cl WS7 6 D8
Radmore Rd LE10 71 D3
Radnor Cl B45 102 B2
Radnor Croft WS5 43 C3
Radnor Ct WS9 15 F4
Radnor Dr CV10 72 E2
Radnor Gn B71 53 C7
Radnor Rd
Birmingham,Brandhall B68 84 B7
Birmingham,Lozells B20 66 B8
Sedgley DY3 50 C8
Radnor Rise WS12 2 B4
Radnor St B18 66 A6
Radnor Wlk CV2 114 F8
Radstock Ave B36 68 C7
Radstock Rd WV12 13 C1
Radway Cl B98 154 B6
Radway Ind Est B90 126 E7
Radway Rd B90 126 E8
Raeburn Rd B43 44 C4
RAF Cotts B35 57 F2
Raford Rd B23 56 D6
Ragees Rd DY6 60 F4
Raglan Ave
Perton WV6 23 F3
Smethwick B66 65 C4
Raglan Cl
Nuneaton CV11 73 D4
Sedgley DY3 50 B7
Sutton Coldfield WS9 30 F3
Raglan Ct
7 Coventry CV1 113 E3
Bromsgrove B60 137 A1
Raglan Gr CV8 148 B5
Raglan Ho B33 69 A2
Raglan Rd
Birmingham,Balsall Heath B5 86 D5
Birmingham,Handsworth B21 65 C8
Smethwick B66 65 C4
Raglan St
Brierley Hill DY5 61 C4
Coventry CV1 165 D3
Wolverhampton WV3 163 A2
Raglan Way B37 70 D1
Ragley Cl
Knowle B93 128 B7
Walsall WS3 14 A1
Ragley Cres B60 151 A8
Ragley Dr
2 Willenhall WV13 40 F8
Birmingham,Grove Vale B43 43 D2
Birmingham,Sheldon B26 89 C6
Ragley Ho 8 B97 153 A4
Ragley Way CV11 73 F2
Ragley Wlk 3 B65 63 C3
Raglis Cl B97 153 A1
Ragnall Ave B33 89 D7
Raikes La WS14 17 C7
Rail Bridge Est B70 53 A1
Railswood Dr WS3 15 B3
Railway Cl B80 159 D4
Railway Dr
Bilston WV14 40 E5
Wolverhampton WV1 163 C3
Railway La WV13 27 A1
Railway Rd
Birmingham B20 55 F2
Sutton Coldfield B73 46 B5
Railwayside Cl B66 64 E7
Railway St
Bilston WV14 40 E5
Cannock WS11 4 E8
Norton Canes WS11 6 A5
Tipton DY4 52 C5
West Bromwich B70 53 B4
Wolverhampton WV1 163 C3
Railway Terr
4 Wednesbury WS10 41 F2
Bedworth CV12 78 C2
Birmingham,Aston B7 67 B6
Birmingham,Hamstead B42 54 F6
Railway View B10 87 C7
Railway Wlk B60 151 A6
Railwharf Sidings DY2 62 D4
Rainbow St
Dudley WV14 40 D2
Wolverhampton WV2 163 C1
Rainford Way B38 123 C8
Rainham Cl DY4 51 D5
Rainsbrook Dr
Nuneaton CV11 74 A1
Solihull B90 126 F6
Rainscar B77 36 B7
Raison Ave CV11 73 F8
Rakegate Prim Sch WV10 11 B1
Rake Hill WS7 7 B8
Rake Way B15 66 B1
Raleigh Cl
Birmingham B21 54 B1
Hinckley LE10 71 D4
Raleigh Croft B43 43 E3
Raleigh Ind Est B21 54 B1
Raleigh Rd
Bilston WV14 41 A3
Birmingham B9 67 D2
Coventry CV2 114 B2
Raleigh St
Walsall WS2 28 C2
West Bromwich B71 53 C4
Ralph Barlow Gdns B44 56 B8
Ralph Rd
Birmingham B8 67 D4
Coventry CV6 112 F5
Solihull B90 106 C4
Ralphs Mdw B32 84 D2
Ralston Cl WS3 14 A4
Rambures Cl CV34 161 F3
Ramillies Cres WS6 4 F1
Ramp Rd B26 90 C5
Ramsay Cl B71 53 F8
Ramsay Cres CV5 112 B7
Ramsay Rd
Oldbury B68 64 C1
Tipton DY4 51 E7
Walsall WS2 28 A5
Ramsden Ave CV10 72 D6
Ramsden Cl B29 103 B7
Ramsden Ct CV10 72 C7
Ramsey Cl
Birmingham B45 101 F1
Hinckley LE10 71 B1
Ramsey Rd
1 Birmingham B7 67 C7
Royal Leamington Spa CV31 162 B7
Ranby Rd CV2 113 F4
Randall Ave B48 139 A6
Randall Cl DY6 60 F4
Randall Rd CV8 147 E8
Randle Dr B75 32 C3
Randle Rd
Nuneaton CV10 72 D4
Stourbridge DY9 81 C4
Randle St CV6 113 B5
Randolph Cl 11 CV31 162 C6
Randwick Gr B44 44 E1
Ranelagh Ho WV2 39 D7
Ranelagh Rd WV2 39 D6
Ranelagh St CV31 162 A6
Ranelagh Terr CV31 161 F6
Range Meadow Cl CV32 156 C3
Rangemoor CV3 134 D6
Rangeview Cl B74 44 F6
Rangeways Rd
Kidderminster DY11 116 A8
Kingswinford DY6 60 F4
Rangeworthy Cl B97 158 C7
Rangifer Rd B78 20 F1
Rangoon Rd B92 89 E4
Ranleigh Ave DY6 60 F4
Rann Cl B16 66 A1
Rannoch Cl
Brierley Hill DY5 81 B8
Hinckley LE10 75 B8
Rannoch Dr CV10 72 C5
Rannock Cl CV3 114 F2
Ranscombe Dr DY3 50 D2
Ransom Rd
Birmingham B23 56 C4
Coventry CV6 113 E8
Ran-tan The B97 158 E5
Ranton Park Area 3 WS11 2 A2
Ranulf Croft CV3 133 C7
Ranulf St CV3 133 C7
Ranworth Rise WV4 39 D4
Raphael Cl CV5 112 C3
Rashwood Cl B94 143 B6
Ratcliffe Ave B30 104 D3
Ratcliffe Cl DY3 50 F6
Ratcliffe Ct CV10 72 C4
Ratcliffe Dr WV13 41 B8
Ratcliffe Rd
Hinckley LE10 75 F6
Solihull B91 107 C7
Wednesfield WV11 27 A6
Ratcliff Way DY4 52 D6
Ratcliff Wlk 3 B69 64 A7
Rathbone Cl
Bilston WV14 40 D5
Birmingham B5 86 E7
Keresley CV7 94 F6
Keresley CV7 95 A6
Rathbone Rd B67 64 F2
Rathlin Cl WV9 11 A3
Rathlin Croft B36 70 B6
Rathmore Cl DY8 80 E2
Rathvilly Sch B31 103 B3
Rathwell Cl WV9 11 A1
Rattle Croft B33 68 E3
Raveloe Dr CV11 73 D1
Ravenall Cl B34 69 B7
Raven Cl
Cannock WS12 2 E4
Cheslyn Hay WS6 4 D2
Huntington WS12 1 C7
Raven Cragg Rd CV5 132 E8
Raven Cres WV11 26 F8
Raven Ct
21 Brierley Hill DY5 61 D2
Wolverhampton WV10 11 B3
Ravenfield Cl B8 68 A5
Ravenhayes La B32 102 A6
Raven Hays Rd B31 102 C2
Ravenhill Dr WV8 10 A4
Ravenhurst Dr B43 43 E3

Ravenhurst Mews B23 ... 56 E3
Ravenhurst Rd B17 ... 85 C6
Ravenhurst St B12 ... 87 A8
Raven Rd WS5 ... 43 B6
Ravens Bank Dr B98 ... 154 E7
Ravens Bank Fst Sch B98 ... 154 D6
Ravensbourne Gr WV13 ... 27 C2
Ravenscroft Rd
Solihull B92 ... 107 A8
Willenhall WV12 ... 27 B5
Ravenscroft DY8 ... 80 C6
Ravens Ct WS8 ... 15 F7
Ravensdale Ave CV32 ... 156 C2
Ravensdale Cl WS5 ... 43 B7
Ravensdale Gdns WS5 ... 43 B7
Ravensdale Prim Sch CV2 ... 114 D4
Ravensdale Rd
Birmingham B10 ... 87 F7
Coventry CV2 ... 114 D3
Ravenshaw La B91 ... 108 A4
Ravenshaw Rd B16 ... 65 C2
Ravenshaw Way B91 ... 108 A3
Ravenshill Rd B14 ... 105 D4
Ravensholme WV6 ... 23 F2
Ravensholt CV4 ... 132 D6
Ravensitch Wlk DY5 ... 61 E1
Ravensmere Rd B98 ... 154 B1
Ravensthorpe Cl CV3 ... 134 E8
Ravenstone B77 ... 36 B8
Ravenswood B15 ... 85 E8
Ravenswood Cl B74 ... 46 B8
Ravenswood Dr B91 ... 106 F1
Ravenswood Dr S B91 ... 106 E1
Ravenswood Hill B46 ... 70 F7
Raven Way CV11 ... 73 F2
Raven Wlk 4 B15 ... 86 C7
Rawdon Gr B44 ... 56 B8
Rawlett Sch B79 ... 21 A8
Rawlings Rd B67 ... 65 A2
Rawlins Croft B35 ... 58 C3
Rawlinson Rd CV32 ... 157 B2
Rawlins St B16 ... 66 A1
Rawnsley Dr CV8 ... 148 C6
Rawnsley Rd WS12 ... 2 E6
Raybolds Bridge Rd WS2 ... 28 C4
Raybon Croft B45 ... 122 A6
Raybould's Fold DY2 ... 62 C5
Rayford Dr B71 ... 43 A2
Raygill B77 ... 36 B8
Ray Hall La
Birmingham B43 ... 54 B8
West Bromwich B43,B71 ... 43 A1
Rayleigh Ho B27 ... 88 D3
Rayleigh Rd WV3 ... 39 A8
Ray Mercer Way DY10 ... 116 F5
Raymond Ave B42 ... 55 B6
Raymond Cl
Coventry CV6 ... 95 F5
Walsall WS2 ... 28 D5
Raymond Gdns WV11 ... 26 E6
Raymond Rd B8 ... 67 E4
Raymont Gr B43 ... 44 B4
Rayners Croft B26 ... 68 F2
Raynor Cres CV12 ... 77 D1
Raynor Rd WV10 ... 25 F6
Raynsford Wlk CV34 ... 155 D1
Raywoods The CV10 ... 72 F3
Rea Ave B45 ... 121 E8
Reabrook Rd B31 ... 122 F8
Rea Bsns Pk B7 ... 67 C4
Rea Cl B31 ... 123 A7
Readers Wlk B43 ... 43 F1
Reading Ave CV11 ... 73 F7
Reading Cl CV2 ... 96 B3
Read St CV1 ... 113 E3
Rea Fordway B45 ... 101 F1
Reansway Sq WV6 ... 25 A4
Reapers Cl WV12 ... 27 D5
Reapers Wlk WV8 ... 10 F1
Rear Cotts B48 ... 138 F6
Rea Rd B31 ... 102 F1
Reardon Ct CV34 ... 155 E1
Rea St S B5 ... 86 F8
Reaside Cres B14 ... 104 B5
Reaside Croft B12 ... 86 E6
Reaside Dr B45 ... 102 B1
Reaside Jun Sch B45 ... 101 E1
Rea St B5 ... 164 D1
Rea Terr B5 ... 66 F2
Rea Twr B19 ... 66 C5
Rea Valley Dr B31 ... 103 B2
Reaview Dr B29 ... 86 B2
Reaymer Cl WS2 ... 28 B6
Reay Nadin Dr B73 ... 45 B4
Rebecca Dr B29 ... 85 E2
Rebecca Gdns WV4 ... 38 F4
Recreation Rd
Bromsgrove B61 ... 136 F3
Coventry CV6 ... 96 A3
Recreation St DY2 ... 62 D5
Rectory Ave WS10 ... 41 D6
Rectory Cl
Allesley CV5 ... 112 C6
Bedworth CV7 ... 78 A1
Drayton Bassett B78 ... 34 E5
Stourbridge DY8 ... 81 B3
Whitnash CV31 ... 162 B4
Rectory Ct B97 ... 153 D1
Rectory Dr CV7 ... 78 A1
Rectory Fields DY8 ... 60 E2
Rectory Gdns
Birmingham B36 ... 69 A8
Oldbury B68 ... 64 C5
Solihull B91 ... 107 D3
Stourbridge DY8 ... 81 B3
Rectory Gr B18 ... 65 E6
Rectory La
Allesley CV5 ... 112 C6
Birmingham B36 ... 69 A8
Upton Warren B61 ... 150 A4
Rectory Park Ave B75 ... 46 E4
Rectory Park Cl B75 ... 46 E4
Rectory Park Ct 7 B75 ... 46 F6
Rectory Park Rd B26 ... 89 C5
Rectory Rd
Birmingham B31 ... 103 B3
Redditch B97 ... 153 D1
Solihull B91 ... 107 C3
Stourbridge DY8 ... 81 B3
Sutton Coldfield B75 ... 46 E6
Rectory St DY8 ... 60 E3
Redacre Rd B73 ... 45 F2
Redacres WV6 ... 24 E6
Redbank Ave B23 ... 56 C3
Redbourn Rd WS3 ... 14 A4
Red Brick Cl B64 ... 82 D7
Redbrook Cl WS12 ... 2 D2
Redbrook Covert 7 B38 ... 123 E8
Red Brook Rd WS2 ... 28 A5
Redbrooks Cl B91 ... 107 A1
Redburn Dr B14 ... 104 D2
Redcap Croft CV6 ... 95 D4
Redcar Cl
Lower Marlbrook B61 ... 121 B1
Royal Leamington Spa CV32 ... 157 C4
Redcar Croft B36 ... 68 C8
Redcar Rd
Coventry CV1 ... 113 E5
Wolverhampton WV10 ... 11 D4
Redcliffe Dr WV5 ... 49 B6
Redcliff B77 ... 21 F5
Redcotts Cl WV10 ... 26 A8
Redcroft Dr B24 ... 57 C5
Redcroft Rd DY2 ... 62 E6
Reddal Hill Prim Sch B64 ... 62 E1
Reddal Hill Rd B64 ... 62 E2
Red Deeps CV11 ... 78 D8
Reddicap Heath Rd B75 ... 46 F4
Reddicap Hill B75 ... 46 E4
Reddicap Trad Est B76 ... 46 D4
Reddicroft B73 ... 46 C5
Reddings Ct B13 ... 86 D3
Reddings La B11,B28 ... 87 E3
Reddings Rd B13 ... 86 E2
Reddings The B47 ... 125 A5
Redditch Ho B33 ... 69 E2
Redditch Rd
Alvechurch,Arrowfield Top B48 ... 139 B8
Alvechurch,Rowney Green B48 ... 139 C3
Birmingham B31,B38 ... 123 C8
Hopwood B48 ... 123 B1
Stoke Heath B60 ... 150 D5
Studley B80 ... 159 D5
Redditch Ringway B97, B98 ... 153 D4
Redditch Sta B97 ... 153 D4
Redditch Wlk 4 CV2 ... 115 A7
Redesdale Ave CV6 ... 112 F5
Redfern Ave CV8 ... 148 A6
Redfern Cl B92 ... 89 B1
Redfern Dr WS7 ... 7 B5
Redfern Park Way B11 ... 88 A5
Redfern Rd B11 ... 88 A5
Redfly La DY5 ... 61 C6
Redford Cl B13 ... 87 B2
Redgate Cl B38 ... 103 D2
Redgrave Cl CV2 ... 115 B8
Red Hall Prim Sch DY3 ... 50 C3
Redhall Rd
Birmingham B32 ... 84 E7
Dudley DY3 ... 50 C2
Redhill Ave WV5 ... 49 A6
Redhill Cl DY8 ... 81 B4
Red Hill Cl B80 ... 159 E6
Redhill Cl B79 ... 21 A7
Redhill Ct DY8 ... 81 B4
Redhill Furrows CV31 ... 162 C5
Red Hill Gr B38 ... 123 F7
Redhill Jun & Inf Sch B25 ... 88 A6
Redhill La B45,B61 ... 121 C5
Red Hill Pl B62 ... 101 A7
Redhill Prim Sch WS11 ... 1 F4
Redhill Rd
Birmingham,King's Norton B38 ... 123 D7
Birmingham,Tyseley B25 ... 88 A6
Cannock WS11 ... 1 F4
Red Hill B98 ... 153 F2
Redhill Sch DY8 ... 81 B4
Red Hill DY8 ... 81 B4
Red Hill St WV1 ... 163 B4
Red House Ave WS10 ... 42 A5
Redhouse Cl B93 ... 127 E4
Redhouse Cone & Mus★ DY8 ... 60 E1
Redhouse Ind Est WS9 ... 29 F6
Red House Ind Est WS9 ... 30 A6
Redhouse JMI Sch WS9 ... 29 E5
Red House La WS9 ... 29 F5
Red House Park Rd B43 ... 43 E2
Red House Rd B33 ... 68 E2
Redhouse Rd WV6 ... 24 B5
Redhouse St WS1 ... 42 E7
Redhurst Dr WV10 ... 11 B3
Red La
Burton Green CV8 ... 131 C2
Coventry CV6 ... 113 F5
Essington WV11 ... 13 C3
Gospel End Village DY3 ... 50 B8
Redlake Dr DY9 ... 99 B8
Red La CV8 ... 147 D8
Redlake Rd DY9 ... 81 B1
Redlake B77 ... 35 E8
Redland Cl
Coventry CV2 ... 96 E2
Lower Marlbrook B60 ... 121 C1
Redland La CV8 ... 135 A2
Redland Rd CV31 ... 162 B5
Redlands Cl B91 ... 107 D5
Redlands Rd B91 ... 107 D5
Redlands Way B74 ... 31 A1
Red Leasowes Rd B63 ... 83 A3
Redliff Ave B36 ... 58 D1
Red Lion Ave WS11 ... 6 A4
Red Lion Cl B69 ... 52 A1
Red Lion Cres WS11 ... 6 A4
Red Lion La WS11 ... 6 B4
Red Lion St
Alvechurch B48 ... 139 B6
Redditch B98 ... 153 E4
Wolverhampton WV1 ... 163 B3
Redlock Field WS14 ... 9 A5
Redmead Cl B30 ... 103 C4
Redmoor Gdns WV4 ... 39 A5
Redmoor High Sch LE10 ... 71 B3
Redmoor Way B76 ... 58 D6
Rednal Hill Jun & Inf Schs B45 ... 122 C7
Rednal Hill La B45 ... 122 A6
Rednall Dr B75 ... 32 C3
Rednal Mill Dr B45 ... 122 C7
Rednal Park Ct B38 ... 103 F2
Rednal Rd B38 ... 103 E1
Rednell Ho B69 ... 63 D6
Redoak Ho WV10 ... 25 F3
Redpine Crest WV12 ... 27 D5
Red River Rd WS2 ... 28 A5
Redruth Cl
Coventry CV6 ... 114 A8
Kingswinford DY6 ... 60 D8
Nuneaton CV11 ... 74 A4
Walsall WS5 ... 43 D7
Redruth Rd WS5 ... 43 D7
Red Sands Rd DY10 ... 116 E8
Redstart Ave DY10 ... 117 B2
Redstone Cl B98 ... 154 C6
Redstone Dr WV11 ... 26 F5
Redstone Farm Rd B28 ... 106 B6
Redstone Way DY3 ... 50 D4
Redthorne Gr CV8 ... 148 B8
Redthorn Gr B33 ... 68 D3
Redvers Rd B9 ... 67 E1
Redway Ct B75 ... 46 E4
Redwell Cl B77 ... 21 D5
Redwing Cl WS7 ... 7 D5
Redwing Ct DY10 ... 117 A1
Redwing Dr WS12 ... 1 C7
Redwing Gr B23 ... 56 B7
Redwing B77 ... 36 A6
Red Wing Wlk B36 ... 70 A8
Redwood Ave DY1 ... 50 F5
Redwood Bsns Pk B66 ... 64 C7
Redwood Cl
Birmingham B30 ... 103 E4
Sutton Coldfield B74 ... 30 F2
Redwood Croft
Birmingham B14 ... 104 E7
Nuneaton CV10 ... 73 A1
Redwood Dr
Burntwood WS7 ... 6 F8
Cannock WS11 ... 2 A3
Tipton B69 ... 52 B2
Redwood Gdns B27 ... 88 B5
Redwood Ho B37 ... 69 F5
Redwood Rd
Birmingham B30 ... 103 E4
Dudley WV14 ... 40 D2
Walsall WS5 ... 43 B4
Redwood Way WV12 ... 27 B8
Reedham Gdns WV4 ... 38 D5
Reedly Rd WV12 ... 13 C1
Reedmace Cl B38 ... 123 F8
Reed Mace Dr B61 ... 137 A5
Reedmace B77 ... 21 C2
Reedswood Cl WS2 ... 28 C3
Reedswood Gdns WS2 ... 28 C3
Reedswood La WS2 ... 28 C3
Reedswood Way WS2 ... 28 B4
Rees Dr
Coventry CV3 ... 133 D4
Wombourne WV5 ... 49 B7
Reeve Ct DY10 ... 117 A1
Reeve Dr CV8 ... 148 A4
Reeve La WS13 ... 9 B8
Reeves Cl DY4 ... 52 B2
Reeves Gdns WV8 ... 10 A4
Reeves Rd
Birmingham B14 ... 104 C6
Hinckley LE10 ... 75 F6
Reeves St WS3 ... 28 B8
Reflex Ind Pk WV13 ... 27 A3
Reform St B70 ... 53 D3
Regal Cl B77 ... 35 C8
Regal Croft B36 ... 68 B8
Regal Dr WS2 ... 42 C8
Regal Ho CV11 ... 73 D3
Regan Ave B90 ... 106 A1
Regan Cres B23 ... 56 E6
Regan Ct B75 ... 47 C5
Regan Dr B69 ... 63 D8
Regan Ho B13 ... 105 D7
Regency Arc 6 CV32 ... 161 F8
Regency Cl
6 Birmingham B9 ... 67 D1
Nuneaton CV10 ... 73 D6
Regency Ct
Coventry CV5 ... 132 F8
Hinckley LE10 ... 76 A7
Walsall WS1 ... 43 A7
Regency Ct *continued*
Wolverhampton WV1 ... 163 B4
Regency Dr
Birmingham B38 ... 103 F2
Coventry CV3 ... 132 F5
Kenilworth CV8 ... 147 F3
Regency Gdns B14 ... 105 C3
Regency Ho
Birmingham B16 ... 66 A1
Royal Leamington Spa CV32 ... 162 A8
Regency Mews CV32 ... 162 A8
Regency Wlk B74 ... 31 D5
Regent Ave B69 ... 52 A1
Regent Cl
Birmingham B5 ... 86 D6
Halesowen B63 ... 83 A4
Kingswinford DY6 ... 60 C6
Oldbury B69 ... 63 A8
Regent Ct
3 Smethwick B66 ... 65 A5
4 Birmingham B62 ... 84 A7
5 Hinckley LE10 ... 75 D8
6 Darlaston WS10 ... 41 D6
Regent Dr B69 ... 52 A1
Regent Gr CV32 ... 161 F8
Regent Ho
6 Walsall WS2 ... 28 D3
Oldbury B68 ... 64 B2
Regent Mews B61 ... 150 E8
Regent Par B1 ... 66 C4
Regent Park Rd B10 ... 67 C1
Regent Pl
4 Royal Leamington Spa CV31 ... 162 A7
Birmingham B1 ... 66 C4
Tipton B69 ... 52 B2
Regent Rd
Birmingham B17 ... 85 D6
Birmingham,Handsworth B21 ... 65 D8
Oldbury B69 ... 63 A8
Wolverhampton WV4 ... 38 E5
Regents Park Com Prim Sch B10 ... 87 B8
Regents Park Rd B60 ... 137 C2
Regent St
Bedworth CV12 ... 78 C4
Bilston WV14 ... 40 D6
Birmingham,Hockley B1 ... 66 C4
Birmingham,Stirchley B30 ... 104 A7
Coventry CV1 ... 165 A2
Cradley Heath B64 ... 62 F2
Dudley DY1 ... 51 C6
Regents The B15 ... 85 D8
Regent St
Hinckley LE10 ... 75 D8
Nuneaton CV11 ... 73 D5
Royal Leamington Spa CV32 ... 161 F8
Smethwick B66 ... 65 A6
Tipton DY4 ... 51 E8
Willenhall WV13 ... 27 A3
Regents Way B75 ... 46 F6
Regent Wlk B8 ... 68 B7
Reg Hadden Ct CV10 ... 73 D6
Regiment Ct CV6 ... 95 A1
Regina Ave B44 ... 55 E8
Regina Cl B45 ... 101 E2
Regina Cres
Coventry CV2 ... 115 A7
Wolverhampton WV6 ... 24 B4
Regina Dr
Birmingham B42 ... 55 D3
Walsall WS4 ... 29 B4
Reginald Rd
Birmingham B8 ... 67 D4
Smethwick B67 ... 64 F2
Regis Beeches WV6 ... 24 C5
Regis Gdns B65 ... 63 C2
Regis Heath Rd B65 ... 63 E2
Regis Rd
Rowley Regis B65 ... 63 C2
Wolverhampton WV6 ... 24 C5
Regis Wlk CV2 ... 114 F7
Reid Ave WV12 ... 27 D6
Reid Cl WS7 ... 7 F7
Reid Rd B68 ... 64 D1
Reigate Ave B8 ... 68 B4
Reignier Pl CV34 ... 161 F2
Reindeer Rd B78 ... 20 E1
Relay Dr B77 ... 36 C7
Reliance Trad Est WV14 ... 40 B5
Relko Dr B36 ... 68 C7
Relton Mews CV6 ... 113 F6
Rembrandt Cl
Cannock WS11 ... 2 D2
Coventry CV5 ... 112 C3
Remburn Gdns CV34 ... 160 F8
Remembrance Rd
Coventry CV3 ... 134 D6
Wednesbury WS10 ... 42 C3
Remington Dr WS11 ... 4 F8
Remington Pl WS2 ... 28 C5
Remington Rd WS2 ... 28 B5
Renaissance Ct 1 B12 ... 67 A1
Rene Rd B77 ... 21 E5
Renfrew Cl DY8 ... 60 C3
Renfrew Gdns DY11 ... 116 C5
Renfrew Sq B35 ... 58 B4
Renfrew Wlk CV4 ... 132 A8
Renison Rd CV12 ... 77 E1
Rennie Gr B32 ... 84 D5
Rennison Dr WV5 ... 49 A6
Renolds Cl CV4 ... 112 C2
Renown Ave CV5 ... 112 C1
Renown Cl DY5 ... 61 B7
Renshaw B91 ... 108 A3
Renshaw Ind Est B80 ... 159 B4
Renton Gr WV10 ... 11 A1
Renton Rd WV10 ... 11 A1
Repington Rd N B77 ... 22 A5
Repington Rd S B77 ... 22 A5
Repington Way B75 ... 47 B5
Repton Ave WV6 ... 23 E3
Repton Cl WS11 ... 4 B8
Repton Dr CV6 ... 96 B2
Repton Gr B9 ... 68 B3
Repton Ho B23 ... 56 F6
Repton Rd B9 ... 68 B3
Reservoir Cl WS2 ... 42 B8
Reservoir Pas WS10 ... 41 F3
Reservoir Pl WS2 ... 42 B8
Reservoir Rd
Birmingham B29 ... 85 C3
Birmingham,Edgbaston B16 ... 65 F2
Birmingham,Rednal B45 ... 122 C3
Birmingham,Stockland Green B23 ... 56 E4
Cannock WS12 ... 2 D4
Kidderminster DY11 ... 116 C3
Oldbury B68 ... 64 C4
Rowley Regis B65 ... 63 D3
Solihull B92 ... 106 F8
Reservoir Retreat B16 ... 65 F1
Reservoir St WS2 ... 42 B8
Reswood Ct 3 B24 ... 56 F3
Retallack Cl B66 ... 65 B8
Retford Dr B76 ... 46 E4
Retford Gr B25 ... 88 C6
Retreat Gdns DY3 ... 50 E7
Retreat St
Astwood Bank B96 ... 158 E1
Wolverhampton WV3 ... 163 A1
Retreat The B64 ... 82 E7
Reuben Ave CV10 ... 72 B6
Revesby Wlk 4 B7 ... 67 A4
Revival St WS3 ... 14 B1
Rex Cl CV4 ... 131 D8
Reyde Cl B97 ... 153 A2
Reynalds Cross Sch B92 ... 106 D7
Reynard Cl B97 ... 152 F3
Reynards Cl DY3 ... 51 A7
Reynolds Cl
Hinckley LE10 ... 71 A3
Lichfield WS13 ... 3 B2
Reynolds Gr WV6 ... 23 F5
Reynolds Ho B19 ... 66 E7
Reynolds Rd
Bedworth CV12 ... 78 A4
Birmingham B21 ... 65 E7
Reynoldstown Rd B36 ... 68 C8
Reynolds Wlk WV11 ... 27 B8
Rhayader Rd B31 ... 102 E5
Rhodes Alms Houses The B21 ... 65 F7
Rhodes Cl DY3 ... 50 A4
Rhone Cl B11 ... 87 C3
Rhoose Croft B35 ... 58 B3
Rhuddlan Way DY10 ... 116 E1
Rhyl Rd CV11 ... 79 F6
Rhys Thomas Cl WV12 ... 27 D4
Rian Ct B64 ... 82 D8
Ribbesford Ave WV10 ... 25 B8
Ribbesford Cl B63 ... 82 D6
Ribbesford Cres WV14 ... 40 D1
Ribble Cl CV12 ... 79 B2
Ribble Ct B73 ... 46 B5
Ribble Rd CV3 ... 113 F2
Ribblesdale Ave LE10 ... 71 E3
Ribblesdale Rd B29,B30 ... 104 A8
Ribblesdale B77 ... 36 B7
Ribble Wlk B36 ... 69 F8
Ribbonbrook CV11 ... 73 D3
Ribbonfields CV11 ... 73 D3
Richard Cooper Rd WS14 ... 17 F5
Richard Joy Cl CV6 ... 95 C2
Richard Lee Prim Sch CV2 ... 114 E3
Richard Lighton Ho 5 B1 ... 66 C3
Richard Pl WS5 ... 43 C8
Richard Rd WS5 ... 43 C8
Richard St S B70 ... 53 C2
Richards Cl
Birmingham B31 ... 122 F6
Kenilworth CV8 ... 147 F5
Rowley Regis B65 ... 63 E4
Richards Ct WS11 ... 5 F6
Richards Gr CV31 ... 162 A5
Richards Ho
2 Walsall WS2 ... 28 D3
3 Oldbury B69 ... 63 E4
Richardson Cl CV34 ... 155 F1
Richardson Ct WS7 ... 6 E8
Richardson Dr DY8 ... 80 E8
Richardson Ho DY4 ... 52 C8
Richardson Way CV2 ... 115 B8
Richards Rd DY4 ... 40 F1
Richards St WS10 ... 41 D7
Richard St B7 ... 66 F5
Richard Street W 1 B70 ... 53 C2
Richard St B70 ... 53 B3
Richard Williams Rd WS10 ... 42 B2
Richborough Dr DY1 ... 50 F4
Rich Cl CV34 ... 161 B7
Riches St WV6 ... 24 F3
Richford Gr B33 ... 69 D2
Richmere Ct WV6 ... 24 B3
Richmond Aston Dr DY4 ... 52 A5
Richmond Ave
Birmingham B12 ... 86 F5
Wolverhampton WV3 ... 24 F1

Richmond Cl
Birmingham B20 .... 55 A3
Cannock WS11 .... 2 A5
Hollywood B47 .... 125 C7
Tamworth B79 .... 21 A5
Richmond Croft B42 ...... 54 F6
Richmond Ct
2 Sutton Coldfield B72 ... 57 B7
4 Birmingham,Weoley Castle B29 .... 103 C7
6 Royal Leamington Spa CV31 .... 162 B7
Birmingham,Calthorpe Fields B15 .... 86 B8
Halesowen B63 .... 82 E3
Oldbury B68 .... 64 C5
Stourbridge DY9 .... 81 B1
Richmond Dr
Lichfield WS14 .... 9 D7
Perton WV6 .... 23 F3
Sutton Coldfield B75 ...... 46 F6
Wolverhampton WV3 ...... 24 E1
Richmond Gdns
Stourbridge DY8 .... 80 F7
Wombourne WV5 .... 49 A5
Richmond Gr DY8 .... 80 E8
Richmond Hill Gdns B15 . 85 E7
Richmond Hill B68 .... 64 C5
Richmond Hill Rd B15 .... 85 F6
Richmond Ho 2 B37 ...... 70 C1
Richmond Mews WV3 .... 25 A1
Richmond Pk DY6 .... 60 C8
Richmond Pl B14 .... 104 F8
Richmond Prim Sch LE10. 71 C3
Richmond Rd
Birmingham B45 .... 121 E7
Birmingham,Hockley B18 ... 66 B6
Birmingham,Yardley B33 ... 68 D2
Dudley DY2 .... 62 C8
Hinckley LE10 .... 71 C3
Nuneaton CV11 .... 73 A4
Sedgley DY3 .... 50 E7
Smethwick B66 .... 65 A2
Solihull B92 .... 88 F2
Sutton Coldfield B73 ...... 46 B6
Wolverhampton WV3 ...... 24 E1
Richmond St S B70 ...... 52 E5
Richmond St
Coventry CV2 .... 114 A3
Halesowen B63 .... 83 A4
Walsall WS1 .... 29 A1
West Bromwich B70 ...... 52 F6
Richmond Way 2 B37 ... 70 C3
Rickard Cl B93 .... 127 E6
Rickman Dr B15 .... 86 D8
Rickyard Cl
Birmingham,Northfield B29 .... 103 A6
Birmingham,Yardley B25 ... 68 D1
Rickyard La B98 .... 154 D5
Rickyard Piece B32 ...... 84 E4
Ricoh Arena (Coventry City FC) CV6 .... 95 E3
Riddfield Rd B36 .... 68 E8
Ridding La WS10 .... 41 F2
Riddings Cres WS3 ...... 14 F4
Riddings Hill CV7 ...... 130 C8
Riddings The
Birmingham B33 .... 68 F4
Coventry CV5 .... 132 E7
Stourbridge DY9 .... 81 D2
Sutton Coldfield B76 ...... 58 B8
Tamworth B77 .... 21 E5
Wolverhampton WV10 .... 26 A7
Riddon Dr LE10 .... 75 B8
Rideswell Gr CV31 ...... 162 A1
Ridgacre Ent Pk B71 ...... 53 B6
Ridgacre La B32 .... 84 C6
Ridgacre Rd B32 .... 84 C6
Ridgacre Rd W B32 ...... 84 A6
Ridgacre Rd B71 .... 53 B6
Ridge Cl
Birmingham B13 .... 105 C6
Willenhall WS2 .... 27 D3
Ridge Ct CV5 .... 112 A6
Ridgefield Rd B62 ...... 83 C7
Ridge Gr DY9 .... 81 C5
Ridge La WV11 .... 26 D7
Ridgeley Cl CV34 ...... 155 E2
Ridgemount Dr B38 ...... 123 D8
Ridge Prim Sch The DY8 . 80 C5
Ridge Rd DY6 .... 60 C5
Ridge St DY8 .... 80 C6
Ridgethorpe CV3 ...... 134 E6
Ridgewater Cl B45 ...... 122 B6
Ridge Way WS9 .... 30 B4
Ridgeway Ave
Birmingham B62 .... 84 A6
Coventry CV3 .... 133 C6
Ridgeway B17 .... 65 B2
Ridgeway Cl B80 ...... 159 E2
Ridgeway Ct WS2 ...... 27 F2
Ridgeway Dr WV4 ...... 38 F3
Ridgeway Prim Sch WS7 . 7 A5
Ridgeway Rd
1 Tipton DY4 .... 52 A8
Stourbridge DY8 .... 60 F2
Ridgeway Sch The CV34 156 A1
Ridgeway DY3 .... 50 D7
Ridgeway The
Birmingham,Quinton B32 ... 84 A4
Birmingham,Upper Witton B23 .... 56 A5
Burntwood WS7 .... 7 A4
Hinckley LE10 .... 75 D6
Ridgeway The *continued*
Warwick CV34 .... 156 A1
Ridgeway Trad Est B96 .. 158 E1
Ridgewood Ave DY8 ...... 80 C7
Ridgewood B34 .... 69 B6
Ridgewood Cl
7 Walsall WS1 .... 42 F8
Royal Leamington Spa CV32 .... 156 C1
Ridgewood Dr B75 ...... 32 B1
Ridgewood Gdns B44 .... 55 F7
Ridgewood High Sch DY8 80 C5
Ridgewood Rise B77 ..... 22 A5
Ridgley Rd CV4 .... 131 E8
Ridgmont Croft B32 ...... 84 E5
Riding Cl B71 .... 53 F7
Ridings Brook Dr 3 WS11 . 2 A2
Ridings La B98 .... 154 B6
Ridings Park Trad Est WS11 .... 2 A3
Ridings The WS11 .... 4 F8
Riding Way WV12 .... 27 D6
Ridley St B1 .... 164 A1
Ridpool Prim Sch B33 .... 69 B3
Ridpool Rd B33 .... 69 B3
Ridware Ho WS13 .... 3 E1
Rifle Range Rd DY11 .... 116 B3
Rifle St WV14 .... 51 A8
Rigby Cl CV34 .... 161 D4
Rigby Dr WS11 .... 1 F4
Rigby Hall B60 .... 151 C8
Rigby Hall Day Specl Sch B60 .... 151 C8
Rigby La B60 .... 151 C8
Rigby St WS10 .... 42 A1
Rigdale Cl CV2 .... 114 E2
Righton Ho B77 .... 21 D1
Riland Ave B75 .... 46 D5
Riland Ct B72 .... 57 C7
Riland Gr B75 .... 46 C5
Riland Ind Est B75 ...... 46 D5
Riland Rd B75 .... 46 D5
Riley Cl CV8 .... 148 D4
Riley Cres WV4 .... 39 A6
Riley Dr B36 .... 59 A1
Riley Ho CV1 .... 165 B2
Riley Rd B14 .... 105 D3
Riley Sq CV2 .... 96 B1
Riley St WV13 .... 27 B2
Riley B77 .... 21 E3
Rills The LE10 .... 71 E2
Rilstone Rd B32 .... 84 F5
Rindleford Ave WV4 ...... 38 C6
Ringhills Rd WV8 .... 10 B2
Ringinglow Rd B44 ...... 44 D2
Ringmere Ave B36 ...... 69 B7
Ring Rd WS7 .... 6 E7
Ring Rd N B15 .... 85 F4
Ring Rd S B15 .... 85 F3
Ring Road St Andrews WV1 .... 163 A3
Ring Road St Davids WV1 .... 163 C3
Ring Road St Georges WV2 .... 163 C2
Ring Road St Johns WV2 .... 163 B2
Ring Road St Marks WV3 .... 163 B2
Ring Road St Patricks WV1 .... 163 C4
Ring Road St Peters WV1 .... 163 B3
Ringswood Rd B92 ...... 88 E4
Ring The B25 .... 88 C8
Ringway WS11 .... 1 E1
Ringway Hill Cross CV1 . 165 A3
Ringway Ind Est WS13 .... 3 C3
Ringway Queens CV1 .... 165 A2
Ringway Rudge CV1 ..... 165 A2
Ringway St Johns CV1 . 165 C2
Ringway St Nicholas CV1 .... 165 B3
Ringway St Patricks CV1 165 B1
Ringway Swanswell CV1. 165 C3
Ringway The DY10 ...... 116 F5
Ringway Whitefriars CV1 .... 165 C3
Ringwood Ave WS9 ...... 30 B5
Ringwood Dr B45 ...... 102 A1
Ringwood Highway CV2 .. 96 E2
Ringwood Rd WV10 ...... 11 D1
Rinhill Gr CV31 .... 162 D6
Ripley Cl B69 .... 62 F8
Ripley Gr B23 .... 56 B5
Riplingham 3 CV32 ...... 156 F2
Ripon Cl CV5 .... 112 B8
Ripon Dr B71 .... 42 D1
Ripon Rd
Birmingham B14 .... 105 C4
Walsall WS2 .... 28 B2
Wolverhampton WV10 .... 25 C7
Rippingille Rd B43 ...... 44 C4
Ripple Rd B30 .... 104 B7
Risborough Cl CV5 ...... 112 C3
Rischale Way WS4 ...... 29 D8
Risdale Cl CV32 .... 156 D2
Rise Ave B45 .... 122 A7
Riseley Cres B5 .... 86 D7
Rise The
Birmingham,Great Barr B42 .... 55 A8
Birmingham,Marston Green B37 .... 90 A7
Hopwood B48 .... 123 B4
Kingswinford DY6 ...... 60 E5
Lichfield WS13 .... 8 F7
Rising Brook WV6 ...... 24 B4
Rising La
Chadwick End B93 ...... 145 B5
Kingswood B94,B93 ...... 144 F5
Rising Rd B94 .... 144 C5
Rissington Ave B29 ...... 104 A8
Ritchie Cl B13 .... 87 A1
Rivendell Ct B28 .... 87 E1
Rivendell Gdns WV6 ..... 24 B5
Riverbank Rd WV13 ...... 27 D2
River Brook Dr B30 ..... 104 B8
River Cl
Bedworth CV12 .... 77 F1
Royal Leamington Spa CV32 .... 161 D8
River Ct 3 CV1 .... 113 B3
Riverdrive B78,B79 ...... 21 B3
Riverfield Gr B77 ...... 21 D5
Riverford Croft CV4 ..... 132 D4
River Lee Rd B11 ...... 87 E5
Rivermead CV11 .... 73 A4
Rivermead Pk B34 ...... 69 A6
Riversdale 6 CV32 ...... 161 E8
Riversdale Rd B14 ...... 105 D3
Riverside Cl
Coventry CV3 .... 134 A7
Lickey End B60 .... 137 C6
Riverside Cres B28 ...... 105 D4
Riverside Ct
1 Coleshill B46 .... 70 F7
Birmingham B38 .... 103 D3
Riverside Dr
Birmingham,Cannon Hill B29 .... 86 C3
Birmingham,Stechford B33 . 68 D4
Solihull B91 .... 107 E2
Riverside Gdns WV8 ..... 10 B5
Riverside Ind Est B78 .... 21 B1
Riverside
Royal Leamington Spa CV32 .... 161 E8
Studley B80 .... 159 F5
Riverslea Rd CV3 ...... 114 C1
Riversleigh Dr DY8 ...... 80 E8
Riversleigh Rd CV32 ..... 156 C1
Riversley Rd CV11 ...... 73 C3
River St B5 .... 67 A2
Riverway WS10 .... 42 B2
River Wlk CV2 .... 96 C2
Rivington Cl DY8 .... 80 E4
Rivington Cres B44 ...... 45 C1
Roach Cl
Birmingham B37 .... 70 C3
Brierley Hill DY5 .... 61 D5
Roach Cres WV11 .... 26 F8
Roach Pool Croft B16 .... 65 C2
Roach B77 .... 35 D6
Road No 1 DY10 .... 116 E2
Road No 2 DY10 .... 116 E2
Road No 3 DY10 .... 116 E2
Roadway Cl CV12 .... 78 B2
Roanne Ringway CV11 ... 73 B4
Robert Ave B23 .... 56 E6
Robert Cl
Coventry CV3 .... 134 C4
Tamworth B79 .... 20 F7
Robert Cramb Ave CV4 .. 131 F8
Robert Ct
5 Birmingham,Wake Green B13 .... 87 B2
Birmingham,Pheasey B44 .. 44 D4
Robert Rd
Bedworth CV7 .... 95 F8
Birmingham B20 .... 55 B1
Tipton DY4 .... 51 F6
Roberts Cl
Brownhills WS9 .... 15 F2
Darlaston WS10 .... 41 B4
Roberts Ct B24 .... 57 C6
Roberts Green Rd DY3 ... 50 E4
Roberts La DY9 .... 99 B8
Robertson Knoll B36 ...... 68 F7
Robertsons Gdns 5 B7 .. 67 C7
Roberts Prim Sch DY3 ... 50 D4
Roberts Rd
Birmingham B27 .... 88 D3
Walsall WS3 .... 28 F5
Wednesbury WS10 ...... 42 E2
Robert St DY3 .... 50 D4
Robert Wynd WV14 ...... 40 A1
Robeson Cl DY4 .... 51 D5
Robey's La B78 .... 22 D3
Robin Cl
Birmingham B36 .... 70 A8
Huntington WS12 .... 1 C7
Kingswinford DY6 .... 61 A6
Tamworth B77 .... 35 C8
Robin Ct DY10 .... 117 A2
Robin Gr WV11 .... 26 C7
Robin Hood Cres B28 ... 105 E7
Robin Hood Croft B28 ... 105 F6
Robin Hood La B28 ...... 105 E7
Robin Hood Rd
Brierley Hill DY5 .... 61 F2
Coventry CV3 .... 134 C6
Robin Hood Sch B28 .... 106 B6
Robinia Cl CV32 .... 157 B2
Robinia B77 .... 22 A4
Robin Rd B23 .... 56 E5
Robins Bsns Pk B70 ...... 52 E7
Robins Cl WS6 .... 4 D1
Robin's Cl DY8 .... 81 A3
Robins Croft WS11 ...... 2 A1
Robins Ct B14 .... 86 F1
Robinsfield Dr B31 ...... 123 A7
Robins Gr CV34 .... 160 C4
Robins Hill Dr B48 ...... 139 A5
Robins La B97 .... 153 C6
Robinson Cl B79 .... 20 E7
Robinson Rd
Bedworth CV12 .... 95 D8
Burntwood WS7 .... 6 F8
Robinson's Way B76 ..... 58 D5
Robinson Way LE10 ...... 75 F4
Robins Rd WS7 .... 6 E7
Robins Way CV10 .... 72 A3
Robin Wlk WS2 .... 27 F3
Robottom Cl WS2 .... 28 B6
Robson Cl WS8 .... 15 F5
Rocester Ave WV11 ...... 26 E7
Rochdale Wlk B10 ...... 87 C7
Roche Rd WS3 .... 13 F1
Rochester Ave WS7 ...... 7 A7
Rochester Cl
Nuneaton CV11 .... 73 B3
Redditch B97 .... 158 C8
Rochester Croft WS2 ..... 28 A4
Rochester Rd
Birmingham B31 .... 103 A4
Coventry CV5 .... 132 E8
Rochester Way WS12 .... 2 C1
Rochester Wlk DY10 .... 117 C5
Roche The WS13 .... 8 A8
Roche Way WS3 .... 13 F1
Rochford Cl
6 Walsall WS2 .... 42 C7
Birmingham B45 .... 121 E7
Halesowen B63 .... 82 F2
Sutton Coldfield B76 ...... 58 A8
Rochford Ct
Royal Leamington Spa CV31 .... 161 E7
Solihull B90 .... 127 A6
Rochford Gr WV4 .... 38 D5
Rock Ave B45 .... 122 C7
Rock Cl CV6 .... 96 B1
Rock Cotts 6 DY11 ..... 116 D6
Rocken End CV6 .... 113 D8
Rocket Pool Dr WV14 .... 41 A2
Rockford Cl B98 .... 158 F5
Rockford Rd B42 .... 55 A7
Rock Gr B92 .... 88 E3
Rock Hill
Bromsgrove B61 .... 150 D7
Weeford B78,WS14 ...... 19 C4
Rockingham Cl
Dorridge B93 .... 127 D2
Dudley DY3 .... 50 B3
Walsall WS3 .... 14 B1
Rockingham Dr
Nuneaton CV11 .... 78 F7
Perton WV6 .... 23 F3
Rockingham Gdns B74 ... 46 B6
Rockingham Hall Gdns DY9 .... 99 D7
Rockingham Rd B25 ..... 88 D8
Rock La CV7 .... 94 C7
Rockland Dr B33 .... 68 E4
Rockland Gdns WV13 .... 40 F8
Rocklands Cres WS13 .... 3 D1
Rocklands Dr B75 .... 46 B8
Rocklands Sch WS13 ...... 9 D8
Rockley Gr B45 .... 122 B7
Rockley Rd B65 .... 63 A6
Rockmead Ave B44 ...... 44 F2
Rock Mill La CV32 ...... 161 C8
Rock Mill CV32 .... 156 C1
Rockmoor Cl B37 .... 69 E3
Rock Rd
Sedgley WV14 .... 50 F8
Solihull B92 .... 88 E3
Rockrose Gdns WV10 .... 12 A7
Rock St DY3 .... 50 E5
Rock The WV6 .... 24 D5
Rockville Rd B8 .... 68 A4
Rockwell La B48 .... 139 E4
Rockwood Rd B27 .... 88 B4
Rocky La
Birmingham,Aston B6 ..... 67 A6
Birmingham,Great Barr B42 55 B5
Birmingham,Nechells Green B7 .... 67 B6
Catshill B61 .... 136 E7
Kenilworth CV8 .... 148 D2
Rodborough Rd
Birmingham B26 .... 89 B7
Dorridge B93 .... 127 E3
Rodbourne Rd B17 ...... 85 C3
Roddis Cl B23 .... 56 D8
Roden Ave DY10 .... 117 A2
Roderick Dr WV11 ...... 26 D7
Roderick Rd B11 .... 87 C5
Rodhouse Cl CV4 .... 111 D1
Rodlington Ave B44 ...... 44 F1
Rodman Cl B15 .... 85 D8
Rodney Cl
Birmingham B16 .... 66 A2
Hinckley LE10 .... 71 D4
Solihull B92 .... 89 B1
Rodney Rd B92 .... 89 B1
Rodway Cl
Birmingham B19 .... 66 E7
Brierley Hill DY5 .... 81 D7
Wolverhampton WV4 ...... 39 D3
Rodway Dr CV5 .... 111 D4
Rodwell Gr B44 .... 56 A8
Rodyard Way CV1 ...... 165 C1
Roebuck Cl B34 .... 69 E5
Roebuck Glade WV12 .... 27 E4
Roebuck La
Smethwick B66 .... 64 F8
West Bromwich B70 ...... 53 E1
Roebuck Pl WS3 .... 28 E6
Roebuck Rd WS3 .... 28 E6
Roebuck St B70 .... 53 F1
Roe Cl CV34 .... 160 F8
Roedean Cl B44 .... 56 B7
Roford Ct DY3 .... 50 E5
Rogerfield Rd B23 ...... 57 A6
Rogers Cl WV11 .... 13 A2
Rogers Rd B8 .... 68 B5
Rogers Way CV34 ...... 160 B4
Rogue's La LE9,LE10 ..... 71 C6
Rokeby Cl B76 .... 46 E4
Rokeby Rd B43 .... 43 F2
Rokeby Wlk B34 .... 69 A6
Rokewood Cl DY6 ...... 49 D1
Rokholt Cres WS11 ...... 1 C1
Roland Ave CV6 .... 95 C3
Roland Gdns 5 B19 ...... 66 C8
Roland Gr 4 B19 .... 66 C8
Roland Mount CV6 ...... 95 C3
Roland Rd B19 .... 66 C8
Rolan Dr B90 .... 125 E8
Roland Terr 3 B19 ...... 66 C8
Roland Vernon Way DY4 . 52 C7
Rolfe St B66 .... 65 A6
Rollason Cl CV6 .... 113 C8
Rollason Rd
5 Dudley DY2 .... 62 D8
Birmingham B24 .... 57 A3
Coventry CV6 .... 113 B8
Rollason's Yd CV6 ...... 96 A3
Rollesby Dr WV13 ...... 40 F8
Rolling Mill Cl B5 ...... 86 E7
Rolling Mill Rd WS11 ...... 5 F4
Rollingmill St WS2 ...... 28 C1
Rollswood Dr B91 ...... 107 A4
Rolvenden Ct WV13 ..... 27 C2
Roman Cl WS8 .... 6 E2
Roman Ct
Birmingham B38 .... 124 B8
Cannock WS11 .... 4 E5
Tamworth B77 .... 35 E7
Romani Cl CV34 .... 160 D7
Roman La B74 .... 31 B4
Roman Pk
Coleshill B46 .... 59 F1
Sutton Coldfield B74 ...... 31 B4
Roman Pl B74 .... 31 B2
Roman Rd CV2 .... 114 B3
Roman Rd (Sandy La) DY8 .... 80 C3
Roman Rd B74 .... 31 C4
Romans Grange B74 ..... 31 C5
Roman View WS11 .... 4 F5
Roman Way
Birmingham B15 .... 85 D3
Bromsgrove B61 .... 137 B4
Coleshill B46 .... 59 F2
Coventry CV3 .... 133 D3
Roman Way Fst Sch B98 154 E3
Roman Way
Lichfield WS14 .... 9 D7
Rowley Regis B65 .... 63 C3
Tamworth B79 .... 20 E7
Roman Wlk WS14 .... 8 D2
Romany Rd B45 .... 101 D1
Romany Way DY8 .... 80 C3
Roma Rd B11 .... 87 E5
Romeo Arbour CV34 .... 161 E3
Romford Cl B26 .... 89 B6
Romford Rd CV6 .... 95 B2
Romilly Ave B20 .... 55 B3
Romilly Cl
Lichfield WS14 .... 9 E7
Stourbridge DY8 .... 80 E6
Sutton Coldfield B76 ...... 47 A4
Romney Cl
Birmingham B28 .... 105 F7
Hinckley LE10 .... 71 A3
Romney House Ind Est WS10 .... 41 B7
Romney B77 .... 35 F8
Romney Way B43 .... 44 D4
Romsey Ave CV10 .... 73 D8
Romsey Gr WV10 .... 11 C3
Romsey Ho WS2 .... 42 C7
Romsey Rd WV10 .... 11 C3
Romsey Way WS3 .... 13 F3
Romsley Cl
Birmingham B45 .... 121 E8
Halesowen B63 .... 83 B2
Redditch B98 .... 154 F3
Walsall WS4 .... 15 C2
Romsley Hill Grange B62 .... 100 F1
Romsley Rd
Birmingham B32 .... 102 B8
Coventry CV6 .... 113 C6
Oldbury B68 .... 64 B2
Stourbridge DY9 .... 81 C5
Romsley,St Kenelm's CE Fst Sch B62 .... 101 A4
Romulus Cl B20 .... 55 B3
Ronald Gr B36 .... 58 D1
Ronald Pl B9 .... 67 E2
Ronald Rd B9 .... 67 D2
Ron Davis Cl B66 .... 65 B5
Ro-Oak Rd CV6 .... 112 F5
Rood End Prim Sch B68 .. 64 C6
Rood End Rd B69 .... 64 C7
Rooker Ave WV2 .... 39 F6
Rooker Cres WV2 .... 39 F6
Rookery Ave
Brierley Hill DY5 .... 61 A2
Wolverhampton WV4 ...... 40 A3
Rookery Cl B97 .... 153 D1
Rookery Ct WS13 .... 8 E7
Rookery La
Aldridge WS9 .... 30 B6
Coventry CV6 .... 95 B4
Weeford B75,B78 .... 19 C2
Wolverhampton WV2 ...... 39 B6
Rookery Par WS9 .... 30 B6

Rookery Pk DY5 ... 61 B5
Rookery Rd
Birmingham B29 ... 85 F2
Birmingham,Handsworth B21 ... 54 E1
Wolverhampton WV14,WV4. 40 A3
Wombourne WV5 ... 49 B6
Rookery Rise WV5 ... 49 B6
Rookery Sch B21 ... 54 E1
Rookery St WV11 ... 26 C5
Rookery The B62 ... 84 A2
Rooks Mdw DY9 ... 99 B6
Rookwood Dr WV6 ... 23 F2
Roosevelt Dr CV4 ... 111 E2
Rooth St WS10 ... 42 B4
Roper Way DY3 ... 50 F6
Roper Wlk DY3 ... 50 F6
Rosafield Ave B62 ... 83 F6
Rosalind Ave DY1 ... 51 B6
Rosalind Gr WV11 ... 27 A5
Rosamond St WS1 ... 42 D7
Rosary RC Prim Sch B8 .. 67 E3
Rosary Rd B23 ... 56 D3
Rosary Villas [1] B11 ... 87 C5
Rosaville Cres CV5 ... 112 A6
Rose Ave
Alvechurch B48 ... 139 A5
Birmingham B68 ... 84 C7
Coventry CV6 ... 112 F5
Kingswinford DY6 ... 60 F5
Rosebank Dr WS3 ... 28 E4
Rosebay Ave B38 ... 123 F8
Rose Bay Mdw [2] WS11 ... 2 C2
Roseberry Ave CV2 ... 96 C1
Rosebery Rd
Smethwick B66 ... 65 C4
Tamworth B77 ... 35 D4
Rosebery St
Birmingham B18 ... 66 A4
Wolverhampton WV3 ... 25 B1
Rosebriars B90 ... 125 E7
Rose Cl B66 ... 65 C5
Rose Cottage Dr [3] DY8 .. 60 D3
Rose Cottage Flats CV5 . 111 D5
Rose Cotts
[6] Birmingham B29 ... 85 F2
Birmingham,Stirchley B30 104 A6
Rose Croft CV8 ... 147 E6
Rosecroft Rd B26 ... 89 C6
Rose Ct
Balsall Common CV7 ... 130 B8
Dudley DY2 ... 51 F1
Rosedale Ave
Birmingham B23 ... 56 E3
Smethwick B66 ... 65 C5
Rosedale CE Inf Sch WV12 ... 27 D5
Rosedale Cl B97 ... 153 A4
Rosedale Gr B25 ... 88 C8
Rosedale Pl WV13 ... 41 A8
Rosedale Rd B25 ... 88 C8
Rosedale Wlk DY6 ... 60 E8
Rosedene Dr B20 ... 54 F2
Rose Dr WS8 ... 15 E5
Rosefield Croft B6 ... 66 F7
Rosefield Ct B67 ... 65 A4
Rosefield Pl [4] CV32 ... 161 F8
Rosefield Rd B67 ... 65 A4
Rosefield St CV32 ... 162 A8
Rosefield Wlk [3] CV32 .. 161 F8
Rosegardens The B63 ... 82 E2
Rosegreen Cl CV3 ... 133 E6
Rosehall Cl
Redditch B98 ... 158 E6
Solihull B91 ... 106 F1
Rose Hill
Barnt Green B45 ... 122 B4
Brierley Hill DY5 ... 62 A1
Rosehill WS12 ... 1 F8
Rose Hill Cl B36 ... 69 B8
Rose Hill WV13 ... 41 A8
Rose Hill Gdns WV13 ... 27 B1
Rose Hill Rd B21 ... 66 A7
Rosehip Cl WS5 ... 43 A3
Rosehip Dr CV2 ... 114 B6
Rose La
Burntwood WS7 ... 7 C7
Dodford B61 ... 136 A6
Roseland Ave DY2 ... 51 F1
Roseland Rd CV8 ... 147 F3
Roselands Ave CV2 ... 114 D8
Roseland Way [7] B15 ... 66 B1
Rose La
Nuneaton CV11 ... 73 C3
Oldbury B69 ... 52 C2
Roseleigh Rd B45 ... 122 B6
Rosemary Ave
Bilston WV14 ... 40 F6
Cheslyn Hay WS6 ... 4 D3
Wolverhampton WV4 ... 39 C6
Rosemary Cl
Brownhills WS8 ... 15 D6
Coventry CV4 ... 111 E3
Rosemary Cres
Dudley DY1 ... 51 A6
Wolverhampton WV4 ... 39 C5
Rosemary Cres W WV4 ... 39 B5
Rosemary Ct B74 ... 31 D4
Rosemary Dr
Huntington WS12 ... 1 D5
Stoke Prior B60 ... 150 C1
Sutton Coldfield B74 ... 31 C3
Rosemary Hill CV8 ... 147 F5
Rosemary Hill Rd B74 ... 31 D4
Rosemary La DY8 ... 80 D3
Rosemary Mews CV8 ... 147 F5
Rosemary Nook B74 ... 31 D5
Rosemary Rd
Birmingham B33 ... 68 F2
Cheslyn Hay WS6 ... 4 D3
Halesowen B63 ... 82 E2
Kidderminster DY10 ... 117 B7
Tamworth B77 ... 21 F4
Tipton DY4 ... 52 A6
Rosemary Way LE10 ... 75 B7
Rosemont Ho B93 ... 127 F3
Rosemoor Dr DY5 ... 81 B7
Rosemount B32 ... 84 E5
Rosemount Cl CV2 ... 114 E7
Rosemount WV6 ... 24 D5
Rosemullion Cl CV7 ... 96 B8
Rose Rd
Birmingham B17 ... 85 D6
Coleshill B46 ... 70 F8
Rose St WV14 ... 40 F2
Rose Terr B45 ... 138 D8
Rosetti Cl DY10 ... 117 C6
Roseville Ct [4] WV14 ... 51 C8
Roseville Gdns WV8 ... 10 A4
Roseville Prec [5] WV14 .. 51 C8
Rosewood Cl
Hinckley LE10 ... 75 F6
Tamworth B77 ... 21 D4
Rosewood Cres CV32 ... 157 B2
Rosewood Ct B77 ... 21 D4
Rosewood Dr
Barnt Green B45 ... 138 C7
Birmingham B23 ... 56 D2
Willenhall WV12 ... 27 B8
Rosewood Gdns WV11 ... 13 B3
Rosewood CV11 ... 73 F1
Rosewood Pk WS6 ... 4 D2
Rosewood Rd DY1 ... 51 B5
Rosewood Sch DY1 ... 50 E1
Roshven Rd B12 ... 87 A4
Roslin Cl B60 ... 137 B1
Roslin Gr B19 ... 66 C6
Roslyn Cl B66 ... 65 A6
Ross Cl
Coventry CV5 ... 112 A5
Wolverhampton WV6 ... 24 E2
Ross Dr DY6 ... 60 C7
Rosse Ct B92 ... 107 F8
Rossendale Cl B63 ... 82 D6
Rossendale Way CV10 ... 72 E2
Ross Hts B65 ... 63 B3
Rosslyn Ave CV6 ... 112 E6
Rosslyn Rd B76 ... 57 F6
Ross Rd WS3 ... 28 F6
Ross B65 ... 63 B2
Ross Way CV11 ... 79 B7
Roston Dr LE10 ... 71 A1
Rostrevor Rd B10 ... 67 F1
Rosy Cross B79 ... 21 B5
Rotary Ct [2] WV3 ... 25 B2
Rotary Ho DY1 ... 50 F1
Rothay B77 ... 35 F8
Rothbury Gn WS12 ... 2 E2
Rotherby Gr B37 ... 90 B7
Rotherfield Cl CV31 ... 162 B7
Rotherfield Rd B26 ... 89 B8
Rotherham Rd CV6 ... 95 C2
Rotherhams Oak La B94. 142 F7
Rothesay Ave CV4 ... 112 B2
Rothesay Cl CV10 ... 73 A2
Rothesay Croft B32 ... 102 B7
Rothesay Dr DY8 ... 60 C3
Rothesay Way WV12 ... 27 B6
Rothley Wlk B38 ... 123 C8
Rothwell Dr B91 ... 106 D4
Rothwell Rd CV34 ... 155 C1
Rotten Row Barns B93 .. 128 C4
Rotten Row WS14 ... 9 C7
Rotton Park Rd B16 ... 65 D2
Rotton Park St B16 ... 65 F3
Rough Coppice Wlk B35 .. 58 A2
Rough Hay Pl WS10 ... 41 C7
Rough Hay Prim Sch WS10 ... 41 C7
Rough Hay Rd WS10 ... 41 C7
Rough Hill Dr
Redditch B98 ... 158 F6
Rowley Regis B65 ... 62 F6
Rough Hills Cl WV2 ... 39 F6
Rough Hills Rd WV2 ... 39 F6
Roughknowles Rd CV4 .. 131 D6
Roughlea Ave B36 ... 68 F7
Roughley Dr B75 ... 32 C2
Roughley Farm Rd B75 ... 32 E3
Rough Rd B44 ... 45 A3
Rough The B97 ... 158 D8
Rough Wood Ctry Pk WV12 ... 27 E6
Rouncil Cl B92 ... 107 D7
Rouncil La CV8 ... 155 C8
Roundabout The B31 ... 102 D1
Round Cl B90 ... 126 A6
Round Croft WV13 ... 27 A2
Round Hill Ave DY9 ... 81 C1
Roundhill Cl B76 ... 46 E4
Round Hill DY3 ... 39 D2
Roundhills Rd B62 ... 83 F8
Roundhill Terr B62 ... 63 E1
Roundhill Way WS8 ... 7 A2
Round Hill Wharf DY11 .. 116 D5
Round House Rd
Coventry CV3 ... 134 B8
Dudley DY3 ... 50 E4
Roundlea Cl WV12 ... 27 B7
Roundlea Rd B31 ... 102 E7
Round Moor Wlk B35 ... 58 A3
Round Oak Sch The CV32 ... 157 A3
Round Rd B24 ... 57 B2
Round Saw Croft B45 ... 121 F8
Rounds Green Prim Sch B69 ... 63 E7
Rounds Green Rd B69 ... 63 F7
Rounds Hill CV8 ... 147 E2
Rounds Hill Rd WV14 ... 51 D8
Rounds Rd WV14 ... 40 D3
Round St DY2 ... 62 C6
Roundway Down WV6 ... 23 F3
Rounton Cl B74 ... 31 D4
Rousay Cl B45 ... 101 F1
Rousdon Gr B43 ... 54 D8
Rover Dr
Birmingham,Acock's Green B27 ... 88 D4
Birmingham,Castle Bromwich B36 ... 58 F1
Rover Rd CV1 ... 165 B2
Rovex Bsns Pk B11 ... 87 F5
Rowallan Rd B75 ... 32 D2
Rowan Cl
Binley Woods CV3 ... 135 D7
Bromsgrove B61 ... 136 E2
Hollywood B47 ... 125 B5
Lichfield WS14 ... 9 D8
Sutton Coldfield B76 ... 46 F2
Rowan Cres
Dudley WV14 ... 40 B1
Redditch B97 ... 153 A4
Wolverhampton WV3 ... 38 E7
Rowan Ct
Birmingham B30 ... 104 A2
Oldbury B66 ... 64 D8
Rowan Dr
[6] Warwick CV34 ... 160 F8
Birmingham B28 ... 106 A5
Essington WV11 ... 13 B3
Rowan Gr
Burntwood WS7 ... 6 F7
Coventry CV2 ... 96 E2
Rowan Rd
Cannock WS11 ... 1 C2
Nuneaton CV10 ... 72 C6
Redditch B97 ... 153 A4
Sedgley DY3 ... 39 F1
Sutton Coldfield B72 ... 46 C3
Walsall WS5 ... 42 F4
Rowan Rise DY6 ... 60 E6
Rowans The CV12 ... 77 E2
Rowantrees B45 ... 122 B5
Rowan Way
Birmingham,Chelmsley Wood B37 ... 70 C1
Birmingham,Longbridge B31 ... 122 F8
Hartshill CV10 ... 72 A8
Roway La B69 ... 52 F1
Rowborough Cl B96 ... 158 E2
Rowbrook Cl B90 ... 125 E8
Rowcroft Covert B14 ... 104 C2
Rowcroft Rd CV2 ... 115 A6
Rowdale Rd B42 ... 55 C6
Rowden Dr
Birmingham B23 ... 57 A6
Solihull B91 ... 106 E2
Rowena Gdns DY3 ... 39 C2
Rowheath Ho B30 ... 103 E5
Rowheath Rd B30 ... 103 F4
Rowington Ave B65 ... 63 D3
Rowington Cl CV6 ... 112 D5
Rowington Gn CV35 ... 144 F1
Rowington Rd B34 ... 69 E6
Rowington Terr B25 ... 88 B7
Rowland Ave B80 ... 159 E3
Rowland Gdns WS2 ... 28 C3
Rowland Hill Ave DY11 .. 116 B5
Rowland Hill Ctr [9] DY10 ... 116 E6
Rowland Hill Dr DY4 ... 52 C5
Rowlands Ave
Walsall WS2 ... 27 E3
Wolverhampton WV1 ... 26 B2
Rowlands Cl WS2 ... 27 E4
Rowlands Cres B91 ... 107 B8
Rowlands Rd B26 ... 88 E7
Rowland St WS2 ... 28 C3
Rowland Way (Road 1a) DY11 ... 116 E1
Rowley Cl WS12 ... 2 B8
Rowley Dr CV3 ... 134 B4
Rowley Gr B33 ... 69 D3
Rowley Hall Ave B65 ... 63 C4
Rowley Hall Prim Sch B65 ... 63 C4
Rowley Hill View B64 ... 82 F8
Rowley La CV3 ... 134 D3
Rowley Pl WS4 ... 29 B7
Rowley Rd
Coventry CV3,CV8 ... 134 B3
Whitnash CV31 ... 162 A2
Rowley Regis Com Hospl B65 ... 63 B2
Rowley Regis Sta B65 ... 63 E2
Rowley's Green La CV6 ... 95 E4
Rowleys Green Lane Ind Est CV6 ... 95 E4
Rowley St WS1 ... 29 A2
Rowley View
Bilston WV14 ... 41 A3
Darlaston WS10 ... 41 C4
West Bromwich B70 ... 53 B3
Rowley Village B65 ... 63 C3
Rowney Croft B28 ... 105 E4
Rowney Green La B48 ... 139 F5
Rowood Dr B91,B92 ... 107 D7
Row The CV7 ... 97 D3
Rowthorn Cl B74 ... 45 A7
Rowthorn Dr B90 ... 127 A6
Rowton Ave WV6 ... 23 E3
Rowton Dr B74 ... 44 F5
Roxall Cl DY10 ... 98 C2
Roxboro Ho B97 ... 153 D2
Roxburgh Croft CV32 ... 157 C6
Roxburgh Gr B43 ... 44 C4
Roxburgh Rd
Nuneaton CV11 ... 73 E1
Sutton Coldfield B73 ... 46 A3
Roxby Gdns WV6 ... 25 A5
Royal Brierley Glassworks* DY5 ... 61 C2
Royal Cl
Brierley Hill DY5 ... 81 C8
Rowley Regis B65 ... 63 C5
Royal Cres CV3 ... 134 C5
Royal Ct
Hinckley LE10 ... 75 D7
Sutton Coldfield B73 ... 46 B2
Royal Gr [3] B23 ... 56 B7
Royal Leamington Spa Rehabilitation Hospl CV34 ... 161 E4
Royal London Bldgs WV1 ... 163 C3
Royal Mail St B1 ... 164 B2
Royal Oak La CV7,CV12 ... 95 C7
Royal Oak Rd
Halesowen B62 ... 83 F5
Rowley Regis B65 ... 62 F5
Royal Oak Yd CV12 ... 78 B4
Royal Orthopaedic Hospl The B31 ... 103 B5
Royal Priors [18] CV32 ... 156 F1
Royal Rd B72 ... 46 C4
Royal Scot Gr WS1 ... 42 D5
Royal Star Cl B33 ... 69 C2
Royal Sta The WV1 ... 163 D2
Royal Way DY4 ... 52 A2
Royal Wolverhampton Sch The WV3 ... 39 B7
Royal Worcester Cres B60 ... 137 C1
Roy Carver Ctr The (St John Ambulance HQ) WV1 ... 163 D2
Roydon Rd B27 ... 106 C8
Roylesden Cres B73 ... 45 C2
Royston Chase B74 ... 31 A3
Royston Cl CV3 ... 115 A3
Royston Croft B12 ... 86 F6
Royston Ct [7] B13 ... 87 B2
Royston Way DY3 ... 50 C8
Rubens Cl
Coventry CV5 ... 112 C3
Dudley DY3 ... 50 D5
Rubery Ct WS10 ... 41 C7
Rubery Farm Gr B45 ... 121 F7
Rubery Field Cl B45 ... 102 B1
Rubery La B45 ... 102 A1
Rubery La S B45 ... 121 F8
Rubery St WS10 ... 41 D8
Ruckleigh Sch B91 ... 107 C4
Ruckley Ave [4] B19 ... 66 C7
Ruckley Rd B29 ... 103 B8
Rudd Gdns WV10 ... 26 B4
Rudgard Rd CV6 ... 96 A4
Rudge Ave WV1 ... 26 B3
Rudge Cl WV12 ... 27 C4
Rudge Croft B33 ... 69 A4
Rudgewick Croft [1] B6 ... 66 F6
Rudge Wlk B18 ... 66 A3
Rudyard Cl WV10 ... 11 E4
Rudyard Gr B33 ... 69 B3
Rudyngfield Dr B33 ... 68 F4
Rufford Cl
Birmingham B23 ... 56 D8
Hinckley LE10 ... 75 D3
Rufford Prim Sch DY9 ... 81 C5
Rufford Rd DY9 ... 81 C4
Rufford St DY9 ... 81 D5
Rufford B79 ... 20 E6
Rufford Way WS9 ... 29 E7
Rugby Rd
Binley Woods CV3 ... 135 D8
Bulkington CV12 ... 79 D2
Cubbington CV32 ... 157 E6
Hinckley LE10 ... 75 D5
Royal Leamington Spa CV32 ... 156 D1
Stourbridge DY8 ... 80 D7
Rugby St WV1 ... 25 B4
Rugeley Ave WV12 ... 27 D8
Rugeley Cl DY4 ... 51 E5
Rugeley Rd
Burntwood,Gorstey Ley WS7 ... 7 C7
Cannock,Hednesford WS12 ... 2 F6
Cannock,West Hill WS12 ... 2 D7
Ruislip Cl B35 ... 58 A4
Ruiton St DY3 ... 50 D4
Rumbow B63 ... 83 B4
Rumbow La B62 ... 100 D3
Rumbush La
Earlswood B90,B94 ... 125 F3
Solihull B90 ... 126 A5
Rumer Hill Bsns Est WS11 .. 4 E7
Rumer Hill Rd WS11 ... 4 F8
Runcorn Cl
Birmingham B37 ... 70 C4
Redditch B98 ... 158 F8
Runcorn Rd B12 ... 87 A5
Runcorn Wlk [10] CV2 ... 115 A7
Runneymede Gdns CV10 .. 72 F3
Runnymede Dr CV7 ... 130 C5
Runnymede Rd B11 ... 87 E3
Rupert Rd CV6 ... 113 B8
Rupert St
Birmingham B7 ... 67 A4
Wolverhampton WV3 ... 25 A2
Rushall Cl
Stourbridge DY8 ... 80 E8
Walsall WS4 ... 29 B4
Rushall Com Coll WS4 ... 29 B6
Rushall Ct B43 ... 54 E7
Rushall JMI Sch WS4 ... 15 B1
Rushall Manor Cl WS4 ... 29 B4
Rushall Manor Rd WS4 ... 29 B4
Rushall Rd WV10 ... 11 E2
Rushbrook Cl
Brownhills WS8 ... 15 D6
Solihull B92 ... 88 E2
Rushbrooke Cl B13 ... 86 F4
Rushbrooke Dr B73 ... 45 C3
Rushbrook Gr B14 ... 104 C4
Rushbrook La B94 ... 141 D3
Rushbury Cl
Bilston WV14 ... 40 B5
Solihull B90 ... 106 D4
Rushden Croft B44 ... 44 F1
Rushes Mill WS3 ... 14 E3
Rushey La B11 ... 88 A4
Rushford Ave WV5 ... 49 A6
Rushford Cl B90 ... 127 A7
Rush Gn B32 ... 84 E2
Rushlake Gn B34 ... 69 B5
Rush La
Redditch B98 ... 154 B6
Tamworth B77,B78 ... 35 D4
Rushleigh Rd B90 ... 125 E8
Rushmead Gr B45 ... 122 A7
Rushmere Rd DY4 ... 52 A8
Rushmoor Cl B74 ... 46 B6
Rushmoor Dr CV5 ... 112 F3
Rushmore St CV31 ... 162 B7
Rushmore Terr [9] CV31 ... 162 B7
Rushock Cl B98 ... 159 C7
Rushton Cl CV7 ... 130 C7
Rushton Hall Sch CV7 ... 95 D5
Rushwick Croft B34 ... 69 D6
Rushwick Ct B23 ... 56 B3
Rushwick Gr B90 ... 127 A6
Rushwood Cl WS4 ... 29 A3
Rushy Piece B32 ... 84 D3
Rusina Ct CV31 ... 161 F6
Ruskin Ave
Dudley DY3 ... 50 A5
Kidderminster DY10 ... 117 C6
Rowley Regis B65 ... 63 D2
Wolverhampton WV4 ... 39 F2
Ruskin Cl
Birmingham B6 ... 66 F7
Coventry CV6 ... 112 D6
Nuneaton CV10 ... 72 A5
Ruskin Ct [5] B68 ... 84 B8
Ruskin Glass Ctr* DY8 ... 80 F7
Ruskin Gr B27 ... 88 B2
Ruskin Hall Gr B6 ... 66 F7
Ruskin Rd WV10 ... 12 A1
Ruskin St B71 ... 53 C5
Russel Croft B60 ... 151 A7
Russell Bank Rd B74 ... 31 E4
Russell Cl
Oldbury B69 ... 52 D2
Tamworth B77 ... 35 E6
Wednesbury DY4 ... 41 C1
Wolverhampton WV11 ... 12 F1
Russell Ct
[7] Royal Leamington Spa CV31 ... 162 A7
Sutton Coldfield B74 ... 31 D3
Wolverhampton WV3 ... 163 A2
Russell Ho
Tamworth B77 ... 21 F2
Wednesbury WS10 ... 41 F2
Russell Rd
Bilston WV14 ... 40 F7
Birmingham,Hall Green B28 87 E1
Birmingham,Moseley B13 .. 86 D3
Kidderminster DY10 ... 116 F4
Russell St N [2] CV1 ... 165 C4
Russells Hall Hospl DY5 .. 61 E7
Russells Hall Prim Sch DY1 ... 50 E1
Russell's Hall Rd DY1 ... 50 F1
Russell St
Coventry CV1 ... 165 C4
Dudley DY1 ... 51 B1
Russells The B13 ... 86 D3
Russell St
Royal Leamington Spa CV32 ... 156 F1
Wednesbury WS10 ... 41 F2
Willenhall WV13 ... 27 B2
Wolverhampton WV3 ... 163 A2
Russell Terr CV31 ... 162 A7
Russet Gr CV4 ... 132 D3
Russett Cl
Burntwood WS7 ... 7 A6
Walsall WS5 ... 43 D8
Russett Way DY5 ... 61 B7
Russet Way B31 ... 102 E6
Russet Wlk WV8 ... 10 E1
Ruston St B16 ... 66 B1
Ruthall Cl B29 ... 103 C7
Ruth Chamberlain Ct [3] DY11 ... 116 D6
Ruth Cl DY4 ... 41 C2
Rutherford Glen CV11 ... 73 F1
Rutherford Rd
Birmingham B23 ... 56 E7
Bromsgrove B60 ... 151 B7
Walsall WS2 ... 28 A5
Rutherglen Ave CV3 ... 134 A6

Rutland Ave
Hinckley LE10 75 C7
Nuneaton CV10 72 F4
Wolverhampton WV4 38 D4
Rutland B17 85 A6
Rutland Cres
Aldridge WS9 16 B1
Bilston WV14 40 E7
Rutland Croft 3 CV3 134 F8
Rutland Ct 2 B29 103 C7
Rutland Dr
Birmingham B26 88 E7
Bromsgrove B60 151 A8
Tamworth B78 21 A1
Rutland Pas 8 DY1 51 C1
Rutland Pl DY8 80 D8
Rutland Rd
Cannock WS12 2 E1
Smethwick B66 65 A1
Wednesbury WS10 42 D4
West Bromwich B71 53 C7
Rutland St WS3 28 E5
Rutland Terr 5 B18 66 A5
Rutley Gr B32 84 F4
Rutters Mdw B32 84 B4
Rutter St WS1 42 E8
Ryan Ave WV11 27 A7
Ryan Pl DY2 62 C6
Rycroft Gr B33 69 C2
Rydal Ave CV11 74 A6
Rydal Cl
Allesley CV5 112 B8
Cannock WS12 2 A8
Hinckley LE10 74 F7
Sutton Coldfield B74 30 F2
Wolverhampton WV11 26 C7
Rydal Dr WV6 23 F4
Rydal Ho 6 B69 63 D5
Rydal B77 36 A7
Rydal Way B28 105 F7
Rydding La B71 53 B8
Rydding Sq B71 53 B8
Ryde Ave CV10 73 D7
Ryde Gr B27 88 A1
Ryde Park Rd B45 122 C7
Ryders Green Prim Sch B70 53 A4
Ryders Green Rd B70 52 F4
Ryders Hayes Com Sch WS3 15 A5
Ryders Hayes La WS3 15 B4
Ryders Hill Cres CV10 72 C7
Ryder St
Birmingham B4 164 C3
Stourbridge DY8 60 D2
West Bromwich B70 52 F5
Ryebank Cl B30 103 C5
Ryeclose Croft B37 70 D3
Rye Croft 7 B27 88 C5
Ryecroft Ave WV4 39 B5
Ryecroft Cl DY3 50 C8
Ryecroft Cotts WV4 39 B5
Ryecroft Dr 3 WS7 7 A8
Rye Croft B47 125 A5
Ryecroft Pk 1 WS2 28 E3
Ryecroft Pl WS3 28 F6
Ryecroft Sh Ctr WS7 7 A8
Ryecroft St 2 WS2 28 E3
Rye Croft DY9 81 E2
Ryefield Cl
Solihull B91 106 E5
West Hagley DY9 99 A4
Ryefield La B76 48 B2
Ryefields Rd B60 150 C3
Ryefield WV8 10 E1
Ryegrass La B97 158 C6
Rye Grass Wlk B35 58 B3
Rye Gr B11 87 F4
Rye Hill CV5 112 A6
Rye Hill Office Pk CV5 112 A7
Ryemarket Sh Ctr 7 DY8 81 A5
Rye Piece Ringway CV12 78 C3
Ryhope Cl CV12 77 C1
Ryhope Wlk WV9 11 A3
Ryknild Cl B74 31 F6
Ryknild Dr B74 45 A7
Ryknild St WS14 9 E6
Ryland Cl
3 Tipton DY4 52 B5
Halesowen B63 82 E2
Royal Leamington Spa CV31 162 C6
Ryland Ho B19 66 D5
Ryland Rd
Birmingham,Edgbaston B15 86 C8
Birmingham,Gravelly Hill B24 56 F1
Rylands Dr WV4 39 A4
Ryland St B16 66 B1
Rylcroft 7 WV4 39 F4
Ryle St WS3 14 D1
Ryley St CV1 165 A3
Rylston Ave CV6 95 A1
Rylstone Way 4 CV34 155 E1
Rymond Rd B34 68 E6
Ryton Cl
Coventry CV4 132 B8
Redditch B98 154 D1
Sutton Coldfield B73 46 B5
Wolverhampton WV10 26 A5
Ryton Gr B34 69 D7
Ryton Organic Gdns* CV8 135 E1
Ryton B77 35 F8

S

Sabell Rd B67 64 F6
Sabrina Rd WV6 23 E1
Sackville Ho 1 CV1 165 D4
Sacred Heart Prim Sch DY4 52 A4
Sacred Heart RC Prim Sch CV2 114 A3
Sacred Heart Sch B20 55 D1
Saddington Rd CV3 134 E8
Saddlers Cl
Halesowen B63 82 B5
Hinckley LE10 75 F6
Lichfield WS14 9 E8
Saddlers Court Ind Est WS2 28 A7
Saddlers Ctr WS1 28 E1
Saddlers Mews B91 107 C1
Saddlestones The WV6 23 D4
Saddleworth Rd WS3 14 A4
Sadler Cres B11 87 D4
Sadler Ctr WS8 16 A8
Sadler Gdns CV12 78 C2
Sadler Ho B19 66 C6
Sadler Rd
Brownhills WS8 16 A8
Coventry CV6 113 A8
Sutton Coldfield B75 46 F7
Sadlers Ct WS2 42 B7
Sadlers Mill WS8 16 A7
Sadlerswell La B94 143 B6
Sadlers Wlk B16 66 A1
Saffron Gdns WV4 39 A4
Saffron Ho 3 B38 123 E8
Saffron B77 22 B4
Sagebury Dr B60 150 C1
Sage Croft B31 102 F5
St Agatha's Rd
Birmingham B8 68 B5
Coventry CV2 114 A3
St Agnes Cl
Birmingham B13 87 B2
Studley B80 159 C4
St Agnes Rd B13 87 B1
St Agnes Way CV11 73 F4
St Aidan's Ct WV4 39 A5
St Aidan's Rd WS11 1 E5
St Aidans Wlk 3 B10 87 C8
St Alban's Ave DY11 116 A7
St Alban's CE Prim Sch WV11 27 B8
St Alban's CE Sch B12 86 F7
St Albans Cl
Royal Leamington Spa CV32 156 C2
Smethwick B67 64 E6
Wednesfield WV11 27 A8
Wolverhampton WV11 13 A1
St Albans Ct WV13 26 E1
St Albans Ho B32 84 F5
St Alban's RC Prim Sch B14 104 F4
St Albans Rd
Birmingham B13 87 A4
Smethwick B67 64 E6
St Alphege CE Inf Sch B91 107 C3
St Alphege CE Jun Sch B91 107 C2
St Alphege Cl B91 107 C3
St Ambrose Barlow RC Prim Sch B28 106 A6
St Ambrose Cl B62,B65 83 C8
St Ambrose RC Prim Sch DY10 116 F6
St Andrews Ave WS3 15 B4
St Andrew's CE Fst Sch B45 138 D8
St Andrew's CE Inf Sch CV5 111 C5
St Andrews CE Prim Sch WV6 24 F4
St Andrews Cl B32 85 A3
St Andrew's Cl DY3 50 A3
St Andrews Cl
Stourbridge DY8 80 F2
Wolverhampton WV6 25 A4
St Andrews Ct 2 B10 67 B1
St Andrews Dr
Nuneaton CV11 74 B1
Oldbury B69 63 B7
Perton WV6 23 D5
St Andrew's Gd (Birmingham City FC) B9 67 C1
St Andrews Gn DY10 116 E4
St Andrews Ho WV6 25 B4
St Andrews Ind Est B9 67 C2
St Andrew's Jun & Inf Sch B9 67 B2
St Andrew's RC Prim Sch B92 89 A2
St Andrew's Rd
Birmingham B9 67 B2
Coventry CV5 132 F8
Royal Leamington Spa CV32 157 B5
St Andrews Rd B75 46 D7
St Andrew's St
Birmingham B9 67 B2
Dudley DY2 62 C5
St Andrews B77 22 B4
St Andrews Way B61 150 D8
St Annes Cl B20 54 F4
St Anne's Cl WS7 6 E4
St Anne's Ct B13 86 E4
St Annes Ct B44 56 A7
St Anne's Ct WV13 27 B1
St Annes Gr B93 128 A6
St Annes Ind Est WV13 27 B3
St Anne's RC Prim Sch
Birmingham B37 70 A2
Birmingham,Deritend B12 87 A8
Coventry CV3 134 C6
Nuneaton CV10 72 D7
Sutton Coldfield B74 44 E8
St Anne's Rd B64 62 C1
St Annes Rd WS13 3 B3
St Anne's Rd
Willenhall WV13 27 B3
Wolverhampton WV10 11 B1
St Annes Way B44 56 A7
St Ann's Cl CV31 162 C7
St Ann's Rd CV2 114 A3
St Anthonys Dr WS3 15 B5
St Anthony's RC Prim Sch
Royal Leamington Spa CV31 162 C7
Wolverhampton WV10 11 D3
St Antony's RC Prim Sch B37 70 A5
St Asaphs Ave B80 159 D4
St Athan Croft B35 58 B3
St Audries Ct B91 106 F2
St Augustine's RC High Sch B97 158 D5
St Augustine's RC Prim Sch
Birmingham B21 54 D2
Coventry CV6 113 A7
Kenilworth CV8 147 E7
Solihull B91 107 A2
St Augustine's Rd B16 65 D1
St Augustine's Wlk CV6 113 A7
St Augustus Cl B70 53 F2
St Austell Cl
Nuneaton CV11 74 A5
Tamworth B79 21 A6
St Austell Rd
Coventry CV2 114 E3
Walsall WS5 43 E7
St Barnabas CE Prim Sch B24 57 A3
St Bartholemews Cl CV3 115 A2
St Bartholomew's CE Prim Sch
Coventry CV3 134 E7
Wolverhampton WV4 38 E3
St Bartholomew Terr 3 WS10 41 F3
St Bede's RC Mid Sch B98 153 F3
St Benedict Bishop CE Prim Sch WV5 49 B7
St Benedict's Cl B70 53 F2
St Benedict's Inf Sch B10 87 F7
St Benedicts Rd B10 87 F8
St Benedict's Rd WS7 7 B6
St Benedicts Rd WV5 49 A6
St Bernadette's RC Prim Sch
Birmingham B25 88 B8
Brownhills WS8 15 F8
St Bernard's RC Prim Sch B13 87 C1
St Bernard's Rd B92 106 E7
St Bernards Rd B72 46 C2
St Bernard's Wlk CV3 134 D6
St Blaise Ave B46 59 C2
St Blaise Rd B75 32 D3
St Brades Cl B69 63 C7
St Bride's Cl CV31 162 C6
St Brides Cl DY3 50 C8
St Brigid's RC Prim Sch B31 102 F3
St Buryan Cl CV11 74 A5
Saintbury Dr B91 127 C8
St Caroline Cl B70 53 F3
St Catharines Cl WS1 43 A7
St Catherine of Siena RC Prim Sch B1 66 D1
St Catherines Cl B60 138 A5
St Catherine's Cl
Coventry CV3 134 B8
Hinckley LE10 75 F7
St Catherines Cl
Oldbury DY2 52 A1
Sutton Coldfield B75 46 F7
St Catherine's Cres
Whitnash CV34 161 F3
Wolverhampton WV4 38 F4
St Catherine's Ct B91 107 B3
St Catherine's Lodge 7 CV6 113 A4
St Catherine's Rd B60 138 A5
St Catherines Rd WS13 3 B3
St Cecilia Cl DY10 116 E2
St Cecilia's WV11 26 C5
St Chad Ct B77 21 F2
St Chad's Cath* B4 164 B4
St Chad's CE Prim Sch WS13 9 C8
St Chad's Circus Queensway B3 164 B3
St Chad's Cl
Cannock WS11 2 A4
Dudley DY3 50 B3
St Chads Cl WS13 3 B1
St Chads Ct 3 WS13 9 B8
St Chads Ind Est B19 66 E5
St Chads Mews B94 144 D3
St Chads Queensway B4 164 C4
St Chad's RC Prim Sch B19 66 D5
St Chads RC Prim Sch DY3 50 D7
St Chad's Rd
Bilston WV14 40 F7
Birmingham B45 121 F7
Lichfield WS13 3 C1
St Chads Rd B80 159 C4
St Chad's Rd
Sutton Coldfield B75 46 F5
Wolverhampton WV10 25 F8
St Christian's Croft CV3 133 E8
St Christian's Rd CV3 133 E8
St Christopher Cl B70 53 E2
St Christopher Dr WS10 42 E3
St Christopher Prim Sch CV5 112 D4
St Christophers B20 54 F4
St Christopher's Cl CV34 160 D8
St Christopher's Dr B77 21 C1
St Christophers RC Prim Sch WV8 10 A3
St Clare's RC Prim Sch B20 55 B1
St Clement's Ave WS3 28 D7
St Clement's CE Prim Sch B7 67 C7
St Clements Ct CV2 114 D8
St Clements Ho 3 B71 53 D4
St Clement's La B71 53 D4
St Clements Rd B7 67 C6
St Columba's Cl CV1 165 B4
St Columbas Dr B45 122 D7
St Columba's RC Prim Sch B45 122 D7
St Cuthbert's Cl B70 53 F2
St Cuthberts RC Prim Sch B8 68 C4
St David Dr WS10 42 E3
St David's Cl CV31 162 C7
St Davids Cl WS3 15 B5
St David's Cl B70 53 F2
St Davids Dr B32 84 B5
St Davids Gr B20 54 F4
St Davids Orch CV3 134 F7
St Davids Pl WS3 14 D2
St Davids Way CV10 78 A6
St Denis Rd B29 103 B7
St Dennis Ho 5 B15 65 D1
St Dominic's Rd B24 56 E1
St Dunstan's RC Prim Sch B14 104 F8
St Edburghs Rd B25 68 E1
St Editha's Cl B79 21 B5
St Editha's Ct B79 21 B7
St Edith's Gn 3 CV34 161 B8
St Edith's Ho 2 CV34 161 B8
St Edmund Campion RC Lower Sch B24 57 C6
St Edmund Campion RC Sch B23 57 B5
St Edmund's Cl
West Bromwich B70 53 F2
Wolverhampton WV6 24 F3
St Edmund's RC Prim Sch B18 66 A4
St Edmunds RC Sch WV3 24 E3
St Edward's RC Prim Sch B29 86 B1
St Edward's Rd B29 85 F2
Sainte Foy Ave WS13 9 A6
SS John & Monica RC Prim Sch B13 86 E4
St Eleanor Cl B70 53 F3
St Elizabeth's RC Prim Sch
Coventry CV6 113 E7
Tamworth B79 20 F8
St Elizabeth's Rd CV6 113 E7
St Foy Ave WS13 8 F5
St Francis Ave B91 106 E6
St Francis CE Prim Sch B30 103 D6
St Francis Cl
Hinckley LE10 71 C3
Walsall WS3 15 B5
St Francis Factory Est B70 53 D2
St Francis of Assisi Tech Coll WS9 30 C5
St Francis RC Prim Sch
Bedworth CV12 78 C3
Birmingham B19 66 B6
Walsall WS4 15 C1
St Francis Xavier RC Sch B69 64 A8
St Fremund Way CV31 162 C5
St Gabriel's RC Prim Sch B77 21 E1
St George Cl WS10 42 E3
St George Dr B66 65 A7
St George & St Teresa RC Prim Sch B93 128 A4
St Georges Ave B23 57 A5
St George's Ave LE10 71 C1
St George's CE Fst Sch
Kidderminster DY10 116 F7
Redditch B98 153 F3
St George's CE Prim Sch
Birmingham B19 164 B5
Birmingham,Ladywood B16 65 F1
St Georges Cl B15 86 A7
St George's Cl
Darlaston WS10 41 D7
Sutton Coldfield B75 46 F6
St Georges Ct
10 Kidderminster DY10 116 E6
5 Walsall WS1 28 F2
St George's Ct
Birmingham B30 103 E7
Darlaston WS10 41 D7
St Georges Ct B74 31 E5
St George's Gdns 3 B98 153 F4
St George's Par WV1 163 C2
St George's Pl
4 Walsall WS1 28 F2
Kidderminster DY10 116 E7
St Georges Pl B70 53 C4
St George's Rd CV1 113 F2
St Georges Rd
Dudley DY2 62 E6
Redditch B98 153 F4
St George's Rd
Royal Leamington Spa CV31 161 F6
Solihull B90 126 D8
Stourbridge DY8 80 D2
St George's Sta WV1 163 C2
St George's St
Birmingham B19 164 B4
Darlaston WS10 41 D7
St George's Terr DY10 116 F6
St Georges Way CV10 78 B8
St George's Way B77 21 F4
St Gerards Ct B91 106 E2
St Gerards RC Prim Sch B35 58 B4
St Gerards Rd B91 106 E2
St Giles Ave B65 63 B4
St Giles' CE Prim Sch WV13 27 B2
St Giles Cl B65 63 C4
St Giles Cres WV1 26 A2
St Giles Ct B65 63 D3
St Gile's Ct WV13 27 B1
St Giles Jun Sch CV7 95 F8
St Giles Rd
Birmingham B33 69 D2
Burntwood WS7 7 B6
Coventry CV7 95 D6
Willenhall WV13 27 B1
Wolverhampton WV1 26 A2
St Giles Row DY8 81 A6
St Giles St DY2 62 C5
St Godwald's Cres B60 151 B8
St Godwald's Rd B60 151 C7
St Govan's Cl 2 CV31 162 C6
St Gregory's RC Prim Sch
Coventry CV2 114 E3
Smethwick B67 64 F2
St Helens Ave DY4 52 C5
St Helens Pas B1 66 C3
St Helens Rd WS13 3 B3
St Helen's Rd
Solihull B91 107 A6
Whitnash CV31 162 A5
St Helen's Way CV5 112 B8
St Heliers Rd B31 102 F4
St Hellier Ho 4 B15 65 D1
St Hubert's RC Prim Sch B68 84 C8
St Ives Cl B79 21 B6
St Ives Rd
Coventry CV2 114 E3
Walsall WS5 43 D7
St Ives Way CV11 73 F5
St James Ave B65 63 B4
St James CE Jun Sch
Bulkington CV12 79 C2
Solihull B90 106 B2
St James CE Prim Sch
Birmingham B21 54 D1
Oldbury B69 63 D5
Stourbridge DY8 80 D7
St James Cl
Walsall WS3 15 B5
West Bromwich B70 53 F2
St James Ct
Bromsgrove B60 137 A3
Coventry CV3 134 E6
St James Gdns
Brownhills WS8 15 F7
Bulkington CV12 79 C2
St James' La CV3 134 D6
St James Meadow Rd CV32 156 C2
St James Pl B15 86 B8
St James' Pl B7 67 A3
St James Pl B90 106 B2
St James Prim Sch WS8 15 F8
St James' RC Jun & Inf Sch B45 122 A7
St James Rd B15 86 B8
St James' Rd B21 65 D8
St James Rd
Cannock WS11 1 C1
Norton Canes WS11 6 B5
Oldbury B69 63 E8
Sutton Coldfield B75 32 C2
St James's Cl LE10 75 D5
St James's Rd DY1 51 B2
St James' St DY3 50 D3
St James's Terr DY1 51 A2
St James St
Wednesbury WS10 41 E2
Wolverhampton WV1 163 D3
St James Wlk WS8 15 F7
St John Bosco RC Jun & Inf Sch B71 53 B7
St John Cl B75 32 D4
St John Fisher RC Prim Sch
Birmingham B31 123 B7
Coventry CV2 114 D5
St John's Arc WV1 163 B2
St John's Ave
Kenilworth CV8 148 A3
Kidderminster DY11 116 B6
St Johns Ave B65 63 B4
St John's CE Foundation Mid Sch B61 136 F1

St John's CE Fst Sch DY11 116 B6
St John's CE Mid Sch DY11 116 B6
St John's CE Prim Sch
Birmingham B11 87 C4
Brownhills WS9 16 A3
Coventry CV5 112 C4
Essington WV11 13 A4
Wednesbury WS10 41 F2
St John's Cl
6 Kidderminster DY11 116 C6
Brownhills WS9 15 F3
Cannock WS11 4 D8
St Johns Cl B93 128 B6
St John's Cl
Lichfield WS13 9 B6
West Bromwich B70 53 F3
St Johns Ct
20 Brierley Hill DY5 61 D2
2 Birmingham,Harborne B17 85 B6
St John's Ct 4 CV34 160 F7
St Johns Ct
5 Wednesbury WS10 41 F2
Birmingham,Turves Green B31 103 B1
St John's Ct
Cannock WS12 2 E1
Walsall WS3 14 B1
St John's Dr WS14 17 F5
St John's Flats CV8 148 A3
St Johns Gr B37 69 F3
St John's Hill WS14 17 F5
St Johns LE10 71 E1
St Johns Ho 2 B74 31 E3
St John's House Mus★ CV34 160 F7
St John's Ladywood CE Prim Sch B16 66 A2
St John's Prim Sch CV8 147 F2
St Johns Rd B11 87 C5
St John's Rd B17 85 D6
St Johns Rd WS8 16 A5
St John's Rd
Cannock WS11 4 E7
Darlaston WS10 41 C5
Dudley DY2 51 E1
St Johns Rd WV11 13 A3
St John's Rd B63 82 E4
St Johns Rd B68 64 C5
St Johns Rd
Royal Leamington Spa CV31 162 A6
Stourbridge DY8 81 A5
Tipton DY4 51 F8
St Johns Rd
Walsall,Pleck WS2 42 B8
Walsall WS3 15 B5
St Johns Ret Pk WV2 163 B1
St Johns Sch WS13 9 B7
St John's Sq WV2 163 B2
St John's St
5 Kidderminster DY11 116 C6
Coventry CV1 165 C2
Dudley DY2 62 C5
Kenilworth CV8 148 A3
Tamworth B79 21 B5
Wolverhampton WV1 163 B2
St John St B61 136 F2
St John's Terr 13 CV31 162 A6
St John St WS13 9 B7
St Johns CV34 160 F7
St Johns Way B93 128 C6
St Johns Wlk B42 55 D4
St Johns Wood
Birmingham B45 122 B5
Shenstone WS14 18 A5
St John the Baptist RC Prim Sch B36 70 B7
St John the Divine CE Prim Sch CV3 134 C5
St John Vianney RC Prim Sch CV5 112 B3
St John Wall RC Sch B21 54 C2
St Joseph & St Theresa RC Prim Sch WS7 6 E6
St Josephs Ave B31 103 B5
St Josephs Cl WS3 15 A4
St Joseph's Convent Sch WV6 24 E6
St Josephs Ct WV4 38 D6
St Joseph's RC Jun Sch CV11 73 C3
St Josephs RC Prim Sch B30 103 F5
St Joseph's RC Prim Sch
Birmingham B7 67 B6
Cannock WS12 2 C4
Darlaston WS10 41 D7
Dudley DY2 51 E1
Lichfield WS14 9 C7
Sutton Coldfield B75 46 C7
Whitnash CV31 162 A3
St Josephs Rd B8 68 C5
St Joseph St 7 DY2 51 D1
St Judes Ave B80 159 D4
St Jude's CE Prim Sch WV3 24 F3
St Judes Cl
4 Sutton Coldfield B75 46 F6
Birmingham B14 104 F2
St Jude's Cres CV3 134 D7
St Jude's Ct 4 WV6 24 F3
St Judes Ct B14 104 F7
St Jude's Pas B5 164 B1
St Judes RC Prim Sch B14 104 F2
St Jude's Rd WV6 24 F3
St Jude's Rd W WV6 24 F3
St Katherine's Rd B68 64 B2
St Kenelms Ave B63 82 E1
St Kenelm's Cl B70 53 F2
St Kenelm's Rd B62 100 E5
St Kilda's Rd B8 67 E5
St Laurence Ave CV34 160 D5
St Laurence CE Inf Sch B31 103 B4
St Laurence CE Jun Sch B31 103 B4
St Laurence Cl B48 139 B6
St Laurence Rd B31 103 B5
St Lawrence Cl
1 Birmingham B5 86 D7
Knowle B93 128 B5
St Lawrence Dr WS11 2 B2
St Lawrence Ho 6 B15 65 D1
St Lawrence Mews B31 103 A3
St Lawrence's Rd CV6 95 F1
St Lawrence Way WS10 41 D6
St Leonards Cl B37 90 A7
St Leonards View B78 36 F8
St Leonard's Wlk CV8 135 A1
St Loye's Cl B62 83 D8
St Luke's CE Fst Sch B97 153 D1
St Luke's CE Prim Sch WV2 39 B7
St Luke's Cl WS11 4 D8
St Lukes Cl B65 63 B4
St Luke's Cotts B97 153 D1
St Lukes Prim Sch (Inf Site) WV2 39 C7
St Luke's Rd
Birmingham B5 86 E7
Burntwood WS7 7 C6
Coventry CV6 95 D3
Wednesbury WS10 42 A3
St Lukes St B64 62 D1
St Luke's Terr DY1 62 A8
St Lukes Way CV10 72 C4
St Margaret Mary RC Jun & Inf Sch B23 56 C6
St Margaret Rd CV1 113 F2
St Margarets Ave B8 68 B6
St Margaret's CE Jun Sch CV31 162 B3
St Margaret's CE Prim Sch
Birmingham B43 43 E4
Solihull B92 88 F2
St Margaret's Ct 3 B92 88 E1
St Margarets Dr B63 82 F2
St Margaret's Ho CV31 162 B4
St Margaret's Rd
2 Solihull B92 88 E1
Birmingham B43 43 F2
St Margarets Rd
Birmingham B8 68 B6
Lichfield WS13 3 B3
St Margaret's Rd B79 21 B7
St Margarets Rd WS3 15 A4
St Margaret's Rd CV31 162 B5
St Margaret's B74 31 C3
St Mark's Annexe (Coventry & Warwickshire Hospl) CV1 165 C4
St Mark's CE Prim Sch DY5 61 C7
St Marks Cl
Great Wyrley WS6 4 F4
Nuneaton CV10 72 C4
St Marks Cres B1 66 B3
St Mark's Ct DY5 61 D7
St Mark's Mews CV32 156 E1
St Mark's RC Prim Sch B42 54 F6
St Marks Rd WS8 16 A5
St Mark's Rd
Burntwood WS7 7 C6
Dudley DY2 51 F1
Royal Leamington Spa CV32 156 D1
Smethwick B67 64 D3
Stourbridge DY9 81 D5
Tipton DY4 52 A8
St Marks Rd WS3 15 A4
St Mark's Rd WV3 25 B1
St Marks St B1 66 B3
St Mark's St WV3 163 A2
St Martin De Porres RC Prim Sch B13 87 A3
St Martins Ave B80 159 D4
St Martin's CE Prim Sch
Bilston WV14 41 A2
Tipton DY4 52 B5
St Martin's Cl
West Bromwich B70 53 F2
Wolverhampton WV2 39 E6
St Martin's Dr DY4 52 A5
St Martin's Cl LE10 75 E6
St Martins Ind Est B69 64 A6
St Martin's Mkt B5 164 C1
St Martin's Queensway B2,B4, B5 164 C2
St Martin's Rd CV3 133 C2
St Martins Rd B75 46 F5
St Martin's Sch B91 107 D3
St Martin's St 6 B15 66 B1
St Martin's Terr WV14 40 E4
St Mary Magdalene CE Jun & Inf Sch B71 53 D6
St Mary of the Angels RC Prim Sch WS9 30 B5
St Mary & St Benedict RC Prim Sch CV1 113 E4
St Mary & St John RC Jun & Inf Sch WV2 163 C1
St Mary & St Jun & Inf Sch B23 56 E3
St Mary & St Margaret's CE Prim Sch B36 69 B8
St Mary's Ave LE9 71 F5
St Mary's CE Fst Sch DY10 116 E8
St Mary's CE Jun & Inf Sch B20 55 B1
St Mary's CE Prim Sch
Birmingham B29 85 D1
Hinckley LE10 75 D8
Kingswinford DY6 60 D7
St Marys Cl B27 88 B3
St Mary's Cl
Sedgley DY3 50 F8
Sutton Coldfield B24 57 D4
Warwick CV34 160 D8
St Mary's Cres CV31 162 B7
St Marys Ct 12 DY5 61 D2
St Mary's Ct
3 Willenhall WV13 27 A2
Kenilworth CV8 147 F2
Nuneaton CV11 73 B5
St Mary's Hall WV1 163 C2
St Mary's Ho 4 B71 53 D4
St Mary's Immaculate RC Prim Sch CV34 160 E8
St Mary's La DY8 81 B3
St Marys Park Cvn Pk B47 124 E2
St Mary's RC Prim Sch
Birmingham B17 85 C5
Brierley Hill DY5 61 E2
Cannock WS11 4 E8
Studley B80 159 E4
Wednesbury WS10 41 F4
Wolverhampton WV10 26 A7
St Marys Rd B17 85 C5
St Mary's Rd
Hinckley LE10 75 D8
Lichfield WS13 3 B3
Nuneaton CV11 73 B5
Royal Leamington Spa CV31 162 B7
Smethwick B67 64 F1
Wednesbury WS10 41 F3
St Marys Ringway DY10 116 E6
St Mary's Row
Birmingham,Moseley B13 86 F3
Birmingham,New Town Row B4 164 C3
St Mary's St WV1 163 C3
St Mary St CV1 165 C2
St Mary's Terr CV31 162 B7
St Mary's The Mount RC Prim Sch WS1 42 F8
St Marys View B23 56 D8
St Mary's Way
Aldridge WS9 30 B5
Tamworth B77 21 E4
St Matthew's Ave WS7 7 F7
St Matthews CE Prim Sch B7 67 A4
St Matthew's CE Prim Sch B66 65 C5
St Matthews Cl CV10 72 C4
St Matthew's Cl WS1 28 F1
St Matthews Cl WS3 15 B5
St Matthew's Rd WS7 7 F7
St Matthews Rd
Oldbury B68 64 A2
Smethwick B66 65 C5
St Matthew St WV1 25 F1
St Mawes Rd WV6 24 A3
St Mawgen Cl B35 58 C4
St Michael Ho 3 B15 65 D1
St Michael Rd WS13 9 C8
St Michael's CE High Sch B65 63 C5
St Michaels CE Inf & Jun Sch B21 66 A7
St Michael's CE Jun & Inf Sch WV6 24 E5
St Michael's CE Prim Sch
Bedworth CV12 78 D3
Birmingham B32 102 C8
Lichfield WS14 9 C7
Lichfield WS14 9 C8
St Michaels CE Prim Sch
Walsall WS3 14 F2
Walsall WS3 15 A3
St Michael's Cl WS3 15 A2
St Michaels Cl CV9 36 C1
St Michael's Cres B69 64 A4
St Michael's Ct 5 B66 65 A5
St Michaels Ct B18 66 B4
St Michael's Ct B68 64 A4
St Michaels Ct B70 53 C3
St Michael's Ct WV6 24 E5
St Michaels Dr WS12 2 F5
St Michael's Gr DY2 52 A1
St Michael's Hill B18 66 A7
St Michael's Hospl
Lichfield WS13 9 D8
Warwick CV34 160 D8
St Michael's Mews B69 52 A2
St Michael's RC Prim Sch WV3 38 D7
St Michael's Rd
Birmingham B18 66 A7
Coventry CV2 114 A3
St Michaels Rd DY3 49 F5
St Michael's Rd
Sutton Coldfield B73 56 F8
Warwick CV34 160 D8
St Michael St
Walsall WS1 42 E8
West Bromwich B70 53 C3
St Michael's Way CV10 72 C4
St Michaels Way DY4 52 A3
St Nicholas Ave CV8 147 F3
St Nicholas CE Com Prim Sch CV8 147 F5
St Nicholas Church St CV34 160 F6
St Nicholas Cl
Coventry CV1 113 C5
Walsall WS3 15 A4
St Nicholas Ct
3 Coventry,Edgwick CV6 113 F7
Coventry,Radford CV6 113 B6
St Nicholas Pk CV34 160 F6
St Nicholas RC Prim Sch B73 45 F2
St Nicholas Rd CV31 162 F5
St Nicholas St CV1 165 B4
St Nicholas Terr CV31 162 E4
St Nicholas Wlk B76 59 B6
St Nicolas CE Prim Sch CV11 73 F6
St Nicolas Gdns B38 103 F2
St Nicolas Park Dr CV11 73 F7
St Nicolas Rd CV11 73 D5
St Osburg's RC Prim Sch CV1 165 A3
St Osburg's Rd CV2 114 A3
St Oswalds Cl DY10 116 F8
St Oswald's Ct B10 87 E8
St Oswalds Rd B10 87 E8
St Patrick's CE Jun & Inf Sch B94 126 C2
St Patricks Cl B14 104 E5
St Patrick's Ct DY11 116 B1
St Patricks RC Prim Sch B18 65 F4
St Patrick's RC Prim Sch
Birmingham B37 70 C2
Coventry CV2 96 D1
St Patricks RC Prim Sch CV31 161 F6
St Patrick's RC Prim Sch
Walsall WS2 28 E3
Wolverhampton WV11 26 C5
St Patrick's Rd CV1 165 B2
St Paul's Ave
Birmingham B12 87 A5
Kidderminster DY11 116 A6
St Paul's CE Prim Sch
Nuneaton CV10 72 C3
Royal Leamington Spa CV32 157 B1
Tipton DY4 51 F6
St Pauls CE Prim Sch WV9 11 A2
St Paul's Cl
5 Walsall WS1 28 E2
Cannock WS11 2 B1
Warwick CV34 160 D6
St Pauls Com Foundation Sch B12 87 A5
St Paul's Cres 5 B46 70 F7
St Pauls Cres WS3 15 B5
St Paul's Cres B70 52 E7
St Pauls Ct B62 63 D1
St Paul's Ct B77 35 C4
St Pauls Ct B46 59 B3
St Pauls Dr B62 63 D1
St Paul's Dr DY4 52 B4
St Pauls Gdns LE10 71 E1
St Paul's RC Prim Sch B38 104 A1
St Paul's Rd
Birmingham B12 87 A5
Burntwood WS7 7 C6
Cannock WS12 2 F3
Coventry CV6 113 E6
Dudley DY2 62 D5
Nuneaton CV10 72 D3
Smethwick B66 64 E7
Wednesbury WS10 42 C5
St Paul's Sch for Girls B16 65 E1
St Paul's Sq
4 Royal Leamington Spa CV32 157 A1
Birmingham B3 164 A4
St Paul's Sta B19 164 B4
St Paul's St WS1 28 E2
St Pauls Terr B3 164 A4
St Paul's Terr CV34 160 D6
St Peter & St Paul RC Prim Sch
Birmingham B24 57 C3
Lichfield WS13 3 B1
St Peter's CE Prim Sch
Birmingham B17 85 B5
Cannock WS12 2 D4
Stonnall WS9 16 E4
St Peters Cl
Birmingham B28 105 D6
Bromsgrove B61 136 E1
St Peter's Cl
Redditch B97 158 E5
Stonnall WS9 16 E4
St Peters Cl B72 46 B3
St Peter's Cl
Tamworth B77 21 D1
Water Orton B46 59 B2
West Bromwich DY4 52 D4
St Peter's Collegiate CE Sch WV3 24 E3
St Peter's Croft B73 46 B3
St Peters Ct 2 LE10 71 E1
St Peter's Ct CV1 165 D4
St Peters Ct
Lichfield WS13 3 B2
Walsall WS3 14 B1
St Peters Dr WS3 15 A4
St Peters La B92 90 D1
St Peter's RC Fst Sch B61 150 E8
St Peters RC Prim Sch B32 84 C1
St Peter's RC Prim Sch
Royal Leamington Spa CV32 161 F8
Walsall WS3 14 B2
St Peter's RC Sch
Hinckley LE10 71 E1
Solihull B91 107 B2
St Peter's Rd 7 CV32 161 F8
St Peters Rd B17 85 B5
St Peter's Rd
Birmingham B20 66 C8
Burntwood WS7 7 C6
Cannock WS12 2 D4
Dudley DY2 62 D5
Stourbridge DY9 81 C1
St Peters Terr WS2 28 E4
St Philip's Cath★ B3 164 B3
St Philip's Pl B2 164 C3
St Philip's RC Prim Sch B66 65 B6
St Phillip's Ave WV3 38 F7
St Phillips Ave WV3 38 F8
St Phillip's Gr WV3 38 F7
St Quentin St WS2 42 C7
St Saviour's CE Prim Sch B8 67 D5
St Saviour's Cl WV2 39 F6
St Saviour's Ct DY9 99 A6
St Saviour's Rd B8 67 D4
St Silas' Sq B19 66 B7
St Simons Cl 3 B75 46 F6
Saint's Peter & Paul RC Prim Sch CV2 114 F7
St Stephen's Ho B97 153 E4
St Stephen's Ave WV13 26 F2
St Stephen's CE Fst Sch B98 153 F5
St Stephen's CE Prim Sch WV10 25 F4
St Stephens Ct WS12 2 C4
St Stephen's Gdns 1 WV13 27 A1
St Stephens Gdns B98 153 F5
St Stephens Rd B29 104 B8
St Stephen's Rd WS7 7 C6
St Stephens Rd B71 65 B8
St Stephens St B6 66 E6
Saints Way CV10 73 D5
St Teresa's RC Prim Sch
Birmingham B20 55 A3
Wolverhampton WV4 39 E5
St Thomas Aquinas RC Sch B38 103 D3
St Thomas' CE Prim Sch B15 86 D8
St Thomas CE Prim Sch WV11 26 D7
St Thomas' Cl WS9 16 B1
St Thomas Cl
Sutton Coldfield B75 46 F5
Walsall WS3 28 E6
St Thomas More RC Fst Sch B98 159 B7
St Thomas More RC Prim Sch
Coventry CV3 133 D5
Great Wyrley WS6 5 A4
St Thomas More RC Sch
Bilston WV14 41 A7
Nuneaton CV10 73 A3
St Thomas More's RC Prim Sch B26 89 B5
St Thomas of Canterbury RC Prim Sch WS3 28 F6
St Thomas' Rd
Birmingham B23 56 D3
Coventry CV6 96 A3
St Thomas's Cl CV10 72 C3
St Thomas's Ct 13 CV1 113 B2
St Thomas's Ho 12 CV1 113 B2
St Thomas St DY2 62 C5
St Valentines Cl B70 53 F2
St Vincent Cres B70 52 F6
St Vincent St W B16 66 A2
St Vincent's RC Prim Sch B7 67 B3
St Vincent St B16 66 B2
St Wilfrid's RC Prim Sch B36 68 F8
Saladin Ave B69 63 E5
Salcombe Ave B26 89 C5
Salcombe Cl
Cannock WS11 4 C7
Coventry CV3 134 D6
Nuneaton CV11 73 F5
Salcombe Dr DY5 81 C7
Salcombe Gr WV14 40 D1
Salcombe Rd 3 B66 65 B5
Saldavian Ct WS2 42 B6
Salem Rd LE10 75 F5
Salem St DY4 52 D5
Salford Cir B23 56 D1
Salford Cl
Coventry CV2 114 A5

Salford Cl *continued*
Redditch B98 159 B6
Salford St B6 67 C8
Salford Trad Est B6 67 C8
Salisbury Ave CV3 133 C6
Salisbury Cl
Birmingham B13 86 E3
Dudley DY1 50 F3
Lichfield WS13 3 C3
Wolston CV8 135 F3
Salisbury Dr
Cannock WS12 2 B1
Kidderminster DY11 116 A6
Nuneaton CV10 72 B7
Water Orton B46 59 C3
Salisbury Gr B72 57 C7
Salisbury Ho
3 Birmingham B24 56 F4
Hinckley LE10 71 C4
Salisbury Pl WV3 25 B1
Salisbury Prim Sch WS10 41 F7
Salisbury Rd
Birmingham,Lozells B19 66 D8
Birmingham,Moseley B13 86 E3
Birmingham,Saltley B8 67 E5
Hinckley LE10 76 B7
Smethwick B66 65 B4
West Bromwich B70 53 E1
Salisbury St
Darlaston WS10 41 E7
Wolverhampton WV3 25 B1
Salisbury Twr B18 66 A3
Sallow Gr WS8 7 A1
Sally Ward Dr WS9 16 A4
Salop Cl B71 53 B6
Salop Dr
Cannock WS11 4 F8
Oldbury B68 64 C2
Salop Rd
Oldbury B68 64 C2
Redditch B97 153 D3
Salop St
Bilston WV14 40 E4
Birmingham B12 86 F8
Dudley DY1 51 B2
Oldbury B69 52 E1
Wolverhampton WV3 163 B2
Salstar Cl B6 66 E6
Saltash Gr B25 68 C1
Saltbrook Rd B63 82 A7
Saltbrook Trad Est B63 82 A7
Salter Rd DY4 51 F7
Salter's La B97 153 B5
Salters La B79 21 B6
Salter's La B71 53 E4
Salter's Rd WS9 16 A3
Salter St B94 126 C2
Salters Vale B70 53 E1
Saltisford Canal Ctr★ CV34 160 C8
Saltisford Gdns CV34 160 C8
Saltisford CV34 160 D7
Salt La CV1 165 B2
Saltley Ind Ctr B8 67 C3
Saltley Rd B7 67 C5
Saltley Sch B9 68 A3
Saltley Trad Est B8 67 D6
Saltley Viaduct B8 67 C5
Saltney Cl B24 57 D5
Salts La B78 34 E5
Saltwells La DY2 62 B2
Saltwells Nature Reserve★ DY5,DY2 62 A3
Saltwells Rd DY2 62 C2
Salwarpe Gr B29 84 F2
Salwarpe Rd B60 150 F8
Sam Barber Ct WS12 2 E1
Sambar Rd B78 20 F1
Sambourn Cl B91 107 E6
Sambourne Dr B34 69 D7
Sambourne La
Astwood Bank B96 158 F1
Sambourne B96 159 A1
Sambourne Park La B96 159 A1
Sambrook Rd WV10 26 A6
Sam Gault Cl CV3 134 E7
Sammons Way CV4 111 D1
Sampson Cl
Birmingham B21 54 C1
Coventry CV2 114 C8
Oldbury B69 63 C7
Sampson Ho B11 87 B8
Sampson Rd B11 87 B7
Sampson Rd N B11 87 B8
Sampson St WS10 42 B3
Samsara Rd B60 137 C1
Sams La B70 53 C1
Sam Spencer Ct DY10 118 A2
Samuel Cl WS13 3 C2
Samuel Hayward Ho 5 CV2 96 B1
Samuel Ho WS3 14 B1
Samuel Johnson's Birthplace Mus★ WS13 9 B8
Samuels Rd B32 84 A5
Samuel St WS3 14 B1
Samuel Vale Ho CV1 165 B4
Sanby Cl CV12 78 A4
Sanda Croft B36 70 B6
Sandalls Cl B31 102 D1
Sandal Rise B91 107 E3
Sandals Rise B62 83 D3
Sandalwood Cl WV12 27 B8
Sand Bank WS3 14 A1
Sandbarn Cl B90 126 F6
Sandbeds Rd WV12 27 C4
Sandbourne Rd B8 68 A4
Sanderling Cl WV10 12 B7
Sanderling Ct DY10 117 A1
Sanderling Rise
Burntwood WS7 7 B8
Kingswinford DY6 61 A6
Sanders Cl
Dudley DY2 62 E7
Redditch B97 153 B4
Sanders Ct CV34 161 C8
Sanders Ind Est 1 B61 136 E1
Sanderson Ct DY11 116 C5
Sanders Rd
Bedworth CV6 96 B6
Bromsgrove B61 136 E1
Sandfield Bridge DY5 50 B1
Sandfield Cl B90 126 B8
Sandfield Gr DY3 50 B2
Sandfield Mdw WS13 9 A6
Sandfield Rd
Stourbridge DY8 60 F2
West Bromwich B71 42 E2
Sandfields Ave B10 87 B8
Sandfields Rd B68 64 C2
Sandford Ave B65 63 C3
Sandford Cl
Coventry CV2 96 E3
Hinckley LE10 71 F1
Sandford Ho WS13 9 A7
Sandford Rd
Birmingham B13 87 A3
Dudley DY1 50 E1
Sandford Rise WV6 24 E6
Sandford St WS13 9 B7
Sandgate Cres CV2 114 E2
Sandgate Rd
Birmingham B28 106 A4
Tipton DY4 52 A8
Sandhill Farm Cl 1 B19 66 D7
Sandhills Cres B91 127 B8
Sandhills Gn B48 138 E7
Sandhills La B45 138 D7
Sandhills Rd B45 138 D8
Sandhill St WS3 14 A1
Sandhurst Ave
Birmingham B36 68 D6
Stourbridge DY9 81 D2
Sandhurst Cl B98 154 C6
Sandhurst Dr WV4 39 A4
Sandhurst Gr
Coventry CV6 113 B5
Stourbridge DY8 60 E3
Sandhurst Ho B38 104 B1
Sandhurst Rd
Birmingham B13 86 F2
Kingswinford DY6 61 A4
Sutton Coldfield B74 31 F5
Sandicliffe Cl DY11 116 C8
Sandilands Cl CV2 114 E4
Sandland Cl WV14 40 F6
Sandland Rd WV12 27 D8
Sandmartin Cl DY2 62 D2
Sandmartin Way DY10 117 A2
Sandmeadow Pl DY6 60 C5
Sandmere Gr B14 105 D3
Sandmere Rd B14 105 D3
Sandmere Rise WV10 11 E1
Sandon Cl B98 154 A3
Sandon Gr B24 57 B4
Sandon Ho WV6 24 E5
Sandon Rd
Birmingham B17 65 B1
Nuneaton CV11 73 B5
Stourbridge DY9 81 F4
Wolverhampton WV10 11 B2
Sandown Ave
Cheslyn Hay WS6 4 E3
Coventry CV6 95 F2
Sandown Cl CV32 157 C4
Sandown Ct 18 B29 103 C7
Sandown Dr
Lower Marlbrook B61 121 B1
Perton WV6 23 F4
Sandown Rd B36 68 D8
Sandown B77 21 F5
Sandown Twr 3 B31 103 A1
Sandpiper Cl
Cannock WS12 2 C7
Kidderminster DY10 117 B2
Stourbridge DY9 81 F5
Sandpiper Gdns B38 123 F7
Sandpiper Rd CV2 96 B3
Sandpiper B77 36 A5
Sandpiper Way B23 56 C6
Sandpit Cl WS10 42 E2
Sand Pits B1 66 B3
Sandpits Cl B76 59 C6
Sandpits Ind Est 4 B1 66 B3
Sandpits La CV6 94 F2
Sandpits The
Birmingham B30 103 E8
Bulkington CV12 79 C2
Sandra Cl WS9 30 B5
Sandringham Ave WV12 27 B6
Sandringham Cl CV4 131 F5
Sandringham Ct
3 Birmingham B43 43 F1
Nuneaton CV10 72 F6
Sandringham Dr
Aldridge WS9 16 B1
Rowley Regis B65 63 C4
Sandringham Ho WV3 163 A1
Sandringham Pl DY8 60 D1
Sandringham Rd
Birmingham B42 55 B6
Halesowen B62 83 B7
Stourbridge DY8 60 D1
Sandringham Rd *continued*
Wolverhampton WV4 39 A4
Sandringham Way DY5 81 C8
Sandstone Ave B45 122 A8
Sandstone Cl DY3 50 D4
Sandstone Ct B77 36 A7
Sand St B70 52 E4
Sandway Gdns B8 67 D6
Sandway Gr B13 105 C7
Sandwell Ave WS10 41 B5
Sandwell Bsns Development Ctr B66 64 C7
Sandwell Bsns Pk B66 64 C8
Sandwell Coll Oldbury Campus B68 64 A3
Sandwell Coll (Smethwick Campus) B66 65 A5
Sandwell Coll (West Bromwich Campus) B70 53 C3
Sandwell Ct B21 65 D8
Sandwell Ctr B70 53 D3
Sandwell & Dudley Sta B70 53 A1
Sandwell General Hospl B71 53 D5
Sandwell Ho 1 WS1 42 F8
Sandwell Park Farm★ B71 53 F3
Sandwell Pl WV12 27 D7
Sandwell Rd B21 54 D1
Sandwell Rd N B71 53 D4
Sandwell Rd
West Bromwich B70 53 C4
Wolverhampton WV10 11 B1
Sandwell Road Pas B70 53 C4
Sandwell St WS1 42 F8
Sandwell Valley Country Pk★ B70,B71 53 F5
Sandwell Valley Ctry Pk B71 54 A5
Sandwell Valley Nature Ctr★ B43 54 C6
Sandwell Wlk 8 WS1 42 F8
Sandwick Cl CV3 134 F8
Sandwood Dr B44 55 F8
Sandyacre Way DY8 81 B5
Sandy Cres
Hinckley LE10 71 C1
Wednesfield WV11 27 A8
Wolverhampton WV11 13 A1
Sandy Croft
Birmingham B13 105 C7
Sutton Coldfield B72 46 C3
Sandyfields Rd DY3 50 B6
Sandygate Cl B97 152 F2
Sandy Gr WS8 6 F1
Sandy Hill Rd B90 106 A4
Sandy Hill Rise B90 106 A4
Sandy Hollow WV6 24 C2
Sandy La
Birmingham,Aston B6 67 B7
Birmingham,Great Barr B42 55 D8
Blackdown CV32 156 F6
Blakedown DY10 118 C7
Cannock WS11 1 B1
Codsall WV8 10 A4
Coventry CV1 113 C5
Madeley Heath B61,B62 120 E5
Sandy Lane Bsns Pk CV1 113 C5
Sandy La
Royal Leamington Spa CV32 156 D4
Wednesbury WS10 42 F3
Wolverhampton,Bushbury WV10 11 E1
Wolverhampton WV6 24 E6
Sandymount Rd WS1 42 F8
Sandy Mount WV5 49 B7
Sandy Rd DY8 80 D1
Sandys Gr DY4 51 E5
Sandythorpe CV3 134 E6
Sandy Way
Birmingham B15 66 B1
Tamworth B77 22 B3
Sandy Wlk LE10 71 B2
Sangwin Rd WV14 51 C7
Sankey Rd WS11 1 F3
Sankey's Cnr WS7 6 F7
Sannders Cres DY4 52 B5
Sansome Rd B90 105 F2
Sansome Rise B90 105 F2
Sanstone Cl WS3 14 C3
Sanstone Rd WS3 14 C3
Santolina Dr WS5 43 A3
Santos Cl CV3 134 F8
Sant Rd B31 123 B7
Santridge Ct B61 137 A4
Santridge La B61 137 A4
Sapcote Bsns Ctr B10 87 E6
Sapcote Gr CV2 96 B4
Sapcote Ind Est B64 62 F3
Sapcote Rd LE10 76 B7
Saplings The B76 58 A8
Sapphire Ct
3 Solihull B92 88 F1
Birmingham B3 164 A4
Sapphire Dr
Cannock WS11 2 C3
Royal Leamington Spa CV31 161 F5
Sapphire Gate CV2 114 C2
Sapphire Hts B1 66 B4
Sapphire Twr 2 B6 66 F6
Saracen Dr
Balsall Common CV7 129 E6
Sutton Coldfield B75 47 A6
Sara Cl B74 32 A3
Sarah Cl WV14 40 E1
Sarah Ct B73 45 D1
Sarah Gdns WS5 42 F4
Sarah Siddons Ho 2 WS13 9 B7
Sarah St B9 67 B2
Saredon Cl WS3 15 A1
Saredon Rd WS6,WS11, WV10 4 B3
Sarehole Mill Mus★ B13 105 D8
Sarehole Rd B28 87 E1
Sargeaunt St CV31 161 F7
Sargent Cl B43 44 D4
Sargent Turner Trad Est DY9 81 F6
Sark Dr B36 70 B6
Satchwell Ct 15 CV32 161 F8
Satchwell Wlk 16 CV32 161 F8
Satellite Ind Pk WV11 26 D4
Saturday Bridge 7 B1 66 C1
Saturn Rd WS11 2 A5
Saumur Way CV34 161 C6
Saunders Ave CV12 78 B2
Saunders Ho 11 CV32 156 F2
Saunton Cl CV5 112 B8
Saunton Way B29 85 C2
Saveker Dr B76 46 E4
Savernake Cl B45 102 A2
Saville Cl
Birmingham B45 122 B7
Hinckley LE10 71 E2
Saville Gr CV8 148 C5
Savoy Cl B32 85 A5
Saw Mill Cl WS4 28 E3
Saxelby Cl B14 104 E2
Saxelby Ho B14 104 E2
Saxifrage Pl DY10 116 F4
Saxon Bsns Pk B60 150 E2
Saxon Cl
Binley Woods CV3 135 D7
Great Wyrley WS6 5 A2
Polesworth B78 22 F1
Studley B80 159 E5
Tamworth B77 35 F6
Saxoncourt WV6 24 C5
Saxon Ct WS13 8 E7
Saxondale Ave B26 88 F6
Saxondrive B79 21 C5
Saxon Dr B65 63 C4
Saxonfields WV6 24 C5
Saxon Hill Sch WS14 9 C6
Saxon Mdws CV32 156 C2
Saxon Mill La B79 21 C4
Saxon Rd CV2 114 B4
Saxons Way B14 105 A2
Saxon Way B37 69 F3
Saxon Wlk WS13 8 E7
Saxon Wood Cl 2 B31 103 A4
Saxon Wood Rd B90 126 D5
Saxton Dr B74 31 F6
Scafell Cl CV5 112 A4
Scafell Dr
Bilston WV14 40 F7
Birmingham B23 56 D5
Scafell Rd DY8 81 B6
Scaife Rd B60 151 B7
Scammerton B77 36 B7
Scampton Cl WV6 23 E5
Scampton Way B79 21 C8
Scar Bank CV34 155 E1
Scarborough Cl 2 WS2 42 B8
Scarborough Rd WS2 42 B8
Scarborough Way CV4 131 F7
Scarecrow La B75 32 E4
Scarfield Hill B48 138 E5
Scarman Rd CV4 132 B5
Scarsdale Rd B42 55 D8
Schofield Ave B71 53 B8
Schofield Bsns Pk B60 151 A7
Schofield Rd B37 70 A5
Scholars Cl B21 66 A7
Scholars Ct DY10 116 E4
Scholars Gate
Birmingham B33 69 B2
Burntwood WS7 7 D7
Scholars Wlk WS4 29 B7
Scholefield Twr B19 66 D5
Scholfield Rd CV7 95 A6
Schoolacre Rd B34 69 B6
Schoolacre Rise B74 30 E1
School Ave WS8 15 F8
School Bell Mews CV8 149 B6
School Cl
Birmingham,Castle Vale B35 58 B3
Birmingham,Kingshurst B37 70 A6
Burntwood WS7 6 D8
Codsall WV8 10 A4
Coventry CV3 113 F2
Hinckley LE10 76 A6
Norton Canes WS11 6 B6
Oldbury B69 63 C7
Wolverhampton WV3 38 B7
School Cotts CV35 145 F3
School Cres WS11 6 A6
School Croft CV35 146 C2
School Ct WS12 2 C6
School Dr
Bilston WV14 41 A2
Bromsgrove B60 137 A3
Stourbridge DY8 80 F8
School Dr The DY2 62 D7
School Dr B47 125 A3
Schoolfields Rd WS14 18 A5
Schoolgate Cl
Birmingham B8 68 A6
Walsall WS4 15 D1
School Gn WV14 40 C8
School Hill CV10 72 A8
School Ho The WS7 7 D7
Schoolhouse Cl B38 104 B2
School House La CV2 115 A6
School La
Alvechurch B48 139 B5
Bedworth CV7 95 F7
Birmingham,Buckland End B34 69 B7
Birmingham,Kitt's Green B33 68 F1
Brierley Hill DY5 61 B4
Burntwood WS7 6 D8
Hagley DY9 99 D6
Halesowen B63 82 F2
Hopwas B78 20 B7
Kenilworth CV8 147 F5
Lickey End B60 137 B6
Little Packington CV7 91 D7
Norton Canes WS3 5 E2
Radford Semele CV31 162 E5
Shuttington B79 22 F7
Solihull B91 107 D4
Tamworth B77 35 D5
Walsall WS3 14 F4
Weeford B78 19 D2
Wolverhampton WV10 11 E2
Wroxall CV35 145 E4
School Rd
Birmingham B45 121 E6
Birmingham,Hall Green B28 106 A8
Birmingham,Moseley B13 86 F1
Birmingham,Yardley Wood B14 105 C4
Brierley Hill DY5 62 A2
Bulkington CV12 79 C2
Himley DY3 49 B3
Hockley Heath B94 143 B7
Norton Canes WS11 6 A6
Solihull B90 106 B2
Trysull WV5 37 C1
Wednesbury WS10 42 D2
Wolverhampton,Nordley Hill WV11 26 C6
Wolverhampton,Tettenhall Wood WV6 24 B3
Wombourne WV5 49 B7
School St W 2 WV14 51 C8
School St
Brierley Hill DY5 61 D7
Cradley Heath B64 62 D1
Darlaston WS10 41 E5
Dudley,Eve Hill DY1 51 B1
Sedgley DY3 50 E8
Stourbridge DY8 80 F6
Tamworth B77 21 E4
Tipton WV14 51 C8
Walsall WS4 15 D1
Willenhall WV13 26 F1
Wolverhampton WV3 163 B2
School Terr 1 B29 85 F2
School Wlk
Bilston WV14 40 C8
Burntwood WS7 6 D8
Nuneaton CV11 73 E2
Tamworth B79 21 B6
Scimitar Cl B79 20 E7
Scorers Cl B90 106 B6
Scotchill The CV6 95 A1
Scotchings The B36 68 E8
Scotch Orchard Prim Sch WS13 3 D1
Scotch Orch WS13 3 D1
Scotia Rd WS11 1 D3
Scotland La B32 102 C7
Scotland St B1 66 C3
Scots Cnr B14 104 E8
Scots La CV6 112 F6
Scott Arms Sh Ctr B43 43 F1
Scott Ave
Nuneaton CV10 73 D8
Wednesbury WS10 42 B2
Wolverhampton WV4 38 E4
Scott Cl
Lichfield WS14 9 B6
West Bromwich B71 53 D5
Scott Gr B92 88 E3
Scott Ho B43 54 F7
Scott Rd
Birmingham B43 43 F2
Kenilworth CV8 147 E2
Redditch B97 158 C8
Royal Leamington Spa CV31 162 B6
Solihull B92 88 E2
Tamworth B77 21 E4
Walsall WS5 43 D6
Scott's Green Cl DY1 62 A8
Scotts Green Island DY1 61 F7
Scott's Rd DY8 80 F6
Scott St WS12 2 F3
Scotwell Cl B65 63 B3
Scout Cl B33 69 C2
Scribban Cl B66 65 B4
Scribers La B28 105 E4
Scribers Mdw B28 105 E4
Scrimshaw Ho 1 WS2 42 C7
Sculthorpe Rd DY10 98 B2
Seacole Ho B97 153 B2
Seacroft Ave B25 68 E1
Seafield Cl DY6 60 E4
Seafield La
Beoley B98 141 A2
Portway B48,B98 140 E4
Seafield B77 21 F5
Seaford Cl CV6 96 B4
Seaforth Dr LE10 71 A1
Seaforth Gr WV11 13 B1
Seagar St B71 53 E4

Seager's La DY5 61 D2
Seagrave Rd CV1 165 D1
Seagull Bay Dr WV14 40 D1
Sealand Dr CV12 78 A3
Seal Cl B76 46 E3
Seals Gn B38 123 D7
Seamless Dr WV11 26 D4
Sear Hills Cl CV7 130 B6
Seaton Cl
Hinckley LE10 76 B7
Nuneaton CV11 73 F5
Wednesfield WV11 26 F5
Seaton Gr B13 86 D1
Seaton Pl DY8 60 C2
Seaton Rd B66 65 B5
Seaton B77 35 F8
Sebastian Cl CV3 134 B5
Seckham Rd 3 WS13 9 A8
Second Ave
Birmingham B29 86 B3
Birmingham,Bordesley Green B9 67 F1
Birmingham,Witton B6 55 F3
Brownhills WS8 7 A1
Coventry CV3 114 C1
Kingswinford,Barrow Hill DY6 61 A7
Kingswinford,Wall Heath DY6 60 F8
Wolverhampton WV10 25 E7
Second Exhibition Ave B40 90 D4
Securehold Bsns Ctr B98 154 B2
Sedge Ave B38 103 F3
Sedgeberrow Covert 4 B38 123 E8
Sedgeberrow Rd B63 83 A2
Sedgebourne Way B31 102 C1
Sedge Dr B61 137 A6
Sedgefield Cl DY1 50 E3
Sedgefield Gr WV6 23 F4
Sedgefield Wlk B61 121 B1
Sedgeford Cl DY5 81 D8
Sedgehill Ave B17 85 B4
Sedgemere Gr
Balsall Common CV7 130 C5
Walsall WS4 29 C8
Sedgemere Rd B26 68 F1
Sedgemoor Ave WS7 7 B5
Sedgemoor Rd CV3 134 B5
Sedgfield Way WS11 6 B4
Sedgley Cl B98 153 F4
Sedgley Gr B20 54 E4
Sedgley Hall Ave DY3 50 C8
Sedgley Rd
Dudley DY1 51 B6
Gospel End Village WV4 38 F2
Sedgley Rd W DY4 51 D5
Sedgley Road E DY4 52 A3
Sedgley St WV2 39 C7
Seed Field Croft CV3 133 E7
Seedhouse Ct B64 83 B8
Seeds La WS8 15 F8
Seekings Dr CV8 148 B4
Seekings The CV31 162 B3
Seeleys Rd B11 87 E5
Seeswood Cl CV10 72 C2
Sefton Dr B65 62 F6
Sefton Gr DY4 41 C2
Sefton Rd
Birmingham B16 65 F2
Coventry CV4 132 E6
Tamworth B77 35 D4
Segbourne Rd B45 121 F8
Segundo Cl WS5 42 F4
Segundo Rd WS5 42 F4
Seisdon Rd WV5 37 A1
Selba Dr DY11 116 A6
Selborne Cl WS1 29 A1
Selborne Gr B13 105 C5
Selborne Rd
Birmingham B20 55 A2
Dudley DY2 62 D7
Selborne St WS1 29 A1
Selbourne Cres WV1 26 B1
Selby Cl B26 68 F1
Selby Gr B13 105 C6
Selby Ho B69 63 D6
Selby Way
Nuneaton CV10 72 B5
Walsall WS3 13 E2
Selcombe Way B38 123 F7
Selco Way B76 58 A5
Selcroft Ave B32 84 F5
Selecta Ave B44 44 D2
Selina Dix Ho CV1 165 C4
Selker Dr B77 21 F5
Selkirk Cl B71 53 C6
Selly Ave B29 86 A2
Selly Cl B29 86 B2
Selly Hall Croft B30 104 A6
Selly Hill Rd B29 85 F2
Selly Manor Mus* B30 103 F7
Selly Oak Colls B29 103 D8
Selly Oak Hospl B29 85 F1
Selly Oak Ind Est B29 85 E1
Selly Oak Rd B30 103 E5
Selly Oak Specl Sch B29 103 E8
Selly Oak Sta B29 85 E2
Selly Park Rd B29 86 A2
Selly Park Tech Coll For Girls B29 86 B1
Selly Wharf B29 85 E2
Selly Wick Dr B29 86 B2
Selly Wick Rd B29 86 B2
Sellywood Rd B29,B30 103 E8
Selma Gr B14 105 D5
Selmans Hill WS3 14 C2
Selman's Par WS3 14 C2
Selsdon Cl
Kidderminster DY11 116 B5
Wythall B47 125 C5
Selsdon Rd WS3 13 F3
Selsey Ave B66 65 B3
Selsey Cl CV3 134 C4
Selsey Rd B17 65 B3
Selston Rd B6 66 E7
Selvey Ave B43 44 C3
Selworthy Rd
Birmingham B36 69 F8
Coventry CV6 95 E3
Selwyn Cl WV2 39 C7
Selwyn Ho B37 70 D3
Selwyn Rd
Bilston WV14 40 F7
Birmingham B16 65 D2
Burntwood WS7 7 F8
Selwyn Wlk B74 31 C4
Semele Cl CV31 162 E5
Seneschal Rd CV3 133 E7
Senior Cl WV11 13 A3
Senneleys Park Rd B31 84 E1
Sennen Cl
Nuneaton CV11 74 A5
Willenhall WV13 26 F1
Sensall Rd DY9 81 F3
Sentry Way B75 46 F6
Sephton Dr CV6 96 C6
Serin Cl DY10 117 A1
Serpentine Rd
Birmingham,Aston B6 56 A1
Birmingham B17 85 C6
Birmingham,Selly Oak B29 86 A2
Serpentine The DY11 116 C4
Servite Ct B14 105 A2
Servite Ho
2 Coleshill B46 70 F7
Kenilworth CV8 147 F3
Seton Ho B74 31 E2
Settle Ave B34 68 F6
Settle Croft B37 69 F1
Setton Dr DY3 50 E7
Seven Acres WS9 30 B5
Seven Acres La B98 154 C5
Seven Acres Rd
Birmingham,Quinton B62 84 A5
Birmingham,Turves Green B31 103 C1
Sevendwellings View DY5 61 C1
Seven Star Rd B91 107 B5
Seven Stars Ind Est CV3 134 A7
Seven Stars Rd B69 64 A7
Severn Ave LE10 75 A8
Severn Cl
Birmingham B36 69 F7
Catshill B61 137 A8
Royal Leamington Spa CV32 157 C3
Tipton DY4 51 F5
Wednesfield WV12 27 A7
Severn Ct
Birmingham B23 56 B3
Sutton Coldfield B73 46 B5
Severn Dr
Brierley Hill DY5 61 B7
Burntwood WS7 7 D6
Perton WV6 23 E4
Severne Gr B27 88 C1
Severne Jun & Inf Sch B27 106 C8
Severne Rd B27 106 C8
Severn Gr
5 Birmingham B19 66 C7
8 Birmingham B19 66 C7
Kidderminster DY11 116 B3
Severn Ho
4 Birmingham B68 84 B8
Dudley DY3 50 D3
Severn Rd
Brownhills WS8 6 C2
Bulkington CV12 79 A3
Coventry CV1 113 F1
Halesowen B63 82 B5
Stourbridge DY8 80 F3
Walsall WS3 14 E1
Severn St B1 164 B1
Severn Twr B7 67 B5
Severn Valley Rly* DY10, DY11 116 D2
Severn Way B47 124 E2
Sevilla Cl CV3 115 A2
Sevington Cl B91 127 C8
Sewall Ct CV6 114 A8
Sewall Highway CV2 114 B6
Seward Cl WS14 9 D6
Seymour Cl
Birmingham B29 86 A2
Cheslyn Hay WS6 4 D1
Coventry CV3 134 C5
Seymour Dr B98 154 A5
Seymour Gdns B74 31 E3
Seymour Gr CV34 161 D6
Seymour Ho CV3 133 C8
Seymour Rd
Kidderminster DY11 116 B8
Nuneaton CV11 73 D3
Oldbury B69 64 C7
Stourbridge DY9 82 A4
Wednesbury DY4 41 C1
Shackleton Dr
Hinckley LE10 75 E4
Perton WV6 23 E5
Shackleton Rd WS3 14 D2
Shadowbrook La B92 108 E7
Shadowbrook Rd CV6 113 A5
Shadwell Dr DY3 50 D3
Shadwell St B4 164 C4
Shady La B44 44 E2
Shadymoor Dr DY5 81 C8
Shaftesbury Ave
Keresley CV7 95 A7
Stourbridge DY9 81 C2
Shaftesbury Cl B60 137 B2
Shaftesbury Dr WS12 2 C7
Shaftesbury Rd
Coventry CV5 132 F8
Wednesbury WS10 42 B2
Shaftesbury Sq B71 53 C5
Shaftesbury St B70,B71 53 C4
Shaft La CV7 93 A4
Shaftmoor Ind Est B28 87 F2
Shaftmoor La B27,B28 87 F2
Shaftsbury Ave B63 82 B7
Shaftsbury Cl WV14 40 F7
Shaftsbury Dr WS7 7 F7
Shaftsbury Rd B26 89 C5
Shahjalal Rd B8 67 D5
Shakels Cl B97 158 E4
Shakespeare Ave
Bedworth CV12 78 D2
Lichfield WS14 9 B6
Redditch B98 154 A2
Warwick CV34 160 C4
Shakespeare Cl
Dudley WV14 40 D2
Tamworth B79 21 A6
Shakespeare Cres WS3 28 F7
Shakespeare Dr
Hinckley LE10 71 C1
Kidderminster DY10 117 B6
Nuneaton CV11 74 A1
Solihull B90 106 B1
Shakespeare Gr WS11 1 D4
Shakespeare Ho B31 123 A8
Shakespeare Pl WS3 28 F7
Shakespeare Rd
Birmingham B23 56 B3
Burntwood WS7 6 F8
Dudley DY3 50 A4
Smethwick B67 64 E4
Solihull B90 126 D8
Tipton DY4 52 A8
Shakespeare St
Birmingham B11 87 C5
Coventry CV2 114 B4
Wolverhampton WV1 163 D2
Shakleton Rd CV5 113 A2
Shaldon Wlk 4 B66 65 B5
Shale St WV14 40 C5
Shalford Rd B92 88 E4
Shallcross La DY3 50 D3
Shalnecote Gr B14 104 C5
Shambles 2 WS10 41 F2
Shandon Cl B32 84 F3
Shanklin Cl WS6 5 A3
Shanklin Dr CV10 73 D6
Shanklin Rd CV3 134 B4
Shannon Dr WS8 6 C2
Shannon Rd B38 123 E7
Shannon's Mill B79 21 A5
Shannon B77 35 F8
Shannon Wlk WS8 6 C2
Shanti Niketan WV2 39 D7
Shapinsay Dr B45 101 F1
Shard End Cres B34 69 C6
Shardlow Rd WV11 26 E8
Shardway The B34 69 C5
Sharesacre St WV13 27 B3
Sharington Cl 3 DY2 62 E8
Sharman Rd WV10 25 E6
Sharmans Cross Jun Sch B91 106 E4
Sharmans Cross Rd B91 106 F4
Sharnford Rd LE10 76 F6
Sharon Cl WV4 39 E5
Sharon Ct B27 88 C3
Sharon Way WS12 2 D3
Sharp Cl CV6 95 C2
Sharpe Cl CV34 160 E8
Sharpe St B77 22 A5
Sharpless Rd LE10 75 F7
Sharpley Ct CV2 115 A8
Sharps Cl B45 122 A7
Sharrat Field B75 32 D2
Sharratt Rd CV12 78 A2
Sharrocks St WV1 163 D2
Shaw Ave DY10 117 B6
Shawbank Rd B98 154 B3
Shawberry Ave B35 58 B4
Shawberry Rd B37 69 F5
Shawbrook Gr 4 B14 105 A3
Shawbury Cl B98 154 E3
Shawbury Gr
Birmingham B12 86 F8
Perton WV6 23 E5
Shawbury Rd WV10 25 F5
Shaw Ct WS11 6 A5
Shaw Dr B33 68 E2
Shawe Ave CV10 73 C7
Shawfield B47 125 A5
Shaw Hall La WV9 11 C7
Shaw Hellier Ave DY5 61 E2
Shaw Hill Gr B8 68 A4
Shaw Hill Prim Sch B8 67 F4
Shaw Hill Rd B8 68 A4
Shawhurst Croft B47 125 A7
Shawhurst Gdns B47 125 B7
Shawhurst La B47 125 A6
Shaw La WS13 9 A8
Shaw Lane Ind Est B60 150 C2
Shaw La
Stoke Prior B60 150 C3
Wolverhampton WV6 24 B3
Shawley Croft B27 88 E4
Shaw Park Bsns Village WV10 25 D6
Shaw Rd
Dudley,Netherton DY2 62 C7
Hurst Hill WV14 40 B1
Tipton DY4 52 C4
Wolverhampton WV4 39 C6
Shaws Cl B97 152 F2
Shawsdale Rd B36 68 F7
Shaw's La WS6 5 A2
Shaw's Pas B5 164 D2
Shaw St B70 52 E7
Shayler Gr WV2 39 D7
Sheaf La B26 89 B4
Sheapecoate Ho 1 B71 42 F1
Shearers Pl 4 B75 32 E3
Shearwater Cl
Birmingham B45 121 F6
Kidderminster DY10 117 B1
Shearwater Ct WV10 11 B3
Shearwater Wlk B23 56 B7
Sheaves Cl WV14 40 B3
Shedden St 3 DY2 62 D8
Sheddington Rd B23 56 D7
Sheen Ho CV2 114 D8
Sheen Rd B44 44 E4
Sheepclose Dr B37 70 A3
Sheepcote Cl CV32 157 A1
Sheepcote Grange B61 136 F5
Sheepcote La B77 21 F4
Sheepcote St B16 66 B2
Sheepcroft Cl B97 152 F2
Sheepfold Cl B65 63 A4
Sheepmoor Cl B17 84 F8
Sheepwash La DY4 52 D5
Sheepy Cl LE10 71 F1
Sheerwater Dr DY5 81 D7
Sheffield Rd B73 57 A7
Sheffield St DY5 62 A1
Shefford Rd B6 66 F5
Sheila Ave WV11 26 E7
Shelah Rd B63 83 A6
Shelbourne Cl B69 52 D2
Sheldon Ave WS10 42 A4
Sheldon Cl WV14 40 D4
Sheldon Ctry Pk* B26 89 E5
Sheldon Dr B31 102 D2
Sheldonfield Rd B26 89 D5
Sheldon Gr
Birmingham B26 89 B5
Warwick CV34 155 F2
Sheldon Hall Ave B33 69 D3
Sheldon Heath Com Arts Coll B26 89 C8
Sheldon Heath Rd B26 89 B8
Sheldon Rd
Redditch B98 159 A8
West Bromwich B71 53 E8
Wolverhampton WV10 11 A1
Sheldon Wlk B33 69 C1
Sheldrake Cl CV3 115 A1
Shelduck Cl DY10 117 B3
Shelfield Cl
Coventry CV5 112 B3
Hockley Heath B94 143 C6
Shelfield Rd B14 104 C3
Shelfield Sports & Com Coll WS4 15 C2
Shell Corner Trad Est B62 83 D8
Shelley Ave
Kidderminster DY10 116 E7
Tipton DY4 52 B8
Warwick CV34 160 C4
Shelley Cl
Bedworth CV12 78 D1
Catshill B61 137 A8
Dudley DY3 50 A5
Redditch B97 158 C8
Stourbridge DY8 81 A8
Shelley Dr
Birmingham B23 56 B3
Sutton Coldfield B74 31 F6
Shelley Gdns LE10 71 E3
Shelley Ho
1 Oldbury B68 64 C4
Halesowen B63 82 B5
Shelley Rd
2 Burntwood WS7 7 A8
Cannock WS11 1 E5
Coventry CV2 114 C3
Tamworth B79 21 A7
Willenhall WV12 27 E7
Wolverhampton WV10 11 D2
Shellon Cl CV3 134 F8
Shelly Cl B37 69 F2
Shelly Cres B90 127 B6
Shelly Croft B33 69 A3
Shelly La B90 127 B6
Shelly Twr B31 103 C3
Shelsley Ave B69 63 D5
Shelsley Dr B13 87 B2
Shelsley Way B91 107 B1
Shelton Cl WS10 42 C5
Shelton La B63 82 E5
Shelton Sq CV1 165 B2
Shelton St B77 35 F7
Sheltwood Cl B97 153 A2
Sheltwood La B60,B97 152 A3
Shelwick Gr B93 127 F4
Shenley Ave DY1 51 C6
Shenley Court Sch B29 102 F7
Shenley Fields Dr B31 102 F8
Shenley Fields Rd B29 103 B8
Shenley Gn B29 102 F6
Shenley Hill B31 102 F6
Shenley La B29 102 F7
Shenstone Ave
Halesowen B62 83 E5
Stourbridge DY8 80 D3
Shenstone Cl
Bromsgrove B60 137 B3
Sutton Coldfield B74 31 E6
Shenstone Ct
Bromsgrove B60 137 B3
Solihull B90 105 D2
Wolverhampton WV3 39 A6
Shenstone Dr
Aldridge WS9 30 A8
Balsall Common CV7 130 A6
Shenstone Flats B62 83 F5
Shenstone Ho WS13 3 E1
Shenstone Lodge Sch WS14 18 A3
Shenstone Rd
Birmingham,Edgbaston B16 65 C3
Birmingham,Great Barr B43 54 E8
Birmingham,Highter's Heath B14 105 A1
Shenstone Sta WS14 17 F6
Shenstone Trad Est B63 83 C4
Shenstone Valley Rd B62 83 F6
Shenton Wlk B37 69 F5
Shepheard Rd B26 89 D5
Shepheards La CV7 92 A3
Shepherd Cl
Coventry CV4 111 F3
Lichfield WS13 3 C3
Shepherd Dr WV12 27 C5
Shepherds Brook Rd DY9 81 D5
Shepherds Fold B65 63 B2
Shepherds Gdns 8 B15 66 B1
Shepherds Green Rd B24 56 F1
Shepherds Pool Rd B75 32 E2
Shepherds Standing B34 69 B6
Shepherds Way B23 56 C8
Shepherds Wlk
Bromsgrove B60 150 E7
Wolverhampton WV8 10 F2
Shepley Mdw B45 138 B8
Shepley Rd
Barnt Green B45 138 A7
Birmingham B45 122 B6
Shepperton Bsns Pk CV11 73 C1
Shepperton Ct CV11 73 C1
Shepperton St CV11 73 C2
Sheppey Dr B36 70 B5
Shepwell Gdns WV10 12 C7
Shepwell Gn WV13 27 C1
Sherard Croft B36 70 B6
Sheraton Cl
Aldridge WS9 30 B6
Cannock WS12 2 A7
Sheraton Dr DY10 117 B6
Sheraton Grange DY8 80 F2
Sheraton Rd B60 137 C1
Sherborne Cl WS3 28 C7
Sherborne Ct WV10 11 E1
Sherborne Gdns WV8 10 A3
Sherborne Gr B1 66 A3
Sherborne Rd
Hinckley LE10 76 B7
Wolverhampton WV10 11 D1
Sherborne St B16 66 B2
Sherbourne Arc CV1 165 B2
Sherbourne Ave
Cannock WS12 2 E4
Nuneaton CV10 72 B4
Sherbourne Cl B98 154 D2
Sherbourne Cres CV5 112 E4
Sherbourne Ct CV1 165 B1
Sherbourne Dr B27 88 C4
Sherbourne Fields Sch CV6 112 D5
Sherbourne Rd
Birmingham,Acock's Green B27 88 C4
Birmingham,Balsall Heath B12 86 F7
Cradley Heath B64 83 B8
Stourbridge DY8 81 B4
Sherbourne St CV1 113 A2
Sherbrooke Ave B77 35 E6
Sherbrook Rd WS11 1 C1
Sherdmore Croft B90 126 F6
Sheridan Cl 3 WS2 42 B7
Sheridan Gdns DY3 49 F5
Sheridan St
Walsall WS2 42 B7
West Bromwich B71 53 D4
Sheridan Wlk B35 58 A3
Sheriff Ave CV4 132 B7
Sheriff Dr DY5 61 F2
Sheriffs Cl WS14 9 E6
Sheriffs Orch CV1 165 B2
Sherifoot La B75 32 B4
Sheringham B15 85 E8
Sheringham Cl CV11 73 F2
Sheringham Rd B30 104 B3
Sherington Ave CV5 112 C4
Sherington Dr WV4 39 D5
Sherlock Cl WV12 27 D5
Sherlock Rd CV5 112 D3
Sherlock St B5 86 E8
Sherrans Dell WV4 39 D4
Sherratt Cl B76 57 F8
Sherringham Dr WV11 13 C1
Sherron Gdns B12 86 F5
Sherston Covert 11 B30 104 C2
Shervale Cl WV4 39 A6
Sherwin Ave WV14 40 A2

Sherwood Ave DY4 .... 51 F4
Sherwood Cl
Birmingham B28 .... 105 F5
Solihull B92 .... 106 F7
Wood End CV9 .... 36 C1
Sherwood Dr
Brierley Hill DY5 .... 61 F2
Cannock WS11 .... 2 A3
Sherwood Ho 1 B64 ..... 82 F8
Sherwood Jones Cl CV6 . 113 B6
Sherwood Mews B28 .... 105 E6
Sherwood Rd
Birmingham B28 .... 105 E7
Bromsgrove B60 .... 151 A6
Smethwick B67 .... 65 A1
Stourbridge DY8 .... 80 E7
Sherwood St WV1 ...... 163 B4
Sherwood Wlk
Birmingham B45 .... 102 B2
Royal Leamington Spa
CV32 .... 157 C4
Walsall WS9 .... 29 E7
Shetland Ave B77 .... 35 F7
Shetland Cl
Birmingham B16 .... 65 F2
Coventry CV5 .... 112 A4
Wolverhampton WV6 ...... 25 B5
Shetland Dr
Nuneaton CV10 .... 73 A2
Smethwick B66 .... 64 D8
Shetland Wlk B36 .... 70 B6
Shevlock Way CV6 ...... 114 A6
Shidas La B69 .... 63 E7
Shifnal Wlk B31 .... 122 F8
Shifrall Way B75 .... 46 F7
Shillcock Gr B19 .... 66 E5
Shillingstone Cl CV2 .... 115 A4
Shillingstone Dr CV10 .... 73 A1
Shilton & Ansty CE Fst Sch
CV7 .... 97 E5
Shilton Cl B90 .... 126 F6
Shilton Gr B29 .... 102 F8
Shilton Ind Est CV7 ...... 97 E7
Shilton La
Barnacle CV2,CV7 .... 97 B4
Bulkington CV12 .... 79 D1
Coventry CV2 .... 96 F3
Shilton CV7,CV12 .... 97 D8
Shinwell Cres B69 .... 52 D2
Shipbourne Cl B32 .... 84 F5
Shipley Fields B24 .... 57 A3
Shipley Gr B29 .... 103 A8
Shipston Rd
Birmingham B31 .... 103 B1
Coventry CV2 .... 114 C6
Shipton Cl
Dudley DY1 .... 50 F3
Redditch B97 .... 153 A5
Shipton Rd B72 .... 46 C3
Shipway Rd B25 .... 88 A7
Shire Brook Cl B6 .... 66 E8
Shirebrook Cl CV2 .... 96 D2
Shire Brook Ct 2 B19 .... 66 D7
Shire Cl
Birmingham B16 .... 65 F2
Coventry CV6 .... 96 B1
Oldbury B68 .... 64 B2
Shirehall Pl WS11 .... 2 B2
Shirehampton Cl B97 ... 152 F2
Shireland Brook Gdns 1
B18 .... 65 D4
Shireland Cl B20 .... 54 F3
Shireland Hall Jun & Inf Sch
B66 .... 65 C3
Shireland Language Coll
B66 .... 65 B3
Shireland La B97 .... 153 A4
Shireland Rd B66 .... 65 B3
Shire Lea WS8 .... 16 B6
Shirelea Cl WS7 .... 7 B8
Shire Oak Sch WS9 .... 16 A5
Shire Ridge WS9 .... 16 B4
Shires Gate Ret Pk CV31 161 E6
Shires Gate Trad Est
CV31 .... 161 E6
Shires Ind Est WS14 .... 9 A6
Shires Ret Pk CV34 ..... 161 D6
Shirestone Com Prim Sch
B33 .... 69 D2
Shirestone Rd B33 .... 69 E2
Shireview Gdns WS3 ..... 15 B4
Shireview Rd WS3 .... 15 B4
Shirewood WS11 .... 1 B2
Shirland Rd B37 .... 70 A1
Shirlett Cl CV2 .... 96 B4
Shirleydale 2 B90 ...... 126 C8
Shirley Dr B72 .... 46 C4
Shirley Heath Jun Sch
B90 .... 106 C1
Shirley La CV7 .... 111 A5
Shirley Park Rd B90 ..... 106 B2
Shirley Rd
Birmingham,Hall Green B27,
B28 .... 106 A7
Birmingham,King's Norton
B30 .... 104 A5
Coventry CV2 .... 115 A7
Dudley DY2 .... 62 E8
Oldbury B68 .... 64 C6
Shirley Sta B90 .... 105 F1
Shirley Wlk B79 .... 20 F7
Shirral Gr B37 .... 69 F5
Shirrall Dr B78 .... 33 E4
Shoal Hill Cl WS11 .... 1 B2
Sholing Cl WV8 .... 10 F1
Shooters Cl B5 .... 86 D6
Shooters Hill B72 .... 46 D2
Shop La WV6 .... 37 B7
Shopping Ctr The CV31 .. 162 B5
Shopping Prec The
CV34 .... 156 A1
Shops The DY6 .... 60 D4
Shopton Rd B34 .... 69 A7
Shoreham Cl WV13 ...... 26 D1
Shorncliffe Rd CV6 ...... 112 E6
Short Acre St WS2 .... 28 D3
Shortbutts La WS14 .... 9 B5
Shorters Ave B14 .... 105 B4
Shortfield Cl CV7 .... 130 B7
Short Heath Ct B23 ...... 56 F5
Short Heath Jun Sch
WV12 .... 27 D5
Short Heath Prim Sch
B23 .... 56 D6
Short Heath Rd B23 ...... 56 E6
Short La WS6 .... 4 E3
Shortland Cl B93 .... 128 A7
Shortlands Cl B30 .... 104 A2
Shortlands CV7 .... 95 D6
Shortlands La WS3 .... 14 F3
Shortley Rd CV3 .... 133 F8
Short Rd
Smethwick B67 .... 64 D3
Wolverhampton WV10 ..... 11 E1
Short St
Bilston WV14 .... 40 D6
Brownhills WS8 .... 15 F7
Cannock WS11 .... 1 F3
Coventry CV1 .... 165 C2
Darlaston WS10 .... 41 F7
Dudley DY1 .... 51 A2
Halesowen B63 .... 82 F5
Nuneaton CV10 .... 72 D4
Rowley Regis B65 .... 63 C2
Solihull B90 .... 126 A5
Stourbridge DY8 .... 80 F5
Tipton DY4 .... 51 E8
Walsall WS2 .... 28 D1
Wednesbury WS10 .... 41 E3
Willenhall WV12 .... 27 C5
Wolverhampton WV1 ..... 163 C3
Shorwell Pl DY5 .... 61 B1
Shottery Cl
Coventry CV5 .... 112 B3
Sutton Coldfield B76 ...... 46 F1
Shottery Gr B76 .... 46 F1
Shottery Rd B90 .... 106 B1
Shotteswell Rd B90 ..... 126 B8
Showell Cir WV10 .... 25 E7
Showell Green La B11 ... 87 C3
Showell Ho 10 B69 .... 64 A7
Showell La
Eaves Green CV7 .... 93 A1
Wombourne WV4 .... 38 B3
Showell Rd WV10 .... 25 D6
Showell Road Ind Est
WV10 .... 25 D6
Showells Gdns B7 .... 67 C7
Showmans Cvn Site WS3 . 14 E2
Shrawley Ave DY11 ..... 116 B3
Shrawley Cl
Birmingham B45 .... 121 F7
Halesowen B63 .... 83 A2
Shrawley Rd B31 .... 103 C2
Shreres Dyche CV34 .... 160 C4
Shrewley Cres B33 .... 69 E1
Shrewsbury Cl WS3 ...... 13 F1
Shrewsbury Rd DY11 .... 116 A6
Shrewton Ave B14 ...... 104 D2
Shrubberies The CV4 .... 132 E4
Shrubbery Ave DY4 ...... 51 D5
Shrubbery Cl
Sutton Coldfield B76 ...... 57 D6
Walsall WS1 .... 29 B1
Shrubbery Ct DY10 ..... 116 F7
Shrubbery Rd B61 ...... 136 E1
Shrubbery Sch The B76 .. 57 F7
Shrubbery St DY10 ..... 116 F7
Shrubbery The
4 Dudley DY1 .... 51 B2
Birmingham B16 .... 65 F3
Shrub La B24 .... 57 B4
Shrublands Ave B68 ..... 84 B7
Shrubland Street Com Prim
Sch CV31 .... 162 A6
Shrubland St CV31 ...... 162 A6
Shuckburgh Gr 5 CV32 . 157 A2
Shugborough Cl WS3 .... 14 B1
Shugborough Dr DY1 .... 50 E2
Shugborough Way WS11 .. 2 C1
Shulman's Wlk CV2 ..... 114 D7
Shultern La CV4 .... 132 D6
Shuna Croft CV2 .... 115 B7
Shustoke La WS5 .... 43 B4
Shustoke Rd
Birmingham B34 .... 69 C6
Solihull B91 .... 107 D5
Shutlock La B13 .... 86 D1
Shut Mill La B62 .... 100 D2
Shuttington Rd B77,B79 .. 22 B6
Shutt La B94 .... 126 B1
Shuttle St CV6 .... 114 B8
Shylock Gr CV34 .... 161 E2
Shyltons Croft B16 ...... 66 A2
Sibdon Gr B31 .... 123 A8
Sibree Rd CV3 .... 134 B4
Sibton Cl CV2 .... 96 C1
Sidaway Cl B65 .... 63 C6
Sidaway St B64 .... 62 E1
Sidbury Gr B93 .... 127 E3
Sidbury Rd CV6 .... 113 C6
Sidcup Cl WV14 .... 40 B3
Sidcup Rd B44 .... 45 A1
Siddeley Ave
Coventry CV3 .... 114 B1
Kenilworth CV8 .... 147 E3
Siddons Factory Est B70 . 52 F8
Siddons Rd WV14 .... 40 D2
Siddons Way B70 .... 53 A7
Sidemoor Fst Sch B61 .. 136 E3
Sidenhill Cl B90 .... 126 B8
Sidestrand WV9 .... 10 F3
Sidford Gdns B24 .... 57 C3
Sidford Gr B23 .... 56 E7
Sidings The
5 West Bromwich B70 .... 53 C2
Birmingham,Gravelly Hill
B23 .... 56 E3
Birmingham,Lozells B20 ... 66 C8
Cannock WS12 .... 2 C7
Sidlaw Cl
Halesowen B63 .... 82 D2
Wolverhampton WV10 ..... 25 C6
Sidmouth Cl
Coventry CV2 .... 114 C7
Nuneaton CV11 .... 73 F5
Sidney Stringer Com Tech
Coll CV1 .... 165 C3
Sidney St WV2 .... 163 B1
Sidon Hill Way WS11 ...... 2 C2
Sidwick Cres WV2 .... 40 B6
Sigmund Cl WV1 .... 26 B3
Signal Gr WS3 .... 14 A1
Signal Hayes Rd B76 ..... 47 A2
Signal Wlk B77 .... 22 A2
Silesbourne Cl B36 ...... 69 C8
Silhill Hall Rd B91 ...... 107 A5
Silica Rd B77 .... 22 B2
Silken Ct CV11 .... 73 B4
Silksby St CV3 .... 133 D8
Sillins Ave B98 .... 154 A3
Silva Ave DY6 .... 60 F4
Silver Birch Ave CV12 .... 77 E2
Silver Birch Cl
Binley Woods CV3 .... 135 D7
Birmingham B8 .... 67 D6
Silverbirch Cl CV10 ...... 72 A7
Silver Birch Coppice B74 . 31 D5
Silverbirch Ct B24 .... 57 B6
Silver Birch Ct DY10 .... 117 A4
Silver Birch Dr
Hollywood B47 .... 125 B6
Kidderminster DY10 ..... 117 C5
Silver Birches Bsns Pk 3
B60 .... 150 F6
Silver Birch Gr 5 CV31 .. 161 F5
Silver Birch Rd
Birmingham,Erdington
B24 .... 57 B6
Birmingham,Kingshurst B37 69 F6
Huntington WS12 .... 1 D8
Norton Canes WS11 .... 6 B5
Silverbirch Rd B91 ..... 107 E3
Silver Birch Rd
Sutton Coldfield B74 ...... 30 F1
Wolverhampton WV2 ...... 39 E7
Silver Court Gdns WS8 ... 15 F7
Silvercroft Ave B21 ...... 54 D3
Silver Ct WS8 .... 15 F7
Silverdale B61 .... 136 F4
Silverdale Cl CV2 .... 96 B4
Silverdale Dr
Burntwood WS7 .... 6 D7
Wolverhampton WV10 ..... 25 E5
Silverdale Gdns DY8 ..... 60 C3
Silverdale Rd B24 .... 57 D5
Silver End Ind Est & Bsns Pk
DY5 .... 61 C1
Silverfield Cl B14 .... 104 E8
Silver Fir Cl WS12 .... 2 A8
Silver Innage B63 .... 82 C7
Silverlands Ave B68 ..... 64 B3
Silverlands Cl B28 .... 87 F1
Silver Link Rd B77 .... 21 F1
Silvermead Ct B47 ..... 124 F5
Silvermead Rd B73 ...... 46 A1
Silvermere Rd B26 .... 89 D6
Silver's Cl WS3 .... 14 F4
Silver St
Birmingham B14 .... 104 E8
Brierley Hill DY5 .... 61 C1
Brownhills WS8 .... 15 F7
Coventry CV1 .... 165 B3
Hollywood B47 .... 124 E5
Kidderminster DY10 ..... 116 E7
Silverstone Ave DY11 ... 116 D8
Silverstone Cl WS2 ...... 27 D3
Silverstone Ct B30 ..... 104 B8
Silverstone Dr
Coventry CV6 .... 95 E5
Sutton Coldfield B74 ...... 44 F6
Silver St
Redditch B97,B98 .... 153 E4
Tamworth B79 .... 21 B5
Silverthorne Ave DY4 .... 51 D5
Silverthorne La B64 ..... 82 B8
Silverton Cres B13 ...... 87 D1
Silverton Hts B67 .... 64 F6
Silverton Rd
Coventry CV6 .... 113 F7
Smethwick B67 .... 64 E6
Silverton Way WV11 ..... 26 F5
Silver Trees Dr CV12 ..... 79 B4
Silvertrees Rd DY4 ...... 51 E5
Silver Wlk CV10 .... 72 F3
Silvester Ct B70 .... 53 E3
Silvester Rd WV14 .... 40 F7
Silvester Way DY5 .... 81 B8
Silvington Cl B29 ...... 103 C7
Simcox Gdns B32 .... 84 D2
Simcox Rd WS10 .... 41 F5
Simcox St WS12 .... 2 D4
Simeon Bissell Cl DY4 .... 52 A5
Simeon's Wlk DY5 .... 81 F7
Simmonds Cl WS3 .... 14 D3
Simmonds Pl WS10 .... 41 F7
Simmonds Rd WS3 .... 14 D3
Simmonds Way WS8 ...... 16 A6
Simmons Cl B78 .... 34 B1
Simmons Dr B32 .... 84 D4
Simmons Leasow B32 .... 84 E2
Simmons Rd WV11 .... 13 B1
Simms La
Dudley DY2 .... 62 C5
Hollywood B47 .... 125 A5
Simon Cl
Nuneaton CV11 .... 73 D2
West Bromwich B71 ...... 42 E1
Simon Ct CV7 .... 96 A8
Simon Rd B47 .... 125 A7
Simon Stone St CV6 ..... 113 F8
Simpkins Cl WS9 .... 16 A3
Simpson Gr
Coventry CV3 .... 134 C6
Wolverhampton WV10 ..... 25 E6
Simpson Rd
Lichfield WS13 .... 3 B2
Sutton Coldfield B72 ...... 46 C1
Walsall WS2 .... 28 B5
Wolverhampton WV10 ..... 25 E6
Simpson St B69 .... 64 A8
Sinclair Ct B13 .... 86 E4
Sinclair Dr CV6 .... 96 C6
Singer Cl CV6 .... 114 B8
Singer Croft B36 .... 58 F1
Singh Cl B21 .... 54 E1
Sion Cl DY5 .... 61 D3
Sir Alfreds Way B76 ..... 46 E3
Sir Frank Whittle Prim Sch
CV2 .... 114 F8
Sir George's Mall 6
DY10 .... 116 E6
Sir Harrys Rd B5 .... 86 C6
Sir Henry Parkes Rd
CV5 .... 132 D7
Sir Hilton's Rd B31 ..... 123 C7
Sir John's Rd B29 .... 86 C3
Sir Richards Dr B17 ...... 84 F7
Sir Robert Peel Hospl
B78 .... 20 D2
Sir Thomas White's Rd
CV5 .... 112 F2
Sir Toby Belch Dr CV34 .. 161 F3
Sir Walter's Mall 8
DY10 .... 116 E6
Sir William Lyons Rd
CV4 .... 132 C6
Sir Winston Churchill Pl
CV3 .... 135 C7
Sisefield Rd B38 .... 104 A1
Siskin Cl
Hammerwich WS7 .... 7 D5
Oldbury B68 .... 64 C2
Siskin Dr
Birmingham B12 .... 86 E6
Coventry CV3 .... 134 C4
Siskin Parkway E CV3 ... 134 C1
Siskin Parkway W CV3 .. 134 C2
Siskin Rd DY9 .... 81 C3
Siskin Way DY10 .... 117 B1
Sisley Way LE10 .... 71 A3
Sister Dora Ave WS7 ...... 7 F7
Sister Dora Bldgs 2 WS1 28 E1
Sister Dora Gdns 1 WS1 . 42 E8
Siviter's Cl B65 .... 63 B3
Siviter's La B65 .... 63 B3
Siviter St B63 .... 83 B4
Six Acres B32 .... 84 C4
Sixth Form Coll Solihull The
B91 .... 107 D2
Six Towers Rd WS2 ...... 28 C4
Six Ways B23 .... 56 F4
Six Ways Ho B23 .... 56 F4
Skelcher Rd B90 .... 106 A3
Skelwith Rise CV11 ...... 74 A6
Skemp Cl WV14 .... 40 D4
Sketchley Cl B66 .... 65 A6
Sketchley Hall Gdns LE10 . 75 C5
Sketchley Hill Prim Sch
LE10 .... 75 E5
Sketchley La LE10 .... 75 C5
Sketchley La Ind Est LE10 75 B5
Sketchley Manor La LE10 . 75 D5
Sketchley Mdws LE10 .... 75 C5
Sketchley Meadows Bsns Pk
LE10 .... 75 C4
Sketchley Old Village
LE10 .... 75 C5
Sketchley Rd LE10 .... 75 E5
Skey Dr CV10 .... 72 B6
Skidmore Ave
Tamworth B77 .... 35 C5
Wolverhampton WV3 ...... 38 F8
Skidmore Dr B70 .... 53 A3
Skidmore Rd WV14 ...... 40 D2
Skilts Ave B98 .... 153 F1
Skinner La B5 .... 66 E1
Skinner St WV1 .... 163 B3
Skip La WS5 .... 43 E6
Skipness B77 .... 21 E5
Skipton Gdns CV2 ...... 114 B6
Skipton Gn WV6 .... 25 A5
Skipton Lodge CV2 ..... 114 B6
Skipton Pl WS11 .... 4 B7
Skipton Rd B16 .... 66 A1
Skipworth Rd CV3 ...... 115 A1
Skomer Cl B45 .... 101 E1
Sky Blue Way CV1 ...... 113 E3
Skydome The CV1 ...... 165 A2
Skye Cl
Birmingham B36 .... 70 B6
Nuneaton CV10 .... 72 F2
Tamworth B77 .... 35 F7
Skye Wlk 5 B64 .... 62 E1
Skylark Cl
Birmingham B23 .... 56 C7
Dudley DY5 .... 50 C1
Huntington WS12 .... 1 C7
Skylark Way DY10 ...... 117 A2
Slack La B20 .... 54 E2
Slacky La WS3 .... 14 F1
Slade Ave WS7 .... 7 A8
Slade Cl
Nuneaton CV11 .... 79 C8
West Bromwich B71 ...... 42 F2
Sladefield Inf Sch B8 .... 68 A5
Sladefield Rd B8 .... 68 A5
Slade Gdns WV8 .... 10 A4
Slade Gr B93 .... 127 F6
Slade Hill 3 WV6 .... 24 F3
Slade Jun & Inf Sch B23 . 56 D2
Slade La B28 .... 105 E3
Slade Lanker B34 .... 69 A5
Slade La
Sutton Coldfield B75 ...... 33 A3
Tamworth B77 .... 35 C4
Slade Mdw CV31 .... 162 E5
Sladen CE Mid Sch The
DY10 .... 116 F7
Sladepool Farm Rd B14 . 105 A2
Slade Rd
Birmingham B23 .... 56 D3
Halesowen B63 .... 82 C6
Sutton Coldfield B75 ...... 32 E3
Wolverhampton WV10 ..... 11 C3
Slaithwaite Rd B71 ...... 53 E4
Slaney Ct WS2 .... 42 C7
Slaney Rd WS2 .... 42 B6
Slatch House Rd B67 ..... 64 E2
Slateley Cres B90 .... 126 F6
Slater Cl B64 .... 62 F1
Slater Rd B93 .... 127 F4
Slaters La WS2 .... 42 B7
Slaters Pl WS2 .... 42 B7
Slater St
Bilston WV14 .... 40 E3
Darlaston WS10 .... 41 D6
Tipton,Dudley Port DY4 ... 52 A4
Tipton,Great Bridge DY4 ... 52 D5
Willenhall WV13 .... 27 C3
Sleaford Gr B28 .... 106 A7
Sleaford Rd B28 .... 106 B7
Sleath's Yd CV12 .... 78 B3
Sledmere Cl CV2 .... 96 B3
Sledmere Prim Sch DY2 .. 62 D6
Sledmore Rd DY2 .... 62 E7
Sleets Yd CV12 .... 78 A2
Slideslow Ave B60 ...... 137 B2
Slideslow Dr B60 .... 137 B3
Slieve The B20 .... 55 A3
Slim Ave WV14 .... 40 E3
Slimbridge Cl
2 Solihull B90 .... 127 A6
Redditch B97 .... 158 E5
Slim Rd WS2 .... 27 E2
Slims Gate B63 .... 83 A4
Slingfield Rd B31 .... 103 C1
Slingsby Cl CV11 .... 73 F2
Slingsby B77 .... 35 C7
Sling The
Dudley DY2 .... 62 C6
Kidderminster DY10 ..... 116 E6
Slitting Mill Cl B21 ...... 65 C8
Sloane Ho 6 B1 .... 66 C3
Sloane St B1 .... 66 C3
Slough The B97,B80 ..... 159 B4
Smallbrook La WV5 ...... 49 B7
Smallbrook Queensway
B5 .... 164 C1
Small Cl B67 .... 64 D5
Smalldale Rd B42 .... 55 D7
Smalley Cl WS11 .... 2 A5
Smalley Pl CV8 .... 147 F4
Small Heath Bridge B10,
B11 .... 87 B8
Small Heath Bsns Pk B10 87 F7
Small Heath Highway B10,
B11 .... 87 D6
Small Heath Sch
Birmingham B10 .... 87 D7
Birmingham B10 .... 87 D8
Small Heath Sta B10 ..... 87 D7
Small Heath Trad Est B11 . 87 D6
Small La B94 .... 141 E6
Smallman Rd CV10 ...... 72 A7
Smallshire Cl WV11 ..... 26 F5
Smallshire Way DY8 ..... 80 E8
Small St
Walsall WS1 .... 42 E8
West Bromwich B71 ...... 53 B5
Smallwood Almshouses
B98 .... 153 E3
Smallwood Arch 5 B98 . 153 E4
Smallwood Cl
Birmingham B24 .... 57 D3
Sutton Coldfield B76 ...... 46 E3
Smallwood Rd WV8 ...... 10 E2
Smallwood St B98 ...... 153 E3
Smarts Ave WS14 .... 32 A7
Smarts Rd CV12 .... 77 F1
Smeaton Gdns B18 ...... 65 E4
Smedley Crooke Pl B48 . 123 C2
Smeed Gr B24 .... 57 B3
Smercote Cl CV12 .... 77 D1
Smestow Ho B68 .... 64 B1
Smestow Sch WV3 .... 24 B1
Smestow St WV10 .... 25 D4

Smethwick Galton Bridge Sta B66 64 E7
Smethwick Rolfe Street Sta B66 65 A6
Smillie Pl WS11 1 F3
Smirrells Rd B28 105 E5
Smith Ave WS10 41 D4
Smith Cl
Smethwick B67 64 D3
Wolverhampton WV14 40 A1
Smithfield Rd WS3 14 D1
Smithfield Rise WS13 9 C8
Smithfields 4 DY8 81 A5
Smithford Way CV1 165 B3
Smith Ho WS3 14 C3
Smithmoor Cres B71 53 F8
Smith Pl DY4 52 B4
Smith Rd
Walsall WS2 42 C6
Wednesbury WS10 41 F1
Smiths Cl B32 84 B1
Smith's Cl WS7 6 D6
Smiths La B93 127 E7
Smith St
2 Royal Leamington Spa CV31 161 F7
Bedworth CV12 77 E1
Bilston WV14 40 D5
Birmingham B19 66 C5
Coventry CV6 113 F5
Dudley DY2 62 D7
Warwick CV34 160 F7
Wood End CV9 36 C1
Smiths Way B46 59 A3
Smiths Wood Sch B36 70 A6
Smithy Dr WS3 15 A4
Smithy La
Aston Flamville LE9 76 C8
Aston Flamville LE9 76 D8
Dudley DY5 50 B1
Lichfield WS13 3 A1
Tamworth B77 35 F7
Smithy The B26 89 C6
Smorrall La CV12 77 C2
Smout Cres WV14 39 F2
Smythe Gr CV34 155 E1
Snake La B48 139 A6
Snakes Lake La B61 136 D6
Snake Terr B48 139 A6
Snapdragon Dr WS5 43 A3
Snape Rd
Coventry CV2 114 F5
Wolverhampton WV11 13 B1
Sneyd Com Sch WS3 13 E2
Sneyd Hall Cl WS3 28 A8
Sneyd Hall Rd WS3 14 A1
Sneyd Ho WS3 13 F1
Sneyd La
Walsall WS3 13 F1
Willenhall WV11 13 C1
Snipe Cl WV10 12 B7
Snowberry Dr DY5 50 C1
Snowberry Gdns 6 B27 88 C5
Snowdon Cl CV10 72 B3
Snowdon Gr B63 82 D1
Snowdon Rd
Cannock WS11 1 E6
Stourbridge DY8 81 B6
Snowdon Rise DY3 50 D6
Snowdon Way
Willenhall WV12 13 B1
Wolverhampton WV10 25 B6
Snowdrop Cl
Bedworth CV12 77 E1
Brownhills WS8 15 D6
Snowford Cl B90 105 F1
Snow Hill Queensway B4 164 C3
Snow Hill Sta B3 164 B3
Snow Hill WV2 163 C2
Snows Drive Hill B90 126 D5
Snowshill Cl
Nuneaton CV11 78 F8
Redditch B98 154 B6
Snowshill Gdns DY1 50 F4
Soar Way LE10 75 A8
Soberton Cl WV11 26 F7
Soden Cl CV3 134 D6
Soden's Ave CV8 135 A1
Soho Ave B18 66 A7
Soho, Benson Road Sta B18 65 F6
Soho Cl B66 65 C6
Soho Hill B19 66 B7
Soho Ho B66 65 C6
Soho House Mus★ B18 66 A7
Soho Pool Way B18 66 A6
Soho Rd B21 65 F8
Soho St B66 65 C6
Soho Way B66 65 B6
Solari Cl DY4 52 C8
Solent Cl WV9 10 F2
Solent Ct B73 46 B5
Solent Dr CV2 96 F1
Solihull By-Pass B91 107 E4
Solihull Coll (Chelmsley Campus) B37 70 C4
Solihull Coll B91 107 A3
Solihull Hospl B91 107 C4
Solihull La B28 106 A6
Solihull Parkway B37 90 E8
Solihull Parkway Hospl B91 107 E5
Solihull Rd
Birmingham B11 87 D3
Hampton-in-A B92 108 E6
Solihull B90 106 D3
Solihull Ret Pk B90 126 C8
Solihull Sch B91 107 D4
Solihull Sta B91 107 A4
Solly Gr DY4 52 D7
Solva Cl WV1 26 B1
Solway Cl
Royal Leamington Spa CV31 162 C6
Tamworth B79 21 A7
Wednesbury WS10 42 C4
Somerby Dr B91 127 A8
Somercotes Rd B42 55 D8
Somerdale Rd B31 103 C4
Somerfield Cl WS4 15 C1
Somerfield Rd WS3 28 C7
Somerford Cl WS6 4 E1
Somerford Gdns WV10 11 E2
Somerford Pl WV13 26 F1
Somerford Rd B29 102 F8
Somerford Way WV14 51 B8
Somerland Rd B26 69 A1
Somerleyton Ave DY10 117 A5
Somerleyton Ct 3 DY10 117 A5
Somerly Cl CV3 134 F8
Somerset Cl B78 21 A1
Somerset Cres WS10 42 D4
Somerset Dr
Birmingham B31 122 F7
Nuneaton CV10 72 E4
Stourbridge DY8 80 D7
Somerset Ho B33 69 A2
Somerset Pl WS11 1 F3
Somerset Rd
Birmingham B15 85 F5
Birmingham,Erdington B23 56 F6
Birmingham,Handsworth B20 54 F2
Coventry CV1 113 C5
Walsall WS4 29 A4
West Bromwich B71 53 D6
Willenhall WV13 27 D2
Somers Pl 4 CV32 161 E8
Somers Rd
Halesowen B62 83 C5
Keresley CV7 95 A6
Meriden CV7 91 F1
Walsall WS2 42 A7
Somers Sq 9 B63 83 B3
Somerton Dr
Birmingham,Erdington B23 57 A6
Birmingham,Marston Green B37 90 B7
Somerville Ct
2 Sutton Coldfield B73 46 A2
Tamworth B79 20 D6
Somerville Ho B37 70 D3
Somerville Prim Sch B10 87 D8
Somerville Rd
Birmingham B10 87 E8
Sutton Coldfield B73 46 A3
Somery Rd
Birmingham B29 85 A2
Dudley DY1 51 C3
Sommerfield Rd B32 84 D3
Sommerville Dr B73 46 A4
Sommerville Rd CV2 114 C4
Sonata Rd B60 137 C1
Sonning Dr WV9 10 F2
Sopwith Croft B35 58 A2
Sorbus B77 22 B4
Soredale Croft CV3 115 A1
Sorrel Cl
Coventry CV4 131 E8
Featherstone WV10 12 B7
Lichfield WS13 8 E6
Tipton B69 52 B2
Sorrel Dr
Birmingham B27 88 B2
Walsall WS5 43 A3
Sorrel Gr B24 57 D3
Sorrel Ho B24 57 D3
Sorrell Pl CV10 78 D8
Sorrell Rd CV10 78 D8
Sorrell Wlk DY5 81 B6
Sorrel B77 22 B5
Sorrento Ct B13 87 A3
Soudan B97 153 D2
Souters Ho B32 102 D8
Southacre Ave B5 86 E8
Southall Cres WV14 40 C1
Southall Rd WV11 27 A8
Southall's La DY1 51 B1
Southam Cl
Birmingham B28 105 E8
Coventry CV4 131 E7
Southam Dr B73 46 B1
Southampton St WV1 163 C4
Southam Rd
Birmingham B28 105 E8
Radford Semele CV31 162 E6
South Ave
Coventry CV2 114 A2
Stourbridge DY8 80 F4
Wolverhampton WV11 26 C5
Southbank Ct CV8 147 F4
Southbank Ho 10 CV34 161 D8
Southbank Rd CV6 112 E5
South Bank Rd B64 82 E8
Southbank Rd
Cradley Heath B64 82 F8
Kenilworth CV8 147 F4
Southbank View DY6 60 E4
South Birmingham Coll (Digbeth Ctr for Arts &Digital Media) B5 66 F1
South Birmingham Coll (Hall Green Campus) B28 105 E8
Southborough Terr 1 CV31 162 A6
Southbourne Ave
Birmingham B34 68 D6
Walsall WS2 28 B1
Southbourne Cl B29 86 A2
Southbourne Pl WS11 1 D2
Southbourne Rd WV10 11 C3
South Bromsgrove Com High Sch (Tech Coll) B60 150 F8
South Car Park Rd B40 90 E3
South Cl WS11 4 C8
Southcote Gr B38 103 D1
Southcott Ave DY5 81 D8
Southcott Way CV2 96 F1
South Cres
Bromsgrove B60 137 A1
Featherstone WV10 12 C6
Southcrest Gdns B97 153 D1
Southcrest Rd B98 154 A2
Southcroft Rd B23 56 E3
South Dene B67 64 F5
Southdown Ave B18 66 A6
Southdown Ct DY6 60 D6
South Dr
Birmingham B5 86 C4
Coleshill B46 70 E6
Sutton Coldfield B75 46 C6
South East Quadrant 8 B98 153 E4
Southern Cl DY6 60 F3
Southern Cross WS14 9 C7
Southerndown Rd DY3 50 B7
Southern Dr B30 104 D3
Southern Ho B13 105 A7
Southern Rd B8 68 C6
Southern Way WS10 41 C3
Southey Cl
Solihull B91 127 B8
Willenhall WV12 27 E8
Southfield Ave
Birmingham,Castle Bromwich B36 69 B8
Birmingham,Edgbaston B16 65 D3
Southfield Cl
Aldridge WS9 30 A6
Nuneaton CV10 73 D5
Southfield Dr
Birmingham B28 106 A5
Kenilworth CV8 148 A6
Southfield Gr WV3 38 C7
Southfield Rd
Birmingham B16 65 D3
Hinckley LE10 75 E7
Wednesfield WV11 26 F5
Southfields Prim Sch CV1 113 E3
Southfields Rd B91 106 F1
Southfields CV32 157 A3
Southfield Way WS6 4 F2
Southgate WS11 4 B7
Southgate Cl DY11 116 A4
Southgate B64 82 D8
Southgate End WS11 4 B7
Southgate Rd B44 44 E2
Southgate Way 3 DY1 51 B2
Southgate WV1 163 A3
South Gdns DY9 99 A4
South Gn WV4 38 D5
South Gr
Birmingham,Aston B6 66 D8
Birmingham,Erdington B23 56 F5
Birmingham,Lozells B19 66 B8
South Holme B9 67 C2
Southlands 8 CV31 162 B7
Southlands Ct B97 153 C1
Southlands Rd B13 87 A1
Southlea Ave CV31 161 E6
Southlea Cl CV31 161 E6
Southleigh Ave CV5 132 F7
Southmead Cres B98 153 F3
Southmead Dr B60 137 B6
Southmead Gdns B80 159 E3
Southminster Dr B14 104 E6
South Moons Moat Ind Est B98 154 D4
South Oval DY3 50 E5
South Park Mews DY5 61 C2
South Par B72 46 C4
Southport Cl CV3 134 B5
South Range 4 B11 87 B6
South Rd
Birmingham,Erdington B23 56 F4
Birmingham,Hockley B18 66 A6
Birmingham,King's Heath B14 104 E8
Birmingham,Northfield B31 102 F2
Birmingham,Sparkbrook B11 87 B7
Bromsgrove B60 151 B7
Smethwick B67 64 F5
Stourbridge DY8 80 E4
Tipton DY4 52 B8
West Hagley DY9 99 A4
Wolverhampton WV4 39 F4
South Ridge CV5 112 B4
South Road Ave B18 66 A6
South Roundhay B33 69 A3
Southside Bsns Ctr B12 87 A5
South St 3 DY10 116 F6
South Staffordshire Bsns Pk WS11 4 C4
South St
Birmingham B17 85 D5
Brierley Hill DY5 61 C2
Coventry CV1 113 E3
South St *continued*
Redditch B98 153 E3
South Street Gdns WS1 42 D8
South St
Walsall WS1 42 D8
Willenhall WV13 26 F1
Wolverhampton WV10 25 C6
South Terr CV31 162 B3
South View B43 54 E7
South View Cl
Codsall WV8 10 B2
Featherstone WV10 12 B6
South View CV35 160 A6
South View Rd
Royal Leamington Spa CV32 157 C5
Sedgley DY3 50 C8
Southview Ridge DY5 81 D7
Southville Bglws For Old People B14 105 B4
Southwark Cl WS13 3 C3
South Way B40 90 F3
Southway Ct DY6 60 F4
Southway CV31 162 A5
Southwick Dr B77 21 C3
Southwick Pl WV14 40 D7
Southwick Rd B62 83 D8
South Wlk B31 103 C1
Southwold Ave B30 104 C3
Southwood Ave B34 69 B7
Southwood Cl DY6 60 E5
Southwood Covert B14 104 C2
Sovereign Cl CV8 147 F1
Sovereign Ct 7 B1 66 C3
Sovereign Dr DY1 50 E2
Sovereign Hts B31 102 C1
Sovereign Rd
Birmingham B30 104 A4
Coventry CV5 113 A2
Sovereign Row CV5 113 A2
Sovereign Way B13 86 F4
Sovereign Wlk 7 WS1 28 F2
Sovereign Works DY1 50 E4
Sowerby March B24 57 D4
Sowers Cl WV12 27 D5
Sowers Ct B75 32 D4
Sowers Gdns WV12 27 D5
Sowe Valley Prim Sch CV3 134 D7
Spa Cl LE10 71 E1
Spadesbourne Rd B60 137 C6
Spa Gr B30 104 C8
Spa La LE10 71 E1
Sparkbrook St CV1 113 F3
Sparkbrook Workshops CV1 113 F3
Spark St B11 87 A7
Sparrey Dr B30 104 A8
Sparrow Cl WS10 42 B5
Sparrow Cock La B93 129 C1
Spartan Cl CV34 161 E4
Spartan Ind Ctr B70 52 E6
Spa View CV31 162 B4
Speakers Cl B69 63 B7
Spearhill WS14 9 E8
Speed Rd DY4 51 E7
Speedway La CV8 135 F7
Speedwell Cl
6 Bedworth CV12 77 D2
Aldridge WS9 30 A5
Birmingham B25 88 A6
Wednesfield WV11 26 E5
Speedwell Dr CV7 130 A6
Speedwell Gdns
Brierley Hill DY5 81 B6
Featherstone WV10 12 B8
Speedwell Ho B38 104 A1
Speedwell Rd
Birmingham,Balsall Heath B5 86 D6
Birmingham,Tyseley B25 88 A6
Speedwell Trad Est B11 88 A6
Speedy Cl WS11 1 E5
Spencer Ave
Coventry CV5 113 A1
Tipton WV14 51 C8
Spencer Cl
5 West Bromwich B71 53 F8
Birmingham B24 57 D4
Dudley DY3 50 A4
Oldbury B69 63 B8
Spencer Dr WS7 6 E8
Spencer Rd
Coventry CV5 165 A1
Lichfield WS14 9 B6
Spencer's La CV7 110 E1
Spencer St
Birmingham B18 66 C4
Hinckley LE10 71 D1
Kidderminster DY11 116 C4
Royal Leamington Spa CV31 161 F7
Spencer Yd CV31 161 F7
Spennells Fst Sch DY10 117 A2
Spennells Valley Nature Reserve★ DY10 117 A3
Spennells Valley Rd DY10 117 A3
Spenser Ave WV6 23 F4
Spenser Cl B79 21 A6
Spenser Wlk B61 137 A8
Spernal Ash B80 159 F1
Spernal La B80 159 F1
Spernall Gr B29 85 A1
Spetchley Cl B97 158 C6
Spey Cl B5 86 D6
Sphinx Dr CV3 114 B1
Spiceland Rd B31 102 F6
Spiers Cl B93 128 A6
Spies Cl B62 83 F6
Spies La B62 83 F5
Spills Mdw DY3 50 E5
Spilsbury Cl CV32 156 E2
Spilsbury Croft B91 127 A8
Spindle La B90 126 A6
Spindle St CV1 113 D6
Spindles The LE10 75 F5
Spindlewood Cl 1 WS12 2 D1
Spinners End Dr B64 62 D1
Spinners End Ind Est B64 82 D8
Spinney Cl
Binley Woods CV3 135 E7
Birmingham B31 103 B3
Kidderminster DY11 116 A7
Norton Canes WS11 5 F5
Polesworth B78 36 F8
Stourbridge DY8 60 C3
Walsall WS3 15 A2
Spinney Dr B90 126 D4
Spinney Farm Rd WS11 4 B7
Spinney Hill CV34 156 A1
Spinney La CV10 72 C4
Spinney Mews B97 153 C1
Spinney Rd LE10 75 C6
Spinney The
Birmingham B15 85 E5
Birmingham,Brown's Green B20 54 E4
Coventry CV4 132 D3
Dudley DY3 50 C2
Royal Leamington Spa CV32 156 D1
Solihull B91 127 C8
Sutton Coldfield B74 31 B6
Wolverhampton WV3 24 D1
Wythall B47 125 B4
Spinning School La B79 21 B5
Spiral Cl B62 83 E8
Spiral Ct
Birmingham B24 56 E2
Dudley DY3 50 D3
Stourbridge DY8 81 A4
Sutton Coldfield B76 46 F3
Wednesfield WV11 26 E7
Spiral Gn B24 57 C4
Spirehouse La B60 137 E5
Spires The
Lichfield WS14 9 E6
Nuneaton CV10 72 C4
Spires View B61 136 F3
Spitfire Cl CV5 112 C1
Spitfire Pk B24 57 C2
Spitfire Rd B24 57 D2
Spitfire Way B35 58 A2
Splash La WS12 2 C3
Spode Pl WS11 2 B2
Spondon Gr B34 69 C5
Spondon Rd WV11 26 E8
Spon End CV1,CV5 113 A3
Spon Gate Ho CV1 113 A2
Spon Gate Prim Sch CV1 113 A3
Spon Lane Ind Est B66 64 D8
Spon Lane S B70 53 D1
Spon Lane Trad Est B70 53 D2
Spon La S B66 64 D8
Spon La B70 53 D1
Spon St CV1 165 A3
Spoon Dr B38 103 D2
Spooner Croft B5 86 E8
Spooners Cl B92 107 F7
Spouthouse La B43 54 F7
Spout La
Walsall WS1 42 E7
Walsall WS1 42 E8
Spreadbury Cl B17 84 F8
Sprig Croft B36 68 C8
Spring Ave B65 63 D2
Springavon Croft B17 85 B6
Springbank B9 68 A3
Springbank Rd B15 86 D7
Springbrook Cl B36 58 D1
Springbrook La B94 142 A7
Spring Cl
6 Coventry CV1 113 E3
Solihull B91 106 F3
Walsall WS4 15 C2
West Hagley DY9 98 F4
Spring Coppice Dr B93 128 A3
Spring Cres B64 82 F7
Springcroft Rd B11 87 F2
Spring Ct
Walsall WS1 43 A8
West Bromwich B70 53 D2
Springdale Ct CV11 73 D3
Springdale Jun & Inf Schs WV4 38 D5
Springfield Ave
6 Birmingham B12 87 A6
Bromsgrove B60 151 A8
Sedgley DY3 39 E1
Stourbridge DY9 81 E4
Springfield B23 56 E3
Springfield Cl B65 63 A5
Springfield Cres
Bedworth CV12 78 B2
Dudley DY2 62 F8
Solihull B92 89 C3
Sutton Coldfield B76 47 A4
West Bromwich B70 53 E1
Springfield Ct
Birmingham B28 105 F8
Sutton Coldfield B75 47 C5

Springfield Ct *continued*
Wolverhampton WV10 11 D4
Springfield Dr
Birmingham B14 86 E1
Halesowen B62 83 D7
Springfield Gn DY3 39 E1
Springfield Gr DY3 39 D1
Springfield Ho DY10 116 F8
Springfield House Com Specl Sch B93 129 A5
Springfield Ind Est B69 64 B7
Springfield La
Kidderminster DY10 116 F8
Rowley Regis B65,DY2 62 F5
Wolverhampton WV10 11 D4
Springfield Mill Ct WS10 41 E6
Springfield Pk LE10 71 A3
Springfield Pl CV1 165 C4
Springfield Prim Sch
Birmingham B13 87 D2
Rowley Regis B65 63 A4
Springfield Rd
Bilston WV14 40 E7
Birmingham,Castle Bromwich B36 69 D8
Birmingham,King's Heath B14 104 F8
Birmingham,Moseley B13 87 D2
Coventry CV1 165 C4
Halesowen B62 83 D7
Hinckley LE10 75 D7
Nuneaton CV11 73 E2
Oldbury B68 64 C4
Sutton Coldfield B75,B76 47 A4
Tamworth B77 35 D8
Wolverhampton WV10 25 E3
Springfield Rise WS12 2 C6
Springfields B46 70 F5
Springfields Rd DY5 61 B2
Springfield St B18 66 A3
Springfields WS4 29 C6
Springfield Terr B65 62 F5
Spring Gdns
4 Dudley DY2 62 D8
Birmingham B21 65 F7
Smethwick B66 65 B3
Spring Gr B19 66 B6
Spring Grove Cres DY11 116 B3
Spring Grove Gdns B18 65 F6
Spring Grove Rd DY11 116 B3
Spring Head WS10 41 F2
Springhill Ave WV4 38 C4
Spring Hill
Birmingham,Erdington B24 56 F3
Birmingham,Hockley B18 66 A4
Springhill Cl
Walsall WS4 15 D1
Willenhall WV12 27 D7
Springhill Ct 5 WS1 42 F8
Springhill Gdns B97 152 F2
Springhill Gr WV4 38 C4
Springhill CV10 72 A8
Spring Hill Ind Est B18 66 A4
Springhill La WV4 38 B4
Spring Hill Pas B18 66 A3
Springhill Pk WV4 38 B3
Springhill Prim Sch WS7 7 B6
Springhill Rd
Brownhills WS8 16 A7
Burntwood WS7 7 A6
Spring Hill Rd CV10 72 C6
Springhill Rd
Walsall WS1 28 F1
Wednesfield WV11 26 E7
Spring La
Birmingham B24 57 A3
Hockley Heath B94 143 B5
Kenilworth CV8 148 A5
Lapworth B94 143 D3
Radford Semele CV31 162 E5
Romsley B62 100 D4
Walsall WS4 15 C2
Willenhall WV12 27 C4
Spring Mdw
3 Cradley Heath B64 62 F1
Cheslyn Hay WS6 4 D1
Halesowen B63 82 F2
Tipton DY4 52 C6
Springmeadow Gr B19 66 D6
Springmeadow Rd B15 86 D7
Spring Meadow Rd DY2 62 C2
Spring Meadows Cl WV8 10 B4
Spring Parklands DY1 62 A8
Spring Pool CV34 160 E7
Spring Rd
Barnacle CV7 97 B6
Birmingham,Balsall Heath B15 86 D7
Birmingham,Tyseley B11 87 F3
Coventry CV6 95 F1
Dudley DY2 62 D6
Lichfield WS13 3 D2
Smethwick B66 64 D8
Walsall WS4 15 D1
Wolverhampton WV4 40 A4
Spring Road Ind Est WV4 40 A4
Spring Road Sta B28 88 A2
Springs Ave B61 121 A1
Springside B98 159 C8
Springslade B32 84 F5
Springslade Dr B24 57 D3
Spring St
Birmingham B15 86 D8
Cannock WS11 4 E8
Spring St *continued*
Halesowen B63 82 D6
Springs The B64 63 A1
Spring St
Stourbridge DY9 81 E4
Tipton DY4 52 C8
Spring Terr WS7 6 E5
Springthorpe Gn B24 57 C4
Springthorpe Rd
Birmingham,Pype Hayes B24 57 D5
Birmingham,Tyburn B24 57 D3
Springvale Ave
Bilston WV14 40 B4
Walsall WS5 43 C7
Springvale Bsns Pk WV14 40 B4
Spring Vale Cl WV14 40 A1
Springvale Dr B97 152 F3
Spring Vale Ind Pk WV14 40 C5
Spring Vale Island WV14 40 C4
Springvale Prim Sch WS11 4 E8
Spring Vale Prim Sch WV4 39 E4
Springvale Rd B97 152 F2
Spring Vale Rd B65 63 A5
Springvale St WV13 27 B3
Springvale Way WV14 40 C4
Springwell Rd CV31 162 D6
Spring Wlk
Halesowen B63 82 D1
Oldbury B69 64 A5
Walsall WS2 28 B3
Sproat Ave WS10 41 C5
Spruce Gr
4 Royal Leamington Spa CV31 161 F5
Birmingham B24 57 B2
Spruce Rd
5 Coventry CV2 96 B2
Nuneaton CV10 72 E7
Walsall WS5 43 B3
Spruces The DY9 98 F4
Spruce B77 22 B4
Spruce Way WV3 24 D1
Spur Tree Ave WV3 24 A1
Squadron Cl B35 58 C4
Square Cl B32 84 C3
Square The
2 Birmingham,Ladywood B15 66 B1
3 Birmingham B17 85 C5
Aldridge WS9 30 B6
Alvechurch B48 139 B6
Birmingham B17 85 B7
Brierley Hill DY2 61 F6
Coventry CV2 115 A7
Fazeley B78 35 A8
Kenilworth CV8 147 F4
Nuneaton CV11 73 E2
Solihull B91 107 C3
Tipton DY4 52 D7
Willenhall WV12 27 D8
Wolverhampton WV2 163 C1
Squires Croft
Coventry CV2 96 F1
Sutton Coldfield B76 47 A2
Squires Ct DY5 81 C8
Squires Gate WS7 7 C8
Squires Gate Rd 4 WV13 27 B2
Squires Gate Wlk B35 58 A3
Squires Gn LE10 75 F6
Squires Way CV4 132 D6
Squire's Wlk 7 WS10 41 F3
Squirhill Pl 1 CV31 162 B7
Squirrel Cl
Cannock WS12 2 D2
Huntington WS12 1 C6
Squirrel Hollow B76 47 A2
Squirrels Hollow B68 84 D7
Squirrels The WS14 9 C7
Squirrel Wlk
Sutton Coldfield B74 31 C5
Wolverhampton WV4 39 A5
Stable Croft B71 53 F7
Stable Ct DY3 50 E6
Stableford Cl
Birmingham B32 84 F3
Redditch B97 158 D7
Stables The
Berkswell CV7 110 C4
Birmingham B29 86 A2
Hinckley LE10 75 D5
Royal Leamington Spa CV32 156 C1
Stable Way B60 150 E6
Stable Wlk CV11 73 F2
Stacey Cl B64 62 E1
Stacey Dr B13 105 A5
Stacey Grange Gdns B45 122 A6
Stackhouse Cl WS9 16 A4
Stackhouse Dr WS3 15 A4
Stadium Cl
Coventry CV6 95 D2
Kidderminster DY10 116 F4
Willenhall WV13 27 B3
Stadium Dr B64 62 C1
Stafford Cl
Bulkington CV12 79 C2
Walsall WS3 14 B2
Stafford Ct
Birmingham B43 54 E7
Wolverhampton WV10 11 C5
Stafford Dr B71 53 B6
Stafford Ho B33 69 E2
Stafford La WS12 2 B5
Stafford Rd
Birmingham B21 65 F8
Stafford Rd *continued*
Cannock WS11 1 D1
Coven Heath WV10 11 D4
Darlaston WS10 41 C6
Huntington WS11,WS12 1 C5
Walsall WS3 14 B4
Staffordshire Pool Cl 2 B6 55 F1
Staffordshire Univ WS13 9 B7
Stafford St
Bilston WV14 40 D5
Birmingham B5 164 D3
Cannock WS12 2 E1
Dudley DY1 51 B1
Walsall WS2 28 E3
Wednesbury WS10 41 F2
Willenhall WV13 27 A2
Wolverhampton WV1 163 C4
Stafford Way B43 54 E7
Staff Way B23 56 E4
Stagborough Way WS12 2 B4
Stag Cres
Norton Canes WS11 6 A6
Walsall WS3 28 E6
Stag Dr WS12 1 C6
Stag Hill Rd WS3 28 E7
Stag Ind Est WV14 40 F4
Stag Wlk B76 57 D7
Staines Cl CV11 73 F7
Stainforth Cl CV11 74 A2
Stainsby Ave B19 66 C5
Stainsby Croft B90 127 B5
Staircase La CV5 112 C7
Stakenbridge La DY10 98 D4
Staley Croft WS12 1 C4
Stalling's La DY6 60 D8
Stambermill Cl DY9 81 D5
Stambermill Ho DY9 81 E5
Stambermill Ind Est DY9 81 D6
Stamford Ave CV3 133 C6
Stamford Cres WS7 7 A8
Stamford Croft B91 107 B2
Stamford Gdns CV32 156 E1
Stamford Gr B20 55 C1
Stamford Rd
Birmingham B20 55 C1
Brierley Hill DY5 81 C6
Stamford St DY8 80 F7
Stamford Way WS9 16 C1
Stanbrook Rd B90 127 A5
Stanbury Ave WS10 41 B6
Stanbury Rd B14 105 B4
Stancroft Gr B26 89 A8
Standard Ave CV4 112 B1
Standard Way B24 67 F8
Standbridge Way DY4 52 F5
Standedge B77 36 B7
Standhills Rd DY6 60 E6
Standish Cl CV2 114 E2
Standlake Ave B36 68 D7
Standlake Mews 14 CV31 162 C6
Standleys Twr B23 57 A6
Stand St CV34 160 D5
Stanfield Rd
Birmingham B32 84 E6
Birmingham,Pheasey B43 44 D5
Stanford Ave B42 55 A7
Stanford Cl B97 158 B6
Stanford Dr B65 63 B4
Stanford Gr B63 82 C1
Stanford Rd WV2 163 B1
Stanford Way 2 B69 63 E4
Stanhoe Cl DY5 81 D8
Stanhope Ho B79 21 A4
Stanhope Rd B67 64 F3
Stanhope St
Birmingham B12 86 F7
Dudley DY2 62 E4
Wolverhampton WV3 163 A2
Stanhope Way B43 44 E4
Stanhurst Way B71 43 A2
Stanier Ave CV1 113 B4
Stanier Cl WS4 29 B7
Stanier Gr B20 55 B2
Staniforth St B4 164 C4
Stanklyn La DY10 117 C1
Stanley Ave
Birmingham B32 84 E7
Solihull B90 106 B4
Sutton Coldfield B75 46 F4
Stanley Cl
Birmingham B28 106 A5
Redditch B98 154 A5
Wednesfield WV11 26 F8
Stanley Ct
9 Birmingham B13 87 B2
Perton WV6 23 E4
Royal Leamington Spa CV31 162 C7
Stanley Gr 2 B11 87 B6
Stanley Pl
Bilston WV14 40 B5
Birmingham B13 86 F3
Walsall WS4 29 B6
Stanley Rd
Birmingham B68 84 C7
Birmingham,King's Heath B14 104 D7
Birmingham,Nechells B7 67 C7
Cannock WS12 2 A6
Coventry CV5 132 F8
Darlaston WS10 41 D5
Hinckley LE10 71 C2
Nuneaton CV11 73 A5
Stourbridge DY8 80 F3
Walsall WS4 29 B6
West Bromwich B71 53 E7
Stanley Rd *continued*
Wolverhampton WV10 11 D1
Stanley St WS3 14 D1
Stanmore Gr B62 84 A3
Stanmore Rd B16 65 C1
Stansbury Ho 3 WS2 42 C8
Stansfield Gr CV8 148 D4
Stanton Ave DY1 51 A6
Stanton Bridge Prim Sch CV6 113 F6
Stanton Gr
Birmingham B26 88 F8
Solihull B90 106 A4
Tipton DY4 52 A5
Stanton Ho 2 B71 42 F1
Stanton Rd
Birmingham B43 54 D8
Royal Leamington Spa CV31 162 C6
Solihull B90 106 A4
Wolverhampton WV1 25 F2
Stanton Wlk CV34 155 D1
Stanville Jun & Inf Sch B26 89 C6
Stanville Rd B26 89 C6
Stanway Gdns B71 53 D6
Stanway Gr B44 44 F3
Stanway Rd
Coventry CV5 133 A8
Solihull B90 106 C4
West Bromwich B71 53 D6
Stanwell Gr B23 56 E6
Stanwick Ave B33 69 E3
Stan Williams Ct CV11 73 D4
Stapenhall Rd B90 127 A5
Staple Flat B60 137 C8
Stapleford Croft B14 104 C2
Stapleford Gdns WS7 7 D6
Stapleford Gr DY8 60 E2
Staple Hall Rd B31 103 B2
Staplehurst Rd B28 105 F8
Staple Lodge Rd B31 103 C2
Staples Cl CV12 79 C3
Stapleton Cl
Redditch B98 154 D3
Studley B80 159 D3
Sutton Coldfield B76 58 B6
Stapleton Dr B37 70 A4
Stapleton La
Barwell LE9 71 F8
Hinckley CV13 71 A8
Stapleton Rd
Aldridge WS9 29 F5
Studley B80 159 D4
Stapylton Ave B17 85 B5
Stapylton Ct 5 B17 85 B5
Starbank Prim Sch (Annexe) B10 68 B1
Starbank Prim Sch B10 88 A8
Starbank Rd B10 88 A8
Starbold Cres B93 128 B5
Starbold Ct B93 128 A6
Star City B7 67 D8
Star Cl
Tipton DY4 52 C5
Willenhall WS2 27 F4
Starcrest Ind Est DY5 61 E1
Starcross Cl CV2 114 C7
Starcross Rd B27 88 C2
Star Ct B91 107 D6
Stare Gn CV4 132 D5
Stareton Cl CV4 132 F6
Star Hill B15 86 B8
Star Ind Pk CV2 114 F5
Starkey Croft B37 70 D2
Starkie Dr B68 64 C4
Starley Ct CV3 135 A7
Starley Pk CV7 96 B8
Starley Rd CV1 165 A2
Starley Way B37 90 C6
Starling Ct WV10 11 B3
Star St
Stourbridge DY9 81 F5
Wolverhampton WV3 38 E8
Startin Cl CV7 95 F7
Startpoint Trad Est B11 87 D4
Statham Dr B16 65 C2
Station App
Barnt Green B45 138 D8
Dorridge B93 127 F2
Kidderminster DY10 116 F5
Lichfield WS13 9 F8
Royal Leamington Spa CV31 161 F7
Solihull B91 107 A4
Sutton Coldfield B74 31 F6
Sutton Coldfield,Maney B73 46 B6
Station Ave
Birmingham B16 65 C1
Coventry CV4 131 D8
Warwick CV34 160 F8
Station Bldgs B46 59 B3
Station Cl WS3 28 B8
Station Cotts
Blackwell B60 138 A4
Shenstone WS14 17 F6
Station Ct WS11 4 F8
Station Dr
Blakedown DY10 98 C2
Brierley Hill,Quarry Bank DY5 61 E2
Brierley Hill,Silver End DY5 61 B1
Earlswood B94 125 D1
Solihull B92 88 E1
Sutton Coldfield B74 46 B8
Tipton DY4 52 B4
West Hagley DY9 99 A6
Stationfields Park Homes B79 21 C5
Station La B94 144 D3
Station Link Rd B26 90 D4
Station Pl WS3 28 B8
Station Rd
Aldridge WS9 30 A5
Alvechurch B48 139 A5
Balsall Common CV7 130 B7
Bilston WV14 40 E5
Birmingham,Acock's Green B27 88 C3
Birmingham,Aston B6 55 F1
Birmingham B17 85 C6
Birmingham,Erdington B23 56 F5
Birmingham,Handsworth B21 65 C8
Birmingham,King's Heath B14 86 E1
Birmingham,King's Norton B30 103 E4
Birmingham,Marston Green B37 90 A8
Birmingham,Northfield B31 103 A2
Birmingham,Stechford B33 68 E3
Blackwell B60 138 A5
Brierley Hill DY5 61 C3
Cannock WS12 2 C6
Coleshill B46 59 F1
Cradley Heath,Haden Cross B64 83 A8
Dorridge B93 128 B4
Great Wyrley WS6 4 F4
Hammerwich WS7 7 E3
Hampton-in-A B92 109 B7
Hinckley LE10 75 D8
Kenilworth CV8 147 F4
Kingswood B94 144 D4
Lichfield WS13 9 C7
Oldbury B69 64 A5
Rowley Regis B65 63 D2
Shenstone WS14 17 F6
Solihull B91 107 B4
Stourbridge DY9 81 E6
Studley B80 159 D4
Sutton Coldfield B73 46 A1
Walsall,Rushall WS4 29 A7
Walsall WS3 15 A3
Warwick CV34 160 F7
West Hagley DY9 99 A6
Wombourne WV5 49 A8
Wythall B47 125 B3
Station Road Ind Est B65 63 D2
Station St E CV6 113 E7
Station St W CV6 113 E7
Station Sq CV1 165 B1
Station St
Birmingham B5 164 B2
Bromsgrove B60 136 F1
Cheslyn Hay WS6 4 E3
Cradley Heath B64 82 C8
Darlaston WS10 41 E7
Station Street W Bsns Pk CV6 113 D7
Station St
Sutton Coldfield B73 46 C5
Tipton DY4 52 B5
Walsall,Blakenall Heath WS3 28 B8
Walsall WS2 28 E1
Station Villas WS10 41 E6
Station Way B97 153 D3
Staulton Gn 5 B69 63 E4
Staunton Rd
Walsall WS3 14 A3
Whitnash CV31 162 A5
Staveley Rd
Birmingham B14 104 D6
Wolverhampton WV1 25 C4
Staverton Cl CV5 112 A3
Stead Cl
Walsall WS2 28 C5
Wednesbury DY4 41 B1
Steadman Croft DY4 52 D8
Stechford La B8 68 D5
Stechford Prim Sch B33 68 D2
Stechford Rd B34 68 E5
Stechford Ret Pk B33 68 E4
Stechford Sta B33 68 D3
Stechford Trad Est B33 68 E3
Steel Bright Rd B66 65 C6
Steel Dr WV10 25 D8
Steel Gr B25 88 C7
Steelhouse La
Birmingham B4 164 C3
Wolverhampton WV2 39 E8
Steelmans Rd WS10 41 F7
Steelpark Rd B62 83 C7
Steelpark Way WV11 26 E4
Steel Rd B31 102 F2
Steel Rdbt WS10 41 E2
Steene Gr B31 102 D3
Steeplefield Rd CV6 113 A5
Steeples The DY8 81 B3
Steepwood Croft B30 103 D4
Steere Ave B79 21 C7
Steetley Ind Est WV14 51 C7
Stella Croft B37 70 C2
Stella Gr B43 54 C8
Stella Rd DY4 51 F6
Stenbury Cl WV10 11 F4
Stencills Dr WS4 29 B3
Stencills Rd WS4 29 B4
Stennels Ave B62 83 E4
Stennels Cl CV6 112 F8
Stennels Cres B62 83 E4
Stephanie Gr B77 22 A6

Stephens Cl WV11 .... 26 F8
Stephens Ct DY4......... 52 A6
Stephens Ind Est B11 .... 87 F4
Stephenson Ave WS2 .... 28 B5
Stephenson Cl
Royal Leamington Spa
CV32................ 156 C1
Tamworth B77........... 22 A2
Stephenson Dr
Birmingham B37 .... 70 B2
Perton WV6............. 23 E5
Stephenson Pl B2....... 164 C2
Stephenson Rd
Bedworth CV7 .... 96 C7
Hinckley LE10 .... 74 E7
Stephenson Sq WS2 ..... 28 B5
Stephenson St
Birmingham B2 .... 164 B2
Wolverhampton WV3..... 163 A2
Stephenson Way WS12.....2 B5
Stephens Rd B76 .... 47 A4
Stephens Wlk WS13....... 3 A2
Stepney Rd CV2......... 114 A4
Stepping Stone Cl WS2... 27 F4
Stepping Stones Rd CV5. 112 F4
Stepping Stones DY8...... 81 B5
Steppingstone St DY1.... 51 B1
Sterling Pk
Brierley Hill DY5 .... 61 F4
Hinckley LE10 .... 74 D8
Tamworth B77........... 35 E7
Sterling Way CV11 .... 78 E8
Sterndale Rd B42 .... 55 C6
Stevenage Wlk 2 CV2 .. 115 A7
Steven Dr WV14 .... 40 E1
Stevens Ave B32 .... 84 D2
Stevens Dr WS12 .... 2 D6
Stevens Gate WV2 ...... 163 B1
Stevens Ho CV1......... 165 C4
Stevenson Ave B98 ..... 153 F3
Stevenson Rd
Coventry CV6.......... 113 A8
Tamworth B79........... 21 A6
Stevenson Wlk WS14.......9 B6
Stevens Rd DY9.......... 81 D2
Steve Roberts Ct DY11 .. 116 A6
Steward St B18.......... 66 A3
Stewart Cl CV4 .... 112 D2
Stewart Ct DY10 .... 116 F5
Stewart Rd
Brownhills WS9.......... 16 A3
Kingswinford DY6 .... 60 D4
Stewarts Rd B62......... 83 D7
Stewart St
Nuneaton CV11 .... 73 C3
Wolverhampton WV2..... 163 B1
Stewkins Ct 4 DY8 ...... 80 E8
Stewkins DY8............ 80 E8
Steyning Rd B26 .... 88 E5
Stickley La DY3 .... 50 C4
Stidfall Gr CV31......... 162 D6
Stilehouse Cres B65 ..... 63 C2
Stilthouse Gr B45....... 122 A7
Stirchley Com Sch B30.. 104 A6
Stirchley Trad Est B30... 104 B6
Stirling Ave
Hinckley LE10 .... 71 A1
Royal Leamington Spa
CV32................ 157 B6
Stirling Cl CV3.......... 134 F8
Stirling Cres WV12....... 27 B6
Stirling Ct B16........... 65 F1
Stirling Ho B75 .... 46 C5
Stirling Pk B90 .... 126 E8
Stirling Pl WS11 ....4 B8
Stirling Rd
Bilston WV14............ 40 F2
Birmingham B16 .... 65 F1
Dudley DY2 .... 62 E6
Solihull B90 .... 126 E8
Sutton Coldfield B73 ...... 45 E2
Stirrup Cl WS5........... 42 F4
Stivichall Croft CV3 ..... 133 B6
Stivichall Prim Sch CV3 . 133 A6
Stockbridge Cl WV6...... 23 F2
Stockdale Pl B15 .... 85 D8
Stockfield Rd B25,B27 .... 88 B5
Stockhay La WS7 .... 7 D5
Stockhill Dr B45 .... 121 F6
Stockingford Inf & Jun Schs
CV10.................... 72 D3
Stocking Leys LE10 ...... 76 A7
Stocking St DY9 .... 81 F5
Stockland Ct B74 .... 44 F8
Stockland Green Sch B23 56 C4
Stockland Rd B23......... 56 D4
Stockley Cres B90 ...... 106 D3
Stockley Rd CV6 .... 96 C6
Stockmans Cl B38 ...... 123 E8
Stocks Wood B30....... 103 F8
Stockton Cl
Dorridge B93........... 128 B4
Sutton Coldfield B76 ...... 58 C5
Walsall WS2 .... 28 D4
Stockton Ct WV14........ 51 B8
Stockton Gr
2 Royal Leamington Spa
CV32................ 157 A2
Birmingham B33 .... 69 D1
Stockton Rd CV1........ 165 D4
Stockwell Ave DY5....... 81 D8
Stockwell End WV6 ...... 24 D6
Stockwell Head LE10..... 71 D1
Stockwell Rd
Birmingham B21 .... 54 E2
Wolverhampton WV6...... 24 D5
Stockwell Rise B92 ..... 107 D7
Stoke Cross B60........ 151 E7
Stoke Gn CV3........... 114 A2
Stoke Green Cres CV3... 114 B1
Stoke Heath Prim Sch
CV2.................. 114 A6
Stoke La B98 .... 154 B7
Stoke Park Mews CV2... 114 A3
Stoke Park Sch & Com Tech
Coll CV2.............. 114 B4
Stoke Pound La
Stoke Pound B60........ 151 A4
Stoke Prior B60......... 150 F3
Stoke Prim Sch CV2..... 114 A4
Stoke Prior Fst Sch B60 150 C3
Stoke Rd
Bromsgrove,Aston Fields
B60.................. 151 A7
Bromsgrove,Charford B60. 150 F7
Hinckley LE10 .... 71 B4
Stoke Row CV2 .... 114 A4
Stokes Ave
7 Tipton DY4 .... 52 A8
Willenhall WV13 .... 40 F8
Stokesay Ave WV6 .... 23 F3
Stokesay Cl
Kidderminster DY10 ..... 116 E2
Nuneaton CV11 .... 73 A3
Oldbury B69.............. 63 A8
Stokesay Gr B31 .... 122 F8
Stokesay Ho B23......... 56 F6
Stokesay Rise DY1 .... 50 E3
Stoke's La WS11 ....5 F7
Stokes St WS3........... 28 B8
Stoke Turn Ct B61 ...... 150 D6
Stoke Way B15 .... 66 C1
Stom Rd WV14............ 40 B5
Stoneacre Cl WV3 .... 24 A1
Stone Ave B75............ 47 A5
Stonebow Ave B91....... 127 B8
Stonebridge Cres B37.... 69 F4
Stonebridge Highway
CV3 .... 133 E4
Stonebridge Rd
Birmingham B46 .... 91 A7
Coleshill B46 .... 70 F5
Stonebridge Trad Est
CV3................... 134 B4
Stonebrook Way
Birmingham B29 .... 84 F2
Coventry CV6............ 95 F3
Stonebury Ave CV5 ..... 111 E4
Stonebury B15............ 85 D8
Stone CE Fst Sch DY10.. 117 E2
Stonechat Cl DY10 ...... 117 B2
Stonechat Dr B23......... 56 C2
Stone Cl B38 .... 103 F2
Stone Cotts B31 .... 103 A3
Stonecroft Ave B45 ..... 122 A7
Stonecrop Cl
Birmingham B38 .... 123 F8
Brownhills WS8........... 15 D6
Stone Cross B46.......... 59 B3
Stonedown Cl WV14 ...... 40 A3
Stonefield Cl CV2 .... 115 A8
Stonefield Dr DY5......... 61 A7
Stonefield Rd WV14....... 40 D5
Stoneford Rd B90....... 106 A4
Stonehaven Dr CV3 ..... 133 C3
Stonehaven Gr B28 ..... 106 B8
Stonehaven B77 .... 21 F5
Stonehenge Croft B14 .. 104 D1
Stonehill Croft B90 ..... 126 F6
Stone Hill DY10 .... 117 E2
Stonehill Wlk 5 B77..... 35 F6
Stonehouse Ave WV13 ... 26 F4
Stonehouse Cl
Cubbington CV32........ 157 D5
Redditch B97........... 153 D1
Stonehouse Cres WS10... 42 B2
Stonehouse Dr B74 ...... 31 C4
Stonehouse Gr B32 .... 84 D2
Stonehouse Hill B29 ..... 85 A3
Stonehouse La
Birmingham B32 .... 84 E2
Birmingham B32 .... 84 F3
Stone House La CV7 ..... 93 F6
Stonehouse La
Coventry CV3........... 134 C4
Hopwood B48 .... 123 E2
Stonehouse Rd
Bromsgrove B60 .... 137 A1
Sutton Coldfield B73 ...... 45 F3
Stonehurst Rd B43........ 44 C3
Stonelea WS9 .... 30 B5
Stonelea Cl B71 .... 53 E8
Stoneleigh Abbey* CV8. 148 F3
Stoneleigh Ave
Coventry CV5........... 132 F7
Kenilworth CV8 .... 148 A6
Stoneleigh Cl
Redditch B98........... 158 F6
Stoneleigh CV8 .... 149 B6
Sutton Coldfield B74 ...... 45 F8
Stoneleigh Ct CV11 ...... 73 C3
Stoneleigh Deer Park Bsns
Village CV8........... 149 D4
Stoneleigh Gdns CV11.... 73 C3
Stoneleigh Ho B32........ 84 F5
Stoneleigh Park National Ag
Ctr* CV8.............. 149 A4
Stoneleigh Rd
Baginton CV8........... 133 F1
Birmingham B20 .... 55 E2
Blackdown CV32 .... 157 A7
Coventry CV4........... 132 E2
Kenilworth CV8 .... 148 A6
Solihull B91 .... 106 E6
Stoneleigh CV8 .... 149 B3
Stoneleigh Way DY3 ..... 50 D6
Stone Mdw CV7.......... 95 A6
Stone Pine Cl WS12........1 F8
Stonepine Pl DY3 .... 50 E6
Stonepits La B97....... 158 D4
Stonepit B77 .... 21 C1
Stone Rd B15............ 86 D7
Stonerwood Ave B28.... 105 E8
Stones Gn B23........... 56 F6
Stone St
Dudley DY1 .... 51 C1
Oldbury B69............. 64 A7
Stoneton Cres CV7...... 130 A6
Stoneton Gr B29........ 103 A8
Stoneway Gr CV31 ..... 162 D6
Stonewell Cres CV11 ..... 79 B8
Stoney Cl B92 .... 107 E7
Stoney Croft WS11.........1 F1
Stoneycroft Twr 4 B36 .. 68 E8
Stoney Ct CV3 .... 135 A7
Stone Yd
Birmingham B12 .... 66 F1
Cradley Heath B64 .... 82 C8
Stoneydelph Prim Sch
B77.................... 22 A1
Stoneyfields Cl 3 WS11....1 F2
Stoneyford Gr B14 ...... 105 B4
Stoneygate Dr LE10 ...... 71 F3
Stoney Hill Cl B60 ...... 137 A1
Stoneyhurst Rd B24...... 56 F1
Stoney La
Birmingham B32 .... 84 B6
Birmingham,Balsall Heath
B12.................... 87 B5
Birmingham,Stechford B25 . 68 E1
Blackwell B60 .... 138 C2
Dudley DY2 .... 62 C3
Kidderminster DY10 ..... 116 E8
Stoney Lane Ind Est
DY10................... 116 E8
Stoney La
Stakenbridge DY10 .... 98 E3
Walsall WS3 .... 14 D3
West Bromwich B71 ...... 53 D4
Wolverhampton WV4...... 39 B5
Stoney Lea Rd WS11 ....1 F1
Stoneymoor Dr B36...... 58 D1
Stoney Rd
Coventry CV1,CV3 .... 165 B1
Nuneaton CV10,CV11...... 73 B6
Stoney Stanton Rd CV1,
CV6 .... 113 E5
Stoneythorpe Cl B91.... 107 B1
Stoneywood Rd CV2 .... 114 F8
Stonnal Gr B23 .... 57 A6
Stonnall Gate WS9....... 30 C8
Stonnall Rd WS9......... 30 C8
Stonor Park Rd B91..... 106 F5
Stonor Rd B28.......... 106 A5
Stonydelph La B77....... 36 A7
Stony La B67 .... 64 F5
Stony St B67............. 64 F6
Stoop The CV3.......... 115 B1
Stornoway Rd B35 .... 58 B4
Storrage La B48 .... 139 E3
Storrs Cl B9 .... 67 D1
Storrs Pl B10 .... 67 D1
Storrs Way The B32..... 102 B7
Stotfold Rd B14......... 104 F2
Stourbridge Coll (Longlands
Ctr) DY8................ 80 E5
Stourbridge Coll DY8 ... 81 A4
Stourbridge Juntion Sta
DY8..................... 81 B3
Stourbridge Rd
Brierley Hill DY1,DY2,DY5 .. 61 E6
Catshill B61 .... 136 F7
Churchill DY10........... 98 A6
Clent DY9................ 99 E3
Dudley DY1 .... 62 A8
Fairfield B61 .... 120 D2
Hackman's Gate DY9...... 98 F1
Hagley DY9 .... 99 C7
Halesowen B63 .... 82 F5
Kidderminster DY10 ..... 116 F8
Madeley Heath DY9...... 120 B7
Stourbridge DY9 .... 81 D5
Wombourne WV5,DY3 ..... 49 B5
Stourbridge Town Sta
DY8..................... 81 A5
Stourbridge Trad Est DY8. 81 A6
Stour Cl
Burntwood WS7........... 7 D6
Halesowen B63 .... 82 E6
Stourdale Rd B64........ 82 C8
Stourdell Rd B63 .... 82 E6
Stour Hill DY5 .... 82 A8
Stour Ho 2 B68 .... 84 B8
Stourminster Specl Sch
DY10................... 117 B4
Stourmore Cl WV12...... 27 D6
Stourport Rd DY11...... 116 C2
Stour St
Birmingham B18 .... 66 A3
West Bromwich B70 ...... 52 E3
Stour B77 .... 36 A5
Stourton Cl
Knowle B93 .... 128 B7
Sutton Coldfield B76 ...... 46 F4
Stourton Dr WV4 .... 38 C5
Stourton Rd B32......... 84 B5
Stourvale Ind Est DY9.... 81 F6
Stour Vale Rd DY9 .... 81 F6
Stourvale Trad Est B63 ... 82 D6
Stour Valley Cl DY5 ...... 81 D7
Stow Dr DY5............. 81 B6
Stowecroft WS13 .... 3 C2
Stowe Hill Gdns WS13..... 3 C1
Stowell Rd B44 .... 55 F8
Stowe Pl CV4 .... 111 C1
Stowe Rd WS13............ 9 C8
Stowe St
Lichfield WS13............ 9 C8
Walsall WS3 .... 28 C7
Stow Gr B36 .... 68 E7
Stowheath Ind Est & New Ent
Ctr WV1................. 40 A8
Stow Heath Jun & Inf Schs
WV13.................... 26 D1
Stow Heath La
Bilston WV1.............. 40 B8
Wolverhampton WV1...... 26 C1
Stow Heath Pl WV1 ...... 40 B7
Stowlawn Jun & Inf Sch
WV14.................... 40 C8
Stowmans Cl WV14 ...... 40 B3
Strachey Ave CV32...... 156 E2
Stradey Cl CV3.......... 115 B1
Straight Rd WV12........ 27 D6
Straits Gn DY3........... 50 B4
Straits Prim Sch DY3..... 50 B5
Straits Rd DY3 .... 50 B3
Straits The DY3.......... 50 A4
Strand The B61 .... 137 A3
Stratford Cl DY1 .... 50 E2
Stratford Ct B72 .... 46 B3
Stratford Dr WS9 .... 30 C8
Stratford Gdns B60 ..... 137 A2
Stratford Pl B12 .... 87 A8
Stratford Rd
Birmingham,Sparkbrook B11,
B28..................... 87 B6
Birmingham,Sparkhill B11 .. 87 D3
Bromsgrove B60 .... 137 A2
Dorridge B94............ 127 B3
Longbridge CV34........ 160 C3
Nuthurst B94 .... 143 C5
Solihull B90 .... 126 D7
Stratford St N B11 .... 87 A8
Stratford St
Birmingham B11 .... 87 C5
Coventry CV2........... 114 A4
Nuneaton CV11 .... 73 C4
Stratford Way WS11 ....1 F5
Stratford Wlk B36 .... 68 C8
Strathdene Gdns B29 .... 85 C1
Strathdene Rd B29....... 85 C1
Strathearn Rd CV32 ..... 156 E1
Strathern Dr WV14....... 40 A1
Strathfield Wlk WV3,WV4 . 38 C6
Strathmore Ave CV1 .... 113 E1
Strathmore Cres WV5.... 38 A1
Strathmore Pl 6 WS11.....1 F2
Strathmore Rd
Hinckley LE10 .... 75 A7
Tipton DY4.............. 52 A8
Stratton St WV10 .... 25 E4
Strawberry Cl B69 .... 63 C7
Strawberry Fields CV7 ... 92 B1
Strawberry La WS6 ...... 13 E8
Strawberry Lane Ind Est
WV13.................... 26 C2
Strawberry La WV13 ..... 26 D3
Strawberry Wlk CV2 ..... 96 D2
Stray The DY5 .... 61 C6
Stream Mdw WS4......... 15 D1
Stream Pk DY6 .... 60 E4
Stream Rd DY6,DY8....... 60 D4
Streamside Cl CV5 ...... 112 A8
Streamside Way
Solihull B92 .... 89 D4
Walsall WS4 .... 29 D8
Streatham Gr B44........ 45 A2
Streather Rd B75 .... 32 C2
Streetly Cres B74 .... 31 D3
Streetly Dr B74 .... 31 D3
Streetly La B74 .... 31 D3
Streetly Rd B23.......... 56 D5
Streetly Sch The B74..... 45 A6
Streetly Wood B74 .... 31 A2
Streetsbrook Inf Sch
B90.................... 106 C4
Streetsbrook Rd B90,B91 106 D5
Streets Corner Gdns WS9 16 A4
Streets La WS6 ....4 F1
Streetway Rd WS14 ...... 18 B7
Strensham Ct B13 .... 86 E4
Strensham Hill B13 ...... 86 E4
Strensham Rd B12 .... 86 E5
Stretton Ave CV3 .... 134 C6
Stretton Cl LE10 .... 75 D6
Stretton Cres CV31...... 162 B5
Stretton Ct
Birmingham B23 .... 56 E2
Hinckley LE10 .... 75 D3
Stretton Dr B45......... 122 A2
Stretton Gr
2 Birmingham,Lozells
B19..................... 66 C7
Birmingham,Sparkbrook
B11..................... 87 C6
Birmingham,Stechford B8 .. 68 C6
Stretton Ho 7 B97...... 153 A4
Stretton Pl
Dudley DY2 .... 62 D5
Wolverhampton WV14...... 40 A1
Stretton Rd
Kidderminster DY11 ..... 116 B4
Nuneaton CV10 .... 73 A3
Solihull B90 .... 126 B8
Willenhall WV12 .... 13 D1
Stretton St B77 .... 21 E3
Stringer Cl B75 .... 32 A4
Stringers Hill WS12 .... 2 D7
Stringes Cl WV13 .... 27 C3
Stringes La WV13 .... 27 B3
Strode Ho B79............ 21 A4
Strode Rd WV2 .... 39 C6
Stroma Way CV10........ 72 F2
Stronsay Cl B45......... 101 F1
Stroud Ave WV12 .... 27 D5
Stroud Cl WV12.......... 27 C4
Stroud Rd B90.......... 105 F2
Strutt Cl B15 .... 85 D8
Strutt Rd LE10 .... 76 A5
Stuart Bathurst RC High Sch
WS10................... 42 B5
Stuart Cl CV34 .... 160 D5
Stuart Cres DY2.......... 51 E1
Stuart Ct
7 Royal Leamington Spa
CV32.................. 156 E1
Coventry CV6........... 114 A8
Stuart Rd
Halesowen B62 .... 83 F5
Rowley Regis B65 .... 63 C4
Stuarts Ct DY9........... 99 A5
Stuart's Dr B33 .... 68 D1
Stuarts Gn DY9 .... 99 B8
Stuarts Rd B33 .... 68 D2
Stuart St
Birmingham B7 .... 67 C7
Walsall WS3 .... 28 B8
Stuarts Way B32........ 102 B7
Stubbers Green Rd
Aldridge WS9............ 30 A7
Walsall WS9 .... 29 E8
Stubbington Cl WV13 .... 26 D1
Stubbs Cl CV12 .... 78 A4
Stubbs Gr CV2.......... 114 B5
Stubbs Rd WV3 .... 39 A6
Stubby La WV11 .... 27 A6
Stubley Dr WV10......... 25 E6
Stud Farm Cotts B78..... 20 E2
Stud La B33 .... 68 F4
Studland Gn CV2......... 115 A4
Studland Rd B28........ 106 A8
Studley Croft B92........ 89 D3
Studley Dr DY5 .... 81 C8
Studley Gate DY8 .... 80 D5
Studley High Sch B80... 159 E3
Studley Inf Sch B80..... 159 E4
Studley Rd
Redditch B98........... 154 A2
Wolverhampton WV3...... 38 C8
Studley St Mary's CE Jun Sch
B80.................... 159 E3
Studley St B12........... 87 B5
Studley Twr B12.......... 86 F7
Sturgeon's Hill WS14...... 9 C7
Sturley Cl CV8 .... 148 B6
Sturman Dr B65 .... 63 C1
Sturminster Cl CV2 ..... 115 A4
Stychbrook Gdns WS13.....3 B2
Styles Cl CV31 .... 162 A7
Styvechale Ave CV5 ..... 133 A8
Suckling Green La WV8 .. 10 A2
Sudbury Cl
Royal Leamington Spa
CV32.................. 157 C3
Wednesfield WV11 .... 26 E7
Sudbury Gr B44.......... 45 B2
Sudeley Cl B36 .... 58 B1
Sudeley Gdns DY1 .... 50 D2
Sudeley Rd CV10......... 78 C8
Sudeley B77.............. 35 C8
Suffield Gr B23 .... 56 B5
Suffolk Cl
Bedworth CV12 .... 78 A3
Coventry CV5........... 112 B3
Nuneaton CV10 .... 72 E3
Oldbury B68............. 64 B4
Wolverhampton WV11...... 26 C6
Suffolk Dr DY5........... 81 C7
Suffolk Gr WS9 .... 30 B8
Suffolk Ho B23 .... 56 F5
Suffolk Pl
Birmingham B5 .... 164 B1
Walsall WS2 .... 28 D5
Suffolk Rd
Dudley DY2 .... 62 A7
Wednesbury WS10 .... 42 C3
Suffolk Street Queensway
B1.................... 164 B2
Suffolk St CV32......... 157 A1
Suffolk Way B78 .... 21 A1
Suffrage St B66.......... 65 B4
Sugarbrook Ct 1 B60.... 150 F6
Sugarbrook La B60 ..... 151 A5
Sugarbrook Rd B60 ..... 151 A7
Sugar Loaf La DY10 ...... 98 B7
Sugden Gr B5 .... 86 E8
Sulgrave Cl
Coventry CV2........... 114 E7
Dudley DY1 .... 51 A3
Sullivan Ct CV6 .... 114 B7
Sullivan Rd CV6......... 114 B7
Sullivan Way WS13........ 3 C2
Sullivan Wlk WS13 .... 3 C2
Sumburgh Croft B35 ..... 58 A3
Summercourt Dr DY6 .... 60 C6
Summercourt Sq DY6 .... 60 C5
Summer Croft B19 .... 66 D6
Summer Dr DY3 .... 50 C3
Summerfield Ave
Kingswinford DY6 .... 60 C7
West Bromwich B70 ...... 53 C4
Summerfield Cl B77 ..... 21 D4
Summerfield Cres B16 ... 65 E3
Summerfield Ct B15 ..... 65 C1
Summerfield Dr 2 B29 . 103 A7
Summerfield Gr 5 B18 .. 65 E4

Summerfield Jun & Inf Sch B18 65 E4
Summerfield Rd
Birmingham B16 65 E3
Burntwood WS7 7 A5
Dudley DY2 62 D7
Holy Cross DY9 99 E2
Solihull B92 89 A1
Tamworth B77 21 D4
Wolverhampton WV1 25 B2
Summerfields Ave B62 83 F7
Summergate DY3 50 C4
Summer Gr WS13 3 D2
Summer Hill 6 B63 83 B3
Summerhill Ave DY11 116 A5
Summer Hill Ind Pk 2 B1 66 B3
Summer Hill DY6 60 C6
Summerhill Prim Sch DY4 52 A6
Summer Hill Rd B1 66 B3
Summerhill Rd
Dudley WV14 40 D1
Tipton DY4 51 F7
Summerhill Sch The DY6 60 B6
Summer Hill St B1 66 B3
Summerhill WS14 16 E8
Summer Hill Terr B1 66 B3
Summerhouse Cl B97 158 A6
Summerhouse Rd WV14 40 A1
Summer La
Birmingham B19 66 D5
Dudley DY3 50 C3
Minworth B76 58 D6
Walsall WS4 15 C2
Summerlee Rd B24 57 B2
Summer Pl DY11 116 C5
Summer Rd
Birmingham,Acock's Green B27 88 A2
Birmingham,Edgbaston B15 86 C7
Birmingham,Erdington B23 56 F5
Dudley DY1 51 A4
Kidderminster DY11 116 C3
Rowley Regis B65 63 D3
Summer Row
Birmingham B3 164 A3
Wolverhampton WV2 163 B2
Summer St
Kingswinford DY6 60 D6
Redditch B98 153 E3
Stourbridge DY8 80 F5
Stourbridge,Lye DY9 81 E5
West Bromwich B71 53 D4
Willenhall WV13 26 F2
Summerton Rd
Oldbury B69 52 D1
Whitnash CV31 162 A3
Summervale Cl DY9 99 A5
Summervale Rd DY9 99 A5
Summerville Terr 4 B17 85 C5
Summit Cres B66 64 E8
Summit Gdns B63 82 F3
Summit Pl DY3 50 B2
Summit The DY9 81 D4
Sumner Rd B46 70 F6
Sunart Way CV10 72 C5
Sunbeam Cl B36 58 F1
Sunbeam Dr WS6 4 F3
Sunbeam St WV2 39 C7
Sunbeam B77 21 E3
Sunbeam Way B33 69 C2
Sunbury Ave WS14 9 E7
Sunbury Cl WV14 40 E1
Sunbury Cotts B31 103 A4
Sunbury Rd
Birmingham B31 122 E7
Coventry CV3 134 C5
Halesowen B63 82 F4
Suncliffe Dr CV8 148 A2
Suncroft B32 84 C5
Sundbury Rise B31 103 B5
Sunderland Dr DY8 81 A8
Sunderton Rd B14 104 E4
Sundew Croft B36 68 D8
Sundew St CV2 96 D2
Sundial La B43 43 F1
Sundorne Cl CV5 112 A4
Sundour Cres WV11 12 B1
Sundridge Prim Sch B44 44 E4
Sundridge Rd B44 44 E4
Sundridge Wlk WV4 38 C6
Sunfield Rd WS11 1 B1
Sunleigh Gr B27 88 E4
Sunley Dr WS12 2 D7
Sunningdale Ave
Coventry CV6 95 D2
Kenilworth CV8 148 B4
Perton WV6 23 D5
Sunningdale B60 137 A1
Sunningdale Cl
Birmingham B20 54 E4
Nuneaton CV11 74 A1
Redditch B98 153 F4
Stourbridge DY8 80 F2
Sutton Coldfield B73 46 A2
Sunningdale Dr B69 63 A7
Sunningdale B62 83 E4
Sunningdale Rd
Birmingham B11 88 A3
Bromsgrove B61 150 D8
Sedgley DY3 39 B1
Sunningdale
Sutton Coldfield B73 46 B1
Tamworth B77 22 C5
Sunningdale Way WS3 14 A3
Sunny Ave B12 87 A5
Sunnybank Ave
Birmingham B44 56 B7
Coventry CV3 134 B5
Sunnybank Cl WS9 30 E2
Sunny Bank CV1 165 A3
Sunny Bank Rd B68 84 C7
Sunnybank Rd
Dudley DY3 50 F5
Sutton Coldfield B73 57 A8
Sunnydale Cres LE10 75 A7
Sunnydale Rd LE10 74 F7
Sunnydale Wlk B71 53 C4
Sunnydene B8 68 A5
Sunny Hill Cl WV5 49 B6
Sunnyhill LE10 75 F7
Sunnyhill S LE10 75 F6
Sunnymead B60 137 A1
Sunnymead Rd
1 Burntwood WS7 7 A8
Birmingham B26 88 F6
Sunnymead Way B74 44 F7
Sunnymede Rd DY6 61 A4
Sunnyside Ave B23 56 E3
Sunnyside WS9 16 A2
Sunnyside Cl
Balsall Common CV7 130 C7
Coventry CV5 112 F3
Sunnyside Ct CV10 72 F3
Sunnyside LE10 71 D3
Sunnyside Hospl LE10 71 D5
Sunnyside Ind Est LE10 71 D4
Sunnyside La CV7 130 C7
Sunnyside B69 63 B7
Sunridge Ave
Birmingham B19 66 D6
Wombourne WV5 49 A7
Sunrise Ct B15 86 D7
Sunrise Hill WS12 2 B6
Sunrise Wlk B68 64 C3
Sunset Cl
Great Wyrley WS6 4 F3
Tamworth B79 21 A5
Sunset Pl WV4 39 F3
Sunshine Cl CV8 148 A2
Sunshine Inf Sch The WS3 28 C8
Sun St
Brierley Hill DY5 61 F1
Walsall WS1 42 E7
Wolverhampton WV10 163 D3
Sunway Gr CV3 133 B6
Surfeit Hill Rd B64 82 D8
Surrey Cl
Cannock WS11 4 F8
Hinckley LE10 75 E4
Nuneaton CV10 72 E3
Surrey Cres B71 53 A8
Surrey Ct CV34 160 E8
Surrey Dr
Kingswinford DY6 60 F3
Tamworth B78 21 A1
Wolverhampton WV3 24 E1
Surrey Ho 2 DY8 80 F8
Surrey Rd
Birmingham B44 44 F4
Dudley DY2 62 A7
Surrey Wlk WS9 16 A1
Sussex Ave
Aldridge WS9 30 A8
Wednesbury WS10 42 D4
West Bromwich B71 53 C6
Sussex Cl CV10 72 E3
Sussex Ct
7 Birmingham B29 103 C7
Warwick CV34 160 E8
Sussex Dr
Cannock WS12 2 B5
Wolverhampton WV3 24 E1
Sussex Rd CV5 112 F4
Sutherland Ave
Coventry CV5 112 A4
Solihull B90 106 C3
Wolverhampton WV2 40 A8
Sutherland Cl
Birmingham B43 44 D4
Warwick CV34 155 E1
Sutherland Dr
Bedworth CV12 78 A4
Birmingham B13 86 F4
Wombourne WV5 38 A1
Sutherland Gr WV6 23 F4
Sutherland Ho WV1 25 A3
Sutherland Pl WV2 163 C2
Sutherland Rd
Cheslyn Hay WS6 4 E2
Cradley Heath B64 82 E8
Wolverhampton WV4 39 B5
Sutherland St B6 67 B8
Sutton App B8 68 A4
Sutton Ave
Coventry CV5 111 D4
Tamworth B78 21 A2
Sutton Cl
Hinckley LE10 71 F3
Redditch B98 154 D2
Sutton Coldfield Coll Design Ctr B72 46 C4
Sutton Coldfield Coll (Erdington Ctr) B24 57 A4
Sutton Coldfield Coll (Great Barr Campus) B44 55 E7
Sutton Coldfield Coll B74 46 C6
Sutton Coldfield Cottage Hospl B72 46 B4
Sutton Coldfield Gram Sch For Girls B73 46 B3
Sutton Coldfield Sta B73 46 B5
Sutton Cres B70 53 A3
Sutton Ct
3 Birmingham,Erdington B24 57 B6
Bedworth CV6 96 C6
Birmingham,Hamstead B43 54 E7
Sutton Coldfield B75 46 B7
Wolverhampton WV4 39 E2
Sutton Lodge B91 107 A3
Sutton New Rd B23 56 F4
Sutton Oak Cnr B73 45 A5
Sutton Oak Rd B73 45 A5
Sutton Park Ct B73 46 B2
Sutton Park Fst Sch DY11 116 B4
Sutton Park Gr DY11 116 C3
Sutton Park Rd DY11 116 B3
Sutton Park Rise DY11 116 B3
Sutton Park Visitor Ctr* B74 46 A5
Sutton Pk
Nuneaton CV10 72 B7
Sutton Coldfield B74 45 D6
Sutton Rd
Aldridge WS9 30 A1
Birmingham B23 57 B6
Darlaston WS10 41 A4
Kidderminster DY11 116 C4
Mile Oak B78 34 A8
Tamworth B78 20 C1
Walsall WS5 43 C8
Sutton's Dr
Birmingham B43 44 A4
Walsall B43 43 F4
Sutton Specl Sch The DY1 61 F8
Sutton Sq B76 58 E6
Sutton St
Birmingham,Aston B6 66 F6
Birmingham B1 66 D1
Sutton Stop CV6 96 B5
Sutton St DY8 60 F1
Swadling St CV31 161 F6
Swaffield Pk WS11 2 B2
Swain Crofts CV31 162 B6
Swains Gn LE10 75 F6
Swains Gr B44 44 F4
Swaledale Cl B60 150 E6
Swaledale CV4 132 D6
Swale Gr
Birmingham B38 103 F1
Willenhall WV13 27 D2
Swale Rd B76 47 A1
Swallow Ave B36 70 A8
Swallow Cl
Birmingham B12 87 B5
Dudley DY2 62 D2
Huntington WS12 1 C7
Wednesbury WS10 42 B4
Swallow Croft WS13 3 A1
Swallow Ct
Bedworth CV12 95 C8
Hinckley LE10 74 F6
Wolverhampton,Fordhouses WV10 11 B3
Wolverhampton,Low Hill WV10 25 D7
Swallowdale
Brownhills WS9 16 B4
Wolverhampton WV6 23 F2
Swallowdean Rd CV6 112 E8
Swallow Dr DY10 117 A2
Swallowfall Ave DY8 80 C4
Swallowfields Dr WS12 2 B3
Swallowfields Rd DY3 39 C2
Swallowfield B79 20 E6
Swallowgate Bsns Pk CV6 95 D1
Swallow Rd CV6 95 C1
Swallows Cl WS3 15 A5
Swallows Ind Est The B90 126 D8
Swallows' Mdw B90 126 D8
Swallows Rise Bsns Pk DY5 61 E3
Swallow St
Birmingham B2 164 B2
West Bromwich B70 53 A4
Swanage Gn CV2 115 A4
Swanage Rd B10 87 D8
Swan Ave B66 64 E7
Swan Bank WV4 38 F4
Swan Cl
Blakedown DY10 98 B1
Cheslyn Hay WS6 4 D2
Swan Copse B25 88 C5
Swan Corner Sh Ctr WS7 7 C6
Swancote Dr WV4 38 C6
Swancote Rd
Birmingham B33 68 F5
Dudley DY1 62 A8
Swan Cres B69 63 F4
Swancroft Ho 11 DY4 52 A8
Swancroft Rd
Coventry CV2 114 A5
Tipton DY4 51 F8
Swan Ctr 7 DY10 116 E6
Swan Ctyd B25 88 D6
Swan Dr WS8 15 E7
Swanfield Rd DY8 61 A2
Swanfields WS7 7 C6
Swan Gdns B23 56 F4
Swan La
Coventry CV2 113 F4
Fairfield B61 120 E3
Swan Lane Ind Est B70 53 A5
Swan La
Stourbridge DY5,DY8 61 A2
Swan La *continued*
Upton Warren B61 150 A3
West Bromwich B70 53 A5
Swanley Cl B62 84 A3
Swan Mews WS13 9 A8
Swanmore Cl WV3 38 E8
Swanmote B79 20 F5
Swann Rd WV14 40 A2
Swann Wlk 10 DY4 52 A8
Swan Pk B77 21 C3
Swan Pool Gr WS4 15 D1
Swan Rdbt B70 52 F5
Swan Rd WS13 9 A7
Swansbrook Gdns 4 B38 104 C2
Swanshurst La B13 105 C8
Swanshurst Sch B13 105 B7
Swans Length B48 139 A7
Swan St
Alvechurch B48 139 B5
Brierley Hill DY5 61 C6
Dudley DY2 62 C6
Royal Leamington Spa CV32 157 A1
Stourbridge DY8 80 E5
Warwick CV34 160 E6
Wolverhampton WV1 25 F2
Swanswell Rd B92 106 D7
Swanswell St CV1 165 C4
Swans Wlk B48 139 A6
Swanswood Gr 3 B37 70 C3
Swan Village Ind Est B70 53 A5
Swarthmore Rd B29 103 B7
Sweetbriar La WV12 27 D5
Sweetbriar Rd WV2 40 A7
Sweetbriar Way WS12 2 D2
Sweetbrier Dr 4 DY8 60 E1
Sweetman Pl WV6 25 A3
Sweetman St
Wolverhampton WV6 24 F4
Wolverhampton WV6 25 A3
Sweetmoor Cl B36 69 C8
Sweetpool La DY8 98 F5
Swift Cl
Birmingham B36 70 A8
Bromsgrove B61 150 E8
Kenilworth CV8 148 A2
Swift Park Gr DY10 117 B2
Swift's Cnr CV3 133 E8
Swift B77 21 E3
Swillington Rd CV6 113 B5
Swinbrook Gr B44 44 E1
Swinbrook Way B90 106 D4
Swinburne Ave CV2 114 D2
Swinburne Cl CV10 72 A5
Swinburne Rd
Hinckley LE10 71 C1
Redditch B97 158 C7
Swincross Rd DY8 81 B3
Swindale Croft CV3 134 F8
Swindale B77 36 B7
Swindell Rd DY9 81 C1
Swindon Rd
Birmingham B17 65 B2
Kingswinford DY6 60 B6
Swinfen Broun Rd WS13 9 A8
Swinford Gr B93 127 E3
Swinford Old Hall DY8 81 B3
Swinford Rd
Birmingham B29 85 B3
Stourbridge DY8 81 A3
Wolverhampton WV10 25 E5
Swiss Dr DY8 60 F2
Swiss Lodge Dr B78 34 F8
Sword Dr LE10 71 B3
Swynnerton Dr WV11 12 F4
Sycamore Ave
Birmingham B12 87 A5
Redditch B98 153 E2
Sycamore Cl
Birmingham B24 56 F3
Hinckley LE10 75 E5
Kidderminster DY10 116 F7
Stourbridge DY8 80 D2
Sutton Coldfield B76 46 F2
Walsall WS4 29 B8
Sycamore Cres
Birmingham,Erdington B24 56 F3
Birmingham,Marston Green B37 90 A8
Sycamore Ct
Allesley CV5 111 F7
Birmingham,Cotteridge B30 103 E4
Birmingham,Perry Common B23 56 C7
Sycamore Dr
Hollywood B47 125 B6
Wolverhampton WV3 24 D1
Sycamore Gn
Cannock WS11 1 E6
Dudley DY1 50 F5
Sycamore Green Prim Sch DY1 50 F5
Sycamore Gr CV34 156 A1
Sycamore Ho
Birmingham B13 87 A3
Redditch B98 158 F8
Sycamore Ind & Trad Est B21 65 D7
Sycamore Paddock 1 DY8 61 A1
Sycamore Pl
Bilston WV14 41 A3
Burntwood WS7 6 F7
Smethwick B67 64 F4
Sycamore Rd
Birmingham,Aston B6 67 A8
Birmingham,Bournville B30 103 F7
Birmingham,Erdington B23 56 F7
Birmingham,Great Barr B43 43 E3
Birmingham,Handsworth B21 65 D7
Burntwood WS7 6 F7
Cannock WS12 2 F4
Coventry CV2 96 B2
Kingswinford DY6 60 E6
Nuneaton CV10 72 D6
Oldbury B69 64 A4
Smethwick B66 65 B3
Tipton DY4 51 F7
Walsall,Shelfield WS4 29 B8
Walsall,The Delves WS5 42 F5
Wednesbury WS10 42 A2
Sycamores The
2 Sutton Coldfield B74 31 F2
Bedworth CV12 77 E2
Lichfield WS14 9 B5
West Hagley DY9 98 F5
Wolverhampton,Elston Hall WV10 25 F8
Wolverhampton WV11 26 B5
Sycamore B77 35 E7
Sycamore Terr B14 104 C7
Sycamore Way
1 Birmingham B27 88 C5
Huntington WS12 1 D8
Sydenham Dr CV31 162 B6
Sydenham Ind Est CV31 162 B6
Sydenham Prim Sch CV31 162 C6
Sydenham Rd
Birmingham B11 87 C6
Smethwick B66 65 A7
Wolverhampton WV1 26 B2
Sydnall Cl B97 152 F2
Sydnall Fields CV6 95 F4
Sydnall Rd CV6 95 F4
Sydney Cl B70 53 A7
Sydney Ct 1 CV12 77 F2
Sydney Ho B34 69 E6
Sydney Rd
Birmingham B9 67 C2
Bromsgrove B61 136 E3
Cradley Heath B64 82 C8
Smethwick B67 64 E2
Sykesmoor B77 36 B7
Sylvan Ave B31 102 F3
Sylvan Dr CV3 132 F6
Sylvan Gn B62 83 D5
Sylvan Gr B90 106 B5
Sylvia Ave B31 123 B8
Symphony Ct B16 66 B2
Synkere Cl CV7 95 A6
Sytch La WV5 49 A5

T

Tabbs Gdns DY10 117 A6
Table Oak La CV8 130 B1
Tachbrook Cl CV2 96 C2
Tachbrook Link CV34 161 E4
Tachbrook Park Dr CV34 161 E5
Tachbrook Rd CV31 161 F4
Tachbrook St CV31 162 A6
Tack Farm Rd DY8 60 D1
Tackford Cl B36 58 D1
Tackford Rd CV6 114 A8
Tackley Cl B90 126 B8
Tadmore Cl WV14 40 D5
Tadworth Cl WV1 26 A2
Tainters Hill CV8 148 A6
Tait Croft B92 107 F8
Talaton Cl WV9 11 A2
Talbot Ave B74 31 B3
Talbot Cl
Birmingham B23 56 D8
Walsall WS2 28 C6
Talbot Ct CV32 157 A1
Talbot Ho
5 Birmingham B24 56 F4
6 Wednesbury WS10 41 F2
Talbot Pass 6 DY8 81 A5
Talbot Pl WV14 40 C6
Talbot Rd
Bromsgrove B60 150 E7
Dudley DY2 62 B4
Smethwick B66 65 A3
Wolverhampton WV2 39 C6
Talbots La DY5 61 F1
Talbot St
Birmingham B18 65 F6
Brierley Hill DY5 61 D3
Halesowen B63 82 C6
Kidderminster DY11 116 C4
Stourbridge,Lye DY9 81 F5
Stourbridge,Stambermill DY8 81 A5
Talbot B77 21 E3
Talbot Way B10 87 F7
Talfourd St B9 67 D1
Talgarth Covert B38 123 E7
Talisman Cl CV8 147 F3
Talisman Sq CV8 147 F4
Talke Rd WS5 42 F5
Talladale B32 102 B7
Talland Ave
Coventry CV6 114 A6
Tamworth B77 21 E5
Tallants Cl CV6 114 A8
Tallants Rd CV6 114 A8
Tallington Rd B33 89 D7

Tall Trees Cl
Catshill B61 136 F8
Sutton Coldfield B74 31 D4
Willenhall WV12 27 D6
Tall Trees Dr DY9 81 D2
Talton Cl B90 127 A5
Tamar Cl WS8 6 C2
Tamar Dr
Birmingham B36 69 F8
Dudley DY3 50 F6
Sutton Coldfield B76 58 B7
Tamar Gr
Perton WV6 23 E4
Willenhall WV13 27 C2
Tamarisk Cl B29 103 B8
Tamar Rd
Bulkington CV12 79 B2
Tamworth B77 36 A5
Tamar Rise DY8 81 A8
Tame Ave
Burntwood WS7 7 D6
Wednesbury WS10 42 C4
Tamebridge Ind Est B42 55 E4
Tame Bridge Sta B71 42 F2
Tame Cl WS1 42 E6
Tame Cres B71 53 C6
Tame Ct
Fazeley B78 35 B8
Tamworth B79 21 A5
Tamedrive B78,B79 21 A4
Tame Dr WS3 15 A1
Tame Gr WS11 4 D8
Tame Rd
Birmingham,Brandhall B68 84 B8
Birmingham,Witton B6 56 A1
Tipton DY4 52 C5
Tame Rise B68 84 B8
Tame Road Ind Est B6 56 B1
Tamerton Rd B32 84 D1
Tame St E WS1 42 F6
Tameside Dr
Birmingham,Castle Bromwich B35 58 A1
Birmingham,Erdington B6 56 A3
Tameside Prim Sch WS10 42 C2
Tame St
Bilston WV14 40 F5
Tamworth B77 21 C3
Walsall WS1 42 E6
West Bromwich B70 52 F8
Tame Valley Bsns Pk B77 35 E6
Tame Valley Com Sch B36 68 D8
Tame Valley Ind Est B77 35 E6
Tame Way LE10 75 A8
Tamora Cl CV34 161 D3
Tamworth Bsns Ctr B77 22 B3
Tamworth Bsns Pk B77 22 B3
Tamworth Castle Mus★ B79 21 B4
Tamworth Castle★ B79 21 B4
Tamworth Cl WS8 6 F2
Tamworth & Lichfield Coll (Tamworth Campus) B79 21 B6
Tamworth Rd (Amington) B77 21 F5
Tamworth Rd B78 35 C2
Tamworth Rd (Dosthill) B77 35 C6
Tamworth Rd
Keresley CV6,CV7 94 D5
Lichfield WS14 9 E5
Polesworth B78 22 E1
Sutton Coldfield B75 33 A2
Tamworth,Mount Pleasant B77 21 C1
Tamworth,Two Gates B77 35 D8
Wood End CV9 36 C1
Tamworth Sta B79 21 C5
Tamworth St WS13 9 B8
Tanacetum Dr WS5 43 B3
Tancred Cl CV31 161 F5
Tandy Ct B14 104 F3
Tandy Dr B14 104 F3
Tandy's La DY10 118 E4
Tanfield Cl WV6 24 B3
Tanfield Rd
Birmingham B33 68 F3
Dudley DY2 62 B7
Tanford Rd B92 89 C3
Tanglewood Cl
Birmingham B32 84 B4
Birmingham,Castle Bromwich B34 69 C5
Blackwell B60 138 A5
Tanglewood Gr DY3 39 C2
Tangmere Cl WV6 23 E5
Tangmere Dr B35 58 A3
Tanhill B77 36 B7
Tanhouse Ave B43 54 C7
Tanhouse Farm Rd B92 89 C2
Tanhouse La
Halesowen B63 82 C5
Redditch B98 154 C6
Tanners Cl B75 46 F7
Tanners Ct WS1 42 E8
Tanners Ctyd CV34 160 D5
Tanners Gr CV6 95 D4
Tanners Green La B47, B94 125 B2
Tanners' La CV4,CV7 111 B1
Tannery Cl WS2 28 D3
Tannery Ct CV8 147 F4
Tansey Ct DY5 61 B7
Tansey Green Rd
Brierley Hill DY5,DY6 61 B8
Tansey Green Rd *continued*
Kingswinford DY6 50 A1
Tansley Cl B93 127 F4
Tansley Gr B44 44 F1
Tansley Hill Ave DY2 62 F8
Tansley Hill Rd DY2 62 E8
Tansley Rd B44 55 F8
Tansley View WV2 39 D7
Tansy
Sutton Coldfield B74 31 F4
Tamworth B77 21 C3
Tantallon Dr B32 84 D1
Tantany La B71 53 C4
Tantarra St
Walsall,The Chuckery WS1 29 A1
Walsall WS1 28 F1
Tanwood Barns DY10 119 B2
Tanwood Cl
Redditch B97 158 A6
Solihull B91 127 B8
Tanwood Cross DY10 119 B2
Tanwood La DY10 119 A2
Tanworth Gr B12 86 F6
Tanworth-in-Arden CE Prim Sch B94 142 A2
Tanworth La B90 126 C5
Tanyard Cl
Alvechurch B48 139 B6
Coventry CV4 111 D1
Tanyard La B48 139 B6
Tanyard WS13 9 C8
Tanyards B27 88 D3
Tapcon Way CV2 114 F5
Tapestries Ave B70 53 A4
Taplow Pl WS11 1 F4
Tappinger Gr CV8 148 C5
Tapster La B94 143 F2
Tapton Cl WS3 14 C3
Tara Ct CV2 114 B4
Tardebigge CE Fst Sch B60 152 B7
Tardebigge Ct B97 152 C6
Tardebigge Ho B60 137 B3
Tarlington Rd CV6 112 E6
Tarmac Rd WV14 40 B5
Tarn Cl CV12 78 A2
Tarquin Cl CV3 134 D7
Tarragon Cl CV2 96 D1
Tarragon Gdns B31 102 C2
Tarrant Gr B32 84 F5
Tarrant B77 35 F8
Tarrant Wlk CV2 115 A5
Tarrington Covert 6 B38 123 E8
Tarry Hollow Rd DY5 61 B7
Tarry Rd B8 67 E5
Tarvin Mews DY5 61 D1
Taryn Dr WS10 41 D7
Tasker St
Walsall WS1 42 D8
West Bromwich B70 52 E4
Tasman Gr WV6 23 E5
Tat Bank Rd B69 64 B6
Tatchbrook Ct 5 CV31 161 F6
Tatnall Gr CV34 160 E8
Taunton Ave WV10 11 D4
Taunton Cl B31 102 C2
Taunton Rd B12 87 B4
Taunton Way CV6 95 A2
Taverners Cl WV12 13 C1
Taverner's Gn B20 54 F3
Tavistock Cl B79 21 C7
Tavistock Rd B27 106 C8
Tavistock St CV32 156 F1
Tavistock Way CV11 73 E5
Tavistock Wlk CV2 114 C7
Taw Cl B36 69 F7
Tay Croft B37 70 C4
Tay Gr
Birmingham B38 123 F8
Halesowen B62 83 E8
Taylor Ave
Royal Leamington Spa CV32 157 B2
Walsall WS3 28 D8
Taylor Cl CV8 148 B6
Taylor Ct CV34 160 D7
Taylor Ho 4 WS2 42 C7
Taylor Rd
Birmingham B13 104 F5
Dudley DY2 62 E2
Wolverhampton WV4 39 F5
Taylors La B69 63 E7
Taylor's La
Smethwick B67 64 F5
West Bromwich B71 53 D4
Taylors Orch B23 56 B4
Taylor St WV11 26 D5
Taylor Way B69 63 B8
Taynton Covert 4 B30 104 C3
Tay Rd
Birmingham B45 102 B1
Coventry CV6 113 B6
Taysfield Rd B31 102 E6
Taywood Dr B10 87 C7
Teachers Cl CV6 113 A5
Tea Gdn The CV12 95 E8
Teal Bsns Ctr LE10 74 D7
Tealby Gr B29 86 A1
Teal Cres DY10 117 B3
Teal Dr
Birmingham B23 56 B3
Hinckley LE10 75 A6
Teal Gr WV14 41 B3
Teall Ct B27 88 C3
Teall Rd B8 67 E5
Teal Rd B80 159 F4
Tean Cl
Birmingham B11 88 A3
Burntwood WS7 7 D6
Teasdale Way DY9 81 D4
Teasel Gr WV10 12 B7
Teasel Rd WV11 26 F5
Teazel Ave B30 103 D6
Tebworth Cl WV9 10 F2
Tedbury Cres B23 56 E6
Tedder Rd WS2 27 F2
Teddesley Ct WS11 1 E3
Teddesley Gr B33 69 C4
Teddesley St WS4 28 F3
Teddesley Way WS12 1 C6
Teddington Cl 4 B73 46 A2
Teddington Gr B42 55 D3
Ted Pitts La CV5 94 B2
Tedstone Rd B32 84 E5
Teesdale Ave B34 68 F6
Teesdale Cl WV1 26 A2
Tees Gr B38 123 F8
Teeswater Cl B60 150 E6
Teign Bank Cl LE10 71 D2
Teign Bank Rd LE10 71 D2
Teignmouth Rd B29 86 A1
Teign B77 36 A5
Telephone Rd CV3 114 C2
Telfer Rd CV6 113 B7
Telford Ave
Great Wyrley WS6 4 F3
Royal Leamington Spa CV32 157 B5
Telford Cl
Burntwood WS7 7 C8
Smethwick B67 64 D1
Walsall WS2 28 A5
West Bromwich B71 53 A8
Telford Gdns WV3 38 D7
Telford Gr WS12 2 B7
Telford Inf & Jun Schs CV32 157 C5
Telford Rd
Bedworth CV7 96 C8
Tamworth B79 20 F8
Walsall WS2 28 A5
Telford Way B66 64 F8
Teme Ave DY11 116 B3
Teme Ct B23 56 B3
Teme Gr WV13 27 D2
Teme Rd
Halesowen B63 82 B5
Stourbridge DY8 80 F3
Tempest St
Tamworth B79 21 A5
Wolverhampton WV2 163 C2
Templar Ave CV4 112 A1
Templar Ct CV11 73 C3
Templars' Fields CV4 132 B7
Templars Prim Sch CV4 112 A1
Templars The
Oldbury B69 63 E5
Warwick CV34 160 F5
Temple Ave
Balsall Common CV7 129 F6
Birmingham B28 106 A6
Temple Bar WV13 27 A2
Temple Cl B98 153 F4
Temple Ct B46 59 F1
Templefield Gdns 2 B9 67 C1
Templefield Sq B15 86 B7
Templefield St B9 67 C1
Temple Gr CV34 160 D5
Temple La B93 129 A4
Temple Meadow Prim Sch B64 63 A1
Temple Meadows Rd B71 53 E6
Templemore Dr B43 54 E7
Temple Pas B2 164 B2
Temple Rd
Dorridge B93 128 A3
Willenhall WV13 27 B3
Temple Row B2 164 C3
Temple Row W B2 164 B3
Temple Sq WV13 27 A3
Temple St
Bilston WV14 40 E5
Birmingham B2 164 B2
Dudley DY3 50 D3
West Bromwich B70 53 C4
Wolverhampton WV2 163 B2
Templeton Cl B93 128 A3
Templeton Rd B44 44 F2
Temple Way
Coleshill B46 59 F1
Oldbury B69 52 D2
Temple Wlk WV13 27 A2
Tenacre La DY3 50 E6
Ten Acres End B30 104 B8
Tenacres Fst Sch B98 154 F3
Tenacres La B98 154 F3
Ten Ashes La B45 122 C4
Tenbury Cl
Aldridge WS9 30 C8
Redditch B98 154 C6
Willenhall WS2 27 D3
Tenbury Ct WV4 38 D5
Tenbury Gdns WV4 38 D5
Tenbury Ho 2 B63 83 A3
Tenbury Rd B14 104 E6
Tenby Cl CV12 77 C1
Tenby Ct CV32 161 E8
Tenby Rd B13 87 D2
Tenby St N B1 66 B4
Tenby St B1 66 B4
Tenby Twr 2 B31 103 A1
Teneriffe Rd CV6 95 F1
Tenlands Rd B63 82 F3
Tenlons Rd CV10 72 F2
Tennal Dr B32 84 F6
Tennal Gr B32 84 F6
Tennal La B32 84 F6
Tennal Rd B32 84 F6
Tennant St
Birmingham B15 66 B1
Nuneaton CV11 73 E3
Tennessee B13 86 E2
Tennis Ct B30 103 D4
Tennis Ct The B15 86 A5
Tennscore Ave WS6 4 E3
Tennyson Ave
Sutton Coldfield B74 31 F6
Tamworth B79 21 A6
Warwick CV34 160 C4
Tennyson Cl CV8 148 C4
Tennyson Ho
3 Oldbury B68 64 C4
Birmingham B31 123 A8
Tennyson Rd
Birmingham B10 87 E7
Coventry CV2 114 C3
Dudley DY3 50 A4
Hinckley LE10 71 C1
Redditch B97 158 C8
Walsall WS3 28 E8
Willenhall WV12 27 E8
Wolverhampton WV10 12 A1
Tennyson St DY5 61 D7
Tennyson Way DY10 117 C6
Ten Shilling Dr CV4 131 E6
Tenter Ct B63 83 B4
Tenter Dr B63 83 C4
Tenterfields B63 83 B4
Tenterfields Prim Sch B63 83 C4
Terminal Rd B26 89 F3
Tern Cl WV4 39 D3
Tern Gr B38 103 E1
Terrace Rd
Birmingham B15 85 F3
Birmingham,Lozells B19 66 B7
Terrace St
Brierley Hill DY5 61 E5
Rowley Regis B65 63 B1
Wednesbury WS10 42 A3
Terrace The
Cradley Heath B64 82 E8
Wolverhampton WV3 24 C1
Terret Cl WS1 28 F2
Terry Ave CV32 156 C1
Terry Dr B76 46 F2
Terry Rd CV1 113 F1
Terrys Cl B98 153 F5
Terrys La B24 57 C3
Terry St DY2 51 E1
Tessall La B31 102 D2
Tetbury Gr B31 102 D3
Tetley Ave WS4 29 B4
Tetley Rd B11 87 E3
Tetnall St DY2 62 D8
Tettenhall Arc WV6 24 D5
Tettenhall Coll WV6 24 D4
Tettenhall Gate 9 WV3 25 A2
Tettenhall Rd WV1,WV3, WV6 24 F4
Tettenhall Wood Sch WV6 24 B3
Teviot Gdns
Brierley Hill DY5 61 B6
Wolverhampton WV8 10 A5
Teviot Gr B38 123 F8
Teviot Twr B19 66 C5
Tewe Pl WS13 9 A6
Tewkesbury Dr
Bedworth CV12 78 C3
Dudley DY2 62 D3
Tewkesbury Rd
Birmingham B20 55 E2
Walsall WS3 13 E2
Tew Park Rd B21 65 E7
Thackeray Cl CV10 72 A4
Thackeray Dr B79 21 A7
Thackeray Rd B30 103 D5
Thackhall St CV2 113 F4
Thame Ct B47 124 E2
Thames Cl
Brierley Hill DY5 61 B7
Bulkington CV12 79 A3
Thames Ct B73 46 B5
Thames Ho DY3 50 D3
Thames Rd WS3 14 E1
Thames Twr B7 67 B5
Thamley Rd CV6 113 A4
Thane Cl B80 159 F4
Thanet Cl DY6 60 C7
Thanet Gr B42 55 C4
Thatchers Ct WV5 37 C1
Thatchers The B62 83 E8
Thatchway Gdns B38 123 E7
Thaxted Rd B33 69 E3
Theatre App B5 164 C1
Theatre Ct CV34 160 D6
Theatre St CV34 160 D7
Thebes Cl CV5 111 B8
Theddingworth Cl CV3 134 E8
Thelbridge Rd B31 122 E6
Thelma Rd DY4 51 E5
Thelma St 1 WS1 42 D7
Thelsford Way B92 107 D8
Theodore Cl
4 Birmingham B17 85 D4
Oldbury B69 52 E1
Theresa Rd B11 87 B7
Thetford Cl DY4 51 D5
Thetford Gdns WV11 26 D6
Thetford Rd B42 55 B7
Thetford Way WS5 43 C3
Thickett Cl WS2 42 B8
Thicknall Dr DY9 81 C2
Thicknall La DY9 99 B3
Thicknall Rise DY9 99 B4
Thickthorn Cl CV8 148 B2
Thickthorn Mews CV8 148 B2
Thickthorn Orchs CV8 148 B2
Thimble Dr B76 46 F1
Thimble End Rd B76 47 A2
Thimble Mill La B6,B7 67 B7
Thimblemill Rd B67 64 E3
Thimbler Rd CV4 132 C7
Thinktank Mus & IMAX Theatre★ B4 66 F3
Third Ave
Birmingham,Bordesley Green B9 67 F2
Birmingham,Selly Oak B29 86 C3
Birmingham,Witton B6 55 F3
Brownhills WS8 7 A1
Kingswinford DY6 60 F8
Wolverhampton WV10 25 F7
Third Exhibition Ave B40 90 D4
Third Rd B61 120 F4
Thirlestane Cl CV8 148 C6
Thirlmere Ave CV11 73 F6
Thirlmere Cl
Cannock WS11 1 E1
Coventry CV4 111 E3
Wolverhampton WV6 24 D8
Thirlmere Dr
Birmingham B13 105 D8
Essington WV11 13 A2
Thirlmere Gr WV6 23 F4
Thirlmere Ho 3 B15 85 D3
Thirlmere Rd
Bedworth CV12 78 A2
Hinckley LE10 75 A7
Wolverhampton WV6 24 D8
Thirlmere Wlk DY5 81 B7
Thirsk Croft B36 68 C8
Thirsk Rd CV3 133 C5
Thirsk Way B61 121 B1
Thirston Cl WV11 27 A5
Thistle Cl DY3 50 F6
Thistle Croft WV11 26 D5
Thistledown Ave WS7 7 A6
Thistle Down Cl B74 31 A2
Thistledown Dr
3 Cannock WS12 2 D1
Featherstone WV10 12 A7
Thistledown Rd B34 69 C7
Thistledown Wlk DY3 39 C1
Thistle Gn B38 123 E7
Thistlegreen Cl B65 62 F5
Thistlegreen Rd DY2 62 E4
Thistle Ho B36 68 D8
Thistle La B32 102 B7
Thistlewood Gr B93 145 B6
Thistley Field E CV6 113 A7
Thistley Field N CV6 113 A7
Thistley Field S CV6 112 F6
Thistley Field W CV6 112 F7
Thistley Nook WS13 3 A1
Thomas Barnes Prim Sch B78 20 B7
Thomas Benson Pl 8 B12 86 F7
Thomas Cres 2 B66 65 C5
Thomas Greenway WS13 3 A2
Thomas Guy Rd B70 52 F6
Thomas Hardy Ct B79 21 A7
Thomas Ho WS3 14 D3
Thomas King Ho 6 CV1 113 E4
Thomas Landsdail St CV3 133 D8
Thomas Lane St CV6 96 A1
Thomas Mason Cl WV11 26 D7
Thomas Naul Croft CV4 111 F3
Thomas Sharp St CV4 132 A7
Thomas St
Bedworth CV12 78 A2
Birmingham B6 66 F6
Royal Leamington Spa CV32 157 A1
Smethwick B66 65 B5
Tamworth B77 21 D4
Walsall WS2 28 D2
West Bromwich B70 53 D2
Wolverhampton WV2 163 B1
Thomas Wlk B35 58 B3
Thompson Ave
Tamworth B77 21 C3
Wolverhampton WV2 39 E6
Thompson Cl
Dudley DY2 62 B2
Willenhall WV13 27 A3
Thompson Dr B24 67 F8
Thompson Gdns B67 64 F4
Thompson Ho DY4 52 C8
Thompson Rd
Oldbury B68 64 B5
Smethwick B67 64 F4
Thompson's La CV7 94 E6
Thompson's Rd CV7 94 F6
Thompson St
Bilston WV14 40 D5
Willenhall WV13 27 A3
Thomson Ave B38 103 D1
Thor Cl WS11 2 A5
Thoresby Croft DY1 50 F3
Thoresby B79 20 E6
Thornberry Dr DY1 61 E8
Thornberry Wlk B7 67 C6
Thornbridge Ave B42 55 D7
Thornbridge Gr WS9 15 F3

Thornbrook Ct 1 WS4 28 F3
Thornbury Ct WV6 24 A3
Thornbury Ho CV8 148 A3
Thornbury La B98 154 C7
Thornbury Rd B20 55 D2
Thornby Ave
Kenilworth CV8 148 B3
Solihull B91 107 B5
Tamworth B77 35 E8
Thornby Rd B23 56 C8
Thorncliffe Cl B97 158 A6
Thorncliffe Rd B44 44 E2
Thorn Cl WS10 41 F4
Thorncroft Way WS5 43 B4
Thorne Ave WV10 25 E7
Thorne Pl B65 63 C2
Thorne Rd WV13 27 A4
Thornes Croft WS9 16 E4
Thorne St WV2 40 A7
Thorneycroft La WV10 26 A6
Thorneycroft Pl WV14 41 B3
Thorneycroft Rd WV14 41 B4
Thorney Rd
Coventry CV2 114 B6
Sutton Coldfield B74 30 F1
Thornfield Cres WS7 7 A8
Thornfield Croft DY3 50 E7
Thornfield Rd B27 88 D2
Thornfield Way LE10 75 E8
Thorngrove Ave 7 B91 127 C8
Thornham Way B14 104 D1
Thornhill Dr CV11 79 C8
Thornhill Gr B21 65 F8
Thornhill Pk B74 45 A8
Thornhill Rd
Birmingham,Handsworth B21 65 F8
Birmingham,Sparkhill B11 87 D3
Brierley Hill DY5 81 E8
Cannock WS12 1 F3
Coventry CV1 113 D5
Dudley DY1 51 C4
Halesowen B63 82 E3
Redditch B98 154 E6
Solihull B91 107 C7
Sutton Coldfield B74 31 B1
Thornhurst Ave B32 84 E7
Thornleigh DY3 50 D5
Thornleigh Trad Est DY2 62 A7
Thornley Cl
Birmingham B13 87 A1
Radford Semele CV31 162 F5
Wolverhampton WV11 12 F1
Thornley Croft WS6 4 D1
Thornley Gr B76 58 C6
Thornley Rd WV11 12 F1
Thornley St WV1 163 C3
Thorn Rd B30 103 E7
Thorns Ave DY5 61 E1
Thorns Com Coll DY5 81 E8
Thorns Com Inf Sch CV8 148 B4
Thornsett Gr B90 106 B6
Thorns Prim Sch DY5 81 E7
Thorns Rd DY5 81 E7
Thorn Stile Cl CV32 157 E6
Thornthwaite Cl B45 102 B2
Thornton Cl
Coventry CV5 111 C4
Oldbury B69 52 C2
Warwick CV34 155 F1
Thornton Dr DY5 61 E1
Thornton Ho B19 66 E5
Thornton Jun Sch B8 68 B5
Thornton Rd
Birmingham B8 68 B5
Solihull B90 126 F6
Wolverhampton WV1 26 B1
Thorntons Way CV10 72 A3
Thornton Way B77 35 C8
Thornwood Cl B68 64 C5
Thornycroft Rd LE10 75 E8
Thornyfield Cl B90 106 D3
Thornyfield Rd B90 106 C3
Thornyhurst La WS14 17 A6
Thorpe Ave WS7 6 D8
Thorpe Cl
Burntwood WS7 6 D8
Sutton Coldfield B75 46 C7
Thorpe Ct B91 106 F6
Thorpe Rd WS1 42 E7
Thorpe St WS7 6 D8
Thorp St B5 164 B1
Threadneedle St CV1 113 D6
Three Acres La B90 125 F6
Three Corner Cl B90 125 E8
Three Cornered Cl CV32 157 E6
Three Crowns Specl Sch WS5 43 F8
Three Oaks Rd B47 125 B4
Three Pots Rd LE10 75 E4
Three Shires Oak Rd B67 64 F2
Three Spires Ave CV6 113 A6
Three Spires Ind Est CV6 96 A5
Three Spires Jct CV6 95 E1
Three Spires Sch CV6 112 D6
Three Spires Sh Ctr WS13 9 B7
Three Tuns La WV10 11 D1
Three Tuns Par WV10 11 C2
Threshers Dr WV12 27 D6
Threshers Way WV12 27 D6
Throckmorton Rd B98 159 A8
Throne Cl B65 63 D5
Throne Cres B65 63 D4
Throne Rd B65 63 D5
Throstles Cl B43 54 E7
Thruppence Cl CV4 131 E6
Thrushel Wlk WV11 26 C5
Thrush Rd B68 63 F2
Thruxton Cl
Birmingham B14 104 F3
Redditch B98 154 E3
Thunderbolt Way DY4 51 D6
Thurcroft Cl B8 67 F4
Thuree Rd B67 64 E2
Thurlby Ct WV1 25 A3
Thurleigh Cl DY9 81 C2
Thurlestone Rd
Birmingham B31 122 E7
Coventry CV6 112 F8
Thurloe Cres B45 101 E1
Thurlston Ave B92 88 F4
Thurlstone Dr WV4 38 F4
Thurlstone Rd WS3 14 B3
Thurne B77 35 F8
Thursfield Rd
Royal Leamington Spa CV32 157 B3
Tipton DY4 52 A6
West Bromwich B71 53 E7
Thurso B77 21 E5
Thurston Ave B69 63 F6
Thynne St B70 53 E2
Tibbats Cl B32 84 C3
Tibberton Cl
Halesowen B63 83 C4
Solihull B91 127 A8
Wolverhampton WV3 38 D7
Tibberton Ct B60 150 E7
Tibbets La B17 85 B4
Tibbington Rd DY4 51 E7
Tibbington Terr DY4 51 F7
Tibbits Ct 8 CV34 160 E6
Tibbits Ho 1 WS2 28 D3
Tibblestone B90 126 A5
Tiber Cl CV5 111 F4
Tiberius Cl B46 59 F1
Tibland Rd B27 88 D2
Ticknall Cl B97 153 A4
Tidbury Cl B97 158 C6
Tidbury Green Sch B90 125 E4
Tiddington Cl B36 58 B1
Tideswell Cl CV3 115 A1
Tideswell Rd B42 55 C7
Tidmarsh Cl CV7 130 A6
Tidmarsh Rd CV35 156 A7
Tidworth Croft 2 B14 105 A3
Tierney Dr DY4 52 C6
Tiffany La WV9 10 F2
Tiffield Rd B25 88 C5
Tigley Ave B32 84 D1
Tilbury Cl WV3 38 A8
Tilbury Gr B13 86 D1
Tildasley St B70 53 B5
Tildesley Dr WV12 27 B5
Tile Cross Rd B33 69 E2
Tile Cross Trad Est B33 69 E1
Tiled House La DY5 61 B6
Tile Gr B37 70 A5
Tile Hill La
Coventry,Allesley CV4, CV5 112 D2
Coventry,Tile Hill CV4 112 B1
Tile Hill Sta CV4 131 C8
Tile Hill Wood Sch & Language Coll CV4 111 D2
Tilehouse Green La B93 127 F6
Tilehouse La B90 125 E6
Tilehouse B97 153 D2
Tilehurst Dr CV4 111 D1
Tilesford Cl B90 127 A6
Tilewood Ave CV5 111 F4
Tilia Rd B77 22 B5
Tiller Gr B75 32 D4
Tilley St WS10 41 E6
Tillington Cl B98 154 E3
Tillyard Croft B29 85 C1
Tilshead Cl B14 104 E3
Tilsley Gr B23 56 B5
Tilston Dr DY5 61 D1
Tilton Rd
Birmingham B9 67 C1
Hinckley LE10 75 E6
Timberdine Cl B63 82 D6
Timberhonger La B61 136 B2
Timberlake Cl B90 127 B6
Timberley Croft B34 69 D7
Timberley La B34 69 C6
Timberley Prim Sch B34 69 D6
Timber Mill Ct 4 B17 85 B6
Timbers Way
Birmingham B11 87 A6
Sutton Coldfield B24 57 F4
Timbertree Cres B64 82 E7
Timbertree Prim Sch B64 82 E7
Timbertree Rd B64 82 F7
Times Square Ave DY5 61 F2
Timmins Cl B91 107 E6
Timmis Cl WV14 40 B3
Timmis Rd DY9 81 C6
Timon View CV34 161 E3
Timothy Gr CV4 112 B1
Timothy Rd B69 63 D7
Tinacre Hill WV6 23 E2
Tinchbourne St 1 DY1 51 C1
Tindal Sch B12 86 F5
Tindal St B12 86 F5
Tink-A-Tank CV34 160 E6
Tinkers Farm Gr B31 102 E3
Tinkers Farm Rd B31 102 E3
Tinkers Green Rd B77 35 F6
Tinkers La
Earlswood B94 142 E7
Lapworth B94 143 E1
Tinmeadow Cres B45 122 C7
Tinsley St DY4 52 E5
Tintagel Cl
Coventry CV3 134 D5
Perton WV6 23 F3
Redditch B98 154 E3
Tintagel Dr DY1 50 E2
Tintagel Gr CV8 148 B4
Tintagel Way
Nuneaton CV11 74 A5
Walsall WS9 29 E7
Tintern Cl
Bromsgrove B61 136 E1
Sutton Coldfield B74 45 A7
Tintern Cres WS3 13 F2
Tintern Ct WV6 23 E4
Tintern Ho B32 84 F5
Tintern Rd B20 55 E1
Tintern Villas 4 B12 87 B5
Tintern Way
Bedworth CV12 78 C3
Walsall WS3 13 F2
Tipperary Cl B36 68 E8
Tipperary Wlk 2 B69 63 F7
Tipper Trad Est DY9 82 A5
Tippett Cl CV11 79 A7
Tipping's Hill B97 158 C5
Tippity Gn B65 63 B4
Tipps Stone Cl DY4 51 E4
Tipton Green Jun Sch DY4 51 F4
Tipton Rd
Dudley,Tipton Green DY1 51 E3
Dudley,Woodsetton DY3 50 F7
Oldbury B69 52 C2
Tipton Sta DY4 51 F6
Tipton St DY3 50 E7
Tirley Rd B33 69 A4
Tisdale Rise CV8 148 B6
Titan Bsns Ctr CV34 161 E4
Titania Cl B45 102 A3
Titan Way WS13 9 F8
Titchfield Cl WV10 11 E4
Titford Cl B69 63 F4
Titford La B65 63 E4
Titford Rd B69 63 F4
Tithe Barn La B94 142 C6
Tithe Croft WV10 25 F3
Tithe Rd WV11 26 D6
Titterstone Rd B31 123 A8
Tiverton Cl DY6 61 A3
Tiverton Dr
Nuneaton CV11 73 F5
West Bromwich B71 53 C6
Tiverton Gr
Coventry CV2 114 D5
Smethwick B67 64 F6
Tiverton Jun & Inf Sch B29 85 F2
Tiverton Rd
Birmingham B29 85 F2
Coventry CV2 114 D5
Smethwick B66 65 B5
Tiverton Sch CV6 112 D5
Tiveycourt Rd CV6 96 A3
Tividale Com Arts Coll B69 52 C1
Tividale Com Prim Sch B69 52 B2
Tividale Rd B69 52 A2
Tividale St DY4 52 A2
Tivoli The B26 88 D6
Tixall Rd B28 105 E5
Tobruk Wlk
Brierley Hill DY5 61 D3
Willenhall WV13 40 E8
Tocil Croft CV4 132 D4
Toledo Cl CV5 112 C1
Toler Rd CV11 73 B5
Tollard Cl CV2 114 F5
Toll End Rd DY4 52 C7
Tolley Rd DY11 116 B1
Tollgate Cl B31 122 F8
Tollgate Dr B20 66 B7
Tollgate Prec B67 64 F6
Toll House Rd B45 122 C7
Tollhouse Rd B60 150 E6
Tollhouse Way B66 64 F6
Tolman Dr B77 21 D3
Tolson Ave B78 35 B8
Tolson Cl B77 35 D5
Tolworth Gdns WV2 39 E7
Tolworth Hall Rd B24 57 B3
Tom Ellis Ct CV7 96 A8
Tomey Rd B11 87 D5
Tom Henderson Cl CV3 134 F7
Tom Hill B94 142 B3
Tomkinson Dr DY11 116 B4
Tomkinson Rd CV10 72 F4
Tomlan Rd B31 123 C7
Tomlinson Rd B36 58 D1
Tompstone Rd B71 53 F8
Tomson Ave CV6 113 B4
Toms Town La B80 159 E3
Tom Ward Cl CV3 134 E7
Tom Williams Way B77 35 C8
Tonadine Cl WV11 13 A1
Tonbridge Rd
Birmingham B24 57 A1
Coventry CV3 134 A6
Tong Ct 9 WV3 25 C4
Tong St WS1 29 A1
Tongue Ave B78 35 A8
Topcliffe Prim Sch B35 58 A3
Top Croft Rd B23 56 F7
Topfield Ho B14 104 E1
Top Field Wlk B14 104 D2
Topland Gr B31 102 C2
Topp's Dr CV12 77 E1
Topp's Heath CV12 77 E1
Top Rd
Barnacle CV7,CV12 97 B7
Upper Catshill B61 121 A4
Topsham Croft B14 104 D5
Topsham Rd B67 64 E6
Torbay Rd CV5 112 C4
Torbay B77 21 E5
Torcastle Cl CV6 113 F7
Torc Ave B77 21 E4
Torc High Sch B77 21 F1
Torcross Ave CV2 114 C6
Torfield WV8 10 E2
Toronto Gdns B32 84 E6
Torpoint Cl CV2 114 C7
Torre Ave B31 102 E2
Torres Cl CV34 160 B4
Torrey Gr B8 68 C4
Torridge Dr WV11 26 C5
Torridge B77 36 A5
Torridon Croft B13 86 D3
Torridon Rd WV11 13 B1
Torridon Way LE10 71 B1
Torrington Ave CV4 131 E8
Torrs Cl B97 153 D2
Torside B77 36 B7
Torvale Rd WV6 24 A2
Tor Way WS3 14 F3
Torwood Cl CV4 131 F6
Totnes Cl CV2 114 C7
Totnes Gr 2 B29 85 F2
Totnes Rd B67 64 F6
Tottenham Cres B44 45 B2
Touchstone Rd CV34 161 F2
Touchwood Hall Cl B91 107 C4
Touchwood Sh Ctr 1 B91 107 C3
Towbury Cl B98 158 F5
Towcester Croft B36 68 D8
Tower Croft B37 70 B4
Tower Dr B61 137 A6
Tower Hill B42 55 A6
Tower Rd
Bedworth CV12 78 B2
Birmingham,Aston B6 67 A7
Birmingham,Aston New Town B6 66 F7
Birmingham B23 56 E4
Oldbury B69 63 C7
Sutton Coldfield B75 32 B3
Tower Rise B69 63 C7
Towers Cl
Kenilworth CV8 147 F2
Kidderminster DY10 117 B5
Tower St
16 Royal Leamington Spa CV31 162 A7
Birmingham B19 164 B5
Coventry CV1 165 B3
Dudley DY1 51 C1
Sedgley DY3 39 D1
Walsall WS1 28 E2
Wolverhampton WV1 163 C3
Tower View Cres CV10 72 B3
Tower View Rd WS6 13 F8
Townend St WS2 28 E2
Townesend Cl CV34 155 F1
Town Feilds Cl CV5 112 B7
Townfields WS13 9 A7
Townfold WS3 15 A4
Town Gate Retail Pk DY1 51 F2
Town Jun Sch B72 46 C4
Townley Gdns B6 55 E1
Townsend Ave
Bromsgrove B61 137 B4
Sedgley DY3 50 D8
Townsend Croft CV3 133 C7
Townsend Dr
Nuneaton CV11 73 F3
Sutton Coldfield B76 57 F7
Townsend Ho B79 21 A4
Townsend Pl DY6 60 D6
Townsend Rd CV3 133 C8
Townsends Cl CV11 75 A1
Townsend Way 5 B1 66 B3
Townshend Gr B37 69 F4
Townson Rd WV11 27 A8
Townwell Fold WV1 163 B3
Town Wharf Bsns Pk WS2 28 D2
Towpath Cl
Bedworth CV6 96 B6
Birmingham B9 67 B2
Towyn Rd B13 87 D2
Toys La B63 82 C5
Tozer St DY4 51 F7
Traceys Mdw B45 122 A7
Tractor Spares Ind Est WV13 26 D2
Trafalgar Cl WS12 2 E4
Trafalgar Ct B69 52 B1
Trafalgar Gr B25 88 A6
Trafalgar Ho
3 Coventry CV1 113 B2
Birmingham B11 87 B8
Cannock WS12 2 E4
Trafalgar Rd
Birmingham,Erdington B24 56 F3
Birmingham,Handsworth B21 65 E8
Birmingham,Moseley B13 86 F4
Oldbury B69 52 B1
Smethwick B66 65 C4
Trafford Dr CV10 72 C6
Trafford Lodge 4 CV31 162 B7
Trafford Pk The B98 153 F3
Trafford Rd LE10 71 F2
Trajan Hill B46 59 F1
Tram St DY10 116 E5
Tramway Cl
1 Bilston WV14 41 A7
Darlaston WS10 41 E7
Tram Way B66 64 C7
Tranter Ave B48 139 A5
Tranter Cres WS11 2 B3
Tranter Rd B8 68 A5
Tranwell Cl WV9 10 F2
Traquain Dr DY1 51 A3
Travellers Cl WS7 7 A5
Travellers Way B37 70 D3
Treaford La B8 68 C4
Treasure Cl B77 21 E2
Treddles La B70 53 D3
Tredington Cl
1 Birmingham B29 103 A7
Redditch B98 159 B7
Tredington Rd CV5 111 F4
Tree Acre Gr B63 82 C4
Treedale Cl CV4 131 D8
Treeford Cl B91 106 F1
Trees Rd WS1 42 F6
Treeton Croft B33 69 A2
Treetops Dr WV12 27 E4
Trefoil Cl B29 103 A7
Trefoil B77 22 B5
Treford Ct DY9 81 B1
Treforest Rd CV3 134 C8
Tregarron Rd B63 82 C5
Tregea Rise B43 54 C7
Tregony Rise WS14 9 D6
Tregorrick Rd CV7 96 A8
Tregullan Rd CV7 96 B8
Trehern Cl B93 128 A5
Treherne Rd CV6 113 B8
Trehernes Dr DY9 81 B1
Trehurst Ave B42 55 C7
Trejon Rd B64 82 E8
Trelawney Rd CV7 96 A7
Tremaine Gdns WV10 25 E4
Tremont Ho WV10 25 E3
Tremont St WV10 25 E3
Trenance Cl WS14 9 D7
Trenance Rd CV7 96 A8
Trenchard Cl B75 46 F5
Treneere Rd CV7 96 B8
Trensale Ave CV6 112 F4
Trent Cl
Burntwood WS7 7 D6
Perton WV6 23 E4
Stourbridge DY8 81 A4
Trent Cres B47 124 E2
Trent Ct B73 46 B5
Trent Dr B36 69 F8
Trentham Ave WV12 27 B5
Trentham Cl
Cannock WS11 2 B1
Nuneaton CV11 78 F8
Trentham Gdns CV8 148 C5
Trentham Gr B26 88 E5
Trentham Rd CV1 113 F4
Trentham Rise WV2 39 F7
Trent Ho
Cannock WS12 2 C5
Dudley DY3 50 E3
Trent Pl WS3 28 D8
Trent Rd
Bulkington CV12 79 A2
Cannock WS11 1 E5
Hinckley LE10 75 A8
Nuneaton CV11 73 D5
Walsall WS3 15 A1
Trent St B5 66 F2
Trent Twr 3 B7 67 A4
Trent Valley Cotts WS13 3 F1
Trent Valley Rd WS13,WS14 9 D8
Trenville Ave B11 87 B5
Tresco Cl B45 101 E1
Trescott Jun & Inf Sch B31 102 D3
Trescott Rd
Birmingham B31 102 D4
Redditch B98 153 F3
Tresham Rd
2 Kingswinford DY6 60 D8
Birmingham B44 44 F1
Tresillian Rd CV7 96 B8
Tressel Croft CV34 161 E2
Trevanie Ave B32 84 C6
Trevelyan Ho 1 B37 70 C1
Treville Cl B98 154 E3
Treviscoe Cl CV7 96 A7
Trevithick Cl WS7 7 C8
Trevor Ave WS6 5 A3
Trevor Cl CV4 131 D8
Trevorne Cl B12 86 F6
Trevor Rd
Hinckley LE10 71 F1
Walsall WS3 14 F5
Trevor St W B7 67 C6
Trevor St B7 67 C6
Trevose Ave CV7 96 B8
Trevose Cl WS3 13 F3
Trevose Retreat B12 86 F5
Trewint Cl CV7 96 A8
Trewman Cl B76 57 F8
Treyamon Rd WS5 43 D7
Treynham Cl WV1 26 C1
Triangle The
Birmingham B18 65 F6
Coventry CV5 112 B4
Trianon Rd B60 137 C1
Tribune Ho 7 LE10 71 D1
Trickley Dr 2 B75 46 F6
Trident Bsns Pk CV11 73 D3
Trident Bvd B35 58 B2

Trident Cl
Sutton Coldfield,Walmley B76 ... 57 F7
Sutton Coldfield,Wylde Green B23 ... 57 A7
Trident Ct
Birmingham,Coleshill Heath B37 ... 90 E8
Birmingham,Handsworth Wood B20 ... 55 A3
Trident Ctr The DY1 ... 51 C1
Trident Dr
Oldbury B68 ... 64 B5
Wednesbury WS10 ... 41 D3
Trident Ho 4 B15 ... 66 C1
Trident Rd B26 ... 90 C4
Trident Ret Pk B9 ... 67 A2
Trigo Croft B36 ... 68 E8
Trimpley Cl B93 ... 127 E3
Trimpley Dr
Coventry CV6 ... 113 C6
Kidderminster DY11 ... 116 A7
Trimpley Gdns WV4 ... 38 E3
Trimpley Rd B32 ... 84 B1
Trinculo Gr CV34 ... 161 F2
Trinder Rd B67 ... 64 D2
Trindle Rd DY2 ... 51 D1
Tring Ct WV6 ... 24 F4
Trinity CE Prim Sch WV10 25 F4
Trinity Churchyard CV1 ... 165 B3
Trinity Cl
1 Birmingham B19 ... 66 D8
Cannock WS11 ... 4 E8
Shenstone WS14 ... 17 F6
Solihull B92 ... 89 B1
Stourbridge DY8 ... 60 D2
Trinity Ct
1 Kidderminster DY10 ... 116 F6
4 Cradley Heath B64 ... 62 E1
Birmingham B6 ... 55 D1
Bromsgrove B60 ... 151 B7
Hinckley LE10 ... 75 C8
Trinity Ctr 1 B64 ... 62 E1
Trinity Ct WV3 ... 25 A2
Trinity Dr B79 ... 20 D6
Trinity Fields DY10 ... 116 F6
Trinity Grange DY10 ... 116 F7
Trinity Gr WS10 ... 42 A3
Trinity High Sch & Sixth Form Ctr B98 ... 153 F4
Trinity Hill B72 ... 46 C5
Trinity Ho B70 ... 53 E1
Trinity La
Coventry CV1 ... 165 B3
Hinckley LE10 ... 71 C1
Trinity Pk B40 ... 90 D3
Trinity RC Sch CV32 ... 156 D2
Trinity RC Sch The CV34 161 C6
Trinity Rd
Bilston WV14 ... 40 F5
Birmingham B6 ... 55 E1
Dudley DY1 ... 51 C1
Freasley B78,CV9 ... 36 B3
Stourbridge DY8 ... 81 A8
Sutton Coldfield B75 ... 32 C1
Willenhall WV12 ... 27 D7
Trinity Road N B70 ... 53 D2
Trinity Road S B70 ... 53 D1
Trinity St
Brierley Hill DY5 ... 61 D3
Coventry CV1 ... 165 B3
Cradley Heath B64 ... 62 E1
Oldbury B69 ... 64 A6
Royal Leamington Spa CV32 ... 156 F1
Smethwick B67 ... 65 A6
West Bromwich B70 ... 53 D2
Trinity Terr 2 B11 ... 87 A8
Trinity Vicarage Rd LE10 ... 75 C8
Trinity Way Sta B70 ... 53 D1
Trinity Way B70 ... 53 D2
Trinity Wlk CV11 ... 73 E3
Trippleton Ave B32 ... 102 B8
Tristram Ave B31 ... 103 B1
Triton Cl WS6 ... 4 F1
Trittiford Rd B13 ... 105 C6
Triumph Cl CV2 ... 114 E3
Triumph Ho CV1 ... 165 B2
Triumph B77 ... 21 E3
Triumph Wlk B36 ... 59 A1
Troilus Ct CV34 ... 161 F3
Trojan B77 ... 21 E3
Tromans Cl B64 ... 82 E7
Tromans Ind Est DY2 ... 62 D3
Troon Cl
Sutton Coldfield B75 ... 46 D8
Walsall WS3 ... 14 A3
Troon Ct WV6 ... 23 D5
Troon Pl DY8 ... 60 C3
Troon B77 ... 22 C4
Troon Way LE10 ... 75 D4
Trossachs Rd CV5 ... 111 F3
Trotter's La B71 ... 53 A7
Troughton Cres CV6 ... 113 A5
Trouse La WS10 ... 41 F3
Troutbeck Ave CV32 ... 156 C2
Troutbeck Dr DY5 ... 81 B8
Troutbeck Rd CV5 ... 111 F4
Troyes Cl CV3 ... 133 E7
Troy Gr B14 ... 104 D4
Troy Ind Est B96 ... 159 A3
Truck Stop Bsns Pk B11 ... 88 B5
Truda St 2 WS1 ... 42 D7
Trueman Cl CV34 ... 160 E8
Truemans Heath La B47, B90 ... 125 C7
Truggist La CV7 ... 130 E8
Trundalls La B90 ... 126 A5
Truro Cl
Hinckley LE10 ... 71 E4
Lichfield WS13 ... 3 B3
Nuneaton CV11 ... 73 F5
Rowley Regis B65 ... 63 E4
Truro Dr DY11 ... 116 A5
Truro Pl WS12 ... 5 C8
Truro Rd WS5 ... 43 D7
Truro Twr 2 B16 ... 66 A2
Truro Wlk B37 ... 70 B2
Trustin Cres B92 ... 107 E8
Tryan Rd CV10 ... 72 E4
Tryon Pl WV14 ... 40 E6
Tryst The B61 ... 137 B5
Trysull Ave B26 ... 89 C4
Trysull Gdns WV3 ... 38 D7
Trysull Holloway WV5 ... 37 C3
Trysull Rd
Orton WV5 ... 37 E1
Wolverhampton WV3 ... 38 D7
Trysull Way DY2 ... 62 C4
Tudbury Rd B31 ... 102 E4
Tudman Cl B76 ... 58 A7
Tudor Ave CV5 ... 111 F4
Tudor Bsns Ctr 9 B98 ... 153 E3
Tudor Cl
Balsall Common CV7 ... 130 A6
Birmingham,Highter's Heath B14 ... 105 A1
Birmingham,King's Heath B13 ... 104 F6
Burntwood WS7 ... 7 C6
Cheslyn Hay WS6 ... 4 E3
Lichfield WS14 ... 9 F6
Sutton Coldfield B73 ... 45 D2
Tudor Cres
Tamworth B77 ... 21 F4
Wolverhampton WV2 ... 39 B6
Tudor Croft B37 ... 69 F1
Tudor Ct
Bedworth CV7 ... 95 E7
Coventry CV3 ... 133 C8
Essington WV11 ... 12 F4
Sutton Coldfield B74 ... 32 A2
Tipton DY4 ... 52 A4
Warwick CV34 ... 160 D5
Tudor Eaves 2 B17 ... 85 C5
Tudor Gdns
Birmingham B23 ... 56 E3
Stourbridge DY8 ... 80 E5
Tudor Grange Sch B91 ... 107 A2
Tudor Gr B74 ... 45 A8
Tudor Hill B73 ... 46 B6
Tudor Ho
Dudley DY2 ... 61 F6
Walsall WS1 ... 28 E2
Tudor Ind Est B11 ... 88 B5
Tudor Park Ct 2 B74 ... 31 F3
Tudor Park Gdns WS7 ... 7 C6
Tudor Pl DY3 ... 50 E6
Tudor Rd
Birmingham B13 ... 86 F3
Burntwood WS7 ... 7 C6
Cannock WS12 ... 1 F8
Darlaston WV14 ... 41 B4
Dudley DY3 ... 50 E6
Hinckley LE10 ... 71 C3
Nuneaton CV10 ... 72 C6
Oldbury B68 ... 64 C4
Rowley Regis B65 ... 63 C5
Sutton Coldfield B73 ... 46 B5
Wolverhampton WV10 ... 26 A4
Tudor Row 3 WS13 ... 9 B7
Tudors Cl 4 B10 ... 87 C8
Tudor St
Birmingham B18 ... 65 E4
Tipton DY4 ... 52 A4
Tudor Terr
Birmingham B17 ... 85 C6
Dudley DY2 ... 51 E1
Tudor Vale DY3 ... 50 E6
Tudor Way
Cheslyn Hay WS6 ... 4 D1
Sutton Coldfield B72 ... 46 B2
Tufnell Gr B8 ... 68 B7
Tugford Rd B29 ... 103 C7
Tuisi Ctr B19 ... 164 A4
Tulip Gdns B29 ... 102 F7
Tulip Tree Ave CV8 ... 148 B5
Tulip Tree Ct CV8 ... 148 B4
Tulip Wlk B37 ... 90 C8
Tulliver Cl CV12 ... 78 B3
Tulliver Rd CV10 ... 73 C1
Tulliver St CV6 ... 113 B5
Tulyar Cl B36 ... 68 C8
Tunnel Dr B98 ... 153 E2
Tunnel La
Birmingham,Brandwood End B14 ... 104 C4
Birmingham,Lifford B30 ... 104 B4
Tunnel Rd B70 ... 53 A7
Tunnel St WV14 ... 51 C8
Tunstall Rd DY6 ... 61 A5
Turchill Dr B76 ... 58 B8
Turf Cl WS11 ... 6 A4
Turf Cotts WV4 ... 38 F2
Turfpits La B23 ... 56 D6
Turf Pitts La B75 ... 32 F4
Turks Head Way B70 ... 53 C2
Turlands Cl CV2 ... 115 A7
Turley St DY1 ... 51 A6
Turls Hill Rd
Sedgley DY3 ... 50 E8
Sedgley WV14 ... 50 F8
Turls St DY3 ... 50 E8
Turnberry Dr CV11 ... 79 C8
Turnberry Gr WV6 ... 23 D5
Turnberry Rd
Birmingham B42 ... 55 B8
Walsall WS3 ... 14 A4
Turnberry B77 ... 22 C5
Turner Ave WV4,WV14 ... 39 F2
Turner Cl
Bedworth CV12 ... 78 A4
Cannock WS11 ... 2 D2
Warwick CV34 ... 160 B4
Turner Dr
Brierley Hill DY5 ... 81 D7
Hinckley LE10 ... 71 A3
Turner Gr WV6 ... 24 A4
Turner Rd CV5 ... 112 D3
Turners Croft B71 ... 54 A8
Turner's Gr DY3 ... 50 C4
Turner's Hill Rd DY3 ... 50 C4
Turner's Hill B65 ... 63 B6
Turner's La DY5 ... 61 D1
Turner St
2 Dudley,Old Dock DY1 ... 62 B8
Birmingham B11 ... 87 A6
Dudley,Gornalwood DY3 ... 50 D3
Tipton DY4 ... 51 F7
West Bromwich B70 ... 53 A4
Turney Rd DY8 ... 80 F6
Turnham Gn WV6 ... 23 E3
Turnhouse Rd B35 ... 58 B4
Turnley Rd B34 ... 69 C6
Turnpike Cl
Balsall Common CV7 ... 130 B7
Birmingham B11 ... 87 A6
Turnpike Dr B46 ... 59 C2
Turnpike La B97 ... 153 A4
Turnstone Dr WV10 ... 12 B7
Turnstone Rd DY10 ... 117 A1
Turpin Ct CV31 ... 161 F6
Turquoise Gr WS11 ... 2 C3
Turton Cl WS3 ... 14 A4
Turton Rd
Tipton DY4 ... 40 F1
West Bromwich B70 ... 53 B2
Turtons Croft WV14 ... 40 B3
Turton St DY10 ... 117 A8
Turton Way CV8 ... 148 C4
Turves Gn
Birmingham,Turves Green B31 ... 103 A1
Birmingham,West Heath B31 ... 122 F8
Turves Green Boys' Tech Coll B31 ... 123 A8
Turves Green Girls Sch & Tech Coll B31 ... 103 A1
Turves Green Prim Sch B31 ... 103 A1
Turville Cl LE10 ... 75 F5
Turville Rd B20 ... 55 C1
Tustin Gr B27 ... 106 C8
Tutbury Ave
Coventry CV4 ... 132 E6
Perton WV6 ... 24 A3
Tutbury Cl WS11 ... 2 C3
Tutbury B77 ... 35 C7
Tutehill B77 ... 36 B7
Tutnall Cl B60 ... 137 F1
Tutnall Dr B94 ... 143 B6
Tutnall Grange B60 ... 138 A1
Tutnall La
Blackwell B60 ... 138 A1
Finstall B60 ... 137 F1
Tutors Way DY10 ... 116 E4
Tuttle Hill CV10 ... 72 F6
Tuxford Cl WV10 ... 25 E4
Twatling Rd B45 ... 122 A2
Tweedside Cl LE10 ... 71 F3
Tweeds Well B32 ... 102 B7
Tweed Twr B20 ... 55 D2
Twickenham Ct DY8 ... 80 C7
Twickenham Dr B13 ... 86 E2
Twickenham Prim Sch B44 ... 45 C1
Twickenham Rd B44 ... 45 C1
Twickenham Way CV3 ... 115 B1
Twiners Rd B98 ... 153 F1
Two Gates Com Prim Sch
Tamworth B77 ... 35 C8
Tamworth,Mount Pleasant B77 ... 21 C1
Two Gates B63 ... 82 C5
Two Gates Ind Est B77 ... 35 D7
Two Gates La B63 ... 82 C5
Two Locks DY5 ... 62 A4
Two Oaks Ave WS7 ... 6 D8
Two Trees Cl B78 ... 20 B6
Two Woods La DY5 ... 61 E1
Two Woods Trad Est DY5 ... 61 F1
Twycross Gr B36 ... 68 D7
Twycross Rd LE10 ... 75 F6
Twycross Wlk CV34 ... 155 D1
Twydale Ave B69 ... 52 C2
Twyford Cl WS9 ... 30 B5
Twyford Gr WV11 ... 26 F7
Twyford Rd B8 ... 68 C5
Twyning Rd
Birmingham,Edgbaston B16 ... 65 D3
Birmingham,Stirchley B30 ... 104 B7
Tybalt Cl
Coventry CV3 ... 134 C5
Royal Leamington Spa CV34 ... 161 D4
Tyber Dr B20 ... 55 B3
Tyberry Cl B90 ... 106 A1
Tyburn Gr B24 ... 57 D3
Tyburn Rd
Birmingham B24 ... 57 C2
Wolverhampton WV1 ... 26 C2
Tyburn Sq B24 ... 57 D3
Tyburn Trad Est B24 ... 57 D2
Tyebeams B34 ... 69 C5
Tye Gdns DY9 ... 81 B1
Tyler Ct B24 ... 56 F3
Tyler Gdns WV13 ... 27 B1
Tyler Gr B43 ... 44 A1
Tyler Rd WV13 ... 27 B1
Tylers Gn B38 ... 104 B1
Tylers Gr B90 ... 126 F6
Tylney Cl
Birmingham B5 ... 86 D7
Coventry CV3 ... 115 B2
Tyndale Cres B43 ... 44 C3
Tyndall Wlk B32 ... 84 A2
Tyne Cl
Birmingham B37 ... 70 C4
Brownhills WS8 ... 6 C2
Tyne Ct B73 ... 46 B5
Tynedale Cres WV4 ... 39 E3
Tynedale Rd B11 ... 87 F3
Tyne Gr B25 ... 88 D8
Tynemouth Cl CV2 ... 96 D5
Tyne Pl DY5 ... 61 F2
Tynes The B60 ... 150 E7
Tyning Cl WV9 ... 11 A2
Tyninghame Ave WV6 ... 24 D7
Tynings La WS9 ... 30 A5
Tynsall Ave B97 ... 152 F2
Tynward Cl CV3 ... 133 B5
Tyrley Cl WV6 ... 24 B2
Tyrol Cl DY8 ... 80 D6
Tyseley Hill Rd B11 ... 88 A4
Tyseley Ind Est B11 ... 87 E5
Tyseley La B11 ... 88 A4
Tyseley Locomotive Wks Visitor Ctr* B11 ... 87 F5
Tyseley Sta B11 ... 88 A5
Tysoe Cl
Hockley Heath B94 ... 143 C6
Redditch B98 ... 154 D2
Tysoe Croft CV3 ... 134 F8
Tysoe Dr B76 ... 46 F4
Tysoe Rd B44 ... 55 F7
Tythe Barn Cl B60 ... 150 D6
Tythebarn Dr DY6 ... 60 A7
Tythe Barn La B90 ... 126 A6
Tyzack Cl DY5 ... 61 C2

U

Udall Rd WV14 ... 40 D3
Uffculme Rd B30 ... 104 D8
Uffculme Specl Sch B13 ... 86 E1
Uffmoor Est B63 ... 82 E2
Uffmoor La B62 ... 100 D7
Ufton Cl B90 ... 106 E3
Ufton Cres B90 ... 106 D3
Ufton Croft CV5 ... 112 A3
Ullapool Cl B97 ... 158 D5
Ullenhall Rd
Dorridge B93 ... 128 A6
Sutton Coldfield B76 ... 57 F8
Ullenwood B21 ... 65 D7
Ulleries Rd B92 ... 89 A2
Ullrik Gn B24 ... 56 F2
Ullswater Ave
Nuneaton CV11 ... 73 F6
Royal Leamington Spa CV32 ... 156 C2
Ullswater Cl B32 ... 84 F2
Ullswater Gdns DY6 ... 60 D6
Ullswater Ho 4 B69 ... 63 D5
Ullswater Pl WS11 ... 1 E1
Ullswater Rd
Bedworth CV12 ... 78 A2
Coventry CV3 ... 114 E1
Willenhall WV11 ... 13 B1
Ullswater Rise DY5 ... 61 E5
Ullswater B77 ... 36 B7
Ulster Cl WS11 ... 2 A3
Ulster Dr DY6 ... 60 E4
Ulverley Cres B92 ... 106 F8
Ulverley Green Rd B92 ... 88 F1
Ulverley Sch B92 ... 89 B1
Ulverscroft Rd CV3 ... 133 D7
Ulwine Dr B31 ... 103 A4
Umberslade Children's Farm* B94 ... 142 C2
Umberslade Rd
Birmingham B29 ... 104 A8
Earlswood B94 ... 142 C7
Tanworth-In-A B94 ... 142 E3
Uncle Ben's Cl 1 B69 ... 63 F4
Underhill Cl
Coventry CV3 ... 133 D3
Redditch B98 ... 158 F6
Underhill La WV10 ... 12 A2
Underhill Prim Sch WV10 12 B1
Underhill Rd
Birmingham B8 ... 67 F3
Tipton DY4 ... 52 C6
Underhill St B69 ... 64 A5
Underhill Wlk B69 ... 64 A5
Underley Cl DY6 ... 60 B7
Underpass The B40 ... 90 E4
Underwood Cl
Birmingham B15 ... 85 D4
Birmingham,Stockland Green B23 ... 56 C4
Redditch B97 ... 158 A7
Underwood Rd B20 ... 54 E5
Unett Ct 9 B66 ... 65 C5
Unett St
Birmingham B19 ... 66 C5
Smethwick B66 ... 65 C4
Unett Wlk B19 ... 66 C5
Unicorn Ave CV5 ... 111 E4
Unicorn Hill B97 ... 153 D4
Unicorn La CV5 ... 111 F4
Union Bldgs CV1 ... 165 B2
Union Dr B73 ... 45 F2
Union Ho B73 ... 45 F2
Union La WV5 ... 37 D2
Union Mill St WV1 ... 163 D3
Union Pas B2 ... 164 C2
Union Pl
Birmingham B29 ... 86 B2
Coventry CV6 ... 95 F4
Union Rd
Birmingham B6 ... 67 B8
Oldbury B69 ... 52 E2
Royal Leamington Spa CV32 ... 156 E1
Solihull,Lode Heath B91 ... 107 C4
Solihull,Shirley B90 ... 106 C2
West Bromwich B70 ... 52 F2
Union Row B21 ... 65 F7
Union St
6 Dudley DY1 ... 51 C1
Bilston WV14 ... 40 C5
Birmingham B2 ... 164 C2
Burntwood WS7 ... 6 E5
Cannock WS11 ... 4 E6
Kidderminster DY10 ... 116 E7
Redditch B98 ... 153 F3
Rowley Regis B65 ... 63 C1
Stourbridge,Lye DY9 ... 81 E5
Stourbridge,Stambermill DY8 ... 81 A4
Tipton,Princes End DY1 ... 51 F8
Tipton,Tipton Green DY4 ... 51 F5
Walsall WS1 ... 28 F1
Wednesbury WS10 ... 41 F2
West Bromwich B70 ... 64 D8
Willenhall WV13 ... 27 A2
Wolverhampton WV1 ... 163 C3
Unisant Trad Est B64 ... 62 F2
United Coll of the Ascension B29 ... 85 C1
Unitt Dr B64 ... 82 E8
Unity Cl WS10 ... 41 C4
Unity Ho CV1 ... 165 C4
Unity Pl
9 Birmingham B29 ... 85 F2
Oldbury B69 ... 64 A8
Unity Wlk DY4 ... 51 F5
University Rd CV4 ... 132 C5
University Road W B15 ... 85 F4
University Sta B15 ... 85 E4
Univ of Birmingham B15 ... 85 F4
Univ of Birmingham The (Halls of Residence) B15 ... 66 C1
Univ of Central England B4 ... 164 D4
Univ of Central England Edgbaston Ctr B15 ... 86 A8
Univ of Central England in Birmingham B42 ... 55 D2
Univ of Warwick CV4 ... 132 C4
Univ of Warwick (Gibbet Hill) CV4 ... 132 D3
Univ of Warwick Science Pk CV4 ... 132 C5
Univ of Warwick (Westwood) CV4 ... 132 B6
Univ of Wolverhampton (Annexe) WV1 ... 163 C3
Univ of Wolverhampton (City Campus North) WV1 ... 163 B4
Univ of Wolverhampton (City Campus South) WV1 ... 163 B3
Univ of Wolverhampton Compton Park Campus WV6 ... 24 E2
Univ of Wolverhampton (Walsall Campus) WS1 ... 43 A7
Unketts Rd B67 ... 64 E3
Unwin Cres DY8 ... 80 E5
Upavon Cl B35 ... 58 A4
Upfield Cotts WS7 ... 7 E7
Upland Gr B61 ... 137 A4
Upland Rd
Birmingham B29 ... 86 B3
Bromsgrove B61 ... 137 B4
Uplands Ave
Rowley Regis B65 ... 63 D3
Willenhall WV13 ... 26 D1
Wolverhampton WV3 ... 38 D8
Uplands Cl DY2 ... 62 E7
Uplands CV2 ... 114 A5
Uplands Dr
Sedgley DY3 ... 50 D8
Wolverhampton WV3 ... 38 E8
Wombourne WV5 ... 49 A6
Uplands Gr WV13 ... 26 C1
Uplands B63 ... 82 E2
Uplands Jun Sch WV3 ... 38 D8
Uplands Manor Prim Sch B67 ... 64 F3
Uplands Rd
Birmingham B21 ... 54 D2
Dudley DY2 ... 62 F7
Wolverhampton WV13 ... 26 C1
Uplands Stop B67 ... 64 F4
Upleadon Cl B97 ... 158 A6
Upper Abbey St CV11 ... 73 B5
Upper Ashley St B62 ... 63 C1
Upper Balsall Heath Rd B12 ... 86 F6
Upper Bond St LE10 ... 71 D1

Upper Brook St WS2 ... 28 D1
Upper Cape CV34 ... 160 D8
Upper Chapel St B69 ... 52 B2
Upper Church La DY4 ... 52 A6
Upper Cl B32 ... 84 D3
Upper Clifton Rd B73 ... 46 B6
Upper Conybere St 6
B12 ... 86 F7
Upper Crossgate Rd B98 159 C8
Upper Dean St B5 ... 164 C1
Upper Eastern Green La
CV5 ... 111 E5
Upper Ettingshall Rd
WV14 ... 51 B8
Upper Field Cl B98 ... 154 C6
Upperfield Way CV3 ... 115 A1
Upper Forster St WS4 ... 28 F3
Upper Gambolds La B60. 151 C5
Upper Gn WV6 ... 24 D5
Upper Gough St B1 ... 164 B1
Upper Green La WS2 ... 28 C4
Upper Grosvenor Rd B20. 55 B2
Upper Grove St 8 CV32. 156 E1
Upper Gungate B79 ... 21 B6
Upper Hall Cl B98 ... 154 D2
Upper Hall La 6 WS1 ... 28 E1
Upper Hattons Cotts WV9 10 D5
Upper Heritage St B12 ... 86 F7
Upper High St
Cradley Heath B64 ... 62 D1
Wednesbury WS10 ... 41 F3
Upper Hill St
Coventry CV1 ... 165 A3
Royal Leamington Spa
CV32 ... 157 A1
Upper Holland Rd B72 ... 46 C4
Upper Holly Wlk CV32 ... 157 A1
Upper Keys Bsns Pk WS12 .. 2 E3
Upper Ladyes Hills CV8 .. 148 A6
Upper Landywood La
Cheslyn Hay WS6 ... 4 D1
Great Wyrley WS6 ... 13 D8
Upper Lichfield St WV13 . 27 A2
Upper Marshall St B1 ... 164 B1
Upper Meadow Rd B32 ... 84 C5
Upper Mill La B5 ... 164 C1
Upper Navigation St WS2 28 D2
Upper Norgrove Ho B97. 152 F1
Upper Pk CV3 ... 134 D6
Upper Portland St B6 ... 67 A7
Upper Prec CV1 ... 165 B3
Upper Ride CV3 ... 134 D5
Upper Rosemary Hill
CV8 ... 147 F5
Upper Rushall St WS1 ... 28 F1
Upper Russell St 1 WS10 41 F2
Upper St John St WS14 ... 9 B6
Upper St Mary's Rd B67 .. 64 F1
Upper Short St WS2 ... 28 D1
Upper Sneyd Rd WV11 ... 13 B2
Upper Spon St CV1 ... 113 A3
Upper Spring La CV8 ... 147 F7
Upper Stone Cl B76 ... 46 E4
Upper St WV6 ... 24 D5
Upper Sutton St B6 ... 66 F7
Upper Thomas St B6 ... 66 F7
Upper Trinity St B9 ... 67 A1
Upper Vauxhall WV1 ... 25 A2
Upper Villiers St WV2 ... 39 C6
Upper Well St CV1 ... 165 B3
Upper William St B1 ... 66 C1
Upper York St CV1 ... 113 B2
Upper Zoar St WV3 ... 163 A1
Upton Cl B98 ... 154 F3
Upton Ct B23 ... 56 B3
Upton Dr CV11 ... 78 F8
Upton Gdns WV14 ... 40 C5
Upton Gr B33 ... 68 C1
Upton Rd B33 ... 68 C2
Upton St DY2 ... 62 C5
Upwey Ave B91 ... 107 A4
Usam Trad Est WV10 ... 11 D2
Usk Cl WS3 ... 28 D8
Usk Way B36 ... 69 F8
Usmere Rd DY10 ... 116 F8
Utrillo Cl CV5 ... 112 C3
Uttoxeter Cl WV6 ... 25 B5
Uxbridge Ave CV3 ... 114 C2
Uxbridge Cl DY3 ... 50 D2
Uxbridge Ct
Burntwood WS7 ... 6 F5
Cannock WS12 ... 2 C5
Kidderminster DY11 ... 116 D5
Uxbridge St
Birmingham B19 ... 66 D5
Cannock WS12 ... 2 C4

V

Valbourne Rd B14 ... 104 C4
Vale Ave
Aldridge WS9 ... 30 D3
Dudley DY3 ... 50 D6
Vale Cl
Birmingham B32 ... 84 F3
Lichfield WS13 ... 3 B1
Vale Ct B64 ... 82 D7
Vale Gr B60 ... 151 A7
Vale Head Dr WV6 ... 24 A2
Vale Ind Est DY11 ... 116 C1
Valencia Croft B35 ... 58 B4
Valencia Rd
Bromsgrove B60 ... 137 D1
Coventry CV3 ... 115 A2
Valentine Cl B74 ... 44 F7
Valentine Ct B14 ... 86 E1
Valentine Rd
Birmingham B14 ... 86 F1
Oldbury B68 ... 64 C2
Valepits Rd B33 ... 69 C1
Vale Rd DY2 ... 62 E4
Valerian
Kidderminster DY10 ... 116 E2
Sutton Coldfield B74 ... 31 F4
Valerie Gr B43 ... 54 C8
Vale Row DY3 ... 50 D5
Vales Cl B76 ... 57 E7
Vale St
Dudley DY3 ... 50 D5
Stourbridge DY8 ... 81 A8
West Bromwich B71 ... 53 E6
Wolverhampton WV2 ... 40 A6
Vale The
Birmingham,Egdbaston
B15 ... 86 A6
Birmingham,Moseley B11 .. 87 B2
Coventry CV3 ... 134 C8
Vale View
Aldridge WS9 ... 30 B4
Nuneaton CV10 ... 72 E4
Valiant Cl LE10 ... 75 E4
Valley Cl B97 ... 158 A6
Valley Farm Rd B45 ... 122 A6
Valley Gn WS6 ... 4 E2
Valley Heritage Ctr* WS12 2 D6
Valley Inf Sch B92 ... 89 D3
Valley La
Kingswood B94 ... 144 E7
Lichfield WS13 ... 9 D8
Tamworth B77 ... 35 E7
Valley Park Nature Reserve*
WV6 ... 24 D3
Valley Rd
Birmingham B43 ... 54 C7
Bournheath B61 ... 136 E7
Cannock,Hednesford WS12 .. 2 D6
Coventry CV2 ... 114 A6
Cradley Heath B64 ... 82 E7
Dudley DY3 ... 50 E6
Earlswood B94 ... 126 A1
Halesowen B62 ... 83 F8
Radford Semele CV31 ... 162 E4
Royal Leamington Spa
CV32 ... 157 C3
Smethwick B67 ... 64 F3
Solihull B92 ... 89 D4
Stourbridge DY9 ... 81 F6
Sutton Coldfield B74 ... 44 F7
Walsall WS3 ... 14 D1
Wolverhampton WV10 ... 25 F5
Valley Side WS3 ... 14 F2
Valley Stad (Redditch FC)
B97 ... 153 C4
Valley The
Burntwood WS7 ... 6 D8
Radford Semele CV31 ... 162 E4
Valley View WS8 ... 16 A7
Vallian Croft B36 ... 68 F7
Vanborough Wlk DY1 ... 51 A2
Vanbrugh Ct WV6 ... 23 E3
Van Dyke Cl CV5 ... 112 C3
Van Gogh Cl WS11 ... 2 D2
Vanguard Ave CV5 ... 112 C1
Vanguard Cl 1 B36 ... 68 E8
Vanguard Ctr CV4 ... 132 C6
Vanguard Rd B26 ... 90 C4
Vanguard B77 ... 35 D6
Vann Cl 2 B10 ... 87 C8
Vantage Point 4 B70 ... 53 C2
Varden Croft B5 ... 86 D7
Vardon Dr CV3 ... 133 D4
Vardon Way B38 ... 103 D1
Varley Rd B24 ... 57 D4
Varley Vale B24 ... 57 D4
Varlins Way B38 ... 123 D6
Varney Ave B70 ... 53 D2
Vaughan Cl B74 ... 31 F6
Vaughan Rd WV13 ... 26 E1
Vaughan Trad Est DY4 ... 52 B3
Vaughton Dr B75 ... 46 E6
Vaughton Ho B15 ... 86 C7
Vaughton St S B12 ... 86 E8
Vaughton St B12 ... 86 F8
Vauxhall Ave 3 WV1 ... 25 A2
Vauxhall Cl 4 CV1 ... 113 E3
Vauxhall Cres B36 ... 58 F1
Vauxhall Gdns DY2 ... 62 E7
Vauxhall Gr B7 ... 67 B3
Vauxhall Ho 2 WV1 ... 25 A2
Vauxhall Pl B7 ... 67 A3
Vauxhall Rd
Birmingham B7 ... 67 A3
Stourbridge DY8 ... 81 A5
Vauxhall St
Coventry CV1 ... 113 E3
Dudley DY1 ... 62 B8
Vauxhall Trad Est B7 ... 67 B4
Vaynor Dr B97 ... 158 D8
Vaynor Fst Sch The B97 . 158 C7
Veasey Cl CV11 ... 73 E3
Vecqueray St CV1 ... 113 E2
Vector Ind Pk B71 ... 53 C6
Velsheda Rd B90 ... 106 A2
Venetia Rd B9 ... 67 C2
Venice Ct 2 B13 ... 87 B2
Venning Gr B43 ... 54 D7
Ventnor Ave
Birmingham,Lozells B19 ... 66 D7
Birmingham,Ward End B36 . 68 D7
Ventnor Cl
Birmingham B68 ... 84 C7
Coventry CV2 ... 114 E3
Ventnor Rd B92 ... 89 C3
Ventnor St CV10 ... 73 D6
Ventura Park Rd B78 ... 20 F3
Ventura Pk Rd B78 ... 21 A3
Ventura Pk B78 ... 21 A3
Venture Ct LE10 ... 74 E8
Venture Way B7 ... 66 F4
Vera Rd B26 ... 88 E7
Vera Roberts Way DY11 . 116 B3
Verbena Cl
Coventry CV2 ... 96 B1
Stoke Prior B60 ... 150 C1
Verbena Gdns B7 ... 67 A5
Verbena Rd B31 ... 102 F6
Vercourt B74 ... 31 B3
Verden Ave CV34 ... 160 B4
Verdi Ct WS13 ... 3 C2
Verdun Cl CV31 ... 162 B2
Verdun Cres DY2 ... 51 F2
Vere St B5 ... 86 D8
Verity Wlk DY8 ... 60 E1
Vermont Gn 4 WS11 ... 2 A3
Vermont Gr CV31 ... 162 D6
Verney Ave B33 ... 89 D7
Vernier Ave DY6 ... 61 A5
Vernolds Croft B5 ... 86 E8
Vernon Ave
Birmingham B20 ... 54 F4
Brownhills WS8 ... 16 A8
Tipton DY4 ... 51 E4
Vernon Cl
5 Coventry CV1 ... 113 E3
Essington WV11 ... 12 F4
Halesowen B62 ... 83 D8
Redditch B98 ... 154 A5
Royal Leamington Spa
CV32 ... 156 E3
Sutton Coldfield B74 ... 31 E5
Willenhall WV13 ... 26 E1
Vernon Ct
9 Coventry CV1 ... 113 E4
Birmingham B16 ... 65 E1
Vernon Rd
Bilston WV14 ... 40 F6
Birmingham B16 ... 65 E1
Halesowen B62 ... 83 C8
Oldbury B68 ... 64 C6
Vernons Ct CV10 ... 72 F4
Vernons La CV10,CV11 ... 72 F4
Vernons Mews CV10 ... 72 F4
Vernon St B70 ... 52 E3
Vernon Trad Est B62 ... 83 C8
Vernon Way WS3 ... 13 E1
Verona Cl CV11 ... 74 A1
Verona Ct WV10 ... 26 A4
Verona Rd B60 ... 137 C1
Veronica Ave WV4 ... 39 E5
Veronica Cl B29 ... 103 A6
Veronica Rd DY6 ... 61 A6
Verstone Croft B31 ... 103 A3
Verstone Rd B90 ... 106 C4
Verwood Cl WV13 ... 26 D1
Vesey Cl
Sutton Coldfield B74 ... 31 F2
Water Orton B46 ... 59 B2
Vesey Rd B73 ... 46 B1
Vesey St B4 ... 164 C4
Vestry Cl B64 ... 62 F1
Vestry Ct DY8 ... 80 E6
Viaduct Dr WV6 ... 25 B6
Viaduct St B7 ... 67 A3
Vibart Rd B26 ... 88 F8
Vicarage Cl
Birmingham,Great Barr
B42 ... 55 D7
Birmingham,Stirchley B30 104 C7
Brierley Hill DY5 ... 81 C8
Bromsgrove B60 ... 151 B8
Brownhills WS8 ... 16 A7
Dordon B78 ... 36 F5
Tipton DY4 ... 51 E5
Vicarage Cres
Kidderminster DY10 ... 116 F5
Redditch B97 ... 153 C3
Vicarage Ct WS7 ... 6 F6
Vicarage Field CV34 ... 161 B8
Vicarage Gdns
Halesowen B62 ... 63 D1
Sutton Coldfield B76 ... 57 F7
Vicarage Hill
Middleton B78 ... 34 B1
Tanworth-In-A B94 ... 141 F3
Vicarage La
Brierley Hill DY5 ... 61 D7
Coventry CV7 ... 95 D7
Longbridge CV35 ... 160 A1
Water Orton B46 ... 59 B2
Vicarage Pl WS1 ... 28 E1
Vicarage Prospect DY1 ... 51 B1
Vicarage Rd
Birmingham,Aston B6 ... 67 A7
Birmingham,Chad Valley
B15 ... 85 F8
Birmingham,Handsworth
B18 ... 66 A7
Birmingham,Harts Green
B17 ... 85 B5
Birmingham,King's Heath
B14 ... 104 D7
Birmingham,Stechford B33 . 68 E1
Brierley Hill DY5 ... 81 C7
Brownhills WS8 ... 16 A7
Cheswick Green B90,B94 . 126 C3
Dudley,West Coseley WV14. 51 C7
Dudley,Woodsetton DY3 ... 50 F5
Halesowen B62 ... 63 C1
Hockley Heath B94 ... 143 F7
Oldbury B68 ... 64 C5
Vicarage Rd *continued*
Royal Leamington Spa
CV32 ... 157 B3
Smethwick B67 ... 64 F5
Vicarage Rd S DY9 ... 81 E5
Vicarage Rd
Stone DY10 ... 117 E2
Stoneleigh CV8 ... 149 B6
Stourbridge DY8 ... 80 D7
Stourbridge,Lye DY9 ... 81 F5
Walsall WS3 ... 15 B2
Vicarage Rd W DY1 ... 51 C6
Vicarage Rd
Wednesbury WS10 ... 42 A4
West Bromwich B71 ... 53 D6
Wolverhampton,Blakenhall
WV2 ... 163 C1
Wolverhampton,Penn WV4 . 38 E3
Wolverhampton WV11 ... 26 B6
Vicarage St
Nuneaton CV11 ... 73 C4
Oldbury B68 ... 64 B5
Vicarage Terr 1 WS2 ... 42 C8
Vicarage View B97 ... 153 D3
Vicarage Wlk 9 WS1 ... 28 E1
Vicar's Cl WS13 ... 9 A8
Vicar St
Dudley DY2 ... 62 C8
Kidderminster DY10 ... 116 E6
Sedgley DY3 ... 50 D8
Wednesbury WS10 ... 42 A3
Vicars Wlk DY9 ... 81 E2
Viceroy Cl
Birmingham B5 ... 86 C6
Kingswinford DY6 ... 61 A5
Victor Bsns Ctr B98 ... 154 B3
Victor Cl WV2 ... 40 B6
Victoria Arc WV1 ... 163 B3
Victoria Ave
Birmingham B21 ... 65 F8
Birmingham,Small Heath
B10 ... 87 D8
Halesowen B62 ... 83 F6
Smethwick B66 ... 65 A5
Walsall,Blakenall Heath
WS3 ... 28 D8
Walsall,Wallington Heath
WS3 ... 14 C1
Victoria Bldgs B16 ... 65 E3
Victoria Bsns Ctr 11
CV31 ... 162 A7
Victoria Colonnade 5
CV31 ... 161 F7
Victoria Com Specl Sch
B31 ... 103 A5
Victoria Ct
2 Birmingham,Showell Green
B13 ... 86 F4
2 Kidderminster DY10 ... 116 F6
6 Birmingham,Hurst Green
B62 ... 84 A7
Brierley Hill DY5 ... 61 D3
Coventry CV5 ... 112 D4
Halesowen B62 ... 83 F6
Norton Canes WS11 ... 6 B5
Victoria Dr B78 ... 35 A8
Victoria Fold WV1 ... 163 B2
Victoria Gdns
Cradley Heath B64 ... 62 F2
Lichfield WS13 ... 8 F6
Victoria Gr
1 Birmingham B18 ... 65 E4
Wombourne WV5 ... 49 A8
Victoria Ho
2 Birmingham B2 ... 164 C2
2 Darlaston WS10 ... 41 C6
4 Birmingham,Ladywood
B16 ... 66 B2
Birmingham,Small Heath
B10 ... 87 D8
Victoria Hospl WS13 ... 9 A6
Victoria Inf Sch DY4 ... 51 F5
Victoria Law Cts B2 ... 164 C3
Victoria Mews
Barnt Green B45 ... 138 D8
Coventry CV3 ... 114 E2
Oldbury B69 ... 63 F3
Walsall WS4 ... 29 A3
Warwick CV34 ... 160 D7
Victoria Park Prim Sch
B66 ... 65 B5
Victoria Park Rd B66 ... 65 B5
Victoria Pass 5 DY8 ... 81 A5
Victoria Pas WV1 ... 163 B3
Victoria Pl DY11 ... 116 B2
Victoria Rd
Birmingham,Acock's Green
B27 ... 88 C2
Birmingham,Aston B6 ... 66 F7
Birmingham B17 ... 85 B5
Birmingham,Handsworth
B21 ... 65 E7
Birmingham,Stechford B33 . 68 D3
Birmingham,Stirchley B30 104 A7
Birmingham,Stockland Green
B23 ... 56 D3
Brierley Hill DY5 ... 62 A1
Bromsgrove B61 ... 137 A3
Cradley Heath B64 ... 62 F2
Darlaston WS10 ... 41 D6
Dodford B61 ... 136 A7
Halesowen B62 ... 83 D8
Hartshill CV10 ... 72 B8
Hinckley LE10 ... 75 F5
Oldbury B68 ... 64 D6
Royal Leamington Spa
CV31 ... 161 E8
Sedgley DY3 ... 50 E8
Victoria Rd *continued*
Sutton Coldfield B72 ... 46 C5
Tamworth B79 ... 21 C5
Tipton DY4 ... 52 A4
Walsall WS3 ... 15 A3
Wolverhampton,Newbolds
WV10 ... 25 F5
Wolverhampton,New Cross
WV11 ... 26 B6
Wolverhampton,Oxbarn
WV3 ... 38 E7
Wolverhampton,Tettenhall
WV6 ... 24 E5
Victoria Sq
Birmingham B3 ... 164 B2
Wolverhampton WV1 ... 163 C3
Victoria St
7 Redditch B98 ... 153 E4
Birmingham B9 ... 67 D1
Brierley Hill,Barrow Hill
DY5 ... 61 C7
Brierley Hill,Merry Hill DY5 . 61 D3
Cannock,Bridgtown WS11 ... 4 D8
Cannock,Broomhill WS11 ... 1 E4
Cannock WS12 ... 2 C6
Coventry CV1 ... 165 D4
Halesowen B63 ... 83 A4
Hinckley LE10 ... 71 D1
Kingswinford DY6 ... 49 B1
Nuneaton CV11 ... 73 C4
Royal Leamington Spa
CV31 ... 161 E8
Stourbridge DY8 ... 81 A5
Warwick CV34 ... 160 D7
Wednesbury WS10 ... 41 E2
West Bromwich,Lambert's End
B70 ... 53 C3
West Bromwich,Swan Village
B70 ... 52 F5
Willenhall WV13 ... 27 B3
Wolverhampton WV1 ... 163 B3
Victoria Terr
4 Walsall WS4 ... 28 F3
Royal Leamington Spa
CV31 ... 161 F7
Victor Rd
Birmingham B18 ... 65 E6
Solihull B92 ... 89 D3
Victor St
Walsall,Caldmore WS1 ... 42 E8
Walsall WS3 ... 15 A1
Victor Twr B7 ... 67 B6
Victory Ave
Burntwood WS7 ... 6 F7
Darlaston WS10 ... 41 C5
Victory Cl WS12 ... 2 F4
Victory Ho 6 B13 ... 86 F4
Victory La WS2 ... 28 A4
Victory Rd CV6 ... 95 E1
Victory Rise B71 ... 53 D5
Victory Terr B78 ... 35 B8
Vienna Ho CV5 ... 112 E2
View Dr DY2 ... 62 E8
Viewfield Ave WS12 ... 1 F7
Viewfield Cres DY3 ... 50 D6
Viewlands Dr WV6 ... 24 A2
View Point B69 ... 63 B7
View St WS12 ... 1 F6
Vigo Cl WS9 ... 15 F2
Vigo Pl WS9 ... 30 A8
Vigo Rd WS9 ... 15 F2
Vigo Terr WS9 ... 15 F2
Viking Rise B65 ... 63 C4
Viking B77 ... 35 D7
Vilia Cl LE10 ... 75 F4
Villa Cl CV12 ... 79 C2
Villa Cotts B19 ... 66 B7
Villa Cres CV12 ... 79 C1
Villa Cross B20 ... 66 B7
Village Mews The WV6 ... 24 C5
Village Rd B6 ... 56 A1
Village The DY6 ... 60 E7
Village Way WV14 ... 40 C5
Village Wlk WS10 ... 42 B3
Villa Park (Aston Villa FC)
B6 ... 55 F1
Villa Rd
Birmingham B19 ... 66 B7
Coventry CV6 ... 113 B6
Villa St
Birmingham B19 ... 66 C6
Stourbridge DY8 ... 81 A8
Villa Wlk B19 ... 66 C6
Villebon Way CV31 ... 162 A2
Villette Gr B14 ... 105 C4
Villiers Ave WV14 ... 40 D7
Villiers Ind Est WV2 ... 39 B7
Villiers Jun & Inf Sch
WV14 ... 40 D7
Villiers Rd
Bromsgrove B60 ... 150 E7
Kenilworth CV8 ... 148 B5
Villiers Sq WV14 ... 40 D7
Villiers St
Birmingham B18 ... 65 E5
Coventry CV2 ... 114 A3
Kidderminster DY10 ... 117 A5
Nuneaton CV11 ... 73 B3
Royal Leamington Spa
CV32 ... 157 A1
Walsall WS1 ... 42 E7
Willenhall WV13 ... 27 B2
Vimy Rd
Birmingham B13 ... 105 B8
Wednesbury WS10 ... 42 A4
Vimy Terr WS10 ... 42 A4
Vincent Cl B12 ... 86 F6
Vincent Dr B15 ... 85 E4

Vincent Par B12 86 F6
Vincent Rd B75 46 E7
Vincent St
Birmingham B12 86 F5
Coventry CV1 113 B2
Royal Leamington Spa CV32 157 A1
Walsall WS1 42 F7
Vincent Wyles Ho CV2 114 E3
Vince St B66 65 A3
Vinculum Way WV13 41 B8
Vine Ave B12 87 A5
Vine Cl WV10 11 D3
Vinecote Rd CV6 95 F4
Vine Cres B71 53 D6
Vine Ct
Cradley Heath B64 82 D8
Warwick CV34 160 F8
Vine Gdns B64 62 F2
Vine La
Cannock WS11 4 D5
Clent DY9 99 F3
Halesowen B63 83 B3
Warwick CV34 160 F8
Vineries The B27 88 E4
Vine St
Birmingham B6 67 B7
Brierley Hill DY2,DY5 61 E5
Coventry CV1 165 C3
Kidderminster DY10 117 A8
Redditch B97 153 D4
Stourbridge DY8 60 E1
Vineyard Rd B31 102 F5
Vinnall Gr B32 102 B8
Vintage Cl B34 69 A5
Vinyard Cl B18 65 F7
Violet Cl
Bedworth CV12 77 E2
Coventry CV2 96 C3
Violet Croft DY4 41 B1
Violet La DY9 99 E4
Virginia Dr WV4 38 F4
Virginia Pl CV10 72 E3
Virginia Rd CV1 113 E3
Viscount Cl
Birmingham B35 58 A2
Royal Leamington Spa CV31 161 F6
Viscount Dr B35 58 B2
Vista Gn B38 104 B1
Vista The DY3 39 D2
Vittle Dr CV34 160 D7
Vittoria St
Birmingham B1 66 C4
Smethwick B66 65 D6
Vittoria Works B1 66 C3
Vivian Cl B17 85 C5
Vivian Rd B17 85 C5
Vixen Cl B76 57 D7
Vodena Ct [5] CV32 156 E1
Vogue Cl CV1 165 D3
Vowchurch Cl B97 153 A5
Voyager Dr WS11 4 F6
Vulcan Ho B91 107 C6
Vulcan House Ind Est B91 107 C6
Vulcan Ind Est WS2 28 C6
Vulcan Rd
Bilston WV14 40 F5
Lichfield WS13 3 E1
Solihull B91 107 C7
Vulcan Road Island WV14 40 F5
Vyrnwy Gr B38 123 E8
Vyse St
Birmingham,Aston B6 67 B8
Birmingham,Hockley B18 66 C4

W

Wackrill Dr CV32 157 C3
Wadbarn B90 126 A5
Waddam's Pool DY2 51 D1
Waddell Cl WV14 39 F2
Waddens Brook La WV11 26 E5
Waddington Ave B43 43 E1
Wade Ave CV3 133 B5
Wadebridge Dr CV11 73 F5
Wade Gr CV34 155 E2
Wades Cl [3] DY4 51 E5
Wadesmill Lawns WV10 11 E4
Wade St WS13 9 B7
Wadham Cl B65 63 C6
Wadham Ho B37 70 D3
Wadham's Fold WV1 163 B3
Wadhurst Rd B17 65 B2
Wadleys Rd B91 106 F6
Waen Cl DY4 52 B8
Waggestaff Dr CV10 72 A7
Waggoners Cl [1] B60 150 E6
Waggoner's La B78 33 E8
Waggon La DY10 98 A3
Waggon St B64 62 F2
Waggon Wlk B38 123 C8
Wagoners Cl B8 67 F6
Wagon La B26,B92 88 F4
Wagstaff Cl WV14 51 D8
Wagstaff Way B37 90 A8
Wainbody Ave N CV3 133 A6
Wainbody Ave S CV3 132 F5
Wainbody Wood Sch CV4 132 D2
Wainrigg B77 36 B7
Wainwright Cl DY6 60 A8
Wainwright St B6 67 A7
Waite Rd WV13 40 E8
Wakefield Cl
Coventry CV3 134 F7
Wakefield Cl *continued*
Sutton Coldfield B73 46 A2
Wakefield Ct B13 87 B2
Wakefield Gr B46 59 B3
Wakeford Rd B31 103 C1
Wake Green Pk B13 87 B2
Wake Green Rd
Birmingham B13 87 A2
Wednesbury DY4 41 A1
Wake Gr CV34 160 B5
Wakehurst Cl CV11 78 F8
Wakelam Gdns B43 43 D1
Wakelams Fold DY3 50 C3
Wakeley Hill WV4 38 F4
Wakelin Rd B90 126 B7
Wakeman Ct WV11 12 F3
Wakeman Dr B69 63 B8
Wakeman Gr B33 89 D7
Wakes Cl WV13 27 B1
Wakes Rd WS10 42 A2
Walcot Cl B75 32 B3
Walcot Dr B43 54 F6
Walcote Cl LE10 74 F8
Walcot Gdns WV14 40 B4
Walcot Gn B93 128 A2
Waldale Cl WV11 13 C1
Walden Gdns WV4 38 E6
Walden Rd B11 88 A3
Waldeve Gr B92 107 F8
Waldley Gr B24 57 D3
Waldon Wlk B36 69 F8
Waldron Ave DY5 61 B2
Waldron Cl WS10 41 F6
Waldrons Moor B14 104 C5
Walford Ave WV3 38 F8
Walford Dr B92 89 D3
Walford Gn B32 102 B7
Walford Gr CV34 155 F1
Walford Rd B11 87 C6
Walford St B69 52 A2
Walford Wlk [6] B97 153 E3
Walhouse CE Jun Sch WS11 1 C1
Walhouse Cl [6] WS1 28 F2
Walhouse Rd WS1 29 A2
Walhouse St WS11 4 E8
Walker Ave
Brierley Hill DY5 81 D7
Oldbury B69 63 C7
Stourbridge DY9 81 E3
Wolverhampton WV10 25 E8
Walker Dr B24 67 E8
Walker Grange DY4 51 F6
Walker Pl WS3 28 E8
Walker Rd WS3 28 E8
Walkers Croft WS13 3 C2
Walkers Fold WV12 27 D6
Walkers Heath Rd B38 104 B1
Walkers Orch CV8 149 B6
Walkers Rd B98 154 E6
Walkers Rise WS12 2 D8
Walker St
Dudley DY2 62 C4
Tipton DY4 52 C7
Walkers Way
Bedworth CV12 77 F1
Kenilworth CV8 147 F2
Walk La WV5 49 A6
Walkmill Bsns Pk WS11 4 D5
Walkmill La WS11 4 D5
Walkmill Way WS11 4 D5
Walk The DY3 39 D1
Walkwood CE Mid Sch B97 158 C8
Walkwood Cres B97 158 C6
Walkwood Rd B97 158 D6
Wallace Cl
Norton Canes WS11 5 F5
Oldbury B69 63 D6
Wallace Ct WS6 4 D1
Wallace Ho
[8] Oldbury B69 63 D5
Warwick CV34 160 D7
Wallace Rd
Bilston WV14 41 A2
Birmingham B29 86 B2
Brownhills WS8 15 E8
Coventry CV6 113 A8
Oldbury B69 63 D6
Wallace Rise B64 82 E7
Wall Ave B46 70 F5
Wallbank Rd B8 68 A6
Wallbrook Prim Sch WV14 51 E8
Wallbrook St WV14 51 D8
Wall Croft WS9 30 B7
Wall Dr B74 31 F4
Wall End Cl WS2 28 A7
Waller Cl CV35 155 F7
Waller St CV32 157 A2
Wallface B71 53 B7
Wallheath Cres WS14 16 E5
Wallheath La WS14 16 F5
Wall Hill Rd CV5,CV7 94 B3
Walling Croft WV14 40 B3
Wallingford Ave CV11 73 F7
Wallington Cl WS3 14 B2
Wallington Heath WS3 14 B2
Wallis Ct [1] B13 87 B2
Wall La WS13,WS14 8 D3
Wall (Letocetvm) Roman Site (Town)★ WS14 8 E2
Wallnut Wlk WS13 8 F6
Wallows Ind Est The DY5 61 D5
Wallows La WS1,WS2 42 C6
Wallows Pl DY5 61 C5
Wallows Rd DY5 61 D5
Wallows Wood DY3 50 A4
Wall Roman Site (Letocetvm) Mus★ WS14 8 D2
Wallsgrove Cl CV32 157 B3
Wall's Rd B60 150 C3
Wall St WV1 26 B2
Wall Well B63 82 F3
Wall Well La B63 82 F3
Wallwin Ct CV34 160 D6
Walmead Croft [1] B17 84 F7
Walmer Ct B16 65 D2
Walmer Gr B23 56 B5
Walmer Mdw WS9 30 B7
Walmers The WS9 30 B7
Walmers Wlk The B31 102 D1
Walmer Way B37 70 C3
Walmesley Way B31 102 E3
Walmley Ash Ct B76 57 F8
Walmley Ash La B76 58 C6
Walmley Ash Rd B76 58 A7
Walmley Cl
Halesowen B63 82 B7
Sutton Coldfield B76 57 F8
Walmley Jun & Inf Schs B76 58 A7
Walmley Park Ct B76 57 F8
Walmley Rd B76 46 F2
Walney Cl LE10 71 B1
Walnut Ave WV8 10 B3
Walnut Cl
Birmingham B37 70 B1
Cannock WS11 1 F3
Hartshill CV10 72 A8
Nuneaton,Camp Hill CV10 72 E6
Stourbridge DY9 81 B1
Walnut Dr
[5] Smethwick B66 65 B5
Cannock WS11 1 F3
Royal Leamington Spa CV32 157 B3
Wolverhampton WV3 24 D1
Walnut Gr WS14 9 F7
Walnut La
Finstall B60 151 D8
Wednesbury WS10 42 A2
Walnut Rd WS5 43 A4
Walnut St CV2 96 B2
Walnut Tree Cl CV8 148 A3
Walnut Way B31 122 F8
Walpole St WV6 25 A3
Walpole Wlk [3] B70 53 D1
Walsal End La B92 108 F3
Walsall Acad WS3 14 C2
Walsall Arboretum★ WS1 29 A2
Walsall Coll of Arts & Tech (Shelley Campus) WS2 28 C1
Walsall Coll of Arts & Tech
Walsall WS1 28 E2
Walsall WS2 28 D3
Walsall Ent Pk WS2 42 C8
Walsall New Firms Ctr WS1 42 D8
Walsall Rd
Aldridge WS9 30 A5
Birmingham B42 55 B6
Brownhills WS9 15 E2
Cannock WS11 4 E7
Darlaston WS10 41 E6
Great Wyrley WS6 5 A2
Leamonsley WS13 8 E6
Lichfield,Christ Church WS13 9 A7
Lichfield,Pipehill WS13,WS14 8 C5
Norton Canes WS11 5 F4
Stonnall WS14 16 E8
Sutton Coldfield B74 31 D4
Walsall,The Delves WS5 42 F4
Walsall WS3 15 A1
Wednesbury WS10,B71, WS5 42 F2
West Bromwich B71 53 E8
Willenhall WV13 27 C2
Walsall Sta WS2 28 E2
Walsall St
Bilston WV14 40 D6
Coventry CV4 132 B7
Darlaston WS10 41 D7
West Bromwich B70 53 D3
Willenhall WV13 27 B1
Wolverhampton WV1 163 D2
Walsall Wood Jun Mix & Inf Sch WS8 16 A4
Walsall Wood Rd WS9 30 B7
Walsgrave CE Prim Sch CV2 115 A6
Walsgrave Cl B92 107 D6
Walsgrave Dr B92 107 D6
Walsgrave Gdns [5] CV2 115 A7
Walsgrave Hospl CV2 115 A5
Walsgrave Rd CV2 114 B3
Walsgrave Ret Pk CV2 115 B7
Walsham Croft B34 69 C5
Walsh Dr B76 46 F4
Walsh Gr B23 56 D8
Walsh La CV7 92 E2
Walsingham Dr CV10 78 A7
Walsingham St WS1 29 A1
Walstead Cl WS5 43 C5
Walstead Rd WS5 43 B5
Walstead Rd W WS5 42 E5
Waltdene Cl B43 43 E3
Walter Burden Ho B66 65 C3
Walter Cobb Dr B73 46 A1
Walter Ct B20 55 C2
Walter Nash Rd E DY11 116 B2
Walter Nash Rd W DY11 116 A1
Walter Rd
Bilston WV14 40 F3
Smethwick B67 64 E6
Walters Cl B31 122 F6
Walter Scott Rd CV12 78 C1
Walters Rd B68 84 B6
Walters Row DY1 51 A1
Walter St
Birmingham B7 67 B6
Walsall WS3 15 A1
West Bromwich B70 53 E2
Waltham Cl B61 136 E1
Waltham Cres CV10 72 B5
Waltham Gr B44 45 B2
Waltham Ho
Birmingham B38 104 B1
West Bromwich B70 53 D3
Walthamstow Ct DY5 61 D1
Walton Ave B65 83 B8
Walton Cl
Coventry CV3 134 E7
Halesowen B63 82 F2
Kidderminster DY11 116 B2
Nuneaton CV11 79 A7
Redditch B98 154 E3
Rowley Regis B65 63 A4
Walton Cres WV4 39 E5
Walton Croft B91 107 B1
Walton Ct B63 82 F3
Walton Dr DY9 81 C5
Walton Gr B30 104 B2
Walton Heath WS3 13 F3
Walton Pool La DY9 99 F2
Walton Rd
Aldridge WS9 16 A1
Bromsgrove B61 137 B4
Oldbury B68 64 C2
Stourbridge DY8 81 A6
Wednesbury WS10 42 C2
Wolverhampton WV4 39 F5
Walton Rise DY9 100 A3
Walton St DY4 51 F5
Wanderers Ave WV2 39 C6
Wanderer Wlk B36 57 E1
Wandle Gr B11 88 A3
Wandsbeck B77 35 E8
Wandsworth Rd B44 44 F3
Wanley Rd CV3 133 D6
Wannerton Rd DY10 98 B1
Wansbeck Gr B38 123 E8
Wansbeck Wlk DY3 50 F6
Wansfell Cl CV4 132 A7
Wanstead Gr B44 45 A1
Wantage Rd B46 59 E1
Wappenbury Cl CV2 96 C2
Wappenbury Rd CV2 96 D2
Warbage La
Belbroughton DY9 119 F1
Dodford B61 136 A7
Warbank Cl B48 139 A6
Warbler Pl DY10 117 A2
Ward Cl B8 68 A5
Warden Ave B73 56 F8
Ward End Cl B8 67 F6
Ward End Hall Gr B8 68 A6
Ward End Park Rd B8 67 F5
Ward End Prim Sch B8 68 B6
Wardend Rd B8 68 A6
Warden Rd
Coventry CV6 113 B6
Sutton Coldfield B73 56 F8
Wardens Ave The CV5 112 B6
Wardens The CV8 148 C5
Ward Gr
Warwick CV34 161 C7
Wolverhampton WV4 39 F3
Wardle Cl B75 32 A4
Wardle Pl WS11 1 E5
Wardles La WS6 4 F2
Wardle St B79 21 A5
Wardlow Cl WV4 39 B6
Wardlow Rd B7 67 B4
Wardour Dr B37 70 C2
Wardour Gr B44 56 C8
Ward Rd WV4 39 D5
Ward St
Bilston WV2 40 B6
Birmingham B19 164 C5
Cannock WS12 1 F6
Dudley WV14 51 B8
Walsall WS1 28 F2
Willenhall WV13 27 B3
Wolverhampton WV1 163 D3
Wareham Cl WS3 28 F5
Wareham Gn CV2 115 A5
Wareham Ho B28 105 E3
Wareham Rd B45 102 B2
Wareing Dr B23 56 D8
Warewell Cl [8] WS1 28 F2
Warewell St [9] WS1 28 F2
Waring Cl DY4 51 E8
Waring Rd DY4 52 A8
Warings Green Rd B94 126 D1
War La B17 85 B5
Warley Croft B68 84 E8
Warley Ct B68 64 B2
Warley Hall Rd B68 64 D1
Warley High Coll of Sport B68 64 A2
Warley Ho B67 64 F2
Warley Inf Sch B68 64 C1
Warley Rd B68 64 C5
Warmington Cl CV3 134 E8
Warmington Dr B73 46 B4
Warmington Gr CV34 160 B8
Warmington Rd
Birmingham B26 89 C5
Hollywood B47 125 A6
Warmley Cl
Solihull B91 107 D5
Wolverhampton WV6 25 B5
Warmstry Rd B60 137 C1
Warmwell Cl CV2 114 F4
Warneford Mews [9] CV31 162 A7
Warner Cl CV34 155 D1
Warner Dr DY5 61 D1
Warner Pl [1] WS3 28 F6
Warner Rd
Walsall WS3 29 A6
Wednesbury WS10 42 C2
Warner Row [2] CV6 113 F7
Warner St [1] B12 87 A8
Warners Wlk [1] B10 87 C8
Warnford Wlk WV4 38 C6
Warple Rd B32 84 C5
Warren Ave
Birmingham B13 86 F2
Wolverhampton WV10 25 F5
Warren Cl
Earlswood B94 142 A8
Lichfield WS14 9 E7
Royal Leamington Spa CV32 157 A3
Ryton-on-D CV8 135 A1
Tipton DY4 52 A7
Warren Dr
Dorridge B93 128 A3
Rowley Regis B65 62 F5
Sedgley DY3 39 C1
Warren Farm Prim Sch B44 56 A8
Warren Farm Rd B44 56 A8
Warren Field CV8 135 A1
Warren Gdns DY6 60 C6
Warren Gn CV4 131 F7
Warren Hill Rd B44 56 A7
Warren House Ct B76 46 F1
Warren House Wlk B76 46 F1
Warren La B45 122 B3
Warren Pl WS8 16 A7
Warren Rd
Birmingham,Perry B44 56 A7
Birmingham,Stirchley B30 104 A6
Birmingham,Washwood Heath B8 67 E6
Burntwood WS7 7 A5
Warrens Croft WS5 43 D5
Warrens End [1] B38 103 F1
Warrens Hall Rd DY2 62 E7
Warrington Cl B76 47 A1
Warrington Dr B23 56 D7
Warsash Cl WV1 40 B8
Warstock La B14 105 A4
Warstock Rd B14 105 A3
Warston Ave B32 84 D3
Warstone Dr B71 53 E4
Warstone La B18 66 B4
Warstone Mews [2] B18 66 C4
Warstone Par E B18 66 B4
Warstone Rd WS6 13 C7
Warstones Cres WV4 38 D5
Warstones Dr WV4 38 C6
Warstones Gdns WV4 38 C6
Warstones Jun & Inf Sch WV4 38 E6
Warstones Rd WV4 38 D5
Warstone Terr B21 65 E8
Warstone Twr B36 68 D8
Wartell Bank Ind Est DY6 60 D7
Wartell Bank DY6 60 D7
Warton Cl CV8 148 C4
Warwards La B29 104 A8
Warwell La B26 88 D6
Warwick Ave
Bromsgrove B60 151 A8
Coventry CV5 133 A8
Perton WV6 23 F3
Wednesbury WS10 42 C4
Willenhall WV13 27 D2
Warwick By-Pass
Hampton Magna CV34, CV35 160 A5
Warwick CV34 161 A1
Warwick Castle★ CV34 160 E6
Warwick Cl
Cannock WS11 4 F8
Oldbury B68 64 B2
Studley B80 159 D3
West Bromwich B70 52 E7
Warwick Crest B15 86 B7
Warwick Ct
[1] Birmingham,Acock's Green B27 88 C2
[1] Birmingham,Weoley Castle B29 103 C7
[5] Birmingham,Chelmsley Wood B37 70 D2
[5] Solihull B91 107 C3
[6] Wolverhampton WV4 39 F4
Birmingham,Moseley B13 87 A2
Coventry CV3 165 B1
Dudley DY3 50 D3
Solihull,Lode Heath B91 107 B4
Warwick Gdns
Hinckley LE10 71 E3
Nuneaton CV10 72 E4
Oldbury B69 52 C2
Willenhall WV13 27 D2
Warwick Gn CV12 79 C1
Warwick Grange B91 106 F7
Warwick Gr B92 88 E1
Warwick Hall Gdns B60 151 A8
Warwick Highway B98 154 C2
Warwick Ho [6] B24 56 F4
Warwick Hospl CV34 160 E8
Warwick Ho B73 46 A3

Warwick La CV1 165 B2
Warwick New Rd CV32 161 C8
Warwick Park Ct B92 106 F8
Warwick Parkway CV35 160 A7
Warwick Pas 3 B2 164 C2
Warwick Pl CV32 156 E1
Warwick Race Course CV34 160 C6
Warwick Rd
Birmingham,Birchfield B42 55 E2
Birmingham,Sparkhill B11 87 D4
Birmingham,Warley Woods B68 84 D7
Chadwick End B93 145 A7
Coventry CV3 165 B1
Dudley DY2 62 E3
Kenilworth CV8 148 A1
Knowle B93 128 D3
Leek Wootton CV35 155 F7
Solihull B27,B91,B92 106 F7
Stourbridge DY8 60 D1
Sutton Coldfield B73 45 C2
Tamworth B77 21 E4
Wolston CV8 135 F3
Warwick Road Trad Est B11 87 D4
Warwick Row CV1 165 B2
Warwick Sch CV34 161 A6
Warwickshire Coll CV32 161 D8
Warwickshire Mus★ CV34 160 E6
Warwickshire Nuffield Hospl The CV32 156 E5
Warwick Sta CV34 160 F7
Warwick St
Bilston WV14 40 E5
Birmingham B12 67 A1
Coventry CV5 112 F1
Royal Leamington Spa CV32 156 F1
Walsall WS4 28 F3
Wolverhampton WV1 163 D2
Warwick Tech Pk CV34 161 B5
Warwick Terr CV32 156 E1
Warwick Way WS9 16 A1
Wasdale Cl CV32 156 C2
Wasdale Dr DY6 60 E6
Wasdale Rd
Birmingham B31 102 F4
Brownhills WS8 15 D6
Waseley Hills Country Pk★ B45 121 C8
Waseley Hills High Sch & Sixth Form Ctr B45 121 D7
Waseley Hills Visitor Ctr★ B45 101 C1
Waseley Rd B45 121 E8
Washbourne Rd CV31 162 A2
Washbrook La
Hawkes End CV5 94 A1
Norton Canes WS11 5 D5
Washbrook Rd B8 68 A6
Washford Dr B98 159 D7
Washford Gr B25 88 B8
Washford Ind Est B98 159 E8
Washford La B98 159 D8
Washington Ct B1 164 A1
Washington Ctr DY2 62 D4
Washington Ct WV3 24 D1
Washington Dr B20 55 B3
Washington St
Birmingham B1 164 A1
Dudley DY2 62 D3
Kidderminster DY11 116 C5
Washington Wharf B1 164 A1
Wash La B25 88 C8
Washwood Heath Rd B8 67 E6
Washwood Heath Tech Coll B8 68 C5
Wasperton Cl
6 Coventry CV3 134 F8
Birmingham B36 69 B8
Wassell Ct B63 82 E2
Wassell Grove Bsns Ctr DY9 82 A2
Wassell Grove Rd
Hagley DY9 99 F8
Halesowen B63 82 A2
Wassell Rd
Bilston WV14 40 D7
Halesowen B63 82 E2
Stourbridge DY9 81 E2
Waste La
Balsall Common CV7 130 F5
Coventry CV6 94 F1
Wast Hill Gr B38 123 F7
Wasthill La B38,B48 123 D5
Wastwater Ct WV6 23 F4
Watchbury Cl B36 58 C1
Watch Cl CV1 165 A3
Watchmaker Ct CV1 165 A2
Watchman Ave DY5 81 F7
Watcombe Rd CV2 114 E8
Waterbrook Way WS11 4 E6
Watercall Ave CV3 133 C6
Waterdale B90 126 D5
Water Dale WV3 24 E2
Waterfall Cl
Meriden CV7 92 C1
Smethwick B66 64 E7
Waterfall La B64 63 A1
Waterfall Lane Ind Est B64 63 A1
Waterfall Rd DY5 81 D7
Waterfall Way LE9 71 F5
Waterfield Cl DY4 51 D5
Waterfield Gdns CV31 162 C7
Waterfield Way
Birmingham B26 89 C7
Hinckley LE10 75 C5
Waterford Ct B23 56 B4
Waterford Pl B33 69 D3
Waterford Rd DY6 60 D7
Waterford Way CV3 114 C1
Waterfront Bsns Pk DY5 61 E4
Waterfront E DY5 61 E4
Waterfront Way
2 Walsall WS2 28 D2
Brierley Hill DY2,DY5 61 F4
Waterfront W DY5 61 E4
Waterglade La WV13 27 A1
Waterhaynes Cl B45 122 A6
Waterhead Cl WV10 12 A2
Waterhead Dr WV10 12 B2
Water La B71 53 F7
Waterlily Cl WS12 2 E3
Water Lily Gr WS8 15 E7
Water Lily Way CV10 78 A8
Waterlinks Bvd B6 67 A7
Waterloo Ave B37 70 B4
Waterloo Bvd WS12 2 E4
Waterloo Ct CV34 161 A8
Waterloo Ind Est B37 70 B5
Waterloo Pl 5 CV32 156 F1
Waterloo Rd
Birmingham,King's Heath B14 104 E8
Birmingham,South Yardley B25 88 C6
Hinckley LE10 75 D8
Smethwick B66 65 A3
Wolverhampton WV1 163 B4
Waterloo St E DY4 51 F5
Waterloo St
8 Coventry CV1 113 E4
Birmingham B2 164 B2
Dudley DY1 62 B8
Kidderminster DY10 116 E6
Royal Leamington Spa CV31 162 B7
Tipton DY4 51 F5
Waterloo Terr WV1 163 A4
Waterman Rd CV6 113 F6
Watermarque 2 B16 66 B2
Watermead Grange WS8 15 E7
Watermeadow Dr WS4 15 D1
Watermere WS4 29 D8
Water Mill Cl B29 85 D3
Watermill Cl WV10 11 D3
Water Mill Cres B76 46 F1
Water Mill Prim Sch B29 85 D3
Watermint Cl WS12 2 E4
Water Orton La B46,B76 58 E4
Water Orton Prim Sch B46 59 B2
Water Orton Rd B36 58 E1
Water Orton Sta B46 59 A3
Water Rd DY3 50 C2
Watersbridge Gdns CV10 73 C1
Waters Dr B74 31 D3
Waters Edge The B1 66 C2
Waterside
1 Birmingham B15 66 C1
Bedworth CV6 96 C6
Birmingham,Egdbaston B15 86 C8
Birmingham,Hamstead B43 54 E7
Waterside Cl
Birmingham,Bordesley B9 67 B2
Birmingham,Pype Hayes B24 58 A5
Wolverhampton WV2 39 D7
Waterside Ct
6 Birmingham B16 66 B2
Hinckley LE10 74 F7
Royal Leamington Spa CV31 162 B6
Tamworth B77 21 F5
Waterside Dr B18 65 F5
Waterside Est DY2 62 C3
Waterside Grange DY10 116 E8
Waterside Ind Est
Rowley Regis B65 62 F4
Wolverhampton WV2 40 A6
Waterside Orch B48 123 B2
Waterside CV31 161 D7
Waterside View
Birmingham B18 66 A5
Brierley Hill DY5 81 B8
Waterside Way
Brownhills WS8 6 D2
Wolverhampton WV9 11 A3
Watersmead Cl WS12 2 F4
Watersmeet Gr CV2 114 B6
Watersmeet Ho B78 35 B8
Watersmeet Rd CV2 114 B6
Waterson Croft B37 70 D3
Water St
Birmingham B3 164 B3
Burntwood WS7 6 E8
Kingswinford DY6 60 D7
West Bromwich B70 53 D2
Wolverhampton WV10 163 D4
Waters View WS3 15 B5
Waterward Cl B17 85 C5
Waterway Ct B14 105 C3
Waterways Dr B69 63 E8
Waterways Gdns DY8 60 E1
Waterworks Dr B31 102 D4
Waterworks Rd B16 65 F1
Waterworks St B6 67 B8
Watery La
Alvechurch B48 124 C1
Watery La *continued*
Birmingham B62 84 A3
Blakedown DY9 118 F7
Cheswick Green B90 126 D4
Codsall WV8 10 A5
Corley Moor CV7 93 D5
Coventry CV6 95 A4
Hopwood B48 123 F2
Keresley CV7 94 F4
Knowle B93 128 E4
Lichfield WS13 3 C4
Longbridge CV35 160 A1
Watery Lane Ind Est WV13 26 E3
Watery Lane Middleway B9 67 B2
Watery La
Portway B47,B48 140 D7
Redditch B98 154 B2
Smethwick B67 65 A5
Stourbridge DY8 60 E2
Tipton DY4 51 F5
Walsall WS1 42 E8
Willenhall WV13 26 E3
Watford Gap Rd WS14 32 A7
Watford Gap WS14 32 A7
Watford Rd B30 103 F5
Wathan Ave WV14 39 F1
Wathen Rd
Royal Leamington Spa CV32 157 A2
Warwick CV34 160 E8
Watkins Gdns B31 103 C4
Watkins Rd WV12 27 C5
Watland Gn B34 69 B5
Watling Cl LE10 75 C4
Watling Ct CV11 73 F3
Watling Dr LE10 75 C4
Watling Rd CV8 148 B6
Watling St
Brownhills WS8 6 D1
Cannock WS11 4 D6
Dordon B77,B78 36 D6
Hinckley CV11,LE10 74 C8
Hints B78 19 D3
Norton Canes WS11 5 D3
Watling Street Bsns Pk WS11 6 A2
Watling Street Prim Sch WS8 6 E1
Watling St
Tamworth,Bonehill B78 20 E1
Tamworth,Wilnecote B77 35 E7
Watney Gr B44 56 C8
Watson Cl
3 Warwick CV34 155 E1
Sutton Coldfield B72 46 C2
Watson Rd
Birmingham B7 67 D7
Birmingham,Nechells B24 67 D8
Birmingham,Saltley B8 67 F5
Coventry CV5 112 D2
Darlaston WS10 41 A5
Watson Rd E B7 67 D7
Watson Rd
Wolverhampton,Pendeford WV10 11 B2
Wolverhampton WV14 39 F2
Watsons Cl DY2 62 E8
Watson's Green Fields DY2 62 F8
Watson's Green Rd DY2 51 E1
Watson Way CV7 130 C8
Watt Cl B60 136 F1
Watt Ho DY6 60 F7
Wattisham Sq B35 58 A4
Wattis Rd B67 65 A2
Wattle Gn B70 53 A3
Wattle Rd B70 53 A4
Watton Cl WV14 40 A1
Watton Ct B6 66 E8
Watton Gn B35 58 A2
Watton La B46 59 D2
Watton St B70 53 D2
Watt Rd
Birmingham B23 56 E4
Tipton DY4 52 B8
Watts Cl DY4 51 D5
Watt's Rd B10 87 D8
Watts Rd B80 159 E2
Watt St
Birmingham B21 65 D7
Smethwick B66 65 B6
Wattville Ave B21 65 C8
Wattville Prim Sch B21 65 B8
Wattville Rd B21 65 C8
Watwood Rd B28,B90 105 F3
Waugh Cl B37 70 B2
Waugh Dr B63 100 D8
Waveley Rd CV1 113 A3
Wavell Rd
Birmingham B8 67 E5
Brierley Hill DY5 81 F7
Walsall WS2 27 E2
Wavendon Cl CV2 96 F1
Waveney Ave WV6 23 E4
Waveney Cl LE10 75 A8
Waveney Croft B36 69 F8
Waveney Gr WS11 1 B1
Waveney B77 35 E8
Wavenham Cl B74 31 E5
Waverhill Rd B21 65 F7
Waverley Ave
Birmingham B43 44 B4
Nuneaton CV11 73 F1
Waverley Cl DY10 117 A8
Waverley Cres
Romsley B62 100 F4
Waverley Cres *continued*
Wolverhampton,Goldthorn Hill WV4 39 B6
Wolverhampton,Lanesfield WV4 39 F3
Waverley Gdns WV5 49 B7
Waverley Gr B91 106 F3
Waverley Rd
Birmingham B10 87 D7
Darlaston WS10 41 D6
Kenilworth CV8 148 A4
Royal Leamington Spa CV31 162 B6
Walsall WS3 13 F2
Waverley Sch B10 88 A8
Waverley Sq CV11 73 F1
Waverley St DY2 62 A8
Waverley Wlk WS14 9 B6
Wavers Marston B37 90 A8
Waverton Mews 15 CV31 162 C6
Wavytree Cl CV34 160 D7
Waxland Rd B63 83 B2
Wayfield Cl B90 106 C3
Wayfield Rd B90 106 C3
Wayford Dr B72 57 D7
Wayford Glade WV13 40 F8
Wayford Gr B8 68 B4
Waynecroft Rd B43 43 E2
Wayside B37 90 A8
Wayside Dr B74 31 C3
Wayside Gdns WV12 27 E5
Wayside Wlk WS2 28 A3
Wayside WV8 10 F2
Waystone La DY9 119 D4
Wealden Hatch WV10 11 E4
Wealdstone Dr DY3 50 D2
Weale Gr CV34 155 F2
Weaman St B4 164 C3
Weates Yd B27 88 C4
Weatheroak Cl B97 153 A1
Weatheroak Hill B48 124 B1
Weatheroak Rd B11 87 C5
Weather Oaks B17 85 B6
Weatheroaks
Birmingham B62 84 A7
Brownhills WS9 16 B4
Weaver Ave
Birmingham B26 89 B6
Sutton Coldfield B76 47 A1
Weaver Cl DY5 61 B6
Weaver Ct 8 B75 32 E3
Weaver Gr WV13 27 D2
Weavers Cl B97 158 D4
Weavers Hill B97 158 D4
Weavers Rise DY2 62 D3
Weavers Wharf DY10 116 D6
Weavers Wlk CV6 114 B8
Weaving Gdns 1 WS11 1 E1
Webb Ave WV6 23 E5
Webbcroft Rd B33 68 F4
Webb La B28 105 E6
Webb Rd DY4 52 C7
Webb St
Dudley WV14 40 C1
Nuneaton CV10 72 D3
Willenhall WV13 26 F2
Webheath Fst Sch B97 153 A2
Webley Rise WV10 11 F4
Webner Ind Est WV2 40 A6
Webster Ave CV8 148 B5
Webster Cl
Birmingham B11 87 B6
Sutton Coldfield B72 57 B7
Webster Rd
Walsall WS2 28 E5
Willenhall WV13 27 A3
Webster St CV6 113 E7
Webster Way B76 58 B8
Webster Wlk WS11 2 A4
Weddell Wynd WV14 40 F1
Weddington Ctry Wlk★ CV10 73 B8
Weddington Prim Sch CV10 73 D7
Weddington Rd CV10 73 C7
Weddington Terr CV10 73 D5
Wedgbury Cl WS10 42 A1
Wedgbury Way DY5 61 B1
Wedge St 10 WS1 28 F2
Wedgewood Ave B70 52 F7
Wedgewood Cl
Burntwood WS7 7 C7
Coventry CV2 114 E8
Wedgewood Ct WS4 15 C1
Wedgewood Dr B20 55 B2
Wedgewood Ho B37 70 B4
Wedgewood Pl B70 52 F7
Wedgewood Rd B32 84 D5
Wedge-Woods CV5 132 F8
Wedgnock Gn CV34 160 D8
Wedgnock Ind Est CV34 160 C8
Wedgnock La CV34 155 C1
Wedgwood Cl WV1 26 A1
Wedmore Rd B73 45 F1
Wednesbury, Great Western Street Sta WS10 41 E2
Wednesbury Mus & Art Gall★ WS10 41 F2
Wednesbury Oak Prim Sch DY4 41 A1
Wednesbury Oak Rd DY4 41 A1
Wednesbury Parkway Sta WS10 41 D2
Wednesbury Rd WS1 42 D7
Wednesbury Trad Est WS10 41 E4
Wednesfield High Sch Specialist Engineering Sch WV11 26 E5
Wednesfield Rd
Willenhall WV13 27 A3
Wolverhampton WV1, WV10 163 D4
Wednesfield Village Prim Sch WV11 26 D5
Wednesfield Way Ind Est WV11 26 D4
Wednesfield Way WV11 26 D4
Wedon Cl CV4 131 E7
Weeford Dell 2 B75 32 E3
Weeford Dr B20 54 F4
Weeford Rd B75 32 F3
Weethley Ho 6 B97 153 A4
Weights Farm B97 153 C7
Weights La B97 153 C7
Weilerswist Dr CV31 161 F4
Weirbrook Cl B29 103 C7
Weland Cl B46 59 B2
Weland Ct B46 59 B2
Welbeck Ave
Hinckley LE10 75 D4
Wolverhampton WV10 25 D7
Welbeck Cl B62 83 E6
Welbeck Dr
Kidderminster DY11 116 B5
Walsall WS4 29 D7
Welbeck Gr B23 56 B5
Welbury Gdns WV6 24 F5
Welby Gate CV7 130 B5
Welby Rd B28 87 F1
Welch Cl DY4 52 B7
Welches Cl B31 103 B5
Welcombe Dr B76 57 F7
Welcombe Gr B91 106 F4
Welcome Dr B61 121 A1
Welford Ave B26 88 F8
Welford Cl B98 158 F5
Welford Gr B74 31 F3
Welford Pl CV6 113 D7
Welford Prim Sch B20 66 A8
Welford Rd
Birmingham B20 66 A8
Solihull B90 106 C4
Sutton Coldfield B73 45 E1
Tamworth B77 35 C5
Welgarth Ave CV6 112 F6
Welham Croft B90 127 A6
Welland Dr DY8 81 A8
Welland Gr
Birmingham B24 57 D3
Willenhall WV13 27 C2
Welland Rd
Coventry CV1 113 F1
Halesowen B63 83 A2
Welland Way B76 58 A7
Well Cl
Birmingham B36 68 E8
Redditch B97 158 E5
Wellcroft Rd B34 69 A7
Wellcroft St WS10 41 F3
Weller Ct WV3 24 D1
Wellesbourne Cl
Redditch B98 153 E4
Wolverhampton WV3 38 B8
Wellesbourne Dr WV14 51 B7
Wellesbourne Rd
Birmingham B20 55 B1
Coventry CV5 112 A3
Wellesbourne B79 21 C8
Wellesbourne Twr 3 B5 86 E8
Wellesley Dr DY4 51 F5
Wellesley Gdns B13 87 D1
Wellesley Rd B68 64 B6
Wellfield Cl
Balsall Common CV7 130 D5
Cannock WS11 4 B7
Wellfield Gdns DY2 62 E6
Wellfield Rd
Aldridge WS9 30 B8
Birmingham B28 106 B6
Wellhead La B42 55 E3
Wellhead Way B42 55 F2
Wellington Ave WV3 38 F7
Wellington Cl
Hinckley LE10 75 E4
Kingswinford DY6 60 E4
Wellington Cres B20 55 B2
Wellington Ct
Birmingham B32 84 F5
Birmingham,Handsworth Wood B20 55 C2
Cradley Heath B64 62 F2
Kidderminster DY11 116 C5
Willenhall WV13 26 F3
Wellington Dr WS11 4 B8
Wellington Gdns 1 CV1 113 B2
Wellington Gr B91 106 F6
Wellington Ho B32 84 F4
Wellington Ind Est WV14 51 C7
Wellington Pl WV13 26 F3
Wellington Rd
Bilston WV14 40 D6
Birmingham B20 55 C2
Birmingham,Edgbaston B15 86 C7
Bromsgrove B60 151 A8
Dudley DY1 51 B1
Royal Leamington Spa CV32 157 C2
Smethwick B67 65 A3
Tipton DY4 52 A4
Walsall WS5 43 C6
Wellington St S B70 53 C4
Wellington St
6 Redditch B98 153 E4

Wellington St *continued*
Birmingham B18 65 D5
Coventry CV1 165 D4
Cradley Heath B64 62 F2
Oldbury B69 64 B6
Walsall WS2 42 B7
West Bromwich B71 53 C4
Wellington Terr 3 B19 66 B7
Wellington Twr 4 B31 103 A1
Wellington Way B35 58 B2
Well La
Birmingham B5 164 D2
Great Wyrley WS6 5 A1
Hinckley LE10 71 D1
Tanworth-In-A B94 142 A1
Walsall,Harden WS3 28 D7
Walsall WS3 28 E8
Wolverhampton WV11 26 C4
Wellman Croft B29 85 D1
Wellman's Rd WV13 27 C1
Well Mdw B45 122 A6
Wellmeadow Gr B92 109 A7
Wellmead Wlk B45 121 F8
Well Pl WS3 28 E8
Wells Ave WS10 41 B6
Wells Cl
Cannock WS11 1 E6
Kidderminster DY11 116 A6
Perton WV6 23 D4
Wednesbury DY4 41 A1
West Bromwich B71 53 D8
Wells Ct
Coventry CV3 133 F7
Dudley DY2 62 C5
Wellsford Ave B92 89 B4
Wells Green Rd B92 89 A4
Wells Rd
Bilston WV14 40 E3
Brierley Hill DY5 61 B3
Rowley Regis B65 63 E4
Solihull B92 89 C4
Wolverhampton WV4 38 F5
Well St
Birmingham B19 66 C5
Coventry CV1 165 B3
Darlaston WS10 41 E6
Wells Twr B16 66 A2
Wells Wlk B37 70 A1
Welney Gdns WV9 11 A3
Welsby Ave B43 54 E7
Welsh Cl CV34 155 E2
Welsh House Farm Com Sch B32 84 F4
Welsh House Farm Rd B32 84 F4
Welshmans Hill B73 45 C3
Welsh Rd
Coventry CV2 114 B4
Cubbington CV32,CV33 157 F2
Welton Cl B76 47 A2
Welton Rd CV34 155 D1
Welwyndale Rd B72 57 C6
Welwyn Rd LE10 71 F1
Wembley Gr B25 88 C8
Wembley La WS7 6 D8
Wembrook Cl CV11 73 D2
Wembrook Ho CV11 73 E2
Wembrook Prim Sch CV11 73 C2
Wembury B77 21 E5
Wem Gdns WV11 26 D6
Wendell Crest WV10 11 F4
Wendiburgh St CV4 132 B7
Wendover Dr LE10 71 E4
Wendover Rd
Birmingham B23 56 C7
Rowley Regis B65 63 A5
Wolverhampton WV4 39 F2
Wendover Rise CV5 112 C4
Wendron Cl B60 137 B2
Wendron Gr B14 104 D4
Wenlock Ave WV3 38 E8
Wenlock Cl
Halesowen B63 82 D2
Sedgley DY3 50 C7
Wenlock Dr B61 137 A5
Wenlock Gdns WS3 28 E5
Wenlock Rd
Birmingham B20 55 F1
Stourbridge DY8 81 B6
Wenlock B77 21 D3
Wenlock Way CV10 72 B3
Wenman St B12 86 F6
Wensley Croft B90 106 B6
Wensleydale Rd B42 55 B6
Wensley Rd B26 88 F6
Wensum Cl LE10 75 B8
Wentbridge Rd WV1 26 C1
Wentworth Ave B36 69 B8
Wentworth Cl
Burntwood WS7 7 C7
Hinckley LE10 71 E3
Wentworth Ct
Birmingham B24 56 F2
Sutton Coldfield B75 32 B1
Wentworth Dr
Blackwell B60 138 A5
Coventry CV6 95 B4
Lichfield WS14 9 D5
Nuneaton CV11 74 A1
Oldbury B69 63 A7
Wentworth Gate B17 85 B6
Wentworth Gr WV6 23 D5
Wentworth Park Ave B17 85 B6
Wentworth Rd
Birmingham B17 85 B6
Royal Leamington Spa CV31 162 D6
Wentworth Rd *continued*
Solihull B92 88 F3
Stourbridge DY8 80 E7
Sutton Coldfield B74 46 A8
Walsall WS3 13 F3
Wolverhampton WV10 11 F3
Wentworth Rise B62 83 D3
Wentworth Way B32 84 F3
Wenyon Cl DY4 52 B4
Weoley Ave B29 85 C2
Weoley Castle Rd B29 84 F1
Weoley Hill B29 103 C8
Weoley Park Rd B29 85 C1
Wergs Dr WV6 24 A7
Wergs Hall WV8 23 F7
Wergs Hall Rd WV6,WV8 24 A7
Wergs Rd
Codsall WV6 23 F7
Wolverhampton WV6 24 B6
Werneth Gr WS3 14 A4
Wesleyan Ct WS4 29 A4
Wesley Ave
Cheslyn Hay WS6 4 D3
Codsall WV8 10 B2
Halesowen B63 82 B8
Wesley Cl B64 62 F1
Wesley Ct
4 Cradley Heath B64 82 F8
5 Wolverhampton WV4 39 F4
Birmingham B16 65 C2
Cannock WS11 1 E1
Wesley Gr WS10 41 E3
Wesley Ho 3 WS2 42 C7
Wesley Pl
Cannock WS12 2 C7
Tipton DY4 52 C7
Wesley Rd
Birmingham B23 56 F5
Brierley Hill DY5 61 B5
Codsall WV8 10 B2
Willenhall WV12 27 C6
Wesley's Fold WS10 41 D6
Wesley St
Bilston WV14 40 E2
Oldbury B69 64 A8
West Bromwich B70 53 B3
Wolverhampton WV2 40 A6
Wesley Way B77 21 F4
Wesley Wlk B60 150 E7
Wessenden B77 36 B7
Wessex Cl
Bedworth CV12 78 A4
Brownhills WS8 15 F7
Wessex Ct B79 22 F7
Wessex Dr WS11 1 F2
Wessex Rd WV2 39 F6
Wesson Gdns B63 83 A3
Wesson Rd WS10 41 C8
Westacre Cres WV3 24 C1
Westacre Dr DY5 81 F8
Westacre Gdns B33 68 F3
Westacre Inf Sch WV3 24 C1
West Acre WV13 26 F1
West Ave
Bedworth CV12 78 D2
Birmingham,Castle Bromwich B36 69 D8
Birmingham,Handsworth B20 55 A4
Coventry CV6,CV7 95 A5
Coventry,Middle Stoke CV2 114 A2
Oldbury B69 63 B7
Redditch B98 153 E3
Wolverhampton WV11 26 C6
Westbourne Ave
Birmingham B34 68 E6
Cannock WS11 1 D3
Cheslyn Hay WS6 4 E3
Westbourne Cl 3 B61 136 E1
Westbourne Cres
Birmingham B15 86 A8
Burntwood WS7 7 B7
Westbourne Ct
Darlaston WS10 41 F7
Walsall WS4 29 A3
Westbourne Gdns B15 86 A7
Westbourne Gr B21 65 F7
Westbourne Rd
Birmingham,Edgbaston B15 86 A8
Birmingham,Handsworth B21 54 D1
Darlaston WS10 41 F7
Halesowen B62 83 E7
Solihull B92 106 F8
Walsall,Ryecroft WS4 28 F4
Walsall WS4 29 A4
West Bromwich B70 53 B2
Wolverhampton WV4 39 A5
Westbourne St WS4 28 F3
Westbourne Terr 2 B61 136 E1
West Bromwich Central Sta B70 53 C2
West Bromwich Rd WS5 42 F5
West Bromwich Ringway B70 53 D2
West Bromwich St
Oldbury B69 52 F1
Walsall WS1 42 E7
Westbrook Ave
Aldridge WS9 29 F5
Aldridge WS9 30 A5
Westbrook Ct CV5 112 A4
Westbury Ave WS10 41 F6
Westbury Ct
22 Brierley Hill DY5 61 D2
Coventry CV2 114 A3
Westbury Ct *continued*
Warwick CV34 161 A7
Westbury Ho B97 153 B2
Westbury Rd
Coventry CV5 112 D5
Nuneaton CV10 72 D3
Smethwick B17 65 B3
Wednesbury WS10 41 F6
Westbury St WV1 163 C3
West Bvd B32 84 F4
West Cl LE10 75 D7
Westcliff Dr CV34 155 E2
Westcliffe Dr CV3 133 B5
Westcliff Pl B31 102 F4
Westcombe Gr B32 84 A1
West Coppice Rd WS8 15 C8
Westcote Ave B31 102 C2
Westcote Cl B92 89 A2
Westcotes CV4 112 B1
Westcott Cl DY6 60 F3
Westcott Rd B26 89 A8
Westcroft Ave WV10 12 A1
Westcroft Gr B38 103 D3
Westcroft Rd
Sedgley DY3 39 B2
Wolverhampton WV6 23 F6
Westcroft Sch & Sports Coll WV10 12 B2
Westcroft Way B14 105 B1
West Cross Sh Ctr B66 64 D7
West Ct B60 150 F6
Westdean Cl B62 83 C4
West Dr
Birmingham,Edgbaston B5 86 C5
Birmingham,Handsworth B20 66 B8
Fazeley B78 20 E2
West End Ave B66 64 D7
West End Ct CV34 160 D6
West End Villas B38 103 F2
Westerdale Cl DY3 51 A7
Westerham Cl B93 127 F6
Westerhope Gr B19 66 C5
Westeria Cl B36 69 C8
Westeria Ho B36 69 C8
Westering Parkway WV10 11 F4
Westerings B20 55 C2
Western Ave
Brierley Hill DY5 61 B2
Halesowen B62 83 E4
Sedgley DY3 50 B8
Willenhall WS2 27 D3
Western Bsns Pk
Birmingham B18 65 E6
Halesowen B62 83 B7
Western By-Pass WS13 8 F8
Western Cl WS2 27 D3
Western Hill Cl B96 158 E1
Western Rd
Birmingham,Edgbaston B18 65 F4
Birmingham,Erdington B24 57 A3
Cannock WS12 2 B6
Cradley Heath B64 82 E8
Oldbury B69 64 B5
Stourbridge DY8 80 F4
Sutton Coldfield B73 46 A1
West Hagley DY9 99 B4
Western Way
Darlaston WS10 41 C3
Kidderminster DY11 116 A5
Westfield Ave B14 105 B1
Westfield Cl
Dorridge B93 127 F2
Nuneaton CV10 73 D5
Westfield Ct LE10 75 C7
Westfield Dr WS9 30 A6
Westfield Grange B14 86 E1
Westfield Gr WV3 38 C8
Westfield Hall 2 B16 65 D1
Westfield Ho B36 70 A7
Westfield Inf Sch LE10 75 B7
Westfield Jun Sch LE10 75 B7
Westfield Manor B75 32 A4
Westfield Prim Sch WV5 49 A7
Westfield Rd
Bilston WV14 40 B7
Birmingham,Acock's Green B27 88 B3
Birmingham B15 85 D7
Birmingham,Moseley B14 86 E1
Brierley Hill DY5 81 F8
Dudley DY2 62 D7
Halesowen B62 63 E1
Hinckley LE10 75 B7
Sedgley DY3 39 E1
Smethwick B67 64 F5
Willenhall WV13 40 E8
Westfields
Birchmoor B78 36 D8
Catshill B61 136 F8
Westford Gr B28 105 E3
Westgate
Aldridge WS9 29 E6
Birmingham B15 85 E4
West Gate B16 65 E3
Westgate WS12 2 F6
Westgate Cl
Sedgley DY3 50 E7
Warwick CV34 160 D6
Westgate Ho 10 CV34 160 E6
Westgate Rd B65 63 E4
Westgate Prim Sch CV34 160 D6
Westgate Trad Est WS9 29 E6
West Gn WV4 38 C5
West Green Cl B15 86 B8
Westgrove Ave 6 B90 127 A6
Westgrove Terr 1 CV32 161 D8
Westhall Gate WS3 14 B2
Westham Ho B37 70 B4
Westhaven Dr B31 102 E7
Westhaven Rd B72 46 C5
Westhay Rd B28 106 B7
West Heath Hospl B38 123 C8
West Heath Prim Sch B38 123 C8
West Heath Rd
2 Birmingham,Edgbaston B18 65 D4
Birmingham,Northfield B31 103 B1
West Hill Ave WS12 2 B6
Westhill Cl B92 106 E8
Westhill Coll of H Ed B29 85 D1
Westhill Coll (Univ Birmingham) B29 103 D8
West Hill Ct B14 104 C4
West Hill Prim Sch WS12 2 B6
Westhill Rd
Birmingham B38 103 F3
Blackdown CV32 157 A6
Coventry CV6 112 F6
Westhill WV3 24 C2
West Holme B9 67 C2
Westholme Croft B30 103 E8
Westhouse Ct B14 104 D4
Westhouse Gr B14 104 D4
West House Sch B15 86 C8
West Hyde LE10 74 F7
Westland Ave WV3 24 F2
Westland Cl B23 56 F5
Westland Gdns
6 Wolverhampton WV3 25 A2
Stourbridge DY8 80 F7
Westland Rd WV6 24 F2
Westlands Rd
Birmingham B13 87 A1
Sutton Coldfield B76 57 F6
Westland Wlk B35 57 F2
Westlea Rd CV31 161 E6
Westleigh Ave CV5 132 F7
Westley Brook Cl B26 89 B5
Westley Cl B28 106 B6
Westley Rd B27 88 B3
Westley St
6 Dudley DY1 62 B8
Birmingham B9 67 A2
West Lodge WV1 25 A3
Westmead Ave B80 159 E4
Westmead Cres B24 57 C4
West Mead Dr B14 104 E6
Westmead Dr B68 64 B4
Westmede Ctr CV5 112 C4
West Mews B44 44 D2
West Midlands Hospl B63 82 D5
West Mill Croft B38 123 E7
Westminster Ave WV4 39 B5
Westminster B37 69 F5
Westminster Cl
Bromsgrove B61 136 D1
Dudley DY1 51 A2
Westminster Ct
3 Bromsgrove B60 137 A2
Birmingham B20 55 C2
Westminster Dr
Birmingham B14 104 E6
Hinckley LE10 75 F4
Nuneaton CV10 72 B7
Westminster Ind Est DY2 62 D2
Westminster Prim Sch B20 55 C1
Westminster Rd
Birmingham,Handsworth B20 55 C1
Birmingham,Stirchley B29 104 A8
Cannock WS11 1 E6
Coventry CV1 165 A1
Kidderminster DY11 116 A6
Stourbridge DY8 60 D2
Walsall WS4 29 B7
West Bromwich B71 53 D8
Westminster Sch The
Smethwick B67 65 A5
West Bromwich B71 53 D8
Westmoreland Ave CV10 72 E4
Westmore Way WS10 42 D5
Westmorland Cl B78 21 A1
Westmorland Ct B71 53 D7
Westmorland Rd
Coventry CV2 114 F4
West Bromwich B71 53 D7
Weston Ave
6 Birmingham,Lozells B19 66 C7
Birmingham,Sparkbrook B11 87 C6
Oldbury B69 52 B1
Westonbirt Cl CV8 148 C6
Weston Cl
5 Royal Leamington Spa CV31 162 C6
Cannock WS11 2 C1
Dorridge B93 128 A2
Hinckley LE10 71 A1
Walsall WS1 42 E6
Warwick CV34 160 F7
Weston Cres WS9 30 B4
Weston Ct 10 WV3 25 C4
Weston Dr
Bilston WV14 40 B5
Great Wyrley WS6 4 F1
Wednesbury DY4 41 C2
Westonhall Rd B60 150 D1
Weston Hall Stables CV12 79 A3
Weston Ho
Birmingham B19 66 E6
Wolverhampton WV6 24 E5
Weston Ind Est B11 87 E4
Weston La
Birmingham B11 87 E4
Bulkington CV12 79 B3
Weston Rd
Birmingham B19 66 B7
Lichfield WS13 3 A2
Smethwick B67 64 F2
Weston St
Coventry CV1 165 C4
Walsall WS1 42 E7
Weston Terr 3 B19 66 D8
West Orchards Sh Ctr CV1 165 B3
Westover Rd B20 54 E4
West Park Ave B31 102 E2
West Park Cl WS9 29 E5
West Park Ct WV1 25 A2
West Park Hospl WV1 25 A2
West Park Prim Sch WV1 163 A4
West Park Rd B67 64 D6
West Pathway B17 85 C6
West Point B17 85 C8
Westport Cres WV11 26 F5
Westray Cl B45 101 F1
Westray Dr LE10 71 C1
West Rd
Birmingham,Hamstead B43 54 E7
Birmingham,Handsworth B6 55 E2
Bromsgrove B60 137 A2
Halesowen B63 82 B6
West Rd S B63 82 B6
West Rd
Tipton DY4 52 B8
Wolverhampton WV4 39 F5
West Ridge CV5 112 A5
Westridge Rd B13 105 C6
Westridge DY3 50 C8
West Rise B75 46 C6
West Rock CV34 160 D7
West Side Bsns Ctr CV4 131 F8
Westside Dr B32 84 D1
West St
17 Royal Leamington Spa CV31 162 A7
Brierley Hill DY5 81 F8
Cannock WS11 4 E6
Coventry CV1 113 E3
Redditch B98 153 E3
Rowley Regis B65 63 C1
Stourbridge DY8 80 F5
Tamworth B79 21 C5
Tamworth,Kettlebrook B77 21 C3
Walsall WS3 28 C7
Warwick CV34 160 D5
Wolverhampton WV6 25 C5
West View B8 68 C4
West View Ct B75 46 E6
West View Dr DY6 60 E5
West View Rd
Royal Leamington Spa CV32 157 C5
Sutton Coldfield B75 46 E6
Westville Ave DY11 116 A5
Westville Rd WS2 28 A3
Westward Cl B44 55 F8
West Way B31 123 B7
Westway Ho WS4 15 B1
West Way WS4 15 B2
Westwick Cl WS9 16 E4
West Winds WV10 12 C7
Westwood Ave
Birmingham B11 87 D4
Stourbridge DY8 80 D3
Westwood Bsns Pk
Birmingham B6 56 B1
Coventry CV4 131 F6
Westwood Cl CV10 72 E3
Westwood Ct B73 45 B4
Westwood Dr B45 102 B1
Westwood Gr B91 106 F2
Westwood Heath Rd CV4 131 E6
Westwood Holdings WS12 1 B6
Westwood Rd
Birmingham,Aston B6 56 A2
Coventry CV5 113 A1
Sutton Coldfield B73 45 A4
Westwoods Hollow WS7 7 B8
Westwood St DY5 61 A1
Westwood View B24 57 C3
Westwood Way CV4 132 A6
Wetherby Cl
Birmingham B36 68 D8
Wolverhampton WV10 11 D5
Wetherby Rd
Birmingham B27 88 C2
Walsall WS3 14 A4
Wetherfield Rd B11 88 A3
Wexford Cl DY1 50 F2
Wexford Rd CV2 96 D1
Weybourne Rd B44 44 E2
Weycroft Rd B23 56 B7
Weyhill Cl WV9 10 F2
Weymoor Rd B17 85 B3
Weymouth Cl CV3 134 D5
Weymouth Dr B74 31 F4
Weymouth Ho B79 21 B5
Whaley's Croft CV6 113 B8
Wharf App WS9 29 F7

…rf Cl WS14 9 C7
Wharfdale Rd B11 88 A5
Wharfedale Cl DY6 60 B7
Wharfedale St WS10 42 A2
Wharf La
Birmingham B18 66 A6
Burntwood WS8 6 F3
Nuthurst B94 143 D4
Solihull B91 107 D6
Tardebigge B60 138 B1
Wharf Lodge CV31 161 D7
Wharf Rd
Birmingham,King's Norton B30 104 A2
Birmingham,Tyseley B11 88 B5
Coventry CV6 113 F5
Wharfside B69 63 F7
Wharf St
Birmingham,Aston B6 67 A7
Birmingham,Hockley B18 66 A6
Walsall WS2 28 C1
Warwick CV34 161 A8
Wolverhampton WV1 163 D2
Wharf The B1 164 A2
Wharf Yd LE10 75 A7
Whar Hall Rd B92 107 E8
Wharrington Cl B98 159 A8
Wharrington Hill B98 159 A8
Wharton Ave B92 107 E7
Wharton St Ind Est B7 67 D8
Wharton St B7 67 D8
Wharwell La WS6 5 A1
Whatcote Gn B92 107 E8
Whatecroft The 3 B17 85 B6
Whateley Ave WS3 28 F6
Whateley Cres B36 69 D8
Whateley Ct CV11 73 B4
Whateley Gn B74 46 A8
Whateley Hall Cl B93 128 C7
Whateley Hall Rd B93 128 B7
Whateley La B77,B78 35 F4
Whateley Lodge Dr B36 69 C8
Whateley Pl WS3 28 F6
Whateley Rd
Birmingham B21 65 E8
Walsall WS3 28 F6
Whateley's Dr CV8 148 A5
Whateley Villas CV9 36 A2
Wheatcroft Cl
3 Sutton Coldfield B75 32 E3
Burntwood WS7 7 A5
Halesowen B62 83 F8
Redditch B97 153 A5
Wheatcroft Dr B37 70 C1
Wheatcroft Gr DY2 51 F1
Wheatcroft Rd B33 68 F2
Wheate Croft CV4 111 F2
Wheaten Cl B37 70 D3
Wheatfield Cl B36 70 A7
Wheatfield View B31 102 D6
Wheatfield Way LE10 71 C4
Wheathill Cl
Royal Leamington Spa CV32 156 E2
Wolverhampton WV4 38 E3
Wheat Hill WS5 43 E8
Wheatland Gr WS9 30 B4
Wheatlands Cl 1 WS12 2 C1
Wheatlands Croft B33 69 E3
Wheatlands The WV6 23 D3
Wheatley Cl
Birmingham B68 84 C8
Solihull B92 107 E8
Sutton Coldfield B75 32 C3
Wheatley Grange B46 70 F6
Wheatley Gr WS6 5 A2
Wheatley Rd B68 84 D8
Wheatley St
West Bromwich B70 53 A3
Wolverhampton WV2 39 F6
Wheatmill Cl DY10 98 B2
Wheatmoor Rd B75 47 A6
Wheatmoor Rise B75 46 E6
Wheaton Cl WV10 25 C7
Wheaton Vale B20 54 E3
Wheatridge Cl DY6 60 A8
Wheatridge Rd B60 150 E6
Wheats Ave B17 85 B3
Wheatsheaf Cl B75 32 E4
Wheatsheaf Rd
Birmingham B16 65 D2
Oldbury B69 63 A8
Wolverhampton WV8 10 E1
Wheat St CV11 73 D4
Wheatstone Cl DY3 50 E6
Wheatstone Gr B33 68 F5
Wheeldon Ho B26 88 E4
Wheeler Cl B93 145 B7
Wheeler Ho 12 B69 64 A7
Wheeler Rd WV11 26 C8
Wheeler's Fold WV1 163 C3
Wheelers La B13 104 F7
Wheeler's La B13 105 A7
Wheelers Lane Prim Sch (Annexe) B13 105 A6
Wheelers Lane Prim Sch B13 104 F7
Wheelers Lane Tech Coll B13 104 F7
Wheelers La B97 153 C6
Wheeler St B19 66 D7
Wheeler Street Sh Ctr B19 66 D6
Wheeler St DY8 80 F5
Wheeley Moor Rd B37 70 A5
Wheeley Rd
Alvechurch B48 138 D5
Solihull B92 107 D7
Wheeley's La B15 66 C1
Wheeleys Rd B15 86 B8
Wheelock Cl B74 44 F7
Wheelwright Cl
4 Darlaston WS10 41 C6
Bromsgrove B60 150 E6
Wheelwright Ct 5 B24 56 E2
Wheelwright La CV6,CV7 95 C4
Wheelwright Lane Prim Sch CV7 95 D5
Wheelwright Rd B24 56 F1
Wheldrake Ave B34 69 C6
Wheler Rd CV3 134 A7
Whernside Dr WV6 25 A5
Wherretts Well La B91 107 E6
Whetstone Cl B15 85 F5
Whetstone Field Prim Sch WS9 30 B4
Whetstone Gn WV10 11 D1
Whetstone Gr WV10 25 D8
Whetstone La WS9 30 B4
Whetstone Rd WV10 25 D8
Whettybridge Rd B45 121 E6
Whetty La B45 121 F7
Whichcote Ave CV7 92 C1
Whichford Cl B76 57 D6
Whichford Gr B9 68 C2
While Rd B72 46 B4
Whilmot Cl WV10 12 B6
Whimbrel Gr DY10 117 A1
Whinberry Rise DY5 50 C1
Whinchat Gr DY10 117 A2
Whinfield Rd B61 136 B6
Whinyates Rise WS11 4 F8
Whisley Brook La B28 87 F2
Whistler Gr WV10 26 A8
Whiston Ave WV11 27 A7
Whiston Gr B29 103 B8
Whiston Ho 9 WS1 28 F1
Whitacre La WS14 16 E7
Whitacre Rd
3 Royal Leamington Spa CV32 157 A2
Birmingham B9 67 F3
Whitacre Rd Ind Est CV11 73 E4
Whitacre Rd
Knowle B93 128 B7
Nuneaton CV11 73 E4
Whitaker Rd CV5 112 C3
Whitbourne Cl B12 87 B5
Whitburn Ave B42 55 A5
Whitburn Cl
Kidderminster DY11 116 B5
Wolverhampton WV9 11 A2
Whitburn Rd CV12 77 C1
Whitby Cl WS3 13 F3
Whitby Rd B12 87 A4
Whitby Way WS11 4 C8
Whitchurch Cl B98 158 F6
Whitchurch Way CV4 131 F8
Whitcot Gr B31 122 F8
White Bark Cl WS12 2 A8
Whitebeam Cl
Brownhills WS8 15 E6
Coventry CV4 111 D1
Dudley DY3 50 C4
Whitebeam Croft 3 B38 103 E1
White Beam Rd B37 90 D8
Whitebeam Way CV10 72 D7
White City Rd DY5 62 A1
White Cl DY9 81 C2
Whitecrest B43 44 A2
Whitecrest Jun & Inf Sch B43 44 A2
Whitecroft Rd B26 89 D5
White Falcon Ct B91 106 F2
White Farm Rd B74 31 E4
White Field Ave B17 85 A6
Whitefield Cl
Codsall WV8 10 B2
Coventry CV4 131 D6
Whitefields Cres B91 107 B2
Whitefields Gate B91 107 A1
Whitefields Rd B91 107 A2
Whitefriars Dr B63 83 A4
White Friars La CV1 165 C2
White Friars St CV1 165 C2
Whitegate Dr DY11 116 A3
Whitegates Rd WV14 40 D2
Whitehall Ct WV3 38 F6
Whitehall Dr
Dudley DY1 51 A2
Halesowen B63 83 B4
Whitehall Ind Pk DY4 52 E5
Whitehall Inf Sch WS1 42 E7
Whitehall Jun Sch WS1 42 F6
Whitehall Rd
2 Walsall WS1 42 E7
Birmingham,Bordesley Green B9 67 E1
Birmingham,Handsworth B21 66 A8
Cradley Heath B64 82 C8
Halesowen B63 83 B4
Kingswinford DY6 60 C6
Stourbridge DY8 81 B2
Tipton DY4,B70 52 E4
Wolverhampton WV4 39 B4
White Hart The 8 WS1 42 E8
Whitehead Dr
Kenilworth CV8 148 C7
Minworth B76 58 D6
Whitehead Gr CV7 130 B7
Whitehead Rd B6 66 E8
Whiteheads Ct 17 CV32 156 F1
Whiteheath Ct 6 B65 63 E4
Whiteheath PRU B65 63 D4
White Hill B31 103 B6
Whitehill La B29,B31 103 A5
Whitehill Rd DY11 116 A4
White Hollies WS3 14 F4
Whitehorse Cl CV6 96 B6
White Horse Rd WS8 6 E2
Whitehouse Ave
Darlaston WS10 41 B7
Wednesbury WS10 41 F3
White House Ave WV11 26 F7
Whitehouse Ave WV3 38 D8
White House Cl B91 106 F3
Whitehouse Common Prim Sch B75 46 D7
Whitehouse Common Rd B75 46 E7
Whitehouse Cres
Burntwood WS7 7 B7
Nuneaton CV10 72 D3
Sutton Coldfield B75 46 E7
Wolverhampton WV11 12 F1
Whitehouse Ct 8 B75 46 F6
White House Dr B45 122 A2
Whitehouse Dr
Lichfield WS13 8 F6
Smethwick B66 65 A7
White House Gn B91 106 F3
Whitehouse La
Codsall WV8 10 A6
Redditch B98 154 E4
Whitehouse Pl B45 121 F6
Whitehouse Rd
Kidderminster DY10 116 D4
Polesworth B78 36 F7
White Houses La WV10 12 B5
Whitehouse St
Birmingham B6 66 F6
Tipton,Burnt Tree DY4 52 A2
Tipton,Wallbrook WV14 51 C8
Walsall WS2 28 D3
Whitehouse Way WS9 29 F4
White House Way B91 107 A3
Whitelaw Cres CV5 112 C6
Whitemoor Dr B90 127 A7
Whitemoor Rd CV8 148 B5
White Oak Dr
Kingswinford DY6 60 C6
Wolverhampton WV3 24 C1
Whitepits La B48 140 F4
Whitepoplars Cl DY5 61 C4
White Rd
Birmingham B32 84 D6
Birmingham,Sparkbrook B11 87 C7
Smethwick B67 64 F6
White Rose Ho 4 CV32 156 F2
White Row WV5 37 C1
Whitesands Cl B77 21 E5
White's Dr DY3 50 E8
Whiteside Cl CV3 134 F8
Whiteslade Cl B93 128 A7
Whitesmith Croft B14 104 E8
Whitesmiths Cl DY3 50 D8
Whitesmore Sch B37 69 F1
White's Rd B71 53 C6
Whites Row CV8 148 A3
White St
Birmingham B12 87 A5
Coventry CV1 165 C3
Whitestitch La CV7 92 C3
Whitestone Inf Sch CV11 79 A8
Whitestone Rd
Halesowen B63 83 A6
Nuneaton CV11 79 B7
White St WS1 42 E8
Whites Wood WV5 49 A5
Whitethorn Cl WS12 2 A8
Whitethorn Cres B74 30 D1
Whitethorn Dr CV32 157 B2
Whitethorn Rd DY8 61 A1
Whitewood Glade WV12 27 E4
Whitfield Gr B15 86 D8
Whitfield Rd WS12 2 C7
Whitford Bridge Rd B60 151 A2
Whitford Cl B61 150 D8
Whitford Dr B90 127 C7
Whitford Gdns B61 136 D2
Whitford Rd B61 136 D2
Whitgreave Ave
Featherstone WV10 12 B7
Wolverhampton WV10 25 F8
Whitgreave Ct WV10 12 B6
Whitgreave Inf Sch WV10 25 E8
Whitgreave Jun Sch WV10 25 E8
Whitgreave Prim Sch WV10 12 B7
Whitgreave St B70 52 E3
Whiting B77 35 D7
Whitland Cl B45 122 B6
Whitland Dr B14 104 F3
Whitley Abbey Com Sch CV3 133 F6
Whitley Abbey Prim Sch CV3 134 A6
Whitley Ave B77 21 E5
Whitley Cl WV6 24 B2
Whitley Court Rd B32 84 D5
Whitley Ct
Birmingham B20 54 E3
Coventry CV3 133 F7
Whitley Dr B74 45 A8
Whitley St WS10 41 E3
Whitley Village CV3 133 F7
Whitlock Gr B14 105 A3
Whitlocks End Halt B90 125 E7
Whitminster Ave B24 57 B3
Whitminster Cl WV12 27 C4
Whitmore Hill WV1 163 B3
Whitmore Ho WV6 25 A4
Whitmore Park Prim Sch CV6 95 A1
Whitmore Park Rd CV6 95 D3
Whitmore Rd
Birmingham B10 87 C8
Stourbridge DY8 80 D5
Whitnash CV31 162 A3
Whitmore St
Birmingham B18 66 B6
Walsall WS1 42 D7
Wolverhampton WV1 163 C3
Whitnash Cl CV7 130 A6
Whitnash Gr CV2 114 D5
Whitnash Prim Sch CV31 162 A4
Whitnash Rd CV31 162 B4
Whitney Ave DY8 80 D6
Whittaker St WV2 39 E6
Whittall Dr E DY11 116 B1
Whittall Dr W DY11 116 A1
Whittall St B4 164 C3
Whittimere St WS1 28 F2
Whittingham Gr WV11 26 F6
Whittingham Rd B63 83 A5
Whittington Cl
4 Warwick CV34 161 B8
Birmingham B14 104 E5
West Bromwich B71 53 F8
Whittington Gr B33 68 F2
Whittington Hall La DY7 80 B3
Whittington Ho WS13 3 E1
Whittington Oval B33 69 A2
Whittington Rd DY8 80 E3
Whittle Cl CV3 134 F8
Whittle Croft B35 57 F3
Whittle Ct 9 CV32 157 A1
Whittleford Gr B36 58 C1
Whittleford Rd CV10 72 C4
Whittle Rd LE10 74 E7
Whittles Ct DY11 116 B8
Whitton St WS10 41 E6
Whitville Cl DY11 116 C7
Whitwell Cl B90 127 A6
Whitworth Ave
Coventry CV3 114 B1
Hinckley LE10 74 F7
Whitworth Cl WS10 41 E7
Whitworth Dr B71 42 E1
Whitworth Ind Pk B9 67 C2
Whoberley Ave CV5 112 D2
Whoberley Hall Prim Sch CV5 112 C3
Whyley St B70 53 A4
Whyley Wlk B69 64 A5
Whynot Cl B60 150 C2
Whynot St B63 82 B5
Whytmore The WS13 8 F5
Wibert Cl B29 86 A1
Wichnor Rd B92 88 F5
Wickets Twr B5 86 C5
Wickham Cl CV6 94 F2
Wickham Ct CV32 157 B3
Wickham Gdns WV11 26 A6
Wickham Rd B80 159 F4
Wickham Sq B70 53 B2
Wicklow Cl B63 82 D1
Wickmans Dr CV4 111 C2
Wiclif Way CV10 72 B3
Widdecombe Cl CV2 114 D7
Widdrington Rd CV1 113 C5
Wideacre Dr B44 55 E7
Wide Acres B45 101 F1
Widgeon Gr WV10 12 B7
Widney Ave
Aldridge WS9 16 B1
Birmingham B29 85 C1
Widney Cl B93 127 F5
Widney Ho B97 153 C4
Widney Jun Sch B91 106 F1
Widney La B91 127 B8
Widney Manor Rd B91, B93 127 D7
Widney Manor Sta B91 127 C8
Widney Rd B93 127 F5
Wigford Rd B77 35 C5
Wiggin Cotts 5 B17 85 C5
Wiggin Ho WS3 14 C3
Wiggins Croft B76 46 F3
Wiggins Hill Rd B76 58 F7
Wigginsmill Rd WS10 41 D1
Wiggin St B16 65 F3
Wigginton Rd B79 21 B7
Wight Croft B36 70 B6
Wightman Cl WS14 9 E6
Wightwick Bank WV6 24 A2
Wightwick Cl WS3 14 B1
Wightwick Ct WV6 24 A2
Wightwick Gr WV6 24 A2
Wightwick Hall Rd WV6 23 E1
Wightwick Hall Sch WV6 23 E2
Wightwick Manor★ WV6 23 F1
Wigland Way B38 104 A1
Wigmore Gr B44 56 B8
Wigmore La B71 54 A8
Wigorn Ho B67 84 F8
Wigorn La DY9 99 B8
Wigorn Rd B67 64 F1
Wigston Rd CV2 96 F1
Wilberforce Way B92 107 F7
Wilbraham Rd WS2 28 C1
Wilcote Gr B27 106 C8
Wilcox Ave WS12 2 B7
Wildacres DY8 80 C6
Wilday Cl DY4 52 A5
Wildcroft Rd CV5 112 C3
Wilde Cl B14 104 D4
Wilden Cl B31 102 C3
Wilden La DY10 116 E1
Wilderness La B43 43 D3
Wildey Rd 1 CV12 77 D2
Wildfell Rd B27 88 D2
Wild Goose La B98 159 D8
Wildmoor Cl CV2 96 B4
Wildmoor La B61 121 A3
Wildmoor Rd B90 106 B5
Wildtree Ave WV10 12 A2
Wiley Ave WS10 41 C5
Wiley Ave S WS10 41 C5
Wilford Gr
Solihull B91 107 B2
Sutton Coldfield B76 58 B6
Wilford Rd B71 53 D6
Wilhelmina Cl CV32 161 E8
Wilkes Ave WS2 27 F2
Wilkes Cl WS3 14 E3
Wilkes Croft DY3 50 D7
Wilkes Green Jun & Inf Sch B21 54 E1
Wilkes St
West Bromwich B71 53 E7
Willenhall WV13 27 A1
Wilkin Rd WS8 6 C2
Wilkins Ho WS3 14 A1
Wilkinson Ave WV14 40 E3
Wilkinson Cl
Burntwood WS7 7 B8
Sutton Coldfield B73 46 A2
Wilkinson Croft B8 68 C6
Wilkinson Jun & Inf Sch WV14 40 F3
Wilkinson Rd WS10 41 A4
Wilkins Rd WV14 40 D7
Wilks Gn B21 54 D3
Willard Rd B25 88 C6
Willaston Rd B33 89 D7
Willclare Rd B26 89 A6
Willcock Rd WV2 39 E7
Willenhall Ind Est WV13 27 C3
Willenhall La CV3 134 F7
Willenhall Lane Cvn Site WS2 27 F7
Willenhall Lane Ind Est WS3 28 A8
Willenhall La WS3 28 A8
Willenhall Mus★ WV13 27 B1
Willenhall Rd
Bilston WV14 40 F7
Darlaston WS10 41 D8
Wolverhampton WV1,WV13 26 C1
Willenhall Sch Sports Coll WV12 27 E5
Willenhall St WS10 41 C7
Willenhall Trad Est WV13 27 A1
Willenhall Wood Prim Sch CV3 134 D6
Willerby Fold WV10 11 F4
Willersey Rd B13 105 D8
Willes Ct
2 Birmingham B62 84 A7
2 Royal Leamington Spa CV31 162 B7
Willes Rd
Birmingham B18 65 E6
Royal Leamington Spa CV31, CV32 162 A8
Willes Terr CV31 162 B8
Willett Ave WS7 6 E5
Willett Rd B71 53 E8
Willetts Dr B63 82 B4
Willetts Rd B31 103 A1
Willetts Way B64 62 F2
Willey Gr B24 57 B2
William Arnold Cl CV2 114 A4
William Batchelor Ho CV1 165 B4
William Baxter Sch WS12 2 A6
William Beesley Cres CV11 79 E6
William Bentley Ct WV11 26 C5
William Booth La B4 164 B4
William Bree Rd CV5 111 C5
William Bristow Rd CV3 133 E7
William Cook Rd B8 68 B5
William Cowper Prim Sch B19 66 E6
William Cree Cl CV8 135 F3
William Ct
7 Birmingham,Showell Green B13 86 F4
Birmingham,Rotton Park B16 65 E1
William Edward St 1 B12 86 F7
William Green Rd WS10 42 C3
William Groubb Cl CV3 134 D7
William Hanke Ind Est DY5 61 E1
William Harper Rd WV13 27 B1
William Henry St B7 67 A6
William Iliffe St LE10 75 B7
William Ker Rd DY4 52 C5
William Kirby Cl CV4 112 A1
William Lunn's Homes 2 WS14 9 C8
William McCool Cl CV3 134 F7
William MacGregor Prim Sch B77 21 D4
William McKee Cl CV3 134 E7
William Malcolm Ho CV2 114 E3
William Morris Gr WS11 1 E4
William Rd
Birmingham B31 102 F1

William Rd *continued*
Smethwick B67 . . . . 64 D3
William St N B19 . . . . 164 B4
William St W B66 . . . . 65 B7
Williams Cl WV12 . . . . 27 C5
William Sheriden Ho
CV2 . . . . 114 E3
Williamson St WV3 . . . . . 163 A2
Williams Rd CV31 . . . . 162 E4
William St
Bedworth CV12 . . . . 78 D2
Birmingham B15 . . . . 66 C1
Brierley Hill DY5 . . . . 61 C3
Nuneaton CV11 . . . . 73 E3
Redditch B97 . . . . 153 E4
Royal Leamington Spa
CV32 . . . . 162 A8
Walsall WS4 . . . . 28 F3
West Bromwich B70 . . . . . . 52 E5
William Tarver Cl CV34 . . 161 A7
William Thomas Ho 7
CV32 . . . . 157 A1
William Thomson Ho 2
CV1 . . . . 165 D4
William Tolson's Ind Est
B78 . . . . 35 A8
William Wiggin Ave WS3 . 14 B2
Willingsworth High Sch
DY4 . . . . 41 B2
Willingsworth Rd WS10 . . 41 D1
Willington Rd B79 . . . . 21 B7
Willington St CV11 . . . . 73 B5
Willingworth Cl WV14 . . . . 40 A3
Willis Gr CV12 . . . . 78 C3
Willis Ho CV11 . . . . 73 E1
Willis Pearson Ave WV14 . 41 A3
Willis St DY11 . . . . 116 C5
Willmore Gr 4 B38 . . . . . 123 F8
Willmore Rd B20 . . . . 55 D2
Willmott Cl B75 . . . . 32 D3
Willmott Rd B75 . . . . 32 D3
Willoughby Ave CV8 . . . . 147 E3
Willoughby Cl CV3 . . . . . . 134 E8
Willoughby Ct B76 . . . . 46 F2
Willoughby Dr B91 . . . . . . 107 B1
Willoughby Gr B29 . . . . 85 A1
Willoughby Rd B79 . . . . 20 E7
Willow Ave
Birmingham B17 . . . . 65 A2
Burntwood WS7 . . . . 7 C6
Wednesbury WS10 . . . . 41 F4
Wolverhampton WV11 . . . . . 26 B8
Willowbank Rd LE10 . . . . . . 75 C7
Willow Bank Rd B93 . . . . 127 F6
Willowbank B78 . . . . 21 B1
Willow Bank WV3 . . . . 24 C1
Willow Brook Rd B48 . . . 139 A7
Willowbud Ho B98 . . . . . . 158 F8
Willow Cl
Bedworth CV12 . . . . 78 A5
Bromsgrove B61 . . . . 136 E2
Cradley Heath B64 . . . . 62 E1
Hinckley LE10 . . . . 75 E5
Nuneaton CV10 . . . . 72 A7
West Hagley DY9 . . . . 98 F5
Whitnash CV31 . . . . 162 B2
Willow Coppice B32 . . . . . 84 C1
Willow Ct
Birmingham B13 . . . . 87 A3
Bromsgrove B61 . . . . 136 E3
Lichfield WS14 . . . . 9 C5
Oldbury B66 . . . . 64 D8
Smethwick B17 . . . . 65 A2
Willow Ctyd CV2 . . . . 114 D7
Willowdale Grange WV6 . 24 E5
Willowdale LE10 . . . . 75 A7
Willow Dr
Birmingham B21 . . . . 54 C1
Cheswick Green B90 . . . . . 126 D4
Codsall WV8 . . . . 10 B3
Oldbury B69 . . . . 63 C7
Willow End DY9 . . . . 81 D3
Willowfield Dr DY11 . . . . 116 C8
Willowfields Rd CV11 . . . . 74 A1
Willow Gdns
Birmingham B16 . . . . 65 F4
Bromsgrove B61 . . . . 136 E3
Willow Gr
Coventry CV4 . . . . 112 B2
Essington WV11 . . . . 13 B3
Willenhall WV13 . . . . 27 B1
Willowherb Cl
4 Walsall WS5 . . . . 43 A3
5 Coventry CV3 . . . . 134 F8
Cannock WS11 . . . . 2 C2
Willowherb Way B90 . . . . 126 A5
Willow Ho
11 Warwick CV34 . . . . 161 D8
Birmingham B7 . . . . 67 B4
Walsall WS4 . . . . 15 D1
Willow Hts B64 . . . . 83 A8
Willow Meer CV8 . . . . 148 B5
Willow Mews B29 . . . . 85 B1
Willow Park Dr DY8 . . . . . . 81 B2
Willow Rd
Birmingham,Bournville B29,
B30 . . . . 103 F8
Birmingham,Great Barr B43 44 A2
Bromsgrove B61 . . . . 136 E3
Dudley DY1 . . . . 51 A4
Nuneaton CV10 . . . . 72 F5
Solihull B91 . . . . 106 E2
Wolverhampton WV3 . . . . . . 38 D8
Willow Rise DY5 . . . . 61 C1
Willowsbrook Rd B62 . . . . 83 F8
Willows Cres B12 . . . . 86 E5
Willow Sheets Mdw
CV32 . . . . 157 E6
Willowside WS4 . . . . 29 C8
Willowsmere Dr WS14 . . . . . 9 F7
Willows Prim Sch WS13 . . . . 3 B2
Willows Rd
Birmingham B12 . . . . 86 E5
Walsall,Shelfield WS4 . . . . . 29 C8
Walsall,The Chuckery WS1 . 29 A1
Willows The
10 Sutton Coldfield B74 . . . 31 F2
Bedworth CV12 . . . . 77 E2
Birmingham B27 . . . . 88 B2
Cannock WS11 . . . . 1 C1
Dudley DY2 . . . . 62 E5
Hollywood B47 . . . . 125 A6
Portway B47 . . . . 140 F7
Sutton Coldfield,Walmley
B76 . . . . 46 F2
Wolverhampton WV11 . . . . . 26 B5
Willowtree Cl WS13 . . . . 3 B2
Willow Tree Dr B45 . . . . . 138 D8
Willow Way
Birmingham B37 . . . . 70 B1
Redditch B97 . . . . 153 B4
Studley B80 . . . . 159 E2
Willow Wlk WS12 . . . . 1 D8
Wills Ave B71 . . . . 53 B7
Willsbridge Covert 8
B14 . . . . 104 C2
Wills Ho B70 . . . . 53 C2
Willson Croft B28 . . . . 105 D3
Wills St B19 . . . . 66 C7
Wills Way B66 . . . . 65 C4
Wilmcote Cl B12 . . . . 86 E6
Wilmcote Ct B61 . . . . 150 D8
Wilmcote Dr B75 . . . . 32 B3
Wilmcote Gn CV5 . . . . 112 A3
Wilmcote Ho B97 . . . . 153 B4
Wilmcote Rd B91 . . . . 106 F6
Wilmcote Twr 5 B12 . . . . 86 F7
Wilmhurst Rd CV34 . . . . . 160 C8
Wilmington Rd B32 . . . . . . 84 B6
Wilmore Ho B20 . . . . 55 D1
Wilmore La B47 . . . . 124 F4
Wilmot Ave B46 . . . . 70 F6
Wilmot Cl CV7 . . . . 130 B8
Wilmot Dr
Birmingham B23 . . . . 57 A6
Tipton DY4 . . . . 51 E6
Wilmot Gdns DY1 . . . . 51 A2
Wilmott Cl WS13 . . . . 9 A7
Wilnecote Gr
Birmingham B42 . . . . 55 D4
Whitnash CV31 . . . . 162 B5
Wilnecote High Sch B77 . 35 F6
Wilnecote Jun Sch B77 . . 35 F7
Wilnecote La B77 . . . . 21 D2
Wilnecote Sta B77 . . . . 35 D7
Wilner's View WS3 . . . . 14 F5
Wilsford Cl
Birmingham B14 . . . . 104 D1
Walsall WS4 . . . . 29 C8
Wilsford Gn B15 . . . . 85 E7
Wilson Dr B75 . . . . 47 A5
Wilson Gn CV3 . . . . 114 F1
Wilson Gr
Cannock WS11 . . . . 2 C2
Kenilworth CV8 . . . . 148 C4
Wilson Rd
Birmingham B19 . . . . 66 D8
Brierley Hill DY5 . . . . 61 C4
Dudley WV14 . . . . 51 C7
Oldbury B68 . . . . 64 D1
Smethwick B66 . . . . 65 B3
Wilsons La CV7 . . . . 96 A6
Wilson's La CV6 . . . . 95 F6
Wilsons Rd B93 . . . . 128 C6
Wilson St DY4 . . . . 52 A5
Wilson Stuart Sch B23 . . . 56 C6
Wilson St WV1 . . . . 163 C4
Wiltell Rd Ind Est WS14 . . . 9 B7
Wiltell Rd WS14 . . . . 9 B6
Wilton Ave DY11 . . . . 116 B8
Wilton Cl DY3 . . . . 50 E7
Wilton Rd
Balsall Common CV7 . . . . . 130 B5
Birmingham,Balsall Heath
B11 . . . . 87 B5
Birmingham,Erdington B23 . 57 A5
Birmingham,Handsworth
B20 . . . . 55 B1
Wilton St B19 . . . . 66 D8
Wiltshire Cl
Bedworth CV12 . . . . 78 A3
Coventry CV5 . . . . 112 B3
Walsall WS2 . . . . 28 D4
Wiltshire Ct 10 B29 . . . . . 103 C7
Wiltshire Dr B63 . . . . 82 B7
Wiltshire Ho 3 DY8 . . . . . . 80 F8
Wiltshire Way B71 . . . . 53 C7
Wimberger Ho 2 B71 . . . . 53 D4
Wimblebury Rd WS12 . . . . . 2 F2
Wimbledon Dr DY8 . . . . 81 B2
Wimborne Dr CV2 . . . . 115 A4
Wimborne Rd WV10 . . . . . . 26 A6
Wimbourne Cl CV10 . . . . . . 72 B5
Wimbourne Rd
Birmingham B16 . . . . 65 D3
Sutton Coldfield B76 . . . . . . 47 A4
Wimperis Way B43 . . . . 44 C4
Wimpole Gr B44 . . . . 56 B7
Wimshurst Mdw WV10 . . . 11 F4
Wincanton Croft B36 . . . . . 68 C8
Winceby Pl CV4 . . . . 111 D1
Winceby Rd WV6 . . . . 23 F3
Winchat Cl CV3 . . . . 114 F1
Winchcombe Cl
Dudley DY1 . . . . 50 E3
Solihull B92 . . . . 89 B2
Winchcombe Rd B92 . . . . . 89 B2
Winchester Ave
Kidderminster DY11 . . . . . 116 A6
Nuneaton CV10 . . . . 73 C7
Winchester Cl
8 Rowley Regis B65 . . . . . 63 E4
Lichfield WS13 . . . . 3 C3
West Hagley DY9 . . . . 99 A6
Winchester Ct 4 B74 . . . . 31 F2
Winchester Dr
Birmingham B37 . . . . 70 A2
Hinckley LE10 . . . . 76 B7
Stourbridge DY8 . . . . 81 A3
Winchester Gdns B31 . . . 103 A3
Winchester Gr B21 . . . . 65 C8
Winchester Mews WS9 . . . 30 B4
Winchester Rd
Birmingham B20 . . . . 55 D1
Cannock WS11 . . . . 2 A3
Tamworth B78 . . . . 20 F3
West Bromwich B71 . . . . . . 53 B8
Wolverhampton WV10 . . . . . 11 C3
Winchester Rise DY1 . . . . . 51 A2
Winchester St CV1 . . . . . . 113 E3
Winchfield Dr B17 . . . . 84 F7
Wincote Dr WV6 . . . . 24 C4
Wincrest Way B34 . . . . 69 C5
Windermere Ave
Coventry,Binley CV3 . . . . . 114 E1
Coventry,Upper Eastern Green
CV5 . . . . 111 E4
Nuneaton CV11 . . . . 73 F6
Windermere Dr
Kingswinford DY6 . . . . 60 D6
Royal Leamington Spa
CV32 . . . . 156 D2
Sutton Coldfield B74 . . . . . . 30 F3
Windermere Ho
11 Oldbury B69 . . . . 63 D5
Kidderminster DY10 . . . . . 116 E7
Windermere Pl WS11 . . . . . . 1 E1
Windermere Rd
Birmingham,Handsworth
B21 . . . . 54 E2
Birmingham,Moseley B13 . . 87 B1
Wolverhampton WV6 . . . . . . 24 D8
Windermere B77 . . . . 36 A7
Windermre Ho 2 B15 . . . . 85 D3
Windfall Ct B24 . . . . 57 D4
Winding House La CV6,
CV7 . . . . 95 C4
Winding Mill N DY5 . . . . . . 81 E7
Winding Mill S DY5 . . . . . . 81 E7
Windings The WS13 . . . . 3 A1
Windleaves Rd B36 . . . . . . 69 E8
Windley Ho B73 . . . . 45 C2
Windmill Ave
4 Coleshill B46 . . . . 70 F7
Birmingham B45 . . . . 121 E8
Windmill Bank WV5 . . . . . . 49 A7
Windmill Cl
Birmingham B31 . . . . 103 C5
Kenilworth CV8 . . . . 148 A6
Lichfield WS13 . . . . 3 A2
Tamworth B79 . . . . 21 A8
Windmill Cres
Smethwick B66 . . . . 65 C5
Wolverhampton WV3 . . . . . . 24 A1
Windmill Croft CV32 . . . . 157 D5
Windmill Ct CV6 . . . . 96 A3
Windmill Dr B97 . . . . 158 C6
Windmill End DY2 . . . . 62 E5
Windmill Gdns B97 . . . . . 158 B6
Windmill Gr DY6 . . . . 60 B8
Windmill Hill
Birmingham B31 . . . . 103 B5
Cubbington CV32 . . . . 157 D5
Halesowen B63 . . . . 82 D5
Windmill Hill The CV5 . . . 112 A7
Windmill Ind Est CV5 . . . . 111 F7
Windmill La
Balsall Common CV7 . . . . . 130 D4
Corley Moor CV7 . . . . 93 D6
Dorridge B93 . . . . 127 F1
Lichfield WS13 . . . . 3 A2
Smethwick B66 . . . . 65 B5
Tanworth-in-A B94 . . . . . . 144 A8
Wolverhampton WV3 . . . . . . 24 A1
Windmill Prec B66 . . . . 65 C5
Windmill Rd
Bedworth CV7 . . . . 96 A8
Coventry CV6 . . . . 96 A3
Nuneaton CV10 . . . . 72 D7
Solihull B90 . . . . 105 E2
Whitnash CV31 . . . . 161 F5
Windmill St
Birmingham B1 . . . . 164 B1
Dudley DY1 . . . . 51 A2
Dudley,Gornalwood DY3 . . . 50 D5
Walsall WS1 . . . . 42 F8
Wednesbury WS10 . . . . 42 A3
Windmill Terr WS10 . . . . . . 42 A3
Windmill View DY1 . . . . 51 B7
Windmill Works Ind Pk
DY2 . . . . 62 B6
Windridge Cl CV3 . . . . 134 C6
Windridge Cres B92 . . . . . 107 F8
Windrow The WV6 . . . . 23 D4
Windrush Cl
Redditch B97 . . . . 158 D6
Solihull B92 . . . . 89 A2
Walsall WS3 . . . . 15 A1
Windrush Dr LE10 . . . . 75 A8
Windrush Gr B29 . . . . 104 A8
Windrush Rd
Cannock WS11 . . . . 1 E6
Hollywood B47 . . . . 125 B7
Windsor Arc B2 . . . . 164 C3
Windsor Ave
Cannock WS12 . . . . 2 B6
Oldbury B68 . . . . 64 A3
Wolverhampton WV4 . . . . . . 38 E6
Windsor Cl
Birmingham,Coft Common
B31 . . . . 123 A6
Birmingham,Frankley B45 102 A2
Dudley DY3 . . . . 50 B2
Halesowen B63 . . . . 82 F3
Rowley Regis B65 . . . . 63 C4
Tamworth B79 . . . . 21 C7
Windsor Cres DY2 . . . . 62 D6
Windsor Ct
12 Royal Leamington Spa
CV32 . . . . 161 F8
Birmingham B38 . . . . 103 F1
Cannock WS12 . . . . 2 B6
Coventry CV4 . . . . 112 B2
Hinckley LE10 . . . . 76 A5
Lichfield WS14 . . . . 9 B6
Nuneaton CV10 . . . . 72 E6
Windsor Dr
Birmingham B24 . . . . 57 C5
Kidderminster DY10 . . . . . 116 E7
Solihull B92 . . . . 89 B2
Windsor Gate WV12 . . . . . . 27 C4
Windsor Gdns
Bromsgrove B60 . . . . 137 A2
Nuneaton CV10 . . . . 72 E4
Wolverhampton WV3 . . . . . . 38 A8
Windsor Gr
Stourbridge DY8 . . . . 60 E1
Walsall WS4 . . . . 15 C2
Windsor High Sch B63 . . . 82 F4
Windsor Ho
Birmingham B23 . . . . 56 F6
Dudley DY2 . . . . 61 F7
Wolverhampton WV3 . . . . . 163 A1
Windsor Ind Est B7 . . . . . . 67 A5
Windsor Lodge B92 . . . . . 106 D8
Windsor Pl
10 Royal Leamington Spa
CV32 . . . . 156 F1
Birmingham B7 . . . . 67 A3
Birmingham,Erdington B23 . 56 E3
Windsor Rd
Birmingham,Castle Bromwich
B36 . . . . 69 F7
Birmingham,New Oscott
B73 . . . . 45 D1
Birmingham,Stirchley B30 . 104 B5
Cheslyn Hay WS6 . . . . 4 E4
Halesowen B63 . . . . 82 F4
Oldbury B68 . . . . 64 A3
Redditch B97 . . . . 153 D5
Rowley Regis B65 . . . . 63 C5
Stourbridge DY8 . . . . 80 E3
Tipton DY4 . . . . 52 A8
West Bromwich B71 . . . . . . 42 B1
Wolverhampton WV4 . . . . . . 39 F5
Windsor St S B7 . . . . 67 A4
Windsor St
Bilston WV14 . . . . 40 C6
Birmingham B7 . . . . 67 A4
Bromsgrove B60 . . . . 137 A2
Coventry CV1 . . . . 113 B2
Hinckley LE10 . . . . 76 A5
Nuneaton CV11 . . . . 73 B4
Royal Leamington Spa
CV32 . . . . 161 F8
Walsall WS1 . . . . 42 E7
Windsor Terr 5 B16 . . . . . 65 F1
Windsor View B32 . . . . . . 102 B7
Windsor Way WS4 . . . . 29 D7
Windsor Wlk WS10 . . . . 41 D8
Winds Point DY9 . . . . 99 A6
Windward Way B36 . . . . . . 70 B6
Windward Way Ind Est
B36 . . . . 69 F8
Windy Arbor Prim Sch
B37 . . . . 70 D2
Windy Arbour CV8 . . . . . . 148 B4
Windyridge Rd B76 . . . . . . 58 A6
Winfield Rd CV11 . . . . 73 B5
Winford Ave DY6 . . . . 60 E4
Winforton Cl B98 . . . . 154 E3
Wingate Cl B30 . . . . 103 F4
Wingate Ct B74 . . . . 31 E4
Wingate Rd WS2 . . . . 27 E2
Wing Cl WS2 . . . . 27 F4
Wingfield Cl B37 . . . . 69 F3
Wingfield Ho B37 . . . . 69 F5
Wingfield Rd
Birmingham B42 . . . . 55 C7
Coleshill B46 . . . . 70 F5
Wingfield Way CV6 . . . . . . 95 A2
Wingfoot Ave WV10 . . . . . . 25 E8
Wingrave Cl CV5 . . . . 112 A6
Winifred Ave CV5 . . . . 113 A1
Winifride Ct B17 . . . . 85 B5
Winkle St B70 . . . . 53 B4
Winleigh Rd B20 . . . . 54 F2
Winnall Cl WV14 . . . . 40 D2
Winnallthorpe CV3 . . . . . . 134 E6
Winn Ho 3 WS2 . . . . 28 D3
Winnie Rd B29 . . . . 85 E1
Winnington Rd B8 . . . . 68 A7
Winnipeg Rd B38 . . . . 124 A8
Winrush Cl DY3 . . . . 50 D3
Winscar Croft DY3 . . . . 50 D3
Winsford Ave CV5 . . . . 112 B4
Winsford Cl
Balsall Common CV7 . . . . . 130 A6
Halesowen B63 . . . . 83 A6
Sutton Coldfield B76 . . . . . . 46 E3
Winsford Ct CV5 . . . . 112 C4
Winsham Gr B21 . . . . 65 E8
Winsham Wlk CV3 . . . . . . 133 C3
Winslow Ave B8 . . . . 68 B4
Winslow Cl
Coventry CV5 . . . . 112 B3
Redditch B98 . . . . 154 F3
Royal Leamington Spa
CV32 . . . . 156 C1
Winslow Dr WV6 . . . . 24 E4
Winslow Ho 11 CV1 . . . . . 113 B2
Winson Green, Outer Circle
Sta B21 . . . . 65 E7
Winson Green Rd B18 . . . . 65 E5
Winson St B18 . . . . 65 D4
Winsor Ave WS12 . . . . 2 B6
Winspear Cl CV7 . . . . 92 B1
Winstanley Rd B33 . . . . 68 D2
Winster Ave B93 . . . . 127 E4
Winster Cl CV7 . . . . 95 A7
Winster Gr B44 . . . . 44 D2
Winster Grove Ind Ctr
B44 . . . . 44 D2
Winster Rd
Birmingham B43 . . . . 54 D8
Wolverhampton WV1 . . . . . . 26 B1
Winston Ave CV2 . . . . 114 D8
Winston Churchill Ct
WV14 . . . . 40 C8
Winston Cl CV2 . . . . 114 D8
Winston Dr
Birmingham B20 . . . . 55 B1
Romsley B62 . . . . 101 A4
Winstone Cl B98 . . . . 154 A4
Winterborne Gdns CV10 . . 73 A2
Winterbourne Botanic Gdn*
B15 . . . . 86 A5
Winterbourne Croft B14 . 104 C1
Winterbourne Rd B91 . . . 106 F4
Winter Cl WS13 . . . . 3 D2
Winterdene CV7 . . . . 130 B7
Winterfold Cl DY10 . . . . . . 117 B6
Winterley Gdns DY3 . . . . . . 50 E6
Winterley La WS4 . . . . 29 C6
Winterton Rd
Birmingham B44 . . . . 45 A3
Bulkington CV12 . . . . 79 C2
Winthorpe Dr B91 . . . . . . 127 C8
Wintney Cl B17 . . . . 85 A7
Winton Gr B76 . . . . 58 A6
Wintour Wlk B60 . . . . 150 E7
Winward Rd B98 . . . . 154 F1
Winwood Ct DY8 . . . . 80 F4
Winwood Heath Rd B62 . 100 E2
Winwood Rd B65 . . . . 63 E3
Winwoods Gr B32 . . . . 102 A8
Winyate Hill B98 . . . . 154 A2
Winyates Crafts Ctr B98 . 154 E3
Winyates Ctr B98 . . . . 154 E3
Winyates Way B98 . . . . . . 154 E4
Wirehill Dr B98 . . . . 153 F1
Wiremill Cl B44 . . . . 55 E6
Wirral Rd B31 . . . . 102 F6
Wiseacre Croft B90 . . . . . 105 E2
Wise Gr CV34 . . . . 155 E2
Wiseman Gr B23 . . . . 45 D1
Wisemore WS2 . . . . 28 E2
Wise St CV31 . . . . 161 F7
Wise Terr CV31 . . . . 161 F7
Wishaw Cl
Redditch B98 . . . . 159 A8
Solihull B90 . . . . 105 E2
Wishaw Gr B37 . . . . 69 F5
Wishaw La
Curdworth B76 . . . . 59 A7
Middleton B76,B78 . . . . 48 C6
Minworth B76 . . . . 58 E7
Wisley Gr CV8 . . . . 148 C5
Wisley Way B32 . . . . 84 F5
Wissage Ct WS13 . . . . 9 D8
Wissage La WS13 . . . . 3 D1
Wissage Rd WS13 . . . . 9 D8
Wistaria Cl
2 Coventry CV2 . . . . 96 B2
Birmingham B31 . . . . 103 A6
Wisteria Dr
2 Walsall WS5 . . . . 42 F4
Brownhills WS8 . . . . 6 C2
Wisteria Gr B44 . . . . 44 E2
Wistmans Cl DY1 . . . . 50 E2
Wistwood Hayes WV10 . . . 11 F4
Witham Cl B76 . . . . 47 A1
Witham Croft B91 . . . . 107 C1
Withdean Cl B11 . . . . 87 D6
Witherford Cl B29 . . . . 103 C8
Witherford Croft B91 . . . 106 E2
Witherford Way B29 . . . . . 103 C8
Withern Way DY3 . . . . 50 D3
Withers Rd WV8 . . . . 10 B3
Withers Way B71 . . . . 53 D4
Withington Covert B14 . . 104 D2
Withington Gr B93 . . . . . . 127 E4
Withybed Cl B48 . . . . 139 A6
Withybed La B48 . . . . 139 A6
Withybrook Cl CV2 . . . . 96 D2
Withybrook La CV7 . . . . 97 F5
Withybrook Rd
Bulkington CV12 . . . . 79 D2
Solihull B90 . . . . 126 B8
Withy Gr B37 . . . . 69 F5
Withy Hill Rd B75 . . . . 47 B8
Withymere La WV5 . . . . 49 C8
Withymoor Prim Sch DY5 61 D1
Withymoor Rd
Dudley DY2 . . . . 62 E4
Stourbridge DY8 . . . . 81 A7
Withymore Ct WV3 . . . . 25 A1

y Rd WV14 40 C3
Withy Road Ind Est WV14. 40 C3
Withywood Cl WV12 13 C1
Witley Ave
Halesowen B63 82 E4
Solihull B91 107 C2
Witley Cl DY11 116 B2
Witley Cres B69 63 E5
Witley Dr 1 WS13 9 E8
Witley Farm Cl B91 107 C2
Witley Rd 1 B31 103 D2
Witnell Rd CV6 113 C6
Witney Cl B79 20 F7
Witney Dr B37 69 F2
Witney Gr WV10 11 B3
Wittersham Ct 5 WV13 27 B2
Witton Bank B62 83 F7
Witton La
Birmingham B6 55 F1
West Bromwich B71 53 B8
Witton Lodge Rd B23 56 D7
Witton Rd
Birmingham B6 66 E8
Wolverhampton WV4 39 A6
Witton Sta B6 55 F1
Witton St
Birmingham B9 67 B2
Stourbridge DY8 80 F4
Wixford Gr B90 106 D2
Wobaston Ct WV10 11 B3
Wobaston Rd
Codsall WV9 10 E4
Wolverhampton WV9,WV10. 11 B4
Woburn Ave WV12 27 B6
Woburn Cl
Bromsgrove B61 136 D1
Hinckley LE10 71 E3
Royal Leamington Spa CV31 162 C6
Woburn Cres B43 43 D1
Woburn Dr
Brierley Hill DY5 81 B8
Cradley Heath B62 83 B7
Nuneaton CV10 73 A2
Woburn Gr B27 88 C1
Woburn Ho B15 86 C7
Woburn B77 21 D3
Wodehouse Cotts WV5 49 D8
Wodehouse La WV5,DY3 49 E8
Woden Ave WV11 26 C6
Woden Cres WV11 26 C6
Woden Prim Sch WV10 25 E4
Woden Rd E WS10 42 B4
Woden Rd N WS10 41 F5
Woden Rd S WS10 42 A1
Woden Rd W WS10 41 D4
Woden Rd WV10 25 F4
Wodensborough Com Tech Coll WS10 42 B2
Wodensfield Prim Sch WV11 26 B6
Wodensfield Twr WV11 26 C5
Woden Way WV11 26 C6
Wold Wlk
Birmingham B13 105 C6
Birmingham B13 105 C6
Wolfe Rd CV4 131 F8
Wolfsbane Dr WS5 43 A3
Wolfson Dr B15 85 E4
Wollaston Cres WV11 26 D6
Wollaston Ct
1 Walsall WS1 28 F2
Stourbridge DY8 80 C6
Wollaston Rd
Stourbridge DY7 80 C7
Stourbridge DY8 80 E8
Wollerton Gr 9 B75 46 F6
Wollescote Bsns Pk 6 DY9 81 F5
Wollescote Dr B91 107 B2
Wollescote Prim Sch DY9 81 F4
Wollescote Rd DY9 81 D3
Wolmer Rd WV11 13 A2
Wolseley Ave B27 88 D4
Wolseley Bank WV10 25 F7
Wolseley Cl
Birmingham B36 59 A1
Wolverhampton WV10 25 F7
Wolseley Dr B8 68 A7
Wolseley Gate WV10 25 F7
Wolseley Rd
Bilston WV14 40 C7
West Bromwich B70 52 F6
Wolseley St B9 67 B2
Wolseley B77 21 F3
Wolston Cl B90 106 B5
Wolston La CV8 135 E2
Wolston Way CV3 134 C6
Wolverhampton Coll Wulfrun Campus WV6 24 E3
Wolverhampton (Dunstall Park) Race Course WV6 25 A6
Wolverhampton Girls' High Sch WV6 24 F3
Wolverhampton Gram Sch WV3 24 F2
Wolverhampton & Midland Cties Eye Infmy WV3 25 A2
Wolverhampton Mus & Art Gall★ WV1 163 B3
Wolverhampton Rd
Cannock WS11 4 D8
Cheslyn Hay WV10,WS6 4 B2
Codsall WV8 10 A3
Essington WV11 13 A3
Wolverhampton Rd E WV4 39 D5
Wolverhampton Rd
Kingswinford DY6 49 C1
Nurton WV6 23 A3
Oldbury B69 63 F4
Wolverhampton Rd S B32 84 E7
Wolverhampton Rd
Sedgley DY3 39 D2
Walsall,Birchills WS2 28 B2
Walsall,Pelsall WS3 14 F3
Walsall,Wallington Heath WS3 14 B1
Wedges Mills WS11 4 B6
Wolverhampton WV10, WV11 26 B4
Wolverhampton Rd W WV13, WS2 27 D2
Wolverhampton Sta WV1 163 C3
Wolverhampton St
Bilston WV14 40 C6
Darlaston WS10 41 C6
Dudley DY1 51 B1
Walsall WS2 28 D2
Willenhall WV13 27 A1
Wolverley Ave
Stourbridge DY8 80 C6
Wolverhampton WV4 38 D5
Wolverley Cres B69 63 E5
Wolverley Rd
Birmingham B32 102 B8
Halesowen B63 82 F2
Solihull B92 89 D2
Wolverson Cl WV12 27 C4
Wolverson Rd WS9 16 A4
Wolverton Cl B98 154 E2
Wolverton Rd
Birmingham,Marston Green B37 90 B7
Birmingham,Rednal B45 122 C6
Coventry CV5 112 A3
Dudley DY2 51 E1
Wolvey Rd
Bulkington CV12 79 E2
Hinckley LE10 75 E4
Wombourne Cl DY3 50 D8
Woodacre Rd B24 57 C4
Woodall Ho WS3 28 C8
Woodall Rd B6 55 F1
Woodall St
Cradley Heath B64 62 C1
Walsall WS3 28 C8
Woodard Rd DY4 52 C7
Wood Ave
Dudley DY3 50 C4
Wednesfield WV11 26 D6
Woodbank Dr B61 136 F8
Woodbank LE10 76 A7
Woodbank Rd DY3 50 C7
Wood Bank Rd WV3 38 A8
Woodberrow La B97 158 D6
Woodberry Dr B76 47 A2
Woodberry Wlk B27 88 D3
Woodbine Ave B10 87 D8
Woodbine Cotts
2 Royal Leamington Spa CV32 161 E8
Kingswood CV35 144 D3
Woodbine Croft B26 89 A6
Woodbine St 1 CV32 161 E8
Woodbine Wlk B37 70 D2
Woodbourne B15 85 D8
Woodbourne Rd
Birmingham B15,B16 85 C8
Smethwick B67 64 E2
Woodbridge Cl
Walsall,Wallington Heath WS3 14 A3
Walsall WS4 15 D1
Woodbridge Rd B13 86 F3
Woodbrooke Gr B31 103 C6
Woodbrooke Rd B30 103 E7
Woodbrook Ho 9 B37 70 B2
Woodburn Cl CV5 112 B4
Woodburn Rd B66 65 D7
Woodbury Cl
Brierley Hill DY5 61 E2
Halesowen B62 83 F8
Redditch B97 158 A6
Woodbury Gr B91 107 B1
Woodbury Rd
Birmingham B62 84 A8
Kidderminster DY11 116 B2
Woodchester Rd B93 127 E2
Woodchester DY9 99 B4
Woodchurch Grange B73 56 F8
Wood Cl B46 70 F7
Woodclose Ave CV6 112 F6
Woodclose Rd B37 69 F3
Woodcock Cl
Birmingham B31 102 C1
Tanworth-In-A B94 141 E3
Woodcock Gdns WV10 12 B7
Woodcock Hill Jun & Inf Sch B31 102 E7
Woodcock La
Birmingham,Acock's Green B27 88 D3
Birmingham,Northfield B31 102 E8
Woodcock La N B27 88 D4
Woodcock St B7 66 F4
Woodcombe Cl DY5 81 B7
Wood Common Grange WS3 14 F4
Woodcote Ave
Kenilworth CV8 147 D6
Woodcote Ave *continued*
Nuneaton CV11 73 F8
Woodcote Cl B98 154 E3
Woodcote Dr
Birmingham B8 67 F5
Dorridge B93 128 B2
Leek Wootton CV35 155 F7
Woodcote La
Belbroughton DY9 119 E1
Leek Wootton CV8,CV35 155 F7
Woodcote Rd
Birmingham B24 57 D5
Royal Leamington Spa CV32 156 F3
Warwick CV34 160 F8
Wolverhampton WV6 24 C4
Woodcote Way
Birmingham B18 66 A4
Sutton Coldfield B74 44 F6
Woodcraft Cl CV4 112 A2
Woodcroft Ave
Birmingham B20 54 E3
Dudley DY4 51 C4
Tamworth B79 21 B6
Woodcroft Cl
Blackwell B60 137 F5
Cradley Heath B64 82 F8
Wood Croft B47 125 B6
Woodcross La WV14 40 A2
Woodcross St WV14 39 F2
Wood Ct
Birmingham B20 55 A2
Coventry CV2 114 D7
Redditch B97 153 C1
Woodend B20 54 E6
Woodend Cl B97 153 B2
Woodend Croft CV4 131 E8
Wood End Dr B45 138 A8
Wood End La
Birmingham B24 56 F3
Lichfield WS13 3 B7
Tanworth-In-A B94 141 F5
Woodend Pl WV6 24 B4
Wood End Prim Sch
Wolverhampton WV11 26 C7
Wood End CV9 36 C1
Wood End Rd
Birmingham B24 56 F3
Walsall WS5 43 D8
Wednesfield WV11 26 D7
Wolverhampton WV11 12 C1
Wood End Sta B94 141 F4
Wood End Way WS9 16 B1
Woodfall Ave B30 103 F5
Woodfield Ave
Brierley Hill DY5 61 B7
Cradley Heath B64 82 D8
Oldbury B69 64 A4
Stourbridge DY9 81 F2
Wolverhampton WV4 38 F6
Woodfield DY9 119 E7
Woodfield Cl
Norton Canes WS11 5 F7
Redditch B98 154 A5
Sutton Coldfield B74 46 B8
Walsall WS5 43 E5
Woodfield Cres
Birmingham B12 87 A6
Kidderminster DY11 116 D5
Woodfield Ct B14 104 F8
Woodfield Dr WS11 5 F7
Woodfield Ho WS3 15 B3
Woodfield Hts WV6 24 D4
Woodfield Jun & Inf Schs WV4 38 F6
Woodfield La B62 120 D8
Woodfield Mid Sch B98 154 A2
Woodfield Rd
Birmingham,Balsall Heath B12 87 A6
Birmingham,King's Heath B13 104 F8
Coventry CV5 132 E8
Dudley DY3 50 C4
Hinckley LE10 75 C6
Solihull B91 107 B6
Woodfields Dr WS14 9 E5
Woodfield St 4 DY11 116 C6
Woodfold Croft WS9 30 B7
Woodford Ave B36 69 B8
Woodford Cl
Coventry CV7 95 D5
Nuneaton CV10 72 D4
Wolverhampton WV9 10 F2
Woodford Cres WS7 7 B7
Woodford End 1 WS11 1 F4
Woodford Green Rd B28 106 B8
Woodford Way WS12 2 D1
Woodfort Rd B43 54 E7
Woodgate Bsns Pk B32 84 B2
Woodgate Dr B32 84 A1
Woodgate Gdns B32 84 A2
Woodgate Ho B97 153 B4
Woodgate La B32 84 A2
Woodgate Prim Sch B32 84 B1
Woodgate Rd
Hinckley LE10 76 A8
Stoke Prior B60 151 B1
Woodgate Valley Ctry Pk★ B32 84 D3
Woodgate Way DY9 119 E7
Woodglade Croft B38 103 E2
Woodgreen WS6 4 E5
Woodgreen Cl B97 158 B7
Woodgreen Croft B68 84 C7
Wood Green High Sch WS10 42 B5
Wood Green Jun Sch WS10 42 A4
Wood Green Rd B18 65 D4
Woodgreen Rd B68 84 C7
Wood Green Rd WS10 42 B4
Woodhall Cl
Nuneaton CV11 74 A2
Tipton DY4 52 A8
Woodhall Croft B92 88 F3
Woodhall Rd WV4 38 E5
Woodham Cl B45 101 E1
Woodhams Rd CV3 134 C3
Woodhaven
Walsall WS4 15 D1
Wedges Mills WS11 4 B5
Wood Hayes Croft WV10 12 C2
Wood Hayes Rd WV11 12 C1
Wood Hill Rise CV6 95 D2
Wood Ho 1 WS1 42 E7
Woodhouse Cl CV3 134 E8
Woodhouse Fold WV11 26 D5
Woodhouse High Sch B77 21 F4
Woodhouse La B77 22 A5
Woodhouse Orch DY9 119 E7
Woodhouse Prim Sch B32 84 E6
Woodhouse Rd B32 84 E5
Woodhouse Rd N WV6 24 B4
Woodhouse Rd WV6 24 B4
Woodhouses La WS7 7 F6
Woodhouses Rd WS7 8 A7
Woodhouse St CV34 160 D6
Woodhouse Way B64 62 C1
Woodhurst Cl B77 21 F5
Woodhurst Rd B13 87 A4
Wooding Cres DY4 41 B1
Woodington Rd B75 47 B5
Wood La
Birmingham,Erdington B24 57 C1
Birmingham,Handsworth B20 55 B2
Birmingham,Marston Green B37 90 A8
Birmingham,Queen's Park B17 85 A6
Birmingham,Woodgate B32 84 A1
Cannock WS12 2 C4
Earlswood B94 125 E1
Eastcote B92 108 F2
Fairfield B61 120 C3
Hartshill CV10 72 A8
Woodland Ave
Brierley Hill DY5 62 A1
Coventry CV5 132 F7
Dudley DY1 51 C3
Hinckley LE10 76 A7
Kidderminster DY11 116 C7
West Hagley DY8 98 F5
Wolverhampton WV6 24 B3
Woodland Cl
Cannock WS12 2 B8
Stourbridge DY9 81 D2
Willenhall WV12 27 D6
Woodland Cres WV3 38 D7
Woodland Ct
Cannock WS12 1 C4
Shenstone WS14 32 A7
Woodland Dr
Barnt Green B45 122 A2
Cheslyn Hay WS6 4 E4
Smethwick B66 64 E7
Woodland Gr
Birmingham B43 43 E3
Dudley DY3 50 B3
Woodland Rd
Birmingham,Handsworth B21 65 C8
Birmingham,Northfield B31 103 B3
Dodford B61 136 A7
Halesowen B62 83 D8
Hinckley LE10 71 F1
Kenilworth CV8 148 B7
Redditch B97 153 B3
Tamworth B77 22 A4
Wolverhampton WV3 38 D7
Woodland Rise
Cradley Heath B64 82 F8
Sutton Coldfield B73 46 B4
Woodlands Ave
Walsall WS5 43 E5
Water Orton B46 59 B2
Woodlands Com Prim Sch The B77 21 E4
Woodlands Cotts WV4 38 F4
Woodlands Cres WS3 14 F5
Woodlands Ct
Binley Woods CV3 135 D7
Coventry CV5 133 A8
Woodlands Farm Rd B24 57 F4
Woodlands Inf Sch B90 126 B8
Woodlands La
Bedworth CV12 77 E4
Solihull B90 126 B8
Woodlands Paddock WV4 38 E4
Woodlands Park Rd B30 103 C5
Woodlands Prim Sch WV12 27 D6
Woodlands Rd
Bedworth CV12 77 F3
Binley Woods CV3 135 D7
Birmingham B45 121 D7
Birmingham,Moseley B11 87 C2
Birmingham,Saltley B8 67 F3
Wombourne WV5 49 A5
Woodlands Sch The CV5 111 D3
Woodlands St B66 65 C5
Woodlands The
Cradley Heath B64 83 A7
Hartshill CV10 72 A8
Lichfield WS13 9 D8
Stourbridge DY8 81 A2
Sutton Coldfield B75 47 A6
Wood End CV9 36 C1
Woodlands Way B37 70 D3
Woodland Way
Burntwood WS7 7 A6
Polesworth B78 36 F8
Wood Lane Cl WV12 27 E7
Wood La
Shenstone WS14 17 B2
Shilton CV7 97 D5
Sutton Coldfield B74 30 E2
Walsall WS3 14 F4
Wedges Mills WS11 4 A6
West Bromwich B70 53 A3
Willenhall WV12 27 E7
Woodlawn Gr DY6 60 D5
Woodlawn B91 107 E4
Wood La WV10 11 D2
Woodlea Dr
Birmingham B24 56 F2
Solihull B91 106 E4
Wood Leasow B32 84 D2
Woodleaves B47 124 F8
Woodleigh Ave B17 85 D4
Wood Leigh Cl B63 83 A6
Woodleigh Ct B38 103 F1
Woodleigh Rd
Coventry CV4 131 F5
Sutton Coldfield B72 46 C1
Woodleys The B14 105 B4
Woodloes Ave N CV34 155 F2
Woodloes Ave S CV34 155 F1
Woodloes Inf Sch CV34 155 E1
Woodloes Jun Sch CV34 155 E1
Woodloes La CV34,CV35 155 F2
Woodloes Rd B90 126 B7
Woodman Cl
Halesowen B63 83 C3
Wednesbury WS10 42 B4
Woodman Gr 5 B75 32 E3
Woodman La
Cheslyn Hay WS6 4 E4
Clent DY9 99 E4
Woodman Rd
Birmingham B14 105 A1
Halesowen B63 83 C3
Woodman Wlk B23 56 A5
Woodmeadow Rd B30 104 B3
Woodmill Mdw CV8 148 B6
Woodnorton Dr B13 86 E2
Woodnorton Rd B65 63 F2
Woodpecker Gr
Birmingham B36 70 A7
Kidderminster DY10 117 B2
Woodpecker Way WS11 2 C3
Woodperry Ave B91 107 C1
Wood Piece La B98 154 D7
Wood Rd
Dudley DY3 50 C4
Wolverhampton WV6 24 C3
Wombourne WV5 49 B7
Woodridge Ave
Birmingham B32 84 B4
Coventry CV5 112 A6
Woodridge B6 55 E1
Woodridge Rd B63 83 A5
Wood Ridings WS13 3 A1
Woodroffe Wlk CV6 96 A4
Woodrough Dr B13 86 F2
Woodrow Cl B61 120 F1
Woodrow Cres B93 128 A5
Woodrow Ctr B98 159 B8
Woodrow Dr B98 159 B6
Woodrow Fst Sch B98 159 B7
Woodrow La
Bluntington DY10 118 E3
Lower Marlbrook B61 121 B2
Woodrow N B98 159 A7
Woodrow S B98 159 B7
Woodrow Wlk B98 159 A7
Woodruff Way WS5 43 A3
Woodrush Com High Sch The B47 125 A6
Woodrush Dr B47 125 A5
Woodsbank Ind Est The WS10 41 D4
Woods Bank Terr WS10 41 C5
Woods Cres DY5 62 A1
Woods Croft WS13 3 A1
Woodsetton Cl DY1 51 B6
Woodsetton Sch The DY3 50 F7
Woodshill Ave B45 122 A2
Woodshires Rd
Coventry CV6 95 F5
Solihull B92 106 E7
Woodside Ave N CV3 132 F6
Woodside Ave B97 153 B2
Woodside Ave S CV3 132 F5
Woodside B37 69 E4
Woodside Cl
Walsall WS5 43 D6
Wood End CV9 36 C1
Woodside Cres B93 128 B4
Woodside Dr
Barnt Green B45 138 B8
Sutton Coldfield B74 31 C5
Woodside Gr WV8 10 B2
Woodside Ind Est DY2 61 F5
Woodside Pk Mobile Homes Pk B94 141 B7
Woodside Pl WS11 1 E5
Woodside Rd
Birmingham B29 86 A1

Woodside Rd continued
Dudley DY2 61 F7
Walsall WS5 43 E6
Woodside B74 31 E2
Woodside Way
Aldridge WS9 30 B5
Birmingham B32 102 A8
Solihull B91 106 E5
Willenhall WV12 27 E7
Wood Side WV11 27 A8
Woods La
Brierley Hill DY5 81 D7
Cradley Heath B64 82 C8
Woodsome Gr B23 56 C7
Woodsorrel Rd DY1 50 F4
Woods Piece CV7 94 F6
Wood St
Bedworth CV12 78 B5
Bilston WV14 40 D5
Birmingham B16 66 A2
Darlaston WS10 41 F6
Dudley DY2 61 F6
Woods The B14 86 F1
Wood St LE10 71 D1
Woodstile B34 69 B6
Woodstile Cl B75 32 D3
Wood St
Kidderminster DY11 116 D5
Nuneaton CV10 72 F4
Woodstock Cl
2 Walsall WS5 43 A3
Dudley DY1 62 A8
Hinckley LE10 76 A5
Stourbridge DY8 60 C1
Woodstock Cres B93 127 F3
Woodstock Ct B13 87 B4
Woodstock Dr
Huntington WS12 1 C7
Stourbridge DY8 60 C2
Sutton Coldfield B74 31 D4
Woodstock Ho B13 105 A7
Woodstock Rd
Birmingham,Handsworth B21 65 F8
Birmingham,Moseley B13 87 B3
Coventry CV3 133 D7
Nuneaton CV11 73 E1
Wolverhampton WV1 26 B1
Woodston Gr B91 127 C8
Wood Street Cl LE10 71 E1
Wood St
Royal Leamington Spa CV32 162 A8
Stourbridge DY8 80 D6
Stourbridge,Lye DY9 81 F5
Tipton DY4 51 E5
Willenhall WV13 27 B2
Wolverhampton,Park Village WV10 25 F5
Woodcross WV4 40 A3
Wood End CV9 36 C1
Wood Terr B96 159 B1
Woodthorne Cl DY1 50 D2
Woodthorne Prim Sch WV6 24 A4
Woodthorne Rd S WV6 24 A5
Woodthorne Rd WV6 24 A6
Woodthorne Wlk DY6 60 E8
Woodthorpe Dr DY9 81 D3
Woodthorpe Gdns B14 104 E5
Woodthorpe Jun & Inf Sch B14 104 E5
Woodthorpe Rd B14 104 E5
Woodvale B13 87 A4
Woodvale Dr B28 105 E4
Woodvale Rd
Birmingham B32 84 A1
Birmingham,Yardley Wood B28 105 E4
Woodview Dr B15 86 C7
Woodview Primary Sch B15 86 C7
Woodville Ct
3 Birmingham B23 56 E2
Warwick CV34 160 F7
Woodville Gdns DY3 39 F1
Woodville Rd
Birmingham B17 85 A6
Birmingham,King's Heath B14 104 F8
Warwick CV34 160 E8
Woodward Cl CV31 162 A2
Woodward Pl DY9 81 C4
Woodward Rd DY11 116 C4
Woodwards Cl WS2 42 B8
Woodwards Pl WS2 42 B8
Woodwards Rd WS2 42 B8
Woodward St B71 53 E4
Woodway B24 57 B5
Woodway Cl CV2 114 F8
Woodway La CV2 96 F1
Woodway Park Sch & Com Coll CV2 96 F1
Woodway Wlk CV2 114 E8
Woodwells Rd B8 68 B5
Woody Bank WS6 4 E2
Woolacombe Lodge Rd B29 85 C2
Woolaston Rd B98 159 C8
Woolgrove St CV6 96 A3
Woolhope Cl B98 154 F3
Woolmore Rd B23 56 C5
Woolpack Cl B65 63 A4
Woolpack St WV1 163 B3
Woolpack The 9 CV34 160 E6
Woolwich Rd CV11 79 F6
Wooton Cl B97 153 A4
Wooton Gr B44 56 C8
Wootton Ave WV11 26 D7
Wootton Cl WS11 2 B3
Wootton Ct
6 Royal Leamington Spa CV32 156 F2
Coventry CV2 114 D7
Wootton Green La CV7 130 A8
Wootton La CV7 109 E1
Wootton Rd
Birmingham B31 123 A6
Wolverhampton WV3 38 D8
Woottons Ct WS11 1 F1
Wootton's Sq WV14 40 E2
Wootton St CV12 78 D3
Worcester Cl
Allesley CV5 112 B7
Cannock WS11 4 F8
Lichfield WS13 3 C3
Sutton Coldfield B75 32 D3
West Hagley DY9 99 A5
Worcester Cross 3 DY10 116 E5
Worcester Ct
Coventry CV6 96 B4
Wolverhampton WV3 39 A6
Worcester Gn B71 53 C7
Worcester Gr WV6 23 D4
Worcester Ho
4 Halesowen B63 83 A3
Birmingham B36 70 A8
Worcester La
Stourbridge DY9 99 B7
Sutton Coldfield B75 32 D4
Worcester Rd
Birmingham,Birchfield B6 55 F2
Birmingham,Brandhall B68 84 A8
Bromsgrove B61 136 F1
Dudley DY2 62 E3
Harvington DY9,DY10 118 C4
Kenilworth CV8 148 B3
Kidderminster DY10 116 E2
Mustow Green DY10 117 F1
Stoke Heath B61 150 B4
West Hagley DY9 99 A5
Willenhall WV13 27 D2
Worcester Rise B29 86 B1
Worcester Sq 1 B97 153 E4
Worcester St
Birmingham B2 164 C2
Kidderminster DY10 116 E6
Stourbridge DY8 81 A4
Wolverhampton WV2 163 B2
Worcester Wlk B37 70 A1
Word Hill B17 84 F7
Wordsley Cl B98 154 B7
Wordsley Ct DY8 60 E3
Wordsley Green Sh Ctr DY8 60 D2
Wordsley Hospl DY8 60 E3
Wordsley Sch The DY8 60 F3
Wordsworth Ave
Redditch B97 158 C8
Tamworth B79 21 A6
Warwick CV34 160 D5
Wolverhampton WV4 39 F4
Wordsworth Cl
Cannock WS11 1 D4
Lichfield WS14 9 B5
Tipton DY4 52 A8
Wordsworth Cres DY10 117 B6
Wordsworth Ct WV6 23 E4
Wordsworth Dr CV8 148 C4
Wordsworth Ho
4 Oldbury B68 64 C4
Birmingham B31 123 A8
Halesowen B63 82 B5
Wordsworth Rd
Bedworth CV12 78 D1
Birmingham B10 87 D7
Burntwood WS7 7 A8
Coventry CV2 114 C4
Dudley DY3 50 B5
Walsall WS3 28 E8
Willenhall WV12 27 E7
Wolverhampton WV10 26 A8
Wordsworth St B71 53 C5
Worfield Cl WS4 29 A4
Worfield Gdns WV3 38 F6
Workhouse La LE10 76 A4
Works Rd B26 90 A3
World's End Ave B32 84 D6
World's End Jun Sch B32 84 D5
World's End La B32 84 D5
Worlds End Rd B20 55 A3
Worleys Wharf Ave WS10 42 E2
Worsdell Cl CV1 113 B4
Worsey Dr DY4 52 D6
Worsfold Cl CV5 112 A7
Worthen Gr B31 123 A8
Worthings The B30 104 B6
Worthy Down WV11 26 F5
Worthy Down Wlk B35 58 B3
Wortley Ave WV10 25 E6
Worton Rd DY9 81 F2
Wragby Cl WV9 11 B3
Wrekin Cl
Halesowen B63 82 C1
Kidderminster DY11 116 B2
Wrekin Ct 9 B74 31 F2
Wrekin Dr
Bromsgrove B61 137 A5
Stourbridge DY9 81 D4
Wolverhampton,Bradmore WV3 38 E8
Wolverhampton,Wergs WV6 24 A5
Wrekin Gr WV11 13 B1
Wrekin La WV6 24 A5
Wrekin Rd
Birmingham B44 56 A6
Sutton Coldfield B73 46 A1
Wrekin View
Brownhills WS8 16 A5
Huntington WS12 1 C7
Wrekin View Rd DY3 50 C8
Wrekin View WV1 163 B3
Wren Ave WV6 23 D3
Wrenbury Dr
Bilston WV14 41 A7
Coventry CV6 96 A4
Wrens Ave
Kingswinford DY6 61 A4
Tipton DY4 51 D4
Wrens Croft WS11 2 B1
Wrens Hill Rd DY1 51 B5
Wren's Nest Cl B90 126 A5
Wren's Nest Nature Reserve★ DY1 51 B4
Wrens Nest Pl DY1 51 A5
Wren's Nest Prim Sch DY1 51 A4
Wrens Nest Rd DY1 51 A4
Wren's Nest Rd DY1 51 A5
Wrens Park Ave B76 57 E7
Wren St
Coventry CV2 113 F3
Dudley DY1 51 C6
Dudley,Netherton DY2 62 B5
Wrentham St B5 86 E8
Wretham Ct B19 66 B7
Wretham Rd B19 66 B6
Wrexham Ave WS2 27 F1
Wright Ave WV11 26 E7
Wrighton Cl WV12 27 C8
Wrighton Dr DY5 50 C1
Wrighton Gr B78 35 A8
Wright Rd B8 67 E5
Wright's Ave WS11 1 F5
Wright's La B64 63 A1
Wright St
Bilston WV14 40 E4
Birmingham B10 87 D8
Coventry CV1 113 E4
Halesowen B63 83 B4
Wolverhampton WV10 25 D4
Wrigsham St CV3 133 D8
Wrottesley Ct WV8 23 C8
Wrottesley Park Rd WV6, WV8 23 D5
Wrottesley Rd
Birmingham B43 43 D1
Wolverhampton WV6 24 B5
Wrottesley Rd W
Perton WV6 23 F6
Wolverhampton WV6 24 A6
Wrottesley St B5 164 C1
Wroxall Cl DY5 81 C8
Wroxall Dr CV3 134 D5
Wroxall Gr B13 105 A6
Wroxall Rd B91 106 E6
Wroxham Glen WV13 40 F8
Wroxton Rd B26 88 E8
Wr Twr La CV8 147 F6
Wulfruna Ct WV3 163 A2
Wulfruna Gdns WV3 24 F1
Wulfruna St WV1 163 B3
Wulfrun Coll Annexe, Newhampton Ctr WV1 163 B4
Wulfrun Ctr WV1 163 C2
Wulfrun Hall★ WV1 163 B3
Wulfrun Sq WV1 163 C2
Wulfrun Trad Est WV6 25 C5
Wulfrun Way WV1 163 B2
Wyatt Cl B5 86 C5
Wyatt Ho CV2 114 D7
Wyatt Rd B75 47 B5
Wyatts Ct CV12 78 B3
Wychall Dr WV10 11 E4
Wychall La B38 103 E2
Wychall Park Gr B38 103 D2
Wychall Prim Sch B31 103 C2
Wychall Rd B31 103 C3
Wychbold Cl
Redditch B97 158 A6
Willenhall WV12 13 D1
Wychbold Cres B33 69 C3
Wychbold Ct DY9 99 C8
Wychbold Way WV12 13 D1
Wychbury Ct B63 83 A3
Wychbury Dr DY9 99 C7
Wychbury Grange DY9 81 C1
Wychbury Rd
Birmingham B32 102 B7
Brierley Hill DY5 81 E8
Stourbridge DY9 81 E2
Wolverhampton WV3 38 C7
Wychbury B76 47 A1
Wyche Ave B14 104 D4
Wyche Cotts B60 150 C1
Wych Elm Dr 6 CV31 161 F5
Wychelm Farm Rd B14 105 A1
Wych Elm Rd WS8 15 E5
Wycherley Way B64 82 E8
Wychnor Gr B71 42 E2
Wychwood Ave
Coventry CV3 133 C3
Knowle B93 128 B8
Wychwood Cres B26 89 A6
Wychwood Dr B97 158 D6
Wyckham Cl B17 85 A4
Wyckham Rd B36 69 F8
Wycliffe Gr CV2 114 B5
Wycliffe Rd W CV2 114 C5
Wycome Rd B28 106 A7
Wye Cl
Bulkington CV12 79 B2
Wye Cl continued
Hinckley LE10 75 A8
Wye Cliff Rd B20 66 B8
Wye Cl
Perton WV6 23 F4
Royal Leamington Spa CV32 157 C3
Sutton Coldfield B76 58 B7
Wyegate Cl B36 69 F8
Wye Ho DY3 50 D3
Wyemanton Cl B43 43 C1
Wye Rd WS3 14 E1
Wykeham Gr WV6 23 D3
Wykeley Rd CV2 114 C4
Wyken Ave CV2 114 D5
Wyken Cl B93 127 E2
Wyken Croft CV2 114 D6
Wyken Croft Nature Pk★ CV2 114 D6
Wyken Croft Prim Sch CV2 114 E5
Wyken Grange Rd CV2 114 C5
Wyken Way CV2 114 B5
Wyke Rd CV2 114 C4
Wykin Rd LE10 71 A3
Wyld Cl B71 53 A8
Wyld Ct CV5 112 B5
Wylde Cres B65 63 C4
Wylde Green Coll B72 46 C1
Wylde Green Prim Sch B73 57 B7
Wylde Green Rd B72,B76 46 D1
Wylde Green Sta B73 46 B1
Wyley Rd CV6 113 B5
Wymering Ave WV11 26 F7
Wynall La S DY9 82 A3
Wynall La DY9 81 F3
Wynbrook Gr B90 127 A6
Wynchcombe Ave WV4 38 D4
Wyncote Cl CV8 148 A4
Wyndcliffe Prim Sch
Birmingham B9 67 C1
Birmingham B9 67 D1
Wyndcliff Rd B9 67 D1
Wyndham Gdns B30 103 D4
Wyndham Rd B16 65 F1
Wyndhurst Rd B33 68 E5
Wyndley Cl B74 31 F6
Wyndley Dr B73 46 B4
Wyndley Gr B72 46 C2
Wyndley La B73 46 A4
Wyndley L Ctr B73 46 A5
Wyndley Manor B74 32 A6
Wyndmill Cres B71 42 F1
Wynds Covert B14 104 D2
Wynds Point B31 103 B5
Wynd The DY3 39 D1
Wynfield Gdns B14 104 F5
Wynford Rd B27 88 C5
Wynford Road Ind Est B27 88 C5
Wyn-Griffith Dr DY4 52 A3
Wynne Cres WV4 38 C3
Wynn Rd WV4 38 F5
Wynn St B15 86 D8
Wynstead Covert 6 B14 104 C2
Wyntor La B71 53 B8
Wynyates B79 20 E6
Wyre Cl
Birmingham B45 102 B1
Brownhills WS9 15 F4
Wyre Rd DY8 80 E7
Wyrley Brook Pk WS11 4 D5
Wyrley Brook Ret Pk WS11 4 D6
Wyrley Cl
Burntwood WS8 6 F3
Lichfield WS14 9 A5
Willenhall WV12 27 D7
Wyrley Ho
Birmingham B23 56 C6
Tipton DY4 52 B3
Wyrley La WS3 14 E8
Wyrley Rd
Birmingham B6 56 A2
Sutton Coldfield B75 32 D1
Wednesfield WV11 27 A6
Wyrley St WV10 25 F2
Wyrley Trad Est B6 56 B2
Wyrley Way B23 56 A6
Wythall Green Way B47 124 E3
Wythall Rd B63 83 A2
Wythall Sta B47 125 C4
Wythwood Cl DY9 81 D1
Wythwood Gr
Hollywood B47 125 C6
Tipton DY4 52 A8
Wythwood Rd B47 125 C6
Wyton Ave B68 64 C2
Wyver Cres CV2 114 C3
Wyvern Cl
Hinckley LE10 75 E4
Oldbury B68 64 B4
Sutton Coldfield B74 46 B7
Wednesfield WV12 27 A7
Wyvern Gr
Birmingham B29 85 C2
Cannock WS12 2 A5
Wyvern Rd B74 46 B7
Wyvern B77 21 F3
Wyvis Cl WV6 24 E2

Y

Yale Dr WV11 26 E5
Yale Rd WV13 41 A7
Yardley Cl
Oldbury B68 64 B1
Yardley Cl continued
Redditch B98 154 E3
Warwick CV34 155 F2
Yardley Fields Rd B33 68 E2
Yardley Green Rd B9,B25, B33 68 A2
Yardley Prim Sch B26 88 D7
Yardley Rd B27 88 C5
Yardleys Sch B11 87 F4
Yardley St
Coventry CV1 113 E4
Darlaston WS10 41 C7
Stourbridge DY9 81 C6
Yardley Wood Com Prim Sch B14 105 D4
Yardley Wood Rd B13, B14 105 B5
Yardley Wood Sta B28 105 D5
Yardley Works DY9 81 C5
Yare Gr WV13 27 D1
Yarmouth Gn CV4 131 E8
Yarnborough Hill DY8 81 A2
Yarnbury Cl B14 104 E1
Yarn Cl B47 125 A5
Yarner Cl DY1 50 E2
Yarnfield Prim Sch B11 88 A3
Yarnfield Rd B11 88 A3
Yarningale Cl B98 158 F6
Yarningale Rd
Birmingham B14 104 D5
Coventry CV3 134 D5
Yarningdale 7 B90 126 C8
Yarn La B90 126 A6
Yarnold La
Bournheath B61 136 C8
Fairfield B61 120 C1
Yarrow Cl
Walsall WS3 15 A5
Wednesfield WV11 26 F5
Yarrow Dr B38 123 F8
Yarwell Cl WV10 163 C4
Yateley Ave B42 55 A7
Yateley Cres B42 55 A7
Yateley Rd B15 85 E7
Yatesbury Ave B35 58 A3
Yates Croft B74 31 F6
Yates Ind Est WS3 5 F2
Yates La B65 63 F2
Yeadon Cl B97 153 A1
Yeadon Gdns WV3 38 D8
Yeames Cl B43 44 C4
Yellowhammer Ct DY10 117 A1
Yelverton Cl WS3 14 B4
Yelverton Dr B15 85 E8
Yelverton Rd CV6 113 D8
Yeman Rd B68 64 D3
Yemscroft WS6 14 A8
Yems Croft WS4 29 A6
Yenton Cl B78 21 A1
Yenton Gr B24 57 C6
Yenton Prim Sch B24 57 C6
Yeoman Cl DY10 116 E3
Yeomanry Cl
12 Warwick CV34 160 F7
Sutton Coldfield B75 47 A6
Yeomans Grange 5 B75 46 F6
Yeomans Way B75 46 F6
Yeomans Wlk B60 150 E8
Yeovil Ct 15 DY5 61 D2
Yeovilton B79 21 C8
Yerbury Gr B23 56 B4
Yew Cl CV3 114 C1
Yew Croft Ave B17 85 B6
Yewdale B17 85 C4
Yewdale Cres CV2 96 E1
Yewdale Ct CV2 96 F1
Yewhurst Rd B91 106 E4
Yews The CV12 77 E2
Yew St WV3 25 A1
Yew Tree Ave
Belbroughton DY9 119 E8
Birmingham B26 88 E7
Lichfield WS14 9 E8
Yew Tree Cl
Kingswood B94 144 D3
Norton Canes WS11 6 A5
Redditch B97 153 A4
Yew Tree Com Jun & Inf Sch B6 56 A1
Yew Tree Ct 1 CV31 161 F5
Yewtree Dr B60 137 B2
Yew Tree Gdns WV8 10 A4
Yew Tree Hills DY2 62 C4
Yew Tree Inf & Jun Sch B91 107 E6
Yew Tree La
Birmingham,Frankley B32 101 E3
Birmingham,Yardley B26 88 E7
Dudley WV14 40 D1
Fairfield B61 120 D2
Lapworth B94 144 B1
Yewtree La B65 63 B2
Yew Tree La
Solihull B91 107 E5
Wednesbury WS10 42 A2
Wolverhampton WV6 24 A5
Yew Tree Pl
Romsley B62 101 A5
Walsall WS3 14 D3
Yew Tree Prim Sch WS5 43 C4
Yew Tree Rd
Birmingham,Castle Bromwich B36 69 E8
Birmingham,Edgbaston B15 86 C8

[Yew] Tree Rd *continued*
Birmingham,Handsworth B6 **56** A1
Birmingham,Moseley B13 . . **86** D2
Dudley DY2 . . . . **62** C4
Halesowen B63 . . . . **82** F3
Kidderminster DY10 . . . . . **116** F5
Smethwick B67 . . . . **64** E4
Yewtree Rd
Sutton Coldfield,Boldmere B73 . . . . **57** A7
Sutton Coldfield,Streetly B74 . . . . **44** D8
Yew Tree Rd
Walsall,The Delves WS5 . . . **43** A5
Walsall WS4 . . . . **15** B1
Yew Tree Ret Pk B25 . . . . . **88** D8
Yew Tree Rise B76 . . . . **46** F3
Yew Tree Villas B73 . . . . . . **57** A7
Yew Wlk B37 . . . . **70** B2
Yockleton Rd B33 . . . . **69** C3
York Ave
Bedworth CV12 . . . . **78** D2
Bromsgrove B61 . . . . **136** E4
Walsall WS2 . . . . **28** B2
Willenhall WV13 . . . . **27** D2
Wolverhampton WV3 . . . . . **24** E1
Yorkbrooke Dr B26 . . . . . . **89** B5
York Cl
Birmingham B30 . . . . **104** A6
Bromsgrove B61 . . . . **136** E4
Coventry CV3 . . . . **134** C5
Lichfield WS13 . . . . **3** C3
Studley B80 . . . . **159** C4
Tipton DY4 . . . . **51** D4
York Cres
Birmingham B34 . . . . **69** E6
Darlaston WS10 . . . . **41** D6
Stourbridge DY8 . . . . **80** D7
West Bromwich B70 . . . . . . **53** A6
Wolverhampton WV3 . . . . . . **24** E1
York Ct DY10 . . . . **116** E7
Yorkdale Cl DY3 . . . . **50** D3
York Dr B36 . . . . **68** B8
Yorke Ave DY5 . . . . **61** A1
York Gdns WV3 . . . . **24** E1
Yorklea Croft B37 . . . . **69** F2
Yorkmead Jun & Inf Sch B28 . . . . **87** F2
Yorkminster Dr B37 . . . . . . **70** D3
York Rd
Birmingham B23 . . . . **56** F4
Birmingham,Edgbaston B16 **65** E1
Birmingham,Handsworth B21 . . . . **65** F8
Birmingham,King's Heath B14 . . . . **104** E8
Birmingham,Tyseley B28 . . . **87** F2
Bromsgrove B61 . . . . **136** F4
Cannock WS11 . . . . **4** F7
Dudley DY2 . . . . **62** E3
Hinckley LE10 . . . . **71** D3
Rowley Regis B65 . . . . **63** E3
Royal Leamington Spa CV31 . . . . **161** F8
Walsall WS4 . . . . **29** D7
Wolverhampton WV3 . . . . . . **38** B8
Yorksand Rd B78 . . . . **34** F8
Yorkshire Way WS7 . . . . **7** F8
York St
Birmingham B17 . . . . **85** D6
Coventry CV1 . . . . **113** B2
Kidderminster DY10 . . . . . **116** E7
Nuneaton CV11 . . . . **73** A4
Wolverhampton WV1 . . . . . **163** D2
Yorks Wood Dr B37 . . . . . . **69** E5
Yorkswood Prim Sch B37 **69** F5
York Terr B18 . . . . **66** C5
Young Cl CV34 . . . . **160** B5
Young St B70 . . . . **53** A3
Yoxall Gr B33 . . . . **69** A3
Yoxall Rd B90 . . . . **106** D2
Yule Rd CV2 . . . . **114** D5
Yvonne Rd B97 . . . . **158** D7

Z

Zealand Cl LE10 . . . . **71** F3
Zion Cl WS6 . . . . **4** D3
Zions Cl B64 . . . . **62** F1
Zion St DY4 . . . . **51** F8
Zoar St
Dudley DY3 . . . . **50** C3
Wolverhampton WV3 . . . . . . **25** B1
Zorrina Cl CV10 . . . . **72** B5
Zouche Cl DY8 . . . . **80** E8

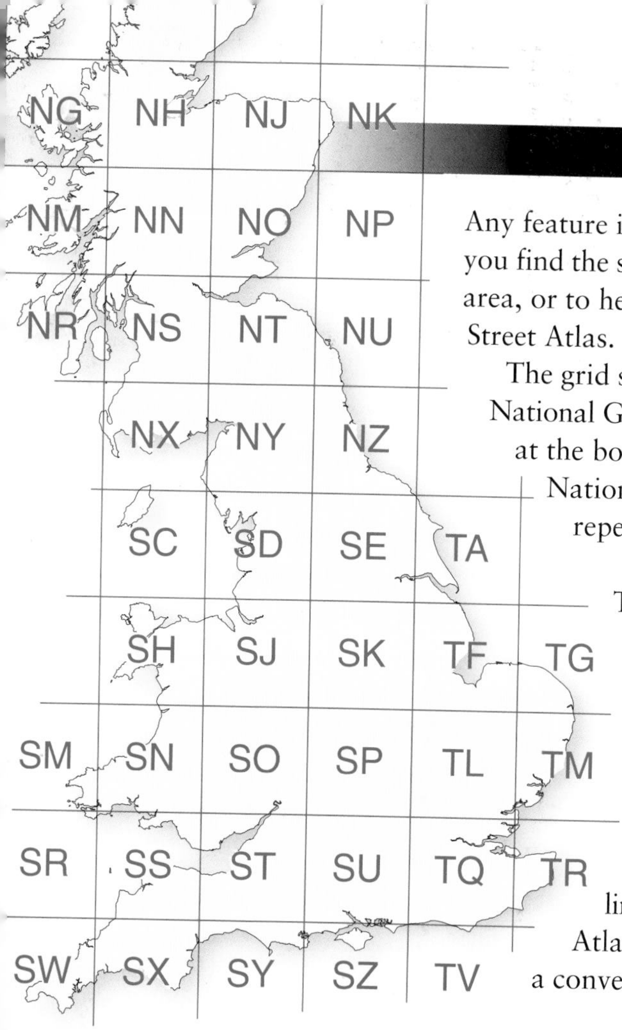

Using the Ordnance Survey National Grid

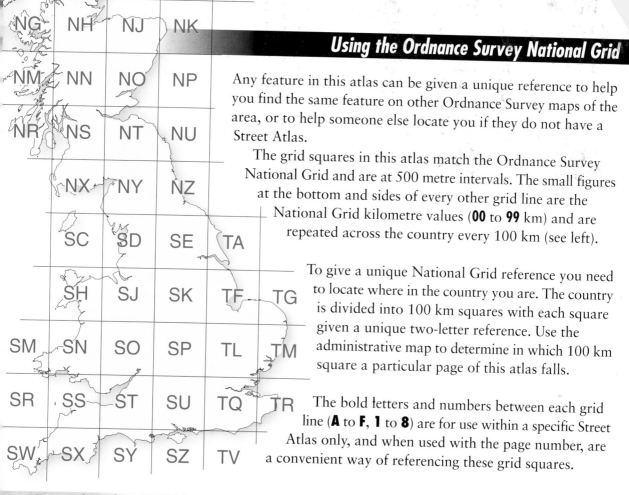

Any feature in this atlas can be given a unique reference to help you find the same feature on other Ordnance Survey maps of the area, or to help someone else locate you if they do not have a Street Atlas.

The grid squares in this atlas match the Ordnance Survey National Grid and are at 500 metre intervals. The small figures at the bottom and sides of every other grid line are the National Grid kilometre values (**00** to **99** km) and are repeated across the country every 100 km (see left).

To give a unique National Grid reference you need to locate where in the country you are. The country is divided into 100 km squares with each square given a unique two-letter reference. Use the administrative map to determine in which 100 km square a particular page of this atlas falls.

The bold letters and numbers between each grid line (**A** to **F**, **1** to **8**) are for use within a specific Street Atlas only, and when used with the page number, are a convenient way of referencing these grid squares.

Example *The railway bridge over DARLEY GREEN RD in grid square B1*

Step 1: Identify the two-letter reference, in this example the page is in **SP**

Step 2: Identify the 1 km square in which the railway bridge falls. Use the figures in the southwest corner of this square: Eastings **17**, Northings **74**. This gives a unique reference: **SP 17 74**, accurate to 1 km.

Step 3: To give a more precise reference accurate to 100 m you need to estimate how many tenths along and how many tenths up this 1 km square the feature is (to help with this the 1 km square is divided into four 500 m squares). This makes the bridge about **8** tenths along and about **1** tenth up from the southwest corner.

This gives a unique reference: **SP 178 741**, accurate to 100 m.

Eastings (read from left to right along the bottom) come before Northings (read from bottom to top). If you have trouble remembering say to yourself "Along the hall, THEN up the stairs"!

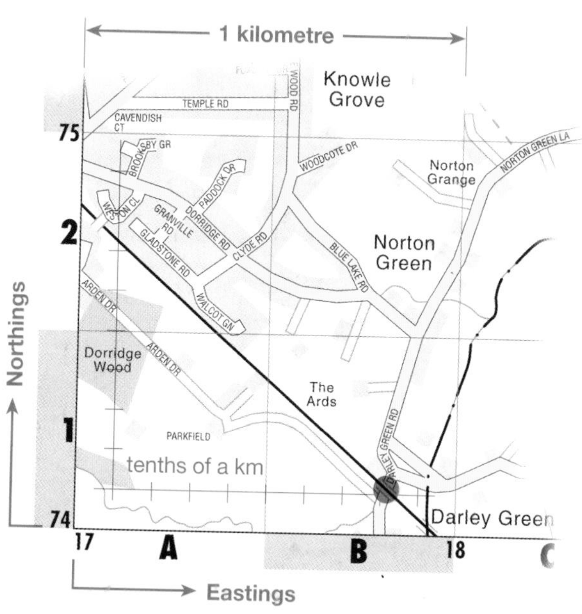

PHILIP'S MAPS

the Gold Standard for serious driving

- Philip's street atlases cover every county in England and Wales, plus much of Scotland
- All our atlases use the same style of mapping, with the same colours and symbols, so you can move with confidence from one atlas to the next
- Widely used by the emergency services, transport companies and local authorities
- Created from the most up-to-date and detailed information available from Ordnance Survey
- Based on the National Grid

BEST BUY • BEST BUY • Auto EXPRESS • BEST BUY • BEST BUY

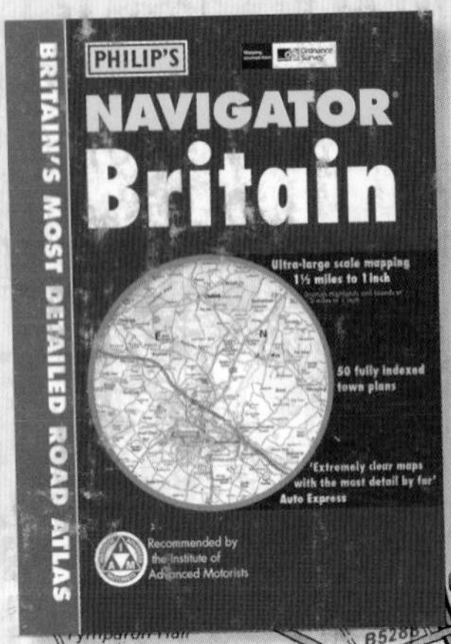

For national mapping, choose **Philip's Navigator Britain** – the most detailed road atlas available of England, Wales and Scotland. Hailed by Auto Express as 'the ultimate road atlas', this is the only one-volume atlas to show every road and lane in Britain.

Street atlases currently available

All England and Wales coverage

England

Bedfordshire
Berkshire
Birmingham and West Midlands
Bristol and Bath
Buckinghamshire
Cambridgeshire
Cheshire
Cornwall
Cumbria
Derbyshire
Devon
Dorset
County Durham and Teesside
Essex
North Essex
South Essex
Gloucestershire
Hampshire
North Hampshire
South Hampshire
Herefordshire Monmouthshire
Hertfordshire
Isle of Wight
Kent
East Kent
West Kent
Lancashire
Leicestershire and Rutland
Lincolnshire
London
Greater Manchester
Merseyside
Norfolk
Northamptonshire
Northumberland
Nottinghamshire
Oxfordshire
Shropshire
Somerset
Staffordshire
Suffolk
Surrey
East Sussex
West Sussex
Tyne and Wear
Warwickshire
Birmingham and West Midlands
Wiltshire and Swindon
Worcestershire
East Yorkshire Northern Lincolnshire
North Yorkshire
South Yorkshire
West Yorkshire

Wales

Anglesey, Conwy and Gwynedd
Cardiff, Swansea and The Valleys
Carmarthenshire, Pembrokeshire and Swansea
Ceredigion and South Gwynedd
Denbighshire, Flintshire, Wrexham
Herefordshire Monmouthshire
Powys

Scotland

Aberdeenshire
Ayrshire
Edinburgh and East Central Scotland
Fife and Tayside
Glasgow and West Central Scotland
Inverness and Moray
Lanarkshire

How to order

Philip's maps and atlases are available from bookshops, motorway services and petrol stations. You can order direct from the publisher by phoning **01903 828503** or online at **www.philips-maps.co.uk**
For bulk orders only, phone 020 7644 6940